food and culture

The classic book that helped to define and legitimize the field of food and culture studies is now available, with major revisions, in an affordable *e-book version* (978-0-203-07975-1).

The *third edition* includes forty *original essays* and reprints of previously published classics under five Sections: **Foundations; Hegemony and Difference; Consumption and Embodiment; Food and Globalization**; and **Challenging, Contesting, and Transforming the Food System.**

Seventeen of the forty chapters included are either new to this edition, rewritten by their original authors, or edited by Counihan and Van Esterik.

A bank of test items applicable to each article in the book is available to instructors interested in selecting this edition for course use. Simply send an email to the publisher at textbooksonline@taylorandfrancis.com.

Carole Counihan is Professor Emerita of Anthropology at Millersville University in Pennsylvania and editor-in-chief of *Food and Foodways*. Her earlier books include *Around the Tuscan Table: Food, Family, and Gender in Twentieth-Century Florence*, *Food in the USA*, and *The Anthropology of Food and Body: Gender, Meaning, and Power*.

Penny Van Esterik is Professor of Anthropology at York University in Toronto, Canada, where she teaches nutritional anthropology, in addition to doing research on food and globalization in Southeast Asia. She is a founding member of WABA (World Alliance for Breastfeeding Action) and writes on infant and young child feeding, including her earlier book, *Beyond the Breast-Bottle Controversy*.

food and culture

a reader

third edition

edited by
carole counihan and
penny van esterik

Routledge
Taylor & Francis Group

NEW YORK AND LONDON

First published 2013
by Routledge
711 Third Avenue, New York, NY 10017

Simultaneously published in the UK
by Routledge
2 Park Square, Milton Park, Abingdon, Oxon OX14 4RN

Routledge is an imprint of the Taylor & Francis Group, an informa business

Library of Congress Cataloging-in-Publication Data
Food and culture : a reader / edited by Carole Counihan and Penny Van Esterik. – 3rd ed.
p. cm.
Includes bibliographical references and index.
1. Food–Social aspects. 2. Food habits. I. Counihan, Carole, 1948- II. Van Esterik, Penny.
GT2850.F64 2012
394.1'2–dc23   2012021989

ISBN: 978-0-415-52103-1 (hbk)
ISBN: 978-0-415-52104-8 (pbk)
ISBN: 978-0-203-07975-1 (ebk)

Typeset in Minion
by Cenveo Publisher Services, Bangalore

Printed and bound in the United States of America by Sheridan Books, Inc. (a Sheridan Group Company).

Contents

Foundations

Hegemony and Difference: Race, Class, and Gender

Food-centered life histories portray the voices and perspectives
of traditionally muted Hispanic women of rural southern Colorado
whose food stories reveal differential behaviors and consciousness
which promote empowerment.

Because feeding work is complex, laborious, and highly gendered,
it is problematic in lesbigay families because a full accounting of it
would destroy illusions of equality and call into question masculinity
of gay men who do it and femininity of lesbians who do not.

By applying feminist materialist theory, Slocum analyses the
embodiment of race and its manifestations through food practices
and behavior displayed at the farmers' market.

Punk cuisine—based on scavenged, rotten, and/or stolen
food—challenges the hierarchy, commodification, toxicity, and
environmental destruction of the capitalist food system.

Consumption and Embodiment

Medieval women used food for personal religious expression,
including giving food away, exuding foods from their bodies,
and undertaking fasts to gain religious and cultural power.

Bordo argues that eating disorders and body image issues are
created through social and media pressures that target all
women regardless of race or class.

This paper offers a biocultural approach to anorexia that stresses how young
people obsess not over beauty but over an ascetic search for self-control.

Challenging, Contesting, and Transforming the Food System

Foreword

People ask me: Why do you write about food, and eating and drinking? Why don't you write about the struggle for power and security, and about love, the way others do?

They ask it accusingly, as if I were somehow gross, unfaithful to the honor of my craft.

The easiest answer is to say that, like most other humans, I am hungry. But there is more than that. It seems to me that our three basic needs, for food and security and love, are so mixed and mingled and entwined that we cannot straightly think of one without the others. So it happens that when I write of hunger, I am really writing about love and the hunger for it . . . and warmth and richness and fine reality of hunger satisfied . . . and it is all one.

I tell about myself, and how I ate bread on a lasting hillside, or drank red wine in a room now blown to bits, and it happens without my willing it that I am telling too about the people with me then, and their other deeper needs for love and happiness.

There is food in the bowl, and more often than not, because of what honesty I have, there is nourishment in the heart, to feed the wilder, more insistent hungers. We must eat. If, in the face of that dread fact, we can find other nourishment, and tolerance and compassion for it, we'll be no less full of human dignity.

There is a communion of more than our bodies when bread is broken and wine drunk. And that is my answer, when people ask me: Why do you write about hunger, and not wars or love?

M. F. K. Fisher
***The Gastronomical Me**,*
originally published 1943

Preface to the Third Edition

In this third edition of *Food and Culture: A Reader,* our aim mirrors that of the previous two editions: to provide a comprehensive introduction to the field that contains classic foundational pieces, a range of outstanding articles reflecting diverse perspectives and topics, and cutting edge new work. This task has become more challenging with each edition as the field has exploded over the sixteen years since the first edition appeared in 1997. To include new work and keep the *Reader* current and lively, we had to omit some pieces that we love, but we hope that the new articles will excite our readers and more than make up for what we dropped.

In this new edition, we have kept almost all of the foundational pieces but cut the article by De Certeau and Giard to include a selection from Pierre Bourdieu. We have modified the section on food consumption and the body by reducing the number of articles on anorexia nervosa, expanding the focus on obesity, and including more diverse approaches to the body. This edition of the *Reader* maintains a broad geographical and multicultural coverage with articles on Euro-Americans, African Americans, and Latinos as well as on Japanese, Greek, Italian, Thai, South Asian, native American, Mexican, and Chinese food cultures. It continues to explore enduring topics of food and gender, consumption and meaning, globalization, and political economy, but introduces new topics with articles on farmers' markets, community food security, the complexities of the organic food market, democracy and food justice, cooking skill and its meanings, gender in food television, and packaged foods in the South Asian diaspora.

Since the first edition of the book, we have been privileged to participate in the creation of the sumptuous covers. From the multihued noodles and fruit of the first edition, to the sensuous chocolate dessert and colorful spices of the second, we have endeavored to combine foods like fish and tomatoes with culturally constructed products like sandwiches. We chose the Thai fruit and vegetable carving for this edition's cover to underscore the skill and effort involved in transforming foods into edible works of art, and the important place of the visual aspects of food in the anthropology of the senses.

We are pleased to publish this third edition not only in standard book format but also as an electronic book. For instructors who adopt the book in courses, we have also prepared test questions which are available on the book's website. We have tried to pay more attention to temporal context in this edition, giving the original date of publication at the beginning of each article, to draw more attention to the scholarly context in which these papers were written.

Acknowledgments

We would like to thank many colleagues who provided feedback on the book, both those who chatted with us informally and those who provided formal reviews for Routledge.

Jonathan Maupin, Arizona State University
Mary Malainey, Brandon University
Janet Alexanian, California State University, Fullerton
Julie Fairbanks, Coe College
Amy Speier, Eckerd College
Thierry Rigogne, Fordham University
Ari Ariel, New York University
Susan C. Rogers, New York University
Susan Cooper, Roosevelt University
Claudia Chang, Sweet Briar College
Sharyn Jones, University of Alabama at Birmingham
Don Pollock, University of Buffalo
J.D. Baker, University of Hawaii at Manoa
Judy Rodriguez, University of North Florida
Frayda Cohen, University of Pittsburgh
Ann Reed, University of Akron

We thank the Boston University Gastronomy MLA students in Carole's Food Anthropology class in spring semester 2012 who wrote reviews of many articles which helped us narrow our selection for this book: Mayling Chung, Aubee Duplesss, Monet Dyer, Jennifer French, Susie Helm, Brad Jones, Joyce Liao, Emily Olson, Katie Peterson, Erin Powell, Jessica Roat, Allison Schultz, Natalie Shmulik, Penny Skalnik, Shannon Streets, Kaylee Vickers, Rachel Wegman, and Chao-Hui (Amy) Young. We express eternal gratitude to Boston University Gastronomy MLA student Alexandre Galimberti for serving as editorial assistant on the project with efficiency and equanimity. We would also like to thank our Routledge editor, Steve Rutter, for his good publishing sense and his unbelievable deadlines, Fred Courtright for help with permissions, Tom Hussey for the cover design, and Samantha Barbaro and Leah Babb-Rosenfeld for their editorial assistance.

Carole would like to thank the Millersville University Sociology-Anthropology Department and Faculty Grants Committee for years of support; the Boston University MLA Gastronomy program and Rachel Black, its coordinator; the University of

Gastronomic Sciences students, faculty and administration for providing the opportunity to teach food anthropology in an international setting for the past eight wonderful years; and the University of Cagliari Visiting Professor program and colleagues Gabriella Da Re, Giovanna Caltagirone, Alessandra Guigoni, and many others. She would also like to thank her patient, smart, supportive husband, Jim Taggart, who has put up with more food anthropology than he ever dreamed of, and her children for their continuing ability to amaze her.

Penny would like to thank Vivian Khouw, Anne Meneley, Paul Antze, and Megan Davies for sharing their resources and experiences teaching about food, and suggesting readings that students enjoy, as well as her husband, John, whose hands and eyes greatly facilitated this project. Penny's efforts on the reader are dedicated to her late mentor, Dr. Michael Latham, founding director of International Nutrition at Cornell, who embodied lasting lessons about how to combine academic integrity with activist social justice around the subject of food and hunger.

Why Food? Why Culture? Why Now?
Introduction to the Third Edition

Carole Counihan and Penny Van Esterik

In 1997, when we proposed the first *Food and Culture Reader*, we had to persuade Routledge of the importance of publishing it. In 2012, Routledge had to persuade us to undertake the arduous task of reviewing the incredibly expanded literature to produce a third edition. We hope that the current selection of articles gives a snapshot of how the field has grown and developed from its early foundations. Cultural anthropology remains the central discipline guiding this field. Food and nutritional anthropology in particular, and food studies generally, manage to rise above the dualisms that threaten to segment most fields of study. This field resists separating biological from cultural, individual from society, and local from global culture, but rather struggles with their entanglements. Food and culture studies have somehow made interdisciplinarity workable. Sometimes co-opting, more often embracing the history and geography of food as part of the holistic emphasis of anthropology, food studies have become increasingly sophisticated theoretically. We hope these papers reveal the roots of contemporary issues in food studies, and we acknowledge our bias towards particular subjects that most engage our interest.

Scholarship in food studies has expanded remarkably over the past decade. A quick and by no means exhaustive bibliographic search turns up scores of recent food books in fields as diverse as philosophy (Heldke 2003, Kaplan 2012, Korsmeyer 2002), psychology (Conner and Armitage 2002, Ogden 2010), geography (Carney 2001, 2010, Friedberg 2009, Guthman 2011, Yasmeen 2006), film studies (Bower 2004, Ferry 2003, Keller 2006)[1], and architecture (Franck 2003, Horwitz and Singley 2006), not to mention the vast literature in food's traditional fields of nutrition, home economics, and agriculture. Countless new texts abound on food in literature—from the study of eating and being eaten in children's literature (Daniel 2006) to food symbols in early modern American fiction (Appelbaum 2006) and classical Arab literature (Van Gelder 2000), to post-Freudian analysis of literary orality (Skubal 2002).

In its more longstanding disciplinary homes, food continues to fascinate, so we find texts exploring the history of food from the Renaissance banquet (Albala 2007a) through the broad sweep of time (Claflin and Scholliers 2012, Parasecoli and Scholliers 2012) to the future of food (Belasco 2006); from the United States (Williams-Forson 2006) to Italy (Capatti and Montanari 2003, Montanari 2010) and all of Europe (Flandrin and Montanari 1999); to the history of many specific foods including tomatoes (Gentilcore 2010), beans (Albala 2007b), turkey (Smith 2006), chocolate (Coe and Coe 2000), salt (Kurlansky 2003), and spices (Turner 2004). Sociologists have not hesitated to stir the food studies pot (Ray 2004), and anthropologists have continued to produce work on topics as varied as hunger in Africa (Flynn 2005), children's eating in China (Jing 2000), the global trade in lamb flaps (Gewertz and Errington 2010), food and memory in Greece (Sutton 2001), the globalization of milk (Wiley 2010), Japan's largest fish market (Bestor 2004), the culture of restaurants (Beriss and Sutton 2007), and the role of cooking in human evolution (Wrangham 2010).

These examples provide some measure of the many texts that have been published in the last decade. Why has the field exploded so? We would like to suggest several reasons for this explosion. Without a doubt, feminism and women's studies have contributed to the growth of food studies by legitimizing a domain of human behavior so heavily associated with women over time and across cultures. A second reason is the politicization of food and the expansion of social movements linked to food. This has created an increased awareness of the links between consumption and production, beginning with books on food and agriculture (e.g. Guthman 2004, Magdoff et al. 2000) as well as more interdisciplinary work on food politics (Guthman 2011, Nestle 2003, Patel 2007, Williams-Forson and Counihan 2012). A third reason is that once food became a legitimate topic of scholarly research, its novelty, richness, and scope provided limitless grist for the scholarly mill, as food links body and soul, self and other, the personal and the political, the material and the symbolic. Moreover, as food shifts from being local and known, to being global and unknown, it has been transformed into a potential symbol of fear and anxiety (Ferrieres 2005), as well as of morality (Pojman 2011, Singer and Mason 2006, Telfer 2005).

Scholars have found food a powerful lens of analysis and written insightful books about a range of compelling contemporary issues: diaspora and immigration (Gabaccia 1998, Ray 2004, Ray and Srinivas 2012); nationalism, globalization, and local manifestations (Barndt 1999, Inglis and Gimlin 2010, Wilk 2006a, 2006b); culinary tourism (Long 2003); gender and race-ethnic identity (Abarca 2006, Williams-Forson 2006); social justice and human rights (Kent 2007, Wenche Barth and Kracht 2005)[2]; modernization and dietary change (Counihan 2004, Watson 1997); food safety and contamination (Friedberg 2004, 2009, Nestle 2004, Schwartz 2004); and taste perception (Howes 2005, Korsmeyer 2002, 2005). Many of these subjects have important material dimensions, which have also been studied by archaeologists, folklorists, and even designers, as food leaves its mark on the human environment.

The explosion of the field of food studies is also reflected in new and continuing interdisciplinary journals such as *Agriculture and Human Values*, *Appetite*, *Culture and Agriculture*, *The Digest*, *Food and Foodways*, *Food, Culture and Society*, *Gastronomica*, *The Anthropology of Food*, and *Nutritional Anthropology*. Hundreds of websites inform food professionals, researchers, and the general public. Groundbreaking documentary films such as *Fast Food Nation*, *The Garden*, *Supersize Me*, *The Future of Food*, *The Real Dirt on Farmer John*, *King Corn*, *Farmageddon*, and *Two Angry Moms* have called attention to problems in our food system and efforts to redress them. Food advocacy is reflected in food movements that promote organic, local, fairly traded, and slow food, revitalizing vegetarianism and freeganism (Van Esterik 2005), and decrying what fast, processed food has done to our bodies and communities. Of particular interest is how food-focused social movements interact with one another, and with academic research (Belasco 2007).

The last few years have also seen a dramatic increase in popular books about food, some by talented journalists such as Michael Pollan, and others by food faddists more closely linked to the diet industry, the latter often relying on hearsay rather than research. It is important that students understand that the papers in this reader come from specific disciplinary perspectives and are based on sound research. We hope that this *Reader* helps students acquire the critical skills to distinguish between the different sources of information about food.

Given the vastness of the food studies repast, there is no way this book can offer up a complete meal. Rather we envision it as an appetizer to introduce the field to the reader—a taste of the diverse array of scrumptious intellectual dishes that await further pursuit. We have chosen articles that are high quality and that explore issues of enduring importance written by some of the leading food studies scholars. "Write a book with legs," our editor urged us in 1997—and we did. But those legs have taken food studies in exciting new directions in the last decade, and this revised *Reader* reflects these changes.

The third edition retains the classic papers reflecting the foundations of food studies, and provides an interdisciplinary collection of cutting-edge articles in the social sciences that combine theory with ethnographic and historical data. We hope our readers will find this third edition engages even more deeply with both past and present scholarship on food and culture.

From the first reader, we retain the wise words of M.F.K. Fisher, and reaffirm that food touches everything and is the foundation of every economy, marking social differences, boundaries, bonds, and contradictions—an endlessly evolving enactment of gender, family, and community relationships.[3]

Foundations

In rethinking and updating the "Foundations" section, we recognize the significant contributions these authors have made to food studies by introducing basic definitions and conceptual tools used by later scholars. The papers we have retained in this edition are considered classics and are fundamental for demonstrating the history of food studies. While we continue to value the pioneering work by Bruch (1979, 2001) and de Certeau (2011) which we included in earlier editions, we have omitted them in this *Reader* to make room for other approaches and because new editions have made their work easily accessible. Our selection demonstrates the centrality of cultural anthropology to the development of the field.[4] We begin with Margaret Mead's 1971 *Redbook* article on "Why Do We Overeat?", in which she explores the very contemporary problem of the relation between overindulgence and guilt. This piece illustrates Mead's commitment to making the insights of anthropologists available to the public and we open with it as a tribute to Mead's pioneering work as one of the earliest anthropologists to articulate the centrality of foodways to human culture and thus to social science.[5] Her article draws attention to the double role of many anthropologists who write about food as both academics and advocates, a topic explored further in the last section of the *Reader*.

The classic articles by Barthes, Bourdieu, and Lévi-Strauss present different approaches to food's ability to convey meaning. Barthes's ruminations on "The Psychosociology of Contemporary Food Consumption" provide an idiosyncratic account of the semiotic and symbolic power of foodways—an account that is not always tightly linked to ethnographic evidence, but is highly provocative and anticipates much later writing on food as communication. In contrast, Bourdieu provides mammoth amounts of ethnographic detail on food in French families in his book, *Distinction*. This challenging author opens up a new world of scholarship to students, particularly around the concept of class. We were concerned that Bourdieu's influence in food studies was not being fully recognized because of the difficulty students and teachers have in accessing and understanding the ethnographic context from which his concepts of life style and habitus emerged. This small excerpt on food and meals gives readers a sample of Bourdieu's contribution.

While many have critiqued the specifics of Lévi-Strauss's "Culinary Triangle," and he himself later revised his formulations in his 1978 book, *The Origin of Table Manners*, this piece remains a classic structuralist statement about food preparation as language. Mary Douglas builds on the work of Barthes and Lévi-Strauss to explain Jewish dietary law, a much debated topic in the field of food and culture and an excellent case study for examining food prohibitions and symbolism. In this edition we have included Douglas's chapter on "The Abominations of Leviticus" from her path-breaking book *Purity and Danger* (1966). Although Douglas later revised her argument in "Deciphering a Meal" (1999) to address subsequent scholarship, we feel that her original formulation has value for its simplicity and elegance. While Douglas explains Jewish food prohibitions on the basis of the religious conception of holiness based on wholeness, Marvin Harris rejects semiotic interpretations of the abomination of pigs and offers a cultural materialist explanation based on economic and ecological utility. The mystery of food taboos—even when the prohibited foods are available, nutritious, and "edible"—is a test case for exploring the gustatory selectivity of all human groups, and a wonderful example of how the same cultural phenomenon can be explained from different theoretical viewpoints.

We have returned to Jack Goody's wonderful article on "Industrial Food" from the first edition, since no other anthropologist frames the historical context of the industrialization of food processing as well. His study of the changes in the British food system that made colonial expeditions possible sets up Mintz's memorable paper on "Time, Sugar and Sweetness" in the Caribbean, an appropriate tribute to his influence on the field. Mintz shows how the rich controlled access to desirable high status sugar, until it was produced in sufficient quantity to become a working class staple rather than a luxury consumed only by the elite; this transformation—and the processes of slavery, global trade, and worker exploitation on which it depended—changed the course of human history.

Categories of Difference: Race, Class, and Gender

Our second section considers the expression of race, class, nation, and personhood through food production and consumption. It recognizes the productive cross-fertilization between food studies, gender studies, and race-ethnic studies marked by a plethora of publications, including Inness's four volumes (2001a, 2001b, 2001c, 2005); Abarca's (2006) study of culinary chats among Mexican and Mexican-American working class women; Witt's (1999), Williams-Forson's (2006), Bower's (2008), and Opie's (2008) books on African-American foodways; and Avakian and Haber's (2005) interdisciplinary edited collection on feminist approaches to food studies.

We open this section with Williams-Forson's paper about food stereotypes which uncovers both the harmful effects of controlling images on African Americans, and also the ways in which Black women have resisted oppression and fostered cultural survival by reversing the stereotypes surrounding chicken and using it as a source of income and community bonding. While the food studies literature is replete with work on the female gender and food, there has still been little research on how food and masculinity construct each other beyond Julier and Lindenfeld's (2005b) edited special issue of *Food and Foodways* on "Masculinities and Food." We have included two papers from that issue—in the next section is Parasecoli's on how fitness magazines construct male bodies and food, and in this section is Holden's on how Japanese food television transmits images of ideal masculinity based on power, authority, and consumerism. Holden's article reveals how television can provide exciting new opportunities for foodways research; Swenson's article demonstrates how programs on the American Food Network both challenge and uphold gender binaries that are increasingly problematic in North American culture.

We follow with Allison's fascinating article on how women reproduce Japanese definitions of subservient femininity through their construction of children's lunch boxes, or *obentos*. Counihan uses food-centered life histories to document the voices of traditionally muted Hispanic women of rural southern Colorado who challenge notions that Mexican American women are compliant housewives complacently accepting subservient feeding roles. They reveal differential behaviors and attitudes towards food work that promote empowerment. To avoid limiting understandings of food and gender to heterosexual populations, we have included Carrington's paper on food, gender identity, and power in gay and lesbian households, one of very few published studies of non-heteronormative populations. Carrington finds that food work is associated with femininity and subservience. While the cooks in both sets of families often enact deference by catering to partners' preferences, lesbigay couples implicitly acknowledge the subordinating dimensions of that practice by denying the extent of the feeders' work and the inequality it implies.[6]

Rachel Slocum's article moves the focus on race and gender outside the home to the farmers' market where she looks at intimate interactions between diverse people and food. She uses corporeal feminist theory to suggest how gender and race are constructed in food purchases. Dylan Clark looks at identity constructions in self-defined punks through their food practices and ideologies enacted in a grubby Seattle restaurant called the Black Cat Café. He uses insights from Lévi-Strauss and Marx to examine punk cuisine as a challenge to the capitalist food system and its entrenched inequalities, environmental destruction, and wastefulness. Punks offer an alternative ethic and practice of consumption to demonstrate how eating is an ideological as well as a physical act.

Consumption and Embodiment

In our third section, we include articles that consider eating and the body from variety of disciplinary and topical perspectives. A key issue in Western women's relationship to food and body for hundreds of years has been their unremitting fasting. We have retained Caroline Bynum's striking discussion of how medieval women used food to gain religious and cultural power. By giving food to the poor, exuding milk from their bodies, and relentlessly fasting, they were able to subvert the economic control of husbands and the religious authority of male priests to commune directly with God.[7] Bynum's article sets the historical stage for the following two very different articles on contemporary eating disorders. Philosopher Susan Bordo challenges the notion that troubled eating is restricted to white women, and describes its permeation through-out United States communities of color and around the globe.[8] Anthropologist Richard O'Connor uses interviews with recovered North American anorexics to question the medicalization of anorexia nervosa which is enacted through an enduring mind body dualism, and to show how young anorexics obsess not over beauty but over self-control, an important value in today's society.

While much work has looked at women's difficult relationship to food and body, men do not escape cultural manipulation through ideologies of food and body, as Parasecoli's article demonstrates. He finds that men's fitness magazines alienate men from cooking except in pursuit of sex, reduce eating to a form of body-building, and propose a nearly unattainable ideal of fitness. David Sutton looks at the body in a very different and more positive way by focusing on corporeal cooking skill as an enactment of practical knowledge, sensory awareness, and memory. Combining ethnographic research in Greece and the United States with an analysis of anthro-pological literature on the senses, he explores how cooking tools and sense organs are repositories of tradition that face challenges from the values and practices of moder-nity. Gisèle Yasmeen's article (a different one from that used in the second edition) also broadens the notion of consumption and embodiment by considering the per-formance of gender through public eating in Thai food stalls. In addition to revealing the changing notions of Thai food, she shows how public eating relates to female labor force participation.

Ethnobotanist Gary Paul Nabhan examines the important health aspect of consumption and embodiment in his study of the desert dwelling Seri Indians of Northern Mexico and their rapidly increasing rates of type-two diabetes. Listening to elders who asserted that diabetes was non-existent two generations earlier, and thus rejecting simple genetic explanations for the disease, Nabhan suggests that dietary changes towards high-sugar, low fiber, rapidly digested foods have caused this major health problem and that traditional "slow release" desert foods are protective against diabetes. This research provides support from a nutritional and health perspective for global efforts to promote local foods and traditional agriculture, a goal also endorsed by Robert Albritton. He engages with concerns over food, body, and health with his interrogation of the paradoxical contemporary situation where rates of hunger and obesity increase simultaneously. He shows how an analysis of the political economy of capitalism can explain this paradox, and can provide a path to reforming the food system to promote healthy bodies and well-nourished consumers while sustaining the earth that feeds us all.

Food and Globalization

Globalization is not new; it is not a one way exchange of items and ideas, and certainly not an expansion of values from Euro-America to peripheries lacking their own culinary identities. But it is probably also true that at no time in history has the pace of change been so rapid and so tied up with new technologies. Neoliberal practices such as deregulation and just-in-time production make our global food system even more vulnerable to abuse. It is a challenge for international and national regulatory agencies to keep up with, let alone solve problems caused by this new economic environment.

Food globalization draws our attention to diasporic identities, authenticity, food nostalgia, and power. Srinivas weaves these themes together through her examination of packaged food consumption in Bangalore, India, and Boston, USA. Transnational instant foods, such as chutneys and spice powders, play interesting roles in the construction of female Indian identity among middle class families in the two locations. The loss of home-cooking also occurs in Belize, where families define themselves and their nation through food consumption. Wilk examines historical transformations in Belizean food resulting from colonialism and globalization. Reversing the lens, Heldke examines how food adventurers at home reproduce "cultural food colonialism" by seeking and cooking ethnic foods to satisfy their taste for the exotic other without actually encountering "real" others on their own terms. She raises important questions about the meaning of "authenticity" in food studies. While there have been many critiques leveled against claims about authentic traditional foods, she brings attention to recipe authorship and ownership, challenging scholars and cookbook writers to think about their responsibility to the native cooks whose recipes they appropriate.

Both Leitch and Pilcher examine the ideology and practices of the Slow Food Movement, and its efforts to foster local, sustainable, and just food production. Leitch looks at Slow Food's work in its country of origin, Italy, through a fascinating case study of pork fat—*lardo di Colonnata*—in the Carrara region famous for its marble on which the lard is cured in humid underground cellars. Achievement of protected status for this traditional product raises questions of national autonomy and identity in the context of the European Union's efforts to impose universal food safety standards. Pilcher investigates the relevance of the Slow Food Movement to Mexico's culinary traditions and sees similar issues to those confronted in Italy, as Mexican peasant producers strive for living wages to produce traditional varieties of maize and hand-made tortillas, in competition with industrially processed versions from global chains like Taco Bell.

Pizza is both authentically local and universal; Thai pizza, German pizza, and Japanese pizza exist as hybrid foods in globalized settings. Rossella Ceccarini draws attention not only to hybrid foods, but also to the transnational experiences of the food workers who create these products in Japan. Much like pizza in Japan, hamburgers in China are modern standardized foods. Yan stresses that the attraction of consuming American fast foods has more to do with their social context and meaning than with their taste in his intriguing ethnographic study of McDonald's in Beijing.

Barndt's article introduces us to three women from her long-term project on the tomato food chain (Barndt 2007). Through their stories, we see how agri-businesses, fast food giants, and supermarket chains increasingly rely on "flexible," part-time, low-wage female labor, which enables them to generate huge profits at the expense of women workers who lack health and other benefits, cannot earn a living wage, and must constantly juggle their lives to accommodate their ever-changing work schedules. Food globalization sets up complex problems in households, communities, NGOs, and UN agencies. But as these papers demonstrate, ethnographers are well prepared to shift directions and pick up on subtle changes that reveal the intricacies of global food practices.

Challenging, Contesting, and Transforming the Food System

If the section on Food and Globalization sets readers up for encountering a food system out of the hands of consumers, this last section renews optimism about how individuals and groups are challenging and contesting globalized food systems. Those activists working to transform the food system, however, are working within a new economic context. This section provides examples of some of the recent food activism undertaken since the publication of the second edition of the *Food and Culture Reader*. It is a reminder that all published work needs to be situated in the decade or even year of its writing (as we have done with the papers in this new edition), and that complex issues underlying food activism remain important long after attention has shifted from *boycott Nestle* to *eat local* or *slow food*. Just as every mouthful has a history, every cause has a past, present, and hopefully, a future.

Food activism has been around longer than food studies. What has changed is that only recently have the activities of activists been observed, analyzed, and reflected upon as subjects/objects of research. Most research remains grounded in the political economy of food, but reflects the ever more sophisticated work done in the last decade on how contemporary food systems are changing. The articles demonstrate that food commodification is deeply implicated in perpetuating and concealing gender, race, and class inequalities while transforming cultures.

Case studies on meat (Schlosser), baby foods (Van Esterik) and "yuppie chow" (Guthman) exemplify some of the social implications of the industrial processing of basic foods. Schlosser carries forward the work he did in his renowned *Fast Food Nation* (2002) to examine the many health dangers suffered by meat-packing workers—including broken bones, muscle strain, burns, and severed limbs—resulting from exhausting and monotonous labor for low wages, few benefits, and high turnover. Worker exploitation results from the concentration of the meatpacking industry, its reliance on immigrant labor, its concerted resistance to unionizing efforts, and its political power.

Guthman's insight into organic farming in California is revealed in her groundbreaking research on the subject (2004, 2011). In her study of the salad mixes known by organic farmers as "yuppie chow," she critiques the dualistic thinking that contrasts alternative farming with industrial farming, fast with slow food, and even good with bad eaters. Her work draws attention to the need for increasing class and gender analysis in food studies, which Van Esterik undertakes in her study of how the commodification of infant food through the international marketing of infant formula has had severe economic and health consequences. Activists have constantly challenged the actions of transnational pharmaceutical and food companies promoting industrially processed baby foods. The addendum shows how current advocacy work must adapt to the new economic climate where conflicts of interest and public–private partnerships with food companies are the new normal.

Even food aid has been affected by the concentration of power in the hands of global food industries. Clapp shows how different African societies exercise their rights to limit the import of genetically modified foods even in the face of famine and extreme hunger. The lens of political economy provides fascinating insights into the current obsession with obesity, as Julier shows. Taking a critical functionalist approach, she shows who benefits from blaming the obese for their weight: the government, the diet food and supplement industries, bariatric medical practitioners, and exercise businesses. Blaming individuals for being obese draws attention away from the broader social and economic causes of obesity, including poverty, inadequate food distribution systems, and the excess of unhealthy food available to the poor.

Following the recession of 2008, hunger and food handouts have played an increasingly important role in North American communities. Poppendieck looks at the role of charity in combating food insecurity in the United States. While charity plays a critical role in temporarily abating hunger, it fails to address the poverty and structural inequality that are its real underlying causes (Berg 2008, Fitchen 1988, Lappé and Collins 1986, Patel 2007, Poppendieck 1998, Winne 2008). Priscilla McCutcheon provides another approach to hunger in examining community empowerment through food in her study of two black nationalist religious organizations—one Christian and the other, the Nation of Islam. Her research brings out the complex entanglements of food and racial identity in the American south where self-reliance in food production offered a means to address both hunger and black identity. Charles Levkoe's prize-winning student essay on "Learning Food Democracy through Food Justice Movements" concludes the section and the *Reader* with more examples of successful community organization around food issues. As a form of adult education that promotes engagement with democratic values, the food justice movement in Canada brings together a wide range of food activists who act not simply as food consumers, but as citizens who advocate for changes in food policy.

Food is a particularly powerful lens on capital, labor, health, and the environment. Taken together, these papers force us to re-examine the interconnections between the availability of cheap food in North America and the conditions of its production in other parts of the world. Food advocacy is a growing arena for political activism, as the success of Italy's Slow Food Movement shows. Food unites all humans; its lack strikes a painful chord among haves and have-nots alike. Progress towards social justice can only come through a concerted effort on the part of social activists everywhere to end world hunger and bring about universal access to nutritious and adequate food.

Cross-Cutting Themes

Throughout the five sections of the reader, several themes emerge that can structure how readers approach the book. Theory and method constitute one important theme. While all of the articles are embedded in theory, some explicitly identify theoretical positions: semiotic (Barthes), structuralist (Lévi-Strauss), symbolic (Douglas), materialist (Harris), Marxist (Clark), critical functionalist (Julier), and liberal, advocacy, corporeal, and Third-World feminist (Bordo, Counihan, Slocum, Van Esterik, Williams-Forson).

Articles also employ different methodologies, providing readers with a wealth of information about the different means of investigating the role of food in history and culture. A number of articles use ethnographic approaches; for example, Allison, Carrington, Sutton, and Yan use interviews and participant-observation, and Counihan uses food-centered life histories.[9] Analysis of cultural symbols and meanings is employed by Douglas and Bordo, the former from an anthropological and the latter from a philosophical perspective. Nabhan uses methods of ethnobotany, and Yasmeen of geography, while Bynum, McCutcheon, and Williams-Forson employ fine-grained historical research, and Srinivas, Sutton, and Williams-Forson examine the material culture of food. Holden, Parasecoli, and Swenson analyze the mass media, while several articles analyze restaurants including fast-food and fancy ones in China (Yan), Taco Bell in Mexico (Pilcher), pizza restaurants in Japan (Ceccarini), and street stalls in Thailand (Yasmeen). Together, these articles provide readers with a rich sampling of diverse theories, approaches, and methods to inspire their own research.

Another cross-cutting theme is food as a means of communication. Because of food's multi-sensorial properties of taste, touch, sight, sound, and smell, it has the ability to communicate in a variety of registers and constitutes a form of language (Barthes). Definitions of acceptable and prohibited foods (Lévi-Strauss, Douglas, Harris), stereotypes associating certain groups with certain foods (Williams-Forson), consumption of foods to express belonging (Clark, Heldke) or attain desired states (Parasecoli, Yan), and use of food narratives to speak about the self (Counihan) are all ways that food communicates.

New forms of communication include information technology and social media. Papers on social media are quickly outdated, as technology and apps change quickly. However, future research will no doubt address the incredible opportunity presented by research in cyberspace. What are the implications of people sharing on Facebook every detail about a just-consumed meal, or of dieters using a smart phone app to instantly document the calories and nutritional content of the dish they are about to eat, or of friends living in different parts of the world sharing a meal in cyberspace?

Is this really commensality when eaters watch each other eating the same meal? Photographs shared quickly on social media can provide instant evidence of food safety violations or advertising that "breaks the rules," such as inappropriate ads directed to children, false health claims for specific foods, or promotions advertising infant formula. These images can be sent to food activists quickly, and possibly be addressed just as quickly both by activists and food corporations.

Food as an index of power relations is another significant theme in several articles. Hierarchy and oppression are themes in Williams-Forson's paper on African American women's contested relationship with chicken, Counihan's exploration of differential consciousness among rural *Mexicanas*, and Barndt's and Schlosser's examination of the exploitation of workers. Complex global power dynamics are explored in different ways in Mintz's treatise on the growth of the sugar industry, Van Esterik's analysis of breast vs. bottle feeding of infants, and Heldke's examination of first world consumers' "adventure cooking and eating." Julier addresses how the excoriation of the obese serves to maintain economic and ideological hegemony of elites, while Clark shows how punks explicitly challenge the power of the agro-industrial food system in their veganism and dumpster diving. Many other articles engage with issues of power in the food economy, ideology, and politics.

Access to food is at the heart of food security and human rights, and its denial is a terrible measure of human powerlessness, an issue addressed in different ways by Nabhan's examination of Native Americans' degraded health, Poppendieck's insightful study of food charity, and McCutcheon's examination of Nation of Islam community feeding programs. With the increasing commodification and globalization of food, power issues are revealed not only in access to food but also in the production of local, culturally meaningful foods whose endurance is key to cultural survival, as Wilk, Nabhan, Leitch, Pilcher, and Clapp demonstrate (see Van Esterik 2006b). Integrating the cultural dimensions of food and eating with the legal discourse on human rights is an ongoing challenge of great significance that Ellen Messer's work addresses (Messer 2004, Messer and Cohen 2008).

Concluding Thoughts

The questions we raised at the end of the second edition are worth asking again, as they still deserve the attention of food researchers. What is it about food that makes it an especially intriguing and insightful lens of analysis? What questions about foodways still need to be addressed? How have food regimes changed through time? How does the universal need for food bind individuals and groups together? What are the most serious problems in the global food system and what causes them? What political, economic, social, and ideological structures enhance food sovereignty and social justice, and what structures contribute to inequitable food systems?

Notes

1.   Some recent articles on food and film are Baron 2003, Johnson 2002, Van Esterik 2006a.
2.   Two insightful articles on food and human rights are Bellows 2003, Van Esterik 1999b.

3. M.F.K. Fisher (1954, 1961, 1983) is one of the most lyrical food writers who has inspired countless others.
4. The development of research interests in food in anthropology is as old as the discipline. Early anthropologists recognized the central role of food in different cultures, most notably Audrey Richards (1932, 1939), but also Raymond Firth (1934), Bronislaw Malinowski (1935), M. and S.L. Fortes (1936), and Cora DuBois (1941). Anthropology continues to make important contributions—both ethnographic and theoretical—to the field today. Some influential books on the anthropology of food are Anderson 1988, 2005, Counihan 1999, 2004, Dettwyler 1994, Fink 1998, Goody 1982, Kahn 1986, Kulick and Meneley 2005, Meigs 1984, Mintz 1985, 1997, Nichter 2000, Ohnuki-Tierney 1993, Pollock 1992, Watson 1997, Weismantel 1988, Wilk 2006a, 2006b.
5. See Spang (1988) on anthropologists' work on food during World War II.
6. On the complex relationship between gender, cooking, and power, see Avakian 1997, Avakian and Haber 2005, Charles and Kerr 1988, Counihan 2004, DeVault 1991, Inness 2001a, 2001b, 2001c, Van Esterik 1996, 1997, 1999a, Williams-Forson 2006, and Witt 1999.
7. Some books that examine the religious and ideological dimensions of fasting and dieting are Adams 1990, Bell 1987, Brumberg 1988, Bynum 1987, Griffith 2004, Sack 2005, and Vandereycken and Van Deth 1994.
8. The following are influential studies of women's food restriction: Bruch 1973, 1978, Brumberg 1988, Nichter 2000, Thompson 1994.
9. Often food and eating become critically important parts of ethnographic fieldwork, even when the research did not originally focus on food (cf. Coleman 2011).

References

Abarca, Meredith. 2006. *Voices in the Kitchen: Views of Food and the World from Working-Class Mexican and Mexican American Women*. College Station: Texas A&M University Press.

Adams, Carol. 1990. *The Sexual Politics of Meat: A Feminist-Vegetarian Critical Theory*. New York: Continuum.

Albala, Ken. 2007a. *The Banquet: Dining in the Great Courts of Late Renaissance Europe*. Champagne-Urbana: University of Illinois Press.

Albala, Ken. 2007b. *Beans: A History*. Oxford: Berg.

Anderson, E. N. 1988. *The Food of China*. New Haven: Yale University Press.

Anderson, E. N. 2005. *Everyone Eats: Understanding Food and Culture*. New York: NYU Press.

Appelbaum, Robert. 2006. *Aguecheek's Beef, Belch's Hiccup, and Other Gastronomic Interjections: Literature, Culture, and Food Among the Early Moderns*. Chicago: University of Chicago Press.

Avakian, Arlene Voski, ed. 1997. *Through the Kitchen Window: Women Explore the Intimate Meanings of Food and Cooking*. Boston: Beacon.

Avakian, Arlene Voski and Barbara Haber, eds. 2005. *From Betty Crocker to Feminist Food Studies: Critical Perspectives on Women and Food*. Amherst: University of Massachusetts Press.

Barndt, Deborah, ed. 1999. *Women Working the NAFTA Food Chain: Women, Food and Globalization*. Toronto: Second Story Press.

Barndt, Deborah. 2007. *Tangled Routes: Women, Work, and Globalization on the Tomato Trail*. Lantham, MD: Rowman and Littlefield, 2nd edition.

Baron, Cynthia. 2003. Food and Gender in *Bagdad Café. Food and Foodways*, 11(1):49–74.

Belasco, Warren. 2006. *Meals to Come: A History of the Future of Food*. Berkeley: University of California Press.

Belasco, Warren. 2007. *Appetite for Change*. Ithaca: Cornell University Press. 2nd edition.

Bell, Rudolph M. 1987. *Holy Anorexia*. Chicago: University of Chicago.

Bell, David and Gill Valentine. 1997. *Consuming Geographies: We Are Where We Eat*. New York: Routledge.

Bellows, Anne. 2003. Exposing Violences: Using Women's Human Rights Theory to Reconceptualize Food Rights. *Journal of Agricultural and Environmental Ethics*, 16:249–279.

Berg, Joel. 2008. *All You Can Eat. How Hungry is America?* New York: Seven Stories Press.

Beriss, David and David Sutton. 2007. *The Restaurants Book: Ethnographies of Where We Eat*. New York: Berg.

Bestor, Theodore C. 2004. *Tsukiji: The Fish Market at the Center of the World*. Berkeley: University of California Press.

Bower, Anne, ed. 2004. *Reel Food: Essays on Food and Film*. New York: Routledge.

Bower, Anne, ed. 2008. *African American Foodways: Explorations of History and Culture*. Urbana: University of Illinois Press.

Bruch, Hilde. 1979. *Eating Disorders: Obesity, Anorexia Nervosa, and the Person Within*. New York: Basic Books.

Bruch, Hilde. 2001. *The Golden Cage: The Enigma of Anorexia Nervosa*, with a New Foreword by Catherine Steiner-Adair, Ed.D. Cambridge: Harvard University Press.

Brumberg, Joan Jacobs. 1988. *Fasting Girls: the Emergence of Anorexia Nervosa as a Modern Disease*. Cambridge, MA: Harvard University Press.

Bynum, Caroline Walker. 1987. *Holy Feast and Holy Fast: The Religious Significance of Food to Medieval Women*. Berkeley: University of California Press.

Capatti, Alberto and Massimo Montanari. 2003. *Italian Cuisine: A Cultural History*. New York: Columbia University Press.

Carney, Judith A. 2001. *Black Rice: The African Origins of Rice Cultivation in the Americas*. Cambridge, MA: Harvard University Press.

Carney, Judith A. 2010. *In the Shadow of Slavery: Africa' s Botanical Legacy in the Atlantic World*. Berkeley: University of California Press.

Charles, Nicki and Marion Kerr. 1988. *Women, Food and Families*. Manchester: Manchester University Press.

Claflin, Kyri W. and Peter Scholliers, eds. 2012. *Writing Food History: A Global Perspective*. Oxford: Berg.

Coe, Sophie D. and Michael D. Coe. 2000. *The True History of Chocolate*. London: Thames and Hudson.

Coleman, Leo, ed. 2011. *Food: Ethnographic Encounters*. London: Berg Press.

Conner, Mark and Christopher Armitage. 2002. *The Social Psychology of Food*. London: Open University.

Counihan, Carole. 1999. *The Anthropology of Food and Body: Gender, Meaning and Power*. New York: Routledge.

Counihan, Carole. 2004. *Around the Tuscan Table: Food, Family and Gender in Twentieth Century Florence*. New York: Routledge.

Daniel, Carolyn. 2006. *Voracious Children: Who Eats Whom in Children's Literature*. New York: Routledge.

De Certeau, Michel. 2011. *The Practice of Everyday Life*. Berkeley: University of California Press.

Dettwyler, Katherine. 1994. *Dancing Skeletons: Life and Death in West Africa*. Prospect Heights, IL: Waveland.

DeVault, Marjorie L. 1991. *Feeding the Family: The Social Organization of Caring as Gendered Work*. Chicago: University of Chicago Press.

Du Bois, Cora. 1941. "Attitudes toward Food and Hunger in Alor," In *Language, Culture, and Personality*, LeslieSpier, et al. eds., Menasha, WI: Sapir Memorial Publication Fund, pp. 272–281.

Ferrieres, Madeleine. 2005. *Sacred Cow, Mad Cow: A History of Food Fears*. New York: Columbia University Press.

Ferry, Jane. 2003. *Food in Film: A Culinary Performance of Communication*. New York: Routledge.

Fink, Deborah. 1998. *Cutting into the Meatpacking Line: Workers and Change in the Rural Midwest*. Chapel Hill: University of North Carolina Press.

Firth, Raymond. 1934. The Sociological Study of Native Diet. *Africa*, 7 (4):401–414.

Fisher, M.F.K. 1954. *The Art of Eating*. Cleveland: World Publishing.

Fisher, M.F.K. 1961. *A Cordiall Water: a Garland of Odd and Old Receipts to Assuage the Ills of Man and Beast*. New York: North Point Press.

Fisher, M.F.K. 1983. *As They Were*. New York: Vintage.

Fitchen, Janet M. 1988. Hunger, Malnutrition and Poverty in the Contemporary United States: Some Observations on Their Social and Cultural Context. *Food and Foodways*, 2(3): 309–333.

Flandrin, Jean Louis and Massimo Montanari, eds. 1999. *Food: A Culinary History*. English edition edited by AlbertSonnenfeld. New York: Penguin.

Flynn, Karen Coen. 2005. Food, Culture and Survival in an African City. New York: Palgrave.

Fortes, Myer and S. L. Fortes. 1936. Food in the Domestic Economy of the Tallensi. *Africa*, 9(2):237–276.

Franck, Karen A. ed. 2003. *Food + Architecture*. Academy Press.

Friedberg, Susanne. 2004. *French Beans and Food Scares: Culture and Commerce in an Anxious Age*. New York: Oxford University Press.

Friedberg, Susanne. 2009. *Fresh: A Perishable History*. Cambridge: Belknap Press.

Gabaccia, Donna. 1998. *We Are What We Eat: Ethnic Foods and the Making of Americans*. Cambridge: Harvard University Press.

Gewertz, Deborah and Fred Errington. 2010. *Cheap Meat: Flap Food Nations in the Pacific Islands*. Berkeley: University of California Press.

Gentilcore, David. 2010. *Pomodoro!: A History of the Tomato in Italy*. New York: Columbia University Press.

Goody, Jack. 1982. *Cooking, Cuisine and Class: A Study in Comparative Sociology*. New York: Cambridge.

Griffith, R. Marie. 2004. *Born Again Bodies: Flesh and Spirit in American Christianity*. Berkeley: University of California Press.

Guthman, Julie. 2004. *Agrarian Dreams: The Paradox of Organic Farming in California*. Berkeley: University of California Press.

Guthman, Julie. 2011. *Weighing In: Obesity, Food Justice, and the Limits of Capitalism*. Berkeley: University of California Press.

Heldke, Lisa. 2003. *Exotic Appetites: Ruminations of a Food Adventurer*. New York: Routledge.

Horwitz, Jamie and Paulette Singley, eds. 2006. Eating Architecture. Cambridge, MA: MIT Press.

Howes, David, ed. 2005. *Empire of the Senses: The Sensual Culture Reader*. Oxford: Berg.

Inglis, David and Debra Gimlin. 2010. *The Globalization of Food*. Oxford: Berg.

Inness, Sherrie A. ed. 2001a. *Cooking Lessons: The Politics of Gender and Food*. New York: Rowman and Littlefield.

Inness, Sherrie A. ed. 2001b. *Pilaf, Pozole, and Pad Thai: American Women and Ethnic Food*. Amherst, MA: University of Massachusetts Press.

Inness, Sherrie A. ed. 2001c. *Kitchen Culture in America: Popular Representations of Food, Gender, and Race*. Philadelphia: University of Pennsylvania Press.

Inness, Sherrie A. 2005. *Secret Ingredients: Race, Gender, and Class at the Dinner Table*. New York: Palgrave Macmillan.

Jing, Jun, ed. 2000. Feeding China's Little Emperoros: Food, Children, and Social Change. Stanford: Stanford University Press.

Johnson, Ruth D. 2002. The Staging of the Bourgeois Imaginary in *The Cook, the Thief, His Wife, and Her Lover* (1990). *Cinema Journal*, 41(2):19–40.

Julier, Alice and Laura Lindenfeld. 2005a. Mapping Men onto the Menu: Masculinities and Food. *Food and Foodways*, 13(1–2):1–16.

Julier, Alice and Laura Lindenfeld, eds. 2005b. Masculinities and Food. Special double issue of *Food and Foodways*, 13:1–2.

Kahn, Miriam. 1986. *Always Hungry, Never Greedy: Food and the Expression of Gender in a Melanesian Society*. Cambridge: Cambridge University Press.

Kaplan, David M., ed. 2012. *Philosophy of Food*. Berkeley: University of California Press.

Keller, James R. 2006. *Food, Film and Culture: A Genre Study*. Jefferson, NC: McFarland.

Kent, George. 2007. *Freedom from Want: The Human Right to Adequate Food*. Washington, DC: Georgetown University Press.

Korsmeyer, Carolyn. 2002. *Making Sense of Taste: Food and Philosophy*. Ithaca, NY: Cornell University Press.

Korsmeyer, Carolyn, ed. 2005. *The Taste Culture Reader: Experiencing Food and Drink*. Oxford: Berg.

Kulick, Don and Anne Meneley, eds. 2005. *Fat: The Anthropology of an Obsession*. New York: Penguin.

Kurlansky, Mark. 2003. *Salt: A World History*. New York: Penguin.

Lappé, Frances Moore and Joseph Collins. 1986. *World Hunger: Twelve Myths*. New York: Grove Press.

Lévi-Strauss, Claude. 1978. *The Origin of Table Manners*. London: Jonathan Cape.

Long, Lucy, ed. 2003. *Culinary Tourism*. Lexington: University of Kentucky Press.

Magdoff, Fred, John Bellamy Foster, and Frederick H. Buttel, eds. 2000. *Hungry for Profit: The Agribusiness Threat to Farmers, Food, and the Environment*. New York: Monthly Review Press.

Malinowski, Bronislaw. 1935. *Coral Gardens and their Magic; a Study of the Methods of Tilling the Soil and of Agricultural Rites in the Trobriand Islands*. New York: American Book Co. 2 volumes.

Messer, Ellen. 2004. "Hunger and Human Rights: Old and New Roles for Anthropologists." In *Human Rights: The Scholar as Activist*, C.Nagengast and C.G.Velez-Ibanez, eds. Oklahoma City: Society for Applied Anthropology, pp. 43–63.

Messer, Ellen and Marc J. Cohen. 2008. U.S. Approaches to Food and Nutrition Rights, 1976–2008. *Hunger Notes* http://www.worldhunger.org/articles/08/hrf/toc.htm.

Mintz, Sidney W. 1985. *Sweetness and Power: The Place of Sugar in Modern History*. New York: Penguin.

Mintz, Sidney. 1997. *Tasting Food, Tasting Freedom: Excursions into Eating, Culture, and the Past*. Boston: Beacon.

Montanari, Massimo. 2010. *Cheese, Pears, and History in a Proverb*. Translated by Beth Archer Brombert. New York: Columbia University Press.

Nestle, Marion. 2003. *Food Politics: How the Food Industry Influences Nutrition and Health*. Berkeley: University of California Press.

Nestle, Marion. 2004. *Safe Food: Bacteria, Biotechnology, and Bioterrorism*. Berkeley: University of California Press.

Nichter, Mimi. 2000. *Fat Talk: What Girls and their Parents Say about Dieting*. Cambridge: Harvard University Press.

Ogden, Jane. 2010. *The Psychology of Eating: From Healthy to Disordered Behavior*. Chichester, UK: Wiley-Blackwell.

Ohnuki-Tierney, Emiko. 1993. *Rice as Self: Japanese Identities through Time*. New Brunswick, NJ: Princeton University Press.

Opie, Frederick Douglass. 2008. *Hog and Hominy: Soul Food from Africa to America*. New York: Columbia University Press.

Parasecoli, Fabio and Peter Scholliers, eds. 2012. *A Cultural History of Food*. Oxford: Berg.

Patel, Raj. 2007. *Stuffed and Starved: The Hidden Battle for the World Food System*. Brooklyn, NY: Melville House.

Pojman, Paul. 2011. *Food Ethics*. Boston: Wadsworth.

Pollock, Nancy. 1992. *These Roots Remain: Food Habits in Islands of the Central and Eastern Pacific since Western Contact*. Honolulu: University of Hawaii Press.

Poppendieck, Janet. 1998. *Sweet Charity? Emergency Food and the End of Entitlement*. New York: Penguin.

Ray, Krishnendu. 2004. *The Migrant's Table: Meals and Memories in Bengali-American Households*. Philadelphia: Temple University Press.

Ray, Krishnendu and Tulasi Srinivas. 2012. Curried Cultures: Globalization, Food, and South Asia. Berkeley: University of California Press.

Richards, Audrey I. 1932. *Hunger and Work in a Savage Tribe*. London: Routledge.

Richards, Audrey I. 1939. *Land, Labour and Diet in Northern Rhodesia: An Economic Study of the Bemba Tribe*. Oxford: Oxford University Press.

Sack, Daniel. 2005. *Whitebread Protestants: Food and Religion in American Culture*. New York: Palgrave.

Schlosser, Eric. 2002. *Fast Food Nation: The Dark Side of the All-American Meal*. New York: Harper Collins.

Schwartz, Maxime. 2004. *How the Cows Turned Mad: Unlocking the Mysteries of Mad Cow Disease*. Berkeley: University of California Press.

Singer, Peter and Jim Mason. 2006. *The Ethics of What We Eat: Why Our Food Choices Matter*. Rodale, PA: Rodale Press.

Skubal, Susan. 2002. *Word of Mouth: Food and Fiction After Freud*. New York: Routledge.

Smith, Andrew. 2006. *The Turkey: An American Story*. Champagne-Urbana: University of Illinois Press.

Spang, Rebecca L. 1988. The Cultural Habits of a Food Committee. *Food and Foodways*, 2(4): 359–391.

Sutton, David E. 2001. *Remembrance of Repasts: An Anthropology of Food and Memory*. Oxford: Berg.

Telfer, Elizabeth. 2005. *Food for Thought: Philosophy and Food*. New York: Routledge.

Thompson, Becky. 1994. *A Hunger So Wide and So Deep: American Women Speak Out on Eating Problems*. Minneapolis: University of Minnesota Press.

Turner, Jack. 2004. *Spice: the History of a Temptation*. New York: Vintage Books.

Van Esterik, Penny. 1996. The Cultural Context of Breastfeeding and Breastfeeding Policy. *Food and Nutrition Bulletin,* 17(4):422–431.

Van Esterik, Penny. 1997. Women and Nurture in Industrial Societies. *Proceedings of the Nutrition Society*, 56(1B): 335–343.

Van Esterik, Penny. 1999a. "Gender and Sustainable Food Systems: a Feminist Critique." In *For Hunger-Proof Cities: Sustainable Urban Food Systems*, M.Koc, R.MacRae, L.Mougeot and J.Welsh, eds. Ottawa: IDRC, pp.157–161.

Van Esterik, Penny. 1999b. Right to Food; Right to Feed; Right to Be Fed. the Intersection of Women's Rights and the Right to Food. *Agriculture and Human Values*, 16:225–232.

Van Esterik, Penny. 2005. No Free Lunch. *Agriculture and Human Values*, 22:207–208.

Van Esterik, Penny. 2006a. Anna and the King: Digesting Difference. *Southeast Asian Research*, 14(2):289–307.

Van Esterik, Penny. 2006b. "From Hunger Foods to Heritage Foods: Challenges to Food Localization in Lao PDR." In *Fast Food/Slow Food: The Cultural Economy of the Global Food System*, R.Wilk, ed., Lanham, Md.: Altimira Press, pp. 83–96.

Vandereycken, Walter and Ron Van Deth. 1994. *From Fasting Saints to Anorexic Girls: The History of Self-Starvation*. New York: New York University Press.

Van Gelder, Geert Jan. 2000. *God's Banquet: Food in Classical Arabic Literature*. New York: Columbia University Press.

Watson, James L., ed. 1997. *Golden Arches East: McDonald's in East Asia*. Stanford: Stanford University Press.

Weismantel, M. J. 1988. *Food, Gender and Poverty in the Ecuadorian Andes*. Philadelphia: University of Pennsylvania Press.

Wenche Barth, Eide and Uwe Kracht, eds. 2005. *Human Rights and Development*. Antwerp: Intersentia.

Wiley, Andrea. 2010. *Re-imagining Milk: Cultural and Biological Perspectives*. New York: Routledge.

Wilk, Richard. 2006a. *Home Cooking in the Global Village: Caribbean Food from Buccaneers to Ecotourists*. Oxford: Berg.

Wilk, Richard, ed. 2006b. *Fast Food/Slow Food: The Cultural Economy of the Global Food System*. Lantham: Altamira.

Williams-Forson, Psyche A. 2006. *Building Houses out of Chicken Legs : Black Women, Food, and Power*. Chapel Hill: University of North Carolina Press.

Williams-Forson, Psyche and Carole Counihan, eds. 2012. *Taking Food Public: Redefining Foodways in a Changing World*. New York: Routledge.

Winne, Mark. 2008. *Closing the Food Gap: Resetting the Table in the Land of Plenty*. Boston: Beacon Press.

Witt, Doris. 1999. *Black Hunger: Food and the Politics of U.S. Identity*. New York: Oxford University Press.

Wrangham, Richard. 2010. *Catching Fire: How Cooking Made Us Human*. New York: Basic Books.

Yasmeen, Gisèle. 2006. *Bangkok's Foodscape*. Bangkok: White Lotus Press.

Foundations

1

Why Do We Overeat?*

Margaret Mead

Holiday cheer inevitably means a great abundance of food and drink—delicious, tempting and for most of us a hazard.

How often during the Christmas holidays have you heard someone say, "Well, just a *little* more—I can't resist"? How often have you yourself said, "I really shouldn't …"? The pressure to enjoy all these varied good things is very great. But in the back of many people's minds there is the thought, After New Year's I'll go on a diet.

Feasting at festivals and eating meagerly in the long intervals between great events is a way of handling food that is very widespread among the peoples of the world who seldom have more than just enough to live on. It is one way of coping with perennial scarcity that allows everyone to share occasionally a very limited supply of foods that are really good.

But this is no longer our way. Daily abundance of food is one of the main characteristics of our very affluent society. So abundant, in fact, is food that many—perhaps most—Americans find it almost impossible to believe that there are millions among us who do not have access to sufficient food.

For the majority of Americans food is omnipresent. Supermarkets, hot-dog stands, candy counters, snack bars, soft-drink machines and a constant stream of highly colored advertisements continually keep the possibility of eating before us. For holidays we make a special effort to buy and prepare foods that take time, effort and thought—foods that demonstrate how far we have come in learning to treat cooking and the enjoyment of eating as an art. But holidays are only a high point. We have contrived to construct a world in which food in great variety is present everywhere at all times of the year.

So the problem for great numbers of Americans is not how to get enough food or how to be well nourished. Instead it is how to fend off the insistent pressure to eat. It has been estimated that at least one in five Americans is ten per cent or more overweight—in most cases the consequence of giving in to that pressure and eating too much. It has been estimated variously, also, that some 10 to 20 million Americans at any one time are dieting—some because they are fat and others because they "feel fat" in relation to current styles.

*Originally published 1971

The vast proliferation of nonfattening and nonnourishing foods in the past decade represents one attempt to cope with the situation—how to eat "harmlessly." There are also the shelves of books on dieting, the books on exercising and the dozens of devices advertised everywhere that are guaranteed to trim one down. All are evidence of good business appreciation of the anxieties we feel and the dilemma we find ourselves in as a result of our present style of eating.

For the truth is, Americans are extremely intolerant of people who, as we see it, "let themselves go." This applies to anyone who neglects to "fix" anything physical that can be remedied. It is the responsibility of parents to make the best of each child; but we believe that adults, as individuals, have control over their own bodies and should demonstrate through the care they exercise both how they see themselves and how they wish to be seen in their relations to others. There are handicaps, clearly, that cannot be overcome. But everyone can try. To make the most of oneself, we say, is good. To give up is wrong.

Today this moral attitude places a very heavy burden on one group—a very mixed group—in our society. This is the group of all those who, for whatever reason, are obese. No fashions are designed for them. No furniture is built for them. Potentially or actually, they are outcasts.

We believe it is wrong to be obese. It shows a lack of character, a disregard for health and a blatant lack of self-discipline. In the light of this belief, all kinds of obesity are lumped together. We treat as similar in kind the overweight of glandular imbalance, weight put on during pregnancy, weight that comes to the lonely girl who eats comforting chocolates that make her fatter and even less likely to get a date and weight that is a response to feelings of unworthiness. Detailed studies have shown that there are many and very different origins of overweight.

But to the average person who is deciding whether to accept a student or whether to hire someone for a job or to promote someone to a higher position, who is anxiously watching the girls a son is dating or (less often) the boys a daughter is dating, obesity is just obesity—unattractive, unacceptable and reprehensible. Back of all the comments, the warnings and the cutting jokes lies the moral reproof "You should lose weight, and you could if you would."

Those who succeed in keeping down their weight—or in getting it down within acceptable limits—count their virtues, suffer for their sins and denigrate others who fail or obviously won't try. Certainly it is important for us to feel that we are in control of our own well-being. But are the obese really sinners? Why today do we still have these puritanical attitudes about eating? Is it necessary to invoke guilt to control our enjoyment of plenty?

The Weight Watchers movement, which has swept the country in the past eight years, gains its greatest strength from the belief that those who try and succeed are good and will be rewarded. Like Alcoholics Anonymous and other groups that use like mindedness as a kind of external conscience to bolster up the will to reform and improve oneself, Weight Watchers expresses a peculiarly American idea. This is the idea that the best way to do something you don't want to do is to get others in the same situation to meet with you and to support you whenever your resolve to kick the habit flickers.

As the obese so often describe themselves (echoing the beliefs and attitudes of those around them), they are people who can't resist indulging their gluttonous greed; who hide their compulsive eating from one another, their families, their spouses and friends; and who come in time to lie even to themselves. Confessing their familiar sins to each other, as is done in all such mutual-support groups, helps them to face themselves and so to take each necessary step in the arduous and painful process of dieting to lose 50,100 or even 200 pounds of cumbersome, misery-making weight. But there is a reward. In the words of Jean Nidetch (the inventor of the movement, who calls herself a Formerly Fat Housewife), getting down to normal size will "make you confident that you are capable of controlling your own body, that you are not the victim of your compulsions."

The system works—after a fashion. Given sufficient support, many of the overweight can suffer their way toward a "normal" figure and perhaps better health. But the various ways we have devised to deal with overweight do not come to grips with the fundamental question: Why do we have this constant struggle with food? Is there no other way?

Recently a movement has been formed called the National Association to Aid Fat Americans (NAAFA), whose founders picture the obese as another persecuted minority. They may well point out some of the injustices suffered by the overweight. But this is likely at best to strengthen the resolve of those who diet to escape the penalties of being fat.

Our peculiar attitudes toward food in this country become even clearer when one looks at another group—the rebellious young. Just as they have rejected so much else that they regard as part of the corrupt adult world, they have rejected the food habits they were taught. In spite of their emphasis on the values of "natural" food, few of them have any real knowledge of sound nutrition. Many are extreme food faddists. Often they are painfully thin, and in many cases seriously malnourished.

We do not condemn them for being thin; most people would like to be thin. But their situation is serious, for their health may be permanently impaired. Even more serious may be the impairment to the health of their children. Very recent studies have shown that adequate prenatal nutrition, which in most cases permits a pregnant woman to gain at least 25 pounds, can mean the difference between a handicapped and a flourishing baby.

Both the obese and the rebellious young are victims—victims of our obsolete attitude toward food and eating. The obese, whom we treat as sinners, are scapegoats for all of us, made to suffer as examples of what many of us fear we might become—if we let ourselves go. They feel left out. For them, getting thinner means a chance to re-enter society—a chance to go to a good college, to get a good job, to make friends, to marry and to be a part of what is going on. The youthful rebels, in contrast, reject our accepted eating habits as part of their search for a new life-style.

But so are we all victims. The real problem is one all of us must face. Most Americans find themselves in the ambiguous situation of having to fight what they enjoy—of feasting and then guiltily fasting in order to be "good." And the question is this: Must the next generation face the same dilemma?

The basic difficulty, I think, is that we have carried over into the present outmoded methods of teaching children how and what to eat, and we back up this teaching with inappropriate moral attitudes toward food.

In the past, when the quantity and variety of foods were much more limited, meals could be extremely monotonous. Then mothers urged and begged and forced children to eat the food set before them three times a day. There was no alternative. The good child dutifully ate the dull food "that is good for you." The reward was dessert, Sunday dinner, holiday fare, the rare treat, all the pleasant and delicious foods that were "good." The child (and the adult too, of course) who uncomplainingly ate the plain, nourishing everyday fare was morally justified in enjoying what came afterward as a sign that all was well.

We still plan our three meals a day in the same way, treating them as if they constituted all the food available to us. We still teach children to be "good" through food—and to express rebellion by not eating the right food. We still treat some foods (the kinds we define as "good, but not really good for you") as rewards and signs of love. There is one major change, but this serves only to reinforce what we teach and believe: Adults, having eaten too much, go on a diet that they treat as difficult, unpleasant and intrinsically unrewarding. Children should be good first; adults do penance afterward.

We punish the obese. But we all have become the victims of this outmoded style.

Recognizing this, we can help our children to eat in a new style.

First I think we can give up using food as a punishment and a reward—as a symbol of a duty performed (or neglected), a consolation or an accolade. Where food is so plentiful, food can be food and the focus of our feeling can be directed toward the pleasure of sharing a meal with others.

Second we can recognize the fact that the rule of "there square meals a day" has become a kind of strait jacket. We would do better to take into account the variations in individual rhythms in the need for food as well as the different rhythms in the working day for different people. A generation ago we began infant feeding on a flexible, self-demand basis—and there we stopped. More realistically, however, eating on the basis of self-demand could be the beginning of self-discovery and flexibility, throughout childhood and on into adulthood.

In the past children were taught to eat. If they were thin, they should eat more; if they stuffed, they were deprived of good things. But in the last generation, those children who were brought up with a genuine sense of self-demand within the bounds of sensible nutrition are the ones who, as adults, have kept a relaxed sense of what their physical need for food is and what they can enjoy. This capacity to follow their individual rhythms in eating would really give people a sense of personal—instead of arbitrarily determined—control over their own bodies. Less punitive toward ourselves, I think, we would become less punitive toward others who differed from us.

Finally, the whole world today is linked through food, the food that some have in superabundance and others urgently need. By freeing our children from the strictures of conscience about their personal consumption of food, they would be freer to think of shared food as a source of well-being for everyone everywhere.

2

Toward a Psychosociology of Contemporary Food Consumption[*]

Roland Barthes

The inhabitants of the United States consume almost twice as much sugar as the French.[1] Such a fact is usually a concern of economics and politics. But this is by no means all. One needs only to take the step from sugar as merchandise, an abstract item in accounts, to sugar as food, a concrete item that is "eaten" rather than "consumed," to get an inkling of the (probably unexplored) depth of the phenomenon. For the Americans must do something with all that sugar. And as a matter of fact, anyone who has spent time in the United States knows that sugar permeates a considerable part of American cooking; that it saturates ordinarily sweet foods, such as pastries; makes for a great variety of sweets served, such as ice creams, jellies, syrups; and is used in many dishes that French people do not sweeten, such as meats, fish, salads, and relishes. This is something that would be of interest to scholars in fields other than economics, to the psychosociologist, for example, who will have something to say about the presumably invariable relation between standard of living and sugar consumption. (But is this relation really invariable today? And if so, why?)[2] It could be of interest to the historian also, who might find it worthwhile to study the ways in which the use of sugar evolved as part of American culture (the influence of Dutch and German immigrants who were used to "sweet-salty" cooking?). Nor is this all. Sugar is not just a foodstuff, even when it is used in conjunction with other foods; it is, if you will, an "attitude," bound to certain usages, certain "protocols," that have to do with more than food. Serving a sweet relish or drinking a Coca-Cola with a meal are things that are confined to eating habits proper; but to go regularly to a dairy bar, where the absence of alcohol coincides with a great abundance of sweet beverages, means more than to consume sugar; through the sugar, it also means to experience the day, periods of rest, traveling, and leisure in a specific fashion that is certain to have its impact on the American. For who would claim that in France wine is only wine? Sugar or wine, these two superabundant substances are also institutions. And these institutions necessarily imply a set of images, dreams, tastes, choices, and values. I remember an American hit song: *Sugar Time*. Sugar is a time, a category of the world.[3]

I have started out with the example of the American use of sugar because it permits us to get outside of what we, as Frenchmen, consider "obvious." For we do not see our own food or, worse, we assume that it is insignificant. Even—or perhaps

[*]*Originally published 1961*

especially—to the scholar, the subject of food connotes triviality or guilt.[4] This may explain in part why the psychosociology of French eating habits is still approached only indirectly and in passing when more weighty subjects, such as life-styles, budgets, and advertising, are under discussion. But at least the sociologists, the historians of the present—since we are talking only about contemporary eating habits here— and the economists are already aware that there is such a thing.

Thus P.H. Chombart de Lauve has made an excellent study of the behavior of French working-class families with respect to food. He was able to define areas of frustration and to outline some of the mechanisms by which needs are transformed into values, necessities into alibis.[5] In her book *Le mode de vie des familles bourgeoises de 1873 à 1953*, M. Perrot came to the conclusion that economic factors played a less important role in the changes that have taken place in middle-class food habits in the last hundred years than changing tastes; and this really means ideas, especially about nutrition.[6] Finally, the development of advertising has enabled the economists to become quite conscious of the ideal nature of consumer goods; by now everyone knows that the product as bought—that is, experienced—by the consumer is by no means the real product; between the former and the latter there is a considerable production of false perceptions and values. By being faithful to a certain brand and by justifying this loyalty with a set of "natural" reasons, the consumer gives diversity to products that are technically so identical that frequently even the manufacturer cannot find any differences. This is notably the case with most cooking oils.[7]

It is obvious that such deformations or reconstructions are not only the manifestation of individual, anomic prejudices, but also elements of a veritable collective imagination showing the outlines of a certain mental framework. All of this, we might say, points to the (necessary) widening of the very notion of food. For what is food? It is not only a collection of products that can be used for statistical or nutritional studies. It is also, and at the same time, a system of communication, a body of images, a protocol of usages, situations, and behavior. Information about food must be gathered wherever it can be found: by direct observation in the economy, in techniques, usages, and advertising; and by indirect observation in the mental life of a given society.[8] And once these data are assembled, they should no doubt be subjected to an internal analysis that should try to establish what is significant about the way in which they have been assembled before any economic or even ideological determinism is brought into play. I should like to give a brief outline of what such an analysis might be.

When he buys an item of food, consumes it, or serves it, modern man does not manipulate a simple object in a purely transitive fashion; this item of food sums up and transmits a situation; it constitutes an information; it signifies. That is to say that it is not just an indicator of a set of more or less conscious motivations, but that it is real sign, perhaps the functional unit of a system of communication. By this I mean not only the elements of *display* in food, such as foods involved in rites of hospitality,[9] for all food serves as a sign among the members of a given society. As soon as a need is satisfied by standardized production and consumption, in short, as soon as it takes on the characteristics of an institution, its function can no longer be dissociated from the sign of that function. This is true for clothing;[10] it is also true for food. No doubt, food is, anthropologically speaking (though very much in the abstract), the first need; but ever since man has ceased living off wild berries, this need has been highly structured. Substances, techniques of preparation, habits, all become part of a system of differences in signification; and as soon as this happens, we have communication by way of food. For the fact that there is communication is proven, not by the more or less vague consciousness that its users may have of it, but by the ease with which all the facts concerning food form a structure analogous to other systems of communication.[11] People may very well continue to believe that food is an immediate reality (necessity or pleasure), but this does not prevent it from carrying a system of communication; it would not be the first thing that people continue to experience as a simple function at the very moment when they constitute it into a sign.

If food is a system, what might be its constituent units? In order to find out, it would obviously be necessary to start out with a complete inventory of all we know of the food in a given society (products, techniques, habits), and then to subject these facts to what the linguists call transformational analysis, that is, to observe whether the passage from one fact to another produces a difference in signification. Here is an example: the changeover from ordinary bread to *pain de mie* involves a difference in what is signified: the former signifies day-to-day life, the latter a party. Similarly, in contemporary terms, the changeover from white to brown bread corresponds to a change in what is signified in social terms, because, paradoxically, brown bread has become a sign of refinement. We are therefore justified in considering the varieties of bread as units of signification—at least these varieties—for the same test can also show that there are insignificant varieties as well, whose use has nothing to do with a collective institution, but simply with individual taste. In this manner, one could, proceeding step by step, make a compendium of the differences in signification regulating the system of our food. In other words, it would be a matter of separating the significant from the insignificant and then of reconstructing the differential system of signification by constructing, if I may be permitted to use such a metaphor, a veritable grammar of foods.

It must be added that the units of our system would probably coincide only rarely with the products in current use in the economy. Within French society, for example, bread as such does not constitute a signifying unit: in order to find these we must go further and look for certain of its varieties. In other words, these signifying units are more subtle than the commercial units and, above all, they have to do with subdivisions with which production is not concerned, so that the sense of the sub-division can differentiate a single product. Thus it is not at the level of its cost that the sense of a food item is elaborated, but at the level of its preparation and use. There is perhaps no natural item of food that signifies anything in itself, except for a few deluxe items such as salmon, caviar, truffles, and so on, whose preparation is less important than their absolute cost.

If the units of our system of food are not the *products* of our economy, can we at least have some preliminary idea of what they might be? In the absence of a systematic inventory, we may risk a few hypotheses. A study by P.F. Lazarsfeld[12] (it is old, concerned with particulars, and I cite it only as an example) has shown that certain sensorial "tastes" can vary according to the income level of the social groups interviewed: lower-income persons like sweet chocolates, smooth materials, strong perfumes; the upper classes, on the other hand, prefer bitter substances, irregular materials, and light perfumes. To remain within the area of food, we can see that signification (which, itself, refers to a twofold social phenomenon: upper classes/lower classes) does not involve kinds of products, but flavors: *sweet* and *bitter* make up the opposition in signification, so that we must place certain units of the system of food on that level. We can imagine other classes of units, for example, opposite substances such as dry, creamy, watery ones, which immediately show their great psychoanalytical potential (and it is obvious that if the subject of food had not been so trivialized and invested with guilt, it could easily be subjected to the kind of "poetic" analysis that G. Bachelard applied to language). As for what is considered tasty, C. Lévi-Strauss has already shown that this might very well constitute a class of oppositions that refers to national characters (French versus English cuisine, French versus Chinese or German cuisine, and so on).[13]

Finally, one can imagine opposites that are even more encompassing, but also more subtle. Why not speak, if the facts are sufficiently numerous and sufficiently clear, of a certain "spirit" of food, if I may be permitted to use this romantic term? By this I mean that a coherent set of food traits and habits can constitute a complex but homogeneous dominant feature useful for defining a general system of tastes and habits. This "spirit" brings together different units (such as flavor or substance), forming a composite unit with a single signification, somewhat analogous to the suprasegmental prosodic units of language. I should like to suggest here two very different examples. The ancient Greeks unified in a single (euphoric) notion the ideas of succulence, brightness, and moistness, and they called it *yávos*. Honey had *yávos*, and wine was the *yávos* of the vineyard.[14] Now this would certainly be a signifying unit if we were to establish the system of food of the Greeks, even though it does not refer to any particular item. And here is another example, modern this time. In the United States, the Americans seem to oppose the category of sweet (and we have already seen to how many different varieties of foods this applies) with an equally general category that is not, however, that of salty—understandably so, since their food is salty and sweet to begin with—but that of *crisp* or *crispy*. *Crisp* designates everything that crunches, crackles, grates, sparkles, from potato chips to certain brands of beer; *crisp*—and this shows that the unit of food can overthrow logical categories—*crisp* may be applied to a product just because it is ice cold, to another because it is sour, to a third because it is brittle. Quite obviously, such a notion goes beyond the purely physical nature of the product; *crispness* in a food designates an almost magical quality, a certain briskness and sharpness, as opposed to the soft, soothing character of sweet foods.

Now then, how will we use the units established in this manner? We will use them to reconstruct systems, syntaxes ("menus"), and styles ("diets")[15] no longer in an empirical but in a semantic way—in a way, that is, that will enable us to compare them to each other. We now must show, not that which is, but that which signifies. Why? Because we are interested in human communication and because communication always implies a system of signification, that is, a body of discrete signs standing out from a mass of indifferent materials. For this reason, sociology must, as soon as it deals with cultural "objects" such as clothing, food, and—not quite as clearly—housing, structure these objects before trying to find out what society does with them. For what society does with them is precisely to structure them in order to make use of them.

To what, then, can these significations of food refer? As I have already pointed out, they refer not only to display,[16] but to a much larger set of themes and situations. One could say that an entire "world" (social environment) is present in and signified by food.

Today we have a tool with which to isolate these themes and situations, namely, advertising. There is no question that advertising provides only a projected image of reality; but the sociology of mass communication has become increasingly inclined to think that large-scale advertising, even though technically the work of a particular group, reflects the collective psychology much more than it shapes it. Furthermore, studies of motivation are now so advanced that it is possible to analyze cases in which the response of the public is negative. (I already mentioned the feelings of guilt fostered by an advertising for sugar which emphasized pure enjoyment. It was bad advertising, but the response of the public was nonetheless psychologically most interesting.)

A rapid glance at food advertising permits us rather easily, I think, to identify three groups of themes. The first of these assigns to food a function that is, in some sense, commemorative: food permits a person (and I am here speaking of French themes) to partake each day of the national past. In this case, this historical quality is obviously linked to food techniques (preparation and cooking). These have long roots, reaching back to the depth of the French past. They are, we are told, the repository of a whole experience, of the accumulated wisdom of our ancestors. French food is never supposed to be innovative, except when it rediscovers long-forgotten secrets. The historical theme, which was so often sounded in our advertising, mobilizes two different values: on the one hand, it implies an aristocratic tradition (dynasties of manufacturers, *moutarde du Roy*, the Brandy of Napoleon); on the other hand, food frequently carries notions of representing the flavorful survival of an old, rural society that is itself highly idealized.[17] In this manner, food brings the memory of the soil into our very contemporary life; hence the paradoxical association of gastronomy and industrialization in the form of canned "gourmet dishes." No doubt the myth of French cooking abroad (or as expressed to foreigners) strengthens this "nostalgic" value of food considerably; but since the French themselves actively participate in this myth (especially when traveling), it is fair to say that through his food the Frenchman experiences a certain national continuity. By way of a thousand detours, food permits him to insert himself daily into his own past and to believe in a certain culinary "being" of France.[18]

A second group of values concerns what we might call the anthropological situation of the French consumer. Motivation studies have shown that feelings of inferiority were attached to certain foods and that people therefore abstained from them.[19] For example, there are supposed to be masculine and feminine kinds of food. Furthermore, visual advertising makes it possible to associate certain kinds of foods with images connoting a sublimated sexuality. In a certain sense, advertising eroticizes food and thereby transforms our consciousness of it, bringing it into a new sphere of situations by means of a pseudocausal relationship.

Finally, a third area of consciousness is constituted by a whole set of ambiguous values of a somatic as well as psychic nature, clustering around the concept of *health*. In a mythical way, health is indeed a simple relay midway between the body and the mind; it is the alibi food gives to itself in order to signify materially a pattern of immaterial realities. Health is thus experienced through food only in the form of "conditioning," which implies that the body is able to cope with a certain number of day-to-day situations. Conditioning originates with the body but goes beyond it. It produces *energy* (sugar, the "powerhouse of foods," at least in France, maintains an "uninterrupted flow of energy"; margarine "builds solid muscles"; coffee "dissolves fatigue");

alertness ("Be alert with Lustucru"), and *relaxation* (coffee, mineral water, fruit juices, Coca-Cola, and so on). In this manner, food does indeed retain its physiological function by giving strength to the organism, but this strength is immediately sublimated and placed into a specific situation (I shall come back to this in a moment). This situation may be one of conquest (alertness, aggressiveness) or a response to the stress of modern life (relaxation). No doubt, the existence of such themes is related to the spectacular development of the science of nutrition, to which, as we have seen, one historian unequivocally attributes the evolution of food budgets over the last fifty years. It seems, then, that the acceptance of this new value by the masses has brought about a new phenomenon, which must be the first item of study in any psychosociology of food: it is what might be called nutritional consciousness. In the developed countries, food is henceforth *thought out*, not by specialists, but by the entire public, even if this thinking is done within a framework of highly mythical notions. Nor is this all. This nutritional rationalizing is aimed in a specific direction. Modern nutritional science (at least according to what can be observed in France) is not bound to any moral values, such as asceticism, wisdom, or purity,[20] but on the contrary, to values of *power*. The energy furnished by a consciously worked out diet is mythically directed, it seems, toward an adaptation of man to the modern world. In the final analysis, therefore, a representation of contemporary existence is implied in the consciousness we have of the function of our food.[21]

For, as we said before, food serves as a sign not only for themes, but also for situations; and this, all told, means for a way of life that is emphasized, much more than expressed, by it. To eat is a behavior that develops beyond its own ends, replacing, summing up, and signalizing other behaviors, and it is precisely for these reasons that it is a sign. What are these other behaviors? Today, we might say all of them: activity, work, sports, effort, leisure, celebration—every one of these situations is expressed through food. We might almost say that this "polysemia" of food characterizes modernity; in the past, only festive occasions were signalized by food in any positive and organized manner. But today, work also has its own kind of food (on the level of a sign, that is): energy-giving and light food is experienced as the very sign of, rather than only a help toward, participation in modern life. The snack bar not only responds to a new need, it also gives a certain dramatic expression to this need and shows those who frequent it to be modern men, managers who exercise power and control over the extreme rapidity of modern life. Let us say that there is an element of "Napoleonism" in this ritually condensed, light, and rapid kind of eating. On the level of institutions, there is also the business lunch, a very different kind of thing, which has become commercialized in the form of special menus: here, on the contrary, the emphasis is placed on comfort and long discussions; there even remains a trace of the mythical conciliatory power of conviviality. Hence, the business lunch emphasizes the gastronomic, and under certain circumstances traditional, value of the dishes served and uses this value to stimulate the euphoria needed to facilitate the transaction of business. Snack bar and business lunch are two very closely related work situations, yet the food connected with them signalizes their differences in a perfectly readable manner. We can imagine many others that should be catalogued.

This much can be said already: today, at least in France, we are witnessing an extraordinary expansion of the areas associated with food: food is becoming incorporated into an ever-lengthening list of situations. This adaptation is usually made in the name of hygiene and better living, but in reality, to stress this fact once more, food is also charged with signifying the situation in which it is used. It has a twofold value, being nutrition as well as protocol, and its value as protocol becomes increasingly more important as soon as the basic needs are satisfied, as they are in France. In other words, we might say that in contemporary French society *food has a constant tendency to transform itself into situation.*

There is no better illustration for this trend than the advertising mythology about coffee. For centuries, coffee was considered a stimulant to the nervous system (recall that Michelet claimed that it led to the Revolution), but contemporary advertising, while not expressly denying this traditional function, paradoxically associates it more and more with images of "breaks," rest, and even relaxation. What is the reason for this shift? It is that coffee is felt to be not so much a substance[22] as a circumstance. It is the recognized occasion for interrupting work and using this respite in a precise protocol of taking sustenance. It stands to reason that if this transferral of the food substance to its use becomes really all-encompassing, the power signification of food will be vastly increased. Food, in short, will lose in substance and gain in function; this function will be general and point to activity (such as the business lunch) or to times of rest (such as coffee); but since there is a very marked opposition between work and relaxation, the traditionally festive function of food is apt to disappear gradually, and society will arrange the signifying system of its food around two major focal points: on the one hand, activity (and no longer work), and on the other hand, leisure (no longer celebration). All of this goes to show, if indeed it needs to be shown, to what extent food is an organic system, organically integrated into its specific type of civilization.

Notes

This article originally appeared in "Vers une psycho-sociologie de l'alimentation moderne" by Roland Barthes, in *Annales: Économies, Sociétés, Civilisations* no. 5 (September–October 1961), pp. 977–986. Reprinted by permission of Annales.

1. Annual sugar consumption in the United States is 43 kg. per person; in France 25 kg. per person.
2. F. Charny, *Le sucre*, Collection "Que sais-je?" (Paris: P. U. F., 1950), p. 8.
3. I do not wish to deal here with the problem of sugar "metaphors" or paradoxes, such as the "sweet" rock singers or the sweet milk beverages of certain "toughs."
4. Motivation studies have shown that food advertisements openly based on enjoyment are apt to fail, since they make the reader feel guilty (J. Marcus-Steiff, *Les études de motivation* [Paris: Hermann, 1961], pp. 44–45).
5. P. H. Chombart de Lauwe, *La vie quotidienne des familles ouvrières* (Paris: C.N.R.S., 1956).
6. Marguerite Perrot, *Le mode de vie des familles bourgeoises, 1873–1953* (Paris: Colin, 1961). "Since the end of the nineteenth century, there has been a very marked evolution in the dietary habits of the middle-class families we have investigated in this study. This evolution seems related, not to a change in the standard of living, but rather to a transformation of individual tastes under the influence of a greater awareness of the rules of nutrition" (p. 292).
7. J. Marcus-Steiff, *Les études de motivation*, p. 28.
8. On the latest techniques of investigation, see again J. Marcus-Steiff, *Les études de motivation*.
9. Yet on this point alone, there are many known facts that should be assembled and systematized: cocktail parties, formal dinners, degrees and kinds of display by way of food according to the different social groups.
10. R. Barthes, "Le bleu est à la mode cette année: Note sur la recherche des unités signifiantes dans le vêtement de mode," *Revue française de sociologie* 1 (1960): 147–162.
11. I am using the word structure in the sense that it has in linguistics: "an autonomous entity of internal dependencies" (L. Hjelnislev, *Essais linguistiques* [Copenhagen, 1959], p. 1).

12. P. F. Lazarsfeld, "The Psychological Aspect of Market Research," *Harvard Business Review* 13 (1934): 54–71.

13. C. Lévi-Strauss, *Anthropologie structurale* (Paris: Plon, 1958), p. 99.

14. H. Jeanmaire, *Dionysos* (Paris: Payot), p. 510.

15. In a semantic analysis, vegetarianism, for example (at least at the level of specialized restaurants), would appear as an attempt to copy the appearance of meat dishes by means of a series of artifices that are somewhat similar to "costume jewelry" in clothing, at least the jewelry that is meant to be seen as such.

16. The idea of social *display* must not be associated purely and simply with vanity; the analysis of motivation, when conducted by indirect questioning, reveals that worry about appearances is part of an extremely subtle reaction and that social strictures are very strong, even with respect to food.

17. The expression *cuisine bourgeoise*, used at first in a literal, then in a metaphoric way, seems to be gradually disappearing while the "peasant stew" is periodically featured in the photographic pages of the major ladies' magazines.

18. The exotic nature of food can, of course, be a value, but in the French public at large, it seems limited to coffee (tropical) and pasta (Italian).

19. This would be the place to ask just what is meant by "strong" food. Obviously, there is no psychic quality inherent in the thing itself. A food becomes "masculine" as soon as women, children, and old people, for nutritional (and thus fairly historical) reasons, do not consume it.

20. We need only to compare the development of vegetarianism in England and France.

21. Right now, in France, there is a conflict between traditional (gastronomic) and modern (nutritional) values.

22. It seems that this stimulating, re-energizing power is now assigned to sugar, at least in France.

3

Distinction: A Social Critique of the Judgement of Taste[*]

Pierre Bourdieu (tr. Richard Nice)

Three Styles of Distinction

The basic opposition between the tastes of luxury and the tastes of necessity is speci-
fied in as many oppositions as there are different ways of asserting one's distinction
vis-à-vis the working class and its primary needs, or—which amounts to the same
thing—different powers whereby necessity can be kept at a distance. Thus, within the
dominant class, one can, for the sake of simplicity, distinguish three structures of the
consumption distributed under three items: food, culture and presentation (clothing,
beauty care, toiletries, domestic servants). These structures take strictly opposite
forms—like the structures of their capital—among the teachers as against the industrial and commercial employers (see Table 3.1). Whereas the latter have exceptionally
high expenditure on food (37 percent of the budget), low cultural costs and medium
spending on presentation and representation, the former, whose total spending is
lower on average, have low expenditure on food (relatively less than manual workers),
limited expenditure on presentation (though their expenditure on health is one of the
highest) and relatively high expenditure on culture (books, papers, entertainments,
sport, toys, music, radio and record-player). Opposed to both these groups are the
members of the professions, who devote the same proportion of their budget to food
as the teachers (24.4 percent), but out of much greater total expenditure (57,122 francs
as against 40,884 francs), and who spend much more on presentation and representation than all other fractions, especially if the costs of domestic service are included,
whereas their cultural expenditure is lower than that of the teachers (or even the engineers
and senior executives, who are situated between the teachers and the professionals,
though nearer the latter, for almost all items).

The system of differences becomes clearer when one looks more closely at the patterns of spending on food. In this respect the industrial and commercial employers
differ markedly from the professionals, and a fortiori from the teachers, by virtue of
the importance they give to cereal-based products (especially cakes and pastries),
wine, meat preserves (foie gras, etc.) and game, and their relatively low spending on
meat, fresh fruit and vegetables. The teachers, whose food purchases are almost

[*]*Originally published 1979*

Table 3.1 Yearly spending by teachers, professionals and industrial and commercial employers, 1972.

Type of spending	Teachers (higher and secondary)		Professionals		Industrial and commercial employers	
	Francs	% of total	Francs	% of total	Francs	% of total
Food[a]	9,969	24.4	13,956	24.4	16,578	37.4
Presentation[b]	4,912	12.0	12,680	22.2	5,616	12.7
Culture[c]	1,753	4.3	1,298	2.3	574	1.3

[a]Includes restaurant or canteen meals.
[b]Clothes, shoes, repairs and cleaning, toiletries, hairdressing, domestic servants.
[c]Books, newspapers and magazines, stationery, records, sport, toys, music, entertainments.
Source: C.S. Ill (1972).

identically structured to those of office workers, spend more than all other fractions on bread, milk products, sugar, fruit preserves and non-alcoholic drinks, less on wine and spirits and distinctly less than the professions on expensive products such as meat—especially the most expensive meats, such as mutton and lamb—and fresh fruit and vegetables. The members of the professions are mainly distinguished by the high proportion of their spending which goes on expensive products, particularly meat (18.3 percent of their food budget), and especially the most expensive meat (veal, lamb, mutton), fresh fruit and vegetables, fish and shellfish, cheese and aperitifs.[1]

Thus, when one moves from the manual workers to the industrial and commercial employers, through foremen, craftsmen and small shopkeepers, economic constraints tend to relax without any fundamental change in the pattern of spending (see Figure 3.1). The opposition between the two extremes is established here between the poor and the rich (nouveau riche), between *la bouffe* and *la grande bouffe*[2] the food consumed is increasingly rich (both in cost and in calories) and increasingly heavy (game, foie gras). By contrast, the taste of the professionals or senior executives defines the popular taste, by negation, as the taste for the heavy, the fat and the coarse, by tending towards the light, the refined and the delicate. The disappearance of economic constraints is accompanied by a strengthening of the social censorships which forbid coarseness and fatness, in favour of slimness and distinction. The taste for rare, aristocratic foods points to a traditional cuisine, rich in expensive or rare products (fresh vegetables, meat). Finally, the teachers, richer in cultural capital than in economic capital, and therefore inclined to ascetic consumption in all areas, pursue originality at the lowest economic cost and go in for exoticism (Italian, Chinese cooking etc.)[3] and culinary populism (peasant dishes). They are thus almost consciously opposed to the (new) rich with their rich food, the buyers and sellers of *grosse bouffe*, the 'fat cats',[4] gross in body and mind, who have the economic means to flaunt, with an arrogance perceived as 'vulgar', a life-style which remains very close to that of the working classes as regards economic and cultural consumption.

Eating habits, especially when represented solely by the produce consumed, cannot of course be considered independently of the whole life-style. The most obvious reason for this is that the taste for particular dishes (of which the statistical

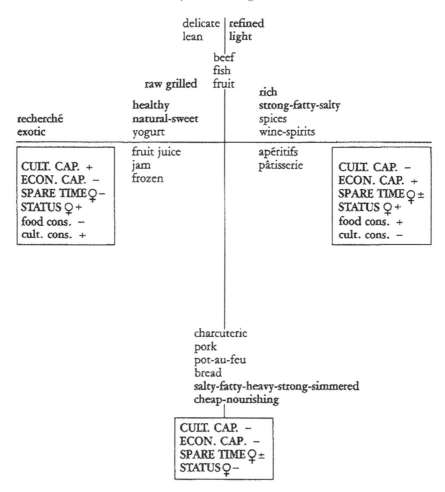

```
                              delicate | refined
                                 lean  | light

                                       beef
                                       fish
                         raw grilled   fruit
                                             rich
                         healthy             strong-fatty-salty
   recherché             natural-sweet       spices
   exotic                yogurt              wine-spirits
 ┌─────────────────┐     fruit juice         apéritifs      ┌─────────────────┐
 │ CULT. CAP.  +   │     jam                 pâtisserie     │ CULT. CAP.  −   │
 │ ECON. CAP.  −   │     frozen                             │ ECON. CAP.  +   │
 │ SPARE TIME ♀ −  │                                        │ SPARE TIME ♀ ±  │
 │ STATUS ♀ +      │                                        │ STATUS ♀ +      │
 │ food cons.  −   │                                        │ food cons.  +   │
 │ cult. cons. +   │                                        │ cult. cons. −   │
 └─────────────────┘                                        └─────────────────┘


                         charcuterie
                         pork
                         pot-au-feu
                         bread
                         salty-fatty-heavy-strong-simmered
                         cheap-nourishing
                       ┌─────────────────┐
                       │ CULT. CAP.  −   │
                       │ ECON. CAP.  −   │
                       │ SPARE TIME ♀ ±  │
                       │ STATUS ♀ −      │
                       └─────────────────┘
```

Figure 3.1 The food space.

shopping-basket gives only the vaguest idea) is associated, through preparation and cooking, with a whole conception of the domestic economy and of the division of labour between the sexes. A taste for elaborate casserole dishes (pot-au-feu, *blanquette*, *daube*), which demand a big investment of time and interest, is linked to a traditional conception of woman's role. Thus there is a particularly strong opposition in this respect between the working classes and the dominated fractions of the dominant class, in which the women, whose labour has a high market value (and who, perhaps as a result, have a higher sense of their own value) tend to devote their spare time rather to child care and the transmission of cultural capital, and to contest the traditional division of domestic labour. The aim of saving time and labour in preparation combines with the search for light, low-calorie products, and points towards grilled meat and fish, raw vegetables (*'salades composées'*), frozen foods, yogurt and other milk products, all of which are diametrically opposed to popular dishes, the most typical of which is pot-au-feu, made with cheap meat that is boiled (as opposed to grilled or roasted), a method of cooking that chiefly demands time. It is no accident that this form of cooking symbolizes one state of female existence and of the sexual division of the labour (a woman entirely devoted to housework is called 'pot-au-feu'), just as the slippers put on before dinner symbolize the complementary male role.

Tastes in food also depend on the idea each class has of the body and of the effects of food on the body, that is, on its strength, health and beauty; and on the categories it uses to evaluate these effects, some of which may be important for one class and ignored by another, and which the different classes may rank in very different ways. Thus, whereas the working classes are more attentive to the strength of the (male) body than its shape, and tend to go for products that are both cheap and nutritious, the professions prefer products that are tasty, health-giving, light and not fattening. Taste, a class culture turned into nature, that is, *embodied*, helps to shape the class body. It is an incorporated principle of classification which governs all forms of incorporation, choosing and modifying everything that the body ingests and digests and assimilates, physiologically and psychologically. It follows that the body is the most indisputable materialization of class taste, which it manifests in several ways. It does this first in the seemingly most natural features of the body, the dimensions (volume, height, weight) and shapes (round or square, stiff or supple, straight or curved) of its visible forms, which express in countless ways a whole relation to the body, i.e., a way of treating it, caring for it, feeding it, maintaining it, which reveals the deepest dispositions of the habitus. It is in fact through preferences with regard to food which may be perpetuated beyond their social conditions of production (as, in other areas, an accent, a walk etc.),[5] and also, of course, through the uses of the body in work and leisure which are bound up with them, that the class distribution of bodily properties is determined.

The quasi-conscious representation of the approved form of the perceived body, and in particular its thinness or fatness, is not the only mediation through which the social definition of appropriate foods is established. At a deeper level, the whole body schema, in particular the physical approach to the act of eating, governs the selection of certain foods. For example, in the working classes, fish tends to be regarded as an unsuitable food for men, not only because it is a light food, insufficiently 'filling', which would only be cooked for health reasons, i.e., for invalids and children, but also because, like fruit (except bananas) it is one of the 'fiddly' things which a man's hands cannot cope with and which make him childlike (the woman, adopting a maternal role, as in all similar cases, will prepare the fish on the plate or peel the pear); but above all, it is because fish has to be eaten in a way which totally contradicts the masculine way of eating, that is, with restraint, in small mouthfuls, chewed gently, with the front of the mouth, on the tips of the teeth (because of the bones). The whole masculine identity—what is called virility—is involved in these two ways of eating, nibbling and picking, as befits a woman, or with whole-hearted male gulps and mouthfuls, just as it is involved in the two (perfectly homologous) ways of talking, with the front of the mouth or the whole mouth, especially the back of the mouth, the throat (in accordance with the opposition, noted in an earlier study, between the manners symbolized by *la bouche* and *la gueule*).[6]

This opposition can be found in each of the uses of the body, especially in the most insignificant-looking ones, which, as such, are predisposed to serve as 'memory joggers' charged with the group's deepest values, its most fundamental 'beliefs'. It would be easy to show, for example, that Kleenex tissues, which have to be used delicately, with a little sniff from the tip of the nose, are to the big cotton handkerchief, which is blown into sharply and loudly, with the eyes closed and the nose held tightly, as repressed laughter is to a belly laugh, with wrinkled nose, wide-open mouth and deep breathing ('doubled up with laughter'), as if to amplify to the utmost an experience which will not suffer containment, not least because it has to be shared, and therefore clearly manifested for the benefit of others.

And the practical philosophy of the male body as a sort of power, big and strong, with enormous, imperative, brutal needs, which is asserted in every male posture, especially when eating, is also the principle of the division of foods between the sexes, a division which both sexes recognize in their practices and their language. It behooves a man to drink and eat more, and to eat and drink stronger things. Thus, men will have two rounds of aperitifs (more on special occasions), big ones in big glasses (the success of Ricard or Pernod is no doubt partly due to its being a drink both strong and copious—not a dainty 'thimbleful'), and they leave the tit-bits (savoury biscuits, peanuts) to the children and the women, who have a small measure (not enough to 'get tipsy') of homemade aperitif (for which they swap recipes). Similarly, among the hors d'oeuvres, the *charcuterie* is more for the men, and later the cheese, especially if it is strong, whereas the *crudités* (raw vegetables) are more for the women, like the salad; and these affinities are marked by taking a second helping or sharing what is left over. Meat, the nourishing food par excellence, strong and strong-making, giving vigour, blood, and health, is the dish for the men, who take a second helping, whereas the women are satisfied with a small portion. It is not that they are stinting themselves; they really don't want what others might need, especially the men, the natural meat-eaters, and they derive a sort of authority from what they do not see as a privation. Besides, they don't have a taste for men's food, which is reputed to be harmful when eaten to excess (for example, a surfeit of meat can 'turn the blood', over-excite, bring you out in spots etc.) and may even arouse a sort of disgust.

Strictly biological differences are underlined and symbolically accentuated by differences in bearing, differences in gesture, posture and behaviour which express a whole relationship to the social world. To these are added all the deliberate modifications of appearance, especially by use of the set of marks—cosmetic (hairstyle, make-up, beard, moustache, whiskers etc.) or vestimentary—which, because they depend on the economic and cultural means that can be invested in them, function as social markers deriving their meaning and value from their position in the system of distinctive signs which they constitute and which is itself homologous with the system of social positions. The sign-bearing, sign-wearing body is also a producer of signs which are physically marked by the relationship to the body: thus the valorization of virility, expressed in a use of the mouth or a pitch of the voice, can determine the whole of working-class pronunciation. The body, a social product which is the only tangible manifestation of the 'person', is commonly perceived as the most natural expression of innermost nature. There are no merely 'physical' facial signs; the colour and thickness of lipstick, or expressions, as well as the shape of the face or the mouth, are immediately read as indices of a 'moral' physiognomy, socially characterized, i.e., of a 'vulgar' or 'distinguished' mind, naturally 'natural' or naturally 'cultivated'. The signs constituting the perceived body, cultural products which differentiate groups by their degree of culture, that is, their distance from nature, seem grounded in nature. The legitimate use of the body is spontaneously perceived as an index of moral uprightness, so that its opposite, a 'natural' body, is seen as an index of *laisser-aller* ('letting oneself go'), a culpable surrender to facility.

Thus one can begin to map out a universe of class bodies, which (biological accidents apart) tends to reproduce in its specific logic the universe of the social structure. It is no accident that bodily properties are perceived through social systems of classification which are not independent of the distribution of these properties among the social classes. The prevailing taxonomies tend to rank and contrast the properties most frequent among the dominant (i.e., the rarest ones) and those most frequent among the dominated.[7] The social representation of his own body which each agent has to reckon with,[8] from the very beginning, in order to build up his subjective image of his body and his bodily hexis, is thus obtained by applying a social system of classification based on the same principle as the social products to which it is applied. Thus, bodies would have every likelihood of receiving a value strictly corresponding to the positions of their owners in the distribution of the other fundamental properties— but for the fact that the logic of social heredity sometimes endows those least endowed in all other respects with the rarest bodily properties, such as beauty (sometimes 'fatally' attractive, because it threatens the other hierarchies), and, conversely, sometimes denies the 'high and mighty' the bodily attributes of their position, such as height or beauty.

Unpretentious Or Uncouth?

It is clear that tastes in food cannot be considered in complete independence of the other dimensions of the relationship to the world, to others and to one's own body, through which the practical philosophy of each class is enacted. To demonstrate this, one would have to make a systematic comparison of the working-class and bourgeois ways of treating food, of serving, presenting and offering it, which are infinitely more revelatory than even the nature of the products involved (especially since most surveys of consumption ignore differences in quality). The analysis is a difficult one, because each life-style can only really be constructed in relation to the other, which is its objective and subjective negation, so that the meaning of behaviour is totally reversed depending on which point of view is adopted and on whether the common words which have to be used to name the conduct (e.g., 'manners') are invested with popular or bourgeois connotations.

Plain speaking, plain eating: the working-class meal is characterized by plenty (which does not exclude restrictions and limits) and above all by freedom. 'Elastic' and 'abundant' dishes are brought to the table—soups or sauces, pasta or potatoes (almost always included among the vegetables)—and served with a ladle or spoon, to avoid too much measuring and counting, in contrast to everything that has to be cut and divided, such as roasts.[9] This impression of abundance, which is the norm on special occasions, and always applies, so far as is possible, for the men, whose plates are filled twice (a privilege which marks a boy's accession to manhood), is often balanced, on ordinary occasions, by restrictions which generally apply to the women, who will share one portion between two, or eat the left-overs of the previous day; a girl's accession to womanhood is marked by doing without. It is part of men's status to eat and to eat well (and also to drink well); it is particularly insisted that they should eat, on the grounds that 'it won't keep', and there is something suspect about a refusal. On Sundays, while the women are on their feet, busily serving, clearing the table, washing up, the men remain seated, still eating and drinking. These strongly marked differences of social status (associated with sex and age) are accompanied by no practical differentiation (such as the bourgeois division between the dining room and the kitchen, where the servants eat and sometimes the children), and strict sequencing of the meal tends to be ignored. Everything may be put on the table at much the same time (which also saves walking), so that the women may have reached the dessert, and also the children, who will take their plates and watch television, while the men are still eating the main dish and the 'lad', who has arrived late, is swallowing his soup.

This freedom, which may be perceived as disorder or slovenliness, is adapted to its function. Firstly, it is labour-saving, which is seen as an advantage. Because men take no part in housework, not least because the women would not allow it—it would be a dishonour to see men step outside their rôle—every economy of effort is welcome. Thus, when the coffee is served, a single spoon may be passed around to stir it. But these short cuts are only permissible because one is and feels at home, among the family, where ceremony would be an affectation. For example, to save washing up, the dessert may be handed out on improvised plates torn from the cake-box (with a joke about 'taking the liberty', to mark the transgression), and the neighbour invited in for a meal will also receive his piece of cardboard (offering a plate would exclude him) as a sign of familiarity. Similarly, the plates are not changed between dishes. The soup plate, wiped with bread, can be used right through the meal. The hostess will certainly offer to 'change the plates', pushing back her chair with one hand and reaching with the other for the plate next to her, but everyone will protest ('It all gets mixed up inside you') and if she were to insist it would look as if she wanted to show off her crockery (which she is allowed to if it is a new present) or to treat her guests as strangers, as is sometimes deliberately done to intruders or 'scroungers' who never return the invitation. These unwanted guests may be frozen out by changing their plates despite their protests, not laughing at their jokes, or scolding the children for their behaviour ('No, no, *we* don't mind', say the guests; 'They ought to know better by now', the parents respond). The common root of all these 'liberties' is no doubt the sense that at least there will not be self-imposed controls, constraints and restrictions—especially not in eating, a primary need and a compensation—and especially not in the heart of domestic life, the one realm of freedom, when everywhere else, and at all other times, necessity prevails.

In opposition to the free-and-easy working-class meal, the bourgeoisie is concerned to eat with all due form. Form is first of all a matter of rhythm, which implies expectations, pauses, restraints; waiting until the last person served has started to eat, taking modest helpings, not appearing over-eager. A strict sequence is observed and all coexistence of dishes which the sequence separates, fish and meat, cheese and dessert, is excluded: for example, before the dessert is served, everything left on the table, even the salt-cellar, is removed, and the crumbs are swept up. This extension of rigorous rules into everyday life (the bourgeois male shaves and dresses first thing every morning, and not just to 'go out'), refusing the division between home and the exterior, the quotidian and the extra-quotidian, is not explained solely by the presence of strangers—servants and guests—in the familiar family world. It is the expression of a habitus of order, restraint and propriety which may not be abdicated. The relation to food—*the* primary need and pleasure—is only one dimension of the bourgeois relation to the social world. The opposition between the immediate and the deferred, the easy and the difficult, substance (or function) and form, which is exposed in a particularly striking fashion in bourgeois ways of eating, is the basis of all aestheticization of practice and every aesthetic. Through all the forms and formalisms imposed on the immediate appetite, what is demanded—and inculcated—is not only a disposition to discipline food consumption by a conventional structuring which is also a gentle, indirect, invisible censorship (quite different from enforced privations) and which is an element in an art of living (correct eating, for example, is a way of paying homage to one's hosts and to the mistress of the house, a tribute to her care and effort). It is also a whole relationship to animal nature, to primary needs and the populace who indulge them without restraint; it is a way of denying the meaning and primary function of consumption, which are essentially common, by making the meal a social ceremony, an affirmation of ethical tone and aesthetic refinement. The manner of presenting and consuming the food, the organization of the meal and setting of the places, strictly differentiated according to the sequence of dishes and arranged to please the eye, the presentation of the dishes, considered as much in terms of shape and colour (like works of art) as of their consumable substance, the etiquette governing posture and gesture, ways of serving oneself and others, of using the different utensils, the seating plan, strictly but discreetly hierarchical, the censorship of all bodily manifestations of the act or pleasure of eating (such as noise or haste), the very refinement of the things consumed, with quality more important than quantity—this whole commitment to stylization tends to shift the emphasis from substance and function to form and manner, and so to deny the crudely material reality of the act of eating and of the things consumed, or, which amounts to the same thing, the basely material vulgarity of those who indulge in the immediate satisfactions of food and drink.[10]

Given the basic opposition between form and substance, one could re-generate each of the oppositions between the two antagonistic approaches to the treatment of food and the act of eating. In one case, food is claimed as a material reality, a nourishing substance which sustains the body and gives strength (hence the emphasis on heavy, fatty, strong foods, of which the paradigm is pork—fatty and salty—the antithesis of fish—light, lean and bland); in the other, the priority given to form (the shape of the body, for example) and social form, formality, puts the pursuit of strength and substance in the background and identifies true freedom with the elective asceticism of a self-imposed rule. And it could be shown that two antagonistic world views, two worlds, two representations of human excellence are contained in this matrix. Substance—or matter—is what is substantial, not only 'filling' but also real, as opposed to all appearances, all the fine words and empty gestures that 'butter no parsnips' and are, as the phrase goes, purely symbolic; reality, as against sham, imitation, window-dressing; the little eating-house with its marble-topped tables and paper napkins where you get an honest square meal and aren't 'paying for the wallpaper' as in fancy restaurants; being, as against seeming, nature and the natural, simplicity (pot-luck, 'take it as it comes', 'no standing on ceremony'), as against embarrassment, mincing and posturing, airs and graces, which are always suspected of being a substitute for substance, i.e., for sincerity, for feeling, for what is felt and proved in actions; it is the free-speech and language of the heart which make the true 'nice guy', blunt, straightforward, unbending, honest, genuine, 'straight down the line' and 'straight as a die', as opposed to everything that is pure form, done only for form's sake; it is freedom and the refusal of complications, as opposed to respect for all the forms and formalities spontaneously perceived as instruments of distinction and power. On these moralities, these world views, there is no neutral viewpoint; what for some is shameless and slovenly, for others is straightforward, unpretentious; familiarity is for some the most absolute form of recognition, the abdication of all distance, a trusting openness, a relation of equal to equal; for others, who shun familiarity, it is an unseemly liberty.

Notes

1. The oppositions are much less clear cut in the middle classes although homologous difference are found between primary teachers and office workers on the one hand and shopkeepers on the other.
2. *La bouffe:* 'grub', 'nosh'; *grande bouffe:* 'blow-out' (translator).
3. The preference for foreign restaurants—Italian, Chinese, Japanese and, to a lesser extent, Russian—rises with level in the social hierarchy. The only exceptions are Spanish restaurants, which are associated with a more popular form of tourism, and North African restaurants, which are most favoured by junior executives.
4. *Les gross:* the rich; *grosse bouffe:* bulk food (cf. *grossiste:* wholesaler; and English 'grocer'). See also note 2 above (translator).
5. That is why the body designates not only present position but also trajectory.
6. In 'The Economics of Linguistic Exchanges', *Social Science Information*, 26 (December 1977), 645–668, Bourdieu develops the opposition between two ways of speaking, rooted in two relations to the body and the world, which have a lexical reflection in the many idioms based on two words for 'mouth': *la bouche* and *la gueule*. *La bouche* is the 'standard' word for the mouth; but in opposition to *la gueule*—a slang or 'vulgar' word except when applied to animals—it tends to be restricted to the lips, whereas *la gueule* can include the whole face or the throat. Most of the idioms using *la bouche* imply fastidiousness, effeminacy or disdain; those with *la gueule* connote vigour, strength or violence (translator's note).
7. This means that the taxonomies applied to the perceived body (fat/thin, strong/weak, big/small etc.) are, as always, at once arbitrary (e.g., the ideal female body may be fat or thin in different economic and social contexts) and necessary, i.e., grounded in the specific reason of a given social order.
8. More than ever, the French possessive pronouns—which do not mark the owner's gender—ought to be translated 'his or her'. The 'sexism' of the text results from the male translator's reluctance to defy the dominant use of a sexist symbolic system (translator).
9. One could similarly contrast the bowl, which is generously filled and held two-handed for unpretentious drinking, and the cup, into which a little is poured, and more later ('Would you care for a little more coffee?'), and which is held between two fingers and sipped from.
10. Formality is a way of denying the truth of the social world and of social relations. Just as popular 'functionalism' is refused as regards food, so too there is a refusal of the realistic vision which leads the working classes to accept social exchanges for what they are (and, for example, to say, without cynicism, of someone who has done a favour or rendered a service, 'She knows I'll pay her back'). Suppressing avowal of the calculation which pervades social relations, there is a striving to see presents, received or given, as 'pure' testimonies of friendship, respect, affection, and equally 'pure' manifestations of generosity and moral worth.

4

The Culinary Triangle*

Claude Lévi-Strauss

Linguistics has familiarized us with concepts like "minimum vocalism" and "minimum consonantism" which refer to systems of oppositions between phonemes of so elementary a nature that every known or unknown language supposes them; they are in fact also the first oppositions to appear in the child's language, and the last to disappear in the speech of people affected by certain forms of aphasia.

The two concepts are moreover not really distinct, since, according to linguists, for every language the fundamental opposition is that between consonant and vowel. The subsequent distinctions among vowels and among consonants result from the application to these derived areas of such contrasts as compact and diffuse, open and closed, acute and grave.

Hence, in all the languages of the world, complex systems of oppositions among phonemes do nothing but elaborate in multiple directions a simpler system common to them all: the contrast between consonant and vowel which, by the workings of a double opposition between compact and diffuse, acute and grave, produces on the one hand what has been called the "vowel triangle":[1]

$$a$$
$$u \quad i$$

and on the other hand the "consonant triangle":

$$k$$
$$p \quad t$$

It would seem that the methodological principle which inspires such distinctions is transposable to other domains, notably that of cooking which, it has never been sufficiently emphasized, is with language a truly universal form of human activity: if there is no society without a language, nor is there any which does not cook in some manner at least some of its food.

We will start from the hypothesis that this activity supposes a system which is located—according to very difficult modalities in function of the particular cultures

*Originally published 1966

one wants to consider—within a triangular semantic field whose three points correspond respectively to the categories of the raw, the cooked and the rotted. It is clear that in respect to cooking the raw constitutes the unmarked pole, while the other two poles are strongly marked, but in different directions: indeed, the cooked is a cultural transformation of the raw, whereas the rotted is a natural transformation. Underlying our original triangle, there is hence a double opposition between *elaborated/unelaborated* on the one hand, and *culture/nature* on the other.

No doubt these notions constitute empty forms: they teach us nothing about the cooking of any specific society, since only observation can tell us what each one means by "raw," "cooked" and "rotted," and we can suppose that it will not be the same for all. Italian cuisine has recently taught us to eat *crudités* rawer than any in traditional French cooking, thereby determining an enlargement of the category of the raw. And we know from some incidents that followed the Allied landings in 1944 that American soldiers conceived the category of the rotted in more extended fashion than we, since the odor given off by Norman cheese dairies seemed to them the smell of corpses, and occasionally prompted them to destroy the dairies.

Consequently, the culinary triangle delimits a semantic field, but from the outside. This is moreover true of the linguistic triangles as well, since there are no phonemes *a, i, u* (or *k, p, t*) in general, and these ideal positions must be occupied, in each language, by the particular phonemes whose distinctive natures are closest to those for which we first gave a symbolic representation: thus we have a sort of concrete triangle inscribed within the abstract triangle. In any cuisine, nothing is simply cooked, but must be cooked in one fashion or another. Nor is there any condition of pure rawness: only certain foods can really be eaten raw, and then only if they have been selected, washed, pared or cut, or even seasoned. Rotting, too, is only allowed to take place in certain specific ways, either spontaneous or controlled.

Let us now consider, for those cuisines whose categories are relatively well-known, the different modes of cooking. There are certainly two principal modes, attested in innumerable societies by myths and rites which emphasize their contrast: the roasted and the boiled. In what does their difference consist? Roasted food is directly exposed to the fire; with the fire it realizes an unmediated conjunction, whereas boiled food is doubly mediated, by the water in which it is immersed, and by the receptacle that holds both water and food.

On two grounds, then, one can say that the roasted is on the side of nature, the boiled on the side of culture: literally, because boiling requires the use of a receptacle, a cultural object; symbolically, in as much as culture is a mediation of the relations between man and the world, and boiling demands a mediation (by water) of the relation between food and fire which is absent in roasting.

The natives of New Caledonia feel this contrast with particular vividness: "Formerly," relates M. J. Barrau, "they only grilled and roasted, they only 'burned' as the natives now say . . . The use of a pot and the consumption of boiled tubers are looked upon with pride . . . as a proof of . . . civilization."

A text of Aristotle, cited by Salomon Reinach (*Cultes, Mythes, Religions*, V, p. 63), indicates that the Greeks also thought that "in ancient times, men roasted everything."

Behind the opposition between roasted and boiled, then, we do in fact find, as we postulated at the outset, the opposition between nature and culture. It remains to

discover the other fundamental opposition which we put forth: that between elaborated and unelaborated.

In this respect, observation establishes a double affinity: the roasted with the raw,
that is to say the unelaborated, and the boiled with the rotted, which is one of the two
modes of the elaborated. The affinity of the roasted with the raw comes from the fact
that it is never uniformly cooked, whether this be on all sides, or on the outside and
the inside. A myth of the Wyandot Indians well evokes what might be called the paradox of the roasted: the Creator struck fire, and ordered the first man to skewer a piece
of meat on a stick and roast it. But man was so ignorant that he left the meat on the
fire until it was black on one side, and still raw on the other . . . Similarly, the Pocon-
achi of Mexico interpret the roasted as a compromise between the raw and the burned.
After the universal fire, they relate, that which had not been burned became white,
that which had been burned turned black, and what had only been singed turned red.
This explanation accounts for the various colors of corn and beans. In British Guiana,
the Waiwai sorcerer must respect two taboos, one directed at roast meat, the other red
paint, and this again puts the roasted on the side of blood and the raw.

If boiling is superior to roasting, notes Aristotle, it is because it takes away the rawness of meat, "roast meats being rawer and drier than boiled meats" (quoted by Reinach, *loc. cit.*).

As for the boiled, its affinity with the rotted is attested in numerous European languages by such locutions as *pot pourri, olla podrida*, denoting different sorts of meat
seasoned and cooked together with vegetables; and in German, *zu Brei zerkochetes
Fleisch*, "meat rotted from cooking." American Indian languages emphasize the same
affinity, and it is significant that this should be so especially in those tribes that show
a strong taste for gamey meat, to the point of preferring, for example, the flesh of a
dead animal whose carcass has been washed down by the stream to that of a freshly
killed buffalo. In the Dakota language, the same stem connotes putrefaction and the
fact of boiling pieces of meat together with some additive.

These distinctions are far from exhausting the richness and complexity of the contrast
between roasted and boiled. The boiled is cooked within a receptacle, while the roasted
is cooked from without: the former thus evokes the concave, the latter the convex. Also
the boiled can most often be ascribed to what might be called an "endo-cuisine," prepared for domestic use, destined to a small closed group, while the roasted belongs to
"exo-cuisine," that which one offers to guests. Formerly in France, boiled chicken was for
the family meal, while roasted meat was for the banquet (and marked its culminating
point, served as it was after the boiled meats and vegetables of the first course, and
accompanied by "extraordinary fruits" such as melons, oranges, olives and capers).

The same opposition is found, differently formulated, in exotic societies. The
extremely primitive Guayaki of Paraguay roast all their game, except when they prepare the meat destined for the rites which determine the name of a new child: this meat
must be boiled. The Caingang of Brazil prohibit boiled meat for the widow and wid-
ower, and also for anyone who has murdered an enemy. In all these cases, prescription
of the boiled accompanies a tightening, prescription of the roasted a loosening of
familial or social ties.

Following this line of argument, one could infer that cannibalism (which by definition is an endo-cuisine in respect to the human race) ordinarily employs boiling

rather than roasting, and that the cases where bodies are roasted—cases vouched for by ethnographic literature—must be more frequent in exo-cannibalism (eating the body of an enemy) than in endo-cannibalism (eating a relative). It would be interesting to carry out statistical research on this point.

Sometimes, too, as is often the case in America, and doubtless elsewhere, the roasted and the boiled will have respective affinities with life in the bush (outside the village community) and sedentary life (inside the village). From this comes a subsidiary association of the roasted with men, the boiled with women. This is notably the case with the Trumai, the Yagua and the Jivaro of South America, and with the Ingalik of Alaska. Or else the relation is reversed: the Assiniboin, on the northern plains of North America, reserve the preparation of boiled food for men engaged in a war expedition, while the women in the villages never use receptacles, and only roast their meat. There are some indications that in certain Eastern European countries one can find the same inversion of affinities between roasted and boiled and feminine and masculine.

The existence of these inverted systems naturally poses a problem, and leads one to think that the axes of opposition are still more numerous than one suspected, and that the peoples where these inversions exist refer to axes different from those we at first singled out. For example, boiling conserves entirely the meat and its juices, whereas roasting is accompanied by destruction and loss. One connotes economy, the other prodigality; the former is plebeian, the latter aristocratic. This aspect takes on primary importance in societies which prescribe differences of status among individuals or groups. In the ancient Maori, says Prytz-Johansen, a noble could himself roast his food, but he avoided all contact with the steaming oven, which was left to the slaves and women of low birth. Thus, when pots and pans were introduced by the whites, they seemed infected utensils; a striking inversion of the attitude which we remarked in the New Caledonians.

These differences in appraisal of the boiled and the roasted, dependent on the democratic or aristocratic perspective of the group, can also be found in the Western tradition. The democratic Encyclopedia of Diderot and d'Alembert goes in for a veritable apology of the boiled: "Boiled meat is one of the most succulent and nourishing foods known to man. . . One could say that boiled meat is to other dishes as bread is to other kinds of nourishment" (Article "Bouilli"). A half-century later, the dandy Brillat-Savarin will take precisely the opposite view: "We professors never eat boiled meat out of respect for principle, and because we have pronounced ex cathedra this incontestable truth: boiled meat is flesh without its juice. . . This truth is beginning to become accepted, and boiled meat has disappeared in truly elegant dinners; it has been replaced by a roast filet, a turbot, or a matelote" (*Physiologie du goût*, VI, 2).

Therefore if the Czechs see in boiled meat a man's nourishment, it is perhaps because their traditional society was of a much more democratic character than that of their Slavonic and Polish neighbors. One could interpret in the same manner distinctions made—respectively by the Greeks, and the Romans and the Hebrews—on the basis of attitudes toward roasted and boiled, distinctions which have been noted by M. Piganiol in a recent article ("Le rôti et le bouilli," *A Pedro Bosch-Gimpera*, Mexico City, 1963).

Other societies make use of the same opposition in a completely different direction. Because boiling takes place without loss of substance, and within a complete enclosure, it is eminently apt to symbolize cosmic totality. In Guiana as well as in the Great Lakes region, it is thought that if the pot where game is boiling were to overflow even a little bit, all the animals of the species being cooked would migrate, and the hunter would catch nothing more. The boiled is life, the roasted death. Does not world folklore offer innumerable examples of the cauldron of immortality? But there has never been a spit of immortality. A Cree Indian rite admirably expresses this character of cosmic totality ascribed to boiled food. According to them, the first man was commanded by the Creator to boil the first berries gathered each season. The cup containing the berries was first presented to the sun, that it might fulfill its office and ripen the berries; then the cup was lifted to the thunder, whence rain is expected; finally the cup was lowered toward the earth, in prayer that it bring forth its fruits.

Hence we rejoin the symbolism of the most distant Indo-European past, as it has been reconstructed by Georges Dumézil: "To Mitra belongs that which breaks of itself, that which is cooked in steam, that which is well sacrificed, milk . . . and to Varuna that which is cut with the axe, that which is snatched from the fire, that which is ill-sacrificed, the intoxicating soma" (*Les dieux des Germains*, p. 60). It is not a little surprising—but highly significant—to find intact in genial mid-nineteenth-century philosophers of cuisine a consciousness of the same contrast between knowledge and inspiration, serenity and violence, measure and lack of measure, still symbolized by the opposition of the boiled and the roasted: "One becomes a cook but one is born a roaster" (Brillat-Savarin); "Roasting is at the same time nothing, and an immensity" (Marquis de Cussy).

Within the basic culinary triangle formed by the categories of raw, cooked and rotted, we have, then, inscribed two terms which are situated: one, the roasted, in the vicinity of the raw; the other, the boiled, near the rotted. We are lacking a third term, illustrating the concrete form of cooking showing the greatest affinity to the abstract category of the cooked. This form seems to us to be smoking, which like roasting implies an unmediated operation (without receptacle and without water) but differs from roasting in that it is, like boiling, a slow form of cooking, both uniform and penetrating in depth.

Let us try to determine the place of this new term in our system of opposition. In the technique of smoking, as in that of roasting, nothing is interposed between meat and fire except air. But the difference between the two techniques comes from the fact that in one the layer of air is reduced to a minimum, whereas in the other it is brought to a maximum. To smoke game, the American Indians (in whose culinary system smoking occupies a particularly important place) construct a wooden frame (a buccan) about five feet high, on top of which they place the meat, while underneath they light a very small fire which is kept burning for forty-eight hours or more. Hence for one constant—the presence of a layer of air—we note two differentials which are expressed by the opposition *close/distant* and *rapid/slow*. A third differential is created by the absence of a utensil in the case of roasting (any stick doing the work of a spit), since the buccan is a constructed framework, that is, a cultural object.

In this last respect, smoking is related to boiling, which also requires a cultural means, the receptacle. But between these two utensils a remarkable difference appears, or more accurately, is instituted by the culture precisely in order, it seems, to create the opposition, which without such a difference might have remained too ill-defined to take on meaning. Pots and pans are carefully cared for and preserved utensils, which one cleans and puts away after use in order to make them serve their purpose as many times as possible; but the buccan *must be destroyed immediately after use*, otherwise the animal will avenge itself, and come in turn to smoke the huntsman. Such, at least, is the belief of those same natives of Guiana whose other symmetrical belief we have already noted: that a poorly conducted boiling, during which the cauldron overflowed, would bring the inverse punishment, flight of the quarry, which the huntsman would no longer succeed in overtaking. On the other hand, as we have already indicated, it is clear that the boiled is opposed both to the smoked and the roasted in respect to the presence or absence of water.

But let us come back for a moment to the opposition between a perishable and a durable utensil which we found in Guiana in connection with smoking and boiling. It will allow us to resolve an apparent difficulty in our system, one which doubtless has not escaped the reader. At the start we characterized one of the oppositions between the roasted and the boiled as reflecting that between nature and culture. Later, however, we proposed an affinity between the boiled and the rotted, the latter defined as the elaboration of the raw by natural means. Is it not contradictory that a cultural method should lead to a natural result? To put it in other terms, what, philosophically, will be the value of the invention of pottery (and hence of culture) if the native's system associates boiling and putrefaction, which is the condition that raw food cannot help but reach spontaneously in the state of nature?

The same type of paradox is implied by the problematics of smoking as formulated by the natives of Guiana. On the one hand, smoking, of all the modes of cooking, comes closest to the abstract category of the cooked; and—since the opposition between raw and cooked is homologous to that between nature and culture—it represents the most "cultural" form of cooking (and also that most esteemed among the natives). And yet, on the other hand, its cultural means, the buccan, is to be immediately destroyed. There is striking parallel to boiling, a method whose cultural means (the receptacles) are preserved, but which is itself assimilated to a sort of process of auto-annihilation, since its definitive result is at least verbally equivalent to that putrefaction which cooking should prevent or retard.

What is the profound sense of this parallelism? In so-called primitive societies, cooking by water and smoking have this in common: one as to its means, the other as to its results, is marked by duration. Cooking by water operates by means of receptacles made of pottery (or of wood with peoples who do not know about pottery, but boil water by immersing hot stones in it): in all cases these receptacles are cared for and repaired, sometimes passed on from generation to generation, and they number among the most durable cultural objects. As for smoking, it gives food that resists spoiling incomparably longer than that cooked by any other method. Everything transpires as if the lasting possession of a cultural acquisition entailed, sometimes in the ritual realm, sometimes in the mythic, a concession made in return to nature: when the result is durable, the means must be precarious, and vice-versa.

This ambiguity, which marks similarly, but in different directions, both the smoked and the boiled, is that same ambiguity which we already know to be inherent to the roasted. Burned on one side and raw on the other, or grilled outside, raw within, the roasted incarnates the ambiguity of the raw and the cooked, of nature and culture, which the smoked and the boiled must illustrate in their turn for the structure to be coherent. But what forces them into this pattern is not purely a reason of form: hence the system demonstrates that the art of cooking is not located entirely on the side of culture. Adapting itself to the exigencies of the body, and determined in its modes by the way man's insertion in nature operates in different parts of the world, placed then between nature and culture, cooking rather represents their necessary articulation. It partakes of both domains, and projects this duality on each of its manifestations.

But it cannot always do so in the same manner. The ambiguity of the roasted is intrinsic, that of the smoked and the boiled extrinsic, since it does not derive from things themselves, but from the way one speaks about them or behaves toward them. For here again a distinction becomes necessary: the quality of naturalness which language confers upon boiled food is purely metaphorical: the "boiled" is not the "spoiled"; it simply resembles it. Inversely, the transfiguration of the smoked into a natural entity does not result from the nonexistence of the buccan, the cultural instrument, but from its voluntary destruction. This transfiguration is thus on the order of metonymy, since it consists in acting as if the effect were really the cause. Consequently, even when the structure is added to or transformed to overcome a disequilibrium, it is only at the price of a new disequilibrium which manifests itself in another domain. To this ineluctable dissymmetry the structure owes its ability to engender myth, which is nothing other than an effort to correct or hide its inherent dissymmetry.

To conclude, let us return to our culinary triangle. Within it we traced another triangle representing recipes, at least the most elementary ones: roasting, boiling and smoking. The smoked and the boiled are opposed as to the nature of the intermediate element between fire and food, which is either air or water. The smoked and the roasted are opposed by the smaller or larger place given to the element air; and the roasted and the boiled by the presence or absence of water. The boundary between nature and culture, which one can imagine as parallel to either the axis of air or the axis of water, puts the roasted and the smoked on the side of nature, the boiled on the side of culture as to means; or, as to results, the smoked on the side of culture, the roasted and the boiled on the side of nature:

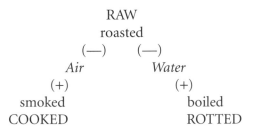

The operational value of our diagram would be very restricted did it not lend itself to all the transformations necessary to admit other categories of cooking. In a culinary system where the category of the roasted is divided into roasted and grilled, it is the latter term (connoting the lesser distance of meat from fire) which will be situated at the apex of the recipe triangle, the roasted then being placed, still on the air-axis, halfway between the grilled and the smoked. We may proceed in similar fashion if the culinary system in question makes a distinction between cooking with water and cooking with steam; the latter, where the water is at a distance from the food, will be located halfway between the boiled and the smoked.

A more complex transformation will be necessary to introduce the category of the fried. A tetrahedron will replace the recipe triangle, making it possible to raise a third axis, that of oil, in addition to those of air and water. The grilled will remain at the apex, but in the middle of the edge joining smoked and fried one can place roasted-in-the-oven (with the addition of fat), which is opposed to roasted-on-the-spit (without this addition). Similarly, on the edge running from fried to boiled will be braising (in a base of water and fat), opposed to steaming (without fat, and at a distance from the water). The plan can be still further developed, if necessary, by addition of the opposition between animal and vegetable foodstuffs (if they entail differentiating methods of cooking), and by the distinction of vegetable foods into cereals and legumes, since unlike the former (which one can simply grill), the latter cannot be cooked without water or fat, or both (unless one were to let the cereals ferment, which requires water but excluded fire during the process of transformation). Finally, seasonings will take their place in the system according to the combinations permitted or excluded with a given type of food.

After elaborating our diagram so as to integrate all the characteristics of a given culinary system (and no doubt there are other factors of a diachronic rather than a synchronic nature; those concerning the order, the presentation and the gestures of the meal), it will be necessary to seek the most economical manner of orienting it as a grille, so that it can be superposed on other contrasts of a sociological, economic, esthetic or religious nature: men and women, family and society, village and bush, economy and prodigality, nobility and commonality, sacred and profane, etc. Thus we can hope to discover for each specific case how the cooking of a society is a language in which it unconsciously translates its structure—or else resigns itself, still unconsciously, to revealing its contradictions.

Note

Translated from the French by Peter Brooks.

1. On these concepts, see Roman Jakobson, *Essais de linguistique générale*. Editions de Minuit, Paris (1963).

5

The Abominations of Leviticus[*]

Mary Douglas

Defilement is never an isolated event. It cannot occur except in view of a systematic ordering of ideas. Hence any piecemeal interpretation of the pollution rules of another culture is bound to fail. For the only way in which pollution ideas make sense is in reference to a total structure of thought whose key-stone, boundaries, margins and internal lines are held in relation by rituals of separation.

To illustrate this I take a hoary old puzzle from biblical scholarship, the abominations of Leviticus, and particularly the dietary rules. Why should the camel, the hare and the rock badger be unclean? Why should some locusts, but not all, be unclean? Why should the frog be clean and the mouse and the hippopotamus unclean? What have chameleons, moles and crocodiles got in common that they should be listed together (Levit. xi, 27)?

To help follow the argument I first quote the relevant versions of Leviticus and Deuteronomy using the text of the New Revised Standard Translation.

Deut. xiv

3. You shall not eat any abominable things. 4. These are the animals you may eat: the ox, the sheep, the goat, 5. the hart, the gazelle, the roebuck, the wild goat, the ibex, the antelope and the mountain-sheep. 6. Every animal that parts the hoof and has the hoof cloven in two, and chews the cud, among the animals you may eat. 7. Yet of those that chew the cud or have the hoof cloven you shall not eat these: The camel, the hare and the rockbadger, because they chew the cud but do not part the hoof, are unclean for you. 8. And the swine, because it parts the hoof but does not chew the cud, is unclean for you. Their flesh you shall not eat, and their carcasses you shall not touch. 9. Of all that are in the waters you may eat these: whatever has fins and scales you may eat. 10. And whatever does not have fins and scales you shall not eat it; it is unclean for you. 11. You may eat all clean birds. 12. But these are the ones which you shall not eat: the eagle, the vulture, the osprey; 13. the buzzard, the kite, after their kinds; 14. every raven after its kind; 15. the ostrich, the night hawk, the sea gull, the hawk, after their kinds; 16. the little owl and the great owl, the water hen; 17. and the pelican, the carrion vulture and the cormorant, 18. the stork, the heron, after their kinds; the hoopoe and the bat. 19. And all winged insects are unclean for you; they shall not be eaten. 20. All clean winged things you may eat.

Lev. xi

2. These are the living things which you may eat among all the beasts that are on the earth. 3. Whatever parts the hoof and is cloven-footed and chews the cud, among the animals you

[*]*Originally published 1966*

may eat. 4. Nevertheless among those that chew the cud or part the hoof, you shall not eat these: The camel, because it chews the cud but does not part the hoof, is unclean to you. 5. And the rock badger, because it chews the cud but does not part the hoof, is unclean to you. 6. And the hare, because it chews the cud but does not part the hoof, is unclean to you. 7. And the swine, because it parts the hoof and is cloven-footed but does not chew the cud, is unclean to you. 8. Of their flesh you shall not eat, and their carcasses you shall not touch; they are unclean to you. 9. These you may eat of all that are in the waters. Everything in the waters that has fins and scales, whether in the seas or in the rivers, you may eat. 10. But anything in the seas or the rivers that has not fins and scales, of the swarming creatures in the waters and of the living creatures that are in the waters, is an abomination to you. 11. They shall remain an abomination to you; of their flesh you shall not eat, and their carcasses you shall have in abomination 12. Everything in the waters that has not fins and scales is an abomination to you. 13. And these you shall have in abomination among the birds, they shall not be eaten, they are an abomination: the eagle, the ossifrage, the osprey, 14. the kite, the falcon according to its kind, 15. every raven according to its kind, 16. the ostrich and the night hawk, the sea gull, the hawk according to its kind, 17. the owl, the cormorant, the ibis, 18. the water hen, the pelican, the vulture, 19. the stork, the heron according to its kind, the hoopoe and the bat. 20. All winged insects that go upon all fours are an abomination to you. 21. Yet among the winged insects that go on all fours you may eat those which have legs above their feet, with which to leap upon the earth. 22. Of them you may eat: the locust according to its kind, the bald locust according to its kind, the cricket according to its kind, and the grasshopper according to its kind. 23. But all other winged insects which have four feet are an abomination to you. 24. And by these you shall become unclean; whoever touches their carcass shall be unclean until the evening, 25. and whoever carries any part of their carcass shall wash his clothes and be unclean until the evening. 26. Every animal which parts the hoof but is not cloven-footed or does not chew the cud is unclean to you: everyone who touches them shall be unclean. 27. And all that go on their paws, among the animals that go on all fours, are unclean to you; whoever touches their carcass shall be unclean until the evening, 28. and he who carries their carcass shall wash his clothes and be unclean until the evening; they are unclean to you. 29, And these are unclean to you among the swarming things that swarm upon the earth; the weasel, the mouse, the great lizard according to its kind, 30. the gecko, the land crocodile, the lizard, the sand lizard and the chameleon. 31. These are unclean to you among all that swarm; whoever touches them when they are dead shall be unclean until the evening. 32. And anything upon which any of them falls when they are dead shall be unclean. 41. Every swarming thing that swarms upon the earth is an abomination; it shall not be eaten. 42. Whatever goes on its belly, and whatever goes on all fours, or whatever has many feet, all the swarming things that swarm upon the earth, you shall not eat; for they are an abomination.

All the interpretations given so far fall into one of two groups: either the rules are meaningless, arbitrary because their intent is disciplinary and not doctrinal, or they are allegories of virtues and vices. Adopting the view that religious prescriptions are largely devoid of symbolism, Maimonides said:

> The Law that sacrifices should be brought is evidently of great use . . . but we cannot say why one offering be a lamb whilst another is a ram, and why a fixed number of these should be brought. Those who trouble themselves to find a cause for any of these detailed rules are in my eyes devoid of sense. . . .

As a mediaeval doctor of medicine, Maimonides was also disposed to believe that the dietary rules had a sound physiological basis, but we have already dismissed the medical approach to symbolism. For a modern version of the view that the dietary rules are not symbolic, but ethical, disciplinary, see Epstein's English notes to the Babylonian Talmud and also his popular history of Judaism (1959, p. 24):

> Both sets of laws have one common aim . . . Holiness. While the positive precepts have been ordained for the cultivation of virtue, and for the promotion of those finer qualities which

distinguish the truly religious and ethical being, the negative precepts are defined to combat vice and suppress other evil tendencies and instincts which stand athwart man's striving towards holiness . . . . The negative religious laws are likewise assigned educational aims and purposes. Foremost among these is the prohibition of eating the flesh of certain animals classed as 'unclean'. The law has nothing totemic about it. It is expressly associated in Scripture with the ideal of holiness. Its real object is to train the Israelite in self-control as the indispensable first step for the attainment of holiness.

According to Professor Stein's *The Dietary Laws in Rabbinic and Patristic Literature,* the ethical interpretation goes back to the time of Alexander the Great and the Hellenic influence on Jewish culture. The first century A.D. letters of Aristeas teaches that not only are the Mosaic rules a valuable discipline which 'prevents the Jews from thoughtless action and injustice', but they also coincide with what natural reason would dictate for achieving the good life. So the Hellenic influence allows the medical and ethical interpretations to run together. Philo held that Moses' principle of selection was precisely to choose the most delicious meats:

> The lawgiver sternly forbade all animals of land, sea or air whose flesh is the finest and fattest, like that of pigs and scaleless fish, knowing that they set a trap for the most slavish of senses, the taste, and that they produced gluttony,

(and here we are led straight into the medical interpretation)

> an evil dangerous to both soul and body, for gluttony begets indigestion, which is the source of all illnesses and infirmities.

In another stream of interpretation, following the tradition of Robertson Smith and Frazer, the Anglo-Saxon Old Testament scholars have tended to say simply that the rules are arbitrary because they are irrational. For example Nathaniel Micklem says:

> Commentators used to give much space to a discussion of the question why such and such creatures, and such or such states and symptoms were unclean. Have we, for instance, primitive rules of hygiene? Or were certain creatures and states unclean because they represented or typified certain sins? It may be taken as certain that neither hygiene, nor any kind of typology, is the basis of uncleanness. These regulations are not by any means to be rationalised. Their origins may be diverse, and go back beyond history . . .

Compare also R. S. Driver (1895):

> The principle, however, determining the line of demarcation between clean animals and unclean, is not stated; and what it is has been much debated. No single principle, embracing all the cases, seems yet to have been found, and not improbably more principles than one co-operated. Some animals may have been prohibited on account of their repulsive appearance or uncleanly habits, others upon sanitary grounds; in other cases, again, the motive of the prohibition may very probably have been a religious one, particularly animals may have been supposed, like the serpent in Arabia, to be animated by superhuman or demoniac beings, or they may have had a sacramental significance in the heathen rites of other nations; and the prohibition may have been intended as a protest against these beliefs. . . .

P. P. Saydon takes the same line in the *Catholic Commentary on Holy Scripture* (1953), acknowledging his debt to Driver and to Robertson Smith. It would seem that when

Robertson Smith applied the ideas of primitive, irrational and unexplainable to some parts of Hebrew religion they remained thus labelled and unexamined to this day.

Needless to say such interpretations are not interpretations at all, since they deny any significance to the rules. They express bafflement in a learned way. Micklem says it more frankly when he says of Leviticus:

> Chapters XI to XV are perhaps the least attractive in the whole Bible. To the modern reader there is much in them that is meaningless or repulsive. They are concerned with ritual 'uncleanness' in respect of animals (11) of childbirth (12), skin diseases and stained garments (13), of the rites for the purgation of skin diseases (14), of leprosy and of various issues or secretions of the human body (15). Of what interest can such subjects be except to the anthropologist? What can all this have to do with religion?

Pfeiffer's general position is to be critical of the priestly and legal elements in the life of Israel. So he too lends his authority to the view that the rules in the Priestly Code are largely arbitrary:

> Only priests who were lawyers could have conceived of religion as a theocracy regulated by a divine law fixing exactly, and therefore arbitrarily, the sacred obligations of the people to their God. They thus sanctified the external, obliterated from religion both the ethical ideals of Amos and the tender emotions of Hosea, and reduced the Universal Creator to the stature of an inflexible despot. . . . From immemorial custom P derived the two fundamental notions which characterise its legislation: physical holiness and arbitrary enactment—archaic conceptions which the reforming prophets had discarded in favour of spiritual holiness and moral law.
>
> (p. 91)

It may be true that lawyers tend to think in precise and codified forms. But is it plausible to argue that they tend to codify sheer nonsense—arbitrary enactments? Pfeiffer tries to have it both ways, insisting on the legalistic rigidity of the priestly authors and pointing to the lack of order in the setting out of the chapter to justify his view that the rules are arbitrary. Arbitrariness is a decidedly unexpected quality to find in Leviticus, as the Rev. Prof. H. J. Richards has pointed out to me. For source criticism attributes Leviticus to the Priestly source, the dominant concern of whose authors was for order. So the weight of source criticism supports us in looking for another interpretation.

As for the idea that the rules are allegories of virtues and vices, Professor Stein derives this vigorous tradition from the same early Alexandrian influence on Jewish thought (p. 145 seq.). Quoting the letter of Aristeas, he says that the High Priest, Eleazan:

> admits that most people find the biblical food restrictions not understandable. If God is the Creator of everything, why should His law be so severe as to exclude some animals even from touch (128 f)? His first answer still links the dietary restrictions with the danger of idolatry . . . . The second answer attempts to refute specific charges by means of allegorical exegesis. Each law about forbidden foods has its deep reason. Moses did not enumerate the mouse or the weasel out of a special consideration for them (143 f). On the contrary, mice are particularly obnoxious because of their destructiveness, and weasels, the very symbol of malicious tale-bearing, conceive through the ear and give birth through the mouth (164 f). Rather have these holy laws been given for the sake of justice to awaken in us devout thoughts and to form our character (161–168). The birds, for instance, the Jews are allowed to eat are all tame and clean, as they live by corn only. Not so the wild and carnivorous birds who fall upon lambs and goats, and even human beings. Moses, by calling the latter unclean, admonished the faithful not to do violence to the weak and not to trust their own power (145–148). Cloven-hoofed animals

which part their hooves symbolise that all our actions must betray proper ethical distinction and be directed towards righteousness. . . . Chewing the cud, on the other hand stands for memory.

Professor Stein goes on to quote Philo's use of allegory to interpret the dietary rules:

Fish with fins and scales, admitted by the law, symbolise endurance and self-control, whilst the forbidden ones are swept away by the current, unable to resist the force of the stream. Reptiles, wriggling along by trailing their belly, signify persons who devote themselves to their ever greedy desires and passions. Creeping things, however, which have legs above their feet, so that they can leap, are clean because they symbolise the success of moral efforts.

Christian teaching has readily followed the allegorising tradition. The first century epistle of Barnabus, written to convince the Jews that their law had found its fulfilment, took the clean and unclean animals to refer to various types of men, leprosy to mean sin, etc. A more recent example of this tradition is in Bishop Challoner's notes on the Westminster Bible in the beginning of this century:

Hoof divided and cheweth the cud. The dividing of the hoof and chewing of the cud signify discretion between good and evil, and meditating on the law of God; and where either of these is wanting, man is unclean. In like manner fishes were reputed unclean that had not fins and scales: that is souls that did not raise themselves up by prayer and cover themselves with the scales of virtue.

                                                                                    Footnote verse 3.

These are not so much interpretations as pious commentaries. They fail as interpretations because they are neither consistent nor comprehensive. A different explanation has to be developed for each animal and there is no end to the number of possible explanations.

Another traditional approach, also dating back to the letter of Aristeas, is the view that what is forbidden to the Israelites is forbidden solely to protect them from foreign influence. For instance, Maimonides held that they were forbidden to seethe the kid in the milk of its dam because this was a cultic act in the religion of the Canaanites. This argument cannot be comprehensive, for it is not held that the Israelites consistently rejected all the elements of foreign religions and invented something entirely original for themselves. Maimonides accepted the view that some of the more mysterious commands of the law had as their object to make a sharp break with heathen practices. Thus the Israelites were forbidden to wear garments woven of linen and wool, to plant different trees together, to have sexual intercourse with animals, to cook meat with milk, simply because these acts figured in the rites of their heathen neighbours. So far, so good: the laws were enacted as barriers to the spread of heathen styles of ritual. But in that case why were some heathen practices allowed? And not only allowed—if sacrifice be taken as a practice common to heathens and Israelites—but given an absolutely central place in the religion. Maimonides' answer, at any rate in *The Guide to the Perplexed,* was to justify sacrifice as a transitional stage, regrettably heathen, but necessarily allowed because it would be impractical to wean the Israelites abruptly from their heathen past. This is an extraordinary statement to come from the pen of a rabbinical scholar, and indeed in his serious rabbinical writings Maimonides did not attempt to maintain the argument: on the contrary, he there counted sacrifice as the most important act of the Jewish religion.

At least Maimonides saw the inconsistency and was led by it into contradiction. But later scholars seem content to use the foreign influence argument one way or the other, according to the mood of the moment. Professor Hooke and his colleagues have clearly established that the Israelites took over some Canaanite styles of worship, and the Canaanites obviously had much in common with Mesopotamian culture (1933). But it is no explanation to represent Israel as a sponge at one moment and as a repellent the next, without explaining why it soaked up this foreign element but repelled that one. What is the value of saying that seething kids in milk and copulating with cows are forbidden in Leviticus because they are the fertility rites of foreign neighbours (1935), since Israelites took over other foreign rites? We are still perplexed to know when the sponge is the right or the wrong metaphor. The same argument is equally puzzling in Eichrodt (pp. 230–1). Of course no culture is created out of nothing. The Israelites absorbed freely from their neighbours, but not quite freely. Some elements of foreign culture were incompatible with the principles of patterning on which they were constructing their universe; others were compatible. For instance, Zaehner suggests that the Jewish abomination of creeping things may have been taken over from Zoroastrianism (p. 162). Whatever the historical evidence for this adoption of a foreign element into Judaism, we shall see that there was in the patterning of their culture a pre-formed compatibility between this particular abomination and the general principles on which their universe was constructed.

Any interpretations will fail which take the Do-nots of the Old Testament in piece-meal fashion. The only sound approach is to forget hygiene, aesthetics, morals and instinctive revulsion, even to forget the Canaanites and the Zoroastrian Magi, and start with the texts. Since each of the injunctions is prefaced by the command to be holy, so they must be explained by that command. There must be contrariness between holiness and abomination which will make over-all sense of all the particular restrictions.

Holiness is the attribute of Godhead. Its root means 'set apart'. What else does it mean? We should start any cosmological enquiry by seeking the principles of power and danger. In the Old Testament we find blessing as the source of all good things, and the withdrawal of blessing as the source of all dangers. The blessing of God makes the land possible for men to live in.

God's work through the blessing is essentially to create order, through which men's affairs prosper. Fertility of women, livestock and fields is promised as a result of the blessing and this is to be obtained by keeping covenant with God and observing all His precepts and ceremonies (Deut. XXXVIII, 1–14). Where the blessing is withdrawn and the power of the curse unleashed, there is barrenness, pestilence, confusion. For Moses said:

> But if you will not obey the voice of the Lord your God or be careful to do all his commandments and his statutes which I command you to this day, then all these curses shall come upon you and overtake you. Cursed shall you be in the city, and cursed shall you be in the field. Cursed shall be your basket and your kneading trough. Cursed shall be the fruit of your body, and the fruit of your ground, the increase of your cattle, and the young of your flock. Cursed shall you be when you come in and cursed shall you be when you go out. The Lord will send upon you curses, confusion, and frustration in all that you undertake to do, until you are destroyed and perish quickly on account of the evil of your doings, because you have forsaken me ... The Lord will smite you with consumption, and with fever, inflammation, and fiery heat, and with drought, and with blasting and with mildew; they shall pursue you till you perish.

And the heavens over your head shall be brass and the earth beyond you shall be iron. The Lord will make the rain of your land powder and dust; from heaven it shall come down upon you until you are destroyed.

(Deut. XXVIII, 15–24)

From this it is clear that the positive and negative precepts are held to be efficacious and not merely expressive: observing them draws down prosperity, infringing them brings danger. We are thus entitled to treat them in the same way as we treat primitive ritual avoidances whose breach unleashes danger to men. The precepts and ceremonies alike are focused on the idea of the holiness of God which men must create in their own lives. So this is a universe in which men prosper by conforming to holiness and perish when they deviate from it. If there were no other clues we should be able to find out the Hebrew idea of the holy by examining the precepts by which men conform to it. It is evidently not goodness in the sense of an all-embracing humane kindness. Justice and moral goodness may well illustrate holiness and form part of it, but holiness embraces other ideas as well.

Granted that its root means separateness, the next idea that emerges is of the Holy as wholeness and completeness. Much of Leviticus is taken up with stating the physical perfection that is required of things presented in the temple and of persons approaching it. The animals offered in sacrifice must be without blemish, women must be purified after childbirth, lepers should be separated and ritually cleansed before being allowed to approach it once they are cured. All bodily discharges are defiling and disqualify from approach to the temple. Priests may only come into contact with death when their own close kin die. But the high priest must never have contact with death.

Levit. xxi

17. Say to Aaron, None of your descendants throughout their generations who has a blemish may approach to offer the bread of his God. 18. For no one who has a blemish shall draw near, a man blind or lame, or one who has a mutilated face or a limb too long. 19. or a man who has an injured foot or an injured hand, 20. or a hunch-back, or a dwarf, or a man with a defect in his sight or an itching disease or scabs, or crushed testicles; 21. no man of the descendants of Aaron the priest who has a blemish shall come near to offer the Lord's offerings by fire; . . . .

In other words, he must be perfect as a man, if he is to be a priest.

This much reiterated idea of physical completeness is also worked out in the social sphere and particularly in the warriors' camp. The culture of the Israelites was brought to the pitch of greatest intensity when they prayed and when they fought. The army could not win without the blessing and to keep the blessing in the camp they had to be specially holy. So the camp was to be preserved from defilement like the Temple. Here again all bodily discharges disqualified a man from entering the camp as they would disqualify a worshipper from approaching the altar. A warrior who had had an issue of the body in the night should keep outside the camp all day and only return after sunset, having washed. Natural functions producing bodily waste were to be performed outside the camp (Deut. XXIII, 10–15). In short the idea of holiness was given an external, physical expression in the wholeness of the body seen as a perfect container.

Wholeness is also extended to signify completeness in a social context. An important enterprise, once begun, must not be left incomplete. This way of lacking wholeness also disqualifies a man from fighting. Before a battle the captains shall proclaim:

Deut. xx
5. What man is there that has built a new house and has not dedicated it? Let him go back to his house, lest he die in the battle and another man dedicate it. 6. What man is there that has planted a vineyard and has not yet enjoyed its fruit? Let him go back to his house, lest he die in the battle and another man enjoy its fruit. 7. And what man is there that hath betrothed a wife and has not taken her? Let him go back to his house, lest he die in the battle and another man take her.

Admittedly there is no suggestion that this rule implies defilement. It is not said that a man with a half-finished project on his hands is defiled in the same way that a leper is defiled. The next verse in fact goes on to say that fearful and faint-hearted men should go home lest they spread their fears. But there is a strong suggestion in other passages that a man should not put his hand to the plough and then turn back. Pedersen goes so far as to say that:

in all these cases a man has started a new important undertaking without having finished it yet... a new totality has come into existence. To make a breach in this prematurely, i.e. before it has attained maturity or has been finished, involves a serious risk of sin.

(Vol. III, p. 9)

If we follow Pedersen, then blessing and success in war required a man to be whole in body, whole-hearted and trailing no uncompleted schemes. There is an echo of this actual passage in the New Testament parable of the man who gave a great feast and whose invited guests incurred his anger by making excuses (Luke XIV, 16–24; Matt. XXII. See Black & Rowley, 1962, p. 836) One of the guests had bought a new farm, one had bought ten oxen and had not yet tried them, and one had married a wife. If according to the old Law each could have validly justified his refusal by reference to Deut. XX, the parable supports Pedersen's view that interruption of new projects was held to be bad in civil as well as military contexts.

Other precepts develop the idea of wholeness in another direction. The metaphors of the physical body and of the new undertaking relate to the perfection and completeness of the individual and his work. Other precepts extend holiness to species and categories. Hybrids and other confusions are abominated.

Lev. xviii
23. And you shall not lie with any beast and defile yourself with it, neither shall any woman give herself to a beast to lie with it: it is perversion.

The word 'perversion' is a significant mistranslation of the rare Hebrew word *tebhel*, which has as its meaning mixing or confusion. The same theme is taken up in Leviticus XIX, 19.

You shall keep my statutes. You shall not let your cattle breed with a different kind; you shall not sow your field with two kinds of seed; nor shall there come upon you a garment of cloth made of two kinds of stuff.

All these injunctions are prefaced by the general command:

Be holy, for I am holy.

We can conclude that holiness is exemplified by completeness. Holiness requires that individuals shall conform to the class to which they belong. And holiness requires that different classes of things shall not be confused.

Another set of precepts refines on this last point. Holiness means keeping distinct the categories of creation. It therefore involves correct definition, discrimination and order. Under this head all the rules of sexual morality exemplify the holy. Incest and adultery (Lev. XVIII, 6–20) are against holiness, in the simple sense of right order. Morality doesnot conflict with holiness, but holiness is more a matter of separating that which should be separated than of protecting the rights of husbands and brothers.

Then follows in chapter XIX another list of actions which are contrary to holiness. Developing the idea of holiness as order, not confusion, this list upholds rectitude and straight-dealing as holy, and contradiction and double-dealing as against holiness. Theft, lying, false witness, cheating in weights and measures, all kinds of dissembling such as speaking ill of the deaf (and presumably smiling to their face), hating your brother in your heart (while presumably speaking kindly to him), these are clearly contradictions between what seems and what is. This chapter also says much about generosity and love, but these are positive commands, while I am concerned with negative rules.

We have now laid a good basis for approaching the laws about clean and unclean meats. To be holy is to be whole, to be one; holiness is unity, integrity, perfection of the individual and of the kind. The dietary rules merely develop the metaphor of holiness on the same lines.

First we should start with livestock, the herds of cattle, camels, sheep and goats which were the livelihood of the Israelites. These animals were clean inasmuch as contact with them did not require purification before approaching the Temple. Livestock, like the inhabited land, received the blessing of God. Both land and livestock were fertile by the blessing, both were drawn into the divine order. The farmer's duty was to preserve the blessing. For one thing, he had to preserve the order of creation. So no hybrids, as we have seen, either in the fields or in the herds or in the clothes made from wool and flax. To some extent men covenanted with their land and cattle in the same way as God covenanted with them. Men respected the first born of their cattle, obliged them to keep the Sabbath. Cattle were literally domesticated as slaves. They had to be brought into the social order in order to enjoy the blessing. The difference between cattle and the wild beasts is that the wild beasts have no covenant to protect them. It is possible that the Israelites were like other pastoralists who do not relish wild game. The Nuer of the South Sudan, for instance, apply a sanction of disapproval of a man who lives by hunting. To be driven to eating wild meat is the sign of a poor herdsman. So it would be probably wrong to think of the Israelites as longing for forbidden meats and finding the restrictions irksome. Driver is surely right in taking the rules as an *a posteriori* generalisation of their habits. Cloven-hoofed, cud-chewing ungulates are the model of the proper kind of food for a pastoralist. If they must eat wild game, they can eat wild game that shares these distinctive characters and is therefore of the same general species. This is a kind of casuistry which permits scope for hunting antelope and wild goats and wild sheep. Everything would be quite straightforward were it not that the legal mind has seen fit to give ruling on some borderline cases. Some animals seem to be ruminant, such as the hare and the hyrax (or rock badger), whose constant grinding of their teeth was held to be cud-chewing. But they are definitely not cloven-hoofed and so are excluded by name. Similarly for animals which are cloven-hoofed but are not ruminant, the pig and the camel. Note that this failure to conform to the two necessary criteria for defining cattle is the only reason given in the Old Testament for avoiding the pig; nothing whatever is said about its dirty scavenging habits. As the pig does not yield milk, hide nor wool, there is no other reason for keeping it except for its flesh. And if the Israelites did not keep pig they would not be familiar with its habits. I suggest that originally the sole reason for its being counted as unclean is its failure as a wild boar to get into the antelope class, and that in this it is on the same footing as the camel and the hyrax, exactly as is stated in the book.

After these borderline cases have been dismissed, the law goes on to deal with creatures according to how they live in the three elements, the water, the air and the earth. The principles here applied are rather different from those covering the camel, the pig, the hare and the hyrax. For the latter are excepted from clean food in having one but not both of the defining characters of livestock. Birds I can say nothing about, because, as I have said, they are named and not described and the translation of the name is open to doubt. But in general the underlying principle of cleanness in animals is that they shall conform fully to their class. Those species are unclean which are imperfect members of their class, or whose class itself confounds the general scheme of the world.

To grasp this scheme we need to go back to Genesis and the creation. Here a three-fold classification unfolds, divided between the earth, the waters and the firmament. Leviticus takes up this scheme and allots to each element its proper kind of animal life. In the firmament two-legged fowls fly with wings. In the water scaly fish swim with fins. On the earth four-legged animals hop, jump or walk. Any class of creatures which is not equipped for the right kind of locomotion in its element is contrary to holiness. Contact with it disqualifies a person from approaching the Temple. Thus anything in the water which has not fins and scales is unclean (XI, 10–12). Nothing is said about predatory habits or of scavenging. The only sure test for cleanness in a fish is its scales and its propulsion by means of fins.

Four-footed creatures which fly (XI, 20–26) are unclean. Any creature which has two legs and two hands and which goes on all fours like a quadruped is unclean (XI, 27). Then follows (V. 29) a much disputed list. On some translations, it would appear to consist precisely of creatures endowed with hands instead of front feet, which perversely use their hands for walking: the weasel, the mouse, the crocodile, the shrew, various kinds of lizards, the chameleon and mole (Danby, 1933), whose forefeet are uncannily hand-like. This feature of this list is lost in the New Revised Standard Translation which uses the word 'paws' instead of hands.

The last kind of unclean animal is that which creeps, crawls or swarms upon the earth. This form of movement is explicitly contrary to holiness (Levit. XI, 41–44). Driver and White use 'swarming' to translate the Hebrew shérec, which is applied to both those which teem in the waters and those which swarm on the ground. Whether we call it teeming, trailing, creeping, crawling or swarming, it is an indeterminate form of movement. Since the main animal categories are defined by their typical movement, 'swarming' which is not a mode of propulsion proper to any particular element, cuts across the basic classification. Swarming things are neither fish, flesh nor fowl. Eels and worms inhabit water, though not as fish; reptiles go on dry land, though not as quadrupeds; some insects fly, though not as birds. There is no order in them. Recall what the Prophecy of Habakkuk says about this form of life:

> For thou makest men like the fish of the sea, like crawling things that have no ruler.
>
> (I, V. 14)

The prototype and model of the swarming things is the worm. As fish belong in the sea so worms belong in the realm of the grave, with death and chaos.

The case of the locusts is interesting and consistent. The test of whether it is a clean and therefore edible kind is how it moves on the earth. If it crawls it is unclean. If it hops it is clean (XI, V. 21). In the Mishnah it is noted that a frog is not listed with creeping things and conveys no uncleanness (Danby, p. 722). I suggest that the frog's hop accounts for it not being listed. If penguins lived in the Near East I would expect them to be ruled unclean as wingless birds. If the list of unclean birds could be retranslated from this point of view, it might well turn out that they are anomalous because they swim and dive as well as they fly, or in some other way they are not fully bird-like.

Surely now it would be difficult to maintain that 'Be ye Holy' means no more than 'Be ye separate'. Moses wanted the children of Israel to keep the commands of God constantly before their minds:

> *Deut. xi*
>
> 18. You shall therefore lay up these words of mine in your heart and in your soul; and you shall bind them as a sign upon your hand, and they shall be as frontlets between your eyes. 19. And you shall teach them to your children, talking of them when you are sitting in your house, and when you are walking by the way, and when you lie down and when you rise. 20. And you shall write them upon the doorposts of your house and upon your gates.

If the proposed interpretation of the forbidden animals is correct, the dietary laws would have been like signs which at every turn inspired meditation on the oneness, purity and completeness of God. By rules of avoidance holiness was given a physical expression in every encounter with the animal kingdom and at every meal. Observance of the dietary rules would thus have been a meaningful part of the great liturgical act of recognition and worship which culminated in the sacrifice in the Temple.

References

Black, M. and Rowley, H.H., 1962. (Eds.) *Peake's Commentary on the Bible*. London.

Driver, R.S., 1895. *International Critical Commentary on Holy Scriptures of the Old and New Testaments: Deuteronomy*.

Eichrodt, W., 1933 (first edit.) *Theology of the Old Testament*. Trans. Baker 1961.

Epstein, I. *Judaism*. London.

Hooke, S.H., ed., 1933. *Myth and Ritual*. Oxford.

Hooke, S.H., C.N. Deedes, E.R. Burrows, A.R. Johnson and W.O.E. Oesterley, 1935. *The Labyrinth: Further Studies in the Relation between Myth and Ritual in the Ancient World*. London.

Maimonides, Moses, 1881. *Guide for the Perplexed*. Translated by M. Friedlander, first edition, London.

Micklem, Nathaniel, 1953. *The Interpreter's Bible, II, Leviticus*.

Pfeifer, R.H., 1957. *Books of the Old Testament*.

Saydon, P.P., 1953. *Catholic Commentary on the Holy Scripture*.

Stein, S., 1957. 'The Dietary Laws in Rabbinic and Patristic Literature'. *Studia Patristica*, Vol. 64, pp. 141 ff.

Zaehner, R.H., 1963. *The Dawn and Twilight of Zoroastrianism*.

6

The Abominable Pig[*]

Marvin Harris

An aversion to pork seems at the outset even more irrational than an aversion to beef. Of all domesticated mammals, pigs possess the greatest potential for swiftly and efficiently changing plants into flesh. Over its lifetime a pig can convert 35 percent of the energy in its feed to meat compared with 13 percent for sheep and a mere 6.5 percent for cattle. A piglet can gain a pound for every three to five pounds it eats while a calf needs to eat ten pounds to gain one. A cow needs nine months to drop a single calf, and under modern conditions the calf needs another four months to reach four hundred pounds. But less than four months after insemination, a single sow can give birth to eight or more piglets, each of which after another six months can weigh over four hundred pounds. Clearly, the whole essence of pig is the production of meat for human nourishment and delectation. Why then did the Lord of the ancient Israelites forbid his people to savor pork or even to touch a pig alive or dead?

> Of their flesh you shall not eat, and their carcasses you shall not touch; they are unclean to you (Lev. 11: 1) . . . everyone who touches them shall be unclean.
>
> (Lev. 11:24)

Unlike the Old Testament, which is a treasure trove of forbidden flesh, the Koran is virtually free of meat taboos. Why is it the pig alone who suffers Allah's disapproval?

> These things only has He forbidden you: carrion, blood, and the flesh of swine.
>
> (Holy Koran 2, 168)

For many observant Jews, the Old Testament's characterization of swine as "unclean" renders the explanation of the taboo self-evident: "Anyone who has seen the filthy habits of the swine will not ask why it is prohibited," says a modern rabbinical authority. The grounding of the fear and loathing of pigs in self-evident piggishness goes back at least to the time of Rabbi Moses Maimonides, court physician to the Islamic emperor Saladin during the twelfth century in Egypt. Maimonides shared with his Islamic hosts a lively disgust for pigs and pig eaters, especially Christian pigs and pig eaters: "The principal reason why the law forbids swine-flesh is to be found in the circumstance that its habits and food are very filthy and loathsome." If the law

[*]*Originally published 1985*

allowed Egyptians and Jews to raise pigs, Cairo's streets and houses would become as filthy as those of Europe, for "the mouth of a swine is as dirty as dung itself." Maimonides could only tell one side of the story. He had never seen a clean pig. The pig's penchant for excrement is not a defect of its nature but of the husbandry of its human masters. Pigs prefer and thrive best on roots, nuts, and grains; they eat excrement only when nothing better presents itself. In fact, let them get hungry enough, and they'll even eat each other, a trait which they share with other omnivores, but most notably with their own masters. Nor is wallowing in filth a natural characteristic of swine. Pigs wallow to keep themselves cool; and they much prefer a fresh, clean mudhole to one that has been soiled by urine and feces.

In condemning the pig as the dirtiest of animals, Jews and Moslems left unexplained their more tolerant attitude toward other dung-eating domesticated species. Chickens and goats, for example, given motivation and opportunity, also readily dine on dung. The dog is another domesticated creature which easily develops an appetite for human feces. And this was especially true in the Middle East, where dung-eating dogs filled the scavenging niche left vacant by the ban on pigs. Jahweh prohibited their flesh, yet dogs were not abominated, bad to touch, or even bad to look at, as were pigs.

Maimonides could not be entirely consistent in his efforts to attribute the abstention from pork to the pig's penchant for feces. The Book of Leviticus prohibits the flesh of many other creatures, such as cats and camels, which are not notably inclined to eat excrement. And with the exception of the pig, had not Allah said all the others were good to eat? The fact that Maimonides's Moslem emperor could eat every kind of meat except pork would have made it impolitic if not dangerous to identify the biblical sense of cleanliness exclusively with freedom from the taint of feces. So instead of adopting a cleaner-than-thou attitude, Maimonides offered a proper court physician's theory of the entire set of biblical aversions: the prohibited items were not good to eat because not only was one of them—the pig—filthy from eating excrement but all of them were not good for you. "I maintain," he said, "that food forbidden by the Law is unwholesome." But in what ways were the forbidden foods unwholesome? The great rabbi was quite specific in the case of pork: it "contained more moisture than necessary and too much superfluous matter." As for the other forbidden foods, their "injurious character" was too self-evident to merit further discussion.

Maimonides's public health theory of pork avoidance had to wait seven hundred years before it acquired what seemed to be a scientific justification. In 1859 the first clinical association between trichinosis and undercooked pork was established, and from then on it became the most popular explanation of the Jewish and Islamic pork taboo. Just as Maimonides said, pork was unwholesome. Eager to reconcile the Bible with the findings of medical science, theologians began to embroider a whole series of additional public health explanations for the other biblical food taboos: wild animals and beasts of burden were prohibited because the flesh gets too tough to be digested properly; shellfish were to be avoided because they serve as vectors of typhoid fever; blood is not good to eat because the bloodstream is a perfect medium for microbes. In the case of pork this line of rationalization had a paradoxical outcome. Reformist Jews began to argue that since they now understood the scientific and medical basis of the taboos, pork avoidance was no longer necessary; all they had to do was to see to it that the meat was thoroughly cooked. Predictably, this provoked a reaction among

Orthodox Jews, who were appalled at the idea that the book of God's law was being relegated to the "class of a minor medical text." They insisted that God's purpose in Leviticus could never be fully comprehended; nonetheless the dietary laws had to be obeyed as a sign of submission to divine will.

Eventually the trichinosis theory of pork avoidance fell out of favor largely on the grounds that a medical discovery made in the nineteenth century could not have been known thousands of years ago. But that is not the part of the theory that bothers me. People do not have to possess a scientific understanding of the ill effects of certain foods in order to put such foods on their bad-to-eat list. If the consequences of eating pork had been exceptionally bad for their health, it would not have been necessary for the Israelites to know about trichinosis in order to ban its consumption. Does one have to understand the molecular chemistry of toxins in order to know that some mushrooms are dangerous? It is essential for my own explanation of the pig taboo that the trichinosis theory be laid to rest on entirely different grounds. My contention is that there is absolutely nothing exceptional about pork as a source of human disease. All domestic animals are potentially hazardous to human health. Undercooked beef, for example, is a prolific source of tapeworms, which can grow to a length of sixteen to twenty feet inside the human gut, induce a severe case of anemia, and lower the body's resistance to other diseases. Cattle, goat, and sheep transmit the bacterial disease known as brucellosis, whose symptoms include fever, aches, pains, and lassitude. The most dangerous disease transmitted by cattle, sheep, and goats is anthrax, a fairly common disease of both animals and humans in Europe and Asia until the introduction of Louis Pasteur's anthrax vaccine in 1881. Unlike trichinosis, which does not produce symptoms in the majority of infected individuals and rarely has a fatal outcome, anthrax runs a swift course that begins with an outbreak of boils and ends in death.

If the taboo on pork was a divinely inspired health ordinance, it is the oldest recorded case of medical malpractice. The way to safeguard against trichinosis was not to taboo pork but to taboo undercooked pork. A simple advisory against undercooking pork would have sufficed: "Flesh of swine thou shalt not eat until the pink has been cooked from it." And come to think of it, the same advisory should have been issued for cattle, sheep, and goats. But the charge of medical malpractice against Jahweh will not stick.

The Old Testament contains a rather precise formula for distinguishing good-to-eat flesh from forbidden flesh. This formula says nothing about dirty habits or unhealthy meat. Instead it directs attention to certain anatomical and physiological features of animals that are good to eat. Here is what Leviticus 11: 1 says:

Whatever parts the hoof and is cloven footed and chews the cud among animals, you may eat.

Any serious attempt to explain why the pig was not good to eat must begin with this formula and not with excrement or wholesomeness, about which not a word is said. Leviticus goes on to state explicitly of the pig that it only satisfies one part of the formula. "It divideth the hoof." But the pig does not satisfy the other part of the formula: "It cheweth not the cud."

To their credit, champions of the good-to-eat school have stressed the importance of the cud-chewing, split-hoof formula as the key to understanding Jahweh's abomination of the pig. But they do not view the formula as an outcome of the way the Israelites used domestic animals. Instead they view the way the Israelites used domestic animals as an outcome of the formula. According to anthropologist Mary Douglas, for example, the cud-chewing, split-hoof formula makes the split-hoof but non-cud-chewing pig a thing that's "out of place." Things that are "out of place" are dirty, she argues, for the essence of dirt is "matter out of place." The pig, however, is more than out of place; it is neither here nor there. Such things are both dirty and dangerous. Therefore the pig is abominated as well as not good to eat. But doesn't the force of this argument lie entirely in its circularity? To observe that the pig is out of place taxonomically is merely to observe that Leviticus classifies good-to-eat animals in such a way as to make the pig bad to eat. This avoids the question of why the taxonomy is what it is.

Let me attend first to the reason why Jahweh wanted edible animals to be cud-chewers. Among animals raised by the ancient Israelites, there were three cud-chewers: cattle, sheep, and goats. These three animals were the most important food-producing species in the ancient Middle East not because the ancients happened capriciously to think that cud-chewing animals were good to eat (and good to milk) but because cattle, sheep, and goats are ruminants, the kind of herbivores which thrive best on diets consisting of plants that have a high cellulose content. Of all domesticated animals, those which are ruminants possess the most efficient system for digesting tough fibrous materials such as grasses and straw. Their stomachs have four compartments which are like big fermentation "vats" in which bacteria break down and soften these materials. While cropping their food, ruminants do little chewing. The food passes directly to the rumen, the first of the compartments, where it soon begins to ferment. From time to time the contents of the rumen are regurgitated into the mouth as a softened bolus—the "cud"—which is then chewed thoroughly and sent on to the other "vats" to undergo further fermentation.

The ruminant's extraordinary ability to digest cellulose was crucial to the relationship between humans and domesticated animals in the Middle East. By raising animals that could "chew the cud," the Israelites and their neighbors were able to obtain meat and milk without having to share with their livestock the crops destined for human consumption. Cattle, sheep, and goats thrive on items like grass, straw, hay, stubble, bushes, and leaves—feeds whose high cellulose content renders them unfit for human consumption even after vigorous boiling. Rather than compete with humans for food, the ruminants further enhanced agricultural productivity by providing dung for fertilizer and traction for pulling plows. And they were also a source of fiber and felt for clothing, and of leather for shoes and harnesses.

I began this puzzle by saying that pigs are the most efficient mammalian converters of plant foods into animal flesh, but I neglected to say what kinds of plant foods. Feed them on wheat, maize, potatoes, soybeans, or anything low in cellulose, and pigs will perform veritable miracles of transubstantiation; feed them on grass, stubble, leaves, or anything high in cellulose, and they will lose weight.

Pigs are omnivores, but they are not ruminants. In fact, in digestive apparatus and nutrient requirements pigs resemble humans in more ways than any mammal except monkeys and apes, which is why pigs are much in demand for medical research concerned with atherosclerosis, calorie-protein malnutrition, nutrient absorption, and metabolism. But there was more to the ban on pork than the pig's inability to thrive on grass and other high-cellulose plants. Pigs carry the additional onus of not being well adapted to the climate and ecology of the Middle East. Unlike the ancestors of cattle, sheep, or goats, which lived in hot, semiarid, sunny grasslands, the pig's ancestors were denizens of well-watered, shady forest glens and riverbanks. Everything about the pig's body heat-regulating system is ill suited for life in the hot, sun-parched habitats which were the homelands of the children of Abraham. Tropical breeds of cattle, sheep, and goats can go for long periods without water, and can either rid their bodies of excess heat through perspiration or are protected from the sun's rays by light-colored, short fleecy coats (heat-trapping heavy wool is a characteristic of cold-climate breeds). Although a perspiring human is said to "sweat like a pig," the expression lacks an anatomical basis. Pigs can't sweat—they have no functional sweat glands. (Humans are actually the sweatiest of all animals.) And the pig's sparse coat offers little protection against the sun's rays. Just how does the pig keep cool? It does a lot of panting, but mostly it depends on wetting itself down with moisture derived from external sources. Here, then, is the explanation for the pig's love of wallowing in mud. By wallowing, it dissipates heat both by evaporation from its skin and by conduction through the cool ground. Experiments show that the cooling effect of mud is superior to that of water. Pigs whose flanks are thoroughly smeared with mud continue to show peak heat-dissipating evaporation for more than twice as long as pigs whose flanks are merely soaked with water, and here also is the explanation for some of the pig's dirty habits. As temperatures rise above thirty degrees celsius (eighty-six degrees Fahrenheit), a pig deprived of clean mudholes will become desperate and begin to wallow in its own feces and urine in order to avoid heat stroke. Incidentally, the larger a pig gets, the more intolerant it becomes of high ambient temperatures.

Raising pigs in the Middle East therefore was and still is a lot costlier than raising ruminants, because pigs must be provided with artificial shade and extra water for wallowing, and their diet must be supplemented with grains and other plant foods that humans themselves can eat.

To offset all these liabilities pigs have less to offer by way of benefits than ruminants. They can't pull plows, their hair is unsuited for fiber and cloth, and they are not suited for milking. Uniquely among large domesticated animals, meat is their most important produce (guinea pigs and rabbits are smaller equivalents; but fowl produce eggs as well as meat).

For a pastoral nomadic people like the Israelites during their years of wandering in search of lands suitable for agriculture, swineherding was out of the question. No arid-land pastoralists herd pigs for the simple reason that it is hard to protect them from exposure to heat, sun, and lack of water while moving from camp to camp over long distances. During their formative years as a nation, therefore, the ancient Israelites could not have consumed significant quantities of pork even had they desired it. This historical experience undoubtedly contributed to the development of a traditional aversion to pig meat as an unknown and alien food. But why was this tradition preserved and strengthened by being written down as God's law long after the Israelites had become settled farmers? The answer as I see it is not that the tradition born of pastoralism continued to prevail by mere inertia and ingrown habit, but that it was preserved because pig raising remained too costly.

Critics have opposed the theory that the ancient Israelite pork taboo was essentially a cost/benefit choice by pointing to evidence of pigs being raised quite successfully in many parts of the Middle East including the Israelite's promised land. The facts are not in dispute. Pigs have indeed been raised for ten thousand years in various parts of the Middle East—as long as sheep and goats, and even longer than cattle. Some of the oldest Neolithic villages excavated by archaeologists—Jericho in Jordan, Jarmo in Iraq, and Argissa-Magulla in Greece—contain pig bones with features indicative of the transition from wild to domesticated varieties. Several Middle Eastern pre-Bronze Age villages (4000 B.C. to 2000 B.C.) contain concentrated masses of pig remains in association with what archaeologists interpret as altars and cultic centers, suggestive of ritual pig slaughter and pig feasting. We know that some pigs were still being raised in the lands of the Bible at the beginning of the Christian era. The New Testament (Luke) tells us that in the country of the Gadarenes near Lake Galilee Jesus cast out devils from a man named Legion into a herd of swine feeding on the mountain. The swine rushed down into the lake and drowned themselves, and Legion was cured. Even modern-day Israelites continue to raise thousands of swine in parts of northern Galilee. But from the very beginning, fewer pigs were raised than cattle, sheep, or goats. And more importantly, as time went on, pig husbandry declined throughout the region.

Carlton Coon, an anthropologist with many years of experience in North America and the Levant, was the first scholar to offer a cogent explanation of why this general decline in pig husbandry had occurred. Coon attributed the fall of the Middle Eastern pig to deforestation and human population increase. At the beginning of the Neolithic period, pigs were able to root in oak and beech forests which provided ample shade and wallows as well as acorns, beechnuts, truffles, and other forest floor products. With an increase in human population density, farm acreage increased and the oak and beech forests were destroyed to make room for planted crops, especially for olive trees, thereby eliminating the pig's ecological niche.

To update Coon's ecological scenario, I would add that as forests were being destroyed, so were marginal farmlands and grazing lands, the general succession being from forest to cropland to grazing land to desert, with each step along the way yielding a greater premium for raising ruminants and a greater penalty for raising swine. Robert Orr Whyte, former director general of the United Nations Food and Agricultural Organization, estimated that in Anatolia the forests shrank from 70 percent to 13 percent of the total land area between 5000 B.C. and the recent past. Only a fourth of the Caspian shore-front forest survived the process of population increase and agricultural intensification; half of the Caspian mountainous humid forest; a fifth to a sixth of the oak and juniper forests of the Zagros Mountains; and only a twentieth of the juniper forests of the Elburz and Khorassan ranges.

If I am right about the subversion of the practical basis of pig production through ecological succession, one does not need to invoke Mary Douglas's "taxonomic anomaly" to understand the peculiarly low status of the pig in the Middle East. The danger it posed to husbandry was very tangible and accounts quite well for its low status. The pig had been domesticated for one purpose only, namely to supply meat. As ecological conditions became unfavorable for pig raising, there was no alternative function which could redeem its existence. The creature became not only useless, but worse than useless—harmful, a curse to touch or merely to see—a pariah animal. This transformation contrasts understandably with that of cattle in India. Subject to a similar series of ecological depletions—deforestation, erosion, and desertification—cattle also became bad to eat. But in other respects, especially for traction power and milk, they became more useful than ever—a blessing to look at or to touch—animal godheads.

In this perspective, the fact that pig raising remained possible for the Israelites at low cost in certain remnant hillside forests or swampy habitats, or at extra expense where shade and water were scarce, does not contradict the ecological basis of the taboo. If there had not been some minimum possibility of raising pigs, there would have been no reason to taboo the practice. As the history of Hindu cow protection shows, religions gain strength when they help people make decisions which are in accord with preexisting useful practices, but which are not so completely self-evident as to preclude doubts and temptations. To judge from the Eight-fold Way or the Ten Commandments, God does not usually waste time prohibiting the impossible or condemning the unthinkable.

Leviticus consistently bans all vertebrate land animals that do not chew the cud. It bans, for example, in addition to swine, equines, felines, canines, rodents, and reptiles, none of which are cud-chewers. But Leviticus contains a maddening complication. It prohibits the consumption of three land-dwelling vertebrates which it specifically identifies as cud-chewers: the camel, the hare, and a third creature whose name in Hebrew is *shāphān*. The reason given for why these three alleged cud-chewers are not good to eat is that they do not "part the hoof":

> Nevertheless, these shall ye not eat of them that chew the cud . . . the camel because he . . . divideth not the hoof. And the *shāphān* because he . . . divideth not the hoof. . . And the hare, because he . . . divideth not the hoof.
>
> (Lev. 11: 4–6)

Although strictly speaking camels are not ruminants, because their cellulose-digesting chambers are anatomically distinct from those of the ruminants, they do ferment, regurgitate, and chew the cud much like cattle, sheep, and goats. But the classification of the hare as a cud-chewer immediately casts a pall over the zoological expertise of the Levite priests. Hares can digest grass but only by eating their own feces—which is a very uncud-like solution to the problem of how to send undigested cellulose through the gut for repeated processing (the technical term for this practice is coprophagy). Now as to the identity of the *shāphān*. As the following stack of Bibles shows, *shāphān* is either the "rock badger," "cherogrillus," or "cony":

Bibles Translating shāphān as "Rock Badger"

> *The Holy Bible*. Berkeley: University of California Press.
> *The Bible*. Chicago: University of Chicago Press, 1931.
> *The New Schofield Reference Library Holy Bible* (Authorized King James Version). New York: Oxford University Press, 1967.
> *The Holy Bible*. London: Catholic Truth Society, 1966.
> *The Holy Bible*. (Revised Standard Version). New York: Thomas Nelson and Sons, 1952.

The American Standard Bible. (Reference Edition). La Habra, CA: Collins World, 1973.

The New World Translation of the Holy Scriptures. Brooklyn, NY: Watchtower Bible and Tract Society of Pennsylvania, 1961.

Bibles Translating *shāphān* as *"Cony"*

The Pentateuch: *The Five Books of Moses.* Edited by William Tyndale. Carbondale: Southern Illinois University Press, 1967.

The Interpreter's Bible: *The Holy Scriptures.* 12 vols. New York: Abingdon Press, 1953.

The Holy Bible. King James Version (Revised Standard Version). Nashville: Thomas Nelson and Sons, 1971.

Holy Bible. Authorized version. New York: Harpers.

Holy Bible. Revised. New York: American Bible Society, 1873.

Modern Readers Bible. Edited by Richard Moulton. New York: Macmillan, 1935.

Bibles Translating *shāphān* as *"Cherogrillus"*

Holy Bible. (Duay, translated from Vulgate.) Boston: John Murphy and Co., 1914.

The Holy Bible. (Translated from the Vulgate by John Wycliffe and his followers.) Edited by Rev. Josiah Forshall and Sir Frederick Madden. Oxford: Oxford University Press, 1850.

All three terms refer to a similar kind of small, furtive, hoofed herbivore about the size of a squirrel that lives in colonies on rocky cliffs or among boulders on hilltops. It has two other popular aliases: "dassie" and "damon." It could have been any of these closely related species: *Hyrax capensia, Hyrax syriacus,* or *Procavia capensis.* Whichever it was, it had no rumen and it did not chew the cud.

This leaves the camel as the only bona fide cud-chewer that the Israelites couldn't eat. Every vertebrate land animal that is not a ruminant was forbidden flesh. And only one vertebrate land animal that is a ruminant, the camel, was forbidden. Let me see if I can explain this exception as well as the peculiar mixup about hares and *shāphān.*

My point of departure is that the food laws in Leviticus were mostly codifications of preexisting traditional food prejudices and avoidances. (The Book of Leviticus was not written until 450 B.C.—very late in Israelite history.) I envision the Levite authorities as undertaking the task of finding some simple feature which good-to-eat vertebrate land species shared in common. Had the Levites possessed a better knowledge of zoology, they could have used the criterion of cud-chewing alone and simply added the proviso, "except for the camel." For, as I have just said, with the exception of the camel, all land animals implicitly or explicitly forbidden in Leviticus—all the equines, felines, canines, rodents, rabbits, reptiles, and so forth—are nonruminants. But given their shaky knowledge of zoology, the codifiers could not be sure that the camel was the only undesirable species which was a cud-chewer. So they added the criterion of split hooves—a feature which camels lacked but which the other familiar cud-chewers possessed (the camel has two large flexible toes on each foot instead of hooves).

But why was the camel not a desirable species? Why spurn camel meat? I think the separation of the camel from the other cud-chewers reflects its highly specialized adaptation to desert habitats. With their remarkable capacity to store water, with-stand heat, and carry heavy burdens over great distances, and with their long eye-lashes and nostrils that shut tight for protection against sandstorms, camels were the most important possession of the Middle Eastern desert nomads. (The camel's hump concentrates fat—not water. It acts as an energy reserve. By concentrating the fat in the hump, the rest of the skin needs only a thin layer of fat, and this facilitates removal of body heat.) But as village farmers, the Israelites had little use for camels. Except under desert conditions, sheep and goats and cattle are more efficient converters of cellulose into meat and milk. In addition, camels reproduce very slowly. The females are not ready to bear offspring and the males are not ready to copulate until six years of age. To slow things down further, the males have a once-a-year rutting season (during which they emit an offensive odor), and gestation takes twelve months. Neither camel meat nor camel milk could ever have constituted a significant portion of the ancient Israelites' food supply. Those few Israelites such as Abraham and Joseph who owned camels would have used them strictly as a means of transport for crossing the desert.

This interpretation gains strength from the Moslem acceptance of camel meat. In the Koran, pork is specifically prohibited while camel flesh is specifically allowed. The whole way of life of Mohammed's desert-dwelling, pastoral Bedouin followers was based on the camel. The camel was their main source of transport and their main source of animal food, primarily in the form of camel milk. While camel meat was not daily fare, the Bedouin were often forced to slaughter pack animals during their desert journeys as emergency rations when their regular supplies of food were depleted. An Islam that banned camel flesh would never have become a great world religion. It would have been unable to conquer the Arabian heartlands, to launch its attack against the Byzantine and Persian empires, and to cross the Sahara to the Sahel and West Africa.

If the Levite priests were trying to rationalize and codify dietary laws, most of which had a basis in preexisting popular belief and practice, they needed a taxonomic principle which connected the existing patterns of preference and avoidance into a comprehensive cognitive and theological system. The preexisting ban on camel meat made it impossible to use cud-chewing as the sole taxonomic principle for identifying land vertebrates that were good to eat. They needed another criterion to exclude camels. And this was how "split hooves" got into the picture. Camels have conspicuously different feet from cattle, sheep, or goats. They have split toes instead of split hooves. So the priests of Leviticus added "parts the hoof" to "chews the cud" to make camels bad to eat. The misclassification of the hare and *shāphān* suggest that these animals were not well known to the codifiers. The authors of Leviticus were right about the feet—hares have paws and *Hyrax* (and *Procavia*) have tiny hooves, three on the front leg and five on the rear leg. But they were wrong about the cud-chewing—perhaps because hares and *shāphān* have their mouths in constant motion.

Once the principle of using feet to distinguish between edible and inedible flesh was established, the pig could not be banned simply by pointing to its nonruminant nature. Both its cud-chewing status and the anatomy of its feet had to be considered, even though the pig's failure to chew the cud was its decisive defect.

This, then, is my theory of why the formula for forbidden vertebrate land animals was elaborated beyond the mere absence of cud-chewing. It is a difficult theory to prove because no one knows who the authors of Leviticus were or what was really going on inside their heads. But regardless of whether or not the good-to-eat formula originated in the way I have described, the fact remains that the application of the expanded formula to hare and *shāphān* (as well as to pig and camel) did not result in any dietary restrictions that adversely affected the balance of nutritional or ecological costs and benefits. Hare and *shāphān* are wild species; it would have been a waste of time to hunt them instead of concentrating on raising far more productive ruminants.

To recall momentarily the case of the Brahman protectors of the cow, I do not doubt the ability of a literate priesthood to codify, build onto, and reshape popular foodways. But I doubt whether such "top-down" codifications generally result in adverse nutritional or ecological consequences or are made with blithe disregard of such consequences. More important than all the zoological errors and flights of taxonomic fancy is that Leviticus correctly identifies the classic domesticated ruminants as the most efficient source of milk and meats for the ancient Israelites. To the extent that abstract theological principles result in flamboyant lists of interdicted species, the results are trivial if not beneficial from a nutritional and ecological viewpoint. Among birds, for example, Leviticus bans the flesh of the eagle, ossifrage, osprey, ostrich, kite, falcon, raven, nighthawk, sea gull, hawk, cormorant, ibis, water-hen, pelican, vulture, stork, hoopoe, and bat (not a bird of course). I suspect but again cannot prove that this list was primarily the result of a priestly attempt to enlarge on a smaller set of prohibited flying creatures. Many of the "birds," especially the sea birds like pelicans and cormorants, would rarely be seen inland. Also, the list seems to be based on a taxonomic principle that has been somewhat overextended: most of the creatures on it are carnivores and "birds of prey." Perhaps the list was generated from this principle applied first to common local "birds" and then extended to the exotic sea birds as a validation of the codifiers' claim to special knowledge of the natural and supernatural worlds. But in any event, the list renders no disservice. Unless they were close to starvation and nothing else was available, the Israelites were well advised not to waste their time trying to catch eagles, ospreys, sea gulls, and the like, supposing they were inclined to dine on creatures that consist of little more than skin, feathers, and well-nigh indestructible gizzards in the first place. Similar remarks are appropriate vis-à-vis the prohibition of such unlikely sources of food for the inland-dwelling Israelites as clams and oysters. And if Jonah is an example of what happened when they took to the sea, the Israelites were well advised not to try to satisfy their meat hunger by hunting whales.

But let me return to the pig. If the Israelites had been alone in their interdictions of pork, I would find it more difficult to choose among alternative explanations of the pig taboo. The recurrence of pig aversions in several different Middle Eastern cultures strongly supports the view that the Israelite ban was a response to recurrent practical conditions rather than to a set of beliefs peculiar to one religion's notions about clean and unclean animals. At least three other important Middle Eastern civilizations—the Phoenicians, Egyptians, and Babylonians—were as disturbed by pigs as were the Israelites. Incidentally, this disposes of the notion that the Israelites banned the pig to "set themselves off from their neighbors," especially their unfriendly neighbors. (Of course, after the Jews dispersed throughout pork-eating Christendom, their abomination of the pig became an ethnic "marker." There was no compelling reason for them to give up their ancient contempt for pork. Prevented from owning land, the basis for their livelihood in Europe had to be crafts and commerce rather than agriculture. Hence there were no ecological or economic penalties associated with their rejection of pork while there were plenty of other sources of animal foods.)

In each of the additional cases, pork had been freely consumed during an earlier epoch. In Egypt, for example, tomb paintings and inscriptions indicate that pigs were the object of increasingly severe opprobrium and religious interdiction during the New Kingdom (1567–1085 B.C.). Toward the end of late dynastic times (1088–332 B.C.) Herodotus visited Egypt and reported that "the pig is regarded among them as an unclean animal so much so that if a man in passing accidentally touches a pig, he instantly hurries to the river and plunges in with all his clothes on." As in Roman Palestine when Jesus drove the Gadarene swine into Lake Galilee, some Egyptians continued to raise pigs. Herodotus described these swineherds as an in-marrying pariah caste who were forbidden to set foot in any of the temples.

One interpretation of the Egyptian pig taboo is that it reflects the conquest of the northern pork-eating followers of the god Seth by the southern pork-abstaining followers of the god Osiris and the imposition of southern Egyptian food preferences on the northerners. The trouble with this explanation is that if such a conquest occurred at all, it took place at the very beginning of the dynastic era and therefore does not account for the evidence that the pig taboo got stronger in late dynastic times.

My own interpretation of the Egyptian pig taboo is that it reflected a basic conflict between the dense human population crowded into the treeless Nile Valley and the demands made by the pig for the plant foods that humans could consume. A text from the Old Kingdom clearly shows how during hard times humans and swine competed for subsistence: "food is robbed from the mouth of the swine, without it being said, as before 'this is better for thee than for me,' for men are so hungry." What kinds of foods were robbed from the swine's mouth? Another text from the Second Intermediate period, boasting of a king's power over the lands, suggests it was grains fit for human consumption: "The finest of their fields are ploughed for us, our oxen are in the Delta, wheat is sent for our swine." And the Roman historian, Pliny, mentions the use of dates as a food used to fatten Egyptian pigs. The kind of preferential treatment needed to raise pigs in Egypt must have engendered strong feelings of antagonism between poor peasants who could not afford pork and the swineherds who catered to the tastes of rich and powerful nobles.

In Mesopotamia, as in Egypt, the pig fell from grace after a long period of popularity. Archaeologists have found clay models of domesticated pigs in the earliest settlements along the lower Tigris and Euphrates rivers. About 30 percent of the animal bones excavated from Tell Asmar (2800–2700 B.C.) came from pigs. Pork was eaten at Ur in predynastic times, and in the earliest Sumerian dynasties there were swineherds and butchers who specialized in pig slaughter. The pig seems to have fallen from favor when the Sumerians' irrigated fields became contaminated with salt, and barley, a salt-tolerant but relatively low-yielding plant, had to be substituted for wheat. These agricultural problems are implicated in the collapse of the Sumerian Empire and the shift after 2000 B.C. of the center of power upstream to Babylon. While pigs continued to be raised during Hammurabi's reign (about 1900 B.C.), they virtually disappear from Mesopotamia's archaeological and historical record thereafter.

The most important recurrence of the pig taboo is that of Islam. To repeat, pork is Allah's only explicitly forbidden flesh. Mohammed's Bedouin followers shared an aversion to pig found everywhere among arid-land nomadic pastoralists. As Islam spread westward from the Arabian Peninsula to the Atlantic, it found its greatest strength among North African peoples for whom pig raising was also a minor or entirely absent component of agriculture and for whom the Koranic ban on pork did not represent a significant dietary or economic deprivation. To the east, Islam again found its greatest strength in the belt of the semiarid lands that stretch from the Mediterranean Sea through Iran, Afghanistan, and Pakistan to India. I don't mean to say that none of the people who adopted Islam had previously relished pork. But for the great mass of early converts, becoming a Moslem did not involve any great upending of dietary or subsistence practices because from Morocco to India people had come to depend primarily on cattle, sheep, and goats for their animal products long before the Koran was written. Where local ecological conditions here and there strongly favored pig raising within the Islamic heartland, pork continued to be produced. Carlton Coon described one such pork-tolerant enclave—a village of Berbers in the oak forests of the Atlas Mountains in Morocco. Although nominally Moslems, the villagers kept pigs which they let loose in the forest during the day and brought home at night. The villagers denied that they raised pigs, never took them to market, and hid them from visitors. These and other examples of pig-tolerant Moslems suggest that one should not overestimate the ability of Islam to stamp out pig eating by religious precept alone if conditions are favorable for pig husbandry.

Wherever Islam has penetrated to regions in which pig raising was a mainstay of the traditional farming systems, it has failed to win over substantial portions of the population. Regions such as Malaysia, Indonesia, the Philippines, and Africa south of the Sahara, parts of which are ecologically well suited for pig raising, constitute the outer limits of the active spread of Islam. All along this frontier the resistance of pig-eating Christians has prevented Islam from becoming the dominant religion. In China, one of the world centers of pig production, Islam has made small inroads and is confined largely to the arid and semiarid western provinces. Islam, in other words, to this very day has a geographical limit which coincides with the ecological zones of transition between forested regions well suited for pig husbandry and regions where too much sun and dry heat make pig husbandry a risky and expensive practice.

While I contend that ecological factors underlie religious definitions of clean and unclean foods, I also hold that the effects do not all flow in a single direction. Religiously sanctioned foodways that have become established as the mark of conversion and as a measure of piety can also exert a force of their own back upon the ecological and economic conditions which gave rise to them. In the case of the Islamic pork taboos, the feedback between religious belief and the practical exigencies of animal husbandry has led to a kind of undeclared ecological war between Christians and Moslems in several parts of the Mediterranean shores of southern Europe. In rejecting the pig, Moslem farmers automatically downgrade the importance of preserving woodlands suitable for pig production. Their secret weapon is the goat, a great devourer of forests, which readily climbs trees to get at a meal of leaves and twigs.

By giving the goat free reign, Islam to some degree spread the conditions of its own success. It enlarged the ecological zones ill suited to pig husbandry and removed one of the chief obstacles to the acceptance of the words of the Prophet. Deforestation is particularly noticeable in the Islamic regions of the Mediterranean. Albania, for example, is divided between distinct Christian pig-keeping and Moslem pig-abominating zones, and as one passes from the Moslem to the Christian sectors, the amount of woodland immediately increases.

It would be wrong to conclude that the Islamic taboo on the pig caused the deforestation wrought by the goat. After all, a preference for cattle, sheep, and goats and the rejection of pigs in the Middle East long antedated the birth of Islam. This preference was based on the cost/benefit advantages of ruminants over other domestic animals as sources of milk, meat, traction, and other services and products in hot, arid climates. It represents an unassailably "correct" ecological and economic decision embodying thousands of years of collective wisdom and practical experience. But as I have already pointed out in relation to the sacred cow, no system is perfect. Just as the combination of population growth and political exploitation led to a deterioration of agriculture in India, so too population growth and political exploitation took their toll in Islamic lands. If the response to demographic and political pressures had been to raise more pigs rather than goats, the adverse effects on living standards would have been even more severe and would have occurred at a much lower level of population density.

All of this is not to say that a proselctyzing religion such as Islam is incapable of getting people to change their foodways purely out of obedience to divine commandments. Priests, monks, and saints do often refuse delectable and nutritious foods out of piety rather than practical necessity. But I have yet to encounter a flourishing religion whose food taboos make it more difficult for ordinary people to be well nourished. On the contrary, in solving the riddle of the sacred cow and abominable pig, I have already shown that the most important food aversions and preferences of four major religions—Hinduism, Buddhism, Judaism, and Islam—are on balance favorable to the nutritional and ecological welfare of their followers.

References

Coon, Carleton (1951) *Caravan*. New York: Henry Holt.
Douglas, Mary (1966) *Purity and Danger: An Analysis of Concepts of Pollution and Taboo*. New York: Praeger.

7

Industrial Food: Towards the Development of a World Cuisine[*]

Jack Goody

The British diet, claims the modern "Platine," went straight "from medieval barbarity to industrial decadence." With the general sentiment one has some sympathy. But as we have seen, medieval barbarity meant culinary differentiation, if not into something as grand as a sophisticated cuisine such as the French established in building on firm Italian foundations, at least into systems of supply, preparation, cooking, serving and consumption of food that resolutely set aside the high from the low. And "industrial decadence," whatever its consequences for the *haute cuisine* (larks' tongues are not promising ingredients for a mass cuisine, canned food is not always the best basis for a gourmet meal), has enormously improved, in quantity, quality and variety, the diet (and usually the cuisine) of the urban working populations of the western world.[1] It is also making a significant impact on the rest of the world, initially on the productive processes, some of which have become geared to supplying those ingredients on a mass scale, and more recently on consumption itself, since the products of the industrial cuisine and of industrialised agriculture are now critical elements in the food supply of the Third World.

But before we consider the impact on the particular corner of the world on which we are concentrating, we need first to look at the world context in which those changes took place, at the rise of an industrial cuisine in the West. The immediate factors that made this possible were developments in four basic areas: (1) preserving; (2) mechanisation; (3) retailing (and wholesaling); and (4) transport. As we have seen, the preservation of food was a feature of relatively simple economics like those of northern Ghana. The drying of fish and meat enabled animal protein to be more widely distributed in time and space; the drying of vegetables such as okra prolonged their use into the dry season when soup ingredients were scarce. The preservation of meat and vegetables, by drying, by pickling, by salting and in some regions by the use of ice, was characteristic of the domestic economy in early Europe.[2] With the developments in navigation that allowed the great sea voyages of the fifteenth century, the use of long-life foods became a matter of major importance; the navies and armies of Europe required considerable quantities of such products to feed their personnel. Werner Sombart has written of the revolution in salting at the end of the fifteenth century that

[*]*Originally published 1982*

permitted the feeding of sailors at sea. In the Mediterranean, salted fish and the ship's biscuit were already long-established (Braudel 1973: 132); in the Atlantic, much use was made of salted beef which came mainly from Ireland. The enormous catches of cod that arrived from Newfoundland by the end of the fifteenth century were mostly salted. Salt was much used by peasants to preserve food during the winter months.[3] Butter and vegetables were also preserved with salt, and until recently the French peasant placed part of the "family pig" in the salting tub, while the rest was made into sausages. But the importance of salt was not only dietary.[4] It was the hunger for salt, both for preserving, which became more common in eighteenth-century France, and for eating, that lay behind the peasant uprisings against the *gabelle,* the salt tax. Such taxes were an important source of revenue in Europe as in Asia, both to the merchants and to the governments; it was against such fiscal impositions, as well as against the alien government imposing them, that Gandhi led the famous march to the sea in British India.

Salting, of course, is only one method of preserving food. It is possible to pickle in vinegar as well as salt, and the production of vinegar was an important aspect of early industrial activity. Sugar was used to preserve fruit in forms such as marmalade and jam, as well as being used for coating ham and other meats. Spreading first from India and then from the eastern Mediterranean at the time of the Crusades, cane-sugar played an increasingly important part in the diets of Western Europe, a demand that led to the establishment of many of the slave plantations of the New World. Imports of sugar increased rapidly in the eighteenth century. It was the fact that supplies of cane-sugar were cut off from continental Europe during the Napoleonic wars that led to the fundamental invention embodied in the canning process, as well as to the use of the beet as a source of sugar, at the same time chicory developed as a substitute for the second of the trio of "junk foods," as Mintz has called them, that is, coffee (the third being tea). It was these "proletarian hunger-killers," to use another of Mintz's forceful phrases, that became such central elements of working-class diet in the nineteenth century and "played a crucial role in the linked contribution that Caribbean slaves, Indian peasants, and European urban proletarians were able to make to the growth of western civilization" (Mintz 1979: 60).

It was this general context of colonialism, overseas trade and long-lasting foods that saw the development of the great British Biscuit Industry. Its product owed much to the ship's biscuit which was known there at least as early as Shakespearean times and was manufactured by small bakeries situated around the many harbours of the kingdom. "Hard-tack" was essentially a substitute for bread (brown or white, depending on class, as had been the case since Roman times), which with ale, cheese and meat, was a basic feature of the diet of the common man (Drummond and Wilbraham 1939: 218). In the course of the eighteenth century the victualling authorities in certain of the king's dockyards such as Portsmouth set up their own large-scale bakeries "creating a human assembly line that economised each workman's movements to the utmost" (Corley 1976: 14). Despite these organisational developments, the fluctuation of demand caused by the various wars meant that dockyard production had to be supplemented by the work of contractors. The situation changed in 1833 when Thomas Grant of the Victualling Office invented steam machinery to mechanise certain of the processes, reducing labour costs, increasing output and improving the quality of the biscuits.

"Fancy biscuits" like "hard-tack" also had a long history, being employed for medicinal purposes as well as for the table, especially at festivals. The earliest proprietary brands were probably the Bath Oliver, invented by Dr. William Oliver (1695–1764) and the Abernethy, called after a doctor of that name (1764–1831). All these biscuits were initially made by hand, but mechanisation was applied to their manufacture not long after the technological changes had taken place in the dock-yards. In the late 1830s a Quaker miller and baker of Carlisle, named Carr, designed machinery for cutting out and stamping biscuits. In 1841 George Palmer, another Quaker, went into partnership with his cousin Thomas Huntley who made biscuits in Reading.

The business that developed into Huntley and Palmers had been founded at a bakery in that town in 1822. Huntley's shop was opposite the Crown Hotel, a posting inn on the main London-Bath road. He had the idea of sending his delivery boy to sell biscuits to the waiting passengers. Their quality led customers to demand Huntley's produce from their grocers at home, opening up the market from a purely local one. So Huntley persuaded his son, who had been apprenticed to a Reading ironmonger and kept a shop nearby, to make tins and tinned boxes in order to keep the biscuits fresh. He also employed a traveller to collect orders for Abernethy, Oliver and other biscuits in the south of England, which he dispatched mainly by the canal system. When Palmer joined the firm, he immediately investigated the application of steam power to mixing the dough, to rolling and cutting, and to providing the oven with a continuous feed. These inventions subsequently led to the development of a whole secondary industry of specialised manufacturers of machinery for the trade, a development that helped to fuel the Industrial Revolution.

The sale of biscuits made rapid headway. The manufactured brands, Carrs, Huntley and Palmers, later Peek Freans, were distributed throughout the nation. In 1859, these firms sold 6 million pounds of their products. Changing eating habits in the shape of earlier breakfasts and later dinners led to a further increase in consumption, and by the late 1870s the figure had risen to 37 million pounds a year. Huntley and Palmers had become one of the forty most important companies in Britain, and within fifty years their biscuits were distributed not only throughout the nation but throughout the world. As with the early canning industry, much of the production of biscuits had first of all been directed to the needs of travellers, explorers and the armed forces. Such produce sustained sailors, traders and colonial officers overseas; only later did industrial production impinge upon the internal market in England or upon the local market overseas, eventually becoming part of the daily diet of the population.

Preserving: Canning

The creation of a long-lasting cereal product, the biscuit, long pre-dated the Industrial Revolution, though its production and distribution were radically transformed by the course of those changes, making the biscuit an important element in the development of the industrial cuisine. But that cuisine was based in a large degree on two processes, the discovery of the techniques of canning and artificial freezing.

The preserving of food in containers again dates back a long way, but the canning on which modern industry depends was invented by Nicolas Appert in response to an appeal of the Directoire in 1795 for contributions to solving the problems created by the war situation in France. During the Napoleonic wars France was cut off from its overseas supplies and this separation stimulated the search for substitutes. At the same time the recruitment of a mass army of citizens raised in a very radical way the problem of supplying food for a large, mobile and non-productive element in the society; in 1811 Napoleon invaded Russia with over a million men. So the aim of the appeal was partly military, though the citation to Appert when he received the award refers to the advantages of the new invention for sea voyages, hospitals and the domestic economy (Bitting 1937).

This invention of "canning," what the English call bottling, was based on earlier practices and earlier devices, such as the "digester," a sort of pressure cooker, invented by Denis Papin in London in 1681, which provided John Evelyn, the diarist, with a "philosophical supper" (Cutting 1955: 5; Teuteberg in E. and R. Forster 1975: 88). A contemporary account of Appert's book in the *Edinburgh Review* (1814, vol. 45) calls the process "neither novel in principle, nor scarcely in any point of practice" (Bitting 1937: 38), and declares that "our fair country women ... unless they have alike forgotten the example and precepts of their ancestors ... must ... be more or less acquainted with the methods" (p. 39). Nevertheless the author goes on to recognise the importance of Appert's contribution, especially as the ladies of 1814, having been relieved of various household tasks by the Industrial Revolution, tend to know too little about such things.

Appert had been a chef, and he worked out his new methods at his business near Paris. It was in 1804 that a series of public tests were made on his produce at Brest, and in the same year he opened his bottling factory at Massy, near Paris. Five years later he was awarded the prize of 12,000 francs by the committee that included Guy-Lussac and Parmentier, on condition that he deliver a description of the process, in 200 copies, printed at his own expense. This description he published in 1810 and proclaimed the use of his method of bottling as a general aid to domestic life. Entitled "Le livre de tous les ménages ... ," the book gave instructions for bottling pot-au-feu, consommé, bouillon or pectoral jelly, fillet of beef, partridge, fresh eggs, milk, vegetables (including tomatoes or love apples, spinach, sorrel and petit pois), fruit and herbs. "No single discovery," declared Bitting, "has contributed more to modern food manufacturer nor to the general welfare of mankind" (1920: 13).

Nor did Appert stop there. Investing his prize money in production and research, he founded the house of Appert in 1812, produced bouillon cubes two years later and experimented with a number of other ideas, turning eventually to the use of the tin can to supplement that of the glass jar.

In England, where as much interest had been displayed in Appert's discoveries as in his own country, the tin can had been in use for some years. An English translation of Appert's book appeared in 1811, a second edition in 1812, and an American edition in the same year. Already in 1807 T. Saddington had been awarded a premium by the London Society for Arts for his work on bottling, and he probably learnt of Appert's process during his travels abroad. In 1810 Peter Durand and de Heine took out patents on the process, but in the former case it was adapted for preserving "food in vessels made of tin and other metals." The potentialities of these inventions aroused the interest of Bryan Donkin who was a partner in the firm of John Hall, founder of the Dartford Iron Works in 1785. Whether he acquired either of the earlier patents is not known, but he appreciated the potential value of Appert's discovery for his firm.[5] After various experiments, Donkin, in association with Hall and Gamble, set up a factory for canning food in metal containers in Blue Anchor Road, Bermondsey. The Navy immediately purchased supplies of "preserved provisions" to form part of their medical stores. These were used for numerous expeditions, by Ross in his voyage to the Far North in 1814, by the Russian von Kotzebue to the North-West Passage in 1815, by Parry to the Arctic in the same year. In 1831 Admiralty Regulations decreed that all ships should carry such provisions as part of their "medical comforts" (Drummond and Wilbraham 1939: 319). This was the prelude to their more general spread into the domestic economy which was still hindered by their great expense compared with other foods.

Glass containers continued to be used for most purposes and had a history dating back many years. At the end of the seventeenth century there were 37 glass-houses in London making only bottles, approximately three million a year, which were used mainly as containers for wine and medicine. The chemist Joseph Priestly gave the industry a further boost when early in the eighteenth century he discovered how to make artificial mineral water which led to a flourishing new industry. By the end of the century, the Swiss, Jacob Schweppe, had set up a factory in London (Wright 1975: 46). But it was with Appert's invention that the glass container came into wide use for preserved foods.

From England the process spread to the United States, where bottles rather than cans were used. William Underwood, who had served his apprenticeship in pickling and preserving with a London house, left for New Orleans in 1817. By 1819 he had made his way to Boston, and in the following year he and one C. Mitchell founded a factory for bottling fruit which by 1821 was shipping goods to South America. Damsons, quinces, currants and cranberries were the main items preserved at the beginning, but the major part of the business had to do with pickles, ketchups, sauces, jellies and jams.

In England these preserved foods did not reach the shops until 1830 and were slow in selling because of the high price. In America too the local trade was initially poor, and most of Underwood's produce went abroad to India, Batavia, Hong Kong, Gibraltar, Manila, the West Indies and South America.[6] Much of it was marketed under an English label to counter the prejudice against American goods (Butterick, 1925). In 1828 Underwood was shipping preserved milk to South America and in 1835, having imported the seed from England, he started to bottle tomatoes, partly for export to Europe.[7] Up to this time the fruit was little known in the States and indeed was regarded as poisonous, even though it had been domesticated in the New World and taken from Mexico to Europe.[8]

In America the local trade developed with the shift from glass to the cheaper metal containers and with the immense boost to sales given by the Civil War (1861–5). Once again the demands of the army were of major significance. But the point of take-off had now been reached for society as a whole. At about the same time as Underwood started his factory in Boston, another English immigrant, Thomas Kensett, and his father-in-law, Ezra Doggett, set up a cannery in New York for salmon, lobsters and oysters. In 1825 Kensett took out a patent for tin cans but they did not become widely used until 1839.

Many of the pioneer factories in the States started with fish as the primary product, and fruit and vegetables as incidental (A. and K. Bitting, 1916: 14). In Europe the canning of sardines, that is, young pilchards, began in Nantes in the early 1820s. By 1836 Joseph Colin was producing 100,000 cans, and the industry spread along the coast of Brittany. But it was not until 1870 that a rapid expansion began. By 1880 50 millions tins of sardines were being packed annually on the west coast of France, three million of which were exported to Britain. The world of industrial food had begun.

The canning of the other major object of fish packaging, the salmon, began about the same time in Aberdeen on a small scale. Others in Scotland followed, in an attempt to save the long haul of salmon, frozen and smoked, to the London market. The first large-scale salmon cannery was established at Cork, in the south of Ireland, in 1849 by Crosse and Blackwell, It was with the development of canneries on the Pacific coast in 1864 that large-scale production began in America.

The canning of meat was especially important for the army, being developed not only in the American Civil War but also by the Anglo-French forces in the Crimea. It continued to be of great military significance, and in the First World War the Germany Army were producing eight million cans of meat per month. The process was less important for the domestic market, especially after the advent of refrigeration techniques in the latter part of the nineteenth century, when frozen produce became widely available and was preferred by the consumers.

Condensed milk was another major product of the canning industry. In Britain Grimwade took out a patent for evaporated milk in 1847 and was supplying some to expeditions at an early date. In 1855 he took out another patent for powdered milk which could be reconstituted with water. A great improvement in milk processing was made possible by Borden's work in the United States. Borden, who had been stimulated by the needs of migrants in the Gold Rush to market pemmican and meat biscuits, applied for his patent in 1853 and his process was used for production not only in America but also by the Anglo-Swiss Company, later Nestlé's. Condensed milk became a major item of diet in Britain, and in 1924 over two million hundredweight of the product was imported, more than the total imports of tinned fruit and the combined imports of beef and fish.

Food was also processed by other techniques than canning, and some of the results played a prominent part in the new cuisine. Meat extract was developed by the Frenchmen, Proust and Parmentier, and after 1830 meat bouillon was boiled down to a stock soup, dried and sold as "bouillon bars" in pharmacies and for use on ships. Large scale production became possible in 1857 as the result of Liebig's research on muscle meat, and in the following years factories were built in Fray Bentos, Uruguay, to process meat into a brown powder for shipping to the growing urban populations of Europe. Soon the process of manufacturing meat foods spread to Australia, New Zealand, Argentina and North America with the result that the soups and gravies of the English kitchen became dominated by the dehydrated products of the international meat industry.

Preserving: Freezing

While the canning of food was the most significant step in the development of an industrial cuisine, other processes of preservation also played an important part, especially the artificial freezing of foodstuffs. In cold climates the technique had been practised since prehistoric times, and natural ice continued to be used until very recently. In the early nineteenth century the Russians were packing chickens in snow for consumption as occasion required, and frozen veal was being sent from Archangel to St Petersburg. In Scotland ice-houses had long been attached to richer homes, and the practice spread into the food trades. By the beginning of the nineteenth century every salmon fishery in Scotland was provided with an ice-house. The fish were packed in long boxes with pounded ice and dispatched to the London market (Bitting 1937: 29).[9]

In America natural ice was also packed in "refrigerators" from the beginning of the nineteenth century. Indeed, ice gathered from the Boston ponds became big business. Beginning in 1806 with the West Indies, Frederic Tudor developed a worldwide operation, which between 1836 and 1850 extended to every large port in South America and the Far East; within thirty years ice had become one of the great trading interests of the city of Boston, and one French source claimed that in 1847 the Asian trade of one house was almost equal in value to the whole of the Bordeaux wine harvest (Prentice 1950: 114ff.).

The demand of Asian countries for Boston ice had a history in the local usage of Chinese society where in pre-imperial times the feudal nobility had the prerogative of storing ice to keep sacrificial objects fresh. In later imperial times eunuchs supervised the cutting of blocks of ice from rivers and ponds, packing it in clean store and keeping it in trenches. The use of ice was not limited to the imperial house, though it helped to supply the court with fresh food. Mote remarks that "refrigerated shipping seems to have been 'taken for granted' in Ming times, long before we hear of such a development in Europe" (1977: 215).[10]

About the time of the development in the Boston trade, ice became widely used in America for transporting food on the railroad. It was in 1851 that the first refrigerated rail car brought butter from Ogdensburg, New York, to Boston, Massachusetts. Of greater significance was the ability to transport frozen meat from the Chicago stockyards to the urban centres of the East, an enterprise associated with the names of Armour and Swift, and providing a parallel development to the international shipment of meat to Europe from America and Australia.

With the development of rail transport around the middle of the century, fresh sea fish began to make its regular appearance in inland markets in England, leading to a decline in the popularity of salted and picked herrings, which had long been a staple food. Fish from rivers and dew ponds had long been available, sometimes being marketed alive by the fishmonger in tanks. Live fish were carried by the wives of sea-fishermen to towns as far inland as Coventry, being transported in brine on pack-horses (Davis 1966: 15). But the expense of such products meant that they were not available to the majority of the population, a situation that rail transport helped to change. Meanwhile in America a great deal of herring had been frozen by exposure since 1846, "providing the masses with a cheap and wholesome food" (Cutting 1955: 296).

In cooler climes and for longer distances the extensive use of refrigeration depended upon the development of artificial rather than natural ice. The newly exploited pastures of Australia and America produced an abundance of livestock, but the problem lay in getting meat to the industrial consumers. Shipping cattle live to Europe presented great difficulties until the length of the voyage had been reduced. Nevertheless American livestock was imported into Europe in appreciable numbers by the early 1870s. The Australian voyage was much longer and, although meat was now canned, its quality left much to be desired. In 1850, James Harrison, a Scottish immigrant to Australia, designed the first practical ice-making machine, using the evaporation and subsequent compression of ether. Ten years later, the French engineer Carré produced a much more efficient machine based on ammonia gas. But the problem of transporting Australian frozen meat to Europe was not solved until 1880 when the S.S. *Strathleven* brought a cargo from Melbourne to London. Meanwhile similar experiments were being carried on in other countries, and frozen meat reached the London market, probably from the United States, as early as 1872. In France, the engineer Charles Tellier had been working on the same problems since 1868, and after several unsuccessful attempts, the S.S. *Frigorifique* brought a cargo of meat from Argentina to Rouen in 1876. These developments led to a rapid diminution in the amounts of canned and salted meat being imported from those countries, just as the use of natural ice in Britain had earlier led to a decrease in the amount of salted and pickled fish.

Not only diet but cooking too responded in significant ways to technological changes. While domestic refrigeration had to wait until the following century, in the later part of the nineteenth century such machines were used in the new catering trades. It was these developments in freezing techniques that enabled Lyons tea-shops to serve their popular cucumber sandwiches all the year round. Started by the successful operators of a tobacco business in 1887, these shops followed the rise of the coffee public houses of the 1870s which had been organised by the temperance societies as an alternative to the pub. Out of these coffee houses developed two sizeable catering concerns, the first multiples of their kind, Lockharts and Pierce & Plenty. The growth of the commercial catering business was the counterpart of the decline of the domestic servant; in 1851 905,000 women in Britain were employed as domestic servants, plus 128,000 servant girls on farms; by the 1961 Census, there were no more than 103,000 resident domestic servants in England and Wales.[11]

Many of the other developments surrounding food in the nineteenth century had little to do with preservation *per se,* but rather with branding, packaging, advertising and marketing. In 1868 Fleischmann provided a standardised yeast for the American market; Heinz bottled horse-radish sauce in 1869. In England, sauces based on vinegar featured early on in the commercial food business; their production was stimulated by the cheaper spices brought back by the East India Company in Elizabethan times, and the demand was later increased by the return of families from abroad. The well-known Worcester sauce, for example, was produced by the analytical chemists Lea and Perrins, who went into partnership in 1823 to run a pharmacy that also dealt in toiletries, cosmetics and groceries. They began to market their own medicinal products, and their first catalogue listed more than three hundred items, such as

Essence of Sarsaparilla for scurvy and Taraxacum (dandelion coffee) for liver complaints. These products were soon in great demand from the new industrial towns of the Birmingham area as well as from abroad; travellers set off with a Lea and Perrins' medical chest, and this publicity led to orders from all over the world. However it was the invention of the sauce which exemplifies the rapid growth of prepared foods, the shift of focus from kitchen to factory, as well as the influence of overseas trade and overseas colonisation.

> Mr. Lea & Mr. Perrins were perfecting their medicines, hair lotions and marrow pomades when Marcus, Lord Sandys visited the shop in Worcester. Late Governor of Bengal, he had retired to his country estate in nearby Ombersley Court, and would be obliged if they would make up one of his favourite Indian sauces. They obliged. Having already arranged their own supplies of spices and dried fruits, from Asia and the Americas, they had the ingredients to hand. Scrupulously following his lordship's recipe, they made the required quantity, plus some for themselves. One taste was enough. The sauce was ghastly: an unpalatable, red hot, fire water. His lordship was entirely satisfied. The remainder however was consigned to a cellar below the shop, and there it stayed until the annual spring-cleaning and stocktaking.

It was on the point of being poured away when Mr. Lea and Mr. Perrins detected its appetising aroma. Tasting it once again they discovered it had matured into a rare and piquant sauce. The sauce was saved, more was made. Customers were persuaded to try the new Worcestershire Sauce, and did not need more persuasion: the sauce was an instant success. Sales rose. In 1842, Lea & Perrins sold 636 bottles. In 1845, a manufactory was set up in Bank Street, Worcester. Ten years later the yearly sales were up to 30,000 bottles of Worcestershire Sauce. Travellers covered Great Britain and there were agencies in Australia and the United States (Wright 1975: 31). The product still adorns the tables of cafés, restaurants and dining rooms the world over.

Another item of processed food which has substantially changed eating habits in many parts of the world, including the new bourgeoisie of Ghana, is the breakfast cereal. Initially these foods were developed in the United States to meet the needs of vegetarian groups like the Seventh Day Adventists, who were experimenting with cereal-based foods at Battle Creek, Michigan, in the 1850s. Dr John Kellogg was director of the "medical boarding house" at Battle Creek where he carried out research in the "dietary problem" and in the development of so-called "natural foods" (Deutch 1961). It was in the 1860s that he produced "Granola," the first ready-cooked cereal food, made from a mixture of oatmeal, wheat and maize baked in a slow oven until thoroughly dextrinised (Collins 1976: 31). It was his brother who later became the promoter of these foods.

The 1890s saw the invention of most of the basic types of pre-cooked cereal and manufacturing process—flaking, toasting, puffing and extrusion: Shredded Wheat appeared in 1892, and in 1898 Grape Nuts, invented by Charles W. Post, an ex-patient of Kellogg's who also produced Post Toasties. It was Post who pioneered the use of advertising techniques employed by the makers of patent medicines to market his products, "selling health foods to well people." Ever since this market has been heavily dependent upon massive publicity campaigns. After the First World War the American foods spread to Britain, whereas elsewhere in the world the market is still dominated by more or less the same products. Pushing aside porridge and other breakfast foods, they owed their success to their ease of preparation, especially important for breakfast in households whose members are all working outside the home; but their widespread use was also due to the vigorous sales campaigns, later directed primarily towards children, to the general shift to lighter meals consistent with the changing nature of "work," and to rising real incomes which made it possible for people to buy "health" foods and so transform them into utility foods.[12]

Mechanisation and Transport

The use of machines in the production of industrial food has already been noted in the case of the biscuit industry. But it was equally important in the whole canning industry at three levels, in the mechanisation of the production of food, especially in agriculture, in the mechanisation of the preparation of the food, cleansing, peeling, podding, etc., and in the mechanisation of the canning itself.

When canned goods first reached the shops about 1830, they made little impact on domestic consumption on account of their price, even with the cheaper metal containers. A skilled man could fill only 50 or 60 cans a day; the cans themselves were made from rolled sheets of wrought iron; their lids were fitted by placing a sheet of metal across the top and then hammering it down at the sides, after which it was soldered on. The early cans were so heavy that they sometimes had to be fitted with rings to lift them, and they could only be opened with a hammer and chisel. During the course of the second half of the nineteenth century these obstacles were gradually overcome; in 1849 came a machine for pressing out the tops and bottoms, then a substitute for the soldering iron, and in 1876 the Howe machine produced a continuous stream of cans for sealing so that two men with assistants could produce 1,500 cans a day (Cummings 1941: 68). The methods of canning themselves improved in 1861 when the addition of calcium chloride to the water increased its temperature and cut down the boiling time required from five hours to thirty minutes, a time that was further reduced by the invention of the autoclave (a closed kettle). The other bottle-neck lay in the preparation of the food itself, a phase that also gradually became dominated by new machinery—washers, graders, peelers, corn huskers and cutters, bean snippers and filling machines. Once again a whole series of subsidiary industries arose to meet the new requirements.

It should be stressed that the manufacture of many processed and packaged foods did not require great advances in techniques of preservation but rather the adaptation of simple machinery for producing standard goods on a large scale. This happened not only with biscuits but with pasta. Possibly coming from China through Germany, this "typical" Italian dish was adopted in the fourteenth century.[13] It spread across the Atlantic with the influx of Italian immigrants late in the nineteenth century, and in 1890 it was manufactured on a large scale by Foulds, wrapped in a sanitary package and advertised as "Cleanly made by Americans." Mechanisation permitted the domestication and purification of foreign foods.

Not only production but distribution too was mechanised, involving a similar massive use of energy. The mechanisation of the process of distribution depended upon the development of a system of transport that could shift the very large quantities of goods involved in the ready-made market; in the United States this amounted to some

700 million cases of canned goods a year in the 1960s, each case including an average of 24 cans. The distribution of processed foods to a mass market was dependent upon the railway boom which in Britain marked the beginning of the second phase of industrialisation (roughly 1840–95). Following the little mania of 1835–7 came the big railway mania of 1845–7; during this period, from 1830, over 6,000 miles of railway were constructed in Britain (Hobsbawn 1968: 88). Here was an opportunity for investment, for employment and for the export of capital goods which laid the basis of working-class prosperity in the third quarter of the century, permitted the growth of the mass markets for preserved and processed foods, and built up the volume of imports from the Colonial (now the Third) World.

Critical to the growth of the overseas trade was the development of large cargo ships capable of transporting the raw materials to the metropolitan country in exchange for the mass export of manufactured goods. These various processes of mechanisation and transportation were essential to the preservation and distribution of food on a mass scale, and so to the industrialisation of the domestic diet of the new proletariat. But more immediately relevant to the domestic level were the social changes that took place in the organisation of the actual distribution of food to the household, since a whole series of agents now intervened between the producer and the consumer.

Retailing

The changes in the English retailing trade were marked by two phases. The first was the shift from open market to closed shop which began in Elizabethan times, although the move to retail shops in the food trade was strongly resisted by many urban authorities. The second retail revolution occurred in the nineteenth century and was associated with industrialisation rather than with urbanisation itself; indeed it affected food and cooking in both town and country.

In medieval England market-places were areas for exchanging the products of the nearby countryside with those made by local craftsmen. Great efforts were made by the authorities to prevent the intervention of any middle men, except in the long-distance trades where their services could not be avoided. Shops for buying food scarcely existed; the town authorities forced the food trade into the street market for the purposes of control.[14] Frequent regulations were made against "forestalling" the market by buying goods outside it, against "regrating" those goods, that is, selling them at a higher price, and against "engrossing," or hoarding. At the same time an attempt was made to control the quality and the price;[15] control lay partly in the hands of the occupational associations and partly in the hands of the collective authority of the corporation. In Chester, butchers and bakers were made to take a public oath that the food they supply to their fellow-citizens shall be wholesome and fair in price.[16] Such regulations also included rules about the use of standard weights and measures, instructing men "not to sell by aime of hand."

It was impossible completely to control the marketing of food, even at this time. In addition to "foreigner" or "stranger" markets (i.e., those catering for country folk) there was a certain amount of hawking. But the move to establishing food shops only developed with the growth of suburban London, the main markets being too far away for their inhabitants. By this time the cornchandler and a few other traders were beginning to act as wholesalers with fixed premises. Nevertheless it was well into the eighteenth century before the big open markets ceased to be the normal place to buy food (Davis 1966: 74).

Apart from the shift from market to shop, little had changed in London as late as 1777, when the country was on the threshold of the great changes in the processing and sale of food that industrialisation brought. In that year, James Fitch, the son of an Essex farmer who, like others in a period of depression following the great agricultural changes of the earliest part of the century, came to London to enter the food trade.

> The only retailers allowed to trade were those who had been apprenticed to a freeman of the City, and who, on completion of their apprenticeship, had themselves taken up the freedom of a City Company or Guild. The Lord Mayor and his Court were still virtual dictators of trade within the City walls and for up to seven miles outside. Price control was exercised from the Guildhall, and it was an offence to offer goods for sale other than in the markets. No one was allowed to own more than one shop selling poultry, butter or eggs. (Keevil 1972: 2)

Control was exercised by the great City companies, and freeman engaged in selling produce had to belong to the appropriate Livery Company, Butchers', Poulterers', Bakers', Fruiterers' or Grocers.'

It was the last of these, the grocers, who were the key to later developments. Originally one of the minor food trades, grocery overtook all the others. For many years grocers were associated with the import of foreign goods. In the fifteenth century they had been general merchants dealing in most goods except fresh food and clothing. But in London they gradually concentrated on the non-perishable items of food arriving in increasing quantities from the Mediterranean, the Far East and the New World. The English (London) Company of Grocers was made up of merchants dealing in spices, dried fruit and similar commodities which they imported or bought in bulk ("gross," *grassier* in French is a wholesaler), and sold in small quantities. Later they added tea, coffee, cocoa and sugar, all of them initially "luxury" goods.[17] One of the most important commodities was sugar, first imported at a high price from Arabia and India but then brought in much more cheaply first from the Canaries and then from the Caribbean, one of the "junk foods" that were key components of colonial plantations and working-class diets.

The grocer was distinguished from the provision merchant who dealt in butter, cheese and bacon, and the distinction obtained until very recently in the larger shops where there was a "provision" counter dealing in these items; the British housewife herself referred to these central foods as "provisions" and to the dry goods as "groceries."

It was the grocer dealing in dry, imported goods who led the second retailing revolution. Authors such as Davis (1966) and Jefferys (1954) have considered this great development in retailing (as distinct from wholesaling) to lie in the growth of multiples, of shops that were organised in branches along national lines. Since this growth was based upon the rise of working-class incomes, it is not surprising that the first such organisation was that of the Rochdale Pioneers whose cooperative was begun in 1844—not the first of its kind but the first commercial success. In 1856, at the request of loyal customers, it opened the first of its many branches. At the same time the cooperative experimented in vertical integration by starting the Wholesale Society in

1855 which moved from purchase and distribution directly into production. It was not until sometime later that private firms entered into the same field.[18] Indeed, the great boom came in the last twenty years of the century, when Coop membership rose from half a million in 1881 to three million in 1914.

One of the first trades to develop a network of chain stores was footwear which had 300 shops in 1875, rising to 2,600 in 1900. Butchers started later, with 10 shops in 1880 and 2,000 in 1900, while grocery branches jumped from 27 to 3,444 over the same period (Hobsbawm 1968: 131). In 1872 Thomas Lipton started his grocery shop in Glasgow; twenty-six years later there were 245 branches scattered all over the kingdom. Selling a limited number of cheaper goods, the new multiples in turn influenced the trade of the old-fashioned grocer who now had to deal with the appearance of "an entirely new style of commodity in the form of manufactured foods" (Davis 1966: 284)—tinned goods, jams, powders for custards, grains and so forth. Just as imported goods became cheaper with the new developments in transport, so too manufactured goods and items packaged before sale came to dominate the market. These products were generally branded goods, "sold" before sale by national advertising.

Advertising in the modern sense was a critical factor in these developments and had begun with printing itself; already in 1479 Caxton printed an advertisement for books from his press. The first newspaper advertisement appeared in 1625, and by the mid-eighteenth century Dr Johnson was complaining of their ubiquity. But the major development of the business came in the nineteenth century with the advent of the wholesale trade which itself derived from the industrialisation of production, as well as with the coming of the mass newspaper dependent upon the rotary press. Large-scale manufacture brought with it an increased gap between producer and consumer so that some new way of communication was required. During the fifty years from 1853 the quality of soap bought in Britain increased fourfold, with the main companies, Levers', Pears', and Hudson's, competing by means of national advertising campaigns of which the use of Sir John Millais' painting "Bubbles" was the most famous example. In America, N.W. Ayer and Son, Inc., the first modern agency, was founded in Philadelphia in 1869, acting as an intermediary between producer and media, and making possible the more complex advertising campaigns which not only enable products to reach a wider market but which to some extent create that market, as in the case of breakfast cereals.

The role of advertising in promoting the Hovis loaf is an interesting example of this process. This patent bread has been the product leader in brown bread since 1890 when it had probably been adapted from a loaf invented by an American vegetarian, Graham, in the 1840s. The problem was to overcome the popular prejudice, in existence since Roman times at least, in favour of white bread.[19]

> In the early years the goal was to acquire a sound reputation with a public that was sceptical of patent foods and wary of adulteration. Thus early advertisements made considerable play of royal patronage, of awards and diplomas for quality and purity, and of the need to beware of cheap imitations. (Collins 1976: 30)

The relics of the system of royal patronage and international diplomas employed by the industry remain with us to this day. They were essential parts of the initial legitimation of processed foods, just as the advertisement and the grocery trade were essential aspects of their distribution.

This whole process led to a considerable degree of homogenisation of food consumption and was dependent upon the effective increase in demand from the "working class', which now had no direct access to foodstuffs, to primary production. Because of this mass demand, mass importation and mass manufacture, grocery, formerly one of the minor food trades, became by far the most important. "The vast majority of consumers of all income groups drink the same brand of tea, and smoke the same cigarettes, and their children eat the same cornflakes just as they wear the same clothes and watch the same television sets" (Davis 1966: 84). Differences in income, class and status have to manifest themselves in other ways.

While some historians see the second retailing revolution as developing with the growth of the multiples, Blackman would place it earlier in the century when processed foods and mass imports began to make an impact on the market as a result of changes in technology that were linked with the new demands of the industrial workers. Cheaper West Indian sugar and less expensive Indian teas became essential items in the improved diets of the working class (when they were employed) in the latter half of the nineteenth century. In the 1860s grocers added other new lines, processed foods, including cornflours, baking powders and dried soups, such as Symingtons'. As we have seen, many of these "processed" foods were not the results of changing techniques of food preservation so much as the advent of national instead of local products, such as soap or "patented" branded foods consisting of established items broken down, packaged and sold through public advertising campaigns. Blackman notes that at this time one grocer in Sheffield was buying dried peas, oatmeal and groats from Symingtons, Steam Mills at Market Harborough, and mustard, cocoa, chicory and other commodities from forty different firms including starch and blue from J. & J. Coleman's, the mustard manufacturers who had a dramatic rise from the time in 1854 when they purchased a windmill in Lincolnshire, before moving to Norwich. In the United States too the national canning industry took off in the mid-1860s when Blue Label canned foods, founded in 1858, started advertising nationally, though items like Borden's condensed milk (1857), Burham and Morrill's sweet corn (c. 1850), Burnett's vanilla essence (1847) and various brands of soap were already available.

By 1880 a grocer in Hull was buying Wotherspoon's cornflour, Brown and Poison's brand of the same commodity, Symingtons' pea flour, Goodall's custard and egg powders, several brands of tinned milk, including Nestlé's, tinned fruit, Crosse & Blackwell jams, and many other items which are still household names. It was the technical revolution of mass-producing and semi-processing foodstuffs in common use together with the increased volume of trade in tea and sugar that now brought the grocer into focus as "the most important food trader for regular family purchases" (Blackman 1976: 151).

Adulteration Under the New Dispensation

Complaints against the adulteration of food are as old as the sale of foodstuffs itself. In Athens protests about the quality of wine led to the appointment of inspectors to control its quality. In Rome wines from Gaul were already accused of adulteration, and local bakers were said to add "white earth" to their bread.[20]

Adulteration is a feature of the growth of urban society, or rather of urban or rural society that is divorced from primary production. The agro-towns of West Africa were not so divorced, while even many of the rural inhabitants of modern England have little or nothing to do with the land. With the growth of a distinct town life in England in the centuries after the Norman Conquest, an increasing number of merchants, artisans and shopkeepers had to rely on others for their supply of food, and it was these non-food producers who were the targets (and sometimes the perpetrators) of adulteration. The quality and price of bread and ale was controlled as early as 1266 and continued to be so for more than five hundred years.

It was that "most revolutionary social change" of the first half of the nineteenth century, the rapid growth of towns, and especially the industrial towns of the midlands and north of England (Burnett 1966: 28), which was based on the development of manufacturing industry in the previous century, that made the adulteration of food a major social problem. Protests against impure food had already taken a literary form by the middle of the eighteenth century and were mainly aimed at millers, bakers and brewers. In 1757 "My Friend," a physician, published a work entitled *Poison Detected;* the next year saw the appearance of *Lying Detected* by Emmanuel Collins, attacking the general trend of this literature, as well as a work by Henry Jackson entitled *An Essay on Bread ... to which is added an Appendix; explaining the vile practices committed in adulterating wines, cider, etc.* In a later period of scarcity and high prices, we find *The Crying Frauds of London Markets, proving their Deadly Influence upon the Two Pillars of Life, Bread and Porter,* by the author of the *Cutting Butcher's Appeal* (1795). But it was the work of Frederick Accum in 1820, *A Treatise on Adulterations of Food and Culinary Poisons, etc.,* that had the greatest influence on the public since he was a respected analytical chemist and a professor at the Surrey Institution. He gave widespread publicity both to the methods adopted and to named individuals until he had to flee to Berlin, possibly as a result of a "a deliberate conspiracy of vested interests" (Burnett 1966: 77).

The adulteration of food continued to be a problem for the industrialisation of cooking, particularly in these early days. While Accum's departure from the country led to a temporary neglect of his work, the fight continued. The main analytic contribution was a series of reports made by Dr. Hassall between 1851 and 1855, published collectively in the latter year. Hassall recounts that within months of coming to live in London in 1850 he saw that "there was something wrong in the state of most of the articles of consumption commonly sold" (1855: xxxvii). So he examined a range of items sold at grocers' shops (coffee, cocoa, mustard, sauces, preserved goods, prepared flour) as well as butter, bread, beer and gin. Some passed the test; many failed. To take a typical example, 22 out of 50 samples of arrowroot were adulterated; one variety advertised on the label as:

Walker's
Arrow-root

sold in packages, "2d the quarter pound," elicited the comment (most were equally lapidary) "Consists entirely of potato-flour" (1855: 41). Much of the produce was packaged in the stores in which it was sold. Some had been wrapped and even produced elsewhere, being labelled with the maker's name. These names were publicised by Hassall so that the brand became a mark of quality, or lack of it. Names like Frys and Cadbury's already appear in the cocoa trade (pp. 264–5), Crosse & Blackwell and Fortnum & Mason's in the sauce trade, J. & J. Coleman for mustard (p. 131). Each of these well-known firms was indicted for selling adulterated products and no doubt took steps to improve the quality. On the other hand a positive recommendation for a branded product was clearly an important aspect of publicity as well as of quality control, as for example in Hassall's conclusion: "That Borden's Patent Meat Biscuit was in a perfectly sound state, and that there is much reason to regard it as a valuable article of diet in the provisioning of ships, garrisons, etc." (1855: xx). Firms soon began to employ the label as a certification.

> Vicker's Genuine Russian Isinglass for invalids and culinary use. . . . Purchasers who are desirous of protecting themselves from the *adulteration* which is now extensively practised are recommended to ask for "Vicker's Genuine Russian Isinglass," in *sealed packets.*

The samples that were tested by Hassall sometimes indicate the foreign provenances of their constituents or recipes. India had an obvious influence on the appearance of chutneys as well as on the fact that three varieties of "King of Oude" Sauce were on the market as well as an "India Soy," consisting of burnt treacle. Hassall tested seven tomato sauces, six of which were adulterated, including two from France, one of which was from Maille ("very much of the red earth," he comments).

The combined contribution of public medical testing, branded goods and widespread advertising brought adulteration under control at the same time as creating a national cuisine, at least as far as processed ingredients and prepared foods were concerned. At the same time the pattern of the grocery trade changed radically. For now the shopkeeper was no longer the one who selected and certified the product; that was done by the producer and packager, by the name and the advertisement. Regional tastes continued to be important, as Allen (1968) has pointed out. But these comprised only a small component of a largely nationalised, even internationalised, repertoire.

Given these developments in retailing, the move towards self-service, even automated service, was the next major step. Consumer services become of less and less importance; small special shops tend to vanish while large general stores prosper. But not altogether. In some European countries the tendency is less marked. So it is in rural areas where the owner-managed general store persists. In towns, smaller shops often specialise in new products, in second-hand and antique goods, filling the spatial interstices created by the supermarkets, the department stores and the discount houses, while market stalls arise in unexpected places to sell objects of craft manufacture or local produce. But in general the larger stores offer lower prices, wider choices and the impersonality of selection that a socially mobile population often appears to prefer.

The effect of these changes on the diet and cuisine was enormous. A great deal of domestic work was now done before the food ever entered the kitchen. Many foods were already partly or fully processed, and even sold in a ready-to-eat form. Consequently not only have the ingredients become standardised but a number of the dishes as well, at least in many homes in England and America where only the festive occasion, either in the house or at the restaurant, requires the food to make some claim to be "home-made." While Ghana is far from attaining this extreme condition, the industrialisation of food has begun to affect the country not only as a supplier (essentially of cocoa) but also as a consumer. Within a relatively short space of time tinned sardines, condensed milk, tomato paste and cartons of lump sugar have become standard features of the small markets throughout Anglophone West Africa. A drain on the limited resources of foreign exchange, the demand for which is continuously expanding while cocoa production remains static, the absence of these items causes hardship and complaint; these industrial foods of the "West" have now become incorporated in the meals of the Third World.

Notes

1. For an example of an attempt to "improve" the diet of the urban proletariat the reader is referred to the booklet of Charles Elmé Francatelli, late maître d'hôtel and chief cook to Her Majesty the Queen, entitled "A Plain Cookery Book for the Working Classes" (1852, reprinted by the Scholar Press, London, 1977). The first entry, Boiled Beef, is described as "an economical dinner, especially where there are many mouths to feed," and, "as children do not require much meat when they have pudding" there should be "enough left to help out the next day's dinner, with potatoes." Such fare contrasts with that of the poorer classes in France and many parts of Europe who "very seldom taste meat in any form" (p. 47). The staples of later English cuisine are already there: Toad in the Hole, Meat Pie, Sausage Roll, Bread Pudding, Rice Pudding, Cocky Leaky, Irish Stew, Bubble and Squeak, Jugged Hare, Fish Curry, Boiled Bacon and Cabbage, Tapioca Pudding, Brown and Polson Pudding, Blancmange, Stewed Prunes, Welsh Rarebit—the list reads like the roll of honour of school catering, and one is surprised to find it reinforced by a cook in royal employ and with such continental credentials as his name and title imply. However, the working classes are also taught how to bake their own bread, brew their own beer, to cure hams, and to make A Pudding of Small Birds. Their potential benefactors are also instructed on how to prepare "economical and substantial soup for distribution to the poor."

2. On the early use of dried food for soldiers and travellers in China, see Yü 1977: 75. Chang points out the many ways in which China made use of preservation techniques, by smoking, salting, sugaring, steeping, pickling, drying, soaking in many kinds of soy sauces, etc. For example, meat (either raw or cooked) was pickled or made into a sauce. It also seems that even human flesh was pickled and even famous historical personages ended up in the sauce jar (Chang 1977: 34). In Turkey dried meat was used by soldiers in the field (Braudel 1973: 134); elsewhere such food was intended for the poor, as with the *carne do sol* of Brazil and the *charque* of Argentina.

3. On the processing of fish see the valuable book, *Fish Saving*, by F. L. Cutting (1955), and for a fascinating catalogue of North Atlantic fish as food, see Alan Davidson's North Atlantic Seafood (1979). Both works contain useful bibliographic information.

4. Butter, cheese, cream and, in Asia, yoghurt were ways of preserving milk. Throughout Eurasia, eggs were preserved by a variety of methods. Butter was salted for preservation, not only for internal use but also for sale. At Isigny in Normandy the inhabitants benefited from the right of "franc salé" which enabled them to set their butter and export it to the capital as early as the twelfth century (Segalen 1980: 88).

5. According to Drummond and Wilbraham (1939). Other authors however are sure that it was Durand's patent that was used by Donkin and Hall. Keevil mentions the figure of £1,000 for the purchase of the invention (1972: 6) and Durand is even referred to as the "father of the tin can." However iron containers coated with tin were already used by the Dutch to preserve salmon, a forerunner of the sardine process (Cutting 1955: 86). Appert himself visited London in 1814 to try and place orders for his bottled goods, and found the English industry more advanced in certain ways.

6. The contribution of canned goods to the running of the colonial regime, or rather to the maintenance of the metropolitican cuisine in foreign parts, is illustrated by Mrs. Boyle's account of her journey to Wenchi in the interior of the Gold Coast in the middle of the First World War. She remarks that a large number of the boxes that had to be headloaded from railhead at Kumasi contained "food supplies of all kinds, provided in those days for so many Colonial officers by Fortnum & Mason, and ranging from soap and candles to tinned peaches, butter, sausages and so on—in fact enough to stock a District Officer's house for at least nine or ten months" (1968: 3).

7. Despite early contributions to the technology of canning, the British industry remained small until the 1930s. Quantities of canned food were imported before the First World War, mainly from America; even in the field of canned vegetables, the share of the home market in 1924 was only 5.1 percent (Johnston 1976: 173).

8. See Doudiet (1975) on coastal Maine cooking from 1760.
9. Drummond and Wilbraham report the case of a London fishmonger who "as early as 1820" used ice to bring Scotch salmon to London (1939: 308–9).
10. On the making and storing of ice among wealthy families in the Indian city of Lucknow, see Sharar 1975: 168.
11. See L. A. Coser, "Domestic Servants: the obsolescence of an occupational role" in *Greedy Institutions* (New York, 1974). According to Hobsbawm (1968: 131), the figure rose to 1.4 million by 1871, of which 90,000 were female cooks and not many more were housemaids. See also Keevil's remark on the growth of the firm of Fitch Lovell:

> Prosperity, high wages and inflation have also had their effect on the food trade. The well-off can no longer obtain domestic servants to cook for them. Attracted by high wages more and more women take jobs outside their homes, so a demand has been created for convenience foods and labour-saving gadgets. Nowadays the typical domestic servant is in a factory making washing machines, the typical shop assistant working in a cannery. A whole new food manufacturing industry has sprung up (1972: 9).

12. Indicative of this change, Collins points out, was the change of names. Post Toasties was formerly "Elijah's Manna," and the Kellogg Co. was the "Sanitas Nut Food Company." "Most breakfast cereals were originally marketed as 'natural,' 'biologic' or, in the case of Grape Nuts, 'brain' foods" (1976: 41).
13. See Anderson 1977: 338; but also Root 1971.
14. A London regulation, revoked in the fourteenth century, ran "Let no baker sell bread in his own house or before his own oven, but let him have a basket with his bread in the King's market" (Davis 1966: 24).
15. See for example the entries from the Chester Mayors' Books reprinted by Furnivall (1897: lxiii).
16. In Chester in 1591 the oath was taken by 33 Butchers and 30 Bakers. The Butchers' oath included the statement that "all such your victuall that you shall utter and sell, to poore and Riche, at reasonable prices" (Furnivall 1897: 153).
17. In German they were originally *Kolonialwarenhändler* (dealers in colonial produce).
18. On the impact of multiples on the retail trade itself, see Keevil's account of the growth of Fitch Lovell:

> Already by 1900 the growth of multiple shops was well under way and in the 1930s great integrated companies like Allied Suppliers, and Unigate began to appear. These companies expanded rapidly, as did multiple shops in every field, helped by the low value of property and low rents. The standardisation of packaging made possible mass advertising of branded food, selling it long before it reached the shop. Traditional wholesaling was becoming an expensive luxury and far-sighted firms like Fitch Lovell diversified out of it as quickly as possible. (1972: 8)

19. McCance and Widdowson note that the distinction between brown and white breads goes back at least to Roman times when "white bread ... was certainly one of the class distinctions" (1956: 6). Indeed in eighteenth-century France white bread was customarily offered to the master and brown to the servants, even when eating at the same table (Flandrin 1979: 105). But the milling and preparation of bread was another, perhaps more basic ground, for class distinction, since both water and wind mills were at first the property of the manor or of the monastery. In Norman times and later, the miller rented the mill, and the other tenants were expected to bring their grain to be ground. Such relations lasted well into the seventeenth century. Like the mill, the bakehouse was also the property of the lord; serfs were compelled to bring their meal or dough to be baked there for a fixed charge, an imposition that they tried to avoid whenever possible for there was never the same need to use the bakehouse as the mill (McCance and Widdowson 1956: 13–14). All monasteries had their own bakehouses until the dissolution under Henry VIII. This basic food of the mass of the British population has shifted from domestic production in the early Middle Ages, to the lord's bakehouse under feudalism, to the local bakery under early capitalism, to the concentration of production in a few firms—four controlling about 70 per cent of bread production, according to Collins (1976: 18)—and its distribution through that contemporary descendant of the grocer's shop, the supermarket.
    The Chinese preference for the less beneficial white rice is also associated with status, partly because the milling was more expensive and partly because it stored better (Anderson 1977: 345). The same preference is found in India and the Middle East.
20. See Vehling 1977: 33 for a comment on Roman adulteration of food.

References

Anderson, E. N. and M. L. 1977. Modern China: South. In K. C. Chang, ed., *Food in Chinese Culture.* New Haven.
Bitting, A. W. and K. G. 1916. *Canning and How to Use Canned foods.* Washington, D.C.

Bitting, A. W. 1937. *Appertizing: Or, The Art of Canning; Its History and Development.* San Francisco.

Bitting, K. G. 1920. Introduction to N. Appert, *The Book for All Households.* Chicago.

Blackman, J. 1976. The Corner Shop: The Development of the Grocery Trade and General Provisions Trade. In D. Oddy and D. Miller, eds., *The Making of the Modern British Diet,* London.

Boyle, L. 1968. *Diary of a Colonial Officer's Wife.* Oxford.

Braudel, F. 1973. *Capitalism and Material Life, 1400–1800.* London.

Burnett, J. 1966. *Plenty and Want: A Social History of Diet in England from 1815 to the Present Day.* London.

Butterick. 1925. *The Story of the Pantry Shelf, An Outline of Grocery Specialties.* New York.

Chang, K. C., ed. 1977. *Food in Chinese Culture: Anthropological and Historical Perspectives.* New Haven.

Collins, E. J. T. 1976. The "Consumer Revolution and the Growth of Factory Foods: Changing Patterns of Bread and Cereal-Eating in Britain in the Twentieth Century." In D. J. Oddy and D. Miller, eds., *The Making of the Modern British Diet.* London.

Corley, T. A. B. 1976. Nutrition, Technology and the Growth of the British Biscuit Industry, 1820–1900. In D. J. Oddy and D. Miller, eds., *The Making of the Modern British Diet.* London.

Coser, L. A. 1974. *Greedy Institutions.* New York.

Cummings, R. O. 1941. *The American and His Food.* Chicago, 2nd ed.

Cutting, C. L. 1955. *Fish Saving: A History of Fish Processing from Ancient to Modern Times.* London.

Davidson, A. 1979. *North Atlantic Seafood.* London.

Davis, D. 1966. *Fairs, Shops and Supermarkets: A History of English Shopping.* Toronto.

Deutch, R. M. 1961. *The Nuts among the Berries.* New York.

Doudiet, E. W. 1975. Coastal Maine Cooking: Foods and Equipment from 1970. In M. L.Arnott, ed. *Gastronomy: The Anthropology of Food and Food Habits.* The Hague.

Drummond, J. C. and A. Wilbraham. 1939. *The Englishmen's Food: A History of Five Centuries of English Diet.* London.

Flandrin, J-L. 1979. *Families in Former Times: Kinship, Household and Sexuality.* Cambridge.

Francatelli, C. E. 1852. *A Plain Cookery Book for the Working Classes.* London.

Furnivall, F. J. 1897. *Child-marriages, Divorces, and Ratifications . . . .* London.

Hassall, A. H. 1855. *Food and Its Adulteration.* London.

Hobsbawm, E. J. 1968. *Industry and Empire.* New York.

Jefferys, J. B. 1954. *Retail Trading in Britain 1880–1950.* London.

Johnston, J. P. 1976. The Development of the Food-Canning Industry in Britain during the Inter-War Period. In D. J. Oddy and D. Miller, eds., *The Making of the Modern British Diet.* London.

Keevil, A. 1972. *The Story of Fitch-Lovell 1784–1970.* London.

McCance, R. A. and E. M. Widdowson. 1956. *Breads Brown and White.* London.

Mintz, S. 1979. Time, Sugar, and Sweetness. *Marxist Perspectives,* 2: 56–73.

Mote, F. W. 1977. Yuan and Ming. In K. C. Chang, ed., *Food in Chinese Culture.* New Haven.

Prentice, E. P. 1950. *Progress: An Episode in the History of Hunger?* New York.

Root, W. 1971. *The Food of Italy.* New York.

Segalen, M. 1980. *Mari et femme dans la société paysanne.* Paris.

Sharar, A. H. 1975. *Lucknow: The Last Phase of an Oriental Culture.* London.

Teuteberg, H. J. 1975. The General Relationship between Diet and Industrialization. In E. and R. Forster, eds., *European Diet from Pre-Industrial to Modern Times.* New York.

Vehling, J. D. trans. 1977. *Apicius: Cookery and Dining in Imperial Rome.* New York.

Wright, L. 1975. *The Road from Aston Cross: An Industrial History, 1875–1975.* Leamington Spa.

Yü, Y-S. 1977. Han. In K. C. Chang, ed., *Food in Chinese Culture.* New Haven.

8

Time, Sugar, and Sweetness[*]

Sidney W. Mintz

Food and eating as subjects of serious inquiry have engaged anthropology from its very beginnings. Varieties of foods and modes of preparation have always evoked the attention, sometimes horrified, of observant travelers, particularly when the processing techniques (e.g., chewing and spitting to encourage fermentation) and the substances (e.g., live larvae, insects, the contents of animal intestines, rotten eggs) have been foreign to their experience and eating habits. At the same time, repeated demonstrations of the intimate relationship between ingestion and sociality among living peoples of all sorts, as well as the importance attributed to it in classic literary accounts, including the Bible, have led to active reflection about the nature of the links that connect them. Long before students of Native America had invented "culture areas," or students of the Old World had formulated evolutionary stages for pastoralism or semiagriculture, W. Robertson Smith had set forth elegantly the concept of commensality and had sought to explain the food prohibitions of the ancient Semites.[1] But food and eating were studies for the most part in their more unusual aspects—food prohibitions and taboos, cannibalism, the consumption of unfamiliar and distasteful items—rather than as everyday and essential features of the life of all humankind.

Food and eating are now becoming actively of interest to anthropologists once more, and in certain new ways. An awakened concern with resources, including variant forms of energy and the relative costs of their trade-offs—the perception of real finitudes that may not always respond to higher prices with increased production—seems to have made some anthropological relativism stylish, and has led to the rediscovery of a treasure-trove of old ideas, mostly bad, about natural, healthful, and energy-saving foods. Interest in the everyday life of everyday people and in categories of the oppressed—women, slaves, serfs, Untouchables, "racial" minorities, as well as those who simply work with their hands—has led, among other things, to interest in women's work, slave food, and discriminations and exclusions. (It is surely no accident that the best early anthropological studies of food should have come from the pens of women, Audrey Richards[2] and Rosemary Firth.[3]) What is more, the upsurge of interest in meaning among anthropologists has also reenlivened the study of any subject matter that can be treated by seeing the patterned relationships between substances and human groups as forms of communication.

[*]*Originally published 1979*

While these and other anthropological trends are resulting in the appearance of much provocative and imaginative scholarship, the anthropology of food and eating remains poorly demarcated, so that there ought still to be room for speculative inquiry. Here, I shall suggest some topics for a study of which the skills of anthropology and history might be usefully combined; and I shall raise questions about the relationship between production and consumption, with respect to some specific ingestible, for some specific time period, in order to see if light may be thrown on what foods mean to those who consume them.

During and after the so-called Age of Discovery and the beginning of the incorporation of Asia, Africa, and the New World within the sphere of European power, Europe experienced a deluge of new substances, including foods, some of them similar to items they then supplemented or supplanted, others not readily comparable to prior dietary components. Among the new items were many imports from the New World, including maize, potatoes, tomatoes, the so-called "hot" peppers (*Capsicum annuum, Capsicum frutescens*, etc.), fruits like the papaya, and the food and beverage base called chocolate or cacao.

Two of what came to rank among the most important post-Columbian introductions, however, did not originate in the New World, but in the non-European Old World: tea and coffee. And one item that originated in the Old World and was already known to Europeans, the sugar cane, was diffused to the New World, where it became, especially after the seventeenth century, an important crop and the source of sugar, molasses, and rum for Europe itself. Sugar, the ingestible of special interest here, cannot easily be discussed without reference to other foods, for it partly supplemented, partly supplanted, alternatives. Moreover, the character of its uses, its association with other items, and, it can be argued, the ways it was perceived, changed greatly over time. Since its uses, interlaced with those of many other substances, expressed or embodied certain continuing changes in the consuming society itself, it would be neither feasible nor convincing to study sugar in isolation. Sweetness is a "taste," sugar a product of seemingly infinite uses and functions; but the foods that satisfy a taste for sweetness vary immensely. Thus, a host of problems arise.

Until the seventeenth century, ordinary folk in Northern Europe secured sweetness in food mostly from honey and from fruit. Lévi-Strauss is quite right to emphasize the "natural" character of honey,[4] for he has in mind the manner of its production. Sugar, molasses, and rum made from the sugar cane require advanced technical processes. Sugar can be extracted from many sources, such as the sugar palm, the sugar beet, and all fruits, but the white granulated product familiar today, which represents the highest technical achievement in sugar processing, is made from sugar cane and sugar beet. The sugar-beet extraction process was developed late, but sugar-cane processing is ancient. When the Europeans came to know the product we call sugar, it was cane sugar. And though we know sugar cane was grown in South Asia at least as early as the fourth century B.C., definite evidence of processing—of boiling, clarification and crystallization—dates from almost a millennium later.

Even so, sugar crudely similar to the modern product was being produced on the southern littoral of the Mediterranean Sea by the eighth century A.D., and thereafter on Mediterranean islands and in Spain as well. During those centuries it remained costly, prized, and less a food than a medicine. It appears to have been regarded much as were spices, and its special place in contemporary European tastes—counterpoised, so to speak, against bitter, sour, and salt, as the opposite of them all—would not be achieved until much later. Those who dealt in imported spices dealt in sugar as well. By the thirteenth century English monarchs had grown fond of sugar, most of it probably from the Eastern Mediterranean. In 1226 Henry III appealed to the Mayor of Winchester to obtain for him three pounds of Alexandrine sugar, if possible; the famous fair near Winchester made it an entrepôt of exotic imports. By 1243, when ordering the purchase of spices at Sandwich for the royal household, Henry III included 300 pounds of *zucre de Roche* (presumably, white sugar). By the end of that century the court was consuming several tons of sugar a year, and early in the fourteenth century a full cargo of sugar reached Britain from Venice. The inventory of a fifteenth-century chapman in York—by which time sugar was beginning to reach England from the Atlantic plantation islands of Spain and Portugal—included not only cinnamon, saffron, ginger, and galingale, but also sugar and "casson sugar." By that time, it appears, sugar had entered into the tastes and recipe books of the rich; and the two fifteenth-century cookbooks edited by Thomas Austin[5] contain many sugar recipes, employing several different kinds of sugar.

Although there is no generally reliable source upon which we can base confident estimates of sugar consumption in Great Britain before the eighteenth century—or even for long after—there is no doubt that it rose spectacularly, in spite of occasional dips and troughs. One authority estimates that English sugar consumption increased about four-fold in the last four decades of the seventeenth century. Consumption trebled again during the first four decades of the eighteenth century; then more than doubled again from 1741–1745 to 1771–1775. If only one-half of the imports were retained in 1663, then English and Welsh consumption increased about twenty times, in the period 1663–1775. Since population increased only from four and one-half million to seven and one-half million, the per capita increase in sugar consumption appears dramatic.[6] By the end of the eighteenth century average annual per capita consumption stood at thirteen pounds. Interesting, then, that the nineteenth century showed equally impressive increases—the more so, when substantial consumption at the start of the nineteenth century is taken into account—and the twentieth century showed no remission until the last decade or so. Present consumption levels in Britain, and in certain other North European countries, are high enough to be nearly unbelievable, much as they are in the United States.

Sugar consumption in Great Britain rose together with the consumption of other tropical ingestibles, though at differing rates for different regions, groups, and classes. France never became the sugar or tea consumer that Britain became, though coffee was more successful in France than in Britain. Yet, the general spread of these substances through the Western world since the seventeenth century has been one of the truly important economic and cultural phenomena of the modern age. These were, it seems, the first edible luxuries to become proletarian commonplaces; they were surely the first luxuries to become regarded as necessities by vast masses of people who had not produced them, and they were probably the first substances to become the basis of advertising campaigns to increase consumption. In all of these ways, they, particularly sugar, have remained unmistakably modern.

Not long ago, economists and geographers, not to mention occasional anthropologists, were in the habit of referring to sugar, tea, coffee, cocoa, and like products as "dessert crops." A more misleading misnomer is hard to imagine, for these were among the most important commodities of the eighteenth- and nineteenth-century world, and my own name for them is somewhat nastier:

> Almost insignificant in Europe's diet before the thirteenth century, sugar gradually changed from a medicine for royalty into a preservative and confectionery ingredient and, finally, into a basic commodity. By the seventeenth century, sugar was becoming a staple in European cities; soon, even the poor knew sugar and prized it. As a relatively cheap source of quick energy, sugar was valuable more as a substitute for food than as a food itself; in western Europe it probably supplanted other food in proletarian diets. In urban centres, it became the perfect accompaniment to tea, and West Indian sugar production kept perfect pace with Indian tea production. Together with other plantation products such as coffee, rum and tobacco, sugar formed part of a complex of "proletarian hunger-killers," and played a crucial role in the linked contribution that Caribbean slaves, Indian peasants, and European urban proletarians were able to make to the growth of western civilization.[7]

If allowance is made for hyperbole, it remains true that these substances, not even known for the most part by ordinary people in Europe before about 1650, had become by 1800 common items of ingestion for members of privileged classes in much of Western Europe—though decidedly not in all—and, well before 1900, were viewed as daily necessities by all classes.

Though research by chemists and physiologists on these substances continues apace, some general statements about them are probably safe. Coffee and tea are stimulants without calories or other food value. Rum and tobacco are both probably best described as drugs, one very high in caloric yield, and the other without any food value at all, though apparently having the effect at times of reducing hunger. Sugar, consisting of about 99.9 percent pure sucrose, is, together with salt, the purest chemical substance human beings ingest and is often labeled "empty calories" by physicians and nutritionists. From a nutritional perspective, all are, in short, rather unusual substances. With the exception of tea, these hunger-killers or "drug foods" destined for European markets were mostly produced in the tropical Americas from the sixteenth century onward until the nineteenth century; and most of them continue to be produced there in substantial amounts. What, one may ask, was the three-hundred-year relationship between the systems of production of these commodities, their political and economic geography, and the steady increase in demand for them?

Though remote from his principal concerns, Marx considered the plantations of the New World among "the chief momenta of primitive accumulation":[8]

> Freedom and slavery constitute an antagonism. . . . We are not dealing with the indirect slavery, the slavery of the proletariat, but with direct slavery, the slavery of the black races in Surinam, in Brazil, in the Southern States of North America. Direct slavery is as much the pivot of our industrialism today as machinery, credit, etc. Without slavery, no cotton; without cotton, no modern industry. Slavery has given their value to the colonies; the colonies have created world trade; world trade is the necessary condition of large-scale machine industry. Before the traffic in Negroes began, the colonies only supplied the Old World with very few products and made no visible change in the face of the earth. Thus slavery is an economic category of the highest importance.[9]

These and similar assertions have been taken up by many scholars, most notably, Eric Williams, who develops the theme in his famous study, *Capitalism and Slavery* (1944). In recent years a lively controversy has developed over the precise contribution of the West India plantations to capitalist growth in the metropolises, particularly Britain. The potential contribution of the plantations has been viewed in two principal ways: fairly direct capital transfers of plantation profits to European banks for reinvestment; and the demand created by the needs of the plantations for such metropolitan products as machinery, cloth, torture instruments, and other industrial commodities. Disputes continue about both of these potential sources of gain to metropolitan capital, at least about their aggregate effect. But there is a third potential contribution, which at the moment amounts only to a hunch: Possibly, European enterprise accumulated considerable savings by the provision of low-cost foods and food substitutes to European working classes. Even if not, an attractive argument may be made that Europeans consumed more and more of these products simply because they were so good to consume. But it hardly seems fair to stop the questions precisely where they might fruitfully begin. Of the items enumerated, it seems likely that sweet things will prove most persuasively "natural" for human consumption—if the word dare be used at all. Hence, a few comments on sweetness may be in order.

Claude Lévi-Strauss in his remarkable *From Honey to Ashes* (1973), writes of the stingless bees of the Tropical Forest and of the astoundingly sweet honeys they produce, which, he says,

> have a richness and subtlety difficult to describe to those who have never tasted them, and indeed can seem almost unbearably exquisite in flavour. A delight more piercing than any normally afforded by taste or smell breaks down the boundaries of sensibility, and blurs its registers, so much so that the eater of honey wonders whether he is savouring a delicacy or burning with the fire of love.[10]

I shall resist an inclination here to rhapsodize about music, sausage, flowers, love and revenge, and the way languages everywhere seem to employ the idiom of sweetness to describe them—and so much else—but only in order to suggest a more important point. The general position on sweetness appears to be that our hominid capacity to identify it had some positive evolutionary significance—that it enabled omnivores to locate and use suitable plant nutrients in the environment. There is no doubt at all that this capacity, which presumably works if the eating experience is coupled with what nutritionists call "a hedonic tone," is everywhere heavily overladen with culturally specific preferences. Indeed, we know well that ingestibles with all four of the principal "tastes"—salt, sweet, sour, and bitter—figure importantly in many if not most cuisines, even if a good argument can be made for the evolutionary value of a capacity to taste sweetness.

Overlaid preferences can run against what appears to be "natural," as well as with it. Sugar-cane cultivation and sugar production flourished in Syria from the seventh century to the sixteenth, and it was there, after the First Crusade, that north Europeans got their first sustained taste of sugar. But the Syrian industry disappeared during the sixteenth century, apparently suppressed by the Turks, who, according to Iban Battuta, "regard as shameful the use of sugar houses." Since no innate predisposition, by itself, explains much about human behavior, and since innate predispositions rarely get studied before social learning occurs—though there is at least some evidence that fetal behavior is intensified by the presence of sucrose, while human newborns apparently show a clear preference for sweetened liquids—how much to weigh the possible significance of a "natural" preference remains moot. For the moment, let it suffice that, whether there exists a natural craving for sweetness, few are the world's peoples who respond negatively to sugar, whatever their prior experience, and countless those who have reacted to it with intensified craving and enthusiasm.

Before Britons had sugar, they had honey. Honey was a common ingredient in prescriptions; in time, sugar supplanted it in many or most of them. (The term "treacle," which came to mean molasses in English usage, originally meant a medical antidote composed of many ingredients, including honey. That it should have come to mean molasses and naught else suggests, in a minor way, how sugar and its byproducts overcame and supplanted honey in most regards.) Honey had also been used as a preservative of sorts; sugar turned out to be much better and, eventually, cheaper. At the time of the marriage of Henry IV and Joan of Navarre (1403), their wedding banquet included among its many courses "Perys in syrippe." "Almost the only way of preserving fruit," write Drummond and Wilbraham, "was to boil it in syrup and flavour it heavily with spices."[11] Such syrup can be made by super-saturating water with sugar by boiling; spices can be added during the preparation. Microorganisms that spoil fruit in the absence of sugar can be controlled by 70 percent sugar solutions, which draw off water from their cells and kill them by dehydration. Sugar is a superior preservative medium—by far.

Honey also provided the basis of such alcohol drinks as mead, metheglin, and hypomel. Sugar used with wine and fruit to make hypocras became an important alternative to these drinks; ciders and other fermented fruit drinks made with English fruit and West Indian sugars represented another; and rum manufactured from molasses represented an important third. Here again, sugar soon bested honey.

The use of spices raises different issues. Until nearly the end of the seventeenth century, a yearly shortage of cattle fodder in Western Europe resulted in heavy fall butchering and the preservation of large quantities of meat by salting, pickling, and other methods. Though some writers consider the emphasis on spices and the spice trade in explanation of European exploration excessive, this much of the received wisdom, at least, seems well founded. Such spices were often used to flavor meat, not simply to conceal its taste; nearly all were of tropical or subtropical origin (e.g., nutmeg, mace, ginger, pepper, coriander, cardamom, turmeric—saffron is an important exception among others). Like these rare flavorings, sugar was a condiment, a preservative, and a medicine; like them, it was sold by Grocers (Grossarii) who garbled (mixed) their precious wares, and was dispensed by apothecaries, who used them in medicines. Sugar was employed, as were spices, with cooked meats, sometimes combined with fruits. Such foods still provide a festive element in modern Western cuisine: ham, goose, the use of crab apples and pineapple slices, coating with brown sugar, spiking with cloves. These uses are evidence of the obvious: that holidays preserve better what ordinary days may lose—just as familial crises reveal the nature of the family in ways that ordinary days do not. Much as the spices of holiday cookies—ginger, mace, cinnamon—suggest the past, so too do the brown sugar, molasses, and cloves of the holiday ham. More than just a hearkening to the past, however, such practices may speak to some of the more common ways that fruit was preserved and meat flavored at an earlier time.

Thus, the uses and functions of sugar are many and interesting. Sugar was a medicine, but it also disguised the bitter taste of other medicines by sweetening. It was a sweetener, which, by 1700, was sweetening tea, chocolate, and coffee, all of them bitter and all of them stimulants. It was a food, rich in calories if little else, though less refined sugars and molasses, far commoner in past centuries, possessed some slight additional food value. It was a preservative, which, when eaten with what it preserved, both made it sweeter and increased its caloric content. Its byproduct molasses (treacle) yielded rum, beyond serving as a food itself. For long, the poorest people ate more treacle than sugar; treacle even turns up in the budget of the English almshouses. Nor is this list by any means complete, for sugar turns out to be a flavor-enhancer, often in rather unexpected ways. Rather than a series of successive replacements, these new and varied uses intersect, overlap, are added on rather than lost or supplanted. Other substances may be eliminated or supplanted; sugar is not. And while there are medical concerns voiced in the historical record, it appears that no one considered sugar sinful, whatever they may have thought of the systems of labor that produced it or its effects on dentition. It may well be that, among all of the "dessert crops," it alone was never perceived as an instrument of the Devil.[12]

By the end of the seventeenth century sugar had become an English food, even if still costly and a delicacy. When Edmund Verney went up to Trinity College, Oxford in 1685, his father packed in his trunk for him eighteen oranges, six lemons, three pounds of brown sugar, one pound of powdered white sugar in quarter-pound bags, one pound of brown sugar candy, one-quarter pound of white sugar candy, one pound of "pickt Raisons, good for a cough," and four nutmegs.[13] If the seventeenth century was the century in which sugar changed in Britain from luxury and medicine to necessity and food, an additional statistic may help to underline this trans-formation. Elizabeth Boody Schumpeter has divided her overseas trade statistics for England into nine groups, of which "groceries," including tea, coffee, sugar, rice, pepper, and other tropical products, is most important. Richard Sheridan points out that in 1700 this group comprised 16.9 percent of all imports by official value; in 1800 it comprised 34.9 percent. The most prominent grocery items were brown sugar and molasses, making up by official value two-thirds of the group in 1700 and two-fifths in 1800. During the same century tea ranked next: The amount imported rose, during that hundred years, from 167,000 pounds to 23 *million* pounds.[14]

The economic and political forces that underlay and supported the remarkable concentration of interest in the West India and East India trade between the seventeenth and nineteenth centuries cannot be discussed here. But it may be enough to note Eric Hobsbawm's admirably succinct summary of the shift of the centers of expansion to the north of Europe, from the seventeenth century onward:

> The shift was not merely geographical, but structural. The new kind of relationship between the "advanced" areas and the rest of the world, unlike the old, tended constantly to intensify and widen the flows of commerce. The powerful, growing and accelerating current of overseas trade which swept the infant industries of Europe with it—which, in fact, sometimes actually *created* them—was hardly conceivable without this change. It rested on three things: in Europe,

the rise of a market for overseas products for everyday use, whose market could be expanded as they became available in larger quantities and more cheaply; and overseas the creation of economic systems for producing such goods (such as, for instance, slave-operated plantations) and the conquest of colonies designed to serve the economic advantage of their European owners.[15]

So remarkably does this statement illuminate the history of sugar—and other "dessert crops"—between 1650 and 1900 that it is almost as if it had been written with sugar in mind. But the argument must be developed to lay bare the relationships between demand and supply, between production and consumption, between urban proletarians in the metropolis and African slaves in the colonies. Precisely how demand "arises"; precisely how supply "stimulates" demand even while filling it—and yielding a profit besides; precisely how "demand" is transformed into the ritual of daily necessity and even into images of daily decency: These are questions, not answers. That mothers' milk is sweet can give rise to many imaginative constructions, but it should be clear by now that the so-called English sweet tooth probably needs—and deserves—more than either Freud or evolutionary predispositions in order to be convincingly explained.

One of Bess Lomax's better-known songs in this country is "Drill, ye Tarriers, Drill."[16] Its chorus goes:

And drill, ye tarriers, drill,
    Drill, ye tarriers, drill,
It's work all day for the sugar in your tay,
    Down behind the railway.

As such, perhaps it has no particular significance. But the last two verses, separated and followed by that chorus, are more pointed:

Now our new foreman was Gene McCann,
    By God, he was a blamey man.
Last week a premature blast went off
    And a mile in the air went Big Jim Goff.
Next time pay day comes around,
    Jim Goff a dollar short was found.
When asked what for, came this reply,
    You're docked for the time you was up in the sky.

The period during which so many new ingestibles became encysted within European diet was also the period when the factory system took root, flourished, and spread. The precise relationships between the emergence of the industrial workday and the substances under consideration remain unclear. But a few guesses may be permissible. Massive increases in consumption of the drug-food complex occurred during the eighteenth and nineteenth centuries. There also appears to have been some sequence of uses in the case of sugar; and there seems no doubt that there were changes in the use, by class, of sugar and these other products over time, much as the substances in association with which sugar was used also changed. Although these are the fundamentals upon which further research might be based, except for the first (the overall increases in consumption) none may be considered demonstrated or proved. Yet, they are so general and obvious that it would be surprising if any turned out to be wrong. Plainly, the more important questions lie concealed behind such assertions. An example may help.

To some degree it could be argued that sugar, which seems to have begun as a medicine in England and then soon became a preservative, much later changed from being a direct-use product into an indirect-use product, reverting in some curious way to an earlier function but on a wholly different scale. In 1403, pears in syrup were served at the feast following the marriage of Henry IV to Joan of Navarre. Nearly two centuries later, we learn from the household book of Lord Middleton, at Woollaton Hall, Nottinghamshire, of the purchase of two pounds and one ounce of "marmalade" at the astronomical price of 5s. 3d., which, say Drummond and Wilbraham, "shows what a luxury such imported preserved fruits were."[17]

Only the privileged few could enjoy these luxuries even in the sixteenth century in England. In subsequent centuries, however, the combination of sugars and fruit became more common, and the cost of jams, jellies, marmalades, and preserved fruits declined. These changes accompanied many other dietary changes, such as the development of ready-made (store-bought) bread, the gradual replacement of milk-drinking by tea-drinking, a sharp decline in the preparation of oatmeal—especially important in Scotland—and a decrease in the use of butter. Just how such changes took place and the nature of their interrelationship require considerable detailed study. But factory production of jams and the increasing use of store-bought (and factory-made) bread plainly go along with the decline in butter use; it seems likely that the replacement of milk with tea and sugar are also connected. All such changes mark the decline of home-prepared food. These observations do not add up to a lament over the passage of some bucolic perfection, and people have certainly been eating what is now fashionably called "junk food" for a very long time. Yet, it is true that the changes mentioned fit well with a reduction in the time which must be spent in the kitchen or in obtaining foodstuffs, and that they have eased the transition to the taking of more and more meals outside the home. "Only in the worst cases," writes Angeliki Torode of the mid-nineteenth-century English working class, "would a mother hesitate to open her jam jar, because her children ate more bread if there was jam on it."[18] The replacement of oatmeal by bread hurt working-class nutrition; so, presumably, did the other changes, including the replacement of butter by jam. Sugar continues to be used in tea—and in coffee, which never became a lower-class staple in England—but its use in tea is direct, its use in jam indirect. Jam, when produced on a factory basis and consumed with bread, provides an efficient, calorie-high and relatively cheap means of feeding people quickly, wherever they are. It fits well with changes in the rhythm of effort, the organisation of the family, and, perhaps, with new ideas about the relationship between ingestion and time.

"What is wanted," wrote Lindsay, a nutritionist of the early twentieth century, about Glasgow, "is a partial return to the national dish of porridge and milk, in place of tea, bread and jam, which have so universally replaced it in the towns, and which are replacing it even in the rural districts."[19] But why, asks R. H. Campbell, the author of the article in which Lindsay is cited, did people fail to retain the more satisfactory yet cheap diet of the rural areas?"[20] Investigators in Glasgow found a ready answer: "When it becomes a question of using the ready cooked bread or the uncooked oatmeal, laziness decides which, and the family suffers." In the city of Dundee, home of famous jams and marmalades, other investigators made an additional observation: The composition of the family diet appears to change sharply when the housewife goes to work. There, it was noted that such time-consuming practices as broth-making and oatmeal-cooking dropped out of domestic cuisine. Bread consumption increases; Campbell cites a statistic for the nineteenth century indicating that one family of seven ate an average of fifty-six pounds of bread per week.[21] Jam goes with bread. The place of laziness in these changes in diet remains to be established; the place of a higher value on women's labor—labor, say, in jam factories (though women worked mainly in jute factories in Dundee)—may matter more.

The rise of industrial production and the introduction of enormous quantities of new ingestibles occurred during the same centuries in Britain. The relationship between these phenomena is, on one level, fairly straightforward: As people produced less and less of their own food, they ate more and more food produced by others, elsewhere. As they spent more and more time away from farm and home, the kinds of foods they ate changed. Those changes reflected changing availabilities of a kind. But the availabilities themselves were functions of economic and political forces remote from the consumers and not at all understood as "forces." People were certainly not compelled to eat the specific foods they ate. But the range of foods they came to eat, and the way they came to see foods and eating, inevitably conformed well with other, vaster changes in the character of daily life—changes over which they plainly had no direct control.

E. P. Thompson has provided an illuminating overview of how industry changed for working people the meaning—nay, the very perception—of the day, of time itself, and of self within time: "If men are to meet both the demands of a highly-synchronized automated industry, and of greatly enlarged areas of 'free time,' they must somehow combine in a new synthesis elements of the old, and the new, finding an imagery based neither upon the seasons nor upon the market but upon human occasions."[22] It is the special character of the substances described here that, like sugar, they provide calories without nutrition; or, like coffee and tea, neither nutrition nor calories, but stimulus to greater effort, or, like tobacco and alcohol, respite from reality. Their study might enable one to see better how an "imagery based . . . upon human occasions" can take shape partly by employing such substances, but not always with much success. Perhaps high tea can one day become a cozy cuppa; perhaps the afternoon sherry can find its equivalent in the grog shop. But a great amount of manufactured sweetness may eventually lubricate only poorly, or even partly take the place of, human relations on all occasions.

The coffee break, which almost always features coffee or tea, frequently sugar, and commonly tobacco, must have had its equivalent before the industrial system arose, just as it has its equivalent outside that system today. I have been accused of seeing an inextricable connection between capitalism and coffee-drinking or sugar use; but coffee and sugar are too seductive, and capitalism too flexible, for the connection to be more than one out of many. It is not that the drug-food habits of the English working classes are the consequence of long-term conspiracies to wreck their nutrition or to make them addicted. But if the changing consumption patterns are the result of class domination, its particular nature and the forms that it has taken require both documentation and specification. What were the ways in which, over time, the changing occupational and class structure of English society was accompanied by, and reflected in, changes in the uses of particular ingestibles? How did those ingestibles come to occupy the paramount place they do in English consumption? Within these processes were, first, innovations and imitations; later, there were ritualizations as well, expressing that imagery based upon human occasions to which Thompson refers. But an understanding of those processes, of those meanings, cannot go forward, I believe, without first understanding how the production of the substances was so brilliantly separated by the workings of the world economy from so-called meanings of the substances themselves.

I have suggested that political and economic "forces" underlay the availabilities of such items as sugar; that these substances gradually percolated downward through the class structure; and that this percolation, in turn, probably fit together social occasion and substance in accord with new conceptions of work and time. And probably, the less privileged and the poorer imitated those above them in the class system. Yet, if one accepts this idea uncritically, it might appear to obviate the research itself. But such "imitation" is, surely, immeasurably more complicated than a bald assertion makes it seem. My research to date is uncovering the ways in which a modern notion of advertising and early conceptions of a large clientele—a mass market, or "target audience" for a mass market—arose, perhaps particularly in connection with sweet things and what I have labeled here "drug-foods." How direct appeals, combined with some tendency on the part of working people to mimic the consumption norms of those more privileged than they, can combine to influence "demand" may turn out to be a significant part of what is meant by meaning, in the history of such foods as sugar.

As anthropologists turn back to the study of food and eating and pursue their interest in meaning, they display a stronger tendency to look at food in its message-bearing, symbolic form. This has resulted in an enlivening of the discipline, as well as in attracting the admiration and attention of scholars in kindred fields. Such development is surely all to the good. But for one interested in history, there is reason to wonder why so few anthropological studies have dealt with long-term changes in such things as food preferences and consumption patterns, to which historians and economic historians have paid much more attention. In part, the relative lack of anthropological interest may be owing to the romanticism of an anthropology once resolutely reluctant to study anything not "primitive." But it appears also to stem from a readiness to look upon symbolic structures as timeless representations of meaning.

Hence, we confront difficult questions about what we take "meaning" to mean and within what limits of space and time we choose to define what things mean. No answers will be ventured here. But if time is defined as outside the sphere of meaning in which we are interested, then certain categories of meaning will remain and may then be considered adequate and complete. In practice, and for the immediate subject-matter, the structure of meaning would in effect be made coterminous with the political economy. For the substances of concern here—plantation products, tropical products, slave products, imported from afar, detached from their producers—the search for meaning can then be confined within convenient boundaries: the boundaries of consumption.

But if one is interested in the world economy created by capitalism from the six-teenth century onward, and in the relationships between the core of that economy and its subsidiary but interdependent outer sectors, then the structure of meaning will not be coterminous with the metropolitan heartland. If one thinks of modern societies as composed of different groups, vertebrated by institutional arrangements for the distribution and maintenance of power, and divided by class interests as well as by perceptions, values and attitudes, then there cannot be a single system of mean-ing for a class-divided society. And if one thinks that meanings arise, then the separa-tion of how goods are produced from how they are consumed, the separation of colony from metropolis, and the separation of proletarian from slave (the splitting in two of the world economy that spawned them both in their modern form) are unjus-tified and spurious.

Such substances as sugar are, from the point of view of the metropolis, raw materi-als, until systems of symbolic extrusion and transformation can operate upon them. But those systems do not bring them forth or make them available; such availabilities are differently determined. To find out what these substances come to mean is to reunite their availabilities with their uses—in space and in time.

For some time now anthropology has been struggling uncomfortably with the recog-nition that so-called primitive society is not what it used to be—if, indeed, it ever was. Betrayed by its own romanticism, it has sought to discover new subject-matters by imputations of a certain sort—as if pimps constituted the best equivalent of "the prim-itive" available for study. Without meaning to impugn in the least the scientific value of such research, I suggest that there is a much more mundane modernity equally in need of study, some of it reposing on supermarket shelves. Anthropological interest in things—material objects—is old and highly respectable. When Alfred Kroeber referred to "the fundamental thing about culture . . . the way in which men relate themselves to one another by relating themselves to their cultural material"[23] he meant objects as well as ideas. Studies of the everyday in modern life, of the changing character of such humble matters as food, viewed from the perspective of production and consumption, use and function, and concerned with the emergence and variation of meaning, might be one way to try to renovate a discipline now dangerously close to losing its purpose.

Notes

Versions of this paper were presented during the past few years at the University of Minnesota, Bryn Mawr College, Rice University, Wellesley College, Cornell University, the University of Pennsylvania, and at Johns Hopkins Univer-sity's Seminar in Atlantic History and Culture. In radically modified form, these materials also formed part of my 1979 Christian Gauss Lectures at Princeton University. I benefited from comments by participants at all of these presenta-tions, and from criticisms from other friends, including Carol Breckinridge, Carol Heim, and Professors Fred Damon, Nancy Dorian, Eugene Genovese, Jane Goodale, Richard Macksey, Kenneth Sharpe, and William Sturtevant.

1.   W. Robertson Smith, *Lectures on the Religion of the Semites* (New York, 1889).
2.   Audrey I. Richards, *Hunger and Work in a Savage Tribe*: A Functional Study of Nutrition Among the Southern *Bantu (London, 1932); Land, Labour and Diet in Northern Rhodesia: An Economic Study of the Bemba Tribe* (London, 1939).
3.   Rosemary Firth, *Housekeeping Among Malay Peasants* (London, 1943).
4.   Claude Lévi-Strauss, *From Honey to Ashes* (New York, 1973).
5.   Thomas Austin, *Two Fifteenth-Century Cookbooks* (London, 1888).

6. Richard Sheridan, *Sugar and Slavery* (Baltimore, 1974).

7. Sidney W. Mintz, "The Caribbean as a Socio-cultural area," *Cahiers d'Histoire Mondiale*, IX (1966), 916–941.

8. Karl Marx, *Capital* (New York, 1939), I, 738.

9. Karl Marx to P. V. Annenkov, Dec. 28, 1846, *Karl Marx to Friedrich Engels: Selected Works* (New York, 1968).

10. Lévi-Strauss, *From Honey to Ashes*, 52.

11. J. C. Drummond and Anne Wilbraham, *The Englishman's Food* (London, 1958), 58.

12. I am indebted to Professor Jane Goodale of Bryn Mawr College, who first suggested to me that I investigate this possibility.

13. Drummond and Wilbraham, *Englishmen's Food*, 111.

14. Sheridan, *Sugar and Slavery*, 19–20. Statistics on tea are somewhat troublesome. Smuggling was common, and figures on exports are not always reliable. That the increases in consumption were staggering during the eighteenth century, however, is not open to argument. See Elizabeth Schumpeter, *English Overseas Trade Statistics, 1697–1808* (Oxford, 1960).

15. Eric Hobsbawm, *Industry and Empire* (London, 1968), 52.

16. See A. Lomax, *The Folk Songs of North America* (Garden City, N.Y., 1975).

17. Drummond and Wilbraham, *Englishmen's Food*, 54.

18. Angeliki Torode, "Trends in Fruit Consumption," in T. C. Barker, J. C. McKenzie, and John Yudkin, eds., *Our Changing Fare* (London, 1966), 122.

19. R. H. Campbell, "Diet in Scotland: An Example of Regional Variation," in ibid., 57.

20. Ibid.

21. Ibid., 58.

22. E. P. Thompson, "Time, Work Discipline and Industrial Capitalism," *Past and Present*, no. 38 (1967), 96.

23. Alfred Kroeber, *Anthropology* (New York, 1948), 68.

Hegemony and Difference:
Race, Class and Gender

9

More than Just the "Big Piece of Chicken": The Power of Race, Class, and Food in American Consciousness*

Psyche Williams-Forson

In 1999 HBO premiered Chris Rock's stand-up comedy routine *Bigger and Blacker*. One of the jokes deals with what Rock humorously calls the "big piece of chicken."[1] Using wit, Chris Rock delivers a semi-serious treatise on parenting and marriage. First, he admonishes the audience for not recognizing that "a real daddy" receives little praise for "making the world a better place . . ." A man, or "daddy", according to Rock, pays bills, provides food, and all of a family's other necessities. Despite his efforts, he rarely receives any praise for his "accomplishments." Although these tasks are clearly part and parcel of adult responsibilities, Rock ignores this truism in an effort to set up his commentary on the intersection of race, class, gender, and food. Continuing, he argues, "Nobody appreciates daddy . . ."

By way of illustrating why a father needs and deserves such concern Rock points out that fathers work hard all day fighting against the stresses of life. Then a father—particularly an African American father—comes home to more stress:

> And what does daddy get for all his work? The *big piece of chicken*. That's all daddy get is the *big piece of chicken*. That's right. And some women don't want to give up the big piece of chicken. Who the fuck is you to keep the *big piece of chicken*? How dare you keep *the big piece of chicken*! A man can't work for 12 hours and come home to a wing! When I was a kid, my momma [would] lose her mind if one of us ate the *big piece of chicken* by accident. "What the fuck? You ate the *big piece of chicken*. Oh Lawd, no, no, no! Now I got to take some chicken and sew it up. Shit! Give me two wings and a poke chop. Daddy'll never know the difference."[2]

Chris Rock's kind of humor has an extensive history as a form of black expressive culture. Physically, he walks back and forth on stage, bobbing and weaving as he shares different versions of his comic narrations, turning out stories from "everyday conversational talk."[3] Rock uses this form of performance or narrativizing to wage social commentary on a variety of issues including stereotypes of black people and chicken. When an artist uses stereotypes there are a number of factors that have to be considered including the purposes to which such oversimplifications are put.

*Originally published 2008

Stated more plainly, the humor of Chris Rock makes us wonder about the subversive ways in which objects like food can be used to contest hegemonic representations of blackness and the ways in which performances of blackness reveal complicated aspects of identity.

Investigating Intersections

As more or less correctly stated, there are roughly two methodological schools of thought when talking about African American foodways. There are those that focus on the food itself and its connections to the African Diaspora. Among them are historians of the American South (e.g., Karen Hess, Joe Gray Taylor and Sam Hilliard) and African American studies (e.g., Tracy Poe and Robert Hall), archeologists (e.g., Theresa Singleton and Anne Yentsch), geographer Judith Carney, anthropologist Tony Whitehead, and independent foodways scholars (e.g., Jessica Harris, Howard Paige, Joyce White, and Diane Spivey). Those who focus generally on the intersections of food and identity, representation, and/or contestation are literary scholars Anne Bower, Kyla Wazana Tompkins, Doris Witt, and Rafia Zafar, sociologist William Whit, anthropologist Charles Joyner, and folklorist Patricia Turner; media specialist Marilyn Kern-Foxworth, and historians Kenneth Goings and M. M. Manring.[4] My research into the realm of African American foods is not only about locating, identifying, and understanding the connections between foods but also the people who consume them. This approach goes beyond the theories that argue we are what we eat and the ways our foods reflect our cultural identity. Rather, the method I employ asks us to consider what we learn about African American life and culture by studying the intersections of food, gender, race, class, and power. How do African American historical, socioeconomic, and political spaces influence the foods that are consumed? How is this consumption a part of the performance of black class? Further-more, what do we learn about African Americans when black people willingly engage in perpetuating the oversimplified images or ideas that are sometimes held by the larger American society?

Black people have long been engaged in ideological warfare involving food, race, and identity. Most commonly known are the stereotypes concerning black people's consumption of fried chicken and watermelon. Though these stereotypes have been around for centuries they are still pervasive in the contemporary American psyche. Consider, for instance, the numerous postcards, invitations, and other ephemera that illustrate African American men, women, and children with watermelon.

Black feminist scholar Patricia Hill Collins suggests the need to be attuned to the ways in which processes of power underlie social interactions and are involved in the process of external definition. These definitions can be challenged, however, through the process of "self-definition." The acts of "challenging the political knowledge-validation process that result[s] in externally defined stereotypical images . . . can be unconscious or conscious acts of resistance."[5] One engages in the process of self-definition by identifying, utilizing, and more importantly, redefining symbols—like chicken or watermelon—that are commonly affiliated with African Americans. By doing this, black people refuse to allow the wider American culture to dictate what represents their expressive culture and thereby what represents blackness. But this process of defining one's self is fraught with complications and complexities particularly if the group fails to understand or acknowledge that there is a power structure at work behind the creation of common affiliations, labels, or stereotypes.

Collins explains these complications further in her delineation of self-valuation or the replacement of negative images with positive ones. This process of replacement can be equally as problematic as the original external definition if we fail to understand and to recognize the stereotype as a controlling image. This concept is perhaps best illustrated by the example of Chris Rock's comedy that opens this essay. Though I will return to Rock's funny side later, Collins' caution is registered here. The exchange of one set of controlling images for another does little to eradicate the defining image itself. Consequently, black people need to be clear about the ways in which historical, social, political, and economic contexts have established reductionist narratives and how these accounts are embedded in food.

One way that blacks can both deal with these narratives and gain independence from them is to begin by taking a close look at the historical basis of various food stereotypes. These stereotypes tend to be distorted portrayals of those cultural behaviors that are and have been used in order to diminish black personal and collective power.

Stereotypes Abound

Stereotypes involving black people have been around for years. Indeed, they continue to exist.[6] Elsewhere I argue extensively for the partial evolution of some of these stereotypes as ideologies shaped from laws and ordinances passed during the seventeenth and eighteenth centuries.[7] It was and continues to be my contention that these depictions partly emerged as a way to control the economic gains of enslaved and free men and women who bartered and traded in the marketplace. Historians often cite newspaper articles, court documents, and travelers' accounts among other critical sources detailing information on early African and African American entrepreneurs of food. Nineteenth-century travelers' diaries, for example, indicate "flocks of poultry [were] numerous" and, "there are very few [slaves] indeed who are denied the privilege of keeping dunghill fowls, ducks, geese, and turkeys." Moreover, some black people would often sit by the wharf for days on end waiting to buy foods like chicken and then sell them for exorbitant prices.[8] Historian Philip Morgan notes a similar practice whereby some travelers would instruct their stewards to hold in reserve various foods like bacon so they would have bartering power with "the Negroes who are the general Chicken Merchants [sic]."[9]

As with any encroachment, the bartering and trading by African Americans ushered in a slew of regulations that sought to limit items being sold door-to-door and in the market. To be sure the ambiguous ownership of goods prior to sale was one of the many reasons for stalling and halting the sale of goods. Foods were not supposed to be sold prior to passing through the town gates, and in particular customers were not supposed to purchase goods whose ownership might be difficult to trace. This included items such as chickens, which were often sold outside the market.

Archeologist Anne Yentsch maintains that foods such as oysters, salted fish in large barrels or casks, cattle, sheep, and hogs that were alive could easily be traced because they were by-and-large produced by small farmers.[10]

Chickens, on the other hand were far harder to pinpoint. Even though several blacks had chickens their masters and neighboring farms had them as well. Sometimes these birds roamed freely and thus were traded or sold in an effort to obtain more favorable goods. Often times, especially during the colonial era, it was difficult to ascertain the exact origins of a bird. Except among the wealthy, most chickens during that time were not kept in hen houses. Chicken and fowl were free to roam finding food and shelter wherever possible, an issue that easily lends support to the charge of theft. Additionally, there was no widespread formalized system of breeding in early America when many Africans and Native Americans were engaged in bartering. Consequently, it was difficult to distinguish most common fowl from one another with the exception of certain kinds of partridges, pheasant, and hens. This reality, however, did little to hinder the accusations of theft, which were not only levied against slaves but also free blacks and fugitives.

These claims were fueled by black people's use of trading practices like forestalling, which legal ordinances did little to reduce. According to the *South Carolina Gazette*, one writer complained that almost on a daily basis, black women could be found huckstering and forestalling "poultry, fruit, eggs," and other goods "in and near the Lower Market . . . from morn till night," buying and selling what and how they pleased to obtain money for both their masters and themselves. Often times their prices were exorbitant and they would use all kinds of marketing strategies to choose which white people to sell to and for how much.[11] Robert Olwell captures this point when he explains: "as slaveholders, Carolina whites felt that slaves should be generally subordinate, but as property holders and capitalists they also had to recognize the legitimacy of the market in which sellers had the right to seek the highest price for their goods."[12]

Many whites viewed blacks with "great prejudice" when they sought to engage in capitalist enterprises. Under slavery's oppression, blacks, regardless of their status, were to be subordinate at all times. Any deviation from this norm was a threat to the social order that had been systematically and institutionally constructed over time. Consequently, any element of freedom recognized and enjoyed by black people, and particularly women, was an affront to white social power. Lawrence McDonnell explains it this way: "The marketplace . . . is a neutral zone, a threshold between buyer and seller . . . . Master and slave confronted each other at the moment of exchange as bearers of commodities, stripped of social dimensions . . . [this] linked black sellers with White buyers, and hence with White society, not only by assertion of black humanity but through White objectification. Slaves appeared here equally purposeful as Whites."[13]

Money and a small measure of market power assaulted the charade played out during slavery that sought to convince black people that freedom would never come. Attributing black economic gain to theft helped to perpetuate the travesty. By attributing stealing by slaves to an inherent nature rather than a condition of their circumstances (or even to a performance of sorts), slave owners were able to deflect attention from their own participation in this aspect of slave victimization.

Morally, it was much better to believe that slaves were natural thieves than to believe that the institution of enslavement contributed to their larceny. Clearly there is some truth to the claim that slaves engaged in thievery; the extent to which this was the case, however, is rooted in white patriarchal ideology.[14]

Though devoid of a disposition toward theft, some slaves did engage in pilfering and stealing. Some scholars however, have referred to these acts as skill and cunning. Eugene Genovese's study of African American life and culture, suggests this when he writes, "for many slaves, stealing from their own or other masters became a science and an art, employed as much for the satisfaction of outwitting Ole' Massa as anything else."[15] In Weevils in the Wheat, for example, ex-slave Charles Grandy tells that hunger was a motivating factor for stealing food. He says, "I got so hungry I stole chickens off de roos' . . . . We would cook de chicken at night, eat him an' bu'n de feathers . . . . We always had a trap in de floor fo' de do' to hide dese chickens in."[16] This is just one example of African American trickster heroism that not only reflects a kinship to African traditions but also views this type of behavior as both morally acceptable and necessary for survival. At the same time, it is a subversive cultural form that uses humor in its expression.

John Roberts' point about early African Americans should be registered here: "Given the desperate and oppressive circumstances under which they lived, enslaved Africans could not be overly concerned with the masters' definition of 'morality' of behaviors that enhanced their prospects for physical survival and material well-being. The task that they confronted, however, was how to make such individually devised solutions to a collective problem function as a behavior strategy for the group without endangering their adaptability or the physical well-being of members of their community."[17] Although the oppressive circumstances of today are nowhere near those of enslavement, the delicate balance of performing individual behavior and yet not suffering collective consequences is still applicable. Teasing out this sense of balance and its complications might become more apparent as I discuss African American performances of stereotypes during the late nineteenth and early twentieth century.

The South suffered a devastating loss of free labor with the end of the Civil War and migrations of newly freed blacks; it found itself in a precarious situation. Its infrastructure was suffering economically, politically, socially, culturally, and physically. Suddenly, the millions of freed blacks became an overwhelming problem. What about their rights? Would they be given rights? How and to what end? How would white Southerners keep their subordinates in line? Was this even possible anymore? These and many other questions played themselves out on the political landscapes of the day. But they were also played out on cultural playing fields as well. According to historian Kenneth Goings, the loss of control over black people registered such a blow among white Southerners that they began using emerging technology as one means of reasserting control and reclaiming power.[18]

Advancing technology, namely the camera, was useful for depicting African Americans—men, women, boys, and girls—as visually conciliatory. As Grant McCracken intimates, such illustrations were useful for alleviating some of the "nervous prostration" brought on by the rapid changes of the time. Goods and commodities were used in an effort to alleviate some of the distress caused by the social, political, economic, and cultural transformations.[19] Goods were particularly useful for helping individuals contemplate the "possession of an emotional condition, a social circumstance, even an entire lifestyle" by making desires concrete.[20] These illustrations, or commodities of racism, were coveted possessions. They enabled their owners not only to possess the physical object but also to mentally covet the pastoral image of the gallant South that whites wished to maintain. This interpretation is certainly not the only reason that people might have purchased these kinds of photos. But for sure these images and their owners were complicit in spreading the network of racial power.

What quickly emerged through this visual communication was an ideology of black inferiority, which assisted in the formulation of racist stereotypes. These stereo-types were perpetuated by advertisements, trading cards, sheet music and stereoviews like that which illustrates an African American baby in a buggy, caption reading: "When I Dit Big, 'Oo'll Have to Roost Hiah." This, and countless other images are clearly staged as if to appear natural. More than likely it was the case of African Americans performing to stay alive. From the thieving child, to the salacious lover of white hens, African Americans—particularly men and boys—were constantly ridiculed; more often than not it was centered on the stereotypical image of the coon.

Kenneth Goings, whose study *Mammy and Uncle Mose* historicizes the cultural and political economy of black collectibles, maintains that the coon image was one of the most offensive stereotypes. M. L. Graham used this coon motif as the mascot for his little-known "Coon Chicken Inn" restaurants. The emblem, a black-faced man with large, extended red lips, was typically symbolic of how whites would stereotype black people with food to endorse various products like fried chicken. Considered a most effective advertising technique, images like these reinforced the stereotypical Old South/New South myth of the loyal, happy servant just waiting to be used by the master—and now the consumer.

The restaurant with all of its accoutrements became a metaphor for whites using and discarding black service. When the meal is complete, the napkins, plates and utensils bearing the black-faced logo are discarded and along with it any remnant of the serviceable "darker" that is no longer needed or desired. This act of symbolic and physical disposal provided whites with what Goings describes in a similar discussion as a sense of "racial superiority" and a "therapeutic sense of comfort."[21] Manipulating these objects of material culture enabled white Americans not only to forge an alliance across class lines, but also to more collectively subjugate and vilify black people. The ideology of black inferiority provided a safeguard for white America during a time when their racial, economic, and political balance was perceived as unstable and threatened.

Unfolding against this backdrop, are the numerous ways that food becomes inter-laced with discourses of power, race, class, and gender in American consciousness. Chicken, for example, which was once championed as a celebrated food of the South prepared by some of the best culinary talent turns into an object of ridicule and defacement. Chicken—both the bird and the food—is fraught then, with paradoxes in the contexts of the historical and economic circumstances of the South. On the one hand, black consumption of chicken was seen as normative; on the other hand, this consumption was also perceived as negative. The issue is made more complex when we read chicken—the food—as a cultural text.

Fried chicken, a largely southern food that emerged out of social institutions shaped by racial complexities, is one of many foods that blurs the lines between the "symbolic separations [of] those who prepare the food and those who consume it."[22] Black women were widely credited with lining "Southern groaning boards." This was their rightful place as loyal cooks—a cultural demarcation that became necessary for symbolically separating the domestic rituals of the South. Black women prepared and cooked fried chicken for white families but they did not consume it; and, thereby they maintained the purity of southern cuisine. Mentally, this belief was important for reinforcing the necessary symbolic distance between cook and consumer. This configuration is made problematic and complicated, however, by the insistence that black people are zealous about their consumption of fried chicken.

What becomes necessary then are carefully coded words and messages. Namely, the word Southern becomes coded for white, while "soul food" is decoded as black. Diane Spivey has labeled this coding phenomenon, "Whites Only Cuisine." She says:

> The end of the [Civil] war also signaled the beginning of the redefining of southern White heritage. Food was a factor in the efforts of southern White elites to hold on to their old way of life. Cooking and cuisine were remade to look uniquely southern . . . . Asserting that the recipes were "southern" made [their] cookbooks exclusionary, and therefore racist, because the cookbooks and recipes contained therein were heralded as the creations of the elite southern White women. In an attempt to promote southern White culture, therefore, the concept of "southern cooking" started out as *Whites Only Cuisine.*[23]

Given the mass exchange of foods and food habits that occurred between early Africans, Europeans, and Native Americans it is almost impossible for one group or another to claim any recipe as original or native to their culture. With the ebb and flow of people across continents, regions, and lands come vast amounts of mutual exchange resulting in multi-amalgamations between and among cultures and foods changing and evolving over time.

The intersections of food with power and other variables enable a reading of the ways in which the idea of blackness as performance boldly emerges. As I have discussed thus far, since their arrival in this country, Africans and Africans born in America have been performing race in myriad ways. Long after the auction block performance African Americans engaged in other racial acts like participating in staged photographs and witnessing their recipes being usurped. A good many of these performances of racial roles for survival involved food. Part of understanding the food and foodways of African Americans asks that we also question what all of these performances had to do with blackness and issues of identity? And how has agency been a part of the performance of this blackness? Turning back to Chris Rock's comedic discussion of the "big piece of chicken" helps us to think a bit more about these questions.

In the vignette that opens this essay Chris Rock is explaining how the children of an African American family have eaten the "big piece of chicken" even though they are aware that this piece of meat belongs to their father. In the comedy, Rock makes manhood and fatherhood synonymous with the right to have the largest piece of chicken not simply as a reward but as a right. Rock argues that this is the father's just portion because "daddy can't work all day and come home to a wing." Implied, of course, is the fact that because the father leaves the home to work and engages in a number of anxieties outside the home, he therefore deserves all of the praise— including culinary recompense.

On the surface one could argue that this routine is simply another of Rock's treatises on the ills of society. Every race of people can identify with this scenario— one of the many aspects of Rock's performances that endear him to diverse audience members. However, my contention is that this scene is multifaceted. Rock is, in effect, performing blackness in ways that can be described as both subversive as well as oppressive, rendering this piece to be about more than "the big piece of chicken." Rock is dissident in that, more or less, he follows the basic formula of delivering an African American trickster folktale. Consider, for example, Jacob Stoyer's slave narrative, *Sketches of My Life in the South*, wherein he tells a story of man named Joe and how he outsmarted the master's wife, Mrs. King. According to the story, Joe killed and dressed a turkey that belonged to the King family. In his haste to get the bird into a pot without being caught, he neglected to cut it leaving its knees to stick out of the pot. To hide his thievery, Joe threw one of his shirts over the pot. When Joe failed to respond to the calling of Mr. King, Mrs. King came into the kitchen to inquire of his whereabouts. Discovering the theft, which Joe declined to know anything about, she saw to it that Joe was punished for "allowing the turkey to get into the pot."[24] The point here is the way in which Joe was able to dupe, if only briefly, the King family. The larger issue is the momentary reversal of power executed by Joe in his performance as a "dumb slave."

Similarly, Rock manages to dupe both white and black audience-goers who usually have paid a somewhat hefty price to enjoy a laugh. By performing racist, sexist, and otherwise problematic comedies Rock proffers the illusion that he buys into these notions as truisms. In doing so, he is a relative trickster, perpetuating the racist perception of black people as chicken lovers.[25] But as E. Patrick Johnson argues, "blackness does not only reside in the theatrical fantasy of the White imaginary that is then projected onto black bodies. Nor is blackness always consciously acted out. It is also the inexpressible yet undeniable racial experience of black people—the ways in which the 'living of blackness' becomes a material way of knowing."[26] Among black audiences then, it is not surprising that Rock's performances are laudatory and celebratory. Many watch the performances of him and other comedians and laugh uproariously knowing that much of what is being performed has all kinds of negative implications. Yet, there is something to be said for these dramatic interludes, which often make audiences momentarily forget about their troubles. The very fact of the matter is that these comedians are enjoyed precisely because they engage in the slipperiness of black cultural politics.

Part of this slipperiness derives from another suggestion offered by Johnson: "The interanimation of blackness and performance and the tension between blackness as 'play' and material reality further complicates the notion of what . . . 'playing black' is and what 'playing black' ain't." Rock engages this question of "black is/black ain't" with his audiences. With white audiences he leads them into thinking that he is per- forming what "black is" as he mocks, mimics, and ridicules black people. With black audiences, he relies upon a number of "in-group" techniques to offer black audiences comic relief while simultaneously playing to a number of 'truth claims.'[27] Later, using a similar coded performance as the trickster hero in African American folktales, Rock turns the tables on this segment of the audience using the rhetoric of race, class, and gender.

The art of verbal play has always been a vehicle of self-expression for black men and women, although women have only recently been recognized as engaging in such. Rock understands the role of signifying in the black community and employs it well in his routines. From Rock's references to the fact that daddy experiences stress all day from working in a "white world," we can assume that daddy feels little or no economic power. Consequently, in order to establish his manhood, he needs to assert his authority at home. One of the ways he is able to affirm his household status is by eating the "big piece of chicken." Here the chicken functions metaphorically and literally as a source and a reflection of masculine power. Rock's subtle explication of this power enables him to dupe his black audience-goers—particularly the women.

Using children as the catalyst, Rock creates the scenario of mama as a culinary artist. After her children consume the forbidden big piece of chicken, she is able to flawlessly recreate it by expertly sewing together two wings and a pork chop. In addition to all of the other work mama has done during the day—caring for children, running a household, cooking and other chores—she now has to make up for the fact that one of her children has eaten the wrong piece of chicken: "Oh Lawd, no, no, no! Now I got to take some chicken and sew it up. Shit! Give me two wings and a poke chop. Daddy'll never know the difference."[28] The challenge posed by this situation is perhaps the cause for Rock acknowledging, "Now mama got the roughest job, I'm not gonna front." Denying daddy his rightful portion is a measure of disrespect that will surely bring wrath upon the children. To avoid this mama tries to make amends. Mama then has not only procured, prepared, and presented the food, she now has to alter and re-prepare the meal while simultaneously protecting her children. After all of this, mama will undoubtedly have to "do a jig" so that daddy does not recognize her necessary handiwork. She then will have to placate him if he discovers the ruse.

The discussion of mama's incredible talents is double-edged because while plentiful, her culinary and household ingenuity must not be celebrated because to do so would reveal that daddy is eating something less than the "big piece of chicken." Equally problematic is that it has gone unnoticed that while mama is not in the paid work force, she is nonetheless very much involved in a system of work. Her work, unfortunately, is largely domestic, economically undervalued, and from the standpoint of this example, aesthetically unappreciated. Because even though mama has created another large portion for daddy she cannot speak of it because it will only make daddy feel that he gets little for all his "hard work." Unspoken are the stories of mama's day of work, her troubles, and her battles—many of which are represented symbolically by the chicken.

It is not surprising that Rock would gender his discussion to include some kind of praise of a mother's culinary abilities. As Pamela Quaggiotto notes, "the mother determines when, what, and how much family members will eat . . . . She controls the symbolic language of food, determining what her dishes and meals will say about herself, her family, and world."[29] And yet his depictions of "mama" are both enlightening and baffling for what they seem to reveal/hide about Rock's gender and racial agenda. Clearly the parody and humor of this situation are evident. Though the audience knows it is a joke, there is uncertainty over whether mama's work is being praised or ridiculed. Moreover, there are the questions of whether or not Rock is waging some sort of commentary on racial stereotypes involving black people and chicken. For example, it is significant to note that Rock never specifies whether the chicken is fried or baked. In fact, he does not have to because he relies upon a certain amount of a priori knowledge that assumes that chicken eating in the company of black people means "fried." Comforted by the fact that black audience members bring to bear their own life experiences and cultural memories surrounding food and thus know what "black is" and "black ain't" he is able to launch into his dramatization.

Maybe it is a similar comfort and ease that Rock attends to when at the end of the routine he admonishes women to remember their "proper" place in dealing with men. Undoubtedly many in the audience see mama's work as a labor of love that is taken for granted, not needing any particular recognition. In fact, Rock half-heartedly suggests this when he implies that daddy has the primary responsibilities in the household. As if rethinking this assertion, Rock soon after backtracks by supplying his one line of praise for mama. Despite all of this backpedaling, by the end of his show Rock is clear about his direction as he definitively reinstates his masculinist stance. He closes his performance with: "Women talk too much. They always want you to be listenin.' Let a man get situated! Let me get my other foot in the door! Let me get somethin' to eat. Let me get somethin' to drink! Let me take a shit! Go in the fuckin' kitchen and get me my *big piece of chicken*!" Having said this, Rock drops the mike and struts off the stage amid the cheers and shouts of approval from men—and women.[30]

Food objects are useful for elucidating the type of obscurities revealed by this kind of close reading. Additionally, they are politicized by the meanings inscribed in their uses and associations historically and contemporarily. This is particularly salient to an article like chicken that is perceived to be generic in its uses among all races and ethnicities of people. The meanings that chicken holds for black people are as diverse as its members. But when chicken is placed in various contexts alongside performances of power and race then it is plentiful for what it reveals beyond being a portion of food.

This essay has attempted to illustrate the importance of moving beyond studying merely the foods of various cultures to include the behaviors, actions, contexts, and histories that involve them. As this article has also suggested foods like chicken, that have been used to stereotype African American people, are often actually undergirded by intersecting variables of race, gender, class, and power. This fact, perhaps more than any other, lends credence to the notion that food is always about more than what it seems.

Notes

1.   For a more detailed analysis of this particular routine of Chris Rock's see Williams-Forson, *Building Houses Out of Chicken Legs: Black Women, Food, and Power* (Chapel Hill: UNC Press, 2006), 178–185.

2. Chris Rock, *Bigger and Blacker*.

3. Geneva Smitherman, "The Chain Remain the Same: Communicative Practices in the Hip Hop Nation." *Journal of Black Studies* 28, 1 (September 1997): 3–25.

4. Though in no way this dichotomous, most of these scholars can be roughly divided into these categories, as Krishnendu Ray observes. See book review by Ray, *Building Houses out of Chicken Legs*, in *Food & Foodways*, 15:1–6, 2007. Also see *African American Foodways: Explorations of History & Culture*, Ed. Anne Bower (Urbana: University of Illinois Press, 2007).

5. Patricia Hill Collins, "Learning from the Outsider Within: The Sociological Significance of Black Feminist Thought," *Social Problems* 33, no. 6 (1986): 516–517.

6. African Americans have long been caricatured as brand mascots for various food and household products. For example, a grinning black chef named Rastus was used to represent Cream of Wheat hot cereal and a pair of black children who were known as the Gold Dust Twins, were used to advertise soap powder. In addition to the now infamous Aunt Jemima, who sold pancake mix, there have been numerous other grinning black women who were "Jemima-like" that were used to sell fried chicken, shortening, and cookware. It also should be noted that other races and ethnicities have also been stereotyped where food is concerned. First there was Frito Bandito, who spoke in an exaggerated Mexican accent and then there was the Chihuahua who muttered ¡Yo Quiero Taco Bell! In March 2007 Masterfoods USA, a unit of Mars Foods attempted to hoist the stereotypical depiction of "Uncle Ben" from servant to chairman of the board. The attempt was met with mixed success. See Stuart Elliott, "Uncle Ben, Board Chairman." *The New York Times*. 30 March 2007, C1.

7. For a more lengthy discussion see Williams-Forson, *Building Houses Out of Chicken Legs*, in particular chapters 1 and 2. See also Williams-Forson, " 'Suckin' the Chicken Bone Dry': African American Women, Fried Chicken, and the Power of a National Narrative." In *Cooking Lessons: The Politics of Gender and Food*. Ed. Sherrie Inness. (Lanham, MD: Rowman & Littlefield, 2000): 200–214.

8. Anne E. Yentsch, *A Chesapeake Family and Their Slaves: A Study in Historical Archaeology* (Great Britain: Cambridge University Press, 1994), 242.

9. Philip D. Morgan, *Slave Counterpoint: Black Culture in the Eighteenth-Century Chesapeake and Lowcountry* (Chapel Hill: University of North Carolina Press for the Omohundro Institute of Early American History and Culture, Williamsburg, Virginia, 1998), 359.

10. Yentsch, 245.

11. Quoted in Robert Olwell, " 'Loose, Idle, and Disorderly': Slave Women in the Eighteenth-Century Charleston Marketplace." In *More Than Chattel: Black Women and Slavery in the Americas*, Eds., David Barry Gaspar and Darlene Clark Hine. (Bloomington: Indiana University Press, 1996): 97–110. See also, Yentsch, 242–243; Phillip Morgan, 368–372.

12. Olwell, 102.

13. McDonnell, "Money Knows No Master: Market Relations and the American Slave Community." In *Developing Dixie: Modernization in a Traditional Society*, ed., Winfred B. Moore, Jr., Joseph F. Tripp, and Lyon G. Tyler, Jr. (Westport: Greenwood Press, 1988): 31–44.

14. Lichtenstein, " 'That Disposition to Theft, With Which They Have Been Branded': Moral Economy, Slave Management, and the Law." *Journal of Social History* 21 (1989): 413–40.

15. Eugene Genovese, *Roll, Jordan, Roll: The World the Slaves Made* (New York: Vintage Books, Inc., 1976), 606.

16. Charles L. Perdue, Jr., Thomas E. Barden, and Robert K. Phillips, Eds. *Weevils in the Wheat* (Charlottesville: University of Virginia Press, 1976), 116.

17. Roberts, *From Trickster to Badman: The Black Folk Hero in Slavery and Freedom*. (Philadelphia: University of Pennsylvania Press, 1989): 33. Lawrence Levine also establishes connections between the African American trickster and the acquisition of food. See "The Slave as Trickster," in *Black Culture, Black Consciousness*. (New York: Oxford University Press, 1977), 121–133.

18. Kenneth W. Goings, *Mammy and Uncle Mose: Black Collectibles and American Stereotyping* (Bloomington: Indiana University Press, 1994), 4–7.

19. Grant McCracken's discussion is a good one on the ways in which consumer goods helped to preserve hopes and ideals during the Victorian era. See "The Evocative Power of Things," *Culture and Consumption* (Bloomington: Indiana University Press, 1990), 104.

20. McCracken, 110.

21. Ibid., 47.

22. Mary Titus, " 'Groaning Tables and Spit in the Kettles': Food and Race in the Nineteenth-Century South," *Southern Quarterly* 20, no. 2–3 (1992), 15.

23. Diane M. Spivey, "Economics, War, and the Northern Migration of the Southern Black Cook," in *The Peppers, Crackling, and Knots of Wool Cookbook: The Global Migration of African Cuisine* (New York: State University of New York Press, 1999), 263.

24. See Jacob Stroyer, *Sketches of My Life, Sketches of My Life in the South*. Part I. 1849–1908. Salem: Salem Press (1879). *Documenting the American South: The Southern Experience in Nineteenth-Century America*, eds. Lee Ann

Morawski and Natalia Smith (2001). Academic Affairs Lib., U. of North Carolina, Chapel Hill. <http://docsouth. unc.edu/neh/storyer/stroyer.html> (June 1, 2007).

25. Williams-Forson, *Building Houses Out of Chicken Legs*, 176–181.

26. E. Patrick Johnson, *Appropriating Blackness: Performance and the Politics of Authenticity* (Durham: Duke University Press, 2003), 8.

27. Patricia Turner and Gary Alan Fine suggest that when rumors and/or stereotypes are based on information that *could be* correct it is considered a truth-claim. Truth claims contain a certain amount of "cultural logic" because they make "cultural sense" (i.e. all black people eat fried chicken) even though no systemic, definitive evidence exists in which to substantiate them. *Whispers on the Color Line: Rumor and Race in America*. (Berkeley: University of California Press, 2001), 18.

28. Chris Rock, *Bigger and Blacker*. Videocassette. HBO Studios (1999).

29. Pamela Quaggiotto as quoted in Carole M. Counihan, "Female Identity, Food, and Power in Contemporary Florence," *Anthropological Quarterly* 61 (1988): 52.

30. It is quite easy to become overcome with laughter by Rock's prose and delivery. The immediacy and dramatic nature of the moment invite this response. It is only later, once you have had a chance to relive the scene that one might realize the sexism inherent in both the rhetoric and the performance as Rock leaves the stage seemingly in command, having said all that he has had to say.

10

The Overcooked and Underdone: Masculinities in Japanese Food Programming[*]

*T. J. M. Holden***

To the Western ear, the phrase "Japanese food show" will likely conjure images of teams of smocked chefs hustling through a rangy in-studio kitchen, racing the clock, concocting ingenious ways to prepare a particular ingredient, thereby pleasing a panel of judges and defeating a crafty culinary rival. In fact, though, food battles are only one genre of food show in Japan; a genre, itself, that is widely represented on television. Moreover, battles are but one way that gender and, in this particular case, masculinities are expressed in Japanese culinary TV. Stated another way, on Japanese television, food shows are manifest—even ubiquitous—and food is a dominant means by which identity discourse transpires (Holden 2003).[1] While masculinity is but one component of identity, it is a major one. It is a discursive formation that emerges prominently at various turns in TV food shows, in multiple ways.

This article's purpose is to demonstrate the degree to which discourse about masculinity courses through Japanese food shows. So, too, does it seek to open for consideration the communication architecture and set of codes through which masculinities are expressed. This is important for at least two reasons: first, because it has not been done before; and second, because (not unlike the false perception that *Iron Chef* is representative of the universe of Japanese food shows) prevailing assumptions about Japanese masculinity are similarly truncated. The paltry range of masculinities depicted on culinary TV must be said to play a part in that. For the most part, masculinity is a narrow, repetitive discourse; hence, the "overcooked" in this article's title. What is underdone is both ironic and intriguing. First, the salary-man—the prototypical version of Japanese masculinity—is virtually invisible; secondly, although a wide range of male characterizations (that is, fashions and mannerisms and lifestyles) may be on display, the actual range of masculinities represented on TV is close to nil. Despite the fact that a more protean set of representations concerning masculinity exist as social text out in the world beyond the screen, inside the box, these masculinities are, like the salaryman, incapable of being found.

*Originally published 2005

Japanese Masculinity in the Academic Literature

What are the prevailing assumptions about Japanese masculinity? Until recently, discourse was nearly univocal, confined to the social type, "salaryman." The urban, middle class, white-collar worker has remained a relatively uncontested figure in both academic literature and public consciousness. Emblematic of the "typical" Japanese male since the 1960s (e.g., Vogel 1963; Plath 1964), this caricature persisted relatively unabated into the 1990s (e.g., Rohlen 1974; Allison 1994). Now, however, that image is beginning to change. As Roberson and Suzuki (2003:8) recently observed, the salaryman is but an idealized version of Japanese masculinity. Its wide currency may be explained because it articulates other powerful "discursive pedagogies," such as the capitalist employee, state taxpayer and family provider. The authors cite Ito (1996), who has argued that past conceptions of Japanese masculinity have been driven by views of hegemony and, in particular, three "inclinations" characterize the dominant discourse concerning masculinity.[2] These inclinations, identified as (interpersonal) authority, power, and possession (especially in relation to women), obviously align easily with conceptions of men as workers, members of power structures, protectors, and "bread-winners."

Importantly, Roberson and Suzuki assert, the salaryman is not the sole version of masculine identity in contemporary Japan. Indeed, there are numerous discourses available regarding what is "male" in contemporary Japan.[3] Such a critique is consistent with a general, quiet revisionism that has transpired in Japanese studies over the past two decades; one that has alleged greater heterogeneity in Japanese identity.[4]

The unitary image of masculine identity in the form of salaryman reflects an association of masculinity with particular institutional sites (for instance, *inside corporation* or *outside home*). This has been a standard, unreflecting, academic trope during the post-Pacific War era. It is also (coincidentally) consistent with the way Hall (1994) has theorized that identity *ought* to be decoded (i.e., within institutional contexts). For most researchers of Japanese masculine identity, those institutional contexts have centered on the state, the workplace, and the school (Connell 1995). By inversion (i.e., reflecting a relative absence or exclusion), the institution of family (and its locus, the home) can also be included in gender-identity discourse.[5]

Perhaps in reaction to the institutional emphasis, Roberson and Suzuki's volume is rich with alternatives: civil movements, transnational information flows, transgender practices, day-laborers. Non-institutional theorization of identity is an important maneuver, but does not minimize the importance of institutions in bounding, framing, and providing meaning to contemporary identity. This is particularly true in an era of "reflexive modernization" (Robertson 1992; Beck 1994), constituted by "late modern" or "post-traditional" societies (Giddens 1994), such as Japan. In this article, in particular, it is the media institution (generally) and television (specifically) through which masculine identity is found to flow. As shown in my previous work on "mediated identity" (2003), such formal institutional sites are heavily implicated in the gender-identity calculus.[6] In a word, media (such as television) are institutions— no different than the state, corporation, or family—that provide the ideational and "physical" context within which masculinity is represented and through which it is reproduced.

In this article, I explore one genre within this institutional site of television communication in Japan: food discourse. Surveying this content, one soon learns that Japanese masculinities are both on-message and beyond-message vis-à-vis past academic framings. Consistent with what has heretofore been alleged about masculine identity in Japan, there is a widespread hegemonic masculinity on display. At the same time (and significantly), that hegemonic masculinity is *not* played out through the aegis of the corporate worker. Despite the pervasive expression of masculine identity through food talk, and despite the fact that such identity tends to be hegemonic in nature, there is nary a salaryman to be found. Japan's televisual masculinity is singularly hegemonic, yet it is not confined to a particular model or "type" of person. It is communicated through any number of people—both male *and* female (as we shall see), people who are both conventional and unconventional in appearance, job designation, or background.

Japanese Television and Food Discourse: A Précis

All of this is important because television is the preeminent medium of communication in Japan. It has a diffusion rate of 100%,[7] is viewed by virtually every Japanese person every day,[8] and outpaces other popular forms of information processing, such as newspapers (86%), cell phones (73%), and the internet (27%). It has been reported that, on average, at least one TV set plays 7 to 8 hours a day in each Japanese dwelling, with personal viewing rates per day approaching 225 minutes.[9] A recent European survey ranks Japan second worldwide in terms of daily TV viewership.[10]

While television is dominant, one might wish to argue that food is not. A conservative accounting—based on genres reported in television guides—suggests that TV food shows comprise but 5% of programming between 6 a.m. and 6 p.m. The reality, though, is quite different. Begin with the fact that, unlike other countries (in which food shows are generally confined to specialty cable channels, or else a particular hour on a particular day), Japan's food shows can be found on at least one commercial station during "golden time"[11] on multiple days of the week. In past years, there has been either a food-themed show or a show with a regular food segment every day of the week in prime time.

The best current embodiment is "*Dochi no Ryāri Syou*" (*Which?! Cooking Show*). Now in its seventh season, it is a highly rated Thursday night offering from 9 to 10 p.m. In this show, seven entertainers must choose between two dishes prepared before their eyes by rival chefs from a prestigious cooking academy. The guests are allowed to sample the food and are given a chance to change "sides" if or when their preferences for the respective dishes shift. Their decisions are often influenced by two hosts—both popular male TV fixtures, one in his late 40s, the other in his early 60s—who interview chefs, cajole the guests, and make impassioned appeals for their support. *Dochi* also serves as a window on the world, with segments on the people and places associated with one of the key ingredients in each dish: a fisherman, for instance, a dairy farmer, or cabbage grower, all toiling away in their respective remote corners of Japan.

In addition to shows that are exclusively about food, a number of golden hour variety shows feature regular segments built around food. For instance, SMAPXS-MAP—now in its sixth year and hosted by Japan's premier "boys band" (SMAP)—includes a "Bistro" segment in which an invited guest (generally a female entertainer) is welcomed into the bistro by the "owner" (generally SMAP's lead singer Masahiro Nakai), interviewed about her life and career, then eats (and judges) rather elaborate, multi-course meals prepared by competing teams (which are comprised of SMAP pairs).[12]

The popular, Thursday night variety show *Tonnerus' Minasan no Okage Deshita* (Tunnel's: Because of Everyone's Good Will) offers a weekly segment in which two guests—usually one male and one female—are invited to sit alongside one member of the (male) comedy duo, *Tonnerus*. Both guests are served four dishes, which they must consume while being interviewed about the food as well as their life histories. Free discussion and casual banter co-mingle with on-camera consumption. At the end of the show, all four participants vote as to which dish the guests consumed and pretended to enjoy, but in actuality detested.

Gotchi Battaru is a third show in which food plays an important, entertaining role. It is actually an elaborate segment of another show, the Friday evening variety hour, *Guru Guru Ninety-Nine*. Four regulars (comedians, usually, and all men) travel each week to a different top-rated (and pricey) restaurant and try to guess the price of a set of dishes prepared for them. An invited guest from the entertainment world accompanies them.[13] After all individual estimates are summed, the guest farthest from the price of the entire meal must pay for everyone. Cumulative, weekly totals are also kept and posted on the show's web site, listing how many times each regular has lost, and how far in arrears he is. Discussion during the show is balanced between good-natured ribbing of individual guestimates, information about how the food is prepared, and comments about how each dish tastes.

These are four examples of food discourse on Japanese TV, reflective of a larger pool of shows in which food plays either a primary or secondary role. Factor in the number of shows in which food appears in an ancillary role (for instance, during morning "wake-up" programs that discuss urban culinary trends or local village festivals, or else travel shows that present the foods of target destinations that can be consumed) and the percentage of food-related discourse on Japanese television increases exponentially. This description does not even begin to tap the great reservoir of "inadvertent food discourse" in which food serves as an incidental, but prominent background feature during dramas, quiz shows, newscasts, sporting events, and the like. Finally, one must not forget the ubiquitous presence of food advertising on TV, which has been found to account for as much as 20% of all ads broadcast in a one month period (Holden 2001).[14]

All considered, it is *impossible* to view food discourse as a trivial or negligible element in Japanese televisual communication. Food is present on virtually every channel, every hour, every day of the week, throughout the broadcast day.

Characteristics of Televisual Masculinities

What then, of gender, in general, and masculinity, in particular, is in these televisual culinary productions? First, these elements are neither invisible, nor insignificant.

Furthermore, scrutiny of the content of food shows supports recent theorization on gender. To wit, rather than simple sets of stereotypical differences between classes tagged as "male" and "female," masculinity and femininity clearly emerge as social constructions, i.e., sets of reproduced practices and performances that mimic and support a system of power.[15] In fact, the ways in which gender identities (in general) and masculinities (in particular) are communicated in these televisual productions faithfully reflect Ito's (1996) trinity of authority, power, and possession. Similarly, there are cases in which femininities are constructed and communicated in such a way as to embody and buttress Ito's hegemonic masculinity. Let's consider concrete examples of these elements, in turn.

Power: Masculinity as Competition

To begin, let's return to *Dochi*, previously introduced, in which rival dishes are hawked by two male hosts. These front-men are combatants who do whatever they can to secure victory: interviewing the competing chefs (who are almost always men), sampling the food, cajoling the guests to join their side, and making impassioned appeals for support. At the end of the contest, one exults in victory, the other despairs in loss. Their win-loss record is updated weekly on *Dochi*'s website. At the close of each show, the victorious host holds court center stage, consuming the favored meal with the winning guests. He gloats and needles the losing host as well as those unfortunate guests who voted incorrectly. These minority members are made to observe and, sometimes, even serve the winners. *Dochi*'s discourse, in short, is one of contestation, of dominance achieved, and of subordination suffered; it operates in the vernacular of power.[16] Its conflictual, competitive discourse is one normally associated with games—not unlike the *Iron Chef* show, with its clock, rival combatants, teams of specialists, sideline announcer, play-by-play and color commentators, and final judges. Such competitive shows adopt the rhetoric, the visual, contextual, and practical tropes of sport, "an institution created by and for men," (Messner and Sabo 1990), whose practices service the reproduction of hegemonic masculinity.[17]

Viewed in this way, shows like *Dochi* and *Iron Chef* support a sporting, contentious masculinity. They conjure constructions of gender in terms of combat—not coincidentally performed almost exclusively by men. And lest one wonder whether this is but an aberration, we must note that this discursive practice is not confined to one or two shows. *Bistro SMAP*, after all, is a competition between teams. The results are not simply points on a weekly chart, but kisses acquired from the female guests. And even in shows where food is used to measure intellect, sophistication, and judgment (e.g., *Gotchi Battaru*), the discursive frame centers on competition to avoid pecuniary loss and, thus, public "face."

In keeping with the notion that gender is not simply reducible to male/female categorizations, there are those Japanese food shows in which women battle one another for judges' approval. When they do, these females adopt the vernacular of (hegemonic) male discourse.[18] They are operating within an authoritative structuration of power, working against rivals for a favorable personal result. In a word, women in the context of Japanese mediated identity are not immune from operating in the rhetoric, manifesting the core trait of hegemonic masculinity.[19]

Authority (I): Masculinity as Executive Function

Among the categories that Goffman identified in his qualitative assessment of *Gender Advertisements* (1976) was "executive function," the role (of elevated position, control, and authoritative action) that men adopt when paired in ads with women. This function was patent in my own content analysis of gender in Japanese television ads (1999); it also seems widely replicated in Japanese television food shows.

Men are executives insofar as they are accorded the lead and the power to direct. All activity flows through them, or else beneath their commanding gaze. In food shows, masculine guidance can take the form of two guises: host and chef.

Host   As *Dochi*'s description suggests, men often appear in the role of host. This is not a hard and fast rule—*Emiko no O-shaberi Kukingu* (Emiko's Cooking Talk)— features a female host. Importantly, though, Emiko defers to the chef who is a man. As is true of all food shows, in the matter of food preparation, culinary direction, and advice, the chef operates as chief executive. For the host, the role is clearly defined and circumscribed: hosts greet guests, interview them about their lives, solicit their opinions about life and food, ensure that attention is accorded to the chef's (often backgrounded) work in the kitchen, and facilitate the flow between and balance these various elements. Important among the latter is timekeeping and scheduling; hosts determine when final judgments will be rendered. As guardians of continuity, they also verbally validate results tendered by chefs or guests. In a word, they exert administrative control over the communication event.

In cases where there are multiple hosts of differing gender, executive function adheres to a "gender order," with males invariably reigning over women. Consider the show *Chūbō Desu Yo* (This is the Kitchen). Airing at 11:30 p.m. on Saturdays, the hosts' job is not only to welcome guests and make them feel at home, but also to prepare a meal with them in an in-studio kitchen. Like *Dochi*, the guest offers judgment on the food prepared, and, like *Dochi*, that decision has the power to make the hosts exult in triumph or deflate in defeat. Unlike *Dochi*, however, the hosts are not rivals, and, importantly, unlike *Dochi*, they stand in a particular (power) relation to one another. The female host of *Chūbō* (Ikumi Kimura) is intro-duced at the outset of each show as an "announcer." Moreover, she wears the same green and yellow sticker on her apron that all newly minted drivers in Japan affix to their car windows—signifier of a beginner. Tellingly, Ms. Kimura has worn that sticker for over three years. By contrast, the male host (formerly a popular singer named Masaaki Sakai) introduces himself as possessor of "three stars"—the highest rating that can be awarded to a prepared dish on the show—and "Master Chef."

Gender ranking does not end there. During the course of the half hour, Sakai provides directions to Kimura in the kitchen, during the interview segments, and at the dinner table when the time comes to ask the guest for his or her evaluation of the completed meal. Often Sakai will interrupt his work in the kitchen to engage the guest in conversation, leaving Kimura to toil on her own, making sure that the preparation moves toward completion. In addition, during the critical moments of the show, when a segment has to be concluded or a result announced, it is Sakai who takes the lead.

"This dish is *finished!*" he will intone after the casserole comes out of the oven. Or, as they consume the food, he will suggest, "Ms. Kimura, please ask the guest for his final evaluation." Kimura-san will then dutifully inquire, "For this dish, how many stars will you give?" Once the guest has responded, it is left to Sakai to affirm the judgment. As the camera focuses tight on his face, he shouts theatrically toward the rafters, "for this dish . . . one and a half stars!"

Chef There are numerous shows in which the chef also adopts the executive function by instructing the host and/or guests in the ways of food preparation. *Chūbō* is emblematic of this, introducing three chefs at the outset, who perform on their own premises. Having viewed three variations on the show's selected meal, the three amateur cooks now follow one of the demonstrated recipes. At various stages of the preparation, the three loosely discuss the method they are following. In particular, though, once the meal has been completed and is being consumed, they discuss where they may have improved on the meal—what ingredient was in too little or too great supply, where the oven or stove was used for too long or too short a time. In short, the amateurs note their deviations from the chef's instructions and chastise themselves for failing to conform to his direction.

In addition, *Chūbō* features a short segment introducing a resident apprentice in one of the chef's kitchens. Almost always, these chefs-in-training are young men in their early twenties. In every case to date, these young men are depicted receiving commands from elder male employers. Here again, then, Japan's food shows cast men and masculinity in a discourse of authority.

With but two exceptions, the featured chefs in all of Japan's food show genres are men—the exceptions being the case of desserts and *katei ryōri* (home cooking).[20] When these dishes are featured, female chefs consistently appear. However, because neither category of food is widely represented on food shows, the female presence tends to be overshadowed by that of the male. As a consequence, viewers are apt to perceive "chef" as a male role and, logically, see men as culinary authorities. It is not a stretch to assert that, on the other side of the gender equation, the significance that flows out of the two areas reserved for female expertise (desserts and home cooking) communicates that women are "sweet," soft, peripheral or decentered (i.e., not associated with main courses), less sophisticated or elaborate, and also are specialists in meals served in private rather than out in the public sphere.

Authority (II): Masculinity in Profession

The executive function is not the only way in which status and authority are communicated in cooking shows. Another is the provision of expert knowledge. And like the direction of stage and culinary activity, this is another function that is performed predominantly by men. The recognition of a chef as an "expert" occurs in numerous ways in food shows.

First, and most obviously, is the invocation of the title "chef" to those who are called upon to perform in these TV productions. The deference hosts show to these culinary workers—soliciting their opinion about preparation, allowing them to explain the peculiarities and secrets of each ingredient—goes a long way toward elevating cooks to a position of authority. Clothes, too, serve as markers of professional association, and guest chefs never fail to appear in the starched white aprons and *toques* of those who cook for a living. Finally, and most importantly, is the chef's resume. In Japan, where organizational affiliation is one of the significant markers of legitimacy, food shows take pains to introduce their kitchen authorities not simply by name or age, but by pedigree. For example, they name the schools in which they have trained, the countries in which have they apprenticed, and under which banner they now wield a spatula. In a word, this discursive formation is framed institutionally, in terms of economy and social sanction.

Dochi serves as exemplar of this intellectual construction, drawing its chefs exclusively from one corporate group, *Tsuji* in Osaka—arguably Japan's most prestigious professional cooking academy. The title "*Tsuji*" (or its offshoot "*Ecole Culinaire Nationale*") flashed beneath the in-studio chef or else on the food show's web page is enough to communicate "expert." To Japanese media consumers, "*Tsuji*" connotes "rigorous training," "knowledge," "competence," "professionalism," and "quality-control."

As mentioned earlier, *Dochi* (not unlike most other food shows) calls upon its professionals to provide advice in between segments of host/guest repartee. Culinary experts explain the "dos and don'ts" associated with particular foods and tricks for preparing a meal to perfection. Hosts are careful to respond with affirmative noises, such as "Oh, I see" or "That makes sense," or even "Incredible!"—clearly stressing the presence of a knowledge hierarchy. In this way, the message is communicated that chefs are "professionals," not merely because they have a title and an impressive uniform, but because they are experts and leaders in their field.

Status in a Binary Universe: The Comparison with Women One of the major areas of contestation in gender studies—appropriated from structuralism and ushered in large part, by Judith Butler (1990)—is the issue of language as totality, a closed system in which signs give rise, by inference, to (often invisible) paired opposites. On these terms, "man" begets "woman" as "feminine" conjures "masculine." As Hughes (2002:15) has observed, "In the male-female binary, to be a woman requires us to have a corresponding concept of man. Without this relation, the terms alone would have no reference point from which to derive their meaning."

Butler's influence—along with Foucault's (1980)[21]—was to move analysis beyond simplistic binaries. At the same time, the structure of meaning in Japanese televisual productions is predominantly dualistic, creating sign-pairs of male/chef and female/not chef. In this way, what is present, what is communicated, and what "exists," is an absence of females in the role of "chief cook," and the banishment of women from public kitchens as either professional or apprentice. All of this can produce the view that women are *not* cooking authorities, and that "chef" is a male identification, rather than a female one.

Probing this possibility further, we find that women who appear as cooks in Japanese cooking shows are often featured in one of two ways: in the primary guise as "*talento*" (entertainer), or else in the capacity as "housewife." In the case of the former, women seldom, if ever, offer culinary advice. Their cooking duties are mere props to their true identity, star, singer, sex symbol, or actress. In the case of the latter, women prepare foods and engage in activities associated with the private domain of the household.

An example of the former is found in the Sunday afternoon show, "*Iron Shufu*."[22] A spin-off of *Iron Chef*, this variety show features female guests, all former entertainers who are now married. The show has a number of components: two rounds of quizzes (one centering on food customs, another concerning ingredients, nutrition, and calories), then a round in which kitchen skills are on display. For instance, housewives might have to run an obstacle course while flipping stir-fry in a wok, or grasp slippery *konyaku* with chopsticks. One week, there aired a task involving whipping cream, after which sticky hands and quivering fingers were made to thread three needles in succession. Following this ordeal, contestants were asked a battery of personal questions regarding life with their husbands (e.g., where was their first date, what was the first present they received from their husband, when is their wedding anniversary).

Once all these tasks are completed, the two highest scoring guests (measured in terms of fastest time through the obstacle course and most correct quiz answers) are pitted against one another in a cook-off. They are given thirty minutes to prepare a meal in the *katei* (or "home-cooking") style. Like its namesake, *Iron Chef*, one featured ingredient must be integrated into the menu. An additional stipulation (since it is *katei* style) is that one of the courses must be served with rice. A panel of celebrity judges—along with the president of a cooking school (i.e., a professional/expert)—offers evaluative comments and scores the two contestants. In numerous ways, then, *Iron Shufu* embodies elements of the masculine hegemonic discourse: competition, expert evaluation, and female cooks associated with private (home-made) food. It also casts women in overtly-domesticated roles that differ in multiple, stereotypical ways from those accorded to men. In this way, patriarchal gendered discourse is reproduced.[23]

Markers of Masculine Identity   It should be observed that there *are* a few food shows in which female chefs prepare foods other than desserts or home cooking. In these cases, however, an interesting designation is attached to the cooks; an appellation that appears to undercut their status as authority. Their title is "*riyōri kenkyu ka*"—literally "food researchers." One tangible effect of this title is that it tends to soften the impression left when a woman is offering advice to a male announcer or host.

This is not so in reverse, of course. Where women are being instructed and a man is in the tutelary role, there is no shying away from affixing the title "chef" or "*sensei*" (teacher), providing his professional affiliation, and clothing him in the garb of the professional cook. A prime example is the after-hours entertainment (Saturday 12:30 a.m.), *Ai no Ēpuron 3* (The Love of Three Aprons), in which three young (generally sexy) *talento* are assigned the task of preparing a particular dish (for instance, apple pie) without the benefit of a recipe. The final product is then presented to a panel of (generally) male entertainers. The program's website explains that the "women must make the dishes for these men with love."

The bulk of the show involves the heaping of (generally critical) judgments by the male hosts upon each of the women's food productions. Thereafter, the dishes are assessed by a professional (male) chef. His comments, though generally respectful, aim at improving the women's effort next time out (with the implicit assumption that there *will* be a next time). Due to the deference paid to him by the guests and hosts, as well as his uniform and title, he comes across as an authority possessing special knowledge; his words are treated as insights beyond reproach.

Possession: Masculinity as Ownership

Punctuating and possibly stoking the go-go era of Japanese socioeconomic development were distinct epochs in which particular trinities of goods were sought. Thus, there were the three Ss of the late 1950s and early 1960s: *senpūki, sentakuki,* and *suihanki* (fan, washing machine, and electric rice cooker); the three Cs of the late 1960s: *kā, kūr ā,* and *karā terebi* (car, air conditioner, and color TV); and the three Js of the late 1970s: *jūeru, jetto, and jūtaku* (jewels, jetting, and house).[24] Aside from travel by jet, all of these items were goods to be owned. They were statuses secured through acquisition and were communicated via conspicuous display.

Of course, these trinities center on consumption; however, they also reflect a discourse of possession. It is this rhetoric that can also be spied in Japanese food productions, particularly in relation to the chefs who appear. In numerous shows, the chefs are introduced on the premises of restaurants they have founded, manage, and maintain. Cameras capture them either outside the door of their business or else inside, in the dining area. Invariably, they proudly bow in greeting and offer some remarks of invitation. Viewers are treated not only to tours of their kitchens, but are shown menus, sample the décor, drink in the ambiance, and even watch the chef as he prepares and then consumes his product.

Chūbō, previously mentioned, is noted for such excursions to the owner-chef's domain. So, too, though, are the numerous shows in which hosts travel to a particular locale (perhaps in a village off the beaten path) or else seek out a particularly special dish. In such cases, the chef becomes something more than a food preparer; he becomes host in his own right, commander of a world of his own invention, and interviewee. His status as owner lends an additional power to his countenance. He is not only executive, not only employer, not only expert, he is also landholder, proprietor, and business owner. In Japan, for historical (social class-based) reasons, these are quite powerful statuses to hold. And, of course, it goes without saying, these are roles that are almost exclusively held by men, at least in the Japanese televisual universe.

Alternative Conceptions of Televisual Masculinity

Thus far, we have explored how masculinity in TV food programming is consistent with past conceptions of Japanese masculinity; in a word, it embodies a hegemonic discourse of authority, power, and possession. Here, I wish to briefly identify two elements that suggest alternative, though not necessarily inconsistent, conceptions of gender identity.

Creation: Masculinity as Production

When Sherry Ortner offered the now-famous assertion (1974) that women are nature and men are culture, she was referring to the notion that the male world is "made"; it is a world invented, produced, rendered, and controlled. Certainly, this is the message from Japan's food shows—where the key producers are generally all male. Production transpires within an institutional context (media) and, within that context, an (generally) organizational structure. Such a structure is "man-made"; it is a humanly constructed, artificial environment, configured to confer status and facilitate the expression of power. The tools wielded and the products crafted on these shows, may or may not belong to the cooks, but the fact that they are produced in audio-visual spaces generally presided over by men and filtered through rhetorical strategies that are often regarded as "hegemonic masculinity" suggests that these productions are, in fact, male; they are possessions of the male producer world and, hence, can be associated with masculine identity.

By contrast, for women—who are so often associated with the "natural realm"— their televisual role is generally one of nurturer or consumer. As such, their job is to *facilitate* food production (as hosts) or else serve as end-users (as guests).[25] Certainly, exceptions can be located as in the case of the *Three Aprons* or the *Iron Shufu* shows, previously described. In each case, however, production is for purposes supportive of a patriarchal frame, namely, satisfying the dictates of male hosts or else proving one's wherewithal in providing an amenable home for a husband. Because competition is involved, the women in these shows subrogate themselves to and adopt the logic of hegemonic male discourse. Even when they are not governed by the male world, they seek to uphold and reproduce the logic of that world.

Freedom: Masculinity as Agency

If the message of some TV food shows is that women exist within a clearly delineated, bounded structure, the same could obviously be said of men. As previously mentioned, chefs are often depicted as members of organizations (as in the case of the *Tsuji* performers) or else (as in the case of the *Chūbō* chefs and a wealth of other shop proprietors) as proud possessors (creators, owners, executives) of structures that, incidentally, are "man-made."

At the same time, this image of attachment must be counterbalanced with the impressions of independence often communicated by Japanese media productions. As Gill (2003:145) has written, "Japanese male fantasies frequently stress the mobile: the sportsman, the traveler, the man of action, the magically endowed superhero." For men, and especially television viewers, the majority are tied to structures of "permanence and stasis" (Ibid:146) and, so, pine for an alternative model of existence—a model offered by the television shows. This is not so much embodied by the chefs who have hung out their shingle and run their own businesses; rather, it is in the aegis of the entertainers and guests who saunter onto the food show stage seemingly unencumbered and free of institutional affiliation or organizational layering.

This is a version of Japanese masculinity that is less well known—one that has few exemplars out in the free world, one that is often relegated to the realm of wish fulfillment (for instance, movies centering on the vagabond peddler "*Tora-san*," leaderless *samurai*, like the "*47 Ronin*," or meandering monks like "*Zatoichi*," or, more recently, daily news about highly-publicized "free agents" who have migrated to play baseball in America). It is a version of masculinity that, far from the quintessential salaryman, views male identity in terms of autonomy and individually-oriented existence. It is a disparate image of masculinity, one which may have little referent in reality, but is, nonetheless, persistently cropping up in televisual productions.

Alternative Masculinities

While the general argument on these pages has been that, with regard to Japan's televisual food shows, little alternative discourse circulates concerning masculinity, this is not completely the case. As we saw in the previous passage, discrepant masculinities *do* exist. And, in fact, these discrepant versions are greater—more extensive and farther reaching—than simply that of the autonomous agent just described. Here, I'd like to consider a few of these deviations, and also what that may tell us about contemporary Japanese society.

TV's Widest Angle: Masculinity's "Multiplicity"

It is not infrequent that alternative genders—transgendered men and female masculinities—surface on Japanese TV.[26] Food shows and food advertising, in particular, often feature performances of multiple genders.[27] Consider, for example, *Dochi*. Generally, six of the seven invitees rotate weekly,[28] often striking a numerical balance between men and women. Among the former, past episodes have included a transvestite, numerous *rikishi* (sumo wrestlers), retired baseball and tennis players, actors, singers, comedians, writers, and producers.

The transvestite, in particular, warrants mention here. His name is Akihiro Miwa, and he is a cultural icon. A former cabaret singer, Miwa is as famous for his elegant gowns as he is for his silky singing voice and his romantic involvement with a famous novelist, the late Yukio Mishima. A writer and TV personality, as well as a regular on variety shows, Miwa is accorded respect, with little hint of derision or disdain. The same can also be said for the homosexual twins "Píco" and "Osugi," the "new half," "Pítā," and the ubiquitous and enormously popular transvestite, Ken'ichi Mikawa. While one would be hard-pressed to claim that transgendered men are widely represented on Japanese television, it would also be impossible to deny their presence. Rarely does a day pass without the appearance of a person embodying an alternative conception of gender on mass-distributed, mass-consumed Japanese television.

Alongside these versions of masculinity are also other "models." On *Dochi* alone, one encounters an obese wrestler from Hawaii; a waif-like singer from Japan's longest-running boy's band, SMAP; a forty-something producer in scruffy beard, blue jeans, signature cowboy boots and ten-gallon hat; a Japan-raised, blond-haired, grungy, earring-studded Canadian; an elderly actor with assiduously trimmed goatee, adorned in *yukata* (traditional male *kimono*). In short, one can hardly claim that what is broadcast is the narrow, repetitive discourse of masculinity embodied by salarymen in gray suits and conservative ties. So, too, could one hardly assert that this motley mélange of free agents fits the profile of power wielding, authoritative, possessive hegemonists—at least on the surface.

The Illusion of Freedom

It must be recognized, however, that while such "models" of masculinity may materialize on-screen, good reasons exist to view their social impact with caution. As guests, these men stand in an asymmetric relationship to those who manage the show, specifically, the hosts and chefs in front of the cameras. For these latter groups, invariably, action is wrapped in the vernacular of masculine hegemony. Significantly, no matter what model of masculinity hosts and chefs may *appear* to communicate via their appearance, they uniformly manage to channel food talk into discourse concerning authority, power, and possession.

It also must be noted that a disjuncture exists between the televisual and the real worlds. Food shows place a plethora of free agents on display and communicate alternative masculinities and femininities in far greater measure than the stereotypical types comprising the world beyond the screen. To wit, in Japan today, organizational work still accounts for upwards of 70% of those employed;[29] day laborers and casual or part-time workers also comprise a significant sector of workers. Nonetheless, in show after show, from the food-centered *Dochi*, *Chubo Desu Yo*, and *Kakurea Gohan*, to the weekly cooking segments on SMAPXSMAP, *Tonnerus'* (*Minasan no Okage Deshita*) and *Gotchi Battaru*, workers—both within and on the margins of "organizational society"—are *never* invited to sit at the TV table.

What's more, while the actors and actresses, athletes, singers, comedians, and the like *appear* to be "free agents," it is also apparent that this is mere illusion; they are far from free. Almost all of the food consuming-performers on screen belong to invisible corporate structures that book them onto these shows, not only to reap money, but more importantly, to gain further exposure for them, their popular cultural product. As such, the consumer-performers on food shows offer the illusion of independence, reproducing a myth of masculine and feminine freedom that in actually doesn't exist. In its stead stands the more hegemonic, structurated model of masculinity that pervades almost all of Japanese society today.

The Absence of Vision

In the same way, although transgendered and alternative masculinities are represented on these shows, it is generally only through the aegis of a handful of prominent entertainers, the few, established well-known, accepted "others" who make the perpetual rounds in what is a finite, hermetic, televisual universe. Today, these performers who began as public curiosities rotate from show to show, appearing in a variety of genres equally distributed across the four major channels and spread throughout the seven day viewing week. The consequence is that the message that they might embody of alternative versions of masculinity stands a very real likelihood of being absorbed into, and even overshadowed by, the intimacy cultivated through repetitive exposures of star and host and encounters between viewer and performer.[30] It is this affective bond, I would aver, that may easily lead to the emotional embrace of the one or three or five alternatively masculine "regulars," without having to inculcate the ontological potentials they actually embody. The result may be that viewers become desensitized to, or even come to ignore, the performativities that these personalities signify, the various transgender potentials of "transvestite," "drag queen," "new half," or "homosexual."[31]

The Tight Focus of Televisual Masculine Identity

There is no end to food shows on Japanese television. No two are exactly identical, but all are broadcast for a purpose. To be sure, they exist to educate and entertain. Occasionally they may carry some deep unspoken or less motivated purpose, for instance, the mediation of identity. When this occurs it might be identity defined in terms of the nation, interest group, or individual (Holden 2001, 2003). Or, as shown here, it may be identity cast in terms of gender.

Televisual food shows clearly play a powerful role in communicating masculine identity in contemporary Japan.[32] Clearly, too, such shows are not amenable to the representation of all aspects of masculinity. Beyond the gender performativities previously mentioned, a number of contexts are absent from the screen in which masculinities are generally reproduced. For instance, save for the simulated kitchens in which chefs toil, workplaces are almost entirely absent. Also missing are homes, sites where parenting occurs.[33] Class also is invisible, as are men who are unemployed or else under-employed. Not surprisingly, the homeless are non-existent. In short, there is so much that bears on masculinity that televisual productions ignore, deny, or banish from public view.

The discourse that does appear in these productions serves to present, interpret, translate, and/or modify masculinities. Interestingly, as pervasive as gendered identifications are, the emblematic masculinity for Japan, the salaryman, is entirely pulled from the frame. In his place are other figures—numerous tropes, codes, characters, social processes, institutions, organizational structures, and human agents—both visible and invisible, who are employed to communicate masculine identity. It is a certain kind of identity, a singular kind of identity that is consistently organized and communicated in terms of authority, power, possession, production, and—only seemingly—autonomy.

Notes

**I wish to thank Takako Tsuruki for the invaluable assistance she provided throughout this research. In particular, her wise counsel, cultural and linguistic interpretations, and apt examples immeasurably improved the original paper.*

1. This work, like two precursors (Holden 1999, 2001), is based on a systematic sampling of the universe of Japanese TV shows. As explained in that earlier work, recording transpired over the course of an entire month and was supplemented with new programming as some shows were retired and others debuted. Analysis was based on the construction of three distinguishable data sets: (1) an "ideal week" of prime time food shows, (2) food-related advertising, and (3) regular programming in which "inadvertent food discourse" was regularly introduced. Especially considering the extensive amount of air-time accorded to the last category, it was concluded that food discourse is ubiquitous on Japanese television, playing virtually every hour, on every channel, every day.

2. Ito's concept was developed in association with his introduction to men's studies—written in Japanese. Clearly, however, the concept is not culturally bound and can be applied to other contexts.

3. Presaging this work, perhaps, was McLelland's (2000), which argues that homosexuality in Japan does not reduce to a neat, unitary discourse.

4. Among a chorus of writers Lebra and Lebra (1986), Moeur and Sugimoto (1986), Harootunian (1989), and Befu (2000) have observed that there is no homogenous Japan, comprised of a single class, gender, geography, ethnicity, occupation, or generation.

5. Iwao (1993:271), while arguing that Japan has witnessed a dramatic opening up of the public sphere (and, attendant institutional sites) for women, discusses how family has remained one institution which an earlier generation of women use to define their identity.

6. In my conceptualization, "mediated identity" is interactive and institutional, involving: (1) significations, (2) conveyed through representations of sameness and difference, (3) by media, and (4) brought into relief by: (a) references to (socially constructed) group-based traits, and (b) the depiction of relationships between: (i) individuals and/or (ii) groups. Even more recent work on cell phone users (Holden forthcoming) suggests that the above definition requires modification to allow for the power of users to communicate representations of themselves and actively construct identities by consciously utilizing media.

7. Japan: Profile of a Nation, Kodansha (1995:247). See also Kazuo Kaifu, "Japan's Broadcasting Digitization Enters the Second Stage: Its present state and prospects," NHK Culture Broadcasting Institute, No.11 (New Year, 2000). In fact, the diffusion rate as early as 1965 was 95%.

8. 95% of the population according to Shuichi Kamimura and Mieko Ida. See: "Will the Internet Take the Place of Television?: From a Public Opinion Survey on 'The Media in Daily Life,' " NHK Culture Broadcasting Institute, No. 19 (New Year, 2002); url: #http://www.nhk.or.jp/bunken/bcri-news/bnls-feature.html.

9. NHK's Research Institute reported a figure of 3 hours and 44 minutes in a 2001 survey. This statistic has consistently topped three hours since 1960. Kato (1998:176), reports that viewer rates averaged three hours and eleven minutes in 1960 and three hours and twenty-six minutes in 1975.

10. Bosnia is the only country to rank ahead of Japan in terms of daily average viewing. See: " '2002'; Une Année de Télévision dans Le Monde; analyse les paysages télévisuels et les programmes préférés de 1.4 milliard de téléspectateurs dans 72 territoires audiovisuals."

11. The Japanese equivalent of "prime time," running from 8 p.m. to 10 p.m., Monday through Sunday.

12. The Bistro SMAP website can be accessed at the following url: http://www.fujitv.co.jp/b_hp/smapsmap/ bistro. html. Pages such as the following (http://www.eonet.ne.jp/~smapy/SMAP-DATA.htm) feature cumulative data on guests, meals prepared, team combinations, winning teams, and number of victories amassed by each SMAP member. Awards are given to the chef (among the 5 SMAP members) who has recorded the most victories in a season.

13. Generally Japanese, although in the first season Chris Carter and Jackie Chan were invited. Carter won and Chan finished last of the four contestants.

14. The actual numbers were 681 out of 3,656 ads. Food was the second most advertised product category—behind "events" and about equal to "cars" and "sundries". This is significant insofar as Japan boasts the world's second largest advertising market, amounting to $223,250,000 just for television. This translates into 957,447 ads, consuming 6,016 broadcasting hours per year. (*Source*: Dentsu Koukoku Nenkan, '02–'03 [Dentsu Advertising Yearbook, 2002–2003], Tokyo: Dentsu, 2002; pp. 57, 90, 89 [respectively]). Advertising serves not only a major motor for consumption-based capitalist societies; it also works as one of the major means by which cultural communication occurs. Through ads, television exerts both a socializing and ideological power, narrowly and repetitiously re/producing images of gender, cultural values, history, nationalism, and political, social and personal identity (among others). I have explored these manifestations in, among other works, studies of gender advertisements (1999) and "adentity" (2000a) in Japan.

15. See, for instance, Hearn and Morgan (1990) and Broad and Kaufman (1994).

16. One might wish to have a "representative" example of masculine hegemony, in the form of one particular host. However, there are any number of "male figures" or "characters" across the TV spectrum who adopt the traits of hegemonic masculinity. The number of cases is so large, and any particular TV personality may accentuate a certain masculine trait over another, that it is best left to work through various cases in which these traits are expressed. In this way, the characteristics constituting hegemony take precedence over the particular "hegemonic representative"; so, too, does this afford us the freedom to recognize cases in which, for instance, women

adopt those characteristics, thereby, serving to "enrich" and strengthen the spread of this masculine hegemonic discursive formation.

17. Indeed, Messner (1992) has argued that sport is one of the primary areas in which hegemonic masculinity is learned and perpetuated. To the degree that food shows adopt sporting rhetoric, then, they serve as such communication vehicles as well.

18. To underscore this point, consider the case of the female chef who finally prevailed on *Dochi*. Having appeared and lost a number of times, when her dessert finally won she gushed: "That's the first time I won!" Reflecting on past efforts, which resulted in her having to sit for the cameras, in a room off center stage, eating the food (by herself) that she had prepared, she explained, "When I lost, that (i.e. sitting alone eating my food) was the hardest thing . . ."

19. Importantly, it is not "female masculinity" (Halberstam 1998) that they manifest, rather a male model of masculinity.

20. Home cooked meals are those served everyday, featuring a soy sauce base and/or rice.

21. See, for instance, Fausto-Sterling (1993) and Halberstam (1998).

22. "Shufu" is the word for "housewife" in Japanese.

23. An example of what Sugimoto (1997) decries as the overarching ideology of the male-centered family in Japan;one that, in his opinion, is deeply sexist and patriarchal.

24. These triplets have, over the years, held currency in the popular culture, from marketers to journalists to everyday citizens, and, hence were widely discussed. The recitation here, however, is from Kelly (1992). In the early 1990s, just prior to the bursting of the "economic bubble," young women talked about searching for mates who possessed the "three kos (highs)": physical height, job status, and salary. In the late 1990s, after half a decade of economic downturn, these same women complained that their salarymen husbands embodied the "three Ks": kitanai, kusai, kirai (dirty, smelly, hateful). Mathews (2003:116), more optimistically, speaks of a new set of three Cs for men: bringing home a *comfortable* income, being *communicative*, and *cooperating* with childcare and housework.

25. In Tobin's (1992:10) words, "consumption is associated with the sphere of women." At the same time, Tobin is careful to observe that, while such associations may exist, they amount to critically under-assessed stereotypes. In fact, in Japan today, women also produce and men consume. Too much emphasis has been accorded to this artificial (and inaccurate) dichotomy—a point to bear in mind when applying Ortner to contemporary Japan.

26. Here I refer to the women of Takarazuka theatre in which an all-female cast plays roles both male and female. These stars have, on occasion, crossed over into TV. According to Nakamura and Matsuo (2003:59), Takarazuka is a "special type of asexual, agendered space," one allowing "both female and male fans, regardless of their sexual orientations, (to) temporarily transcend their everyday gender expectations and roles." A recent, quite different, example of female masculinity was the 2003–04 Georgia (canned coffee) TV ad campaign in which women, dressed Takarazuka-style, as salarymen, wreak havoc in their office space, tormenting their (male) boss, while dancing, rapping, taunting, and laughing with delight.

27. Here I invoke Lunsing (2003:20) who employs " 'transgender' in the broadest sense possible". In his words, "the majority of people have at least some attributes ascribed to the opposite gender and thereby can be seen to engage in transgender activity."

28. One guest holds near-permanent status: Tsuyoshi Kusanagi, singer for the J-pop mega-group, SMAP. Kusanagi's appeal may lie in his asexual, if not effeminate, countenance. As a character with a blurry gender identity, he appears to comfortably rest between the weekly groups of three males and three females. It is not uncommon to see Kusanagi among the winning side in a 4 to 3 split, often in cases when the food choice cleaves panelists along traditional gender lines.

29. Precise statistical confirmation can be illusory. One such study—from a Marxist/worker's perspective (Voice of Electricity Workers) can be found at the following url: http://www.eefi.org/0702/070215.htm. Its data is culled from numerous official and unofficial studies in the mid-1990s which, combined, work the figure toward the 70% threshold. More recent reports from the Ministry of Health, Labour and Welfare (1999) speak to dramatic decline in the number of employees in blue collar jobs (due to economic downturn), as well as a glut of professional and technical workers.

30. English-language studies of Japanese television are rather sparse. One of the best, by Painter (1996), argues that TV productions seek to produce "quasi-intimacy" by "emphasiz(ing) themes related to unity (national, local, cultural, or racial) and unanimity (consensus, common sense, identity) . . ." (198). I would go further. Theorization I am currently completing suggests that affective bonds are formed among a national community via the hermetic circulatory process I described earlier. The result, in the first instance, is a fusing of affective ties between viewer, performer, host, production team, and TV station. In the second instance, it is the dislodging and transfer of such bonds (as the performers and viewers jump from program to program and station to station, day after day). In the final instance, it is the creation of a sort of seamless, floating family locked in an on-going communal conversation. Although Painter doesn't suggest as much, it would seem that the intimacy he first described today serves increasingly as a stepping stone in the forging of solidarity among TV's national viewers;

a solidarity that in contemporary Japan, exerts greater unifying power than that of corporate, legal, religious or ritualistic activities and formations.

31. On these categories—"the various tropes constructing transgender" in contemporary Japan—see Lunsing (2003).

32. Female identity, to be sure, is just as rich an area of inquiry. Femininities are more variegated than masculinities. There are so many "types" of women on-screen; at the same time, ultimately, the range of female motion is less extensive. For, as we have seen in this research (at least when it comes to food shows) so much of feminine discourse is subrogated to expressions of masculine hegemony. Women end up operating within those terms, either employing such tools of power, themselves or deferring to them.

33. In fact, men are rarely, if ever, depicted cooking in homes. Male culinary acts are: always for show (i.e., in the studio); associated with work (i.e., in the role of chef); or else at play (i.e., during seasonal picnics, generally in commercials).

References

Allison, A. (1994) *Nightwork: Sexuality, Pleasure and Corporate Masculinity in a Tokyo Hostess Club.* Chicago: University of Chicago Press.

Baudrillard, J. (1994) (1981) *Simulacra and Simulation,* S.F. Glaser (ed.). Ann Arbor: The University of Michigan Press.

Beck, U. (1994) "The Reinvention of Politics: Towards a Theory of Reflexive Modernization." In U. Beck, A. Giddens and S. Lash (eds.) *Reflexive Modernization: Politics, Tradition and Aesthetics in the Modern Social Order,* Oxford: Polity Press, pp. 1–55.

Befu, H. (2001) *Hegemony of Heterogeneity: An Anthropological Analysis of Nihonjinron.* Melbourne: Trans Pacific Press.

Brod, H., and Kaufman, M. (eds.) (1994) *Theorizing Masculinities, Thousand Oaks:* Sage Publications.

Butler, J. (1990) *Gender Trouble: Feminism and the Subversion of Identity.* London and New York: Routledge.

Clammer, J. (2000) "Received Dreams: Consumer Capitalism, Social Process, and the management of the emotions in contemporary Japan." In J.S. Eades, T. Gill, and H. Befu (eds.). *Globalization and Social Change in Contemporary Japan.* Melbourne: Trans Pacific Press. pp. 203–223.

Connell, R. W. (1995*) Masculinities.* Berkeley: University of California Press.

Fausto-Sterling, A. (1993) "The Five Sexes: Why Male and Female are not Enough." *The Sciences* (March –April): pp. 20–25.

Foucault, M. (1980) *Power/Knowledge: Selected Interviews and Other Writings,* 1972–77. C. Gordeon, (ed.) Brighton: Harvester.

Giddens, A. (1994) "Living in a Post-Traditional Society," in U. Beck, A. Giddens and S. Lash (eds.). *Reflexive Modernization: Politics, Tradition and Aesthetics in the Modern Social Order.* Oxford: Polity Press, pp. 56–109.

Gill, T. (2003) "When Pillars Evaporate: Structuring Masculinity on the Japanese Margins." In J.E. Roberson and N. Suzuki (eds.). *Men and Masculinities in Contemporary Japan: Dislocating the Salaryman Doxa.* London and New York: RoutledgeCurzon, pp. 144–161.

Goffman, E. (1976) *Gender Advertisements.* New York: Harper and Row Publishers.

Halberstam, J. (1988) *Female Masculinity.* Durham, N.C. and London: Duke University Press.

Hall, S. (1994) "Introduction: Who Needs 'Identity'?" In S. Hall and P. du Gay (eds.). *Questions of Cultural Identity.* London and Thousand Oaks: Sage Publishing, pp. 1–17.

—— (1980) "Encoding/Decoding in Television Discourse." In S. During (ed.). *The Cultural Studies Reader.* London and New York: Routledge, pp. 90–103.

Harootunian, H. D. (1989) "Visible Discourses/Invisible Ideologies." In M. Miyoshi and H. D. Harootunian (eds.). *Postmodernism and Japan.* Durham and London: Duke University Press.

Hearn, J., and Morgan, D. (eds.) (1990) *Men, Masculinities and Social Theory.* London: Unwin Hyman.

Holden, T.J.M. (1999) " 'And Now for the Main (Dis)course . . .' or: Food as Entree in Contemporary Japanese Television." *M/C: A Journal of Media and Culture,* Volume 2, Issue 7 (October 20).

—— (2000a) "*Adentity:* Images of Self in Japanese Television Advertising." *The International Scope Review.* Volume 2, Issue 4 (Winter).

—— (2000b) " 'I'm Your Venus'/You're a Rake: Gender and the Grand Narrative in Japanese Television Advertising." *Intersections: Gender, History and Culture in the Asian Context.* Issue 3 (February).

—— (2001) "Food on Japanese Television: The Entree and the Discourse." Presented at the 3rd Annual Meeting of *Anthropology of Japan in Japan,* National Museum of Ethnology, Osaka, Japan. May 12th and 13th.

—— (2003) "Japan's 'Mediated' Global Identities." In T.J. Scrase, T.J.M. Holden, and S. Baum (eds.). *Globalization, Culture and Inequality in Asia.* Melbourne: Trans Pacific Press, pp. 144–167.

—— Forthcoming. "The Social Life of Japan's Adolphenic." In P. Nilan and C. Feixa (eds.). *Global Youth? Hybrid Identities: Plural Worlds.* London: Routledge.

Hughes, C. (2002) *Key Concepts in Feminist Theory and Research.* London and Thousand Oaks: Sage Publications.

Ito, K. (1996) *Danseigaku Nyumon* (Introduction to Men's Studies). Tokyo: Sakuhinsha.

Iwao, S. (1993) *The Japanese Woman: Traditional Image and Changing Reality.* New York: The Free Press.

Kelly, W. W. (1992). "Tractors, Television and Telephones: Reach out and Touch Someone in Rural Japan." In J. J. Tobin (ed.). *Re-Made in Japan: Everyday Life and Consumer Taste in a Changing Society.* New Haven and London: Yale University Press, pp. 77–88.

Lebra, T.S., and Lebra, W.P. (1986) (1974) *Japanese Culture and Behavior: Selected Readings.* Honolulu: University of Hawaii Press.

Lunsing, W. (2003) "What Masculinity?: Transgender Practices Among Japanese 'Men.' " In J. E. Roberson and N. Suzuki (eds.). *Men and Masculinities in Contemporary Japan: Dislocating the Salaryman Doxa.* London and New York: RoutledgeCurzon, pp. 20–36.

Mathews, G. (2003) "Can a 'Real Man' Live for his Family?: *Ikigai* and Masculinity in Today's Japan." In J. E. Roberson and N. Suzuki (eds.). *Men and Masculinities in Contemporary Japan: Dislocating the Salaryman Doxa.* London and New York: RoutledgeCurzon, pp. 109–125.

McLelland, M. (2000). *Male Homosexuality in Modern Japan: Cultural Myths and Social Realities.* Richmond, Surrey: Curzon.

Messner, M. (1992) *Power at Play: Sports and the Problem of Masculinity.* Boston: Beacon Press.

Messner, M., and Sabo, D. (1990) "Introduction: Toward a Critical Feminist Reappraisal of Sport, Men and the Gender Order." In M. Messner and D. Sabo (eds.). *Sport, Men and the Gender Order: Critical Feminist Perspectives.* Champagne, Il: Human Kinetics, pp. 1–15.

Moeur, R., and Sugimoto, Y. (1986) *Images of Japanese Society.* London and New York: Kegan Paul International.

Nakamura, K., and Matsuo, H. (2003) "Female Masculinity and Fantasy Spaces: Transcending Genders in the Takarazuka Theatre and Japanese Popular Culture." In J. E. Roberson and N. Suzuki (eds.). *Men and Masculinities in Contemporary Japan: Dislocating the Salaryman Doxa.* London and New York: RoutledgeCurzon, pp. 59–76.

Ortner, S. (1974) "Is Female to Male as Nature is to Culture?" *In Woman, Culture, and Society.* Michelle Zimbalist Rosaldo and Louise Lamphere (eds.). Stanford University Press.

Painter, A.A. (1996) "Japanese Popular Daytime Television, Popular Culture, and Ideology," In J. W. Treat (ed.). *Contemporary Japan and Popular Culture.* Surrey: Curzon Press.

Plath, D. (1964) *The After Hours: Modern Japan and the Search for Enjoyment.* Berkeley: University of California Press.

Roberson, J. E., and N. Suzuki (eds.) (2003). *Men and Masculinities in Contemporary Japan: Dislocating the Salaryman Doxa.* London and New York: RoutledgeCurzon.

Robertson, R. (1992) *Globalization: Social Theory and Global Culture.* London and Thousand Oaks: Sage Publications.

Rohlen, T. P. (1974) *For Harmony and Strength: Japanese White-Collar Organization in Anthropological Perspective.* Berkeley: University of California Press.

Sugimoto, Y. (1997) *An Introduction to Japanese Society.* Cambridge: Cambridge University Press.

Tobin, J. J. (ed.) (1992) *Re-made in Japan: Everyday Life and Consumer Taste in a Changing Society.* New Haven and London: Yale University Press.

Vogel, E. F. (1963) *Japan's New Middle Class: The Salary Man and His Family in a Tokyo Suburb.* Berkeley: University of California Press.

11

Domestic Divo? Televised Treatments of Masculinity, Femininity, and Food*

Rebecca Swenson

Over the sound of clashing knives, television host Mark Dacascos warns the audience that they are about to witness a "battle of masters" in which a "band of brothers" will be put to the ultimate test. The lights dim and floor opens to reveal three shadowy figures slowly rising from beneath the stage. As the music swells and spotlights flash, Dacascos cries, "Gentlemen, prepare for battle!" (Episode IANS03). The scene carries the same masculine intensity and drama of a boxing match; however, combat takes place in "kitchen stadium" and focuses on culinary—not martial—art. Here, on the Food Network's *Iron Chef America*, food preparation is sport, and chefs are athletes.

With high production budgets, scriptwriters, and lucrative marketing contracts, food television has come a long way since the days of Julia Child's simmer-and-stir type programming that introduced French cuisine to American homemakers. Yet, at other moments, food television appears to have not changed at all. Before battles commence on *Iron Chef America*, peppy Food Network star Ingrid Hoffman spends the morning chopping-and-blending her way through *Simply Delicioso*, an instructional cooking show dedicated to introducing viewers to Latin-inspired dishes. Like Julia, and a long line of feminine cooks, Hoffman digs through the refrigerator while explaining to the camera that she has decided to do something fun for her girlfriends and loved ones: mix up her "Yummy Avocado Sopita" and host a "Spa Day" luncheon (Episode IY0201).

The easy mix of masculine "battles" and feminine "spa days" on the Food Network reflects important assumptions about audiences and beliefs about gender, food, and the rewards of labor. The division of labor—in and outside of the kitchen—is no longer as definite as it was in Julia Child's day. A gender segregation of tasks within the domestic domain still exists; however, there are signs of a convergence in certain areas of the home—especially in the kitchen (Bianchi, Milkie, Sayer, & Robinson, 2000). If men are doing more work in the kitchen, our cultural ideas about what is and is not strictly "women's work" might also be shifting. The way cooking tasks are divided within the home and described on television is important, for as West and Zimmerman (1987) write, issues of allocation—such as "who is going to do what" or

*Originally published 2009

"who is going to get what"—often reflect our beliefs about the "essential" nature of significant social categories, such as "man" and "woman" (p. 143). Yet, there have been very few academic analyses of how ideologies surrounding women, men and food are changing (Julier & Lindenfeld, 2005, pp. 2–3).

The Food Network is an important site that articulates discourses about gender and cooking, as it is one of the most widely viewed channels devoted to instructing viewers about how to buy, prepare, and consume food. It is also part of the underanalyzed genre of television programming that seeks to make over the domestic sphere (Ketchum, 2005, p. 218). The Food Network's audience and profits have continued to grow since its 1993 launch, and as of January 18, 2008, the network was available in 96 million coverage area homes (Barnes, 2006; Food Network "Facts and Figures" document). Although the network's core audience is in the United States and Canada, some Food Network shows are also available in Australia, Korea, Japan, Egypt, Thailand, Singapore, the Philippines, Monaco, Andorra, Africa, France, and the Caribbean (Robinson, 2006; Keeler, 2006).

In this article, I examine how the relationship between masculinity, femininity, and cooking has been historically constructed, describe current presentations of gender on the Food Network, and then discuss the implications of these mediated constructions on social change and equality. My analysis is guided by the following research questions: does the Food Network present cooking as gendered "work"? If so, are these constructions different from the masculinities and femininities previously identified in popular discourse around cooking? These questions are important as challenges and revisions to cultural texts about the kitchen shape and reshape gendered divisions between the public and private sphere.

To analyze the Food Network, I look at how production, social and ideological codes within each program, work together to construct the work of cooking. I also compare male and female hosts to illustrate how cooking activities uphold and challenge the traditional masculine and feminine binary. I argue that the Food Network is one channel of discourse in which cooking is no longer defined solely as women's work. White men are prominent in the Food Network kitchen; however, channel programming carefully protects the concept of White masculinity by separating it from feminine, family-centered domestic labor in subtle and nuanced ways.

Doing Dinner, Doing Gender

In the last 30 years or so, feminists—and other researchers—have challenged conventional wisdom by conceptualizing the link between biological sex, gender norms, and sexuality in diverse ways. Postmodern conceptualizations further the flexibility and freedom of categories like "feminine" and "masculine" by separating biological sex from gender norms. Judith Butler (2004) takes these conceptualizations one-step further by calling into question the strict, binary division of gender and pointing to the wide range and breadth of both biological sex and gender manifesta-tions (p. 42). Weedon (1997) also describes gender as a socially produced and historically changing aspect of identity that is shaped by cultural and institutional discourse within a society. She writes: "As children we learn what girls and boys should be and later, what women and men should be" from social institutions, such as "the family, schools, colleges, teenage fashion, pop culture, the church and worlds of work and leisure" (Weedon, 1997, p. 3).

Social institutions and popular culture, as described by Weedon, have made the kitchen a gendered space in which deeply held ideologies about "natural" feminine or masculine behaviors are evident. Inness (2001b) writes that kitchen culture transcends the "passing down of Aunt Matilda's recipe for Swedish meatballs" to include recipes on "how to behave like 'correctly' gendered beings" (p. 4). The idea that food preparation is fun and pleasurable has its roots in its assignment to the happy homemaker, a wife and mother whose unpaid labor is done for loved ones because of natural, altruistic, and maternal instincts. For example, Neuhaus (2003) describes how cookbooks in the late 1940s and 1950s urged women to focus entirely on their family's welfare "for the good of their families and for the nation" (p. 223). Devault (1991) also writes that the image of women "doing for others" is a powerful, central image in American society of what a woman should be (p. 1). She argues that household tasks, like cooking, are events in which we mark ourselves as acceptable men and women (Devault, 1991, p. 118). Household tasks are often continually associated with one gender and become viewed as natural expressions of "one's gendered relations to the work and to the world" (Beck 204 quoted in Devault, 1991, p. 118).

Devault's (1991) concept of gender as something that is "done" for others is borrowed from West and Zimmerman (1987), who describe "doing gender" as a social activity unconsciously performed with or for another. For the purpose of this research, I also borrow West and Zimmerman's (1987) definition of gender as a situated performance that is "carried out in the virtual or real presence of others who are presumed to be oriented to its production" (p. 126). In this conceptualization, gender becomes an interactional and institutional phenomenon, instead of simply a property of individuals. This is important, as viewing gender as an individual attribute or as a role often obscures how gender is produced in everyday activities, like cooking (West and Fenstermaker, 1993, p. 151). I am interested in exploring gender as an activity that is performed in response to institutional and social norms and is capable of pluralities—both masculinities and femininities. I am also interested in the contradictions that might surface within these pluralities and the ways in which masculinities and femininities might be disrupted from a historical perspective (Connell, 1995, p. 73).

With this definition of gender, masculinities and femininities are both an "outcome of and a rationale for various social arrangements and as a means of legitimizing one of the most fundamental divisions of society" (West & Zimmerman, 1987, p. 126). As such, it is important to connect moments of "doing gender" with hegemonic power structures and institutions that legitimate "normal" and "deviant" constructions of personhood. Butler (2004) notes that gendered discourses enable and constrain how an individual defines himself or herself and constitute subjects while Foucault (1976) notes that these discourses are always framed within particular relations of power. The disciplinary practices of enacting and reenacting of gender norms regulate the body until its gestures, postures, and movements are recognizably feminine or masculine. Discourse gains power through its ability to repeat or reiterate an idea until it seems natural and normal. Below, I describe how cooking culture has made gender a natural and normal part of discourse about the kitchen.

The Way to a Man's Heart

The private kitchen is a feminized space and female domain; however, men have not been totally absent from kitchen culture. Neuhaus (2003) points out that at least thirteen cookbooks intended for men appeared in the United States from 1946 to 1960 (p. 195). Most of these cookbook writers told men how to prepare meat over a roaring fire, assuming an innate, caveman-like connection between men and barbequed meat (Neuhaus, 2003, p. 194). As Adams (1990) argues, meat has long been a symbol of masculinity and male power. If he was not next to the BBQ, the male cook was portrayed as a hobbyist, easily preparing dishes with creativity and flair for occasional fun rather than as an everyday task (Neuhaus, 2003, p. 74). Hollows (2002) writes about an alternative masculinity in her research on the meaning of the "bachelor dinner" in *Playboy*'s regular food pages from 1953 to the early 1960s (p. 143). *Playboy* did not exactly conform to the 1950s vision of tradition; instead, the imagined reader was an urban "glamorized bum" who rejected the married, suburban, and female-centered life of his "breadwinner" counterpart (Hollows, 2002, p. 144). Not surprising, *Playboy*'s food columnists made explicit connections between food, cooking, and sex and frequently referred to the sensual pleasures of eating, the seductive effect of entertaining, and the aphrodisiac qualities of certain foods (Hollows, 2002, p.146). *Playboy* also negotiates unease at integrating cooking into a masculine lifestyle by suggesting recipes in a "travelogue" format, where the dish is connected to a tale of adventure in an exotic locale (Hollows, 2002, p. 144). Hollows (2002) concludes that the *Playboy* chef is not obligated to cook, does not shape his cooking to satisfy the tastes of others, and views cooking as an enjoyable leisure activity (p. 152).

Within the public sphere, the professional chef has long been male. Even today, restaurant kitchens are notoriously sexist and macho (Pratten, 2003, p. 455). Women still hold less than 10% of the top positions in the culinary industry (Cooper 1998). Roche (2004) writes the United Kingdom's Equal Opportunities Commission receives more complaints of bullying and sexual harassment from those in the hospitality industry than any other employment sector. The separation between the discourse of feminine cooks who prepare food everyday out of necessity and the haute culinary discourse of male professionals has a long history in both the United States and Europe. Trubek (2000) writes that the founding masters of French cuisine saw themselves as educators and "a combination of elitism and missionary zeal characterized the attitude of male French chefs towards French women" (p. 12).

Visions of masculinity within American culture are always relational and exist only by depending on an "other"—in this case femininity (Connell, 1995, p. 68). The female cook described by Devault (1991) in *Feeding the Family* and the professional or Playboy chef described by Hollows (2002) and Trubek (2000) both invest "care" in an imagined other by preparing meals; however, female labor demonstrates love for the family and is a gift to a husband or children, while the male laborer aims to produce more fleeting sexual encounters, put on a glamorous show for others, develop a career, or pursue the pleasures of eating for himself (Devault, 1991, p. 118; Hollows, 2002, p. 151; Trubek, 2000, p. 12).

Overall, the main message to men in cooking literature during the first half of the twentieth century was that despite being masters of the professional kitchen, the private kitchen was not their lair (Inness, 2001b, p. 12). If men did wander into the home kitchen, cooking must be negotiated in very specific ways to protect the concept of masculinity (Inness, 2001b, pp. 18–19). The "male cooking mystique" is based on the following assumptions about the relationship between men and cooking: "if men choose to cook, they must make sure their masculinity isn't diminished;" men's taste in food is antithetical to women's taste in food; men should cook manly food, like wild game and other types of meat; if men cook meals besides meat it should be a rare event and cause for applause; if a woman wants to keep a man she should adapt to his tastes in food, not the reverse (Inness, 2001b, pp. 18–19).

Inness (2001b) writes that the male mystique has far-reaching implications for how our society uses gender to separate and justify the larger division of labor: "Women are the ones responsible for a double shift, working a full-time job and then rushing home to cook a meal for the family. Since cooking in our society remains deeply linked to gender, if a wife decides not to cook, this frequently is perceived as a sign that she is 'abnormal' and 'bad'" (pp. 35–36). It also eliminates expectations that men share second shift responsibilities with working women.

However, if the division of labor is shifting— albeit in limited and subtle ways—is the male mystique shifting as well? If so, this might help society redefine 'normal' and 'deviant' forms of masculinity and femininity and allow both genders to continue to question what appears to be natural and inevitable divisions between the public and private sphere.

Method

As discussed above, the purpose of this research is to examine how masculinities and femininities presented in popular cooking culture might be shifting and to investigate if the male mystique, as described by Inness, still holds true today. I conducted an initial textual analysis of Food Network programs that ran during October 20 to October 27, 2006. In addition, the tapes were supplemented with additional viewings of significant programs during November and December 2006. After identifying core themes, I analyzed Food Network programs that ran during January 2 to January 23, 2008 from 8:30 am to 11 pm CST weekdays and from 6 am to 11 pm CST weekends. These time periods captured multiple episodes of the Food Network's most popular and current programs.[1] Many blocks of programming were repetitive, as the network frequently rebroadcasts shows and often plays food-related infomercials during the overnight hours. Overall, total viewing resulted in approximately 200 hr of original programming.

As of January 2008, the Food Network's Web site lists 57 celebrity hosts and 71 shows as part of their current line-up.[2] Network hosts are predominately White and male. Of the 57 celebrity hosts listed on the Web site, 38 hosts are male, 19 are female, 42 hosts are Caucasian, 7 are Japanese, and 8 are African American. It is important to note that the gendered portrayals discussed here focus on White masculinity and White femininity.[3]

Overall analysis focuses on narratives and key themes, social cues in the host's language, action and appearance, and production conventions used to convey the relationship between the host and imagined viewer.

Cooking Codes

Food Network programming combines food preparation with travel, adventure, history, trivia, pop culture, and competition. To potential viewers and advertisers, the Food Network divides programming into two major blocks: daytime "in the kitchen" and evening "way more than cooking" programs.[4] Within daytime "in the kitchen" programs, two themes were prominent in shows featuring men as hosts: *cooking as way to flex professional muscles* and *cooking as leisurely entertainment.* Conversely, female hosts tend to portray *cooking as domestic work done for family and friends.* During evening "way more than cooking" programs hosts construct *cooking as competitive contest* and *cooking as a journey.*

Cooking As Way to Flex Professional Muscles

By adopting the role of chef, instructor or scientist, male hosts construct cooking *as a way to flex professional muscles*, a theme which rejects situating the male cook as an everyday provider of the personal, domestic care that is a hallmark of family life. This masculine performance relates to work done by Adams and Coltrane (2005), who write that men and boys remain ambivalent about family life because "achieving manhood" is typically based on accomplishments in extrafamilial settings, such as business, sports or politics (p. 230). This creates a situation in which "boys and men 'come from' or 'have' families" but "they often experience profound difficulties being 'in' them" (Adams & Coltrane, 2005, p. 230). By giving cooking an aura of professionalism, hosts reify masculine autonomy from domestic responsibilities and maintain the masculine ideal of "breadwinner" and "good provider."

In shows like *Molto Mario, Party Line with the Hearty Boys,* and *Tyler's Ultimate,* the hosts often make casual references to previous business experience and culinary training. For example, in the "Sweets and Coffee" episode of *Party Line with the Hearty Boys*, Dan Smith and Steve McDonagh are arranging food on a table for a party and digging in cupboards for props. Smith turns to the camera and says: "This is what we do as caterers—go through your stuff!" (Episode DS0105). Similarly, in *Boy Meets Grill*, as Bobby Flay prepares a pot of homemade chicken stock, he tells the camera, "This is how I was taught in culinary school, crazy, I know!" (Episode GL0612). Florence also peppers his speech with phrases like "this is an old classic restaurant cooking tip" (Episode BW0510). Other male hosts mark their professionalism by wearing the traditional white jacket used by chefs. A few male hosts don the jacket during the entire program while others, such as Emeril Lagasse in *Essence of Emeril,* only wear it during the introduction.

Mario Batali, who also wears a chef jacket, frequently pulls down maps and other props to educate viewers and his audience. During the "Messy Polenta" episode,

Batali compares culinary history and techniques from different regions of Italy and describes how difficult it is for chefs to educate American restaurant customers about the proper way to combine seafood and dairy within a dish (Episode MB2G18). Batali's recipes are time-consuming and complex, for example, he tells viewers that his Baccala alla Veneta has to soak for 2 days in water that must be changed three times a day. At one point in another episode, an audience member points out a heavily smoking pan on the stove. Mario assures him it is fine, as "things smoke up in a professional kitchen." At the end of shows hosted by Mario Batali, Tyler Florence, Bobby Flay, and Emeril Lagasse a reference to their restaurants often appears on the screen.

In comparison, female personalities with instructional programs position themselves as approachable, domestic cooks that prepare meals for friends and family members, rather than as professional chefs or artists. Despite some impressive credentials, female hosts rarely mention cooking professionally and dress in casual clothes, usually with an apron.[5] Female hosts, such as Rachael Ray in *30-Minute Meals* and Robin Miller in *Quick Fix Meals* directly address the challenges of efficiently preparing weeknight meals for families. Robin assures viewers that "cooking three weekday meals is a cinch as long as you plan ahead" (Episode RM0209). During the introduction to *Healthy Appetite* host Ellie Krieger tells viewers that she understands eating healthy is hard when you are juggling everyday life. At the end of the "Mood Food" episode, Krieger adds, "you can put this together when you get home for work —it is super energizing" (Episode EK0307). In every episode of *30-Minute Meals*, Ray cranks out dinner in 30 minutes from start to finish so viewers "can put great food on the table, and still have time to enjoy your family, friends or tackle that home improvement project you've been waiting to get your hands on" (Food Network Web site).

Food Network also uses subtle costuming, positioning, and camera work to create a masculine professional and feminine domestic frame. *Paula's Party* and *Emeril Live*[6] are both high-energy "new domestic cooking shows" which look like talk shows with loud, excited and adoring studio audiences, music, and an overall "party" atmosphere (Ketchum, 2005, p. 225). In these shows, the host alternates between talking directly to the camera and interacting with a live studio audience that claps and cheers back at the host on cue, creating a social atmosphere. Like other programs in the talk show genre, select audience members become part of the host's routine and have to shift from viewer to performer. Although Deen and Lagasse host similar shows, they differentiate themselves in subtle ways that construct cooking as professional labor for Lagasse and as domestic labor for Deen.

During *Emeril Live*, Lagasse wears a professional chef jacket with a towel casually slung over his shoulder and some episodes open with Lagasse coming into the studio in street clothes and waiting while two assistants help him into the professional garb. Like a president, athlete, or actor, Lagasse jogs into the studio amidst cheers, shakes hands with those in the front of the studio audience and waves to those in the back. This works to position Emeril as an expert who is on stage and ready to entertain fans. Paula enters the studio in a much more casual way, stands close to her audience, hugs her guests, and leaves her street clothes on during the entire show.

Despite an impressive business background that includes restaurant and catering success, Deen portrays herself as a bawdy but home-spun, grandmotherly figure. She blends cooking demonstrations with family anecdotes, self-help mantras, humor, sexual innuendos, and advice. Deen creates the feeling of an intimate women's circle by referring to audience members as "us girls," inviting audience members to join her behind the stove and answering personal questions about her life and family. Deen also says things like, "How good are you going to look when you serve this? You will have him eating out of your hand for weeks." Conversely, Lagasse's interaction with audience members is much less intimate. Audience members tend to sit facing the stove and dialogue is more call-and-response, in which Emeril shouts "Bam" or "Should we go for it?" and the audience mimics him, replies "Oh, yeah baby" and cheers.

In other programs, especially shows like *Food 911* and *How to Boil Water* hosted by Tyler Florence, the male host establishes professional authority by more directly adopting a "chef-and-student" model with guests and cohosts. In *Food 911*, Florence comes to the rescue of a viewer by traveling to their home kitchen in order to help revamp and prepare a specific dish. In *How to Boil Water*, Florence conducts short classes during which he teaches his "cooking challenged" cohost actress Jack Hourigan how to prepare basic meals. She mimics Florence, asks questions, and presses him for explanations as he cooks. During the introduction to the "Healthy Helpings" episode, Hourigan says, "this is the show where beginners like me learn just how easy it is to cook with confidence." Florence chimes in, "That's right, Jack. I'm going to show you and everyone at home how to become an accomplished cook" (Episode BW0510).

Within this theme, masculinity can also be protected using other areas of professional skill besides formal culinary training and business expertise. For example, in *Good Eats*, Alton Brown enters the kitchen as a scientist and a historian who often treats cooking as an opportunity for an educational lecture or experiment. Poniewozik (2005) describes Brown as "the MacGyver of mackerel" who explores how food works from "the chemistry of cured salmon" to "the physics of pressure cookers." In the "Dr. Strangeloaf "episode, Brown uses pie charts, rockets, magnifying glasses, and other props to educate viewers about the properties of wheat kernel, yeast, and bacteria. Like a botanist, he traces the evolutionary development of plants that produce key ingredients used by craft bakers (Episode EA1H15). Other male hosts also reference the "science" of cooking. For example, Batali tells guests, "this is what emulsification looks like in science books" (Episode MB2G18). Flay also assures viewers that making pastries requires a lot of chemistry and math (BFIE13).

Science, business, and professional training function to separate the work done behind the stove by masculine hosts from that of "women's work." Instead of using cooking to explore science or reenact broad strokes of culinary history, female hosts describe recipes as valued personal possessions that preserve family history, values, and generational legacy. "The family that eats together stays together" is the opening line for *Sara's Secrets* "Sunday Dinner with Aunt Fanny" episode (Episode SS1B83). Moulton has Fanny di Giovanni on as a guest, who helps make a Sunday dinner that is guaranteed to "get everyone to the table." Aunt Fanny, who appears to be over

60 years old, talks about how her mother prepared similar dishes. In *Semi-Homemade with Sandra Lee*, Lee says, "I have been cooking and entertaining for years, in the way that my grandmother did. It takes so much time, so I created shortcuts and shared them with my girlfriends—they love them and so will you." Nigella Lawson's "Fun Food" episode focuses on cooking for her children, which she described as both fun and dreamy (Episode NL0104). Similarly, in the "Gourmet Fiesta" episode, Amy Finley of The *Gourmet Next Door* tells viewers that she enjoys preparing Mexican recipes because her kids love the food (GY0105). *Everyday Italian* with Giada De Laurentiis and *Barefoot Contessa* with Ina Garten also frequently refer to making meals as "gifts" for loved ones. Preserving the familial chain of cooking expertise has long been a feminine task; these hosts reify their femininity by coding cooking as a fulfilling act of love and intimacy done for others.

Shapiro (2004) writes that "nothing in the long history of women doing what used to be man's work has ever seemed to Americans as unnervingly radical as the notion of men wholeheartedly engaged in woman's work" (p. 253). The above programs illustrate how male hosts draw upon a professional ethos to resist being classified with the feminine, family-centered domestic cook. However, not all instructional programs hosted by a male personality fit a professional frame. Cooking was also constructed as *leisurely entertainment*, a theme that implies a temporary slippage into the domestic lair. The temporal nature of this frame protects the concept of masculinity, for as Shapiro (2004) writes, "to help out is noble; to place domestic responsibilities on a par with one's job is suspect" (p. 253).

Cooking As Leisurely Entertainment

Thomas Adler (1981) reports that as late as the 1930s, men who went into the kitchen to cook for the fun of it "were in danger of being a laughingstock" (p. 45). This stereotype began to erode as the amateur male cook gained popularity along with the post-World War II backyard barbequing trend in the United States (Adler, 1981, p. 47). To make cooking an acceptable masculine activity, Adler (1981) writes that it is important to designate special meals and tools to the male chef (p. 50). This keeps masculine cooking "festal" and separate from mundane and "ferial" feminine cooking habits (Adler, 1981, p. 50).

On the Food Network, male hosts separate the "festal" and "ferial" by making cooking a special event. For example, host Tyler Florence often uses a professional frame to reify masculine authority in the kitchen; however, *Tyler's Ultimate* "Sunday Dinner" is one episode that embraces the domestic, family-centered realm (Episode TU0204). Florence is careful to position Sunday dinner as a special event, different from weekday meals. He tells viewers that he orders takeout during the week and goes out on the weekends; however, Florence believes Sunday dinner is a special time to cook and guides viewers on how to create the "ultimate" pot roast to get the family together. Other programs like *Easy Entertaining with Michael Chiarello, Good Deal with Dave Lieberman*, and *Guy's Big Bite* also closely resemble the feminine, domestic, family-centered frame yet are careful to position cooking as a fun, temporary, and voluntary leisure activity. These male hosts do not discuss the challenges of routinely cooking for a family but do show viewers how easy and enjoyable it is to prepare meals for friends on occasion.

For Michael Chiarello of *Easy Entertaining*, cooking is a pleasurable hobby. He prepares a full dinner in every episode and is always extremely relaxed and in control while at the stove. He owns a vineyard and often strolls among grapevines with a glass of wine as pots simmer on the range. The "Fireplace Cooking" episode opens with Michael in a lumberman jacket chopping wood before his guests arrive (Episode MO1A02). Chiarello changes out of his lumberman jacket into casual clothes to cook; and then, as his guest's arrive, Chiarello dons a professional chef jacket. During this same episode, the camera cuts to Michael sipping coffee at a sidewalk café after doing some initial prep work in the kitchen, and later, he takes another break by chatting on the telephone with his feet propped up on his desk while the meal cooks. As usual, guests applaud Chiarello during the meal, toast him with their wine glasses and enthusiastically tell him how wonderful and talented he is.

Good Deal with David Lieberman also positions the host as an experienced and leisurely entertainer but for a much younger, urban, and hip demographic. A promo for Lieberman's show says the young host has a style that is focused on "a budget minded twenty-something audience with social-driven calendars. Without sacrificing taste (or cash), [Lieberman] could fill something of a void in talking to Gen Ys who are increasingly adopting more 'domestic' lifestyles, often opting to stay in and host a dinner party rather than spending the evening bar hopping" (Trendcentral.com, 2005). During the opening of the show, host Lieberman assures viewers that he spares no expense during his day job as food writer and professional gourmet chef. At night, however, he finds a way to entertain his friends "like a king" while keeping costs down. Entertaining is both a hobby and economic necessity for Lieberman. For example, in the opening to the "Lite-N-Healthy" episode, Lieberman tells the camera that he is going on a vacation with his friends and everyone has resolved to save money, exercise more and eat healthy to get ready for the beach. In order to "help us all out," Lieberman tells viewers that he is going to cook up a light and healthy meal that costs less than $8 a person. As in most episodes, Lieberman invites a group of friends over to enjoy the food at the end of the show. As with Chiarello, the guests praise Lieberman and rave about the meal (Episode DA0203).

Like Chiarello and Lieberman, Fieri, the Gen-X inspired host of *Guy's Big Bite* who has spiky blond hair, tattoos, a goatee, and dresses in bowling shirts and skateboarder shorts, occasionally cooks for his "posse" and has male friends join him in the kitchen. Although the "posse" isn't present on all episodes, the party is ready to start at any moment. The kitchen looks like a recreation room with a full bar, a stage with drums and guitars, a pinball machine, a bumper pool table, a giant television screen, and a bright orange racecar-themed fridge. While turning on the stove, Fieri says things like, "let's get this party started!" While shuffling pots around, Fieri is trying to "keep the party going," and as he plates the food, Fieri is "putting the party together" (Episode GI0306).

Related to *cooking as leisurely entertainment*, another interesting theme surfaced at a few points—cooking as male bonding activity. Unlike the feminine cook who ties bonding in the kitchen to generational legacy and her role as mother, wife, daughter and friend, this narrative about male camaraderie was supported by references to manual work and vocational fraternity. For example, in the "Cooking Club for Men" episode, a group of guys gets together in Chiarello's kitchen to cook a meal (Episode MOIB08). Chiarello raises his glass at the end of the episode and says, "Here's to men that cook!" He also assures the men while making dinner, "what guys have to remember is that cooking is more like construction than an art." In another show, Flay goes to the Seattle Pike's Place fish market to interview a group of "buddies" who work the market. Flay interviews one young man who describes how the "guys" throw BBQ parties after work as a way to keep the camaraderie up and talk about things besides fish (Episode BQ0304). Similarly, in *Emeril Live's* "Firehouse Thanksgiving" episode, a group of New York firefighters are shown bonding like a family by cooking and eating together (Episode EM0310). Emeril talks about the importance of bonding as a team while working together—both in the kitchen and while battling a fire. As the men prepare a turkey for Emeril, they talk about being comrades in the kitchen and refer to their peers as a "family."

When cooking is constructed as leisurely entertainment, food television adopts a "masculine domesticity" that helps redefine the private kitchen in ways that give men a place at the stove. However, this place remains only partially and temporarily tied to the rewards and responsibilities of family life. Marsh (1988), who coined the term, refers to masculine domesticity as a redefinition of manliness to include some traditional female activities (p. 180). She argues that advice literature, architectural design, recreational patterns and personal papers from the turn of the twentieth century suggest men started to draw themselves into the domestic circle by assuming more day-to-day responsibilities of child-rearing and household maintenance while still rejecting the feminist notion that these tasks should be shared equally (Marsh, 1988, p. 166). Gelber (2000) applies Marsh's term to the 1950s "do-it-yourself "trend of home maintenance yet calls it "domestic masculinity" to recognize the creation of a male sphere inside the house. He writes, "unlike masculine domesticity, which had men doing jobs that had once belonged to women, domestic masculinity was practiced in areas that had been the purview of professional (male) craftsmen, and therefore retained the aura of preindustrial vocational masculinity" (p. 73). Household maintenance, and related trappings like heavy tools and workshops, eventually became defined as a masculine domain and shifted how suburban masculinity was idealized within the United States (Gelber, 2000, p. 87). Similarly, with food television, the vocational roots of professional chefs allow male hosts to embrace the private kitchen as an important site of work. However, themes such as *cooking as leisurely entertainment* limit the masculinities and femininities performed in the kitchen by defining work done by men for families as temporary, voluntary, and peripheral to the rewards and responsibilities of their roles as fathers, sons, and husbands.

Cooking As Journey

In touring series, both male and female hosts go "on the road" to showcase unusual dishes and sights in restaurants, bakeries, and backyards around the globe. Here, the domestic kitchen disappears, as the focus is on eating, traveling, buying and selling food rather than on meal planning and preparation techniques.

For some shows featuring a female host, the purpose of the journey is to provide trip-planning services for viewers, often with a focus on being economical. Budgeting has long been associated with the "thrifty homemaker," and Hollows (2002) points out how writers of the *Playboy* column refused to be concerned with economy in order to distinguish between the single, self-focused, bachelor, and the family-centered housewife. Hollows (2002) contrasted *Playboy's* rejection of budgetary constraints with Helen Brown's (1962) *Sex and the Single Girl*, written during the same time period, in which Brown gives single girls tips on how to be more economical while cooking and wrote "being smart about money is sexy" (Brown, p. 105 quoted in Hollows, p. 149).

This feminine "thrifty homemaker" theme is present in shows like Rachael Ray's *$40 a Day* and *Rachael's Tasty Travels*. The premise of *$40 a Day* is to see if Ray can complete her quest to find good meals in different cities while staying under the "paltry" $40 per diem budget. A receipt appears on the screen at the end of show so viewers can tally up what Ray was able to buy for her money. In *Tasty Travels*, Ray doesn't have to stick to a budget but continually talks about the inexpensive nature of the food. "What a bargain!" she often exclaims. During the introduction to the "Austin" episode, Ray says, "For years, I've been traveling the globe, discovering incredible deals and finding the best food—all with an eye for value. Now, I'm returning to my favorite places to bring you more of my money-saving tips!" (Episode RY0108). Ray works for viewers so they can "turn any next vacation into a delicious, affordable adventure!" (Episode RY0202).

However, not all female-hosted programs focus on being "thrifty." In *Rachael's Vacation* and *Weekend Getaways*, Ray and Laurentiis also perform trip-planning work for viewers yet do so without focusing on a budget. In *Weekend Getaways*, Laurentiis describes extravagant activities, restaurants, and lodging options for different locales; for example, in the "Las Vegas" episode, she takes a helicopter ride around the city and tries racecar driving (Episode WG0206). In media interviews, Giada describes her role on *Weekend Getaways*: "I want to be sort of a travel guide. What to see, how to get there, what activities you can do, where to eat, it's a combination of all those things" (Huff, 2007).

Rather than perform trip-planning or budgeting services for viewers, male hosts of touring series are portrayed as down-to-earth, "everyman" food critics who want to satisfy their "manly appetites" with "real" American food or as "cultural anthropologists" who can unlock the secrets of exotic locales by eating local cuisine, like the *Playboy* adventurer. Fieri of *Diners, Drive-ins and Dives eats*, chats with customers and employees, and gets dirty in the kitchens of greasy spoons across the United States. Like other hosts of these "manly appetite" segments, Fieri relies upon American themes that valorize small, family-owned businesses and self-made mom- and-pop type restaurateurs who are "living the dream." For example, on the "24/7" diner episode, Fieri chats with owner George Liakopoulos, who fulfilled his life-long dream of following his immigrant father into the restaurant business by purchasing the White Palace Grill in Chicago from the original owner (who established the diner in 1939). Fieri tells viewers that if they need to "chow down" in the middle of the night, they would be lucky to find a "real deal" diner like the White Palace that serves big plates of "down-home," "scratch-made" food (Episode DV0210). Similarly, in *Road Tasted*, the Deen brothers are perpetually positive and hungry food connoisseurs who "hit the road" to sample edible fare from local specialty shops and family-owned craft manufacturers.

The travelogue goes global in shows hosted by maverick "cultural anthropologists," like Lamprey of *Have Fork Will Travel* and Bourdain of *A Cook's Tour*, who enjoy extreme cuisine in exotic settings.[7] In the "Cobra Heart: Food That Makes You Manly" episode, Bourdain is "willing to try anything, risk everything" as he travels to Vietnam in search of "the extremes of experience." Bourdain seeks out unusual fare, including a fetal duck egg, which is supposed to enhance male virility, and a beating cobra heart, which is supposed to strengthen the diner. At the end of the episode, Bourdain tells viewers that he is not disappointed in his Asian adventure as it was "even more scary" than he anticipated, yet strangely enough, he was "feeling stronger" (Episode TB1A03). Although the domestic kitchen is not present in these touring series, the journey of cooking is still presented as gendered work. "Thrifty homemakers" journey in order to perform budgeting or planning services to others while adventurers and those with "manly appetites" journey to satisfy themselves or indulge in fleeting, exotic escapades.

Cooking As Competitive Contest

In an article written by Janet Keeler (2006), Food Network's vice president of network programming Bob Tuschman is quoted as saying, "Viewers have different needs at different times of day. We don't do any less cooking shows than we ever did, but we just put them on at different times of day. At night, people want information in a gentler way."

Ironically, to portray cooking information in a "gentler way," shows like *Iron Chef*, *Iron Chef America*, *ThrowDown with Bobby Flay*, *Dinner Impossible*, *Glutton for Punishment* use a competitive sports format. In these programs the hosts are athletes competing against other chefs, racing against the clock and performing for judges. For example, in *ThrowDown* Flay finds a master chef or local expert and shows up unannounced to "challenge the best of the best" to a cook-off. In the Phillyb "cheesesteak" episode, the screen splits to position heads shots of challenger Tony Luke and host Flay as boxers going head to head (Episode BT0111). Flay jogs into the area where they are going to compete and cooks in front of a crowd of spectators who are chanting his name. At the end of the cooking session, a panel of judges crowns Luke the "Throw Down Philly Cheesesteak" winner.

Although there aren't two contenders competing directly, *Dinner: Impossible* also has a competitive field, as host Robert Irvine receives his "mission assignment" at the beginning of each episode and struggles to create a dinner party for a large group of people with a team of local assistants and limited resources in 6 hours or less. In the "Ice Hotel Impossible" episode, the introduction plays off the show "Knight Rider," as Irvine receives challenge details on a computer screen mounted in a "talking" car. Here, he learns he must create a "blazing feast" in arctic conditions for 75 people and immediately speeds off to the Ice Hotel in Quebec, Canada.

These competitive contests place cooking firmly in the public sphere and promote a version of masculinity tied to hierarchy, success, power, speed, and stamina. As Birrell and McDonald (2000) write, "sport is best understood as a male preserve, a major site for the creation of male bonding, privilege and hegemonic masculinity" (p. 5). By supporting hegemonic masculinity rather than a domestic masculinity, competitive contests counter constructions of cooking as nurturing, democratic, and family-centered labor.

Yet, it is important to recognize that both male and female chefs participate in competitive contests as hosts, contenders, supporting staff, and judges. Many *Food Network Challenges* allow both male and female professional chefs to compete in bake-offs and other contests for prize money in front of a live studio audience. In the "Ice Hotel" episode, Irvine barks orders to a staff of men and women from a local culinary school who help him shop, prepare, and serve the food. Female chef Cat Cora is one of three main "Iron Chefs" who battles in *Iron Chef America's* "kitchen stadium" and often prevails over her male challengers; for example, Cora beat experienced restaurateur Joey Campanero in the "Venison" face-off, bringing her battle record to 7–3 (Episode IA0313). Overall, competitive contests function to normalize the "manly" nature of professional cooking and to remove cooking from the cooperative ethos of family life; however, the sports orientation of these programs does not completely work against a nongendered division of labor. In small ways the network does resist the classification of separate spheres when female hosts become active participants in the public sport of cooking and the performance of hegemonic masculinity. According to Adams and Coltrane (2005), "There is a direct correspondence between sharing power in more public domains and sharing the care and drudgery of domestic life in the family realm" (p. 243).

Conclusion

Spigel (2004) points to a strategy used by modern art museums to negotiate their affiliation with television in the postwar culture. She writes "here, as elsewhere, the gender of the highbrow was male, even while his tastes seemed to be in the traditionally feminine realm of domesticity" (Spigel, 2004, p. 361). The Food Network is a similar cultural institution that uses gendered notions of taste and the highbrow sensibilities of the culinary arts to negotiate the tension between masculinity and feminine domesticity within the televised home kitchen.

As the themes above illustrate, the Food Network does construct food preparation as gendered work, and cooking is negotiated in ways that protect traditional under-standings of masculinity and femininity. For women, "kitchen culture" is still strongly tied to the domestic family, generational legacy, and care for others. For the mascu-line cook, the "cooking mystique" has shifted, in that cooking discourse no longer warns men that the kitchen is not their lair; yet, to protect the concept of masculinity, men enter the kitchen as scientists, chefs, athletes, and entertainers.

The most striking way in which the binary between the genders is maintained is through the absence of discussion by male hosts of cooking as everyday, family-centered labor. Many female hosts of "instructional" cooking shows, such as Rachael

Ray in *30 minute meals*, offer viewers "quick" solutions to meal preparation and situate cooking firmly in the private, domestic kitchen. Conversely, many male hosts of instructional programs, such as Batali or Lagasse, differentiate themselves from the feminine cook by constructing cooking as a professional, public challenge rather than as a domestic chore. The rewards of cooking are blurred with pleasure, recognition, and leisure for these male chefs and their constructed viewers. By tying men's work in the kitchen to rewards outside of the family, the Food Network furthers a "domestic masculinity" that allows men to be at the stove without fully engaging in "women's work" and prevents men from acknowledging the benefits of "achieving manhood" through nurturing, family-centered labor.

At the same time, it is important to acknowledge moments of convergence or slippage between these gendered distinctions—for example, when Michael Chiarello addresses the masculine, domestic cook and suggests men set up "cooking clubs" on *Easy Entertaining* or when Cat Cora battles on *Iron Chef*. Most importantly, these shows do assume that viewers of both genders are domestic cooks who are going to download recipes and purchase products for use in the kitchen at home, rather than within a professional kitchen or for competition. Food television should pursue these moments of convergence in the kitchen and expand the gendered rewards of cooking. For example, Tyler Florence could address the challenge of cranking out a set of "ultimate" weeknight dinners at home for his wife and kids while keeping it efficient, budget-friendly, and interesting. Similarly, spunky Guy Fieri could demonstrate the rewards of teaching his two sons how to prepare family recipes (that don't involve grilling meat). Ellie Krieger, who is a dietician and adjunct professor, could dissect the science behind food preparation. Paula Deen could have a show that allows viewers to go behind the scenes to see how she manages her professional kitchen and staff.

By situating the contemporary "instructional" genre of television within the larger cultural history of the kitchen, this research helps further our understanding of media's role in constructing and sustaining the social values and roles that order society. As more male cooks join female cooks in the kitchen at home and on television, it is important to continue examining how kitchen culture treats "doing dinner" as gendered work. Policy makers have begun to identify those conflicting demands of economy and family as a "problem" for society. The divide between the public and private sphere is no longer feasible or desirable for most men and women. Identifying individual and institutional-level solutions is in the best interest of both genders, and to do this, it is necessary to continue to examining the masculinities and femininities constructed around specific household tasks.

Notes

1. I eliminated late night programming from my analysis (11 pm to 4:30 am CST) in order to focus on daytime, primetime, and weekend programming when viewership is high and the network broadcasts new shows. January 2008 was the most-watched month in network history with viewing levels among adults aged 25–54 at 454,000 during primetime, up 21 percent versus 2007, and at 308,000 during total day programming, up 2007 levels by 11 percent (Food Network Press Release).
2. From FoodNetwork.com on January 2, 2008.

3. Al Roker's *Roker on the Road* and Marlie Hall/Eric McLendon's *Recipe for Success* are the only shows with an African American host that ran during the studied 6:30 am to 11 pm time period during January 2008. Other shows featuring a Black host, including Warren Brown's *Sugar Rush*, Sandra Pinckey's *Food Finds*, and Bobby River's *Top 5*, were sporadically aired during January 2008 in the 4:00 am CST timeslot and so were outside the parameters set for this study. The two other African American hosts, Pat and Gina Neely, have a new show, titled *Down Home with the Neelys*, which is set to premier Saturday, February 2, 2008 at 11:00 am CST. All of the Japanese hosts are associated with the *Iron Chef* and *Iron Chef America* series, which is included in my analysis. With new programs featuring African American hosts premiering in 2008 portrayals of race within food television are promising areas for future research.

4. The network runs commercials promoting these two blocks to viewers and mentions them in media kit materials to potential advertisers. In the quarter one schedule for 2008, the "in the kitchen" block appears to run from 10:30 am to 8:00 pm EST weekdays and from 7:30 am to 2 pm EST weekends. The "way more than cooking" block appears to run from 8:00 pm to 11 pm weeknights and from 2 pm to 11 pm weekends. Weekday mornings from 9:30 am to 10:30 am mixes both types of programming.

5. However, women participating in "competitive contests," which are discussed below, are an exception to this statement.

6. The Food Network cancelled *Emeril Live* in November of 2007 after a 10-year run. Reruns of the show remain prominent on the programming schedule. Unlike most of the other "in the kitchen" programs, these shows run during the evening; During January of 2008, *Emeril Live* is on at 7:00 pm EST and *Paula's Party* is on at 10:00 pm EST.

7. Some touring series used the travelogue format to highlight a business, entrepreneur, or unique food manufacturing process and did not fit into either the "thrifty homemaker" or "manly appetite" theme. In shows like *Recipe for Success*, *The Secret Life of*, *Unwrapped*, *Behind the Bash*, *On the Road*, and *Inside Dish with Rachael Ray*, both male and female hosts become pop culture journalists who interview experts, owners and workers and illustrate how their stories are intertwined with American history, contemporary food trends, and culture.

References

Adams, C. (1990). *The sexual politics of meat: A feminist-vegetarian critical theory.* New York: Continuum.

Adams, M., & Coltrane, S. (2005). Boys and men in families. In M. Kimmel, J. Hearn & R. W. Connell (Eds), *Handbook of studies on men and masculinities* (pp. 230–248). Thousand Oaks, CA: Sage.

Adler, T. (1981). Making pancakes on Sunday: The male cook in family tradition. *Foodways and Eating Habits: Directions for Research, 40,* 45–54.

Barnes, B. (23 August 2006). As stars lose their spice, Food network bets on sassy southerner. *Wall Street Journal,* p. B1.

Bianchi, S., Milkie, M., Sayer, L., & Robinson, J. (2000). Is anyone doing the housework? *Social Forces, 79,* 191–228.

Birrell, S., & McDonald, M. (2000). *Reading sport.* Boston: Northeastern University Press.

Butler, J. (2004). *Undoing gender.* New York: Routledge.

Connell, R. W. (1995). *Masculinities.* Berkley: University of California Press.

Cooper, A. (1998). *A woman's place is in the kitchen: The evolution of women chefs.* New York: Van Nostrand Reinhold.

Devault, M. (1991). *Feeding the family.* Chicago: University of Chicago Press.

Foucault, M. (1976). *The history of sexuality.* New York: Random House.

Gelber, S. (2000). Do-it-yourself: Constructing, repairing, and maintaining domestic masculinity. In J. Scanlon (Ed), *The gender and consumer culture reader.* New York: New York University Press.

Hollows, J. (2002). The bachelor dinner: Masculinities, class and cooking in *Playboy*, 1953–1961. *Journal of Media and Cultural Studies, 16,* 142–155.

Huff, R. (18 January 2007). *Food network series not Giada's usual fare.* New York: Associated Press.

Inness, S. (2001a). *Kitchen culture in America.* Philadelphia: University of Pennsylvania Press.

Inness, S. (2001b). *Dinner roles: American women and culinary culture.* Iowa City: University of Iowa Press.

Julier, A., & Lindenfeld, L. (2005). Mapping men onto the menu: Masculinities and food. *Food and Foodways, 13,* 1–16.

Keeler, J. (13 September 2006). Food network: Night & day. *St. Petersburg Times,* p. 1E.

Ketchum, C. (July 2005). The essence of cooking shows: How the food network constructs consumer fantasies. *Journal of Communication Inquiry, 29,* 217–234.

Marsh, M. (1988). Suburban men and masculine domesticity, 1870–1915. *American Quarterly, 40,* 165–186.

Neuhaus, J. (2003). *Manly meals and mom's home cooking.* Baltimore, MD: Johns Hopkinsn University Press.

Poniewozik, J. (July 24, 2005). Six shows worth their salt. Retrieved January 19, 2009, from Time magazine Website: http://www.time.com/time/magazine/article/0,9171,1086152.00.html

Robinson, A. (2006). Changing Channels. Retrieved January 19, 2009, from Frozen Food Age Website: http://www.frozenfoodage.com/publication/article.jsp?siteSection=0&id=169&pageNum=6

Pratten, J. D. (2003). What makes a good chef? *British Food Journal, 105,* 454–459.

Roche, E. (28 January 2004). If you can't stand the heat, get some balls. *The Guardian.* Retrieved December 31, 2008, from http://www.guardian.co.uk/g2/story/0,3604,1132605,00.html

Shapiro, L. (2004). *Something from the oven: Reinventing dinner in 1950s America.* New York: Penguin Books.

Spigel, L. (2004). Television, the housewife, and the Museum of Modern Art. In L.Spigel&J.Olsson (Eds), *Television after TV: Essays on a medium in transition.* Durham, NC: Duke University Press.

Trendcentral.com. (May 2005). Chef makes cooking fun and easy. IG Intelligence Group. Retrieved December 31, 2008, from http://www.trendcentral.com/trends/trendarticle.asp?tcArticleId=1341

Trubek, A. (2000). *Haute cuisine: How the French invented the culinary profession.* Philadelphia: University of Pennsylvania Press.

Weedon, C. (1997). *Feminist practice and poststructuralist theory.* Malden, MA: Blackwell.

West, C., & Fenstermaker, S. (1993). Power, inequality and the accomplishment of gender: An ethnomethodological view. In P. England (Ed.), *Theory on gender/feminism on theory* (pp. 151–174). New York: Aldine De Gruyter.

West, C., & Zimmerman, D. (1987). Doing gender. *Gender and Society, 1*(2), 125–151.

12

Japanese Mothers and *Obentōs*: The Lunch-Box as Ideological State Apparatus[*]

Anne Allison

Introduction

Japanese nursery school children, going off to school for the first time, carry with them a boxed lunch (*obentō*) prepared by their mothers at home. Customarily these *obentōs* are highly crafted elaborations of food: a multitude of miniature portions, artistically designed and precisely arranged, in a container that is sturdy and cute. Mothers tend to expend inordinate time and attention on these *obentōs* in efforts both to please their children and to affirm that they are good mothers. Children at nursery school are taught in turn that they must consume their entire meal according to school rituals.

Food in an *obentō* is an everyday practice of Japanese life. While its adoption at the nursery school level may seem only natural to Japanese and unremarkable to outsiders, I will argue in this article that the *obentō* is invested with a gendered state ideology. Overseen by the authorities of the nursery school, an institution which is linked to, if not directly monitored by, the state, the practice of the *obentō* situates the producer as a woman and mother, and the consumer as a child of a mother and a student of a school. Food in this context is neither casual nor arbitrary. Eaten quickly in its entirety by the student, the *obentō* must be fashioned by the mother so as to expedite this chore for the child. Both mother and child are being watched, judged, and constructed; and it is only through their joint effort that the goal can be accomplished.

I use Althusser's concept of the Ideological State Apparatus (1971) to frame my argument. I will briefly describe how food is coded as a cultural and aesthetic apparatus in Japan, and what authority the state holds over schools in Japanese society. Thus situating the parameters within which the *obentō* is regulated and structured in the nursery school setting, I will examine the practice both of making and eating *obentō* within the context of one nursery school in Tokyo. As an anthropologist and mother of a child who attended this school for fifteen months, my analysis is based on my observations, on discussions with other mothers, daily conversations and an interview with my son's teacher, examination of *obentō* magazines and cookbooks, participation in school rituals, outings, and Mothers'

*Originally published 1991

Association meetings, and the multifarious experiences of my son and myself as we faced the *obentō* process every day.

I conclude that *obentō* as a routine, task, and art form of nursery school culture are endowed with ideological and gendered meanings that the state indirectly manipulates. The manipulation is neither total nor totally coercive, however, and I argue that pleasure and creativity for both mother and child are also products of the *obentō*.

Cultural Ritual and State Ideology

As anthropologists have long understood, not only are the worlds we inhabit sym-bolically constructed, but also the constructions of our cultural symbols are endowed with, or have the potential for, power. How we see reality, in other words, is also how we live it. So the conventions by which we recognize our universe are also those by which each of us assumes our place and behavior within that universe. Culture is, in this sense, doubly constructive: constructing both the world for people and people for specific worlds.

The fact that culture is not necessarily innocent, and power not necessarily transparent, has been revealed by much theoretical work conducted both inside and outside the discipline of anthropology. The scholarship of the neo-Marxist Louis Althusser (1971), for example, has encouraged the conceptualization of power as a force which operates in ways that are subtle, disguised, and accepted as everyday social practice. Althusser differentiated between two major structures of power in modern capitalist societies. The first, he called (Repressive) State Apparatus (SA), which is power that the state wields and manages primarily through the threat of force. Here the state sanctions the usage of power and repression through such legitimized mechanisms as the law and police (1971: 143–5).

Contrasted with this is a second structure of power—Ideological State Apparatus(es) (ISA). These are institutions which have some overt function other than a political and/or administrative one: mass media, education, health and welfare, for example. More numerous, disparate, and functionally polymorphous than the SA, the ISA exert power not primarily through repression but through ideology. Designed and accepted as practices with another purpose—to educate (the school system), entertain (film industry), inform (news media), the ISA serve not only their stated objective but also an unstated one—that of indoctrinating people into seeing the world a certain way and of accepting certain identities as their own within that world (1971: 143–7).

While both structures of power operate simultaneously and complementarily, it is the ISA, according to Althusser, which in capitalist societies is the more influential of the two. Disguised and screened by another operation, the power of ideology in ISA can be both more far-reaching and insidious than the SA's power of coercion. Hidden in the movies we watch, the music we hear, the liquor we drink, the textbooks we read, it is overlooked because it is protected and its protection—or its alibi (Barthes 1957: 109–111)—allows the terms and relations of ideology to spill into and infiltrate our everyday lives.

A world of commodities, gender inequalities, and power differentials is seen not therefore in these terms but as a naturalized environment, one that makes sense because it has become our experience to live it and accept it in precisely this way. This commonsense acceptance of a particular world is the work of ideology, and it works by concealing the coercive and repressive elements of our everyday routines but also by making these routines of everyday familiar, desirable, and simply our own. This is the critical element of Althusser's notion of ideological power: ideology is so potent because it becomes not only ours but us—the terms and machinery by which we structure ourselves and identify who we are.

Japanese Food as Cultural Myth

An author in one *obentō* magazine, the type of medium-sized publication that, filled with glossy pictures of *obentōs* and ideas and recipes for successfully recreating them, sells in the bookstores across Japan, declares, "the making of the *obentō* is the one most worrisome concern facing the mother of a child going off to school for the first time" (*Shufunotomo* 1980: inside cover). Another *obentō* journal, this one heftier and packaged in the encyclopedic series of the prolific women's publishing firm, *Shufunotomo*, articulates the same social fact: "first-time *obentōs* are a strain on both parent and child" ("*hajimete no obentō wa, oya mo ko mo kinchoshimasu*") (*Shufunotomo* 1981: 55).

An outside observer might ask: What is the real source of worry over *obentō*? Is it the food itself or the entrance of the young child into school for the first time? Yet, as one look at a typical child's *obentō*—a small box packaged with a five- or six-course miniaturized meal whose pieces and parts are artistically arranged, perfectly cut, and neatly arranged—would immediately reveal, no food is "just" food in Japan. What is not so immediately apparent, however, is why a small child with limited appetite and perhaps scant interest in food is the recipient of a meal as elaborate and as elaborately prepared as any made for an entire family or invited guests?

Certainly, in Japan much attention is focused on the *obentō*, investing it with a significance far beyond that of the merely pragmatic, functional one of sustaining a child with nutritional foodstuffs. Since this investment beyond the pragmatic is true of any food prepared in Japan, it is helpful to examine culinary codes for food preparation that operate generally in the society before focusing on children's *obentōs*.

As has been remarked often about Japanese food, the key element is appearance. Food must be organized, reorganized, arranged, rearranged, stylized, and restylized to appear in a design that is visually attractive. Presentation is critical: not to the extent that taste and nutrition are displaced, as has been sometimes attributed to Japanese food, but to the degree that how food looks is at least as important as how it tastes and how good and sustaining it is for one's body.

As Donald Richie has pointed out in his eloquent and informative book *A Taste of Japan* (1985), presentational style is the guiding principle by which food is prepared in Japan, and the style is conditioned by a number of codes. One code is for smallness, separation, and fragmentation. Nothing large is allowed, so portions are all cut to be bite-sized, served in small amounts on tiny individual dishes, and arranged on a table (or on a tray, or in an *obentō* box) in an array of small, separate containers.[1] There is no one big dinner plate with three large portions of vegetable, starch, and meat as in American cuisine. Consequently the eye is pulled not toward one totalizing center but away to a multiplicity of de-centered parts.[2]

Visually, food substances are presented according to a structural principle not only of segmentation but also of opposition. Foods are broken or cut to make contrasts of color, texture, and shape. Foods are meant to oppose one another and clash; pink against green, roundish foods against angular ones, smooth substances next to rough ones. This oppositional code operates not only within and between the foodstuffs themselves, but also between the attributes of the food and those of the containers in or on which they are placed: a circular mound in a square dish, a bland-colored food set against a bright plate, a translucent sweet in a heavily textured bowl (Richie 1985: 40–41).

The container is as important as what is contained in Japanese cuisine, but it is really the containment that is stressed, that is, how food has been (re)constructed and (re)arranged from nature to appear, in both beauty and freshness, perfectly natural. This stylizing of nature is a third code by which presentation is directed; the injunction is not only to retain, as much as possible, the innate naturalness of ingredients—shopping daily so food is fresh and leaving much of it either raw or only minimally cooked—but also to recreate in prepared food the promise and appearance of being "natural." As Richie writes, "the emphasis is on presentation of the natural rather than the natural itself. It is not what nature has wrought that excites admiration but what man has wrought with what nature has wrought" (1985: 11).

This naturalization of food is rendered through two main devices. One is by constantly hinting at and appropriating the nature that comes from outside—decorating food with season reminders, such as a maple leaf in the fall or a flower in the spring, serving in-season fruits and vegetables, and using season-coordinated dishes such as glass-ware in the summer and heavy pottery in the winter. The other device, to some degree the inverse of the first, is to accentuate and perfect the preparation process to such an extent that the food appears not only to be natural, but more nearly perfect than nature without human intervention ever could be. This is nature made artificial. Thus, by naturalization, nature is not only taken in by Japanese cuisine, but taken over.

It is this ability both to appropriate "real" nature (the maple leaf on the tray) and to stamp the human reconstruction of that nature as "natural" that lends Japanese food its potential for cultural and ideological manipulation. It is what Barthes calls a second-order myth (1957: 114–17): a language that has a function people accept as only pragmatic—the sending of roses to lovers, the consumption of wine with one's dinner, the cleaning up a mother does for her child—which is taken over by some interest or agenda to serve a different end—florists who can sell roses, liquor companies that can market wine, conservative politicians who campaign for a gendered division of labor with women kept at home. The first order of language ("language-object"), thus emptied of its original meaning, is converted into an empty form by which it can assume a new, additional, second order of signification ("metalanguage" or "second-order semiological system"). As Barthes points out, however, the primary meaning is never lost. Rather, it remains and stands as an alibi, the cover under which the second, politicized meaning can hide. Roses sell better, for example, when lovers view them as a vehicle to express love rather than the means by which a company stays in business.

At one level, food is just food in Japan—the medium by which humans sustain their nature and health. Yet under and through this code of pragmatics, Japanese cuisine carries other meanings that in Barthes' terms are mythological. One of these is national identity: food being appropriated as a sign of the culture. To be Japanese is to eat Japanese food, as so many Japanese confirm when they travel to other countries and cite the greatest problem they encounter to be the absence of "real" Japanese food. Stated the other way around, rice is so symbolically central to Japanese culture (meals and *obentōs* often being assembled with rice as the core and all other dishes, multifarious as they may be, as mere compliments or side dishes) that Japanese say they can never feel full until they have consumed their rice at a particular meal or at least once during the day.[3]

Embedded within this insistence on eating Japanese food, thereby reconfirming one as a member of the culture, are the principles by which Japanese food is customarily prepared: perfection, labor, small distinguishable parts, opposing segments, beauty, and the stamp of nature. Overarching all these more detailed codings are two that guide the making and ideological appropriation of the nursery school *obentō* most directly: 1) there is an order to the food: a right way to do things, with everything in its place and each place coordinated with every other, and 2) the one who prepares the food takes on the responsibility of producing food to the standards of perfection and exactness that Japanese cuisine demands. Food may not be casual, in other words, nor the producer casual in her production. In these two rules is a message both about social order and the role gender plays in sustaining and nourishing that order.

School, State, and Subjectivity

In addition to language and second-order meanings I suggest that the rituals and routines surrounding *obentōs* in Japanese nursery schools present, as it were, a third order, manipulation. This order is a use of a currency already established—one that has already appropriated a language of utility (food feeds hunger) to express and implant cultural behaviors. State-guided schools borrow this coded apparatus: using the natural convenience and cover of food not only to code a cultural order, but also to socialize children and mothers into the gendered roles and subjectivities they are expected to assume in a political order desired and directed by the state.

In modern capitalist societies such as Japan, it is the school, according to Althusser, which assumes the primary role of ideological state apparatus. A greater segment of the population spends longer hours and more years here than in previous historical periods. Also education has now taken over from other institutions, such as religion, the pedagogical function of being the major shaper and inculcator of knowledge for the society. Concurrently, as Althusser has pointed out for capitalist modernism (1971: 152, 156), there is the gradual replacement of repression by ideology as the prime mechanism for behavior enforcement. Influenced less by the threat of force and more by the devices that present and inform us of the world we live in and the subjectivities that world demands, knowledge and ideology become fused, and education emerges as the apparatus for pedagogical and ideological indoctrination.

In practice, as school teaches children how and what to think, it also shapes them for the roles and positions they will later assume as adult members of the society. How the social order is organized through vectors of gender, power, labor, and/or class, in other words, is not only as important a lesson as the basics of reading and writing, but is transmitted through and embedded in those classroom lessons. Knowledge thus is not only socially constructed, but also differentially acquired according to who one is or will be in the political society one will enter in later years. What precisely society requires in the way of workers, citizens, and parents will be the condition determining or influencing instruction in the schools.

This latter equation, of course, depends on two factors: 1) the convergence or divergence of different interests in what is desired as subjectivities, and 2) the power any particular interest, including that of the state, has in exerting its desires for subjects on or through the system of education. In the case of Japan, the state wields enormous control over the systematization of education. Through its Ministry of Education (Monbusho), one of the most powerful and influential ministries in the government, education is centralized and managed by a state bureaucracy that regulates almost every aspect of the educational process. On any given day, for example, what is taught in every public school follows the same curriculum, adheres to the same structure, and is informed by textbooks from the prescribed list. Teachers are nationally screened, school boards uniformly appointed (rather than elected), and students institutionally exhorted to obey teachers given their legal authority, for example, to write secret reports (*naishinsho*) that may obstruct a student's entrance into high school.[4]

The role of the state in Japanese education is not limited, however, to such extensive but codified authorities granted to the Ministry of Education. Even more powerful is the principle of the "*gakureki shakkai*" (lit., academic pedigree society), by which careers of adults are determined by the schools they attend as youth. A reflection and construction of the new economic order of post-war Japan,[5] school attendance has become the single most important determinant of who will achieve the most desirable positions in industry, government, and the professions. School attendance itself is based on a single criterion: a system of entrance exams which determines entrance selection, and it is to this end—preparation for exams—that school, even at the nursery-school level, is increasingly oriented. Learning to follow directions, do as one is told, and "*ganbaru*" (Asanuma 1987) are social imperatives, sanctioned by the state, and taught in the schools.

Nursery School and Ideological Appropriation of the *obentō*

The nursery school stands outside the structure of compulsory education in Japan. Most nursery schools are private; and, though not compelled by the state, a greater proportion of the three- to six-year-old population of Japan attends pre-school than in any other industrialized nation (Tobin 1989; Hendry 1986; Boocock 1989).

Differentiated from the *hoikuen*, another pre-school institution with longer hours which is more like daycare than school,[6] the *yochien* (nursery school) is widely perceived as instructional, not necessarily in a formal curriculum but more in indoctrination to attitudes and structure of Japanese schooling. Children learn less about reading and writing than they do about how to become a Japanese student, and both parts of this formula—Japanese and student—are equally stressed. As Rohlen has written, "social order is generated" in the nursery school, first and foremost, by a system of routines (1989: 10, 21). Educational routines and rituals are therefore of heightened importance in *yochien*, for whereas these routines and rituals may be the format through which subjects are taught in higher grades, they are both form and subject in the *yochien*.

While the state (through its agency, the Ministry of Education) has no direct mandate over nursery-school attendance, its influence is nevertheless significant. First, authority over how the *yochien* is run is in the hands of the Ministry of Education. Second, most parents and teachers see the *yochien* as the first step to the system of compulsory education that starts in the first grade and is closely controlled by Monbusho. The principal of the *yochien* my son attended, for example, stated that he saw his main duty to be preparing children to enter more easily the rigors of public education soon to come. Third, the rules and patterns of "group living" (*shudanseikatsu*), a Japanese social ideal that is reiterated nationwide by political leaders, corporate management, and marriage counselors, is first introduced to the child in nursery school.[7]

The entry into nursery school marks a transition both away from home and into the "real world," which is generally judged to be difficult, even traumatic, for the Japanese child (Peak 1989). The *obentō* is intended to ease a child's discomfiture and to allow a child's mother to manufacture something of herself and the home to accompany the child as s/he moves into the potentially threatening outside world. Japanese use the cultural categories of *soto* and *uchi*; *soto* connotes the outside, which in being distanced and other, is dirty and hostile; and *uchi* identifies as clean and comfortable what is inside and familiar. The school falls initially and, to some degree, perpetually, into a category of *soto*. What is ultimately the definition and location of *uchi*, by contrast, is the home, where family and mother reside.[8] By producing something from the home, a mother both girds and goads her child to face what is inevitable in the world that lies beyond. This is the mother's role and her gift; by giving of herself and the home (which she both symbolically represents and in reality manages[9]), the *soto* of the school is, if not transformed into the *uchi* of the home, made more bearable by this sign of domestic and maternal hearth a child can bring to it.

The *obentō* is filled with the meaning of mother and home in a number of ways. The first is by sheer labor. Women spend what seems to be an inordinate amount of time on the production of this one item. As an experienced *obentō* maker, I can attest to the intense attention and energy devoted to this one chore. On the average, mothers spend 20–45 minutes every morning cooking, preparing, and assembling the contents of one *obentō* for one nursery school-aged child. In addition, the previous day they have planned, shopped, and often organized a supper meal with left-overs in mind for the next day's *obentō*. Frequently women[10] discuss *obentō* ideas with other mothers, scan *obentō* cook-books or magazines for recipes, buy or make objects with which to decorate or contain (part of) the *obentō*, and perhaps make small food portions to freeze and retrieve for future *obentōs*.[11]

Of course, effort alone does not necessarily produce a successful *obentō*. Casualness was never indulged, I observed, and even mothers with children who would eat anything prepared *obentōs* as elaborate as anyone else's. Such labor is intended for the child but also the mother: it is a sign of a woman's commitment as a mother and her inspiring her child to being similarly committed as a student. The *obentō* is thus a representation of what the mother is and what the child should become. A model for school is added to what is gift and reminder from home.

This equation is spelled out more precisely in a nursery school rule—all of the *obentō* must be eaten. Though on the face of it this is petty and mundane, the injunction is taken very seriously by nursery school teachers and is one not easily realized by very small children. The logic is that it is time for the child to meet certain expectations. One of the main agendas of the nursery school, after all, is to introduce and indoctrinate children into the patterns and rigors of Japanese education (Rohlen 1989; Sano 1989; Lewis 1989). And Japanese education, by all accounts, is not about fun (Duke 1986).

Learning is hard work with few choices or pleasures. Even *obentōs* from home stop once the child enters first grade.[12] The meals there are institutional: largely bland, unappealing, and prepared with only nutrition in mind. To ease a youngster into these upcoming (educational, social, disciplinary, culinary) routines, *yochien obentōs* are designed to be pleasing and personal. The *obentō* is also designed, however, as a test for the child. And the double meaning is not unintentional. A structure already filled with a signification of mother and home is then emptied to provide a new form: one now also written with the ideological demands of being a member of Japanese culture as well as a viable and successful Japanese in the realms of school and later work.

The exhortation to consume one's entire *obentō*[13] is articulated and enforced by the nursery school teacher. Making high drama out of eating by, for example, singing a song; collectively thanking Buddha (in the case of Buddhist nursery schools), one's mother for making the *obentō*, and one's father for providing the means to make the *obentō*; having two assigned class helpers pour the tea, the class eats together until everyone has finished. The teacher examines the children's *obentōs*, making sure the food is all consumed, and encouraging, sometimes scolding, children who are taking too long. Slow eaters do not fare well in this ritual, because they hold up the other students, who as a peer group also monitor a child's eating. My son often complained about a child whose slowness over food meant that the others were kept inside (rather than being allowed to play on the playground) for much of the lunch period.

Ultimately and officially, it is the teacher, however, whose role and authority it is to watch over food consumption and to judge the person consuming food. Her surveillance covers both the student and the mother, who in the matter of the *obentō* must work together. The child's job is to eat the food and the mother's to prepare it. Hence, the responsibility and execution of one's task is not only shared but conditioned by the other. My son's teacher would talk with me daily about the progress he was making finishing his *obentōs*. Although the overt subject of discussion was my child, most of what was said was directed to me: what I could do in order to get David to consume his lunch more easily.

The intensity of these talks struck me at the time as curious. We had just settled in Japan and David, a highly verbal child, was attending a foreign school in a foreign language he had not yet mastered; he was the only non-Japanese child in the school. Many of his behaviors during this time were disruptive: for example, he went up and down the line of children during morning exercises hitting each child on the head. Hamadasensei (the teacher), however, chose to discuss the *obentōs*. I thought surely David's survival in and adjustment to this environment depended much more on other factors, such as learning Japanese. Yet it was the *obentō* that was discussed with such recall of detail ("David ate all his peas today, but not a single carrot until I asked him to do so three times") and seriousness that I assumed her attention was being misplaced. The manifest reference was to boxed lunches, but was not the latent reference to something else?[14]

Of course, there was another message for me and my child. It was an injunction to follow directions, obey rules, and accept the authority of the school system. All of the latter were embedded in and inculcated through certain rituals: the nursery school, as any school (except such nonconventional ones as Waldorf and Montessori) and practically any social or institutional practice in Japan, was so heavily ritualized and ritualistic that the very form of ritual took on a meaning and value in and of itself (Rohlen 1989: 21, 27–28). Both the school day and the school year of the nursery school were organized by these rituals. The day, apart from two free periods, for example, was broken by discrete routines—morning exercises, arts and crafts, gym instruction, singing—most of which were named and scheduled. The school year was also segmented into and marked by three annual events—sports day (*undokai*) in the fall, winter assembly (*seikatsu happyokai*) in December, and dance festival (*bon odori*) in the summer. Energy was galvanized by these rituals, which demanded a degree of order as well as a discipline and self-control that non-Japanese would find remarkable.

Significantly, David's teacher marked his successful integration into the school system by his mastery not of the language or other cultural skills, but of the school's daily routines—walking in line, brushing his teeth after eating, arriving at school early, eagerly participating in greeting and departure ceremonies, and completing all of his *obentō* on time. Not only had he adjusted to the school structure, but he had also become assimilated to the other children. Or, restated, what once had been externally enforced now became ideologically desirable; the everyday practices had moved from being alien (*soto*) to being familiar (*uchi*) to him, that is, from being someone else's to being his own. My American child had to become, in some sense, Japanese, and where his teacher recognized this Japaneseness was in the daily routines such as finishing his *obentō*. The lesson learned early, which David learned as well, is that not adhering to routines such as completing one's *obentō* on time results not only in admonishment from the teacher, but in rejection from the other students.

The nursery-school system differentiates between the child who does and the child who does not manage the multifarious and constant rituals of nursery school. And for those who do not manage, there is a penalty, which the child learns to either avoid or wish to avoid. Seeking the acceptance of his peers, the student develops the aptitude, willingness, and in the case of my son—whose outspokenness and individuality were the characteristics most noted in this culture—even the desire to conform to the highly ordered and structured practices of nursery-school life. As Althusser (1971) wrote about ideology: the mechanism works when and because ideas about the world and particular roles in that world that serve other (social, political, economic, state) agendas become familiar and one's own.

Rohlen makes a similar point: that what is taught and learned in nursery school is social order. Called *shudanseikatsu* or group life, it means organization into a group where a person's subjectivity is determined by group membership and not "the assumption of choice and rational self-interest" (1989: 30). A child learns in nursery school to be with others, think like others, and act in tandem with others. This lesson is taught primarily through the precision and constancy of basic routines: "Order is shaped gradually by repeated practice of selected daily tasks ... that socialize the children to high degrees of neatness and uniformity" (p. 21). Yet a feeling of coerciveness is rarely experienced by the child when three principles of nursery-school instruction are in place: (1) school routines are made "desirable and pleasant" (p. 30), (2) the teacher disguises her authority by trying to make the group the voice and unity of authority, and (3) the regimentation of the school is administered by an attitude of "intimacy" on the part of the teachers and administrators (p. 30). In short, when the desire and routines of the school are made into the desires and routines of the child, they are made acceptable.

Mothering as Gendered Ideological State Apparatus

The rituals surrounding the *obentō*'s consumption in the school situate what ideological meanings the *obentō* transmits to the child. The process of production within the home, by contrast, organizes its somewhat different ideological package for the mother. While the two sets of meanings are intertwined, the mother is faced with different expectations in the preparation of the *obentō* than the child is in its consumption. At a pragmatic level the child must simply eat the lunch box, whereas the mother's job is far more complicated. The onus for her is getting the child to consume what she has made, and the general attitude is that this is far more the mother's responsibility (at this nursery school, transitional stage) than the child's. And this is no simple or easy task.

Much of what is written, advised, and discussed about the *obentō* has this aim explicitly in mind: that is making food in such a way as to facilitate the child's duty to eat it. One magazine advises:

> The first day of taking *obentō* is a worrisome thing for mother and *boku* (child[15]) too. Put in easy-to-eat foods that your child likes and is already used to and prepare this food in small portions. (*Shufunotomo* 1980: 28)

Filled with pages of recipes, hints, pictures, and ideas, the magazine codes each page with "helpful" headings:

- First off, easy-to-eat is step one.
- Next is being able to consume the *obentō* without leaving anything behind.
- Make it in such a way for the child to become proficient in the use of chopsticks.

- Decorate and fill it with cute dreams (*kawairashi yume*).
- For older classes (*nencho*), make *obentō* filled with variety.
- Once he's become used to it, balance foods your child likes with those he dislikes.
- For kids who hate vegetables …
- For kids who hate fish …
- For kids who hate meat … (pp. 28–53)

Laced throughout cookbooks and other magazines devoted to *obentō*, the *obentō* guidelines issued by the school and sent home in the school flier every two weeks, and the words of Japanese mothers and teachers discussing *obentō*, are a number of principles: 1) food should be made easy to eat: portions cut or made small and manipulated with fingers or chopsticks, (child-size) spoons and forks, skewers, toothpicks, muffin tins, containers, 2) portions should be kept small so the *obentō* can be consumed quickly and without any left-overs, 3) food that a child does not yet like should be eventually added so as to remove fussiness (*sukikirai*) in food habits, 4) make the *obentō* pretty, cute, and visually changeable by presenting the food attractively and by adding non-food objects such as silver paper, foil, toothpick flags, paper napkins, cute handkerchiefs, and variously shaped containers for soy sauce and ketchup, and 5) design *obentō*-related items as much as possible by the mother's own hands including the *obentō* bag (*obentōfukuro*) in which the *obentō* is carried.

The strictures propounded by publications seem to be endless. In practice I found that visual appearance and appeal were stressed by the mothers. By contrast, the directive to use *obentō* as a training process—adding new foods and getting older children to use chopsticks and learn to tie the *furoshiki* [16]—was emphasized by those judging the *obentō* at the school. Where these two sets of concerns met was, of course, in the child's success or failure completing the *obentō*. Ultimately this outcome and the mother's role in it, was how the *obentō* was judged in my experience.

The aestheticization of the *obentō* is by far its most intriguing aspect for a cultural anthropologist. Aesthetic categories and codes that operate generally for Japanese cuisine are applied, though adjusted, to the nursery school format. Substances are many but petite, kept segmented and opposed, and manipulated intensively to achieve an appearance that often changes or disguises the food. As a mother insisted to me, the creation of a bear out of miniature hamburgers and rice, or a flower from an apple or peach, is meant to sustain a child's interest in the underlying food. Yet my child, at least, rarely noticed or appreciated the art I had so laboriously contrived. As for other children, I observed that even for those who ate with no obvious "fussiness," mothers' efforts to create food as style continued all year long.

Thus much of a woman's labor over *obentō* stems from some agenda other than that of getting the child to eat an entire lunch-box. The latter is certainly a consideration and it is the rationale as well as cover for women being scrutinized by the school's authority figure—the teacher. Yet two other factors are important. One is that the *obentō* is but one aspect of the far more expansive and continuous commitment a mother is expected to make for and to her child. "*Kyoiku mama*" (education mother) is the term given to a mother who executes her responsibility to oversee and manage the education of her children with excessive vigor. And yet this excess is not only demanded by the state even at the level of the nursery school; it is conventionally given by mothers. Mothers who manage the home and children, often in virtual absence of a husband/father, are considered the factor that may make or break a child as s/he advances towards that pivotal point of the entrance examinations.[17]

In this sense, just as the *obentō* is meant as a device to assist a child in the struggles of first adjusting to school, the mother's role is generally perceived as that of support, goad, and cushion for the child. She will perform endless tasks to assist in her child's study: sharpen pencils and make midnight snacks as the child studies, attend cram schools to verse herself in subjects her child is weak in, make inquiries as to what school is most appropriate for her child, and consult with her child's teachers. If the child succeeds, a mother is complimented; if the child fails, a mother is blamed.

Thus, at the nursery-school level, the mother starts her own preparation for this upcoming role. Yet the jobs and energies demanded of a nursery-school mother are, in themselves, surprisingly consuming. Just as the mother of an entering student is given a book listing all the pre-entry tasks she must complete—for example, making various bags and containers, affixing labels to all clothes in precisely the right place and of precisely the right size—she will be continually expected thereafter to attend Mothers' Association meetings, accompany children on field trips, wash her child's clothes and indoor shoes every week, add required items to her child's bag on a day's notice, and generally be available. Few mothers at the school my son attended could afford to work in even part-time or temporary jobs. Those women who did tended either to keep their outside work a secret or be reprimanded by a teacher for insufficient devotion to their child. Motherhood, in other words, is institutionalized through the child's school and such routines as making the *obentō* as a full-time, kept-at-home job.[18]

The second factor in a woman's devotion to over-elaborating her child's lunch box is that her experience doing this becomes a part of her and a statement, in some sense, of who she is. Marx writes that labor is the most "essential" aspect to our species-being and that the products we produce are the encapsulation of us and therefore our productivity (1970: 71–76). Likewise, women are what they are through the products they produce. An *obentō* therefore is not only a gift or test for a child, but a representation and product of the woman herself. Of course, the two ideologically converge, as has been stated already, but I would also suggest that there is a potential disjoining. I sensed that the women were laboring for themselves apart from the agenda the *obentō* was expected to fill at school. Or stated alternatively in the role that females in Japan are highly pressured and encouraged to assume as domestic manager, mother, and wife, there is, besides the endless and onerous responsibilities, also an opportunity for play. Significantly, women find play and creativity not outside their social roles but within them.

Saying this is not to deny the constraints and surveillance under which Japanese women labor at their *obentō*. Like their children at school, they are watched not only by the teacher but by each other, and they perfect what they create, at least partially, so as to be confirmed as a good and dutiful mother in the eyes of other mothers. The enthusiasm with which they absorb this task, then, is like my son's acceptance and internalization of the nursery-school routines; no longer enforced from outside, it is adopted as one's own.

The making of the *obentō* is, I would thus argue, a double-edged sword for women. By relishing its creation (for all the intense labor expended, only once or twice did I hear a mother voice any complaint about this task), a woman is ensconcing herself in the ritualization and subjectivity (subjection) of being a mother in Japan. She is alienated in the sense that others will dictate, inspect, and manage her work. On the reverse side, however, it is precisely through this work that the woman expresses, identifies, and constitutes herself. As Althusser pointed out, ideology can never be totally abolished (1971: 170); the elaborations that women work on "natural" food produce an *obentō* that is creative and, to some degree, a fulfilling and personal statement of themselves.

Minami, an informant, revealed how both restrictive and pleasurable the daily rituals of motherhood can be. The mother of two children—one aged three and one a nursery school student—Minami had been a professional opera singer before marrying at the relatively late age of 32. Now, her daily schedule was organized by routines associated with her child's nursery school: for example, making the *obentō*, taking her daughter to school and picking her up, attending Mothers' Association meetings, arranging daily play dates, and keeping the school uniform clean. While Minami wished to return to singing, if only on a part-time basis, she said that the demands of motherhood, particularly those imposed by her child's attendance at nursery school, frustrated this desire. Secretly snatching only minutes out of any day to practice, Minami missed singing and told me that being a mother in Japan means the exclusion of almost anything else.[19]

Despite this frustration, however, Minami did not behave like a frustrated woman. Rather she devoted to her mothering an energy, creativity, and intelligence I found to be standard in the Japanese mothers I knew. She planned special outings for her children at least two or three times a week, organized games that she knew they would like and would teach them cognitive skills, created her own stories and designed costumes for afternoon play, and shopped daily for the meals she prepared with her children's favorite foods in mind. Minami told me often that she wished she could sing more, but never once did she complain about her children, the chores of child raising, or being a mother. The attentiveness displayed otherwise in her mothering was exemplified most fully in Minami's *obentōs*. No two were ever alike, each had at least four or five parts, and she kept trying out new ideas for both new foods and new designs. She took pride as well as pleasure in her *obentō* handicraft; but while Minami's *obentō* creativity was impressive, it was not unusual.

Examples of such extraordinary *obentō* creations from an *obentō* magazine include: 1) ("donut *obentō*"): two donuts, two wieners cut to look like a worm, two cut pieces of apple, two small cheese rolls, one hard-boiled egg made to look like a rabbit with leaf ears and pickle eyes and set in an aluminum muffin tin, cute paper napkin added, 2) (wiener doll *obentō*): a bed of rice with two doll creations made out of wiener parts (each consists of eight pieces comprising hat, hair, head, arms, body, legs), a line of pink ginger, a line of green parsley, paper flag of France added, 3) (vegetable flower and tulip *obentō*): a bed of rice laced with chopped hard-boiled egg, three tulip flowers made out of cut wieners with spinach precisely arranged as stem and leaves, a fruit salad with two raisins, three cooked peaches, three pieces of cooked apple, 4) (sweetheart doll *obentō—abekku ningyo no obentō*): in a two-section *obentō* box there are four rice balls on one side, each with a different center, on the other side are two dolls made of quail's eggs for heads, eyes and mouth added, bodies of cucumber, arranged as if lying down with two raw carrots for the pillow, covers made of one flower—cut cooked carrot, two pieces of ham, pieces of cooked spinach, and with different colored plastic skewers holding the dolls together (*Shufunotomo* 1980: 27, 30).

The impulse to work and re-work nature in these *obentōs* is most obvious perhaps in the strategies used to transform, shape, and/or disguise foods. Every mother I knew came up with her own repertoire of such techniques, and every *obentō* magazine or cookbook I examined offered a special section on these devices. It is important to keep in mind that these are treated as only flourishes: embellishments added to parts of an *obentō* composed of many parts. The following is a list from one magazine: lemon pieces made into butterflies, hard-boiled eggs into *daruma* (popular Japanese legendary figure of a monk without his eyes), sausage cut into flowers, a hard-boiled egg decorated as a baby, an apple piece cut into a leaf, a radish flaked into a flower, a cucumber cut like a flower, a *mikan* (nectarine orange) piece arranged into a basket, a boat with a sail made from a cucumber, skewered sausage, radish shaped like a mushroom, a quail egg flaked into a cherry, twisted *mikan* piece, sausage cut to become a crab, a patterned cucumber, a ribboned carrot, a flowered tomato, cabbage leaf flower, a potato cut to be a worm, a carrot designed as a red shoe, an apple cut to simulate a pineapple (pp. 57–60).

Nature is not only transformed but also supplemented by store-bought or mother-made objects which are precisely arranged in the *obentō*. The former come from an entire industry and commodification of the *obentō* process: complete racks or sections in stores selling *obentō* boxes, additional small containers, *obentō* bags, cups, chop-sticks and utensil containers (all these with various cute characters or designs on the front), cloth and paper napkins, foil, aluminum tins, colored ribbon or string, plastic skewers, toothpicks with paper flags, and paper dividers. The latter are the objects mothers are encouraged and praised for making themselves: *obentō* bags, napkins, and handkerchiefs with appliqued designs or the child's name embroidered. These supplements to the food, the arrangement of the food, and the *obentō* box's dividing walls (removable and adjustable) furnish the order of the *obentō*. Everything appears crisp and neat with each part kept in its own place: two tiny hamburgers set firmly atop a bed of rice; vegetables in a separate compartment in the box; fruit arranged in a muffin tin.

How the specific forms of *obentō* artistry—for example, a wiener cut to look like a worm and set within a muffin tin—are encoded symbolically is a fascinating subject. Limited here by space, however, I will only offer initial suggestions. Arranging food into a scene recognizable by the child was an ideal mentioned by many mothers and cook-books. Why those of animals, human beings, and other food forms (making a pineapple out of an apple, for example) predominate may have no other rationale than being familiar to children and easily re-produced by mothers. Yet it is also true that this tendency to use a trope of realism—casting food into realistic figures—is most prevalent in the meals Japanese prepare for their children. Mothers I knew created animals and faces in supper meals and/or *obentōs* made for other outings, yet their impulse to do this seemed not only heightened in the *obentō* that were sent to school but also played down in food prepared for other age groups.

What is consistent in Japanese cooking generally, as stated earlier, are the dual principles of manipulation and order. Food is manipulated into some other form than it assumes either naturally or upon being cooked: lines are put into mashed potatoes, carrots are flaked, wieners are twisted and sliced. Also, food is ordered by some human rather than natural principle; everything must have neat boundaries and be placed precisely so those boundaries do not merge. These two structures are the ones most important in shaping the nursery school *obentō* as well, and the inclination to design realistic imagery is primarily a means by which these other culinary codes are learned by and made pleasurable for the child. The simulacrum of a pineapple recreated from an apple therefore is less about seeing the pineapple in an apple (a particular form) and more about reconstructing the apple into something else (the process of transformation).

The intense labor, management, commodification, and attentiveness that goes into the making of an *obentō* laces it, however, with many and various meanings. Overarching all is the potential to aestheticize a certain social order, a social order that is coded (in cultural and culinary terms) as Japanese. Not only is a mother making food more palatable to her nursery-school child, but she is creating food as a more aesthetic and pleasing social structure. The *obentō*'s message is that the world is constructed very precisely and that the role of any single Japanese in that world must be carried out with the same degree of precision. Production is demanding; and the producer must both keep within the borders of her/his role and work hard.

The message is also that it is women, not men, who are not only sustaining a child through food but carrying the ideological support of the culture that this food embeds. No Japanese man I spoke with had or desired the experience of making a nursery-school *obentō* even once, and few were more than peripherally engaged in their children's education. The male is assigned a position in the outside world, where he labors at a job for money and is expected to be primarily identified by and committed to his place of work.[20] Helping in the management of home and the raising of children has not become an obvious male concern or interest in Japan, even as more and more women enter what was previously the male domain of work. Females have remained at and as the center of home in Japan, and this message too is explicitly transmitted in both the production and consumption of entirely female-produced *obentō*.

The state accrues benefits from this arrangement. With children depending on the labor women devote to their mothering to such a degree, and women being pressured as well as pleasurized in such routine maternal productions as making the *obentō*— both effects encouraged and promoted by institutional features of the educational system, which is heavily state-run and at least ideologically guided at even the nursery-school level—a gendered division of labor is firmly set in place. Labor from males, socialized to be compliant and hardworking, is more extractable when they have wives to rely on for almost all domestic and familial management. And females become a source of cheap labor, as they are increasingly forced to enter the labor market to pay domestic costs (including those vast debts incurred in educating children) yet are increasingly constrained to low-paying part-time jobs because of the domestic duties they must also bear almost totally as mothers.

Hence, not only do females, as mothers, operate within the ideological state apparatus of Japan's school system, which starts semi-officially with the nursery school, they also operate as an ideological state apparatus unto themselves. Motherhood *is* state ideology, working through children at home and at school and through such mother-imprinted labor that a child carries from home to school as the *obentō*. Hence the post-World War II conception of Japanese education as egalitarian, democratic, and with no agenda of or for gender differentiation, does not in practice stand up. Concealed within such cultural practices as culinary style and child-focused mothering is a worldview in which the position and behavior an adult will assume has everything to do with the anatomy she/he was born with.

At the end, however, I am left with one question. If motherhood is not only watched and manipulated by the state but made by it into a conduit for ideological indoctrination, could not women subvert the political order by redesigning *obentō*? Asking this question, a Japanese friend, upon reading this paper, recalled her own experiences. Though her mother had been conventional in most other respects, she made her children *obentōs* that did not conform to the prevailing conventions. Basic, simple, and rarely artistic, Sawa also noted, in this connection, that the lines of these *obentōs* resembled those by which she was generally raised: as gender-neutral, treated as a person not "just as a girl," and being allowed a margin to think for herself. Today she is an exceptionally independent woman who has created a life for herself in America, away from homeland and parents, almost entirely on her own. She loves Japanese food, but the plain *obentōs* her mother made for her as a child, she is newly appreciative of now, as an adult. The *obentōs* fed her, but did not keep her culturally or ideologically attached. For this, Sawa says today, she is glad.

Notes

The fieldwork on which this article is based was supported by a Japan Foundation Postdoctoral Fellowship. I am grateful to Charles Piot for a thoughtful reading and useful suggestions for revision and to Jennifer Robertson for inviting my contribution to this issue. I would also like to thank Sawa Kurotani for her many ethnographic stories and input, and Phyllis Chock and two anonymous readers for the valuable contributions they made to revision of the manuscript.

1. As Dorinne Kondo has pointed out, however, these cuisinal principles may be conditioned by factors of both class and circumstance. Her *shitamachi* (more traditional area of Tokyo) informants, for example, adhered only casually to this coding and other Japanese she knew followed them more carefully when preparing food for guests rather than family and when eating outside rather than inside the home (Kondo 1990: 61–2).
2. Rice is often, if not always, included in a meal; and it may substantially as well as symbolically constitute the core of the meal. When served at a table it is put in a large pot or electric rice maker and will be spooned into a bowl, still no bigger or predominant than the many other containers from which a person eats. In an *obentō* rice may be in one, perhaps the largest, section of a multi-sectioned *obentō* box, yet it will be arranged with a variety of other foods. In a sense rice provides the syntactic and substantial center to a meal yet the presentation of the food rarely emphasizes this core. The rice bowl is refilled rather than heaped as in the preformed *obentō* box, and in the *obentō* rice is often embroidered, supplemented, and/or covered with other foodstuffs.
3. Japanese will both endure a high price for rice at home and resist American attempts to export rice to Japan in order to stay domestically self-sufficient in this national food *qua* cultural symbol. Rice is the only foodstuff in which the Japanese have retained self-sufficient production.

4. The primary sources on education used are Horio 1988; Duke 1986; Rohlen 1983; Cummings 1980.

5. Neither the state's role in overseeing education nor a system of standardized tests is a new development in post-World War II Japan. What is new is the national standardization of tests and, in this sense, the intensified role the state has thus assumed in overseeing them. See Dore (1965) and Horio (1988).

6. Boocock (1989) differs from Tobin *et al.* (1989) on this point and asserts that the institutional differences are insignificant. She describes extensively how both *yochien* and *hoikuen* are administered (*yochien* are under the authority of Monbusho and *hoikuen* are under the authority of the Koseisho, the Ministry of Health and Welfare) and how both feed into the larger system of education. She emphasizes diversity: though certain trends are common amongst pre-schools, differences in teaching styles and philosophies are plentiful as well.

7. According to Rohlen (1989), families are incapable of indoctrinating the child into this social pattern of *shundanseikatsu* by their very structure and particularly by the relationship (of indulgence and dependence) between mother and child. For this reason and the importance placed on group structures in Japan, the nursery school's primary objective, argues Rohlen, is teaching children how to assimilate into groups. For further discussion of this point see also Peak 1989; Lewis 1989; Sano 1989; and the *Journal of Japanese Studies* issue [15(1)] devoted to Japanese pre-school education in which these articles, including Boocock's, are published.

8. For a succinct anthropological discussion of these concepts, see Hendry (1987: 39–41). For an architectural study of Japan's management and organization of space in terms of such cultural categories as *uchi* and *soto*, see Greenbie (1988).

9. Endless studies, reports, surveys, and narratives document the close tie between women and home, domesticity and femininity in Japan. A recent international survey conducted for a Japanese housing construction firm, for example, polled couples with working wives in three cities, finding that 97 percent (of those polled) in Tokyo prepared breakfast for their families almost daily (compared with 43 percent in New York and 34 percent in London); 70 percent shopped for groceries on a daily basis (3 percent in New York, 14 percent in London), and only 22 percent of them had husbands who assisted or were willing to assist with housework (62 percent in New York, 77 percent in London) (quoted in *Chicago Tribune* 1991). For a recent anthropological study of Japanese housewives in English, see Imamura (1987). Japanese sources include *Juristo zokan sogo tokushu* 1985; *Mirai shakan* 1979; *Ohirasori no seifu kenkyukai* 3.

10. My comments pertain directly, of course, to only the women I observed, interviewed, and interacted with at the one private nursery school serving middle-class families in urban Tokyo. The profusion of *obentō*-related materials in the press plus the revelations made to me by Japanese and observations made by other researchers in Japan (for example, Tobin 1989; Fallows 1990), however, substantiate this as a more general phenomenon.

11. To illustrate this preoccupation and consciousness: during the time my son was not eating all his *obentō*, many fellow mothers gave me suggestions, one mother lent me a magazine, my son's teacher gave me a full set of *obentō* cookbooks (one per season), and another mother gave me a set of small frozen-food portions she had made in advance for future *obentōs*.

12. My son's teacher, Hamada-sensei, cited this explicitly as one of the reasons why the *obentō* was such an important training device for nursery-school children. "Once they become *ichinensei* [first-graders], they'll be faced with a variety of food, prepared without elaboration or much spice, and will need to eat it within a delimited time period."

13. An anonymous reviewer questioned whether such emphasis placed on consumption of food in nursery school leads to food problems and anxieties in later years. Although I have heard that anorexia is now a phenomenon in Japan, I question its connection to nursery-school *obentōs*. Much of the meaning of the latter practice, as I interpret it, has to do with the interface between production and consumption, and its gender linkage comes from the production end (mothers making it) rather than the consumption end (children eating it). Hence, while control is taught through food, it is not a control linked primarily to females or bodily appearance, as anorexia may tend to be in this culture.

14. Fujita argues, from her experience as a working mother of a daycare (*hoikuen*) child, that the substance of these daily talks between teacher and mother is intentionally insignificant. Her interpretation is that the mother is not to be overly involved in nor too informed about matters of the school (1989).

15. "*Boku*" is a personal pronoun that males in Japan use as a familiar reference to themselves. Those in close relationship with males—mothers and wives, for example—can use *boku* to refer to their sons or husbands. Its use in this context is telling.

16. In the upper third grade of the nursery school (the *nencho* class; children aged five to six) that my son attended, children were ordered to bring their *obentō* with chopsticks rather than forks and spoons (considered easier to use) and in the traditional *furoshiki* (piece of cloth that enwraps items and is double-tied to close it) instead of the easier-to-manage *obentō* bags with drawstrings. Both *furoshiki* and chopsticks (*o-hashi*) are considered traditionally Japanese, and their usage marks not only greater effort and skills on the part of the children but their enculturation into being Japanese.

17. For the mother's role in the education of her child, see, for example, White (1987). For an analysis, by a Japanese, of the intense dependence on the mother that is created and cultivated in a child, see Doi (1971). For Japanese sources on the mother-child relationship and the ideology (some say pathology) of Japanese motherhood, see Yamamura (1971); Kawai (1976); Kyutoku (1981); *Sorifu seihonen taisaku honbuhen* (1981); *Kadeshobo shinsha* (1981). Fujita's account of the ideology of motherhood at the nursery-school level is particularly interesting in this connection (1989).

18. Women are entering the labor market in increasing numbers, yet the proportion who do so in the capacity of part-time workers (legally constituting as much as thirty-five hours per week but without the benefits accorded to full-time workers) has also increased. The choice of part-time over full-time employment has much to do with a woman's simultaneous and almost total responsibility for the domestic realm (Juristo 1985; see also Kondo 1990).

19. As Fujita (1989: 72–79) points out, working mothers are treated as a separate category of mothers, and non-working mothers are expected, by definition, to be mothers full-time.

20. Nakane's much-quoted text on Japanese society states this male position in structuralist terms (1970). Though dated, see also Vogel (1963) and Rohlen (1974) for descriptions of the social roles for middle-class, urban Japanese males. For a succinct recent discussion of gender roles within the family, see Lock (1990).

References

Althusser, Louis (1971) *Ideology and ideological state apparatuses (Notes toward an investigation in Lenin and philosophy and other essays)*. New York: Monthly Review Press.

Asanuma, Kaoru (1987) *"Ganbari" no kozo (Structure of "Ganbari")*. Tokyo: Kikkawa Kobunkan.

Barthes, Roland (1957) *Mythologies*. Trans. Annette Lavers. New York: Noonday Press.

Boocock, Sarane Spence (1989) Controlled diversity: An overview of the Japanese preschool system. *The Journal of Japanese Studies* 15(1): 41–65.

Chicago Tribune (1991) Burdens of working wives weigh heavily in Japan. January 27, section 6, p. 7.

Cummings, William K. (1980) *Education and equality in Japan*. Princeton, NJ: Princeton University Press.

Doi, Takeo (1971) *The anatomy of dependence: The key analysis of Japanese behavior*. Trans. John Becker. Tokyo: Kodansha International, Ltd.

Dore, Ronald P. (1965) *Education in Tokugawa Japan*. London: Routledge and Kegan Paul.

Duke, Benjamin (1986) *The Japanese school: Lessons for industrial America*. New York: Praeger.

Fallows, Deborah (1990) Japanese women. *National Geographic* 177(4): 52–83.

Fujita, Mariko (1989) "It's all mother's fault": Childcare and the socialization of working mothers in Japan. *The Journal of Japanese Studies* 15(1): 67–91.

Greenbie, Barrie B. (1988) *Space and spirit in modern Japan*. New Haven, CT: Yale University Press.

Hendry, Joy (1986) *Becoming Japanese: The world of the pre-school child*. Honolulu: University of Hawaii Press.

—— (1987) *Understanding Japanese society*. London: Croom Helm.

Horio, Teruhisa (1988) *Educational thought and ideology in modern Japan: State authority and intellectual freedom*. Trans. Steven Platzer. Tokyo: University of Tokyo Press.

Imamura, Anne E. (1987) *Urban Japanese housewives: At home and in the community*. Honolulu: University of Hawaii Press.

Juristo zokan Sogotokushu (1985) Josei no Gensai to Mirai (The present and future of women). 39.

Kadeshobo shinsha (1981) *Hahaoya (Mother)*. Tokyo: Kadeshobo shinsha.

Kawai, Jayao (1976) *Bosei shakai nihon no Byori (The pathology of the mother society—Japan)*. Tokyo: Chuo koronsha.

Kondo, Dorinne K. (1990) *Crafting selves: Power, gender, and discourses of identity in a Japanese workplace*. Chicago, IL: University of Chicago Press.

Kyutoku, Shigemori (1981) *Bogenbyo (Disease rooted in motherhood)*. Vol II. Tokyo: Sanma Kushuppan.

Lewis, Catherine C. (1989) From indulgence to internalization: Social control in the early school years. *Journal of Japanese Studies* 15(1): 139–157.

Lock, Margaret (1990) Restoring order to the house of Japan. *The Wilson Quarterly* 14(4): 42–49.

Marx, Karl and Frederick Engels (1970) (1947). *Economic and philosophic manuscripts*, ed. C. J. Arthur. New York: International Publishers.

Mirai shakan (1979) Shufu to onna (Housewives and women). Kunitachishi Komininkan Shimindaigaku Semina— no Kiroku. Tokyo: Miraisha.

Mouer, Ross and Yoshio Sugimoto (1986) *Images of Japanese society: A study in the social construction of reality*. London: Routledge and Kegan.

Nakane, Chie (1970) *Japanese society*. Berkeley: University of California Press.

Ohirasori no Seifu kenkyukai (1980) Katei kiban no jujitsu (The fullness of family foundations). (Ohirasori no Seifu kenkyukai—3). Tokyo: Okurasho Insatsukyoku.

Peak, Lois (1989) Learning to become part of the group: The Japanese child's transition to preschool life. *The Journal of Japanese Studies* 15(1): 93–123.

Richie, Donald (1985) *A taste of Japan: Food fact and fable, customs and etiquette, what the people eat.* Tokyo: Kodansha International Ltd.

Rohlen, Thomas P. (1974) *The harmony and strength: Japanese white-collar organization in anthropological perspective.* Berkeley: University of California Press.

—— (1983) *Japan's high schools.* Berkeley: University of California Press.

—— (1989) Order in Japanese society: attachment, authority, and routine. *The Journal of Japanese Studies* 15(1): 5–40.

Sano, Toshiyuki (1989) Methods of social control and socialization in Japanese day-care centers. *The Journal of Japanese Studies* 15(1): 125–138.

Shufunotomo Besutoserekushon shiri-zu (1980) *Obentō* 500 sen. Tokyo: Shufunotomo Co., Ltd.

Shufunotomohyakka shiri-zu (1981) 365 nichi no *obentō* hyakka. Tokyo: Shufunotomo Co.

Sorifu Seihonen Taisaku Honbuhen (1981) Nihon no kodomo to hahaoya (Japanese mothers and children): koku-saihikaku (international comparisons). Tokyo: Sorifu Seishonen Taisaku Honbuhen.

Tobin, Joseph J., David Y. H. Wu, and Dana H. Davidson (1989) *Preschool in three cultures: Japan, China, and the United States.* New Haven CT: Yale University Press.

Vogel, Erza (1963) *Japan's new middle class: The salary man and his family in a Tokyo suburb.* Berkeley: University of California Press.

White, Merry (1987) *The Japanese educational challenge: A commitment to children.* New York: Free Press.

Yamamura, Yoshiaki (1971) *Nihonjin to haha: Bunka toshite no haha no kannen ni tsuite no kenkyu (The Japanese and mother: Research on the conceptualization of mother as culture).* Tokyo: Toyo-shuppansha.

13

Mexicanas' Food Voice and Differential Consciousness in the San Luis Valley of Colorado[*1]

Carole Counihan

I never cooked you know. I was always a bookworm. Ever since I was a growing up. When it was time for the dishes, they couldn't find me, so my poor sister had to do them by herself. ... We had an outhouse—a soldiers', a government toilet outside—and I'd take a book, you know, and I'd go there, and they'd say, "Where's Helen?" And somebody would pop up and say, "Oh she's in the toilet reading, she could be." And when I thought the dishes were half done or done I'd pop up. I never was responsible for them, they never depended on me, and my sister was such a good cook. She was a good cook and she griped about me not taking turns on the dishes but she didn't fight, she didn't mind. She was grown up on the job, you know, it was natural for her.[2]

These words of Helen Ruybal, a ninety-nine-year-old widow, mother of two, and former teacher, are part of a long-term ethnographic project I have been conducting since 1996 in the Mexican-American town of Antonito in rural Southern Colorado. I collected food-centered life histories from nineteen women, including Ruybal, and suggest that they reveal women's voice, identity, and worldview.

Antonito is six miles north of the New Mexico state line in the San Luis Valley, an eight thousand square-mile cold desert valley lying at approximately eight thousand feet above sea level between the San Juan and Sangre de Cristo mountains. Antonito is located in Conejos County in the Upper Rio Grande region on the northern frontier of greater Mexico.[3] The population of Antonito is 90% Hispanic and thus it is an excellent site to study the contemporary experience of rural Chicanas and Chicanos. My forthcoming book, tentatively titled *Mexicanas' Stories of Food, Identity and Land in the San Luis Valley of Colorado*,[4] gives a full exposition of how my nineteen interviewees described land and water, defined food and meals, and enacted family, gender, and community relations. In this paper, I use excerpts from one woman's interviews to make two points—first, to affirm the value of the food-centered life history methodology, and second, to suggest how women can display differential consciousness through their practices and beliefs surrounding food.

Food Voice, Feminist Anthropology and *Testimonios*

For over two decades, I have been using a food-centered life history methodology in Italy and the United States to present women's food voices.[5] Food-centered life

[*]Originally published 2008

histories are semi-structured tape-recorded interviews with willing participants, on their beliefs and behaviors surrounding food production, preparation, distribution, and consumption. I developed this methodology out of a feminist goal of fore-grounding the words and perspectives of women who have long been absent in recorded history. In the interviews women describe material culture as well as their subjective remembrances and perceptions. Topics include gardening, preserving food, past and present diets, recipes, everyday and ritual meals, eating out, foods for heal-ing, eating in pregnancy, breast-feeding, and many other subjects (see Appendix 1 for a list of interview themes). For many women (and some men), food is a significant voice of self-expression. In the meals they cook, the rituals they observe, and the memories they preserve, women communicate powerful meanings and emotions.

Like other feminist ethnographers, I have grappled with how to present an authen-tic picture of my respondents, one that is as much theirs as possible.[6] I used a tape-recorder so I could begin the process of representation with their words. Before doing interviews, I established informed consent, telling people in Antonito who I was and what I was doing there, promising confidentiality, and giving them the choice to participate or not.[7] I asked for their permission to tape-record, explaining that I wanted to have their verbatim descriptions of their experiences, but I also assured them that they could turn the tape recorder off at any time and decline to answer any questions, both of which they did on occasion. While I tried eventually to address all of the topics on my list (see Appendix 1), interviews were conversations with their own momentum and wandered into many non-food topics.

I have not followed the practice of some ethnographers of citing transcriptions verbatim, but at the urging of participants, I have edited the transcriptions to achieve readability, while staying as close to their original language as possible. I eliminated repetition and filler expressions (e.g. "like," "you know"), edited lightly for grammar, and moved around phrases and sections to achieve greater coherence.

My methodology coheres with two linked intellectual traditions—feminist anthro-pology and *testimonios*. It shares feminist anthropology's goals of placing women at the center, foregrounding women's diversity, challenging gender oppression, and reconstructing theory based on women's experiences (Moore 1988). My use of food-centered life histories to give voice to marginalized women links with the research of other feminists who have examined food as women's voice[8]—particularly Hauck-Lawson's (1998) research on immigrants in New York City, Pérez's (2004) "Kitchen Table Ethnography" with women on both sides of the U.S.-Mexico border, and Abarca's (2001, 2004, 2006) "culinary chats" with Mexican and Mexican-American working class women—all of which use women's food stories to theorize about their identity, agency, and power.[9]

Like the *testimonios* gathered by the Latina Feminist Group, food-centered life histories are about "telling to live." *Testimonios* involve participants speaking for themselves about events they have witnessed, events centered on "a story that *needs* to be told—involving a problem of repression, poverty, subalternity, exploitation, or simply survival" (Beverly 1993: 73). *Testimonios* are personal narratives that reveal individual subjectivity while calling attention to broad political and economic forces. They grew out of Latin American liberation movements at the same time that feminism was emerging in politics and scholarship. Sternbach (1991) highlighted the fact that these movements shared "breaking silences, raising consciousness, envisioning a new future, and seeking collective action" (Sternbach 1991: 95). Both feminism and *testimonios*, she said, linked the personal and the political, the "private, domestic or intimate sphere" with the "public, historic or collective one" (Sternbach 1991: 97). This is also the aim of food-centered life histories: to thrust the traditionally private sphere of cooking and feeding into the public arena and show the impact of women's experiences on culture and history. The experiences and voices of rural Colorado *Mexicanas* have been left out of the historical record for too long,[10] and recuperating them enhances understanding of the diversity of Mexican and Mexican American women. It fulfills a central goal in feminist ethnography, enriches our understanding of American culture, and makes possible more inclusive political policy.

Food and Differential Consciousness

Across cultures and history, food work can represent drudgery and oppression but also power and creativity. My second goal in this article is to show how women can challenge subordination and strive for agency through their food-centered life histories by evincing what Chela Sandoval (1991) calls "differential consciousness." Differential consciousness is a key strategy used by dominated peoples to survive demeaning and disempowering structures and ideologies. It is the ability to acknowledge and operate within those structures and ideologies but at the same time to generate alternative beliefs and tactics that resist domination.[11] Differential consciousness is akin to Scott's (1990) idea of the "hidden transcripts" developed by oppressed peoples to undermine public discourses upholding power structures. Ruybal and other women in her community took diverse stances towards food and were able, in Sandoval's words, to function "within yet beyond the demands of the dominant ideology" (1991: 3).

Women can develop differential consciousness in their relationship to food, as Ruybal did, by challenging the dichotomy between production and reproduction that has been so detrimental to women's social status.[12] As Engels originally pointed out in *The Origin of the Family, Private Property and the State*, and feminist anthropologists have elaborated upon,[13] the splitting of production and reproduction led to the privatization and devaluation of women's labor both inside and outside the home, and, to quote Engels (1972: 120), the "world historical defeat of the female sex." Interpreting Engels, Eleanor Leacock (1972: 41) argued that a major force in the subjugation of women has been "the transformation of their socially necessary labor into a private service." This process has characterized much of women's food work with the global decline of subsistence farming and the separation of production and consumption, but women in Antonito have resisted it in several ways.

Ruybal pursued three strategies throughout her life that displayed differential consciousness and enabled her to overcome the production–reproduction dichotomy surrounding food. First, she rejected cooking as pillar of her own identity yet respected women who did it—especially her sister Lila. Second, she welcomed and legitimized her husband's cooking, and thus reduced the dichotomization of male and female labor. Third, she produced and sold *queso*—a fresh, white cow's milk cheese—and, thus, transformed kitchen work into paid, productive labor. In these ways, Ruybal minimized food's oppressive dimensions and enhanced its empowering ones. I focus on Ruybal's experience but place it into the broader cultural context by referring to other women I have interviewed in Antonito, some of whom shared Ruybal's strategies of publicly valuing women's domestic labor, enlisting men's help in the home, and making money from food. In contrast, other women in Antonito found cooking to be a symbol and channel of oppression (Counihan 2002, 2005). Food work offered diverse and conflicting avenues of self-realization for *Mexicanas* in Antonito as it has for women everywhere.

Antonito, Colorado

Antonito is a small town running six blocks east to west and twelve blocks south to north along U.S. Route 285 and State Highway 17 in Southern Colorado. Several Indian groups, especially the Ute, Navaho, and Apache, originally inhabited the region around Antonito in what is today Conejos County. This area was claimed by Spain until Mexican independence in 1821 and by Mexico until the Treaty of Guadalupe Hidalgo in 1848, when it became part of the United States. In the mid-1850s, the earliest Hispanic settlers immigrated from Rio Arriba County, New Mexico and settled in the agricultural hamlets of Conejos, Guadalupe, Mogote, Las Mesitas, San Rafael, San Antonio, Ortiz, La Florida, and Lobatos on the Conejos, San Antonio, and Los Pinos rivers. When the Denver and Rio Grande Railroad tried to build a depot in 1881 in the county seat of Conejos, landowners refused to sell their property, so the railroad established its station and a new town in Antonito.[14]

The town grew steadily due to its commercial importance, saw mills, perlite mines, ranching, and agriculture through and after World War II, with its population peaking at 1255 in 1950 and then dropping steadily to 873 in 2000. In the 2000 census, ninety percent of residents declared themselves "Hispanic." Today the town hosts a pharmacy, a locally owned supermarket, three restaurants, a seasonal food stand, two gas stations, a video store, a hair salon, and several gift and used-goods stores. The climate is cold, dry, and dusty with average annual rainfall a meager eight inches and only two frost-free months a year. Traditional agriculture and ranching depended on the complex ditch or *acequia* system that channeled water from the rivers into the fields, but today commercial agriculture relying on center-pivot irrigation is increasingly common.

Today, poverty is widespread in Antonito, Conejos County, and the predominantly Hispanic rural region of Northern New Mexico and Southern Colorado that Martínez (1998: 70) calls the *siete condados del Norte*, the seven rural counties of northern New Mexico and southern Colorado with Chicano/a majorities.[15] In the Antonito area, important employers are the town, the county, the perlite mine, the schools, the hospitals in La Jara and Alamosa, and the service economy in Alamosa thirty miles north. Many people get by on odd jobs, baby-sitting, trading in used goods, home health care work, public assistance jobs, and welfare. In the summer and fall there is a small tourist economy due to the popular Cumbres and Toltec Scenic Railroad, and to hunting, fishing, and vacationing in the nearby San Juan Mountains.

Helen Ruybal

Helen Gallegos Ruybal grew up with her parents, two brothers, and one sister in the small farming and ranching hamlet of Lobatos, four miles east of Antonito. They owned a modest five acres of land that Helen's mother inherited from her parents. Helen's father used the land to raise some crops and farm animals to provide for their subsistence. She said, *My father used to milk four or five cows, to get around, to get going. And we had two or three pigs and he took care of them and butchered them at the right time, and we had lots of pork.* Helen was not born into the local elite, called *ricos*, whom she defined as those having *money and ranches and animals and cows and water*, but she did achieve membership in the Hispanic elite through education, work, and accumulation of wealth.

Ruybal's parents followed the traditional division of labor: *he provided and she raised the children*. When her father was young, Ruybal said, *He was a common laborer*. But later he opened a small store and also taught school for a while. She remarked: *My father opened up a little convenience store just in a room of the house because the school was there and the kids would go buy candy and go buy peanuts. And they had cigarettes and tobacco and all those things … And my mother just cooked and sewed and raised the kids and put up the garden food.* Ruybal's mother was like most women in the community, including her sister Lila, whose primary work was gardening, preserving food, cooking for the family, caring for children, sewing, quilting, cleaning, washing clothes, and other forms of reproductive labor.

Rejecting Cooking, Respecting Women Who Cooked

But Ruybal diverged from the norm represented by her mother and sister and spent as little time as possible on domestic chores throughout her life, while maximizing her productive paid work outside the home. Her food-centered life history revealed both the tactics she followed and the ideologies she developed to support her choices—ideologies grounded in differential consciousness. Ruybal eschewed the housewife role and cooked as little as possible, but valued and benefited from the help of her mother, sister, and husband. Her strategy minimized the subordinating dimensions of reproductive labor.

Even as a girl Ruybal had ambitions beyond the traditional female role: *I wanted to be different. I wanted to go my own way*, she said. She aspired to *education, earning money, and doing some good to people*. Assistance from her sister and parents was critical to Ruybal's ability to study and work: *I had my likes and dislikes supported at home. … My parents were interested in education for all of us … and my folks believed in going without so we could have supplies and go to school and we never missed it.* By running a store and raising their own food, Ruybal's parents were able to send her to Loretto Academy, a Catholic boarding school in Santa Fe, New Mexico, where she completed high school and teacher certification. She returned home and began teaching while she went part-time and summers to Adams State College in nearby Alamosa. She achieved a BA in 1954, which enhanced her credentials and earning power. She was employed steadily, first in several different hamlets around Antonito, and later in the better paying Chama, New Mexico public schools forty miles away over the San Juan Mountains.

Ruybal's employment gave her financial independence, which meant that she did not have to marry for economic reasons as many girls did. Helen's future husband, Carlos Ruybal, courted her for years and both families supported the match, but Helen resisted marriage: *I wanted to be free to do what I wanted. ... I didn't want to be tied down. ... I didn't want to get married, and I refused to all the time, for the sake of not having a family to keep. ... I wanted to work, and I felt like if I had children, I wasn't going to be able to work. I skipped marriage for a long time.*

Not only did she avoid marriage, but Ruybal also rejected cooking and the prominent role it played in many women's identity: *I never cooked you know. I was always a bookworm. Ever since I was a growing up.* For Ruybal food production, preparation, and clean-up were marginal activities she avoided if she could: *I'm not really a kitchen guy, you know what I mean, a provider in the kitchen.* Nonetheless, she could not escape cooking entirely but made it clear that she was a haphazard and indifferent cook. For example, one day she visited me and brought a gift of bread she had just made, saying, *Is it good? I thought it was kind of good. Sometimes it doesn't come out right. . ... I'm not a good cook [laughs], I'm not a steady cook.* Another time Ruybal spoke about making home-made tortillas, which she and everyone else in town thought were superior to store-bought ones, but she acknowledged her own uncertain skill: *Sometimes I make tortillas. And sometimes they come out good and sometimes they don't, not so good. And oh well.*

Ruybal eventually succumbed to cultural pressure to marry and she had to manage the household and the two children who came soon after her marriage. Crucially important was the support of her mother and sister: *My sister Lila was my right hand; she raised my kids. I'd come from my home, one mile, and I'd leave my kids there. What they didn't have, they had it there, and what they had, well they used it. She took care of them, fed them, and cleaned them up, and when I came in the evening I visited with her, and I picked them up, and I went home.*

Ruybal respected her sister's domestic identity, proficiency in the home, and accomplished cooking: *Lila had six children. ... She used to sew and crochet and knit and make quilts, pretty ones. ... And she cooked and she baked. ... Her children still remember the jelly rolls, and they came out perfect like the ones in the store. ... She used to make pies, a table full of pies, apple pies. ... And she had such a good heart, and she was a good cook, she was a good housekeeper.*

Throughout her life Ruybal valued her sister and worked hard to stay on good terms with her: *We got along fine until she died. We were in favor of each other always, since we were growing up. ... And we never got mad at each other, and we never got into a fight. ... If it was for my side, she'd go out of her way to do it, and I'd go out of my way to appreciate it. I gave her a lot of things. ... If she needed twenty dollars, I gave it to her. ... I always would give her every gift like that, any amount. And she would accept It. ... I had a good job in the first place, and I had less children, and more money, more money coming in. I was working and I couldn't miss a day and she never earned money. She just cooked, and washed and ironed, and took care of her kids and my kids.*

Even though she said her sister "just" cooked, Ruybal was able to appreciate and benefit from her sister's assumption of traditional female duties while at the same time she rejected them for herself. Not all women in Antonito were able to forge mutual respect out of difference, and public criticism of other women's choices was not uncommon. But Ruybal and her sister displayed differential consciousness by valuing and benefiting from each other's different choices vis-à-vis domestic labor and public work.

Blending Gender Roles: Involving Husband in Cooking

Ruybal's food-centered life history revealed how she improved her status by involving her husband Carlos in domestic chores and thus challenged the splitting of male and female labor so instrumental to women's subordination.[16] Ruybal did not marry until she was sure that Carlos would support her career as a teacher. She said, *He thought of me. If I was going to work, he didn't want to put any objections, just go ahead and work. And ... the first thing, [my daughter] Carla came. And Carlos helped me a lot and I helped him a lot. ... And then, not even two years later, [my son] Benito came. I wondered how far I was going that way. And I didn't want a large family. ... So after that, well, we just didn't let our family grow bigger. ... We were both combined. We both wanted the same thing.*

Because of her economic contributions to the marriage and busy work schedule, Ruybal was able to secure her husband's help at home and to skirt some of the domestic labor that fell to most women: *I never had to cook. ... I had kids, but they went to boarding school. I had them in the summer and Carlos used to help me a lot. In fact, they'd be with him at the ranch. ... He would [cook] when I wasn't home. On Fridays when I came from school he had supper ready. He did fried potatoes, he did fried beans, and he did everything fried quickly, because he didn't want to be at the stove watching it. ... And he cooked and he had a good meal and I helped him too, we both cooked.* Carlos learned to cook as many men did during summers in the all-male sheep and cattle camps, but unlike most, he utilized his skills at home.

Ruybal described the prevailing gender ideology based on clear and separate male/female work and the differential strategies and consciousness that she—and some others—upheld: *People just wanted to go that a lady's job is a lady's job. ... They didn't expect the wife to go out and plow the garden or to pick up the plants or brush. They didn't like for them to do men's jobs. ... And a man's job would be a man's job. ... But I knew husbands that did all the housework ... and they took care of the babies, put them to bed and fed them, changed them, dressed them, and changed the diapers, and people would laugh at that, for me they did too. ... People would be nasty about it—some would—they were jealous. ... They didn't want men to be that soft and kind-hearted. ... But others said, well, she deserves it, that he be considerate. She deserves that help. ... They would consider it right, she deserves it if she works and earns the bread and butter, why not do the dishes for her and do the floor, and make the beds and things like that? And others would think that that's ladies work—make the beds and wash the floor, some men didn't do anything but eat and provide—provide flour, provide money, provide salt and pepper. All those things but they wouldn't do anything in the kitchen.*

Carlos liked to be a helper always. ... I always had some other little thing to do, understand? I didn't have it to sit down here and watch. I did other things that had to be done, even little things and bigger things in the home, or in my job, my duty. Because I had to be prepared for that every day and I saw that I was before I tackled anything else. In the

mornings, when I went to Taos [to teach], he'd get up early in the morning and run my
car, warm and ready to go and he'd come in and prepare breakfast for me. … He saw me
out and the dishes were left on the table and buying more bread was left on the table and
he'd get those things ready for the week, he'd do it.

Ruybal's relatively egalitarian marriage went against the publicly stated value of
men controlling family and budget. One man told me that he knew several marriages
that fell apart when the women bettered themselves through education, attained jobs
outside the home, and gained financial independence. Husbands did not always
define their wives' economic success as a boon, but according to Ruybal, Carlos
respected her brains and business acumen, and they worked together as successful
business partners, with Helen bringing in a steady salary and Carlos managing the
growing ranch. Their cooperation allowed them to maximize their economic position
and accumulate land and cattle, attaining the status of *ricos*.

Ruybal's economic power outside the home raised her value in the home. Involving
her husband in the family cooking and admiring him for it improved the status of
food work, reduced her domestic workload, established reciprocity, and challenged
the subordination implicit in the expectations that women feed and serve men
(cf. DeVault 1991). In contrast, another Antonito woman, Bernadette Vigil, described
how her Puerto Rican husband humiliated her by forcing her to cook rice his way, and
threw her creations against the wall until she "*got it right*" (Counihan 2002, 2005).
Vigil's was an extreme situation, and most women fell somewhere in between Ruybal
and Vigil, cooking—sometimes willingly and sometimes not—and spending much of
their time on domestic chores, especially feeding men and children.

Transforming Reproduction to Production: Making and Selling Cheese

Ruybal's food-centered life history detailed how she transformed food work from
"private service" to public gain by selling cheese she made from the milk of the
family's cows. She said, *For ten years, at least ten years, maybe more, I made cheese,*
white cheese. My husband and my son used to milk at the ranch and bring it from there
to town. … Cheese was a luxury item, like ice cream on a cake. … Oh, that used to be my
job, and I'd use that money for a lot of little things. Even big things, I'd just put it with the
rest of the money. … That was a job, but I liked the idea, I didn't work hard. Even when
I went to school, I'd leave the cheese hanging and I'd go away and come back and it was
all ready to take it out and put it in the pan in the refrigerator. … As long as I had the
milk, instead of throwing it away, I made cheese. That's what I did it for more than for an
income. But I loved to get the money that I got from my work.

Converting reproductive labor to productive work enhanced Ruybal's pride,
money, and power—in her culture and in her marriage—and enabled her to develop
differential consciousness towards food work as she simultaneously minimized its
importance in her identity and valued its economic contribution. Many other women
in Antonito used their food preparation skills to make money. For example, Ramona
Valdez grew up on a ranch in Guadalupe with her parents and two siblings, and from
the 1930s through the 1950s, she regularly made cheese and butter, which she sold for
fifty cents a pound. Valdez also raised and sold turkeys. Through these activities, she
was able to accumulate $800, a lot of money in the 1950s. Pat Gallegos made and

sold cheese in the 1990s. Flora Romero was renowned for planning and cooking the food for funeral dinners and weddings. Gloria Garcia and Dora Sandoval both owned and ran local restaurants, and they catered weddings and parties as well. Several women made and sold tortillas, burritos, *empanaditas*, or tamales. Selling food in public gave what they ate in the home a monetary value and transformed food work from undervalued "reproduction" into remunerated "production." By holding differential attitudes towards these diverse forms of food preparation women were able to value their own work and that of others.

Conclusion

Ruybal's food-centered life history showed how she used food as a path to dignity and power, key issues in women's mediation of gender roles. She was among a minority of women in her community who achieved a college degree, a steady career, and a reduced domestic workload; nonetheless she was not unique but rather fell on a continuum of acceptable roles for women. Indeed almost all of the nineteen women I interviewed worked for money for varying periods of time. As they went in and out of the work force, their domestic roles contracted and expanded. Their experiences showed the permeability of the boundaries between public and private, production and reproduction, a permeability that some women, like Ruybal, were able to exploit to gain social prestige and economic power.

Ruybal's food-centered life history revealed her differential consciousness. She functioned "within yet beyond" dominant beliefs about women's food roles—*within* by valuing domestic labor and those who did it, *beyond* by curtailing cooking and using food to further her identity as a worker: *within* by recognizing the gender-dichotomized power structure of her culture, *beyond* by transcending gender oppositions. She, more than many women in her community, managed to shape "the relationship between women's reproductive and productive labor" (Moore 1988: 53), an essential step toward gender equality. Ruybal's flexible attitudes and activities surrounding food enabled her to be economically empowered and socially valued, and to attain the sense of belonging and respect that are hallmarks of what scholars have called cultural citizenship (Flores & Benmayor 1997).

Food-centered life histories are a valuable means to gather information that may otherwise be inaccessible (Hauck-Lawson 1998). They can reveal women's nutritional status, economic realities, psycho-emotional states, social networks, family concerns, and even spouse abuse (Ellis 1983). This information can buttress public policies relevant to women's needs, such as the WIC program, food stamps, and meals for senior citizens; small-business loans for women to start up food-based enterprises; and publicly funded child-care programs to permit women to work and attain parity with men.

I have used food-centered life histories to project Ruybal's voice into the public arena and counter the silencing that has been a central weapon in women's oppression (hooks 1989). Ruybal and other *Mexicanas'* food stories are *testimonios* that counteract erasure and affirm the value of women's labor, memory, and resourcefulness. They increase understanding of Chicanas' diversity in the United States, and challenge universalizing and demeaning portrayals (Zavella 1991).

Appendix 1 Food Centered Life Histories

Food-centered life histories consist of tape-recorded semi-structured interviews with willing participants, focusing on behaviors, experiences, beliefs, and memories centered on food production, preservation, preparation, cooking, distribution, and consumption. The following is a list of key topics presented in condensed form. In an interview, questions are not nearly so condensed and they follow the flow of conversation. Many lead naturally to further topics without prompting.

(1) Consumption
What are people/you/your family eating?
   (a)   Where do foods come from, local vs. imported foods?
   (b)   Diversity of cuisines?
   (c)   Vegetarianism?
   (d)   Picky eaters?
   (e)   Processed foods?
   (f)   Fast vs. slow foods?
   (g)   Dietary make-up?
   (h)   Nutritional composition?
   (i)   Seasonal, weekly variation?
Describe the quality of food.
Describe your meals: names, when, what, where, with whom.
   (a)   Describe eating at home.
   (b)   Describe eating out—school, daycare, restaurants, fast food, etc.
Describe the atmosphere and social relations of the eating experience.
Describe the current practices about outsiders eating in the home.
Describe the most important holidays and the role of food and commensality.
Do you know anyone with fussy eating habits, eating disorders, body image issues?
Do you know anyone suffering hunger, malnutrition, or food-related health problems?
How do individuals and the community deal with hunger and malnutrition?
Describe the relationship between food and health. Are foods used in healing?
Describe beliefs and practices surrounding eating in pregnancy.
Describe beliefs and practices surrounding eating during the post-partum period.
Describe the beliefs and practices surrounding infant feeding.
Over your lifetime, what are the most important changes in foodways? Their causes? Effects?
Describe outstanding food memories, good or bad.
Describe symbolic foods and their meanings.

(2) Production
How and by whom are foods produced, processed, and prepared?
Who cooks with what principal foods, ingredients, spices, and combinations?
What are some key recipes?
How are singles, couples or families handling the division of labor at home and at work?
   (a)   Who does the meal planning, shopping, cooking, serving, clearing, dish-washing?
   (b)   Who does other chores—bathroom, floors, clothes-washing, ironing, child-care?
How are boy and girl children being raised vis-à-vis food chores?
Describe the kitchen, place in the home, appliances, cooking tools, and technology.
Is there home gardening, canning, drying, freezing, brewing, baking, etc.? Recipes?
Describe the garden, layout, plants, labor, yearly cycle.

(3) Distribution
Describe your food acquisition.
Who procures food, by what means, where, when, and at what cost?
Do you shop in a grocery store, supermarket, farmers' market, coop, or CSA?
Is food exchanged or shared? How, with whom, when, why?
Is there a food bank, food pantry or soup kitchen in the community? Describe.

(4) Ideology
Describe food uses in popular culture, literature, films, art, advertising, music, etc.
Is food used in religion, magic, or witchcraft?

(5) Demographic Data:
Describe date of birth, marriage, children, parents, occupations, residences, etc.

Notes

1. An earlier version of this paper was published as "Food as Mediating Voice and Oppositional Consciousness for Chicanas in Colorado's San Luis Valley," in *Mediating Chicana/o Culture: Multicultural American Vernacular*, ed. Scott Baugh, Cambridge, England: Cambridge Scholars Press, 2006, pp. 72–84. I thank Scott Baugh for offering new ways of thinking about my work. I thank Penny Van Esterik for helpful comments and my husband, Jim Taggart, for his support and insights. I thank the people of Antonito for their hospitality and all the women who participated in my research for their generosity, especially Helen Ruybal, an extraordinary woman who passed away at the age of 100 in 2006. This paper is dedicated to her memory.
2. Direct quotations from my interviews with Helen Ruybal appear in italics throughout the paper.
3. Paredes (1976: xiv) defined Greater Mexico as "all the areas inhabited by people of a Mexican culture" in the U.S. and Mexico. See also Limón (1998). "*Mexicano*" is one of the most common terms that the people of Antonito use to describe themselves, along with Hispanic, Spanish, and Chicana/o. The life story of Helen Ruybal, like the lives of other women living in rural areas of Greater Mexico, differs in many ways from those of the urban Mexican and Mexican-American women of her generation explored by Ruiz (1993).
4. This book is under contract with the University of Texas Press.
5. See especially my book *Around the Tuscan Table: Food, Family and Gender in Twentieth Century Florence* (2004) as well as Counihan (1999, 2002, 2005).
6. See Behar and Gordon (1995), Gluck and Patai (1991), and Wolf (1992).
7. The American Anthropological Association Code of Ethics guided my research: http://www.aaanet.org/committees/ethics/ethcode.htm
8. On the food voice see Brumberg (1988), especially in her chapter "Appetite as Voice" reprinted in this volume. See also Avakian (1997) who collected personal accounts of cooking and eating from women of various class and ethnic groups. Thompson (1994) collected stories from eighteen women of color and lesbians who used food to cry out against racism, poverty, abuse, and injustice. Hauck-Lawson (1998) showed how one Polish American woman expressed through food her social isolation, depression, and declining self image—issues that she was unable to speak about directly and that affected her health and diet.
9. Historically, the production, preservation and preparation of food were central to women's roles and identity in the Hispanic Southwest (Deutsch 1987). See Cabeza de Baca (1949, 1954), Gilbert (1942) and Jaramillo (1939, 1955) on the recipes, cooking, and culture of Hispanic New Mexico. Many of the Mexican American women interviewed by Elsasser et al. (1980) in New Mexico and by Patricia Preciado Martin (1992, 2004) in Arizona described foodways and dishes similar to those of Antonito. Williams (1985) and Blend (2001a, b) used a feminist perspective to uncover both the liberating and oppressive dimensions of women's food work and responsibility. Abarca (2001, 2004, 2006) used "culinary chats" and Pérez used "kitchen-table ethnography" to explore Mexican and Mexican-American women's diverse lives. See also Bentley (1998), Montaño (1992), Taggart (2002, 2003), and Taylor and Taggart (2003). For fascinating analyses of literary representations of Chicanas and food, see Ehrhardt (2006), Goldman (1992), and Rebolledo (1995).
10. Deutsch (1987: 11) wrote, "Written history of female minorities or 'ethnics' is rare, that of Chicanas or Hispanic women rarer though increasing, and of Chicanas or Hispanic women in Colorado virtually non-existent."
11. See Segura and Pesquera (1999) on diverse oppositional consciousness among Chicana clerical workers in California. Gloria Anzaldúa's "*Oyé como ladra: el lenguaje de la frontera*" is a wonderful example of differential consciousness expressed through language use (1987: 55–6).
12. Two recent discussions of Latinas' role in transnational food production that undermine the production/reproduction, male/female dichotomy are Barndt (2002) and Zavella (2002).
13. See Lamphere (2000), Leacock (1972), Moore (1988), Rosaldo (1974), Sacks (1974), Sargent (1981).
14. On the history, culture, and land use of the San Luis Valley, see Aguilar (2002), Bean (1975), Deutsch (1987), García (1998), Gutierrez and Eckert (1991), Martínez (1987, 1998), Peña (1998), Simmons (1979), Stoller (1982), Swadesh (1974), Taggart (2002, 2003), Taylor and Taggart (2003), Tushar (1992), Weber (1991), and Weigle (1975).
15. The *siete condados del norte* are Costilla and Conejos Counties in Colorado, and Taos, Río Arriba, San Miguel, Mora, and Guadalupe Counties in New Mexico (Martínez 1998: 70).
16. See Ybarra (1982) and Pesquera (1993) on the relationship of Chicanas' earning power and work to husbands' sharing of household labor.

References

Abarca, Meredith (2001) "*Los Chilaquiles de mi 'ama*: The Language of Everyday Cooking." In Sherrie A. Inness, ed., *Pilaf, Pozole and Pad Thai: American Women and Ethnic Food*. Amherst: University of Massachusetts Press, pp. 119–44.

—— (2004) "Authentic or Not, It's Original," *Food and Foodways* 12, 1: 1–25.

—— (2006) *Voices in the Kitchen: Views of Food and the World from Mexican and Mexican American Working-Class Women. College* Station: Texas A & M UP.

Aguilar, Louis (2002) "Drying Up: drought pushes 169-year-old family-owned ranch in southern Colorado to the edge of extinction." *The Denver Post*, July 29, 2002.

Anzaldúa, Gloria (1987) *Borderlands/La Frontera: The New Mestiza*. San Francisco: Aunt Lute.

Avakian, Arlene Voski (ed.) (1997) *Through the Kitchen Window: Women Explore the Intimate Meanings of Food and Cooking*. Boston: Beacon Press.

Barndt, Deborah (2002) *Tangled Routes: Women, Work, and Globalization on the Tomato Trail*. Lanham: Rowmanand Littlefield.

Bean, Luther E. (1975) *Land of the Blue Sky People*. Alamosa, CO: Ye Olde Print Shoppe.

Behar, Ruth, and Deborah A. Gordon (eds) (1995) *Women Writing Culture*. Berkeley: University of California Press.

Bentley, Amy (1998) "From Culinary Other to Mainstream America: Meanings and Uses of Southwestern Cuisine." *Southern Folklore* 55, 3: 238–52.

Beverly, John (1993) *Against Literature*. Minneapolis: University of Minnesota Press.

Blend, Benay (2001a) "I am the Act of Kneading: Food and the making of Chicana Identity." In Sherrie A. Inness, ed., *Cooking Lessons: The Politics of Gender and Food*. New York: Rowman and Littlefield, pp. 41–61.

—— (2001b) " 'In the Kitchen Family Bread is Always Rising!' Women's Culture and the Politics of Food." In Sherrie A. Inness, ed., *Pilaf, Pozole and Pad Thai: American Women and Ethnic Food*. Amherst: University of Massachusetts Press, pp. 119–144.

Brumberg, Joan Jacobs (1988) *Fasting Girls: The Emergence of Anorexia Nervosa as a Modern Disease*. Cambridge: Harvard UP.

Cabeza de Baca, Fabiola (1982 [1949]) *The Good Life*. Santa Fe: Museum of New Mexico Press.

—— (1994 [1954]) *We Fed Them Cactus*. Albuquerque: University of New Mexico Press.

Counihan, Carole (1999) *The Anthropology of Food and Body: Gender, Meaning and Power*. New York: Routledge.

—— (2002) "Food as Women's Voice in the San Luis Valley of Colorado." In Carole Counihan ed., *Food in the USA: A Reader*. New York: Routledge, pp. 295–304.

—— (2004) *Around the Tuscan Table: Food, Family and Gender in Twentieth Century Florence*. New York: Routledge.

—— (2005) "Food as Border, Barrier and Bridge in the San Luis Valley of Colorado." In Arlene Voski Avakian, and Barbara Haber, eds, *From Betty Crocker to Feminist Food Studies: Critical Perspectives on Women and Food*. Amherst: University of Massachusetts Press.

Deutsch, Sarah (1987) *No Separate Refuge: Culture, Class, and Gender on an Anglo-Hispanic Frontier in the American Southwest , 1880–1940*. New York: Oxford.

DeVault, Marjorie (1991) *Feeding the Family: The Social Organization of Caring as Gendered Work*. Chicago: University of Chicago Press.

Ehrhardt, Julia C. (2006) "Towards Queering Food Studies: Foodways, Heteronormativity, and Hungry Women in Chicana Lesbian Writing." *Food and Foodways* 14, 2: 91–109.

Ellis, Rhian (1983) "The Way to a Man's Heart: Food in the Violent Home." In Anne Murcott, ed., *The Sociology of Food and Eating*. Aldershot: Gower Publishing, pp. 164–171.

Elsasser, Nan, et al. (eds) (1980) *Las Mujeres: Conversations from a Hispanic Community*. New York: Feminist Press.

Engels, Frederick (1972 [1942]) *The Origin of the Family, Private Property and the State*. New York: International.

Flores, William V., and Rina Benmayor (eds) (1997) *Latino Cultural Citizenship: Claiming Identity, Space and Rights*. Boston: Beacon.

García, Reyes (1998) "Notes on (Home) Land Ethics: Ideas, Values and the Land." In Devon Peña, ed., *Chicano Culture, Ecology, Politics: Subversive Kin*. Tucson: University of Arizona Press, pp. 79–118.

Gilbert, Fabiola Cabeza de Baca (1970 [1942]) *Historic Cookery*. Santa Fe: Ancient City.

Gluck, Sherna Berger, and Daphne Patai (1991) *Women's Words: The Feminist Practice of Oral History*. New York: Routledge.

Goldman, Anne (1992) " 'I Yam What I Yam': Cooking, Culture and Colonialism." In Sidonie Smith and Julia Watson, eds, *De/Colonizing the Subject: The Politics of Gender in Women's Autobiography*. Minneapolis: University of Minnesota Press, 169–95.

Gutierrez, Paul, and Jerry Eckert (1991) "Contrasts and Commonalities: Hispanic and Anglo Farming in Conejos County, Colorado." *Rural Sociology* 56, 2: 247–63.

Hauck-Lawson, Annie (1998) "When Food is the Voice: A Case-Study of a Polish-American Woman." *Journal for the Study of Food and Society* 2, 1: 21–8.

hooks, bell (1989) *Talking Back: Thinking Feminist, Thinking Black*. Boston: South End.

Jaramillo, Cleofas (1981) (orig. 1939) *The Genuine New Mexico Tasty Recipes*. Santa Fe: Ancient City Press.

—— (2000) (orig. 1955) *Romance of a Little Village Girl*. Albuquerque: University of New Mexico Press.

Lamphere, Louise (2000) "The Domestic Sphere of Women and the Public World of Men: The Strengths and Limitations of an Anthropological Dichotomy." In Caroline B. Brettell and Carolyn F. Sargent, eds, *Gender in Cross-Cultural Perspective*. Upper Saddle River: Prentice, pp. 100–109.

Latina Feminist Group (2001) *Telling to Live: Latina Feminist Testimonios*. Durham: Duke UP.

Leacock, Eleanor Burke (1972) " 'Introduction.' Frederick Engels." *The Origin of the Family, Private Property and the State*. New York: International, pp. 7–67.

Limón, José E. (1998) *American Encounters: Greater Mexico, the United States, and Erotics of Culture*. Boston: Beacon.

Marsh, Charles (1991) *People of the Shining Mountains: The Utes of Colorado*. Boulder: Pruett.

Martin, Patricia Preciado (1992) *Songs My Mother Sang to Me: An Oral History of Mexican American Women*. Tucson: University of Arizona Press.

—— (2004) *Beloved Land: An Oral History of Mexican Americans in Southern Arizona*. Collected and edited by Patricia Preciado Martin. With photographs by José Galvez, Tucson: University of Arizona Press.

Martínez, Rubén O. (1987) "Chicano Lands: Acquisition and Loss." *Wisconsin Sociologist* 24, 2–3: 89–98.

—— (1998) "Social Action Research, Bioregionalism, and the Upper Rio Grande." In Devon Peña, ed., *Chicano Culture, Ecology, Politics: Subversive Kin*. Tucson: University of Arizona Press, pp. 58–78.

Montaño, Mario (1992) *The History of Mexican Folk Foodways of South Texas: Street Vendors, Offal Foods, and Barbacoa de Cabeza*. Ph.D. Dissertation, University of Pennsylvania.

Moore, Henrietta (1988) *Feminism and Anthropology*. Minneapolis: University of Minnesota Press.

Paredes, Américo (1976) *A Texas-Mexican Cancionero*. Urbana: University of Illinois Press.

Peña, Devon (ed) (1998) *Chicano Culture, Ecology, Politics: Subversive Kin*. Tucson: University of Arizona Press.

Pérez, Ramona Lee (2004) "Kitchen Table Ethnography and Feminist Anthropology." Paper presented at the Association for the Study of Food and Society Annual Conference, Hyde Park, NY, June 12.

Pesquera, Beatríz M. (1993) " 'In the Beginning, He Wouldn't Lift Even a Spoon': The Division of Household Labor." In Adela Torre and Beatríz M. Pesquera, eds, *Building with Our Hands: New Directions in Chicana Studies*. Berkeley: University of California Press, 181–95.

Rebolledo, Tey Diana (1995) *Women Singing in the Snow: A Cultural Analysis of Chicana Literature*. Tucson: University of Arizona Press.

Rosaldo, Michelle Zimbalist (1974) "Women, Culture and Society: A Theoretical Overview." In Michelle Zimbalist Rosaldo and Louise Lamphere, eds, *Women, Culture and Society*. Stanford: Stanford University Press, pp. 17–42.

Ruiz, Vicki L. (1993) " 'Star Struck': Acculturation, Adolescence, and the Mexican American Woman, 1920–1950." In Adela Torre and Beatríz M. Pesquera, eds, *Building with Our Hands: New Directions in Chicana Studies*. Berkeley: University of California Press, 109–29.

Sacks, Karen (1974) "Engels Revisited: Women, the Organization of Production, and Private Property." In Michelle Zimbalist Rosaldo and Louise Lamphere, eds, *Women, Culture and Society*. Stanford: Stanford University Press, pp. 207–22.

Sandoval, Chela (1991) "U.S. Third World Feminism: The Theory and Method of Oppositional Consciousness in the Postmodern World." *Genders* 10, 1: 1–24.

Sargent, Lydia (ed.) (1981) *Women and Revolution: The Unhappy Marriage between Marxism and Feminism*. Boston: South End.

Scott, James C. (1990) *Domination and the Arts of Resistance: Hidden Transcripts*. New Haven: Yale UP.

Segura, Denise A., and Beatríz M. Pesquera (1999) "Chicana Political Consciousness: Re-negotiating Culture, Class, and Gender with Oppositional Practices." *Aztlán* 24, 1: 7–32.

Simmons, Virginia McConnell (1979) *The San Luis Valley: Land of the Six-Armed Cross*. Boulder: Pruett.

Sternbach, Nancy Saporta (1991) "Re-membering the Dead: Latin American Women's 'Testimonial' Discourse." *Latin American Perspectives* 70, 18, 3: 91–102.

Stoller, Marianne L. (1982) "The Setting and Historical Background of the Conejos Area." In Marianne L. Stoller and Thomas J. Steele, eds, *Diary of the Jesuit Residence of Our Lady of Guadalupe Parish, Conejos, Colorado, December 1871–December 1875*. Colorado Springs, CO: Colorado College, pp. xvii–xxviii.

Swadesh, Frances León (1974) *Los Primeros Pobladores: Hispanic Americans of the Ute Frontier*. Notre Dame: University of Notre Dame Press.

Taggart, James M. (2002) "Food, Masculinity and Place in the Hispanic Southwest." In Carole Counihan ed., *Food in the USA: A Reader*. New York: Routledge, pp. 305–13.

—— (2003) "José Inez Taylor." *Slow* 31: 46–49.

Taylor, José Inez, and James M. Taggart (2003) *Alex and the Hobo: A Chicano Life and Story*. Austin: University of Texas Press.

Thompson, Becky W. (1994) *A Hunger So Wide and So Deep: American Women Speak Out on Eating Problems*. Minneapolis: University of Minnesota Press.

Tushar, Olibama López (1992) *The People of El Valle: a History of the Spanish Colonials in the San Luis Valley.* Pueblo: Escritorio.

Weber, Kenneth R. (1991) "Necessary but Insufficient: Land, Water, and Economic Development in Hispanic Southern Colorado." *Journal of Ethnic Studies* 19, 2: 127–142.

Weigle, Marta (ed.) (1975) *Hispanic Villages of Northern New Mexico.* A Reprint of vol. II of the 1935 Tewa Basin Study, with Supplementary Materials. Edited, with introduction, notes and bibliography by Marta Weigle. Santa Fe, NM: The Lightning Tree.

Williams, Brett (1985) "Why Migrant Women Feed Their Husbands Tamales: Foodways as a Basis for a Revisionist View of Tejano Family Life." In Linda Keller Bown and Kay Mussell, eds, *Ethnic and Regional Foodways in the United States.* Knoxville: University of Tennessee Press, pp. 113–126.

Wolf, Margery (1992) A *Thrice Told Tale: Feminism, Postmodernism, and Ethnographic Responsibility.* Stanford: Stanford University Press.

Ybarra, L. (1982) "When Wives Work: The Impact on the Chicano Family." *Journal of Marriage and the Family* 44: 169–178.

Zavella, Patricia (1991) "Reflections on Diversity among Chicanas." *Frontiers* 12, 2: 73–85.

—— (2002) "Engendering Transnationalism in Food Processing: Peripheral Vision on Both Sides of the U.S.-Mexican Border." In C. G.Vélez-Ibañez, and Anna Sampaio, eds, *Transnational Latina/o Communities: Politics, Processes, and Cultures.* Lanham: Rowman. pp. 225–45.

14

Feeding Lesbigay Families*

Christopher Carrington

> To housekeep, one had to plan ahead and carry items of motley nature around in the mind and at the same time preside, as mother had, at the table, just as if everything from the liver and bacon, to the succotash, to the French toast and strawberry jam, had not been matters of forethought and speculation.
>
> *Fannie Hurst*, Imitation of Life

> Life's riches other rooms adorn. But in a kitchen home is born.
>
> *Epigram hanging in the kitchen of a lesbian family*

Preparing a meal occurs within an elaborate set of social, economic, and cultural frameworks that determine when and with whom we eat, what and how much we eat, what we buy and where we go buy it, and when and with what tools and techniques we prepare a meal. [...] As sociologist Marjorie DeVault convincingly argues in *Feeding the Family* (1991), the work of preparing and sharing meals creates family. Many lesbigay families point to the continuous preparation of daily meals and/or the occasional preparation of elaborate meals as evidence of their status as families. The labor involved in planning and preparing meals enables family to happen in both heterosexual and in lesbigay households. However, both the extent and the character of feeding activities can vary dramatically from one household to the next and often reflects the influence of socioeconomic factors like social class, occupation, and gender, among others.

In this chapter I pursue two objectives in the investigation of feeding work in lesbigay families. First, I explore feeding work through analyzing its character and revealing its often hidden dimensions. This entails some discussion of how families conceive of and articulate the work of feeding. For instance, participants use a number of rhetorical strategies to portray the organization of feeding in their households. Many participants use two distinctions: cooking/cleaning and cooking/shopping. I will show how these distinctions function to create a sense of egalitarianism and to obfuscate rather than clarify the process of feeding. This inevitably leads to questions about the division of feeding work in lesbigay households. [...] Second, in

*Originally published 1999

this chapter I explore how socioeconomic differences among lesbigay households influence feeding activities, and vice-versa. Therein, just as feeding work can create family identity for participants, so too can feeding work create gender, ethnic, class, and sexual identities.

The Character of Feeding Work

As DeVault (1991) so aptly describes in her study of feeding work in heterosexual families, the people who do feeding work often find it difficult to describe the task. Commonly held definitions and most sociological investigations of domestic labor often reduce feeding work to cooking, shopping, and cleaning up the kitchen—the most apparent expressions of feeding. But when interviewing and engaging in participant observation with people who perform these functions, it becomes clear that cooking and shopping refer to a wide range of dispersed activities that punctuate the days of those who feed. It includes things like knowledge of what family members like to eat, nutritional concerns, a sense of work and recreation schedules, a mental list of stock ingredients in the cupboard, a mental time line of how long fruits and vegetables will last, etc. Frequently, these activities go unnoticed because they often happen residually and unreflectively. For instance, the way that one comes to know about the character and qualities of food stuffs—through experimentation, through conversations with colleagues, through browsing in a cookbook at a bookstore, through reading the food section in the newspaper—these activities often appear as recreation or as an expression of personal interest and not as forms of work. Yet, to successfully feed a family, such activities must occur and consume the energy and time of those who do them. In order to illuminate the full character of feeding work in lesbigay families, I want to look behind the traditional typologies of cooking, shopping, and cleaning and reveal the dynamic and invisible character of much of the work involved in feeding these families.

Planning Meals

Feeding actually consists of a number of distinct processes including planning, shopping, preparation, and management of meals. Planning presumes the possession of several forms of knowledge about food, about the household, about significant others, and about cultural rules and practices toward food. In most of the lesbigay families in this study, one person emerges as a fairly easily identified meal planner; hereafter I refer to such persons as planners. Planning for most families means thinking ahead, perhaps a day or two or even a week, but in many cases just a few hours before a meal. For those who decide what to eat on a day-to-day basis, they often decide and plan meals while at work. Matthew Corrigan, an office administrator, put it like this:

> Usually we decide something at the last minute. Or sometimes we go out with someone. We rarely go out with just us two, but with others as well. If Greg is home in time and has an

inspiration, he will make something, but the general pattern is for me to throw something
together when I get home. I usually decide at work what to make.

A retail clerk, Scott McKendrick, reports: "We decide right before we eat. We go out
to the store and buy enough brown rice for several days or a package of chicken breasts
or broccoli. We shop every three days." "We" actually refers to Scott's partner, Gary
Hosokawa, a thirty-six-year-old bookkeeper who works for a small hotel. Earlier in
the interview, Scott reports that his partner cooks 75 percent of the time, and later
in the interview he indicates that his partner stops at the store several days a week. In
fact, Scott makes few planning decisions. His partner Gray makes most of them. [...]

Many times the partner who pulls together meals on a daily basis does not consider
what they do as planning. One computer engineer, Brad O'Neil, explains: "I hardly
ever plan. It just happens at the last minute." Further questioning reveals he often
decides at work what to make and often stops at the store to buy missing ingredients.
Like the other planners, Brad knows the foodstuffs available at home, he knows where
to go to get what he needs, and he knows how to prepare the food. Mentally, he draws
the connections between things at home, the things he needs, and a potential meal.
He plans, through he fails to recognize his efforts as such.

In some instances, someone plans for a longer period of time, often a week. Those
partners who plan by the week more readily recognize the planning they do. While
some planners find the effort enriching and pleasant, many others express a certain
amount of frustration with the process, particularly in deciding what to make. Randy
Ambert, an airline flight attendant, expresses the frustration this way:

> I find that he doesn't give me any input. I rarely make things he doesn't like, but he doesn't
> tell me what he wants to have, I have to do that every single week. I am constantly searching
> for clues as to what he likes and doesn't like. I don't think he truly appreciates how much effort
> it takes.

Sucheng Kyutaro, an office manager for a real estate agency, explains:

> I also find it hard to figure out what she likes to eat, I think. It's a pain to get her to tell me
> what she will eat and then she becomes annoyed when I forget it the next time. I think about
> her every time I try to come up with some dinner items.

These comments illustrate one of the hidden forms of work involved in feeding:
learning what others will and will not eat and learning to predict their responses.
Hochschild (1983) uses the terms *emotion work* or *emotion management* to refer to
this kind of empathetic activity, quite often performed by women, but as my research
suggests, by many gay men as well. When thinking about domestic work, most people
conjure up images of cleaning bathrooms, buying groceries and cooking meals.
Emotion management involves the process of establishing empathy with another,
interpreting behavior and conducting yourself in a way that "produces the proper
state of mind in others" (Hochschild 1983, 7). Emotion management involves the
management of feelings, both of your own and those of others. For example, it
involves efforts to soothe feelings of anger in another or to enhance feelings of
self-worth when someone "feels down." Sucheng's effort to "think about her partner
every time" she plans a meal, in order to avoid producing "annoyance" in her partner,

constitutes emotion work. Sucheng hope to create an emotional state of satisfaction and happiness in her partner through her feeding efforts.

Most lesbigay families, just like most heterosexual families, do not engage in the emotion work of feeding in an egalitarian way. For example, partners in lesbigay relationships do not share equal knowledge of the food tastes and preferences of each other. Queries about the food preference of partners reveal a highly differentiated pattern, where the planners possess extensive and detailed knowledge of their partner's preference and food concerns, while their partners know comparatively little about the planner's tastes. In response to a question about his partner's food preference, Steven Beckett, a retired real estate agent, reports that "he will not eat 'undercooked' or what the rest of us call normally cooked chicken, if he finds any red near the bone he will throw it across the room. Milk has to be low fat. Pork has to be quite cooked. He likes things quite spiced. He doesn't like peas or Brussels sprouts." Steven's partners, Anthony Manlapit, answers, "I think he likes a lot of things, I know he likes to eat out a lot." In response to the same question, Robert Bachafen, a school librarian, responds, "Yes. I stay away from radishes, shellfish, and certain soups. It's basically trail and error. He won't touch barbecued meats. I have learned over the years what he will and will not eat." His partner, Greg Sandwater, an architect, says, "I can't think of anything. He is not too fussy." Emily Fortune, a homemaker and mother of infant twins, as well as an accountant who works at home replies, "She doesn't care for pork. She has a reaction to shrimp. She doesn't like fish that much. Used to be that she wouldn't eat chicken. She doesn't like bell peppers. She doesn't like milk." Her partner, Alice Lauer, a rapid transit driver, says, "There aren't too many things she doesn't like." A finance manager for a savings and loan company, Joan Kelsey, replies, "Liver, brussels sprouts, she doesn't like things with white sauces. She is not as fond of junk food as I am." Her partner, Kathy Atwood, an accountant, responds, "I can't think of much of anything she doesn't like."

Steven, Robert, Alice, and Joan all plan meals and hold responsibility for the lion's share of feeding work. The partners of these meal planners confidently assert that their partners tend to like most things. Not true. In interviews I asked explicit questions about food likes and dislikes and found that planners indeed hold food preferences though their partners often do not readily know them. The ease with which planners cite detailed accounts of their partner's food likes and dislikes suggests that they use such knowledge with some frequency. Coming to know a partner's food preferences takes work: questioning, listening, and remembering. Successful feeding depends on this effort. [...]

Nutritional Concerns as Feeding Work

While the planners need to learn the food preferences of family members and continuously learn about food and its preparation from a variety of sources, they must also take into consideration a whole set of concerns about nutrition. Such concerns seem omnipresent in our society, through my research indicates some significant variation by both gender and age regarding this issue. Many of the planners work within fairly stringent guidelines regarding the nutritional content of the meals they prepare. [...] Many lesbian and gay-male (in particular) families fight over the nutritional content of food. These concerns cast a long shadow over the entire feeding process for some of the male planners. Joe McFarland, an attorney, states:

> We constantly fight about it. I am more conscious of fat and calorie content and seem to have to remind Richard constantly about it. He prepares great meals, but I am trying desperately to stay in shape. He gets upset because sometimes I just won't eat what he made or very much of it. I don't see why it's so hard for him to make low-fat stuff.

His partner, Richard Neibuhr, who does the feeding work, perceives it this way:

> Yes. Well, we try to cut fat. We eat a lot less red meat. We eat fish and poultry and we always skin the poultry because that's not too good for you. We eat a lot of rice and potatoes and avoid white cheese and butter. It all boils down to him trying to sustain his sexual attractiveness, I think. It would be easier for me to tell you things he will eat. He will not eat pork, no sausage. He eats one or two types of fish, he eats chicken and pasta. Anything other than that, it's a battle royal to get him to eat. It's too fat! He won't eat Greek, Mexican, Chinese—forget it. He will eat Italian, but only with light marinara sauces, sea bass, sole, skinless chicken, and that's about it. He is very picky and it all comes down to his effort to look beautiful. It's a lot of work to come up with meals that meet his dietary standards and yet still taste good and don't bore you to death.

Note the extent of Richard's knowledge about his partner's food preferences. Also note that Richard carries the burden of making sure the meals remain nutritionally sound.

Lesbian households also report conflicts over the nutritional quality of meals. Deborah James, a daycare worker, shares the following thoughts:

> Yeah, she doesn't want me to fry things because it makes such a mess and she has to clean it up. She would rather that I stir-fry and make more vegetables. She likes my cooking because it tastes good, but she would rather eat healthier than I would. I think my cooking sort of reminds her of her growing up. She partly likes that and she partly doesn't because it reminds her of being poor and I think the food I make sometimes, she thinks she's too good for it, that she should eat like rich people eat. I try to keep her happy, though.

Emily Fortune, a work-at-home accountant in her early thirties who recently became the mother of twins, maintains concern over both her partner's nutrition and her newborn children's nutrition. Emily, in response to a question about conflict over food states:

> Yes, I am still nursing, so I watch out for what the babies are going to get. We are no longer vegetarians. We both were at one time, but I eat a lot of protein for the babies. I think Alice would prefer a more vegetarian diet that was better for her. I try to think up meals that are healthy for all of them, both Alice and the babies. It's hard, though.

In most cases the meal planner becomes responsible for preparing meals that conform to dietary preferences and nutritional regimes.

In sum, planning meals, learning about foodstuffs and techniques, considering the preferences and emotions of significant others, and overseeing nutritional strategies frame the essential yet invisible precursor work to the actual daily process of preparing a meal. However, before the preparation begins, one must shop.

Provisioning Work

Shopping includes much more than the weekly trips to buy food products. DeVault (1991) recommends the use of the term *provisioning* to capture the character of the work involved in shopping. Provisioning assumes several forms of mental work that precede the actual purchase of food, including determining family members' food preferences, dietary concerns, as well as culturally specific concerns about food. Further, provisioning depends upon the following additional activities: developing a standard stock of food, learning where to buy the "appropriate" food, monitoring current supplies, scheduling grocery trips, making purchases within particular financial constraints and building flexibility into the process. Each of these components appears in lesbigay households and most often fall to the planner to orchestrate and perform.

Quite often these dimensions of provisioning go unrecognized and get subsumed in the rhetorical strategies participants use to describe the division of feeding work. More than half of the lesbigay family members use the distinction cooking/shopping to describe the division of tasks in meal preparation. This distinction creates an egalitarian impression, as in the phrase "She cooks and I shop." But the distinction conceals. In most cases the person with responsibility for cooking either did the actual shopping himself or herself or they prepared a list for the other person to use at the market. Responses to queries about who writes grocery lists illustrate this dynamic, as Carey Becker, a part-time radiologist, put it: "I write the list for major shopping for the most part, as well. She knows what brand to buy, so I don't tell her that. But I am the one who knows what we need and I make the list up for her." Daniel SenYung, a health educator, speaks of a similar pattern: "During the week when *we* are cooking, *we* write things on the list. He is more likely to do that, I guess, because he is cooking and will run out of stuff, so I get it at the store. He knows what we need." Note the recurrence of the phrase "knows what we need." In both instances the phrase refers to the possession of a stock knowledge of foodstuffs. Planners develop and possess an extensive mental list of standard ingredients used in their kitchens. In the research I asked to see the current grocery list, should one exist. I saw thirty-two such lists. In the wide majority of cases, just one person wrote the list or wrote more than three-quarters of the items on the list. In those relationships where participants make a distinction between shopping and cooking meals, lists become longer and more detailed. For instance, many planners specify brand names or write down terms like *ripe avocado* instead of just *avocado*. The cumulative effect of such detailed list writing greatly simplifies the work of shopping and undermines the seeming egalitarianism of the cooking/shopping distinction.

The Significance of Small Grocery Trips

In most households, shopping includes a number of smaller trips to supplement throughout the week. In the wide majority of lesbigay families, one person makes these supplemental trips. In most cases, the person who bears responsibility for meal preparation does this type of shopping. They often stop at the store at lunch or, more often, on their way home from work. While many families initially indicate that they split cooking from shopping, in reality the person who cooks often shops throughout the week while the other partner makes "major" shopping trips, usually on weekends and often using a shopping list prepared by the planner at home. At first glance the intermittent shopping trips during the week appear ad hoc and supplemental in character. Yet for many lesbigay households, particularly in the lesbian and gay enclaves of San Francisco, these little trips constitute the essential core of feeding. Many planners shop at corner markets near their homes or places of work, frequently purchasing the central ingredients for the meal that evening—fresh meats and vegetables, breads, and pastas. In many respects the weekend shopping actually looks more supplemental. Again, the grocery lists prove instructive. They contain many more entries for items like cereals, granola bars, sugar, mustard, yogurt, and soda than for the central elements in evening meals: vegetables, fresh pasta, fish, chicken, bread, potatoes, corn, prepared sauces, and often milk.

The intermittent shopper often operates with a great degree of foresight. Alma Duarte, a bookkeeper for a small business, belies the ad hoc characterization of daily grocery trips:

> Every couple of days, I go to the store. I do the in-between shopping. Every couple of days, I run down and pick up stuff we need or are running out of. I buy vegetables, fish, and bread. I buy the heavy items at Calla Market because she has a back problem, so I buy like soda and detergent and kitty litter, but she does the big shopping on weekends. I almost always go and buy fish on Monday afternoons at a fish market near where I work and then I stop at the produce market near home. And I have to go and get fresh vegetables every couple days over there.

Alma speaks of at least three destinations, and she obviously organizes her schedule to accommodate these different trips. One might think that this kind of shopping appears rather routine, after all, she describes it as "in between." Note that she does not consider this effort major, rather her partner does "big" shopping. Yet each of Alma's little shopping trips consists of a rather large number of choices about feeding. She must decide on what kind of fish and conceive of other items to serve with it. She decides when to go for vegetables and chooses among myriad varieties, making sure not to buy the same ones over and over yet also measuring the quality of the produce. Interestingly, she identifies her partner as the shopper, though she actually makes most of the feeding and provisioning decisions for her family. [...]

Monitoring: Supplies, Schedules, and Finances

Another component of feeding work revolves around the efforts of planners to monitor the supply of foods and other household products. DeVault suggests the complexity of monitoring work:

> Routines for provisioning evolve gradually out of decisions that are linked to the resources and characteristics of particular households and to features of the market. ... Monitoring also provides a continual testing of typical practices. This testing occurs as shoppers keep track of changes on both sides of the relation: household needs and products available. (1991, 71)

Lesbigay family members, both planners and others, attest to clear patterns of specialization when it comes to who keeps tabs on both food products and other household products like cleaning supplies, toiletries, and items like dinner candles. Very few families reported splitting this effort up equally, and even those that did, did so gingerly. Susan Posner, an employment recruiter in the computer industry, recounts: "Neither one of us keeps track. It just kind of surfaces that we need something. We don't have a list or anything. I guess whoever runs out of toilet paper first. And I guess I run out of toilet paper a lot. [*Laughter*] Okay, so maybe I do it." Susan's comments should give pause to students of domestic labor. Her comments reveal not only that she does the work of monitoring supplies, but also that she seems either unaware or perhaps to be attempting to deny that she does it. The planners, who do much of the monitoring, frequently speak of the dynamic character of the work. Tim Cisneros, a registered nurse, describes how he needed to change his routine in order to get the right deodorant for his partner:

> I mostly shop at Diamond Heights Safeway, though now I go over to Tower Market as well, at least once a month. 1 started doing that because Paul is hyperallergic to most deodorants, and he needs to use one special kind, and Safeway stopped carrying it. I tried to get it at the drugstore next to Safeway, but they don't carry it, either. So now, I go to Tower to get it. I buy other stuff while I'm there, so it's not really a big deal.

Tim captures the dynamic quality of provisioning. As demands change in the household or products change in the market, he comes up with new strategies to maintain equilibrium. Among roughly half of the families reporting a shopping/cooking division, more discussion of products occurs. Narvin Wong, a financial consultant in healthcare, comments:

> We sometimes get our wires crossed. I buy what he puts on the list, and that's almost always what we usually buy. I mean, I know what we need, but sometimes he changes his mind about what he needs and I don't always remember him telling me. Like a few weeks ago, he put olive oil on the list, and 1 bought olive oil. He says he told me that he wanted to start using extra-virgin olive oil. Well, I didn't hear that, and he yelled and steamed about it when he unpacked the groceries.

Narvin's comments suggest that perhaps less of this kind of conflict takes place in households where one person performs both the actual shopping and the provisioning work behind the trips to the store. Further, Narvin's partner, Lawrence Shoong, says that he often tries to go with Narvin to the store. Why?

> Because it gives me a chance to see what's out there. Narvin doesn't look for new things. Even if he does, he doesn't tell me about them. I like to know what's in season and just to see what's new. And inevitably, he forgets stuff. I know I should write it on the list, which is what he says, but when I go to the store, I can go up and down the rows and remember what we have and what we need.

Again, this points to the interdependent and dynamic character of feeding work. To do it successfully, given the way our society distributes foodstuffs and defines appropriate eating, the meal planner needs to stay in contact with the marketplace. Many planners do this through reading grocery flyers in the paper or in the mail, but many also try to stay in contact with the store itself. As Lawrence's comments suggest, much of provisioning work takes place in one's mind, the place where much of the hidden work of monitoring takes place.

Just as the work of monitoring the household and the marketplace come into view as highly dynamic processes, so too does the planner monitor the dynamic schedules of family members as a part of provisioning work. This means that many planners shop with the goal of providing a great deal of flexibility in meal options. For instance, many planners report selecting at least some dinner items that they can easily move to another night of the week should something come up. Sarah Lynch, a graphic artist who works in a studio at home, captures the dynamic circumstances under which she provisions meals:

> I never have any idea when Andrea will get here. She may stay at the bank until 11:00 at night. Sometimes, she doesn't know up until right before 5:00 whether she will be able to come home. So I still want us to eat together and I want her to get a decent meal, so I try to buy things that I can make quickly and that still taste good. She will call me from her car phone as soon as she is leaving the city. That gives me about an hour. I often will make something like a lasagna that I can then heat up when she calls, or I buy a lot of fresh pastas, in packages, you know the ones, and I will start that when she calls. I also try to buy a lot of snacklike items, healthy ones, but things like crackers and trail mix and dried fruit so that she can eat those things if she is really hungry and went without lunch or something, and so I can eat while I am waiting for her to get here.

Similarly, Matthew Corrigan, an office administrator, provisions meals to accommodate the schedule of his partner:

> I sometimes find it hard to keep a handle on things. Greg is active in a number of voluntary things—our church and a hospice for PWAs—and he serves on a City task force on housing issues. I am never completely sure he will be here for the meals I plan. So I try to have a lot of food around that we can make quickly and easily, like soups, veggie burgers, and pastas. If it gets too tight, and it often does, we will eat out, or just he will eat out and then I eat something at home, and hopefully I have something here to make.

Both Matthew and Sarah provision their households in light of the need to build in flexibility around the work and social schedules of their partners and themselves. The effort they put into this kind of dynamic provisioning frequently goes unnoticed and often appears routine, but they clearly think about these scheduling concerns in the work of provisioning for their families.

In addition to the efforts planners make in monitoring schedules, supplies, and markets, many also report concerns about monitoring finances. Participants refer to financial concerns in deciding what to eat and where to shop. The cutting of coupons both illustrates financial concerns and demonstrates the de facto division of provisioning work in many lesbigay families. Rarely do all family members report cutting coupons. For the most part, one partner, the planner/provisioner, cuts coupons. Tim Reskin, a clerk in a law firm, describes his use of coupons:

> Over time I have developed a sense of the brands that I know that we prefer. Sometimes I have coupons that I use. It's not like I will use any coupon, but if there's something that seems interesting or we don't have an opinion about, I might use that to decide. I always go through the Sunday paper and cut out the usable coupons. Cost is a big criterion for us.

In addition to cutting coupons, the less affluent households more often report that they compare prices, watch for sales and buy large-portioned products at discount stores like Costco and Food for Less. Lower-income planners also report spending more time reading grocery advertisements and going to different stores to buy sale items with the purpose of saving money in mind.

The estimates provided by participants regarding food expenditures provide additional insight into the division and character of feeding work. Weekly grocery expenditures vary significantly for lesbigay families, ranging from thirty dollars a week in the less affluent households to over two hundred and fifty dollars a week in the wealthier ones. Not that family members always agree on the cost of groceries. Planners estimate spending roughly thirty dollars more per week on groceries than their partners estimate. The thirty-dollar figure functions both as the mean and the median among the one hundred and three adult participants.

This knowledge gap in food expenditures points to several interesting dynamics. First, it reflects planners' knowledge of the cost of the many small trips to the store during the week. Second, it indicates planners' greater attentiveness to the cost of food items. Finally, it often points to the expectation of family members that planners should monitor and limit the cost of food. Consider the following examples. Tim Reskin and Philip Norris live in a distant East Bay suburb in a modest apartment. While they both work in the city, they live in the suburbs to avoid the high cost of housing in the city. Phillip performs much of the work of feeding their family. He plans the meals and creates much of the grocery list. In explaining why Tim does the bigger shopping on weekends, they both speak about financial concerns. Tim puts it this way: "Money, that's a major part of the reason why he doesn't go to the store. For Tim, he doesn't take price into consideration as much as he should. I use coupons and don't get distracted by advertising gimmicks at the store. I am more conscious of money." Philip sees things somewhat differently, but points to the issue of cost as well.

> He shops. He feels he has more control at the store. He feels he's a smarter shopper. I tend to look for high quality, whereas he tends to look for the best price. He does seem sharper. Well, he thinks he has a better handle on excessive spending. I don't know, though. You know, he does limit things during the major shopping, but then I have to go out and get things during the week. I am very, very careful about watching the cost. But you know what? Partly I have to go out and get things because of his complaints. He says that I cook blandly, like an Englishman. But the fact is, I work with what he brings home, and if he won't buy spices or sauces or whatever, in order to save money, then the food will taste bland. He denies that's what happens, but it is.

Phillip actually bears a significant part of the responsibility for monitoring food costs. Note the phrase "I am very, very careful about watching the cost." Philip's comments illustrate the interdependent character of monitoring costs and planning meals, but further, he also must consider his partner's satisfaction with the meals.

A strikingly similar example emerges within a lesbian household. Marilyn Kemp and Letty Bartky live in one of the lesbigay neighborhoods of San Francisco. They both work in lower-level administrative jobs and find themselves struggling financially. They talk about the high cost of housing and how to cut corners in order to stay living in San Francisco. Letty, who performs much of the feeding work in the family, comments on Marilyn's approach to weekend shopping:

> Marilyn likes to shop like a Mormon—you know, be prepared for six months. She buys these huge boxes of stuff. I think it's silly. I am more into going two or three times a week. Also, I like to take time to make up my mind, while she just wants to get through the store as fast as possible. She bitches that I don't make interesting things to eat, but what does she expect given our financial constraints and her shopping regimen.

Marilyn sees it differently: "We don't disagree much at all about shopping. I do it because I am more cost-conscious than she is."

Both of the above families suggest that it is one thing to manage the cost of groceries while shopping, but another matter entirely to manage the cost of groceries in the broader context of feeding the family.

Preparing Meals

The actual physical work of preparing meals each day requires thorough analysis. In some instances, the physical preparation of the meal occasionally begins in the morning when meal planners take items from the freezer to defrost for the evening meal. Some planners report other early morning efforts such as marinating meats, vegetables, of tofu. Most planners begin the meal preparation shortly after arriving home from work. Many report emptying the dishwasher or putting away dry dishes from the rack as one of the first steps in getting ready to prepare the evening meal. This point to the ambiguity of the cooking/cleaning distinction offered by many participants. The majority of meal planners arrive home from work earlier than their partners, more than an hour earlier in most cases. Depending on the menu items, which vary widely, participant's estimate that meal preparation takes approximately an hour. The preparation of the meal involves mastering a number of different tasks, including coordinating the completion time of different elements of the meal, managing unexpected exigencies like telephone calls or conversations with family members, coping with missing ingredients or short supplies, and engaging in all of the techniques of food preparation, from cutting vegetables to kneading pizza dough to deboning fish to barbecuing meats.

Many meal preparers find it difficult to capture the character of the process involved in creating meals. Even those who seem well versed in cooking find it difficult to characterize the process in its true fullness and complexity. Clyde Duesenberry, who prepares most of the meals in the house, comments:

> We make pesto quite a bit. We have that with fried chicken or some sausage or whatever. We like breaded foods. We like Wienerschnitzel. We will have blue cheese on burgers. We roast chickens quite often. We watch cooking shows quite a bit. The story about Mike, he can do it if he wants to, he knows the basics of cooking. One time I got called out on a call on a Sunday evening and he took over and we never had chicken as good as he made it. He cooks the broccoli. He knows how to do that. It isn't the recipe that makes a cook, it's the mastery of techniques. I can't even begin to cover all the territory of cooking you are asking about.

The meal preparer realizes the complexity of the work involved and struggles to put it into words. Usually their words belie the full extent of their effort as they struggle to express what they do. Another participant, Daniel Sen Yung, says:

> I tend to steam things a lot. I use dressings. A lot of salads and stuff. I don't know [said with exasperation], it's hard to describe, I just do it. Each time it seems like there are different things to do. I call someone and ask them, or I look at a cookbook, or I just experiment and hope for the best. I make some things over and over and each thing has its own routine.

The daily physical process of meal preparation takes on a highly dynamic and thoughtful quality. While some meals take on a routine quality in some households, for most the process appears much more vigorous and multifaceted. It requires the constant attention, the knowledge, and the physical labor of meal prepares.

Feeding and Cleaning

In contrast to meal preparation, the cleanup of the evening meal appears much more routine, requiring less mental effort, less time, less knowledge, and less work. As previously indicated, many lesbigay households use a cooking/cleaning distinction to explain the organization and division of feeding work. However, in close to one-third of the sample, the person who prepares the meal also cleans up after the meal. The cleaning component deserves closer analysis. Those who clean up the kitchen estimate a median time of thirty minutes. They talk about clearing the dishes, loading the dishwasher, putting away leftover food, and wiping the counters and the stovetop. Some include taking out trash or wiping floors, but not most. Among the less affluent families, participants include washing and drying the dishes. As I briefly noted earlier, meal preparers often empty the dishwasher or put away dry dishes when they begin preparing the evening meal. The work of cleaning up is highly routinized in most lesbigay households, requiring little decision making and little emotional work. Barbara Cho, a shift supervisor for a hotel, notes that the cleanup actually allows her time to think and unwind from her day: "It's not a big deal. I clean off the table. Sandy helps bring in the dishes. I load the dishwasher, wipe off the counter, and put stuff away. It's a great time for me to think about things, I often reflect on my day or decide what I'm going to do that night. It helps me unwind." Rarely do meal planners/preparers conceive of their feeding work in these terms. Most spoke of the importance of staying focused on meal preparation in order to avoid burning meats or overcooking vegetables, and of coordinating meal items so they reach completion at the same time.

Several meal preparers also note that they make some effort to limit the mess caused by meal preparation and actually do a lot of cleaning as they go. Sucheng Kyutaro, who prepares most meals eaten at home, notes:

> She complains a lot if I make too much of a mess during cooking. So I kind of watch it as I go. I try to clean the major things as I cook. I will rinse out pans, like if I make spaghetti sauce, I will run all the remains from the vegetables down the garbage disposal and rinse out the sauce pan and I always wipe off the stove. She really doesn't like cleaning that up at all.

Gary Hosokawa, a payroll supervisor who does much of the feeding work in his family, remarks: "Usually I cook and he cleans. Although I am really anal about keeping a clean kitchen, so I clean a lot while I am cooking. There is not that much for him to do."

The preceding comments demonstrate the limited character of cleaning up after meals in many lesbigay households, and they further undermine the salience of the cooking/cleaning distinction employed by many participants to indicate the egalitarianism of their household arrangements.

Feeding Work and the Creation of Gender, Class, Ethnic, and Family Identities

Feeding and the Production of Gender Identity

Recent empirical and theoretical work on the sociology of gender conceives of the production or achievement of gender identity as resulting from routine and continuous engagement in certain kinds of work and activities socially defined as gendered (Berk 1985; Coltrane 1989; West and Zimmerman 1987). This perspective emerges from a school of thought in sociology that understands gender as a dynamic and purposeful accomplishment: something people produce in social interaction (Cahill 1989; Goffman 1977; Kessler and McKenna 1978). West and Zimmerman point to the significance of action, interaction, and display in the process of "doing gender": "a person's gender is not simply an aspect of what one is, but, more fundamentally, it is something that one does, and does recurrently, in interaction with others" (1987, 140). Gender is not the product of socialized roles in which individuals continually recast themselves. Rather, gender requires continual effort to reproduce in everyday life. Since in this society and many others gender constitutes an essential component or the system of social classification, "doing gender" results in keeping social relationships orderly, comprehensible, and stratified. Frequently, individuals possess an awareness of doing gender while deciding how to conduct themselves in daily life. How masculine should one appear while observing a sports event? How feminine should one appear in a television interview? Berk demonstrates how household tasks function as occasions for creating and sustaining gender identity (1985, 204). Coltrane (1989), in his study of fathers who become extensively involved in the work of childcare, shows how such men must manage the threats to gender identity that such work poses to them. To violate the gendered expectations of others often lends to stigma and to challenges to the gender identity of the violator. Coltrane found that men who care for (feed, clean, teach, hold) infants often face stigma from coworkers and biological relatives, and that oftentimes the men hide their caring activities from these people to avoid conflict and challenges to their masculine identity. Men performing domestic labor—or women who fail to—produce the potential for stigma, a matter of great significance for gay and lesbian couples, where the reality of household life clashes with cultural gender expectations.

Accordingly, managing the gendered identity of members of lesbigay families becomes a central dynamic in the portrayal of feeding work both within the family and to outsiders. In general, feeding work in the household constitutes women's work, even when men engage in the work. That link of feeding with the production of womanly status persists and presents dilemmas for lesbigay families. Let me begin my analysis of this dynamic by pointing to a rather odd thing that happened in interviews with lesbigay family members. I interviewed family members separately to prevent participants from constructing seamless accounts of household activities. In so doing, inconsistencies occurred in the portrayal of domestic work, including feeding work. In six of the twenty-six male families, both claim that they last cooked dinner. In four of the twenty-six female couples, both claim that the other person last cooked dinner. How can one explain this? Were the participants simply confused? Why a persistent gendered pattern of confusion? Lesbian families do more often report sharing in the tasks of meal preparation than do gay-male families, so here the confusion may reflect the presence of both partners in the kitchen. Participant observation confirms such a pattern. For instance, in two of the four female households observed in depth, both women spent the majority of time during meal preparation together in the kitchen. I do not mean to imply that they share every task or divide meal preparation equally. Frequently, they engage in conversation and one person assists by getting things out the refrigerator, chopping celery, or pulling something out of the oven. Mostly, one person prepares and manages the meal while the other helps. The question remains, Why do men who did not prepare a meal claim to have done so, and why do women report that their partners who assisted actually prepared the meal?

The answer looks different for female and male households. In some lesbian couples the partner who performs much of the feeding work seems to also concern herself with preventing threats to the gender identity of her less domestically involved partner. This pattern seems most persistent among lesbian couples where one of the partners pursues a higher-paying, higher-status occupation. Consider the following examples. Cindy Pence and Ruth Cohen have been together for eleven years. Cindy works as a nurse, and she does much of the feeding work in the family. Ruth works as a healthcare executive. Ruth works extensive hours, and it often spills over into their family life, something Cindy dislikes. Ruth acknowledges that Cindy does much of the domestic work in their relationship, including the feeding work. Ruth says that she tries to help out when she can, and she tries to get home to help with dinner. They each claim that the other person cooked the last meal at home. During my interview with Ruth I asked about work and family conflicts, and how work might impinge on family life. Ruth comments:

RUTH: Cindy's great about my work. She does so much. I don't think I could handle it all without her. She sort of covers for me, I guess and I feel guilty about it, but I also know that she appreciates how hard I work for us.
CC: What do you mean, she covers up for you?
RUTH: I mean, she gives me credit for doing a lot of stuff at home that I don't really do. I mean, I help her, but it's not really my show. She does it and I really appreciate it. But I feel terrible about it.

The same kind of feelings emerged in an interview with Dolores Bettenson and Arlene Wentworth. Both women work as attorneys for public entities, though Dolores's job requires less overtime and allows for a more flexible schedule. Dolores reports working for wages forty hours per week, while Arlene reports working for wages around sixty hours per week, including frequent trips to the office on Saturdays and on Sunday evenings. Dolores handles much of the feeding work of the family, while the couple pays a housekeeper to do much of the house cleaning. Both Dolores and Arlene initially report that they split responsibility for cooking. Arlene, in response to a question about conflicts over meal preparation, says:

> I think things are pretty fifty-fifty, we are pretty equal: I guess she does things more thoroughly than I do, and she complains about that, but she always gives me a lot of credit for the stuff I do. Sometimes, I think she gives me too much credit, though, and I feel guilty about it, because, as I said, she takes that kind of stuff more seriously than I do, I just don't have as much time.

Both Ruth's and Arlene's comments reveal a pattern of the more domestically involved partner assigning credit for completing domestic work that the less domestically involved partner did not do. I suspect that this occurs in part to provide "cover" for women who spend less time doing domestic work, less time "doing gender."

In a similar vein, the pattern among gay males appears the opposite, and more intensely so, in some respects. Engaging in routine feeding work violates gendered expectations for men. I emphasize routine because men can and do participate in ceremonial public cooking such as the family barbecue. Yet the reality of household life requires that someone do feeding work. In heterosexual family life, men are usually capable of avoiding feeding work, but in gay-male families, someone must feed. Only in a very few, quite affluent households did feeding work seem particularly diminished and replaced by eating most meals in the marketplace. Most gay-male, couples eat at home, and among many of them I detect a pattern of men colluding to protect the masculine status of the meal planner/preparer. The conflicted claims of who last prepared an evening meal illustrate this dynamic and also reveal the ambiguous feelings held by men who feed about their status and their work. Bill Regan and Rich Chesebro have been together for three years. Rich works at a large software company and Bill works as an artist. Bill often works at home and carries much of the responsibility for domestic work, including feeding work. Both men claim that they last prepared the evening meal. Other questions in the interview reveal that, in fact, Bill prepared the last meal. When I asked about the last time they invited people over for dinner, Bill replied that it was two days before the interview, on Saturday night. When asking about what he prepared, he responded: "Well, let us see, *last night I made lasagna*. Oh, and that night, Saturday, I broiled tuna." It turns out that Bill made the last meal, though Rich claims that he did: Why should Rich make such a claim? Part of the answer lies in Rich's concern, expressed several times, that Bill not become overly identified with domestic work. When asking Rich about who last went to the grocery store, Rich replies: "I think that Bill might have, but it is not that big of a deal really. He really likes his work as an artist and that's *where his true interest lies*" (emphasis added). This response initially confused me. I ask about a trip to the store, and I receive an answer emphasizing Bill's work as an artist. I let this response pass, but later in the interview, I ask Rich about who last invited someone over to dinner, and who typically does this. In a similar rhetorical move, Rich says: "Well, I suspect Bill might be the one to do that, but I don't think it is that significant to him, really: *His real love* is his work as an artist, that's where he puts most of his energy" (emphasis added). At this point in the interview I decide to pursue Rich's intent in moving us from matters of domesticity to Bill's status as an artist. I ask Rich why he brought up Bill's work as an artist in the context of who most likely invites people to dinner. "Well, because I worry that people will get the wrong idea about Bill. I know that he does a lot of stuff around here, but he really wants to become an artist, and I don't want people to think of him as a housewife or something. He has other interests." As these comments disclose, Rich attempts here to manage the identity of his partner. This interpretation receives further confirmation on the basis of Rich's answer to a question about how he would feel about his partner engaging in home-making full-time and working for wages only partly or not at all:

> Well, I wouldn't like it at all. I don't see how that could be fair, for one person to contribute everything and the other to give little or nothing to the relationship. Plus, what about one's self-respect? I don't see how one could live with oneself by not doing something for a living. I would not be comfortable at all telling people that Bill is just a housewife. If he wanted to do his artwork and do more of the housework, that would be okay, I guess, but that's kind of how we do it already.

While Rich attempts to shield Bill from identification with domestic work, both in order to protect Bill from the status of "a housewife or something" but also to confirm his own *belief that domestic work holds little value*, the reality remains that Bill does much of the domestic work, including feeding work. Doing feeding work ties Bill to a more feminine identity. Bill put it like this in response to a question about whether the roles of heterosexual society influence the character of his relationship with Rich:

> I think that the functions all need to be handled. There is a certain amount of mothering that is required and whether that is done by a man or a woman does not matter. But mothering per se is an important function. And there is a certain amount of fathering having to do with setting goals and directions and creating focus. I guess people do think of me as more of the mother in our relationship, because I cook and invest a lot in our home, but that's their problem. Sometimes I feel strange about it, but I like to do it and I like the family life that we have together.

Bill's words capture the ambiguity of feelings about feeding work and other domestic work that I heard frequently in many lesbigay households. On the one hand, Bill recognizes the importance of such work (mothering) to creating a family life. On the other hand, he feels strange about his participation in domestic work. Bill's partner worries about people identifying Bill with domestic work and emphasizes Bill's identity as artist.

Another gay-male household illustrates a similar set of dynamics. Nolan Ruether and Joe Mosse have been together just under two decades. They live in an affluent suburban community outside the city. They both work in healthcare, though in very different settings and with quite different responsibilities. Nolan is a registered nurse and reports working forty hours per week. Joe works in a medical research lab and reports working closer to fifty hours per week. He also has a part-time job on the weekends. Nolan handles much of the domestic life of the family, including much of the feeding work. Both partners claim that they last cooked an evening meal. They actually eat separately more often than not, with Nolan eating a meal at home in the early evening that he cooks for himself and Joe either eating something on the run or eating something late when he arrives home. Joe indicates that he does the major shopping on weekends, though Nolan makes frequent trips to the market during the week and says that "I often pick up things that will be easy for him to prepare when he gets home from work, and I frequently will make something that he can simply warm up when he gets in." Nolan actually cooked the last meal, while Joe warmed up the meal when he arrived home late. Throughout the interview Joe emphasizes the egalitarian character of their relationship and diminishes the amount and significance of domestic work in the household. When I ask about conflicts over meals or meal preparation, Joe responds, "Um, well, we hardly ever eat meals at all. There is no work to conflict about. I eat out and he tends after his own." Nolan reports that they eat at home half the week, while they go out the other half. Nolan reports that they do not plan meals, though he says that they do communicate on the subject: "We don't plan meals, really. We either are both at home and I ask him what he wants or I call him at work and then I just go to the store and buy it. We don't keep a lot of food here, because I tend to run out to the store most every day." Nolan does much of the feeding work. He engages in routine provisioning work for the family, and he plans many of the family's social occasions that involve food. He also does most of the emotional labor related to food. Now consider Nolan's responses to questions about his feelings toward traditional gender roles for men and women in American Society:

> I certainly see the value in it, in ways I never did before I was in a relationship. There's a lot of work to be done to keep a house nice and to make life pleasant. I get pretty tired sometimes, I don't think Joe has any sense of it, really. He is off so much doing work, but he works so much by choice. You know, I think I said, we don't really need the money, but he couldn't imagine being around here doing this stuff.

Does he think that traditional gender roles influence the pattern of domestic life in your relationship?

> Well, in the sense that I do everything and he does very little, yes, I think it resembles the traditional pattern. He would of course deny it and get angry if I pushed the topic, so I don't bring it up, and I feel it's kind of difficult to talk to anyone about it because, well, because they might think of me as a complaining housewife or something, and I don't think most people can understand a man doing what I do. So when he says there isn't that much to do around here, I just sort of let him believe what he wants. It isn't worth the trouble.

Notice the ambiguity of feeling Nolan expresses about talking to others about his situation. Nolan's restraint (emotion work) actually enables Joe to diminish the importance of the work that Nolan does to maintain family life. Joe's approach to his household life closely resembles the pattern of need reduction detected by Hochschild (1989, 202) among some men in her study of heterosexual couples. Consider the following excerpts from our interview:

> CC: Tell me about your feelings toward traditional roles for men and women in the family in American society.
> JOE: I think those roles have declined a lot. It's more diverse now. I am really glad that such roles have declined. I feel that there should be two people out earning incomes. I don't think that people should stay at home. I can't see the value in it. Everyone should have outside interests. And I especially don't think that a man should be stuck in the home, cooking and stuff like that. Nolan works full-time, and we mostly eat out.
> CC: Do you feel like the prescriptions for such roles influence or shape your relationship? Why or why not?

JOE: Definitely not. We are both men and we both work for a living, and so we don't really fit those images. We don't have much domestic work here, especially since I am not here that much.

CC: What would you think of your partner or yourself engaging in homemaking full-time and working for wages only partly or not at all?

JOE: I would not be too pleased with it. There has to be a common goal that you both work toward. For one to contribute everything would not be fair. I don't make that much of a mess, and so I don't think that there would be anything for him to do.

Throughout this exchange Joe not only diminishes the presence of domestic work through emphasizing how often he is gone but also expresses his concern that his partner not become overly identified with domestic work. Nolan's own feelings of ambiguity about doing domestic work, and the threat it poses to his gender identity, actually keep him from talking about his circumstances.

One observes another example of the salience of gender to the portrayal of feeding work in dinner parties. Using Goffman's conceptions of "frontstage" and "backstage" work, sociologist Randall Collins suggests that cooking meals for dinner parties constitutes a frontstage activity that "generally culminates with the housewife calling the family or guests to the table and presiding there to receive compliments on the results of her stage (or rather table) setting" (1992, 220). The backstage work, much more arduous and time intensive, consists of a wide array of different kinds of invisible work: planning, provisioning, and monitoring. The work is often invisible in the sense that these forms of work receive little public recognition during dinner parties. In most lesbigay families the responsibility for both the elaborateness and the exoticness of foods for dinner parties becomes the responsibility of the meal planner/preparer, and often this person takes front stage at the dinner party.

However, in ten of the lesbigay households, and in contrast to the normative pattern in heterosexual families described by Collins, the person who cooks for dinner parties often only engages in the frontstage work while the other partner performs much of the backstage or more hidden forms of work. These ten households share a common pattern. In the male families the person who performs routine feeding work and performs the backstage work for dinner parties also works for wages in somewhat female-identified occupations: two nurses, a primary education teacher, a legal secretary, a social worker, and an administrative assistant. The frontstage males work in male-identified occupations: two accountants, an engineer, an attorney, a physician, and a midlevel manager. In the female families exhibiting a split between frontstage and backstage feeding, frontstage women work in male-identified occupations: two attorneys, a higher-level manager, and a college professor. The occupations of the backstage females include two retail sales workers, a nurse, and an artist. Taking the front stage in such dinner parties may well function as a strategy on the part of these lesbigay couples to manage threats to the gender identity of the domestically engaged men or the less domestically engaged women.

Confirming this pattern in the words of participants proves somewhat elusive. None of the women who do backstage feeding work for dinner parties expressed dissatisfaction about this. And while several of the men complain that they do not receive credit for the backstage work they do in preparation for such dinners, they also seem reluctant to make much of a fuss about it. Tim Cisneros, who works as a nurse and does much of the routine feeding work, responds to a question about who last prepared a meal for dinner guests, and why, by saying, "Well, I guess you would have to say he did. Though, I am the one who did most of the prep work for it. He gets a lot of pleasure out of cooking fancy stuff for others, and while I think I should get some credit, I don't make a big deal about it. I would feel kind of weird pointing it out, so I just let him take the credit. It's easier that way." Tim's observations convey his awareness of an inconsistency between frontstage and backstage, and his assertion of the ease of maintaining that inconsistency makes it plausible to think that there is little to gain, and there may even be a cost, in disclosing the inconsistency.

As evidenced by the above cases, gender operates as a continuous concern for lesbigay families, but in ways more complex than many accounts of lesbigay family life indicate. The gender strategies deployed by the different participants suggest an abiding concern about maintaining traditional gender categories, and particularly of avoiding the stigma that comes with either failing to engage in domestic work for lesbian families or through engaging in domestic work for gay-male families. The portrayal of feeding work by lesbigay households conforms to these gender-related concerns, and partners tend to manage the identity of their respective partners.

Feeding Work and the Production of Class Identity

Feeding work in lesbigay families both reflects and perpetuates social-class distinctions. Patterns of meal preparation and patterns of sociability forged through the sharing of meals across families reflect the presence of social-class distinctions among lesbigay families. These social-class distinctions seem quite apparent but, historically, sociologists have found it difficult to find such class differences among lesbigay people. Two decades ago, when sociologist Carol Warren conducted a study of gay life, she concluded:

> It is clear that members tend to think of themselves, no matter what the abstract criteria, as members of an elite class .... since an elegant upper-middle-class lifestyle is one of the status hallmarks of the gay community, it is quite difficult to tell, and especially in the context of secrecy, what socioeconomic status people actually have. (1974, 85)

The families in this study do not lead secret lives: only five of the 103 adults interviewed completely hid their identities from coworkers, and only six hid their identities from biological relatives. It seems that as the lesbigay community becomes more visible, so too do differences among lesbigay people become more visible. Gender and racial distinctions pervade lesbigay life. Social-class distinctions also pervade lesbigay life and patterns of feeding often reflect and reproduce such distinctions.

The organization, preparation, and hosting of dinner parties plays a significant role in the production of class distinctions among lesbians and gays. Upper-middle-class lesbigay families report organizing and participating in dinner parties for friends and coworkers with much greater frequency than middle- and working/service-class families, except for some ethnically identified families, to whom I will return shortly. In terms of household income, the top 25 percent of families report either holding or attending a dinner party at least two times per month. In the bottom 25 percent, families rarely report any such occasion.

These meals function to reproduce social-class alliances and identities. For example, these meals become occasions for professionals to identify potential clients, learn of potential job opportunities, learn of new technologies, or stay abreast of organizational politics. During election cycles, these dinner parties among the affluent can take on political significance. Many lesbian and gay politicians in the city of San Francisco use such occasions as fundraisers. The lesbigay politician attends the gathering and the campaign charges between $50 and $500 per person. Among the wealthier participants living in San Francisco proper and earning household incomes of over $80,000, nearly every household reports either attending or hosting such a meal. These dinner parties provide access to power and influence on policy, and they play a crucial role in the political order of San Francisco lesbigay politics.

In a wider sense, dinner parties contribute to the creation of social-class identities. As DeVault comments on the function of hosting dinner parties, "it also has significance in the mobilization of these individuals as actors in their class: it brings together 'insiders' to a dominant class, and marks their common interests" (1991, 207). Given DeVault's observation, what does it mean to claim that these shared meals "mark their common interests"?

Beyond the more obvious career advantages and the sheer social enjoyment of such occasions, part of the answer lies in the symbolic meaning people attach to cuisine and the Style in which hosts present it. Collins conceives of the symbolic meanings people attach to such occasions as an example of "household status presentation" (1992, 219). In other words, the choice of cuisine and the style of serving constructs social-class identity for the participants. Further, dinner parties function as occasions for the display and sharing of "cultural capital" (Bourdieu 1984). Bourdieu conceives of cultural capital as knowledge and familiarity with socially valued forms of music, art, literature, fashion, and cuisine, in other words, a sense of "class" or "good taste." Bourdieu distinguishes cultural capital from economic capital, therein arguing that some members of society may possess higher levels of cultural capital yet possess less wealth, and vice-versa. The household often functions as the site where cultural capital or good taste finds expression. Dinner parties often operate as a stage upon which the hosts display and call attention to various forms of cultural capital, including everything from works of art to home furnishings, from musical selections to displays of literature, from table settings to the food itself. The elaborate and the exotic quality of meals plays a central role in the upper-middle-class lesbigay dinner party. The higher-status participants often speak of specializing in a particular cuisine. Joe Mosse speaks of his interest in Indian cuisine:

> We often have Indian food when guests come over. I started cooking Indian food as a hobby many years ago. We've collected lots of Indian cookbooks, and I do a lot of different dishes. People generally love it. It's unusual and people remember that. You can get Indian food when you go out, especially in San Francisco, but how many people actually serve it at home?

Such dinner parties become elaborate both through the featuring of exotic menus and through the serving of a succession of courses throughout the meal: appetizers, soups, salads, main courses, coffee and tea, desserts, and after-dinner drinks. These dinner parties often feature higher-quality wines, and the higher-status participants often know something about the wine; this becomes part of the conversation of the evening.

In sum, the dinner party serves as an opportunity for the creation and maintenance of class distinction.

Class differences impact the character and extent of everyday meals as well. More affluent families spend less time in preparing meals for everyday consumption than do the less affluent. A number of factors contribute to this. First, the more affluent eat out quite frequently. One in five lesbigay families report eating four or more meals per week in restaurants. Those who eat out more often earn higher incomes. Second, the more affluent use labor-saving devices like microwaves and food processors more frequently. Third, they often purchase prepared meals from upscale delis and fresh pasta shops. All of this purchasing feeding work in the marketplace enables more affluent couples to achieve a greater degree of egalitarianism in their relationships. These couples resemble the dual-career heterosexual couples studied by Hertz (1986). To the outside observer, and to the participants, affluent lesbigay families are more egalitarian in terms of feeding work, and they purchase that equality in the marketplace. As Hertz so eloquently argues:

> On the surface, dual-career couples appear to be able to operate as a self-sufficient nuclear family. Nonetheless, they are dependent as a group and as individuals on a category of people external to the family. Couples view their ability to purchase this service as another indication of their self-sufficiency (or "making it"). Yet, appearances are deceptive. … What appears to be self-sufficiency for one category of workers relies on the existence of a category of less advantaged workers (p. 194).

Accordingly, scanning the lesbian and particularly the gay-male enclaves of San Francisco one discovers a preponderance of food service establishments offering relatively cheap and convenient meals: taquerias, Thai restaurants, pasta shops, hamburger joints, Chinese restaurants, and delis. Most of these establishments employ women, ethnic and racial minorities, and less educated, less affluent gay men. The low wages earned by these workers enable more affluent lesbigay families to purchase meals in the marketplace and to avoid conflicts over feeding work. Many affluent lesbigay families report deciding to simply eat out rather than face the hassle of planning, preparing, and cleaning up after meals. Less affluent families may not make that choice, and thus they spend much more time and effort in the production of routine meals.

Feeding Work and the Production of Ethnic Identity

While one's social-class status influences whether one attends dinner parties with much frequency, those families with strong ethnic identifications do report more shared meals. Among these groups the sharing of food, and the ethnic character of that food, becomes an important expression of ethnic heritage and cultural identity. Gary Hosokowa, an Asian-American of Hawaiian descent, speaks of the centrality of his *hula* group to his social life and understands that group in familial terms. In response to a question about how he thinks about family, Gary replies:

> It's really strange, hard to explain. In Hawaiian culture, your *hula* group is family. In ancient times, the *hula* teacher would choose students to become *hula* dancers and they would live

together and become family. They ate together, slept together. They were picked from their own family groups and became part of another family group. *My hula* group is my family, we eat together, we dance together. It is very deep, spiritual thing for me.

For Gary, the sharing of meals functions to create and sustain ethnic identity.

In like manner, Michael Herrera and Frederico Monterosa, a Latino couple together for three years who live with a young lesbian women, Jenny Dumont, consider themselves a family. They also speak of a larger family, consisting of other Latino and non-Latino friends, as well as Federico's cousins. Michael and Frederico report recurrent dinner and brunch gatherings, often featuring Mexican foods. Michael remarks:

> We like to make enchiladas a lot, and sometimes we have meat, like beef or something, but always with a Mexican soup for our family gatherings. We get together every couple of weeks. It's very important to me. It's one thing that I think a lot of my Anglo friends feel really envious about, we sort of have a family and many of them don't.

When comparing the appeal of ethnically identified foods to the upper strata of the lesbigay community (mostly Euro-Americans) with the appeal of such foods to the Asian and Latino participants it becomes clear that the food symbolizes very different things for each group. For the affluent lesbigay families the food represents creativity and contributes to the entertaining atmosphere of the dinner party. It carries status due to its exoticness and the difficulty of its preparation.

In contrast, among Asian and Latino lesbigay participants, food expresses ethnic heritage and symbolizes ethnic solidarity, and sometimes resistance to cultural assimilation. Many Asian and Latino participants pride themselves not on the variety of cuisine but on the consistent replication of the same cuisine and even the same meals.

Feeding Work and the Production of Family

Feeding work plays a pivotal role in the construction of lesbigay families. The comments of meal planners/preparers suggest a conscious effort to create a sense of family through their feeding work. For instance, Kathy Atwood and Joan Kelsey, a lesbian couple in their mid-thirties and living in a sort of lesbian enclave in the Oakland neighborhood of Rockridge, both speak of sharing meals as constitutive of family. Kathy, talking about why she considers some of her close friends as family, says, "Well, we eat with them and talk to them frequently. I have known one of them for a very long time. They are people we could turn to in need. They are people who invite us over for dinner and people with whom we spend our fun times and because of that, I think of them as family."

Other participants point to sharing meals, as well as jointly preparing the meals, as evidence of family. Fanny Gomez and Melinda Rodriguez have been together for nine years. Fanny does much of the feeding work for the family. Fanny tells of how she and a close friend, Jenny, whom she considers a part of the family, actually get together to prepare meals for holidays and birthdays.

> I certainly think of Jenny as family. She is the partner of the couple friend that I mentioned earlier. She and I get together to plan meals and celebrations. It feels like family to me when we

talk, go shop together, and then cook the meals. I mean, it's like family when we eat the meal together, too, it's just that preparing the meal, I guess, it reminds me of working with my mother in her kitchen.

For Fanny, the planning, provisioning, and preparation of the meal constitutes family. The feeding work of Fanny and Kathy links material and interpersonal needs together and results in the creation of family.

We have seen that feeding work within lesbigay families is neither inconsequential nor simple. Strangely, much conversation and academic analysis concerning feeding work reduces the complexity of the enterprise, minimizes its significance, and legitimates the view held by many participants that they don't really do very much feeding work—a view held by those who do it as well as by those who don't. In part we can explain this sentiment by remembering that those who feed often lack the vocabulary to articulate their efforts to others. Few people will tell others that they spent part of their day monitoring the contents of their refrigerator, but they do. Such work remains invisible. We must also understand that many participants diminish feeding because they don't want to face the conflict that a thorough accounting, as I have just provided, might produce in their relationship. Moreover, given the potential for stigma that exists for the men who feed, and the women who don't, it becomes even clearer why the work of feeding remains particularly hidden in lesbigay households.

Finally, concealing the labors of feeding reflects the cultural tendency to romanticize domestic activities as well as to romanticize the relationships such activities create. Spotlighting the labor involved tarnishes the romantic luster that people attach to domesticity. I can't count how many times I have heard people who feed respond to compliments saying, "Oh, it was nothing really." Perhaps this is just a matter of self-deprecation, but it might also suggest a cultural cover-up of the laborious character of such efforts. The dinner guests don't really want to hear about the three different stores one went to in search of the ingredients, nor the process of planning and preparing the meal, nor the fight one had with one's spouse about whom to invite or what to serve. A thorough investigation of the labors involved in feeding the family reveals that feeding is work. Recognizing feeding as work raises the impertinent question of why the effort goes uncompensated, a question that leads directly to issues of exploitation and inequality, issues ripe with the potential for social and family conflict.

Given the social precariousness of lesbian and gay relationships, mostly due to the lack of social, political, and economic resources, the tendency of the participants to avoid such conflicts is probably essential to their long-term survival. When some resources exist, as in the case of economic resources, assuaging such conflicts becomes easier. When ample economic resources exist, feeding becomes less arduous with affluent families turning to the marketplace for meals and preparing meals at home teaming with creativity, quality, symbolic meaning, and nutritional content. When lesbigay families lack economic resources, as is the case among many of the working/service-class families, feeding looks different: routine, fatiguing, nutritionally compromised, and symbolically arid (in the sense that the capacity of feeding to produce a sense of family is compromised). Participants rarely conceive of eating ramen noodle soup on the couch as constitutive of their claim to family status, but they frequently conceive of eating a nutritionally complete meal at dining-room table as constitutive of such a claim.

References

Berk, S. Fenstermacher (1985) *The Gender Factory: The Apportionment of Work in American Households*. New York: Plenum Press.

Bourdieu, P. (1984) *Distinction: A Social Critique of the Judgment of Taste*. Cambridge, Mass.: Harvard University Press.

Cahill, S. (1989) Fashioning males and females: Appearance management and the social reproduction of gender. *Symbolic Interaction*, 12 (2): 281–98.

Collins, R. (1992) Women and the production of status cultures. In M. Lamont and M. Fournier, eds., *Cultivating Differences: Symbolic Boundaries and the Making of Inequality*. Chicago: University of Chicago Press.

Coltrane, S. (1989) Household labor and the routine production of gender. *Social Problems*, 36 (5): 473–90.

DeVault, M. (1991) *Feeding the Family: The Social Organization of Caring as Gendered Work*. Chicago: University of Chicago Press.

Goffman, E. (1977) The arrangement between the sexes. *Theory and Society*, 4 (Fall): 301–31.

Hertz, R. (1986). *More Equal Than Others: Women and Men in Dual-Career Marriages*. Berkeley: University of California Press.

Hochschild, A. (1983) *The Managed Heart: Commercialization of Human Feeling*. Berkley: University of California Press.

Kessler, S. and W. McKenna (1978) *Gender: An Ethnomethodological Approach*. Chicago: University of Chicago Press.

Warren, C. (1974) *Identity and Community in the Gay World*. New York: John Wiley.

West, C. and D. Zimmerman (1987) Doing Gender. *Gender and Society*, 1 (2): 125–51.

15

Thinking Race Through Corporeal Feminist Theory: Divisions and Intimacies at the Minneapolis Farmers' Market*

Rachel Slocum

Introduction

The Minneapolis Farmers' Market is simultaneously constituted by connections made through difference as well as multiple forms of exclusion, by bigoted ideas but also clear curiosity and pleasure. A theory of race that rests on the raced body's practices in connection to food, market space and different visitors needs to recognize racial inequality, non-racist acts and anti-racist encounters. Drawing from an ongoing ethnography, this paper explores the divisions and intimacies of everyday practice that produce the embodied racial geography of the Market. It does so in order to explain how racialized bodies emerge through this food space.

Opening in 1876 as a wholesale market with over 400 growers, the Minneapolis Farmers' Market (hereafter the MFM or the Market) is now a retail enterprise scaled back to 240 vendors, including both producers and 'dealers' who resell goods purchased whole-sale. The Market's three red-roofed, open sheds stand opposite the interstate. When not in full swing, it is a desolate location absent of pedestrians, dwellings or shops; its soundscape, the hiss of cars rushing by on the highway ramps above. The Market provides space for vendors through permanent places, some of them handed down through generations. 'Dailies', vendors without a permanent spot, get assigned different locations depending on the availability of temporarily unused stalls. The market manager answers to the board consisting of ten older men and two women who govern the MFM. The majority European-white population of growers, some of whose families have been at the market for five generations, was augmented by the arrival in the 1970s of Hmong immigrants.[1] Hmong people now constitute almost 1 per cent of the Minnesota population, but approximately 40 per cent of the vendors, and two of the twelve board members.

To some, the Market is a crowded, bustling, confusing urban space on the weekends. It serves a diverse group of urban and suburban customers. In this diversity

*Originally published 2008

are Latinos, Russians, Eastern Europeans, Scandinavians and various other white ethnicities, Vietnamese, Hmong, Chinese, South Asian, Somalis, East Africans and American Indians. On summer weekends up to Labor Day, in addition to being a shopping place, the MFM is also a tourist attraction during which time the throngs of people are noticeably more white. But prices at the MFM for local and non-local goods are typically not high and the fact that the MFM is *not* a growers-only market makes it more inviting to a greater race- and class-diverse population.

This space is also constituted by the globalization of food production, transport and consumption that pushed the MFM from wholesale into retail and which today makes it more difficult for some smaller vendors to market their goods. In the context of the neoliberal discourse of personal responsibility (for one's body size, health and welfare), the new urbanism and alternative food, the Market's presence is awkward. The Twin Cities is home to newer immigrant communities, arriving under different terms, including peoples from Laos, Somalia and Latin America. The nostalgia for quiet, safe 'American' communities meets the Market: a rambunctious place for Minnesota, with diverse customers and, for some publics, strange vegetables. The Market troubles the pervasiveness of hyper-commodified, sanitized and segregated public spaces (which is not to suggest it is not itself sanitized, commodified and segregated).

This paper contributes in three areas. First, the literature on embodied geographies has tended to focus on representations of bodies, revealing how bodies are inscribed by society, or has relied on the concept of performativity. In contrast, this paper deploys corporeal feminist theory in which the body's materiality is foregrounded. Second, the paper enhances scholarship on race by claiming, through this materialist framework, that it is important to speak of race through phenotypic differentiations, connections, tendencies and what bodies do. Third, by focusing on embodied racial geographies in a farmers' market, this study contributes to a growing body of work on such markets in the Global North.

Farmers' Markets, Corporeality, Race

Farmers' Markets

To the sites of the dinner table, the kitchen, recipe books and supermarkets (Bell and Valentine 1997), this paper adds a less studied area: the farmers' market. Farmers' markets have recently experienced a renaissance in the USA and their numbers have burgeoned (Brown 2002). A valuable public space, the market is a crossroads for different foods, bodies and discourses that shape the city and the agro-ecological region. Spatial processes and varying mobilities of people and goods converge to constitute the MFM within uneven relations of power (Massey 1994). Here, there are brief, pleasurable meeting points that need to be recognized along-side the comparatively invisible violence of systemic processes.

Farmers' markets have been constituted by discourses of quality and nationalism as well as consumer distrust of the state (Ilbery and Kneafsey 2000). Ideals of localness and quality become conflated as consumers assume something local is more authentic or healthier (Futamura 2007; Holloway and Kneafsey 2000). Some research suggests that these markets may encourage social networks (Gerbasi 2006) through the 'relations of regard' that develop (Sage 2003) or via consumer requests for sustainable practices (Hunt 2007). While the farmers' market could enable practices that change social relations, they may also reaffirm entrepreneurialism and individualism (see Gregson and Crewe 1997). Markets should not be seen as only the location of celebration and community; such nostalgia renders invisible the conditions that shape the market (Stallybrass and White 1986). This nostalgia is deeply racialized (Watson and Wells 2005).

The alternative food movement uses farmers' markets as vehicles to improve food access and encourage sustainable farming. Organizations and consumers interested in local food and sustainable farming tend to be wealthier, more educated and white (Allen 2004). As vehicles to augment grower incomes through better prices, some markets cater implicitly (organic-only, location, music, classes) to a well-off, educated and often white demographic, which I have argued (2007) produces white food space (see also Alkon 2008; Guthman 2008). These accounts undertake important analyses showing how farmers' markets are formed through various discourses and what work these meanings do. This paper is concerned, instead, with the bodies, things, movements and clustering, that are necessary to meaning.

A sensual space where connections among particular natures and certain foods are more deeply valorized (Kirwan 2004; Parrott, Wilson and Murdoch 2002), farmers' markets are spaces of intimacy. Considering intimacy between the human and more than human brings the materiality of both into focus. Sarah Whatmore (2002: 162), for instance, writes that 'the rhythms and motions of inter-corporeal practices [growing, provisioning, cooking and eating] configure spaces of connectivity between more-than-human life worlds; topologies of intimacy and affectivity that confound conventional cartographies of distance and proximity, and local and global scales'. Similarly, Emma Roe (2006) suggests attention to the visceral relations and embodied practices involved in eating and being eaten as a means to understand food fear or interest in organic. The biochemical and physical properties of vegetables sold at the MFM intimately shape human bodies and the city. The gut, after all, 'allows the outside world to pass through us' and in so doing, it maintains relationships with others (Wilson 2004: 44). In this public space, 'negotiation is forced upon us' (Massey 2005: 114). The paper is interested in those spoken and silent negotiations and even more so in the frisson of contact,[2] the mix of fear, surprise and wonder.

Embodiment, to which I turn next, is indispensable to this analysis of race, division and intimacy. Sensory exchange constitutes much of the sense of place of the Market. Different bodies brush against one another, smell tomatoes, exclaim with curiosity and lean with heavy bags. Bodies respond differently to the properties of foods—their taste, smell, color, consistency, temperature, vitamin content, calories and ripeness. What counts as embodied in this paper encompasses *what* people do, say, sense and feel as well as *how* they do any of these things.

Embodiment in Feminist Materialist Theory

Geographers have expressed great interest in the body, contributing to feminist philosophy by showing how space and embodied difference are co-constitutive processes (e.g. Ainley 1998; Bell et al. 2001; Butler and Parr 1999; Teather 1999; Nast and Pile 1998; Pile 1996; Rose 1995). Bodies become gendered through activities in place and the place itself is active in the production of capacities. But despite the apparent enthusiasm for the concept of embodiment, Robyn Longhurst (1997, 2001) proposes that in geography bodies continue to be represented while their fleshiness is held at bay. Yet the ways bodies fit snugly into airplane seats (Longhurst 2005), throw a ball (Young 2005) or are leaky, messy and rubbery are important to consider as part of a political as well as a conceptual argument.

A contentious point within feminist theory has been the question of how to talk about physically different bodies without reifying that difference (Williams and Bendelow 1998). One means was to focus on how society's norms shape bodies. But social constructionism understood matter as pre-existing and unintelligible and had not theorized how sexual oppression occurs at the 'level of the constitution of bodily materiality as sexed' (Cheah 1996: 111). The importance and sophistication of performativity as a response to these inadequacies cannot be overstated. But as it has been articulated by Judith Butler (1993), the matter of bodies is mediated by discourse and therefore comprehensible only through that mediation. Pheng Cheah (1996) finds that Butler excludes natural materiality and instead confines matter to human morphology which the latter understands as already cultural. For Butler, 'materiality becomes present, is given body, … only in being … signified in language' (1996: 116). Yet, asks Jacinta Kerin,

> If we insist on conflating ontological inquiry *per se* with the way in which it has worked historically within dominant knowledges then the possibility of thinking otherwise is foreclosed How can we decide what it means to affirm an array of materialities unless we are permitted some, however contingent, ontological concept of what those materialities are? (1999: 99–100)

Kerin points out that feminists cannot afford *not* to engage with matter—its existence, its necessity and its bearing on interpretation. For Elizabeth Wilson (2004: 8), engaging with matter means not sidestepping the neurological and biochemical, as she claims many humanities and social science accounts of the body have done. Exploring what may, at first glance, appear essentialist or reductionist is useful, she argues, to the feminist project.

Far from being a tired topic, the discussion of nature and culture has only just begun. Some of the most interesting contributions to that conversation have come from Elizabeth Grosz. Her philosophical positioning of nature and culture provides the ground from which to speak of the body's mattering.[3] No dismissal of work concerned with epistemology occurs; the question for Grosz (2005: 5) is the debt representation owes to ontology. Culture, she writes, drawing on Darwin, is not the completion of an incomplete nature. Instead, nature 'enables and actively facilitates cultural variation and change'; the biological incites culture, but nature does not limit the cultural. Culture and representation have an outside that impinges on the plans of the living (see Clark 2005). The competing forces of this outside induce subjectivity and make culture act and change (Grosz 2005: 30–31, 43, 47–49).

Earlier, Grosz (1994) had argued that all aspects of the subject can be just as adequately explained through bodies as through the mind or consciousness. Bodies are biological and sensory, not merely blank slates for inscription by society and not biologically-given entities with particular destinies. Generating 'what is new, surprising, unpredictable' (Grosz 1994: xi), bodies are the 'passage from being to becoming', thus what bodies do is to continually form themselves ('positive becoming') (Colebrook 2000: 86–87). Bodies become through what they do, the relations of which they are a part and the formations in which they act. Corporeality, then, refers to a dynamic capacity of human bodies to emerge in relation to each other and to things, within social and physical limits, and thereby to form sexual and racial identities (Grosz 2005). While these differences are not limited to those forms we currently acknowledge, they are not 'open to self conscious manipulation, identification or control by subjects' (2005: 89). A body's capacities, finally, are always enabled or limited by the socio-physical space in which they are located (Saldanha 2007).

In geography, an interest in ethics and particularly affect and emotion has emerged to focus attention on material bodies. For instance, Sarah Whatmore (2002) argues that without the body being understood in terms of its corporeality, it will be difficult to develop ethical relationships within more-than-human worlds. Some of this work has emerged from non-representational theory (see Harrison 2008; Obrador-Pons 2007) and some is explicitly feminist (Ahmed 2004; Bondi, Davidson and Smith 2005; Tolia-Kelly 2006). The paper draws on the latter's work, which Grosz refers to as 'a phenomenology of everyday life' (Kontturi and Tiainen 2007: 252). Thus the examples I provide can be situated in both the realm of the intentional (disdain for those who bargain) and the unintentional: 'the impersonal or pre-personal, subhuman or inhuman forces ... competing microagencies' beyond the control of the subject (Grosz 2005: 6).

The feminist materialist scholarship that provides the inspiration for this paper can be read as arguing for an appraisal of race as embodied, non-essentialist being, not only that which is discursive or performed. I am not making the claim that this theory is useful because I think that what is true for sex/gender is also true for race. Sex, even though it is many, differentiates people biologically and socially in a way that is not true for race. But the point is that these feminist theorists have taken the important step of engaging with the body's matter rather than dismissing such an interest as pre-critical and dangerously essentialist.

The Materiality of Race

Race tends to be understood as a consequence of societies' ideas that become productive truths about people. Significant work has gone into underscoring the racist history, genetic irrelevance and arbitrariness of racial categories. From this, many have argued *'there is no such thing as race'* (Nayak 2006, his italics) and further, that the fiction that is race must be abolished (Gilroy 2000). Different approaches to race and racism rely on these ideas. From sociology and legal studies, critical race scholars argue that racism has been perpetuated by institutions of law and emphasize deconstruction to undermine racist narratives, relying on personal experience and storytelling to build others (Delgado and Stefancic 2001). Drawing on the concept of performativity, Anoop Nayak finds that in some critical race writing, racial groups are positioned as at once fictional, relational and tangibly irreducible ... [unable to] 'escape the body politic' (2006: 416). He argues that figures such as 'white women' have to be understood as part of historically and geographically specific processes (see Kobayashi and Peake 1994) 'that constitute this subjectivity as intelligible, and [as part of] the symbolic regimes of language that summon this representation to life' (Nayak 2006: 417). Whether using the language of construction (Jackson 1998) and reconstruction (of whiteness) (Gallaher 2002), memories and performance (Hoelscher 2003), or performance and space (Thomas 2005), there is an emphasis on the social, on representations of the real and implicit or explicit use of the work of Judith Butler. Even a work dedicated to 'making race matter' (Alexander and Knowles 2005) is still primarily about performance and the dangers of linking race in any way to biology.

Building on these important contributions, the paper argues that it is not enough to talk about constructions or performance, leaving the body's matter out of the analysis (Saldanha 2006; see also Moore, Pandian and Kosek 2003). Indeed, fictionalizing race makes some of the most interesting aspects of race disappear, whether the focus is an affective historiography of race (Anderson 2007), the embodied experience of displacement and segregation (Delaney 2002) or the embedding of race in the body (Wade 2004). Writing on white hyper-sensitivity to smell in the Ecuadorian Andes, Weismantel claims:

> It is in the interactions between bodies and the substances they ingest, the possessions they accumulate, and the tools they use to act on the world [that] we can really see race being made, and making the society around it. This kind of race is neither genetic nor symbolic, but organic: a constant, physical process of interaction between living things. Little surprise then that it has a distinct smell. (2001: 266)

I turn now to the emphasis of this paper: the tendencies and actions of raced bodies.

Race becomes material through the body. Groupings of bodies do things and are 'done to', becoming racialized in the process (Grosz 2005). From this perspective, bodies are not only inscribed; they actively participate in the material production of themselves and other bodies. Race takes shape out of the physical gathering of bodies in which phenotype matters in its connection to material objects, practices and processes (Saldanha 2007). The term phenotype does *not* indicate any essential connections, but it and other visible characteristics (e.g. clothes) are recognized in real, everyday interactions and so play a role in what people do. Bodies stare at each other, or are glimpsed or ignored; they are moved or forced to stop; some meander, others stride; giving way and standing ground, they prevent and enable. In this sense, what happens to bodies, what they do and the fact that they tend to be white or brown in certain places are all important to consider with the aim of understanding how and why that happened. Race, then, is a process, made and remade not just by exclusions and erasures, but by its ongoing connections (Saldanha 2006).

Skin is 'a site of subjectivity, crisis, desire, instability' and thus has productive potential in day-to-day practices (Ahmed 1998 cited by Johnston 2005: 112). In Lynda Johnston's example, beach space and the activities that take place there produce bodies with specific desires and capacities. Skin changes color, confusing one's sense of 'who's who'. Some white bodies lying on beaches became darker and were taken for Maori. Phenotype, of course, should not be understood as referring to the visible form of an interior essence. Phenotypic differences produce mobile and gradual groups, made through processes that change these groupings of bodies—their color, shape, size and health. Such change may occur over a lifetime, with inter-racial off-spring, through generations or because of wealth or poverty. Equally, bodily changes may be a consequence of not having enough food or enough of certain foods and it may be due to how bodies are physically implicated in and shaped by capitalism, patriarchy, neocolonialism and so on. People are phenotypically different and structurally organized into populations that are endlessly disrupted, and therefore temporary, contingent upon class, sexuality, nationality, age and gender. The materiality of race does not refer to innate differences nor does it map phenotype, posture, clothes, language, accent, gestures or gait to 'a race', because there are no 'races', but it does refer to bodies.

The ways people sense worlds is part of how differences are shaped. Mark Smith (2006) proposes that restoring hearing, smell, touch and taste to an understanding of racial difference might shed some new light on how unthinkingly race is made and racism learned. In his account, white southerners had ways of determining whether someone was 'black' by smell, touch, taste and sound—because vision was not always reliable. Yet it is clear that 'seeing remains ... extraordinarily important for locating racial identity' (Smith 2006: 3). Rather than posit the visual as an 'all determining foundation of race' (Brown 2005: 273, n14–16), the claim I make is that (observed) bodies are one part in a series of intersections. These bodily differences are noticed (in particular ways in this racist society) and they enable what occurs at the Market, in ways that limit and open avenues, supporting ethical engagement, mobilizing confusion, activating prejudice or reinforcing inequality. Though I acknowledge sound, smell and touch, vision remains central to this account. I also use vendor and customer vision because it is unreliable, contributing to raced imaginaries and productive uncertainty about raced bodies. That a physical knot of whiteness around some foods, for instance, happens is something that should be discussed. Equally, when diverse bodies encounter each other through leafy greens when they ordinarily might not, race should not be left out of the analysis.

When I use the term 'Hmong growers', rather than suggesting that this group 'has' a discrete and pre-formed identity, I understand 'Hmongness' as a process of becoming. Instead of an argument that makes uncritical use of descriptive demographic facts, I propose using the term 'white farmer' or 'Hmong grower' as something dynamic that includes phenotype and land ownership, clothes and speech, types of vegetables sold and generations at the market. I recognize that Hmong farmers are seen as different by some customers and known as Hmong by many vendors. Emergent 'Hmongness' is embodied through, for instance, the sale of bitter green and collards, facial features, wearing 'traditional' dress or a tie, having a CIA identity card. It becomes through the suggestion that I watch *The Fast and the Furious: Tokyo Drift* to understand Asian/Hmong fast car culture. 'Hmong' means vending for fifteen years compared to four generations, renting as opposed to owning land, and, according to some white vendors, it means 'under-pricing the market'. Race is an active process in which Hmong emerges as the object of white liberal interest which wants to help Hmong people through land donations. Hmong becoming at the Market is active in a question about my 'racial background' which arises because I have 'such blue eyes'.

The aim here is to be able to talk about the material tendencies racially differentiating bodies without making racist statements or authorizing essentialist identity politics. Understanding how racially different bodies emerge through practices provides different insights into race. What follows is an attempt to work through the particular challenges that arise in talking about racial embodiment and to demonstrate how the Market makes sense through this lens.

Methods

Observation, inclusive of vision, sense of smell, hearing and touch, is a method necessary for this paper's argument. I draw on participant observation as well as informal and formal interviews conducted from May 2006 to March 2008. The research has moved between naturalistic observation and participant observation—in other words it has ranged from conversation, interview, peripheral membership and active membership in a social crowd (Adler and Adler 1998). My observations have noted routines, rituals, spaces, organization, interactions, behavior and clothing (Denzin 1989). I took photos to study later and tried vegetables unfamiliar to me. I undertook naturalistic observation of the Market on most weekends in 2006 during the late spring, summer and fall months from 6 a.m. until 2 p.m. as well as during the week at different times and on different days. I have attended one board meeting, at which I discussed the research and one annual membership meeting in March 2008. The research also involves making sense of overheard exclamations and questions.

I have done structured interviews with the market manager, several vendors, a member of the Minnesota State Department of Agriculture, the Minneapolis mayor and a close associate, four local non-profit leaders and a researcher working on Hmong agriculture. Additionally, I have followed Twin Cities food activism and visited other markets. Unstructured interviews took place at the Market with resellers, growers, customers and custodial staff as well as by email and letter with some vendors over the 2006 2008 seasons and off season as well. Typically, I speak to several of the same people each week. All told, I have done informal interviews with about sixty people (vendors and customers). Some of the quotes in the paper are from handwritten notes taken while vendors talked to me or while I listened to others' conversations. Others are from taped and transcribed interviews. The interviews and observations that I draw on are illustrative of themes that have emerged so far in the research. The paper is not an exhaustive statement on the Market but instead offers a way of thinking about these collected observations.

Race as Bodily Practice

Racial difference in the context of the Market is a corporeal relationship to growing, selling and eating food. It emerges through what can be called 'racial practices': the production and marketing of certain plants, the location and quality of someone's land, ideas about 'good' food and the gathering of racially identified people around some vendors and vegetables but not others. Thus food practices that may not usually be associated with race can be called racial practices, but not any fixed sense. At the market, bodies are not just inscribed by food practices; they are materially produced through what people buy, who they talk to, where they grow vegetables, as well as through phenotypic differences (Saldanha 2007). The materiality of practice does not deny that meanings circulate through these actions, but wants to show how it is the matter of race and operating policies, land ownership, vegetables, laughter, pesticide use and touch within the space of the Market that is necessary to meaning.

In the following two sections (racial divisions and public intimacy), I attempt to show how bodies moving around the Market, attaching themselves to some foods, brushing shoulders and being propelled by curiosity are all ways of talking about race as bodily practice.

Racial Divisions at the Market

Race emerges at the Market through four spatial processes: the clustering of bodies around tables; the avoidance of markets with resellers; dress and comportment; and racial imaginaries. As a zone of encounter in a racist society, it would be surprising if race did *not* emerge in this market space through prejudice and separation and so I first consider racial divisions.

Roots and Leaves

Race emerges spatially as bodies ebb and eddy around vendors' stalls. Some bodies search for organic eggs, others move towards amaranth leaves and still others cluster around basil in a neat bunch, without roots, shut inside a hard plastic container. Clear cohesions of white people are evident around the enclosed herbs laid out on a red and white checked tablecloth. Opposite this permanent stall is often a Hmong daily vendor selling much larger bunches of basil, fastened with a rubber band. Desiring food in plastic indicates a particular expectation of how food arrives and what quality means. Other customers come because they have established a relationship with these growers, whose produce also appears in area supermarkets. These clumps of white people are also visible around the locally grown asparagus laid in short, upright, brown paper bags that sells at $6 for one pound, and later, the heirloom[4] melons and potatoes (six dollars for about eight finger potatoes). The expense plus the relationship of these particular foods to the desire for local, fresh, non-conventional food is part of why white people are evident here. Finally, some trust and comfort may come from engaging with a white vendor.

There is something to be learned about race through plants. Racial divisions occur through greens and roots. Hmong tables carry cilantro and onions with bristling roots. These growers have learned that there are Asian and African populations who come to the Market seeking certain vegetables and demanding roots attached. Race emerges through connections among visible difference, a plant, its nutrients and politics, the soil it requires, the land used and the care given its growth. Thus one could say that race is in the leaves. Hmong growers have verdant cascades of amaranth, black nightshade, sweet potato leaves and pigweed. Most white growers do not leave the roots on and they do not supply amaranth or pigweed ('no I don't sell it, it's a weed').

In the third shed, white vendors are clumped at the western end, while most of the rest are Hmong permanent or daily vendors, hence among vendors, it is called the 'Hmong shed'. There are white vendors here who enjoy the company of non-white people and also those who refuse to be situated next to Hmong vendors. In the third shed, as well, are the two Hmong resellers, the only African American vendor and a white flower reseller who employs two African American men. This grizzled reseller spends the morning shouting at customers, one minute cajoling them with a bouquet, and the next, daring them to look away from his aging blossoms. In 2006 a white wild rice daily vendor was situated next to the sole African American vendor in the third aisle, but in 2007 moved to a place in the middle shed. Regardless of how vendors have come to be positioned in the sheds, the cohesions of bodies among the three reveals a racial division of the space.

Caring Where Your Food Comes From

The movement of people at the MFM is also toward other food spaces and this is partly due to the presence of six larger food resellers at the MFM. While vendors of asparagus, certain herbs and meat receive greater concentrations of white customers, a markedly diverse gathering of racialized and classed populations is evident around reseller tables. Some MFM vendors I have spoken with accept the resellers in their midst but some customers do not. Nationwide, farmers' markets are typically for growers only. Alternative food consumers denigrate the resale of non-local foods, going so far as to shop at other markets to avoid the MFM because it allows the practice. One middle-aged white man at the local-only St. Paul market explained to his friends that unlike St. Paul, the goods at the MFM looked like they had 'fallen off the truck on the way to the market'. On the Nicollet Mall downtown (Thursday's MFM location), an older white man in a suit asked a strawberry vendor if he knew where pineapples grew in Minnesota, indicating, with his head, the Hmong-owned reseller behind them. The vendor replied, shaking his head, 'yeah, I call them banana sellers'. This vendor was working for a fairly large-scale conventional farmer—but a more local one.

What I am describing is not as simple as a distaste for resellers or prejudice against the more mixed (class and race) clientele that comes to the MFM, drawn, in part by resellers. Whiteness emerges through the thinking that local is necessarily best and that the St. Paul market is 'more local' as well as through the fact that alternative food tends to be a white movement. It comes into being through the spatial separation of a more white and more middle-class (socially and economically) group from more brown and more working-class people.

There is a sense that the products available and the prices at the MFM bring people who do not recognize the close-to-the-edge profitability and the work involved in sustainable, organic or smaller-scale farming. The fierce demand for cheaply priced food has been observed by some customers and vendors as coming particularly from newer immigrant non-white populations. Indicating toward the flow of people around a reseller, another vendor told me, 'they don't care where their food comes from'. White growers claim that Hmong farmers encourage ignorance of the difficulty of farming by typically charging one dollar for ample bunches of vegetables. But for some it is the established members of the Market whose habits participate in the preference for cheap. Referring to the white, longer-term vendors, one grower remarked, 'they shop at Cub [a local, conventional, low-cost supermarket] and eat at McDonalds'. Finally, a white grower recounted how a white, woman customer told him 'I don't know if I feel like peeling potatoes tonight'. The grower said to me, shaking his head, 'if people don't even want to *peel potatoes*, that's it, I'm finished'. It should be pointed out here that the gendered division of labor is a factor that should not be discounted in discussions of such shopping practices.

Baby Strollers and Lattés

Bodies present themselves differently at the Market. Few shoppers I have seen charge through the Market intent on getting through in minimum time; the experience tends to be more exploratory. Some Asian and African visitors wear high heels, skirts, dress pants or wax prints. Others go to the Market in shorts, sneakers and oversized t-shirts, with coffee in one hand—and these people tend to be white. This same group tends to stroll through the market as they talk with their companions. Advises Beth Dooley (2001), 'Nearly twice as big and much busier than St. Paul's, [the MFM] can be downright daunting. My strategy is this: First, go to Neon Coffee in the northwest corner for a latte′ … '. White people can be differentiated as middle class because they have a canvas bag from the expensive organic chain, Whole Foods, over their shoulder. Elderly bodies are also here, but I have seen only a few with wheeled baskets to tote food. Women originally from an African nation in bright cotton prints come at 5:30–7 a.m. to negotiate for large bags of greens, moving these to the trunks of cars and coming back for more. In a quantity sufficient to last the winter, these greens will be cooked and frozen. This group may come so early because it suits their schedule, because the leaves are more fresh or it may have something to do with the increasing presence of white bodies the later it gets. Regardless of the reason, the composition of bodies changes and changes the meaning of this space over the hours of the morning.

Children are brought to the Market as part of a shopping or a tourist experience. Strollers pushed by men and women of color tend to have bags full of produce slung over the handles of strollers and under the seat. Strollers are evident even during the busiest part of the day when the aisles are nearly impassable. One white middle-class father, pushing his child in a baby carriage, said, 'We're going to see lots today'. He falls into the tourist category. Vendors call tourists 'basket kickers'—people who come to look but not to buy. While not always a white practice, basket kicking is the domain of those who have the leisure time and no need or wish to purchase anything from a farmers' market. Market tourism is also associated with cooking demonstrations and musical guests. Having fun at the farmers' market is encouraged as one of the key aims of the Mill City Market. Last year its website called on residents to '[j]oin local healing art practitioners for health lectures, demos & mini-sessions exploring mind and body work such as Qi Gong, Tibetan medicine, Thai yoga massage, herbalogy, homeopathy, meditation, acupuncture, dance, boot camp fitness and eating like food matters'.[5] The Eastern emphasis often associated with the new age movement can be loosely linked with a white, middle-class demographic.

Comfort Zones and Confusion

Constituting this space are racial imaginaries in which the perceived clarity of race is brought into relief through observations that are sometimes prejudicial. Vendors mistaking East Africans for African Americans appears to be the norm, but a woman vendor observes that she can clearly pick out features of African American, Somali and Ethiopian customers. One vendor suggested, with considerable enthusiasm, that the 'Somali' women who come early to buy large bags of 'okra' (noted in previous sub-section) might be engaged in something illicit. An older white vendor, told me that there are lots of African Americans who come to the Market, contrary to what I had noticed. When I said as much, he told me, 'if you turn around, I think you'll see they're here'. I did and there were people standing further down the aisle, but they were from an African country. I could tell because of how they were dressed (button down shirt, tucked in, slacks), what they were buying (bitter green) and the quantities they were purchasing. Had I been closer I might have discerned differences in gestures, stance or accents. There is no point calling this ignorance. Instead, I am intrigued by the wish to see, the act of seeing something else and the inexorable fuzziness of race.

   People of color from global non-US cultures are said to disturb the 'comfort zone' of white customers and thus the lower sales volume can be attributed, in part, to their presence. This (racist) comfort zone is placed with equanimity alongside other reasons for fewer sales like gas prices, the weather or construction. A young white vendor with whom I was talking about the purchase of greens by Africans asked me if I saw whether they used cash. He proposed that I would 'see a lot of them using food stamps'. His statement is familiarly prejudiced as it connects skin color to something opprobrious in the mainstream national imaginary—the use of government support. Some white farmers claim that Hmong growers get special assistance, which they do not deserve and are able to succeed largely through this and the help of children. A customer remarked, as she walked by some mong kids behind a table, 'I thought child labor was illegal'. Other imaginaries mobilized are claims made by Hmong people that farming is something Hmong women and elderly Hmong do. An African American man complained that Somalis refuse to talk with blacks ('we got bombed by Somalis'), Asians always want cheap produce and Latinos are 'not invasives', implying that others are. One middle-aged white male farmer noted that it is people from the Middle East who bargain most fiercely. 'Those people', he said, pointing in an obvious way to what appeared to be a South Asian family walking past at that moment. As he pointed, they looked back at him.

This section has offered examples of how racial division emerges through stereotypes, movement, location and production of plants—bodily practices. If embodiment concerns the characteristics of bodies and what people do, race is embodied at the Market through attractions to vegetables that segregate the space as well as the ways some racialized groups think other racialized groups act.

Public Intimacy and Encounter

So far I have discussed racial divisions and essentialist productions of racial difference. Now I turn to a public intimacy that also constitutes the Market and could be productive of other, non-racist ways of living and doing race. Writing about race and domestic intimacy, Ann Laura Stoler suggests that 'strangely familiar "uncanny" intimacies. … may leave room for relations that promise something else, that activate desires and imaginaries less easily named' (2006: 14). Guiding this section is Stoler's point that intimacy provides a view into both structures of dominance *and* the promise of 'something else'. Race emerges through the encounters I discuss below as well as through the separations outlined above.

Intimacy, a spatial process of tense and tender ties, does not require proximity but needs to consider alterity (Thien 2005, see also Fortier 2007). The world becomes intimate with the gut through the alterity of food; stomach problems indicate the breakdown of relations with others (Wilson 2004). Echoing this, a local food advocate at a Twin Cities gathering to 'build community and dismantle racism' suggests 'we have two things in common: food and isolation'. In this paper, intimacy refers to the domestic, public act of food provisioning. It is embodied through the seemingly mundane yet critically important acts of seeing, smelling, touching, anticipating, wondering about food, all of which are shared in public space by different bodies. A practical politics of the intimate reveals the home in the world, a realm of untidy, unruly bodiliness (Fidecaro 2006: 255).

The Market enables an intimacy absent in other spaces of consumption such as malls, supermarkets and gas stations. Alphonso Lingis (1998) writes of encounter through travel (even to a market), which people undertake to lose their identity. Travel forces the imprisoning skin of privilege to become recognizable to some. The more meanings we ascribe to others' ways, the more bodies become hidden and the violence of stereotype arises. It is the inexpressiveness of the body, unconnected from the lines of inscription that excites.

The intimacy present at the Market is one of contact, connecting people's lives outside the Market to this food moment through small talk, questions asked about food, seeing the same farmer, the smell of earth on the wind and touching vegetables. Pleasure, in this context, is not only an individual experience; it emerges among bodies and things in place. Looking at pleasure shows the intimacy of human contact in which race matters though it may not be the only or primary organizing feature. I will cover four types of public intimacy: public eating and desire, curiosity about foods, chatting and bargaining. These minutiae are food practices that are also racial, bodily practices.

Roasted Corn and Honey Space

One of the most popular sites for public eating is the roasted corn stand. On one end of the stall next to boxes of Florida-grown sweet corn, an eight-foot roaster stands, slowly rotating unhusked corn up and out of sight until they return, blackened on the outside and brilliant cooked yellow on the inside. The corn is removed from the roaster, a green ear taking its place, the cooked corn moves on to be husked, dry leaves pulled back to hug the stalk, then to the butterer, a woman who also collects your two dollars and then finally to the customer who goes off to shake cayenne, lemon or just salt on the redolent, dripping ear. The corn is sweet, crunchy and hot. The workers are usually one Latino man and two Latina women. On summer weekends there is a line of ten to twelve people waiting patiently. Standing in the scent of hot butter and corn, people bite into their ears, or, cob in hand they walk through the Market. Sharing in this pleasurable intimacy of eating publicly, market goers make this stand the most racially diverse place in the Market.[6] Because the stand is here and because it is corn that is sold (which appears to appeal to different populations), different bodies are concentrated and thus come into eating contact when the other spaces of their lives would probably not enable such interaction.

Honey space is also more fractured: the single-source raw honey vendor with the more labor-intensive honey-collecting practice and the more expensive glass jars has high racial diversity. Standing by his stall, I heard people driven to seek honeys similar to those from other places they called home. I listened to conversations the vendor initiates about the epidemic of bee deaths and the low quality of heated honey sourced from China and sold in conventional supermarkets. He knows about the shades and tastes of honeys from other parts of the world and suggests which of his honeys—the dark amber Buckwheat to the lighter Basswood—might be similar. He provides samples to taste. With a good location, a range of products (pollen, dried apples, candles, honey comb) and a glass case full of bees at a child's eye level, this honey vendor draws many older and younger bodies. In 2006 I heard a woman from a European country talking with the vendor about how the honey is like that from her country of origin. I recognized her again in 2007. We talked about honey, the coarse, brown bread that is no longer available in her other country, and then about blue eggs that were once sold at the Market. Honey space and the conversations that shape it suggest that the MFM is potentially a zone of interaction in which different bodies meet through desire for foods lost and found.

Curiosity Toward the Unknown

The pleasure of curiosity can be associated with some bodies. Curiosity about growing practices and unknown vegetables is mostly a white middle-class tendency at the Market. They ask, 'What's this?' as they touch the bitter melon, feeling its chartreuse ridges. It is more often than not someone white who asks a Hmong grower, 'Did you grow these? Did you pick these this morning? Where do you farm? Where is your garden? How big is it? Do you use pesticides?' These questions may be provoked in part by skepticism about the Market's localness because resellers also vend there.

They may indicate the intensity of alternative food fervor. A discourse productive of the Market is Hmong misuse of pesticides ('Hmong growers think if some is good, more is better'), which may also explain these questions. Alternatively, the questions may emerge from customers' interest or desire to talk.

It is true, as some vendors claim, that white people shop at white vendors' stalls. But white people shop at Hmong tables as well and those that do may want to interact with different people, hold 'foreign' objects and try vegetables that are strange to them. Some middle-class white people may travel more, fear less, be more curious and more enabled to try new things than some non-white people. Whiteness at the Market is the security of having all of your vegetables available in many venues. But there is something more going on than security and availability, something more than the impulse to appropriate that moves white shoppers to reach for unknown fruit. Through that reaching, is it possible that other ideas about people and food that open more avenues for ethical engagement might obtain? Of course white people are not the only ones who try new plants. For instance, I watched a Hmong vendor attempting to get a Latina woman to try basil. He told her 'it's used in Italian food'. 'Italian food?' she said dubiously, taking it, smelling the leaves and passing it to an older woman shopping with her. 'Just try it', the grower said, giving it to her. She took it.

The Joy of Small Talk

Pleasure is part of the sensuousness of bodies in this space. People walking in the aisles meet the eyes of people passing. They smile, they look interested or their faces are blank because one can be non-reactive, unthinking, guided forward, without effort, by the swell of the crowd. One woman recounted how she sometimes visits a farmers' market near her home twice during its hours of operation. Her emotional attachment to this market is so great that she felt left out when she overheard the vendors talking of meeting for dinner but did not invite customers. A white MFM producer whose spouse died recently tells me details of the spouse's death and burial during our first conversation. I watched her tell the story to other customers, using an album of photos of her spouse's burial site. She can do this in part because she is a woman and maybe because she has the confidence of middle-class whiteness supporting her. She seemed to think that customers would want to know, would want an explanation. Another white vendor brings beer every weekend, keeping it cold in his refrigerated truck in order to drink and talk with homeless African Americans after the Market closes. His black friends, he tells me, say he's 'black on the inside and white on the outside'. The Market is also one of the few public places in Minneapolis in which I have seen white gay men walking hand in hand and pausing to smell soap.

People are drawn to markets for the opportunity to have conversations with growers. The market is one of a few places where one can speak easily with someone who is not a friend or relative. This opportunity to converse with vendors is routinely mentioned by denizens of farmers' markets as the part of the experience they love. Hmong growers came to realize the importance of this conversational interaction— the possibility of small talk and the desire of consumers to converse with the person who has actually grown the food they buy (Kerr 2007). Hmong farmers bring their children who have grown up using English. It is the youth who call out, asking shoppers to try something new. Through small talk, race emerges in connection to age, English fluency, time and farming practices. If there are not younger people present, it will be more difficult for customers to have the interaction some desire, but curiosity, as noted earlier, and willingness on the part of the vendor, propels the encounter forward.

There are different sensibilities toward the joy of chatting. Some farmers view these conversations as a chore, a job that must be done to make a living. Not surprisingly, vendors seem to find more pleasure in their relationships with other vendors and long-term customers. Intimate knowledge about people's lives is conveyed, particularly among vendors, especially within racialized groups (but not entirely) and to some extent with customers. Vendors know who is ill and recovering or who has died as well as who has retired and not been replaced by family members. An older white woman vendor comes to the Market for the company of other vendors (not the customers), not for the money she might or might not make. An African American vendor's father came 'for the people' and suggested that his sons understand that this was what the Market was about, not necessarily for making a profit. For one middle-aged vendor, the Market used to bring regular customers with whom he established friendships, but he laments the fact that there are fewer and fewer of such customers.

The Time of Bargaining

Hmong and white vendors have conveyed to me their distaste for bargaining, another type of intimate interaction. They claim prices are already low. To bargain or not to bargain is a racial practice that varies over time. One white grower said his father's best customers were 'the blacks, because they never argued about the price'. It is possible that in white, largely rural 1950s Minnesota, African Americans did not feel comfortable haggling or did not do so for reasons that are more complicated than fear. His father sold them mustard greens, which his family grew but never ate. Organic eggs sell for $4.50 a dozen but one Asian woman asks the white woman vendor, 'for four dollars, right?' Vendor: 'Well I need $4.50 so I won't lose money'. Customer: 'These are so good, you know I always buy from you'. The vendor, clearly reluctant said, 'Ok, this time, Ok. But don't tell anyone'. Having lost her husband and being unable to pay for organic certification, the price this vendor asked is critical to economic survival. I listened as a Hmong grower told two South Asian customers asking for a lower price, 'I grow these [fenugreek plants] for thirty days and at the end of that time, I ask for a dollar a bunch'. He told me 'I don't sell my vegetables for less than a dollar. That's the price. They can try to get it cheaper somewhere else'.

This section has suggested that the public intimacy afforded by the Market is a site for potentially productive encounter. These intimacies are part of racial embodiment at the Market. Intimacy is not separate from racial division; plants racially divide the Market but they also invite curiosity and spur encounter.

Conclusions

I focused on the scale of bodies to suggest that the concept of racial embodiment as an emergent process of connection is a means to understand race, food and the Market. I argued that despite the importance of social construction and performativity to thinking race, these frameworks do not enable a discussion of matter. Rather, the work of feminist materialists, particularly Elizabeth Grosz, allows an exploration of racial embodiment through phenotypic difference and the things that bodies do. Embodied differences among racialized groups emerge through practices—growing, selling, purchasing and eating food. These are partially observable tendencies of bodies that exist dynamically in social and physical space. To think about race as what (phenotypically differentiated) bodies do helps to analyze this food space as one in which people are racially divided and brought together. Racial embodiment can be a means to catalog the obvious, subtle, creative and changing forms of racism as well as note 'what else' happens in this place. I argued that racial divisions can be seen through the production of certain plants by one racialized group and the clustering of bodies around some tables and products. Playing out the intimate human acts of food sale and consumption, different bodies display dismay, wonder, frustration and delight. Race is one important part in the act of the encounter in which bodies are central. The process that is race consists of bodies interacting with amaranth, Market sheds, honey, other bodies and the Minnesota fields.

Elizabeth Grosz proposes that the task of feminist theory is to formulate questions that generate inventiveness. Feminist materialist theorists have been on the forefront of theorizing the body in ways that acknowledge biology and society. They have done so towards other politics. Exploring how race emerges, embodied, strengthens politics by expanding the discussion of race to include more than representation, recognition and intentional actions. What (anti-racist) politics would follow when bodies, formations in which they act and bodily practices are foregrounded?[7] Grosz suggests that identity could be understood in terms of bodily practices. Thus a politics of bodily practices against oppression should be undertaken as a struggle of endless 'becoming other' in which categories of action, not the struggle for recognition, are affirmed. She writes,

> Without an adequate acknowledgement of the material, natural, biological status of bodies (these terms being understood as vectors of change rather than as forms of fixity), we lose the resources to understand how to best harness these forces which invariably direct us to the future; we lose an understanding of our place in the world as beings open to becoming, open to activities, if not identities, of all types. (Grosz 2005: 89)

Acknowledgments

This paper developed through the questions and comments I received when I presented parts of this paper at the 2007 AAG meeting, in a number of other academic settings and finally at the University of Minnesota's Institute for Advanced Study in May 2008. I thank these commentators. I am also grateful to Arun Saldanha for his insights and suggestions. The encouragement and criticism of three reviewers for Social & Cultural Geography and Editor Michael Brown pushed the paper still further. Many thanks, finally, to Minneapolis Farmers' Market vendors who gave me their time and thoughts.

Notes

1. The Hmong, indigenous peoples of China, left their lands in the mid to late 1800s, eventually coming to reside in the mountainous regions of Laos. They were involved in various acts of resistance against the French and Laotian governments. Some provided assistance to the USA in its war against Vietnam and persisted in attacks against the government of Laos after the USA withdrew from the region. Many Hmong people fled Laotian retaliation and now live in refugee camps in Thailand. Since then, some have been relocated to other countries, including the USA (Yia 2000). US Hmong populations are concentrated around the Twin Cities, MN and Fresno, CA.
2. This phrase thanks to an anonymous reviewer who read an earlier version of the paper when it was under review at *Cultural Geographies*.
3. This term from Cheah (1996).
4. Heirlooms are cultivars preserved by passing seeds down through generations. Often they have been selected for flavor and have not been grown using industrial agricultural production methods (Kingsolver 2007).
5. See <www.millcityfarmersmarket.org> (accessed 9 June 2007).
6. Technically, this stand is in the Farmer's Market Annex, a privately owned space that rents to vendors of food and other goods that covers the block adjacent to the MFM. Together they make this Market space.
7. M. C. Emad, Institute for Advanced Study, University of Minnesota, personal communication, 5 May 2008.

References

Adler, P.A. and Adler, P. (1998) Observational techniques, in Denzin, N.K. and Lincoln, Y.S. (eds) *Collecting and Interpreting Qualitative Materials*. London: Sage, pp. 79–109.

Ahmed, S. (1998) Animated borders: Skin, colour and tanning, in Shildrick, M. and Price, J. (eds) *Vital Signs. Feminist Reconfigurations of the Bio/logical Body*. Edinburgh: Edinburgh University Press, pp. 45–65.

Ahmed, S. (2004) *The Cultural Politics of Emotion*. New York: Routledge.

Ainley, R. (ed.) (1998) *New Frontiers of Space, Bodies and Gender*. London: Routledge.

Alexander, C. and Knowles, C. (eds) (2005) *Making Race Matter: Bodies, Space and Identity*. New York: Palgrave Macmillan.

Alkon, A.H. (2008) Paradise or pavement: the social constructions of the environment in two urban farmers' markets and their implications for environmental justice and sustainability, *Local Environment: The Inter- national Journal of Justice and Sustainability*, 13(3): 271–289.

Allen, P. (2004) *Together at the Table*. University Park: The Pennsylvania State University Press.

Anderson, K. (2007) *Race and the Crisis of Humanism*. London: Routledge.

Bell, D. and Valentine, G. (1997) *Consuming Geographies*. London: Routledge.

Bell, D., Binnie, J., Holliday, R., Longhurst, R. and Peace, R. (eds) (2001) *Pleasure Zones: Bodies, Cities, Spaces*. New York: Syracuse University Press.

Bondi, L., Davidson, J. and Smith, M. (2005) Introduction: geography's emotional turn, in Davidson, J., Bondi, L. and Smith, M. (eds) *Emotional Geographies*. Aldershot: Ashgate, pp. 1–18.

Brown, A. (2002) Farmers' market research 1940–2000: an inventory and review, *American Journal of Alternative Agriculture* 17: 167–176.

Brown, J.N. (2005) *Dropping Anchor Setting Sail: Geographies of Race in Black Liverpool*. Princeton, NJ: Princeton University Press.

Butler, J. (1993) *Bodies that Matter: On the Discursive Limits of 'Sex'*. New York: Routledge.

Butler, R. and Parr, H. (eds) (1999) *Mind and Body Spaces: Geographies of Illness, Impairment and Disability*. London: Routledge.

Cheah, P. (1996) Mattering, *Diacritics* 26: 108–139.

Clark, N. (2005) Ex-orbitant globality, *Theory, Culture and Society* 22: 165–185.

Colebrook, C. (2000) From radical representations to corporeal becomings: the feminist philosophy of Lloyd, Grosz and Gatens, *Hypatia* 15: 76–93.

Delaney, D. (2002) The space that race makes, *The Professional Geographer* 54: 6–14.

Delgado, R. and Stefancic, J. (2001) *Critical Race Theory*. New York: New York University Press.

Denzin, N.K. (1989) *The Research Act*. Englewood Cliffs, NJ: Prentice Hall.

Dooley, B. (2001) A tale of two markets, *Eaters Digest* 22(1075), 11 July, City Pages, <www.citypages.com/databank/22/1075/article9694.asp> (accessed 17 July 2006).

Fidecaro, A. (2006) Jamaica Kincaid's practical politics of the intimate in *My Garden* (book), *Women's Studies Quarterly* 34: 250–270.

Fortier, A. (2007) Too close for comfort: loving thy neighbor and the management of multicultural intimacies, *Environment and Planning D: Society and Space* 25: 104–119.

Futamura, T. (2007) Made in Kentucky: the meanings of 'local' food products in Kentucky's farmers' markets, *Japanese Journal of American Studies* 18: 209–228.

Gallaher, C. (2002) On the fault line: race, class and the US Patriot Movement, *Cultural Studies* 16: 673–703.

Gerbasi, G.T. (2006) Athens farmers' market: evolving dynamics and hidden benefits to a Southeast Ohio Rural Community, *Focus on Geography* 49: 1–6.

Gilroy, P. (2000) *Against Race: Imagining Political Culture Beyond the Color Line*. Cambridge, MA: Harvard University Press.

Gregson, N. and Crewe, L. (1997) The bargain, the knowledge and the spectacle: making sense of consumption in the space of the car-boot sale, *Environment and Planning D: Society and Space* 15: 87–112.

Grosz, E. (1994) *Volatile Bodies: Toward a Corporeal Feminism*. Bloomington: Indiana University Press.

Grosz, E. (2005) *Time Travels: Feminism, Nature, Power*. Durham, NC: Duke University Press.

Guthman, J. (2008) 'If they only knew': colorblindness and universalism in California alternative food institutions, *The Professional Geographer* 60: 387–397.

Harrison, P. (2008) Corporeal remains: vulnerability, proximity, and living-on after the end of the world, *Environment and Planning A*, 40: 423–445.

Hoelscher, S. (2003) Making place, making race: performances of whiteness in the Jim Crow south, *Annals of the Association of American Geographers* 93: 657–686.

Holloway, L. and Kneafsey, M. (2000) Reading the space of the farmers' market: a preliminary investigation from the UK, *Sociologia Ruralis* 40: 285–299.

Hunt, A.R. (2007) Consumer interactions and influences on farmers' market vendors, *Renewable Agriculture and Food Systems* 22: 54–66.

Ilbery, B. and Kneafsey, M. (2000) Producer constructions of quality in regional specialty food production: a case study from southwest England, *Journal of Rural Studies* 16: 217–230.

Jackson, P. (1998) Constructions of whiteness in the geographical imagination, *Area* 30: 99–106.

Johnston, L. (2005) Transformative tans? Gendered and raced bodies on beaches, *New Zealand Geographer* 61: 110–116.

Kerin, J. (1999) The matter at hand: Butler, ontology and the natural sciences, *Australian Feminist Studies* 14: 91–104.

Kerr, L.M. (2007) *Resisting Agricultural Assimilation: The Political Ecology of Hmong Growers in the Twin Cities Metropolitan Region*. St. Paul, MN: Department of Geography. Macalester College.

Kingsolver, B. (2007) *Animal, Vegetable, Miracle: A Year of Food Life*. New York: HarperCollins.

Kirwan, J. (2004) Alternative strategies in the UK agro food system: interrogating the alterity of farmers' markets, *Sociologia Ruralis* 44: 396–415.

Kobayashi, A. and Peake, L. (1994) Unnatural discourse: 'race' and gender in geography, *Gender, Place and Culture* 1: 225–243.

Kontturi, K. and Tiainen, M. (2007) Feminism, art, Deleuze, and Darwin: an interview with Elizabeth Grosz, *Nordic Journal of Feminist and Gender Research* 15: 246–256.

Lingis, A. (1998) Schizoanalysis of race, in Lane, C. (ed.) *The Psychoanalysis of Race*. New York: Columbia University Press, pp. 176–189.

Longhurst, R. (1997) (Dis)embodied geographies, *Progress in Human Geography* 21: 486–501.

Longhurst, R. (2001) *Bodies: Exploring Fluid Boundaries*. London: Routledge.

Longhurst, R. (2005) Fat bodies: developing geographical research agendas, *Progress in Human Geography* 29: 247–259.

Massey, D. (1994) *Space, Place and Gender*. Minneapolis: University of Minnesota Press.

Massey, D. (2005) *For Space*. London: Sage.

Moore, D.S., Pandian, A. and Kosek, J. (2003) The cultural politics of race and nature: terrains of power and practice, in Moore, D.S., Kosek, J. and Pandian, A. (eds) *Race, Nature and the Politics of Difference*. Durham, NC: Duke University Press, pp. 1–70.

Nast, H.J. and Pile, S. (eds) (1998) *Places Through the Body*. London: Routledge.

Nayak, A. (2006) After race: ethnography, race and post-race theory, *Ethnic and Racial Studies* 29: 411–430.

Obrador-Pons, P. (2007) A haptic geography of the beach: naked bodies, vision and touch, *Social & Cultural Geography* 8: 123–141.

Parrott, N., Wilson, N. and Murdoch, J. (2002) Spatializing quality: regional protection and the alternative geography of food, *European Urban and Regional Studies* 9: 241–261.

Pile, S. (1996) *The Body and the City.* London: Routledge.

Roe, E.J. (2006) Things becoming food and the embodied, material practices of an organic food consumer, *Sociologia Ruralis* 46: 104–121.

Rose, G. (1995) Geography and gender, cartographies and corporealities, *Progress in Human Geography* 19: 544–548.

Sage, C. (2003) Social embeddedness and relations of regard: alternative 'good food' networks in south-west Ireland, *Journal of Rural Studies* 19: 47–60.

Saldanha, A. (2006) Re-ontologizing race, *Environment and Planning D: Society and Space* 24: 9–24.

Saldanha, A. (2007) *Psychedelic White: Goa Trance and the Viscosity of Race.* Minneapolis: University of Minnesota Press.

Slocum, R. (2007) Whiteness, space and alternative food practice, *Geoforum* 38: 520–533.

Smith, M.M. (2006) *How Race is Made: Slavery, Segregation and the Senses.* Chapel Hill: University of North Carolina Press.

Stallybrass, P. and White, A. (1986) *The Politics and Poetics of Transgression.* Ithaca, NY: Cornell University Press.

Stoler, A.L. (2006) Intimidations of empire: predicaments of the tactile and unseen, in Stoler, A.L. (ed.) *Haunted by Empire: Geographies of Intimacy in North American History.* Durham, NC: Duke University Press, pp. 1–22.

Teather, E.K. (ed.) (1999) *Embodied Geographies: Spaces, Bodies and Rites of Passage.* London: Routledge.

Thien, D. (2005) Intimate distances: considering questions of 'us', in Davidson, J., Bondi, L. and Smith, M. (eds) *Emotional Geographies.* Aldershot: Ashgate, pp. 191–204.

Thomas, M.E. (2005) 'I think it's just natural': the spatiality of racial segregation at a US high school, *Environment and Planning A* 37: 1233–1248.

Tolia-Kelly, D. (2006) Affect–an ethnocentric encounter? Exploring the 'universalist' imperative of emotional/affectual geographies, *Area* 38: 213–217.

Wade, P. (2004) Human nature and race, *Anthropological Theory* 4: 157–172.

Watson, S. and Wells, K. (2005) Spaces of nostalgia: the hollowing out of a London market, *Social & Cultural Geography* 6: 17–30.

Weismantel, M. (2001) *Cholas and Pishtacos: Stories of Race and Sex in the Andes.* Chicago: University of Chicago Press.

Whatmore, S. (2002) *Hybrid Geographies: Natures, Cultures, Spaces.* London: Sage.

Williams, S.J. and Bendelow, G. (eds) (1998) *The Lived Body: Sociological Themes, Embodied Issues.* London: Routledge.

Wilson, E.A. (2004) *Psychosomatic: Feminism and the Neurological Body.* Durham, NC: Duke University Press.

Yia, G.L. (2000) Bandits or rebels? Hmong resistance in the new Lao state, *Indigenous Affairs* 4: 6–15.

Young, I.M. (2005) *On Female Body Experience.* Oxford: Oxford University Press.

16

The Raw and the Rotten: Punk Cuisine*[1]

Dylan Clark

Having been moved 2,000 miles to the north of its original home on the Rio Grande, a steel government sign was placed along the colorful fence of the Black Cat Café in Seattle, and there it retained something of its original meaning. It was a small white sign with black letters which announced, "U.S. Border." On one side, land administered by the United States; on the other, the sign implied, a space beyond the reach of the American state: an autonomous region.

For five years, this zone was a haven for people called punks and their kindred spirits,[2] an assortment of young adults who exercised and debated punk praxis in and through the premises. At the Cat, punks read, talked, smoked, and ate. They chewed ideas and articulated dietary practices, and rehashed their experiences with one another. Being punk is a way of critiquing privileges and challenging social hierarchies. Contemporary punks are generally inspired by anarchism, which they understand to be a way of life in favor of egalitarianism and environ-mentalism and against sexism, racism, and corporate domination. This ideology shows up in punk routines: in their conversations, their travels, and in their approach to food.

Food practices mark ideological moments: eating is a cauldron for the domination of states, races, genders, ideologies, and the practice through which these discourses are resisted. Indeed, as Weiss (1996: 130) argues, "Certain qualities of food make it *the* most appropriate vehicle for describing alienation." The theory and practice of punk cuisine gain clarity when they are viewed through the work of Claude Lévi-Strauss (1969), who saw the process of cooking food as the quintessential means through which humans differentiate themselves from animals, and through which they make culture and civilization. Lévi-Strauss's tripolar gastronomic system defines raw, cooked, and rotten as categories basic to all human cuisines. This model is useful for analyzing punk cuisine, and thereby punk culture. Yet this article also toys with the model, using it to give voice to the ardent critics of "civilization." Many punks associate the "civilizing" process of producing and transforming food with the human domination of nature and with White, male, corporate supremacy. Punks believe that industrial food fills a person's body with the norms, rationales, and moral pollution of corporate capitalism and imperialism. Punks reject such "poisons" and do not

*Originally published 2004

want to be mistaken for being White or part of American mainstream society. A variety of practices, many dietary, provide a powerful critique against the status quo.

A Punk Culinary Triangle

In the punk community, food serves to elaborate and structure ideologies about how the world works. Through a complex system of rules, suggestions, and arguments, punk cuisine is a code like those posited by Lévi-Strauss (1969, 1997). But punk cuisine is best discussed as a cultural mechanism responsible to its own logic, and in dialogue with what punks perceive to be the normative culture. Lévi-Strauss's ideas about food are insightful, especially when placed in a locally defined context (Douglas 1984). His culinary triangle (Figure 16.1) provides a helpful way to think about how the transformations of food can be cognitively mapped. For example, American food geographies have shifted toward processing (or cooking) food. Industrial food products are milled, refined, butchered, baked, packaged, branded, and advertised. They are often composed of ingredients shipped from remote places, only to be processed and sent once more around the globe. From a Lévi-Strauss perspective, then, punks consider industrial food to be extraordinarily cooked. Punks, in turn, preferentially seek food that is more "raw"; i.e., closer to its wild, organic, uncultured state; and punks even enjoy food that has, from an American perspective, become rotten—disposed of or stolen.

For punks, mainstream food is epitomized by corporate-capitalist "junk food." Punks regularly liken mainstream food geographies to colonialism because of their association with the Third World: destruction of rainforests (allegedly cleared for beef production), the creation of cash-cropping (to service World Bank debts), and cancer (in the use of banned pesticides on unprotected workers and water supplies). Furthermore, punks allege that large-scale stock-raising (cattle, chickens, pigs) and agribusiness destroy whole ecosystems. A representative of this point of view states, "Ultimately this vortex brings about the complete objectification of nature.

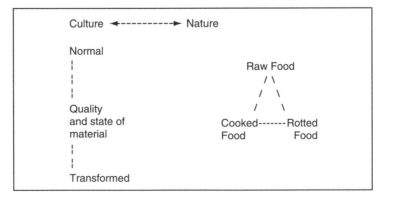

Figure 16.1 Lévi-Strauss' (1969) culinary triangle (Adopted from Wood (1995: 11)).

Every relationship is increasingly instrumentalized and technicized. Mechanization and industrialization have rapidly transformed the planet, exploding ecosystems and human communities with monoculture, industrial degradation, and mass markets" (Watson 1999: 164; see also CrimethInc. Workers' Collective 2001: 122).

Punk food attempts to break free from the fetishism of food as a commodity. As such, it is ideally purchased in brandless bulk or directly from farmers, self-made or home-grown, and otherwise less commodified, which is to say stolen or reclaimed from a garbage dumpster. By bathing corporate food in a dumpster or by stealing natural foods from an upscale grocery store, punk food is, in a sense, decommodified, stripped of its alienating qualities, and restored to a kind of pure use-value as bodily sustenance. In their organic, unmediated forms, such foods come closer to a "wild" diet, free of commodification and hierarchical relations of production, and closer to Lévi-Strauss' "raw" and "rotten" and further from his "cooked." Comments anarchist Bey (1991: 54), "Food, cooked or raw, cannot escape from symbolism. ... But in the airless vault of our civilization, where nearly every experience is mediated ... we lose touch with food as nourishment; we begin to construct for ourselves personae based on what we consume, treating *products* as projections of our yearning for the authentic."

The Order of Signs at the Black Cat Café

Hardly a quaint place sweetly nestled in a booming urban landscape, the Black Cat was a boxy structure enclosed by a jagged rampart of fencing and discarded materials. Part of the fence was topped with a tangled line of bicycle frames, reminiscent of a wall of thorns. It enclosed a café yard of scattered benches, tables, and cigarette butts. Against the side of the café a mass of bicycle frames and parts made a tangled mound of metal. To beautify the courtyard, scrap-wood planters held salvaged greenery. The place looked more like a junkyard than a restaurant, for it violated normal aesthetic conventions associated with dining. Unlike other restaurants, the café did not strive to declare sanitation and safety. If the space of modern authority is clean, empty, and clearly marked (Sennett 1990: 38), the façade and decor of the Black Cat Café suggested the antithesis. The café was cluttered, soiled, its interior covered with posters, art, and canvas coffee sacks: packed with bulky, dilapidated furniture, it felt cramped.

This ambiance was precisely what drew punks to the Black Cat collective. On a dirty cement floor that would offend mainstream good taste, punks tossed their rucksacks holding all their worldly possessions. Where others were repelled by the body odors of the unwashed, punks recognized kindred spirits. Where others feared to eat food prepared by grimy, garishly pierced cooks, patrons appreciated the ambiance of food lovingly prepared.

Food itself was one of the centrally reversed signs here, perhaps because food was the ostensible *raison d'être* for the restaurant. Black Cat food, like the café itself, was a declaration of autonomy and organic creation, a rejection of commodification. Meat and dairy products were proudly excluded. Vegetables with peanut sauce, tofu scrambles, and other vegan creations served as entrees. The place and the food rejected strict adherence to conventional conceptions of hygiene, where even the appearance of filth somehow infects the object or the body. Here hygiene was associated with bleached teeth, carcinogenic chemicals, and freshly waxed cars, and operated as a code for sterility, automation, and alienation. Hygiene meant "idiot box" sitcoms and suburban fears of dark bodies. At the café, hygiene was a projection of Whiteness, and rejected.[3]

In rejecting the image of sterility, the Black Cat collective scorned decades of market research, and refuted dominant mantras of modernity. Marketing doctrine in the United States urges restaurants to emphasize scrubbed surfaces, clarity, and predictability. As a rule, the food industry seeks to provide a product so clean and neat that its human creation is not readily apparent. In this sense, the commodity fetishism as a corporate mandate is more apparent to the senses than is the migrant laborer in the field or the minimum-wage dishwasher. For the greater punk community, interchangeability, consistency, and hygienic food represent food that is utterly cooked and gastronomically problematic: "When we accept their definition of 'cleanliness,' we are accepting their economic domination of our lives" (CrimethInc. Workers' Collective 2001: 123).

What to make, then, of a restaurant which rarely produces a tahini salad dressing the same way twice or a pile of home fries without a good many charred? What of a restaurant with spotty service, spotty dishes, where the roof leaks, and the bathroom reeks? For five years, the Black Cat found a way to thrive in spite of, or because of, its unorthodox practices. The workers and patrons of the café are a different breed who seek out what is "rotten" in mainstream society. One worker-owner, Ketan, talked about how the marginality of the Black Cat scared away many potential patrons, but noted with a laugh:

> I hope … people realize that this not a café. This is not a café. This is not a restaurant. … That's not what this place is about. This is a safe space. It is a haven for people who want to live their lives away from the bullshit of corporate oppression. That's what this space is about. It's not about anything else other than that. It's for people who want to believe what they want to believe and not be ridiculed, and be free from control by governments or other forms of systematic, abusive power things.

Food as Gender/Power

As a site of resource allocation, food tends to recapitulate power relations. Around the globe, unequal allocations of food according to a patriarchal system are common. A working-class male comes of age in France when he is able to help himself to large volumes of food (Bourdieu 1984). Men, and sometimes boys, often receive larger amounts of food and have culinary choices catered to their taste (see Narotzky 1997: 136–37; Mintz 1985: 144–45; Appadurai 1981). Thus, food displays practices through which unequal gender power is acted out, resisted, and reproduced (Counihan 1999). Punks, too, play out gender/power relations in their diets. In recent years, the punk ethic has become more committed to anarchist, egalitarian principles that celebrate and practice an antihierarchical social order, including one that prohibits a hierarchy of gender.

Feminist praxis in punk explicitly critiques food as a site of repression, using the Victorian age as an example of a discourse disciplining female bodies through food

(Mennell 1985). This discourse was fostered in part by capitalist food and pharmaceutical industries eager to create new products for dieting and beauty (Bordo 1993;
Chapkis 1986). Feminists identify this discourse as a form of control over women that
at times leaves them malnourished, anorexic, or bulimic, and fixated on manipulating
their body shape and diets. As a gendered and specifically American national project,
by the early twentieth century, through women's magazines, newspapers, churches,
cookbooks, and civic societies, native-born and immigrant women were educated in
"home economics," a correlated set of technologies intended to produce an idealized
femininity schooled in Whiteness, to produce the right kind of patriarchy and racial
order of the U.S. nation-state. Such ideological uses of food are routinely referenced
in punk food discourse, in everyday talk, by bands such as Tribe 8, and in "zines" (the
popular broadsheets of punk) such as *Fat Girl*.

Thus, many punks identify the body as a place where hegemony is both made and
resisted. Punks are critical of the beauty industry and of the commodification of the
body. They argue that food is part of a disciplinary order in which women are taught
to diet and manage their bodies so as to publicly communicate in the grammar of
patriarchy. "Riot girl" punks, in particular, have produced a large volume of zines,
music, conversations, and practices that challenge the sexist politics of food. In the
ongoing evolution and critique of punk culture, diet is one of the many places where
feminist ideas have been advanced and largely won out.

Indeed, vegetarianism for many punks is partly a feminist practice, but it also
reveals ideological fissures within punk culture. Meat, with its prestige, caloric content, and proximity to physical violence, has been widely associated with masculinity
(Adams 1990; Rifkin 1992). Yet even within punk culture, which is critical of
both sexism and meat-eating (O'Hara 1999), some punks continue to produce an
overtly sexist, masculine presence (Nguyen 1999) and one associated with eating
meat. Meat for some punks is a way to challenge feminism in punk and to reassert
masculine power. Other punk meat-eating falls into the categories of those who
are apolitical about food, and those who flaunt meat-eating as a way of challenging
punk orthodoxy.

For most punks, however, meat-eating is collaborative with an unjust social order,
which punks typically portray as a patriarchy. Opposing social hierarchies, and living
in staunchly patriarchal societies, they need to subvert male supremacy in everyday
life, and vegetarianism, widely stigmatized as an oriental and feminine practice, helps
to differentiate punks from the mainstream.

Punk Veganism

In punk veganism, the daily politics of consumption and the ethical quandaries of
everyday life are intensified. In part, the decade-long struggle to make food and animal
products overtly political was carried out by bands such as Vegan Reich and in zines.
Zines regularly comment on animal rights, industrial food, and veganism. Often
drawing upon Rifkin (1992) and Robbins (1987), many zines recount details of
cruelty toward animals, contaminated meat, and the unhealthful effects of meat and
dairy products on the human body. Other punk writing describes environmental
consequences of industrial food production. "Even Punks who do not acknowledge

the concept of animal rights and hold strong anthropocentric views have been known to change their diet purely for environmental reasons" (O'Hara 1999: 135). In the daily praxis of punk, vegetarianism and veganism are strategies through which many punks combat corporate capitalism, patriarchy, and environmental collapse.

The emphasis on a radical diet was not always a dominant part of punk cultures. But by the 1990s, veganism was a rapidly ascending force within the greater punk landscape in North America. Led by the "straight edge" punk movement, veganism gained credence across the punk spectrum, including those who scorned the drug-abstaining politics of straight edge, as did most Seattle punks in this study.

At the Black Cat Café, punks said that to eat animal-based products was not only unhealthful, it participated in the bondage and murder of animals. Many punks were concerned about the cruel conditions of factory farms, where animals were kept in cramped quarters, pumped with hormones and antibiotics, and "tortured" in sundry ways. Near the middle of its tenure, the Black Cat discontinued its use of milk and eggs. A vegetarian café from its outset, the Cat became more orthodox when its menu was made completely vegan. The transition to a vegan menu marked a turning point for the collective. The original members had dropped out, and a younger, more militant membership had taken control. The café became less tolerant, less compromising, and more thoroughly punk in its clientele and ambiance. Ketan expressed the urgency that many punks feel about veganism:

> There's this line that occurs with being vegan and being activist: at what point does the freedom of people who believe what they believe cross over to the point where people are being harmed? You know? Like, yeah: people are free to eat meat. But actually, in this day and age, they *can't* eat meat because it's killing animals. Because someone is eating meat, land that could potentially benefit all of us is being destroyed. I have a lot of problems with that line: I don't want to impede people's freedom, but what everyone does affects everyone else. … I honestly believe that people have to stop eating meat now. Now! I'm not gonna force anyone to stop eating meat, but they're hurting me, my children's future, my friends, my family—because they're eating meat. And they're hurting the Earth, which is most important of all.

Many punks around the nation were part of the growing politicization of the culture, with veganism at the forefront of the politics. To be vegan in America is to perpetually find oneself in the minority, chastised, excluded, challenged, and reminded of one's difference. In this sense, veganism also served as an incessant critique of the mainstream, a marker of Otherness, and an enactment of punk.

Raw as a Critique of Cooked

In punk cuisine, the degree to which food is processed, sterilized, brand named, and fetishized is the degree to which it is corrupted, distanced from nature, and "cooked." Punks describe a world under the assault of homogenized foods and culture, a world of vast monocropped cornfields and televisions lit with prefabricated corporate "infotainment." Whereas industrial agriculture is associated with genetic engineering, monocropping, pesticides, animal cages, chemical fertilizers, and commodification, "raw" food tends toward wildness and complexity.

Punks perceive in everyday American food an abject modernity, a synthetic destroyer of locality and diversity. The "cooking" of foods, to which punks vociferously object, is an outcome of the industrialization and commercialization of modern food production, which are made visible and critiqued through punk culinary practices. The following trends in modern food manufacture and consumption comprise the increasingly cooked qualities of food against which punks can be said to form their culinary triangle.

From a punk perspective, American food has reached an unprecedented and remarkable state: nearly all the food that Americans eat is received in the form of a commodity, and the fetishism of food goes far beyond the simple erasure of labor. Lears (1994: 171) describes the emergence of the industrialization of eating:

> By the 1920s and 1930s, advertisements for food displayed an almost panicky reassertion of culture over nature—an anxious impulse to extirpate all signs of biological life from one's immediate personal environment. That impulse has been spreading widely for decades, as methods of mass production were brought to food processing and distribution.

Such logics, for example, are apparent in the segregated meat products, in which the animal carcass is hidden. The animal's head, feet, and tongue (its recognizable body parts) have disappeared from most American butcher displays.

Through the most sophisticated branding, packaging, and advertising, American food commodities work hard to conceal the labor, spatial divides, and resources that went into making the food. Or, as Weiss (1996: 131) shows, "the effects of encompassing transformations in political economy (colonialism, wage labor, commoditization and the like) … [have] their greatest and gravest consequences for food." In modern advertising, images of food often divert attention from the industrialized production of food, and draw attention to its consumption (DuPuis 2000). Rather than depict the mechanized dairy factory, ads show celebrities and athletes wearing smiles and milk mustaches. Notes Harvey (1989: 300):

> The whole world's cuisine is now assembled in one place. … The general implication is that through the experience of everything from food, to culinary habits, music, television, entertainment, and cinema, it is now possible to experience the world's geography vicariously, as a simulacrum. The interweaving of simulacra in daily life brings together different worlds (of commodities) in the same space and time. But it does so in such a way as to conceal almost perfectly any trace of origin, of the labour processes that produced them, or of the social relations implicated in their production.

Perhaps these postmodern geographies, along with relentless commodification, heighten the fetishism of the commodity, hiding as much as possible the making of a product; the alienating conditions of production, cooking in the extreme.

Punks see industrialized food production not as a desired convenience, but as one of the hallmarks of monoculture. The anarchist idea of monoculture plays on the "culture" part of the term, thus expanding it to cover not only modern industrial agriculture, but also mainstream culture. For punks, monoculture encapsulates the idea that societies around the world are being devoured and homogenized by consumerism; it invokes the idea that humans everywhere increasingly eat, dream, work, are gendered, and otherwise live according to a narrow and hegemonic culture sold to them by global capitalism. Across the globe, punks argue, humans are losing their cultural, ecological, temporal, and regional specificity. Among other things, this means that people are often eating foods grown and flavored elsewhere: people everywhere are increasingly alienated from that which keeps them alive.

"Raw" food, which is to say, organic, home-grown, bartered food, was one way punks resisted the spread of monoculture. At the Black Cat Café, customers could trade home-grown organic produce for meal credits, they could trade their dishwashing labor for meals, and they could drink "fair trade" coffee. Moreover, the café strove to subvert profiteering at every step in the food's production. At the Cat, people who might be called punks contrasted the synthetic, processed, and destructive diet of the mainstream with their own, and declared that their bodies and minds were healthier for it, unpolluted by toxic chemicals and capitalist culture.

Stealing Yuppie-Natural Foods

Not far from the Black Cat Café, Seattle hosted a variety of natural-foods retailers, who attracted both the contempt and the palates of punks. Such places offered organically grown foods marketed to an upscale clientele. Indeed, the natural-foods industry in 1990s Seattle was part of a vast reconfiguration of food in America, which witnessed a hitherto unprecedented niche marketing of what punks saw as foods which fed egos more than bodies. The punk narrative critique of the natural-foods movement was extended by stealing, for by this the food was remade.

Punk discourses of food are partly a response to the heightening of identity marketing in foods over the last few decades of the twentieth century. Although locating identity and prestige in food is an ancient practice, it has historically been limited by income, tradition, and spatial divides. But in contemporary America, the bewildering array of food choices challenges the consumer, whose choices are understood to "express" or manufacture him- or herself. Americans have reached the point at which food as essential for survival has been sublimated under the ideology of food as self-gratification and consumer identity.

Such formulas were apparent to punks in the commercial discourse on natural foods. Punks regard these foods, while ostensibly pure and simple, as much commodities as the food products that preceded them, and derisively locate "yuppie," "individualistic," and "White" behavior in an expensive obsession about one's own purity and health (see Bey 1991: 53). The natural-foods industry, then, is a target of punk critical practices. In Seattle, the Puget Consumers' Co-op (PCC) bore the brunt of the punk natural-foods critique. Fashionable, expensive, and allegedly catering to a mostly White and upscale clientele, the PCC was scorned by punks.

While commodified natural foods were repulsively overcooked, they were simultaneously closer to the raw forms of food that punks preferred: organic, bulk, and whole grain. So, while the PCC market offered the organic products that punks preferred (as well as a relatively tolerable and tolerant workplace for those who opted for wage labor), the high prices and upscale marketing represented the cooking of foods; the heightened state of gastronomic fetishism from which punks felt alienated. Cleansed of their commodification, these foods would be perfectly suited to the punk culinary system. Thus, many punks, whether as workers or customers, targeted natural-foods supermarkets for theft (c.f. Himelstein and Schweser 1998: 18–21, 24). In this manner, the kitchen of the Black Cat Café was routinely stocked with products stolen from chain supermarkets and natural-foods stores. This behavior suggests an axiom of punk culinary geometry: in the act of being stolen, heavily cooked food is transformed into a more nutritive, gustative state. Stolen foods are outlaw foods, contaminated or rotten to the mainstream, but a delicacy in punk cuisine.

The Rotten Logic of Dumpster Diving

Each night American supermarkets and restaurants fill their dumpsters with food, and each night punks arrive to claim some of it. A host of foods become rotten in corporate-capitalist food production: food with an advanced expiration date, cosmetically damaged produce, food in dented packaging, day-old baked goods, and the like. As punks saw it, people were hungry in Seattle, in America, and around the world. To punks it was obscene that businesses were trashing good food (Resist 2003: 67).

Unlike raw foods, dumped food tends to be commercialized, nonorganic, and highly processed. Baked goods, donuts, produce, vegetables, pizza, and an array of junk foods are foraged by punks, who otherwise disdain such products. Yet in the process of passing through a dumpster, such foods are cleansed or rotted, as it were, and made nutritious and attractive to the punk being.

It was ironic to punks that people are hassled by security guards, store employees, and police merely for taking things out of a dumpster. Not only did the mainstream waste food, it protected its garbage with armed guards. Commented one punk: "There is the odd paradox—the casualness with which they will throw something into the dumpster, and the lengths they will go to protect it once it's there. How an innocent and harmless act—dumpster diving—will be confronted by greedy shop-keepers, store managers, and employees with scathing words, rage, and violence" (Anonymous 2001: 72). Taken in tandem, the waste of food and the protection of waste were seen by punks as the avaricious gluttony of American society. Food in dumpsters is, for most Americans, garbage and repulsive. It goes beyond the pale of Whiteness to eat food classified as garbage: only untouchables, such as the homeless, eat trash. So for those punks who were raised White or middle class, dump-sters and dumped food dirty their bodies and tarnish their affiliation with a White, bourgeois power structure. In this sense, the downward descent into a dumpster is literally an act of downward mobility. Moreover, eating garbage (food deemed rotten) is a forceful condemnation of societal injustices. On an ecologically strained planet home to two billion hungry people, punks see their reclamation of rotten food as a profoundly radical act.

Gastro-Politics in Punk Activism

For its five years of existence, the Black Cat Café was the kitchen of Seattle's punk scene. It was a decidedly anticorporate environment, where mainstream types were not always welcomed, and where there was always room for young wayfarers. As with many cultures, punk food practices helped shape community, symbolize values, and foster group solidarity. The Black Cat was a place where anarcho-punk "disorganizations" could put up flyers, recruit members, and keep their limited dollars circulating. At the café, feelings of alienation from the mainstream were converted into punk sentiments and channeled into anarchist practices.

Various activist groups were associated with punk culture. One of the foremost was Food Not Bombs, an anarchist dis-organization. It served to collect, prepare, and distribute free food to the homeless and the hungry. The hostility of the Seattle City Council and Seattle police toward Food Not Bombs was received at the Cat as another sign of American class warfare and a coercive attempt to force even the homeless to turn to commodities for their survival (see also Narotzky 1997: 114). When Food Not Bombs was cited for giving meals to the poor, this revealed the militancy of the ruling class to punks. Despite—and because of—the hassles from authorities, Food Not Bombs drew many volunteer hours from people who were affiliated with the Black Cat. Ketan mentioned Food Not Bombs as inspiring him to become a punk:

> I think the reason I chose not to [be a part of the mainstream] is … empathy … empathy and recognition of … what we're going through. I myself have been helping out with Food Not Bombs for a year straight, and [so] I've got a pretty good idea of what [poor] people go through. And I myself have [suffered] in the sense that I've not had my own space, and it's drove me crazy—you know, not knowing where I was going to sleep the next night. … Certainly I can't say that I know exactly what's going on [with the homeless], but I'm just trying to say that I have some understanding of it, you know? Just knowing that [poverty's] happening. And knowing that that's happening in the midst of that CEO making 109 million dollars [a year] … just knowing that makes me not want to be a part of that [wealth]. And that's happened with a lot of people here. I don't want to say what they believe, but—people here try to be as aware as they can of what's going on.

Another member of the scene, Karma, said that the "sense of family" drew her to the Cat.

> I like the fact that it's not run to make money. It's run for people, not profit. There's always some cause happening, some flyer up about something to go to: Books to Prisoners or Food Not Bombs or the Art and Revolution thing. … I think [activism] has a lot to do with it— certainly not the majority of why people come here. I think the majority of why people come here is because there's cheap food that's damn good. But because the food is specifically vegan, and that on a level by itself is activism, a lot of activists are vegan so they end up coming here. [Laughs.] And that kind of spurs the whole activism-crowd thing. Because they're all coming here, leaving their flyers, more people are coming, they're seeing the flyers, "Oh yeah, look: this is going on."

By making its political content explicit, food became a primary site of discussion and recruitment. In these movements, punk cuisine took shape and with it punks at the Black Cat concocted a daily life of meaningful situations, anarchist discourse, and resistance to "the System."

Conclusions

Contemporary punks—largely anarchist, antiracist, and feminist—use food as a medium to make themselves, and to theorize and contest the status quo. As an integral part of their daily practice, punks politicize food. For punks, everyday

American food choices are not only nutritionally deficient, they are filled with a commodified, homogenous culture, and are based in White-male domination over nature, animals, and people around the world. Punk cuisine is one way punks critique these power relations, and one substance with which to remake themselves outside of those relations. Punk cuisine is a way to make punk ideas knowable, ritualized, and edible; a way to favor the less mediated anarchist food over the capitalist product: the raw over the cooked. From punk vantage points, modern American food is transformed to a cultural extreme; its origins in nature and labor are cooked away, leaving a fetishized byproduct. Punk cuisine aspires toward food that is free of brand names, pesticides, and exploited labor, and toward food that is as raw as possible. In punk poesis, raw is a metaphor for wild, and one of the most important tropes in punk culture. Where mainstream society is said to control, exploit, and homogenize foods and people, punks idealize freedom, autonomy, and diversity.

For five years, the Black Cat Café brought punks together in a cultural space where they critiqued modernity, capitalism, Whiteness, and mainstream America. In their cuisine, punks identify and challenge Fordism, sexism, greed, cruelty, and environmental destruction. They choose to avoid eating American cuisine, for they see the act of eating everyday American food as a complicit endorsement of White-male corporate power. Reared White and middle class, and raised on foods that are seemingly nonideological in American culture, punks come to reject their ethno-class identities and cuisine, for they believe that mainstream American foods recapitulate a violent and unjust society. Mainstream American food, with its labor and natural components cooked beyond recognition, is countered with the raw and rotten foods of punks; foods that are ideally natural, home grown, stolen, discarded, and uncommodified. These foodways define punk cuisine and punks themselves.

Notes

1. My deep gratitude goes to Ratna Saptari, Marcel van der Linden, and to the International Instituut voor Sociale Geschiedenis (International Institute for Social History) of Amsterdam for support during the writing of this paper. Many thanks also to the Bushuis Bibliotheek in Amsterdam.
2. Research for this article stems from my participant-observation in the Black Cat Café in Seattle from 1993 to 1998. The café was owned and operated by people called "punk" in their culture for their anarchist philosophy. Punks are diverse, and though these punks might be called "anarcho-punks" (to distinguish them from gutter punks, straight-edge punks, and other types), all punk ideologies are related. The cuisine of punks is always changing, always being argued over, and always responding to new circumstances and ideologies.
3. The restaurant was never in violation of health codes except for minor offenses (once, for example, an inspector prohibited leaving rice in the rice cooker and the collective grudgingly had to buy a food warmer). Dishes, food, and hands were washed, and no customer ever reported suffering from food poisoning.

References

Adams, C. J. (1990) *The Sexual Politics of Meat: A Feminist-Vegetarian Critical Theory*. New York.
Anonymous (2001) Evasion. Atlanta.
Appadurai, A. (1981) Gastro-Politics in Hindu South-Asia. *American Ethnologist* 8: 494–511.
Bey, H. (1991) *T.A.Z.: The Temporary Autonomous Zone, Ontological Anarchy, Poetic Terrorism*. Brooklyn.
Bordo, S. (1993) *Unbearable Weight: Feminism, Western Culture and the Body*. Berkeley.
Bourdieu, P. (1984) *Distinction: A Social Critique of the Judgment of Taste*, transl. R. Nice. Cambridge MA.
Chapkis, W. (1986) *Beauty Secrets: Women and Politics of Appearance*. Boston.
Counihan, C. M. (1999) *The Anthropology of Food and the Body: Gender, Meaning, and Power*. New York.

CrimethInc. Workers' Collective (2001) *Days of War, Nights of Love: Crimethink for Beginners.* Atlanta.

Douglas, M. (ed.) (1984) *Food in the Social Order: Studies of Food and Festivities in Three American Communities.* New York.

DuPuis, E. M. (2000) *The Body and the Country: A Political Ecology of Consumption. New Forms of Consumption: Consumers, Culture, and Commodification* ed. M. Gottdiener, pp. 131–52. New York.

Harvey, D. (1989) *The Condition of Postmodernity: An Enquiry into the Origins of Cultural Change.* Oxford.

Himelstein, A. S., and J. Schweser (1998) *Tales of a Punk Rock Nothing.* New Orleans.

Lears, J. (1994) *Fables of Abundance: A Cultural History of Advertising in America.* New York.

Lévi-Strauss, C. (1969) (1964). *The Raw and the Cooked*, transl. J. Weightman and D. Weightman. New York.

Mennell, S. (1985) *All Manners of Food.* London.

Mintz, S. W. (1985) *Sweetness and Power: The Place of Sugar in Modern History.* New York.

Narotzky, S. (1997) *New Dimensions in Economic Anthropology.* London.

Nguyen, M. (1999) It's (Not) a White World: Looking for Race in Punk. *Punk Planet*, Nov/Dec. Also available at: www.worsethanqueer.com.

O'Hara, C. (1999) *The Philosophy of Punk: More Than Noise.* San Francisco.

Resist, M. (2003) *Resist #44.* Minneapolis.

Rifkin, J. (1992) *Beyond Beef: The Rise and Fall of the Cattle Culture.* New York.

Robbins, J. (1987) *Diet for a New America.* Walpole NH.

Sennett, R. (1990) *The Conscience of the Eye: The Design and Social Life of Cities.* New York.

Watson, D. (1999) (1991) *Civilization in Bulk. Against Civilization: Readings and Reflections*, ed. J. Zerzan, pp. 155–64. Eugene.

Weiss, B. (1996) *The Making and Unmaking of the Haya Lived World: Consumption, Commoditization, and Everyday Practice.* Durham.

Wood, R. C. (1995) *The Sociology of the Meal.* Edinburgh.

Consumption and Embodiment

17

Fast, Feast, and Flesh: The Religious Significance of Food to Medieval Women[*]

Caroline Walker Bynum

> In reading the lives of the [ancients] our lukewarm blood curdles at the thought of their austerities, but we remain strangely unimpressed by the essential point, namely, their determination to do God's will in all things, painful or pleasant.
>
> Henry Suso,[1] German mystic of the fourteenth century

> Strange to say the ability to live on the eucharist and to resist starvation by diabolical power died out in the Middle Ages and was replaced by "fasting girls" who still continue to amuse us with their vagaries.
>
> William Hammond,[2] nineteenth-century American physician and founder of the New York Neurological Society

Scholars have recently devoted much attention to the spirituality of the thirteenth, fourteenth, and fifteenth centuries. In studying late medieval spirituality they have concentrated on the ideals of chastity and poverty—that is, on the renunciation, for religious reasons, of sex and family, money and property. It may be, however, that modern scholarship has focused so tenaciously on sex and money because sex and money are such crucial symbols and sources of power in our own culture. Whatever the motives, modern scholars have ignored a religious symbol that had tremendous force in the lives of medieval Christians. They have ignored the religious significance of food. Yet, when we look at what medieval people themselves wrote, we find that they often spoke of gluttony as the major form of lust, of fasting as the most painful renunciation, and of eating as the most basic and literal way of encountering God. Theologians and spiritual directors from the early church to the sixteenth century reminded penitents that sin had entered the world when Eve ate the forbidden fruit and that salvation comes when Christians eat their God in the ritual of the communion table.[3]

In the Europe of the late thirteenth and fourteenth centuries, famine was on the increase again, after several centuries of agricultural growth and relative plenty. Vicious stories of food hoarding, of cannibalism, of infanticide, or of ill adolescents left to die when they could no longer do agricultural labor sometimes survive in the sources, suggesting a world in which hunger and even starvation were not

[*]*Originally published 1984*

uncommon experiences. The possibility of overeating and of giving away food to the unfortunate was a mark of privilege, of aristocratic or patrician status—a particularly visible form of what we call conspicuous consumption, what medieval people called magnanimity or largesse. Small wonder then that gorging and vomiting, luxuriating in food until food and body were almost synonymous, became in folk literature an image of unbridled sensual pleasure; that magic vessels which forever brim over with food and drink were staples of European folktales; that one of the most common charities enjoined on religious orders was to feed the poor and ill; or that sharing one's own meager food with a stranger (who might turn out to be an angel, a fairy, or Christ himself) was, in hagiography and folk story alike, a standard indication of heroic or saintly generosity. Small wonder too that voluntary starvation, deliberate and extreme renunciation of food and drink, seemed to medieval people the most basic asceticism, requiring the kind of courage and holy foolishness that marked the saints.[4]

Food was not only a fundamental material concern to medieval people; food practices—fasting and feasting—were at the very heart of the Christian tradition. A Christian in the thirteenth and fourteenth centuries was required by church law to fast on certain days and to receive communion at least once a year.[5] Thus, the behavior that defined a Christian was food-related behavior. This point is clearly illustrated in a twelfth-century story of a young man (of the house of Ardres) who returned from the crusades claiming that he had become a Saracen in the East; he was, however, accepted back by his family, and no one paid much attention to his claim until he insisted on eating meat on Friday. The full impact of his apostasy was then brought home, and his family kicked him out.[6]

Food was, moreover, a central metaphor and symbol in Christian poetry, devotional literature, and theology because a meal (the eucharist) was the central Christian ritual, the most direct way of encountering God. And we should note that this meal was a frugal repast, not a banquet but simply the two basic foodstuffs of the Mediterranean world: bread and wine. Although older Mediterranean traditions of religious feasting did come, in a peripheral way, into Christianity, indeed lasting right through the Middle Ages in various kinds of carnival, the central religious meal was reception of the two basic supports of human life. Indeed Christians believed it was human life. Already hundreds of years before transubstantiation was defined as doctrine, most Christians thought that they quite literally ate Christ's body and blood in the sacrament.[7] Medieval people themselves knew how strange this all might sound. A fourteenth-century preacher, Johann Tauler, wrote:

> St. Bernard compared this sacrament [the eucharist] with the human processes of eating when he used the similes of chewing, swallowing, assimilation and digestion. To some people this will seem crude, but let such refined persons beware of pride, which come from the devil: a humble spirit will not take offense at simple things.[8]

Thus food, as practice and as symbol, was crucial in medieval spirituality. But in the period from 1200 to 1500 it was more prominent in the piety of women than in that of men. Although it is difficult and risky to make any quantitative arguments about the Middle Ages, so much work has been done on saints' lives, miracle stories, and vision literature that certain conclusions are possible about the relative popularity of various practices and symbols. Recent work by André Vauchez, Richard Kieckhefer,

Donald Weinstein, and Rudolph M. Bell demonstrates that, although women were only about 18 percent of those canonized or revered as saints between 1000 and 1700, they were 30 percent of those in whose lives extreme austerities were a central aspect of holiness and over 50 percent of those in whose lives illness (often brought on by fasting and other penitential practices) was the major factor in reputation for sanctity.[9] In addition, Vauchez has shown that most males who were revered for fasting fit into one model of sanctity—the hermit saint (usually a layman)—and this was hardly the most popular male model, whereas fasting characterized female saints generally. Between late antiquity and the fifteenth century there are at least thirty cases of women who were reputed to eat nothing at all except the eucharist,[10] but I have been able to find only one or possibly two male examples of such behavior before the well-publicized fifteenth-century case of the hermit Nicholas of Flüe.[11] Moreover, miracles in which food is miraculously multiplied are told at least as frequently of women as of men, and giving away food is so common a theme in the lives of holy women that it is very difficult to find a story in which this particular charitable activity does not occur.[12] The story of a woman's basket of bread for the poor turning into roses when her husband (or father) protests her almsgiving was attached by hagiographers to at least five different women saints.[13]

If we look specifically at practices connected with Christianity's holy meal, we find that eucharistic visions and miracles occurred far more frequently to women, particularly certain types of miracles in which the quality of the eucharist as food is underlined. It is far more common, for example, for the wafer to turn into honey or meat in the mouth of a woman. Miracles in which an unconsecrated host is vomited out or in which the recipient can tell by tasting the wafer that the Priest who consecrated it is immoral happen almost exclusively to women. Of fifty-five people from the later Middle Ages who supposedly received the holy food directly from Christ's hand in a vision, forty-five are women. In contrast, the only two types of eucharistic miracle that occur primarily to men are miracles that underline not the fact that the wafer is food but the power of the priest.[14] Moreover, when we study medieval miracles, we note that miraculous abstinence and extravagant eucharistic visions tend to occur together and are frequently accompanied by miraculous bodily changes. Such changes are found almost exclusively in women. Miraculous elongation of parts of the body, the appearance on the body of marks imitating the various wounds of Christ (called stigmata), and the exuding of wondrous fluids (which smell sweet and heal and sometimes are food—for example, manna or milk) are usually female miracles.[15]

If we consider a different kind of evidence—the *exempla* or moral tales that preachers used to educate their audiences, both monastic and lay—we find that, according to Frederic Tubach's index, only about 10 percent of such stories are about women. But when we look at those stories that treat specifically fasting, abstinence, and reception of the eucharist, 30 to 50 percent are about women.[16] The only type of religious literature in which food is more frequently associated with men is the genre of satires on monastic life, in which there is some suggestion that monks are more prone to greed.[17] But this pattern probably reflects the fact that monasteries for men were in general wealthier than women's houses and therefore more capable of mounting elaborate banquets and tempting palates with delicacies.[18]

Taken together, this evidence demonstrates two things. First, food practices were more central in women's piety than in men's. Second, both men and women associated food—especially fasting and the eucharist—with women. There are however, a number of problems with this sort of evidence. In addition to the obvious problems of the paucity of material and of the nature of hagiographical accounts—problems to which scholars since the seventeenth century have devoted much sophisticated discussion—there is the problem inherent in quantifying data. In order to count phenomena the historian must divide them up, put them into categories. Yet the most telling argument for the prominence of food in women's spirituality is the way in which food motifs interweave in women's lives and writings until even phenomena not normally thought of as eating, feeding, or fasting seem to become food-related. In other words, food becomes such a pervasive concern that it provides both a literary and a psychological unity to the woman's way of seeing the world. And this cannot be demonstrated by statistics. Let me therefore tell in some detail one of the many stories from the later Middle Ages in which food becomes a leitmotif of stunning complexity and power. It is the story of Lidwina of the town of Schiedam in the Netherlands, who died in 1433 at the age of 53.[19]

Several hagiographical accounts of Lidwina exist, incorporating information provided by her confessors; moreover, the town officials of Schiedam, who had her watched for three months, promulgated a testimonial that suggests that Lidwina's miraculous abstinence attracted more public attention than any other aspect of her life. The document solemnly attests to her complete lack of food and sleep and to the sweet odor given off by the bits of skin she supposedly shed.

The accounts of Lidwina's life suggest that there may have been early conflict between mother and daughter. When her terrible illness put a burden on her family's resources and patience, it took a miracle to convince her mother of her sanctity. One of the few incidents that survives from her childhood shows her mother annoyed with her childish dawdling. Lidwina was required to carry food to her brothers at school, and on the way home she slipped into church to say a prayer to the Virgin. The incident shows how girlish piety could provide a respite from household tasks—in this case, as in so many cases, the task of feeding men. We also learn that Lidwina was upset to discover that she was pretty, that she threatened to pray for a deformity when plans were broached for her marriage, and that, after an illness at age fifteen, she grew weak and did not want to get up from her sickbed. The accounts thus suggest that she may have been cultivating illness—perhaps even rejecting food—before the skating accident some weeks later that produced severe internal injuries. In any event, Lidwina never recovered from her fall on the ice. Her hagiographers report that she was paralyzed except for her left hand. She burned with fever and vomited convulsively. Her body putrefied so that great pieces fell off. From mouth, ears, and nose, she poured blood. And she stopped eating.

Lidwina's hagiographers go into considerable detail about her abstinence. At first she supposedly ate a little piece of apple each day, although bread dipped into liquid caused her much pain. Then she reduced her intake to a bit of date and watered wine flavored with spices and sugar; later she survived on watered wine alone—only half a pint a week—and she preferred it when the water came from the river and was contaminated with salt from the tides. When she ceased to take any solid food, she also ceased to sleep. And finally she ceased to swallow anything at all. Although Lidwina's biographers present her abstinence as evidence of saintliness, she was suspected by some during her lifetime of being possessed by a devil instead; she herself appears to have claimed that her fasting was natural. When people accused her of hypocrisy, she replied that it is no sin to eat and therefore no glory to be incapable of eating.[20]

Fasting and illness were thus a single phenomenon to Lidwina. And since she perceived them as redemptive suffering, she urged both on others. We are told that a certain Gerard from Cologne, at her urging, became a hermit and lived in a tree, fed only on manna sent from God. We are also told that Lidwina prayed for her twelve-year-old nephew to be afflicted with an illness so that he would be reminded of God's mercy. Not surprisingly, the illness itself then came from miraculous feeding. The nephew became sick by drinking several drops from a pitcher of unnaturally sweet beer on a table by Lidwina's bedside.

Like the bodies of many other women saints, Lidwina's body was closed to ordinary intake and excreting but produced extraordinary effluvia.[21] The authenticating document from the town officials of Schiedam testifies that her body shed skin, bones, and even portions of intestines, which her parents kept in a vase; and these gave off a sweet odor until Lidwina, worried by the gossip that they excited, insisted that her mother bury them. Moreover, Lidwina's effluvia cured others. A man in England sent for her wash water to cure his ill leg. The sweet smell from her left hand led one of her confessors to confess sins. And Lidwina actually nursed others in an act that she herself explicitly saw as a parallel to the Virgin's nursing of Christ.

One Christmas season, so all her biographers tell us, a certain Catherine, who took care of her, had a vision that Lidwina's breasts would fill with milk, like Mary's, on the night of the Nativity. When she told Lidwina, Lidwina warned her to prepare herself. Then Lidwina saw a vision of Mary surrounded by a host of female virgins; and the breasts of Mary and of all the company filled with milk, which poured out from their open tunics, filling the sky. When Catherine entered Lidwina's room, Lidwina rubbed her own breast and the milk came out, and Catherine drank three times and was satisfied (nor did she want any corporeal food for many days thereafter).[22] One of Lidwina's hagiographers adds that, when the same grace was given to her again, she fed her confessor, but the other accounts say that the confessor was unworthy and did not receive the gift.

Lidwina also fed others by charity and by food multiplication miracles. Although she did not eat herself, she charged the widow Catherine to buy fine fish and make fragrant sauces and give these to the poor. The meat and fish she gave as alms sometimes, by a miracle, went much further than anyone had expected. She gave water and wine and money for beer to an epileptic burning with thirst; she sent a whole pork shoulder to a poor man's family; she regularly sent food to poor or sick children, forcing her servants to spend or use for others money or food she would not herself consume. When she shared the wine in her bedside jug with others it seemed inexhaustible. So pleased was God with her charity that he sent her a vision of a heavenly banquet, and the food she had given away was on the table.

Lidwina clearly felt that her suffering was service—that it was one with Christ's suffering and that it therefore substituted for the suffering of others, both their bodily ills and their time in purgatory. Indeed her body quite literally became Christ's macerated and saving flesh, for, like many other female saints she received stigmata (or so one—but only one—of her hagiographers claims).[23] John Brugman, in *Vita posterior*, not only underlines the parallel between her wounds and those on a miraculous bleeding host she received; he also states explicitly that, in her stigmata, Christ "transformed his lover into his likeness."[24] Her hagiographers state that the fevers she suffered almost daily from 1421 until her death were suffered in order to release souls in purgatory.[25] And we see this notion of substitution reflected quite clearly in the story of a very evil man, in whose stead Lidwina made confession; she then took upon herself his punishment, to the increment of her own bodily anguish. We see substitution of another kind in the story of Lidwina taking over the toothache of a woman who wailed outside her door.

Thus, in Lidwina's story, fasting, illness, suffering, and feeding fuse together. Lidwina becomes the food she rejects. Her body, closed to ordinary intake and excretion but spilling over in milk and sweet putrefaction, becomes the sustenance and the cure—both earthly and heavenly—of her followers. But holy eating is a theme in her story as well. The eucharist is at the core of Lidwina's devotion. During her pathetic final years, when she had almost ceased to swallow, she received frequent communion (indeed as often as every two days). Her biographers claim that, during this period, only the holy food kept her alive.[26] But much of her life was plagued by conflict with the local clergy over her eucharistic visions and hunger. One incident in particular shows not only the centrality of Christ's body as food in Lidwina's spirituality but also the way in which a woman's craving for the host, although it kept her under the control of the clergy, could seem to that same clergy a threat, both because it criticized their behavior and because, if thwarted, it could bypass their power.[27]

Once an angel came to Lidwina and warned her that the priest would, the next day, bring her an unconsecrated host to test her. When the priest came and pretended to adore the host, Lidwina vomited it out and said that she could easily tell our Lord's body from unconsecrated bread. But the priest swore that the host was consecrated and returned, angry, to the church. Lidwina then languished for a long time, craving communion but unable to receive it. About three and a half months later, Christ appeared to her, first as a baby, then as a bleeding and suffering youth. Angels appeared, bearing the instruments of the passion, and (according to one account) rays from Christ's wounded body pierced Lidwina with stigmata. When she subsequently asked for a sign, a host hovered over Christ's head and a napkin descended onto her bed, containing a miraculous host, which remained and was seen by many people for days after. The priest returned and ordered Lidwina to keep quiet about the miracle but finally agreed, at her insistence, to feed her the miraculous host as communion. Lidwina was convinced that it was truly Christ because she, who was usually stifled by food, ate this bread without pain. The next day the priest preached in church that Lidwina was deluded and that her host was a fraud of the devil. But, he claimed, Christ was present in the bread he offered because it was consecrated with all the majesty of the priesthood. Lidwina protested his interpretation of her host, but she agreed to accept a consecrated wafer from him and to pray for his sins. Subsequently the priest claimed that he had cured Lidwina from possession by the devil, while

Lidwina's supporters called her host a miracle. Although Lidwina's hagiographers do not give full details, they claim that the bishop came to investigate the matter, that he blessed the napkin for the service of the altar, and that the priest henceforth gave Lidwina the sacrament without tests or resistance.

As this story worked its way out, its theme was not subversive of clerical authority. The conflict began, after all, because Lidwina wanted a consecrated host, and it resulted in her receiving frequent communion, in humility and piety. According to one of her hagiographers, the moral of the story is that the faithful can always substitute "spiritual communion" (i.e., meditation) if the actual host is not given.[28] But the story had radical implications as well. It suggested that Jesus might come directly to the faithful if priests were negligent or skeptical, that a priest's word might not be authoritative on the difference between demonic possession and sanctity, that visionary women might test priests. Other stories in Lidwina's life had similar implications. She forbade a sinning priest to celebrate mass; she read the heart of another priest and learned of his adultery. Her visions of souls in purgatory especially concerned priests, and she substituted her sufferings for theirs. One Ash Wednesday an angel came to bring ashes for her forehead before the priest arrived. Even if Lidwina did not reject the clergy, she sometimes quietly bypassed or judged them.

Lidwina focused her love of God on the eucharist. In receiving it, in vision and in communion, she became one with the body on the cross. Eating her God, she received his wounds and offered her suffering for the salvation of the world. Denying herself ordinary food, she sent that food to others, and her body gave milk to nurse her friends. Food is the basic theme in Lidwina's story: self as food and God as food. For Lidwina, therefore, eating and not-eating were finally one theme. To fast, that is, to deny oneself earthly food, and yet to eat the broken body of Christ—both acts were to suffer. And to suffer was to save and to be saved.

Lidwina did not write herself, but some pious women did. And many of these women not only lived lives in which miraculous abstinence, charitable feeding of others, wondrous bodily changes, and eucharistic devotion were central; they also elaborated in prose and poetry a spirituality in which hungering, feeding, and eating were central metaphors for suffering, for service, and for encounter with God. For example, the great Italian theorist of purgatory, Catherine of Genoa (d. 1510)—whose extreme abstinence began in response to an unhappy marriage and who eventually persuaded her husband to join her in a life of continence and charitable feeding of the poor and sick—said that the annihilation of ordinary food by a devouring body is the best metaphor for the annihilation of the soul by God in mystical ecstasy.[29] She also wrote that, although no simile can adequately convey the joy in God that is the goal of all souls, nonetheless the image that comes most readily to mind is to describe God as the only bread available in a world of the starving.[30] Another Italian Catherine, Catherine of Siena (d. 1380), in whose saintly reputation fasting, food miracles, eucharistic devotion, and (invisible) stigmata were central,[31] regularly chose to describe Christian duty as "eating at the table of the cross the food of the honor of God and the salvation of souls."[32] To Catherine, "to eat" and "to hunger" have the same fundamental meaning, for one eats but is never full, desires but is never satiated.[33] "Eating" and "hungering" are active, not passive, images. They stress pain more than joy. They mean most basically to suffer and to serve—to suffer because in hunger one joins with Christ's suffering on the cross; to serve because to hunger is to expiate the sins of the world. Catherine wrote:

> And then the soul becomes drunk. And after it . . . has reached the place [of the teaching of the crucified Christ] and drunk to the full, it tastes the food of patience, the odor of virtue, and such a desire to bear the cross that it does not seem that it could ever be satiated . . . . And then the soul becomes like a drunken man; the more he drinks the more he wants to drink; the more it bears the cross the more it wants to bear it. And the pains are its refreshment and the tears which it has shed for the memory of the blood are its drink. And the sighs are its food.[34]

And again:

> Dearest mother and sisters in sweet Jesus Christ, I, Catherine, slave of the slaves of Jesus Christ, write to you in his precious blood, with the desire to see you confirmed in true and perfect charity so that you be true nurses of your souls. For we cannot nourish others if first we do not nourish our own souls with true and real virtues . . . . Do as the child does who, wanting to take milk, takes the mother's breast and places it in his mouth and draws to himself the milk by means of the flesh. So . . . we must attach ourselves to the breast of the crucified Christ, in whom we find the mother of charity, and draw from there by means of his flesh (that is, the humanity) the milk that nourishes our soul . . . . For it is Christ's humanity that suffered, not his divinity; and, without suffering, we cannot nourish ourselves with this milk which we draw from charity.[35]

To the stories and writings of Lidwina and the two Catherines—with their insistent and complex food motifs—I could add dozens of others. Among the most obvious examples would be the beguine Mary of Oignies (d. 1213) from the Low Countries, the princess Elisabeth of Hungary (d. 1231), the famous reformer of French and Flemish religious houses Colette of Corbie (d. 1447), and the thirteenth-century poets Hadewijch and Mechtild of Magdeburg. But if we look closely at the lives and writings of those men from the period whose spirituality is in general closest to women's and who were deeply influenced by women—for example, Francis of Assisi in Italy, Henry Suso and Johann Tauler in the Rhineland, Jan van Ruysbroeck of Flanders, or the English hermit Richard Rolle—we find that even to these men food asceticism is not the central ascetic practice. Nor are food metaphors central in their poetry and prose.[36] Food then is much more important to women than to men as a religious symbol. The question is why?

Modern scholars who have noticed the phenomena I have just described have sometimes suggested in an offhand way that miraculous abstinence and eucharistic frenzy are simply "eating disorders."[37] The implication of such remarks is usually that food disorders are characteristic of women rather than men, perhaps for biological reasons, and that these medieval eating disorders are different from nineteenth- and twentieth-century ones only because medieval people "theologized" what we today "medicalize."[38] While I cannot deal here with all the implications of such analysis, I want to point to two problems with it. First, the evidence we have indicates that extended abstinence was almost exclusively a male phenomenon in early Christianity and a female phenomenon in the high Middle Ages.[39] The cause of such a distribution of cases cannot be primarily biological.[40] Second, medieval people did not treat all refusal to eat as a sign of holiness. They sometimes treated it as demonic possession, but they sometimes also treated it as illness.[41] Interestingly enough, some of the holy women whose fasting was taken as miraculous (for example, Colette of Corbie) functioned as healers of ordinary individuals, both male and female, who could not eat.[42] Thus, for most of the Middle Ages, it was only in the case of some unusually devout women that not-eating was both supposedly total and religiously significant. Such behavior must have a cultural explanation.

On one level, the cultural explanation is obvious. Food was important to women religiously because it was important socially. In medieval Europe (as in many countries today) women were associated with food preparation and distribution rather than food consumption. The culture suggested that women cook and serve, men eat. Chronicle accounts of medieval banquets, for example, indicate that the sexes were often segregated and that women were sometimes relegated to watching from the balconies while gorgeous foods were rolled out to please the eyes as well as the palates of men.[43] Indeed men were rather afraid of women's control of food. Canon lawyers suggested, in the codes they drew up, that a major danger posed by women was their manipulation of male virility by charms and potions added to food.[44] Moreover, food was not merely a resource women controlled; it was the resource women controlled. Economic resources were controlled by husbands, fathers, uncles, or brothers. In an obvious sense, therefore, fasting and charitable food distribution (and their miraculous counterparts) were natural religious activities for women. In fasting and charity women renounced and distributed the one resource that was theirs. Several scholars have pointed out that late twelfth- and early thirteenth-century women who wished to follow the new ideal of poverty and begging (for example, Clare of Assisi and Mary of Oignies) were simply not permitted either by their families or by religious authorities to do so.[45] They substituted fasting for other ways of stripping the self of support. Indeed a thirteenth-century hagiographer commented explicitly that one holy woman gave up food because she had nothing else to give up.[46] Between the thirteenth and fifteenth centuries, many devout laywomen who resided in the homes of fathers or spouses were able to renounce the world in the midst of abundance because they did not eat or drink the food that was paid for by family wealth. Moreover, women's almsgiving and abstinence appeared culturally acceptable forms of asceticism because what women ordinarily did, as housewives, mothers, or mistresses of great castles, was to prepare and serve food rather than to eat it.

The issue of control is, however, more basic than this analysis suggests. Food-related behavior was central to women socially and religiously not only because food was a resource women controlled but also because, by means of food, women controlled themselves and their world.

First and most obviously, women controlled their bodies by fasting. Although a negative or dualist concept of body does not seem to have been the most fundamental notion of body to either women or men, some sense that body was to be disciplined, defeated, occasionally even destroyed, in order to release or protect spirit is present in women's piety. Some holy women seem to have developed an extravagant fear of any bodily contact.[47] Clare of Montefalco (d. 1308), for example, said she would rather spend days in hell than be touched by a man.[48] Lutgard of Aywières panicked at an abbot's insistence on giving her the kiss of peace, and Jesus had to interpose his hand in a vision so that she was not reached by the abbot's lips. She even asked to have her own gift of healing by touch taken away.[49] Christina of Stommeln (d. 1312), who fell into a latrine while in a trance, was furious at the laybrothers who rescued her because they touched her in order to do so.[50]

Many women were profoundly fearful of the sensations of their bodies, especially hunger and thirst. Mary of Oignies, for example, was so afraid of taking pleasure in food that Christ had to make her unable to taste.[51] From the late twelfth century comes a sad story of a dreadfully sick girl named Alpaïs who sent away the few morsels of pork given her to suck, because she feared that any enjoyment of eating might mushroom madly into gluttony or lust.[52] Women like Ida of Louvain (d. perhaps 1300), Elsbeth Achler of Reute (d. 1420), Catherine of Genoa, or Columba of Rieti (d. 1501), who sometimes snatched up food and ate without knowing what they were doing, focused their hunger on the eucharist partly because it was an acceptable object of craving and partly because it was a self-limiting food.[53] Some of women's asceticism was clearly directed toward destroying bodily needs, before which women felt vulnerable.

Some fasting may have had as a goal other sorts of bodily control. There is some suggestion in the accounts of hagiographers that fasting women were admired for suppressing excretory functions. Several biographers comment with approval that holy women who do not eat cease also to excrete, and several point out explicitly that the menstruation of saintly women ceases.[54] Medieval theology—profoundly ambivalent about body as physicality—was ambivalent about menstruation also, seeing it both as the polluting "curse of Eve" and as a natural function that, like all natural functions, was redeemed in the humanity of Christ. Theologians even debated whether or not the Virgin Mary menstruated.[55] But natural philosophers and theologians were aware that, in fact, fasting suppresses menstruation. Albert the Great noted that some holy women ceased to menstruate because of their fasts and austerities and commented that their health did not appear to suffer as a consequence.[56]

Moreover, in controlling eating and hunger, medieval women were also explicitly controlling sexuality. Ever since Tertullian and Jerome, male writers had warned religious women that food was dangerous because it excited lust.[57] Although there is reason to suspect that male biographers exaggerated women's sexual temptations, some women themselves connected food abstinence with chastity and greed with sexual desire.[58]

Women's heightened reaction to food, however, controlled far more than their physicality. It also controlled their social environment. As the story of Lidwina of Schiedam makes clear, women often coerced both families and religious authorities through fasting and through feeding. To an aristocratic or rising merchant family of late medieval Europe, the self-starvation of a daughter or spouse could be deeply perplexing and humiliating. It could therefore be an effective means of manipulating, educating, or converting family members. In one of the most charming passages of Margery Kempe's autobiography, for example, Christ and Margery consult together about her asceticism and decide that, although she wishes to practice both food abstention and sexual continence, she should perhaps offer to trade one behavior for the other. Her husband, who had married Margery in an effort to rise socially in the town of Lynn and who was obviously ashamed of her queer penitential clothes and food practices, finally agreed to grant her sexual abstinence in private if she would return to normal cooking and eating in front of the neighbors.[59] Catherine of Siena's sister, Bonaventura, and the Italian saint Rita of Cascia (d. 1456) both reacted to profligate young husbands by wasting away and managed thereby to tame disorderly male behavior.[60] Columba of Rieti and Catherine of Siena expressed what was clearly adolescent conflict with their mothers and riveted family attention on their every move by their refusal to eat. Since fasting so successfully manipulated and embarrassed families, it is not surprising that self-starvation often originated or escalated at puberty, the moment at which families usually began negotiations for husbands for their daughters. Both Catherine and Columba, for example, established themselves as unpromising marital material by their extreme food and sleep deprivation, their frenetic giving away of paternal resources, and their compulsive service of family members in what were not necessarily welcome ways. (Catherine insisted on doing the family laundry in the middle of the night.)[61]

Fasting was not only a useful weapon in the battle of adolescent girls to change their families' plans for them. It also provided for both wives and daughters an excuse for neglecting food preparation and family responsibilities. Dorothy of Montau, for example, made elementary mistakes of cookery (like forgetting to scale the fish before frying them) or forgot entirely to cook and shop while she was in ecstasy. Margaret of Cortona refused to cook for her illegitimate son (about whom she felt agonizing ambivalence) because, she said, it would distract her from prayer.[62]

Moreover, women clearly both influenced and rejected their families' values by food distribution. Ida of Louvain, Catherine of Siena, and Elisabeth of Hungary, each in her own way, expressed distaste for family wealth and coopted the entire household into Christian charity by giving away family resources, sometimes surreptitiously or even at night. Elisabeth, who gave away her husband's property, refused to eat any food except that paid for by her own dowry because the wealth of her husband's family came, she said, from exploiting the poor.[63]

Food-related behavior—charity, fasting, eucharistic devotion, and miracles—manipulated religious authorities as well.[64] Women's eucharistic miracles—especially the ability to identify unconsecrated hosts or unchaste priests—functioned to expose and castigate clerical corruption. The Viennese woman Agnes Blannbekin, knowing that her priest was not chaste, prayed that he be deprived of the host, which then flew away from him and into her own mouth.[65] Margaret of Cortona saw the hands of an unchaste priest turn black when he held the host.[66] Saints' lives and chronicles contain many stories, like that told of Lidwina of Schiedam, of women who vomited out unconsecrated wafers, sometimes to the considerable discomfiture of local authorities.[67]

The intimate and direct relationship that holy women claimed to the eucharist was often a way of bypassing ecclesiastical control. Late medieval confessors and theologians attempted to inculcate awe as well as craving for the eucharist; and women not only received ambiguous advice about frequent communion, they were also sometimes barred from receiving it at exactly the point at which their fasting and hunger reached fever pitch.[68] In such circumstances many women simply received in vision what the celebrant or confessor withheld. Imelda Lambertini, denied communion because she was too young, and Ida of Léau, denied because she was subject to "fits," were given the host by Christ.[69] And some women received, again in visions, either Christ's blood, which they were regularly denied because of their lay status, or the power to consecrate and distribute, which they were denied because of their gender. Angela of Foligno and Mechtild of Hackeborn were each, in a vision, given the chalice to distribute.[70] Catherine of Siena received blood in her mouth when she ate the wafer.[71]

It is thus apparent that women's concentration on food enabled them to control and manipulate both their bodies and their environment. We must not under-estimate the effectiveness of such manipulation in a world where it was often extraordinarily difficult for women to avoid marriage or to choose a religious vocation.[72] But such a conclusion concentrates on the function of fasting and feasting, and function is not meaning. Food did not "mean" to medieval women the control it provided. It is time, finally, to consider explicitly what it meant.

As the behavior of Lidwina of Schiedam or the theological insights of Catherine of Siena suggest, fasting, eating, and feeding all meant suffering, and suffering meant redemption. These complex meanings were embedded in and engendered by the theological doctrine of the Incarnation. Late medieval theology, as is well known, located the saving moment of Christian history less in Christ's resurrection than in his crucifixion. Although some ambivalence about physicality, some sharp and agonized dualism, was present, no other period in the history of Christian spirituality has placed so positive a value on Christ's humanity as physicality. Fasting was thus flight not so much *from* as *into* physicality. Communion was consuming—i.e., becoming—a God who saved the world through physical, human agony. Food to medieval women meant flesh and suffering and, through suffering, salvation: salvation of self and salvation of neighbor. Although all thirteenth- and fourteenth-century Christians emphasized Christ as suffering and Christ's suffering body as food, women were espe-cially drawn to such a devotional emphasis. The reason seems to lie in the way in which late medieval culture understood "the female."

Drawing on traditions that went back even before the origins of Christianity, both men and women in the later Middle Ages argued that "woman is to man as matter is to spirit." Thus "woman" or "the feminine" was seen as symbolizing the physical part of human nature, whereas man symbolized the spiritual or rational.[73] Male theologi-ans and biographers of women frequently used this idea to comment on female weak-ness. They also inverted the image and saw "woman" as not merely below but also above reason. Thus they somewhat sentimentally saw Mary's love for souls and her mercy toward even the wicked as an apotheosis of female unreason and weakness, and they frequently used female images to describe themselves in their dependence on God.[74] Women writers, equally aware of the male/female dichotomy, saw it somewhat differently. They tended to use the notion of "the female" as "flesh" to associate Christ's humanity with "the female" and therefore to suggest that women imitate Christ through physicality.

Women theologians saw "woman" as the symbol of humanity, where humanity was understood as including bodiliness. To the twelfth-century prophet, Elisabeth of Schönau, the humanity of Christ appeared in a vision as a female virgin. To Hilde-gard of Bingen (d. 1179), "woman" was the symbol of humankind, fallen in Eve, restored in Mary and church. She stated explicitly: "Man signifies the divinity of the Son of God and woman his humanity."[75] Moreover, to a number of women writers,

Mary was the source and container of Christ's physicality; the flesh Christ put on was in some sense female, because it was his mother's. Indeed whatever physiological theory of reproduction a medieval theologian held, Christ (who had no human father) had to be seen as taking his physicality from his mother. Mechtild of Magdeburg went further and implied that Mary was a kind of preexistent humanity of Christ as the Logos was his preexistent divinity. Marguerite of Oingt, like Hildegard of Bingen, wrote that Mary was the *tunica humanitatis*, the clothing of humanity, that Christ puts on.[76] And to Julian of Norwich, God himself was a mother exactly in that our humanity in its full physicality was not merely loved and saved but even given being by and from him. Julian wrote:

> For in the same time that God joined himself to our body in the maiden's womb, he took our soul, which is sensual, and in taking it, having enclosed us all in himself, he united it to our substance . . . . So our Lady is our mother, in whom we are all enclosed and born of her in Christ, for she who is mother of our saviour is mother of all who are saved in our saviour; and our saviour is our true mother, in whom we are endlessly born and out of whom we shall never come.[77]

Although male writers were apt to see God's motherhood in his nursing and loving rather than in the fact of creation, they too associated the flesh of Christ with Mary and therefore with woman.[78]

Not only did medieval people associate humanity as body with woman; they also associated woman's body with food. Woman was food because breast milk was the human being's first nourishment—the one food essential for survival. Late medieval culture was extraordinarily concerned with milk as symbol. Writers and artists were fond of the theme, borrowed from antiquity, of lactation offered to a father or other adult male as an act of filial piety. The cult of the Virgin's milk was one of the most extensive cults in late medieval Europe. A favorite motif in art was the lactating Virgin.[79] Even the bodies of evil women were seen as food. Witches were supposed to have queer marks on their bodies (sort of super-numerary breasts) from which they nursed incubi.

Quite naturally, male and female writers used nursing imagery in somewhat different ways. Men were more likely to use images of being nursed, women metaphors of nursing. Thus when male writers spoke of God's motherhood, they focused more narrowly on the soul being nursed at Christ's breast, whereas women were apt to associate mothering with punishing, educating, or giving birth as well.[80] Most visions of drinking from the breast of Mary were received by men.[81] In contrast, women (like Lidwina) often identified with Mary as she nursed Jesus or received visions of taking the Christchild to their own breasts.[82] Both men and women, however, drank from the breast of Christ, in vision and image.[83] Both men and women wove together—from Pauline references to milk and meat and from the rich breast and food images of the Song of Songs—a complex sense of Christ's blood as the nourishment and intoxication of the soul. Both men and women therefore saw the body on the cross, which in dying fed the world, as in some sense female. Again, physiological theory reinforced image. For, to medieval natural philosophers, breast milk was transmuted blood, and a human mother (like the pelican that also symbolized Christ) fed her children from the fluid of life that coursed through her veins.[84]

Since Christ's body itself was a body that nursed the hungry, both men and women naturally assimilated the ordinary female body to it. A number of stories are told of female saints who exuded holy fluid from breasts or fingertips, either during life or after death. These fluids often cured the sick.[85] The union of mouth to mouth, which many women gained with Christ, became also a way of feeding. Lutgard's saliva cured the ill; Lukardis of Oberweimar (d. 1309) blew the eucharist into another nun's mouth; Colette of Corbie regularly cured others with crumbs she chewed.[86] Indeed one suspects that stigmata—so overwhelmingly a female phenomenon—appeared on women's bodies because they (like the marks on the bodies of witches and the wounds in the body of Christ) were not merely wounds but also breasts.

Thus many assumptions in the theology and the culture of late medieval Europe associated woman with flesh and with food. But the same theology also taught that the redemption of all humanity lay in the fact that Christ was flesh and food. A God who fed his children from his own body, a God whose humanity was his children's humanity, was a God with whom women found it easy to identify. In mystical ecstasy as in communion, women ate and became a God who was food and flesh. And in eating a God whose flesh was holy food, women both transcended and became more fully the flesh and the food their own bodies were.

Eucharist and mystical union were, for women, both reversals and continuations of all the culture saw them to be.[87] In one sense, the roles of priest and lay recipient reversed normal social roles. The priest became the food preparer, the generator and server of food. The woman recipient ate a holy food she did not exude or prepare. Woman's jubilant, vision-inducing, inebriated eating of God was the opposite of the ordinary female acts of food preparation or of bearing and nursing children. But in another and, I think, deeper sense, the eating was not a reversal at all. Women became, in mystical eating, a fuller version of the food and the flesh they were assumed by their culture to be. In union with Christ, woman became a fully fleshly and feeding self—at one with the generative suffering of God.

Symbol does not determine behavior. Women's imitation of Christ, their assimilation to the suffering and feeding body on the cross, was not uniform. Although most religious women seem to have understood their devotional practice as in some sense serving as well as suffering, they acted in very different ways. Some, like Catherine of Genoa and Elisabeth of Hungary, expressed their piety in feeding and caring for the poor. Some, like Alpaïs, lay rapt in mystical contemplation as their own bodies decayed in disease or in self-induced starvation that was offered for the salvation of others. Many, like Lidwina of Schiedam and Catherine of Siena, did both. Some of these women are, to our modern eyes, pathological and pathetic. Others seem to us, as they did to their contemporaries, magnificent. But they all dealt, in feast and fast, with certain fundamental realities for which all cultures must find symbols—the realities of suffering and the realities of service and generativity.

Notes

This paper was originally given as the Solomon Katz Lecture in the Humanities at the University of Washington, March 1984. It summarizes several themes that will be elaborated in detail in my forthcoming book, *Holy Feast and*

Holy Fast: Food Motifs in the Piety of Late Medieval Women. I am grateful to Rudolph M. Bell, Peter Brown, Joan Jacobs Brumberg, Rachel Jacoff, Richard Kieckhefer, Paul Meyvaert, Guenther Roth, and Judith Van Herik for their suggestions and for sharing with me their unpublished work.

1. Quoted from Suso's letter to Elsbet Stagel in Henry Suso, *Deutsche Schriften im Auftrag der Württembergischen Kommission für Landesgeschichte*, ed. Karl Bihlmeyer (Stuttgart, 1907), 107; trans. (with minor changes) M. Ann Edward in *The Exemplar: Life and Writings of Blessed Henry Suso, O.P*, ed. Nicholas Heller, 2 vols. (Dubuque, Ia., 1962), 1:103.

2. William A. Hammond, *Fasting Girls: Their Physiology and Pathology* (New York, 1879), 6. Quoted in Joan J. Brumberg, " 'Fasting Girls': Nineteenth-Century Medicine and the Public Debate over 'Anorexia,' " paper delivered at the Sixth Berkshire Conference on the History of Women, 1–3 June 1984.

3. On the patristic notion that the sin of our first parents was gluttony, see Herbert Musurillo, "The Problem of Ascetical Fasting in the Greek Patristic Writers," *Traditio* 12 (1956): 17, n. 43. For a medieval discussion, see Thomas Aquinas *Summa theologiae* 2-2.148.3. For several examples of very explicit discussion of "eating God" in communion or of "being eaten" by him, see Augustine of Hippo (d. 430). *De civitate Dei, in Patrologiae cursus completus: Series latina*, ed. J.-P. Migne [hereafter *PL*], 41, col. 284c; Hilary of Poitiers (d. 367), *Tractatus in CXXV psalmum*, in PL 9, col. 688b-c; idem, *De Trinitate*, PL 10, cols. 246–47; Mechtild of Magdeburg (d. about 1282 or 1297), *Offenbarungen der Schwester Mechtild von Magdeburg oder Das Fliessende Licht der Gottheit*, ed. Gall Morel (Regensburg, 1869; reprint ed., Darmstadt, 1963), 43; Hadewijch (thirteenth century), *Mengeldichten*, ed. J. Van Mierlo (Antwerp, 1954), poem 16, p. 79; Johann Tauler, sermon 30, *Die Predigten Taulers*, ed. Ferdinand Vetter (Berlin, 1910), 293.

4. See Fritz Curschmann, *Hungersnöte im Mittelalter: Ein Beitrag zur Deutschen Wirtschaftsgeschichte des 8. bis 13. Jahrhunderts* (Leipzig, 1900); Mikhail M. Bakhtin, *Rabelais and His World*, trans. Hélène Iswolsky (Cambridge, Mass., 1968); and Piero Camporesi, *Il pane selvaggio* (Bologna, 1980).

5. For a brief discussion, see P M. J. Clancy, "Fast and Abstinence," *New Catholic Encyclopedia* (New York, 1967), 5:846–50.

6. Lambert, "History of the Counts of Guines," in *Monumenta Germaniae historica: Scriptorum* (hereafter MGH. SS), vol. 24 (Hanover, 1879), 615.

7. See Peter Brown, "A Response to Robert M. Grant: The Problem of Miraculous Feedings in the Graeco-Roman World," in *The Center for Hermeneutical Studies* 42 (1982): 16–24; Édouard Dumoutet, *Corpus Domini: Aux sources de la piété eucharistique médiévale* (Paris, 1942).

8. Tauler, sermon 31, in *Die Predigten*, 310; trans. E. Colledge and Sister M. Jane, *Spiritual Conferences* (St. Louis, 1961), 258.

9. André Vauchez, *La Sainteté en Occident aux derniers siècles du moyen âge d'après les procès de canonisation et les documents hagiographiques* (Rome, 1981); Donald Weinstein and Rudolph M. Bell, *Saints and Society: The Two Worlds of Western Christendom, 1000–1700* (Chicago, 1982); Richard Kieckhefer, *Unquiet Souls: Fourteenth-Century Saints and Their Religious Milieu* (Chicago, 1984). See also Ernst Benz, *Die Vision: Erfahrungsformen und Bilderwelt* (Stuttgart, 1969), 17–34.

10. For partial (and not always very accurate) lists of miraculous abstainers, see T E. Bridgett, *History of the Holy Eucharist in Great Britain*, 2 vols. (London, 1881), 2:195ff.; Ebenezer Cobham Brewer, *A Dictionary of Miracles: Imitative, Realistic and Dogmatic* (Philadelphia, 1884), 508–10; Peter Browe, *Die Eucharistischen Wunder des Mittelalters* (Breslau, 1938), 49-54; Thomas Pater, *Miraculous Abstinence: A Study of One of the Extraordinary Mystical Phenomena* (Washington, D.C., 1964); and Herbert Thurston, *The Physical Phenomena of Mysticism* (Chicago, 1952), 341–83 and passim. My own list includes ten cases that are merely mentioned in passing in saints' lives or chronicles. In addition, the following women are described in the sources as eating "nothing" or "almost nothing" for various periods and as focusing their sense of hunger on the eucharist: Mary of Oignies, Juliana of Cornillon, Ida of Louvain, Elisabeth of Spalbeek, Margaret of Ypres, Lidwina of Schiedam, Lukardis of Oberweimar, Jane Mary of Maillé, Alpaïs of Cudot, Elisabeth of Hungary, Margaret of Hungary, Dorothy of Montau (or Prussia), Elsbeth Achler of Reute, Colette of Corbie, Catherine of Siena, Columba of Rieti, and Catherine of Genoa. Several others—Angela of Foligno, Margaret of Cortona, Beatrice of Nazareth, Beatrice of Ornacieux, Lutgard of Aywières, and Flora of Beaulieu—experienced at times what the nineteenth century would have called a "hysterical condition" that left them unable to swallow.

11. Possible male exceptions include the visionary monk of Evesham and Aelred of Rievaulx in the twelfth century and Facio of Cremona in the thirteenth; see *The Revelation to the Monk of Evesham Abbey*, trans. Valerian Paget (New York, 1909), 35, 61; *The Life of Aelred of Rievaulx by Walter Daniel*, ed. and trans. F. M. Powicke (New York, 1951), 48ff.; *Chronica pontificum et imperatorum Mantuana* for the year 1256, MGH.SS 24: 216. In general those males whose fasting was most extreme—for example, Henry Suso, Peter of Luxembourg (d. 1386), and John the Good of Mantua (d. 1249)—show quite clearly in their *vitae* that, although they starved themselves and wrecked their digestions, they did *not* claim to cease eating entirely nor did they lose their *desire* for food. See Life of Suso in *Deutsche Schriften*, 7–195; John of Mantua, Process of Canonization, in *Acta sanctorum*,

ed. the Bollandists [hereafter *AASS*], October: 9 (Paris and Rome, 1868), 816, 840; Life of Peter of Luxemburg, in *AASS*, July: 1 (Venice, 1746), 513, and Process of Canonization, in ibid., 534–39. James Oldo (d. 1404), who began an extreme fast, returned to eating when commanded by his superiors; life of James Oldo, in AASS, April: 2 (Paris and Rome, 1865), 603–4.

12. On food multiplication miracles, see Thurston, *Physical Phenomena*, 385–91. According to the tables in Weinstein and Bell, *Saints and Society*, women are 22 percent of the saints important for aiding the poor and 25 percent of those important for curing the sick, although a little less than 18 percent of the total.

13. Elisabeth of Hungary, Rose of Viterbo, Elisabeth of Portugal, Margaret of Fontana, and Flora of Beaulieu; see Jeanne Ancelet-Hustache, *Sainte Elisabeth de Hongrie* (Paris, 1946), 39–42, n. 1; life of Margaret of Fontana, in *AASS*, September: 4 (Antwerp, 1753), 137; and Clovis Brunel, "Vida e Miracles de Sancta Flor," *Analecta Bollandiana* 64 (1946): 8, n. 4. We owe the story, first attached to Elisabeth of Hungary but apocryphal, to an anonymous Tuscan Franciscan of the thirteenth century; see Paul G. Schmidt, "Die zeitgenössische Überlieferung zum Leben und zur Heiligsprechung der heiligen Elisabeth," in *Sankt Elisabeth: Fürstin, Dienerin, Heilige: Aufsätze, Dokumentation, Katalog*, ed. the University of Marburg (Sigmaringen, 1981), 1, 5.

14. Browe, *Die Wunder*, and Antoine Imbert-Gourbeyre, *La Stigmatisation: L'Extase divine et les miracles de Lourdes: Réponse aux libres-penseurs*, 2 vols. (Clermont-Ferrand, 1894), 2:183, 408–9. The work of Imbert-Gourbeyre is on one level inaccurate and credulous, but for my purposes it provides a good index of stories medieval people were willing to circulate, if not of events that in fact happened. See also Caroline W. Bynum, "Women Mystics and Eucharistic Devotion in the Thirteenth Century," *Women's Studies* 11 (1984): 179–214.

15. See Thurston, *Physical Phenomena*, passim; E. Amann, "Stigmatisation," in *Dictionnaire de théologie catholique*, vol. 14, part I (Paris, 1939), col. 2617–19; Imbert-Gourbeyre, "La Stigmatisation"; and Pierre Debongnie, "Essai critique sur l'histoire des stigmatisations au moyen âge," *Études carmélitaines* 21.2 (1936): 22–59. According to the tables in Weinstein and Bell, women provide 27 percent of the wonder-working relics although only 18 percent of the saints. Women also seem to provide the largest number of myroblytes (oil-exuding saints), although more work needs to be done on this topic. Of the most famous medieval myroblytes—Nicolas of Myra, Catherine of Alexandria, and Elisabeth of Hungary—two were women. On myroblytes, see Charles W. Jones, *Saint Nicolas of Myra, Bari and Manhattan: Biography of a Legend* (Chicago, 1978), 144–53; J.-K. Huysmans, *Sainte Lydwine de Schiedam* (Paris, 1901), 288–91 (which must, however, be used with caution); and n. 85 below.

16. Frederic C. Tubach, *Index Exemplorum: A Handbook of Medieval Religious Tales* (Helsinki, 1969); see entries for "abstinence," "fasting," "bread," "loaves and fishes," "meat," "host," and "chalice."

17. See, for example, *Tractatus beati Gregorii pape contra religionis simulatores*, ed. Marvin Colker, in *Analecta Dublinensia: Three Medieval Latin Texts in the Library of Trinity College, Dublin* (Cambridge, Mass., 1975), 47, 57; and A. George Rigg, " 'Metra de monachis carnalibus': The Three Versions," *Mittellateinisches Jahrbuch* 15 (1980): 134–42, which gives three versions of an antimonastic parody and shows that the adaptation for nuns eliminates most of the discussion of food as temptation.

18. See David Knowles, "The Diet of Black Monks," *Downside Review* 52 [n.s. 33] (1934), 273–90; and Eileen Power, *Medieval English Nunneries, c. 1275 to 1535* (Cambridge, 1922), 161–236.

19. There are four near-contemporary *vitae* of Lidwina, one in Dutch by John Gerlac, two in Latin by John Brugman, and one by Thomas à Kempis. (Both Gerlac and Brugman knew her well: Gerlac was her relative and Brugman her confessor.) See *AASS*, April: 2, 267–360, which gives Brugman's Latin translation of Gerlac's Life with Gerlac's additions indicated in brackets (the *Vita prior*) and Brugman's longer Life (the *Vita posterior*); and Thomas à Kempis, *Opera omnia*, ed. H. Sommalius, vol. 3 (Cologne, 1759), 114–64. See also Huysmans, *Lydwine*.

20. Brugman, *Vita posterior*, 320; see also ibid., 313. It is also important to note that Lidwina at first responded to her terrible illness with anger and despair and had to be convinced that it was a saving imitation of Christ's passion; see *Vita prior*, 280–82, and Thomas à Kempis, Life of Lidwina, in *Opera omnia*, 132–33.

21. For parallel lives from the Low Countries, see Thomas of Cantimpré, Life of Lutgard of Aywières (d. 1246), in *AASS*, June: 4 (Paris and Rome, 1867), 189–210; and G. Hendrix, "Primitive Versions of Thomas of Cantimpré's *Vita Lutgardis*," *Cîteaux: Commentarii cistercienses* 29 (1978): 153–206; Thomas of Cantimpré, Life of Christina Mirabilis (d. 1224), in *AASS*, July: 5 (Paris, 1868), 637–60; Life of Gertrude van Oosten (d. 1358), in *AASS*, January: 1 (Antwerp, 1643), 348–53; and Philip of Clairvaux, Life of Elisabeth of Spalbeek (or Herkenrode) (d. after 1274), *Catalogus codicum hagiographicorum Bibliothecae regiae Bruxellensis*, vol. 1, part 1, ed. the Bollandists, in *Subsidia hagiographica*, vol. 1 (Brussels, 1886), 362–78.

22. *Vita prior*, 283; *Vita posterior*, 344; Thomas à Kempis, Life of Lidwina, 135–36.

23. *Vita posterior*, 331–32, 334–35. See Debongnie, "Stigmatisations," 55–56.

24. *Vita posterior*, 335.

25. See, for example, *Vita prior*, 277, 297. We are told that her relatives and friends benefited especially.

26. See *Vita prior*, 297; see also ibid., 280. And see Thomas à Kempis, Life of Lidwina, 155–56.

27. *Vita prior*, 295–97; *Vita posterior*, 329–35; Thomas à Kempis, Life of Lidwina, 155–56.

28. *Vita posterior*, 330.

29. *Vita mirabile et doctrina santa della beata Caterina da Genova . . .* (Florence, 1568; reprint ed., 1580), 106–7.

30. *Trattato del Purgatorio,* in Umile Bonzi da Genova, *S. Caterina Fieschi Adorno,* 2 vols. (Marietta, 1960), vol. 2, *Edizione critica dei manoscritti cateriniani,* 332–33. Catherine's "works" were compiled after her death, and there is some controversy about their "authorship" but all agree that the treatise on purgatory represents her own teaching.

31. It is quite easy to establish striking parallels between Catherine's behavior and modern descriptions of anorexia/bulimia. For accounts of Catherine's extended inedia, bingeing, and vomiting, see Raymond of Capua, Life of Catherine, in *AASS,* April: 3 (Paris and Rome, 1866), 872, 876–77, 903–7, 960; and the anonymous *I miracoli di Caterina di Jacopo da Siena di Anonimo Fiorentino a cura di Francesco Valli* (Siena, 1936), 5–9, 23–35. On Catherine's eucharistic devotion, see Raymond, Life of Catherine, 904–5, 907, and 909.

32. See, for example, letter 208, *Le lettere de S. Caterina da Siena, ridotte a miglior lezione, e in ordine nuovo disposte con note di Niccolò Tommaseo,* ed. Piero Misciattelli, 6 vols. (Siena, 1913–22), 3: 255–58; letter 11, ibid., 1:44; letter 340, ibid., 5:158–66; and *Catherine of Siena: The Dialogue,* trans. Suzanne Noffke (New York, 1980), 140.

33. See, for example, *Dialogue,* 170; letter 34, *Le lettere,* 1:157; letter 8, ibid., 1:34–38; letter 75, ibid., 2:21–24.

34. Letter 87, ibid., 2:92.

35. Letter 2* (a separately numbered series), in ibid., 6:5–6. Catherine is fond of nursing images to describe God: see letter 86, ibid., 2:81–88; letter 260, ibid., 4:139–40; letter 1*, ibid., 6:1–4; letter 81 (Tommaseo-Misciattelli no. 239) in *Epistolario di Santa Caterina da Siena,* ed. Eugenio Dupré Theseider, vol. 1 (Rome, 1940), 332–33; Dialogue, 52, 179–80, 292, and 323–24; and Raymond of Capua, Life of Catherine, 909.

36. On Hadewijch and Mechtild, see n. 3 above. On Mary of Oignies, see Bynum, "Women Mystics and Eucharistic Devotion." For Elisabeth, see Albert Huyskens, *Quellenstudien zur Geschichte der hl. Elisabeth Landgräfin von Thüringen* (Marburg, 1908); and Ancelet-Hustache, *Elisabeth.* For Colette, see the Lives in *AASS,* March: 1 (Antwerp, 1668), 539–619. For an analysis of the extent of food asceticism and food metaphors in the lives and writings of Francis, Suso, Tauler, Ruysbroeck, and Rolle, see my forthcoming book, *Holy Feast and Holy Fast.* Tauler and Rolle (like Catherine of Siena's confessor, Raymond of Capua) were actually apologetic about their inability to fast. And Tauler and Ruysbroeck, despite intense eucharistic piety, use little food language outside a eucharistic context. See also n. 11 above.

37. See, for example, Thurston, *Physical Phenomena,* passim; Benedict J. Groeschel, introduction to *Catherine of Genoa: Purgation and Purgatory . . .,* trans. Serge Hughes (New York, 1979), 11; J. Hubert Lacey, "Anorexia Nervosa and a Bearded Female Saint," *British Medical Journal* 285 (18–25 December 1982): 1816–17. Rudolph M. Bell is at work on a sophisticated study, the thesis of which is that a number of late medieval Italian religious women suffered from anorexia nervosa.

38. There is good evidence for biological factors in women's greater propensity for fasting and "eating disorders." See Harrison G. Pope and James Hudson, *New Hope for Binge Eaters: Advances in the Understanding and Treatment of Bulimia* (New York, 1984), which argues that anorexia and bulimia are types of biologically caused depression, which have a pharmacological cure. See also "Appendix B: Sex Differences in Death, Disease and Diet" in Katharine B. Hoyenga and K. T. Hoyenga, *The Question of Sex Differences: Psychological, Cultural and Biological Issues* (Boston, 1979), 372–90, which demonstrates that, for reasons of differences in metabolism between men and women, women's bodies tolerate fasting better than men's. For a sophisticated discussion of continuities and discontinuities in women's fasting practices, see Joan Jacobs Brumberg, " 'Fasting Girls': Reflections on Writing the History of Anorexia Nervosa," *Proceedings of the Society for Research on Child Development* (forthcoming).

39. See Browe, Die Wunder, 49–50; *Jules Corblet, Histoire dogmatique, liturgique et archéologique du sacrement de l'eucharistie,* 2 vols. (Paris, 1885–86), 1:188–91; and n. 10 above.

40. Even for the modern period there is much evidence that confutes a rigidly biochemical explanation of women's inedia. Most researchers agree that incidents of anorexia and bulimia are in fact increasing rapidly, although recent talk of an "epidemic" may be journalistic over-reaction. See Hilde Bruch, "Anorexia Nervosa: Therapy and Theory," *American Journal of Psychiatry* 139, no. 12 (December 1982): 1531–38; and A. H. Crisp, et al., "How Common Is Anorexia Nervosa? A Prevalence Study," *British Journal of Psychiatry* 128 (1976): 549–54.

41. Lidwina, Catherine of Siena, and Alpaïs of Cudot (d. 1211) apparently saw their inedia as illness, although all three were accused of demonic possession. See n. 20 above; Catherine of Siena, letter 19 (Tommaseo-Misciattelli no. 92), Epistolario, 1:80–82, where she calls her inability to eat an infermità; Raymond of Capua, Life of Catherine, 906; and Life of Alpaïs, in *AASS,* November: 2.1 (Brussels, 1894), 178, 180, 182–83, and 200.

42. Peter of Vaux, Life of Colette, 576, and account of miracles performed at Ghent after her death, ibid., 594–95. See also the two healing miracles recounted in the ninth-century life of Walburga (d. 779) by Wolfhard of Eichstadt, in *AASS,* February: 3 (Antwerp, 1658), 528 and 540–42. Holy women also sometimes cured people who could not fast; see the Life of Juliana of Cornillon, in *AASS,* April: 1 (Paris and Rome, 1866), 475, and Thomas of Cantimpré, Life of Lutgard, 200–201.

43. Barbara K. Wheaton, *Savouring the Past: The French Kitchen and Table from 1300 to 1789* (Philadelphia, 1983), 1–26.

44. Georges Duby, *The Knight, the Lady and the Priest: The Making of Modern Marriage in Medieval France*, trans. Barbara Bray (New York, 1984), 72, 106

45. On Mary of Oignies, see Brenda M. Bolton, "*Vitae Matrum*: A Further Aspect of the *Frauenfrage*," in *Medieval Women: Dedicated and Presented to Professor Rosalind M. T. Hill* . . . ed. D. Baker, Studies in Church History, subsidia 1 (Oxford, 1978), 257–59; on Clare, see Rosalind B. Brooke and Christopher N. L. Brooke, "St. Clare," in ibid., 275–87. And on this point generally see my essay, "Women's Stories, Women's Symbols: A Critique of Victor Turner's Theory of Liminality," in Frank Reynolds and Robert Moore, eds., *Anthropology and the Study of Religion* (Chicago, 1984), 105–25.

46. Life of Christina *Mirabilis*, 654.

47. On this point, see Claude Carozzi, "Douceline et les autres," *in La religion populaire en Languedoc du XIIIᵉ siècle à la moitié du XIVᵉ siècle*, Cahiers de Fanjeaux, no. 11 (Toulouse, 1976), 251–67; and Martinus Cawley, "Lutgard of Aywières: Life and Journal," *Vox Benedictina: A Journal of Translations from Monastic Sources* 1.1 (1984): 20–48.

48. See Vauchez, *La Sainteté*, 406. For Francesca Romana de' Ponziani (d. 1440) and Jutta of Huy (d. 1228), who found the act of sexual intercourse repulsive, see Weinstein and Bell, 39–40, 88–89.

49. Life of Lutgard, 193–95. To interpret these incidents more psychologically, one might say that it is hardly surprising that Lutgard, a victim of attempted rape in adolescence, should feel anesthetized when kissed, over her protests, by a man. Nor is it surprising that the "mouth" and "breast" of Christ should figure so centrally in her visions, providing partial healing for her painful experience of the mouths of men; see Life of Lutgard, 192–94, and Hendrix, "Primitive Versions," 180.

50. Ernest W. McDonnell, *The Beguines and Beghards in Medieval Culture with Special Emphasis on the Belgian Scene* (Rutgers, 1954; reprint ed., New York, 1969), 354–55.

51. James of Vitry, Life of Mary of Oignies, in AASS, June: 5 (Paris and Rome, 1867), 551–56.

52. Addendum to the life of Alpaïs, 207–8.

53. See above n. 29; Life of Ida of Louvain, in AASS, April: 2, 156–89, esp. 167; Anton Birlinger, ed., "Leben Heiliger Alemannischer Frauen des XIV–XV Jahrhunderts, 1: Dit erst Büchlyn ist von der Seligen Kluseneryn von Rüthy, die genant waz Elizabeth," *Alemannia* 9 (1881): 275–92, esp. 280–83; Life of Columba of Rieti, in AASS, May: 5 (Paris and Rome, 1866), 149*–222*, esp. 159*, 162*–164*, 187*, and 200*. This would also appear to be true of Dorothy of Montau (or of Prussia) (d. 1394); see Kieckhefer, *Unquiet Souls*, 22–33.

54. See, for example, Life of Lutgard, 200; Life of Elisabeth of Spalbeek, 378; Peter of Vaux, Life of Colette, 554–55; Life of Columba of Rieti, 188*. This emphasis on the closing of the body is also found in early modern accounts of "fasting girls." Jane Balan (d. 1603) supposedly did not excrete, menstruate, sweat, or produce sputum, tears, or even dandruff; see Hyder E. Rollins, "Notes on Some English Accounts of Miraculous Fasts," *The Journal of American Folk-lore* 34.134 (1921): 363–64.

55. See Charles T. Wood, "The Doctors' Dilemma: Sin, Salvation and the Menstrual Cycle in Medieval Thought," *Speculum* 56 (1981): 710–27.

56. Albert the Great, *De animalibus libri XXVI. nach der Cölner Urschrift*, vol. 1 (Münster, 1916), 682. Hildegard of Bingen, *Hildegardis Causae et Curae*, ed. P. Kaiser (Leipzig, 1903), 102–3, comments that the menstrual flow of virgins is less than that of nonvirgins, but she does not relate this to diet.

57. See, for example, Jerome, letter 22 *ad Eustochium*, PL 22, cols. 404–5, and *contra Jovinianum*, PL 23, cols. 290–312; Fulgentius of Ruspé, letter 3, PL 65, col. 332; John Cassian, *Institutions cénobitiques*, ed. Jean-Claude Guy (Paris, 1965), 206; and Musurillo, "Ascetical Fasting," 13–19. For a medieval preacher who repeats these warnings, see Peter the Chanter, *Verbum abbreviatum*, PL 205, cols. 327–28.

58. See Life of Margaret of Cortona, in AASS, February: 3 (Paris, 1865), 313, and Life of Catherine of Sweden, in *AASS*, March: 3 (Paris and Rome, 1865), 504. On the tendency of male writers to depict women as sexual beings, see Weinstein and Bell, 233–36.

59. *The Book of Margery Kempe*, trans. W. Butler-Bowdon (London, 1936), 48–49.

60. Raymond, Life of Catherine, 869; Life of Rita of Cascia, in AASS, May: 5 (Paris and Rome, 1866), 226–28. (There is no contemporary life of Rita extant.)

61. Raymond, Life of Catherine, 868–91 passim; Life of Columba, 153*–161*.

62. On Dorothy, see *Vita Lindana*, in AASS, October: 13 (Paris, 1883), 505, 515, 523, and 535–43; see also John Marienwerder, *Vita Latina*, ed. Hans Westpfahl, in *Vita Dorotheae Montoviensis Magistri Johannis Marienwerder* (Cologne, 1964), 236–45, and Kieckhefer, *Unquiet Souls*, 22–33. On Margaret, see Father Cuthbert, *A Tuscan Penitent: The Life and Legend of St. Margaret of Cortona* (London, n.d.), 94–95.

63. See above nn. 36, 53, and 61. On Elisabeth, see the depositions of 1235 in Huyskens, *Quellenstudien*, 112–40, and Conrad of Marburg's letter (1233) concerning her life in ibid., 155–60. See also Ancelet-Hustache, *Elisabeth*, 201–6 and 314–18. The importance of Elisabeth's tyrannical confessor, Conrad of Marburg, in inducing her obsession with food is impossible at this distance to determine. It was Conrad who ordered her not to eat

food gained by exploitation of the poor; at times, to break her will, he forbade her to indulge in charitable food distribution.

64. On this point, see Bynum, "Women Mystics and Eucharistic Devotion," and idem, *Jesus as Mother: Studies in the Spirituality of the High Middle Ages* (Berkeley, 1982), chap. 5.

65. See Browe, *Die Wunder* 34.

66. Life of Margaret of Cortona, 341; see also 343, where she recognizes an unconsecrated host.

67. See, for example, Life of Ida of Louvain, 178–79, and account of "Joan the Meatless" in Thomas Netter [Waldensis], *Opus de sacramentis* . . . (Salamanca, 1557), fols. 111v–112r. See also life of Mary of Oignies, 566, where James of Vitry claims that Mary saw angels when virtuous priests celebrated.

68. See Joseph Duhr, "Communion fréquente," *Dictionnaire de spiritualité, ascétique et mystique, doctrine et histoire*, vol. 2 (Paris, 1953), cols. 1234–92, esp. col. 1260.

69. For Imelda, see Browe, *Die Wunder*, 27–28; for Ida of Léau, see Life, in AASS, October: 13, 113–14. See also Life of Alice of Schaerbeke (d. 1250), in AASS, June: 2 (Paris and Rome, 1867), 473–74; and Life of Juliana of Cornillon, 445–46.

70. Life of Angela of Foligno, in *AASS*, January: 1, 204. For Mechtild's vision, see Bynum, *Jesus as Mother*, 210, n. 129.

71. See Catherine's own account of such a miracle, *Dialogue*, 239.

72. The work of David Herlihy and Diane Owen Hughes, which argues that, in the thirteenth and fourteenth centuries, the age discrepancy between husband and wife increased and the dowry, provided by the girl's family, became increasingly a way of excluding her from other forms of inheritance and from her natal family, suggests some particular reasons for a high level of antagonism between girls and their families in this period. The antagonism would stem less from the failure of families to find husbands for daughters (as Herlihy suggests) than from the tendency of families to marry girls off early and thereby buy them out of the family when they were little more than children (as Hughes suggests). See David Herlihy, "Alienation in Medieval Culture and Society," reprinted in *The Social History of Italy and Western Europe, 700–1500: Collected Studies* (London, 1978); idem, "The Making of the Medieval Family: Symmetry, Structure and Sentiment," *Journal of Family History* 8.2 (1983): 116–30; and Diane Owen Hughes, "From Brideprice to Dowry in Mediterranean Europe," *Journal of Family History* 3 (1978): 262–96.

73. Vern Bullough, "Medieval Medical and Scientific Views of Women," *Viator* 4 (1973): 487–93; Eleanor McLaughlin, "Equality of Souls, Inequality of Sexes: Women in Medieval Theology," *Religion and Sexism: Images of Woman in the Jewish and Christian Traditions*, ed. R. Ruether (New York, 1974), 213–66; and M.-T d'Alverny, "Comment les théologiens et les philosophes voient la femme?" *Cahiers de civilisation médiévale* 20 (1977): 105–29.

74. See Bynum, *Jesus as Mother*, chap. 4, and idem, " 'And Woman His Humanity': Female Imagery in the Religious Writing of the Later Middle Ages," in *New Perspectives on Religion and Gender*, ed. Caroline Bynum, Stevan Harrell, and Paula Richman, to appear.

75. *Die Visionen der hl. Elisabeth und die Schriften der Aebte Ekbert und Emecho von Schönau*, ed. F W. E. Roth (Brunn, 1884), 60; Hildegard, *Liber divinorum operum*, PL 197, col. 885; and idem, *Scivias*, ed. Adelgundis Führkötter and A. Carlevaris, 2 vols. (Turnhout, 1978), 1:225–306, esp. 231 and plate 15.

76. On Mechtild, see *Jesus as Mother*, 229, 233–34, and 244; and on Hildegard, see Barbara Jane Newman, "O *Feminea Forma*: God and Woman in the Works of St. Hildegard (1098–1179)," Ph.D. diss., Yale, 1981, 131–34. And see Marguerite of Oingt, *Speculum, in Les Oeuvres de Marguerite d'Oingt*, ed. and trans. A. Duraffour, R. Gardette, and R. Durdilly (Paris, 1965), 98–99.

77. *Julian of Norwich: Showings*, trans. Edmund Colledge and James Walsh (New York, 1978), long text: 292, 294.

78. See *Jesus as Mother*, chap. 4, and Jan van Ruysbroeck, *The Spiritual Espousals*, trans. E. Colledge (New York, n.d.), 43; idem, "Le Miroir du salut éternel," in *Oeuvres de Ruysbroeck l'Admirable*, trans. by the Benedictines of St.-Paul de Wisques, vol. 3 (3rd ed., Brussels, 1921), 82–83; Francis of Assisi, "Salutation of the Blessed Virgin," trans. B. Fahy, in *St. Francis of Assisi: Writings and Early Biographies: English Omnibus of Sources*, ed. Marion Habig (3rd ed., Chicago, 1973), 135–36; and Henry Suso, *Büchlein der Ewigen Weisheit*, in *Deutsche Schriften*, 264.

79. See P. V. Bétérous, "A propos d'une des légendes mariales les plus répandues: Le 'Lait de la Vierge,' " *Bulletin de l'Association Guillaume Budé* 4 (1975): 403–11; Léon Dewez and Albert van Iterson, "La Lactation de saint Bernard: Légende et iconographie," *Cîteaux in de Nederlanden* 7 (1956): 165–89.

80. See Bynum, " 'And Woman His Humanity.' "

81. On the lactation of Bernard of Clairvaux, see E. Vacandard, *Vie de saint Bernard, abbé de Clairvaux*, 2 vols. (1895; reprint ed., Paris, 1920), 2:78; and Dewez and van Iterson, "La Lactation." Suso received the same vision; see Life, in *Deutsche Schriften*, 49–50. Alanus de Rupe (or Alan de la Roche, d. 1475), founder of the modern rosary devotion, tells a similar story of himself in his Revelations; see Heribert Holzapfel, *St. Dominikus und der Rosenkranz* (Munich, 1903), 21. See also Alb. Poncelet, "Index miraculorum B. V. Mariae quae saec. VI–XV latine conscripta sunt," *Analecta Bollandiana* 21 (1902): 359, which lists four stories of sick men healed by the Virgin's milk. Vincent of Beauvais, *Speculum historiale* (Venice, 1494), fol. 80r, tells of a sick cleric who nursed

from the Virgin. Elizabeth Petroff, *Consolation of the Blessed* (New York, 1979), 74, points out that the Italian women saints she has studied nurse only from Christ, never from Mary, in vision. A nun of Töss, however, supposedly received the "pure, tender breast" of Mary into her mouth to suck because she helped Mary rear the Christchild; Ferdinand Vetter, ed., *Das Leben der Schwestern zu Töss beschrieben von Elsbet Stagel* (Berlin, 1906), 55–56. And Lukardis of Oberweimar nursed from Mary; see her Life in *Analecta Bollandiana* 18 (1899): 318–19.

82. See, for example, Life of Gertrude van Oosten (or of Delft), 350. For Gertrude of Helfta's vision of nursing the Christchild, see *Jesus as Mother*, 208, n. 123. There is one example of a man nursing Christ; see McDonnell, *Beguines*, 328, and Browe, *Die Wunder*, 106.

83. See *Jesus as Mother*, chap. 4, and nn. 35 and 49 above. Clare of Assisi supposedly received a vision in which she nursed from Francis; see "Il Processo di canonizzazione di S. Chiara d'Assisi," ed. Zeffirino Lazzeri, *Archivum Franciscanum Historicum* 13 (1920), 458, 466.

84. See Mary Martin McLaughlin, "Survivors and Surrogates: Children and Parents from the Ninth to the Thirteenth Centuries," *The History of Childhood*, ed. L. DeMause (New York, 1974): 115–18, and *Jesus as Mother*, 131–35.

85. See above nn. 15 and 82. Examples of women who exuded healing oil, in life or after death, include Lutgard of Aywières, Christina *Mirabilis*, Elisabeth of Hungary, Agnes of Montepulciano, and Margaret of Città di Castello (d. 1320). See Life of Lutgard, 193–94; Life of Christina *Mirabilis* 652–54; Huyskens, *Quellenstudien*, 51–52; Raymond of Capua, Life of Agnes, in AASS, April: 2, 806, Life of Margaret of Città di Castello, Analecta Bollandiana 19 (1900): 27–28, and see also AASS, April: 2, 192.

86. Life of Lutgard, 193; Life of Lukardis of Oberweimar, *Analecta Bollandiana* 18 (1899): 337–38; Peter of Vaux, Life of Colette, 563, 576, 585, and 588.

87. For a general discussion of reversed images in women's spirituality, see Bynum, "Women's Stories, Women's Symbols."

18

Not Just "a White Girl's Thing": The Changing Face of Food and Body Image Problems*

Susan Bordo

When You Think of Eating Disorders, Whom Do You Picture?

If your images of girls and women with eating and body image problems have been shaped by *People* magazine and *Lifetime* movies, she's probably white, heterosexual, North American, and economically secure. If you're familiar with the classic psychological literature on eating disorders, you may also have read that she's an extreme 'perfectionist' with a hyper-demanding mother, and that she suffers from 'body-image distortion syndrome' and other severe perceptual and cognitive problems that 'normal' girls don't share. You probably don't picture her as Black, Asian, or Latina. Consider, then, Tenisha Williamson. Tenisha is black, suffers from anorexia, and has described her struggle on 'Colors of Ana,' a website specifically devoted to the stories of non-white women dealing with eating and body image problems. Tenisha, who was raised believing that it was a mark of racial superiority that Black women are comfortable with larger bodies, feels like a traitor to her race. 'From an African-American standpoint, she writes, 'we as a people are encouraged to "embrace our big, voluptuous bodies" This makes me feel terrible because *I don't want a big, voluptuous body!* I would rather die from starvation than gain a single pound' (Colors of Ana, http:colorsofana.com//ss8.asp).

Also on the 'Colors of Ana' site is the story of 15-year-old Sami Schalk. Sami is biracial, and attended a virtually all-white grade school: 'At school, stick-skinny models were the norm,' she writes, 'and I was quickly convinced that my curves and butt weren't beautiful. Instead of seeking help, I turned to binge and emotional eating, and at around 11 years old began purging after I ate' (ibid.). When Sami's mom finally took her to a doctor, he put her on a 'safer' diet. The diet only made Sami gain more weight -which in turn led to diet pills and laxative abuse.

Eighteen-year-old Jun Sasaki's eating problems developed after her father was transferred from Japan to the United States. Sasaki, who like many Japanese girls was naturally slim, did not have a problem until one day. when she was 12, a friend hit her slightly protruding stomach playfully and said. 'You look like you're pregnant.' Jun was appalled. She intended at first to lose only a few pounds, but when she began to receive compliments from friends and neighbors, she started a regime of

*Originally published 2009

800 calories a day. Ultimately, as Jun describes it, she lost the ability to 'eat normally.' 'I ate from day to night, searching for every piece of food in the house, consuming every piece of fat I could find. I was never hungry, but I ate, I ate and ate and ate' (ibid.).

As someone who has tracked the world of popular culture for the last 25 years, I'm not surprised to see that clinicians are seeing more and more ethnic, racial, and sexual diversity among their anorexic patients (see Renfrew Center Foundation for Eating Disorders, 2003; see also Franko et al., 2007, for discussion of statistics). When I wrote *Unbearable Weight* (1993) however—one of the first multi-dimensional, interdisciplinary studies to take a cultural approach to eating problems (see below for a summary of my arguments)—I was virtually alone in viewing eating and body image problems as belonging to anyone except privileged, heterosexual white girls.

Where Did This Idea Come From? Several Factors Played a Role

As with many other scientific and social–scientific explanations of various disorders, the first paradigms for understanding eating problems were based on populations that were extremely skewed, both in terms of race and in terms of class. Most of the initial clinical data came from the treatment of white, middle, and upper middle-class patients (see also Saukko, 2009). They were the first ones to seek out treatment; the ones with the money to do so; the ones with the cultural support for doing so. And so, the way their eating problems presented themselves became the standard—of diagnosis, profiling, and explanation. This, of course, resulted in a very limited picture. Most of these patients were brought in by their parents, which meant that the problem had become desperate—which is to say, among other things, highly visible, and an enormous source of family struggle. Emaciated, refusing to eat in circumstances of plenty, often engaged in fierce battles with parents at dinner-time, these girls presented with what would become stamped in many people's mind as a rich, spoiled, white girl's disease: anorexia nervosa.

From this initial paradigm, a number of ideas about eating problems flowed. Dysfunctional family dynamics began to be defined as paradigmatic of eating disorders. So did physical, perceptual, and psychological criteria that reflected the extreme nature of the classical anorexic syndrome. Emaciation. Never seeing oneself as thin enough, even when skeletal—a Perceptual distortion that came to be picked up in the popular media as the hallmark of this 'bizarre' disease. An 'addiction to perfection'. And so on.

Who was left out of this picture? For one thing, the many young college women, of all races and ethnicities, who looked just fine, but were privately throwing up and abusing laxatives regularly to keep their weight under control. Ultimately, this type of disordered eating became better known. But because of the dominant anorexic paradigm, within which hinging and purging was subsumed as a variant—called bulimia nervosa—clinicians failed to see how normative such behavior had become. More than half of all college girls were doing it; and it was still conceptualized as a 'disease' to which only certain kinds of young women—with the expected family profile, 'anorexic thinking,' 'body image distortion syndrome,' and so on—were vulnerable.

Also left out of the picture were the growing numbers of young black women who were struggling with body-image issues. Early research *had* shown a much lower incidence of eating disorders among African American women, and both black women *and* black men, in interviews and studies, have consistently expressed distaste for the hyper-skinny models that many anorexics emulate. From this, many specialists postulated that black women were permanently 'immune' to eating problems. The conclusion was based on a perspective that viewed eating problems as cast in an unchanging mold, rather than the dynamic and shape-shifting phenomena that we have witnessed over the past decade, as more voluptuous styles of bodily beauty that had been excluded from the dominant culture have gained ascendancy, due to the popularity of stars such as Beyonce Knowles and Jennifer Lopez. As video director, Little X, maintains, 'Black folks . . . now have influence, and we're able to set a new standard of beauty. We've flipped the mirror. The old standard of the superskinny white woman doesn't really apply.'

The new standards, however, can be equally self-punishing, and have expanded the repertoire of eating problems from starvation diets and the dream of a body as slender as a reed, to exercise addictions and the dream of a body that is curvaceous but rigorously toned. Probably more college girls today—of *all* races and ethnicities—aspire to some version of this body than they do to the hyper-skinny body. Here, the rise of the female athlete as beauty icon has played as significant a role as racial aesthetics. Ours is now a culture in which our sports superstars are no longer just tiny gymnasts but powerful soccer and softball players, broad-shouldered track stars: Mia Hamm, Sarah Walden, Marion Jones, Serena Williams. It's also a culture, however, in which female athletes are presented as sex goddesses by Nike and *Vogue,* their muscular bodies feminized and trivialized, turned into fashion accessories and erotic magnets for male eyes. The young girls who emulate these bodies are 'passing'—they look great and many may seem to be eating healthfully, too. It's hard to see that there's anything wrong. But the hours spent at the gym are excessive, and when the girls miss a day they are plunged into deep depression. Their sense of self-acceptance, although you can't tell just from looking, in fact hangs on a very slender thread.

In believing Black, Latina, and other ethnicities to be 'immune,' the medical literature often conflated class and race. Poor people didn't get eating disorders—so how could black people get eating disorders, they reasoned—fallaciously. For of course there are plenty of young black women who come from privileged families, attend private schools, and are subjected to the same competitive pressures as their white counterparts—a fact which slipped by those eating disorders specialists who declared eating problems to be 'virtually unknown' in their homogeneous notion of 'the black community.'

Some also may have been unconsciously influenced by the image of the plump, maternal Mammy as the prototype of black womanhood. Only Scarlet has to worry about fitting into a corset; mammy's job is to cook the fried chicken and lace her baby in. Her own girth is of no consequence—she has no romantic life of her own; her body exists only to provide comfort. Does this sound like a relic of a time long gone? In an article in *Essence,* Retha Powers (1989) describes how she went to her high-school guidance counselor, seeking help managing her weight, and was told she shouldn't worry because 'black women aren't seen as sex objects.' It's highly unlikely, of course, that such a comment would be made today in the era of Beyonce and L'il Kim, but many people *do* still believe that just because a woman is black, she has greater cultural permission to be large. Here, generational as well as class differences are being ignored—differences that are highlighted in a piece by Sirena Riley (2002: 358–359):

> As a teenager, I remember watching a newsmagazine piece on a survey comparing black and white women's body satisfaction. When asked to describe the 'perfect woman,' white women said she'd be about five foot ten, less than 120 pounds, blond and so on. Black women described this ideal woman as intelligent, independent and self-confident, never mentioning her looks. After the survey results were revealed ... the white women stood, embarrassed and humiliated that they could be so petty and shallow. They told stories of starving themselves before dates and even before sex. The black women were aghast! What the hell were these white women talking about?
>
> I was so proud . . . Black women being praised on national television! There they were telling the whole country that their black men loved the 'extra meat on their bones.' Unfortunately, my pride also had a twinge of envy. In my own experience.I couldn't quite identify with either the black women or the white women.
>
> Raised by a single mother, independence was basically in my blood. But in a neighborhood of successful, often bourgeois black families, it was obvious that the 'perfect woman' was smart, pretty and certainly not overweight. As a child, no one loved the 'extra meat' on my bones. I was eight years old when I first started exercising to Jane Fonda and the cadre of other leotard-clad fitness gurus. I now have a sister around that age. and when I look at her and real-ize how young that is, it breaks my heart that I was so concerned about weight back then.
>
> [. . .] If we really want to start talking more honestly about all women's relationships with our bodies, we need to start asking the right questions. Just because women of color aren't expressing their body dissatisfaction in the same way as heterosexual, middle-class white women, it doesn't mean that everything is hunky-dory and we should just move on. If we are so sure that images of rail-thin fashion models, actresses and video chicks have contributed to white girls' poor body image, why aren't we addressing the half-naked black female bodies that have replaced the half-naked white female bodies on MTV?

Also left out of the 'anorexic paradigm' were compulsive or binge eaters who do *not* purge, or whose repeated attempts to diet are unsuccessful. To have an 'eating disorder,' according to the anorexic paradigm, means being thin—and since most compulsive eaters are overweight, it took a long time for clinicians to recognize that compulsive eaters, too, are suffering from an eating disorder. Class bias played a role here, too, for a growing body of research has shown that people who have gained the most weight in the last decade—and the largest population of bingers—have tended to have the lowest incomes. The reasons, once you know them, make enormous sense: people who work long, hard hours have little time or energy for cooking, and feeding a family at McDonald's, although it may not be the most nutritious way to go, is the most affordable alternative for many people. Processed foods rich in sugar and fat are now far cheaper than fresh fruits and vegetables. In the ads, they beckon with the promise of pleasure, good times, and satisfaction, to lives which have very little of those in any other domain.

I include myself among compulsive eaters. Although I have never binged to the degree of excess represented in media depictions of bulimics, I, like many women, especially those from cultures for whom food represents comfort, safety, home— Black women, Jewish women, Latinas—often find myself unable to control my end-of-day longings to be soothed and pleasured by food. I may not empty the cupboards, but as I watch late night junk-television, my daughter asleep and my immediate pressures dealt with, every commercial becomes a cue to leap up and go to the kitchen. My choices are benign at first—a slice of rolled up lo-fat ham, some leftover tabouli, fat-free chips. Then, a slice of fat-free cheese makes its way into the ham roll-up. I have a couple of those, dipped in honey mustard. Fat free or not, cheese is a trigger for me; soon I am microwaving it with salsa, and dipping the chips, then my fingers, into it. The creaminess unhinges me and I'm at the freezer, after the Edy's slow-churned (50 percent less fat) French silk ice cream. I eat so much of it that 'less fat' becomes laughable; by the next commercial my rational mind has been put fully on hold. I sprint into my office, open my desk drawer, and make it back to my chair with the chocolate truffles that 1 bought for my daughter's teacher.

Probably the most significant factor, however, in the failure to conceptualize eating problems in an inclusive way has been ignorance of (or, in some cases, resistance to acknowledging) the awesome power of cultural imagery. Fiji is a striking example of that power. Because of their remote location, the Fiji islands did not have access to television until 1995. when a single station was introduced. It broadcasts programs from the United States, the UK, and Australia. Until that time. Fiji had no reported cases of eating disorders, and a study conducted by anthropologist Anne Becker (Becker et al., 2002, reported in Snyderman, 2002: 84; Becker, 2004) showed that most Fijian girls and women, no matter how large, were comfortable with their bodies (see also Nasser and Malson). In 1998, just three years after the station began broadcasting, 11 percent of girls reported vomiting to control weight, and 62 percent of the girls surveyed reported dieting during the previous months. Becker was surprised by the change; she had thought that Fijian cultural traditions, which celebrate eating and favor voluptuous bodies, would 'withstand' the influence of media images. Becker hadn't yet understood that we live in an empire of images, and that there are no protective borders.

Asia is another example. Among the members of audiences at my talks. Asian women had for years been among the most insistent that eating and body image weren't problems for their people, and indeed, my initial research showed that eating disorders were virtually unknown in Asia. But when, a few years ago, a Korean translation of *Unbearable Weight* was published, and several translations of chapters appeared in Chinese publications (a Chinese edition of the book is currently in preparation), I felt I needed to revisit the situation. I discovered multiple reports (see also Nasser and Malson) on dramatic increases in eating disorders in China, South Korea, and Japan. Eunice Park, in *Asian Week* magazine, writes: 'As many Asian countries become Westernized and infused with the Western aesthetic of a tall, thin, lean body, a virtual tsunami of eating disorders has swamped Asian countries' (reported in Rosenthal, 1999).

The spread of eating problems, of course, is not just about aesthetics. Rather, as I argued in *Unbearable Weight,* the emergence of eating disorders is a complex, multi-layered cultural 'symptom,' reflecting problems that are historical as well as contemporary, accelerating in our time because of the confluence of a number of factors. Eating problems, as I theorize them, are over determined in this culture. They have not only to do with new social expectations of women and the resulting ambivalence toward the plush, maternal body, but also with more general anxieties about the body as the source of hungers, needs, and physical vulnerabilities not within our control. These anxieties are deep and long-standing in western philosophy and religion, and they are especially acute in our own time. Eating problems are also linked to the contradictions of consumer culture (see also Gard, 2009), which continually encourages us to binge on our desires at the same time as it glamorizes self-discipline and scorns fat as a symbol of laziness and lack of willpower. And they reflect, too, our increasing 'postmodern' fascination with the possibilities of reshaping our bodies in radical ways, creating new selves that are unlimited by our genetic inheritance.

The relationship between problems such as these and cultural images is complex. On the one hand, the idealization of certain kinds of bodies foments and perpetuates our anxieties and insecurities—that's clear. But, on the other hand, such images carry fantasized solutions *to* our anxieties and insecurities, and that's part of the reason why they are powerful. As I argued in *Twilight Zones* (1997), cultural images are never 'just pictures.' as the fashion magazines continually maintain (disingenuously) in their own defense. They speak to young people not just about how to be beautiful but also about how to become what the dominant culture admires, values, rewards. They tell them how to be cool, 'get it together,' overcome their shame. To girls and young women who have been abused they may offer a fantasy of control and invulnerability, and immunity from pain and hurt. For racial and ethnic groups whose bodies have been deemed 'foreign,' earthy, and primitive, and considered unattractive by Anglo-Saxon norms, they may cast the lure of being accepted by the dominant culture. And it is images, too, that teach us how to *see,* that educate our vision in what is a defect and what is *normal,* that give us the models against which our own bodies and the bodies of others are measured. Perceptual pedagogy: 'How TO Interpret Your Body 101.' It's become a global requirement.

A good example, both of the power of perceptual pedagogy and of the deeper meaning of images is the case of Central Africa. There, traditional cultures still celebrate voluptuous women. In some regions, brides are sent to fattening farms, to be plumped and massaged into shape for their wedding night. In a country plagued by AIDS, the skinny body has meant—as it used to among Italian, Jewish, and Black Americans—poverty, sickness, death. 'An African girl must have hips,' says dress designer, Frank Osodi, 'We have hips. We have bums. We like flesh in Africa.' For years, Nigeria sent its local version of beautiful to the Miss World Competition. The contestants did very poorly. Then a savvy entrepreneur went against local ideals and entered Agbani Darego, a light-skinned, hyper-skinny beauty. Agbani Darego won the Miss World Pageant, the first black African to do so. Now, Nigerian teenagers fast and exercise, trying to become 'lepa'—a popular slang phrase for the thin 'it' girls that are all the rage. Said one: 'People have realized that slim is beautiful' (Onishi, 2002).

It's incorrect, however, to imagine that this is simply about beauty. When I presented the example at a college whose faculty included a Nigerian, she pointed out that Nigerian girls were dieting well before Agbani Darego won her crown, and that, in her opinion, the allure of western body ideals had to do primarily with the rejection of traditional identities and the system of male dominance that they were anchored in. It was for men, she explained, that Nigerian women were encouraged to be full-bottomed, for men that they were often sent to fattening farms to be plumped into shape for the wedding night. Now, modern young women were insisting on the right of their bodies to be less voluptuous, less domestically 'engineered' for the sexual pleasure and comfort of men. Hearing this was fascinating and illuminating. Here was a major similarity in the 'deep' meaning of slenderness for both the young Nigerian dieters and the first generation of (twentieth-century) anorexics in this country. Many of them, like the young Nigerian women, were also in rebellion against a voluptuous, male-oriented, sexualized ideal—that of the post-World War II generation (see also Saukko, 2009). Significant numbers of them had been sexually abused, or witnessed their mothers being treated badly. To be a soft sexual plaything, a Marilyn Monroe, was their horror; Kate Moss and others (like Agbani Darego for the young Nigerians) provided an alternative cultural paradigm to aspire to.

Clearly, body insecurity can be exported, imported, and marketed—just like any other profitable commodity. In this respect, what's happened with men and boys is illustrative. Ten years ago men tended, if anything, to see themselves as better looking than they (perhaps) actually were. And then the menswear manufacturers, the diet industries, and the plastic surgeons 'discovered' the male body (see Bordo, 1999). And now, young guys are looking in their mirrors, finding themselves soft and ill defined, no matter how muscular they are. Now they are developing the eating and body image disorders that we once thought only girls had. Now they are abusing steroids, measuring their own muscularity against the oiled and perfected images of professional athletes, body-builders, and *Men's Health* models.

Let me be clear here. I've got nothing against beautiful, toned, bodies. I also realize that many people come by their slenderness naturally, by virtue of genetics, and that not all models are anorexics. Nor am I anti-fitness. I know that I am happier and healthier when I'm exercising regularly and trim enough to feel comfortable and confident in the form-fitting clothes that I like to wear when my husband and I, who have been doing ballroom dancing for three years, do our rumbas and mambos. The issue for me is not fat versus fitness, but moderation, realism and appreciation of human diversity versus the excesses, the obsessions, the unrealistic expectations that make people sick and treat others as cultural pariahs. Unfortunately, it's the extremes, excesses, and obsessions that our culture fosters. It's a breeder of disorder.

In 2009, I would think this should be obvious. And yet, the prevailing medical wisdom about eating disorders has failed, over and over, to acknowledge, finally and decisively, that we are dealing here with a *cultural* problem. Initially, in the early 1980s, when I first began attending conferences on the subject, eating disorder specialists were very grudging—and most designers and fashion magazine editors in downright denial, and still are—about the role played by cultural images in the spread of eating and body image problems (see Bordo, 1997, 2004). In the early 1990s, when Kate Moss and Calista Flockhart were in ascendancy, we saw a brief flurry of accusations against the fashion industry and the media. But astonishingly (or perhaps predictably), the more indisputable the evidence of the central role played by culture, the more the medical focus has drifted toward genetic and bio-chemical explanations—as, for example, in this *Newsweek* story on anorexia:

> In the past decade, psychiatrists have begun to see surprising diversity among their anorexic patients. Not only are [they] younger, they're also more likely to be black, Hispanic or Asian, more likely to be boys, more likely to be middle-aged. All of which caused doctors to question their core assumption: if anorexia isn't a disease of A-type girls from privileged backgrounds,

then what is it? Although no one can yet say for certain, new science is offering tantalizing clues. Doctors now compare anorexia to alcoholism and depression . . . diseases that may be set off by environmental factors such as stress or trauma, but have their roots in a complex combination of genes and brain chemistry. . . . The environment 'pulls the trigger,' says Cynthia Bulik, director of the eating-disorder program at the University of North Carolina at Chapel Hill. But it's a child's latent vulnerabilities that 'load' the gun.

(Tyre, 2005)

It doesn't make sense; you have to torture logic to come to this conclusion. But although logic is tortured, the empire of images is let off the hook; the culture is merely a 'trigger'; 'it's the child's latent vulnerabilities that load the gun.' Well, I don't buy it. I'd put it this way instead: 'Some studies show that genetic vulnerabilities may play a role in which children develop the most serious forms of eating problems. But the incredible spread of these problems to extraordinarily diverse groups of genetic populations, over a strikingly short period of time, and coincident with the mass globalization of media imagery, strongly suggests that culture is the "smoking gun" that is killing people, and that the situation will not change until the culture does.'

What do I mean by 'the culture'? I mean many things. 'Culture' includes those who made the decision to present an actress like Tony Collete as the 'fat sister' in the otherwise charming film, *In Her Shoes*. Collette gained 25 pounds for that role, and even so, there's nothing remotely fat about her body in the movie. 'Culture' includes directors like David Kelley, who pressure their actresses into losing weight (see Gumbel, 2000; Keck, 2000; Van Meter, 2006). 'Culture' includes the manufacturers of Barbie who, despite a brief flurry of interest some years back in making a more 'realistic' body for the doll, are now making her skinnier than ever. 'Culture' includes those companies that would have us believe that computer-generated thighs are ours for the price of a jar of cellulite control cream. 'Culture' includes *Men's Health* magazine, and all the merchandisers and advertisers who have suddenly recognized that men can be induced to worry about their bodies, too (see Bordo, 1999). 'Culture' includes the contradictory and extreme messages we are constantly receiving about eating, dieting, and fitness. Open most magazines and you'll see them side-by-side. On the one hand, ads for luscious—and usually highly processed—foods, urging us to give in, let go, indulge. On the other hand, the admonitions of the exercise and fitness industries—to get in shape, get it together, prove you've got willpower, show that you have the right stuff. And don't settle for mere cardiovascular fitness, but insist on the sculpted body of your dreams—go for the gold, make it your new religion, your life. It's easy to see why so many of us experience our lives as a tug-of-war between radically conflicting messages, and why it's not a 'paradox,' as it is often represented, that we have an epidemic of obesity alongside increases in anorexia, bulimia, and exercise addictions in this culture.

'Culture,' is, of course, the fashion industry. The average model is 5'10" and weighs 107 pounds; the average American woman is 5'4" and weighs 143 pounds. With a gap like this, it's a set up for the development of eating disorders, as girls and women try to achieve bodies that their genetics, for the most part, just won't support. It's true that more and more merchandisers are beginning to realize that there are lots of size 12 and over girls and women out there, with money to spend, who will respond positively to ad campaigns that celebrate our bodies. But as potentially transformative images, campaigns that single us out as 'special' still mark us as outside the dominant norms of beauty, requiring special accommodation.

What we need, instead, is a transformation similar to what has been going on in the world of children's movies and books, which have normalized racial diversity far more consistently and strikingly than their adult counterparts. Disney's *Cinderella,* for example, without presenting it as remarkable in any way, has Whoopi Goldberg and Victor Garber—a white actor—married, as the queen and king; their son is Asian. Brandi plays Cinderella; her mother is Bernadette Peters. One of her stepsisters is black and the other is white. This is a movie that tells my Cassie, the biracial daughter of two white parents, that there is nothing unusual or improbable about her own family. From this, and from many of her books, she's learned that families are made in many different ways, and that looking like each other is not a prerequisite for loving each other. I would like to see a visual world that will tell her, similarly, that healthy bodies are made in many different ways, and that looking like Beyonce or Halle Berry– or even Marion Jones—is not a prerequisite for loving oneself. A world in which voluptuous models are not only found in 'Lane Bryant' and 'Just My Size' ads.

Unfortunately, and with a few notable exceptions—such as Dove's Campaign for Real Beauty, for example, and the brave, and quite unique, resistance of teenage television fashionista Raven Simone—instead of this happening, I'm seeing a lot of backsliding among once-progressive forces. *Essence* and *Oprah* magazine used to have fashion spreads that featured a range of bodies; they hardly ever do anymore. In 2002, *YM* magazine, an up-beat fashion magazine for teen readers, conducted a survey that revealed that 86 percent of its young readers were dissatisfied with the way their bodies looked. New editor, Christina Kelley, immediately announced an editorial policy against the publishing of diet-pieces and said *YM* would henceforth deliberately seek out full-size models for all its fashion spreads (www.womensnews.org/article.cfm/dyn/aid/833/context/journalistofthemonth; Carmichael, 2002. For an interview with Christina Kelley, see NPR, 2002). It hasn't.

'The culture' includes parents, too. A study in the *Journal of the American Dietetic Associations* found that five-year-old girls whose mothers dieted were twice as likely to be aware of dieting and weight-loss strategies as girls whose mothers didn't diet (Abramovitz and Birch, 2000). 'It's like trying on Mom's high heels,' says Carolyn Costin, spokeswoman for the National Eating Disorders Association, 'They're trying on their diets, too' (Choi, 2006). But this is even to put it too benignly. 'Self-deprecating remarks about bulging thighs or squealing with delight over a few lost pounds can send the message that thinness is to be prized above all else,' says Alison Field (Field et al., 2001), lead author of another study, from Harvard, that found that girls with mothers who had weight concerns were more likely to develop anxieties about their own bodies.

I've been guilty of this. A lifelong dieter, I've tried to explain to my eight-year-old daughter that the word diet doesn't necessarily mean losing weight to look different, but eating foods that are good for you, to make your body more healthy. But the lectures paled beside the pleasure I radiated as I looked at my shrinking body in the mirror, or my depression when I gained it back, or my overheard conversations with my friend Althea, about the difficulties we were facing, as a Jewish and Black woman respectively, who had habitually used food for comfort. When Cassie saw me eat a bowl of ice cream and asked me if I wrote down my points, I knew she understood exactly what was going on.

So far, Cassie has not yet entered the danger zone. A marvelous athlete, she has a muscular, strong body that can do just about anything she wants it to do; she loves it for how far she can jump with it, throw a ball with it, stop a goal with it. Looking at her and the joy she takes in her physical abilities, the uninhibited pleasure with which she does her own version of hip-hop, the innocent, exuberant way she flaunts her little booty, it's hard to imagine her ever becoming ashamed of her body.

Yet, as I was about to serve the cake at her last birthday party, I overheard the children at the table, laughingly discussing the topic of fat. The conversation was apparently inspired by the serving of the cake. 'I want to get fat!' one of them said, laughingly. But it was clearly a goad, meant for shock and amusement value, just as my daughter will sometimes merrily tell me 'I want to get smashed by a big tank!' and then wait for my nose to wrinkle in reaction. That's what happened at the party. 'Uggh! Fat! Uggh!' 'You do not want to be fat!' 'Nyuh, huh, yes, I do!' 'You do not!' And then there was general laughter and descent into gross-talk, 'Fat! Fat! Big fat butt!' and so on.

No one was pointing fingers at anyone—not yet—and no one was turning down cake – not yet. But the 'fat thing' has become a part of their consciousness, even at eight, and I know it's just a matter of time. I know the stats—that 57 percent of girls have fasted, used food substitutes or smoked cigarettes to lose weight, that one-third of all girls in grades nine to 12 think they are overweight, and that only 56 percent of seventh graders say they like the way they look. I also know, as someone who is active at my daughter's school—a public school, with a diverse student population—that it actually begins much, much earlier.

Already, Cassie sometimes tells me that she's fat, pointing to her stomach—a tummy we all would *die* to have. Recently, we were watching TV, and she sucked in her gut and said, 'This is what I'd like my stomach to look like.' At such moments, the madness of our culture hits me full force. I know that I am up against something that cannot be fought with reason or reassurance alone—or even, I'm afraid, with body-image workshops. As gargantuan as the task may seem, as helpless as we may all feel to do much to change things, we cannot let our culture off the hook.

No one strategy will suffice, because the powers that have created and continue to promote body image disorders—and here I refer to not only eating disorders, but the over-use and abuse of cosmetic surgery, steroids, exercise addictions, our cultural obsession with youth, and on and on—are multi-faceted and multiply 'deployed,' as Foucault would put it. That is, they are spread out and sustained in myriad ways, mostly with the cooperation of all of us. There is no king to depose, no government to overthrow, no conspiracy to unmask. Moreover, the very same practices that can lead to disorder are also, when not carried to extremes, the wellsprings of health and great deal of pleasure—exercise for example. This is one reason why it has been so difficult to create coalitions—for example, between different generations of feminists—to work for change. But there is also tremendous potential for inclusiveness here; for, as I've argued, these are issues that are far from limited to the problems of rich, spoiled white girls, but that reach across race, class, ethnicity, nationality, age, and (as I've shown elsewhere) gender. I don't have a master plan for how to alter or resist what seems to be our inexorable drift into this culture in which it *seems* as if our choices to do what we want with our bodies are expanding all the time, but in which we increasingly exercise those 'choices' under tremendous normalizing pressure. But then, neither do I know what can be done to alter some of the larger social and political injustices, dangers, and absurdities of our lives today. Not knowing what to do about those, however, doesn't prevent people from analyzing, complaining, organizing, protesting, working to create a better world. I'd like to see more of that sort of spirit operating in this arena too—if not for ourselves, then for our children.

References

Abramovitz, B. and Birch, L. (2000) Five-year-old girls' ideas about dieting are predicted by their mothers' dieting, *Journal of the American Dietetic Association,* 100(10): 1157–1163.

Becker, A.E. (2004) Television, disordered eating, and young women in Fiji: negotiating body image and identity during rapid social change, *Culture, Medicine and Psychiatry,* 28(4): 533–559.

Becker, A.E., Burwell, R.A., Herzog, D.B., Hamburg, P., Gilman and Stephen, E. (2002) Eating behaviours and attitudes following prolonged exposure to television among ethnic Fijian adolescent girls, *British Journal of Psychiatry,* 180(6): 509–514.

Bordo, S. (1993) *Unbearable Weight: Feminism, Western Culture and the Body,* Berkeley: University of California Press.

Bordo, S. (1997) Never just pictures, in S. Bordo, *Twilight Zones: The Hidden Life of Cultural Images From Plato to O.J.,* Berkeley: University of California Press.

Bordo, S. (1999) Beauty re-discovers the male body, in S. Bordo, *The Male Body: A New Look at Men in Public and in Private,* New York: Farrar, Straus and Giroux.

Bordo, S. (2004) Whose body is this?, in S. Bordo, *Unbearable Weight: Feminism, Western Culture and the Body,* 10th anniversary edition, Berkeley: University of California Press.

Carmichael, A. (2002) Teen magazine takes stand against diet, weight obsession, *Ottawa Citizen,* 11 February.

Choi, C. (2006) Mother's dieting also affects her daughter, *Lexington Herald Leader,* 11 August, p. B6.

Field, A. et al. (2001) Peer, parent, and media influences on the development of weight concerns and frequent dieting among preadolescent and adolescent girls and boys. *Pediatrics,* 107: 54–60, at: www.pediatrics.org/cgi/content/full/107/l/54.

Franko, D.L. et al. (2007) Cross-ethnic differences in eating disorder symptoms and related distress. *International Journal of Eating Disorders,* 40(2): 156–164.

Gard, M. (2009). Understanding Obesity by understanding desire, in H. Malson and M. Burns (eds), *Critical Feminist Approaches to Eating Dis/Orders,* New York: Routledge, pp. 35–45.

Gumbel, A. (2000) Survival of the thinnest, *The Independent,* 21 December.

Keck, W. (2000) *Ally Mc Beal's* Courtney Thorne-Smith says she's fed up with the pressure to be thin, *US weekly.* 11 December, at http://www.geocities.com/cthorne_smith/us_121100.html.

NPR (2002) On the media, 26 January.

Onishi, N. (2002) Globalization of beauty makes slimness trendy, *New York Times,* 3 October.

Powers, R. (1989) Fat is a black woman's issue. *Essence,* October: 75–78, 134–146.

Renfrew Center Foundation for Eating Disorders (2003) *Eating Disorders 101 Guide: A Summary of Issues, Statistics and Resources,* October, at: http://www.renfrew.org.

Riley, S. (2002) The black beauty myth, in D. Hernandez and B. Rehman (eds), *Colonize This!,* Emeryville, CA: Seal Press, pp. 357–369.

Rosenthal, E. (1999) *Beijing Journal:* China's chic waistline: convex to concave, *New York Times,* 9 December.

Saukko, P. (2009) A critical discussion of normativity in discussions of eating disorders, in H. Malson and M. Burns (eds), *Critical Feminist Approaches to Eating Dis/Orders,* New York: Routledge, pp. 63–73.

Snyderman, N. (2002) *The Girl in the Mirror,* New York: Hyperion.

Tyre, P. (2005) No one to blame, *Newsweek,* 5 December, 52–53.

Van Meter, J. (2006) Disappearing act: how did Portia De Rossi withstand the pressure of Hollywood, *Vogue,* 1 April, at: www.advocate.com/newsdetailektid28186.asp.

19

De-medicalizing Anorexia: Opening a New Dialogue[*][1]

Richard A. O'Connor

Anorexia mystified Becca:

> To this day, I really don't know why, all of a sudden, I decided to have these weird eating pat-
> terns and not eat at all. Exercise so much. I think that I was just a perfectionist, just wanting to
> make my body even more perfect. But the thing is, a skeleton as a body really isn't perfect. So
> I don't know exactly what my train of thinking was.

The usual explanations didn't work: she had no weight to lose (*"people would always tell me how skinny I was"*), no festering trauma, no troubled psyche. To the contrary, an upbeat person (*"I'm very energetic and very bubbly"*), she got along well at home (*"I have really loving and supportive parents"*) and school. A top athlete who made excellent grades and had good friends, life was going great when anorexia suddenly came out of nowhere. Neither Becca nor her therapists could explain how it all happened.

Becca's story isn't exceptional. Although a clinician would rightly diagnose "atypical anorexia nervosa", her type-denying case is anything but atypical. Through in-depth interviews with 22 recovered anorexics (20 female, 2 male) in Tennessee and Toronto, we repeatedly heard type-denying cases.[2] So did Garrett (1998) who, in interviewing 34 Australian anorexics, found vanity did not explain the disease; and Warin (2010) whose 46 anorexics at three sites (Australia, Scotland, Canada) repeatedly told her "anorexia was not solely concerned with food and weight". It's the same for clinicians in Asia (Khandelwal, Sharan and Saxena 1995; Lee, Ho and Hsu 1993), not to mention the U.S. (Katzman and Lee 1997; Palmer 1993), who find many patients neither fear fat nor crave thinness as "typical" anorexics should. Indeed, what the public and many professionals have come to expect—women dieting madly for appearance—does not adequately explain cases on either side of the globe.

Instead of adolescent girls literally dying for looks, we found youthful ascetics— male as well as female—obsessing over virtue, not beauty. Their restricting was never just instrumental (the means to weight loss) but always also expressive or adventur-ous or even accidental. Most felt transcendence or grace, echoing the "distorted form of spirituality" that Garrett (1998, 110) found in Australia. That said, today's pathol-ogy is neither specifically religious as anorexia once was (Bynum 1987) nor the per-formance of tradition as monastic asceticism still is (Flood 2004). Indeed, precisely

[*]*Originally published here*

because our interviewees' self-imposed asceticism developed outside established religious institutions, it had no community or tradition to regulate it, to reign in excess. Initially exhilarating, their virtuous eating and exercising eventually became addictive. That, anyway, was what our interviewees described—the anorexic's anorexia.

Shockingly, that isn't the disease that many institutions are treating. Although most professionals know it's not as simple as beauty-mad dieting, research has yet to capture the complexity that practitioners actually face. Take a distorted body image: it's still an official diagnostic criterion but that cliché collapsed under contradictory evidence by the early 1990s (Hsu and Sobkiewicz 1991). Or take categorizing anorexia as an *eating* disorder: many cases might more readily be called *exercise* disorders and every case is an ascetic disorder. Or slighting adolescence. Or the unsettled issue of gender: while most sociocultural explanations treat anorexia as a woman's disease (e.g. Bordo 1997), men make up from one-fifth (full syndrome) to one-third (full or partial syndrome) of the sufferers (Woodside et al. 2001). Over the years the explanation has changed—from hysteria or pituitary dysfunction a century ago to malignant mothering or sexual abuse today—but the one constant is how these supposed causes look *through* rather than *at* the anorexic as a whole person. The discourse on anorexia thereby detaches from that anorexic's experience and values. No wonder treatment programs are so unsuccessful (Agras et al. 2004; Ben-Tovin et al. 2001)!

Medicalizing—and Mystifying—Anorexia

How has healthcare gotten so far from the anorexic's anorexia? The larger intellectual answer is Cartesian dualism: in dividing mind from body and individual from society, modern thought fights any realistic social and cultural understanding of disease. The more immediate institutional answer is medicalization: over two centuries, by isolating the sick and sickness from their surroundings, biomedicine has complicated diseases like anorexia and obscured their causes. An emerging literature shows how treatment programs can exercise a Foucauldian power over anorexics (Eckermann 1997), replicate conditions that support and possibly cause the disease (Gremillion 2003; Warin 2010) and, by labeling the person an anorexic, inspire efforts to live up to that diagnosis (Warin 2010). Our interviewees supported these findings, testifying to how treatment sometimes aggravated their affliction and inspired resistance. While medicalizing can also save lives, in this regard its hegemony hurt patients.

Our findings stress how medicalizing hurts research: it obscures anorexia's causes. We set out to contextualize anorexia only to end up demedicalizing the syndrome. Take the mind/body split. In imposing this arbitrary Cartesian distinction, medicalizing makes anorexia into a mental illness—the mind's war on the body. That sounds reasonable—and if we ignore the "mindful body" (Scheper-Hughes and Lock 1987) and neuroscience it might be—but how and why this happens becomes a total mystery. Yet all we had to do was erase this Cartesian line to see how an intense mind-with-body activity (restrictive eating and rigorous exercise) bootstrapped anorexics into anorexia much as boot camp makes civilians into soldiers. Or take the individual/society distinction. In isolating anorexics as abnormal, medicalizing takes them out of the surroundings that gives them social and moral reasons to restrict. Suddenly their actions look completely senseless, inviting out-of-the-blue psychological and biological guesswork. Yet all we had to do was put the person back in context for the obvious evidence to suggest that anorexics were misguided moralists, not cognitive cripples. Warin (2010) makes a similar point: seen in context, anorexics are following cultural rules for hygiene, not obsessing randomly or venting secret traumas. Again and again, contextualizing challenges how medicalizing constructs anorexia by isolating it.

One disease, two approaches—who has it right? We don't deny that anorexics need medical attention—indeed, it's the most deadly mental illness of all—but medicalizing anorexics and pathologizing their asceticism and other cultural practices have a miserable record of repeated failure. Today, over 130 years after physicians first isolated self-starvation as a disease, biomedicine can neither adequately explain nor reliably cure nor even rigorously define anorexia (Agras et al. 2004). As medicine's isolating has failed so spectacularly, perhaps anthropology's contexualizing can do better.

Contextualizing Anorexia

What's striking about reconnecting anorexia to the light of day is just how much the obvious evidence can explain. Once interviewing gave us life-course and life-world details, anorexia was anything but exotic. Its extraordinary asceticism had ordinary roots: schooling, sports, work and healthy eating all taught self-denial that these overachievers took to heart. Anorexics simply exaggerated—and eventually incarnated—the deferred gratification that's so widely preached for the young. Anorexia, then, did not come out of the blue. It came out of perfectly obvious surrounding values and local bodily practices.

Take Becca's case. Although anorexia blindsides her, it develops out of obvious life-course patterns that she readily describes. In her words, *"I'm a real big perfectionist"*. In growing up,

> I kind of had this image of Becca. When people referred to me it was because of something that had been done quite well. That's what perfection came to. I wanted every little thing about me to just—I guess—be an example. That people would look at me and, like "Wow, There goes Becca! Oh that's the perfect child!"

What Becca describes is a virtuous identity, not a mental pathology. What goes wrong is that she applies this to eating. Her diet thereby takes on a moral character where fat is evil and she chooses good relentlessly.

> In third grade I almost had an eating disorder. For some reason I just got scared of fat. I would look at nutrition panels and I would observe the fat, what it said, and I really got scared of fat. I would only eat Kellogg's cereal. Mom was like, "I just cooked dinner and you're eating Kellogg's cereal!" "I like Kellogg's!" My mom got to the point where like, 'Rebecca, if you don't stop eating just Kellogg's corn flakes I'm going to take you to see a doctor". And that scared me. I didn't want anyone to think that there was something the matter with me. So how my mom and I approached the problem was we started going to this health food grocery store called Whole Foods. They have a lot of organic products. We would go every Sunday. It was quite a distance. I would get really upset when we didn't get food from Whole Foods.

Was Becca idealizing supermodels? No—and neither was Jim. He reports the same third-grade aversion to fat (*"I remember I stopped drinking whole milk and eating red meat in third grade . . . . That was back when the big health trend was fat. We didn't eat anything fat. No fat at all. Never. None".*). Only much later, as a high school runner, does this health-obsessed athlete train himself into anorexia.

Anorexia's Cultural Connection

Becca's restricted eating copies her mother directly (*"I look up to my mom a lot and my mom eats really small portions because she gets full easily"*) whereas Jim's regimen develops mutually with his mother (*"we pushed each other into having these athletic, healthy lifestyles"*). That familial link was typical: nearly three-quarters of our interviewees (16 of 22) grew up valuing healthy eating and living. Then, as anorexics, all obsessively exaggerated how healthy eating restricts. And now, in recovery, all of them watch what they eat, a reasonable yet distant echo of their earlier obsession.

Are these fringe attitudes, the delusions of a few health fanatics? No, our informants echo how contemporary culture moralizes eating. Witness the popular prejudice where fat people, in "letting themselves go", get stigmatized as weak or even bad; and slim people, in being strict with themselves, exemplify strength and goodness. Or consider how people readily judge their own eating, speaking of "sinning" with dessert, "being good" with veggies, or "confessing" a late-night binge. What's at stake here is virtue, not beauty. Over roughly the last century, as the body has increasingly become a moral arena, eating and exercise have come to test our mettle (Brumberg 1997; Stearns 1999).

Anything but marginal, this discourse of individual responsibility is heavily promoted by health agencies and widely accepted by the public. It urges the good person to eat sparely and nutritiously, exercise regularly, avoid all health risks, and—as a matter of self-respect—keep a slim and attractive body. True, few people live up to this demanding discipline, but fewer still contest it is "right", the proper way to live. So it's a bit like a Sunday sermon where the lifestyle urgings are scientific, not religious—or are they? Healthy eating's discourse cherry-picks science. A more realistic perspective would recognize that health is broadly social, not narrowly individual, and that the "domain of personal health over which the individual has direct control is *very* small when compared to heredity, culture, environment, and chance". So says Marshall Becker (1986, 21, 20), a public health school dean. He goes on to characterize today's faith in healthy living as "a new religion, in which we worship ourselves, attribute good health to our devoutness, and view illness as just punishment for those who have not yet seen the Way". Well, it is religious—evangelical even—but it's not very new. Early 19th-century health and fitness movements developed this moralizing discourse (Green 1988), but it took until the turn of the 20th century to become mainstream (Stearns 1999).

What draws people into this discourse? Our interviewees gave us two answers: a bodily predisposition and identity politics. Here's Becca on identity:

> My best friend's family—whenever I would come to their lake house or something—they would always, "Goodness Gracious, we gotta have fruit for this child! We have to have carrots. Here we have all the other little girls that are having cookies and this kid's eating carrots and fruits and healthy peanut butter snacks".

Becca restricts and, given today's cultural concerns, others notice. Their feedback makes this a point of pride, an arena for further achieving. This isn't exceptional. Most of our informants described how a slim body, strict eating, rigorous exercise, or even being anorexic became an identity that they began to value and build into their youthful sense of self. Here age matters: our informants all develop anorexia during adolescence, a transitional time that intensifies the need to find and express one's identity.

The Anorexic's Constitution

A further anorexia-explaining factor appeared once we looked at our informants historically rather than just situationally. Here, in shifting from a life-world to a life-course context, we found a biocultural "flywheel" carried them into anorexia. To make sense of this evidence, we had to revive the old fashioned and decidedly non-Cartesian idea that each person has a distinctive constitution. Our update is biocultural.

Anorexics are not culturally but bioculturally constructed. To starve oneself taps capacities and inclinations that develop only over years. From conception to adolescence, each person's initially wide possibilities progressively narrow as the organism grows and adapts to a particular environment. Day-by-day, the interaction of biology, culture and chance fix points that shape later interactions; and, bit-by-bit, this biocultural hybrid—a constitution—grows in guiding force. Our informants had developed constitutions as children that later predisposed them to anorexia as adolescents. Three dispositions stood out:

- *A performative disposition:* Although most kids perform for parents and teachers to admire, our informants had long built who they were and how they thought, felt and acted around sustained superior performance. All had records of high achievement and roughly a third called themselves perfectionists. Almost all excelled academically; four-fifths grew up not just with but through dance, athletics or both; and, out of that subset, over half were so good that they competed regionally or nationally.
- *An ascetic disposition:* As determined achievers, our interviewees had mastered deferred gratification long before they took up restrictive eating in adolescence. Some developed self-denial as a bodily mode through sports. Molly, for example, says *"athletics actually taught me self-discipline. So I knew how to push myself and I knew how to be mentally tough. I learned you can always push yourself further. What you think you can do, you can do more"*. That attitude got her into anorexia as well as state tournaments.
- *A virtuous disposition:* A major figure in the study of anorexia, Hilde Bruch (1962, 192) characterized her anorexic patients as "'outstandingly good and quiet children, obedient, clean, eager to please, helpful at home, precociously dependable, and excelling in school work". That fit how our interviewees saw themselves. Although we had no way to confirm that they were as good as they said, a virtuous disposition is the single most consistent explanation for their remarkable success as children, students and athletes.

Were someone to take up dieting, healthy eating or training for any reason, these dispositions would intensify their practice. In this sense our informants were primed for anorexia. All of this was quite obvious once we looked at life-course.

Reviving Empiricism

None of what we've attributed to constitution, identity and healthy living is guess-work. It's what our informants reported, each speaking independently. With remark-able consistency they describe paths into anorexia that are obvious and rather ordinary—at least until the last step. That final exceptional step—becoming anorexic—is mysterious. None of our informants could say how or even when it happened. So perhaps here, as the change comes invisibly, clinical inference might reasonably replace everyday evidence. And yet, when we pieced together what our informants said separately, we discovered that even the final move into anorexia had left empirical tracks. We found eight recurring features that, taken together, suggested how intense restricting and exercising integrated into a self-sustaining system. That's not to say facts speak for themselves—in this instance Foucault's (1988) technologies of the self elucidated the dynamics; it's to say that, taken seriously, empiricism can penetrate even the enigmatic.

Empiricism has answers that medicalizing dismisses. Instead of making the most of what's obvious, specialists *assume* anorexia has an *underlying* pathology, that the cause is deeper than what the surface suggests.[3] And that might eventually prove right—surely we can't rule out what's still undiscovered—but for now it's better to reason with the obvious rather than guess at the obscure. That's better science: by Ockham's razor (the principle of parsimony) simple and direct explanations should take precedence over the complex inferences the now "explain" anorexia. And it's better medicine: addressing the obvious—by showing anorexia's everyday dimen-sions—would allow anorexics to participate in their own recovery, quite unlike some treatment programs where specialists take control (cf. Gremillion 2003).

Negotiating Recovery

What a culture knows about an illness can help sufferers interpret the experience, share it with others and work towards recovery. Yet with anorexia what today's cul-ture supposedly knows—stereotypes about media excess, gender inequity, sexual abuse, dysfunctional families—stigmatizes sufferers and their families. As this dis-torted picture has little or nothing to do with the experience of anorexia and its causes, it misdirects self-help as well as treatment. No wonder anorexics resist therapy and nothing seems to work!

To do better at treating anorexia we should stop searching the shadows for hidden causes when the sunlight reveals so much. By this standard everyone—family, friends, clinicians, sufferers—should consider four facts. First, what outsiders see as stubborn self-destruction is not what the anorexic experiences. Quite the contrary, inside the regimen, restricted eating and intense exercise prove moral worth, showing one has world-class willpower and self-control. Here, to open a dialogue, outsiders must first appreciate this achievement. Then, and only then, can one help anorexics see the vice in their virtues.

Second, once established, the syndrome has all the visceral momentum of an addiction. So anorexics may want to change long before they can break free of the body's discipline. Some credited their recovery to loved ones or friends who kept trying to help them break free, refusing to give up hope or to accept rejection.

Third, long before anorexia, our interviewees had set a constitutional course for the disease. We asked them how they stayed healthy after recovery returned them to their earlier inclinations and immersed them in a society that moralizes eating. Three suggestions emerged: develop activities with mind/body integration (e.g. playing piano, nature walks), reverse anorexic inclinations (e.g. seek friends rather than solitude) and cultivate balance in everyday life.

Fourth, the disease develops through training. That suggests the need for retraining, perhaps in healthy practices described above, and it argues against digging up deeper pathologies. The latter unleashes doubt and blaming that can impede recovery.

Notes

1. Based on the book *How Virtue Becomes Vice: Explaining Anorexia as an Activity* by Richard A. O'Connor and Penny Van Esterik [under review]. From age 13 to 16, O'Connor's daughter was anorexic. Researching how she and other anorexics embodied ascetic values raised larger biocultural questions about nurturance and society that we explore in *The Dance of Nurture: Embodying Infant Feeding* [in preparation].

2. Use of "we" throughout this article recognizes the collaboration of our interviewees as well as the contribution of Penny Van Esterik, second author in the original *Anthropology Today* article (2008, Vol. 24, No. 5, pp. 6–9) entitled "Demedicalizing anorexia: A new cultural brokering". We would also like to acknowledge the help and insights of Anne Becker, John O'Connor, Leeat Granek, Jim Peterman and *Anthropology Today*'s editor and reviewers.

3. In the 19th century, as modern medicine developed its scientific authority, rationalism theorizing often trumped empiricism's everyday evidence. Where the former was Platonic, seeing reality *behind* appearances, the latter followed Aristotle in learning from direct observation. At one point calling a physician an "empiricist" implied he was a quack who practiced by personal observation rather than scientific theory (*Oxford English Dictionary* 1989).

References

Agras, W. S., Brandt, H. A., Bulik, C. M., Dolan-Sewell, R., Fairburn, C. G., Halmi, K. A., Herzog, D. B., Jimerson, D. C., Kaplan, A. S., Kaye, W. H., le Grange, D., Lock, J., Mitchell, J. E., Rodorfer, M. V., Street, L. L., Striegel-Moore, R., Vitousek, K. M., Walsh, B. T. and Wilfley, D. E. 2004. Report of the National Institutes of Health Workshop on overcoming barriers to treatment research in anorexia nervosa. *International Journal of Eating Disorders* 35: 509–521.

Becker, M. H. 1986. The tyranny of health promotion. *Public Health Review* 14: 15–25.

Ben-Tovin, D., Walker, K., Gilchrist, P., Freeman, R., Kalucy, R. and Esterman, A. 2001. Outcome in patients with eating disorders: A 5-year study. *The Lancet* 357: 1254–1257.

Bordo, S. 1997. Anorexia nervosa: Psychopathology as the crystallization of culture. In: Counihan, C. and Van Esterik, P. (eds) *Food and culture, A reader*, pp. 226–250. New York: Routledge.

Bruch, H. 1962. Perceptual and conceptual disturbances in anorexia nervosa. *Psychosomatic Medicine* 24(2): 187–194.

Brumberg, J. J. 1997. *The body project: An intimate history of American girls*. New York: Random House.

Bynum, C. W. 1987. *Holy feast and holy fast: The religious significance of food to medieval women*. Berkeley: University of California Press.

Eckermann, L. 1997. Foucault, embodiment and gendered subjectivities: The case of voluntary self-starvation. In: Petersen, A. and Bunton, R. (eds) *Foucault, health and medicine*. London: Routledge.

Flood, G. 2004. *The ascetic self: Subjectivity, memory and tradition*. Cambridge, UK: Cambridge University Press.

Foucault, M. 1988. *The care of the self: The history of sexuality*, v.3. New York: Vintage Books.

Garrett, C. 1998. *Beyond anorexia: Narrative, spirituality and recovery*. Cambridge, UK: Cambridge University Press.

Green, H. 1988. *Fit for America: Health, fitness, sport and American society*. Baltimore: Johns Hopkins University Press.

Gremillion, H. 2003. *Feeding anorexia: Gender and power at a treatment center*. Durham: Duke University Press.

Hsu, L. K. G. and Sobkiewicz, T. A. 1991. Body image disturbance: Time to abandon the concept for eating disorders? *International Journal of Eating Disorders* 10: 15–30.

Katzman, M. A. and Lee, S. 1997. Beyond body image: The integration of feminist and transcultural theories in the understanding of self starvation. *International Journal of Eating Disorders* 22: 385–394.

Khandelwal, S. K., Sharan, P. and Saxena, S. 1995. Eating disorders: An Indian perspective. *International Journal of Social Psychiatry* 41(2): 132–146.

Lee, S., Ho, P. and Hsu, L. K. G. 1993. Fat phobic and non-fat phobic anorexia nervosa: A comparative study of 70 Chinese patients in Hong Kong. *Psychological Medicine* 23: 999–1017.

Oxford English dictionary. 1989. 2nd edition. New York: Oxford University Press.

Palmer, R. L. 1993. Weight concern should not be a necessary criterion for eating disorders: A polemic. *International Journal of Eating Disorders* 14: 459–465.

Scheper-Hughes, N. and Lock, M. M. 1987. The mindful body: A prolegomenon to future work in medical anthropology. *Medical Anthropology Quarterly* 1: 6–41.

Stearns, P. N. 1999. *Battleground of desire: The struggle for self-control in modern America*. New York: New York University Press.

Warin, M. 2010. *Abject relations: Everyday worlds of anorexia*. New Brunswick: Rutgers University Press.

Woodside, D. B., Garfinkel, P. E., Lin, E., Goering, P., Kaplan, A. S., Goldbloom, D. S. and Kennedy, S. H. 2001. Comparisons of men with full or partial eating disorders, men without eating disorders, and women with eating disorders in the community. *American Journal of Psychiatry* 158(4): 570–574.

20

Feeding Hard Bodies: Food and Masculinities in Men's Fitness Magazines[*]

Fabio Parasecoli

Plural Masculinities

All over the Western world, a new breed of leisure publications that deal with various intimate aspects of men's lives have recently invaded kiosks: men's fitness magazines. These publications have now abandoned the closets of gay men and the lockers of professional body builders to be conspicuously displayed in dentist's waiting rooms or on coffee tables next to football magazines.

Amongst these, *Men's Health, Men's Fitness,* and *Muscle and Fitness* have proved to be particularly successful over time, in terms of popularity and sheer sales.[1] They constitute a particularly significant segment in this kind of literature and deserve closer examination. I will examine the differences in both editorial and advertising materials that assume a certain range of diversity within the target readership. *Muscle and Fitness* is more specifically geared toward professional body builders, while the other two are geared toward an audience of men who, although conscious of their bodies, are also interested in other aspects of their masculinities. Launched in 1988, *Men's Health,* owned by Rodale, is definitely the most popular, claiming a circulation of 1.7 million, with 22 editions in 30 countries.[2] Rodale, a family owned company, publishes magazines, such as Organic Gardening, Prevention, Bicycling, Runner's World, and Backpacker, and has established a public image of health consciousness and commitment against tobacco and hard liquor. At the end of 2002, both *Men's Fitness* and *Muscles and Fitness,* originally owned by Weider Publications Inc. and founded by the bodybuilder Joe Weider in the 1940s, were bought by American Media, which already owns many tabloids, such as *National Enquirer* and *Star,* and also operates Distribution Services to place these periodicals in supermarkets. In other words, bodybuilding has gone mainstream.

The enthrallment with the body image, previously imposed mostly on women, is now becoming a common feature in masculine practices and identification processes, to the point that the expression "the Adonis complex" has been created, referring to the more pathological, obsessive forms of this phenomenon.[3] Recent literature on

[*]*Originally published 2005*

body images has developed in the frame of theories that consider multiple masculinities as constructed collectively in culture and sustained in all kinds of institutions (the school, the gym, the army, the workplace). Connell writes,

> Men's bodies are addressed, defined and disciplined, and given outlet and pleasures, by the gendered order of society. Masculinities are neither programmed in our genes, nor fixed by social structure, prior to social interaction. They come into existence as people act. They are actively produced, using the resources and strategies available in a given social setting.[4]

Masculinities are not fixed or defined once and for all; they do not represent embodiments of discrete states of being. They vary in time and place, in different historical, social, and cultural environments. As practices, they sometimes articulate contradictory desires, emotions, and ideals, denying the very notion of a static and defined identity. These concurrent masculinities are not equivalent: some tend to be considered more desirable than others, even when they are not the most common, and thus become "hegemonic," a standard against which men embodying other kinds of masculinities assess their self perception and often also their self-esteem.[5] Body images play a fundamental role in defining what the dominant masculinity model should look like. Nevertheless, men's bodies are not blank pages that become the receptacle for all kinds of power and social determinations: they are actual agents, and they interact with other aspects of the social practices determining masculinities. As Connell emphasizes,

> To understand how men's bodies are actually involved in masculinities we must abandon the conventional dichotomy between changing culture and unchanging bodies . . . Through social institutions and discourses, bodies are given social meaning. Society has a range of "body practices" which address, sort and modify bodies. These practices range from deportment and dress to sexuality, surgery and sport.[6]

The growing attention to the male body—it has sometime been argued—is, at least partially, a result of the mainstreaming and the normalization of gay culture.[7] Nevertheless, also in heterosexual contexts, male strong bodies have traditionally served as metaphors for sexual potency, power, productivity, dominance, independence, and control. Both discourses are somehow articulated in the contemporary hegemony of the muscular body type (also known as mesomorphic, as opposed to ectomorphic, slim, and endomorphic, overweight), often in connection with a phenomenon sometimes defined as "re-masculinization."[8] Until a few decades ago, the aspiration for a muscular build was a prerogative of a small circle of professional and amateur bodybuilders, who were also involved in different forms of competition, giving to the whole scene the veneer of a sport. In time, after large sections of the gay community embraced the muscular body as desirable and prestigious, the same attitude became more and more visible, also in heterosexual—or should we now say metrosexual—circles. A renewed attention to the body and its appearance goes well beyond the concern for its athletic potential, which was a normal element of the sport subculture, uniting all men, gay and straight, in the same awe for the bulging muscle. These phenomena explain the growing success of men's fitness magazines, which, at any rate, carefully avoid dealing with issues of sexual preference, and ban any hint of homoeroticism, which is, nevertheless, always lurking behind the glossy pages of the magazines.

The growing prestige granted to the muscular body places increasing pressure on men to take greater care of their looks.[9] Men seem to adopt different strategies to make sense of their bodies when they do not meet the hegemonic expectations; the three predominant ways to adjust the discrepancy between the ideal and the real body have been defined as reliance, where the individual works on his body to reach the model; reformulation, where each individual adjusts his conception of hegemonic masculinity to meet his abilities; rejection, where the individual totally refuses the hegemonic model.[10] In the case of reliance, usually great amounts of energy, money, and time are invested in gaining the desired body image, often with anxious undertones that reveal a certain preoccupation with control over one's body. In this context, food plays a fundamental, though often concealed, role. Diets and eating habits are interpreted as a key element in the construction of a fit body.

Advertising to the Hardliners

Needless to say, the food and supplement industry has tapped into these trends to acquire new consumers for highly processed products that ensure growing revenues for a sector structurally plagued by intense competition.[11] Many of the advertising pages in these magazines often play with a sense of inadequacy, or with a desire for emulation in order to increase sales, proposing behaviors and values. These constructs hinge on dedication and effort that help to form the constructs of hegemonic masculinities.[12]

On the first page of *Muscle and Fitness,* we find an ad page by Animal for "Hardcore Training Packs." Next to a hip bodybuilder, wearing a woolen hat and a grungy sweater, we read the sentence: "Shut up and train," followed by a small print copy text:

> Every day you train is judgment day. Each rep, each plate matters. You don't make time for talk. All you care about is moving weight. Nothing else. This is hardcore. This is Animal. Can you handle it?[13]

A few pages later, the same man is shown, while lifting heavy weights, with an expression of near pain on his face. The text states:

> Go hard . . . or go home. Balls-to-the-wall training. You sweat. You push. It hurts. In here, there's no room for crybabies, no place for talking trash. Just raw lifting. This is the real deal. This is Animal. Can you handle it?[14]

In the same magazine, another ad shows a weight lifting bench with pillows and a blanket in an empty room. The text reads, "Obsessed is just a rod the lazy use to describe the dedicated."[15] Amen, one would fervently respond. What we face here is a fullblown cult. The new religion requires total dedication, in anticipation of the final ordeal when all believers will present themselves to the Big Trainer to have their thighs and deltoids carefully measured. Good results can be attained only by severe, unrelenting, and even painful workouts.

Nevertheless, followers are offered ways to cheat a little, as in any religion. The magazine pages are full of ads for protein drinks, integrators, engineered nutrition items, and dietary supplements that can help adepts to reach their goals. Exercising is necessary, but science can help to the point that one can grow muscle while sleeping, as with products such as SomnaBol-PM, Night charger, or NitroVarin-PLS.[16] Nonetheless, the ad specifies that there is absolutely no need to stop taking regular proteins during the day.

As a matter of fact, most advertising in *Muscle & Fitness* is related to nutrition, meeting the readers' needs to ensure the correct intake of substances required to bulk up, and expressing the food and supplement industry's necessity to increase sales. The technical terminology it uses aims itself at readers who are supposedly familiar with choline bitartrate (for serious mental energy and acuity, we are told) or glutamine peptides, who are extremely aware of their daily protein intake, and who would never ingest the wrong kind of proteins. We are made privy of "the ugly truth behind the collagen."

> Pigs feet, cattle hide, crushed bone, fish skin. How did they ever end up in your chocolate protein bar? Easy. After those bones and skins get soaked in lime to remove all hair and grease, seared with acid until they disintegrate and then molded into edible gelatin or collagen, they become part of countless protein bars, even the best sellers.[17]

The text, advertising the VHT 100% real Protein Chocolate Rum Cake, is placed next to a full page picture of a meat grinder where a cow skull, a not-at-all-bad-looking fish, a bone, and a pig foot are being cranked in what is clearly an impossible fashion. The effect is quite overwhelming, even if for a non-American, the pig foot and the fish actually look appetizing. But the correlation with death, clearly expressed by the skull and the bone, would make even the most adventurous eater flinch. To balance the disturbing effect of the image, the text is followed by a very reassuring chart that explains how the protein efficiency ratio is much lower in collagen than in, say, milk protein, beef protein, or best of all, in whole eggs. The advertisement clearly tries to convince the potential consumers to buy a product that provides the necessary nutrients, all the while avoiding any contamination with the less appealing aspects of food, namely death and corruption.

The assumed goal for this magazine's target readers, it is clear, is gaining muscle mass. The three page advertisement for Cytodine, "The Single Most Revolutionary Advancement in Bodybuilding History," recurs to the old routine of the before and after pictures, except that the before pictures portray bodies that would make the average male seethe in sheer envy. The same trick is deployed a few pages later, where we are told that an Idrise Ward-El was able to lose 20 pounds of fat and gain 25 pounds of muscle with the help of Muscle Tech supplements, like Cell-tech.[18] The before picture of Mr. Ward-El shows us a stocky but muscular and good looking black man, who, in the after picture, actually boasts huge muscles (and no longer wears glasses). At this point, it is necessary to note that Asian men are conspicuously absent from these magazines, both in the editorial and the advertising material. The underlying but unexpressed assumption is that Asian men are either not interested in achieving a muscular body for cultural reasons, or physically not able to do so.

Buy a Better Body

Muscle & Fitness readers are hardliners and dedicated body-builders. The advertising is overwhelmingly concentrated on nutritional items. The few exceptions are pages for sports gear. On the other hand, advertising in both *Men's Fitness* and *Men's Health,* with a greater emphasis on fitness and general well-being, also promotes colognes, after shave moisturizer, razors, a juice processor, trekking shoes, even cars, fashion and hi-tech. The advertising in *Men's Health* definitely appeals to needs other than fitness or muscle building. As we will see, even women become a center of interest. It is relevant to point out that in all three magazines, the advertising pages for nutritional products can be classified in two typologies: the ones where each item is promoted exclusively for its nutritional value without any reference to taste, and others where flavor plays a certain, if peculiar, role.

Only one advertisement in the three magazines refers to the idea of actually cooking food. The headline is: "Trim, tone, define, & sculpt! Your complete Diet, Training, Nutrition and Fat Free Cook Book Collection." We are informed that the cook, a black woman who smilingly displays her amazing biceps, besides being a master chef, was a contender in the Miss Olympia body building competition. She's not alone: the other author is a white nutrition consultant with a health science degree. The ad interestingly uses a woman, as muscled as she is, to evoke the idea of the kitchen, while the scientific side of the cookbooks, guaranteeing good results, is the work of a man.[19] This element—as we will see—often recurs when the preparation of food is mentioned. The fact that the cook is black and the scientist is white adds further layers to this advertisement, revealing race biases that are otherwise invisible in this kind of literature, probably based on the assumption that part of the readership is composed of black males.

The scientific seal that seems fundamental to these ads is particularly evident in those belonging to the first typology, advertising nutritional supplements. Long lists of components are given in uncompromising terminology, aimed at convincing readers that the products are actually systematically engineered to improve their muscle mass. Pictures and details of muscled persons, and images of the advertised items, usually accompany written texts. Since their names are difficult to remember, and in the end they all sound the same, it is important to display the actual box or flacon in the ad, to make sure that readers will be able to recognize it when they are shopping at their local health shop. Most of the products in this typology do not make any reference to the act of eating. Sometimes a flavor is given to them, especially when it comes to drinks and bars, but it is not relevant in the economy of most ads.

On the other hand, the second typology employs the element of taste to make the advertised products more appealing, even if only to ensure a certain variety of flavors for the same product. The important elements are still nutritional, but consumers can turn to taste to avoid boredom. Even in this second category, there is little, if any, reference to actual food. Some ads display fruit, milk, or chocolate next to the supplement. Designer Whey promotes a peach flavored bar with the catching title "Finally! Because we're so sick and tired of chocolate." The paradox is that the ad does not refer to real chocolate, of course, but the ersatz flavor that can be found in other bars.[20] The Maxxon bar ad boldly refers to the actual act of eating and munching, usually not even considered, almost repressed. We see four images of the bar. In the first one, it has just been bitten, then more and more chunks of it disappear, supposedly in the watering mouth of a reader. Under each image, we read "Crunch . . . crunch . . . crunch . . ." and finally "Mmmmm!" In this unusual case, the supplement is not mysteriously incorporated in the body to increase muscle mass, but it is actually chewed.[21]

Labrada Nutrition promotes a Carb Watchers Lean Body Banana Split Meal Replacement Bar. In the ad, the bar is actually dipped in a banana split, with whipped cream, cherries, and even chocolate prominently displayed. This is probably the most risqué image in the three magazines, but the impact is, of course, balanced by the copy that points out that the bar provides 30 g of proteins and just 4 g of sugar. The suggestion is that, by choosing that product, health conscious consumers are allowed to sin with their minds and mouths, but their bodies will not even notice it.[22] Pages promoting everyday food products that one would find at a corner store or a supermarket are absent in *Muscle & Fitness*. While in *Men's Fitness*, we find only a few representations, *Men's Health* publishes ads for Heinz Tomato Ketchup, Wendy's, V8 vegetable juice, and Stouffer's frozen meals, and nutrition supplements become much less frequent. The readers of the latter magazine appear to be considered by the advertisers as full blown eating creatures, even if the products, not necessarily flat-belly friendly, refer to a kind of food consumption that does not include any actual cooking.

From this semiotic analysis of the advertising pages, we can already draw a few conclusions about the relationships among food, nutrition, masculinities, and muscle building, with body images playing a paramount role in the choices of what these men—for whom the magazines are meant—eat. Taste and sensual appreciation don't play a central role. Different flavorings are added only to ensure variety to meals that otherwise would be always the same. The key element here is nutrition: how much protein the body absorbs, and how much fat it is able to burn. Readers seem to show a certain need to be reassured in their quest for fitness, and the agency that guarantees this sense of protection is science, connoted as exact, matter of fact, serious, and above all, masculine.

Science, considered as a legitimate masculine way of thinking and approaching reality, also plays a very important role in the editorial features concerning food and nutrition, second in importance only to the stories about fitness and muscle building. In the three magazines, we find sections with nutrition advice: all of them quote the sources the news is taken from, and in *Men's Fitness*, we even see the face of the experts that give the tips.[23] Despite the continuous reference to science, the general discourse is far from adopting an actual scientific approach: tips are just tips. Readers are offered bits and pieces of unrelated news about this specific nutrient or the other, without any systematic connection.[24] As it often happens in diet and nutrition communication, editorial staffs opt for clear, simple, and ready-to-apply pieces of advice, avoiding any difficulty intrinsic in the subject matter.

In *Muscle & Fitness,* readers are told to decrease their consumption of Java coffee for a leaner diet, since in an experiment made in Norway, "the intake of chocolate, sweets, cakes, sweet biscuits, pastry, and jams increased when coffee intake was higher, and decreased when coffee intake was lower. The opposite effect occurred with fish dishes, other drinks, as well as with physical activity."[25] No explanation is given about the phenomenon, not even tentatively. On the other hand, in *Men's Fitness*, we readers are told to take caffeine before a workout, because "caffeine stimulates the release of free fatty acids, which are utilized for energy when you exercise, leading to fat loss."[26]

Another feature in *Men's Fitness* is dedicated to soy, endorsed for its muscle-building and protecting capacity.[27] The whole story is an attempt to explain that eating soy and soy-derived products will not transform readers into "bandy-legged yogis with torsos the shape of Coke bottles." As a matter of fact, after reassuring bodybuilders that the phytoestrogens, contained in soy and similar to estrogens, do not constitute a problem for masculinity, the author affirms, "real men eat tofu, in moderation." In the Nutrition Bulletin section, *Men's Health* invites readers to add fish oil to their diet to avoid the risk of developing both an irregular heartbeat and insulin resistance, to eat strawberry and black raspberries to reduce risks of cancer, to drink soda to help quench appetite, milk to reduce the risk of colon cancer, and wine for better breath.[28] Readers are presented a mass of unrelated information that seems to play with their health fears. "Smart strategies" are proposed to fight any kind of problem connected with food.

In the Weight Loss Section of *Men's Health*, readers are taught what to order at an Italian restaurant by two juxtaposed pictures.[29] One is a serving of lasagna with antipasto and two breadsticks (959 calories), the other is eggplant parmigiana with a side of spaghetti with marinara sauce and two slices of garlic bread (1,246 calories). Frankly, both look quite unappetizing. The text states the obvious, underlying the necessity of limiting caloric intake, without providing the reader with any actual advice or information about better and healthier eating.

Lose Fat, Build Muscle, Eat Smart

As in the case of the advertising pages, the goal of editorial features dealing with nutritional models and attitudes is usually not to follow a balanced and constant diet that can ensure body fitness in the long run, but rather to obtain fast results that are immediately visible on the body. The focus is on food as building material for a better-looking, longer-living body, rather than as a source of pleasurable experiences or a marker of cultural identity, let alone a cherished and hated instrument for caring and nurturing. Each magazine presents some sort of diet. For example, *Muscle & Fitness* introduces King Kamali, a 6 meal, 7 snack daily program that has, at its core, heavy and hard training. The program mixes fresh food, such as fruit or chicken breast, with protein powders and meal replacements.

The same issue of *Muscle & Fitness* also dedicates a long feature to a Crash Course in Nutrition for college students, with a strong caveat against consuming fast food and, in general, "sweet, salty, and fatty temptations."[30] Fast food is not bad, per se, as it often solves time and budget, problems common to many students. As a matter of fact, the editor lists many snacks, categorized into "crunchy," "fruity," and "substantial," that can help youngsters fight their hunger without fattening them up. The aim is, once again, to bulk up, to add muscle, and to lose fat. Male students are not supposed to waste time cooking, which might make them look effeminate. They are advised to "stock up on canned beans, frozen vegetables, bagged pasta, and even canned tuna to provide a basis for many nutritious meals." One single recipe is given, and that is for batches of pasta "made ahead of time and refrigerated in a sealed container until you're ready to assemble the meal." As a matter of fact, all that students are supposed to do is toss some precooked or canned food in the pasta.

Men's Fitness presents us with the 15/21 Quickstart Plan to lose up to 15 pounds in 21 days.[31] For each week, a daily diet is prescribed (not proposed) that has to be repeated, unchanged, for seven days. The diet is composed of 6 meals, with two main intakes and 4 snacks. Readers are also given eight "ground rules for maximal fat loss," such as "Eat the meals in order," "Eat all the food prescribed," "Don't cheat." The language transpires sheer severity: If you want to lose fat, you have to be totally dedicated, even ready to sacrifice yourself on the kitchen stove, for you are required to boil eggs, steam vegetables and fish, and bake potatoes. The feature is illustrated with pictures of fresh, if unappetizing, food, in light yellow dishes and bowls.

The same magazine, nevertheless, deals with the issue of daily food intake, in an article aimed at teaching readers to maintain the muscle they have earned in months of training without losing definition.[32] The story features appetizing pictures of simple and nourishing dishes, just like those one could see in a food magazine. Readers are given another series of clear rules. "The idea is to control as much as possible of what goes into what you eat." The control issue is paramount: If one does not keep one's otherwise wild appetites in check, one can neither lose fat and build muscle, nor maintain one's body frame. Once again, most of the dishes proposed in the maintenance menu require little or no preparation. If they do, it's not mentioned. So readers are told to eat lean turkey, chicken breasts, or salmon, but no information is given about how to fix them.

Do Real Men Cook?

When actual food is advertised, it is ready-made or fast food. Potential readers are not supposed to have any connection with buying, storing, and cooking food, all activities apparently belonging to the feminine. Male subjects cannot perform activities related to the preparation of food without affecting their masculine traits and the inscription of these in a cultural order that is deeply gendered. By reiteration, the norms intrinsic to these practices and processes, highly regulated and ritualized, are likely to be incorporated in the very body of the individual, which thus enters the domain of cultural intelligibility.[33] They constitute the conditions of emergence and operation, the boundaries and stability of the gendered subject. Thus, the production or materialization of a masculine subject is also its subjection, its submission to rules and norms, including the ones regulating the kitchen. The embodiment of gender through reiterated practices, including food related activities, reveals the influence of power structures that, in Foucaultian fashion, are omnipresent and pervasive, not necessarily connected with specific institutions, and not always imposed on the subject from the outside.[34] At any rate, the food and supplement industry seems eager to and capable of exploiting these elements to encourage readers to buy products that reinforce their perceived masculinities by avoiding gendered activities, such as buying food and cooking, while turning them into better consumers of high added value, hence more expensive, products.

Usually, no cooking is required from readers. In *Muscle & Fitness,* we find a feature about eating fish.[35] "Bodybuilders, grab your can openers—try these 10 scrumptious, high-protein seafood recipes you can prepare in minutes." Readers are given alternatives to the boring old tuna, such as canned or preserved salmon, clams, crab, and shrimp. Again, these dishes can be assembled more than cooked, saving time and sparing the readers' self-esteem. On the pages in *Men's Fitness,* triple-deckers become "a tower of muscle-building power."[36] The title is reinforced by the picture of a never-ending series of superposed layers of sandwich, filled with a scrumptious bounty of food. The abundance is so overwhelming that the sandwich passes the limits of the page and continues on the next one. Then, of course, limitations are given about what kind of bread, cheese, and condiments are to be used. Again, there is no cooking involved. This is real men's food, even if it gingerly avoids mayonnaise, full-fat cheese, and fattening bread (described as "bullets to be dodged").

Men's Health has a section called, "A man, a can, a plan," that gives a recipe for "Beer-n-sausage bake: a tasty, filling, and alcohol-tinged meal."[37] This is the quintessential macho meal: cans, beer, and no cooking. Well, actually there is some cooking involved. A sausage has to be grilled in a skillet and then put into the oven with the other ingredients, but we are still at a manageable level of assemblage. Anyway, everybody knows that cooking meat, as on the occasion of barbecues, is a man's thing. Exceptions are rare. In a story aimed at promoting pork, after reassuring readers of its leanness, *Muscle & Fitness* entices its readers with tips for making it tastier ("fruits go well with pork") and even gives instructions for a tropical stir-fried pork tenderloin, re-inforced by an inviting picture of the dish. It goes without saying, we are given the exact quantity of calories and nutrients per serving.[38]

In another section of *Muscle & Fitness,* Laura Creavalle (the author of the above mentioned cookbooks advertised in the same magazine) gives the recipe for a home-baked and healthy fruit and nut bread.[39] The recipe is simple and quick, and while the text refers to "moist, delicious cakes that warm the hearts of young and old alike," it also warns against the excess of fat in baked goods. It is interesting that the cook is a woman, and while she refers to the emotional connotations of food, she also puts herself under the banners of the fight against inordinate consumption of victuals.

Again, dedicating time and effort in fixing meals is perceived as connected to the nurturing role that is considered typical of females. Women re-affirm their nature by performing their role of caregiver. They are responsible with feeding not only their own, but also others' bodies, ensuring their survival, but submitting them to the constant temptation of the unchecked, always invading flesh. This short examination of food preparation practices, as explained in the feature articles, reconfirms the conclusions deducted from the analysis of the advertising pages. Cooking is perceived as one of the most identifiable performative traits of femininity. Men should avoid participating in the transformation of food at the stove, an almost alchemical activity dangerously close to the growth of flesh, inherently difficult to keep in check.

How to Feed a Naked Woman

As a matter of fact, according to *Men's Health Guide to Women*, there is an occasion when a man is supposed to cook: When he wakes up after a night of sex, and he wants to fix breakfast for the naked woman dozing in his bed.[40] "Once you get her into bed, these breakfasts will keep her there," affirms the writer, who, being a woman, knows what she is talking about. The five recipes she gives are simple and quite fast. The point is to nourish the body in ways that are propitious to more sex, obviously the sole goal of all the cooking. So readers are told that the crustless quiche they are taught to prepare is "high in protein to help control SHBG, a substance that makes it harder for your body to use testosterone and arginine. Argigine is an amino acid that improves the blood flow to your penis and may also improve sexual stamina for both men and women." In the introduction to Eggs Benedict with Broiled Grapefruit the author states:

> Eggs, bacon, English muffin: the combination provides extra zinc, a mineral that she needs to stay well lubricated and that you need to keep producing semen; You'll pick up niacin, too—a B vitamin essential for the secretion of histamine, a chemical that helps trigger explosive orgasms. And since studies have found that too much or too little dietary fat can decrease levels of libido-boosting testosterone, the recipe has been tweaked to provide an optimal 28 percent of calories from fat. The pink grapefruit? It's for her; women like pink stuff.

Is that not a known fact? Nevertheless, readers are clearly advised to avoid thinking about women, except as objects of sexual desire, waiting in bed to be fed. "Remember when your mom used to make French toasts on Saturday mornings? Try not to think about it. Instead, think about thiamin and riboflavin." Thank goodness science is there to help men achieve their goals and, to some extent, to reassure their apparently wobbling self-confidence. Recipes have more the function of a placebo that works like Viagra, rather than a sensual, sexual experience to be shared with one's partner. Taste is not mentioned once.

Herbs and other natural ingredients are also supposed to help with one's sex life.[41] They surely will not hurt, and they might actually help, "whether you're an old man battling occasional bouts of impotence or a younger man whose sex drive is sometimes slowed by stress." A whole list is given, with specific explanations for each substance. A similar approach is evident in a feature in *Men's Health*, "The Sex for Life Diet."[42]

> The article you are about to read is based on the simple notion that a) men like food and b) men like sex, so c) wouldn't it be great if you could actually eat your way to more fun in the

bedroom? Grunt if you agree. Or maybe just sharpen your knife and fork. With help from nutritionists and the latest research, we've discovered 10 superfoods that can help you at every age and stage of sex life—whether it's seducing women in your 20s, producing Mini-Me's in your 30s, or inducing your equipment to keep working in your 40s and beyond.

Science is invoked not only in the content of the story, but the whole argument is presented like a robust, if actually fake, Aristotelian syllogism. Men act according to logic, even when their bodies crave sex and food, and live their lives according to neat plans. In your 20s, you have fun; in your 30s, you concentrate on reproduction (not out of love, but with the goal of creating replicas of your narcissistic self); in your 40s, there is nothing much left to do but worry about your faltering pleasure tools.

In the pictures, we see a handsome couple engaged in various activities. In one, the smiling, blond, thin, and cute woman feeds pizza to her muscle-bound, tight T-shirt wearing partner. In the second, he has just dipped a strawberry in whipped cream, while she coyly averts her gaze from him, with a finger in her mouth. In the third, she holds a glass of red wine in her hand, while he smiles and leans on her. The images make a clear distinction between male food (pizza) and female food (strawberries, whipped cream, wine). Wine seems to haunt men as a dangerous world, often perceived as intrinsically feminine, that they are obliged to cope with and that causes performance anxieties. Men wander in uncharted territories, far from the reassuring haven of beer. In the article, "22 Ways to Make an Impression," readers are given a few basic tips:[43] "11. Never bring out a half-consumed bottle of wine sealed with aluminum foil. 12. When choosing a bottle of wine to take to a dinner party, spend between $10 and $15. That's for a bottle, not a gallon. 13. When a wine steward gives you a cork, sniff it. Don't check it by plunging it rapidly in and out of your pursed lips."

In other words, never mimic fellatio in front of your date, as allusive to future pleasure as that may be. Why is the "wine steward" supposed to give you the cork to sniff? If that operation needs to be done, it should be his task, and he will pour some wine in your glass to swirl and, yes, sniff. The story is written for men who clearly are not used to ordering wine, and prefer eating at the local diner, or even greasy spoon, rather than at a restaurant where a somehow menacing and mysterious "wine steward" might embarrass them. We find another hint to the anxiety provoked by dining experiences in "24 Rules for a Successful Relationship," which interestingly mentions dinner in the same sentence with the choice of living quarters or, even, reproduction.[44]

> Put your foot down the next time both of you are making plans for dinner—or, heck, deciding where to live and whether to have children. Women rate agreeable men as more attractive than stubborn ones, but only if the nicer guys have a dominant streak. If strength and decisiveness are missing, nice guys come off as meek.

In only one instance taste is mentioned together with sex. In "9 Tricks of Domestic Bliss," giving tips on where to have sex when at home, we read:

> Use a sturdy wooden table, which is more comfortable than the floor and a better height than the kitchen counter, says Louanne Cole Weston, Ph.D., a sex therapist in Fair Oaks, California. Have your partner lie back on the table with her pelvis near the edge. Then reach for some

food—anything that can be licked off is fair game. Giving your tongue something tasty to aim for can help you dwell in one spot longer—and she'll love that.[45]

Cunnilingus can be fun, but it is better to give it more taste. Here, women are equaled to food, put on a table, and eaten. They don't necessarily taste good though.

Balanced Diets, Controlled Bodies

In all the examined material, a strong desire to control not only one's body appearance, but also to curb one's desires and appetites is evident. A fit male body becomes the material expression of one's dominion over the self. *Muscle & Fitness* features a story about "taming the craving for sugary treats."[46] Sweets are interestingly connected with women, either because they supposedly yearn for them more than men do, "especially during that week of the month," or because they control the administration of sweets in the household, and not only for children. The professional bodybuilder, Garrett Downing, tells readers,

> Since I have problems with portion control, I put my wife in charge. She's the keeper of the sweets. She'll give me one or two cookies and hide the rest from me. Otherwise, I could actually sit down and eat an entire box . . . I think if you try to eat clean all the time, you get to a point where you get a little insane. Having that bit of a sweet treat brings a little sanity back into your life. If you're training consistently and the rest of your diet is intact, occasional treats won't do damage. When you don't train consistently but cheat frequently, that's when they catch up. Even when you're dieting, you can allow yourself a treat—a couple of cookies, a slice of pie or cake.[46]

The woman as the "keeper of the sweet" is quite a powerful, if involuntary, metaphor. The phrase reveals an ongoing struggle between a "clean" diet and the unrelenting desire for sensory satisfaction that can lead the more dedicated man to "cheating." Sweets—and appetite in general—are clearly perceived as feminine. This is a recurrent—though often latent and disguised—element that plays an important role in structuring the nutritional discourse in these magazines. As a matter of fact, only women appear capable of keeping men's desire in check, probably because they are supposed to deal constantly with their own. The agency of desire, thus, becomes the agency controlling desire. This ambivalence reminds us of Melanie Klein's theories on the ambivalent desires and fears of devouring and being devoured in infants.[47] According to the famed psychoanalyst, the mother's breast, and any other source of nourishment, that ensures satisfaction and then disappears, is perceived as both good and bad, creating frustrations in infants and cannibalistic drives aiming at the destruction and ingestion of the desired objects. Since infants experience their own cannibalistic drives as dangerous, they protect themselves by externalizing and projecting them outside, on to the breast, from which they fear retaliation in the form of ingestion. Thus, desire and hunger are perceived as potentially destructive and, for that reason, projected on the outside. This anxiety ridden dualism that characterizes the first months of life—defined by Klein as "paranoid-schizoid"— appears to be successively sublimated in the dichotomy that, according to the feminist theorist Susan Bordo, haunts Western civilization from Plato on. She writes, "the construction of the body as something apart from the true self (whether conceived as soul, mind, spirit, will, creativity, freedom . . .) and as undermining the best efforts of that self."[48] As it happens, when gender is applied to this dualism, women are on the side of the lower bodily drives, embodying appetites and desires that weigh down men in their attempt to achieve freedom from materiality. In the passage from the feature, "Taming the Craving for Sugary Treats," we quoted, women are the keepers of the occasional but controlled treats that allow men to attain the perfect trained body by freeing them of excessive stress about food.[46] If we follow the Kleinian hypothesis, sweet treats, of which the writer acknowledges the irresistible appeal, materialize the schizoid attitude of infants desiring their mothers' breast and being frustrated at them when they do not get total satisfaction. The desire for limitless enjoyment cannot be met; the craved symbiosis between the child and the mother, where the infant fantasizes to get rid of all individuality, is unattainable and intrinsically impossible, because the body is always already inscribed as singular and autonomous in the cultural order, despite its inherent fragmentation.[49] Similarly, the alluring and threatening sweets, symbolizing unbridled pleasure, must be kept at a distance, submitted to the woman who knows how to deal with this kind of danger.

In the development of these dynamics leading to a loss of the individual distinction that is clearly perceived as a masculine trait, women coincide with the dimension that has been defined by Julia Kristeva as the abject, "a threat that seems to emanate from an exorbitant outside or inside, ejected beyond the scope of the possible, the tolerable, the thinkable . . . The abject has only one quality of the object—that of being opposed to I."[50] As Mary Douglas has shown in her study on purity and danger, the abject is what subverts order, codified systems, and stable identities. In this specific context, sweets endanger the whole effort to build a distinctively masculine, muscular body. They belong to a dimension both wanted and, precisely for this reason, demonized, in that it could condemn the male body to lose its frontiers that were gained with such great difficulty.

As Susan Bordo has pointed out, the body is identified "as animal, as appetite, as deceiver, as prison of the soul and confounder of its projects." It is always in opposition with the spiritual self and rationality that mirror the divine.[51] Historically, Bordo argues, women have been identified with the debasing dimension of the body, chaotic and undisciplined. Men, on the other side, are supposed to reflect the spirit. Masculinity is embodied in their control over the flesh, a metaphorical equivalent of their dominion over female unchecked carnality. The dichotomy is inscribed in the male body as a series of clear oppositions between hard and soft, thick and thin, and, of course, fit and flabby. Food is a temptation that can make man fall, unless it is stripped down to its nutritional components, purified by the intervention of scientific rationality. Within these nutrients, the main contest is between protein, the building material for good muscle, and fat, the symbol of the uncontrollable flesh. Carbohydrates are in a middle ground; they are the fuel that allows us to work out, but they can easily fall in the realm of the enemy if they are consumed in excessive quantity. The battle is fought in every man's body, and it takes strenuous efforts. Food and nutrition often play an important role in the discourse proposed in this literature, deploying scientific language to reassure readers of the effectiveness of the advice given. This rhetoric proposes a strong desire to control not only one's body appearance, but also to curb one's desires and appetites. A fit body becomes the material expression of one's dominion over the self, over the flesh and appetites that often appear as tainted by a definite feminine character. Control clearly does not imply cooking; most of the dishes proposed in those magazines require little or no preparation. Cooking food seems to constitute a threat to the reader's masculinity; men consume, they do not get involved with the chores related to food. Men's fitness magazines present themselves as scientific weapons, offering practical advice and helping readers to discern when food is a friend and when, more often, a foe.

Notes

1. See also Connell, R. W. (1995) *Masculinities*. University of California Press. Connell, R.W. (2000) *The Men and the Boys*. University of California Press. Bordo, S. *The Male Body: A New Look at Men in Public and in Private*. New York: Farrar, Straus and Giroux, 1999.
2. See the company's official website, www.rodale.com
3. Harrison, G., Pope, Katharine, A., Phillips, R. O. (2000) *The Adonis Complex*. Touchstone Books, New York.
4. Connell, R. W. (2000), *The Men and the Boys*. Polity, Cambridge, p. 12.
5. Connell, R. W. (1995) *Masculinities*. University of California Press, Berkeley CA.
6. Connell, R. W. (2000) *The Men and the Boys*. Polity, Cambridge, p. 57.
7. Bronki, M. (1998) "The Male Body in the Western Mind." *Harvard Gay and Lesbian Review*, 5(4):28.
8. Jeffords, S. (1989) *The Remasculinization of America: Gender and the Vietnam War*. Indiana University Press, loomington.
9. Wienke, C. (1998) Negotiating the male body: Men, masculinity, and cultural ideas. *The Journal of Men's Studies*, (3):255.
10. Gerschick T. and Miller, A. (1994) Gender Identities at the Crossroads of Masculinity and Physical Disability. *Masculinites*, 2:34–55.
11. Marion Nestle (2002) Food Politics. Berkeley: University of California Press, pp. 1–30.
12. Naomi Wolf (1991) The Beauty Myth: How images of beauty are used against women. New York: W. Morrow.
13. *Muscle & Fitness*, November 2002, p. 1.
14. *Muscle & Fitness*, November 2002, pp. 138–139.
15. *Muscle & Fitness*, November 2002, p. 87.
16. *Muscle & Fitness*, November 2002, pp. 58–60.
17. *Muscle & Fitness*, November 2002, pp. 20–21.
18. *Muscle & Fitness*, November 2002, p. 204.
19. *Muscle & Fitness*, November 2002, p. 17.
20. *Muscle & Fitness*, November 2002, p. 65.
21. *Muscle & Fitness*, November 2002, p. 70.
22. *Muscle & Fitness*, November 2002, p. 57.
23. Men's Fitness, "10 ways to leave your blubber," October 2002, pp. 46–50.
24. For the reasons behind this approach, see Marion Nestle (2002). *Food Politics*. University of California Press.
25. *Muscle & Fitness*, "Cut back on Java for a leaner, healthier diet," November 2002, p. 44.
26. *Men's Fitness*, "Expert's tip: Cut the bad stuff in half," October 2002, p. 50.
27. *Men's Fitness*, "The power of soy," October 2002, pp. 134–136.
28. *Men's Health*, "Nutrition bulletin," October 2002, p. 52.
29. *Men's Health*, "Eat this not that," October 2002, p. 72.
30. *Muscle & Fitness*, "Crash course in nutrition," October 2002, pp. 158–162.
31. *Men's Fitness*, "Quick start three week program," October 2002, p. 77.
32. *Men's Fitness*, "Going the distance," October 2002, pp. 118–121.
33. Judith Butler, *Bodies that Matter*. Routledge, New York (1993), pp. 1–23. Butler limits herself to sex, but I do think that also food can be approached in the same way. She wonders: "Given that normative heterosexuality is clearly not the only regulatory regime operative in the production of bodily contours or setting the limits of bodily intelligibility, it makes sense to ask what other regimes of regulatory production contour the materiality of bodies." p. 17.

34. "Power must be understood in the first instance as a multiplicity of force relations, as the process which, through ceaseless struggles and confrontations, transforms, strengthens or reverses them: as the support which these force relations find in one another, thus forming a chain or a system, or on the contrary, the disjunction and contradictions which isolate them from one another; and lastly, as the strategies in which they take effect, whose general design or institutional crystallization is embodied in the state apparatus, in the formulations of the law, in the various social hegemonies." Michel Foucault (1990). *The History of Sexuality Vol. I.* Vintage Books, New York, p. 93.

35. *Muscle & Fitness,* "Go fish," November 2002, pp. 168–174.

36. *Men's Fitness,* "Science of sandwich," October 2002, 96–98.

37. *Men's Health,* "A man, a can, a plan," October 2002, pp. 66.

38. *Muscle & Fitness,* "Pork slims down," November 2002, p. 68.

39. *Muscle & Fitness,* "Home-baked and healthy," November 2002, p. 206.

40. *Men's Health Guide to Women,* "How to feed a naked woman," October 2002, pp. 56–59.

41. *Men's Health Guide to Women,* "Better sex naturally," October 2002, pp. 146–151.

42. *Men's Health,* "The sex for life diet," October 2002, pp. 156–159.

43. *Men's Health Guide to Women,* "22 ways to make an impression," October 2002, pp. 4–5.

44. *Men's Health Guide to Women,* "24 rules for a successful relationship," October 2002, pp. 166–167.

45. *Men's Health Guide to Women,* "9 tricks of domestic bliss," October 2002, pp. 208–209.

46. *Men's Fitness,* "Sweet tooth?" November 2002, p. 210.

47. *The Selected Melanie Klein* (1986) Edited by Juliet Mitchell, The Free Press.

48. Bordo, S. (1993) *Unbearable weight.* University of California Press, p. 3.

49. Jacques Lacan, "Le stade du miroir comme formateur de la fonction du Je." In *Ecrits*, Editions du Seuil, Paris (1966) See also Slavoj Zizek (1989) *The Supreme Object of Ideology.* Verso, London, pp. 121–129.

50. Kristeva, J. (1982) *Powers of Horror.* Columbia University Press, New York, p. 1.

51. Bordo, S. (1993) *Unbearable Weight.* University of California Press, p. 3.

21

Cooking Skills, the Senses, and Memory: The Fate of Practical Knowledge*

David Sutton

> How, after all, did my grandmother acquire her culinary magic? It required an elder not just willing but determined to share her powers with a neophyte. And it required an upstart who craved to follow the path treaded by forebears. Is it possible that as much as my grandmother's eighteen progeny revered her, that none of them wanted to be her?
>
> Stephen Steinberg, 1998, "Bubbie's Challah"

How might we think of ordinary food preparation as a site that brings together skilled practice, the senses, and memory? In reflecting on his grandmother's *challah* bread, Steinberg suggests some of the larger identity issues embedded in the relationship between people and their socio-material environment, in this case a set of relatives and a set of kitchen tools, flavors, and ingredients. He evokes an image of "traditional" cooking, without recipes, cookbooks, cuisinarts, or bread machines, but with the implied hierarchy of gerontocratic authority passed in a female line. He further suggests that loss of tradition, which is, in fact, loss of particular *skills*, is a necessary part of becoming the modern, individualistic Americans that his family members aspired to be. Is this image, then, a relic of grandmothers past? How do people face the task of everyday cooking under conditions of "modernity," and what might this mean for issues of skill, memory, and embodied sensory knowledge, particular given the uncomfortable relationship with the "lower senses" associated with modernity and modernization projects and the devaluation of practical knowledge, tradition, and social embeddedness. How have recent times changed people's relationship to the various kinds of cooking tools, ranging from their sense organs (the nose, the tongue) to pots and pans, knives, even bread machines, with which they populate and structure their kitchen environment?

Recent debates within anthropology and the social sciences more broadly have taken opposing views on the question of the homogenization of cultural knowledge potentially brought about by "globalization." While some support the "McDonaldization" thesis implicit in changing relations of production and distribution that have allowed Western hegemony to extend consumer capitalism to the far reaches of the globe, others argue for an endless proliferation of individual creativity and cultural meanings and reinterpretations of Western processes and products. In a sense, however, the two sides may be talking past each other, one focusing on production and distribution, the other tending to put more emphasis on the endless diversity of consumption practices.

*Originally published 2006

Cooking provides an interesting, transgressive object in this regard for a number of reasons. First, and perhaps less importantly, the products of cooking partake in some sense of both production and consumption, and nearly simultaneously; indeed, consumption itself (through tasting) is part of the process of skilled food production.[1] Yet there has been relatively little research on consumption as not simply a creative, but a *skilled* process, involving judgment and the reasoned use of the senses. More significantly, by focusing attention on skill as opposed to abstract cultural knowledge, we are encouraged to think of practices as embedded in particular contexts, as skill is always in relation to a particular task at hand. Thus skill-based ethnography forces us to examine the complex processes by which practices are produced and reproduced, rather than positing vague forces of "the global" and "the local." A focus on skill also raises questions of memory in a very direct way as well. In thinking about cooking, attention to memory is important in connecting the senses to the kind of embodied practices that we see in the kitchen. Skill raises issues of apprenticeship and repetition, and the education of the senses that allow for the comparisons necessary to judge the successful dish.

Habit Memory and the Social Nature of the Senses

I begin my consideration of cooking with a focus on the senses.[2] The senses are once again matters of theoretical and ethnographic concern, after what David Howes (2003: xii) refers to as "a long, dry period in which the senses and sensuality were bypassed by most academics as antithetical to intellectual investigation." But what does this mean in the case of "taste," perhaps the most ethnographically neglected of the senses? Taste, of course, has a double meaning in English, and in one of its senses, it has been explored by a number of authors, most extensively Bourdieu, who examines the ways that "good taste" is turned into cultural capital in the pursuit of class distinction. While Bourdieu is dealing with taste in the "social" sense, with peoples' "taste" in home furnishings, clothing and recreation, he does in this context touch on actual practices of eating. "Taste" he says "is class culture ... embodied" (1982:19). With echoes of Levi-Strauss in the background, and perhaps because he focused on a thoroughly "modern Western" society, Bourdieu argues that the middle-class perform their freedom from need, necessity and nature by consuming small portions of light, less-filling food, chewed carefully. While working class (men here) shun such eating practices "the whole body schema ... governs the selection of certain foods ... in the working classes fish tends to be regarded as an unsuitable food for men, not only because it is a light food, insufficiently 'filling', ... but above all, it is because fish has to be eaten in a way which totally contradicts the masculine way of eating, that is, with restraint, in small mouthfuls, chewed gently, with the front of the mouth ..." (1982:190). Which is another way of saying that apparently real French men don't eat quiche either! Connerton develops Bourdieu's argument in developing a notion of skill as fluid performance. For the European nobility (here in contradistinction to the bourgeoisie), such performance is evidenced in skills which *take time* to acquire (like Steinberg's grandmother's *challah*) and cannot be simply reproduced or copied:

> To own a chateau or manor house is not primarily to display disposal over money; one must
> appropriate also the skill of bottling and tasting fine wines, the secrets of fishing ... the

knowledge of the hunt. All these competencies are ancient, they can be learned only slowly, they can be enjoyed only by those who take their time, they … require that one occupy one's time not economically but ceremonially

(Connerton 1989: 87).

For Connerton, the key point about such practices is that they are not simply signs which everyone can recognize, but skills, which few can incorporate into their bodies (1989:87; 90). Thus Connerton makes the dimension of memory more explicit than Bourdieu, referring to these skills as habit memories "acquired in such a way as not to require explicit reflection on their performance" (102). In the case of a fluid piano performance, Connerton refers to such skills as "a remembrance in the hands" (93). Thus Connerton directs us to questions of enculturation and enskillment, the process by which taste is learned, mobilized, and repeatedly practiced, so that it gains the aura of naturalization which makes it such a critical marker of class distinction.

But there is the other meaning of taste, that of a sensory experience, which is neglected, or at least not ethnographically explored in the studies above. How are we to approach that? I think a consensus (no pun intended) has begun to develop in studies of the senses that we are not dealing with radical cultural difference, but with shifting emphases, with cultural elaborations on a continuum of experience. How and in what ways are sensory registers elaborated in different societies? The study of taste or smell might lead one to look at the realm of myth and the afterlife in one society (Bubant 1998), in another to issues of healing (Rasmussen 1999), and to the domain of advertising in a third (Classen, Howes and Synnott 1994). In some cases a specific sensory domain may be elaborated to the detriment of other domains, and in other cases the study of one domain may by necessity lead into others, the phenomenon of synesthesia that characterizes many aspects of non-hierarchized sensory perception that has not undergone the discipline of modernity. These parameters form a set of ethnographic questions for exploration. In studying taste and other senses in the context of Greece I have been led to focus on Orthodox ritual on the one hand and cooking on the other. In looking at Greek sense scapes one must be attentive to both linguistic and non-linguistic elaborations. Non-linguistic include such multi-sensory practices as the Orthodox liturgy, involving the smells of myrrh and frankincense that are spread by the priests swinging censers rhythmically back and forth, the flicker of the candles that each person lights and places in front of the painted icon when entering the church, the kinesthetics of making the cross and kissing the icon, the press of bodies in the often confined space of small chapels, the reverberating nasal pitch of the cantors, and of course the multicolored sight of the icons illustrating key biblical stories and the taste of communion bread and wine mixed together to the consistency of gruel and presented by the priest on a spoon. "An Orthodox Church service is a synesthetic experience: every sense is conveying the same message" (Kenna 2005). The sensory experiences extend out into the community in numerous ways as well, such as the incense, basil and blessed bread which are brought home by women church attendees to pervade the home with the tastes and smells of Orthodoxy.

Linguistic elaboration of the senses take numerous forms. One particularly striking one is the expression "listen to that smell" which is used approvingly to refer to the odor of food cooking, and is often accompanied by a noisy intake of breath through the nose. The opposite, to indicate the failure to taste a dish, is "it is not hearable," a seemingly direct appreciation of the process of synesthesia, even if coded in everyday metaphor. Other metaphors tie one taste to another: A man tells his friend that he ate prickly pears the other day and they were tasteless, but today "they were honey!" A woman refers to fresh-caught tuna as "souvlaki!" and a man describes a batch of sweet oranges as "banana." Tilley has suggested a connection here between vivid metaphors and the facilitation of memory (Tilley 1999:8). In these cases we have some sense of the basis for the Proustian phenomenon of remembering through evocation of a powerful sensory image. The sweetness of a banana hardly seems similar to that of an orange, and yet, as an image of a food with a strikingly sweet flavor, "banana" does have a certain evocative power. In these cases and others the sensory *intensity* of the experience is stressed, and used as a sort of aid in the storage and retrieval of memory.

Against this background of everyday practices, we can begin to understand the role of sensory experiences and sensory images in more extended social memories of the type mentioned above. But implicit in these sensory distinctions is our other meaning of taste as well: taste as the ability to judge and compare. Just as wine tasting involves the cultivation of certain practices, as well as an elaborated metaphorical vocabulary, the sensory practices of food consumption on Kalymnos meant that Kalymnians have elaborated schemata by which they can compare foods present with meals past (see Sutton 2011).

On Practical Knowledge or Skill

Connerton and Bourdieu pose the question of taste as embodied knowledge or incorporated skill. Thinking about it in these terms lead to a series of questions about *how* such skill is transmitted, deployed in daily practice and in our relationship to material objects in our environment. To think about these issues I suggest we develop the notion of skill or practical knowledge through looking at the phenomenological approach of Tim Ingold. Ingold's work fits well with Bourdieu and Connerton, in that all three take as their starting point a critique of lingering structuralist assumptions that in practice can be seen as the execution of a preexistent code. But Ingold takes us closer to understanding the mechanics of everyday practice through his approach to the emergent qualities of action.

For Ingold, as for Connerton, skilled practice involves not the mind telling the body what to do according to a preconceived plan, but rather a mobilization of the mind/body within an environment of "objects" which "afford" different possibilities for human use. Skill, then, involves much more than the application of a sort of mechanical force to objects (what he sees is the model of technology), but an extension of the mind/body, often through the use of tools, requiring constant and shifting use of judgment and dexterity within a changing environment. The environment is not objectified as a "problem" that humans must "adapt" to, it itself is part of the total field of activity, as in the example of a woodsman who in chopping wood, consults the world with his senses for guidance, not a picture in his head. "The world is its own best model" (Ingold 2001:12; see also Lave 1988). It is through such skilled practices, then, that forms are generated, rather than through the execution of a mental plan, though mental plans may provide guideposts for practices, i.e., they can allow you to assess your work at various moments. This approach has implications for the transmission of skill as well, which, as with Connerton, is seen as impossible to objectify into a set of rules. Skill must be learned through the sensuous and sensory engagement of a novice with the environment and/or with a skilled practitioner. What we tend to refer to as "enculturation" is seen by Ingold as an "education of attention," or, as he puts it, speaking of his father, "His manner of teaching was to show me things, literally to point them out. If I would but notice the things to which he directed my attention, and recognize the sights, smells and tastes that he wanted me to experience … then I would discover for myself much of what he already knew" (2000: 20). Learning from others involves copying, but it is the copying of Connerton's "incorporation" rather than a transcription of knowledge from one head to another, of "guided rediscovery" (2001: 11) in a sensorily-rich environment. One can see here why Ingold's view of skilled practice might be compatible with an anthropology of the senses. Like recent studies in material culture, Ingold does not view objects or the "environment" as passive ciphers to which humans simply add symbolic meaning (see e.g., Myers 2001). Rather objects, because of their sensual properties, afford certain possibilities for human use, the semiotic and the material constantly cross-cut and convert into each other. Hiking boots, for example, by their material nature "afford" certain possibilities in relation to nature by "expanding the range of possible actions available to the body" (Michael 2000: 112). This in no way limits the meaning or uses of hiking boots, any more than recognizing distinctions between the proximate senses (taste, smell, touch) and the distance senses (vision, hearing) limits the cultural elaborations of these different domains, as discussed above.

Ingold argues that the abstraction of knowledge and the senses characteristic of modernity is in a sense counter to our social natures, insofar as it subordinates skill and the senses to the rational paradigm of plans and mental operations. Similarly, modern technology is seen as very different from tool use. A traditional tool is "not a mere mechanical adjunction to the body, serving to deliver a set of commands issued to it by the mind, rather it extends the whole person [into the environment]" (Ingold 1993: 440). Modern technology, by contrast, disembeds the tool from a social context and a context of skilled practice, and treats the workman as a mere operator. If the tool draws its power from and extends the human body, the logic of technology's operation lies outside human bodies (1993: 434–5). He notes that "Throughout history, at least in the western world, the project of technology has been to capture the skills of craftsmen or artisans, and to reconfigure their practice as the application of rational principles whose specification has no regard for human experience and sensibility" (2011: 61). However, Ingold argues that the advent of technological projects definitively does not spell "the end of skill." This is because new skills are constantly developing around new technologies, despite, perhaps, the intentions of technology's makers. "The essence of skill, then, comes to lie in the improvisational ability with which practitioners are able to disassemble the constructions of technology, and creatively to reincorporate the pieces into their own walks of life" (2011: 62). Thus people adapt technologies to their own "rules of thumb" (2000:332).

In the Kitchen

How do these issues and oppositions apply to food and cooking processes? As argued above, cooking is interesting in part because it seems to blur the line between production and consumption, allowing for no hard-and-fast distinction, and implicating the processes discussed by Ingold. I believe these issues have been too long mired in stereotypes, and an endless bombardment of newspaper articles about the "death of cooking," in the replacement of techniques with technologies and the loss of cooking "knowledge" and transmission, similar to the loss of Steinberg's grandmother's *challah* bread. The only way to advance research is through sustained ethnographic treatment, an ethnography of everyday cooking. A number of areas of investigation seem to be indicated.

Cooking Tools

Clearly the above issues can be applied to the tools of the kitchen. Michel de Certeau's *Practice of Everyday Life, Vol. II* contains many examples of the "loss of many ancient gestures" as the woman/cook "has become the unskilled spectator who watches the machine function in her place" (Giard et al. 1998: 212). The measuring cup and spoon is a different sort of technological innovation which does not disembody as much as it standardizes, another specter of modernity that I will take up below. The microwave is another such device which seems to deskill the cook in relation to the traditional oven. But a more nuanced view explores the "use" of these technologies, the way the microwave, bread machine etc., in fact, require many reasoned judgments, new skills to manipulate (think VCR remotes here).[3] The microwave and the bread machine could also be found ethnographically to be supplemental, as Suchman argues above, good for some things, but not replacing older skills. Finally, one has to consider the potential social implications, including the freedoms afforded by such cooking technologies to the intensive labors that traditionally have fallen on women (see Sutton 2001 for a much fuller discussion). As material possessions, kitchen tools themselves may carry family histories and multiple, layered stories, is this also the case for kitchen technologies? These are some of the questions that my research has begun to address.[4]

Plans and Recipes (and their Transmission)

Ingold himself contrasts his view and that of Dan Sperber (1996) in relation to the question of recipes. Sperber's view of a recipe for mornay sauce is that it is a prototypical cultural representation or meme that can be transmitted to others containing all the information one needs to produce the sauce by simply converting the instructions into bodily behavior. But as Ingold (2001: 10) argues, such conversion is not generally such a simple matter, unless the recipe speaks to skills already acquired from melting, stirring, handling different substances, to finding the relevant ingredients and utensils within the layout of the kitchen (no mean feat, those of you with children untrained in kitchen skills no doubt know). Then there are the sensory components, from the kinesthetics of various cooking procedures, chopping, mixing, etc., to the use of the tongue and nose as "tools" to mark the progress of the dish and make the constant judgments and adjustments that are part and parcel of skillful cooking. The recipe may provide certain "critical junctures" in the process, but "between these points ... the cook is expected to be able to find her way around, attentively and responsively, but without further recourse to explicit rules of procedure – or in a word, skillfully" (2001: 11; see also Schlanger 1990). Planning itself is a type of "situated action" and plans are simply one among a number of resources for actions which still take place *in situ* (Leudar & Costall 1996). Recipes in such a view, act more as memory-jogs for previous learning that has acquired through experience (see Heldke 1992: 219). It will be of small surprise to those who cook that cooking is best learned through embodied experience, or even apprenticeship (as it is in most societies, a fully social apprenticeship of a younger generation to a set of female relatives, in which one learns much more than how to get dinner on). But what this "experience" consists of has had minimal ethnographic elaboration. In other words, how do people learn to cook in different societies, who teaches them, under what circumstances, and with how much stress on observation, participation, positive or negative reinforcement, "play-frames," challenges to elders (see e.g., Herzfeld 1995: 137). There is a substantial literature on apprenticeship in anthropology and archaeology which has developed concepts such as scaffolding, distributive competencies, etc. Surprisingly, none of this has been applied to the homely craft of cooking. Another set of questions is raised by the *lack of* cooking apprenticeship that seems to characterize modern, or even more post-modern society, where transmission of knowledge from experienced elders to juniors is explicitly and in practice often eschewed. Once again, cooking seems to be increasingly socially disembedded if not disembodied, though we mustn't neglect new sources of cooking apprenticeship such as the ubiquitous cooking shows.[5] What kind of implications does all this have for an Ingold-type approach?

To conclude this section I once again want to pose the question, are there new narratives to tell this story which avoid the opposition between loss of traditional knowledge or recuperation and invention, especially when these narratives seem to have salience to my ethnographic subjects? One of the goals of my research is to find such new narratives, or I hope to find such narratives, or at least new metaphors that would push us beyond the stale antinomies of the past (as Fernandez [1973] puts it). Before turning to my ethnographic research it will be helpful to present a short history of cooking's relationship to modernity and post-modernity in the US, in order to give a sense of how we have come to some of the current predicaments in our thinking about cooking, and hopefully how we might emerge from them.

Cooking 101: The Not Very Tasty Culture of Scientific Feeding

An offshoot of first-wave feminism, though going in a direction which seems to lead more toward Martha Stewart than it does to grrl power, the development of the "domestic science" movement at the turn of the twentieth century is richly chronicled in Laura Shapiro's book *Perfection Salad* (1986). Here I attempt to present some of the highlights of this history to suggest some of the tensions that led to the present. Shapiro chronicles the rise of the domestic science movement at a time when "science and technology were gaining the aura of divinity: such forces could do no wrong, and their very presence lent dignity to otherwise humble lives" (1986: 4), while "the nation's eating habits underwent their most definitive turn toward modernity" (48). The women reformers who founded this movement were committed to claiming the prestige of heretofore "male" science for housework and cooking, to move cooking, nutrition, and hygiene into the public sphere in its importance for the nation. Thus the interest of the domestic science movement in food was "because it offered the easiest and most immediate access to the homes of the nation" (1986: 5). And through this scientific cookery, women would be able to alleviate not just malnutrition, but the key social problems of the day: poverty, worker discontent, alcoholism, criminality were all put down to improper diet and improper knowledge of scientific householding principles.

In order to making cooking scientific, the women in the movement, initially associated with the Boston Cooking School, made "tradition," which included all kinds of things from the kind of transmission from grandmother to mother to daughter discussed above, to ethnic differences in food habits, to the home as a center for productive activity (Carrier 1998). All of these past practices were stamped as backwards: women who hewed to tradition were labeled as "drudges," "stuck in the past." As Ellen Richards, one such reformer, put it: "'One feels a peg higher in the scale of intelligence for using even a dishwashing machine … The woman who boils potatoes year after year, with no thought of how or why, is a drudge … but the cook who can compute the calories of heat which a potato of given weight will yield, is no drudge'" (Shapiro, 1986: 42). While the cooking schools they established, some to train servants and aspiring working class women, some for the middle-classes, did not ignore issues of skill and manual dexterity, they held the occupations of the mind and "theory" as crucial to their goal,[6] not just how to make a cream sauce "but the abiding reasons why heat acts upon starch in such a way as to produce cream sauce" (68). Thus cooking was a science of the transformation of food substances to create the optimal nutrition, digestion, and hygiene. Standardization and measurement were key components of such a project. Indeed, Fannie Farmer, a leading figure in this movement, was known as "the mother of level measurements." "Exact measurement was the foundation of everything else that happened in the scientific kitchen" (Shapiro, 1986: 115). In this she was aided by the development of measuring cups and spoons in the late nineteenth century, which added a new precision to previous vague recipes for "a teacupful of flour." Farmer added more precision by calling for "level" measurements, and dispensing with imagery in her recipes and cookbooks, such as "butter the size of an egg." She encouraged cooks to use a knife to level the surface of their measured ingredients for additional precision. There should be no "margin for error" (or imagination for that matter) in recipes, and she was known to specify that strips of pimento be cut "three quarters of an inch long and half an inch wide" and to measure out spices by the grain! (Shapiro, 1986: 116). In all this she was guided as much by a business model of standardization as by the scientific model, as discussed below.

What was left out of this course in scientific cookery, of course, was taste, or any of the lower senses for that matter. The food itself was uninteresting except as a route to nutrition and to a better society. While this movement was hardly the first to see good tasting food as problematic in American society, this had a much longer history tied to Christianity and notions of sin (see, for example Mintz 1996 on the threat of ice cream to public morals), they were certainly influenced by this tradition, as well as one that saw middle-class women as a key force in taming the "natural" and "primitive" instincts of middle-class men and the lower classes in general (Shapiro, 1986: 73; 139).[7] Appetite was too low a sense to fit with the "nobler purposes" to which these women aspired (Shapiro, 1986: 71). Cooking schools saw eating as problematic, and rarely allowed their students to consume their finished products; these were sometimes disposed of, or sold to the poor at cost. Food itself was, in pure Levi-Straussian fashion, brought under control by science and careful hygiene. Appeal to the sense of sight was permitted, and considerable imagination was allowed in decorating and arranging the food: shaping it into various objects, color-coordinating it, miniaturizing it: "Food that could be appreciated most fully without being eaten was a special achievement in scientific cookery ... Croquettes, timbales, creamed foods served in pastry shells or ramekins, molded desserts [it's at this time that Jell-O-cooking comes into fashion]—anything that could be encapsulated, or made smaller and prettier than life, became a recurring favorite" (Shapiro, 1986: 102). The key was to contain and *disguise* food, to control its "volatility," and thus to make highly nutritious food *visually* palatable, to wean Americans away from their unhealthy reliance on fried foods, cakes, and pies. Even touch was seen as problematic, partly for hygiene reasons, hence the popularity of the innovation at this time the chafing dish, which allowed meals to be prepared by women "who hardly seemed to be cooking, so distant [were they] from the intimation of raw food" (Shapiro, 1986: 103).

Fannie Farmer was an important transition figure in this movement, as her reliance on business imperatives—standardization and novelty—was much stronger than in other women in the movement. She published so many cookbooks through her constant search for diversity, new combinations of ingredients and preparations, of course within the bounds of scientific principles, although she did tend to pay somewhat more attention to taste than many of her colleagues, perhaps accounting for her enduring popularity. The rise of the food industry in the early twentieth century, however, found a strong ally in rhetoric and in practice, in the domestic science movement. Novelty itself, of course, always has had the ring of "progress," as many of us remember from childhood bombardments of products promising to be "new and improved." Processed foods seemed to offer possibilities for sterility unavailable in individual kitchens. They also promised standardization in the sense of invariability, each bottle of Catsup the same as the previous one, which was later one of the key aspects of the rise of the fast food industry. Indeed, machinery promised to remove human hands, and once again, the senses or simply messiness from the process of cooking. One innovator of the time, in a prelude to the modern day bread machine, introduced a series of devices which would produce bread "which no human hand has touched from the time the wheat was planted until it was taken from the pan in which the loaf was baked" (Shapiro, 1986: 151), leading some movement women to hope that "'home cooking as we now know it' would soon be a thing of the past, at least for city dwellers" (Shapiro, 1986: 210). While another movement leader foresaw the scientific kitchen of the future through the motor of commerce: "Every new scientific device that might save steps and labor was installed in the kitchen, the pantry held a large stock of prepared foods, and a pneumatic tube connected the kitchen with a supply station" (Shapiro, 1986: 170). While these predictions have not all been borne out, Shapiro suggests that they were successful insofar as the home cook came to measure her culinary success "in conviction, not skill" (Shapiro, 1986: 215). Indeed, well into the 1970s the popularity of the notion of "the meal in a pill" as the promise of the future (see Belasco 2000) argues for the long term appeal of these ideals. However, the food industry and the domestic science movement parted company in the 1950s, when increasingly cooking was portrayed popularly as drudgery to be combated with TV dinners and "convenience" foods, involving not only a bodily deskilling in Ingold's sense, but a loss of even the kind of theoretical knowledge of nutrition and ingredients which the movement valued. The homemaker of the 1950s was told that femininity and coy sexuality were the key to their husband's faithfulness, in the kitchen, she became an assembler, not a cook: "Scientific cooks had anticipated the era of culinary regimentation but not the intellectual collapse that would accompany it" (Shapiro, 1986: 229).

But in another sense capitalism's need for innovation also no doubt led us away from these ideals and to a present where flavor, in ever diverse combinations and "authentic origins" is once again on the menu. Shapiro does not document this shift, but suggests that the liberation movements of the 1960s also liberated our appetites to appreciate the sensory again (and to distrust the food industry). The ethnic revival and the rise of multiculturalism have also no doubt played a role, and many have written on the politics of "tasting the other." Zygmunt Baumann sees the shift in terms of a larger scale societal shift from concern for the "producer body," the soldier, the worker, to the "consuming body," the seeker of new experiences or "sensations-gatherer" (Baumann 1996: 115) so amicable to a flexible capitalism, which Bauman sees epitomized in cookbooks: "not just ordinary cookbooks—but collections of ever more refined, exotic, out-of-this-world, exclusive, fastidious and finical recipes; promises of taste-bud delights never experienced before and of new heights of ecstasy for the eyes, nose and palate" (1996: 121). Whether this shift in taste practices was a result of the demands of capitalism or simply a "happy" coincidence is an open question. But Baumann suggests that the post-modern politics of the "Other" has some advantages over the modern. No longer is the "Other" (in this case other foodways) something to be brought under control, ordered and normalized, changed beyond recognition, as the domestic science movement hoped to do for all "traditional" and immigrant foodways. The sensations-gatherer demands that the other be preserved in its otherness. The sensations-gatherer would have to be skilled at consumption, to have "taste," as well as "taste," as I have been arguing throughout this chapter. But has the sensations-gatherer irrevocably undone the link between food production and consumption, transferring production, as in the rest of flexible capitalism, to the "third world" and to immigrants, who labor to create the objects of first world skilled consumption?

It is important to note that this characterization of our post-modern food condition is meant to be in broad strokes, and that we need to be attentive to the many historical strands of experience that go into making the present moment, the domestic science movement, the food industry and the multicultural/pleasure nexus being three prominent ones. In the final section I consider some of these issues ethnographically through a beginning ethnography of everyday cooking that I have been pursuing in Greece and Southern Illinois.[8]

Toward an Ethnography of Everyday Cooking

> Demetra would make most of the basic Greek items with ruthless efficiency, hacking up her ingredients by the bunch and then seeming to measure them solely according to how much she managed to grab in one hand ... I, on the other hand, would place my cookbook on a little stand I had brought for the purpose and carefully measure out everything spoon by spoon and cup by cup.
>
> Tom Stone, 2003, *The Summer of my Greek Taverna*

One way that we have been approaching such an ethnography is through intensive filming of a small number of subjects as they go about cooking "ordinary" and "special" dishes. This allows us to develop a profile and also a sort of culinary biography of some of the key experiences and values that have led people to their current cooking practices. Such biographies, I hope, will help avoid the problem of dichotomies discussed above, although given that "tradition" and "modernity" are very much part of our informants' discourse, we inevitably have to confront these categories. In this section I present some preliminary findings based on two subjects, one a Greek woman, Georgia Vourneli, from the city of Thessaloniki, a middle-class housewife, born and raised in a village in Northern Greece, whom we filmed while she was visiting her son in Southern Illinois; the other, Jane Adams, a Professor of Anthropology, native of Southern Illinois, and longtime political activist. Georgia and Jane provide interesting comparisons and contrasts, as they share similar gender and relative income levels, but very different cultural contexts and educational levels—Georgia having grown up in a village in northern Greece but living most of her adult life in urban Thessaloniki, while Jane has lived most of her life in semi-rural Southern Illinois. For reasons of space I will limit my discussion to issues of tool use and measurement, as well as judgment and taste. Other issues that I am considering include: shopping, structuring of the kitchen environment, recipe and cookbook use, and teaching and learning.

Georgia's relationship to Greek tradition is like her relationship to Greek modernity, a hybrid one. She works out at a private gym twice a day, owns her own car (which for her is a potent symbol of personal independence), and has western-European based sense of fashion and style, including permed, dyed-blond hair. According to her son Leo Vourneli, she has a large collection of "modern" kitchen utensils and appliances. Even though her kitchen is filled with utensils of modernity, when it comes to matters of food and food preparation, Georgia seems to spurn modern technology. She embraces nativistic values of the superiority of things "Greek," in both tools and food, as well as the techniques of cooking she learned from her mother and her grandmother.

Georgia prepared the dish leek pie. *During the time the leeks were cooking and reducing, Georgia began the process of making the Philo for the Prasopita. She began by pouring a large amount of bleached flour into a large bowl. At first we believed that Georgia was measuring the flour by sight, but rather she folded the bag and measured the amount of flour by the size and weight of the flour remaining in the bag. After the desired amount of flour was placed in the bowl, Georgia used the back of her hand to create a hole for future ingredients. She made several passes through the center to create the right depth, so that the liquid ingredients could be contained.*

At no point in the process does she employ measuring spoons or cups. In this case the ingredients themselves become "tools" and perform the role of "measuring" other ingredients. In a *sense the use of ingredients as tool can be seen as part* of the structuring of the cooking environment itself as a mnemonic, or memory-jog, which we have documented in other cooking practices. For example, cooking implements in much of Greece are hung on the wall, in plain sight, rather than in a cupboard or under a counter, reminding the cook of their potential for use (cf. Keller & Dixon-Keller 1999). This would fit well with Ingold's view of using the environment as a form of memory storage—"the world is its own best model."

Georgia placed the following ingredients within the hole in the flour: olive oil (Figure 21.2), vinegar, salt, egg yolk, and water. In this recipe all but two ingredients were measured by sight. The two excluded from this were vinegar and an egg. Drawing her fingers together and pulling up slightly to create a cup of her right hand with her thumb forming the outer edge of the bowl by being crooked against her first finger, she poured the vinegar into her left hand to measure the correct amount (Figure 21.3). She allowed the vinegar to drizzle over the ingredient holding area as well as the rest of the bowl. When it came to adding the egg yolk, Georgia used her left hand, formed as a shallow bowl, as a strainer separating the white from the yolk The egg white was strained into another bowl and discarded. The yolk remaining in her hand was then added to the hole in the center of the bowl of flour.

In this case it is not the environment, but the body which becomes a measuring tool, much more directly than in the metaphoric gauge "three fingers." It is interesting that Georgia's embrace of middle-class, "modern" values (health club, Walmart) does not extend to this embodied aspect of the cooking she had learned from her grandmother. As she puts it when asked about her preference for hand kneading of the dough: "The tools are not good. The traditional way is the right way … before tools." She complains about the limited tools at her son's house. In response to the question "where do you get your tools," she doesn't mention the fancy store-purchased machines, but instead "I got my tools from my mother's home place. In the village where she had a carpenter make for her a rolling pin and table that was low. Mother would sit with her legs under the table and roll Phyllo."

Figure 21.1 Georgia Vourneli.

Figure 21.2 Pouring oil into the flour hole.

Figure 21.3 Measuring the vinegar.

Figure 21.4 Rolling the Phyllo.

Michael: "How do you know when the Phyllo is done?"
Georgia: "When it happens, not worry, I can tell."
Michael: "It is the thinness ..."
Georgia: "not worry, I know. If I had my own roller, the dough would be better."
Michael: "How do you know if the Phyllo is thin enough?"
Georgia: "You can tell. You can feel that it is right."

Georgia complains that she does not have her own rolling pin. And yet the rolling pin she uses is the same "traditional" type as the one she has at home. A conventional, "modern" rolling pin (i.e., the ultra-smooth model with low-friction ball bearings, and a larger, heavier dowel) is eschewed in this case for a smooth stick, which allows one to feel every nuance of the rolling action and its effect on the elasticity of the dough. In contrast the "modern" rolling pin construction disconnects the cook from the dough by being designed to produce uniform strokes. The "traditional" type of rolling pin allows Georgia once again to "feel" when the dough is right (without being able to verbalize the process), since this type of roller is once again a simple extension of the hands, not a tool meant to achieve the rolling process with minimal human effort. At one point she cast her eyes around her son's apartment, and her gaze fell on his wooden-handled broom. Deciding that this was the right width for the task, she asked her son to cut up the broom to create a proper rolling pin. Once again, improvisation, the importance of responding to the problem of the moment rather than executing a preestablished plan, seems to be a thread running through Georgia's cooking practices and her explicit philosophy, where tradition isn't static, but rather constantly adaptable.[9] Clearly Georgia illustrates many aspects of the relationship to tool use described by Ingold, in which tools of production simply extend the body and the senses into the environment. Georgia's case also shows that such practices can exist alongside a self-conscious modernity that characterizes Georgia's relationship to other aspects of her life, such as home decoration and female body-image. In part this may reflect the fact that contemporary Greek discourse on food, reflecting perhaps global trends, places a high value on the "authentic" (see, for example, Gefou-Madianou 1999; Wilk 2006).

Jane Adams also learned to cook from her mother. But, unlike Georgia, who did not encounter any of the modernizing discourses discussed above, Jane also learned to cook in 4-H classes, where they would learn to follow recipes and create menus. Jane notes, "My mother was very modern and I learned from her the use of measurements. She would convert recipes she did by 'feel' into measurements: ¼ tsp. thyme, ½ tsp. oregano, etc. And she was a stickler about using level measurements for cakes and other similar baked goods." Jane also notes that since her mother was working outside of the home, she would often leave written instructions for Jane to follow, giving her early on a textualized mediation of cooking. "I used cookbooks from the time I could read. Mother got me one for children and I made things from it." Jane's mother also taught Jane to can vegetables, "I was a pair of hands," something that Jane continues to this day, producing a hot pepper sauce from ingredients bought at the local farmers' market. Jane defines "authentic" food as having a connection to the ingredients or to the place where the dish came from. But she also believes in eating globally, suggesting that the environmental movement is mistaken to limit their eating to what is available locally, indeed that the availability of foods from around the world is one of the benefits of globalization that we should appreciate. Georgia is, of course, also a global consumer, as reflected in her idolization of Walmart. Her embrace of global commodities, however, does not by and large extend to food items, but rather to those items oriented toward display: thus the global is not "internalized" in the same way for Georgia as it is for Jane.

In one session Jane was preparing several loaves of French bread to accompany a meal of pork loin. She was assisted in cooking by her husband D. Gorton. Jane eschews bread makers, saying that they only used one when they lived far from a grocery store, but otherwise "if you're going to use a bread maker you might as well buy it from the store, the only advantage is that you get to eat it hot." For French bread she used a set of aluminum mold pans, which she had found when she had moved into a house, as well as the recipe that accompanied the pans. She noted that with other breads she experiments but with this one she follows the recipe exactly, measuring out the ingredients using standard cups and spoons, though carelessly measuring the flour, since this, she said, is added till it feels right. As she prepared the dough she reminisced about women in the community who used to make their own yeast out of hops, noting that she always wanted to make a sourdough starter, but felt the climate would not be right for it in Southern Illinois. She kneaded the dough by pulling from the back and folding over in a motion that quickly became automatic. As she kneaded she noted that the recipe calls for using four pans but she only used three because she liked the loaves to be larger. She also noted that the recipe called for letting it rise on a towel and then sliding it into the pans, but she found that too cumbersome and didn't know the reason for it. Her husband interjected that the pans cooled the dough and thus would affect the yeast, but she shrugged and said that she hadn't seen any difference.

David: Can the dough be underkneaded or overkneaded?
Jane: Certainly underkneaded, but overkneaded? I don't think so.
D.:   Overkneaded would get the glutens too worked up, make the bread stringy.

Jane: I don't know. The recipe says to knead for ten minutes, but I just use a trick: you put
         your hand on the dough and count to 10 and if it doesn't stick then the dough is done.
David: Where did you learn that?
Jane: I don't remember. I think in 4-H club.

Jane then prepared a rub for the pork loin, using a number of different spices. The rub was a family recipe that her uncle had taught her mother. First she chopped garlic, then mixed herbs and spices with it in a mortar. While she used measuring spoons to put the spices in the mortar, it was used more as a scoop than a measurer. She measured the herbs by hand, grinding them between her palms. Once ground, she added water and used her finger to mix it and to distribute it on the pork. She chopped the garlic rather than using a press, noting that she could never find a press that gets the garlic the way she wants it, which produces the right flavor. This leads D. to raise the question of why Jane won't use sage in her rub.

Jane: I'm not crazy about the taste of sage. I like growing it.
D.:   To me sage and pork go together. But not to Jane. This is the way she grew up making it.
Jane: This is the way it's supposed to taste. This is the way it should taste. This is the moral
         way (laughing).

In the interview that accompanied the session, Jane and D. spoke of the relationship of food, morality, and politics, which they see as having been basically altered by the 1960s. They identify this period as marking a shift from the Boston Cooking School approach (of which they were knowledgeable) to a valorization of pleasure in cooking and eating as well as in other spheres of life.[10] While Jane clearly valued the sensory and pleasureful aspects of the food she prepared, in an interview session a year later Jane and D. had gone on a no-carb diet, and thus homemade bread was, at least for a time, off the menu.

Figure 21.5 Jane Adams.

Figure 21.6   Applying the rub to the pork loin.

Figure 21.7   Kneading the dough.

Like Georgia, Jane is a hybrid of practices, judgments, and values in relation to cooking. Georgia's hybridity, as noted, seems to lie less in her cooking practices than in her outfitting of the kitchen with the expensive, but unused, marks of distinction. Jane's hybridity lies more in a combination of influences in her learning to cook: her mother, 4-H club, and cookbooks, as well as in the values she sees as expressed in her practice: cosmopolitanism, local history, pleasure, and moderation. Standardized measurements and writing (recipes) play somewhat more of a role in Jane's cooking. Recipes and cookbooks form a backup reference for things that she can't remember (e.g., the correct temperature to cook the pork loin). But at the same time there are also many "rules of thumb" (Ingold 2000: 332) (for judging the bread dough) and sensory memories—the automaticity of kneading as a kind of memory in the hands, the tastes of childhood which form the tastescape of the present, the set of unarticulated taste memories which allow for comparison and judgment, and which can determine the choice of tools (knife vs. garlic press), or of spices. Furthermore, cooking technologies like the bread machine are explicitly rejected.

The connection of all these small gestures to Jane's goals and values is encapsulated in her joking reference to "the moral way of preparing the dish," that is, by duplicating past tastes she is preserving something of her mother's commitment to good food (and social justice: her mother was a leading community social activist, and Jane has been involved in politics her entire adult life).[11] Thus both Georgia and Jane refer back to childhood as a key touchstone for their cooking. But while Georgia frames her cooking in terms of being true to her mother (and to Greece), Jane's explicit discourse speaks of innovation as well, learning new tastes as part of her life course—time spent in Mexico began a long-term passion for Mexican food, for example. In spite of this more "globalized" influence, certain dishes for Jane can be a source of stories about the local past, family and community as well. Both express hybrid desires and feelings, as Georgia's "traditional" cooking sits side by side with her fancy, unused gadgets, and Jane's "moral cooking" has room for a cosmopolitan tasting of what the world has to offer, as well as for dietary fads. Both preserve the gestures and judgments of the past, even if Jane in some cases defers to measuring spoons and recipes (at least as memory jogs), part, perhaps of the legacy of 4-H and other normalizing discourses as described by Shapiro. Much of their similarities, no doubt, can be traced to the fact that both learned the basics of cooking largely in a social context, from their mothers and other relatives. But neither of them has passed on this tradition, Georgia because she had no daughters. Jane has a daughter, who has continued Jane's political activism, but rejected this type of embodied knowledge: "My greatest disappointment was not teaching my daughter how to cook, but she never took an interest and I never made her." Thus the fact that there are fewer milieus for cultural transmission of cooking knowledge through families raises questions which can only be answered by studying the next generation: Jane and Georgia's children.

This short ethnography is meant to be suggestive rather than conclusive. It provides a taste of how we might operationalize the different concepts discussed in this chapter. While it does not resolve the many issues raised, I hope it begins to suggest the fruitfulness of wedding a concern with "taste" to one with "taste." That is, in each case I have tried to suggest that such cooking biographies need to be attentive to both the technical skills and sensory aspects of cooking, and its more explicitly social dimensions.

The latter is reflected in my discussion of Georgia and Jane's individual goals and values, as well as the ways in which these goals and values interact with the larger totalities (culturally inflected notions of authenticity, morality, globality, and locality) in which they are enmeshed. This chapter, then is also meant as a critique of food studies that have focused on symbols rather than on processes ("food as a symbol of identity"), suggesting here that meaning, like cooking, is very much "in the making."[12]

Acknowledgments

Thanks to Georgia and Jane for their delightful and open participation in this research project. I am grateful to Richard Fox and the Wenner-Gren Foundation for hosting the symposium for which the material in this chapter was written, as well as the organizers of the symposium, Elizabeth Edwards, Chris Gosden, and Ruth Phillips, and the other participants, for a most stimulating week. Thanks to Michael Hernandez for his superlative filming and general collaboration on the research for this chapter. Thanks also to a number of people who read and commented on various drafts of this chapter: Janet Dixon Keller, Linda Smith, Constance Sutton, Amy Trubek, Leo Vournelis, and Peter Wogan.

Notes

1. Indeed, Graeber (2011) has recently argued that the terms production and consumption are themselves a false dichotomy set in place by capitalist modernity, and that we need to look into the genealogy of these concepts.
2. See Sutton 2010a, for a review of the anthropological literature on food and the senses.
3. On microwaves, see Ormrod 1994.
4. See Sutton & Hernandez 2007; Sutton 2010b.
5. See Sutton & Vournelis 2009.
6. Indeed, as Shapiro documents, they established Domestic Science as part of many university curricula based on persuading universities that theirs was a theoretical discipline.
7. Middle-class women were generally thought to have a minimal appetite for food, among other things.
8. I have been pursuing this project in conjunction with Michael Hernandez. See Hernandez & Sutton 2003. Thus I use the first person plural to discuss this research in the next section.
9. Note that this trick may be a rediscovery of a common technique used by Greek migrants in the U.S., as described by Papanikolas (1987: 7).
10. See Sutton & Hernandez 2007 for more discussion of D.'s cooking in relation to his historical consciousness.
11. On reading a version of this chapter, Jane commented "I think the link between food and social justice is complicated: My mother was very much into good nutrition, and in that sense (and many others) fully in line with scientific housekeeping, but it was also inflected with an aesthetic sensibility that was more connected to the socialist movement, of arts and crafts (which has now moved to Martha Stewart—the ironies of history!). So menus were in fact 'moral'—a 'balanced diet.' But appropriate herbs hearkened more to a sense of good eating which was probably Jewish—it certainly wasn't local. So there was a degree of snobbery, of 'taste' in Bourdieu's sense in there as well."
12. Quote from Dobres 2001; see also Pfaffenberger 2001; Sutton 2001.

References

Baumann, Zygmunt. 1996. *Life in Fragments: Essays in Postmodern Morality*. Oxford: Blackwell.
Belasco, Warren. 2000. "Future Notes: The Meal-in-a-Pill." *Food and Foodways* 8: 253–71.
Bourdieu, Pierre. 1982. *Distinction: A Social Critique of the Judgement of Taste*. Trans. Richard Nice. Cambridge: Harvard University Press.

Bubant, Nils. 1998. "The Odour of Things: Smell and the Cultural Elaboration of Disgust in Eastern Indonesia." *Ethnos* 63: 48–80.

Carrier, James. 1998. Abstraction in Western Economic Practice. In *Virtualism: A New Political Economy*. J. Carrier & D. Miller (eds.) Oxford: Berg, 25–47.

Classen, Constance, David Howes and Anthony Synnott. 1994. *Aroma: The Cultural History of Smell*. London: Routledge.

Connerton, Paul. 1989. *How Societies Remember*. Cambridge: Cambridge University Press.

Dobres, Marcia-Anne. 2001. Meaning in the Making: Agency and the Social Embodiment of Technology and Art. In *Anthropological Perspectives on Technology*. M. B. Schiffer (ed.) Albuquerque: University of New Mexico Press, 47–76.

Fernandez, James. 1973. "Analysis of Ritual: Metaphoric Correspondences as the Elementary Forms." *Science* 182: 1366–67.

Gefou-Madianou, Dimitra. 1999. "Cultural Polyphony and Identity Formation: Negotiating Tradition in Attica." *American Ethnologist* 26: 412–39.

Giard, Luce. 1998. Part II: Doing-Cooking. In *The Practice of Everyday Life, Volume 2: Living and Cooking*. Luce Giard (ed.) In association with Michel de Certeau and Pierre Mayol. Trans. Timothy J. Tomasik. Minneapolis: University of Minnesota Press, 149–248.

Graeber, David. 2011. "Consumption." *Current Anthropology* 52: 489–511.

Heldke, Lisa. 1992. Foodmaking as Thoughtful Practice. In *Cooking, Eating, Thinking: Transformative Philosophies of Food*. Deane Curtin & Lisa Heldke (eds.) Bloomington, IN: Indiana University Press, 203–29.

Hernandez, Michael and David Sutton. 2003. "Hands that Remember: An Ethnography of Everyday Cooking." *Expedition: Journal of the University of Pennsylvania Museum* 45: 30–7.

Herzfeld, Michael. 1995. It Takes One to Know One: Collective Resentment and Mutual Recognition among Greeks in Local and Global Contexts. In *Counterworks: Managing the Diversity of Knowledge*. Richard Fardon (ed.) London: Routledge, 124–42.

Howes, David. 2003. *Sensual Relations: Engaging the Senses in Culture and Social Theory*. Ann Arbor: University of Michigan Press.

Ingold, Tim. 1993. Tool-Use, Sociality and Intelligence. In *Tools, Language and Cognition in Human Evolution*. K. Gibson & T. Ingold (eds.) Cambridge: Cambridge University Press, 429–45.

Ingold, Tim. 2000. *The Perception of the Environment: Essays in Livelihood, Dwelling and Skill*. London: Routledge.

Ingold, Tim. 2001. From the Transmission of Representations to the Education of Attention. Paper Archive. Mind, Culture and Activity. http://lchc.ucsd.edu/MCA

Ingold, Tim. 2011. *Being Alive: Essays on Movement, Knowledge and Description*. London: Routledge.

Keller, Charles and Janet Dixon-Keller. 1999. "Imagery in Cultural Tradition and Innovation." *Mind, Culture and Activity* 6: 3–32.

Kenna, Margaret. 2005. "Why Does Incense Smell Religious? The Anthropology of Smell Meets Greek Orthodoxy." *Journal of Mediterranean Studies* 15: 51–70.

Lave, Jean. 1988. *Cognition in Practice: Mind, Mathematics and Culture in Everyday Life*. Cambridge: Cambridge University Press.

Leudar, Ivan and Alan Costall. 1996. "Situating Action IV: Planning as Situated Action." *Ecological Psychology* 8: 153–70.

Michael, Mike. 2000. "'These Boots Are Made for Walking …' Mundane Technology, the Body and Human–Environment Relations." *Body and Society* 6: 107–26.

Mintz, Sidney. 1996. *Tasting Food, Tasting Freedom*. Boston: Beacon.

Myers, Fred. 2001. *The Empire of Things: Regimes of Value and Material Culture*. Santa Fe, NM: School of American Research Press.

Ormrod, S. 1994. 'Let's Nuke the Dinner': Discursive Practices of Gender in the Creation of a New Cooking Process. In *Bringing Technology Home: Gender and Technology in a Changing Europe*. C. Cockburn & R. Furst-Dilic (eds.) Buckingham, UK: Open University Press.

Papanikolas, Helen. 1987. *Amilia-Yeiorgos*. Salt Lake City, UT: University of Utah Press.

Pfaffenberger, Bryan. 2001. Symbols Do Not Create Meanings—Activities Do: Or, Why Symbolic Anthropology Needs the Anthropology of Technology. In *Anthropological Perspectives on Technology*. M. B. Schiffer (ed.) Albuquerque, NM: University of New Mexico Press, 77–85.

Rasmussen, Susan. 1999. "Making Better 'Scents' in Anthropology: Aroma in Tuareg Sociocultural Systems and the Shaping of Ethnography." *Anthropological Quarterly* 72: 55–73.

Schlanger, Nathan. 1990. "The Making of a Soufflé: Practical Knowledge and Social Senses." *Techniques et Culture* 15: 29–52.

Shapiro, Laura. 1986. *Perfection Salad: Women and Cooking at the Turn of the Century*. New York: Farrar, Straus & Giroux.

Sperber, Dan. 1996. *Explaining Culture: A Naturalistic Approach*. Oxford: Blackwell.

Steinberg, Stephen. 1998. "Bubbie's Challah." In *Eating Culture*. R. Scapp & B. Seitz (ed.) Albany, NY: SUNY Press.

Stone, Tom. 2003. *The Summer of My Greek Taverna: A Memoir*. New York: Simon & Schuster.

——, David. 2001. *Remembrance of Repasts: An Anthropology of Food and Memory.* Oxford: Berg.

——, David. 2010a ."Food and the Senses." *Annual Review of Anthropology* 39: 209–23.

——, David. 2010b. "The Mindful Kitchen, The Embodied Cook: Tools, Technology and Knowledge Transmission on a Greek Island." *Canadian Material Culture Review* 70: 63–8.

Sutton, David. 2011. "Memory as a Sense: A Gustemological Approach." *Food, Culture and Society* 14: 468–75.

Sutton, David and Michael Hernandez. 2007. "Voices in the Kitchen: Cooking Tools as Inalienable Possessions." *Oral History* 35: 67–76.

Sutton, David and Leonidas Vournelis. 2009. "Vefa or Mamalakis: Cooking up Nostalgia in Contemporary Greece." *South European Society & Politics* 14(2): 147–66.

Tilley, Christopher. 1999. *Metaphor and Material Culture.* Oxford: Basil Blackwell.

Wilk, Richard. 2006. *Home Cooking in the Global Village: From Buccaneers to Ecotourists.* Oxford: Berg.

22

Not "From Scratch": Thai Food Systems and "Public Eating"*

Gisèle Yasmeen

The goal of this paper is to explain Thai patterns of 'public eating'—or the purchasing and consumption of prepared food in public places, namely: sidewalks, lanes and the growing number of indoor spaces such as educational institutions and office/shopping complexes. This is done through a historically contextualised gender analysis. Remarkably few Thai urbanites cook meals at home regularly, especially 'from scratch'. It is not absolutely necessary to prepare meals given the ubiquitous presence of inexpensive cooked food around the clock as well as semi-prepared food now available (Napat and Szanton, 1986; Tinker, 1987, 1997).

The significance in this paper lies in its focus on the interrelationship between gender and foodways—a topic that is often ignored or taken for granted in mainstream scholarship. Fortunately, recent research attests to the growing interest in the study of food in general and its link with gender (Van Esterik, 1992). The Thai case in particular highlights the unusual dominance of women in a commercial aspect of the food system, namely small-scale food-retailing, which is highly related to the fact that Thai and Southeast Asian women are overwhelmingly involved in the paid labour force compared to other regions of the world. The specific contribution of this paper is the attention paid to the spatially gendered dimension of foodways in the case of Thailand.[1] This analytical framework serves to open up the discussion on the spatial gendering of foodways cross-culturally (Breckenridge, 1995; Conlon, 1995).

To begin, I explore the Thai diet and eating habits to provide a broader context for the later examination of public eating. I then outline how the food system has been modified subsequent to the penetration of capital into agricultural production and food processing. Attention is paid to patterns of food retailing in Bangkok—including the system of public markets—and the changes which have taken place in distribution over the past 20 years.

Finally, I explore in some detail the role of the household and gender in public eating as a complement to what I have done elsewhere (Yasmeen, 1996b). I then provide explanations for the purchasing of cooked food and will outline diverse strategies for obtaining prepared food on a daily basis. The paper concludes by forecasting the future of public eating in urban Thailand given the current food marketing trends

*Originally published 2000

and a general commentary on the impact of the recent economic crisis which is dealt with substantially in a recent paper (Yasmeen, 1999).[2]

Rice, Fish and Foundations of Southeast Asian Eating

> Villagers in Thailand, as well as parts of Burma, Malaysia, Bali, and Vietnam, see themselves as physically and psychically made up of rice. The Christian God made man and woman in His own image; Southeast Asians think in the same general way, but their self-image is one of rice. For them, rice is literally 'the bones of the people'. (MacClancy, 1992, p. 24)

One of the defining characteristics of Southeast Asia as a region is that its diverse societies share basic characteristics related to diet. Rice is a primary staple. Most Southeast Asian languages equate the word for rice with food and/or eating.[3] Indeed, the region is considered home to the domestication of rice, and its wet-rice agricultural system has been regarded with fascination because of its efficiency (Bray, 1986) complex irrigation schemes (Lansing, 1991) and the ability of the system to support high population densities (Geertz, 1963). Historically, there were hundreds of varieties of rice in Southeast Asia, but much of the diversity has been lost in the past hundred years due to 'modernisation' and the standardisation of production (McGee, 1992).[4]

The Thai Diet

Rice is so important to Southeast Asians that it is an almost sacred substance associated with life essence (Thai = *khwan*). As explained by Jane Hanks, femininity—specifically women's bodies—is associated with rice and with this essence (Hanks, 1960).

> Thus the *khwan* is sustained by, and its incarnation grows from, the physical nourishment of a woman's body. What is to sustain it after a woman's milk gives out? Rice, because rice, too, is nourishment from a maternal figure. 'Every grain is part of the body of Mother Rice (*Mae Posop*) and contains a bit of her *khwan*.' When weaning is to rice, there is no break in female nurture for body and *khwan*. (Hanks, 1960, p. 299)

Indeed, pre-Buddhist fertility rituals persist in the Thai countryside and principally involve women during rice planting (Sharp and Hanks, 1978). Keyes has characterised the Southeast Asian region as subscribing to the cult of 'women, earth and rice' (Keyes, 1977, p. 132).

Fish is also a substantial element in the Southeast Asian diet, and a distinguishing characteristic of the region is the preparation of spicy fermented fish paste which is served as a condiment (Thai = *namprik*).[5] Thai cuisine also includes a great variety of vegetables—some introduced by the Chinese—as well as indigenous varieties of yams, eggplants and the characteristic fragrant herbs and pungent spices. The familiar combination of fish sauce (a Chinese invention), garlic, lime juice and chillies (introduced by the Portuguese in the 16th century) is considered the essence of Thai flavour although tamarind (sweet and sour varieties), palm sugar, lemon grass and galangal also play a crucial role.

Traditional Retailing

Prior to the introduction of the automobile and other forms of land-based transport in central Thailand, food retailing most often took place on canals (Chira *et al.*, 1986, p. 9). Floating markets (*talad nam*) were the dominant type of food market and persist today in parts of central Thailand and often cater to tourists. Women dominate these traditional markets of central Thailand as vendors. Land-based markets (*talad din*) selling fresh produce, meat and fish have replaced the quintessential central Thai form of retailing (Chira *et al.*, 1986, p. 9), Land-based markets are considered by many to be originally a Chinese commercial form and, thus, are traditionally male controlled; '… in those days the Chinese were the pioneers of street-living hence the *talad* or food markets usually resembled the fresh food market pattern in China' (Chira *et al.*, 1986, p. 9). Today, Thai and Sino-Thai women are widely represented as vendors in land markets.

Today, Bangkok continues to have the same basic system of public markets but—as the next section demonstrates—élite shopping practices now include regular trips to North American style supermarkets. The city has one large wholesale market (*pakklong talad*) which supplies many of the smaller neighbourhood *talad* with fresh fruit, vegetables and flowers (Warren and Lloyd, 1989, pp. 48–49).

Neighbourhood markets involve both male and female entrepreneurs who work in the middle of the night to get the food ready for dawn. The markets sell semi-prepared items such as curry pastes and coconut milk—labour saving devices for both house-wives and employed women. Owners of foodshops (Thai = *raan ahaan*) or small restaurants and stalls also sometimes make use of these shortcuts.[6]

The (Post)Industrial Palate?

Now that traditional retailing systems have been introduced, I shall try to summarise the impact of urbanisation and modernisation on the food system. Following Goody (1982), it is clear that, as a society industrialises and urbanises, it becomes uprooted from its agricultural way of life, and food becomes a commodity purchased from the market. With the involvement of both women and men in the paid labour force, an opportunity for the sale of value-added food arises (Goodman and Redclift, 1991). This demand can be fulfilled in several ways: through neighbourhood catering networks or the hiring of a cook; however, it is in the interests of large-scale business to direct the consumer's spending to a standardised range of value-added goods. The classic theatre for the sale of these goods is the supermarket where highly processed foods are the most vigorously promoted due to their commercial profitability.

The term 'industrial palate' refers to the growing share of value-added, often mass-produced, processed food products in the diet of the average consumer (Salih *et al.*, 1988, p. 4). Urbanites figure prominently in this shift from family-based food production to the commodization of 'people's most basic requirement—food—from a part of their place to a placeless industrial commodity' (MacLeod, 1989, p. 4), The social and environmental implications of these changes are alarming as documented elsewhere (Sanitsuda, 1993; Sinith, 1998).

Profitable Palates: New Food Retailing

In the, 1980s and early 1990s, Thailand experienced spectacular levels of economic growth, 'The Asian food market could be worth over $450 billion a year by the end of the century' wrote *The Economist* (1993, p. 15). Asians were and sometimes still are seen as a profitable target population by large food multi-nationals because of their supposed brand consciousness, 'At the luxury end of the market, especially, Asian consumers seem to be more conscious of the snob value of brands than their western counterparts' *(The Economist,* 1993, p 16), The appearance and diffusion of supermarkets, related retail outlets such as convenience stores, Western-style fast food chains and the newest addition, the mega-wholesale outlet (Costco, Makro and/or Wal-Mart) is a burgeoning feature of the Asian urban landscape (Robison and Goodman, 1996).

In Thailand convenience stores such as 7–11 have made impressive inroads. These are new institutions that have multiplied rapidly in the last ten years. They are generally open 24 hours and sell household products, Western and Thai fast food and fountain drinks. Customers include schoolchildren, the increasing number of people working late and commuters *(The Nation,* 1992, pp. B1–B3).[7] Managers of some of these stores (such as 7–11 and Central mini-mart) claim that their clientèle includes lower income groups as well as the wealthier urbanites.

It would be spurious to attribute these changes simply to the infiltration of 'Third World' economies by Western and Japanese capital. More precisely in the case of Thailand, locally owned conglomerates control the largest share of the domestic industrial palate and have expanded their operations to China and other parts of Southeast Asia. This is typical of the region's food distribution system.

> Take Thailand's Charoen Pokphand, Asia's biggest animal-feed supplier and the country's largest conglomerate, with sales of about $5 billion. Boasting that 'from the farmyard to the dinner table it's Charoen Pokphand all the way', the company, which was set up by Chinese emigrants, produces feed for and then raises and processes broiler chickens. It also handles prawns and pigs. One of its greatest assets is a network of feedmills and poultry-processing plants sprinkled across China. These and Charoen Pokphand's fast-food joint ventures with America's Kentucky Fried Chicken should allow it to cash in on the country's culinary revolution. (*The Economist,* 1993, p. 17)

Charoen Pokphand (CP) also controls the nation's 7–11s, numerous motorcycle and automobile manufacturing operations, and is the major shareholder of Telecom Asia. CP, being essentially a Sino-Thai conglomerate, is also one of the biggest foreign investors in China.

The expansion of the well-heeled classes and accompanying automobile culture has resulted in the proliferation of scores of large shopping centres throughout the Bangkok Metropolitan Region. These new cathedrals of commerce are expected to erode traditional retailing business and ultimately carve out 50% of market share according to a Siam Retail Development executive quoted in the above article. Since the 1980s, many mega-malls have appeared—especially on the urban periphery (*Asia Magazine,* 1992).

Some of these mega-malls resemble the 'West Edmonton Mall' phenomenon with a focus on leisure activities (Hopkins, 1991). Most have extensive and elaborate food-centres and food floors. Much of Bangkok's retailing activity in the food-sector is clearly expanding from public places (streets and lanes) to privately owned and controlled indoor places (shopping centres and new air-conditioned restaurants) in food centres and on 'food floors' where 'street food'—as well as semi-prepared food— is available for take-home consumption.

The divisions appearing within Thai society as a whole mirror the shift from public eating from truly public places to privately owned spaces. As the gap continually widens between the rich and the poor in Bangkok, we are witnessing the emergence of a dual food system resembling trends identified in neighbouring Malaysia (Salih *et al.*, 1988). One, for the wealthy, consists of eating at home in comfortable surroundings (with food prepared by servants, catering networks, neighbourhood food shops and increasingly food centres in shopping plazas) and eating out in 'food courts', subur-ban 'food gardens' (large restaurants with a monolithic *sala thai*[8] design) and upscale restaurants. The working poor staff the second system, which includes those who actually transport, sell and prepare the food. Their eating places include their humble living quarters and shops and, in some cases, cafeterias provided by their employers. Though there are layers of differentiation which cannot be enumerated here, gener-ally speaking, the inhabitants of these two separate worlds need only come together for the purpose of a transaction between vendor and customer, maid and employer. As summarised by Askew and Paritta (1992):

> The shopping centres of the outer areas symbolise the development of a newer culture based on modern convenience, shopping and transportation by private motor vehicle. At the same time, the neighbourhood markets and the cheap street-side restaurants in the *soi* [lanes] and more congested neighbourhoods point to the persistence of a less modernised life-style reflect-ing the continuing significance of public life in less formally regulated public spaces, especially for the urban poor (p. 164)

The shift in retailing structure toward the growing availability of convenience and ready-to-eat foods, as the next section will explain, has been associated with the high number of women in the workforce (*Bangkok Post*, 1992, p. 20).

Why Eat Out?

The major contemporary impetus for buying prepared food in Thailand and Southeast Asia comes from rapid urbanisation, industrialisation and concomitant changes in family structure, affecting, in turn, the roles played by women (cf. Horton, 1995). Thailand has experienced a rise in the nuclear family—displacing extended kinship relations—and has also seen a rise in the number of single people, particularly in the cities. Changes in women's roles are related to these demographic trends. As Suntaree Komin explains, socio-economic change has completely altered the food system:

> The decline of family functions is clearly visible in Bangkok. As there is an increase of women working outside households, this trend is almost inevitable. Family functions have been taken over by various specialised organisations. For example, working mothers leave their household chores to the servants. Meals preparation [*sic*] are taken care of either by servants, or by sub-scription to the meal-catering services (*Ipintol*),[9] or by buying those ready-made foods each day on the way home. (Suntaree, 1989, p. 86)

Suntaree is primarily describing middle-class food habits. Few people in Bangkok can afford to hire servants. The general explanation for the growth of public eating, nevertheless, is the changing roles and occupations of women.

Thailand boasts the highest female labour force participation rates (FLFPR) in Southeast Asia—a region already known for the high economic activity levels of women. Compared with other Southeast Asian countries, Thai FLFPR is consistently the highest and peaks at 87% (International Labour Organization, 1999). The Thai pattern demonstrates that women do not withdraw from the labour force during their child-bearing/rearing years (Jones, 1984, p. 28), This is characteristic of the Malay and Tai[10] cultural realms where women play an important role in local commerce, as office workers and in many other professions.

There are several other interrelated explanations for the general emergence of public eating in Bangkok. These include: the labour- and skill-intensivity of Thai cuisine; demographic change—specifically migration to the cities of large numbers of single and young people; kitchenless housing (20% of Bangkok's housing is kitchenless); and general 'cultural' preferences for eating out and entertaining outside the home. According to Walker's *Food Consumption Survey*, 11% of Bangkokians *never* cook at all. NSO figures are given higher at 27% (National Statistical Office, 1994).

Public Eating

As already established, high male and female labour force participation rates in Thailand mean that neither women nor men have time to cook. The statistical profile of public eating in Bangkok has been demonstrated elsewhere (Yasmeen, 1996a, b). This section therefore simply provides an overview of the phenomenon.

Studies have shown that expenditures on prepared food consumed *outside the home* are mainly for lunch, with breakfast coming in second place at (Walker, 1990, 1991). Concerns about the impact of eating away from home on family life need not be exaggerated, because evenings are still reserved for eating at home with the family.

Prepared food is therefore a frequent substitute for home-cooked meals, whether or not the food is actually eaten at *home* or *elsewhere*. The following section will define and describe the various food strategies employed by Bangkokians to obtain cooked food outside the home.

Everyday Food Strategies

A traditional strategy common throughout Southeast Asia is the subscription to neighbourhood catering networks, in which food—normally one soup, one vegetable and one dish (often a curry)—is delivered at a regular time every day in a tiffin *(pinto)*. The tiffin-network strategy is seemingly being eclipsed by the small foodshop sector where food is available anywhere, anytime—an important attribute in a city where traffic is gridlocked during rush hours. Women can be seen stopping at a food shop in the evenings on their way home from work to pick up dinner for the family, main courses are placed in small plastic bags with rice being prepared easily at home in a rice cooker. Bangkok residents hence refer to *mae baan tung plastic* or 'plastic bag housewives' (Van Esterik, 1992; Yasmeen, 1996a).

For typically middle-class Bangkokians—particularly women who tend to be impeccably dressed—frequenting cool, comfortable establishments is the most desirable option. Their male cohorts—stereotypically government officials on Friday evenings—enjoy 'slumming' in stalls and outdoor restaurants where they can sit at long tables, eat spicy meat dishes and drink vast quantities of whiskey. Working-class men, such as tuk-tuk drivers, do the same but are limited to less expensive venues. Since 'proper' Thai women do not drink alcohol in public, they engage in a slightly different pattern. Their habit is to go out with a group of friends, women or mixed-company, to a *suan ahaan* or a restaurant in a shopping centre. The urban masses are, for the most part, of humble economic means and purchase food on the streets and *soi* from vendors both mobile and stationary, and small food-shops specialising in noodles, curried dishes or other fare (cf. Yasmeen, 1992).[11]

Bangkok is therefore one of the homes of small ubiquitous food-shops which act as a life-support system for many urbanites. Small restaurants serve a number of latent social functions in addition to providing meals. For example, children are often cared for in these environments, young people spend time and 'help' thereby learning skills and meeting others. Foodshops are meeting places where information can be gleaned on local affairs such as jobs.

The Future of Streetfoods and Public Eating

> The worst thing that could happen in the future, in my opinion, would be the disappearance of working-class street food. The street stalls and tiny hole-in-the-wall restaurants that used to make noodles, won ton, pao, congee, stuffed dumplings, steamed meatballs, fried pastries, and thousands of other snack items could be at risk in the new, affluent world of the future. (Andersen, 1988, p. 300)

Anderson wrote this critique of the emerging industrial palate in 1980s Hong Kong, Bangkok's foodscape is, to a certain extent, being threatened in similar ways due to the emerging middle-class and its tastes. To aggravate the situation, quite often, the food served in more expensive Thai restaurants and the growing number of food-centres is of much poorer quality than the comestibles in the humblest foodshop. Nevertheless, I do not believe that the types of food sold on the streets and lanes of the city are under threat *per se*. Rather the *informal context* in which the food is usually sold is apparently being eclipsed by indoor food-centres and highly commercialised restaurants. However, recent work on the impact of the economic crisis gives one hope for the survival of 'small cats' in Southeast Asia (Yasmeen, 1999).

What is equally alarming with respect to the 'privatisation' of public caring-places is the potential effects on civil society and urban culture. Bangkok's small foodshops are instrumental in establishing contemporary Thai public life similar to the roles played by pubs and coffeehouses in industrialising Europe.

> Habermas argues that … it was the growth of an urban culture—of meeting houses, concert halls, opera houses, press and publishing ventures, coffee houses, taverns and clubs, and the like—… which represents the expansion of the public sphere. (Howell, 1993, p. 310)

Small foodshops are products of urbanisation and industrialisation and concomitant social change but, at the same time, reproduce traditional social relations. As such, they represent the simultaneous modernisation and postmodernisation of Thai urban society. Foodshops and streetfoods play a crucial social and cultural function in Thai society and all efforts must be made to preserve them.

The risk associated with trying to preserve streetfoods is their potential 'museumification'. Even prior to the economic crisis, residents of Bangkok and visitors to the city began to take an interest in 'discovering' streetfoods in up-scale hotels and plazas rather than on the street, where they fear the possibility of food poisoning and general discomfort. 'Streetfood festivals' are therefore held in what appear to be controlled situations. For example, the Stable Lodge Hotel on Sukhumvit Soi 8 used to hold a 'traditional' Thai streetfood buffet every Saturday evening, 'but with the Stable's special flair' (*Bangkok Post*, n.d.). The Martino Coffee Lounge, located in The Mandarin Hotel, advertised its addition of 'Authentic Thai coffee prepared from our coffee cart as you watch' (*Bangkok Post*, 1992). Like the postmodern *Sala Thai* (traditional pavillion) style 'food gardens'—or open air restaurants—the nostalgia of the Martino Coffee lounge is a simulacrum of a place that never really existed (Baudrillard, 1981). Meanwhile, few 'traditional' coffee carts are found on the streets of Bangkok. I recall all of one or two from years of fieldwork in the city. Ironically, as in other parts of Asia, Thai working and middle-classes increasingly consume Nescafé as a status symbol, following years of vigorous advertising. In the past five years, Starbucks has made inroads into the region, which is stimulating demand for gourmet and speciality coffees.

The interest in streetfoods is also borne out by the publication of handbooks for foreigners such as *Thai Hawker Food* where 'authentic' streetfood is the object of interest (Pranom, 1993). The guidebook contains colourful drawings of the different types of street vendors and their goods as well as Thai phrases designed to help negotiate the foreigner through Bangkok's foodscape. This paper is yet another attempt to negotiate through the complex maze of Thai foodways in transition.

Acknowledgements

I am grateful to the Social Sciences and Humanities Research Council, the International Development Research Centre, the Canada-Asean Centre, the CUC-AFT partnership project and the Northwest Consortium for Southeast Asian Studies for providing funding. I would like to thank Marilyn Walker and Terry McGee for useful comments. Thanks also to the Chulalongkom University Social Research Institute, and the Asian Institute of Technology, which hosted my field research in Thailand. Most of all, my gratitude extends to the many informants who gave me their time and shared their life experience.

Notes

1. See Simoons (1994) and Bell and Valentine (1997) for a baseline work on the geography of food.
2. Data for this paper are based primarily on fieldwork for my Ph.D. dissertation, which took place from 1992 to 1994a, supplemented by recent fieldwork pertaining to the economic crisis which tool place from 1997 to 1999.

A variety of data-gathering techniques were used, including participant observation, interviews (both structured and semi-structured), questionnaires, mapping and reference to numerous secondary sources. An earlier version of this paper was published as a working paper of the Centre for Southeast Asia Research, Institute of Asian Research, University of British Columbia.

3. In Thai, *khaaw* means rice but also means to eat (*kin khaaw*, literally 'eat rice').

4. Recently, however, Southeast Asians and others have rediscovered 'lost' grains and re-incorporated them into their diets. An example is red rice. Several varieties of glutinous rice (white, red and black) are still cultivated, however, and used extensively in Northeastern food and in sweets.

5. In Malay and Bahasa Indonesia, this pounded mixture is known as *sambal*. Fermented fish paste has a few basic ingredients but is prepared differently by every cook.

6. I will use the term 'food shop' synonymously with restaurant throughout this paper Here, I am referring to establishments with a stationary location where food can be consumed on the premises.

7. The near grid-lock traffic situation in Bangkok has been identified as contributing to the success of convenience stores which are located on major routes.

8   A *sala thai* is a traditional pavilion in which community activities customarily take place. Roofs are sloped in the manner of Thai architecture and the entire structure is usually made of wood.

9. *Pinto* is the Thai expression for a 'tiffin', or tiered lunch kit, which is commonly used throughout Asia. It has an agricultural origin and is referred to by Hauck *et al.* (1958). They describe how lunch was often transported to the fields in this three- or four-tiered metal container.

10. By Tai, I am referring to the societies which share a common linguistic heritage in the Tai language family, notably Thailand, Laos, Burma and Cambodia,

11. It is difficult to ascertain how economically viable this system of 'contracting out' is at the household budget level. Certainly, it is clear that individuals are trading potential monetary savings for convenience and time, which can be used to earn extra income.

References

Anderson, E.N. (1988) *The Food of China* (New Haven and London, Yale University Press).

Askew, M. and Ko-Anantakul Paritta (1992). "Bangkok: The Evolving Urban Landscape". In A Pongsapich, M. Howard and J AmyotRegional (eds), *Development and Change in Southeast Asia in the 1990*s. Bangkok: Chulalongkorn University Social Research Institute, Bangkok, Thailand.

Bangkok Post (1992) Authentic Thai Coffee at the Martino coffee lounge (Advertisement), 11 November, p. 1.

Bangkok Post (n.d.) Scandinavian food at the Stable: Bangkok's new dining option.

Baudrillard, J. (1981) *Simulacres et Simulation* (Paris, Editions Galilée).

Bell, D. & Valentine, G. (1997) *Consuming Geographies: we are where we eat* (London and New York, Routledge).

Bray, F. (1986) *The Rice Economies: technology and development in Asian societies* (Oxford and New York, Blackwell).

Breckenridge, C. (Ed.) (1995). *Consuming Modernity: public culture in a South Asian world* (Minneapolis, University of Minnesota).

Chira H. *et al.* (1986) *Urban Food Market in Bangkok* (Ottawa, International Development Research Centre).

Conlon, F. (1995) Dining out in Bombay, in: C. Breckenridge (Ed.) *Consuming Modernity: public culture in a South Asian World*, pp. 90–127 (Minneapolis, University of Minnesota).

Geerktz, C. (1963) *Agricultural Involution; The process of ecological change in Indonesia* (Berkeley, Published for the Association of Asian Studies by University of California Press).

Goodman, D. & Redclift, M. (1991) *Refashioning Nature: food, ecology and culture* (London and New York, Routledge).

Goody, J. (1982) *Cooking, cuisine, and class: a study in comparative sociology cambridge* (New York: Cambridge University Press).

Hanks, J.R. (1960) Reflections on the ontology of rice, in: S. Diamond (Ed.,) *Culture in History: essays in Honor of Paul Radin*, pp. 298–301 (New York and London, Columbia University Press).

Hauck, H.M, Saovanee, S. & Hanks, J.R. (1958) *Food Habits and Nutrient Intakes in a Siamese Rice Village: studies in Bang Chan*, 1952–54, Data Paper No. 29 (Ithaca, Cornell University Southeast Asia Program).

Hopkins, J.S.P. (1991) West Edmonton Mall as a centre for social interaction, *Canadian Geographer*, 35(3), pp. 268–279.

Horton, S. (Ed), (1995) *Women and Industrialization in Asia* (London, Routledge).

Howell, P. (1993) Public space and the public sphere: political theory and the historical geography of modernity. *Environment and Planning D: Society and Spaces*, 11, pp. 303–322.

International Labour organization (1999) *Labour Force Statistics, 1998* (Geneva, ILO).

Jones, G.W. (Ed.) (1984) *Women in the Urban and Industrial Workforce: Southeast and East Asia* (Honolulu, University of Hawai'i Press).

Keyes, C.F. (1977) *The Golden Peninsula: culture and adaptation in mainland Southeast Asia* (New York and London, Macmillan-Collier).

Lansing, J.S. (1991) *Priests and Programmers: technologies of power in the engineered landscapes of Bali* (Princeton, Princeton University Press).

Macclancy, J. (1992) *Consuming Culture* (London, Chapmans).

MacLeod, S. (1989) *A Fortune in Cookies? Changing contexts of consumption and the emergence of the industrial palate in Hong Kong.* Working paper No. 3 (Vancouver: Institute of Asian Research).

McGee, T.G. (1992) *The Geography of Southeast Asia.* Course notes (Vancouver, University of British Columbia).

Napat, S. & Szanton, C. (1986) *Thailand's Street Food Vending: the sellers and consumers of 'traditional fast* foods'. Publication No. 5/1990 (Bangkok, Chulalongkorn University Social Research Institute).

National Statistical Office (1992) *Preliminary Report of the 1990 Household Socio-Economic Survey, Whole Kingdom* (Office of the Prime Minister), Bangkok, Thailand.

National Statistical Office (1994) *Report of the 1990 Household Socio-Economic Survey: Greater Bangkok, Samut Prakarn and Nonthaburi* (Office of the Prime Minister).

Pranom, S. (1993) *Thai Hawker Food* (Bangkok, Book Promotion and Service).

Robison, R. & Goodman, D.S.G. (Eds) (1996) *The New Rich in Asia: mobile phones, McDonalds and middle-class revolution* (London and New York: Routledge).

Salih, K. *et al.* (1988) *A Preliminary Review of Changes in the Malaysian Food System.* Occasional Paper No. 6. (Vancouver, Institute of Asian Research, University of British Columbia).

Sanitsuda, E. (1993) A poisonous problem. *Bangkok Post*, 6 February, Section Three, p. 1.

Sharp, L. & Hanks, L. (1978) *Bang Chan: serial history of a rural community in Thailand.* (Ithaca and London, Cornell University Press).

Simoons, F. (1994) *Eat Not This Flesh: food avoidances from prehistory to the present* (2nd ed, revised and enlarged) (Madison, University of Wisconsin Press).

Sinith, S. (1998) *The Daughters of Development: women and the changing environment* (London, Zed Books).

Suntaree, K. (1989) *Social Dimensions of Industrialization in Thailand* (Bangkok, National Institute of Development Administration).

The Economist (1993) A survey of the food industry ... indigestion, 4 December, special section.

The Nation (1992) A marriage of convenience, 18 October, pp. B1–B3.

Tinker, I. (1987) Street foods: testing assumptions about informal sector activity by women and men. *Current Sociology*, 35, entire issue.

Tinker, I. (1997) Street foods: urban food and employment in developing countries (New York and Oxford, Oxford University Press).

Van Esterik, P. (1992) From Marco Polo to McDonald's: Thai cuisine in transition. *Food and Foodways*, 5, pp. 177–193.

Walker, M. (1990) Food Consumption Survey. Unpublished survey of food habits in Thailand, undertaken in conjunction with Peter Snell of Frank Small and Associates Marketing and Research Consultants, (Bangkok, Thailand).

Walker, M. (1991) *Thai Elites and the Construction of Socio-Cultural Identity.* Unpublished Ph.D. Dissertation (North York, York University, Social Anthropology).

Warren W. & Lloyd, R. I. (1989) *Bangkok's Waterways: an explorer's handbook* (Bangkok, Asia Books).

Yasmeen, G. (1992) Bangkok's restaurant sector: gender, employment and consumption. *Journal of Social Research*, 15, pp. 69–81.

Yasmeen, G. (1996a) Plastic bag housewives and postmodern restaurants: public and private in Bangkok's foodscape. *Urban Geography* (Special issue on 'The City and the New Cultural Geography' edited by David Ley), 17(6), pp. 526–544.

Yasmeen, G. (1996b) Bangkok's foodscape: public eating, gender relations and urban change, unpublished Ph.D. Dissertation (Vancouver, Department of Geography, University of British Columbia).

Yasmeen, G. (1999) Stockbrokers turned sandwich vendors: the economic crisis and food-retailing in the Philippines and Thailand. Final Report submitted to Dr David DeWitt, Project Director—Development and Security in Southeast Asia (York University). Truncated version forthcoming in a special issue of *Geoforum*.

23

Rooting Out the Causes of Disease: Why Diabetes is So Common Among Desert Dwellers*

Gary Paul Nabhan

From the land of the Navajo, let us go southward into Mexico once again, to a coastal community of another indigenous people. Although genetically unrelated, the Navajo of the United States and the Seri of Mexico share a problem that has both a genetic and a nutritional component: adult-onset diabetes. This nutrition-related disease is one of the three top causes of death among these two Native American groups and among many other indigenous communities as well. Ironically, a half century ago, its presence as a health risk was so minor in these communities that more Indians were dying each year of accidental snake bite than of diabetes. To understand why that change occurred, and what it means for all of us, we must listen not just to epidemiologists, but to the native peoples themselves.

It was in a small, run-down health clinic on a beach of Mexico's Sea of Cortés that an Indian elder gave me a memorable lesson about gene-food interactions. It was a lesson nested in place—the hot desert coastline studded with giant cactus; that particular Indian village, where people cooked most of their food on small campfires in the sandy spaces between shabby government-built houses; and in that clinic, with no windows and no equipment, so rarely frequented by a doctor that we had planted a garden of healing herbs around it in case there was ever a medical emergency. It was in this place that Seri Indian Alfredo López Blanco challenged me—and Western-trained scientists in general—to pay protracted attention to diet change and its role in disease.

I had accompanied my wife Laurie Monti, nurse-practitioner turned medical anthropologist, who was screening Seri families for adult-onset diabetes. The disease was already running rampant through neighboring tribes, but because the Seri are the last culture in Mexico to have retained hunting, fishing, and foraging traditions instead of adopting agriculture, there was some hope that they could stave it off. Only a few of the some 650 tribal members had ever been screened for the non-insulin-dependent form of diabetes, and that smaller, earlier sample had suggested that only 8 percent of the tribe suffered from chronically high blood-sugar levels and low insulin sensitivity.

While Laurie was screening Seri families in the sole office that contained any semblance of sanitary surfaces, I was in the "waiting room"—a sort of stripped-down

* Originally published 2004

echo chamber full of barking dogs and crying babies—trying to interview the elders of each family about their genealogical histories. I was attempting to ascertain whether the genetic susceptibility to diabetes of individuals with 100 percent Seri ancestry might be different from those who claimed that some of their ancestors came from among the neighboring Pima and Papago (O'odham) tribes in Arizona, the ethnic populations reputed to have the highest incidence of diabetes in the world.

Alfredo López Blanco returned to the waiting room after Laurie confirmed that his blood-sugar levels were unusually high. Alfredo, who had worked as a fisherman since he was a boy, had late in life become boatman and guide for marine and island biologists. In his late sixties, Alfredo often taught younger Seri about the days when their people had subsisted on seafood, wild game, and desert plants like cactus fruit and mesquite pods. He was keenly aware of the traditional diet of his own people, and of his neighbors as well. When he sat down with me, I asked him if any of his forefathers happened to be from other tribes. He answered that one of his great grandmothers was from a Papago-Pima community.

"But *Hant Coáaxoj*," he called me by my Seri nickname, Horned Lizard, "I have a question for you. What does that have to do to my diabetes?"

"Well, I'm not yet sure that it does. But here's why I'm asking. The Pima and Papago suffer from diabetes more than any other tribes. It might be in their blood," I conjectured, groping for a way to explain the concept of *genetic predisposition* to a person whose native language does not contain the exact concept of "genes." "If people have Pima blood in them, maybe they are more prone to diabetes."

"*Hant Coáaxoj*," he said dryly, "sometimes you scientists don't know much history. If diabetes is in their blood—or for that matter, in our blood—why did their grandparents not have it? Why were the old-time Pima and Papago who I knew skinny and healthy? It is a change in the diet, not their blood. They are no longer eating the bighorn sheep, mule deer, desert tortoise, cactus fruit, and mesquite pods. *Pan Bimbo* bread, Coke, sandwiches, and *chicharrones* are the problem!"

The old man—whose sister died within a year of that conversation due to circulatory complications from her own diabetes—was pretty much right on the mark. Or at least that is what Laurie's interpretation of her screening and my genealogical interviews later showed. Diabetes, aggravated by diet change, was clearly on the rise among the Seri, with more than 27 percent of the adults screened by Laurie showing impaired glucose tolerance. But there were also interesting differences between the village where Alfredo lived, Punta Chueca, and the more remote Seri village to the north, Desemboque, where Western foods and other signs of acculturation were much less prominent. While diabetes prevalence in Desemboque had only recently reached 20 percent of the adults in Laurie's sample, it exceeded 40 percent in Punta Chueca.

Other public-health surveys of the Seri suggested why this might be the case. Punta Chueca's residents had easier access to fast-food restaurants and minimarts than did Desemboque dwellers. Roughly 15 percent more of Punta Chueca's residents consumed groceries purchased in nearby Mexican towns on a daily basis, rather than relying more heavily on native foods from the desert and sea. The people of Punta Chueca consumed significantly more store-bought fats (such as lard), alcohol, and cigarettes.

When data from both villages were pooled, Seri individuals with some Papago-Pima ancestry did not show up as suffering from diabetes any more than those with 100 percent Seri ancestry. And yet, comparing the villages, there was one telling difference: those with Papago-Pima ancestry who ate more acculturated, modernized diets in Punta Chueca had the highest probability of the disease. As long as the Desemboque dwellers with Papago-Pima blood remained close to their traditional diet, diabetes among them was held more in check.

This trend held even though traditional Seri individuals in Desemboque appeared to weigh somewhat more than their counterparts in Punta Chueca. This suggests that it may not be the sheer quantity of food metabolized that triggers diabetes as much as the qualities of the foods the Seri now eat—especially the kinds of fats and carbohydrates regularly consumed.

This key distinction has slipped past the U.S. National Institutes of Health Indian Diabetes Project in the Sonoran Desert, which for nearly four decades has spent hundreds of millions of dollars trying to identify the underlying cause of the diabetes epidemic among the Pima and other indigenous communities. Its scientists and educators have all but ignored qualitative differences between Native American diets, preferring to seek a quick genetic fix to everyone's problem at the same time. Several years ago, *New Yorker* writer Malcolm Gladwell called it the "Pima paradox": "All told, the collaboration between the NIH and the Pima is one of the most fruitful relationships in modern medical science—with one fateful exception. After thirty-five years, no one has had any success in helping the Pima lose weight [and control diabetes]. For all the prodding and poking, the hundreds of research papers describing their bodily processes, and the determined efforts of health workers, year after year the tribe grows fatter."

At most, the NIH epidemiologists have quantified how the contemporary Pima and their Indian neighbors eat more fast foods than ever before, especially ones detrimentally high in animal fats and simple sugars. But what the NIH has failed to discuss with Native Americans are the countless studies, including my own collaborations with nutritionists, that demonstrate how traditional diets of desert peoples formerly *protected* them from diabetes and other life-threatening afflictions now known as Syndrome X. This Syndrome X is not some sinister new disease, but rather a cluster of conditions that, when expressed together, may reflect a predisposition to diabetes, hypertension, and heart disease. The term—first coined by members of a Stanford University biomedical team—describes a cluster of symptoms, including high blood pressure, high triglycerides, decreased HDL ("good" cholesterol), and obesity. These symptoms tend to appear together in some individuals, increasing their risk for both diabetes and heart disease. And of course, all of these symptoms are influenced by diet, but what kind of diet most effectively reduces their expression was something that I seemed more interested in than anyone at the NIH or at Stanford.

In the 1980s, I began to collect traditionally prepared desert foods for nutritional analysis by Chuck Weber and Jim Berry in their University of Arizona Nutrition and Food Sciences lab, and for glycemic analysis by Jennie Brand-Miller and her colleagues who had already done similar work analyzing the desert foods traditionally consumed by Australian aborigines. By glycemic analysis, I refer to a simple finger-prick test for blood-sugar and insulin levels done as soon as a particular food is eaten, and every half hour afterwards; the test determines whether the food in question causes blood-sugar levels to rapidly spike after its ingestion, thereby causing pancreatic stress and asynchronies with insulin production.

Jennie Brand-Miller, a good friend as well as colleague, determined with her students that native desert foods—desert legumes, cacti, and acorns in particular—were so slowly digested and absorbed that blood-sugar levels remained in sync with insulin production, without any adverse health effects generated. Jennie called these native edible plants "slow-release foods" to contrast them with spike-inducing fast foods such as potato chips, sponge cakes, ice cream, and fry breads. The fast foods had glycemic values two to four times higher than the native desert foods, whose slow-release qualities Weber and Berry had shown to be derived from the foods' higher content of soluble fiber, tannins, and complex carbohydrates.

Jennie had found the same trend when comparing Western fast foods with the native desert foods that Aussies call "bush tuckers"—the mainstays of aboriginal diets up until a half century ago, before which diabetes was virtually absent in indigenous communities of Australia. As with the desert tribes of North America, once these protective foods were displaced from aboriginal diets, the incidence of diabetes skyrocketed.

Back on an autumn night in 1985, Jennie and I were sipping prickly pear punch, having spent the day comparing the qualities of Australian and American desert foods. I could see that she was brewing over some large question, and she finally teased it out.

"Gary, I've wondered if there might be some explanation [for why desert peoples are vulnerable to diabetes, other than what the NIH promotes], one that you as a desert plant ecologist might help me figure out. I don't know if I'm framing this question precisely enough, but let me give it a try: is there something that helps a number of desert plants adapt to arid conditions which might help control bloodsugar and insulin levels in the humans that consume them?"

"*What?*" I blurted out. "Could you say that again?" Much later, I thought of a famous comment about the heart of science: "Ask an impertinent question and you are on your way to a pertinent answer."

Jennie laughed, aware that she was asking a question far too complex to consider in the midst of the frivolity of a dinner party. "Oh, that's OK," she said quietly. "I just wondered if desert plants from around the world could have evolved the same protective mechanism against drought that somehow . . . ."

"Oh, I think I get it now, some kind of convergent evolution," I said. "If the same drought-adapted chemical substances show up in plants from various deserts that are scattered around the world, perhaps these substances formerly protected the people who consumed them from the risk of diabetes . . ." Then, once diets changed, the desert peoples who once had the best dietary protection from diabetes suddenly had their genetic susceptibility expressed!

Although Jennie posed it in passing, I could not forget her impertinent question, not that night, not that week, and not for a long time. Friends like Gabriel, as well as Alfredo López's sister, Eva, had died of diabetes, but they still inhabited my memory. I mused over Jennie's question whenever I was out studying plants in the desert, and I brought it to the attention of some physiological ecologists who had a far deeper understanding of plant adaptations to drought than I did. They reminded me that desert plants and animals adapted to drought conditions by many different anatomical, physiological, and chemical means, and that there was probably not a single protective substance found in all arid-adapted biota.

In other words, the flora and the fauna from different deserts emphasized distinctive sets of these adaptive strategies. It was simply too much for these ecologists to imagine that a cactus from American deserts and a *wichitty* grub from the Australian outback might all share some dietary chemical that controlled diabetes among the Pima, Papago, and Seri of American deserts as well as among the Warlpiri and Pinkjanjara of Australian deserts.

Still, Jennie's question was rooted in a valid observation: there was an apparent correlation between the extraordinarily high susceptibility of diabetes among desert peoples and the quantity of drought-adapted plants in their diets. If some aboriginal cultures had subsisted on drought-adapted plants and associated wildlife for upwards of 40,000 years, was it not plausible that these people's metabolisms had adapted to the prevailing substances in these foodstuffs? And if, within the last fifty years, the prevalence of these foodstuffs had declined precipitously in their diets, was it not just as plausible that they had suddenly become susceptible to nutrition-related diseases because they had *lost their protection*? The question to pursue, then, was what dietary chemicals—nutrients or even antinutritional factors —might be more common in drought-adapted plants than those occurring in wetter environments?

With the help of ecophysiologist Suzanne Morse, I tried to imagine how water loss from a plant's tissue was slowed by the adaptations developed by a desert-dwelling organism to deal with scant and unpredictable rainfall. At the time, I was involved in a number of field evaluations of drought tolerance in desert legumes, cacti, and century plants. I soon learned that prickly pear cactus pads contain *extracellular mucilage,* that is, gooey globs of soluble fiber that holds onto water longer and stronger than the moisture held within photosynthesizing cells. If a cactus is terribly stressed by drought, it may shut down its photosynthetic apparatus, shut its stomatal pores, and shed most of its root mass, going "dormant" until rain returns. But if stress is not so severe, the cactus will instead gradually shunt the moisture in its extracellular mucilage into photosynthetically active but water-limited cells, thereby slowing the plant's total water loss while keeping active tissues turgid.

In explaining this concept—called "leaf capacitance"—to me, Morse offered me a parallel to slow (sugar) release foods: slow (water) release plant tissues. The very mucilage and pectin that slow down the digestion and absorption of sugars in our guts are produced by prickly pears to slow water loss during times of drought. And prickly pear, it turns out, has been among the most effective slow-release foods in terms of helping diabetes-prone native peoples slow the rise in their blood-glucose levels after a sugar-rich meal. In fact, it was among the first foods native to the Americas demonstrated to lower the blood glucose and cholesterol of indigenous people susceptible to diabetes. As Morse and I followed up on that research, we documented that most of the twenty-two species of cacti traditionally used by the Seri have the same slow-release qualities and are available along the desert coast much of the year.

Soon, Jennie Brand-Miller, in Sydney, and Boyd Swinburn, an endocrinologist from New Zealand, gave me greater insight into how slow-release foods differ from conventional foodstuffs in they way they are digested and absorbed. As I read reports about the "low gastric motility" of slow-release foods, I began to imagine how these foods make a viscous, gooey mass in our bellies. Even when our digestive juices cleave them into simpler sugars, the sugars have a tough time moving through the goo to reach the linings of our guts, to be absorbed and then transported to where they fuel our cells.

Here then, in the prickly pear—one of the food plants in the Americas with the greatest antiquity of use—was the convergence that Jennie had been seeking: the existence of slow-water-release mucilage in cactus pads and fruit explained why desert food plants were likely to produce slow-sugar-release foods. Five years after our conversation over prickly pear punch, I found a potential answer in the very plant Jennie and I had been consuming at the time she asked her impertinent question! The trouble was, prickly pear and other cacti are not native to Australian deserts; I began to investigate if there were plants in other deserts that also contained slow-water-release mucilages.

I soon learned that cacti are not special cases that occur only in the diets of desertdwelling Native Americans; there are dozens of other plants in both American and Australian deserts that have similar slow-sugar-release/slow-water-loss qualities, albeit with different morphologies and different chemical mechanisms. Given that desert peoples have been exposed to such plants for upwards of 10,000 years—more than 40,000 years in Australia—is there any evidence that these people's metabolisms have adapted over time to the presence of these protective foods?

With regard to the Seri, the only general genetic survey comparing them to neighboring agricultural tribes indicates that the Seri exhibit "several micro-polymorphisms [that] may be important in conferring a biological advantage" in their desert coastal homeland. The study claimed that "these may emphasize the relevance of interactions between genes and environment," for Seri hunter-gatherers express several alleles not found in more agriculture-dependent U.S. and Mexican indigenous peoples (Infante et al. 1999).

But do long-time hunter-gatherers with such polymorphisms respond to certain desert and marine foods differently than other people do? The answer can be found in research that Jennie and colleagues have done contrasting various ethnic populations' responses to foods common to one group's traditional diet, but not the other's. As Jennie and her fellow researcher Anne Thorburn have explained:

> the aim of [our] next series of experiments was to compare the responses of healthy Aboriginal and Caucasian subjects to two foods, one a slow release Aboriginal bush food—bush potato (*Ipomoea costata*)—and the other a fast release Western food—[the domesticated] potato (*Solanum tuberosum*). Both Aborigines and Caucasians were found to produce lower plasma insulin responses to the slow release bush food than to the fast release Western food. But the differences were more marked in Aborigines, with the areas under the glucose and insulin curves being one-third smaller after bush potato than potato (Brand-Miller and Thorburn 1987).

In other words, the Aborigines were protected from diabetic-inducing pancreatic stress by a bush food that their metabolisms had genetically adapted to over

40,000 years. Caucasians, with hardly any exposure to this or similar bush foods since colonizing Australia, did not experience such marked benefits.

When many scientists learn of these differences, they recall the theory of a *thrifty gene* that indigenous hunter-gatherers are presumed to maintain as an adaptation to a feast-or-famine existence, and they attribute the differences in insulin response to that gene. As originally hypothesized by James Neel in 1962, hunter-gatherers were likely to exhibit a thrifty genotype that was a vestigial survival mechanism from eras during which they suffered from irregular food availability. "During the first 99 percent or more of man's life on earth while he existed as a hunter-gatherer," Neel wrote, "it was often feast or famine. Periods of gorging alternated with periods of greatly reduced food intake" (Neel 1962).

Neel persuasively argued that repeated cycles of feast and famine over the course of human evolution had selected for a genotype that promoted excessive weight gain during times of food abundance and gradual weight loss of those "reserves" during times of drought. Neel focused on food quantity—the evenness of calories over time—and not food quality, arguing that when former hunter-gatherers were assured regular food quantities over time, the previously adaptive genetic predisposition to weight gain became maladaptive.

However, the only early NIH attempt to characterize the diets of Pima women with traditional versus acculturated (modern) lifestyles found insignificant differences between the calorie amounts consumed by the two groups, nor was there much difference when both groups' diets were compared to what surrounding Anglo populations ate. In other words, despite Neel's hypothesis, food quantity alone did not account for the rise in diabetes among acculturated Pima Indian women.

Nevertheless, Neel's argument has been cited by hundreds of scientific papers on diabetes and other diseases and has reached millions of other readers through "popular science" magazine essays written by such science-literate writers as the *New Yorker's* Malcolm Gladwell, *Harper's* Greg Cristner, *Outside's* David Quammen, and *Natural History's* Jared Diamond. What's more, Neel's hypothesis essentially drove the first thirty-five years of research at the NIH Indian Diabetes Project in Phoenix, Arizona, whose director and staff set their sights on becoming the first to discover the thrifty gene. Hundreds of millions of research dollars later, it is clear that their focus on a single gene and on sheer food *quantity* has blinded researchers to a variety of gene-food-culture interactions that may trigger or prevent diabetes.

Thirty-six years after proposing his famous hypothesis, Neel himself conceded that "the term 'thrifty genotype' has [already] served its purpose, overtaken by the growing complexity of modern genetic medicine," adding that while type 2 diabetes may still be "a multifactorial or oligogenic trait, the enormous range of individual or group socioeconomic circumstances in industrialized nations badly interferes with an estimate of genetic susceptibilities" (Neel 1998).

Neel's colleagues in biomedical research are much more direct in their assertion that there is no single thrifty gene that confers susceptibility to type 2 diabetes among all ethnic populations, or even among all hunter-gatherers. Assessing the recent identification of several genes that heighten or trigger diabetes, geneticist Alan Shuldiner of the University of Maryland School of Medicine told *Science News,*

"I expect there would be dozens of diabetes-susceptibility genes [and that] specific combinations of these genes will identify risk" (Seppa 2002).

What these genes actually do is also different from what Neel and other pro-ponents of the thrifty genotype suspected they would do. When the NIH worked to determine whether *the* thrifty gene they had identified in the Pima was actually a gene for insulin resistance—which causes reduced metabolic sensitivity to sugar loads—researchers found this gene's true function to be weight maintenance and *not* weight gain.

As molecular biologist Morris White of the Joslin Diabetes Center recently concluded in the pages of *Science,* "We used to think type 2 diabetes was an insulin receptor problem, and it's not. We used to think it was solely a problem of insulin resistance, and it's not. We used to think that muscle and fat were the primary tissues involved, and they are not. Nearly every feature of this disease that we thought was true 10 years ago turned out to be wrong" (White 2000).

Once again, it was my friend Jennie Brand-Miller who hammered the coffin closed on the thrifty gene hypothesis by refuting its very underpinnings—that famines were more frequent among hunter-gatherers than among agriculturists, leading to the former's extraordinary capacity to accumulate fat reserves. In scanning the historic anthropological literature on periodic famine and starvation among various ethnic groups, Jennie and her colleagues found scant evidence that hunter-gatherers suffered from these stresses anywhere near as frequently as agriculturalists did. In fact, periodic starvation and wide-spread famines increased in frequency less than 10,000 years ago, after various ethnic groups became fully dependent on agricultural yields. In particular, Jennie noted, since Caucasians living in Europe have repeatedly suffered from famines in historic times, they ought to be predisposed to insulin resistance and diabetes if Neel's hypothesis is correct. And yet, Caucasians are one of the few groups that do not exhibit much insulin resistance or heightened susceptibility to type 2 diabetes when they consume modern industrialized agricultural diets.

"The challenge," Jennie and her colleagues argue, "is to explain how Europeans came to have a low prevalence and low susceptibility to adult-onset diabetes . . ." (Cordain et al. 2000). Indeed, Europe harbors most of the world's ethnic populations who have *not* suffered dramatic rises in this nutrition-related disease since 1950.

At an international workshop that Jennie and I hosted at Kims Toowoon Bay on the coast of New South Wales in May of 1993, we elucidated four factors that could explain why individuals of European descent appear to be less vulnerable to Syndrome X maladies—including diabetes—than do ethnic populations that have adopted agricultural and industrial economies more recently. With colleagues from four countries, including Australian Aborigines and Native Americans, we identified that the incidence of diabetes rapidly increases under the following four circumstances.

First, when an ethnic population shifts to an agricultural diet and abandons a diverse cornucopia of wild foods, its members lose many secondary plant compounds that formerly protected them from impaired glucose tolerance. This is particularly true for populations that have coevolved with a certain set of wild foods over millennia, ones that are rich in antioxidants.

Second, when the remaining beneficial compounds in traditional crops and free-ranging livestock are selected out of a people's diet through breeding and restricted livestock management practices, their diet is further depleted of protective factors. For instance, modern bean cultivars have been bred to contain less soluble fiber, and livestock raised on cereal grains under feedlot conditions lack omega-3 fatty acids.

Third, the industrial revolution that began in Europe in the seventeenth century changed the quality of carbohydrates in staple foods by milling away most of the fiber in them. High-speed roller mills now grind grains into easily digested and rapidly absorbed cereals and flours, which results in blood-sugar and insulin responses two to three times higher than those reported from whole grains or coarse-milled products like bulgur wheat.

Fourth, the last fifty years of highly industrialized foods has introduced additives such as trans-fatty acids, fiber-depleted gelatinous starches, and sugary syrups, which ensure that most fast foods are truly *fast-release* foods. Jennie estimates that the typical fast-food meal raises blood-sugar and insulin levels three times higher than humans ever experienced during preagricultural periods in our evolution. Combined with the trend toward oversize servings of convenience foods and a more sedentary lifestyle, the dominance of fast foods in modern diets has made contemporary humans less fit than ever.

Although nearly all ethnic populations have come to suffer from fast foods over the last quarter century, the other changes took place in European societies over thousands of years. Whereas the genetic constituency of European peoples may have slowly shifted with these technological and agricultural changes as they emerged, the Seri and Warlpiri have had less than fifty years to accommodate these changes, and their genes are not in sync with them. Significant adaptation through evolutionary processes to new diets rarely occurs over the course of two to three generations.

And yet, most people now living in the world fall somewhere between the French and German farmers on the one hand, and the Seri and Warlpiri hunter-gatherers on the other. The majority of traditional diets have historically been more like the Pima and Papago in the Arizona deserts, where perhaps 60 percent of foods were harvested from domesticated crops in wet years while the rest came from wild and weedy plants and free-ranging game or fish. In dry years, the Papago-Pima diet shifted more toward the reliable harvests of drought-tolerant wild perennials.

While details richly vary around the world—from coastal habitats where fish were once abundant to rain forests where birds and root crops proliferated—most indigenous peoples in developing countries have maintained, until recently, a healthy mix of wild foods and diverse cultivated crops. Today, following dramatic economic shifts that have favored a few cereal grains and livestock production for export over mixed cropping, the bulk of the world's population has been left vulnerable to diabetes. One recent reckoning suggests that upwards of 200 million people are now susceptible to diabetes and the other killers associated with Syndrome X. This is not the exception among the diverse peoples of the world; it is a pathology that has become the norm.

But while fast foods lead to rapid deterioration of healthy carbohydrate metabolism in most people—with or without the existence of a thrifty gene—a return to the traditional foods of one's own ancestry leads to rapid recovery. This is what New Zealand endocrinologist Boyd Swinburn found when he asked me to help him reconstruct a semblance of the nineteenth-century dietary regime for the Pima and Papago. Swinburn wanted to compare the effects of a traditional versus a fast-food diet, both consisting of the same number of calories and percentages of carbohydrate and fats.

When twenty-two Pima Indians in his study were exposed to the fast-food diet, their insulin metabolism deteriorated enough to trigger diabetic stress without the need to conjure up any other explanation to explain it. Yet when the same individuals were placed on the traditional diet rich in soluble fiber and other secondary plant compounds, their insulin sensitivity and glucose tolerance improved. Swinburn and his coworkers concluded that "the influence of Westernization on the prevalence of diabetes may in part be due to changes in dietary composition [as opposed to food quantity]" (Swinburn et al. 1993).

I followed Swinburn's clinical study with a demonstration project at the National Institute for Fitness outside St. George, Utah, where eight Pima, Papago, Hopi, and Southern Paiute friends suffering from diabetes came together for ten days of all-you-can-eat slow-release foods and outdoor exercise. Within ten days, their weight and their blood-sugar levels had been dramatically reduced, and everyone felt healthier. The changes began so immediately that several participants had to seek medical advice to figure out how to reduce the hypoglycemic medications they had been self-administering for years.

In yet another example, in what may be one of the most dramatic gains in health conditions ever witnessed in a short period of time, Kieran O'Dea documented the marked improvement in diabetic Australian aborigines after they reverted for a month to a nomadic foraging lifestyle in western Australia. Even though study subjects "poached" several free-ranging cows as part of their meat consumption, their diet primarily consisted of bush foods that their ancestors had long eaten. The aboriginal participants moved frequently to take advantage of hunting and plant-gathering opportunities, and they lost considerable weight while doing so.

Their consumption of calories from macronutrients was 54 percent protein, about 20 percent plant carbohydrates, and 26 percent fat. These proportions had a dramatic effect on lowering blood-sugar levels and increasing insulin sensitivity. While some critics have conjectured that their insulin sensitivity, glucose tolerance, and cholesterol levels improved merely because of the subjects' weight loss, others have pointed out that the ratio of macronutrients they consumed certainly did not worsen their condition. While not necessarily optimal for all ethnic populations, a diet with this mixture of macronutrients clearly brought health benefits to the Australian desert dwellers that participated.

Inspired by O'Dea's collaboration with indigenous sufferers of diabetes, I organized a similar moveable feast in the spring of 1999, engaging more than twenty Seri, Papago, and Pima individuals who also suffered from diabetes. We walked 220 miles through the Sonoran Desert during a twelve-day pilgrimage, fueled only by native slow-release foods and beverages. Although we did not measure our blood-sugar and insulin levels each day to compare our health status before and after our journey, we took note of something perhaps far more significant: the native foods we ate were considered by all the participants to be nutritious, satisfying, and filling enough to sustain our arduous pilgrimage. These foods enabled us to hike across rugged terrain for ten hours a day, followed by another hour or two of celebratory dancing.

Our collective effort made us more deeply aware that our own energy levels could be sustained for hours by slow-release foods. At the same time, we took a good hard look at the health of our neighbors and of the land itself. The pilgrimage allowed us to clearly see for the first time all the damage that had been done to our homeland and its food system, damage that was echoed in our very own bodies.

There was something else going on among my Native American companions during that walk. The Seri, Papago, and Pima pilgrims frequently expressed that their cultural pride, spiritual identity, and sense of curiosity were being renewed. And so, a return to a more traditional diet of their ancestral foods was not merely some trip to fantasy land for nostalgia's sake; it provided them with a deep motivation for improving their own health by blending modern and traditional medical knowledge in a way that made them feel whole. They were not eating native slow-release foods merely to benefit a single gene—thrifty or not. Instead, they were communing to keep their entire bodies, their entire communities, and the entire Earth healthy.

Yes, genes matter, but diverse diets and exercise patterns matter just as much. And when the positive interaction among all three of these factors is reinforced by strong cultural traditions, our physical health improves, as does our determination to keep it that way. The Native American folks I walked with on that pilgrimage have re-doubled their commitments to keep their traditional slow-release foods accessible in their communities; they serve them at village feasts and at wakes honoring those who have succumbed to the complications of diabetes for lack of earlier access to these foods. When the persistence of traditional foods is more widely recognized as a source of both cultural pride and as an aid to physical survival and well-being, I doubt that many Native American communities will abandon what many of them feel to be a true gift from their Creator.

References

Brand-Miller, J. C., J. Snow, G. P. Nabhan, and A. S. Truswell (1990) Plasma glucose and insulin responses to traditional Pima Indian meals. *American Journal of Clinical Nutrition* 51:416–420.

Brand-Miller, J. C., and A. W. Thorburn (1987) Traditional foods of Australian aborigines and Pacific Islanders. In *Nutrition and health in the tropics*, ed. C. Rae and J. Green, 262–270. Canberra, Australia: Menzies Symposium.

Brand-Miller, J. C., and S. Colaguiri (1994) The carnivore connection: Dietary carbohydrate and the evolution of NIDDM. *Diabetologica* 37:1280–1286.

——— (1999) Evolutionary aspects of diet and insulin resistance. In *Evolutionary aspects of nutrition and health: diet, exercise, genetics, and chronic disease*. Vol. 84 of *World review of nutrition and diet*. Basel, Switzerland: Karger.

Cordain, L., J. C. Brand-Miller, and N. Mann (2000) Scant evidence of periodic starvation among hunter-gatherers. *Diabetologica* 24(3):2400–2408.

Cowen, R. (1991) Desert foods offer protection from diabetes. *Science News* 32:12–14.

Diamond, J. (1992) Sweet death. *Natural History* 2:2–7.

Gladwell, M. (1998) The Pima paradox. *New Yorker*, February 2:41–53.

Infante, E., A. Olivo, C. Alaez, F. Williams, D. Middleton, G. de la Rosa, M. J. Pujo, C. Duran, J. L. Navarro, and C. Gorodezky (1999) Molecular analysis of HLA class I alleles in Mexican Seri Indians: Implications for their origin. *Tissue Antigens* 54:35–42.

Nabhan, G. P. (2004) Cross-pollinations: The marriage of science and poetry. Minneapolis: Milkweed Editions.

Nabhan, G. P., C. W. Weber, and J. Berry (1979) Legumes in the Papago-Pima Indian diet and ecological niche. *Kiva* 44:173–178.

Neel, J. V. (1962) Diabetes mellitus: A "thrifty genotype" rendered detrimental by progress. *American Journal of Human Genetics* 14(4):353–362.

—— (1998) The "thrifty genotype" in 1998. *Perspectives in Biology and Medicine* 42:44–74.

O'Dea, K. (1984) Marked improvement in carbohydrate metabolism in diabetic Australian aborigines after temporary reversion to traditional lifestyle. *Diabetes* 33:596–603.

Seppa, N. (2002) Gene tied to heightened diabetes risk. *Science News* 158:212.

Swinburn, B. A., V. L. Boyce, R. N. Bergman, B. V. Howard, and C. Borgardus (1993) Deterioration in carbohydrate metabolism and lipoprotein changes induced by a modern, high fat diet in Pima Indians and Caucasians. *Journal of Clinical Endrocrinology and Metabolism* 73(1):156–164.

Villela, G. J., and L. A. Palinkas (2000) Sociocultural change and health status among the Seri Indians of Sonora, Mexico. *Medical Anthropology* 19:147–172.

Weber, C. W., R. B. Arrifin, G. P. Nabhan, A. Idouraine, and E. A. Kohlhepp (1996) Composition of Sonoran Desert foods used by Tohono O'odham and Pima Indians. *Journal of the Ecology of Food and Nutrition* 26:63–66.

White, M. (2000) New insights into type 2 diabetes. *Science* 289:37–39.

24

Between Obesity and Hunger: The Capitalist Food Industry*

Robert Albritton

We live in a world capable, in principle, of providing a diverse and healthy diet for all, and yet one quarter of its people suffer from frequent hunger and ill health generated by a diet that is poor in quantity or quality or both. Another quarter of the world's population eats too much food, food that is often heavy with calories and low on nutrients (colloquially called 'junk food'). This quarter of the world's population risks diabetes and all of the other chronic illnesses generated by obesity. In Mexico, for example, 14 per cent of the population have diabetes, and in India, 11 per cent of city-dwellers over 15.[1] In the US it has been estimated that one-third of the children born in the year 2000 will develop diabetes—a truly sad prospect, given that most of this is entirely preventable.[2] Study after study in recent years has come to the conclusion that the single most important factor in human health is diet, and diet is something we can shape.

Cheap food is important to capitalism because it allows wages to be lower (and thus profits to be higher) and yet leave workers with more disposable income available to buy other commodities. For these and other reasons, early in the history of capitalism, the food system became tied to colonialism, where various forms of forced or semi-forced labour were common. After the civil war ended slavery in the US, the domestically-produced food system came to rest primarily on the family farm. But after the Second World War the increasing mechanization and chemicalisation of agriculture favoured larger farms. In the early 1970s the US Secretary of Agriculture Earl Butz got Congress to pass a programme of subsidies that rewarded high yields. As a result, the larger the farm and the higher the yield, the larger became the subsidy. Nearly all the subsidies went to large farms, and for a few basic crops: tobacco, cotton, corn, wheat, and eventually soy. Moreover the large farms that could benefit the most from mechanization and chemicalisation became increasingly subservient to the gigantic corporations that supplied the inputs and bought the outputs of these factory farms.[3]

This situation remains essentially unchanged today. In 2005 alone the US government spent over $20 billion in agricultural subsidies (46 per cent of this went for corn production, 23 per cent for cotton, 10 per cent for wheat, and 6 per cent

*Originally published 2010

for soybeans).[4] The largest 10 per cent of the farms got 72 per cent of the subsidies and 60 per cent of all farms got no subsidy at all. For the most part, fruit and vegetable crops received no subsidies, and the same could be said for most small and medium sized farms. In short, the subsidy program rewards the large yields that result from very large, highly industrialized farms.

Today, while there are still many family farms in the US, the older mixed family farm that utilized manure from its animals to fertilize the land, and practised crop rotation and other techniques to control pests, has been largely wiped out. The giant capitalist farm of today is dependent on cheap oil and government subsidies. David Pimentel, professor of ecology at Cornell University and a globally recognized expert on food systems and energy, has argued that if the entire world adopted the American food system, all known sources of fossil fuel would be exhausted in seven years.[5] At the same time, utilizing such huge amounts of petroleum-based chemicals (fertilizers and pesticides) would not only contribute enormously to global warming, but also would make our toxic environment even more toxic.

In this short essay most of my examples come from the US, because, as the most hegemonic capitalist power in the world, it has done the most to shape the global food system. But I don't want to give the impression that there is one tightly integrated capitalist world food system. Even in the US, capitalism has not entirely subsumed the whole food system, and while there are few places in the world untouched by capitalism, its degree of hegemony may vary a great deal. Still, up to the present, capitalism has been the single strongest force shaping the global food system, and much of that shaping power has flowed outward from the US.[6]

The Profits of Obesity

It is scandalous that in the academic world many professors of economics still teach the doctrine of consumer sovereignty when it is so clear that on the contrary, corporations are the far greater sovereign force. Coca-Cola, for example, is the most universally recognized brand name, and is one of the world's largest and most profitable corporations. But Coke got this way with a little help from its friends. According to food political economist Raj Patel:

> ... the US taste for Coca-Cola was first chorused in the theatre of the Second World War. The drink itself wasn't given away during the conflict, but General Marshall went to great lengths to make sure that it was freely available to buy wherever US troops were stationed. The Coca-Cola Company was exempted from sugar rationing [Pepsi was not] so that it might produce a drink that came, for US soldiers, to signify the very lifeblood of the country.[7]

According to nutritionist Marion Nestle, Americans consume on average 31 teaspoons of added sugars a day, 40 per cent of which comes from soft drinks.[8] American teenage boys drink on average 800 12-ounce cans of soft drink a year, while the standard soft drink in vending machines has gone from 8 to 12 to 20 ounces (on average there are 15 teaspoons of sugar in a 20-ounce bottle).[9] No wonder the number of overweight children in the US has tripled since 1980. Given that fat and sugar constitute 50 per cent of the caloric intake of the average American, it is also not surprising to find that over two-thirds of all Americans are overweight, while the very obese (at least 100 pounds overweight) are the fastest-growing group.[10] Obesity is a risk factor for many chronic diseases, but is most closely connected to diabetes. In the seven years from 1997 to 2004 type 2 diabetes increased 41 per cent in the US. Globally the six-fold increase in cases of diabetes since 1985 almost exactly parallels the global increase in high fructose corn syrup (HFCS) consumption.[11]

The ideal food ingredient for profit purposes is something that is cheap and that consumers crave. Sweetness is the most desired taste to the point that many if not most people can easily be caught up in an 'excessive appetite' for it.[12] A craving for sugar is widespread, and recent tests suggest that sugar may be addictive.[13] It also happens that many of the widely used sugars in the food industry are among the cheapest inputs to food processing. The cheapness of HFCS makes soft drinks—that typically consist of artificial flavour, artificial colouring, water, and HFCS—among the most profitable commodities produced by the capitalist food industry.[14] A common way of classifying foods contrasts calorie density to nutrient density. While some foods may be both calorie dense and nutrient dense, food that we usually call 'junk food' tends to be very high in calories relative to nutrients.[15] Many soft drinks contain lots of calories but no other nutrients whatever.

The addictive quality of sugar can be compared to that of cigarettes. In part because of the marketing power of corporations like Philip Morris, cigarette smoking is now common amongst children as young as thirteen in places like Latin America, the former Soviet Union, China, and India, and it is estimated that over one billion people will die from smoking cigarettes in the twenty-first century.[16] But the so-called 'obesity pandemic' with its frequent sugar fix may end up damaging more lives than the rapid spread of smoking cigarettes amongst the youth of developing and post-communist societies. Tobacco often kills after the age of sixty, while sugar attacks the teeth of the young and may in many cases be the main cause of obesity and all of its related chronic illnesses throughout life.[17]

Warren Buffet, among the top five richest men in the world, once said: 'I'll tell you why I like the cigarette business. It costs a penny to make. Sell it for a dollar. It's addictive. And there's fantastic brand loyalty.[18] One could say that the same for sugar. It is very cheap and it produces a craving, and in the case of Pepsi and Coca-Cola there is often strong brand loyalty too—a sure formula for fabulous profits in the food industry. It should also be noted that the cost of food inputs (in many cases of 'value added' processed foods) constitutes a small fraction of the total price. This is certainly the case with soft drinks, as it is also for most breakfast cereals. For example, the grain in a 12 ounce box of cereal that sells for $3.50 may only cost 25 cents.[19] The rest of the $3.50 reflects the costs of transporting, processing, packaging, and retailing, plus a very sweet profit.

It happens that the sugars, fats, and salts that are so central to junk food, are not only the foods that humans most crave, but also are among the cheapest food inputs. With such cheap inputs it is tempting to increase portion sizes, since the increased cost to the consumer of the larger portion then becomes almost pure profit. While McDonalds led the way, the entire food industry has now followed. Many studies show that as portions get larger, people eat more, and since food itself is a small portion of the costs in food items like french fries, or soda pop, much of the extra cost to the consumer of larger portions is pure profit for the fast food outlet. Indeed, the difference between what the farmer gets and the final selling price of food items sometimes reaches obscene proportions as when on average the potato farmer gets 2 cents out of an order of fries that sells for $1.50.[20] No wonder some burger chains have found it profitable to serve larger and larger orders of fries.

In response to recent criticisms, fast food chains have made a few cosmetic changes, but overall their commitment to deliver large portions of junk food cheap is continuing. For example, in the summer of 2008, Pizza Hut began to aggressively market its new one pound P'zone pizza and dipping sauce, which contains 1,560 calories (the average daily intake of calories should be 2,100 calories) and twice the recommended daily intake of sodium.[21] Indeed, salt consumption in the US increased by a striking 20 per cent over the ten-year period between 1992 and 2002.[22] Salt itself is not fattening, but it does increase thirst, which in the US is very often slaked by high calorie soft drinks or beer. Further, salt contributes to high blood pressure, a major risk factor in heart disease and strokes. It has been estimated that reducing salt consumption by half in the US would prevent 150,000 deaths a year.[23]

The growth of meat and dairy consumption, with their saturated fats, along with the conversion of various vegetable oils into trans fats, have also contributed to the obesity epidemic and other health problems. The percentage of fat in the average American diet increased from 19 per cent in 1977 to 40 per cent in 2005.[24] French fries drenched in fat and salt constitute 25 per cent of all vegetables consumed in the US,[25] and the per capita consumption of cheese has nearly tripled since 1970.[26]

And this meatification and junkification of diet is now spreading to the rest of the world with dire long term consequences to human and environmental health. The world's poorer countries already carry immense burdens of infectious diseases. Now they have to contend with the junkification of their diets, plus increased tobacco use, both of which have escalated the incidence in these countries of chronic illnesses such as diabetes, heart disease, and cancer.

The United Nations International Codex Alimentarius Commission, which sets international food norms, is heavily influenced by the food industry. This influence was demonstrated at its November 2006 meeting where it was proposed to lower the limit of sugar in baby foods from the existing 30 per cent to 10 per cent. The proposal was defeated by the combined forces of the European and American sugar industries.[27] In a similar case, the UN's World Health Organization (WHO) and Food and Agriculture Organization (FAO) proposed, in their 2003 report, *Diet, Nutrition and the Prevention of Chronic Diseases*, a guideline, widely supported by nutritionists, that recommended that added sugars should not exceed 10 per cent of daily calorie intake. This was too much for the US sugar industry to swallow, and they threatened to lobby Congress to cut off its $400,000 annual funding of the WHO and FAO if they did not remove the offending norm from their report.[28] Under the circumstances, it was hardly surprising, if nevertheless still shameful, that the UN bodies gave in.

According to Patti Rundall, policy director of Baby Milk Action Group, 'A bottle-fed baby consumes 30,000 more calories over its first eight months than a breast-fed one. That's the calorie equivalent of 120 average size chocolate bars.[29]' 'Several research studies have shown correlations between bottle-feeding and subsequent obesity', which is what would be expected given the early age at which tastes may be formed.[30] And yet despite these findings, baby formula is aggressively marketed around the world. The soy lobby in the US has convinced the government to buy its soy formula and give it away to mothers on welfare—despite the fact that giving a baby soy formula with its powerful oestrogen is equivalent to an adult woman taking 5 birth control pills a day.[31]

At the same time, because the American sugar industry is protected by high tariffs blocking the import of sugar, it can charge consumers up to three times the going international price, which typically amounts to a subsidy of $1–3 billion a year.[32] This subsidy paid by American consumers of sugar is given to very large and profitable corporations that grow a crop high in calories and low in other nutrients (refined sugar typically has no other nutrients), a crop that consumed in large quantities endangers the health of the world. At the same time, sugar laden food is marketed with a vengeance.[33]

'Brand loyalty from cradle to grave' is the aim of current marketing strategies that seem to be achieving just that. Toddlers are requesting brands early in life, with 60 per cent of American children under two watching television (and with 26 per cent having their own television!).[34] According to Schor, children request on average over 3,000 products a year.[35] The food brands that can tap into the human craving for sugar, fat, and salt the earliest end up being the big winners, for kids' number one spending category (at one-third of the total) is sweets, snacks, and beverages.[36] American children get on average over 25 per cent of their total calorie intake from snacks,[37] and 50 per cent of their calories from sugars and fats added to their food.[38] The incidence of diabetes among children and teenagers is to say the least alarming: besides the one-third of the babies born in the US in the year 2000 who are likely to become diabetic, about 6 per cent suffer from fatty liver disease,[39] and about 25 per cent have risk factors, such as elevated blood pressure, for heart disease.[40]

The private sector has developed numerous marketing strategies for getting at the impressionable minds of today's youth by exploiting the underfunding of schools. McDonalds and other fast food chains utilize sets of toys made by children in China to entice American children to want to come back repeatedly in order to complete their set.[41] The hunger and exploitation of children in one part of the world feeds 'the toxic food environment' offered children in another part, where soft drink companies gain exclusive 'pouring rights' in educational institutions in return for a modest monetary contribution, junk foods find their ways into cafeterias in similar fashion, and some schools even receive free televisions for having students watch ten minutes of news and two minutes of commercials a day on Channel One in the US.[42] Since so much of this advertising is for junk foods, it would indeed appear that so long as this continues—however many pledges we hear today to turn around the massive increase in healthcare spending in recent decades—we may expect an even greater expansion of healthcare spending in the future.[43]

The Hunger of Capitalism

Almost as a hallmark of its dysfunctionality, the same capitalist food system that produces obesity also produces hunger, which in terms of immediate suffering is far more serious than obesity. One of the UN's Millennium Development Goals is to reduce hunger from the previous 800 million (in 2000) to 400 million by the end of 2015. Yet, since this goal was enunciated, the number of hungry people in the world has *grown*, to over a billion.

Why is it that the term 'obesity epidemic' has wide currency and 'starvation epidemic' does not? One reason is that capitalists would rather not call attention to hunger, because its widespread existence stands in such jarring contrast to the 'chicken in every pot' pretensions of capitalism. A second reason is that to medicalise starvation with the term 'epidemic' seems out of place in connection with something so obviously connected, except for natural disasters, to institutions of human design. A third reason is that capitalistic rationality dictates profit maximisation, and the 'starvation sector' of the economy is not one where profits can be made. A fourth reason is that from the point of view of distributive justice or of ethics, the global massacre that is starvation is totally preventable and totally unjustifiable.

Defenders of the capitalist system might point out that hunger and starvation have always been problems, and that we must accept them as we do the law of gravity. But we have the knowledge and technical means to provide a good diet for everyone in the world, and failing to do so stems from radically unjust institutions of distribution. Good intentions continually arise from the grass roots, but more often than not they get deflected away from altering the capitalist institutions that lie at the base of the hunger and starvation. Hunger is basically a problem of poverty, a poverty created primarily by capitalism, colonialism, imperialism, racism, and patriarchy.

Agriculture remains the main source of income for 2.5 billion people, 96 per cent of them living in developing countries. In the late 1970s the World Bank and International Monetary Fund developed increasingly invasive structural adjustment policies (SAPs) which set conditions for developing countries to get further loans, or get better repayment schedules for existing loans, in response to the capitalist-generated 'debt crisis'. Many of these countries were forced to develop export-oriented cash crops to pay off debts. With many tropical countries expanding their export crops (such as tea, coffee, tobacco, sugar, flowers, peanuts, cotton, and cocoa) at the same time, the resulting glut on the market produced falling prices. Given that agriculture is the weightiest sector in the economies of over 80 developing countries, the result was devastating. According to Peter Robbins, 'The collapse of tropical commodity prices represents the most formidable obstacle to efforts to lift huge numbers of people out of poverty and yet, mysteriously, the problem has received almost no attention from the world's mainstream media'.[44] For example, by 2002 coffee prices were 14 per cent of their already low 1980 price, while cocoa had fallen to 19 per cent and cotton to 21 per cent. Is it really so surprising that a class-biased media would neglect such phenomena?

Worse still, while one might think that coffee farmers would be better off if the price of coffee went up this does not necessarily follow. Kraft and Nestlé, which control 49 per cent of the roasting, are among the small number of importers and roasters that control 78 per cent of the total revenues received from selling coffee.[45] History has shown that when the price of coffee increases it is the large corporations that rake in extra profits, while the money received by the direct producers changes little if at all; just as when the price of coffee falls, it often does not fall for the consumer, the large corporations grabbing the difference.[46]

Developing countries cannot compete with crops grown in the US or Europe because they are so highly subsidized. The North American Free Trade Agreement (NAFTA) between Canada, Mexico, and the US has had a similar impact on Mexico as SAPs and the 'green revolution' have had in other parts of the world. During the first ten years of the agreement, 1.7 million Mexicans were displaced from agriculture largely as a result of highly subsidised US food commodities (especially corn) flooding into Mexico.[47] Because US corn farmers receive on average half of their income in subsidies, they can sell their corn on the international market under the cost of production and still make a profit. For instance, in 2002 US corn cost $2.66 a bushel to produce and was sold on the international market for $1.74 a bushel.[48] Many of the Mexican farmers displaced by the dumping of cheap US corn into the Mexican market crossed the border to the US. Before the NAFTA 7 per cent of the 900,000 migrant farm workers in the US were undocumented. Ten years later 50 per cent of the 2 million migrant farm workers in the US were undocumented.[49]

The struggle of farm households is not limited to developing countries. By 1990 20 per cent of farm households in the US had incomes that put them below the poverty line.[50] And with up to 20,000 family farms shutting down each year, many low income farm families no longer farm.[51] These trends largely account for the fact that the average Iowa farmer is now approaching 60, and that suicide is the leading cause of death amongst US farmers, three times higher than for the population as a whole.[52]

It is the rising incidence of hunger and starvation among children that bodes so ill for the future. More than 18 per cent of hungry people are children under five, and many of them do not make it to five. For those who do survive, physical and/or mental stunting affects 31 per cent of all children in developing countries.[53] Current trends indicate that soon one billion people in the world will suffer impaired mental development because of malnutrition.[54] According to the FAO, malnutrition plays a role in more than 50 per cent of the annual 12 million deaths of children under five.[55] In developing countries 25 per cent of men and 45 per cent of women have anaemia, which is also far more dangerous to women, of whom an estimated 300 die during childbirth each day.[56] Clearly gender relations that disadvantage women play a huge role in the continuation of global poverty. A more thorough analysis of global poverty would need to make gender issues much more visible.

The UN estimates that 1.2 billion people live on less than $1 a day, while 2.8 billion, or 40 per cent of the world's population, live on less than $2 a day.[57] When food prices spike, as they did in the first half of 2008, the survival of many of these 2.8 billion people is jeopardised, as many of them were already spending 90 per cent or more of their income on food. The deepening global depression has since reduced all commodity prices, including food, but the price of food has still gone up 28 per cent since 2006.[58] Though many prices may fluctuate in the short term, there are several reasons why the price of food is bound to go up in the long run unless some radical changes are made.

- Fertile land that could grow food crops is being utilized for non-food crops, including tobacco, agro-fuels, illegal drugs, and trees for pulp and paper.

- Fertile land is being lost to suburban sprawl, golf courses, roads, parking lots, and mega shopping malls.
- Land is being degraded by industrial farming techniques.
- Global warming will sharply decrease crop yields due to higher temperatures and extreme weather.[59]
- The globalisation of a meat-based diet will divert food grains to animals.
- Speculators, seeing all of these pressures on the global food supply, will bid up the price of basic grains on commodity futures markets.

All of this adds up to rising food prices and increasing hunger for nearly half of the world's population. It is unlikely that the poor farmers who produce the food will benefit much from higher prices, since they will mostly be skimmed off by the transnational corporations that control the international trade and processing.

The Irrationality of Capitalist Rationality

What could be more foolhardy than placing food, the basis of all human flourishing, in the hands of giant corporations, which are obliged to pursue profits in order to further enrich an elite of wealthy stockholders? Indeed, within the framework of existing company law, units of capital must continually attempt to expand by maximizing profits, no matter what the social or environmental costs. The absurdity of our capitalist economic system emerges clearly when our understanding is not blinded by the ideology of market fundamentalism. The two basic institutions of our capitalist system are corporations and markets, and without radical reform neither has the capability of rationally responding to the mounting crises that we face now (and will increasingly face in the future) as the ecological and energy crises compound the economic crisis. Immense corporations whose decisions affect everyone in the world are fundamentally only accountable to a small number of wealthy shareholders, and even to them only in accord with the narrow criteria of profit maximisation. Markets, that in theory are supposed to satisfy social needs, treat enormous and ever-mounting social costs as 'externalities' that corporations can ignore and simply pass on to taxpayers, or to future generations.

In India, Coca-Cola's bottling companies are running down aquifers that farmers desperately need to irrigate crops.[60] Banana corporations have knowingly exposed third world workers to highly toxic pesticides, because the companies figured that they would not have to pick up any medical bills and because poor people desperate for jobs abound, so that sick or dying workers can always be replaced.[61] Meatpacking companies prey upon the vulnerability of undocumented workers, paying them low wages and speeding up the line to the point where injuries become routine.[62] Sugar companies oppose a norm which would lower the 30 per cent sugar now allowed in baby foods to 10 per cent.[63] Giant feedlots (Confined Animal Feeding Operations or CAFOs) pollute the surrounding earth, air, and water with foul odours and toxic substances.[64] Highly subsidised and therefore profitable ethanol producers buy up much of America's corn crop (as much as 50 per cent in the near future, on current predictions), and, as a result, raise the cost of food while the world's poor starve.[65]

Cocoa farmers in Ivory Coast receive so little for their crop that some have had to turn to child slavery in order to survive.[66]

All of the above examples are taken from our actually existing capitalist system of food provision, and what needs to be emphasized is that they are all perfectly rational from the point of view of profit-maximising capitalism. But this only confirms the extreme irrationality of capitalist 'rationality', and the urgent need to bring about radical changes via democratic long-term planning from the local level to the global. It is precisely because today's global capitalist food system promotes both hunger and obesity while at the same time undermining the earth's capacity to support us, that we need to fight to replace it at every link of the food chain with a system that is democratically planned to meet the human need for nutritious food and ensure that everyone has access to it, while at the same time leaving the environment— in so far as this is possible, given the damage already done—in an improved state for future generations.

Notes

1. B. Popkin, 'The world is fat', *Scientific American*, September, 2007, pp. 94–5; 'By 2020, 7 million Indians may die of lifestyle diseases', *Times of India*, 24 September 2007.
2. Cited in M. Pollan, *The Omnivores Dilemma*, New York: Penguin, 2006, p. 102.
3. Another aim of Butz's subsidies was that by enabling the dumping of basic grains on international markets at below cost of production, the growing US balance of trade deficit could be lessened, and developing countries would become more dependent on the US for food.
4. 'Uncle Sam's teat', *The Economist*, 9 September 2006, p. 35.
5. Cited in R. Manning, 'The oil we eat', *Harpers*, February, 2004.
6. For a much more inclusive analysis of how the current food system is integrated into global capitalism in ways that undermines not only human and environmental health, but also social justice and democracy, see my recently published book: *Let Them Eat Junk: How Capitalism Creates Hunger and Obesity*, London: Pluto Press, 2009 and Winnipeg: Arbeiter Ring Press, 2009.
7. Raj Patel, *Stuffed and Starved: Markets, Power, and the Hidden Battle for the World Food System*, Toronto: Harper Collins, 2007, p. 258; see also B. Popkin, *The World is Fat*, New York: Avery, 2009, p. 59.
8. M. Nestle, *What to Eat?*, New York: North Point Press, 2006, pp. 321, 327.
9. Global Dump Soft Drinks Campaign, http://www.dumpsoda.org, 2007. See also, Center for Science in the Public Interest, 'Consumer groups in 20 countries urge Coke and Pepsi to limit soft drink marketing to children', 3 January 2008, available from http://www.cspinet.org/new/index.html.
10. J. Schor, *Born to Buy*, New York: Scribner, 2004, p. 35. See also E. Schlosser, *Fast Food Nation*, New York: Harper Collins, 2002, p. 53; G. Gardner and B. Halweil, 'Overfed and underfed, the global epidemic of malnutrition', *Worldwatch Institute*, No. 150, March, 2000.
11. T. Philpott, 'How the feds make bad-for-you-food cheaper than healthful fare', 22 February 2006, available from http://www.grist.org.
12. J. Orford, *Excessive Appetites: A Psychological View of Addictions*, Toronto: Wiley, 2001.
13. See C. Colantuoni, 'Evidence that intermittent, excessive sugar intake causes endogenous opioid dependence', *Obesity Research*, No. 10, pp. 478–88; See also 'A survey of food', *The Economist*, 13 December, 2003, p. 16.
14. HFCS constitutes 50 per cent of all caloric sweeteners in processed foods. There is considerable debate over whether or not HFCS is more likely to cause diabetes than other sugars. There is some evidence that high levels of HFCS consumption may contribute to heart attacks, kidney and liver disease, high blood pressure, systemic inflammation and increased formation of cell-damaging free radicals. Two things are well established: never has the level of fructose consumption in the human diet increased so rapidly and to such a high level, and HFCS does not trigger the body's satiation reflex as much as other sugars. P. Roberts, *The End of Food*, New York: Houghton Mifflin, 2008, pp. 97–8. T. Talago, 'Too poor to avert diabetes', *Toronto Star*, 27 December 2007, p. A27.
15. Popkin, *The World is Fat*, pp. 33–4.
16. A. Brandt, *The Cigarette Century*, New York: Basic Books, 2007, pp. 451, 459, 486–7.
17. I. Loefler, 'No sweet surrender', *British Medical Journal (BMJ)*, 330(7495), 2005.
18. Brandt, *The Cigarette Century*, p. 448.

19. Roberts, *The End of Food*, p. 37.
20. Schlosser, *Fast Food Nation*, p. 117.
21. A triple thick 32 ounce milk shake has 1,110 calories. J. Wells, 'Chewing the fat about what's really in fast food', *Toronto Star*, 29 January 2005, p. L1. See also *Toronto Star*, 1 September 2008.
22. *Economist*, 'A survey of food', p. 9.
23. Nestle, *What to Eat?*, p. 367.
24. G. Critser, *Fat Land: How Americans Became the Fattest People in the World*, New York: Houghton Mifflin, 2003, p. 32.
25. Ibid., p. 75.
26. Nestle, *What to Eat?*, p. 63.
27. Ibid.
28. G. Dyer, 'Sugar lobby copies big tobacco', *Toronto Star*, 29 April 2003.
29. F. Lawrence, 'Sugar rush', *Guardian*, 15 February 2007.
30. Ibid.
31. F. Lawrence, *Eat Your Heart Out: Why the Food Business is bad for the Planet and your Health*, London: Penguin, 2008, p. 283.
32. *The New Internationalist*, No. 363, December, 2003, p. 23.
33. The health of workers on sugar plantations also needs to be considered. There are approximately 650,000 field workers on American-owned sugar plantations in the Dominican Republic, where in 2004 they received on average $2 for a twelve hour day working in the hot sun cutting cane. See Brian McKenna's documentary film, *Big Sugar* (2005), produced by Galafilm.
34. S. Linn, *Consuming Kids: Protecting Our Children from the Onslaught of Marketing and Advertising*, New York: New Press, 2004, p. 49.
35. J. Schor, *Born to Buy*, p. 20.
36. Ibid., p. 23.
37. Popkin, *The World is Fat*, p. 33.
38. Gardner and Halweil, 'Overfed and underfed', p. 15. See also M. Nestle, *Food Politics*, Berkeley: University of California Press, 2002, p. 175.
39. This condition can lead to cirrhosis, liver cancer, and liver failure. A. Johnson, 'Liver disease plagues obese adolescents', *Associated Press*, 9 November 2008, available from http://abcnews.go.com.
40. Center for Science in the Public Interest, 'Obesity on the kids' menus at top chains', 4 August 2008, available from http://www.cspinet.org/new/index.html.
41. McDonalds, for example, sells or gives away more than 1.5 billion toys a year. Most are made in China, often by children paid as little as 20 cents an hour. See E. Schlosser and C. Wilson, *Chew On This: Everything You Don't Know About Fast Food*, Boston: Houghton Mifflin, 2006, p. 59.
42. K. Brownell and K. Horgen, *Food Fight: The Inside Story of the Food Industry, America's Obesity Crisis, and What You can Do About It*, New York: McGraw-Hill, 2004, pp. 86-8.
43. J. Califano, *High Society: How Substance Abuse Ravages America and What to do about it*, New York: Public Affairs, 2007, p. 80.
44. P. Robbins, *Stolen Fruit*, Halifax: Fernwood, 2003, p. 3.
45. World Vision (2006), 'Slave to coffee and chocolate', available from http://www.worldvision.com.au.
46. J. M. Talbot, *Grounds for Agreement*, New York: Rowman & Littlefield, 2004, p. 115.
47. P. Rosset, *Food is Different: Why We Must Get the WTO out of Agriculture*, Halifax: Fernwood, 2006, p. 62.
48. Patel, *Stuffed and Starved*, p. 74.
49. C. Ahn, M. Moore and N. Parker, 'Migrant farmworkers: America's new plantation workers', *Backgrounder*, Food First, 10(2), available online via http://www.foodfirst.org.
50. T. Weis, *The Global Food Economy: The Battle for the Future of Farming*, Halifax: Fernwood, 2007, p. 83.
51. P. Rosset, *Food is Different*, p. 49.
52. *The New Internationalist*, 2003, No. 353, p. 10.
53. P. Pinstrup-Andersen and F. Cheng, 'Still hungry', *Scientific American*, 297(3), September 2007, pp. 96–8.
54. T. Lang and M. Heasman, *Food Wars: The Global Battle for Mouths, Minds, and Markets*, London: Earthscan, 2004, p. 61.
55. Cited in Pinstrup-Andersen and Cheng, 'Still hungry', p. 101.
56. Ibid., p. 98.
57. FAO, *The State of Food Insecurity in the World 2006*, Rome: FAO, 2006, p. 32.
58. J. Berger & J. Jowitt, 'Nearly a billion people worldwide are starving, UN agency warns', *The Guardian*, 10 December, 2008, p. 1.
59. E. deCarbonnel, 'Catastrophic fall in 2009 global economy food production', available from http://www.marketskeptics.com; see also T. Engelhardt, 'What does economic "recovery" mean on an extreme weather planet?', 18 February 2009, available from http://www.countercurrents.org.

60. 'Campaign to hold Coca-Cola accountable', *India Resource Center*, available at http://www.indiaresource.org/campaigns/coke.

61. N. Berube, 'Chiquita's children', *In These Times*, May 2005.

62. This has occurred throughout the US meatpacking industry. See S. Striffler, *Chicken, The Dangerous Transformation of America's Favourite Food*, New Haven: Yale University Press, 2005, p. 8; S. Parker, 'Finger-lickin bad', 21 February 2006, available from http://www.grist.org; Schlosser, *Fast Food Nation*, p. 174.

63. Lawrence, 'Sugar rush'.

64. The smell of CAFOs is repellent, and schools near to CAFOs have a higher incidence of asthma. S. Cox, *Sick Planet: Corporate Food and Medicine*, London: Pluto Press, 2009, p. 71. One study found that 25 per cent of hog house workers had breathing obstructions that could cause long-term lung damage. See T. Pawlick, *The End of Food*, Toronto: Greystone, 2006, p. 132.

65. L. Brown, 'Distillery demand for grain to fuel cars vastly understated: world may be facing highest grain prices in history', *Earth Policy Institute*, No. 5, January 2007, available from http://www.earth-policy.org.

66. C. Off, *Bitter Chocolate*, Toronto: Random House, 2006.

Food and Globalization

25

"As Mother Made It": The Cosmopolitan Indian Family, "Authentic" Food, and the Construction of Cultural Utopia[*]

Tulasi Srinivas

If America is a melting-pot, then to me India is a thali, a selection of sumptuous dishes in different bowls. Each tastes different, and does not necessarily mix with the next, but they belong together on the same plate... That, to me, is the notion or metaphor of the Indian identity.

—Shashi Tharoor. Under Secretary United Nations, author. 1997.

As we get to know Europe slowly, tasting the wines, cheeses, and characters of different countries you begin to realize that the important determinant of any culture is after all—the spirit of place...

—Lawrence Durrell. *N.Y.Times Magazine,* June 12, 1960.

Introduction

When I went to do fieldwork in Bangalore city in South India in the spring of 1998 I found middle class housewives and working women excited about packaged foods that had begun to flood the urban Indian market.[1] When I returned to Boston in the fall of 1999, I found working women of the Indian diaspora equally excited about the same products that had begun to enter the "Indian" markets in the United States. My fascination with why these women were so attracted to these "instant" foods has led me to a questioning of how global food flows construct identity in a cosmopolitan and multicultural world and the social and symbolic contours of transnational food consumption (Appadurai, 1981, 1986). So here, in a context devoted to understanding the family in a transnational world, I revisit the question that has bothered social theorists since the time of Marx: How are relations among people shaped by relations between people and things? In this exploratory paper, the focus is upon recent trends of consuming a variety of packaged and pre-prepared "Indian" food among (Achaya, 2005) Indian families, and the convergent symbolic trends among two twinned transnational Indian communities—urban, middle class professionals, and their families in the South Indian city of Bangalore, and the same urban, middle class, diasporic professionals and their families in the city of Boston, in the United States. This article addresses two interrelated questions, one pragmatic and the other affective—the radical transformation in

[*]*Originally published 2006*

the manner of food consumption occurring due to globalization and concordant development of the packaged food industry in India; and the anxiety over identity loss experienced by South Asians both in urban India and abroad.

Globalization (Hannerz, 1996; Tomlinson, 1991, 1999), the consequent warping of time and space through media, travel, and other modes of access, perforce leads to pluralism. This in turn leads to a consequent and important questioning of identity. Identity is no longer a "taken for granted" (Berger, 1961) but becomes an all absorbing project that is often enacted through consumption. Recent ethnographic work describes cultural consumption among the Indian middle classes (Osella and Osella, 2000; Mankekar, 1999; Varma, 1998; Kothari, 1991) link it repeatedly, to the shaping of a nation, imagined or otherwise. But how this consumption actually plays out in the everyday lives of the middle class (see Wessel, 2004), whether in urban India or among the Indian diaspora, and what it means to them, is rarely explored.

Globalization has been seen by theorists as the dominance of the culture of Euro-America (Appadurai, 1996; Barber, 1996; Berger, 1997; Friedman, 2006) i.e. the center upon the periphery. This paper seeks to expand on an understanding of a network form of cultural globalization—where goods and ideologies move through the network in many directions, leading perforce to plural forms of cultural globalization—that I have argued for earlier (T. Srinivas in Berger and Huntington, 2001) which stands in opposition to this cultural homogeneity model. In her discussion of the globalization of Bombay cinema, Lakshmi Srinivas argues that Bombay films "convey sensual and emotional experiences-the most immediate and embodied effects of globalization," through what she terms "feeling rules." She suggests that the films act as "a medium of translation," where the local as opposed to the global, is communicated through "a structure of feeling," where the local is "the known, the taken for granted and the tacit" (L. Srinivas, 2005: 324). Following her lead, I conceptually "map" (L. Srinivas, 2005) the affective contours of cultural globalization through an examination of how Indians, particularly *women* in urban India, (in Bangalore) and in diasporic contexts (Boston) (Theophano, 2002), engage this emergent world of prepared packaged foods. This article argues that food provisioning is fuelled by what I term a "meta-narrative of loss" engaging several narratives within it. Food consumption is seen as a "narrative of affiliative desire" that affectively recreates caste, micro regional and other social identity groupings for the cosmopolitan Indian family. Fuelled by a "narrative of anxiety" over "authentic" foods—"as mother made them"—the act of eating is transformed into a performance of "gastro-nostalgia" that attempts to create a cultural utopia of ethnic Indian-ness that is conceptually de-linked from the Indian nation state. Finally, "narratives of subterfuge," often invest the preparation of these packaged heat-and-eat "home made" foods, as South Asian women attempt to become socially acceptable models of domesticity. I further argue that a two habits are powerful paradigms in shaping the women's emotions over food; one is the nostalgic desire to prepare food as their mother or their spouse's mother made it, and to keep tradition alive in the hope of giving their children a sense of their "Indian self" by cooking the foods of their particular local caste and ethnic group in India; and secondly, and somehow oppositionally, to engage the transnational world of speed and economy that they live in, where the emphasis is on work and play and where food preparation and eating is the rapid "heat and eat" variety.

The data suggests that women in Bangalore and Boston are torn over the "right" thing to do for themselves and their families, and I explore what these conflicting changes in food preparation and eating mean for the role of the mother in the South Asian family. What are the desires that these foods articulate and fulfill? How do Indian women see these foods? What emotions do these foods create or engage? And most importantly, what is the dynamic between women and family that these foods articulate? These and other such questions form the central framework of the paper.

I suggest that the movement of Indian packaged prepared foods across international borders allows for a "utopic consumption" by cosmopolitan Indian families, where "local" food is culturally inserted into the "global" space (Appadurai, 1996; Hannerz, 1992). This insertion enables South Asian families to conceptually "sidestep" the confrontation between the local and the global, and engage what Lakshmi Srinivas calls, the "translocal" (L. Srinivas, 2005: 319–21). I agree with Appadurai (1996) that cultural mediation lies at the center of the problem of transnationalism. I suggest that the packaged food becomes—in its familiarity and its distance—a mediating model for these cosmopolitan families and is, simultaneously seen as of a place, and placeless (Giddens, 1991: 26) leading one not only to question the empirical value of these categories,[2] but also to question the nature of embeddedness and authenticity.

Much of the material for this chapter is based on ethnographic work in Boston and in Bangalore, both in observation of families and what they eat, as well as in informal and formal interviews of women as they shopped, cooked, and fed their families. I began the study of Indian packaged food in 1998 as part of a ten nation study on globalization,[3] but it is only in the past three years that I have actively thought about the world of packaged food in India primarily because of the growing number of packaged products both in Bangalore and in Boston. Secondly, my Indian friends and colleagues, are at an age when they all have young children, and I find that Indian mothers, both in urban India and in America, struggle to find foods that their children will eat, that have what they consider both nutritive and "cultural" content.

The comparison between the urban Indian and diasporic Indian community is useful since both the Bangalore community and the Boston community are dealing with similar problems of cosmopolitanism arising from being an integral part of a transnational world (Bourdieu, 1984). From an outsider's perspective one may say that these two communities are roughly similar. Both these cities are central to the global economy through their dynamic participation in knowledge capital industries, software and IT services and biotech advancements. But the similarity between the two communities holds up only in a first approximation. The local patterning of the diasporic community is in its complex relationship to the dominant Western Judeo-Christian culture of the United States (Appadurai, 1986, 2005). As a group one could argue that Indians in America are marginalized, both politically and socially by the dominant culture,[4] even though they, according to Kibria, suffer from (Breckenridge, 1995) the label of a "model minority," derived from their "cultural programming for economic success" (2003: 11). Nationally, their median income in $68,500, double that of the national average income.[5] This "programming for success" has made South Asian immigrants "a part yet apart" of the larger society; separate even from other Asian immigrant groups.[6] In the 1980s and 1990s, with increasing visibility due to the overwhelming successes of Indians in Silicon valley, in academia, in literature, and a few in the political arena and in films, this marginal position has been contested in the public arena. (Mintz, 1996; Nestle, 2002).

Boston is the academic Mecca in the United States, and has its fair share of South Asian intellectuals, along with a substantial community of venture capitalists, software engineers, biotechnologists, doctors, and technology specialists. By and large, immigrants to the New England region tend to be well educated, middle class, cosmopolitan professionals, and their families. According to the U.S. census for the year 2000 the city of Boston showed growth in the immigrant groups to the point of—"a minority as majority"—where minorities were over 50 percent of the total population.[7] Asian Indians were in fact the fastest growing ethnic minority in New England—up 110 percent in 2000 from a decade previously, and numbering roughly 76,000 in 2000 (Allis, 2005). This expansion in Asian Indian population increases as one moves towards the suburbs where the hi-tech industries are located. Asian Indians gravitate between the technology firms on Rt. 128, the Massachusetts Institute of Technology, the medical research complexes and hospitals, and the many laboratories and research facilities in the region. Indians in Boston lead a cosmopolitan life, often meeting for Mexican dinners accompanied by margaritas during the week, and for South Asian dance and cultural recitals on the weekend.

The middle class professionals in Bangalore lead a similar cosmopolitan life in which they too are an essential part of transnational culture. In the late 1980s Bangalore became one of the "hot zones" (Heitzman, 2004) of technology in the country attracting the new software companies and their employees.[8] Today Bangalore is a center for all those interested in engineering, software technology, chip building, information technology, and related fields (Heitzman, 2004). Engineers and other professionals have poured into the city, and the population of Bangalore has grown from 3.4 million in 1985 to 5.5 million in 2000[9] and is projected to reach 7 million in 2011 (Heitzman, 2004 quoting Bangalore Development Authority, 2000 statistics). There are believed to be more information technology engineers in Bangalore (150,000) than in Silicon valley USA (120,000) (see Kripalani and Engardio, 2003: 69–70). As a result of this economic spurt and increased monetization, a significant and growing Indian middle class[10] has been created with the power and cultural capital for global consumption. It is important to note that this middle class is a minority as over one third of the Indian population is illiterate and the country's per capita income is $460.00 per annum (Kripalani and Engardio, 2003).

But this middle class has significant social and economic clout as they loom large in the public imagination of urban India. Journalists often extol this new "consumer revolution" in India. *The Wall Street Journal* writes: "a thriving middle class is changing the face of India in land of poverty; its buying spree promises economic growth" (19th May 1988). Popular news magazines have focused several stories on the consumption mores of the new India—for example; "The New Middle Class" (*Hindustan Times*, 7 June 1987), and "The New Millionaires and How They Made it" (*India Today*, 31 October 1987), and "The New Gold Rush" (*Sunday*, 13 December 1987). The popularity of new Italian restaurants, Thai food restaurants, and ubiquitous bars, discotheques, coffee shops and pubs, has created the image of Bangalore as a cosmopolitan location within India. The new Bangalore[11] cosmopolitans are often single people or young couples who often find themselves far from their home and larger family. This "spatially mobile class of professionals" (Appadurai, 1988) creates a small (by Indian standards) but culturally important consumer base known for their knowledgeable often "westernized" (Srinivas, 1962; 1989) taste and is characterized by its "multi ethnic, multi caste, polyglot" (Appadurai, 1988: 6) taste.

But I have strayed far from the issue with which I began; the complex links between culture, motherhood, family dynamics, food consumption, identity and loss. Excavating these hidden links, the paper traces the social history of these packaged foods.[12] Since there are few sources on the social history of food in India (Goody, 1982), and even fewer on the eating habits of the Indian middle class or the Indian diaspora, much of this data comes from an analysis of "unorthodox" primary texts such as community based newspapers for the South Asian community in the United States, English language newspapers in Bangalore that carry food product and restaurant reviews, and the internet sites of many of these growing food corporations. This reconstructed gastronomic social history centres on the problem of home; How is the concept of "home made" constructed in an increasingly industrialized, corporatized and urban world of packaged foods in India? How is the "home" constructed in the increasingly plural and transnational world of food for the Indian diaspora? And how does the eating of packaged Indian food relate to identity? (Ferro-Luzzi, 1977). I consider this problem in emic terms and conclude with the way in which this peculiar and rich form of consumption can expand and enrich our understandings of the family, motherhood, and the construction of a cultural utopia (Counihan and Van Esterik, 1997).

The Indian Family: Mothers, Domesticity, and Commodity

According to Lamb and Mines (2002), co-editors of a volume titled *Everyday Life in South Asia*, the family is "*the* site of everyday life in South Asia" (italics mine). A familiar term for family in India is *samsara,* which means "that which flows together" in which "flows" is used to denote relationships between family members, as well as the flow of daily events. The assumption commonly made and not incorrect is that South Asians, particularly Indians in India, live in joint families comprising of many members related by networks of kinship. According to Shah, the family in India has undergone rapid change in the past fifty years. A "patterned widening of the connubial field" (1998: 10) had led to "contextual" marriages rather than "caste circumscribed" ones. Thus, inter-caste, inter-regional, and inter-religious marriages form new alliances and "create a new class which is cosmopolitan" (1998: 11). As time goes on, this class widens. Shah suggests that Hindu joint family (HJF) while enduring in surprising ways is giving way, especially in urban areas and in non business castes, to the nuclear family.[13]

The family in America is also changing. As more and more immigrant families from Latin America and Asia become part of the United States, family structures change. Add to that the aging population of the United States, and the economic instability that these elders face, and American families will, according to Zolli (2006), "get bigger and bigger." Zolli suggests that the American family will be redefined from being a single parent, or two co-parents and their children—a "nuclear family"—to being multi generational, sometimes even "a three- or even four-generation affair," a return to the beginning of the 20th century, ironically like the Indian joint family.

But in all these families, multi-generational or otherwise, the image of the good mother is conceptualized as a nurturing relationship between the mother and child, where this dyad is a metaphor for relations of caretaking and dependency (Counihan, 1999; Lupton, 1996). It is obvious that mothering relationships are much like other social relationships and, like them, are bound to take shape from the broader political and economic order within which they are forged. In South Asia, as elsewhere, feeding the child and provisioning the family are key components of the role of mother and wife. The "good" mother is one who feeds the child on demand with wholesome home made complex foods of the particular ethnic and caste based group of the patriliny. Renowned Indian psychologist Sudhir Kakar states:

> The Indian mother is intensely attached to the child ... From the moment of birth the Indian infant is greeted and surrounded by ... relentless physical ministrations the emotional sensuality of nurturing in traditional Indian families serves to amplify the effects of physical gratification. An Indian mother is inclined towards a total indulgence of her infant's wants and demands whether these be related to feeding, cleaning, sleeping or being kept company. Moreover she tends to extend this sort of mothering to well beyond the time when the 'infant' is ready for independent functioning in many areas. Thus, feeding at all times of night and day and 'on demand' (81).

With the growing economy in India from the 1970s, the Indian family has undergone rapid and enduring change, and more women have entered the work force in urban India (Theophano, 2002). One would assume that the expectations of motherhood and wifeliness would have shifted (Elias, 2000). But Desai (1996: 100) argues that while employment for women increased rapidly in the 1970s outside the home, there was little if no change in home management.[14] Desai states:

> Traditionally food processing was women's work. Women have been involved in cleaning grinding, and powdering grains and condiments: cleaning salting and drying of fish once it comes ashore; and preserving fruits and vegetables. Thus in spite of increasing education citizenry rights and employment in the workforce the familial role still gets precedence over the work role (1996: 107)

Echoing Desai, the economist Amartya Sen (2005: 235) states that unequal sharing of household *chores* has remained part of the Indian family tradition. Women were, and are, still primarily responsible to looking after the home, the children, the provisioning of the household and the preparation of food. Sen says:

> It is quite common in many societies to take for granted that while man will naturally work outside the home, it is acceptable for women to do this if, and only if, they can engage in the work in addition to their inescapable and unequally shared household duties (2005: 238).

However Sen does concede that "in reality women working outside the home and earning an income tends to have powerful impact on enhancing women's standing and voice in decision making, both within the household, and in society" (2005: 238). While the Indian family has remained resistant to change, and the primary roles for women in India are as wives and mothers, it almost appears as though working women in Bangalore have read Sen, for in Bangalore city, in the past five years, there have been signs of more men learning to look after children and keeping house.[15] But still, domestic cooking and family provisioning remains, by and large, a female realm.

As Dharamjit Singh, chef and expert on Indian food notes, Indian recipes are complex, often using many ingredients and spices, and many different cooking methods, such as roasting, baking, flash frying, steaming, and so on, in combination so they fuse into complex, layered flavours (Singh, 1970). Often, in traditional joint families in India, many women of the family would gather together; sisters-in-law, mothers-in-law, young adult women, and aged female relatives, to create the meal for the family. Faced with the daunting task of preparing a complex, many tiered meal of time consuming preparation alone, contemporary Indian women find themselves ordering food from local restaurants, or relying on "heat and eat" foods or asking family members such as mothers and elderly relatives to cook and servants to help them.

In the diasporic Indian family, the links between motherhood and provisioning (Taylor, Layne and Wozniak, 2004) are engaged somewhat differently as nuclear Indian families find themselves with no family members, extended kin or servants to help. With most Indian families having two working parents, and children engaged in extracurricular activities required to get them into "good" colleges, the family is constantly harassed for time. But Indian women, in the diasporic context, are usually expected both by their families and by themselves, to run the household whether they work outside the home or not. In Boston, Indian women often tried to cook Indian dishes but chose easy recipes that could be done in a few minutes often substituting frozen vegetables for fresh, to cut the preparation time. Some women I interviewed confessed to preparing a whole week's worth of food on Sunday, and freezing it so that an Indian meal was just microwave seconds away during the hectic weekday schedule.

The "time crunch" for both urban Indian women and their diasporic counterparts is very real, and food manufacturers are tapping into this demand. Food manufacturer Amin states, "We recognized that more and more couples were working and had less time to spend in the kitchen. Now we get so much fan mail saying that these prepared meals are a lifesaver."[16] The overwhelming pressure that most Indian woman feel to get an Indian meal on the table in a few minutes, is underlined by author Lavina Melwani in her article titled "Retouch of Curry." Melwani (2004) says:

> Indeed, it must be hard for Indian families to give up the cultural tradition of cooking fresh food every day, but in this new world you don't have the retinue of servants nor do you have the time to always whip up an elaborate meal from scratch, weeping as you chop the onions.[17]

The fear of loss of the "real" food that this "quickie" cuisine implies is poignantly echoed in Melwani's article. She states:

> But what about "real" food—that authentic home cuisine, those heavenly delights which each Indian American family hands down, those wonderful pots of comfort food that tastes like no other food in the world? What about those flavorful South Indian rasams..? The layered, perfumed Hyderabadi biryani that has been made for generations in your family? Are all these an endangered species in the frenetic hustle bustle of America where time and

attention spans are short and where for many cooking means simply pressing the microwave button? Will the cooking of authentic regional home food become a lost language?[18]

As we can see from the excerpts what I term "meta-narratives of loss," invest the provisioning of the South Asian families. Fears of loss of a rather loose concept of "Indian" culture and family values tends to drive food choices. It is better to eat Indian food than any other food. This explains the ready acceptance of pre-packaged foods by the cosmopolitan Indian family. Melwani ends her article with a paen to the grocer who stocks ready to eat Indian food.

> So the next time you're on deadline and have no time to cook and don't have the desire to eat yet another turkey sandwich or slice of pizza, holler for your invisible personal chef. No need to chop and cut; all the exercise your fingers have to do is open up the boxes and zap the microwave button. Huge succulent *samosas* stuffed with cheese and jalapeno peppers, plates of steaming *daal makhani*, *palak paneer* and an array of crisp *parathas*, *rotis* and *naan*. Or perhaps you'd prefer fluffy *idlis*, golden *dosas*, *uttampams* and some spicy *rasam*? No problem, it's all in the box. Spread out your fit for a king feast on the dining table and then say a silent prayer of thanks to your Indian grocer![19]

Prepared and packaged Indian food has become the food of the everyday in the cosmopolitan Indian urban family, in Bangalore and in Boston. That these foods are consumed within loosely knit "ethnic" communities in diasporic or urban contexts allows for a fluid semiotics open to innovation to invest the consumption of the food (Douglas, 1972; 1975). These are changes that are legitimated because they allow for the travel of the food across the world, and the foods are not subject to regulatory strictures of purity and pollution of caste and religion based authenticity (Toomey, 1992) and "orthodox" consumption of their "original" sending contexts.

The Social History of Indian Packaged Foods

A whole range of social, economic, and cultural changes have taken place in India over the past fifty years, culminating in the economic boom of the past decade.[20] In 1989 the Indian economy was "liberalized" after nearly fifty years of independence and Soviet style protectionism. Perhaps by design or perhaps coincidentally, since then the Indian economy has seen significant growth rising from 2 percent in 1990 to 7.8 percent in 2001.[21] Emergent during this sudden liberalization, was a new packaged prepared food industry that has grown rapidly in the past decade and a half. However, the prepared food market in India is still in its nascent stage, with only 5 percent of the food market is packaged and branded. Indian players see a staggering 95 percent of product still to be packaged and enormous profits to be made. The Indian Tobacco Industry,[22] a recent entrant into the world of packaged foods, announced that they see a huge market potential for these foods among the middle classes of urban India and among NRIs (Non Resident Indians, the local term for the diaspora). Ravi Naware, head of the Indian Tobacco Industry (ITC) food development sector projected the growth of the ITC segment alone of the packaged food industry to be Rs 500 *crores* (approximately $10 million). He stated in a press conference:

> Certainly, there is a close linkage (between economic development and food). As the disposable income goes up, standard of life improves and consumers . . . start looking for packed food that are reliable and of good quality'. . . . Firstly, the market for food is simply huge and estimated to be Rs 500,000 *crore* annually. It is also growing for two main reasons: population growth and improvement in consumers' spending ability. Consumers, more and more, are looking for packaged food because of hygiene, nutrition and convenience.[23]

The indigenous packaged food industry takes Indian recipes, simplifies them for fast production, and decreases the time and cost to the consumer. The industry includes food products for immediate consumption, as well as pre-prepared foods such snacks, spice powders, lentil wafers, pickles, and chutneys. The Indian pre-prepared food industry is divided along caste and ethnic and micro regional lines of affiliations. Preparation of these indigenous prepared foods has become a local cottage industry for cooperatives of women (many of them home makers and widows) who are subcontracted to work for larger local food preparation companies (Srinivas, 2002). Local entrepreneurs, many of them women, often employ poor women from the targeted caste or ethnic group to prepare the product so it has an authentic taste. Today in local markets in urban India over three hundred companies do business and middle and lower middle class housewives rely on these mixes and snacks to provide food for the family.

The prepared food industry has an eager large clientele in urban America in the South Asian diaspora. According to Neil Soni, vice president of House of Spices, for "wholesalers to retailers, it's possibly a $15 million market, while for the retailers it could be a $25 million market. It's a good component with lots of growth opportunities." The February 2006 issue of *Little India* the self proclaimed "largest circulated Indian publication in the USA," aimed at the South Asian diasporic readership ran a feature article titled "The Immigrant *Thali*" by Lavinia Melwani. In the article Melwani quotes Madhu Gadia, the health editor of "Diabetes Living" the article states that Indians have started eating far more prepared foods than ever before. Gadia states that Indian food is catching on even in the "heartland" of America. In her home town of Ames, Iowa where "many of the supermarkets and coops carry frozen and canned Indian foods," Gadia states: "these are becoming part of the everyday home food of busy Indian families." She says that she knows of many friends who "carry the shelf stabilized ready Indian meals to work often." In the same article, Julie Sahni, chef, author, food historian, and culinary celebrity, states:

> I think what has happened is that they (Indians) are buying a tremendous amount of ready made foods because people with busy schedules still need to have something nice to put on the dinner table...These are family people buying ready made food. So there is a need and it is being fulfilled. There are some very good products out there very tasty and authentic tasting in both shelf stabilized and frozen.

Food manufacturers in India and in the US scour the Indian food market for prepared foods that can be marketed to the growing Indian diaspora. Shwetal Patel of Raja Foods says:

> Our best bread is going to be something we discovered in Delhi, called the *Papad Paratha*, a *paratha* with *papad* inside it. Trust me, it's unbelievable! We're also coming out with *paneer* and potato wraps. These will be great for people on the go, such as college students,

and the taste is really good. It's solid Indian *paneer* (home made cheese) which tastes delicious.

Most of the packaged food in the urban India and diasporic market is sourced in India. MTR (The Mavalli Tiffin Rooms) one of the oldest players in the packaged food market specializes in South Indian cuisine. The Bangalore based[24] MTR prepared food line is owned and operated by the Mayya family; an Udupi Brahmin family from coastal western Karnataka.[25] Members of the Mayya family have gone through rigorous hospitality and hotel management courses in Europe and America, and bring modern ideas and technologies to increase the MTR market share (Kohn, 1999). In the past few years MTR has come to dominate the South Indian niche of the prepared food market. With their wide range of product categories and with a consistent track record of good quality products, the brands of MTR have made substantial in-roads to markets overseas such as U.S.A., U.K., Gulf, Far East (Singapore, Malaysia), Australia etc. Other Indian companies that have product lines that are sold transnationally are Gits (ready mixes), MDH (for curry powders), Maya, Mothers, and Priya (pickles and sauces).[26]

But not all Indian food packaged food comes from India or even from the subcontinent. Patak is an international family owned packaged food company started by a twice immigrant in London, UK, that exports packaged Indian food all over the world. Patak's owns several manufacturing facilities—a frozen food factory in Dundee, an Indian bread factory in Glasgow, the head office in Haydock, Lancashire and an £18 million investment in a new state of the art food processing factory in London which at 164,000 sq ft, is believed to be the largest Indian food factory in the world. Within a year Patak's project that they will manufacture 30 million jars of Indian sauce, produce over 1.5 million ready meals, over 1 million Indian snacks, and use 2,700 tons of spice from around the world. Patak's states that it manufactures its products primarily for the Indian women "who needs more time." The Patak's website states:

> Patak's, a household brand name in the UK, is fast becoming recognised around the world for creating authentic Indian food that is quick and easy to prepare. Our popular cooking sauces, curry pastes, *chutneys*, pickles, *naan* bread and *pappadums* make it easy for food lovers everywhere to prepare authentic Indian dishes at home *in less than 35 minutes.*[27] (Italics mine).

The biggest overseas manufacturer of Indian food in the USA is believed to be Deep Foods. Deep Foods has a 100,000 square feet facility in Union, NJ, where it produces several lines—*Mirch Masala*, Deep and Curry Classics, as well as the Green Guru International Cuisine line, other frozen food lines such as Maharani and Kawon Malaysian *parathas*. Raja Foods, based in Skokie, Ill, a suburb of Chicago has been in business since 1992 and imports frozen foods from India under the ubiquitous Swad label. According to Swetal Patel of Raja Foods, Swad has the largest variety of frozen vegetables in the market, especially ethnic products like, *tindora, papdi lilva, valor papdi, chauri and tandal jo ni bhaji*, vegetables which are a part of traditional Gujarati cuisine. These come fresh from the farms in Gujarat and are much easier to prepare since they are already cleaned and cut.[28] Swad is part of the latest trend in prepared frozen Indian food and ingredients. According to Ms. Melwani in her essay titled, "The Cold Revolution," flash freezing techniques delivers "fresh" Indian food to your door in any part of the world making Indian food quick and easy to prepare.[29] "Ethnic" grocery stores, which previously stocked varieties of raw ingredients are turning more rapidly to flash frozen, packaged, and prepared foods. According to Neil Soni, vice president of "House of Spices," frozen prepared foods are the "next big thing;" "Wholesalers to retailers, it's possibly a $15 million market, while for the retailers it could be a $25 million market. It's a good component with lots of growth opportunities." Soni believes that the Indian market is evolving into what the mainstream consumers already expect from their supermarkets.[30]

The Anxieties and Unintended Consequences of Cosmopolitan Consumption

Multiculturalism and cosmopolitanism creates anxiety because they expose us to new ways of being in, and seeing the world. In the contemporary world, large populations of people live in diasporas, in exile, in migration for all sorts of reasons, self-chosen or not. Clifford describes this condition as a world where syncretism and parodic invention have become the rule rather than the exception, where everyone's "roots" are in some degree cut, and therefore it has become *"increasingly difficult to attach human identity and meaning to a coherent 'culture'"* (Clifford, 1988: 95). The paradox of the cosmopolitan in an existing multicultural context is that as the local becomes less significant physically, the memory and the imagination of that place become stronger. As people are living abroad or away from what they consider their "home culture", the idea of "homeland" becomes an important nucleus for nostalgic sentiment.

The anxiety of cosmopolitanism in the case of the Indian family appears to be centered on food consumption. Food provisioning and food consumption in South Asian families are couched in what I call "narratives of anxiety"—who is eating, how much, and what they are eating—are questions laced with anxiety for South Asian parents.

When I interviewed Prabhakar and his wife Sathya, both from the city of Chennai in South India, they expressed anxiety about their children's eating habits. Prabhakar said: "Pasta, that's all they eat. Night and day…pasta. How can they eat it, I don't know." The second problem parents encounter is cultural and aesthetic—getting children to eat caste and regionally based appropriate Indian food. Sathya, Prabhakars' wife, spoke to this concern: "The children don't eat Indian food at all, let alone South Indian food. They want macaroni and cheese all the time. Or pizza." When I attended a Diwali party for Indian couples and their children, in November 2005, the talk turned naturally among the women to the "problem" of getting their children to eat the "right" Indian food. Uma, a South Indian upper caste woman said of her six year old son Vijay: "He will eat Indian food only if it is from the packages, so Kannan (her husband) and I go every weekend to the Indian store and we stock up on *palak panner*, *malai kofta*, *chola puri* and all that. All North Indian food he likes. My mother was shocked when she came to visit us. She also tried convincing him to eat "home" food (i.e. South Indian Brahmin food) but he refused. She told me "How can you let him do this?" Uma voiced her disappointment that her child not only refused to eat home cooked food, preferring the packaged alternatives, but that he refused to eat *South Indian* food. She felt she was a bad mother, and had not provided proper direction to his choices of ethnic affiliation, allowing him to eat North Indian Punjabi food when he was a South Indian Tamil Brahmin. These "narratives of affili-ative desire" where South Asian mothers see their children's choice of food as a desire for affiliation with another ethnic community, are contentious. With adult children, Indian parents often feel that they have lost the battle to inculcate the children into eating "their" food. Sanjay, a young adult lives with his parents while he goes to college. While his parents come from a strict Brahmin vegetarian family, Sanjay eats only non vegetarian food. His mother Saraswati often buys him food from Indian restaurants, and packaged food of the "heat and eat" variety from the Indian grocery stores. "That's all he eats," she said matter-of-factly while picking up twenty frozen Indian chicken and lamb entree dinners at the local Indian store. "He won't eat our south Indian *rasam, sambhar. Avanakei ishtame illai.* He does not like it. If he doesn't have this, he'll heat up a pepperoni pizza."

For the children on the other hand, the eating of Indian food, especially in the company of others, either not of your own culture or ethnic type, or those who are "hipper" and more westernized than you, presents a series of shameful moments. For example, Anjana Mathur editor of "Food Matters" recounts her own shame filled tale of desiring a tuna salad sandwich in her lunchbox in the hope that it would make her just like her white Australian classmates. She states:

> In April 1982, my family moved away from Penang, Malaysia. When I first started carrying lunch to school, my mother would pack a lunch consisting of rice and *dahl* and rice and yogurt into a *tiffin-dubba*, a split-level metal lunch container. My white Australian classmates would look on in curiosity at my "weird" lunch in a "strange" container. My rice and *dahl* were nothing like the tuna fish sandwiches they would carry in their pink plastic lunchboxes adorned by the likes of Strawberry Shortcake. Over time, the snickering and odd looks became too much, and I begged my mother to buy me a plastic lunchbox and to let me have tuna fish sandwiches. Eventually she relented, and when the day finally arrived that I had tuna for lunch, I was visibly excited; I was that much closer to losing my status as "Other" and becoming like my white classmates, or so I believed. But upon opening my lunchbox, I found something entirely different. My mother had "Indianized" my lunch and created a bright yellow tuna fish sandwich filling spiced with green chilies, cilantro, chopped onion, and turmeric.

Anjana's chagrin at the Indianized tuna is captured in a poignant paragraph about her "otherness."

> In my school setting, food was a visible way to mark ethnicity and difference. When I look back on my curried tuna sandwiches, they were my mother's attempt to combine Indianness with apparently "Western" fare. I wanted them to help me try to assimilate, but ironically, they merely reinforced my otherness.

As the cultural critic Frank Wu (2002) notes, our ideas of diversity conflict with our actual practices of tolerating diversity, and what the mainstream might consider intolerable, unethical, unpalatable, and inedible, determines what we eat. The articu-lation of the real difficulties involved in confronting difference in understanding foodways is central to the story of the negotiation of cosmopolitanism (Bestor, 2001). Wu concludes, "Our festivals of diversity tend toward the superficial, as if America were a stomach-turning combination plate of grits, tacos, sushi, and humus. We fail to consider the dilemma of diversity where our principles conflict with our practices" (216).

So in a multi cultural arena, the Indian packaged food becomes, as Appadurai states, "*chimerical, aesthetic, even fantastic objects*" (Appadurai, 1996: 35) where strong feelings of longing are located for the displaced. The food represents "an important symbolic anchor to imagined homelands."[31] Consumption of these foods becomes in some sense "sacramental" (Berger, 2001)—a return to a "taken for granted" identity of the homeland. So as cosmopolitanism increases, a hyper caste based local Indian identity asserts itself in consumption located affectively in gastro-nostalgia. In this globalized state of re-territorialization, imagination and fantasy become a necessary alternative for "the real thing" (which is also imagined as Anderson [2005] points out). I want to emphasise that, in multicultural cities, "parodic" inventions such as these packaged foods have substituted for the real food of the homeland. It would appear that authenticity is not questioned, as long as the copies that appear authentic are provided, as symbolic anchors on which identification can unfold.

Authentic Mothers, Narratives of Subterfuge, and False Memories

But authenticity is central to the problem of multiculturalism in more ways than one. In Bangalore the packaged Indian foods serve other social desires linked in part to anxiety over authenticity. In May 2004, when I was in Bangalore, I was invited to a dinner party at the home of an old friend, Rashmi, who is now a manager at a Fortune 500 software company. She had invited several, elderly, family members, and some friends for dinner. The food was excellent; cooked in a traditional manner, and the meal comprised of many of the traditional South Indian, Iyengar, Brahmin, vegetarian dishes that were part of festival menus such as *Bisibelebhath, Puliyogare, Kootu, Kosambari,* and so on. I was surprised at her choices since I knew her to be a cosmopolitan eater who was not very interested in traditional cooking. Everyone complimented her on the meal discussing how well cooked all the dishes were, and how they tasted "just like her grandmother used to make them." They asked for her recipes, which she coyly refused to divulge. When all the guests had left, I helped her clean up and went into her kitchen where I found twenty opened packages from MTR Packaged food division, known for their "authentic" tasting South Indian cuisine, strewn all over the kitchen counter. Rashmi winked at me to keep the secret of her "home cooked" meal. I found Rashmi was not the only young working woman who resorted to MTR packaged foods when they wanted to create an impression of having cooked authentic, traditional, home cooked meals for their in-laws and other visitors. Kalpana, was Punjabi woman from Delhi in North India, had lived in Bangalore for twenty years. In 2004, her in-laws visited her from Delhi, and for weeks before their visit she asked all her South Indian friends for recipes. Apparently, Kalpana's in-laws were convinced that since she lived in Bangalore, she must know how to cook South Indian food. But Kalpana herself never bothered to learn the intricacies of South Indian cuisine because she was surrounded by it everyday. When her in-laws arrived, I found that Kalpana had made an enormous breakfast of *idlis, dosas,* and other South Indian delicacies for her guests and they praised her "authentic Madrasi" food—"*Kithni acchi hai na?* So good … almost she can start Madrasi restaurant in Dilli (Delhi)." Kalpana herself confided in me that she had bought the whole MTR line of packaged instant South Indian food before they arrived, and had spent the past week mastering the amount of water and *ghee* (clarified butter) she needed to add to each dish.

In Bangalore the MTR "heat and eat" south Indian line of dishes have become the modern housewife's guilty secret. The MTR packaged food promotes secrecy and subterfuge among certain women whereby a façade of authenticity and traditional eating is maintained when in fact multiculturalism and cosmopolitanism have changed both eating and cooking habits (Cwiertka, 1998; Curtin and Heidke, 1992). These "narratives of subterfuge" allow South Asian women to remain socially acceptable models of domesticity, when in actuality the loss of traditional knowledge of recipes, cooking ingredients, and methods, is wide spread and inter-generational. When I asked an older friend of mine for her *rasam* (lentil broth) spice powder that I thought she made from scratch at home, she told me that she got it made to order by a caterer and had never even thought to ask the recipe. She added: "Oh, now I don't even bother to ask him. I just go to Food World (the local supermarket) and buy the MTR *rasam* powder mix." However, in the larger society, the expectations of women still being able to produce an "authentic," micro regional, caste based meal, is still evident. The disjuncture between societal expectations and the reality are bridged by the readily available, culturally accurate, packaged foods. The parody of a continuous tradition is kept alive for these cosmopolitans (James, 1996; Nestle, 2002).

Authentic Mothers and Gastro-Nostalgia

So this raises the problem of the authentic in cosmopolitan consumption: to most people authenticity resides in the ability to recognise it. Regina Bendix (1997), a folklorist who argues for a legitimation of the discipline of folklore, states that; "in an increasingly transcultural world, where Zulu singers back up Paul Simon and where indigenous artists seek copyright for their traditional crafts, the politics of authenticity mingles with the forces of the market," and that declaring that something is "authentic," legitimates it, and by reflection, adds more status and legitimacy to the authenticator as well (Bendix, 1997: 10). The problem for Bendix is "what does authenticity do?" both for the authenticator and the authenticated. So while authenticity can be the search for something lost as in the case of Shaila, it is also, paradoxically, the legitimation of something existant such as in the case of Rashmi and Kalpana.

The question of the authentic (Handler, 1986) arises primarily about how it is created or manufactured. Rachel Laudan argues that culinary authenticity, (Laudan, 2000) is framed in the terms espoused by the viewer, or eater: as she says, Americans tend to say it's authentic if it is artisanal, pre-industrial, uses indigenous ingredients, and no processed foods. It is also to us "historical"—meaning, what people used to eat, preferably familial, rural, regional foods, and now, natural and organic are added to the list of requirements. We set up this checklist, she says, because we contrast the "sunny days of yore with the grey industrial present." Italians too, according to Alessandra Guignoni, travel to Sardinia for a taste of an imagined past, for what she calls "naïve" cooking, simple, genuine, the core of "what Italians really are" (Guignoni, 2001). The retrieving of a pre-modern self located in earlier caste based and agricultural rhythms located in the highly local through cuisine, is part of the push against the anxiety that modernity and globalization bring. As globalization erodes the traditional notions of hierarchy, breaking down caste barriers through commensality and marriage (see M.N. Srinivas, 2003), the anxiety over identity becomes rooted in the symbolic value of consumption (Giddens, 1991). The retrieving of the self through the eating of the cuisine of one's caste, ethnic group, region, and locale, becomes a precious experience. So in Bangalore as in Boston, foodways and the eating of ethnic Indian food epitomizes a personal, a local, or a caste based utopia, a cultural utopia that can be either the pure and simple peasant like (whether Tamil *rasam*[32] or Gujarati *rotli nu shaak*[33]), or the high aesthetic culture of the elite (*Mughlai* cream *Burra kebab*). The utopian ideal of a lost time is engaged through gastro nostalgia and the eating of foods (Roy, 2004) that symbolize this lost golden era, thereby catering to the gestalt of loss and memory that is part of the cosmopolitan's narrative. Loss and retrieval are built on the idea that there is something to retrieve that is unchanged; that is essential, and essentializing the narrative of self and other is at the core of fighting anomie in a multicultural space.[34] As Lindholm argues so convincingly in his work on authenticity, the search for new taste becomes a "moral imperative as the performance of difference through new and authentic foods is seen as valuable in itself." Further, recovering and maintaining the authentic food of any ethnic group, caste, family, locale, region etc. is seen as a "good" enterprise leading to knowledge and awareness.[35] Creating and exploiting nostalgia yearning, for a local culture and cuisine perceived as all but lost makes travel to such places both a pleasure and an urgent duty.

One of the key ingredients of the descriptions of foods that appeal to gastro-nostalgia is the evoking of "home cooking" or as "mother made it." The Indian diasporic market and the urban Indian market are dynamic because Indians like Indian food. Melwani argues that Indian immigrants "cling to the food as talisman and mantras, substituting mother and father. How vitalized they feel when they cook *daal chaval* just like mother! Or the *kaju barfi* that grandma specialty. They hold that wonderful taste in their mouths, lose their eyes and are transported back home." Melwani states: "millions and millions of *samosas, kachoris, dosas* and *idlis*—made in India and quick frozen—delivered to your door in California, London or Dubai, almost as fresh as those made by your dear *Amma!*"[36]

Besides the prepared food industry, Indian internet sites have chat rooms devoted to "foods as my mother made them." One of the largest internet sites with over 36,000 recipes is called "Ammas.com" (*amma* meaning Mother). Ammas.com begins with a narrative about this "authentic" grandmotherly character behind all the recipes for south Indian cooking on the site.

> *Amma* is the original Amma on the Internet—having started her web site in 1996. Her advice and recipes are authentic, culled from the mind of an authentic "Amma." "Amma" in South India (and many other parts of Asia) means "mother." Amma was born in a small village (by Indian standards) near Vijayawada, in the South Indian State of Andhra Pradesh. In fact, *Amma* comes from a long line of powerful women, known for their strength both in and

outside the kitchen. Her grandmother ("*Ammama*") was a freedom fighter and revolutionary. She is especially remembered for her efforts to protect women's rights. She was well-known for her *Kalagoora Pulusu* (mixed vegetables in tamarind sauce) and dry fish or mutton curries which she would prepare for the field hands during the rice-threshing season (known as Kuppalu)." (Excerpt from ammas.com)

The familial link of mother and grandmother are mentioned to authenticate and legitimate the recipes and the food. Food and its emotional association with mothers and grandmothers, is the fodder for eager food merchants, as they recreate in a public realm what was previously the food of the home. Images of mothers become touchstones for the authenticity of thee cuisine. Gastro nostalgia as related to mothers' home cooking is paradoxically the crux of the prepared food industry, as the symbolic and affective value of "foods as mother made them" is invaluable. As more and more cosmopolitan women are haunted by a sense of loss of what they cannot reclaim, they turn to "authentic" food to reclaim their identity (Kurien, 2003; Yalman, 1989; Khare, 1976).

Shashi Tharoor states that Indian expatriates and migrants live in a nostalgic world: ". . . nostalgia is based on the selectiveness of memory . . . his (the immigrants) perspective is distorted by exile . . . his view of what used to be home is divorced from the experience of home. They are no longer an organic part of the culture, but severed digits that, in their yearning for the hand, can only twist themselves into a clenched fist" (Tharoor, 1993). He writes with sensitivity of the migrants' response to a dominant culture is a reiteration of the latter's own culture. Tharoor says: "But his nostalgia is based on the selectiveness of memory; it is a simplified, idealized recollection of his roots, often reduced to their most elemental—family, caste, region, religion. In exile amongst foreigners, he clings to a vision of what he really is that admits no foreignness" (Tharoor, 1993).

Salman Rushdie argues that fantasy helps the Indian living in diaspora and migrant Indians to relive the India of the imagination (Kakar, 1996) based on semi truths, stories and heard accounts that are strongly based on the local. For the Indian cosmopolitan, fantasy is an important narrative structure to assuage the ambivalence of the cosmopolitan over the loss of family and place. As growing number of groups claim cosmopolitan status, cosmopolitanism gets broadened to include the growth of particularistic cultural identities of all kinds. Therefore the "cosmopolitan" has come to "signify a transnationally situated subject who is nonetheless rooted in particular histories, localities, and community allegiances."[37] It means the world (or a big part of it) is a field of interaction where people's identities can escape the confines of nationalism, allowing for both a local and a global identity simultaneously.

Are We What We Eat? Some Thoughts By Way of a Conclusion

So, paradoxically, as the local fades further and further away for cosmopolitans, the memory and the imagination of family, mother and place become more powerful. Self consciously searching for their roots—ethnic, local, and caste based—these memories become located in the emotional and gustatory link between mother and family, symbolically located in a cultural utopia of loss. The prepared food industry packages authentic foods of their particular caste and ethnic, regional group, so that cosmopolitan working women can come home and cook a "home cooked meal" to reclaim their identity for themselves and their children. This produces a limited and circumscribed authentic experience. While these food companies cater to gastro-nostalgics, and support the diversity of caste and regional foods, they (unwittingly) support a conceptual division of India, into micro regions, religious and caste based groups, which runs counter to the discourse of nationalism that pervades the anthropological literature on South Asia (Appadurai, 1988; Inden, 1990; Mankekar, 1999).

The overriding narrative of loss for cosmopolitans is detailed through the emotional loss of "home cooked" food that migrants feel. The availability of packaged "authentic" Indian food that echoes micro regional, caste, and ethnic variation of India enable urban Indians and diasporic Indians alike to indulge in "gastro-nostalgia" where the food recreates a cultural utopia exemplified by mothers' home cooking, located in the collective imagination of the ethnic community (Schivelbusch, 1992; Sahlins, 1990). The "narrative of affiliative desire"—of wanting one's child to eat the food of one's ethnic group is a powerful desire for these mothers.

It is clear that in the spaces of a global consumer-capitalist cosmopolitan society, mothers provide for their children primarily by providing purchased food. Motherhood offers unique practices that resist ready analysis since they reveal, by the "very manner in which they transgress,"[38] the contours of a deeply rooted ideological opposition between that which is recognized as "real," good motherhood and the "corrupting" influence of consumption. Because of this "deep rooted belief in the opposition between consumption and motherhood," the rules governing consumption, especially the choices made by the mother on behalf of the child, are often the "cause of much anxiety for mothers" (Warner, 2005). South Asian mothers I have shown, are no different in their anxieties over consumption and they face new challenges in a cosmopolitan world as they attempt to retain a sense, not of nationality; i.e., of Indianness or Pakistaniness, but more of regional and local identity i.e., Punjabi-ness or Bengali-ness, through food consumption. The "narrative of subterfuge" that runs through the preparation of a "traditional" meal points to the complete pragmatic acceptance of caste and regional based packaged foods by South Asian women, while they attempt to remain socially acceptable models of feminine domesticity.

Rephrasing the nineteenth century gourmand Billat-Savarin's assertion—"you are what you eat"—I have attempted to shed new light on consumption, memory and identity, through stories that might speak to the ways in which migrants and their families use food to explore the classed, ethnic, caste based, regional, and gendered dimensions of their personal and collective identities. The consuming of these packaged foods point to a new way of "being" Indian in a transnational space.

Notes

1. This essay is dedicated to my mother, Rukmini Srinivas, who is not only a great cook, but is also interested in culinary and cultural landscapes.
2. See L. Srinivas (2005) for a comprehensive and thought provoking argument on the locally situated and the global.

3. This research was supported in part by the Pew Charitable Trust and the Smith Richardson Foundation. I thank Peter Berger of the Center for the Study of Religion and World Affairs of Boston University for his support of my interest in food in Bangalore and his encouragement when I decided to study the gastro-scapes of Bangalore as part of a ten nation comparative study of cultural globalization that he directed in 1998 and 1999. Subsequent data collection has been funded in part by Wheaton College. I thank my colleagues at Boston University, Merry White and Charles Lindholm for supporting me in writing this paper and for reading its many incarnations. I have benefited enormously through discussions with Lakshmi Srinivas and many of these discussions were the fuel for this paper. I also would like to thank Professor Gopal Karanth of Institute of Social and Economic Change, Bangalore, for his unstinting help in understanding the Bangalore food industry. Dhanvanti Nayak did the initial research on food in Bangalore that led me to look at packaged food. Jyothi Kadambi and Aruna and Krishna Chidambi brought some of these packaged foods to my attention. Kala Sunder helped me enormously by pointing out interesting articles on food in the Bangalore newspapers and sending me newspaper clippings.

4. See Kibria (2003).

5. Statistics drawn from Kibria (2003).

6. I borrow this phrase from the title of a book on South Asian Americans by Shankar and Srikanth (1998) brought to my attention by Nazli Kibria.

7. For a more detailed account of the US census as related to the city of Boston refer http://www.ci.boston.ma.us/BRA/pdf/publications//pdr_547.pdf

8. Altogether it is estimated that there are about between 150 and 300 software firms in Bangalore, the majority of which are medium-sized, i.e. between 100 and 150 employees and only about 10 per cent of which have over 500 employees (interviews). More than two-thirds of the companies in Bangalore are Indian. The foreign component of total investment in the software industry, however, is about 70 percent (*Economist*, March 23rd, 1996: 67). For a comprehensive history of Bangalore city, refer to S. Srinivas (2001).

9. Population statistics derived from Megacities Taskforce of the International Geographical Union. http://www.megacities.uni-koeln.de/internet/

10. Scholars put the number of the Indian middle class anywhere between 100 to 250 million, a significant number by any standard.

11. In a recent paper I chart the changes in the cosmopolitan gastro-scape of Bangalore (Srinivas to be published 2007 in Food, Culture and Society) from the early 1990s to the present. I suggested that non domestic eating for Bangaloreans has become a moral quest in which adaptive creativity and innovation in the face of the attempted domination of multi national food firms—socio historical processes that I examine in the paper cited above. Here, however, what is important to note is that the moral quest for identity in the transnational frame is central to gustatory activity in Bangalore.

12. I have benefited greatly from conversations I have had with my colleague Lakshmi Srinivas.

13. Shah (1998) argues that the decline of the joint family while accepted by sociologists in India is not quite the case. The situation is far more complex and the joint family endures and in fact many new joint families are created. Yet it appears that the cosmopolitan nuclear family is growing especially in urban India. For a fuller scholarly exposition on the Indian family see Shah (1998).

14. But while women worked outside the home less than 1 percent had a long term career strategy, because they felt these positions conflicted with their roles as wives and mothers in the home.

15. See Nair, Deepti. "Behind every Successful Woman…" *Deccan Herald*. *Metrolife* March 7, 2005. "Amit Heri, musician, is married to noted dancer Madhu Heri Natraj. When Madhu is away travelling, Heri has always chipped in with the housework and believes it is but a natural thing. "What is meant by traditional? I don't go by what you'd call traditional."

16. Melwani, Lavina. *Little India*. "Hot and Cold". http://www.littleindia.com/october2004/hotcold.htm

17. Melwani, Lavina. *Little India*. "Hot and Cold". http://www.littleindia.com/october2004/hotcold.htm

18. Melwani, Lavina. *Little India*. "Re Touch of Curry". September 2003. http://littleindia.com/september2003/Retouch%20of%20Curry.htm

19. Melwani, Lavina. *Little India*. "Hot and Cold". http://www.littleindia.com/october2004/hotcold.htm

20. The Indian economy has reached a growth rate of about 5 percent and inflation has fallen to under 2.8 percent in November 1999, the lowest in the decade. The latest Asian Development Bank figures report India's potential growth at over 7 percent whereby the Indian economy will be on a par with China in another two years, something that has not occurred since 1990.

21. Specialists in Indian economics, such as Jagdish Bhagwati, Deepak Lal, and Ashutosh Varshney warn that the bubble of this economy may well burst unless pursued thoroughly by the Indian government. But India has pursued the free trade alternatively vigorously though cautiously opening the economy carefully and instituting new economic policies that are market friendly, private investment driven, and that cover internal and external trade relations.

22. Historically this parallels the entry of tobacco interests into prepared food in the 1970s and 1980s in the United States as RJR Reynolds and other tobacco companies diversified into prepared foods.

23. *Deccan Herald* July 21 http://www.itcportal.com/newsroom/press_july21.htm
24. "Mavalli Tiffin Rooms" as it was known was famous all over south India for cooking their food in clarified butter and serving their customers in silver utensils, practices associated with "good" and "pure" upper caste Brahmin food ways. Rumours swirled that the Mayya's recipes came from the kitchens of the famous Krishna temple at Udipi where over 5000 pilgrims are fed everyday with fifty different kinds of rice, salads, vegetarian curries, fruit chutneys, and accompaniments. MTR's cuisine was and is very micro region specific and is located in what is called Dakshina Kannada on the western coast of Karnataka. This region is famous in south India both for their innovative mixing of sweet, hot, and sour ingredients and the business acumen of their chefs. The popular joke in Karnataka acknowledging their ability is that if one climbs to the top of Mt. Everest one would find an Udipi hotelier there ready with a cup of steaming coffee to greet you in a spotless cotton dhoti. The cleanliness, commitment to quality and the business acumen, characterize the Udupi Brahmin food enterprise.
25. During the political Emergency in India the mid seventies, when Indira Gandhi suspended Individual rights one of the populist measures that the government brought in was to standardize and control the price for a cup of coffee. MTR hotel found it impossible to maintain its very high food standards at the ridiculously low prices enforced by the Food Control Act. But in order to keep funds flowing into his business, and to keep the cooks occupied, Sadanand got into the instant food business, and started experimenting with packaged mixes, a range of sambar and rasam powders, instant idli, dosa, chutney, and other mixes.
26. This is not an exhaustive list but merely illustrative.
27. http://www.pataks.co.uk/about/index.php
28. Melwani, Lavina. "Hot and Cold." http://www.littleindia.com/october2004/hotcold.htm
29. http://www.littleindia.com/october2004/hotcold.htm
30. Ethnic Indian prepared food is also considered the next big niche market in the USA to go mainline. Pillsbury is now actually making *naans* in India, and Kostos International is national distributor for the Pillsbury line. Says Kostos Vice President Jay Parikh, "Pillsbury has many ethnic lines, and one of them is Indian. They have a factory near Bombay and they have the experts in the field of Indian food and that's how they developed the recipes." Pillsbury has seven frozen products coming into the USA—a ready to puff *roti*, spring onion *parathas*, layered *Malabar parathas*, Adraki Alu parathas, tawa whole wheat parathas, stuffed spicy alu *masaledaar naan*, and a paneer-filled naan for the regular American market.
31. See "Imagining other places" by Rebecca Graversen. November 2001 at http://www.geocities.com/udeifelten/imaginingotherplaces
32. Lentil spicy soup eaten with rice.
33. Unleavened bread eaten with lentil (*dhal*) soup.
34. Robbins (1998) argues that the alternative to cosmopolitanism is not a romantic idea of strongly rooted belonging, but "a reality of (re)attachment, multiple attachment, or attachment at a distance" (1998: 3).
35. Thanks to Charles Lindholm (forthcoming, 2007).
36. Melwani Lavina. "The Cold Revolution." *Little India*.
37. See a review of Rajan and Sharma (2006) by Frances Assissi. March 17, 2006. http://www.indolink.com/displayArticleS.php?id=030106070622
38. For a complete analysis of consumption and motherhood see Tayler et al. (2004)

References

Achaya, K.T. (1994 [2005]), *Indian Food: A Historical Companion*. Delhi: Oxford University Press.
Allis, Sam. (2005), The Infancy of an Empire. *The Boston Globe*. November 6. Pg A3.
Anderson, E.N. (2005), *Everyone Eats: Understanding Food and Culture*. New York: New York University Press.
Appadurai, Arjun. (1981), Gastro Politics in Hindu South Asia. *American Ethnologist*, 8 (3): 494–511.
Appadurai, Arjun. (1986), *The Social Life of Things: Commodities in a Cultural Perspective*. Cambridge: Cambridge University Press.
Appadurai, Arjun. (1988), How to Make a National Cuisine: Cookbooks in Contemporary India. *Comparative Studies in Society and History*, 30 (10): 3–24
Appadurai, Arjun. (1996), *Modernity at Large: Cultural Dimensions of Globalization*. Minneapolis: University of Minnesota Press.
Bendix, Regina. (1997), *In Search of Authenticity*. Madison: University of Wisconsin Press.
Berger, Peter L. (1961), *The Precarious Vision: A Sociologist Looks at Social Fictions and Christian Faith*. Garden City, NY: Doubleday.
Berger, Peter. (1997), The Four Faces of Global Culture. *The National Interest*, 49 Fall: 23–9.
Berger, Peter ed. (2001), *Many Globalizations*. New York: Oxford University Press.
Bestor, Theodore C. (2001), Supply Side Sushi: Commodity Market and the Global City. *American Anthropologist*, 103 (1): 76–95.

Bourdieu, Pierre. (1984), *Distinction: A Social Critique of the Judgement of Taste*. Cambridge: MA. Harvard University Press.

Breckenridge, Carol, A. (1995), *Consuming Modernity: Public Culture in a South Asian World*. Minneapolis: University of Minnesota Press.

Clifford, James.(1988). The Predicament of Culture:Twentieth- Century Ethnography, Literature and Art. Cambridge, Harvard University press.

Counihan, C. and Van Esterik, P. (eds.) (1997), *Food and Culture: A Reader*. New York: Routledge.

Counihan, C. M. (1999), *The Anthropology of Food and the Body: Gender Meaning and Power*. New York: Routledge.

Curtin, D. and Heidke, L. eds. (1992), *Cooking Eating Thinking: Transformative Philosophies of Food*. Bloomington: Indiana University Press.

Cwiertka, K. J. (1998), How Cooking Became a Hobby: Changes in Attitude Toward Cooking in Early Twentieth Century Japan. In S. Fruhstuck and S. Linhart (eds.), *The Culture of Japan As Through Its Leisure*, (pp. 41–58). Albany: SUNY Press.

Desai, N. (1996), Women's Employment and their Familial Role in India. In A.M. Shah, B.S. Baviskar and E.A. Ramaswamy (eds.), *Social Structure and Change: Women in Indian Society*, (pp. 98–113). Delhi: Sage Publications.

Douglas, Mary. (1975), *Implicit Meanings*. London: Routledge and Paul.

Douglas, Mary. (1972), Deciphering a Meal. *Deadalus,* Winter 10: 61–81.

Elias, Norbert. (2000 [1939]), *The Civilising Process*. Oxford: Blackwell Publishers.

Ferro-Luzzi, G. (1977), Ritual As Language: The Case of South Indian Food Offerings. *Current Anthropology*, 18: 507–514.

Fuller, C. J. (1992), *The Camphor Flame: Popular Hinduism and Society in India*. Princeton: Princeton University Press.

Giddens, Anthony. (1991), *Modernity and Self-Identity: Self and Society in the Late Modern Age*. Palo Alto: Stanford University Press.

Goody, Jack. (1982), *Cooking Cuisine and Class. A Study in Comparative Sociology*. Cambridge: Cambridge University Press.

Guigoni, Alexandra. (2001). 'Food, drink and identity.' Europæa(1/2), 209–211.

Handler, Richard. (1986), Authenticity. *Anthropology Today* 2 (1): 2–4.

Hannerz, Ulf. (1992), *Cultural Complexity*. New York: Columbia University Press.

Hannerz, Ulf. (1996), *Transnational Connections*. London: Routledge.

Heitzman, James. (2004), *Network City. Planning the Information Society in Bangalore*. Oxford University Press.

Howes, David. (1996), *Cross Cultural Consumption: Global Markets Local Realities*. London: Routledge.

Inden, Ronald. (1990), *Imagining India*. Oxford: Basil Blackwell.

James, Alison. (1996), Cooking the Books: Global and Local Identities in Food Cultures. In Howes D. (ed.), *Cross-Cultural Consumption: Global Markets and Local Realities*. London: Routledge.

Kakar, Sudhir. (1996), *The Indian Psyche*. Delhi: Oxford University Press.

Khare, R. S. (1976), *The Hindu Hearth and Home*. Delhi: Vikas Publishing House.

Khare, R.S. (1992), *The Eternal Food: Gastronomic Ideas and Experiences of Hindus and Buddhists*. Albany: SUNY Press.

Kibria, Nazli. (2003), *Becoming Asian American: Second Generation Chinese and Korean American Identities*. Baltimore: Johns Hopkins University Press.

Kohn, Nancy, F. (1999), Henry Heinz and Brand Creation in the Late Nineteenth Century: Making Markets for Processed Food. *The Business History Review*, 73: 349–393.

Kothari, Rajni. (1991), State and Statelessness in our Time. *Economic and Political* Weekly, 11/12: 553–8.

Kripalani, Manjeet, and Engardio, Pete. (2003), The Rise of India. *Businessweek,* (8 December): 66–76.

Kurien, Prema. (2003), To be or not to be South Asian: Contemporary IndianAmerican Politics. *Journal of Asian American Studies*, 6 (3): 261–88.

Lamb, Sarah and Diane, Mines. (2002), *Everyday Life in South Asia*. Bloomington: Indiana University Press.

Laudan, R. (2000), Birth of the Modern Diet. *Scientific American,* 283 (2): 76–81.

Lindholm, Charles. (Forthcoming, 2007), *Eating the Queen's Rat and other Tales of Authenticity*. Boston: Basil Blackwell.

Lupton, Deborah. (1996), *Food, the Body and the Self*. London: Sage Publications.

Mankekar, Poornima. (1999), *Screening Culture Viewing Politics; An Ethnography of Television Womanhood and Nation in Postcolonial India*. Durham, NC: Duke University Press.

Melwani, Lavinia. (2004), *Hot and Cold: The hottest thing on Indian grocery shelves is Frozen*. October 5, 2004. http://www.littleindia.com/arts-entertainment/1508-hot-and-cold.html?print

Mintz, Sidney, W. (1996), *Tasting Food, Tasting Freedom: Excursions into Eating, Culture and the Past*. Boston: Beacon Press.

Nestle, Marion. (2002), *The Politics of Food. How the Food Industry influences Nutrition and Health*. CA: University of California Press.

Osella, Fillipo and Caroline, Osella. (2000), *Social Mobility in Kerala: Modernity and Identity in Conflict*. London: Pluto Press.

Rajan, Gita and Shailja, Sharma. (2006), *New Cosmopolitanisms: South Asians in the U.S.* Palo Alto: Stanford University Press.

Robbins, Bruce. (1998), Actually Existing Cosmopolitanism. In Pheng Cheah and Bruce Robbins (eds.), *Cosmopolitics: Thinking and Feeling Beyond the Nation*. Minneapolis: University of Minnesota Press.

Roy, Nilanjana. (2004), *A Matter of Taste: The Penguin Book of Indian Writing on Food*. Delhi: Penguin.

Sahlins, Marshall. (1990), Food as a Symbolic Code. In Jeffrey Alexander and Steven Seidman (eds.), *Culture and Society: Contemporary Debates*, (pp. 94–101). Cambridge: Cambridge University Press.

Schivelbusch, Wolfgang. (1992), Translated by David Jacobson. *Tastes of Paradise: A Social History of Spices, Stimulants and Intoxicants*. New York: Pantheon.

Sen, Amartya. (2005), *The Argumentative Indian; Writings on Indian History Culture and Identity*. New York: Farrar Strous and Giroux.

Shah, A.M. (1998), *The Family in India: Critical Essays*. Hyderabad: Orient Longman.

Shankar, Lavinia, Rajini Srikanth, eds. (1998), *A Part Yet Apart: South Asians in Asian America*. Philadelphia: Temple University Press.

Singh, Dharamjit. (1970), *Indian Cookery*. London: Penguin.

Srinivas, Lakshmi. (2005), Communicating Globalization in Bombay Cinema: Everyday Life, Imagination and the Persistence of the Local. *Comparative American Studies*, 3 (3): 319–44.

Srinivas, M.N. (1962), *Caste in Modern India*. Bombay: Media Publishers.

Srinivas, M.N. (1989), *The Cohesive Role of Sanskritization*. Delhi: Oxford.

Srinivas, M.N. (2003), An Obituary on Caste as a System. *Economic and Political Weekly*, 38 (5)· February 1.

Srinivas, Smriti. (2001), *Landscapes of Urban Memory; The Sacred and the Civic in India's High City*. Minneapolis: University of Minnesota Press.

Taylor, Janelle, Linda L. Layne and Danielle F. Wozniak. (2004), *Consuming Motherhood*. Piscataway, NJ: Rutgers University Press.

Tharoor, Shashi. (1997), Growing Up Extreme: On the Peculiarly Vicious Fanatacism of [Indian] Expatriates. http://www.sacw.net/i_aii/tharoor.html [Originally from The Washington Post].

Theophano, Janet. (2002), *Eat My Words: Reading Women's Lives Through The Cookbooks They Wrote*. London: Palgrave Macmillan.

Tomlinson, John. (1991), *Cultural Imperialism*. London: Printer Publishers.

Tomlinson, John. (1999), *Cultural Globalization*. Chicago: University of Chicago Press.

Toomey, Paul. (1992), Mountain of Food, Mountain of Love: Ritual Inversion of the Annakuta Feast at Mount Govardhan. In R.S. Khare (ed.), *Eternal Food: Gastronomic Ideas and Experiences of Hindus and Buddhists*, (pp. 117–145). Albany: SUNY Press.

Van, Wessel Margit. (2004), Talking about Consumption: How an Indian Middle Class Disassociates from Middle Class Life. *Cultural Dynamic*, 16 (1): 93–116.

Varma Pavan, K. (1998), *The Great Indian Middle Class*. Delhi: Penguin.

Warner, Judith. (2005), *Perfect Madness: Motherhood in and Age of Anxiety*. New York: Riverhead Books.

Wu, Frank. (2002), *Yellow: Race in America Beyond Black and White*. New York: Basic Books.

Yalman, Nur. (1969), On the Meaning of Food Offerings in Ceylon. In Robert Spencer (ed.), *Forms of Symbolic Action*, (pp. 81–96). Seattle: University of Washington Press.

Zolli, Andrew. (2006), *The US's future is Older, Browner, and Feminine*. 16 March. Rediff.com.

26

"Real Belizean Food": Building Local Identity in the Transnational Caribbean[*]

Richard Wilk

It is an anthropological truism that food is both substance and symbol, providing physical nourishment and a key mode of communication that carries many kinds of meaning (Counihan and Van Esterik 1997). Many studies have demonstrated that food is a particularly potent symbol of personal and group identity, forming one of the foundations of both individuality and a sense of common membership in a larger, bounded group. What is much less well understood is how such a stable pillar of identity can also be so fluid and changeable, how the seemingly insurmountable boundaries between each group's unique dietary practices and habits can be maintained, while diets, recipes, and cuisines are in a constant state of flux (Warde 1997:57–77).

In a world of constant cultural contact, international media, and marketing, the process of change in diets seems to have accelerated, but the boundaries that separate cultures have not disappeared. The difficult conundrum of stability and change, of borrowing and diffusion, without growing similarity or loss of identity, which we find in the world's food consumption, appears in many other realms of culture too (Appadurai 1996; Friedman 1994). It is clear that older modernization and acculturation theories that predicted a growing homogenization and Westernization of the world's cultures are inadequate in a world that seems to constantly generate new diversities, new political and social divisions, and a host of new fundamentalisms.

Many social scientists have pointed to the resurgence of nationalism and ethnicity in the last two decades, and some argue that strengthened local identities are a direct challenge to globalizing diffusion of consumer culture (Jenkins 1994; Tobin 1992). Popular discourse also opposes the authentic local or national culture or cuisine with an anonymous artificial mass-marketed global culture of McDonalds and Disney. These arguments reproduce a diffusionary model of history as Westernization or cultural imperialism. In this paper I continue to build an alternative approach, recognizing that the strengthening of local and national identities and global mass-market capitalism are not contradictory trends but are in fact two aspects of the same process (Beckett 1996; Miller 1997). I will further this argument through an analysis of recent changes in the cuisine of a tiny and marginal place, a mere dot on the globe, which may in some ways be unique, but which is in other ways typical of many tiny and unique places that are increasingly integrated into the world market for consumer goods.

[*]*Originally published 1999*

I have worked in the Central American and Caribbean nation of Belize since 1973. Belize is a wonderful place to study the relationship between food and national identity because nationhood is such a recent construct there. Belize only attained independence in 1981, and until that time nationhood was primarily a matter of political rhetoric, government commissions, and debate among the educated elite. Since that time foreign media, tourism, and migration have spread a broad awareness that Belize needs a national culture, cuisine, and identity to flesh out the bare institutional bones of nationhood provided by the British. Belizeans know their flag, anthem, capital, and great founding father, and they now know they should have a culture to go with them.[1]

Belizean nationalism contends with a variety of other forms of identification, including regional, familial, class, language, and ethnicity. Many, but not all, Belizeans identify with a language or ethnic group, what are usually called "races" or "cultures." The "Creole" category was once applied to local Europeans, then was extended to those of mixed European and African ancestry, and now it has become a general term for people with multiple or overlapping ethnic backgrounds (see Stone 1994). Diverse groups of migrants from neighboring Spanish-speaking countries are usually labeled "Spanish," though many are of Amerindian origins. In addition there are relatively bounded ethnic groups defined by language, residence, and liveli-hood, including Mopan, Kekchi, East Indians, Mennonites, Chinese, and Garifuna. Of course, in a country of only 200,000 people, all "ethnic" boundaries are crosscut by multiple personal and familial relationships.

Most of the puzzles and problems of uniqueness and sameness, of boundaries and open flows, of imperialism and resistance, which we find in other parts of the developing world, are also found in Belize. While it does not always occupy center stage, food and cooking are an important and sometimes dramatic entry into understanding this uneven process. To show how rapidly Belize has been transformed, and to argue for the crucial importance of foreign influence in the growth of local culture, I begin with a contrast between two meals, separated by 17 years.

Eating Culture: A Tale of Two Meals

Meal One: Tea with the Gentles. May 1973, Orange Walk Town (a predominantly Hispanic community in the northern sugar zone).

Henry and Alva Gentle, both schoolteachers in the Creole lower middle class, invited a 19-year-old archaeology student to their home for a meal. I showed up one evening about 5 p.m., just as the family sat down to the evening meal. "Dinner" at midday was the main meal of the day in Belize; evening "Tea" was usually leftovers from dinner, with some bread or buns and coffee or tea.

Everyone was excited about having a foreign visitor in the house and stopped eating when I entered. I was ushered into the uninhabited and unused front "parlor" for a few minutes while furious activity took place in the kitchen, and children were sent running out of the back door to the local shops. Then we all went back to the kitchen table to finish tea. Everyone sat before small plates of fish and plantain dumplings simmered in coconut milk, with homemade coconut bread, and either fresh fruit juice or tea.

After six weeks on archaeological camp food (most of which had been sent out in a large crate from England), my mouth watered at the prospect of tasting something authentically Belizean. Instead, as an honored guest I was treated to the best food the house could afford, food they thought I would be comfortable with: a plate of greasy fried canned corned beef (packed, as I later found out, in Zimbabwe), accompanied by six slices of stale Mexican "Pan Bimbo" white bread, a small tin of sardines in tomato sauce, and a cool Seven-up with a straw. When this was presented, the whole family paused in their own meal to smile shyly and expectantly, waiting for my pleased reaction. I did as well as I could, given that I dislike both sardines and canned meat.

Despite the food, the meal was relaxed and fun, with a lot of joking between family members. There was no formal beginning or end to the meal; late arrivals were seated and served. People got up and went to the kitchen to fill their plates when they wanted more food. Gradually people drifted out to the verandah to sit and discuss the day, and see who was walking by on the street.

Meal Two: Dinner with the Lambeys. August 1990, Belmopan (a small town of about 3,000, also the nation's capital, with a mixed population).

Lisbeth and Mike Lambey lived across the street from us in a nice part of town, populated mostly by middle-rank civil servants. Mike worked in the refugee office, and Lisbeth was an assistant to a permanent secretary. A bit more educated than the Gentles and better paid, they still belonged to the same salaried middle class. Lisbeth was born into an old Creole family in Belize City, while Mike's family included Creole and East Indians from the southern part of Belize. All of Mike's family live in various parts of Belize, but all of Lisbeth's seven siblings have emigrated to the United States.

When Mike invited us to dinner, over the front wall of his yard one morning, he said, "I want you to taste some good local food." By 1990, many younger Belizeans, especially those with both spouses working for wages, had shifted to what was seen as an "American" practice of eating a light lunch and the main family meal in the evening.

When my wife and I arrived, we were seated in front of the TV, handed large glasses of rum & Coke (made with local rum and "local" Coke), and were shown a videotape about the refugee situation in Belize, produced by the United Nations. Then we sat down to a formal set table; all the food was laid out on platters, and it was passed from hand to hand. Everything we ate, both Mike and Lisbeth said, was produced in Belize and cooked to Belizean recipes. We had tortillas (from the Guatemalan-owned factory down the road), stewed beans (which I later found were imported from the United States, but sold without labeling), stewed chicken (from nearby Mennonite farms), salad (some of the lettuce was from Mexico) with bottled French dressing (Kraft from England), and an avocado with sliced white cheese (made locally by Salvadoran refugees). We drank an "old-fashioned" homemade pineapple wine.

The meal was formal, with a single common conversation about local politics to which each of us contributed. When everyone was finished, Lisbeth circulated a small dish of imported chocolate candies, and we all rose together and went back to the TV. Mike proudly produced a videocassette on which a friend had taped Eddie Murphy's "Coming to America" from a satellite broadcast. Both Lisbeth and Mike found the film hilarious and especially liked the parts where the two unsophisticated bumbling Africans show their ignorance of New York and American ways. We had seen the film before, and pleading the need to put our daughter to bed, went home before it was over.

That same week Radio Belize carried advertisements for the grand opening of the first self-proclaimed "Belizean Restaurant."[2] Owned by a Belize-born couple who had recently returned from a 20-year sojourn in the United States, the advertisement asked customers to "Treat yourself to a Belizean Feast. Authentic Belizean dishes—Garnachas, Tamales, Rice and Beans, Stew Chicken, Fried Chicken." All these foods were already served in numerous restaurants all over the country; the only other kind of food available in most places is Chinese. But this was the first time they had been granted the public distinction of being the national cuisine.[3]

In the next two years the notion of Belizean restaurants and Belizean cuisine became commonplace, and most people accepted that there was indeed a national and traditional lexicon of recipes. In fact, as an anthropologist running around the country asking questions about Belizean food, I often found that my very efforts loaned legitimacy to the idea of a national cuisine. How is it that British and Mexican dishes, and global standards like stewed and fried chicken, emerged so quickly as an emblematic Belizean cuisine? This is a clear example of nation building, as a contextualized and nonreflective set of practices was codified and labeled as characteristic of the nation as a whole (Lofgren 1993).

In Belize, cuisine has been nationalized in a process quite distinct from that described by Appadurai in India (1988). There, cookbooks were crucial instruments, and regional diversity has been the main theme. National cuisine explicitly incorporates and crosscuts local traditions, which are simultaneously codified as each local group finds a significant contrastive "other" in neighboring areas and in the superordinate national melange. In Belizean cuisine the internal contention over how different ethnic and regional groups will be incorporated in the national has been quite muted. Instead, Belizean cooking has emerged through an explicit contrast with an externalized "other." The crucible of Belizean national cooking has been the *transnational* arena: the flow of migrants, sojourners, tourists, and media that increasingly links the Caribbean with the United States. Caribbean nationalism and identity is now problematized and contested, debated and asserted, in this shifting transnational terrain (Basch et al. 1994; Olwig 1993).

Belizean National Culture

The emergence of Belizean cuisine is just a small part of a general process, which has unevenly and imperfectly established and legitimized Belizean national culture (Everitt 1987; Medina 1997; Wilk 1993b). Just twenty years ago, the concept of Belizean Culture" was no more than politicians' rhetoric and a project for a small group of foreign-trained intellectuals. Official national dance troupes, endless patriotic speeches, history textbooks, and border disputes with neighboring Guatemala have helped establish the existence of a category of "Belizean Culture," but they have not filled it with meaning. It does not take a social scientist to define or observe the ways Belizeans contest the meaning of the category of local culture; this is the stuff of daily conversation and debate. The process is contrastive, defining the self through defining difference. Belizeans speak of "floods" and "invasions" of foreign goods, television, preachers, tourists, money, entrepreneurs, music, language, drugs, gangs, tastes, and ideas (Wilk 1993a). Contrasts between the local and the foreign are on everyone's lips, though there are many shades of opinion about which is good or bad, and about where it will all end up. People constantly talk about authenticity and tradition, contrasting the old "befo' time" with everything new, foreign, and "modan."

Popular ideas about how the foreign is affecting "little Belize" are dramatized in jokes and stories about Belizeans who mimic or affect foreign ways. The traveler who returns after a few weeks in the States with an American accent is a common figure of fun. So is the returned cook who no longer recognizes a catfish, and the shopper who buys pepper sauce from an American supermarket to bring home, and pays a hefty import duty before looking at the label and seeing that it was made in Belize.

Opportunities for drawing contrasts appear often. Estimates of the number of Belizeans living in the United States range widely, but 60,000 seems a reasonable low estimate, or 30% of the total living in Belize (Vernon 1990). Los Angeles is the second-largest Belizean settlement. There is constant flow of people, goods, and money between domestic and foreign communities (Wilk and Miller 1997). At the same time, more than 140,000 foreign tourists visit Belize every year. Belize is flooded with American media, from books and magazines to a barrage of cable and satellite television.

Elsewhere I have argued that one effect of the increasing prominence of the foreign in Belize has been the objectification of the local (Wilk 1993a, 1995). Many issues that were once seen as localized, ethnic, and even familial are now interpreted in a global context. The problems of youth, social welfare, ethnicity, and gender roles, for example, are now placed in a global contrast of "our way" or "our Belizean traditions" with "those in the States." This has led to the emergence of a political and cultural discourse about otherness and sameness. During colonial times, foreign culture was received indirectly, with the expatriate and local colonial elite acting as selective agents and gatekeepers. Now all classes have direct access to foreign culture, and the foreign is no longer as closely associated with wealth and power (Wilk 1990).

This suggests an important way of reading the differences between the two meals I discussed above. While class differences between my two hosts account for some of the variation, the most dramatic differences between the Gentles and the Lambeys have little to do with changes in the content of Belizean culture or identity. Instead, they result from changing knowledge about foreigners and increased consciousness of culture itself. The Gentles, despite (or maybe even because of) their education really knew very little about Americans or American culture. Travelers were rare; personal contact with foreigners was sought for the very purpose of learning. The Gentles wanted to please me—they just did not know how Americans were different from the British. They could not know that young Americans wanted something "local," "cultural," and "authentic"—the very things they knew educated and rich people looked down upon. No wonder that our relationship did not flourish; I felt like I was a disappointment to them, and they probably felt the same way about me. My zeal to teach them to value their indigenous culture probably sounded false and condescending, if not just incoherent and weird.

Seventeen years later, the Lambeys know how to play this game properly. They are Belizean nationalists who know that they are supposed to have something authentic and local to offer. They have been abroad and have learned to perceive and categorize differences as "national" and "cultural." They have learned that foreigners expect them to be Belizean, and they know how to do the job. They are as busy creating traditions and national culture as the itinerant Belizean woodcarvers who now tell tourists that their craft was handed down from their African ancestors (rather than taught by Peace Corps volunteers). Serving an authentic Belizean meal, for the Lambeys, is a performance of modernity and sophistication. The emotion it evokes for them is closer to pride or defiance than to nostalgia, the warmth of memory, or the comfort of repeated family habits. On the contrary, the meal expresses a sense of distance. A Belizean student, home for the summer from Jamaica, expressed this distanced, critical stance when, discussing his feeling about Belizean nationalism and ethnic identity, he told me "you can respect something without believing in it." Belizeans often express a similar sophisticated tolerance toward the stereotypes of their country that appear constantly in travel guides and tourist magazines—"Belize the unspoiled wilderness," etc. (Munt and Higinio 1993).

To sneer at this accomplishment, at the Lambeys' dinner, by laughing at its shallowness or inauthenticity, is to miss its point (Friedman 1992). Mastering the performance and the role asserts a claim to categorical equality, to knowledge and power. I did not really understand how important a step this was until I talked with older Belizeans about their first trips to America.

A newspaper editor told me that as a child he and his friends looked at the names of cities on the labels of American products, at the goods advertised on the pages of magazines plastered on their house walls, and fantasized about what the United States was like. He thought the advertisements depicted a real world. So on his first trip to the United States, he was excited about going to the places where the products came from. And it was a shock to find how ignorant he had been—and that so many of the things people ate and used in the United States actually came from Japan and other countries. He felt humiliated and foolish for having confused fantasy with reality.

He related that even recently Belizeans were relatively unsophisticated consumers and were "easy marks" for advertising—bad loans and credit terms and shoddy goods—because they lacked the experience and sophistication of Americans. As an ardent and radical nationalist, he decried the effects of television on local culture, but in the same breath praised the way TV has "raised Belizeans' consciousness," making them knowledgeable and aware of the rest of the world. No longer were they blinded by surface appearances. He, and other Belizeans I spoke with, expressed an optimistic hope that in seeing more clearly the problems of the rest of the world, Belizeans would learn to value what they had at home (Salzman [1996] finds this same effect on the island of Sardinia).[4]

The invasion of foreign media and goods and increased knowledge and sophistication are two sides of the same coin, two elements of the same process.[5] Outsiders tend to focus attention on the former, on the ways that certain meanings, messages, and practices are imparted and forced on powerless consumers of media and advertising (e.g., Lundgren 1988). We may see this as seduction or as a transformation of consciousness. But at the same time, it leads to an accumulation of knowledge about the world. By putting this knowledge into play in their everyday consuming lives, by performing and enacting and using unfamiliar goods, Belizean consumers transform abstract images, words, and names into the familiar appliances of life in Belize.

Through consumption the foreign is made part of local existence, and it therefore comes under the same sorts of (albeit limited) control.

Belizeans are becoming sophisticated consumers, and in the process they are gaining a form of power that was previously denied, or was rationed and controlled by the local elite. Now Belizeans can penetrate deceit and "comparison shop," by playing one message off against another, and break away from the "brand loyalty" of the colonial consumer who had limited information. Furthermore, Belizeans have become more aware that they use and manipulate goods to their own social ends; they have acquired the distance necessary to view goods as tools to be manipulated rather than signs to be accepted or rejected. This sort of distance, of course, does not necessarily diminish desire or emotional longing for the foreign. For example, when in my 1990 survey I asked 1,136 high school students what they would buy with $50, 28% chose imported tennis shoes, usually by brand, color, and type of lacing.

When I first went to Belize I was asked many strange questions about the United States—was it true that people in California had sex in public? Did Indians still attack travelers in the West? Today I am more likely to be engaged in debate about Los Angeles street gangs or Bill Clinton's troubles with his cabinet. Through media, Belizeans tap more levels of American discourse—they get the "official" word on CNN news, and the gossip from the *National Enquirer, Life-Styles of the Rich and Famous* (which has featured a Belizean resort twice), and *A Current Affair*.

Belize has always had a lively network of gossip and rumor about local politics and goings-on, but for England and America there was only the official word. While Belizeans do not usually feel equal to Americans in most political and material ways, they now know more of the dimensions of their perceived inferiority. This is very different from the more pervasive, generalized, and threatening inferiority that people felt during colonial times. Their new depth of knowledge of the world does not in and of itself create tastes for foreign things. Knowledge "of" the world is not the same as knowledge of how it works, but it lends new textures of significance to foreign things and imparts a much richer field of meaning to them. The taste for foreign goods over local equivalents so often observed in developing countries (e.g., Orlove 1997) can then be seen as a consequence of the desire to know more about the world, to become more sophisticated, to acquire new forms of knowledge, and to make that knowledge material.

I am not arguing that having access to the American tabloid press has been a great boon to Belize and has changed the global balance of culture and power. But this access does indicate a series of shifts in the relationship between Belize and the rest of the world, which transforms Belizeans as consumers. In the process, a colonial-era hierarchical discourse that opposed the backward local against the modern and foreign has begun to crumble. One way to describe this process is through the metaphor of drama.

The Drama of Local vs. Global

The many manifestations of the "global ecumene" in different places often appear to be chaotic, a pastiche of shreds and patches (Foster 1991:251). One place to seek structure in the flow of goods and meanings is to look for an underlying power and interest groups, focusing for example on the interests of the state, or of multinational corporations (see critique in Miller 1994). A complementary approach can instead seek an emerging structure in the form of a narrative or story, played over and over in different settings with new characters and variations—a repetitious drama instead of a social or spatial order.

Observers of global cultural process find tendencies toward both homogenization and heterogeneity (Arizpe 1996; Friedman 1990; Hannerz 1987; Howes 1996; Lofgren 1993; Tobin 1992). If we think of the global culture as constituted by drama, we can perhaps locate the homogeneity in a common dramatic structure of encounter, while the local actors, symbols, and performances of the drama proliferate in splendid diversity. In this way, the global ecumene becomes a unifying drama, rather than a uniform culture, a constant array of goods or a constellation of meanings.

One unifying dramatic theme is a struggle that reads as "the local against the foreign," or *our* culture vs. the powerful and dangerous *other*. This drama is played out in many permutations, at many different levels, often nested within each other. What is universal is the drama itself, not its outcome. And this is in itself a significant opening for both cross-cultural communication and misunderstanding, for example, in the trade disputes between the United States and Japan, or the long-standing cultural ambivalence of the French toward Americans (Kuisel 1993).

If we follow this argument in Belize, we see that participation in the global ecumene is not so much a matter of acquiring goods or building a nation. Instead, there is a process of learning to share and participate in a core drama, in which national identity is essential costume. Social scientists studying consumption have been actors—sometimes scriptwriters—for this performance. We tend to force debate into two positions—hegemony and resistance. On one hand there is capitalism's need for expansion of markets, the breakdown of community and local economies, and the capacity of advertising to create envy, social composition, and new needs. Consumer goods are essential components of new market-oriented systems of ranking and hierarchy.

On the other hand, we can emphasize the ways objects are used to resist capitalism, to maintain local systems, to forge links with an authentic past, to build identities defined by local systems of meaning and nonmarket social relationships. The moral of this story is that the technological apparatus of capitalism, including television and other media, has been turned to very local and anti-hegemonic purposes. New gardens of cultural diversity will continue to spring up from the leveled and furrowed fields of international capitalism; even corporate icons of homogeneity like McDonalds can become local institutions (Watson 1997).

This contrast of seductive globalism and authentic localism is an extremely potent drama because it has no solution—it is an eternal struggle, where each pole defines its opposite, where every value carries its own negation. The players in the drama are always taking positions as advocates for one pole or the other, but they are actually locked in a dance—dependent on each other for the support of opposition. Anthropologists and folklorists tend to embrace this drama, attached to both its tragedy (ethnocide) and its comedic moments (bumbling development bureaucrats out-witted by canny natives). The key development in the last 20 years is that the drama has escaped from academic confinement and is no longer the province of the educated.

Everyone in Belize is now concerned with foreign influence, local authenticity, and the interpretation of various kinds of domination and resistance (Wilk 1993a).

Colonial to Global Drama: An Example

To bring the discussion back to earth in Belize, we need to begin with the colonial regime of consumption and describe the way it set the stage and provided scenery for the drama of local vs. global. To stretch my metaphor, this section is a brief look "backstage" at local political economic reality. My data come from extensive archival work with newspapers and documents and from numerous personal histories. For contemporary consumption practices and tastes I draw on a survey of 1,136 high school students from four diverse institutions (Babcock and Wilk 1998) and a door-to-door survey of 389 people in Belize City, Belmopan, and a large village in the Belize District, both conducted in 1990. The latter survey replicated parts of Bourdieu's French work that was the basis of *Distinction* (1984), with a focus on likes and dislikes for a wide variety of foods, music, television, and reading material.[6] These data and my interviews were focused on people's likes and dislikes for particular dishes. I have much less material on the presentation, serving, and context of consumption of foods, though this topic is also very important.

The Colonial Taste for Imports

During the nineteenth century Belize was a logging colony, the source of famous "Honduras mahogany" that was used to build European railway cars and furniture. The colony was dependent on imported foods of all kinds. While scattered rural subsistence farmers produced most of their own food, the standard diet of mahogany cutters and working-class urban dwellers was imported flour and salt meat. A weekly ration for workers was four pounds of pork and seven of flour, eaten as dishes like "pork and doughboys."[7] The managerial and mercantile European and Creole middle and upper classes consumed a wide variety of imported foods and drink and limited amounts of a few local vegetables, fish, poultry, and game. Given the very uneven quality of imported goods, consumers who could afford packaged and branded foodstuffs became highly "brand loyal" to established lines and companies. Brands were ranked according to both price and quality, with the highest ranks from Britain and lower ranks from the United States and Latin America. Access to the best brands was tightly controlled both through price and a strict system of exclusive distributorships that kept them in only the "best" shops. Branding was a key element of cultural capital, and it came to connote quality (see Burke 1996 on soap in Zimbabwe). The poor bought generic goods, often dipped out of barrels, and had little choice when compelled to purchase in company stores through various forms of debt-servitude and payments of wages in goods.

Diet was highly class stratified. A single scale of values placed local products at the bottom and increasingly expensive and rare imports at the top. Imports were available to anyone who had the money, but in practice people did not usually consume above their class, whatever their economic resources. These strictures were only relaxed during the Christmas season, when the most exclusive products circulated at every kind of festivity. At this time the elite placed special emphasis on rare delicacies obtained directly from England through private networks of friends and relatives. Among the laboring class, almost any kind of store-bought food was considered superior to the rural diet based on root crops, rice, game, fruits, and vegetables.

This relatively simple hierarchy put the greatest pressure on the thin middle class of local petty merchants, low-level officials, tradespeople, and clerical workers. They did not have the resources for an exclusively imported diet but had to work hard to distance themselves from the kind of cheap and local foods that were the rural and working-class staple. One consequence was that they shunned local foods like fresh fish and game meat. These were common fare for the rural poor (for whom they were part of a subsistence lifestyle) and the upper elite (for whom selected varieties were considered exotic delicacies as long as they were prepared according to European recipes and smothered with imported sauces).

While the middle class depended most heavily on imports, menus from elite ceremonial meals included local snapper fillets in fish courses, garnished with oysters imported fresh from New Orleans. Venison, duck, and a few other local game animals with European analogs also appeared on the tables of the local gentry. Lobster is a good example of a stratified taste "sandwich": eaten by the poor because it was cheap, by the elite because it was prized in Europe, but shunned by the middle class as a "trash fish." Older Belizeans from middle-class backgrounds say that their mothers would not allow a lobster in the house; some of these people never ate lobster until it became a major export commodity in the 1970s, and then they had to stop when the price skyrocketed in the 80s.

The middle class built dietary diversity by borrowing foods from the Hispanic mercantile and managerial elites in the northern part of the country. "Spanish" food, especially festive dishes like tamales, relleno (a stuffed chicken stew), and tacos, entered the middle-class diet as a safely exotic option—associated neither with the class below nor the class above. "Spanish" food quickly became naturalized as part of the middle-class Creole diet. In this case, the "foreign" quickly became "local" and authentic.

There was some local resistance to or evasion of colonial food hierarchy. Foreign dishes were often localized or made affordable by substituting ingredients, renaming, and recombination. Kin ties cut across class and ethnic boundaries, and local produce therefore circulated between classes through networks of extended kin. Certain kinds of rare "country foods," especially wild game, honey, hearts of palm and the like, came to carry a connotation of familism and embeddedness; of belonging to place, even for the urban middle class. Some rustic dishes were enjoyed only in privacy, or on special occasions or during visits to country relatives. Festivals and celebrations also provided sites for the legitimate consumption of local products as holiday foods, especially fruit wines and snacks like cashew and pumpkin seed. But while neighboring countries like Mexico had a substantial indigenous population whose dishes could be adapted and co-opted by an educated elite, Mayan cooking entered Belize only indirectly, mainly through the influence of the refugees from Yucatan's caste war in the 1850s.

The colonial regime of consumption in Belize, therefore, was similar to that seen by Bourdieu in modern France (1984). A relatively stable social hierarchy was defined by differential access to economic and cultural capital, which takes the form of "taste" and thoroughly naturalized predisposition and preference. Goods were positional markers within the hierarchy, both the means by which culture is internalized as taste and an external symbolic field through which groups identify boundaries and define differences among classes. There was a slow flow downward, as lower ranks emulated the elite and the elite found new markers. There was also a stable degree of resistance, as some local products and practices were regenerated and adopted upwards through kin ties.

Of course, in France the hierarchy is much more elaborate, with a clear division between economic and cultural elites and a dynamic and innovative upper middle class. In Belize the fashion system was more firmly controlled by an elite that tended to combine political, economic, and cultural power through the media, government, schools, and shops. They managed and censored the flow of goods and information into and around the colony and enforced quite uniform standards within the elite class through many of the same exclusive social practices used in London at the time (Mennell 1984:200–228). Boundaries with lower classes were policed through many forms of class and racial discrimination. Up until the 1970s there were racially exclusive clubs, and working-class people were not welcome and subject to humiliation in the few shops that catered to the elite (Conroy 1997).

Elite power was embodied in practices of consumption, and through roles as cultural gatekeepers, the elite were arbiters of taste in everything. The choices of the middle and working classes were limited to accepting or rejecting what was offered. They could not find alternative sources of goods, information, or taste, except in the immediately neighboring Hispanic republics.

Pupsi and Crana; The Beginning of the End

This hierarchy of taste remained remarkably stable until the early 1960s. An incident, where food entered national political debate, illustrates one of the ways the colonial order began to unravel. In 1963 the British finally granted Belize limited local self-government. The anticolonial Peoples United Party was promptly elected, led by George Price, who had been imprisoned for nationalist activity in the 1950s (Shoman 1985). With limited legislative power, Price began to make symbolic changes in flags, official dress, and the names of towns and landmarks. He chose to de-emphasize some colonial holidays and changed the name of the country from British Honduras to Belize. There was a lot of popular support for most of these measures.

Then he gave a speech about the local economy, which exposed the country's ambivalence about the depth of the decolonizing project. In the speech he suggested that it was time to stop aping the food standards of the colonial masters. Belizeans would have to become self-sufficient in food and value the "traditional" local foods instead of copying foreign models and continuing to depend on imported foodstuff. He told his audience they should eat less imported wheat bread and more of their own products, drinking fever-grass tea and sweet potato wine, and eating pupsi and crana (abundant local river fish) instead of imported sardines. Like a number of colonial agricultural officers, he argued that it was unreasonable for a country rich in fertile soil, surrounded by abundant sea life, to import grain and fish from Europe.

The pro-British opposition, which had unsuccessfully fought Price's other cultural initiatives, now found an issue that aroused popular support that threatened Price's whole nationalist project.

> When the PUP started they promised you ham and eggs, etc., if you put them in power. They also promised you self government. But today when they get Self Government, they tell you to boil fever grass and eat pupsi and other river fishes. What will they tell you to eat when they get independence? [Belize Billboard, January 5, 1964]

> The human body is like a machine, and it must have fuel to keep it running. And the fuel of the human machine is food, protective and sustaining foods such as milk and other dairy products, eggs, vegetables, fruits, whole grain and enriched bread and other cereals, just to name a few. Food must supply the vitamins needed, along with other essential nutrients such as proteins to keep the body running in high gear . . . . It is obvious that pupsi and crana, which live mostly in polluted swamps[,] cannot replace, as our premier advises, our sources of vitamin rich food and proteins, the most important ingredients in our diet. Conditions such as pellagra and ariboflavinosis (disease dues [sic] to lack of vitamin B) occur in people who live continuously on restricted diets such as corn and salt pork only. [Belize Billboard, January 11, 1964]

While the PUP's previous nationalist program challenged British political authority, the suggestion about diet turned the entire edifice of colonial cultural values and hierarchy literally upside-down. The words *pupsi* and *crana* became a rallying point for the formation of an opposition party. Price's suggestion was also unpopular among working-and middle-class people, who felt that they were being told to be satisfied with poverty instead of "improving" their lot. Many who had supported Price had seen his goal in terms of equity—a society where everyone would eat "high table" imported foods, sardines, and wine, not one where even the elite would be eating "bush food." Surprised by the reaction, Price moderated his position to one of import substitution, particularly supporting local rice and bean production, and he never publicly again called for a change in the national diet.[8] The violent reaction to his speech shows just how resistant to change the cultural order of colonial taste had become. It brought home to Belizeans the realization that the end of colonialism would mean more than a new flag and new street names. The "Pupsi and Crana" speech was the point where the colonial regime of taste was no longer part of the taken-for-granted of everyday life.

The Royal Rat

Queen Elizabeth's 1985 visit to Belize marked a major symbolic recognition of Belize's independence, at a time when Belizeans were increasingly worried about the veracity of British defense guarantees against Guatemalan aggression (the result of a long-standing border dispute). A major event during the visit, the first by a reigning Monarch, was a state banquet at the residence of the British High Commissioner in Belmopan, the new capital city built by the British. A selection of Belizean delicacies was prepared for the royal party by the best local cooks.

One of the tastiest wild mammals of the Belizean rain forest is a large rodent called a *gibnut* or *paca* (*Agouti paca*). Highly prized in the rural diet, it was never widely eaten by the urban middle class. At the suggestion of local cooks and officials, but with the approval of the High Commissioner, roast gibnut was given the place of national honor as a main meat course at the Queen's banquet. She did not eat very much of it, but as a graceful veteran of hundreds of inedible feasts of local specialties, she still praised it to the cook. There the story would have ended, but for the British tabloid press. The Sun and other British newspapers produced a slew of outraged headlines, variations on the theme of "Queen Served Rat by Wogs." Angry letters were printed in the British press by citizens who were enraged by this assault on HRH's dignity.

The press reports were quickly transmitted back to Belize, where they provoked outrage and widespread anger, even among those who had never eaten gibnut. A few conciliatory conservative writers tried to explain to the British that the gibnut was *not* a rat and suggested that the incident was merely a misunderstanding. But most Belizeans saw this as an example of British arrogance and racism. For the first time, a Belizean dish became a matter of public pride. Nationalist chefs and nutritionists defended the Belizean gibnut as tasty, healthful, and nutritious. Reinterpreted as a national delicacy, today it often appears on restaurant menus as "Royal Rat," and its high price and legitimacy in national cuisine place heavy hunting pressure on remaining populations.

The incident of the royal rat came at a crucial time, just after political independence was granted in 1981. A legitimate category of Belizean food was beginning to emerge. The government, interested in cutting down food imports, had halfheartedly sponsored several campaigns through the Ministry of Education aimed at promoting production and consumption of local foods with help from CARE and the Peace Corps. During the 1970s the thrust was one of substituting local products for imports in familiar recipes: making bread with plantain flour, jams with local fruits. During the eighties the emphasis shifted to rediscovering (or reinventing) traditional foods; eating pupsi and crana was no longer unthinkable.

Belizean restaurants in the United States, cookbooks, public festivities where food is served, and the expensive dining rooms of foreign-owned luxury hotels were all crucial stages where ideas about Belizean food were tried out. By 1990, many dishes that were once markers of rural poverty had been converted into national cuisine. Others had quietly disappeared. Foreigners, expatriates, tourists, and emigrants were crucial agents in formulating and valuing the local.

Taste and Hierarchy Today

Colonial Belize had a clear hierarchy of social and economic strata, marked by their food practices and preferences. As Bourdieu points out (1984), these class tastes are bound together into systems, with internal logic and structure, by sentiments and dispositions rooted in childhood and a lifetime of learning. He focuses on schools as crucial institutions where these tastes are transmitted and ordered.

The social and economic stratification of Belize has not changed drastically since the 1950s. There are still quite exclusive and cosmopolitan mercantile economic and bureaucrat-technocrat elites, a diverse petit-bourgeoisie and functionary middle class, and a large and partially destitute working class. This hierarchy is crosscut in complex ways by ethnicity, family ties, political alliances, regional loyalties, and rural/urban differences.

Under the colonial regime, diversity was managed and regulated through the flows of fashion and taste, which entered through the gatekeepers at the top who were legitimate models for emulation or resistance. Today this hierarchy has been drastically undercut by new flows of information and goods. Travel, once the province of the privileged elite, is now practical for most Belizeans. My survey shows that 73% of Belizean adults have traveled out of their country, while 34% have lived abroad for three months or more. Variation by class is not high. For example, 45% of skilled manual workers have lived abroad, compared to 54% of business managers. The average Belizean has 2.6 immediate consanguineal relatives living abroad, again with little difference broken down by class, education, or wealth.

The worlds these travelers encounter are quite diverse; some end up in middleclass suburbs, others in urban ghettos. Some bring back luxury cars, high fashion clothing, and silverware, some display diplomas and stereos, others bring the latest rap tunes, BK basketball shoes, Gumby haircuts, and dread belts.

Similarly, tourists who once concentrated in a few oceanside resorts are now diffusing through the countryside and cities as ecotourists in search of unspoiled nature, ancient ruins, and authentic folk culture. A growing portion of the population has direct contact with foreigners; Belizeans now make sophisticated distinctions between different kinds of foreigners, and see them as representing diverse cultural backgrounds.

Finally, greater access to electronic and print media has vastly broadened the images that Belizeans have of the world and has destroyed much of the gate-keeping role of the elite. Satellite-fed cable television had reached 35% of the urban population by 1990, and broadcast stations served almost all of the rest. Forty-six percent of high school students reported that they watched TV every day. Belizeans now have a diversity of models, fantasies, and dramas to choose from, in a kind of "global menu" (Petch 1987; Wilk 1993a, 1995). People are now faced with the need to contrast, weigh, and choose. What seems to be emerging is both a clearer definition of the national and local, and a less hierarchical diversification of lifestyles.

In one survey I asked 389 Belizeans to rate 21 main course dishes on a four-point scale from love to hate (Wilk 1997). Eight were clearly Belizean Creole food, and the other 13 were foreign in varying ways (Hispanic, Chinese, and Indian dishes represented Belizean minority ethnic groups, while dishes like macaroni and cheese or pizza have no local constituency). The responses were striking in their lack of clear order or hierarchy; tastes did not cluster together, nor did they help disaggregate the population by class or education.

In a correlation matrix of preferences for each dish with various socioeconomic measures, differences in gender and age were as strongly correlated with food preferences (r^2 ranging from .08 to .12) as were differences in wealth, job status, and education. Ethnicity was a surprisingly weak variable in explaining differences in taste, especially so among the young. All ethnic, age, and income groups showed a high degree of agreement in their preferences for basic nationalized dishes like rice and beans or tamales. 41% of high school students, for example, volunteered rice and beans with stewed chicken as their favourite dish on an open-ended question. Most important, there was little difference between ethnic/language categories.

The neat orderings of taste that Bourdieu found in France are absent from the Belizean data on food or other kinds of preferences for art, clothing, and music. I tried numerous measures of cultural and economic capital, but could not make simple directional patterns out of taste. There was no consensus on "highbrow," "middle-brow," and "lowbrow" that was more pronounced than the differences based on basic demographic categories like age and gender. Belize is a mosaic when it comes to consumer preferences, not a simple hierarchy. Recent investigation in developed countries also finds the connection between taste and class to be attenuated (Land 1998; Warde 1997; though also see Featherstone 1990).

Conclusion: Cultural Capital Revisited

When Bourdieu uses the metaphor of capital he implies something stored up, acquired, and kept. The stability of high culture is perhaps this kind of capital—knowledge of Shakespeare remains a class signifier for a whole lifetime. But in Belize this kind of stable regime of taste is literally a thing of the past, either in the form of indigenous cultures that are increasingly marginalized as "traditional," or as an imperfectly translated and assimilated colonial high culture. What remains is fluid and changeable; this year's imported high culture (e.g., Lambada) is next year's street music. In such a small population, where kin ties crosscut wealth and class, exclusivity is very difficult to maintain. Belize may simply not be big enough for the exclusive economic and cultural elites or the challenging and mobile middle class that maintain the fashion system in France. The constant drain of emigration, the flow of media, and arrival of expatriates and returned migrants do not eliminate local tastes or fashions, but do prevent these tastes from crystallizing and forming a fashion system of their own.

If consumption and taste are reflections of and constitutive of power, what are the sources of power in Belize? First and foremost is economic capital in the form of ownership of business, next is ownership of land (though this has been very uneven historically). Another important source of power is education, both schooling and the knowledge and practices of a class. In Belize these knowledges and practices have usually been of two kinds: access to foreign goods, objects, styles, and knowledge; and family connections.

But now these are far from the only sources of power in Belize. Today knowledge of the foreign is no longer the monopoly of either the economic or cultural elite; it is accessible to many people directly through travel and indirectly through television and the movement of relatives back and forth. The knowledge of things foreign can be seen as a kind of cultural capital, but its source lies only partially within the family or the educational systems, and it has no legitimizing institution like a university or a social register. It can be obtained in many ways, and so loses some of its power to make social distinctions.

Bourdieu's analysis concentrates on the cultural means that reflect, constitute, and enforce the power of dominant classes. In his scheme, the rest of society belongs to the dominated classes. "It must never be forgotten that the working-class 'aesthetic' is a dominated 'aesthetic' which is constantly obliged to define itself in terms of the dominant aesthetic" (1984:41). In colonial Belize this dominance was complete among the small Bourgeoisie, but the scheme excluded the working classes to a degree that prevented them from completely accepting its dominance. Alternative systems of power grew in the working-class majority milieu that have been seen in other parts of the Caribbean as "reputation" or "the transient mode" (Austin 1983; Miller 1990; Wilson 1973). Power in this working-class context emerges from personal ability, personal knowledge, and a personal history. There are many arenas in which this kind of power can be gained through particular forms of competence: in verbal play, sexual prowess, violence, dancing, making music, having babies (Abrahams 1983). These forms of cultural capital are obtained through shared and lived experience, informal education, and social and economic commitment. Forms of consumption that legitimize and reflect this kind of power are not the simple opposites of the dominant forms. They include: foreign kinds of music (dub, rap); forms of dress (today derived from U.S. street-gang fashion), drinks, and foods; and local speech styles, vocabulary, and music.

Is this kind of capital totally antithetical to the "dominant" mode? In the past colonial society, perhaps. Today, however, it is possible to blend and meld the two in new and creative ways. For example, the educated middle class have now adopted local, "Caribbean" or pan-African styles and practices that are self-consciously similar to working-class fashions (though not dangerously similar). They can eat "roots food," listen to Caribbean music, and wear dreadlocks, but they are neat and clean dreadlocks. The hierarchy of power and capital is not gone, but it is no longer mirrored by simple hierarchies of taste.

Tastes and preferences are therefore always polysemic in Belize; there is no overwhelming order imposed by a strict hierarchy of capital. Fashion exists not in Bourdieu's two-dimensional space, linked to underlying variation in class, but in a multidimensional space tied to a series of different sources of power inside and outside of Belizean society. These other kinds of power include access to foreign culture through relatives, visits, tourism, or temporary emigration. As Basch et al. (1994) point out, transnational migration is now at least partially motivated by what the emigrant can bring and *send home*. Foreign goods create local identity on a global stage.

The paradoxical result is that in an increasingly open, global society like Belize, tastes and preferences are now more deeply localized than ever before. Local knowledge of history, people, personalities, and politics determine taste, much more than they ever did under the protective boundaries of the British empire.

Notes

Acknowledgments. An early version of this paper was presented at the conference "Defining the National," organized by Ulf Hannerz and Orvar Lofgren, in Lund, Sweden during April of 1992. I thank the participants in that conference for their comments. I also thank James Carrier, Beverly Stoeltje, Danny Miller, Anne Pyburn, and four excellent anonymous reviewers for comments that have improved this paper in many ways. Small portions of this paper previously appeared in *Ethnos* (Wilk 1993b). The research for this paper was supported by a grant from the Wenner-Gren

Foundation and a Fulbright research fellowship. Special thanks to Inez Sanchez and Gloria Crawford who taught me most of what I know and appreciate about Belizean cuisine.

1. The national flag and symbols were chosen in 1973 through a public contest; the struggle over them is a good story in itself. Medina (1997) and Judd (1989) provide excellent material on the historical emergence of ethnic categories in Belize, while Bolland (1988) defines the broader political economic context of ethnicity and class in the country.

2. Belizean restaurants appeared first in New York, then Los Angeles; Belizean cuisine is a concept invented almost entirely outside of Belize. Under a national label it submerges ethnic distinctions between what Belizeans call "Spanish" food (tamales, garnachas, chirmole), Garifuna dishes like cassava bread and fish stew (sere), and Creole foods like boil-up and rice-and-beans.

3. There was, at this time, a "Belizean dish of the day" on the menu at the most expensive and exclusive hotel in town; but this was clearly a performance for tourists, since few Belizeans could afford to eat there.

4. To illustrate we have the following quotes from the 1990 Miss Universe Belize, over nationwide radio at the opening of the annual agricultural show. "While foreigners rush to take advantage of our resources, exhibited here today, fellow Belizeans, the prosperity you seek is right before your eyes." The columnist "Smokey Joe," in the Amandala newspaper, Feb. 23, 1990, says, "I wonder why it is that everyone who comes to this country can see the beauty, but we who live here can't. They see the same garbage that we lovingly put all over the place. They see the beauty that we refuse to see. They bless us; we curse ourselves. They praise us: we condemn ourselves. Is this a better land for them, and a plague to us?"

5. Many Belizeans tell jokes and stories about ignorant bumpkins who went to the States full of wild dreams. But in 30 interviews and discussions with high school students in 1990, I never found such innocence, though Lundgren (1988) did find many naive fantasies among Belizean elementary school children.

6. The full presentation of the data from my national and high school surveys would require far more space than is available here. Extensive correlation, partial correlation, and multivariate analysis was done on this large data set; full results will be reported elsewhere.

7. This diet of flour and salt meat was common among nonagricultural hand laborers in many parts of the world in the nineteenth century. Like sugar and dried codfish, these were cheap commodities produced by relatively standardized means, which could be shipped long distances and provided cheaply by employers where there was no ready local source of foodstuff (see Mennell 1984). The early cuisine of Belize is clearly derived from the preserved rations served to sailors on board ships, whereas more agricultural parts of the Caribbean developed dishes based on local products (Mintz 1996).

8. It is interesting that today most government appeals for people to consume local foods are couched in the language of health once again. Now Belizean foods are touted as fresh and natural, as opposed to preserved and processed imports.

References

Abrahams, Roger (1983) *The Man-of-Words in the West Indies*. Baltimore: Johns Hopkins University Press.

Appadurai, Arjun (1988) How to Make a National Cuisine: Cookbooks in *Contemporary India. Comparative Studies in Society and History* 30(1):3–24.

———(1996) *Modernity at Large*. Minneapolis: University of Minnesota Press.

Arizpe, Lourdes (ed.) (1996) *The Cultural Dimensions of Global Change: An Anthropological Approach*. Vendôme, France: UNESCO.

Austin, Diane (1983) Culture and Ideology in the English-Speaking Caribbean: A View from Jamaica. *American Ethnologist* 10(2): 223–240.

Babcock, Elizabeth, and Richard Wilk (1998) International Travel and Consumer Preferences among Secondary School Students in Belize, Central America. *Caribbean Geography* 8(1):32–45.

Basch, Linda, Nina Schiller, and Cristina Blanc (1994) *Nations Unbound*. Langhorne, PA: Gordon & Breach.

Beckett, Jeremy (1996) Contested Images: Perspectives on the Indigenous Terrain in the Late 20th Century. *Identities* 3(1–2):1–13.

Bolland, Nigel (1988) *Colonialism and Resistance in Belize*. Belize City: Cubola Productions.

Bourdieu, P. (1984) *Distinction: A Social Critique of the Judgment of Taste*. Cambridge, MA: Harvard University Press.

Burke, Timothy (1996) *Lifebuoy Men, Lux Women*. Durham, NC: Duke University Press.

Conroy Richard (1997) *Our Man in Belize: A Memoir*. New York: St. Martin's Press.

Counihan, C., and P. Van Esterik (1997) Introduction. In *Food and Culture: A Reader*. C.Counihan and P. VanEsterik, eds. Pp. 1–1. New York: Routledge.

Everitt, J. C. (1987) The Torch Is Passed: Neocolonialism in Belize. *Caribbean Quarterly* 33(3&4):42–59.

Featherstone, M. (1990) Perspectives on Consumer Culture. *Sociology* 24(1): 5–22.

Foster, Robert J. (1991) Making National Cultures in the Global Ecumene. *Annual Review of Anthropology* 20: 235–260.

Friedman, Jonathan (1990) Being in the World: Globalization and Localization. *Theory, Culture and Society* 7: 311–328.

——— (1992) The Past in the Future: History and the Politics of Identity. *American Anthropologist* 94(4):837–859.

——— (1994) *Cultural Identity and Global Process.* London: Sage.

Hannerz, Ulf (1987) The World in Creolization. *Africa* 57(4):546–559.

Howes David (1996) Introduction: Commodities and Cultural Borders. In *Cross Cultural Consumption: Global Markets, Local Realities.* DavidHowes, ed. Pp. 1–16. London: Routledge.

Jenkins, Richard (1994) Rethinking Ethnicity: Identity, Categorization and Power. *Ethnic and Racial Studies* 17(2):197–223.

Judd, Karen (1989) Cultural Synthesis or Ethnic Struggle? Creolization in Belize. *Cimarron* 1–2:103–118.

Kuisel, Richard (1993) *Seducing the French: The Dilemma of Americanization.* Berkeley: University of California Press.

Land, Birgit (1998) *Consumer's Dietary Patterns and Desires for Change.* Working Paper 31, Center for Market Surveillance, Research and Strategy for the Food Sector, Aarhus, Denmark.

Lofgren, Orvar (1993) Materializing the Nation in Sweden and America. *Ethnos* 58(3–4):161–196.

Lundgren, Nancy (1988) When I Grow Up I Want a Trans Am: Children in Belize Talk about Themselves and the Impact of the World Capitalist System. *Dialectical Anthropology* 13:269–276.

Medina, Laurie (1997) Defining Difference, Forging Unity: The Construction of Race, *Ethnicity and Nation in Belize. Ethnic and Racial Studies* 20(4):757–780.

Mennell, S. (1984) *All Manners of Food: Eating and Taste in England and France from the Middle Ages to the Present.* Oxford: Blackwell.

Miller, Daniel (1990) Fashion and Ontology in Trinidad. *Culture and History* 7:49–78.

——— (1994) *Modernity: An Ethnographic Approach.* London: Berg Publishers.

——— (1997) *Capitalism: An Ethnographic Approach.* Oxford: Berg Publishers.

Mintz, Sidney (1996) *Tasting Food, Tasting Freedom,* Boston: Beacon Press.

Munt, Ian, and Egbert Higinio (1993) Eco-Tourism Waves in Belize. In *Globalization and Development: Challenges and Prospects for Belize. Speareports 9.* Society for the Promotion of Education and Research, Belize City. pp. 34–48.

Olwig, Karen (1993) Defining the National in the Transnational: Cultural Identity in the Afro-Caribbean Diaspora. *Ethnos* 58(3–4): 361–376.

Orlove, Benjamin (ed.) (1997) *The Allure of the Foreign: Imported Goods in Post-Colonial Latin America.* Ann Arbor: The University of Michigan Press.

Petch, T. (1987) Television and Video Ownership in Belize. *Belizean Studies* 15(1):12–14.

Salzman, Philip (1996) The Electronic Trojan Horse: Television in the Globalization of Paramodern Cultures. In *The Cultural Dimensions of Global Change: An Anthropological Approach.* LourdesArizpe, ed. Pp. 197–216. Vendôme, France: UNESCO.

Shoman, Assad (1985) *Party Politics in Belize.* Benque Viejo, Belize: Cubola.

Stone, Michael (1994) Caribbean Nation, Central American State: Ethnicity, Race, and National Formation in Belize, 1798–1990. Ph.D. dissertation, University of Texas, Austin.

Tobin, Joseph (1992) Introduction: Domesticating the West. In *Re-made in Japan: Everyday Life and Consumer Taste in a Changing Society.* JamesTobin (ed.), pp. 1–41. New Haven, CT: Yale University Press.

Vernon, Dylan (1990) Belizean Exodus to the United States: For Better or Worse. In *Speareport 4,* Society for the Promotion of Education and Research, Belize City. Pp. 6–28.

Warde, Alan (1997) *Consumption, Food and Taste.* London: Sage Publications.

Watson, James, (ed.) (1997) *Golden Arches East: McDonald's in East Asia.* Stanford: Stanford University Press.

Wilk, Richard (1990) Consumer Goods as Dialogue about Development: Research in Progress in Belize. *Culture and History* 7: 79–100.

——— (1993a) "It's Destroying a Whole Generation": Television and Moral Discourse in Belize. *Visual Anthropology* 5:229–244.

——— (1993b). Beauty and the Feast: Official and Visceral Nationalism in Belize. *Ethnos* 53(3–4):1–25.

——— (1995) Colonial Time and TV Time: Television and Temporality in Belize. *Visual Anthropology Review* 10(1). 94–102.

——— (1997) A Critique of Desire: Distaste and Dislike in Consumer Behavior. *Consumption, Markets and Culture* 1(2):175–196.

Wilk, Richard, and Stephen Miller (1997) Some Methodological Issues in Counting Communities and Households. *Human Organization* 56(1):64–71.

Wilson, Peter (1973) *Crab Antics.* New Haven, CT: Yale University Press.

27

Let's Cook Thai: Recipes for Colonialism*

Lisa Heldke

I think I've finally figured out why I like Thanksgiving dinner so much, why I enjoy having it at my house, cooking all the food myself, and eating it—sometimes for days afterward. It's because I never wonder what to fix. I prepare virtually the same meal every year. It's a ritual for me; turkey, stuffing, mashed potatoes, gravy, squash, and pumpkin and mince pie appear every year. I like it this way. It's comfortable. It's delicious. I do it only once a year. And my mom does it that way. And there, perhaps, lies the crux of the matter. I have been eating this meal one day a year for my entire life, and over the years, it has come to be virtually the only full meal that my mother and I cook in common.

When I went away to graduate school some fifteen years ago, I entered a world of experimental cooking and eating, a world heavily populated with academics and people with disposable incomes who like to travel. It's a world in which entire cuisines can go in and out of vogue in a calendar year. Where lists of "in" ingredients are published in the glamorous food magazines to which some of us subscribe. In which people whisper conspiratorially about this place that just opened serving Hmong cuisine. It's a wonderful world, full of tastes I never tasted growing up in Rice Lake, Wisconsin, textures I never experienced in the land of hot dish. I love cooking and eating in that world.

However, I never know what to cook when I invite people over for dinner. Sometimes I get paralyzed with indecision. The night before the event, the floor of my living room is covered with cookbooks bristling with book-marks. There are cookbooks by my bed and next to the bathtub, even some actually in the kitchen. I've sketched out five possible menus, each featuring foods of a different nationality, most of them consisting of several dishes I've never cooked before. My mom doesn't do this. When she invites guests for dinner, she selects a menu from among her standards, preparing foods she's prepared and enjoyed countless times before, knowing that once again they will turn out well and everyone will enjoy the meal. I miss that. I envy that—especially when I spend three hours trying to decide on a menu, or when I try a new dish for company and it turns out to be awful and everyone at the meal has to try to pretend they are enjoying it.

So why do I do it? Surely no one holds a freshly sharpened carving knife to my throat and says "cook Indonesian next week when those people you barely know

*Originally published 2001

come over for dinner!" What's my motivation, anyway? Excellent question. And, as it turns out, disturbing answer—an answer of which I've come to be deeply suspicious.

After years of adventurous eating in graduate school and now as a professor, I have come to be seriously uncomfortable about the easy acquisitiveness with which I approach a new kind of food, the tenacity with which I collect eating adventures—as one might collect ritual artifacts from another culture without thinking about the appropriateness of removing them from their cultural setting. Other eating experiences have made me reflect on the circumstances that conspired to bring such far-flung cuisines into my world. On my first visit to an Eritrean restaurant, for example, I found myself thinking about how disturbing and how complicated it was to be eating the food of people who were in the middle of yet another politically and militarily induced famine. On another occasion, an offhand remark in a murder mystery I was reading started me thinking about the reasons there were so many Vietnamese restaurants in Minneapolis/St. Paul, reasons directly connected to the U.S. war in Vietnam and the resultant dislocation of Vietnamese, Laotian, and Hmong people.[1]

Cultural Colonialism

Eventually, I put a name to my penchant for ethnic foods—particularly the foods of economically dominated cultures. The name I chose was "cultural food colonialism." I had come to see my adventure cooking and eating as strongly motivated by an attitude bearing deep connections to Western colonialism and imperialism. When I began to examine my tendency to go culture hopping in the kitchen, I found that the attitude with which I approached such activities bore an uncomfortable resemblance to the attitude of various nineteenth- and early twentieth-century European painters, anthropologists, and explorers who set out in search of ever "newer," ever more "remote" cultures they could co-opt, borrow from freely and out of context, and use as the raw materials for their own efforts at creation and discovery.[2]

Of course, my eating was not simply colonizing; it was also an effort to play and to learn about other cultures in ways that I intended to be respectful. But underneath, or alongside, or over and above these other reasons, I could not deny that I was motivated by a deep desire to have contact with—to somehow own an experience of—an exotic Other as a way of making myself more interesting. Food adventuring, I was coming to decide, made me a participant in cultural colonialism, just as surely as eating Mexican strawberries in January made me a participant in economic colonialism.

This chapter is part of a larger work, *Let's Eat Chinese*, which explores the nature of cultural food colonialism: What is it? What are its symptoms, its manifestations, its cures? Who does it? Where? Why? In that work, I consider a range of activities in which food adventurers participate—everything from dining out to cooking to food journalism—and how these activities manifest and reproduce cultural food colonialism. Here I look specifically at ethnic cookbooks. Cookbooks, like restaurant reviews, and like dining in ethnic restaurants, manifest cultural food colonialism in two ways: first, they speak to the food adventurer's never-ending quest for novel eating experiences—where novelty is also read as exoticism, and second, they turn the ethnic Other into a resource for the food adventurer's own use.

Before plunging further into an exploration of these two features of cultural colonialism, I pause to situate my project within the field of feminist thought. I see it as a feminist project on at least two levels. At the first, most banal level, my field of inquiry—food and cooking—is something traditionally regarded as "women's arena." For at least several decades now, feminist theorists have been exploring those domains of human experience traditionally identified as "belonging" to women. Reproductive issues, childbirth, the work of mothering, sexuality, sex work, pornography, women's health, and any number of other features of human life have come to be examined by scholars because of the efforts of feminists who have seen these "women's issues" as relevant *theoretical* issues. Feminist theorists have now begun to turn serious attention to food and eating—for nearly the first time since that original food theorist Plato took it up.[3]

I also understand this as a feminist project because of my theoretical approach; my work attempts to take up challenges posed by various strands of feminist theory, most notably those strands developed by feminists of color and Third World feminists (for example, bell hooks, Trinh T. Min-ha, Joanna Kadi). One of the most important lessons white feminists learned from the work of feminists of color in the 1980s was that oppression—women's oppression—always exists along multiple axes simultaneously. Feminists must therefore take racism and classism seriously as central features of *women's* oppression—not as add-ons that can be considered after the "real" challenges of "women's" oppression have been met.

In the 1990s that lesson further evolved to emphasize the importance of investigating one's own privilege within systems of oppression—consider, for example, Ruth Frankenburg's analyses of the nature of whiteness. My work takes up the feminist project of interrogating my own location in systems of privilege and oppression—systems that variously privilege and marginalize me.[4] I explore cultural food colonialism, in part, in an attempt to understand my racial/ethnic and class privilege.

Let's Cook Thai

Take a walk through the cookbook section of your local book supermarket and you will confront a gigantic subsection of books promising to teach their readers how to cook some ethnic cuisine. The shelves will hold several works that have become classics in the field, such as Claudia Roden's *A Book of Middle Eastern Food and An Invitation to Indian Cooking* by Madhur Jaffrey. It will also include a significant number of new arrivals—new both in the sense of their publication dates and in terms of the cuisine they tout. (In the past fifteen years, for example, mainstream America has "discovered" the cuisines of Southeast Asia—especially Thailand, Vietnam, and Indonesia—and, even more recently, the foods of both East and West Africa.) You will also find a number of books that are the culinary equivalent of *If This Is Tuesday, It Must Be Belgium*—cookbooks that give you a smattering of recipes from every region of the globe, along with a winsome anecdote or two about the people of that region. The ethnic cookbook market has exploded in the United States, as has the market for the equipment, ingredients, and spices to cook the foods of the world. How does this explosion of interest in ethnic cooking feed into the phenomenon of cultural food colonialism?

Consider one example, *The Original Thai Cookbook* by Jennifer Brennan. Brennan opens her book with these lines: "It is dusk in Bangkok and you are going out to dinner. The chauffeured Mercedes 280 sweeps you from your luxury hotel through streets lined with large, spreading trees and picturesque tile-roofed wooden shops and houses." Brennan goes on to describe "your" arrival at an elegant Thai home— where you are greeted by an "exquisite, delicately boned Thai woman, youthful but of indeterminate age"—and also your meal—a "parade of unfamiliar and exotic dishes" (3–4).

Renato Rosaldo has coined the phrase "imperialist nostalgia" to describe the long-ing of the colonizer for that which he perceives to be destroyed by imperialism. Brennan here evokes what might be called nostalgia *for* imperialism when she invites her readers to imagine themselves as wealthy and privileged visitors in a culture not their own, and in which they are treated with great deference and respect by some of the wealthiest, most important people in the culture.

Brennan invites her readers to *be* the protagonist of this colonialist story. Her descriptions invite those readers to luxuriate in a fantasy of wealth and also beauty; she suggests that her readers—who are primarily women—should see themselves as "tall and angular" (5), a description that manifests long-standing Euro-American standards of feminine beauty emphasizing long, thin limbs. Reading this description, I find myself seduced by the glamorous role she has assigned me, a middle-class Euro-American woman who has never even been in a Mercedes, let alone traveled to Thailand, and whose body, while fairly tall, would never be described as angular. Just throw in some high cheekbones and a tousled mop of thick, blond hair while you're at it, and I'll sign up for this fantasy tour.

Brennan's description also effectively reduces the identity of the imaginary Thai hostess to her relationship with her guests; Brennan has invented this woman expressly to provide us Western "dinner guests" with pleasure, both visual and gustatory. The "exotic woman" provides just the right touch of beauty, mystery, and servility to get us Western gals into the spirit of imagining ourselves as the heroines of this colonial-ist culinary tale.[5]

Although she eventually gets down to the business of telling her readers how to cook their own food (a detail that acknowledges that we do not in fact have a Thai cook of our own), Brennan never completely dismisses the colonialist fantasy she has created. Her introduction to this book is just one illustration of the ways that ethnic cookbooks manifest and foster cultural colonization—in this case, by perpetu-ating a view of the Other as existing to serve and please the reader, and by creating a vision of this Other culture as exotic and alluring.

The Quest for the Exotic

Modern Western colonizing societies have been characterized in part by an obsessive attraction to the new, the unique, the obscure, and the unknown, where "new" is understood in relation to the colonizing society. Desire for new territory, new goods, new trade routes, and new sources of slaves sent European colonizers out to capture and control the rest of the world. The desire to understand the essence of human nature sent European and American anthropologists on a quest to find new, primitive societies not yet exposed to (Western) culture. The desire for new, unadulterated inspiration prompted European painters to move to places far from home. And today, desires for new flavors, new textures, and new styles of dining send us adventuring eaters flipping through the Yellow Pages, scouring the ads in ethnic and alternative newspapers, and wandering down unfamiliar streets in our cities, looking for restaurants featuring cuisines we've not yet experienced—"exotic" cuisines. For the food adventurer, the allure and attraction of such cuisines often consists quite simply in their unfamiliarity and unusualness.

Why does the novel hold such fascination for the food adventurer in American culture? We adventurers come to demand a continual supply of novelty in our diets in part simply to remain entertained. We crave the new just because it is unusual, unexpected, different; differentness is something we have come to expect and require. Of course, it is in the nature of novelty that it is quickly exhausted; if what we crave is novelty per se, our quest will be never-ending. Food magazines often feature articles informing their readers (in all seriousness) about which cuisines and ingredients are now "out" and which have come "in." In a single article, the daily diet of the people of Thailand can be declared passé in the United States.

Novelty is also attractive to adventuring food colonizers because it marks the presence of the exotic, where exotic is understood to mean not only "not local" but also "excitingly unusual." The exotic, in turn, we read as an indication of authenticity. Exotic food is understood as authentic precisely *because* of its strangeness, its novelty. Because it is unfamiliar to me, I assume it must be a genuine or essential part of that other culture; it becomes the marker of what distinguishes my culture from another. Whatever is so evidently not a part of my own culture must truly be a part of this other one. So, in a three-step process, that which is novel to me ends up being exotic, and that which is exotic I end up defining as most authentic to a culture.

How does the quest for the novel-exotic-authentic show up in ethnic cookbooks? Ethnic cookbooks teach their readers how to make the strange familiar by teaching them how to replicate unknown dishes. But how can the cookbook writer achieve this goal without sacrificing the exoticism of the food, given that exoticism has its roots in novelty—in unfamiliarity?

One answer is that for the cook, casual familiarity with a cuisine still radically unfamiliar to most of "us" represents a relationship to the exotic that is itself worth considerable cultural capital, in Pierre Bourdieu's term. A person who achieves such familiarity in a sense becomes the exotic—or at least the exotic once removed. If I can make Indonesian dishes that other food adventurers can only eat in restaurants, I become a kind of exotic myself. Jennifer Brennan—the cookbook author who took us for a ride in Bangkok in her Mercedes—approaches novelty this way in her cookbook.

Jennifer Brennan: The Exotic as Familiar

In the preface to *The Original Thai Cookbook*, Brennan writes that although there are now "Oriental" and Thai markets in "nearly every town," they are filled with "a dazzling and, sometimes, baffling array of foodstuffs: native herbs and spices . . . unusual species of fish; unlabeled cuts of meat; vegetables you might consider weeding from your garden; assortments of strange canned foods and sauces—all with exotic names, sometimes foreign language labels—all purveyed by shopkeepers unfamiliar with English."[6] In other words, although ingredients for Thai food are readily available to non-Thai cooks, availability does not automatically spell familiarity. Brennan emphasizes that language is of little help to the cook here; things are unlabeled, or labeled in a "foreign language," and the people in the stores speak another language too.[7]

Recall Brennan's invitation to imagine yourself visiting an elegant Thai home and being served a banquet. Brennan's lengthy description of this imaginary event highlights the glamorous novelty of everything from the street scenes to the clothing to the way the foods are presented. Her "reassurance of exoticism" serves two related purposes. First, it assures the nervous home cook, perhaps preparing a meal with which to impress her coworkers, that she is not simply naive or ignorant or overly cautious. This food really is strange! You don't have to be embarrassed about finding it so, because it really is! Second, it may confirm for the cook that the food she will learn to make is, in some apparently objective sense, exotic, and even familiarity with it cannot alter that fact. Its exoticism means that a cook will definitely earn cultural capital if she serves it to her dinner guests, for whom home-cooked Thai food is still likely to be a novelty.

Another example illustrates both purposes. It comes from a cookbook published twenty years before Brennan's, titled *Japanese Food and Cooking*. In the foreword, author Stuart Griffin describes the respective experiences of "Mrs. American Housewife" and "Mr. American Husband," who have moved to Japan. Mr. American Husband's arrival predates that of his wife, so he has had time to explore Japanese cuisine and to determine that he "could leave a lot of Japanese food alone," specifically the "big, briny tubs of pickles, the fish stands where every species eyed him, and the small stool-and-counter shops with the stomach-turning cooking-oil smells. . . . But he found lots of things that he wanted to eat and did like" (xii). When Mrs. American Housewife arrives, her husband and her Japanese cook enter into a conspiracy to get her to try Japanese dishes. By the end of the foreword, Mrs. American Housewife is hosting dinner parties for her (American) friends, featuring an "entirely Japanese" menu (xiv)—prepared, of course, by her cook. In presenting such foods to her guests, Mrs. A. becomes to her friends a kind of exotic herself.

When Brennan and Griffin describe food as "strange" and "stomach-turning," to whom are they speaking? Brennan identifies her audience as English-speaking people in the United States. (Notably, the gender references have disappeared by the time Brennan published her cookbook; nevertheless, it is still safe to assume that the person wielding the cookbook in a kitchen is a woman.) But in emphasizing the "unfamiliarity" of the foods, Brennan actually specifies her audience much further. Presumably, Thai Americans would find many of the ingredients in Thai food quite familiar. The same would likely be true of many Vietnamese Americans, Chinese Americans, Indian Americans, Malaysian Americans—any people whose heritage foods have influenced and been influenced by Thai foods. The ingredients Brennan describes would, in fact, be deeply unfamiliar only to *certain* English speakers in the United States. But Brennan's description of the Asian grocery recognizes no such distinctions; "you" will find things strange in such a store, she notes. "Strange," like "exotic," comes to mean strange in principle because strange to us.

Even authors who are insiders to the cuisines about which they write come to use words evincing novelty and exoticism to describe their own cuisines. Claudia Roden, for example, evokes notions of the exotic Middle East when she variously describes certain salads as "rich and exotic" (59), baba ghanoush as "exciting and vulgarly seductive" (46), and Turkish Delight as a food "no harem film scene could be without" (423). That such descriptions also often employ sexual imagery is, of course, no accident; as we saw earlier in Brennan's description, linking food with sexuality or the sexual attractiveness of women is one way to emphasize the exoticism of a food. Women reading this cookbook may feel as though we are being invited to see ourselves as "vulgarly seductive" by extension, when we cook this food.

The Other as Resource

Middle-class members of a colonizing society such as the United States inhabit an atmosphere in which it becomes customary to regard members of a colonized culture as "resources," sources of materials to be extracted to enhance one's own life. In the case of cultural colonialism, the materials are cultural ones. It is no coincidence that the cultures most likely to undergo such treatment at the hands of food adventurers are those described as Third World or nonwhite. There is a tangled interconnection in Euro-American culture between those cultures defined as exotic and Other, and those identified as Third World.

In the world of the ethnic cookbook, the cooking techniques of the Other become marvelous resources that can be scooped up, "developed," and sold to Us, without giving much attention or credit to the women actually responsible for preserving and expanding this cuisine. Recipes become commodities we are entitled to possess when they are taken up into the Western cookbook industry; foods become "developed" when they can be prepared in the West.

In her book *Imperial Eyes*, Mary Louise Pratt suggests that to treat the Other as a resource for one's own use can take many forms—even veneration and admiration.[8] This observation is well worth keeping in mind when one examines ethnic cookbooks, because many of them exhibit appreciation for a food tradition even as they preserve an "essential colonized quality" (163) in the relationship between the cookbook writer and her cook/informant. The case of recipe collecting provides one excellent illustration of this.

Borrowing or Stealing?

Where do recipes come from? And when is it proper to say that a recipe was "stolen," or inadequately credited? When it comes to cookbooks in general, and "ethnic" cookbooks in particular, the definitions of these terms decidedly favor the interests of colonizers. A cookbook author is described as having "stolen" recipes only if they have previously appeared in *published* form—a form of communicating that privileges people on the basis of class and education as well as race, and often sex. Consider the following case: Ann Barr and Paul Levy in *The Foodie Handbook* praise Claudia Roden for her careful "anthropological" work to credit sources of her recipes in *A Book of Middle Eastern Food* (110). But although Roden is careful to identify the sources of the recipes she reproduces when those sources are cookbooks, she acknowledges unpublished sources by name only in the acknowledgments to her book—and then only in a brief, general list of those women to whom she is "particularly indebted."

Barr and Levy's praise for the integrity of "scholar cooks"[9] such as Roden rests on the unstated assumption that only published sources require crediting—an assumption validated by and codified in copyright laws and institutional policies regarding plagiarism. This assumption allows them to regard as highly principled Roden's practice of sometimes describing, but almost never naming, the Middle Eastern women cooks from whom she receives these previously unpublished recipes. But when coupled with her careful crediting of previously published recipes, her practices actually create cookbooks that reflect and reinforce the colonialist and classist societies into which they are received and from which they come. (By "societies from which they come," I mean primarily colonialist Western societies. Their work comes from these societies in a complex manner because Roden is an Egyptian Jew who was educated and has spent much of her adult life in Europe; she is a kind of "insider outsider" who, in part because of her class position, did not in fact learn to cook until she went to Europe.)

In Roden's cookbook, the unpublished women who contributed recipes become interchangeable parts, relevant only for the (universalizable) quality of their being "native cooks." She tells "colorful" stories about some of them in the body of the book, but the reader can match their names to their stories (or their recipes) in only a few cases—and then only with assiduous detective work. They need not be identified definitively, because they cannot be stolen from; they do not own their creations in any genuine (read: legally binding) sense of the word. On the other hand, the creations of cookbook authors, who have access to the machinery of publishing, must be respected and properly attributed.

Barr and Levy's praise of Roden is situated in the context of their discussion of a case of recipe plagiarism. For cookbook writers, the ethics of recipe "borrowing" versus "theft" seem to follow the rules governing plagiarism. According to these, borrowing only becomes theft if a recipe has already appeared in print and one fails explicitly to acknowledge it. Cookbook writers express shock, dismay, or anger when another writer reproduces one of their published recipes without citing its source. However, they waste no emotion over the writer who reproduces recipes gathered "in the field" from unpublished "sources" who go unnamed and uncredited.[10]

Taking up the legal issue, Barr and Levy argue that it is both "mad" and "unenforceable" to suggest that an individual ought to have the right to copyright the directions for an omelet or a traditional French casserole (108); how could any individual "own" the procedure for making dishes so ubiquitous? On the other hand, they favorably report that in a 1984 case Richard Olney successfully sued Richard Nelson for copyright infringement, claiming that Nelson had reproduced thirty-nine of Olney's published recipes in one of his own cookbooks. Thus, while they are uncomfortable with the idea of copyrighting some kinds of recipes, Barr and Levy suggest that justice was served in the Olney case, because Olney is an "originator" of recipes (110)—as opposed to an anthologist (like Nelson) or an anthropologist (like Roden).

In support of their view, Barr and Levy quote passages of the relevant recipes to show that Nelson copied ingredients, procedures, even stylistic touches from Olney.

Olney "owned" his recipes in a way that no one can own the omelet recipe because he both "invented" and published them. The latter step apparently is necessary; Barr and Levy have no pity for the author who prints recipes on index cards and distributes them to her friends and then cries "thief."[11] But in the end, it doesn't matter; just because you receive in the mail an unsigned copy of *On the Road*, written in pencil on paper torn from a wide-ruled spiral notebook, you cannot publish Jack Kerouac's words under your own name.

But what of other cases, in which the recipes in question are not originals, but are the "ethnic" equivalents of the omelet? How are we to understand the "ownership rights" of an "anthropologist cook" who publishes the recipes she has "collected in the field," only to have someone else republish those recipes in their own book? Does the anthropologist have the right to complain about theft? Barr and Levy suggest that she does, in their sympathetic consideration of Claudia Roden, whose work has been the site of much borrowing by other cookbook authors. Barr and Levy report that Roden is pleased to see people using the recipes she gathered but not so pleased to see those recipes reappearing in print. In particular, she is "hurt and angry that Arto der Haroutunian, in his books . . . has a great many of the same recipes as hers (*some of which had never been in print before*), similarly described and including some of the mistakes. . . . As a writer who gathered her material physically, Mrs. Roden feels 'He has stolen my shadow' " (112, emphasis added). Roden's anger here suggests that it is not only the originator of a recipe whose work can be stolen; you are also a victim of theft if the recipes you collect and publish are subsequently published by someone else.

That Roden is the victim of a theft of "original material" seems obvious on one level. In a context defined by copyright law, der Haroutunian's acts do constitute a kind of plagiarism of Roden's original work. But consider the matter again; what he stole were, for the most part, recipes she gathered from other women—along with published texts she excerpted and organized in a particular way. Publishing, in this context, comes to be its own kind of originality—or comes to mean originality.

Furthermore, publishing a thing seems to make it one's own, regardless of who "owned" it in the first place. Roden does not claim that she created the recipes; indeed she expressly describes them as belonging to the particular towns, villages, communities, countries in which she located them (Barr and Levy 112). Nevertheless, she says that *her* shadow has been stolen by der Haroutunian.

While I agree that some kind of harm has been done to Roden by those who have republished parts of her book, I want to redirect the discussion to the kinds of harm that her explanation obscures—namely, harm done to the Middle Eastern women at whose stoves Roden stood and from whom she learned the recipes she reproduced in her cookbook. This harm does not fall neatly under the category of theft, because the women cannot be regarded as the owners of recipes in the sense required. The language of property does not help us to understand such harm for at least two reasons: first, these cooks have not laid any claim to the recipes (say, by publishing them themselves or by cooking them in a restaurant for paying customers), nor will they likely do so, because, second, the recipes from which they cook are often as common to them as the omelet is to a French cook, and thus not the sort of thing they would be inclined to think could be owned. It is not appropriate to describe Claudia Roden as "stealing" recipes from the women with whom she studied. She could not rectify the harm done to them simply by documenting the "originators" of her recipes.

Roden erases or generalizes the identities of most of the women who give her recipes.[12] She does identify various of her relatives as the sources of recipes; she notes, for example, that "my mother discovered [this recipe] in the Sudan, and has made it ever since" (43). But in most cases, she mentions only the primary region in which a dish is served and says nothing about the particular woman or women from whom she got the recipe. (Recipes are peppered with phrases such as "A Greek favorite," and "Found in different versions in Tunisia and Morocco.") By contrast, she carefully notes the dishes she found in particular published cookbooks. (For example, with respect to a chicken recipe, she notes: "A splendid dish described to me by an aunt in Paris, the origin of which I was thrilled to discover in al-Baghdadi's medieval cooking manual" [184].) The effect of this differential treatment is to blur the "ordinary" women who contributed to this cookbook into a mass of interchangeable parts. She renders invisible the work done by members of this mass to create, modify, adapt, and compile recipes; it does not matter which individual was responsible for which modification. Only her own work on these tasks is visible in her text.

A critic could reasonably respond that, in fact, these recipes have no originators: "You have already pointed out that many of them are as ubiquitous in the Middle East as the omelet is in France. Are you advocating that Roden give credit to particular women for their contributions of a particular recipe? Why would that make sense, given their ubiquity?" My first answer would be that it makes as much sense to credit these conduits as it does to credit Roden herself; their participation in making these recipes available is certainly as relevant as hers. Her interaction with the publishing industry should not alone give her special, superior claims to ownership.

Furthermore, I do not advocate making particular women, or even their communities, the owners of recipes any more than I advocate allowing Roden to make that claim. The problem emerges from the fact that Roden and other anthropologist cooks transform "traditional" recipes into commodities. They treat the recipes they gather as resources—raw materials onto which they put their creative stamp—by surrounding the recipes with scholarly background information, a personal anecdote, or a relevant quotation from a work of poetry or literature. With this creative transformation, the recipes become property that can be stolen.

Roden has gathered the creative productions of various peoples to make her own cultural creation. Other women's (often other cultures') recipes are the raw materials she harvested and "refined" into a work of "genuine culture." In her case, this refinement involved situating the recipes alongside erudite quotations from Middle Eastern texts, stories she collected about the various dishes, or accounts of the pro-cesses by which she came into possession of the recipes. Because she regards her work as a genuine cultural product—not just a "natural outgrowth" of a culture, as is the case with the recipes she collects—she expresses outrage at its being plagiarized.

I want to look at the issue of recipe originality, borrowing, and theft in one final way before leaving it. Another factor contributing to the complexity of this issue is that everyday recipe creation has traditionally been women's work done in the home, whereas the harms that are identified and codified by law tend to be those that befall the creative work men have traditionally done in more public arenas.

Like other kinds of women's creative work, such as quilting and weaving, recipe creation tends to be social. By this I mean not only that the physical work may be done in groups, but also that the creation is frequently the result of many women's contributing their own ideas to the general plan, often over considerable spans of time. A recipe that passes from one cook to another may undergo slight modifications to accommodate differences in taste or unavailability of an ingredient, to streamline or complicate a process, or for unidentifiable reasons.[13] We might say that such a recipe is "original" to everyone and no one; its beginning is unknown, but the contributions of particular cooks may be read in it by someone who knows how to decipher such an "evolutionary" record. (I once heard a food expert analyze the Thanksgiving dinners of several families living in different parts of the United States. On the basis of the foods present in the meal, and the way that those foods were prepared, she was able to identify, with accuracy, the areas of the country in which that family had lived over the past generations.) Cooks who have contributed to the evolution of a recipe may well be pleased and proud when someone else takes up their modification—whether or not the other cook knows who is responsible for it.

The categories originality and plagiarism pertain to more individualistic art forms, such as novel writing and painting—which have been regarded as "high art" and have primarily been the purview of a privileged minority of men. These terms cannot be applied so aptly to other art forms, particularly collective and cumulative ones. However, they often are (awkwardly) applied to these forms, perhaps as an attempt to gain legitimacy for them. For example, women often have (in reality and in fiction) appealed to claims of originality and ownership, to accuse others of "stealing" their recipes. Of course, the women who have done so are often subjected to mockery. (My morning radio station regularly plays the song "Lime Jello, Marshmallow, Cottage Cheese Surprise," in which a woman discusses the dishes that have been brought to a "ladies' " potluck luncheon. The singer, who brought the title dish to the potluck, at one point exclaims, "I did not steal that recipe, it's lies, I tell you, lies!" The line is greeted with guffaws of laughter from the audience.) I suggest that such mockery reflects both the pervasive sense that an individual's recipes are not original to them and thus cannot be owned by them and the sense that, even if recipes could be stolen, their theft would be no crime since recipes simply aren't important enough to be the objects of moral concern.[14]

Recipes for Anticolonialism

When I began exploring cultural food colonialism, I naively believed that cooking was an unambiguously anticolonialist activity, one that could be employed by anyone who wished to develop a way of living in the world that resisted colonialism. Although I no longer think of cooking as magically resistant and am deeply critical of much that goes on in the pages of various ethnic cookbooks, I still believe that cooking has important potential as a site for anticolonialist activity. Food is a wonderful medium for this because culinary diversity is already so much a part of the daily life of many Americans—and because food in general is an essential part of everyone's daily life. Because we must eat, opportunities for becoming anticolonialist in the kitchen present themselves to us with tremendous frequency. Most of us don't go to art museums or concerts every day of the week—but we do eat dinner every night, and we often cook it ourselves.

The question for me is, How can one enact anticolonialist resistance in the kitchen, the grocery story, the cookbook? How can I transform my ethnic cooking into what bell hooks calls a critical intervention in the machinery of colonialism? We who would be anticolonialists must learn how to engage with cuisines, cooks, and eaters from cultures other than our own—not as resources but as conversation partners. We must also recognize that our privilege (racial, ethnic, class, gender) is something food adventurers cannot simply give up, that while I have the luxury of experimenting with other cuisines in the kitchen, my privilege—and my guilt about it—will not be banished simply by my forsaking this luxury.

Writing on the subject of white racism against blacks, bell hooks argues, "Subject to subject contact between white and black which signals the absence of domination . . . must emerge through mutual choice and negotiation . . . [S]imply by expressing their desire for 'intimate' contact with black people, white people do not eradicate the politics of racial domination" (28). Cookbook author Jennifer Brennan does not magically neutralize the colonialist dynamic between herself and her private cook simply by making herself at home in the kitchen and cozying up to the cook to ask sincere, well-meaning questions about whether the Thai really use ketchup in their *paad thai*. Such presumed intimacy can in fact reinforce the dynamic, because it highlights the unreciprocated ways Brennan has access to her cook.

What would mutual choice and negotiation require in such an interaction, what must happen in order to change this into a subject-to-subject exchange? At the very least, Brennan and her "changing parade of household cooks" (preface) would have to discuss the terms under which it would be justifiable for her to publish their work— to take their skills and recipes and market them under her own name. It would require that the cooks be able to make an informed choice about whether or not to participate in this cookbook-making enterprise in the first place—that they understand the larger, long-term consequences of participating in it. Would they still want to participate in the project if they knew how angry Claudia Roden was about Middle Eastern cuisine's unfortunate transformation in the pages of Euro-American cookbooks? They may; my point is that mutual choice would require that both parties making the choices have sufficient information on which to base their choices. Given that Brennan has the publishing power—and more access to information about how these recipes will be used in the United States—she has a particular obligation to exchange that information with her cooks.

"Mutual recognition of racism," hooks continues, "its impact both on those who are dominated and those who dominate, is the only standpoint that makes possible an encounter between races that is not based on denial and fantasy" (28). Such a requirement would transform the way in which Euro-American cookbook writers such as Brennan collect their materials for ethnic cookbooks; it would also result in cookbooks with a very different format. Perhaps ethnic cookbooks written by out-siders to a cuisine could be constructed in ways that actually acknowledge and grapple with the fact of continued colonialist domination by Western cultures. Perhaps cookbooks could be written as genuine collaborations, as opposed to the de facto collaborations they so often are now. (It's worth nothing, in this regard, that collaboration is already highly developed and appreciated in one arena—namely, the community fund-raising cookbook. In such cookbooks, one often finds multiple, nearly identical, copies of a recipe, each credited to a different cook. Such repetition may seem ridiculous to someone who just wants to know how to make a dish, but when it is considered as a record of how a community cooks, it becomes a valuable source of information.)

Hooks' message, translated into the realm of food adventuring, is that our only hope for becoming anticolonialists lies in our placing the colonizing relationship squarely in the center of the dining table; only by addressing colonialism directly through our cooking and eating can we possibly transform them into activities that resist exploitation. If "eating ethnic" cannot remain pleasurable once we acknowledge how domination shapes our exchanges with the Other, then we must acknowledge that it is a pleasure well lost.[15]

The anticolonialist aims to disengage from an attitude and a way of life that exploit and oppress and to develop alternatives that subvert the colonizing order. We need to learn how to participate in anticolonialist exchanges of food. We need to find useful, anticolonialist ways to make dinner.

Notes

This article is an earlier version of an argument that eventually appeared in *Exotic Appetites: Ruminations of a Food Adventurer* (Routledge 2004).

1. Sara Paretsky, in her 1985 novel *Killing Orders*, writes, "I stopped for a breakfast falafel sandwich at a storefront lebanese restaurant. The decimation of Lebanon was showing up in Chicago as a series of restaurants and little shops, just as the destruction of Vietnam had been visible here a decade earlier. If you never read the news but ate out a lot you should be able to tell who was getting beaten up around the world" (36).
2. Explorers Richard Burton and Henry Schoolcraft, for example, "discovered" the headwaters of the Nile and the Mississippi, respectively—with the help of local folks who already knew what Burton and Schoolcraft had come to discover. For an analysis of Burton's much-aided journey to the headwaters of the Nile, see Mary Louise Pratt, *Imperial Eyes*. For an analysis of Schoolcraft's use of Ojibwe experts to locate the headwaters of the Mississippi, see Gerald Vizenor, *The People Named the Chippewa*.
    The painter Paul Gauguin went to Tahiti to "immerse [him]self in virgin nature, see no one but savages, live their life" so that he might make "simple, very simple art"—using their lives and art as his raw material (qtd. in Guerin 48).
3. Plato makes such frequent use of food to illustrate his claims that one is forced to conclude that the references are anything but accidental. For two considerations of Plato's conceptions of food, see my "Foodmaking as a Thoughtful Practice" and "Do You Really Know How to Cook?"
4. In what may seem an ironic turn, it is the centrality of feminist theory to my own way of doing theory—the centrality of challenges, questions, and critiques from feminists of color—that makes it sometimes appear as if my work "isn't about women at all." My work is *not* about women, when that phrase is understood to mean "about women by not being about men, about women by talking about women and gender exclusively." But it is precisely this notion of feminism—and of being "about women"—that I wish to undermine, following in the path of Third World feminist theorists. Such "aboutness" necessarily brackets or erases race, class, and other markers of difference, as not being central to "women's" identities.
5. Trinh T. Min-ha notes: "Today, the unspoiled parts of Japan, the far-flung locations in the archipelago, are those that tourism officials actively promote for the more venturesome visitors. Similarly, the Third World representative the modern sophisticated public ideally seeks is the *unspoiled* African, Asian, or Native American, who remains more preoccupied with her/his image of the *real* native—the *truly different*—than with the issues of

hegemony, racism, feminism, and social change (which s/he lightly touches on in conformance to the reigning fashion of liberal discourse)" (88).

6. There is something more than a little odd about the name of this cookbook. What does it mean for a Westerner to lay a claim to the "territory" of Thai food, by describing as "original" a book that records a culture not her own? The book jacket explains the meaning *original* is to have in this context: this is the first Thai cookbook published in English in the United States. This explanation of the word *original* tends to invite the conclusion that something comes into existence only when it does so in the United States.

7. It is worth noting that the situation with respect to Thai foods has changed dramatically since Brennan published this book in 1981. Now, not only are there more Asian groceries in the United States, but also one can buy many of the ingredients for Thai foods in food cooperatives and upscale supermarkets. One can even buy various pre-mixed "Thai spices" in foil packets and glass jars, with directions clearly labeled in idiomatically flawless American English. They are considerably more expensive and less accessible than the ubiquitous taco seasoning packets, but I have little doubt that these spice packets will one day be every bit as common, as Thai food becomes a part of the mainstream U.S. consumer economy.

8. Discussing Maria Graham Callcott's *Journal of a Residence in Chile during the Year 1822*—a section of the book in which Graham describes learning to make pottery—Pratt writes: "Rather than treating the artisanal pottery works as a deplorable instance of backwardness in need of correction, Graham presents it in this episode almost as a utopia, and a matriarchal one at that. The family-based, non-mechanized production is presided over by a female authority figure. Yet even as she affirms non-industrial and feminocentric values, Graham also affirms European privilege. In relation to her, the potters retain the essential colonized quality of *disponibilité*—they unquestioningly accept Graham's intrusion and spontaneously take up the roles Graham wishes them to" (163). As Pratt suggests, to treat the Other as a resource for one's own use can take many forms, some of which even involve veneration and admiration. This observation is well worth keeping in mind when one examines ethnic cookbooks; many of them exhibit appreciation for a food tradition, even as they preserve the "essential colonized quality" of the relationship between the cookbook writer and her cook/informant.

9. Levy describes Elizabeth David as the inspiration for—and the original example of—a group of people he names "scholar cooks" (31). Among the scholar cooks, presumably, the anthropologist cooks are just one subspecies. Other scholar cooks include diplomat-turned-fish-specialist Alan Davidson, and Jane Grigson.

10. If we consider cooking itself—rather than cookbook writing—we may locate another, similar definition of theft, one very much rooted in class and gender. Chefs can be thought of as stealing one another's dishes, particularly "signature dishes" they have invented, even if those dishes have never been published. (They cannot, so far as I know, sue for such theft, their primary recourse is probably ridicule.) Famous chefs, who get paid for their work, can most easily make this claim, because they can produce the most evidence for it. Unknown chefs—like unknown songwriters—will have more difficulty proving that they've been robbed of a culinary idea. And women who are not chefs for pay but simply cook at home for their families will have insurmountable difficulty; a recipe must become a commodity before it can be stolen. The thing to note is that with cooking, as with cookbooks, proving originality is important—but having the power to reinforce a claim to originality is crucial.

11. Indeed, the prevalence of recipe-card exchanges serves to temper some of their outrage over the Olney-Nelson case; it seems that Nelson got his recipes not out of Olney's book but from a set of recipe cards he had received in the mail and used for years in his cooking class with no idea of their origin.

12. Lutz and Collins, in *Reading National Geographic*, examine the similar ways that *National Geographic* transforms the individuals in its photographs into "types," nearly interchangeable members of the group known as Other (see esp. chap. 4).

13. Not all recipes change, of course, some foods are temperamental enough that cooks feel disinclined to change them, for fear that they will fail. Not all cooks feel comfortable modifying recipes either. In my own family, for example, my mother and I are much more likely to tinker with a recipe than are my two sisters. (Interestingly enough, both of them are trained as scientists.) For one philosophical discussion of the processes of recipe creation and exchange, see my "Recipes for Theory Making."

14. I would contrast this to the respect, bordering on reverence, with which recipes used in restaurants are often treated, the deference with which a customer asks for the recipe for a particular dish and the gratitude they heap on the cook/chef willing to pass it along. In food magazines, this difference is sometimes manifested in the presence of two separate recipe columns. In one, readers ask other readers to share a recipe for some particular food ("I'm looking for a good recipe for pumpkin bread. Does anyone have one that uses orange juice?"). In the other, readers write in to ask for specific recipes they have tasted in restaurants (recipes they perhaps were too intimidated to request in person), and almost invariably, they couch their requests in the language of a supplicant: "Do you think you could ever possibly get them to release the recipe for this chicken dish I had?"

15. Wendell Berry, in "The Pleasures of Eating," describes an extensive pleasure in one's food, which "does not depend on ignorance" of the conditions under which that food is grown, harvested, and brought to you. For him, this pleasure is not "merely aesthetic" but ethical, political, and environmental as well (378).

References

Barr, Ann, and Paul Levy. *The Official Foodie Handbook: Be Modern—Worship Food*. New York: Timber House (1984).

Berry, Wendell. "The Pleasures of Eating." *Cooking, Eating, Thinking: Transformative Philosophies of Food*. Ed. Deane-Curtin and LisaHeldke. Bloomington: Indiana UP (1992) 374–79.

Bourdieu, Pierre. *Distinction: A Social Critique of the Judgment of Taste*. Trans. Richard Nice. Cambridge: Harvard UP (1984).

Brennan, Jennifer. *The Original Thai Cookbook*. New York: Perigee (1981).

Frankenberg, Ruth. *White Women, Race Matters: The Social Construction of Whiteness*. Minneapolis: U of Minnesota P (1993).

Griffin, Stuart. *Japanese Food and Cooking*. Rutland, Vt.: Charles E. Tuttle (1959).

Guerin, Daniel, ed. *The Writings of a Savage Paul Gauguin*. Trans. Eleanor Levieux. New York: Viking (1978).

Heldke, Lisa. "Do You Really Know How to Cook? A Discussion of Plato's Gorgias." Unpublished paper.

———— "Foodmaking as a Thoughtful Practice." *Cooking, Eating, Thinking: Transformative Philosophies of Food*. Ed. Deane Curtin and Lisa Heldke. Bloomington: Indiana UP (1992).

———— "Recipes for Theory Making." *Hypatia* 3.2 (1988): 15–31.

hooks, bell. *Black Looks: Race and Representation*. Boston: South End (1992).

Iyer, Pico. *Video Night in Kathmandu*. New York: Knopf (1988).

Jaffrey, Madhur. *An Invitation to Indian Cooking*. New York: Vintage (1973).

Kadi, Joanna. *Thinking Class*. Boston: South End (1996).

Lutz, Catherine A., and Jane L. Collins. *Reading National Geographic*. Chicago: U of Chicago P (1993).

Min-ha, Trinh T. *Woman Native Other: Writing Postcoloniality and Feminism*. Bloomington: Indiana UP (1989).

Paretsky, Sara. *Killing Orders*. New York: Ballantine (1985).

Pratt, Mary Louise. *Imperial Eyes: Travel Writing and Transculturation*. New York: Routledge (1992).

Roden, Claudia. *A Book of Middle Eastern Food*. New York: Vintage (1974).

Rosaldo, Renato. *Culture and Truth*. Boston: Beacon (1989).

Vizenor, Gerald. *The People Named the Chippewa: Narrative Histories*. Minneapolis: U of Minnesota P (1984).

28

Slow Food and the Politics
of "Virtuous Globalization"*

Alison Leitch

In 1987, a group of Italian writers and journalists produced a provocative manifesto announcing the official launch of a new movement for the Defense of and the Right to Pleasure. Published in *Gambero Rosso*—an eight-page monthly 'lifestyle' supplement of *Il Manifesto*—a widely circulating national independent communist daily newspaper the manifesto began with the assertion that 'we are enslaved by speed and have all succumbed to the same insidious virus: Fast Life, which disrupts our habits, pervades the privacy of our homes and forces us to eat Fast Foods'. It followed with a number of statements declaring the necessity of founding a new international movement called Slow Food, which was 'the only truly progressive answer' to the 'universal folly of the Fast Life'. Defending oneself against the speed of modernity, according to the manifesto, began at the table, through the rediscovery of 'the flavours and savours of regional cooking', the banishment of 'the degrading effect of Fast Foods' and the 'development of taste' through the 'international exchange of experiences, knowledge, projects'. Not surprisingly, the manifesto immediately attracted a great deal of public attention although, initially, many commentators regarded the idea of an international organization dedicated to the sensual pleasure of slow food and the 'slow life' as something of a joke. Yet, only two decades later, Slow Food has emerged as a highly visible and politically influential international organization whose dedication to changing consumers' attitudes towards the foods they eat has had some quite remarkable practical effects.

The founder of Slow Food—Carlo Petrini—has famously dubbed his project as a new form of 'virtuous globalization'(Stille 2001; Petrini 2001b). In other words, Slow Food promotes itself as providing a model for imagining alternate modes of global connectedness, in which members of minority cultures—including niche-food producers —are encouraged to network and thrive. While Slow Food has already amply demonstrated considerable organizational acumen in building an international movement around the revitalization of artisanally produced foods, its strategies and cultural politics have also been widely critiqued. This chapter traces the history of the emergence of the Slow Food movement from its origins as a lobby group engaged with the politics of food within Italy to its more recent manifestations as an international organization devoted to global biodiversity. In outlining key moments in this

*Originally published 2009

history, I hope to highlight some of the reasons why Slow Food politics have become so controversial.

Revolutionary Gourmets: The Origins of the 'Little Snail'

The original Slow Food manifesto demanding an end to our 'enslavement by speed' was inspired by a loose coalition of public intellectuals opposed to the introduction in Italy of American style fast food chains. Led by food and wine journalist, Carlo Petrini, this relatively small, though culturally influential group had already garnered a great deal of attention through a spirited media campaign conducted against the installation of a McDonald's franchise near the Spanish Steps in the mid 1980s. According to the *Italy Daily* (1998), it was almost an anti-Proustian moment of the smell of French fries that first stirred Petrini into action:

> Walking in Rome one day, he [Petrini] found himself gazing at the splendid Spanish Steps when the overwhelming odor of French fries disturbed his reverie. To his horror he discovered that not twenty meters along the piazza loomed the infamous golden arches of a well-known food chain. '*Basta!*' he cried. And thus began a project that would take him all over the world in order to promote and protect local culinary traditions. As a symbol for his cause he chose the snail because it was the slowest food he could think of (11/3/1998).

But, if we dig a little deeper, it is clear that the origins of the Slow Food movement are located elsewhere.

The organization now called Slow Food emerged out of a specific Italian cultural context: the 1970s. Popularly dubbed 'the years of lead' in reference to the activities of terrorist groups such as the Red Brigades, the decade of the 1970s was a period in which the radical ideals of the student movements of the late 1960s had ended in disillusionment. While some members of this generation had turned in frustration to the power of bullets, others abandoned revolutionary ideals for alternative forms of transformational cultural politics. The intellectual biography of Slow Food's most famous protagonist, Carlo Petrini, is forged within this milieu. Alongside his collaborators, Petrini came of age within younger leftist critiques of the Italian Communist Party which at this time was itself in crisis (see Leitch 2003).

The son of a teacher and an artisan, Carlo Petrini was born in 1948, in Bra—a provincial town located in the heart of the agricultural region of Piedmont, known as Le Langhe. As its name suggests, this is a landscape of rolling hills that appear as a series of elongated tongues disappearing and reappearing with mirage-like qualities across the hazy horizon, dotted here and there with the villas and castles that still belong to the descendents of the Italian aristocracy. Made famous in the luminous prose of distinguished postwar literary figures such as Cesare Pavese, as well as the detailed documentation of peasant life in the work of noted Italian oral historian, Nuto Revelli (1977), the region is acclaimed for the production of some of Italy's finest agricultural produce, including truffles and prestigious wines, such as Barolo and Barbaresco. With strong connections to the aristocracy, the area is also known for its deeply entrenched working class traditions, particularly left-Catholicism. Once a centre for the leather industry, Bra's main other industries are now the production of laminated plastics and agricultural machinery.[1]

Petrini graduated from high school in 1968, first studying to become a mechanic, but later enrolling in sociology at the University of Trento, a department which, perhaps not coincidentally, was at the epicenter of 1970s extra-parliamentarian politics. After completing his studies, Petrini dedicated himself to local cultural politics, becoming a key protagonist in the foundation of a number of co-operative ventures including a bookshop, a food co-op and one of Italy's first radical-left pirate radio stations called *Radio Bra Onde Rosse* or 'Red Waves'[2] Like many young Italians of his generation, during these years, Petrini also immersed himself in the rediscovery of the region's rural traditions, its festivals and popular songs, as well as its food and wine culture. Indeed, according to Petrini, initially, wine, rather than food was the focus of his attention. He notes, for example, that an early encounter with Italy's most well-known wine journalist and theorist of peasant life, Luigi Veronelli, had nurtured his love of gastronomy and its political potential. A self-avowed anarchist oenologist, Veronelli is famous for publishing a nine-volume work dedicated to Italian wines in the 1960s, as well as for his essays on the importance of rural and culinary traditions to the preservation of specific localities and cultural economies (Veronelli 2004). These works subsequently became a source of inspiration to an entire generation, including, the eventual founders of the Slow Food movement. As Petrini recalls:

> Once I read the texts by Renato Ratti and Gino Veronelli and learned about wine tasting, my world became one with the wine producers, vineyards and wine cellars . . . we wandered through the Langhe looking for inns and new restaurants, but there was not an awful lot . . . there was no wine list, and the Dolcetto was the one and only wine that the innkeeper would serve you. Hardly anyone served Barolo. So it was inevitable that we developed the gastronomic project before the environmental one, although we had the basic idea for it.
>
> (Petrini and Padovani 2006: 61–62)

By the early 1980s, Petrini was contributing articles to *La Gola*, a magazine published in Milan by a group of young intellectuals—philosophers, artists and poets—dedicated to epicurean philosophy. And it was out of this group that a new organization called Arci Gola—the forerunner of the Slow Food Movement—was founded in the mid 1980s.

In Italian *gola* means 'throat' as well as the 'desire for food'. Although it is commonly translated as 'gluttonous' implying a negative state of excess or greed, to be *goloso* has a more positive connotation of craving with pleasure a particular food. As Carole Counihan (1999:180) aptly observes, because *gola* implies both 'desire' and 'voice', it suggests that desire for food is a voice—a central vehicle for self expression in Italian social life. In turn, Arci is an acronym for Recreative Association of Italian Communists: a national network of recreational and cultural clubs first established in 1957 by the Italian Communist party to counter the influence of ENAL, the state recreational organization that supplanted the Fascist OND at the end of the Second World War. In the 1960s and 70s, as political goals became increasingly divided within the Italian left, the Arci network spawned a wide variety of clubs and associations dedicated to particular topical interests such as hunting, sport, women's rights, music, film and the environment. Arci Gola was one of these groups. It emerged out of the desire to create a less hierarchical, youthful alternative to existing gourmet associations that Petrini and his collaborators viewed as linked to chauvinistic and elitist cultural politics. And although the aim of the new association was to raise the profile of regional cuisine and produce, the principle of conviviality combined with an insistence on the right to pleasure and to enjoy oneself through the consumption of good food and wine was always central to the group's philosophy.

However, it is worth noting that the formation of the first Arci Gola groups also took place within the context of a number of other food scandals and environmental catastrophes that led to emerging public discussions on the fate of Italian agriculture and its oeno-gastronomical culture. For example, in March of 1986, there was a public outcry over the revelation of methanol-tainted wine that was eventually discovered to be the cause of nineteen deaths across northern Italy. The deaths resulted from the unscrupulous practices of some bulk wine vendors who had deliberately adulterated wine with methyl alcohol in order to increase the alcoholic content thereby ensuring higher prices. But before the public authorities were able to uncover the chain of contamination, much of this adulterated wine stock had already been sold to large supermarket chains. The consequences of this event were devastating. The scandal not only created wide scale panic among local consumers, but it also resulted in significant damage to the reputation of the Italian wine industry and to its export markets. Later that year, yet another crisis emerged for Italian agriculture: the contamination of the aqueducts of the Po valley with a herbicide called atrazina. Residents of major cities such as Ferrara, Mantua and Bergamo were ordered to turn off their taps as health authorities investigated the damage done to local water supplies from toxic runoff caused, apparently, by the overuse of pesticides (Petrini and Padovani 2006:49). In addition, the Chernobyl disaster occurred in April of 1986. The meltdown of the Russian nuclear plant released a huge plume of radioactive haze over much of Europe, creating widespread panic over the consumption of leafy greens, milk and meat products, as well as wild mushrooms gathered from European forests.

The roots of the slow food movement are located within this political and cultural context: in the growing public outcry over future scandalous scenarios of environmental contamination and in the micro history of a particular group of left activists, who were deeply engaged with transformations to their own regional cultural landscapes, as well as with the utopian possibilities of alternative cultural politics in an era of rapid social change. By the end of the 1980s, the original Arci Gola network was consolidated into a new organization called Slow Food.

Slow Food and the 'Endangered Foods' Project: The Case of *lardo di Colonnata*

In 1989, two years after the appearance of the first Slow Food manifesto, the International Slow Food Movement was launched at the Opéra Comique in Paris. Over the next decade, as its membership base expanded with new offices opening in France, Switzerland and Germany, Slow Food began broadening its political agenda, to include discussions on the importance of food as a cultural artifact linked to the preservation of a distinctive European cultural heritage. This project became known as the 'endangered foods' campaign.

The 'endangered foods' campaign was designed as a polemical intervention into the growing circuits of a vigorous national debate concerning the potential disappearance of regional tastes and idiosyncratic products due to trends such as: the increasing drift towards farming monocultures; the disintegration of traditional rural foodways; environmental threats to national fisheries; and the dearth of alternate distribution networks for small-scale agricultural enterprises. Another, widely perceived threat was the rapid pace of Europeanization in the wake of the 1992 Maastricht Accord. Slow Food argued that the introduction of new European Union standardizing protocols for the manufacture of cured meat products and cheeses posed particular dangers. The application of uniform European hygiene rules designed for large manufacturers would, they argued, lead inevitably to the decline of traditional production techniques, as well as diminishing the economic viability of the small-scale producers of these foods. In response, Slow Food began to compile dossiers on particular products that the organization considered in special need of protection.

One example of an 'endangered food' that later became particularly noteworthy in this debate was the case of a unique type of cured pork fat: *lardo di Colonnata*. As its name suggests, *lardo di Colonnata* is produced in Colonnata, a tiny village located at the end of a windy mountain road several kilometers from the marble quarrying town of Carrara in central Italy, where I had also conducted ethnographic research on the subject of craft identity among quarry workers in the late 1980s. At this time, *lardo di Colonnata* was mainly marketed as a culinary delight —even a curiosity— to the odd bus tour and Italian tourists on weekend excursions to the quarries. Since the 1970s, it had also been celebrated at an annual pork fat festival held in the village over the late summer months. And it was certainly well known to culinary experts who reputedly made pilgrimages to eat what some gourmets referred to as 'one of the most divine foods ever produced on this earth' (Manetti 1996) at Venanzio, a local restaurant, named eponymously after its owner, a local gourmet and *lardo* purveyor. But regardless of its appreciation as a festive food or its reputation among aficionados, pork fat was not commonly eaten in any of the households I regularly visited for meals while conducting fieldwork. It was, however, almost always nominated in the oral histories I collected detailing the conditions of work over past generations (Leitch 1996).

In many of these narratives, the past was distinguished from the present through tales of food scarcity and physical hardship. Until quite recently, meat was a luxury item in diets that consisted predominantly of various grains, legumes and vegetables, as well as produce gathered from the woods and forests, such as chestnuts and mushrooms, wild, edible roots and herbs. Many households also maintained small vegetable gardens which kept them going during periods of unemployment, and some households, with access to land, kept pigs. One of the by-products of these pigs, *lardo* or cured pork fat, thus constituted a kind of food safe for families in the region and was an essential source of calorific energy in the quarry worker's diet. Like sugar or coffee, *lardo* was a 'proletarian hunger killer' (Mintz 1979). Eaten with a tomato and a piece of onion on dry bread, it was a taken-for-granted element in the worker's lunch. *Lardo* was thought to quell thirst as well as hunger and was appreciated for its coolness on hot summer days. It was also adopted as a cure for a number of common health ailments, ranging from an upset stomach to a bad back. As one local *lardo* maker and restaurateur once remarked to me: 'When you went to the butcher and asked for *lardo*, everyone knew there was someone ill at home'.

Although these days, *lardo* producers living in the village of Colonnata claim to have 'invented' the recipe for the product now known as *lardo di Colonnata*, in reality, cured pork fat was not unique to Colonnata. During the 1950s and 1960s, many local people cured their own batches of pork fat at home according to individual recipes that included varying proportions of raw fat, salt, herbs and spices. However, marble, preferably quarried from near Colonnata at Canalone, was almost always cited as an essential ingredient. Apparently, the unique crystalline structure of Canalone marble allows the pork fat to 'breathe' while at the same time containing the curing brine. If at any stage the *lardo* 'went bad' it was simply thrown out. And just like the marble workers who often reported to me that marble dust is actually beneficial to the body because it is 'pure calcium', people who made *lardo* suggested that the chemical composition of marble, calcium carbonate was a purificatory medium that extracted harmful substances from the raw pork fat, including cholesterol.

Traditionally the curing process began with the raw fat—cut from the back of select pigs—and then layered in rectangular marble troughs resembling small sarcophagi called *conche*. The *conche* were placed in the cellar, always the coolest part of the house. At the time of my fieldwork, many of these cellars were quite dank and mouldy. Some still contained underground cisterns that in the past supplied water to households without plumbing. Cellars were used to store firewood, as well as other household equipment, as laundries and, occasionally, to butcher wild boar. Once placed in the troughs, the pork fat was covered with layers of salt and herbs to start the pickling process and six to nine months later the pork fat was ready to eat. Translucent, white, veined with pink, cool and soft to touch, the end product mimics the exact aesthetic qualities prized in high-quality stone.

In 1996, Slow Food nominated *lardo di Colonnata* as one of Italy's ten most endangered foods. As I have detailed elsewhere (Leitch 2000; 2003), this event resulted in some surprising, possibly unintended, consequences. Not only did Colonnata's pork fat suddenly achieve new found fame promoted as far afield as the food columns of the *New York Times* (18/2/1997) and *Bon Appétit* (Spender 2000), the village itself was catapulted into the limelight as a major centre for international culinary tourism. There were also quite profound consequences for local producers, many of whom have now found new ways of making a livelihood out of *lardo* production. But the question remains: Why did the Slow Food movement nominate *lardo di Colonnata* as a key symbol for its endangered foods campaign?

I argue that Slow Food took up the cause of pork fat for a variety of reasons. One was certainly timing. In March of 1996, the local police force had descended on what one newspaper called 'the temple of lardo' (La Nazione 1/4/1996), namely the Venanzio restaurant in Colonnata. Protected by the local constabulary, regional health authority personnel proceeded to remove several samples of Venanzio's *lardo* and subsequently placed all his *conche* under quarantine. Later, samples were also taken from other small *lardo* makers in the village, but Venanzio and one other wholesaler, Fausto Guadagni, were singled out for special attention. The reasons for the quarantine were never entirely clear to the *lardo* makers involved. When I asked them later, they flatly denied it had anything to do with the spread of Bovine Spongiform

Encephalopathy (BSE), which, nevertheless, was a topic of immense anxiety at the time. Obviously, BSE has little to do with pigs, but collective hysteria over the spread of the disease had already provoked numerous articles in the local press about the benefits of vegetarianism. And, in the wake of this hysteria, it may not have been entirely coincidental that regional health authorities had decided to take a closer look at *lardo*, a product that, after all, had never undergone scientific analysis of any kind. However, local *lardo* makers simply interpreted the whole affair as a completely unreasonable attack on their autonomy to make a product that they had been producing without a single problem for many years.

This quarantine resulted in a barrage of media commentary that soon reached the national dailies. Apart from the predictable tones of conspiracy theory, at the local level, the main preoccupation was the possible threat to the 1996 *lardo* festival. Nationally, the issue led to debates over the power of the European Union to impose standardized hygiene legislation regulating Italian food production thereby determining Italian eating habits. Writing for the national daily *La Repubblica*, Sergio Manetti responded to the quarantine with an article entitled 'The European Union ruins Italian Cuisine'. In a somewhat satirical tone he reported that:

> My friend Venanzio introduced *lardo di Colonnata* to the world . . . For centuries *lardo* has been preserved in marble basins and stored in cellars carved out of the rock where the natural humidity and porosity of the walls create the perfect conditions for its maturation and where it can keep for months, even years. Now all this has gone. The cave walls must be tiled up just like the floor and you need a toilet . . . *Lardo* will probably become quite disgusting. All this has happened because some poor functionary from the health authority has to carry out their duty enforcing the bureaucratic rules of the European Union. These poor people have probably never even tasted *lardo*, let alone visited a cellar. Perhaps, like most city children they have never even seen a chicken, a lamb or a live pig. And so, soon, we must bid farewell to the *formaggio di fossa* ('ditch' cheese) and the cheeses of Castelmagno, to the *mocetta valdostana* (a type of fruit chutney). And then we will be forced to eat the industrial products that are made according to strict hygienic laws (but can we be sure?), but which are absolutely tasteless and with no smell . . . and all of this because of the European Union. All of us are facing the end of the world. Or at least that is what Nostradamus predicted in four years time. For God's sake, just let us eat what we want over these last years!
>
> (Manetti 1996; my translation)

According to Carlo Petrini (2001a), coinage of the term 'endangered foods' dated to the mid 1990s, just before the pork fat controversy erupted. As I have already outlined, up until then Slow Food had been perceived by the public as an association of gourmets, mostly concerned with the protection of national cuisines. But by the mid-1990s, Slow Food began to imagine itself as an international organization concerned with the global protection of food tastes. The eruption of the *lardo* quarantine controversy thus proved entirely fortuitous, providing a perfect media opportunity for the organization to promote its new international agenda of eco-gastronomy, and in this regard, Petrini was certainly *not* slow to exploit *lardo*'s proletarian exoticism.

A second reason was that the case of *lardo* presented an unambiguous test case for challenging new standardized European food rules that insisted on the utilization of non-porous materials for the production of cheeses and cured meats. Although there are certainly good techniques for sterilizing the *conche*, marble is porous and its porosity is clearly essential to the curing process as well as to *lardo*'s claims to authenticity and its taste. Local *lardo* makers involved in this dispute thus had a vested interest in lobbying for exceptions to the generic rules designed for large food manufacturers. At *this* particular moment, their interests perfectly coincided with Slow Food's own political agenda, in particular its campaign to widen the debate over food rules to include cultural issues.

A third reason has to do with the discursive strategies used in Slow Food's endangered foods campaign. In the numerous publicity materials that subsequently appeared in the press, Petrini frequently likened the protection of pork fat made by local people in dank and mouldy cellars to other objects of significant national heritage, including major works of art or buildings of national architectural note. In valorizing the traditional techniques of *lardo* producers, Petrini was rhetorically distancing himself from accusations of gourmet elitism, while simultaneously challenging normalizing hierarchies of expert scientific knowledge, including, most importantly, those of the European health authorities. In this kind of strategic symbolic reversal, the food artisan is envisaged not as a backward-thinking conservative standing in the way of progress, but rather, as a quintessential modern subject, holder par excellence of national heritage. A food item once associated with pre-modern culinary otherness was reinterpreted symbolically as the culinary pinnacle of a national cuisine.

From the Ark of Taste to the Terre Madre Meetings

The campaign to protect nationally 'endangered foods' led to the compilation of the Ark of Taste in 1997; a compendium that proposed the documentation of disappearing agricultural and food products on a global scale. With its explicit biblical imagery of deluge and salvation, the Ark project thus represented a new focus for the organization that determined on making more explicit links between gourmets and environmentalists. This campaign eventually spread to include international activists working on issues of food sustainability in countries outside Europe (Meneley 2004; Kummer 2002). As Petrini himself was fond of repeating in numerous interviews he conducted at this time: 'An environmentalist who not a gastronomist is sad; a gastronomist who is not an environmentalist is silly . . . [to include] the environment where food is created . . . has allowed us to overcome the real taboo of every gastronomist: hunger' (Petrini and Padovani 2006:118).

A second initiative linked to the Ark of Taste was the Presidia: a noun derived from the Italian verb *presidiare* meaning to 'garrison' or 'to protect'. These were grassroots organizations of direct producers who worked in collaboration with Slow Food 'research commissions' to identify and promote local Ark foods to the public. With the launch of the Presidia, Slow Food began mixing politics with business even more explicitly, actively intervening in the promotion and distribution of Presidia products and organizing public events such as the *Salone del Gusto* or Hall of Tastes: giant biennial food trade fairs held in the converted ex-Fiat factory exhibition space at Lingotto in Torino. Following from this, in 2000, Slow Food sponsored its first Slow Food award for the Defense of Biodiversity—a star-studded food Oscar—honoring outstanding contributions to the Defense of Biodiversity. Not long after, in 2003, the organization launched its own Foundation for Diversity: a nonprofit organization devoted to the defense of agricultural diversity around the world that has recently gained official recognition by the Food and Agricultural Organization (Donati 2005:237).

In 2004, after almost two decades focusing on the protection of culinary diversity in Europe, Slow Food undertook an even more ambitious new project: the Terre Madre: World Meeting of Food Communities An idea that apparently had emerged some years before in the context of discussions at the Commission for the future of food in Florence, this event brought together 5,000 food producers from 131 nations around the world (Donati 2005:237). Its purpose was to deepen the links between communities of farmers around the globe—the so-called 'destiny communities'—that Slow Food imagined as sharing common feelings and problems but which were separated from each other, as well as from potential global food distribution networks. Thus, according to Donati (2005), the Terre Madre initiative represented the building of a new eco-gastronomic agenda for Slow Food that for the first time explicitly recognized issues of social justice within the global economy. While it was certainly not without controversy (Chrzan 2004), the Terra Madre meeting clearly demonstrated Slow Food's remarkable organizational and financial capacities to bring together large numbers of individuals and groups from diverse cultures, attracting, as well, internationally influential figures engaged in food politics from very diverse ideological spectrums.[3]

While the majority of its members still reside in Europe, Slow Food is now represented in over 122 nations, including Europe, the Americas, Asia, Oceania, as well as a small number in Africa. And while its headquarters remain in Bra—the small town in Piedmont where the movement originated—Slow Food currently has six other national associations with autonomous offices in the United States, Switzerland, Germany, France, Japan and the United Kingdom (Petrini and Padovani 2006). Slow Food has also been active as a lobby group on food and agricultural policy within the European Union, fostering transnational alliances, for example the 2003 joint agreement with the Brazilian government to revive local food traditions using indigenous knowledge (Labelle 2004:88). In addition, Slow Food has successfully lobbied the Italian government to provide funding for the opening of two universities dedicated to teaching its eco-gastronomic philosophy.

What accounts for Slow Food's rapid expansion and increased international visibility over the last two decades? According to Donati (2005) one explanation lies in Slow Food's organizational capacities and its extraordinary knack for securing funding for its activities though growth in membership, as well as though corporate and government sponsorship. Another key to Slow Food's success is its ingenious use of the media. From its inception, Slow Food has cultivated an ever expanding international network of journalists and writers to promote its programs, while also developing an extremely successful commercial wing, publishing books and travel guides on cultural tourism, food and wine. And, as Julie Labelle (2004:88) notes, Slow Food's more recent strategic merging of gastronomy with ecological issues has resulted in a further expansion of this communication network, for example, the establishment in 2004 of a publishing collaboration between Slow Food and *Ecologist* magazine.

For Labelle, it is Slow Food's commitment to knowledge dissemination that is crucial. The breadth of the movement's communication networks enables individual members to connect with one another but, perhaps more importantly it also makes visible how all actors in the food system are linked in a network of food relations

(Labelle 2004:90). Labelle is referring here to the shift from Slow Food's early focus on spreading knowledge to consumers about local and typical foods to the organization's new emphasis on sharing knowledge among food producers as evidenced at the Terra Madre meetings. Slow Food's official web site makes this link explicit. It now promotes the concept of a 'co-producer', that is: 'going beyond the passive role of a consumer' to take an interest in 'those that produce our food, how they produce it and the problems they face in doing so'. As a co-producers, the organization asserts, consumers become part of and partners in the production process.

However, some writers have been rather more critical of Slow Food's well-oiled publicity machine. Acknowledging the popularity of Slow Food activities among upper middle class professional communities in the United States, Janet Chrzan suggests, for example, that Slow Food is, in reality, an organization that relies more on rhetoric than substance. It is, she argues, little more than a 'gourmandizing fan club for celebrity food personalities and their followers' (2004:129). Thus for Chrzan, Slow Food has become a cliché; a phrase that is repeated with 'mantra-like rhythmic repetition' to mean all that is positive to people, societies and the globe. She asks: 'Is Slow Food a movement, or is it an artfully-named organization situated at the right place and the right time ...?' (2004:122). But artful names, these days, are central to modern politics. And despite this critique of Slow Food's attention to media politics and its rhetorical strategies, I argue that Slow Food has undoubtedly struck a chord because the language it adopts quite clearly taps into real concerns about the pace of modern life and its potential erasures.

Beyond Culinary Utopianism: The Critique of the Cult of Speed

One recent analysis of the Slow Food movement has argued that although the origins of Slow Food may have begun with specific campaigns devoted to the preservation of regional cuisines and traditional systems of production linked to the material cultures of local communities, mostly in Italy, its politics were never just about food. Rather, the Slow Food Movement has a much broader agenda linked to a critical re-examination of the politics of time in contemporary society. Drawing for their analysis on the texts of the Slow Food quarterly magazine and various other Slow Food manifestos, Wendy Parkins and Geoffrey Craig (2006) have highlighted the links made between Slow Food and what writers for the magazine call the 'Slow Life'. They argue that in opposing fast to slow, slow food is not just about the opposition to the idea of speed in modernity, but rather its opposite, slowness. In other words, the slowness promoted by the Slow Food movement is not just a negative polemical stance towards the idea of speed and its material manifestations, such as fast food, but rather a more positive assertion of a program for everyday living associated with valuing 'pleasure, authenticity, connectedness, tranquility and deliberation' (2006:52). Slow Living, they assert, is a direct response to the processes of individualization, globalization and the 'radically uneven and heterogeneous production of space and time in post-traditional societies' (Parkins and Craig 2006:12).

Regardless of these debates, Slow Food's philosophical position on the ethics of food as pleasure and eating as a kind of reflective cultural politics of resistance to the role of speed in modernity have quite clearly tapped into the public nerve of current debates on the busyness of everyday life in many Western nations. Apart from the huge publishing success of popular books on this theme,[4] discussions over the organization of time, including the degree to which everyday life is increasingly colonized by work rather than leisure are currently also hotly debated topics within academic discourse (Pocock 2003). Moreover, these debates appear to have generated significant sociological repercussions in the growing phenomena of 'downshifting' (Schor 1998) and sea-changing (Salter 2001), in affluent Western nations. Indeed, in the contemporary context, there is, I suggest, an eerie mirroring of earlier, less well-remembered 'time wars', such as the late nineteenth-century international labor movement's pressing demand for the 'three eights': the division of the day into three equal eight-hour intervals of work, pleasure and rest. And just as Paul Lafargue (1989 [1883]) irreverent treatise, *The Right to be Lazy* critiquing the 'disastrous dogma of work' as the 'cause of all intellectual degeneracy, of all organic deformity' captivated a new audience in the counterculture and student movements of the 1960s and 70s, so too have Slow Food manifestos demanding an end to the 'universal folly of the Fast Life' reverberated in quite unexpected social domains.

In Australia, elements of the Slow Food program have now entered into the realm of public policy. For example, Slow Food's campaign for the creation of Slow Cities has caught the attention of local councils in key metropolitan centers. In both Australia and the United States, prominent celebrity chefs are currently fostering the expansion of other Slow Food agendas, such as its program for taste education though the promotion of school gardens in state primary schools. In addition, the Slow Food philosophy has become something of an international brand, a marketing tool for editors of lifestyle guides to various cities, such as the recently published *Slow Guide to Sydney*, the first in a series, apparently, of guides to some of the 'fastest places on earth' (Hawkes and Keen 2007:3). And judging by the number of people I see wearing 'Slow Life' T-shirts walking around the coastal path where I live in Bondi Beach, the slow brand has the potential for considerable commercial success.

Revolutionary Gourmets or Culinary Luddites?

Slow Food has recently been the subject of a great deal of critical commentary. While some writers, as already mentioned, have criticized Slow Food's marketing strategies as vacuous (Chrzan 2004; Lauden 2004) or based on a corporate vision of food as simply a commodity (Paxson 2006), others have accused the organization of promoting a form of 'culinary luddism' (Lauden 2001) that deliberately obscures the democratizing benefits of modern food production over much of the 20th century (Lauden 2001; 2004). Thus, for Rachel Lauden, Slow Food's program for the defense of high quality local products and regional cuisines has little to say about the plight of the hungry worldwide. By following Slow Food agendas privileging artisanal produced foods over mass production 'The poor' as Lauden puts it, are simply 'stuck with the tyranny of the local' (2004:143). Jeffrey Pilcher's (2006) detailed discussion of the history of the Mexican tortilla production is a case in point. He argues that in Mexico, culinary modernism in the form of mass produced corn tortillas, continues to be essential to the survival of tortillas as the daily bread of the majority of Mexican wage laborers. While middle class Mexican elites, Slow Food activists and environmentalists are prompt to condemn factory produced maize flour as the antithesis of traditional cooking, bags of *masa harina* have nevertheless become essential care packages for Mexican immigrants and other aficionados of Mexican food in the United States, while in Mexico, a large parastatal corporation—the *grupo Maseca*—has emerged as the unlikely champion of authentic Mexican cuisine.

At the heart of these critiques is the accusation that Slow Food is disingenuous when it comes to issues of class. For example, in her fascinating study of the marketing and production of Tuscan olive oil, Anne Meneley (2004) notes that while olive oil producers of all classes displayed an affective attachment to their cold pressed extra virgin olive oil and were vitally concerned with the purity of their product as well as with authenticating markers, in reality sophisticated international marketing strategies were not available to all producers. Indeed, somewhat paradoxically, Slow Food's involvement in the marketing of olive oil has mostly benefited larger consortiums. Thus, while Slow Food claims to champion small producers, it often ends up favoring elites (Meneley 2004:173). Other authors have raised the issue of class in respect to Slow Food's membership base in wealthy nations. Chrzan (2004), for example, questions the high cost of Slow Food activities in the North American context, and Labelle (2004) similarly observes that Slow Food fails to recognize that locally sourced high-quality foods are in reality luxuries for the privileged few. Such critiques, however, are in danger of reproducing ethnocentric accounts of slow food politics that are rather narrowly enmeshed within localized fields of power. While Slow Food politics does at times elide class issues, especially in respect to the assumption of the buying power of consumers, it is equally true that the social and cultural contexts in which Slow Politics now operate vary quite considerably.

Perhaps a more trenchant observation is that in wealthy nations the popularity of Slow Food reifies forms of 'imperialist nostalgia' (Rosaldo 1989:90) that sentimentalize peasant traditions within and outside Europe (Jones et al 2003). Pilcher (2006), for example, asserts that while Slow Food has recognized some key individual Mexican contributions to agricultural bio diversity, as a whole, in Mexico the Slow Food project bears more than a passing resemblance to the European civilizing mission of the 19th century. Maria Gaytán (2004) similarly observes that Californian Slow Food members often draw upon deeply essentialized notions of Italian artisanal traditions that tend to romanticize the past: a process that is reflective of the current mood towards what might be called 'Tuscanopia' (Leitch 2000: 105), in which Tuscan peasant cuisines, house renovation projects and picturesque rurality all seem to have become key fantasy spaces of modern urban alienation.

These critiques not withstanding, a large part of Slow Food's success, I suggest, is due to its promotional politics, with its imaginative use of the media and discursive strategies intended to reevaluate specific foods, not simply as economic commodities, but as cultural artifacts linked to salient notions of the past. By way of comparison, I would like to turn, briefly, to another example of a movement in Europe that similarly succeeded in reframing debates about food as a commodity—in this case genetically modified crops—to debates about taste as cultural heritage.[5]

The French Peasant's Confederation

Between 1997 and 2000 there was a public discussion in France about the future of agricultural biotechnology in France. According to Chaia Heller (2004), during the initial phase of the debate, between 1996 and 1998, the 'risk' frame and scientific expertise played a primary role in shaping public discussion. During the second phase of the debate, between 1998 and 2000, there was a remarkable shift in which an organization of small farmers—(the *Confederation Paysanne* (CP) or the Peasants Confederation) —reframed the debate about GMOs in France from issues of scientific risk, to questions of food quality and culture.

How did this happen? As background to this issue, Heller points out that the CP's formation in 1987 represented the culmination of a decade-long struggle to create an autonomous voice for family farmers in a milieu largely dominated by France's number one union of industrial farmers, the National Federated Union of Agricultural Enterprises (FNSEA). Since its inception, the CP had struggled to become a contending counter-power to the FNSEA, representing a network of socialist leaning family farmers contesting the agricultural policy that intensified during France's post-war period. During this period, the CP was engaged in a strategic campaign to reclaim the historically contested and pejorative term *paysan* or peasant, in order to align itself with an international network of peasant movements, such as the European Peasant Coordination and Via Campesina. And in 1997, the CP launched its own anti-GMO campaign, presenting an anti-globalization message that defended the rights of peasant workers and indigenous peoples against agricultural biotechnology worldwide (Heller 2004:86).

In 1998, a radical sector of the CP, headed by Rene Reisal and the now infamous Jose Bové of anti-MacDonald's fame, organized their first major anti-GMO event that involved a group of about 100 farmers destroying three tons of Novartis transgenetic corn in a storage plant in the southern town of Nerac by spraying it with fire hoses (Heller 2004:87). At the subsequent trial, Bové and Reisal countered the expert scientific witnesses on the subject of GMO related risk, with their own expertise as peasant farmers and union workers, asserting that they were uniquely situated to speak about food quality, farmers' duties to protect and develop French seeds, as well as the implications of industrialized agriculture on rural peoples and cultures worldwide. According to Heller, by invoking both *paysan* expertise and the plight of the small farmer in the face of industrialized agriculture, the CP was able to appeal to a widely shared collective sense of regret felt by many French about the continued dispossession of the peasant farmer in the post-war period; a discussion that, in turn, draws upon a very long history of alternate constructions of the peasant in France (Rogers 1987). In this most recent resuscitation of the peasant as a key symbol of French culture, the CP draws upon the trade unionist discourse of the worker, articulating not a pre-social idea of nature as wilderness but rather, a 'socialized nature whose value is not only historical, cultural, or aesthetic, but also *economic*, providing *paysans* with a viable and productive way of life' (Heller 2004: 89). This, as Heller aptly points out is illustrated in the CP's key slogan 'To Produce, To Employ, To Preserve'. Thus in contrast to environmentalist understandings of conserving nature as wilderness, the CP promotes the idea that nature is best preserved by peasant workers whose expertise in knowing and caring for the land as a productive and meaningful landscape is of vital national importance.

In addition to advocating a view of nature as socialized, Jose Bové has also been instrumental in promoting good food as good taste, a rhetorical position quite akin to that of the Slow Food Movement. For example, in many of his discussions over the negative effects of industrialized agriculture, Bové uses the symbol of *la malbouffe*, a word that is close to the idea of bad or junk food (Heller 2004:92). As Heller observes, *La Bouffe*, or 'good food', on the other hand, brings together notions of pleasure, tradition and French cuisine, synonymous with French culture itself. To be cultured in France is to be 'cultivated' or to have 'good taste'. Taste here, of course, has a double meaning. Both people and food may be regarded as having good or bad taste. As Heller puts it 'While a food is well cultivated when produced according to regional agricultural traditions, an individual is considered cultivated when capable of recognizing, and taking pleasure in well-cultivated, good-tasting food or *la Bouffe*' (2004:92). That which is not traditionally cultivated, in other words, foods produced without reference to cultural expertise and history, for example, fast foods and GMO foods, are seen as having no taste, and people who consume these foods are thus viewed as being without culture.

Conclusion

What are we to make of all these discussions on food and politics? Despite the fact that they are being conducted with reference to distinct national contexts involving particular social actors working within specific historical trajectories, one of the things that interests me in all these debates about food and identity, at least in Europe, is that they are managing to galvanize large numbers of people, and within a very short time frame have become remarkably effective lobby groups for environmental biodiversity and the protection of both cultural landscapes and niche-food producers internationally. Slow Food has been particularly influential in this regard, partly, I believe, because the organization maintains, quite self-consciously, a strategic distance from the radical guerilla strategies utilized by some of the more infamous actors in groups such as CP. Petrini's response to the Jose Bové's acts of sabotage against McDonald's in France is quite explicit: it is against 'slow style'. As he puts it ' we prefer to concentrate our efforts on what we are losing, rather than trying to stop what we don't like' (2001a: 28).

This difference in style can be illustrated by Petrini's manifestos on fast food. Whereas Bové linked fast food to bad taste as well as to an explicitly anti-corporate and anti-globalization agenda, Petrini has always preferred to work in the positive, denying that Slow Food is simply anti-fast food. Rather, he suggests that Slow Food is against the homogenization of taste that fast food symbolizes. In other words, for Petrini, fast food does not necessarily represent bad taste although he certainly argues that it is a sign of the more negative effects of modern market rationalities on cultural difference. Slowness in this formulation becomes a metaphor for a politics of place complexly concerned, like the CP, with the defense of local cultural heritage, regional landscapes and idiosyncratic material cultures of production. Whereas, Bové and the CP lobbied within international networks of anti-globalization activists promoting anti-corporate agendas, from its inception Slow Food has mixed business and politics and none of its public manifestos advocating slowness and the benefits of the slow life or slow cities are explicitly anti-capitalist or anti-corporate. Rather, slowness is employed ideologically in order to promote Petrini's idiosyncratic brand of 'virtuous globalization': a new figuring of cosmopolitanism that seeks to rupture binary oppositions—rural/metropolitan, local/global—refiguring the idea of locality as a kind of 'ethical glocalism' (Tomlinson 1999; Parkins and Craig 2006; Parasecoli 2003).

There are, however, significant convergences between the politics of the two movements. Both are engaged with the protection of cultural landscapes, local traditions and economies within debates about cultural homogenization in the context of Europeanization. Both are, in other words, political responses to what Nadia Seremetakis has called a massive 'reorganization of public memory' (1994:3) accompanying the intensifications of market rationalities in European peripheries. Both utilize rhetorical strategies reframing scientific knowledge in terms of artisanal or peasant expertise, adding further weight to the thesis that political struggles in the contemporary era focus on struggles over meanings, as well as over political and economic conditions (McClagan 2000). Although I have not been able to explore this in great detail, both Slow Food and CP are also caught up in a kind of generational politics in which the interpretive and cultural frames of the main protagonists are deeply influential. Both, I suggest, are intimately involved with socially productive uses of nostalgia. This is to say, following the imaginative work of literary theorist Svetlana Boym (2001), that both movements invoke a *reflective* rather than a *restorative* nostalgia: a nostalgia that 'dwells on the ambivalences of human longing and belonging, [a nostalgia] that does not avoid the contradictions of modernity' (2001: xviii); a nostalgia that explores ways of inhabiting many places at once and imagining different time zones; a nostalgia that hopefully in the end, can, as Boym suggests 'present an ethical and creative challenge, not merely a pretext for midnight melancholias' (2001: xviii).

Just as CP interpreted its struggle over the future of agricultural biotechnology in France in terms of the struggles for the survival of *other* farmers in *other* places, Slow Food is also deeply engaged in public debates *beyond* the politics of food in Italy, intervening in emerging discussions about the ethics and repercussions of speed in the current era. I might add here that in this sense Slow Food draws attention to some very interesting parallels between 19th century rejections of machine time and current debates repudiating the orthodoxy of speed in everyday life. But this is a whole new topic. In this chapter, I have tried to indicate the ways in which food has emerged as a political topic par excellence, capable of connecting individual bodies to abstract communities, techno-scientific innovations and moral concerns. In Italy, Slow Food's campaign to protect 'endangered foods' taps into quite crucial questions about the fate of place and the taste of culture on the margins of Europe. 'Slow Life' says Petrini with typical sound-bite finesse, is not just 'Slow Food'. What I hope I have shown here is that debates about food, at least in Europe, specifically Italy and France, are debates about moral economies, not just economics. Food, in other words, is not just food.

Notes

1. Bra is both a commercial center and a working class town with a long history of Mutual Aid associations launched by local craftspeople: cobblers, market vendors and tanners. In reference to Bra's main commercial activity in the immediate postwar period, Padovani and Petrini note that in the 1950s ' the smell of tannin coming from the leather factories prevailed over the aroma of cheese' (2006: 23).
2. Petrini himself notes that his social and political upbringing did not take place in the University's sociology department, but rather in a 'Catholic organization of which I had become president in 1966, at the age of seventeen' (Petrini and Padovani 2006: 26).
3. For example, the Slow Food Terre Madre meeting attracted a wide range of prominent figures including Prince Charles, the environmental activist, Vandana Shiva, ministers from the Berlusconi government and Mikhail Gorbechev (Donati 2005: 237).
4. A recent example is Carl Honoré's (2004) *In Praise of Slow*.
5. I draw here extensively from Chaia Heller's chapter in *The Politics of Food* (2004).

References

Boym, Svetlana. 2001. *The Future of Nostalgia*. New York: Basic Books.

Chrzan, Janet. 2004. Slow Food: What, Why and to Where? *Food, Culture and Society*. 7(2): 117–131.

Counihan, Carole, M. 1999. *The Anthropology of Food and the Body*. New York/London: Routledge.

Donati, Kelly. 2005. The Pleasure of Diversity in Slow Food's Ethics of Taste. *Food Culture and Society*. 8(2): 228–240.

Gaytán, Maria Sarita. 2004. Globalizing Resistance: Slow Food and New Local Imaginaries. *Food Culture and Society*. 7(2): 97–116.

Hawkes and Keen. 2007. *Slow Guide to Sydney*. Mugrave, Vic: Affirm Press.

Heller, Chaia. 2004. Risky Science and Savoir-faire: Peasant Expertise in the French Debate over Genetically Modified Crops. In *The Politics of Food*, edited by MarianneElisabeth Lien and BrigitteNerlich. Oxford/New York: Berg.

Honoré, Carl. 2004. *In Praise of Slow*. London: Orion Books.

Jones, P., Shears, P., Hillier, D., Comfort, D., and Lowell, J. 2003. Return to Traditional Values? A Case Study of Slow Food. *British Food Journal* 105: 297–304.

Italy Daily. 1998. Slow Food an Antidote to Modern Times. November 3.

Kummer, Corby. 2002. *The Pleasures of Slow Food*. San Francisco, CA: Chronicle Books.

Labelle, Julie. 2004. A Recipe for Connectedness: Bridging Production and Consumption with Slow Food. *Food, Culture and Society*. 7(2): 81–96.

Lafargue, Paul. 1989 [1883]. *The Right to be Lazy*. Translated by Charles H. Kerr. Chicago:Charles H. Kerr Publishing Company.

Laudan, Rachel. 2001. A Plea for Culinary Modernism. Why We Should Love New, Fast, Processed Food. *Gastronomica*. 1: 36–44.

———. 2004. Slow Food, The French Terroir Strategy, and Culinary Modernism. *Food, Culture and Society*. 7(2): 133–144.

La Nazione. 1996. Sequestrati 200 chili di lardo. Carenti I documenti sanitari. *La Nazione*. 1 April

Leitch, Alison. 1996. The Life of Marble: the Experience and Meaning of Work in the Marble Quarries of Carrara. *The Australian Journal of Anthropology*. 7(3): 325–357.

Manetti, Sergio. 1996. La Cee porta la rovina sulla tavola Italiana. *La Repubblica*. April 21

———. 2000. The Social Life of *Lardo*: Slow Food in Fast Times. *The Asia Pacific Journal of Anthropology*. 1(1): 103–118.

———. 2003. Slow Food and the Politics of Pork Fat. *Ethnos*. 68(4): 437–462.

McClagan, Margaret. 2000. Spectacles of Difference: Buddhism, Media Management and Contemporary Tibet Activism. *Polygraph*. 12: 101–120.

Meneley, Anne. 2004. Extra Virgin Olive Oil and Slow Food. *Anthropologica*. 46: 165–176.

Mintz, Sidney. 1979. Sugar and Sweetness. *Marxist Perspectives*. 2: 56–73.

Parasecoli, F. 2003. Postrevolutionary Chowhounds: Food, Globalisation, and the Italian Left. *Gastronomica*. 3(3): 29–39.

Parkins, Wendy and Craig, Geoffrey. 2006. *Slow Living*. Sydney: UNSW Press

Paxson, Heather. 2006. Artisanal Cheese and Economies of Sentiment in New England. In *Fast Food/Slow Food: The Cultural Economy of the Global Food System*. ed. RichardWilk. Lanham, MD: Altamira Press

Petrini, Carlo. 2001a. *Slow Food: le Ragioni del Gusto*. Roma/Bari: Editori Laterza.

———. 2001b. *Slow Food: Collected Thoughts on Taste, Tradition, and the Honest Pleasures of Food*. White River Junction, VT: Chelsea Green.

Petrini, Carlo and Padovani, Gigi. 2006. *Slow Food Revolution*. NewYork: Rizzoli.

Pilcher, Jeffrey. 2006. Taco Bell, Maseca and Slow Food: A Postmodern Apocalypse for Mexico's Peasant Cuisine? in *Fast Food/Slow Food: The Cultural Economy of the Global Food System*, ed. RichardWilk. Lanham. MD: Altamira Press.

Pocock, Barbara. 2003. *The Work/Life Collision*. Sydney: The Federation Press.

Revelli, N. *Il Mondo dei Vinti*. Torino: Einaudi.

Rogers, Susan, Carol. 1987. Good to Think: The 'Peasant' in Contemporary France. *Anthropological Quarterly*. 60(2): 56–62.

Rosaldo, Renato. 1989. *Culture and Truth: The Remaking of Social Analysis*. Boston: Beacon Press.

Salter, Bernard. 2001. *The Big Shift*. Hardie Grant Publishing.

Schor, J. 1998. *The Overspent American. Why We Want What We Don't Need*. New York: Harper Perennial.

Seremetakis, C. Nadia. 1994. The Memory of the Senses, pts. 1&2. In *The Senses Still: Perception and Memory as Material Culture in Modernity*, ed. C. N.Seremetakis, pp. 1–43. Boulder: Westview Press.

Spender, Mathew. 2000. The Politics of Pork Fat. *Bon Appétit*. May, pp. 54–55.

Stille, Alexander. 2001. Slow Food. *The Nation*. August 20–27, pp. 11–16.

Tomlinson, J. 1999. *Globalization and Culture*. Cambridge: Polity.

Veronelli, Luigi. 2004. *Alla Ricerca dei Cibi Perduti*. Rome: Derive/Approdi.

29

Taco Bell, Maseca, and Slow Food: A Postmodern Apocalypse for Mexico's Peasant Cuisine?[*]

Jeffrey M. Pilcher

Mexico has a distinguished revolutionary tradition, but is the land of Emiliano Zapata ready for the "delicious revolution" of Slow Food? The question may sound a bit facetious at first, but given the movement's origins in the Italian Communist Party, a disquisition on class consciousness in a postmodern era seems appropriate. Of course, class has been virtually banished from postmodern academic discourse, perhaps from the sheer embarrassment of an intellectual vanguard discovering itself to be a petit bourgeoisie on the brink of proletarianization by the forces of global capital. In the script of contemporary revolution, only the villain—global capital—retains its traditional role. Slow Food speaks the lines of the reformist Social Democratic Party (SDP) to José Bové's militant Bolshevism, the international proletariat is now politically suspect for its consumerist tendencies, and the peasantry has become the progressive motor of history. Although Slow Food offers an admirable program for personal life, it will never represent a genuine revolution until it confronts the dilemmas of class that have been complicated but not obviated by increasing globalization. Indeed, the Mexican case reveals the impossibility of drawing a clear dichotomy between slow and fast food in markets where global and local capital compete for the trade of middle-class tourists and equally cosmopolitan "peasants."

The Slow Food snail mascot would no doubt bask contentedly in the shade of Emiliano Zapata's sombrero, for the Mexican agrarian revolution of 1910 likewise sought to preserve traditional agrarian livelihoods. Emerging from the crisis of Italian leftist politics in the late 1980s, Slow Food exalted leisure and pleasure as an antidote to the blind pursuit of efficiency within the United States (Parasecoli 2003). The movement sought to revive artisanal production and to preserve vanishing biodiversity against the homogenizing influence of multinational agribusiness. Nevertheless, tensions remained between the elitism of the official manifesto—"preserve us from the contagion of the multitude" (Parasecoli 2003:xxiii)—and the democratizing ideal of affordable but tasty *osterie* (regional restaurants).

Recent work on the history of Italian cuisine demonstrates that the traditions Slow Food seeks to preserve are largely invented, a point acknowledged by the movement's leaders (Hobsbawn 1983; Petrini 2003). Well into the twentieth century, peasants subsisted on monotonous porridges of maize, chestnuts, broad beans, or rice,

[*]*Originally published 2006*

depending on the region and the season (Camporesi 1993; Diner 2001; Helstosky 2004). Italy's regional cuisines are not only modern inventions, they may even have been created in the Americas through the industrial production and canning of olive oil, tomato paste, and cheeses to satisfy migrant workers who could afford foods unavailable to peasants at home (Teti 1992; Gabaccia 2004). More research is needed on the nineteenth-century bourgeois diet, but it seems that contemporary Italian cuisine emerged largely from festival foods such as *maccheroni*, which became items of everyday consumption in the United States. The traditional *osteria* that Slow Food seeks to encourage likewise grew out of the *cucina casalinga*, meals served in urban homes to unattached male workers; they only became restaurants with the postwar growth of tourism. The Italian experience in turn provides a useful model for the emergence of Mexico's regional cuisines.

There can be few foods slower than Mexican peasant cooking. For thousands of years, the preparation of the staple maize tortillas required hours of hard, physical labor each day. Women rose before dawn to grind corn (*masa*) on a basalt stone (*metate*), then patted out tortillas by hand and cooked them on an earthenware griddle (*comal*)—all this before men went out to the fields (Redfield 1929; Lewis 1951). Festivals multiplied the workload of women; in addition to preparing special tortillas and masa dumplings (*tamales*), they labored over the metate grinding chile sauces (*moles*) and cacao while men sat around drinking (Stephen 1991). The metate was so intrinsic to Mexican patriarchy that when mechanical mills capable of adequately grinding masa finally reached the countryside in the first half of the twentieth century, one villager described it as a "revolution of the women against the authority of the men" (Lewis 1951:108). As women transferred their labor from domestic reproduction to market production, tamales and moles were gentrified by restaurants catering to national and international tourists (Pilcher 2004).

Mexico has had two competing visions for the modernization of its cuisine. Attempts by local investors and engineers to industrialize tortilla production have culminated in the rise of Grupo Maseca, a multinational producer of *masa harina* (dehydrated tortilla flour), which can be reconstituted with water to save the trouble of making fresh masa, thus making them popular among migrant workers. Although connoisseurs can distinguish fresh from industrial corn tortillas, both are quite different from the wheat flour tortillas most common in the United States. Meanwhile, Taco Bell has led the way in applying North American fast food technology to Mexican cooking. Neither approach proved satisfactory to aficionados, leaving a space for Slow Food to catch on among middle-class Mexicans and foreign tourists. Yet attempts to save traditional Mexican cuisine have been plagued by the same contradictions of elitism, gender bias, and even a measure of imperial arrogance—treating Native Americans like southern Italians—that typified the movement at home.

Maseca

Although the industrialization of Mexico was generally characterized by imported technology and capital, the modernization of the tortilla was a uniquely national enterprise. The complex skills involved in making tortillas were mechanized in three distinct stages at roughly fifty-year intervals around the beginning, middle, and end of the twentieth century. The arduous task of hand grinding maize at the metate was first replaced by forged steel mills. Next came the technology for automatically pressing out and cooking tortillas, which facilitated the spread of small-scale tortilla factories throughout the country. Finally, the industrial production of masa harina allowed the vertical integration of food processing under Grupo Maseca. Tortilla futurists envisioned these technologies as a complete package, but the three distinct processes could in fact be combined or separated according to circumstances, and each was tied into complex culinary, social, and political relationships. Ultimately, the fate of the tortilla resulted more from questions of political economy than of consumer choice.

Corn mills arrived in Mexican cities by the late nineteenth century but took decades to spread through the countryside, in part because of concern among women about their position within the family. The ability to make tortillas was long considered essential to a rural woman seeking marriage, and any who neglected the metate risked unfavorable gossip. Even the few centavos charged by the mills posed a significant cost in subsistence communities, but poor women often had the greatest incentive to grind corn mechanically because the time saved could be used to engage in artisanal crafts or petty trade. Wealthy families, by contrast, were among the last to give up the metate on a daily basis; this form of slow food offered a status symbol, in part because the rich could pay others to do the actual work. As the benefits of milling gained acceptance, women often organized cooperatives to purchase the machines. By midcentury, corn mills had arrived in virtually every community in Mexico, transforming social relationships and helping to incorporate rural dwellers into the monetary economy (Lewis 1951; Bauer 1990).

The mechanization of the tortilla and the development of masa harina posed more technological than social problems. Conveyer belt cookers were first introduced around 1900, but only at midcentury could they produce a tortilla that satisfied Mexican consumers. Once these machines were created, a cottage industry of tortilla factories quickly spread to all but the most remote rural communities. Although these shops generally sold tortillas by the kilo made from commercially purchased maize, they also ground corn for customers who wished to prepare their own tortillas at home. Both small-scale tortilla factories and their eventual corporate challenger developed under the aegis of a welfare program intended to subsidize food for poor urban consumers. The first masa harina factories were established in 1949 by Molinas Azteca, S.A. (Maseca) and a parastatal corporation, Maíz Industrializado, S.A. (Minsa). The two firms collaborated on research and development for more than a decade before arriving at a suitable formulation that could be transformed into tortilla masa with just the addition of water. By the 1970s, tortilla flour accounted for 5 percent of the maize consumed in Mexico. Sales grew steadily over the next two decades until Maseca alone held 27 percent of the national corn market. Neverthe-less, the subsidy on maize supplied to small-scale tortilla factories slowed the firm's expansion.

The dismantling of the state food agency in the 1990s assured Maseca's triumph. President Carlos Salinas de Gortari (1988–994) first curtailed the corn subsidy while also selling Minsa to a consortium rivaling Maseca. For the fifty-one thousand small-scale tortilla factories, subsidized corn had been essential for their commercial viability. Led by a trade organization, the Association of Proprietors of Tortilla Factories, and Nixtamal Mills, they launched a vocal political campaign to retain the subsidy, citing scientific studies concluding that traditional tortillas were more nutritive than those made with Maseca, which they dubbed "MAsaSECA" ("dry masa"). They also accused Maseca of manipulating corn markets and attempting to monopolize supplies, thereby tapping popular memories of hunger that remain vivid in many sectors of Mexican society. But the proprietors found themselves on the wrong side of a neoliberal political avalanche, and the subsidy was eliminated in January 1999. The sudden change left tortilla factories unable to establish competitive sources of supply, and they were reduced to mere vendors for the multinational company, as masa harina quickly cornered an estimated 80 percent of the national tortilla market. Maseca, in turn, claimed nearly three quarters of these sales (Pilcher 1998; Ochoa 2000; Cebreros, n.d.).

The results of this change have been mixed. Proponents of modernization considered tortillas to be essentially tasteless, anyway, and found no difference in the new product. Journalist Alma Guillermoprieto (1999:46) took a different view, claiming that "when the privatization program of Mexico's notorious former President Carlos Salinas delivered the future of the tortilla into their hands . . . [the tortilla magnates] served up to the Mexican people the rounds of grilled cardboard that at present constitute the nation's basic foodstuff." Campesinos are quite sensitive to tortilla quality, and many have resisted Maseca (see, for example, González 2001:173). Nevertheless, the exigencies of subsistence often require small farmers to sell their best produce to urban markets. Meanwhile, Mexican food faced a still more uncertain fate abroad.

Taco Bell

Even as the tortilla market evolved under government protection at home, tacos slipped across the border into greater Los Angeles, where they fell into the hands of scientists and industrialists. While migrants labored in corporate agribusiness, their foods underwent a process of Taylorization to become more standardized and efficient. Neatly packaged under the trademark of Taco Bell, these brave new tacos subsequently traveled around the world, ultimately colonizing their native land. But despite their best efforts, the food formulators and advertising executives could not determine the global reception of the cyborgs they had created.

Sociologist George Ritzer (1993) has examined most comprehensively the threat of corporate fast food to local traditions, extending Max Weber's theory of rationalization, the process whereby modern technology has made society more efficient, predictable, and controlled. One would, indeed, be hard pressed to find a better example of those values than the Big Mac. The result of this process has been, first, the standardization of food, replacing the endless variety of local cuisines with the artificial choice of numbered selections from a "value menu." The creation of so-called McJobs has further alienated labor by requiring only minimally skilled workers who respond to the commands of machinery. By stifling the social inter-actions customarily associated with dining, fast food has supposedly dehumanized the process of eating.

The McDonaldized taco, like the hamburger, had its origins in southern California in the mid-1950s. Glen Bell, a telephone repairman from San Bernardino, was impressed by the original McDonald's restaurant, but rather than compete head-on for the hamburger trade, he applied the new industrial techniques to a separate market segment, the Mexican American taco stand. As he described it: "If you wanted a dozen, you were in for a wait. They stuffed them first, quickly fried them and stuck them together with a toothpick. I thought they were delicious, but something had to be done about the method of preparation" (Taco Bell 2001). That something was to pre-fry the tortillas, anathema to any Mexican, but a blessing to Anglos who preferred to drive off with their food rather than eat at the stand while the other tacos were freshly cooked.

Corporate mythology attributing the North American taco to Glen Bell is questionable, but whatever the origins of the pre-fried taco, precursor to the industrial taco shell, it made possible the globalization of Mexican food by freeing it from its ethnic roots. No longer would restaurateurs or home cooks need a local supply of fresh corn tortillas to make tacos; the shells could henceforth be mass-produced and shipped around the world, albeit with some breakage. The extent to which the taco has been alienated from the Mexican community can be seen in the job description given by a Taco Bell employee in *The New Yorker* (2000): "My job is I, like, basically make the tacos! The meat comes in boxes that have bags inside, and those bags you boil to heat up the meat. That's how you make tacos."

By the mid-1990s, as the Tex-Mex fad spread worldwide, restaurants in Europe and East Asia abandoned even the pretense of serving Mexican food. Nevertheless, critics have questioned the homogenizing effects of the McDonaldization thesis by emphasizing the diverse ways in which people around the world experience restaurants. Although travelers may find the bland uniformity of the Golden Arches disturbing, locals embrace the new choices made possible by the arrival of fast food. The protests of burger-Luddite José Bové notwithstanding, French cuisine has little to fear from the spread of McDonalds, as sociologist Rick Fantasia (1995) has pointed out, because the fast food chains and upscale restaurants cater to quite different markets. The contributors to James Watson's (1997) volume, *Golden Arches East*, found the experience of U.S. culture, rather than actual food, to be the chain's biggest selling point in Asia. Customers were enthralled by the democratizing influence of waiting in line, the freedom from the social demands of competitive banqueting, and the novelty of clean public bathrooms.

The opening of Taco Bell's first Mexican outlet in 1992 illustrates the divergent expectations of corporate executives and local consumers. The Tricon conglomerate already operated a number of fast food restaurants in the country, and it tested the market by offering a selection of tacos at a Kentucky Fried Chicken location in an upscale mall in the suburbs of Mexico City. Skeptics murmured about "coals to Newcastle," but company spokesmen blithely applied the usual justification for fast food in the United States that "the one thing Mexico lacks is somewhere to get a clean, cheap, fast taco" (quoted in Guillermoprieto 1994:248). In fact, countless *taquerías* offered precisely that, although Guillermoprieto conceded that "no Mexican taco stand looks like a NASA food-preparation station." Even the company acknowledged its doubts by obtaining a supply of fresh tortillas and offering the standard taquería fare of the 1990s, pork *carnitas* and shredded beef. But middle-class customers responded with disappointment, for they could get Mexican tacos anywhere. One woman complained: "This doesn't taste like the real thing, does it? What I wanted was those big taco shells stuffed with salad and Kraft cheese and all *kinds* of stuff, like what you get in Texas" (quoted in Guillermoprieto 1994).

Mexico thus replicates the global experience of fast food as a middle-class privilege, with its own versions of authenticity. The initial opening of Taco Bell in Mexico in 1992 failed due to the economic crisis of that year, but by the end of the decade the company had opened a number of successful outlets. Even in the United States, fast food need not entail the complete obliteration of local culture; witness the spread of "fresh Mex" restaurants such as Chipotle, a subsidiary of the McDonald's corporation. Moreover, by introducing customers to an artificial version of Mexican food, chains may well have expanded opportunities for marketing the genuine article.

Slow Food

In its mission to preserve and advertise distinctive regional foods, Slow Food created an "Ark of Taste" along with awards for biodiversity to promote awareness of and support for ecologically beneficial practices around the world. Despite their relatively small size, organizations from developed nations wield disproportionate power in a country such as Mexico, and as a result, they slant local activist movements toward middle-class agendas with little relevance for the needs of common people. Moreover, the fascination with Mexico's folkloric and Native American heritage diverts attention from the *mestizo* (mixed-race) majority, who do not speak an indigenous language but still suffer economic and political marginalization.

Mexico has done very well through the Slow Food movement, although it is unclear how much of this attention is due to its rich culinary heritage and how much to the Zapatista rebellion in Chiapas. The indigenous uprising gained international acclaim almost from the first shots fired on January 1, 1994, the day the North American Free Trade Agreement (NAFTA) went into effect. While brandishing an AK-47, the charismatic Subcomandante Marcos shunned terrorist bombings and instead waged his campaign with anti-globalization *pronunciamientos* fired across the World Wide Web. Stylish, balaclava-clad guerrillas held particular fascination for the Italian left.

Regardless of the inspiration, Mexicans have topped the list of Slow Food's Award for the Defense of Biodiversity. The jury consists of about five hundred food writers and other culinary authorities from around the world, although the United States and Italy provide the largest number. In the first four years, Mexicans received five out of fifty nominations, worth 3,500 each, and three out of twenty jury prizes, providing an additional 7,500. The United States, by comparison, received four nominations but no jury prize winners. The first Mexican jury prize, in 2000, went to Raúl Manuel Antonio, from Rancho Grande, Oaxaca, for establishing an indigenous vanilla-growing cooperative to supplement the incomes of small coffee producers. The following year, Doña Sebastiana Juárez Broca, known in her Tabasco community as Tía Tana, won a prize for reviving traditional cacao production techniques as an alternative to an official marketing organization that had impoverished farmers. Finally, in 2003, the jury honored historian José Iturriaga de la Fuente for organizing a fifty-four-volume series documenting Mexico's regional and indigenous cuisines (Slow Food n.d.).

Just as Slow Food began in Italy with a 1986 protest against the opening of a McDonald's restaurant below the historic Spanish Steps in Rome, Mexico has had its own showdown with McDonald's on the main square in Oaxaca City, the mecca of indigenous gastronomy. The company had already had one restaurant in a middle-class shopping mall on the outskirts of the city, like hundreds of others from Cancún to Tijuana, but when the local franchise holder sought permission for an outlet on the Zócalo in the summer of 2002, the intelligentsia mobilized its opposition. The campaign, led by renowned Oaxacan artist Francisco Toledo, asserted that burgers and fries were simply too different from the indigenous version of fast food, *chapulines*, fried grasshoppers sold from baskets and eaten with tortillas and guacamole. Bowing to the complaints of such high-profile figures, the government withdrew the permit, but the controversy had little importance, either culturally or economically, for ordinary Oaxacans who could not afford a Big Mac (Weiner 2002).

A similar protest had already played out in Mexico City against Maseca. As masa harina became ubiquitous in tortilla factories throughout the capital, the local branch of Greenpeace began issuing warnings about the use of GM-maize. In September 2001, self-styled ecological guerrillas changed the slogan on a giant bill-board depicting flute-shaped crispy tacos from "Flautas with Maseca are tastier," to "Flautas with Maseca are genetically modified." Héctor Magallón explained the action by pointing out that in a recent survey, 88 percent of Mexicans indicated that they wanted GM-food to be labeled as such, and as a significant importer of maize from the United States, Maseca made an obvious target (Greenpeace 2001). While the desire for accurate labeling is certainly understandable, the protest movement has traveled a long way from the struggles of family-owned tortilla shops against a multinational giant.

For most poor Mexicans, surviving the shock of neoliberal reforms meant increased labor migration. Oaxacans were relative latecomers to the United States, but by the 1970s, Zapotecs and Mixtecs had become an important source of seasonal labor for California agriculture, and many lived year-round in Los Angeles. Despite difficult working conditions and vulnerability due to their undocumented status, migrants generally succeeded in improving their economic position and their remittances were vital for the survival of their families in Mexico. Over time, patterns of migration changed, from predominantly single males to include women and children as well, creating complicated transnational family networks. Higher incomes and tastes for consumer goods have caused significant cultural changes among migrants, especially those who settle permanently in the United States, but ties to home communities often remain strong nevertheless (Kearney 1996; Cohen 1999).

Migrant remittances form only one part of broader family survival strategies based on precarious subsistence agriculture in rural Oaxaca, as elsewhere. Farming has always been difficult in this region, but population growth and revenue from migrant labor has fostered urbanization, placing even greater pressure on cultivable land (Cohen 1999). Even successful artisans catering to the tourist trade spend much of their time in agriculture and depend on local food production (Chibnik 2003). Although often unlettered, these peasant farmers possess an extraordinary empirical understanding of their land and crops (González 2001). Nevertheless, such local knowledge may count for little if the economic necessities of competing with agribusiness cause a downward spiral of ecologically devastating practices, a sort of Gresham's Law of farming (Raikes 1988:62).

In seeking to encourage sustainable agriculture, Slow Food recognized a crucial problem for poor commodity-producing nations, the failure of branding. Mexico exports high-quality pork and vegetables but gains relatively little value from them because of the lack of global cachet associated with, for example, prosciutto ham or Tuscan olive oil. The case of cacao is symptomatic; once the drink of Maya lords, it is now a commodity subject to cutthroat international competition. Small farmers in Mexico suffered further exploitation, having just two options for marketing their harvest, a corrupt monopoly union or multinational buyers, both of which paid desperately low prices. With the assistance of two Mexican biologists and the Dutch organic certifying organization NOVIB, Sebastiana Juárez Broca parlayed her indigenous origins into a valuable brand name, Tia Tana Chocolate. But the adoption of capitalist advertising techniques conferred de facto property rights to a single individual rather than a village cooperative. As the Slow Food citation reads, Tia Tana "produces chocolate using traditional methods employing village women and encouraging the expansion of biological and economically compatible cultivation" (Slow Food n.d.). Yet the picturesque image of local production for tourists can conceal exploitative class relations within indigenous communities. Néstor García Canclini (1993) has observed that profits from craft sales to foreigners generally end up in the hands of local merchants and intermediaries.

Corporate control of international marketing further complicates the prospects for such ecological initiatives. Warren Belasco (1993) has shown the skill with which the food industry has co-opted counterculture movements and created its own forms of ersatz authenticity. Cookbook publishers likewise shared in the bonanza, offering up picturesque images of peasant cuisine to affluent readers (Pilcher 2004). The complicated recipes for traditional festival dishes may even be prepared occasionally by the leisured elite, but slow food offers little to single parents working overtime to support a family in the collapsing ruins of the U.S. welfare state.

Apocalypse Now?

The United States' campaign to spread GM food represents only the latest version of the "white man's burden" to uplift backward peoples through modern agricultural technology, although in practice the so-called Green Revolution has succeeded in promoting capitalist farming, rural unemployment, and urban shantytowns. Yet the Slow Food program likewise bears more than a passing resemblance to the *mission civilisatrice* of nineteenth-century imperialism. While more benign than military intervention, the missionary approach still conceals uneven power relationships that limit the opportunities available to the Mexican people. Moreover, the movement's goal of reducing agricultural overproduction resonates clearly with the dilemmas of the European Union's Common Agricultural Policy, with its mountains of surplus foods. International commodity markets can have complex implications for developing countries (see Raikes 1988), but the agricultural trade wars between Europe and the United States have caused tremendous harm to poor farmers around the world. One of the latest victims of this imperial struggle has been famine-ridden Zambia, the subject of widespread criticism for rejecting U.S. food aid out of fear that GM grain would contaminate domestic crops and forfeit European sales (Annear 2004). Viewed at this level, Sebastiana Juárez Broca appears as simply a colorful indigenous brand to sell Mexican chocolate to upscale consumers.

From the global struggles of industrial food retailers, Grupo Maseca has emerged as an unlikely champion of authentic Mexican cuisine. Mechanization has been essential to the survival of tortillas as the daily bread of Mexican wage laborers, who cannot afford the luxury of slow food on an everyday basis. In foreign markets, the company has launched ambitious expansion plans, and United States and Europe make up nearly 50 percent of total sales (Vega 2003). Occupying foreign territory has meant using local knowledge of fresh corn tortillas to challenge taco shell stereotypes. Although condemned at home as the antithesis of traditional cooking, bags of masa harina have become essential care packages for migrants and aficionados in exile from Aztlán.

With multinational corporations increasingly determining the availability and even the authenticity of food, class-based issues of market power become ever more crucial. While in many European countries restaurant service is an honorable trade paying a living wage, in Mexico it is often the last resort of the most impoverished people. Self-exploitation ultimately makes possible the Slow Food ideal of "good regional cuisine at moderate prices" (Petrini 2003:15). Moreover, Michael Kearney (1996:107) has offered a cautionary note about the conservative embrace of ecological projects generally: "one need not be cynical to see in official support of sustainable development and appropriate technology a de facto recognition that rural poverty in the Third World is not going to be developed out of existence. All peoples will not be brought up to the comfort level of the affluent classes and must therefore adapt to conditions of persistent poverty in ways that are not ecologically, economically, or politically disruptive." He concludes that "the de facto project of such right romantics is to sustain existing relations of inequality." Historically minded observers will note also that much of the program and even the slogan of "alimentary sovereignty" adopted by José Bové was promoted earlier by the fascist regime of Benito Mussolini (Parasecoli 2003:37; Helstosky n.d.). Slow Food has likewise replaced the developmental ideal of Prometheus with the more defensive symbol of Noah. As Petrini (2003:86) explains: "Faced with the excesses of modernization, we are not trying to change the world anymore, just to save it." Yet Oaxacan migrant workers, who must cross a militarized frontier in order to save their own communities, may ask themselves: will they find a place on the Ark?

This is not to deny that Slow Food offers hope for the survival of peasant cuisines. Indeed, the contemporary situation in Mexico parallels that of Italy a century ago. Just as half of all Italian labor migrants ultimately returned home, with new attitudes and more money but still part of their old communities, so do Mexican sojourners continue to follow their circular routes, notwithstanding hysterical media accounts of "a border out of control." Of course, it would be absurd to think that NAFTA will ever lead to income redistribution programs comparable to those of the European Union. Nevertheless, attempts to improve conditions in Oaxaca, like those in the Mezzogiorno, must adopt a continental vision. The indigenous political revival, with roots in both southern California and southern Mexico, offers a model for revalorizing ethnic communities (Kearney 1996). Those who sympathize can help most by allowing transnational families to flourish in their own neighborhoods rather than by indulging in exotic tourism to distant lands. The true foundation of sustainable agriculture in Mexico is outside labor paying decent wages—as it is for any American family farm.

Note

Acknowledgments. This essay was inspired by Martín González de la Vara and greatly improved by the suggestions of Richard Wilk, Donna Gabaccia, William Beezley, Sterling Evans, Glen Kuecker, and the anthropologists of SEA, who graciously welcomed an imposter in their midst.

References

Annear, Christopher M. (2004) "GM or Death": Food and Choice in Zambia. *Gastronomica* 4(2):16–23.

Bauer, Arnold J. (1990) Millers and Grinders: Technology and Household Economy in Meso-America. *Agricultural History* 64(1):1–17.

Belasco, Warren (1993) *Appetite for Change: How the Counterculture Took on the Food Industry.* Ithaca: Cornell University Press.

Camporesi, Piero (1993 [1989]) *The Magic Harvest: Food, Folklore, and Society*, Joan Krakover Hall, trans. Cambridge, U.K.: Polity Press.

Cebreros, Alfonso, n.d. Grupo MASECA: Un Caso Exitoso de Transnacionalización Agroalimentaria. Electronic document. http://ciat-library.ciat.cgiar.org/Alacea/v_congreso_memorias/V_grupo_maseca.htm, accessed September 6, 2003.

Chibnik, Michael (2003) *Crafting Tradition: The Making and Marketing of Oaxacan Wood Carvings.* Austin: University of Texas Press.

Cohen, Jeffrey A. (1999) *Cooperation and Community: Economy and Society in Oaxaca.* Austin: University of Texas Press.

Diner, Hasia (2001) *Hungering for America: Italian, Irish, and Jewish Foodways in the Age of Migration.* Cambridge, MA: Harvard University Press.

Fantasia, Rick (1995) Fast Food in France. *Theory and Society* 24:201–43.

Gabaccia, Donna (2004) *The Atlantic Origins of Italian Food. Conference on American Popular Culture.* Toronto, Ontario.

García Canclini, Néstor (1993) *Transforming Modernity: Popular Culture in Mexico.* Lidia Lozano, trans. Austin: University of Texas Press.

González, Roberto J. (2001) *Zapotec Science: Farming and Food in the Northern Sierra of Oaxaca.* Austin: University of Texas Press.

Greenpeace (2001) Greenpeace etiqueta anuncio espectacular de Maseca. Boletín 173, September. Electronic document. http://www.greenpeace.org.mx/php/gp.php?target=%2Fphp%2Fboletines.php%3Fc%3Dtrans%26n%3D173, accessed April 22, 2004.

Guillermoprieto, Alma (1994) *The Heart That Bleeds.* New York: Vintage.

——— (1999) In Search of the Tortilla. *The New Yorker*, November 26:46.

Helstosky, Carol (2004) *Garlic and Oil: The Politics of Italian Food.* London: Berg.

——— n.d. In press. Mussolini's Alimentary Sovereignty.

Hobsbawm, Eric (1983) Introduction: Inventing Traditions. In *The Invention of Tradition.* EricHobsbawm and TerenceRanger, eds. Pp. 1–14. Cambridge: Cambridge University Press.

Kearney, Michael (1996) *Reconceptualizing the Peasantry: Anthropology in Global Perspective.* Boulder, CO: Westview Press.

Lewis, Oscar (1951) *Life in a Mexican Village: Tepoztlán Revisited.* Urbana: University of Illinois Press. The New Yorker (2000) *Day Job: Taco Bell Employee.* April 24–May 1:185.

Ochoa, Enrique C. (2000) *Feeding Mexico: The Politics of Food Since 1910.* Wilmington, DE: Scholarly Resources.

Parasecoli, Fabio (2003) Postrevolutionary Chowhounds: Food, Globalization, and the Italian Left. *Gastronomica* 3(3):29–39.

Petrini, Carlo (2003) *Slow Food: The Case for Taste.* William McCuaig, trans. New York: Columbia University Press.

Pilcher, Jeffrey M. (1998) *¡Que vivan los tamales! Food and the Making of Mexican Identity*. Albuquerque: University of New Mexico Press.

Pilcher, Jeffrey M. (2004) From "Montezuma's Revenge" to "Mexican Truffles": Culinary Tourism across the Rio Grande. In *Culinary Tourism*. LucyM.Long, ed. Pp. 76–96. Lexington: University Press of Kentucky.

Raikes, Philip (1988) *Modernising Hunger: Famine, Food Surplus and Farm Policy in the EEC and Africa*. London: James Currey.

Redfield, Margaret Park (1929) Notes on the Cookery of Tepoztlan, Morelos. *American Journal of Folklore* 42(164):167–96.

Ritzer, George (1993) *The McDonaldization of Society*. Thousand Oaks, CA: Pine Forge Press.

Slow Food (n.d.) Premio Slow Food. Electronic document. http://www.slowfood.com/eng/sf_premio/sf_premio. lasso, accessed April 22, 2004.

Stephen, Lynn (1991) *Zapotec Women*. Austin: University of Texas Press.

Taco Bell (2001) History. Electronic document. http://www.tacobell.com, accessed March 17, 2004.

Teti, Vito (1992) La cucina calabrese: è un'invenzione americana *I viaggi di Erodoto* 6(14):58–73.

Vega, Marielena (2003) Grupo Industrial Maseca. *El Economista*, September 3.

Watson, James L. (ed.) (1997) *Golden Arches East: McDonald's in East Asia*. Palo Alto: Stanford University Press.

Weiner, Tim (2002) *Mexicans Resisting McDonald's Fast Food Invasion*. New York Times, August 24.

30

Food Workers as Individual Agents of Culinary Globalization: Pizza and Pizzaioli in Japan*

Rossella Ceccarini

According to the Italian Restaurant Guide of Japan, published in 2006 by the Italian Trade Commission, there are 3,974 restaurants serving Italian cuisine, or at least dishes inspired by Italian cuisine all over the Japanese archipelago. Pizza is among the most popular dishes. The purpose of this paper is to give an overview of the status of pizza production in Japan based on the experiences and knowledge of the people who prepare these pizzas, namely "pizzaiolos," and the Italian restaurateurs who work in Tokyo.

This emphasis on the food producer's experience is based on the assumption that researchers on food consumption in Japan have paid considerable attention to the Japanese customer and the way their eating habits have changed since the introduction of new foods (Ohonuki-Tierney 1997; Ashkenazi and Jacob 2000; Cwiertka 2006) but little is known about those who produce it. The paper also notes the way foreign food has become "glocalized," that is, how international foods have become domesticated or tailored to local contexts (Tobin et al. 1994). Prior to being consumed, food and cuisine must be crafted and prepared. Thus, this paper looks at the glocalization of foreign culinary products from the perspective of the food creator, in other words, how the worker as an individual agent of globalization, plays an important role in spreading glocalization and making the culinary product desirable. The first part of the paper introduces the background of pizza restaurants in Tokyo, and the second part focuses on the pizzaiolos.

Before moving to the above issues, let me first write about the qualitative data rendered in this paper. All quotes are based on open-ended interviews with pizzaiolos and restaurateurs involved in the Italian restaurant business. The interviews were held in Tokyo between winter and autumn 2008 and have been digitally recorded and transcribed. The interviews were held in Italian, Japanese, and English, but due to limited space and other practical reasons, I'm presenting only English translations of the original-language quotes. I have tried to respect the privacy of my informants by omitting their names where possible. Some of the informants are popular actors in the restaurant business and easily recognizable; hence their names have not been changed. Information has also been obtained from printed and on-line sources as well as from personal visits to Italian restaurants in and around Tokyo.

*Originally published 2010

Pizza and Pizzerias in Tokyo

A fast search on Google will show that pizza, as a food and a term, has truly gone global. However, the thousands of pizza titles popping out from the Internet as a search result evokes in the reader different images and tastes. One person could be thinking of wedge-shaped slices topped with cheese and pepperoni, while someone else could be thinking of red tomatoes and white mozzarella covering a soft crust; then another person might be thinking of some kind of crunchy Italian food.

To categorize the variations, we can begin by distinguishing between a standardized pizza and a handcrafted one (Helstosky 2008). The standardized pizza originated in the United States, and for this reason I will refer to it as American pizza in this paper, even if there are hand-made American pizza establishments as well. Generally, the American pizza uses industrial preparation techniques and is sold by pizza chain restaurants that usually deliver to their customers. It is a large sliced pizza, heavily garnished, baked in pans, and the taste is homogeneous, so a Domino's pepperoni pizza ordered in Chicago should taste the same as one ordered in London or in Paris. The handcrafted pizza, on the other hand, originated in Italy as the food of the poor and slowly became an emblem of Italian national cuisine. It is made by an expert pizzaiolo using artisanal methods. The pizza is baked directly on the stone of a wood-burning oven, and is garnished with only a few fresh ingredients. There are precise rules to be followed in the making of the artisanal pizza, so no pizza will taste exactly the same. Flavor and crust texture depends upon the pizzaiolo him or herself, the quality of the ingredients, the oven, and other elements. As noted by Helstosky (2008), McDonald's & Co. have left no room for small, independent hamburger shops, but pizza chains have not replaced the artisanal pizza. All over the world, including Japan, standardized and handcrafted pizza seem to coexist without any particular problems.

The escalation of the pizza's popularity in Japan and its link to the Italian restaurant scene, can be broadly traced through three main periods: the 1950–60s, 1970–1980s, and 1990s to the present.

1950–1960s

The darker side of Tokyo's underworld can account for much that happened during the post-war period, as seen through the eyes and the questionable life of Nicola Zappetti. As written by Robert Whiting (1999), Mr. Zappetti was an American marine of Italian descendants who made his way into the Japanese underground economy and became involved with the *yakuza*. In 1956, following his release from jail, he opened "Nicola's pizza house" in the Roppongi area. He was neither a chef nor a restaurateur. Thus he built his knowledge of pizza relying on his sense of taste, a few cookbooks, and what he used to eat back home in New York. While he lost his restaurants through a series of unfortunate events (e.g. gambling losses, wrong investments, wrong business partners, divorce), his name and his mustached figure holding a stack of pizzas is still prevalent. Part of his pizza parlor business went to his ex-wife and another part to Nihon Kotsu, one of the largest taxi companies in Tokyo. Nevertheless Zappetti played an important part in spreading the popularity of pizza in Japan.

In the same area and period, Mr. Antonio Cancemi opened his Italian restaurant. Antonio was a trained chef, born in Sicily in 1916. He graduated from a culinary school and joined the Italian navy as a chef. In 1943 he reached Japan onboard an Italian military vessel during the month of September, when Italy surrendered. As a Japanese ally, Antonio was by classification an enemy to the U.S., but his cooking expertise led him to cook for General McArthur on a train trip around Japan in 1946. In 1957, Antonio moved his operations from Kobe to Tokyo, and almost immediately pizza became one of his restaurant's most popular dishes. Today, Antonio's is the oldest family owned Italian restaurant in Japan. Its flagship restaurant is in Aoyama accompanied by many other restaurants, delicatessens, and cafes throughout Japan.

1970–1980s

In the 1970s and 1980s pizza chains began to make their way into Japan, taking advantage, we can assume, of the Foreign Capital Law, which was revised as follows in 1969:

> In March 1969, Japanese Foreign Capital Law was revised so that foreign-capital restaurants in Japan could operate freely. Restaurant businesses from abroad penetrated the Japanese market openly through direct investment or by operating agreements. Under that law, it became easy for Japanese companies to make an alliance of technology and capital with foreign corporations. From the end of World War II until 1969, Japan made it impossible for private retailers and restaurant businesses to take in foreign capital, because Japan promoted national-sector businesses rather strongly. The revised Foreign Capital Law was welcomed by the restaurant industry. (Doi 1992, 73)

We can learn through various corporate websites that Shakey's Pizza and Pizza Hut opened in 1973, followed by Domino's pizza in 1985. The first *Japanese* shop called "Pizza La," opened in the Mejiro area of Tokyo in 1986.[1] To the present day, American chains are marketing an American pizza style while Pizza La seems to favor the Italian style. Even if Pizza La sells a product that no Italian would recognize as Italian, Pizza La's TV commercials use the word "*buono*," the Italian term for "good." In one television ad, three young Japanese girls place their index fingers under their cheek bones, twisting them while saying, "*Buono*." It is a gesture usually used in Italy when addressing children to indicate something delicious.

In the 1970s and mid 1980s we could witness the continued spread of pizza chains, and along with it the success of Italian cuisine in general. Such terms as イタ飯 (*itameshi*) and イタ飯ブーム (*itameshi* boom), indicated that Italian food and Italian cuisine were now popular and friendly words of the 1980s. Among the restaurants and people partly responsible for the boom was Carmine Cozzolino.

Carmine Cozzolino was born in Calabria, southern Italy, and arrived in Japan in 1978, holding a cultural visa and a lifetime ambition to become an *aikido* master. He first lived in a monastery near Mount Fuji and then moved to Tokyo. Though *aikido* remained his main interest, he started working in various Tokyo restaurants in order to make a living. But he was not satisfied with the dishes he was required to make:

> In those days, most Japanese restaurant owners requested you to put some sort of sauce in the Milanese [fried cutlet dipped in egg and breadcrumbs] because it was the French way. I mean, yes, French do cook in that way, but we don't! So it was something like … I was taken by a sort

of anger like ... "I will show you how it is supposed to be in the restaurants" ... At the end ... I opened up my own restaurant and it became a boom. ... It was bizarre. You needed months and months of reservations. (Interview with Carmine Cozzolino, April 2008)

Because of this sort of prejudice towards the Italian cuisine that prevailed in most Japanese owned restaurants, Carmine opened his own business in a Tokyo area known as Kagurazaka in 1987. Though small (in fact a hole in the wall), that is how he likes to talk about it. There were only twenty-five miniature tables around which students, "salary-men," dating couples, and occasionally show-business people crowded. According to Carmine, the popularity of the place was due to low prices, a friendly atmosphere and, of course, the Italian food itself. Even if different from Japanese food, it proved to share the rule of simplicity: few natural ingredients and not too many rules of etiquette. Earnings were so high each year that finally he had to move to more spacious accommodations on the opposite side of the street.

The business spirit of Carmine has always been to open a restaurant with an image of himself as the first customer of the place. In 1987 he opened his restaurant according the needs of a single, thirty-year-old man, wishing to dine with his friends or take his fiancée to a foreign restaurant without having to go through all his savings. In the 1990s being a forty-year-old man with a family and children, he was thinking of a place to dine without having to worry about noisy youngsters, broken glasses, or high prices. With this "forty-year-old married man with children" idea in mind, he opened Pizzeria La Volpaia (The Fox's Lair) in 1995. Again it became a boom. Little foxes were drawn on the walls, and the room(s) contained long tables with benches to sit on. Importantly, it was easy to clean the concrete flooring. Moreover, it was a self-service environment. Unable to install a wood-burning oven in a wooden structure, he brought an electric oven from Italy. Though his initial idea was to make the restaurant a fun place for kids, it became, once again, a place to take someone on a date. Thanks to the self-service system, the restaurant required fewer personnel, and so the profit margin rose to 40%. The restaurant closed in 2005 because the old wooden house had to be torn down to build a typical Japanese mansion, but Pizza Carmine is still to be found in and around Tokyo.

1990s–present

As observed during the years following the war, the pizza scene was dominated by pioneers of Italian cuisine. In the 70s and 80s there followed a boom in Italian cuisine on one hand, and the birth of pizza chains on the other, mostly standardized pizza. Beginning with the 1990s, we can see the rise of pizzerias as well as a rise in popularity of Napoli style pizza.

Pizzerias are sometimes run by Italians and marketed in a traditional, family-oriented Italian environment, but very often they are owned by Japanese food corporations. For instance, the big Nisshin Seifun Group owns the pizzeria chain "Partenope,"[2] taking the name after a mermaid that, according to the legend, died in the gulf of Napoli. Similarly, Still Food Corporation holds a number of "Pizzeria 1830" establishments.[3]. This name refers to the year in which "Pizzeria Port'Alba" (founded in Napoli in 1738) became the first modern pizzeria with tables and chairs (Levine 2005).

In the past, the pizzeria was a small workshop where peddlers bought the pizza to be sold on the street. Eventually, take-away pizza was sold directly to customers, and by the end of the 18th century, some benches found their way into the pizzeria, enabling customers to sit and eat (Benincasa 1992; Capatti 2001).

Along with pizzerias held by Japanese food corporations, there are also family-owned pizzerias run by Japanese pizzaiolos, who are sometimes assisted in the business by their wives. Two examples are "Pizzeria Dream Factory" (opened in 1994) and "Pizzeria Il Pentito" (opened in 1998). Both are owned and run by Japanese men who left their old jobs to become pizzaiolos. One was a laundry shop owner and the other a fashion buyer.

Beginning with the 1990s the pizzaiolo sometimes became a figure of celebrity status in the restaurant scene, the most popular being Salvatore Cuomo.[4] He was born in Italy and moved to Japan with his family in the late 1980s and for a while traveled back and forth between Italy and Japan. His father ran a restaurant in Kichijoji, an area slightly west of Tokyo that continues to be very popular among foreigners and the younger generation. When his father fell ill, Salvatore had to work alone in the restaurant business with the help of his younger brothers. Being continually exposed to his father's work, and since Italian cuisine was blooming all over Tokyo, it was not difficult for Salvatore to find work as a pizzaiolo and chef. He started teaching Italian cuisine at a popular Italian language school and after working at several locations he began to appear in popular magazines. In 1995, Salvatore conducted what was called "the tomato battle" on the Iron Chef TV Show along with his younger brother. With this, his name grew until he was "scouted" to manage Salvatore Cuomo Brothers and Pizza Salvatore Cuomo, which today is known as "Y's Table corporation." This corporation also holds a number of Asian and French cuisine restaurants. PIZZA SALVATORE CUOMO is advertised as follows:

> PIZZA SALVATORE CUOMO, produced by Chef Salvatore Cuomo, is an Italian-style pizzeria. Thin-crafted but chewy Neapolitan pizza is baked quickly in the wood-fired oven built by a Neapolitan Craftsman. Now delivery service enables this real taste to be enjoyed at households and offices. Gather your family and friends and enjoy the party in Italian style with PIZZA SALVATORE CUOMO's Neapolitan pizza.[5]

Today the trade mark, Salvatore Cuomo, and his restaurants are not only known in Kanto, Tokai and Kinki regions of Japan but are also making their way into Shanghai. Moreover, there are plans to open locations in Seoul.

The pizza of Napoli is also promoted by the Japanese branch of the Italian Associazione Verace Pizza Napoletana. The association was founded in Italy in 1984 to promote and safeguard the traditional pizza of Napoli as a response to the rise of fast-food pizza chains and industrially-made pizzas often marketed as "Pizza from Napoli." Pizzerias making their pizza in accordance to the Napoli system can become members of the association and display the trademark of "Verace Pizza Napoletana (VPN)." The goals of the association are also supported at the local level by the Municipality of Napoli and at national level by the Italian Ministry of Food and Agriculture. The association has members all over the world. As for Japan, the first pizzerias to display the trademark VPN in Tokyo were the "Ristorante Pizzeria Marechiaro"[6] in 1996, followed by "La Piccola Tavola"in 1998.[7] Today the association has members in the northern city of Sapporo and has its own independent branch in Tokyo, established in 2006. It should be noted that in Italy the various pizza associations do not always agree on the pizza recipe and regulations promoted by the VPN. However, this does not diminish the importance of the association's role in spreading traditional, hand-crafted pizza throughout Japan. The association frequently promotes seminars conducted by master pizzaiolos coming directly from Italy, and in 2007 the association published the book *The veracious pizza of Napoli, craft book* (真の ポリピッツァ技術教本). The book features a short history of pizza, the Napoli style pizzerias of Tokyo, the pizzaiolos who studied in Italy to learn how to make pizza, and includes several recipes with colorful photographs.

The Pizzaiolo

So why did pizza become so popular in Japan and other parts of the world? Probably it is because of the simple idea that a dish of bread with tasty toppings, simple in shape and size, has potential roots everywhere. Perhaps it is the pizza's adaptability to a variety of ingredients (first reflecting the regions of Italy and now the world) that has enabled the development of local pizzas. The pizza's initial popularity doubtless has roots in American society's mass production and consumption market (La Cecla 1998; Capatti 2001; Helstosky 2008), but as noted by Sanchez, the role of the pizzaiolo should not be underestimated:

> During the 1930s, the years of the American prohibition, it is to him [the pizzaiolo] that we owe the merit of having attracted the Americans. Americans ventured into the various Italian neighborhoods to buy alcohol, and while allowing themselves to be tempted by a dish of spaghetti, they observed from a distance an amazing worker making a circular shape, dough flying into the air. (Sanchez 2007, 170, author's translation)

The establishment of pizza as the everyday dish of the poor has its roots in Napoli (Capatti 2001), which is also true for the origin of the pizzaiolo (Benincasa 1992). The occupation has evolved to such an extent that in recent years (2005, 2006, and 2008) a bill (in draft form) has been presented to the Italian parliament intended to discipline the trade and to create a sort of European certification for pizzaiolos.[8] Meanwhile, to deal with growing requests for pizzaiolos in Italy and abroad, pizza schools have mushroomed all over Italy, supported by dozens of pizza associations. Nevertheless, the craft of making pizza is still, as a rule, learned through apprenticeships in a pizzeria.

As mentioned by my sources, in traditional pizzerias the roles (preparation duties) are fundamentally comprised of three persons working around a wood-oven in a hierarchical order: the pizzaiolo who makes the dough, rolls it out, and prepares the topping; the baker who is in charge of baking the pizza; and the table assistant who is in charge of such tasks as slicing the mozzarella and placing the ingredients in their respective containers. After a long apprenticeship, the table assistant is expected to become a baker and then pizzaiolo. Nowadays, the task divisions are becoming less common in the sense that assistants are also involved in making pizza. Italian pizzaiolos acquire their skills from an early age, usually through the perpetuation of family tradition. In fact, all of my Italian informants started their pizzaiolo apprenticeships before the age of fifteen. The following excerpts illustrate how deeply embedded—from youth—the pizzeria system is:

> I come from Ischia Ponte, the oldest village of Ischia Island. My house is surrounded by pizzerias. Just for play, at the age of 7, I started unconsciously learning the craft at Pizzeria Di Massa. Relatives, same family ... but in that place there used to be a great maestro pizzaiolo, Tonino Troncone, and from age 7 until I turned thirteen I just played, always inside that place. Always... Neapolitans joke, the oven, and of course, the pizza that is so delicious ... and is among kids' preferred food. ... Anyway, I ended up at age thirteen being completely autonomous, quite able by myself to run a pizzeria and make every single part of the pizza: the dough, setting the working table ... the oven, which is the most complicated part. (Interview with Italian pizzaiolo A, March 2008)
>
> ... I gradually entered this kind of occupation in 1977 during the school summer breaks. Instead of letting me go out with friends to play soccer or to ride the bike, or to go to the country side to steal oranges or fruits, my mother would send me to the shop so I could learn a job. (Italian pizzaiolo B, February 2008)

Having worked all over Italy and Europe, pizzaiolos often find work in Japan through word of mouth and other casual networks. For instance:

> I did not know anyone who had working experience in Japan. I became familiar with this country thanks to a Japanese friend of mine living in Milan with his Italian wife and two children. He proposed that I work independently here in Japan for one of his friends in an area called Saitama. I was about to decide between Russia and China but I chose Japan because of its peacefulness. (Italian pizzaiolo B, February 2008)

In short, when an Italian pizzaiolo arrives in Japan he already has a job, some kind of accommodation, and visa sponsorship. But he doesn't have a strong knowledge of the local culture and does not speak Japanese. Nevertheless, he has the job skills and knowledge, or more specifically, what could be called in Bourdiean terms, cultural capital. In short, he has what it takes to ply his trade in Japan. Such knowledge and the skill can be illustrated through this story by one of my sources. He found a job in a restaurant that was already employing a Japanese pizzaiolo. While the Japanese pizzaiolo could make 50–60 pizzas in one day, the Italian pizzaiolo could make up to 140–150 pizzas by himself. Eventually, the Japanese pizzaiolo quit the job and looked for a different restaurant. But my informant made clear that he did not mean to oust the Japanese pizzaiolo from his work place:

> He quit on his own because I became the first pizzaiolo. But by now, I had already taught him several Napoli-style tools of the trade. Towards the end, we competed against each other, but he just couldn't keep up, falling behind by thirty pizzas within a two-hour period. Finally he gave up! (Italian pizzaiolo C, April 2008)

Dealing with Japanese flour, water and atmospheric conditions that are different from Italy also requires special knowledge and skill. Japanese humidity is so high during the summer that it is necessary to pay careful attention to the leavening process. Without this precaution the dough could, in a sense, "explode." The oven must also be carefully cleaned and cared for. As pointed out by one pizzaiolo residing in

Japan for about 10 years (and having nearly 30 years of business experience), a pizzaiolo's occupation is:

> … a very particular job, it is a sense. When I make the dough or check the oven temperature … I do not use a thermometer or such similar device. I just use my hands. (Italian pizzaiolo A, March 2008)

To develop such a sense, the Japanese pizzaiolo goes to Italy and studies the craft. The pizzaiolos I have met with so far went to Italy starting from the 1990s, but the chances that some Japanese traveled to Italy for this purpose before the 1990s cannot be discounted. This is because Pizzaiolos are not formally trained in culinary schools as is usually the case for chefs. Most of the "want to be" pizzaiolos go to Italy on tourist visas and search for on-the-spot training at a pizzeria. This informal condition of flux and lack of official data make exact training time, or starting points, difficult to account for.

Some of my Japanese informants had worked in restaurants as Italian cooks and then moved to Italy to improve themselves. Such was the case with Makoto Onishi, now a pizzaiolo and chef at Salvatore Cuomo. Below, he recalls his first encounter with Napoli style pizza in Tokyo:

> When I ate [that pizza] I was struck by how delicious it was. So impressive! That cornicione [pizza frame] and that dough were delicious. Even as a cook trained in Italian cuisine, I could not understand how the pizza dough could be so soft and could have both a pleasant soft and springy [もち もち *mochi mochi*] texture in the mouth. Such a good taste. … I then realized that if that is the way a good pizza should taste, I would have much to learn. … That taste! How to get it would be my goal. That is when Italy became a part of my life-long project—to go to Italy to learn the real art of making pizza. (Interview with Makoto Onishi, June 2008)

After spending about two years learning how to make pizza, he also participated in—and won—a pizza competition, as we will see later. Onishi brought with him a basic grasp of the Italian language, which he studied by himself, but there was no job waiting for him. Upon his arrival in Napoli, he met an Italian doctor at the train station who helped him find a job as a pizzaiolo on the island of Ischia. He was not the only person with lucky encounters. Another informant who, having studied European Philosophy, travelled to Europe after his graduation in 1994. At that time he had no interest in pizza or the possibility of becoming a pizzaiolo. But one day as he was walking on the streets of Napoli he was approached by a young Italian man who was studying Japanese at a university. The man asked,

> "Are you Japanese?" "Yes, I am Japanese, not Chinese." Then he invited me to his house and made me dinner. He talked a lot because he was very interested in Japanese culture. Then we went together to that pizzeria … how is it called? The most famous pizzeria of Napoli, Pizzeria Da Michele. He said that I must have pizza in Napoli, and so we went to eat pizza. Pizzeria Michele surprised me. It was something new. I felt something new, even the atmosphere of the pizzeria. (Japanese pizzaiolo B, July 2008)

So impressed was he by this event that decided to learn how to make pizza and was introduced by his new Italian friend to the owner of a pizzeria. He recalls his new part-time job:

> I asked to work. Even washing the dishes would be fine. So I worked only during the weekends, but this way I could also see the work of the pizzaiolo and what kind of job it was. It was fascinating:

the atmosphere of the pizzeria, the laughing and the telling of jokes. The atmosphere of Italian restaurants in Japan were, how would you say, completely different. I don't know how it is now, but 14 years ago Italian restaurants [in Japan] were like conservative French restaurants. (Japanese pizzaiolo B, July 2008)

One way to find a job in Italy is to seek out the various pizzerias. But, given the growing links and network connections between the Italian and Japanese regarding the pizza trade (thanks to the first young Japanese going to Italy and vice versa), we can assume that Japanese who now go to Italy already have pizzeria employment connections. Also, language schools probably play a role in making connections. For instance, a young Japanese working in a Tokyo pizzeria, when asked, "How might you find a place to work in Italy?" he replied that he would be helped by the Italian owner of the Italian language school he is attending.

When the training in Italy is over, the Japanese pizzaiolo returns to Japan having acquired job skills and cultural knowledge. Not only has he learned how to make pizza, but he has also learned that there are different kinds of pizza and pizza tastes around Italy. Such is the case of a Japanese pizzaiolo who was asked by a restaurant manager to move from Napoli to a holiday town in Calabria and to work there alone during the summer. Here is his reaction to the experience:

> There is a difference. For instance, in the region of Calabria basil is not used in the pizza Margherita. They only use oregano and tomato when they make pizza Margherita but include spicy condiments. Yes there are differences. Also they like it kind of crispy. ... Well, Neapolitans also like it crispy but let's say, a little softer. (Japanese pizzaiolo B, July 2008)

Once back in Japan, the pizzaiolo will easily find a job in one of the local pizzerias and will likely be responsible for the training of new pizzaiolos. Some Japanese pizzaiolos who trained in Italy have won important pizza competitions. For example, the Italian and Japanese press paid considerable attention to Makoto Onishi who won the Pizzafest Competition in Napoli in 2003, and in 2006. Likewise, Hisanori Yamamoto won a trophy for the most creative and artistic pizza in 2007, and in 2008. However, Japanese do not go to Napoli only to learn how to make pizza. They also study the regional pizza markets of Italy where the number of pizzerias is relatively high, such as in Emilia Romagna. Takeshi Morita, for instance, worked and received his training near the city of Ravenna for about three years. In 2001, he won the "Gusto della Pizza" (The taste of pizza) prize in a competition held at the Padua Pizza Show. There is also the acrobatic pizza team of Japan that consistently places among the best three (first in 2004) at the world competition held annually in the city of Salsomaggiore, in northern Italy. One might conclude that sometimes the trophies won by Japanese are seen by Italian pizzaiolos as the result of a certain marketing strategy; that is, through media exposure the pizza festival gains in popularity outside of Italy and accordingly, the Japanese companies acquire more recognition and credibility if their pizzaiolos have won a competition in Italy. This might, or might not, be the case, but the basic fact that young Japanese go to Italy by themselves to learn how to make pizza is unquestionable. They acquire the necessary knowledge to become pizzaiolos, thus helping to spread an interest in pizza and pizza cooks throughout Japan. The experience of working in Italy and having won pizza awards can easily lead to television appearances, including major shows, and appearances in popular magazines.

As we have seen, prior to the 1990s, the making of Italian pizzas in Japan was mostly done by Italian chefs, such as the pioneer, Antonio Cancemi in the 1950s. From the 1990s, there was a need for pizzaiolos, which led to a search for pizzaiolos in Japanese restaurants. This employment is now recognized as a specific occupation. That can be inferred, for instance, from the advertisement of Granada, a Corporation holding the various pizzerias "Isola" around Japan. Granada Corporation has a web page dedicated to the occupation of pizzaiolo and to the search for new ones. The company stresses that the image of the pizzaiolo is different from "cook," as is the case in Italy. Granada offers an attractive three year apprenticeship contract for aspiring pizzaiolos whose participants learn the basics of the job in the first six month and earn a salary between 180,000–200,000 yen per month. By the third year they become competent pizzaiolos, often responsible for a shop, and earn between 250,000–500,000 yen a month.[9] As we can see, the globalization of pizza has not only introduced a new food but also a new occupation into Japan. Today the word, ピッツァ職人 (pizza *shokunin*), is used to indicate a pizza artisan and the word, ピッツァイオーロ (pizzaiolo), has entered the Japanese *katakana* dictionary (Sanseido's concise dictionary of katakana words 2005, 865).

Conclusion

While most studies on foreign food in Japan have been considered from the customer's perspective and how they react to the new food, this paper has focused on the food worker's perspective. The paper has shown that by looking at food from the worker's point of view we can see at least two significant issues:

a. That food is not as a mere commodity but an artifact of human ingenuity. It is a creative product shaped through the accumulation of knowledge, skills, and human experience. The paper further shows that food does not depend only on responses to consumer demands or influences by multinational corporations, but also on food creators.

b. Through this perspective we can also see a double-flow of transnational food workers. One is the flow of Italian pizzaiolos traveling to Japan to ply their trade and provide the cultural and human capital necessary to recreate Italian food in Japan (while coping with environmental differences and the use of non-traditional ingredients in craft pizza). The other is the flow of young Japanese traveling to Italy to learn how to make pizza and to build or reinforce their culinary knowledge. Upon returning to Japan they have acquired the necessary forms of capital (i.e., cultural, symbolic and institutionalized, as in the Bourdiean perspective) to enter Japan's world of Italian restaurants.

Acknowledgements

I would like to extend my thanks to Professor David Wank and to Professor James Farrer in guiding my thoughts on this topic. Thanks also to the anonymous reviewer.

I have not been able to incorporate all his valuable suggestions in this paper, but I will keep them in mind in the course of my research. Finally thanks to my Ph.D. colleagues for their comments, and to Ms Miwa Higashiura for organizing the conference out of which this paper came. My gratitude, as well, to the people who dedicated their precious time to the interviews.

Notes

1. For the first opening dates see the following websites: Shakey's http://www.rkfs.co.jp/shakeys/ history.html#35th; Pizza Hut http://www.pizzahut.co.uk/restaurants/our-history.aspx and http:// www.pizzahut.jp/more/effort. php; Domino's http://www.dominoseastgrinstead.co.uk/funfacts.htm; Pizza La http://www.four-seeds.co.jp/ corporate/history_1980.html
2. http://www.nisshin.com/english/english32.html
3. http://www.stillfoods.com/1830/index.html
4. Information drawn from an informal interview with Mr. Raffaele Cuomo in February 2008 and from printed and on-line press articles (See references).
5. salvatore.jp/restaurant/index.html
6. Information from http://www.bellavita.co.jp/company.html
7. Information from http://www.pizzanapoletana.org/showassoc.php?id=94
8. Italian Parliament.
   Draft Bill 426, XVI legislature (2008).
   http://www.senato.it/japp/bgt/showdoc/frame.jsp?tipodoc=Ddlpres&leg=16&id=302278
   Draft Bill 382 , XV legislature (2006).
   http://www.senato.it/japp/bgt/showdoc/frame.jsp?tipodoc=Ddlpres&leg=15&id=209067
   Draft Bill 3380 , XIV legislature (2005).
   http://www.senato.it/japp/bgt/showdoc/frame.jsp?tipodoc=Ddlpres&leg=14&id=135709
9. Information from http://www.granada-jp.net/saiyo/pizza.html

References

Ashkenazi, Michael, and Jeanne, Jacob. 2000. *The Essence of Japanese Cuisine: An Essay on Food and Culture*. Philadelphia: University of Pennsylvania Press.

Benincasa, Gabriele. 1992. *La pizza napoletana: mito, storia e poesia*. Napoli: Alfredo Guida Editore.

Bourdieu, Pierre. 1986. "The forms of capital." In *Readings in Economic Sociology*, ed. Nicole Woolsey Biggart, 280–291. Malden MA: Blackwell Publishers.

Bourdieu, Pierre. 1989. "Social Space and Symbolic Power." *Sociological Theory* 7 (Spring): 14–25.

Capatti, Alberto. 2001. "La pizza: quand le casse-croute des misérables passe à table." *Autrement* 206: 52–63.

Chetta, Alessandro. 2008. "Il sol levante a forma di pizza." *Corriere della Sera,* September 10. #http://corrieredelmez-zogiorno.corriere.it/notizie/a_tavola/2008/10-settembre-2008/sol-levante-forma-pizza-140473588202.shtml

Corriere della sera. 2001. "E' giapponese il <<re>> dei pizzaioli Lavora in un locale di Ravenna." Feb. 1. http://archiv-iostorico.corriere.it/2001/febbraio/01/giapponese_dei_pizzaioli_Lavora_locale_co_0_0102011597.shtml

Cwiertka, Katarzyna J. 2006. *Modern Japanese Cuisine: Food, Power and National Identity*. London: Reaktion Books.

Doi, Toshio. 1992. "An Inside Look at Japanese Food Service." *Cornell Hotel & Restaurant Administration Quarterly*, 33 (6): 73–83. www.allbusiness.com/accommodation-food-services/344991-1.html

Helstosky, Carol. 2008. *Pizza: A Global History*. London: Reaktion books.

Italian Trade Commission. 2006. *Italian Restaurant Guide 2006*. Tokyo: Italian Trade Commission.

Levine, Ed. 2005. *Pizza: A Slice of Heaven*. New York: Universe Publishing.

Ohonuki-Thiernei, Emiko. 1997. "McDonald's in Japan: Changing Manners and Etiquette." In *Golden Arches East: McDonald's in East Asia,* ed. JamesWatson, 161–82. Stanford: Stanford University Press.

Sanchez, Sylvie. 2007. *Pizza Connexion, Une séduction transculturelle*. Paris: Edition CNRS.

Sanseido's Concise Dictionary of Katakana Words. 2005. (大きな活字のコンサイスカタカナ語辞典. 2005. 東京：三省堂). Tokyo: Sanseido.

The Japan Times. 1985. "Italian cooking means more than macaroni. Homemade food and 40 years of hard work make Antonio's the top Italian restaurant." Dec. 12.

Tobin, Joseph J. 1994. *Re-made in Japan: Everyday Life and Consumer Taste in a Changing Society*. New Haven: Yale University Press.

Verace Pizza Napoletana. 真のナポリピッツァ技術教本 (The veracious pizza of Napoli, craft book). 2007. Tokyo: Asahiya Shuppan.

Whiting, Robert. 1999. *Tokyo Underworld: The Fast Times and Hard Life of an American Gangster in Japan*. New York: Pantheon Books.

31

Of Hamburger and Social Space: Consuming McDonald's in Beijing[*]

Yungxiang Yan

In a 1996 news report on dietary changes in the cities of Beijing, Tianjin, and Shang-hai, fast-food consumption was called the most salient development in the national capital: "The development of a fast-food industry with Chinese characteristics has become a hot topic in Beijing's dietary sector. This is underscored by the slogan 'challenge the Western fast food!'"[1] Indeed, with the instant success of Kentucky Fried Chicken after its grand opening in 1987, followed by the sweeping dominance of McDonald's and the introduction of other fast-food chains in the early 1990s, West-ern-style fast food has played a leading role in the restaurant boom and in the rapid change in the culinary culture of Beijing. A "war of fried chicken" broke out when local businesses tried to recapture the Beijing market from the Western fast-food chains by introducing Chinese-style fast foods. The "fast-food fever" in Beijing, as it is called by local observers, has given restaurant frequenters a stronger consumer con-sciousness and has created a Chinese notion of fast food and an associated culture.

From an anthropological perspective, this chapter aims to unpack the rich mean-ings of fast-food consumption in Beijing by focusing on the fast-food restaurants as a social space. Food and eating have long been a central concern in anthropological studies.[2] While nutritional anthropologists emphasize the practical functions of foods and food ways in cultural settings,[3] social and cultural anthropologists try to explore the links between food (and eating) and other dimensions of a given culture. From Lévi-Strauss's attempt to establish a universal system of meanings in the language of foods to Mary Douglas's effort to decipher the social codes of meals and Marshal Sahlins's analysis of the inner/outer, human/inhuman metaphors of food, there is a tradition of symbolic analysis of dietary cultures, whereby foods are treated as mes-sages and eating as a way of social communication.[4] The great variety of food habits can be understood as human responses to material conditions, or as a way to draw boundaries between "us" and "them" in order to construct group identity and thus to engage in "gastro-politics."[5] According to Pierre Bourdieu, the different attitudes toward foods, different ways of eating, and food taste itself all express and define the structure of class relations in French society.[6] Although in Chinese society ceremonial banqueting is frequently used to display and reinforce the existing social structure, James Watson's analysis of the *sihk puhn* among Hong Kong villagers—a special type

[*]*Originally published 1999*

of ritualized banquet that requires participants to share foods from the same pot—demonstrates that foods can also be used as a leveling device to blur class boundaries.[7]

As Joseph Gusfield notes, the context of food consumption (the participants and the social settings of eating) is as important as the text (the foods that are to be consumed).[8] Restaurants thus should be regarded as part of a system of social codes; as institutionalized and commercialized venues, restaurants also provide a valuable window through which to explore the social meanings of food consumption. In her recent study of dining out and social manners, Joanne Finkelstein classifies restaurants into three grand categories: (1) "formal spectacular" restaurants, where "dining has been elevated to an event of extraordinary stature"; (2) "amusement" restaurants, which add entertainment to dining; and (3) convenience restaurants such as cafes and fast-food outlets.[9] Although Finkelstein recognizes the importance of restaurants as a public space for socialization, she also emphasizes the antisocial aspect of dining out. She argues that, because interactions in restaurants are conditioned by existing manners and customs, "dining out allows us to act in imitation of others, in accord with images, in responses to fashions, out of habit, without need for thought or self-scrutiny." The result is that the styles of interaction that are encouraged in restaurants produce sociality without much individuality, which is an "uncivilized sociality."[10] Concurring with Finkelstein's classification of restaurants, Allen Shelton proceeds further to analyze how restaurants as a theater can shape customers' thoughts and actions. Shelton argues that the cultural codes of restaurants are just as important as the food codes analyzed by Mary Douglas, Lévi-Strauss, and many others. He concludes that the "restaurant is an organized experience using and transforming the raw objects of space, words, and tastes into a coded experience of social structures."[11] Rick Fantasia's analysis of the fast-food industry in France is also illuminating in this respect. He points out that because McDonald's represents an exotic "Other" its outlets attract many young French customers who want to explore a different kind of social space—an "American place."[12]

In light of the studies of both the text and context of food consumption, I first review the development of Western fast food and the local responses in Beijing during the period 1987 to 1996. Next I examine the cultural symbolism of American fast food, the meanings of objects and physical place in fast-food restaurants, the consumer groups, and the use of public space in fast-food outlets. I then discuss the creation of a new social space in fast-food restaurants. In my opinion, the trans-formation of fast-food establishments from eating place to social space is the key to understanding the popularity of fast-food consumption in Beijing, and it is the major reason why local competitors have yet to successfully challenge the American fast-food chains. This study is based on both ethnographic evidence collected during my fieldwork in 1994 (August to October) and documentary data published in Chinese newspapers, popular magazines, and academic journals during the 1987–96 period. Since McDonald's is the ultimate icon of American fast food abroad and the most successful competitor in Beijing's fast-food market, McDonald's restaurants were the primary place and object for my research, although I also consider other fast-food outlets and compare them with McDonald's in certain respects.[13]

Fast-food Fever in Beijing, 1987–1996

Fast food is not indigenous to Chinese society. It first appeared as an exotic phenomenon in novels and movies imported from abroad and then entered the everyday life
of ordinary consumers when Western fast-food chains opened restaurants in the Beijing market. *Kuaican*, the Chinese translation for fast food, which literally means "fast
meal" or "fast eating," contradicts the ancient principle in Chinese culinary culture
that regards slow eating as healthy and elegant. There are a great variety of traditional
snack foods called *xiaochi* (small eats), but the term "small eats" implies that they
cannot be taken as meals. During the late 1970s, *hefan* (boxed rice) was introduced to
solve the serious "dining problems" created by the lack of public dining facilities and
the record number of visitors to Beijing. The inexpensive and convenient *hefan*—rice
with a small quantity of vegetables or meat in a styrofoam box—quickly became popular in train stations, in commercial areas, and at tourist attractions. However, thus
far boxed rice remains a special category of convenience food—it does not fall into
the category of *kuaican* (fast food), even though it is consumed much faster than any
of the fast foods discussed in the following pages. The intriguing point here is that
in Beijing the notion of fast food refers only to Western-style fast food and the new
Chinese imitations. More important, as a new cultural construct, the notion of fast
food includes nonfood elements such as eating manners, environment, and patterns
of social interaction. The popularity of fast food among Beijing consumers has little
to do with either the food itself or the speed with which it is consumed.

American fast-food chains began to display interest in the huge market in China in
the early 1980s. As early as 1983, McDonald's used apples from China to supply its restaurants in Japan; thereafter it began to build up distribution and processing facilities in
northern China.[14] However, Kentucky Fried Chicken took the lead in the Beijing market.
On October 6, 1987, KFC opened its first outlet at a commercial center just one block
from Tiananmen Square. The three-story building, which seats more than 500 customers, at the time was the largest KFC restaurant. On the day of the grand opening, hundreds of customers stood in line outside the restaurant, waiting to taste the world-famous
American food. Although few were really impressed with the food itself, they were all
thrilled by the eating experience: the encounter with friendly employees, quick service,
spotless floors, climate-controlled and brightly-lit dining areas, and of course, smiling
Colonel Sanders standing in front of the main gate. From 1987 to 1991, KFC restaurants
in Beijing enjoyed celebrity status, and the flagship outlet scored first for both single-day
and annual sales in 1988 among the more than 9,000 KFC outlets throughout the world.

In the restaurant business in Beijing during the early 1980s, architecture and internal decoration had to match the rank of a restaurant in an officially prescribed hierarchy, ranging from star-rated hotel restaurants for foreigners to formal restaurants,
mass eateries, and simple street stalls. There were strict codes regarding what a restaurant should provide, at what price, and what kind of customers it should serve in
accordance with its position in this hierarchy. Therefore, some authorities in the local
dietary sector deemed that the KFC decision to sell only fried chicken in such an
elegant environment was absurd.[15] Beijing consumers, however, soon learned that
a clean, bright, and comfortable environment was a common feature of all

Western-style fast-food restaurants that opened in the Beijing market after KFC. Among them, McDonald's has been the most popular and the most successful.

The first McDonald's restaurant in Beijing was built at the southern end of Wangfujing Street, Beijing's Fifth Avenue. With 700 seats and 29 cash registers, the restaurant served more than 40,000 customers on its grand opening day of April 23, 1992.[16] The Wangfujing McDonald's quickly became an important landmark in Beijing, and its image appeared frequently on national television programs. It also became an attraction for domestic tourists, a place where ordinary people could literally taste a piece of American culture. Although not the first to introduce American fast food to Beijing consumers, the McDonald's chain has been the most aggressive in expanding its business and the most influential in developing the fast-food market. Additional McDonald's restaurants appeared in Beijing one after another: two were opened in 1993, four in 1994, and ten more in 1995. There were 35 by August 1997, and according to the general manager the Beijing market is big enough to support more than a hundred McDonald's restaurants.[17] At the same time, Pizza Hut, Bony Fried Chicken (of Canada), and Dunkin' Donuts all made their way into the Beijing market. The most interesting newcomer is a noodle shop chain called Californian Beef Noodle King. Although the restaurant sells Chinese noodle soup, it has managed to portray itself as an American fast-food eatery and competes with McDonald's and KFC with lower prices and its appeal to Chinese tastes.

The instant success of Western fast-food chains surprised those in the local restaurant industry. Soon thereafter, many articles in newspapers and journals called for the invention of Chinese-style fast food and the development of a local fast-food industry. April 1992 was a particularly difficult month for those involved in this sector: two weeks after the largest McDonald's restaurant opened at the southern end of Wangfujing Street, Wu Fang Zhai, an old, prestigious restaurant at the northern end of Wangfujing Street, went out of business; in its stead opened International Fast Food City, which sold Japanese fast food, American hamburgers, fried chicken, and ice cream. This was seen as an alarming threat to both the local food industry and the national pride of Chinese culinary culture.[18]

Actually, the local response to the "invasion" of Western fast food began in the late 1980s, right after the initial success of KFC. It quickly developed into what some reporters called a "war of fried chickens" in Beijing. Following the model of KFC, nearly a hundred local fast-food shops featuring more than a dozen kinds of fried chicken appeared between 1989 and 1990. One of the earliest such establishments was Lingzhi Roast Chicken, which began business in 1989; this was followed by Chinese Garden Chicken, Huaxiang Chicken, and Xiangfei Chicken in 1990. The chicken war reached its peak when the Ronghua Fried Chicken company of Shanghai opened its first chain store directly opposite one of the KFC restaurants in Beijing. The manager of Ronghua Chicken proudly announced a challenge to KFC: "Wherever KFC opens a store, we will open another Ronghua Fried Chicken next door."

All of the local fried chicken variations were no more than simple imitations of the KFC food. Their only localizing strategy was to emphasize special Chinese species and sacred recipes that supposedly added an extra medicinal value to their dishes. Thus, consumers were told that the Chinese Garden Chicken might prevent cancer and that Huaxiang Chicken could strengthen the yin-yang balance inside one's body.[19]

This strategy did not work well; KFC and McDonald's won out in that first wave of competition. Only a small proportion of the local fried chicken shops managed to survive, while KFC and McDonald's became more and more popular.

Realizing that simply imitating Western fast food was a dead end, the emerging local fast-food industry turned to exploring resources within Chinese cuisine. Among the pioneers, Jinghua Shaomai Restaurant in 1991 tried to transform some traditional Beijing foods into fast foods. This was followed by the entry of a large number of local fast-food restaurants, such as the Beijing Beef Noodle King (not to be confused with the California Beef Noodle King). The Jinghe Kuaican company made the first domestic attempt to develop a fast-food business on a large scale. With the support of the Beijing municipal government, this company built its own farms and processing facilities, but it chose to sell boxed fast foods in mobile vans parked on streets and in residential areas.[20] Thus it fell into the pre-existing category of *hefan* (boxed rice) purveyors. Although the price of boxed fast foods was much lower than that of imported fast food, the boxed fast foods did not meet consumers' expectations of fast food. The Jinghe Kuaican Company disappeared as quickly as it had emerged. In October 1992, nearly a thousand state-owned restaurants united under the flag of the Jingshi Fast Food Company, offering five sets of value meals and more than 50 fast-foods items, all of which were derived from traditional Chinese cuisines. This company was also the first fast-food enterprise to be run by the Beijing municipal government, thus indicating the importance of this growing sector to the government.[21] The Henan Province Red Sorghum Restaurant opened on Wangfujing Street in March 1996, immediately across the street from the McDonald's flagship restaurant. Specializing in country-style lamb noodles, the manager of Red Sorghum announced that twelve more restaurants were to be opened in Beijing by the end of 1996, all of which would be next to a McDonald's outlet. "We want to fight McDonald's," the manager claimed, "we want to take back the fast-food market."[22]

By 1996 the fast-food sector in Beijing consisted of three groups: The main group was made up of McDonald's, KFC, and other Western fast-food chains. Although they no longer attracted the keen attention of the news media, their numbers were still growing. The second group consisted of the local KFC imitations, which managed to survive the 1991 "chicken war." The most successful in this group is the Ronghua Chicken restaurant chain, which in 1995 had eleven stores in several cities and more than 500 employees.[23] The third group included restaurants selling newly created Chinese fast foods, from simple noodle soups to Beijing roast duck meals. Many believe that the long tradition of a national cuisine will win out over the consumers' temporary curiosity about Western-style fast food.

Thus far, however, Chinese fast food has not been able to compete with Western fast food, even though it is cheaper and more appealing to the tastes of ordinary citizens in Beijing. Red Sorghum was the third business to announce in public the ambitious goal of beating McDonald's and KFC (after the Shanghai Ronghua Chicken and Beijing Xiangfei Chicken), but so far none have come close. By August 1996 it was clear that Red Sorghum's lamb noodle soup could not compete in the hot summer with Big Mac, which was popular year-round.[24]

The lack of competitiveness of Chinese fast food has drawn official attention at high levels, and in 1996 efforts were made to support the development of a local fast-food sector.[25] Concerned experts in the restaurant industry and commentators in the media attribute the bad showing of the Chinese fast-food restaurants to several things. In the mid-1990s, at least: (1) the quality, nutritional values, and preparation of Western fast foods were highly standardized, while Chinese fast foods were still prepared in traditional ways; (2) Chinese fast-food establishments did not offer the friendly, quick service of Western fast-food restaurants; (3) the local establishments were not as clean and comfortable as the Western fast-food restaurants; and (4) most important, unlike McDonald's or KFC, Chinese restaurants did not employ advanced technologies or modern management methods.[26] From a Marxist perspective, Ling Dawei has concluded that the race between imported and local fast foods in Beijing is a race between advanced and backward forces of production; hence the development of the local fast-food industry will rest ultimately on modernization.[27]

There is no doubt that these views have a basis in everyday practice; yet they all regard food consumption as purely economic behavior and fast-food restaurants as mere eating places. A more complete understanding of the fast-food fever in Beijing also requires close scrutiny of the social context of consumption—the participants and social settings, because "The specific nature of the consumed substances surely matters; but it cannot, by itself, explain why such substances may seem irresistible."[28]

The Spatial Context of Fast-food Consumption

As Giddens points out, most social life occurs in the context of the "fading away" of time and the "shading off" of space.[29] This is certainly true for fast-food consumption. Fast-food restaurants, therefore, need to be examined both as eating places and as social spaces where social interactions occur. A physical place accommodates objects and human agents and provides an arena for social interactions, and it follows that the use of space cannot be separated from the objects and the physical environment.[30] However, space functions only as a context, not a determinant, of social interactions, and the space itself in some way is also socially constructed.[31] In the following pages I consider, on the one hand, how spatial context shapes consumers' behavior and social relations, and how, on the other hand, consumers appropriate fast-food restaurants into their own space. Such an inquiry must begin with a brief review of Beijing's restaurant sector in the late 1970s in order to assess the extent to which Western fast-food outlets differ from existing local restaurants.

Socialist Canteens and Restaurants in the 1970s

Eating out used to be a difficult venture for ordinary people in Beijing because few restaurants were designed for mass consumption. As mentioned earlier, the restaurants in Beijing were hierarchically ranked by architecture, function, and the type and quality of foods provided. More important, before the economic reforms almost all restaurants and eateries were state-owned businesses, which meant that a restaurant was first and foremost a work unit, just like any factory, shop, or government agency.[32]

Thus a restaurant's position and function were also determined by its administrative status as a work unit.

Generally speaking, the restaurant hierarchy consisted of three layers. At the top were luxury and exclusive restaurants in star-rated hotels, such as the Beijing Hotel, which served only foreigners and privileged domestic guests. At the next level were well-established formal restaurants, many of which specialized in a particular style of cuisine and had been in business for many years, even before the 1949 revolution. Unlike the exclusive hotel restaurants, the formal restaurants were open to the public and served two major functions: (1) as public spaces in which small groups of elites could socialize and hold meetings; and (2) as places for ordinary citizens to hold family banquets on special, ritualized occasions such as weddings. At the bottom of the hierarchy were small eateries that provided common family-style foods; these were hardly restaurants (they were actually called *shitang*, meaning canteens). The small eateries were frequented primarily by visitors from outlying provinces and some Beijing residents who had to eat outside their homes because of special job requirements. The majority of Beijing residents rarely ate out—they normally had their meals at home or in their work-unit canteens.

In the 1950s the development of internal canteens (*neibu shitang*) not only constituted an alternative to conventional restaurants but also had a great impact on the latter. Most work units had (and still have) their own canteens, in order to provide employees with relatively inexpensive food and, more important, to control the time allotted for meals. Because canteens were subsidized by the work units and were considered part of employees' benefits, they were run in a manner similar to a family kitchen, only on an enlarged scale. The central message delivered through the canteen facilities was that the work unit, as the representative of the party-state, provided food to its employees, just as a mother feeds her children (without the affectionate component of real parental care). The relationship between the canteen workers and those who ate at the canteens was thus a patronized relationship between the feeder and the fed, rather than a relationship of service provider and customers. The tasteless foods, unfriendly service, and uncomfortable environment were therefore natural components at such public canteens, which prevailed for more than three decades and still exist in many work units today.

The work-unit mentality of "feeding" instead of "serving" people also made its way into restaurants in Beijing because, after all, the restaurants were also work units and thus had the same core features as all other work units—that is, the dominating influence of the state bureaucracy and the planned economy. Commercial restaurants also shared with the work-unit canteens the poor maintenance of internal space, a limited choice of foods, the requirement that the diner pay in advance, fixed times for meals (most restaurants were open only during the short prescribed lunch and dinner times), and of course, ill-tempered workers who acted as if they were distributing food to hungry beggars instead of paying customers.[33] It is true that the higher one moved up the ladder of the restaurant hierarchy the better dining environment and service one could find. But in the famous traditional restaurants and the star-rated hotel restaurants, formality and ritual were most likely the dominating themes. Still, until the late 1980s it was not easy for ordinary people to enjoy dining out in restaurants.

In contrast, Western fast-food restaurants offered local consumers a new cultural experience symbolized by foreign fast food, enjoyable spatial arrangements of objects and people, and American-style service and social interactions.

The Cultural Symbolism of Fast Food

It is perhaps a truism to note that food is not only good to eat but also good for the mind. The (Western) fast-food fever in Beijing provides another example of how in certain circumstances customers may care less about the food and more about the cultural messages it delivers. During my fieldwork in 1994 I discovered that although children were great fans of the Big Mac and french fries, most adult customers did not particularly like those fast foods. Many people commented that the taste was not good and that the flavor of cheese was strange. The most common complaint from adult customers was *chi bu bao*, meaning that McDonald's hamburgers and fries did not make one feel full: they were more like snacks than like meals.[34] It is also interesting to note that both McDonald's and KFC emphasized the freshness, purity, and nutritional value of their foods (instead of their appealing tastes). According to a high-level manager of Beijing McDonald's, the recipes for McDonald's foods were designed to meet modern scientific specifications and thus differed from the recipes for Chinese foods, which were based on cultural expectations.[35] Through advertisements and news media reports, this idea that fast foods use nutritious ingredients and are prepared using scientific cooking methods has been accepted by the public. This may help to explain why few customers compared the taste of fast foods to that of traditional Chinese cuisine; instead customers focused on something other than the food.

If people do not like the imported fast food, why are they still keen on going to Western fast-food restaurants? Most informants said that they liked the atmosphere, the style of eating, and the experience of being there. According to an early report on KFC, customers did not go to KFC to eat the chicken but to enjoy "eating" (consuming) the culture associated with KFC. Most customers spent hours talking to each other and gazing out the huge glass windows onto busy commercial streets—and feeling more sophisticated than the people who passed by.[36] Some local observers argued that the appeal of Chinese cuisine was the taste of the food itself and that, in contrast, Western food relied on the manner of presentation. Thus consumers would seem to be interested in the spectacle created by this new form of eating.[37] In other words, what Beijing customers find satisfying about Western fast-food restaurants is not the food but the experience.

The cultural symbolism that McDonald's, KFC, and other fast-food chains carry with them certainly plays an important role in constructing this nonedible yet fulfilling experience. Fast food, particularly McDonald's fast food, is considered quintessentially American in many parts of the contemporary world. In France, the most commonly agreed "American thing" among teenagers is McDonald's, followed by Coca-Cola and "military and space technologies."[38] In Moscow, a local journalist described the opening of the first McDonald's restaurant as the arrival of the "ultimate icon of Americana."[39] The same is true in Beijing, although the official news media have emphasized the element of modernity instead of Americana. The high efficiency of the service and management, fresh ingredients, friendly service, and spotless dining environment in Western fast-food restaurants have been repeatedly reported by the Beijing media as concrete examples of modernity.[40]

Ordinary consumers are interested in the stories told in news reports, popular magazines, and movies that the Big Mac and fried chicken are what make Americans American. According to a well-known commentator on popular culture in Beijing, because of the modernity inherent in the McDonald's fast-food chain, many American youths prefer to work first at McDonald's before finding other jobs on the market. The experience of working at McDonald's, he argues, prepares American youth for any kind of job in a modern society.[41] To many Beijing residents, "American" also means "modern," and thus to eat at McDonald's is to experience modernity. During my fieldwork I talked with many parents who appreciated their children's fondness for imported fast food because they believed it was in good taste to be modern. A mother told me that she had made great efforts to adapt to the strange flavor of McDonald's food so that she could take her daughter to McDonald's twice a week. She explained: "I want my daughter to learn more about American culture. She is taking an English typing class now, and I will buy her a computer next year." Apparently, eating a Big Mac and frics, like learning typing and computer skills, is part of the mother's plan to prepare her daughter for a modern society.

Inspired by the success of the cultural symbolism of McDonald's and KFC, many Chinese fast-food restaurants have tried to use traditional Chinese culture to lure customers. As I mentioned in the preceding section, almost all local fried-chicken outlets during 1990–91 emphasized the use of traditional medicinal ingredients and the idea of health-enhancing food.[42] Others used ethnic and local flavors to stress the Chineseness of their fast foods, such as the Red Sorghum's promotion of its lamb noodle soup.[43] And some directly invoked the nationalist feelings of the customers. For instance, Happy Chopsticks, a new fast-food chain in Shenzhen, adopted "Chinese people eat Chinese food" as the leading slogan in its market promotion.[44] The power of cultural symbolism in the fast-food sector also has made an impact on the restaurant industry in general: the cultural position of the restaurant business is regarded as an important issue, and the debate about the differences between Western and Chinese cuisine continues in professional journals.[45]

A Place of Entertainment for Equals

According to older residents, in addition to different cuisine styles, traditional restaurants in pre-1949 Beijing also differed in their interior decorations, seating arrangements, and interactions between restaurant employees and customers. During the Maoist era, such features were considered inappropriate to the needs of working-class people and thus gradually disappeared. Under the brutal attack on traditional culture during the Cultural Revolution period, some famous restaurants even replaced their old names with new, revolutionary names, such as Workers and Peasants Canteen (*Gongnong shitang*). As a result, by the late 1970s most restaurants looked similar both inside and out, which, combined with the canteen mentality in restaurant management and poor service, turned Beijing restaurants into unpleasant eating places.

When KFC and McDonald's opened their outlets in Beijing, what most impressed Beijing consumers was their beautiful appearance. As mentioned earlier, both the first KFC and first McDonald's are located near Tiananmen Square in the heart of Beijing, and both boast that they are the largest outlets of their kind in the world, one with a three-floor, 500-seat building and the other with a two-floor, 700-seat building. The statues of Colonel Sanders and Ronald McDonald in front of the two establishments immediately became national tourist attractions.

Once inside the restaurants, Beijing customers found other surprises. First, both McDonald's and the KFC restaurants were brightly lit and climate-controlled. The seats, tables, and walls were painted in light colors, which, together with the shiny counters, stainless-steel kitchenware, and soft music in the background, created an open and cheerful physical environment—a sharp contrast to traditional Chinese restaurants. Moreover, social interaction at McDonald's or KFC was highly ritualized and dramatized,[46] representing a radical departure from the canteen-like restaurants in Beijing. Employees wore neat, brightly colored uniforms, and they smiled at customers while working conscientiously and efficiently. As one observant informant remarked, even the employee responsible for cleaning the toilets worked in a disciplined manner. In his study of restaurants in Athens, Georgia, Allen Shelton commented: "The spectacle of McDonald's is work: the chutes filling up with hamburgers; the restaurant and the other diners are secondary views."[47] In contrast, both the work and the restaurant itself constituted the spectacle at McDonald's and KFC in Beijing.

One of the things that most impressed new customers of the fast-food outlets was the menu, which is displayed above and behind the counter, with soft backlighting and photographic images of the food. The menu delivers a clear message about the public, affordable eating experience that the establishment offers. This was particularly important for first-timers, who did not know anything about the exotic food. Another feature is the open, clean, kitchen area, which clearly shows the customers how the hamburgers and fried chickens are prepared. To emphasize this feature, Beijing's McDonald's also provides a five-minute tour of the kitchen area on customer request.

The Western fast-food restaurants also gave customers a sense of equality. Both employees and customers remain standing during the ordering process, creating an equal relationship between the two parties. More important, the friendly service and the smiling employees give customers the impression that no matter who you are you will be treated with equal warmth and friendliness. Accordingly, many people patronize McDonald's to experience a moment of equality.[48] The restaurants also seem to convey gender equality and have attracted a large number of female customers (I will return to this point later).

All these details in internal space are important in understanding the success of McDonald's and KFC in Beijing: objects have a voice that originates in those who use them, just as the scenery on a stage shapes the movements of an actor.[49] The impact of spatial context on people's behavior in McDonald's restaurants is well addressed by Peter Stephenson. He observed that some Dutch customers lost their cultural "self" in such a culturally decontextualized place because "there is a kind of instant emigration that occurs the moment one walks through the doors, where Dutch rules rather obviously don't apply."[50] Rick Fantasia observed that French customers undergo similar changes or adjustments in behavior in McDonald's outlets in Paris.[51] Given the sharper and deeper cultural differences between American and Chinese societies, it is natural to expect the cultural decontextualization to be even stronger in Beijing's McDonald's and KFC restaurants.

The interesting point is that, owing to the powerful appeal of modernity and Americana projected by McDonald's and KFC, when experiencing the same "instant emigration," Beijing customers seem to be more willing to observe the rules of American fast-food restaurants than their counterparts in Leiden or Paris. For instance, in 1992 and 1993 customers in Beijing (as in Hong Kong and Taiwan) usually left their rubbish on the table for the restaurant employees to clean up: people regarded McDonald's as a formal establishment at which they had paid for full service. However, during the summer of 1994 I observed that about one-fifth of the customers, many of them fashionably dressed youth, carried their own trays to the waste bins. From subsequent interviews I discovered that most of these people were regular customers, and they had learned to clean up their tables by observing the foreigners' behavior. Several informants told me that when they disposed of their own rubbish they felt more "civilized" (*wenming*) than the other customers because they knew the proper behavior. My random check of customer behavior in McDonald's and in comparably priced and more expensive Chinese restaurants shows that people in McDonald's were, on the whole, more self-restrained and polite toward one another, spoke in lower tones, and were more careful not to throw their trash on the ground. Unfortunately, when they returned to a Chinese context, many also returned to their previous patterns of behavior. As a result, the overall atmosphere in a Western fast-food outlet is always nicer than that in Chinese restaurants of the same or even higher quality.[52]

A Multidimensional Social Space

In part because of the cultural symbolism of Americana and modernity and in part because of the exotic, cheerful, and comfortable physical environment, McDonald's, KFC, and other foreign fast-food restaurants attract customers from all walks of life in Beijing. Unlike in the United States, where the frequenters of fast-food restaurants are generally associated with low income and simple tastes, most frequenters of fast-food restaurants in Beijing are middle-class professionals, trendy yuppies, and well-educated youths. Unfortunately, there has yet to be a systematic social survey of Chinese fast-food customers. Nevertheless, according to my field observations in 1994, a clear distinction can be drawn between those who occasionally partake of the imported fast foods and those who regularly frequent fast-food restaurants.

Occasional adventurers include both Beijing residents and visitors from outlying provinces and cities. It should be noted that a standard one-person meal at McDonald's (including a hamburger, a soft drink, and an order of French fries, which is the equivalent of a value-meal at McDonald's in the United States) cost 17 renminbi (rmb) ($2.10) in 1994 and 21 rmb ($2.60) in 1996.[53] This may not be expensive by American standards, but it is not an insignificant amount of money for ordinary workers in Beijing, who typically made less than 500 rmb ($60) per month in 1994. Thus, many people, especially those with moderate incomes, visited McDonald's restaurants only once or twice, primarily to satisfy their curiosity about American food and culinary culture. A considerable proportion of the customers were tourists from other provinces who had only heard of McDonald's or seen its Golden Arches in the movies. The tasting of American food has recently become an important part of the tourist beat in Beijing; and those who partake of the experience are able to boast about it to their relatives and friends back home.

There are also local customers who frequent foreign fast-food outlets on a regular basis. A survey conducted by Beijing McDonald's management in one of its stores showed that 10.2 percent of the customers frequented the restaurant four times per month in 1992, in 1993 the figure was 38.3 percent.[54] The majority of customers fell into three categories: professionals and white-collar workers; young couples and teenagers; and children accompanied by their parents. Moreover, women of all age groups tended to frequent McDonald's restaurants more than men.

For younger Beijing residents who worked in joint-venture enterprises or foreign firms and had higher incomes, eating at McDonald's, Kentucky Fried Chicken, and Pizza Hut had become an integral part of their new lifestyle, a way for them to be connected to the outside world. As one informant commented: "The Big Mac doesn't taste great; but the experience of eating in this place makes me feel good. Sometimes I even imagine that I am sitting in a restaurant in New York or Paris." Although some emphasized that they only went to save time, none finished their meals within twenty minutes. Like other customers, these young professionals arrived in small groups or accompanied by girl/boy friends to enjoy the restaurant for an hour or more. Eating foreign food, and consuming other foreign goods, had become an important way for Chinese yuppies to define themselves as middle-class professionals. By 1996, however, this group had found other types of activities (such as nightclubs or bars), and gradually they were beginning to visit foreign fast-food restaurants for convenience rather than for status.

Young couples and teenagers from all social strata were also regular frequenters of McDonald's and KFC outlets because the dining environment is considered to be romantic and comfortable. The restaurants are brightly-lit, clean, and feature light Western music; and except during busy periods they are relatively quiet, making them ideal for courtship. In 1994, McDonald's seven Beijing restaurants had all created relatively isolated and private service areas with tables for two. In some, these areas were nicknamed "lovers' corners." Many teenagers also considered that, with only the minimum consumption of a soft drink or an ice cream, fast-food establishments were good places simply to hang out.

As in many other parts of the world, children in Beijing had become loyal fans of Western fast food. They were so fond of it that some parents even suspected that Big Mac or fried chicken contained a special, hidden ingredient. The fast-food restaurants also made special efforts to attract children by offering birthday parties, dispensing souvenirs, and holding essay contests, because young customers usually did not come alone: they were brought to McDonald's and KFC by their parents or grandparents. Once a middle-aged woman told me that she did not like the taste of hamburgers and that her husband simply hated them. But their daughter loved hamburgers and milkshakes so much that their entire family had to visit McDonald's three to five times a month. It is common among Beijing families for children to choose the restaurant in which the whole family dines out. Fast-food outlets were frequently the first choice of children.

A gender aspect of fast-food consumption is highlighted in He Yupeng's 1996 study of McDonald's popularity among female customers. In conducting a small-scale survey at four restaurants in Beijing—a formal Chinese restaurant, a local fast-food outlet, and two McDonald's outlets—He found that women were more likely than men to enjoy dining at fast-food restaurants. According to his survey, while 66 percent of the customers (N=68) at the formal Chinese restaurant were men, 64 percent of the customers (N=423) at the local fast-food outlet were women. Similar patterns were observed in the two McDonald's restaurants, where women constituted 57 percent of a total of 784 adult customers.[55] The most intriguing finding of this survey was that women chose McDonald's because they enjoyed ordering their own food and participating in the conversation while dining. Many female customers pointed out that in formal Chinese restaurants men usually order the food for their female companions and control the conversation. In contrast, they said, at a McDonald's everyone can make his or her own choices and, because smoking and alcohol are prohibited, men dominate less of the conversation.[56]

Furthermore, the imported fast-food restaurants provide a venue where women feel comfortable alone or with female friends. Formal Chinese restaurants are customarily used by elite groups as places to socialize and by middle-class people as places to hold ritual family events such as wedding banquets. In both circumstances, women must subordinate themselves to rules and manners that are androcentric, either explicitly or implicitly (the men order the dishes; the women do not partake of the liquor). These customs reflect the traditional view that women's place is in the household and that men should take charge of all public events. There is a clear division between the private (inside) and the public (outside) along gender lines.

A woman who eats alone in a formal Chinese restaurant is considered abnormal; such behavior often leads to public suspicion about her morality and her occupation. For instance, a young woman I interviewed in a McDonald's outlet in 1994 recalled having lunch alone in a well-known Chinese restaurant frequented mostly by successful businessmen. "Several men gazed at me with lascivious eyes," she said, "and some others exchanged a few words secretly and laughed among themselves. They must have thought I was a prostitute or at least a loose woman. Knowing their evil thoughts, I felt extremely uncomfortable and left the place as quickly as I could." She also commented that even going to a formal Chinese restaurant with female friends would make her feel somewhat improper about herself, because the "normal" customers were men or men with women. But she said that she felt comfortable visiting a McDonald's alone or with her female friends, because "many people do the same." This young woman's experience is by no means unique, and a number of female customers in McDonald's offered similar explanations for liking the foreign fast-food restaurants. Several elderly women also noted the impropriety of women dining in formal Chinese restaurants, although they were less worried about accusations about their morals.[57]

In his survey, He Yupeng asked his respondents where they would choose to eat if there were only a formal Chinese restaurant and a McDonald's outlet. Almost all the male respondents chose the former, and all the female respondents chose the latter.

One of the main reasons for such a sharp gender difference, He argues, is the concern of contemporary women for gender equality.[58] The new table manners allowed in fast-food restaurants, and more important, the newly appropriate gender roles in those public places, seem to have enhanced the image of foreign fast-food restaurants as an open place for equals, thus attracting female customers.

The Appropriation of Social Space

Finally, I would point out that Beijing customers do not passively accept everything offered by the American fast-food chains. The American fast-food restaurants have been localized in many aspects, and what Beijing customers enjoy is actually a Chinese version of American culture and fast foods.[59] One aspect of this localization process is the consumers' appropriation of the social space.

My research confirms the impression that most customers in Beijing claim their tables for longer periods of time than Americans do. The average dining time in Beijing (in autumn 1994) was 25 minutes during busy hours and 51 minutes during slack hours. In Beijing, "fastness" does not seem to be particularly important. The cheerful, comfortable, and climate-controlled environment inside McDonald's and KFC restaurants encourages many customers to linger, a practice that seems to contradict the original purpose of the American fast-food business. During off-peak hours it is common for people to walk into McDonald's for a leisurely drink or snack. Sitting with a milk-shake or an order of fries, such customers often spend 30 minutes to an hour, and sometimes longer, chatting, reading newspapers, or holding business meetings. As indicated earlier, young couples and teenagers are particularly fond of frequenting foreign fast-food outlets because they consider the environment to be romantic. Women in all age groups tend to spend the longest time in these establishments, whether they are alone or with friends. In contrast, unaccompanied men rarely linger after finishing their meals. The main reason for this gender difference, according to my informants, is the absence of alcoholic beverages. An interesting footnote in this connection is that 32 percent of my informants in a survey among college students (N=97) regarded McDonald's as a symbol of leisure and emphasized that they went there to relax.

Beijing consumers have appropriated the restaurants not only as places of leisure but also as public arenas for personal and family ritual events. The most popular such event is of course the child's birthday party, which has been institutionalized in Beijing McDonald's restaurants. Arriving with five or more guests, a child can expect an elaborate ritual performed in a special enclosure called "Children's paradise," free of extra charge. The ritual begins with an announcement over the restaurant's loudspeakers—in both Chinese and English—giving the child's name and age, together with congratulations from Ronald McDonald (who is called Uncle McDonald in Beijing). This is followed by the recorded song "Happy Birthday," again in two languages. A female employee in the role of Aunt McDonald then entertains the children with games and presents each child with a small gift from Uncle McDonald. Although less formalized (and without the restaurant's active promotion), private ceremonies are also held in the restaurants for adult customers, particularly for young women in peer groups (the absence of alcohol makes the site attractive to them). Of the 97 college students in my survey, 32 (including nine men) had attended personal celebrations at McDonald's: birthday parties, farewell parties, celebrations for receiving scholarships to American universities, and end-of-term parties.

The multifunctional use of McDonald's space is due in part to the lack of cafes, tea houses, and ice-cream shops in Beijing; it is also a consequence of the management's efforts to attract as many customers as possible by engendering an inviting environment. Although most McDonald's outlets in the United States are designed specifically to prevent socializing (with less-comfortable seats than formal restaurants, for instance) it is clear that the managers of Beijing's McDonald's have accepted their customers' perceptions of McDonald's as a special place that does not fit into pre-existing categories of public eateries. They have not tried to educate Beijing consumers to accept the American view that "fast food" means that one must eat fast and leave quickly.[60] When I wondered how the management accommodated every-one during busy periods, I was told that the problem often resolved itself. A crowd of customers naturally created pressures on those who had finished their meals, and more important, during busy hours the environment was no longer appropriate for relaxation.

In contrast, managers in Chinese fast-food outlets tend to be less tolerant of customers who linger. During my fieldwork in 1994 I conducted several experimental tests by going to Chinese fast-food outlets and ordering only a soft drink but staying for more than an hour. Three out of four times I was indirectly urged to leave by the restaurant employees; they either took away my empty cup or asked if I needed anything else. Given the fact that I was in a fast-food outlet and did all the service for myself, the disturbing "service" in the middle of my stay was clearly a message to urge lingering customers to leave. I once discussed this issue with the manager of a Chinese fast-food restaurant. He openly admitted that he did not like customers claiming a table for long periods of time and certainly did not encourage attempts to turn the fast-food outlet into a coffee shop. As he explained: "If you want to enjoy nice coffee and music then you should go to a fancy hotel cafe, not here."

Concluding Remarks: Dining Place, Social Space, and Mass Consumption

In the United States, fast-food outlets are regarded as "fuel stations" for hungry yet busy people and as family restaurants for low-income groups. Therefore, efficiency (speed) and economic value (low prices) are the two most important reasons why fast foods emerged as a kind of "industrial food" and remain successful in American society today. These features, however, do not apply in Beijing. A Beijing worker who loads the whole family into a taxi to go to McDonald's may spend one-sixth of his monthly income; efficiency and economy are perhaps the least of his concerns. When consumers stay in McDonald's or KFC restaurants for hours, relaxing, chatting, reading, enjoying the music, or celebrating birthdays, they take the "fastness" out of fast food. In Beijing, the fastness of American fast food is reflected mainly in the service provided; for consumers, the dining experience is too meaningful to be shortened. As a result, the American fast-food outlets in China are fashionable, middle-class establishments—a new kind of social space where people can enjoy their leisure time and experience a Chinese version of American culture.

As I emphasize repeatedly throughout this chapter, eating at a foreign fast-food restaurant is an important social event, although it means different things to different people. McDonald's, KFC, and other fast-food restaurants in Beijing carry the symbolism of Americana and modernity, which makes them unsurpassable by existing standards of the social hierarchy in Chinese culture. They represent an emerging tradition where new values, behavior patterns, and social relationships are still being created. People from different social backgrounds may enter the same eating place/social space without worrying about losing face; on the contrary, they may find new ways to better define their positions. For instance, white-collar professionals may display their new class status, youngsters may show their special taste for leisure, and parents may want to "modernize" their children. Women of all ages are able to enjoy their independence when they choose to eat alone; and when they eat with male companions, they enjoy a sexual equality that is absent in formal Chinese restaurants. The fast-food restaurants, therefore, constitute a multivocal, multidimensional, and open social space. This kind of all-inclusive social space met a particular need in the 1990s, when Beijing residents had to work harder than ever to define their positions in a rapidly changing society.[61]

By contrast, almost all local competitors in the fast-food sector tend to regard fast-food restaurants merely as eating places, and accordingly, they try to compete with the foreign fast-food restaurants by offering lower prices and local flavors or by appealing to nationalist sentiments. Although they also realize the importance of hygiene, food quality, friendly service, and a pleasant physical environment, they regard these features as isolated technical factors. A local observer pointed out that it is easy to build the "hardware" of a fast-food industry (the restaurants) but that the "software" (service and management) cannot be adopted overnight.[62] To borrow from this metaphor, I would argue that an understanding of fast-food outlets not only as eating places but also as social space is one of the "software problems" waiting to be resolved by the local competitors in the fast-food business.

Why is the issue of social space so important for fast-food development in Beijing? It would take another essay to answer this question completely; here I want to highlight three major factors that contribute to fast-food fever and are closely related to consumers' demands for a new kind of social space.

First, the trend of mass consumption that arose in the second half of the 1980s created new demands for dining out as well as new expectations of the restaurant industry. According to 1994 statistics released by the China Consumer Society, the average expenditure per capita has increased 4.1 times since 1984. The ratio of "hard consumption" (on food, clothes, and other necessities of daily life) to "soft consumption" (entertainment, tourism, fashion, and socializing) went from 3:1 in 1984 to 1:1.2 in 1994.[63] In 1990, consumers began spending money as never before on such goods and services as interior decoration, private telephones and pagers, air conditioners, bodybuilding machines, and tourism.[64] As part of this trend toward consumerism, dining out has become a popular form of entertainment among virtually all social groups, and people are particularly interested in experimenting with different cuisines.[65] In response to a survey conducted by the Beijing Statistics Bureau in early 1993, nearly half of the respondents said they had eaten at Western-style restaurants (including fast-food outlets) at least once.[66] A central feature of this development in culinary culture is that people want to dine out as active consumers, and they want the dining experience to be relaxed, fun, and healthful.

In response to increasing consumer demands, thousands of restaurants and eateries have appeared in recent years. By early 1993 there were more than 19,000 eating establishments in Beijing, ranging from elegant five-star hotel restaurants to simple street eateries. Of these, about 5,000 were state-owned, 55 were joint ventures or foreign-owned, and the remaining 14,000 or so were owned by private entrepreneurs or independent vendors (*getihu*).[67]

These figures show that the private sector has played an increasingly important role in the restaurant business. Unlike the state-owned restaurants, some private restaurants have used creativity to meet consumers' demands for a new kind of dining experience. The best example is the emergence of country-style, nostalgic restaurants set up by and for the former sent-down urban youths. In these places customers retaste their experience of youth in the countryside: customers choose from country-style foods in rooms and among objects that remind them of the past. Like customers in McDonald's or KFC, they are also consuming part of the subculture and redefining themselves in a purchased social space. The difference is that the nostalgic restaurants appeal only to a particular social group, while the American fast-food outlets are multivocal and multidimensional and thus attract people from many different social strata.

The rise of new consumer groups is the second major factor that has made the issue of social space so important to understanding fast-food fever in Beijing. Urban youth, children, and women of all ages constitute the majority of the regular frequenters of American fast-food restaurants. It is not by accident that these people are all newcomers as restaurant customers—there was no proper place for them in the pre-existing restaurant system, and the only social role that women, youth, and children could play in a formal Chinese restaurant was as the dependents of men. Women's effort to gain an equal place in restaurant subculture was discussed earlier, so here I briefly examine the place of youth and children.

Young professionals emerged along with the development of the market economy, especially with the expansion of joint-venture and foreign-owned business in Beijing in the 1990s. To prove and further secure their newly obtained social status and prestige, the young elite have taken the construction of a different lifestyle seriously, and they often lead the trend of contemporary consumerism in Chinese cities. Urban youth may be less well off than young professionals, but they are equally eager to embrace a new way of personal life. According to a 1994 survey, the purchasing power of Beijing youth increased dramatically over the previous decade, and nearly half of the 1,000 respondents in the survey had more than 500 rmb per month to spend on discretionary items.[68] With more freedom to determine their lifestyles and more economic independence, these youngsters were eager to establish their own social space in many aspects of life, including dining out.[69] A good example in this connection is the astonishing popularity among young people in mainland China of pop music, films, and romance novels from Hong Kong and Taiwan.[70]

The importance of teenagers and children in effecting social change also emerged in the late twentieth century, along with the growth of the national economy, the increase in family wealth, and the decline of the birth rate. The single-child policy—which is most strictly implemented in the big cities—has created a generation of little emperors and empresses, each demanding the attention and economic support of his or her parents and grandparents. Parental indulgence of children has become a national obsession, making children and teenagers one of the most active groups of consumers. Beijing is by no means exceptional in this respect. According to Deborah Davis and Julia Sensenbrenner, ordinary working-class parents in Shanghai normally spend one-third of their monthly wages to provide their children with a lifestyle that is distinctly upper middle class in its patterns of consumption. For many parents, toys, trips, fashionable clothes, music lessons, and restaurant meals have become necessities in raising their children. This suggests a significant change in patterns of household expenditure, and accordingly there is an urgent need to meet the market demands and special tastes of this important group of consumers.

The emerging importance of women, youth, and children as consumers results from a significant transformation of the family institution in contemporary Chinese society, which is characterized by the nuclearization of the household, the centrality of conjugality in family relations, the rising awareness of independence and sexual equality among women, the waning of the patriarchy, and the rediscovery of the value of children.[71] As far as fast-food consumption is concerned, the link between new groups of independent consumers and shifts in family values is found in other East Asian societies as well. After analyzing the relationship between the McDonald's "takeoff" in five cities (Tokyo, Hong Kong, Taipei, Seoul, and Beijing) and the changes in family values (especially the rising status of teenagers and children), Watson concluded: "More than any other factor . . . McDonald's success is attributable to the revolution in family values that has transformed East Asia."[72]

A third important factor in the success of Western fast-food enterprises is the new form of sociality that has been developing in market-controlled public places such as restaurants. A significant change in public life during the post-Mao era has been the disappearance of frequent mass rallies, voluntary work, collective parties, and other forms of "organized sociality" in which the state (through its agents) played the central role. In its place are new forms of private gatherings in public venues. Whereas "organized sociality" emphasized the centrality of the state, the official ideology, and the submission of individuals to an officially endorsed collectivity, the new sociality celebrates individuality and private desires in unofficial social and spatial contexts. The center of public life and socializing, accordingly, has shifted from large state-controlled public spaces (such as city squares, auditoriums, and workers' clubs) to smaller, commercialized arenas such as dancing halls, bowling alleys, and even imaginary spaces provided by radio call-in shows. The new sociality has even emerged in conventionally state-controlled public spaces, such as parks, and has thus transformed them into multidimensional spaces in which the state, the public, and the private may coexist.

Restaurants similarly meet the demand for a new kind of sociality outside state control—that is, the public celebration of individual desires, life aspirations, and personal communications in a social context. As indicated above, in earlier decades the socialist state did not encourage the use of restaurants as a social space in which to celebrate private desires or perform family rituals. Rather, by institutionalizing public canteens in the workplace, the state tried to control meal time and also change the meaning of social dining itself. This is particularly true in Beijing, which has been the center of national politics and socialist transformation since 1949. Any new form of social dining was unlikely to develop from the previous restaurant sector in Beijing, which consisted primarily of socialist canteens. It is thus not accidental that by 1993 nearly three-quarters of the more than 19,000 eating establishments in Beijing were owned by private entrepreneurs (local and foreign) or were operating as joint ventures.[73] McDonald's and other foreign fast-food restaurants have been appropriated by Beijing consumers as especially attractive social spaces for a new kind of socializing and for the celebration of individuality in public. Moreover, consuming at McDonald's and other foreign fast-food outlets is also a way of embracing modernity and foreign culture in public.

To sum up, there is a close link between the development of fast-food consumption and changes in social structure, especially the emergence of new social groups.[74] The new groups of agents demand the creation of new space for socialization in every aspect of public life, including dining out. Fast-food restaurants provide just such a space for a number of social groups. The new kind of sociality facilitated by fast-food restaurants in turn further stimulates consumers' demands for both the food and the space. Hence the fast-food fever in Beijing during the 1990s.

Notes

1. Liu Fen and Long Zaizu 1996.
2. For a general review, see Messer 1984.
3. See, e.g., Jerome 1980.
4. See Douglas 1975; Lévi-Strauss 1983; and Sahlins 1976.
5. See Harris 1985; Murphy 1986; and Appadurai 1981.
6. Bourdieu 1984, pp. 175–200.
7. Watson 1987. For more systematic studies of food in China, see Chang 1977 and E. Anderson 1988.
8. See Gusfield 1992, p. 80.
9. Finkelstein 1989, pp. 68–71.
10. Ibid. p. 5.
11. Shelton 1990, p. 525.
12. See Fantasia 1995, pp. 213–15.
13. For an anthropological study of sociocultural encounters at McDonald's in Hong Kong, Taipei, Beijing, Seoul, and Tokyo, see chapters in Watson, ed., 1997.
14. See Love 1986, p. 448.
15. See Zhang Yubin 1992.
16. See New York Times, April 24, 1992. For a detailed account, see Yan 1997a.
17. See China Daily, September 12, 1994; and Service Bridge, August 12, 1994.
18. See Liu Ming 1992; Mian Zhi 1993.
19. Duan Gang 1991.
20. Zhang Zhaonan 1992a.
21. See Zhang Zhaonan 1992b; You Zi 1994; and Zhang Guoyun 1995.
22. Yu Bin 1996; "Honggaoliang yuyan zhongshi kuaican da qushi" 1996.
23. Yu Weize 1995.
24. See Liu Fen and Long Zaizu 1996.
25. The development of Chinese fast food is incorporated into the eighth national five-year plan for scientific research. See Bi Yuhua 1994; see also Ling Dawei 1996.
26. For representative views on this issue, see Guo Jianying 1995; Huang Shengbing 1995; Jian Feng 1992; Xiao Hua 1993; Ye Xianning 1993; Yan Zhenguo and Liu Yinsheng 1992a; and Zhong Zhe 1993.

27. Ling Dawei 1995.
28. Mintz 1993, p. 271.
29. Giddens 1984, p. 132.
30. See Sayer 1985, pp. 30–31.
31. See Lechner 1991; Urry 1985.
32. For a comprehensive study of the work-unit system, see Walder 1986.
33. In preform Beijing even the hotel restaurants and guesthouse canteens were open only during "proper" meal times. So if a visitor missed the meal time, the only alternative was to buy bread and soft drinks from a grocery store.
34. For more details on the results of the survey, see Yan 1997a.
35. See discussions in Xu Chengbei 1994.
36. *Zhongguo shipinbao* (Chinese food newspaper), November 6, 1991.
37. *Jingji ribao*, September 15, 1991.
38. Fantasia 1995, p. 219.
39. Ritzer 1993, pp. 4–5.
40. Every time McDonald's opened a new restaurant in the early 1990s, it was featured in the Chinese media. See e.g., *Tianjin qingnianbao* (Tianjin youth news), June 8, 1994; *Shanghai jingji ribao* (Shanghai economic news), July 22, 1994; *Wenhui bao* (Wenhui daily), July 22, 1994. See also Han Shu 1994; Xu Chengbei 1993, p. 3.
41. Xu Chengbei 1992. In fact, I applied to work in a McDonald's outlet in Beijing but was turned down. The manager told me that the recruitment of employees in McDonald's involves a long and strict review process, in order to make sure that the applicants' qualifications are competitive.
42. The relationship between medicine and food has long been an important concern in Chinese culinary culture. See E. Anderson 1988, pp. 53–56.
43. See Yu Bin 1996; and "Honggaoliang yuyan" 1996.
44. Liu Guoyue 1996.
45. See Zhao Huanyan 1995; Xu Wangsheng 1995; Xie Dingyuan 1996; and Tao Wentai 1996.
46. For an excellent account, see Kottak 1978.
47. Shelton 1990, p. 520.
48. *Gaige Daobao* (Reform herald), no. 1 (1994), p. 34.
49. See Douglas and Isherwood 1979.
50. Stephenson 1989, p. 237.
51. Fantasia 1995, pp. 221–22.
52. For an interesting study of eating etiquette in southern China, see Cooper 1986, pp. 179–84. As mentioned near the beginning of this chapter, Finkelstein offers an interesting and radically different view of existing manners and custom in restaurants. Since manners and behavior patterns are socially constructed and imposed on customers, they make the "restaurant a diorama that emphasizes the aspects of sociality assumed to be the most valued and attractive" (Finkelstein 1989, p. 52). Accordingly, customers give up their individuality and spontaneity and thus cannot explore their real inner world in this kind of socially constructed spatial context (ibid., pp. 4–17).
53. The 1994 figure comes from my fieldwork; the 1996 figure is taken from Beijing Dashiye Jingji Diaocha Gongsi (Beijing big perspective economic survey company), quoted in "Kuaican zoujin gongxin jieceng" (Fast food is coming closer to salaried groups), *Zhongguo jingyingbao*, June 21, 1996.
54. Interview with General Manager Tim Lai, September 28, 1994.
55. He Yupeng 1996.
56. Ibid. p. 8.
57 See Yan 1997a.
58. He Yupeng 1996, pp. 8–9.
59. See Yan 1997a.
60. According to John Love, when Den Fujita, the founder and owner of McDonald's chain stores in Japan, began introducing McDonald's foods to Japanese customers, particularly the youngsters, he bent the rules by allowing his McDonald's outlets to be a hangout place for teenagers. He decorated one of the early stores with poster-sized pictures of leather-jacketed members of a motorcycle gang "one shade removed" from Hell's Angels. Fujita's experiment horrified the McDonald's chairman when he visited the company's new branches in Japan. See Love 1986, p. 429.
61. Elsewhere I have argued that Chinese society in the 1990s underwent a process of restructuring. The entire Chinese population—not only the peasants—was on the move: some physically, some socially, and some in both ways. An interesting indicator of the increased social mobility and changing patterns of social stratification was the booming business of name-card printing, because so many people changed jobs and titles frequently and quickly. Thus consumption and lifestyle decisions became more important than ever as ways for individuals to define their positions. For more details, see Yan 1994.

62. Yan Zhenguo and Liu Yinshing 1992b.
63. See Xiao Yan 1994.
64. See, e.g., Gao Changli 1992, p. 6; Dong Fang 1994, p. 22.
65. Gu Bingshu 1994.
66. *Beijing wanbao*, January 27, 1993.
67. *Beijing qingnianbao* (Beijing youth daily), December 18, 1993.
68. Pian Ming 1994.
69. For a review of changes in consumption and lifestyles among Chinese youth, see Huang Zhijian 1994.
70. See Gold 1993.
71. On changing family values and household structure, see chapters in Davis and Harrell 1993. For a detailed study of the rising importance of conjugality in rural family life, see Yan 1997b.
72. Watson 1997, p. 19.
73. See *Beijing qingnianbao*, December 18, 1993.
74. See especially Mintz 1994; see also sources cited in notes 2 to 13.

References

Anderson, Eugene. 1988. *The Food of China*. New Haven, Conn.: Yale University Press.

Appadurai, Arjun. 1981. "Gastro-Politics in Hindu South Asia." *American Ethnologist* 8, no. 3: 494–511.

Bi Yuhua. 1994. "Kuaicanye zhengshi chengwei xin de redianhangye" (Fast food officially becoming a new hot sector). *Shichang bao* (Market news), September 19.

Bourdieu, Pierre. 1984. *Distinction: A Social Critique of the Judgement of Taste*. Cambridge, Mass.: Harvard University Press.

Chang, Kwang-chih, ed. 1977. *Food in Chinese Culture: Anthropological and Historical Perspectives*. New Haven, Conn.: Yale University Press.

Cooper, Eugene. 1986. "Chinese Table Manners: You Are How You Eat." *Human Organization* 45: 179–84.

Davis, Deborah, and Stevan Harrell, eds. 1993. *Chinese Families in the Post Mao Era*. Berkeley: University of California Press.

Dong Fang. 1994. "Zhongguo chengshi xiaofei wuda redian" (The five hot points in Chinese urban consumption). *Jingji shijie*, no. 1.

Douglas, Mary. 1975. "Deciphering a Meal." In *Myth, Symbol, and Culture*, edited by Clifford Geertz. New York: W. W. Norton.

Douglas, Mary, and Baron Isherwood. 1979. *The World of Goods*. New York: Basic Books.

Duan Gang. 1991. "Kuaican quanji hanzhan jingcheng" (Fast food chickens are fighting with each other in Beijing). *Beijing Youth Daily*, April 2.

Fantasia, Rick. 1995. "Fast Food in France." *Theory and Society* 24: 201–43.

Finkelstein, Joanne. 1989. *Dining Out: A Sociology of Modern Manners*. New York: New York University Press. *Gaige daobao* (Reform herald), no. 1 (1994), p. 34.

Gao Changli. 1992. "Woguo jiushi niandai chengxian duoyuanhua xiaofei qushi". (Consumption trends are diversified in China during the 1990s). *Shangpin pingjie* (Review of commodities), no. 10.

Giddens, Anthony. 1984. *The Constitution of Society: Outline of the Theory of Structuration*. Berkeley: University of California Press.

Gold, Thomas B. 1993. "Go with Your Feelings: Hong Kong and Taiwan Popular Culture in Greater China." *China Quarterly* 136 (December): 907–25.

Gu Bingshu. 1994. "Waican: dushi xin shishang" (Eating out: a new fashion in cities), *Xiaofeizhe*, no. 3: 14–15.

Guo Jianying. 1995. "Tantan kuaican de fuwu" (On service in the fast food sector) *Fuwu jingji* (Service economy), no. 2: 27–8.

Gusfield, Joseph. 1992. "Nature's Body and the Metaphors of Food." In *Cultivating Differences: Symbolic Boundaries and the Making of Inequality*, edited by Michele Lamont and Marcel Fournier. Chicago: University of Chicago Press.

Han Shu. 1994. "M: changsheng jiangjun" (M [McDonald's]: the undefeated general). *Xiaofei zhinan* (Consumption guide), no. 2: 10–11.

Harris, Marvin. 1985. *Good to Eat: Riddles of Food and Culture*. New York: Simon and Schuster.

He Yupeng. 1996. "Zuowei nuxin ripin de Beijing maidanglao" (McDonald's as feminine food in Beijing). Paper presented at the conference "Changing Diet and Foodways in Chinese Culture," Chinese University of Hong Kong, Hong Kong, June 12–14.

"Honggaoliang yuyan zhongshi kuaican da qushi" (The red sorghum predicts the trend of Chinese fast food). 1996. *Zhongguo jingyingbao* (Chinese business). June 11.

Huang Shengbing. 1995. "Kuaican xiaofie xingwei de bijiao yanjiu" (Comparative study of fast food consumption behavior). *Xiaofei jingji*, no. 5: 33–4.

Huang Zhijian. 1994. "Yi ge juda de qingnian xiaofei shichang" (A huge market of youth consumers). *Zhongguo qingnina yanjiu* (China youth studies), no. 2: 12–16.

Jerome, N. W., ed. 1980. *Nutritional Anthropology: Contemporary Approaches to Diet and Culture*. New York: Redgrave.

Jian Feng. 1992. "Zhongshi kuaican, na chu ni de mingpai" (Chinese fast food, show your best brand). *Shichang bao*, November 10.

Kottak, Conrad. 1978. "Rituals at McDonald's." *Journal of American Culture* 1: 370–86.

Lechner, Frank. 1991. "Simmel on Social Space." *Theory, Culture and Society* 8: 195–201.

Lévi-Strauss, Claude. 1983. *The Raw and the Cooked*. Chicago: University of Chicago Press.

Ling Dawei. 1996. "Nuli ba zhongshi kuaican gao shang qu" (Endeavor to develop Chinese fast food). *Zhongguo pengren*, no. 6: 4–5.

——. 1995. "Zhongxi kuaican jingzheng zhi wo jian" (My views on the competition between Chinese and Western fast foods). *Xinshiji zhoukan* (New century weekly), November.

Liu Fen and Long Zaizu. 1986. "Jing, jin, hu chi shenmo?" (What are people eating in Beijing, Tianjin, and Shanghai?). *People's Daily* (overseas edition), August 9.

Liu Guoyue. 1996. "Shenzhen kuaican shichang jiqi fazhan" (The fast food market in Shenzhen and its development). *Zhongguo pengren*, no. 8: 20–2.

Liu Ming. 1992. "Guoji kuaicancheng de meili" (The charming international fast food city). *Zhongguo shipinbao* (Chinese food newspaper), July 13.

Love, John. 1986. *McDonald's: Behind the Arches*. New York: Bantam Books.

Messer, Ellen. 1984. "Anthropological Perspectives on Diet." *Annual Review of Anthropology* 13: 205–49.

Mian Zhi. 1993. "Xishi kuaican fengmi jingcheng; zhongshi kuaican zemmaban?" (Western fast food is the fashion; what about Chinese fast food?). *Lianai, hunyin, jiating* (Love, marriage, and family), no. 6: 10–11.

Mintz, Sidney. 1994. "The Changing Role of Food in the Study of Consumption." In *Consumption and the World of Goods*, edited by John Brewer and Roy Porter. London: Routledge.

Murphy, Christopher. 1986. "Piety and Honor: The Meaning of Muslim Feasts in Old Delhi." In *Food, Society, and Culture*, edited by R. S.Khare and M. S. A.Rao. Durham, NC: Carolina Academic Press.

Pian Ming. 1994. "Jingcheng qingnian qingxin gaojia shangpin" (Beijing youth are keen on expensive commodities). *Zhonghua gongshang shibao* (China industrial and commercial times), July 16.

Ritzer, George. 1993. *The McDonaldization of Society*. Newbury Park, Calif.: Pine Forge.

Sahlins, Marshall. 1976. *Culture and Practical Reason*. Chicago: University of Chicago Press.

Sayer, Andrew. 1985. "The Difference That Space Makes." In *Social Relations and Spatial Structures*, edited by Derrek Gregory and John Urry. London: Macmillan.

Shelton, Allen. 1990. "A Theater for Eating, Looking, and Thinking: The Restaurant as Symbolic Space." *Sociological Spectrum* 10: 507–26.

Stephenson, Peter. 1989. "Going to McDonald's in Leiden: Reflections on the Concept of Self and Society in the Netherlands." *Ethos* 17, no. 2: 226–47.

Tao Wentai. 1996. "Guanyu zhongwai yinshi wenhua bijiao de ji ge wenti" (Issues in comparing Chinese and foreign culinary cultures). *Zhongguo pengren*, no. 8: 26–8.

Urry, John. 1985. "Social Relations, Space and Time." In *Social Relations and Spatial Structures*, edited by Derek Gregory and John Urry. London: Macmillan.

Walder, Andrew G. 1986. *Communist Neo-Traditionalism: Work and Authority in Chinese Industry*. Berkeley: University of California Press.

Watson, James. 1997. "Introduction: Transnationalism, Localization, and Fast Foods in East Asia." In *Golden Arches East: McDonald's in East Asia*, edited by James Watson. Stanford, Calif.: Stanford University Press.

——. 1987. "From the Common Pot: Feasting with Equals in Chinese Society." *Anthropos* 82: 389–401.

——, ed. 1997. *Golden Arches East: McDonald's in East Asia*. Stanford University Press.

Xiao Hua. 1993. "Da ru Zhongguo de yangkuaican" (The invasion of Western fast food), *Jianting shenghuo zhinan* (Guidance of family life), no. 5.

Xiao Yan. 1994. "Xiaofei guannian xin qingxie" (New orientations of consumption perception). *Zhongguo xiaofeizhe bao* (China consumer news), September 12.

Xie Dingyuan. 1996. "Pengren wangguo mianlin tiaozhan" (The kingdom of cuisine is facing a challenge). *Zhongguo pengren*, no. 2: 27–9.

Xu Chengbei. 1994. "Kuaican, dacai, yu xinlao zihao" (Fast food, formal dishes, and the new and old restaurants). *Jingji ribao* (Economic daily), September 17.

——. 1993. "Cong Maidanglao kan shijie" (Seeing the world from McDonald's). *Zhongguo pengren*, no. 8.

——. 1992. "Maidanglao de faluu" (McDonald's law). *Fazhi ribao* (Legal system daily), September 9.

Xu Wangsheng. 1995. "Zhongxi yinshi wenhua de qubie" (The differences between Chinese and Western culinary cultures). *Zhongguo pengren*, no. 8: 28–30.

Yan, Yunxiang. 1997a. "McDonald's in Beijing: The Localization of Americana." In *Golden Arches East: McDonald's in East Asia*, edited by James Watson. Stanford, Calif.: Stanford University Press.

———. 1997b. "The Triumph of Conjugality: Structural Transformation of Family Relations in a Chinese Village." *Ethnology* 36, no. 3: 191–212.

———. 1994. "Dislocation, Reposition and Restratification: Structural Changes in Chinese Society." In *China Review 1994*, edited by Maurice Brosseau and Lo Chi Kin. Hong Kong: Chinese University Press.

Yan Zhenguo and Liu Yinsheng. 1992a. "Yangkuaican chongjipo hou de chensi" (Pondering thoughts after the shock wave of Western fast food). *Shoudu jingji xinxibao* (Capital economic information news), December 3.

———. 1992b. "Zhongguo kuaican shichang shu zhu chenfu?" (Who will control the fast food market in China?). *Shoudu jingji xinxibao*, December 8.

Ye Xianning. 1993. "Jingcheng kuaican yi pie" (An overview of fast food in Beijing), *Fuwu jingji*, no. 4.

You Zi. 1994. "Jingcheng zhongshi kuaican re qi lai le" (Chinese fast food has become hot in Beijing). *Jingji shijie* (Economic world), no. 6: 60–1.

Yu Bin. 1996. "Zhongwai kuaican zai jingcheng" (Chinese and foreign fast foods in Beijing). *Zhongguo shangbao* (Chinese commercial news), June 20.

Yu Weize. 1995. "Shanghai Ronghuaji kuaican liansuo de jingying zouxiang" (The management directions of the Shanghai Ronghua Chicken fast food chain). *Zhongguo pengren* (Chinese culinary art), no. 9: 19–20.

Zhang Guoyun. 1995. "Zhongshi kuaican, dengni dao chuntian" (Chinese fast food, waiting for you in the spring). *Xiaofei jingji* (Consumer economy), no. 3: 54–6.

Zhang Yubin. 1992. "Xishi kuaican jishi lu" (Inspirations from Western fast food) *Zhongguo shipinbao* (Chinese food newspaper), September 4.

Zhang Zhaonan. 1992a. "Gan yu yangfan bi gaodi" (Dare to challenge the foreign fast food). *Beijing wanbao* (Beijing evening news), September 13.

———. 1992b. "Kuaicanye kai jin Zhongguo budui" (The "Chinese troops" entering the fast food sector). *Beijing wanbao*, October 9.

Zhao Huanyan. 1995. "Shilun fandian yingxiao zhong de wenhua dingwei" (On the cultural position of the restaurant business). *Fuwu jingji* (Service economy), no. 8: 10–11.

Zhong Zhe. 1993. "Meishi kuaican – gongfu zai shi wai" (American fast food–something beyond foods). *Xiaofeizhe* (Consumers), no. 2.

32

On the Move for Food: Three Women Behind the Tomato's Journey*

Deborah Barndt

Conversations Across Borders

As we sat on the hay wagon, with our lunch spread out before us, Irena proposed a Mexican toast: "Arriba, abajo, afuera, adentro! . . ." She moved her cup of cranberry juice to mimic the words "Up, down, outside, inside" as we swallowed the juice, and learned four words of Spanish at the same time. Irena, a Mexican farmworker, has learned a bit of English over the eleven years she has been coming to southern Ontario to pick vegetables from June to October. But not enough to really converse with Marissa, the Loblaws' cashier, who had brought her two daughters along for a visit to the farm. So we exchanged a few words of Spanish and English as we exchanged our mixed spread of Mexican and Canadian food, an array revealing various cultural histories and fusions, from the President's Choice dips and cheeses that we brought along to almond chicken and rice made by Irena the night before after twelve hours of working in the fields.

The "Up, down, outside, inside" toast is perhaps a good metaphor for the Tomasita Project, a cross-border research venture that traces the journey of the tomato from the Mexican field to the Canadian fast-food restaurant, and focuses on women's experiences within the various stages of food production, distribution, and consumption. The "up and down" metaphor frames not only the tomato's journey but also the power relations (varying interactions of nation, class, race, and gender) upon which the food system is built as well as the contrasting perspectives of what Richard Falk (quoted in Brecher, Childs, and Cutler 1993, ix) calls "globalization-from-above," or the corporate view of multinationals that control the tomato's transformation as opposed to "globalization-from-below," the views of the women workers whose hands move it along its journey.

"Outside and inside" dynamics are also reflected in the project's methodology, combining corporate research and *global* analysis (outside) with the gathering of life histories of women workers in specific *local* contexts (inside); I try to connect them conceptually through the concept of the *glocal*. "Outsider/insider" can also refer to the different relationships to the food system we have as women academics compared with the women who work inside the system (thus acknowledging not only our power

*Originally published 2001

within the research process but also the "epistemic privilege" the women workers can claim as they "know" their experience in a way we can never know). I agree with Ruth Hubbard and Margaret Randall (1988), that "insider" and "outsider" are not clean and neat categories, as we constantly shift between them from one moment, category, and relationship to another.

Although it has been easier for the women academics in the three NAFTA countries to meet and talk with each other, connecting the women workers themselves is more complicated because of differential privilege, time, and resources. Still, we have tried to find ways to make those links. Marissa, the Canadian cashier, has taken a keen interest in the project, digesting a photo story on Tomasa, a tomato worker in Mexico, and commenting on any article I pass to her. Although it would be hard to get her to Mexico to meet Tomasa, I figured she could at least meet Irena, a Mexican working in the fields only two hours west of her home, which is north of Toronto.

There are both differences and similarities in the experiences of Wanda, Irena, and Tomasa. Their most common ground, as Marissa suggested, is that they are all "trying to survive" as women workers in the globalized economy of the 1990s. And they are forced to move to find work in the food system, as they struggle to feed their families in increasingly hard times. Tomasa gets picked up in the early morning by a truck that takes her an hour from her village to pick tomatoes at an agribusiness in Jalisco, Mexico; Marissa drives her car an hour into Toronto where she scans tomatoes at a Loblaws' supermarket checkout lane; and Irena is brought by plane annually to southern Ontario to pick and pack the local tomatoes we eat in the summer.

Theoretical Frames: An Outside View

I'd like to use three interrelated theoretical frames for comparing the experiences of these three women and their roles in the food system: (1) the "distancing" that is central to global food production; (2) the "feminization of labor," which is often synonymous with the "feminization of poverty"; and (3) a "flexibility of labor" characterizing the restructured economy, involving both spatial and temporal migration and featuring women as central actors.

Distancing

Brewster Kneen (1993, 39) first coined the term "distancing" to characterize the dominant logic of the current food system, capturing not only the increasing distance between production and consumption, but also the distancing from natural products and processes inherent in biotechnology, processing, preservation, and packaging. Ecologists have used the concept to illustrate the deepening separation of humans from nature, and political economists have expanded on Marx's original notion of alienation to analyze the disconnectedness workers in agribusiness and the retail sector feel from the "fruits of their labor." I'd like to focus here on the distancing of food-system workers from their own roots, home bases, and cultural practices as well as their resistance to this disconnection.

Feminization of Labor and of Poverty

Although there has been considerable attention paid to the centrality of female labor (increasingly young and nonwhite) in the new global economy (Mitter 1986), particularly in manufacturing and export-processing or free-trade zones, there has been little comparison of women's labor in all sectors of the food system, from production to consumption, from agribusiness and food processing to the commercial and retail sectors. The Tomasita Project has attempted to link studies by women academics in Mexico, for example, that analyze the increasing number of married and single women in salaried agribusiness (as a response to the need for more family members working to survive as well as an exploitation of traditionally lower-paid women workers) (Barren 1999; Appendini 1995) with studies by Canadian feminist scholars (Reiter 1991; Kainer 1999) that reveal the dependency of the dominant service sector (such as supermarkets and restaurants) on part-time, low-wage female labor with limited opportunities for unionization. It is clear that the architects of global restructuring (multinational corporate executives as well as the managers of the producers and retailers they contract) have built the increasingly globalized food system on historical and cultural practices of sexism, racism, and classism, relegating the poor, people of color, indigenous peoples, and women to the most marginalized tasks in the food chain (Lara 1994; Martinez-Salazar 1999).

Flexibility and Migration

Mexican scholar Sara Lara (1994, 41) suggests that the expansion of the agro-export industry in Mexico, facilitated by NAFTA, deepens a basic North-South contradiction between "negotiated flexibility" and "primitive flexibility." Transnational corporations, primarily in the North, as well as privileged sectors in the South, employ skilled workers managed through "negotiated flexibility" while the labor-intensive processes of agribusinesses, for example, remain in the South and exploit women, children, and indigenous peoples, the most flexible workers in the rural labor market, through a "primitive flexibility."

Flexible labor is central to post-Fordist, just-in-time production practices increasingly adopted worldwide, and in the NAFTA food chain, this flexibility is both spatial and temporal. Agricultural production has always depended on migrant labor, particularly during peak season harvest times, but internal as well as international migration has increased since NAFTA. And migration, in the form of commuting, is also a phenomenon in the North, not only in the agricultural sector, but also in the service sector. Finally, the migrant labor force is increasingly female. For most of these women workers, part-time work in the food system is combined with part-time work in other paid jobs or the informal sector, as well as the relentless unpaid domestic work of caring for their families. Flexible labor strategies have forced these women to continually reorganize their time, or movement through days, weeks, and months, in new ways, as seasons begin and end, and shifts expand and contract.

Three Women/Three Stories: An Inside View

Three women can help ground this discussion of distancing, the feminization of labor and poverty, and flexibility and migration work in different sectors of the tomato food chain. But none of them is actually typical of the women workers in their sector. This may be just as well, because they will remind us that there are very real differences within each sector, and no one case can encompass the reality of all women workers. Tomasa, for example, is a seventy-year-old field-worker, while the majority of women agricultural workers in Mexico are between fifteen and twenty-four, the heartiest and most desirable age group, and thus, the first selected when there is an oversupply of labor (Barron, in Dabat 1994, 272). Tomasa is a local mestiza peasant, while a majority of tomato pickers are indigenous peasant families, including women and children, migrating from the poorer states. Irena, the farmworker brought to Ontario to pick our summer vegetables, is also not typical; she is almost fifty, while the official cap for these temporary workers is thirty-five. And Marissa, the supermarket cashier, is older as well, with twenty-five years' seniority as a part-time worker, giving her much more choice of her working hours than the younger majority of cashiers—often high school and university students.

Vignettes of the three women will make the proposed theoretical frames come alive and may even blur their boundaries, while allowing us to know these women a bit, to be able to consider the similarities and differences of their working and living conditions.

Tomasa, Tomato Worker: From Gomez Farias to Sayula, Mexico

Agricultural work in Mexico has always depended on migrant labor, but women's participation as salaried workers in agribusiness has increased in the 1990s due to several interrelated factors. First, the fruit and vegetable sector has expanded with NAFTA, and large domestic producers such as Santa Anita Packers have become primarily export oriented (80 percent of tomatoes head north, with 100 percent of greenhouse production for export). Mexico's almost wholesale adoption of the neoliberal model, pressured by structural adjustment in the 1980s and NAFTA in the 1990s, has meant privatization of *ejido* lands, reduction of small producer credits and food subsidies, and the expansion of monocultural cash crop production, affecting both the environment and the organization of work. Peasant and indigenous communities have suffered the most, and their traditional family-wage economies now require three or more members working to survive. While women's participation in paid work outside the home has become necessary and thus more accepted, domestic chores have not lightened and remain a female domain.

Survival for workers like Tomasa has meant combining strategies of the wage economy and the subsistence economy, picking tomatoes for a large agribusiness while still producing some of their own food on a nearby rented plot. And given the seasonal nature of agricultural work, she has had to seek other income-producing activities during off season such as making and selling straw mats.

The daily wage of twenty pesos (in 1997, just over five dollars) is clearly insufficient, even with both Tomasa and Pablo working as foremen for Santa Anita Packers. Their large family (nine of their sixteen children are still alive) remains an economic asset as they receive remittances from their two sons working in the United States, as well as support from other children working in the area. Migration *al norte* is central to their survival as it is to most Mexican peasant families. Tomasa, Pablo, and their family fit Lara's definition of "primitive flexibility," filling the need for unskilled seasonal labor. But they don't have to move as far for work as the even more marginalized indigenous families, who end up in horrendous migrant labor camps around the tomato plantation and follow harvests from one production site to another (now on the move for food most of the year, and thus torn from their own home bases and possible subsistence production). Tomasa must rise at 5:00 a.m. to make lunch and be on the truck by 6:00 a.m. where she stands up for the hour-long trip to the fields. When she returns at 2:30 p.m., she may accompany Pablo to the *milpa,* where they still practice the more ecological rotational method of planting corn, beans, and squash (the three sisters in indigenous agricultural practice), using minimal chemical inputs, in sharp contrast to their agribusiness employer who sprays fields massively and regularly with an ever-changing array of pesticides, herbicides, and fungicides. This field yields more than enough corn, which we found stacked in their kitchen, to feed the family for a year. Although she used to make tortillas from scratch, during the harvest season she often buys ready-made tortillas, rather than rise at 3:00 a.m. to make them.

Her connection to the corn they grow in their *milpa* is quite different from her connection to the tomatoes she picks at the plantation. Though she may bring some home for domestic consumption, she realizes that "the tomatoes don't stay here" (except for the second-rate ones kept for the Mexican market), but go off on big trailer trucks, which "come from far away and go far away, we don't know where" (personal interview 1997). In this sense, she reflects on the distancing of production from consumption, and typifies other agribusiness workers, most of whom have little sense of where the fruits of their labor end up.

Irena, Migrant Farmworker: From Miacatlán, Mexico, to Wilsonville, Ontario

Irena has a broader view of this process because, like the tomatoes, she too is moved farther north to meet the demands of a more-privileged foreign market. Her rhythm, however, follows the seasonal production of vegetables in Canada, where she is hired under the FARMS program to pick tomatoes during our harvest season. Building on a Canadian government-sponsored program for Temporary Agricultural Workers set up for Caribbean offshore workers in 1966 and expanded to include Mexicans in 1974, the FARMS (or Foreign Agricultural Resource Management Services) program is considered the créme de la créme of migrant worker schemes in North America. While it clearly exploits the asymmetry between Mexico and Canada in terms of wages, it provides a quick way for Mexican workers to amass an income, earning in one hour at minimum wage more than they would in one day for similar work back home. Because these temporary migrant workers migrate alone, they are "freed" from family responsibilities for those few months, have minimal costs, and can work long hours.

Women have only been included in recent years (in 1998 there were 150 women out of 5,000 workers), and widows and single mothers are preferred, because they are sure to return home and will endure this temporary sacrifice for their families. Irena has left her children (mostly older) at home with her parents, and for the past eleven years, has spent four months a year on Ontario farms. For the past eight years, she has worked at the same farm, because the farmer has asked her back again and again. The FARMS program clearly meets a need for Canadian farmers; as Basok (1997) argues, "Agriculture in Ontario is characterized by vulnerability related to competition from abroad and instability related to season and market price fluctuations," and temporary migrant workers are ideally suited to the need for seasonal workers "willing to work long hours during peak season for low remuneration" (4). While official contracts stipulate eight-hour work days, workers may agree to work overtime without overtime pay; and for women like Irena, every hour spent here earning money for her family is time well spent. She works mostly twelve-hour days six and a half days a week, and boasted of working a few years back for nineteen hours a day; "I cleared $1,000 in two weeks," she justified, as that might be almost a year's salary for a Mexican farmworker (personal interview 1999).

Many migrant workers are ignorant of their rights, though Irena is aware of inequities, such as the fact that Canadian workers are paid more; she still receives only minimum wage, after eleven years. Although they do get health care and pension payments, they do not get unemployment insurance, overtime, or vacation pay; they are not covered by the Occupational Safety and Health Act; and they are not allowed to unionize. Nonetheless, they are willing to put up with these inequities, the long hours of grueling work, the social isolation, and often substandard housing conditions because they know it is temporary and lucrative (Basok 1997, 5).

Ironically, although they have moved great distances to take advantage of this program, once in Canada, they rarely move beyond the fields and packing houses. Irena, for example, has come to Canada for eleven years, but had never visited Toronto, which is two hours away from the farm where she worked. On their half-day off, the farmer takes the workers shopping in a nearby town. The farmworkers are totally dependent on the farmer—not only for transportation but also for permission to leave the premises—and thus live almost like indentured workers. This *patron* relationship is central to the program: they dare not displease their farmer/boss or he may not request their return the following summer. Wall (1992, 269) suggests that this paternalistic relationship, where migrant workers are housed on their employers' property, and may depend on them for translation, filling out forms, transportation, communications home, etc., also makes it difficult for workers across farms to develop any solidarity around their common situation, let alone form some kind of workers' organization. This paternalism often incorporates classist, racist, and sexist behaviors. "Flexibility" thus takes on a much broader meaning in this context, as workers not only change countries and work from dawn to dusk, but endure poor labor relations because they know this is temporary and economic gain is their primary motive.

I found myself wondering how women like Irena survived during their eight months back home in Mexico. So, in December 1997, I visited Irena in Miacatlán, an hour from Cuernavaca, south of Mexico City. There I saw some fruits of her twelve-hour Canadian workdays: such appliances as a television, a sewing machine, a stereo, and building materials for adding rooms to her house for her children and their families. But any notion that her cushy Canadian job might allow her to relax for the rest of the year was shattered as I learned that she worked five days a week as a live-in domestic in Cuernavaca, taking care of middle-class Mexican invalids. And when at home on the weekends, she made and sold tamales in the street. This combination of work in the informal sector, piecing together part-time jobs, is the norm for most Mexican women. And, as with Tomasa, this patchwork of jobs is a family affair; her two older sons contribute to the family earnings as migrant farmworkers in the North as well, one slipping in illegally to the States, and the other to Québec, also through the FARMS program. The economic crisis of recent years has increased the gap between a small minority of wealthy Mexicans who have benefited from the neoliberal entrenchment and the poor majority, making the family-wage economy central to their survival.

I was struck by how Irena's survival depended upon work in different parts of the food system—picking tomatoes in Ontario, cooking meals in Cuernavaca, and selling food in her village—and how all of these jobs took her away from her own land and family. Yet I've also been intrigued by the way she maintains her own cultural culinary practices during her short annual stay in Canada. While she identifies little with the tomatoes she picks for our tables, she resists the distancing from her own plot and kitchen at home, bringing herbs, spices, even canned milk, to be able to reproduce her favorite meals, and the farmer has allowed her to grow hot peppers and coriander in small plots around their trailer. Food, ironically, both has distanced her and has provided some comfort and connection to her roots.

Marissa, Supermarket Cashier: From Bolton to Toronto, Ontario

At the other end of the tomato chain, Marissa lives in relative privilege. As she has read Tomasa's story and visited Irena on the Ontario farm, she has recognized her role in the larger global food system, which exploits her "sisters," as she calls them, even more than herself. But she, too, is forced by the reorganization of the economy to "migrate" to work and to move through her days and weeks (what I'm calling the temporal migration of shift work) with a flexibility that suits the corporate agenda. In Lara's (1994) terms, Marissa might be seen as part of a more-skilled labor force, regulated by a "negotiated flexibility," with greater skill and job security, as opposed to the "primitive flexibility" of migrant farmworkers, who must either move seasonally to nearby towns, like Tomasa, or to northern countries, like Irena.

First of all, it's important to recognize that the retail sector where Marissa works increasingly controls agricultural and food production in Canada (Winson 1993), not only dictating what Canadian farmers produce and how, but also bringing foods in from all corners of the world to meet our seemingly insatiable demand for fresh and diverse produce. (The Loblaws' warehouse is the epitome of Kneen's [1993] distancing concept, receiving daily flights of tomatoes from seven countries). And supermarkets represent, too, the increasingly dominant service sector economy, where most Canadians now work and women workers predominate; as Kainer (1999, 176) points out, there are now more people employed in the retail food sector than in auto manufacturing, and most of them are women. Of all the sectors we are studying in the tomato food chain, supermarkets are the only workplaces that are unionized. But recent negotiations have not been able to stem the (very gendered) tide of increasing part-time positions and lowering wage levels, and some suggest that male-run unions have not been the best advocates for female positions such as supermarket cashiers.

Marissa started as a part-time cashier twenty-four years ago when she was a high school student, and the irregular shifts actually suited her as well as her employer. Students will take the evening and weekend shifts that older women, especially mothers, try to avoid. Because of her high seniority (third in her store), she now has first choice in her hours. She chooses to work three eight-hour days, because she must commute an hour to work; this "choice" has some contradictions, however: she commutes only because if she requested a transfer to a Loblaws' closer to her house she would lose her seniority. And much to her employer's delight, she "chooses" to work on most weekends, because her two daughters are with her ex-husband then, saving child-care expenses.

The most recent (1996) collective bargaining of their union, United Food and Commerical Workers, with Loblaws' focused on job security, but increased the part-time cohort and lowered wage floors and ceilings, creating a two-tiered workforce (Kainer 1999, 183). There are now only two full-time cashiers with more than fifty part-timers (all women), some of whom were offered buy-offs to eliminate more jobs with higher wages and benefits, while hiring new cashiers at minimum wage and with the requirement to work 750 hours before receiving a raise, and a new cap of $12.50 per hour. Those at the bottom of the seniority list are "lucky to get four hours a week," as Marissa calculates, "so it is a year before you get that first increment, and they (Loblaws') start paying benefits out to you" (personal interview 1997).

So, although Marissa is among the more privileged part-time cashiers, her gendered flexible labor definitely benefits the company. She, in turn, chooses shifts that fit her children's schedule, and tries to be home for them. But on her weekday workdays, she must drop them at a babysitter at 7:45 a.m., along with the lunches she has made the night before, and heads down the highway, downing a banana for breakfast in the car. "Some women put their makeup on, I'm eating," she laughs, reflecting an increasing reality that workers in our commuting society eat on the run. She takes an hour and a half to get to work, and an hour to get home, by 6:30 or 7:00 p.m., often after her children have eaten at the sitter's.

Even though she is at the top of the wage scale at Loblaws' ($15/hour, twenty-four hours a week) and gets child support from her former husband, Marissa still must supplement her income to make ends meet. She used to do babysitting on her days off, and for the past few years has done home-order catalog sales. These jobs reflect gendered aspects of the informal-sector economy in the North, where women are picking up home-based child care as the state shirks this responsibility, and homework such as sewing and sales becomes increasingly common. And both are built on the notion of women taking primary responsibility for their families and households—their other area of work—still unpaid.

As a frontline worker in the supermarket, Marissa experiences the "distancing" of food in a way quite different from Tomasa and Irena. Cashiers have direct and intimate contact not only with the customers, but also with an increasingly sophisticated and controlling technology. Although technology has contributed to distancing in other jobs within the tomato chain, this change is most dramatic at the consumption end, in supermarkets and fast-food restaurants. The electronic cash register combined with scanning technology not only offers the company an instantly updated inventory to facilitate buying and restocking, but also monitors every move of the women who scan the bar codes and punch in the product lookup codes (PLUs) on fresh produce such as tomatoes.

Marissa showed me a weekly report of her productivity, which calculated to the second how much time she had spent scanning, tendering, and in "idle time," how many items she had sold, and how much money she had gathered. Although cashiers in the past might have known more about the food they sold, their scanning contact now limits them to a quick swipe and a beep; fresh produce requires more consciousness, as the PLU number on the sticker must be punched in, and sometimes must be checked with the computerized illustrated inventory. Either way, their relationship with food gets reduced to a number, as Marissa poignantly illustrated when we visited Irena and the farm, and she quickly identified the peppers, eggplants, and tomatoes by their PLU numbers: 4711 for red sheppard peppers, 4603 for Sicilian eggplant, etc. But a contradiction here is that cashiers are nonetheless introduced to a lot of new foods and, through conversations with customers, too, may learn a lot about them. There is not much time for chatting, however, when the scanning quota is five hundred items per hour.

Inside and Outside, Up and Down: Three Women/Three Concepts

NAFTA, as one more pillar in the neoliberal model that is increasingly being applied hemispherically, is built on a historical asymmetry between the United States, Canada, and Mexico, and on historical inequities within each of those countries that have marginalized poor, peasant, and working class; indigenous and people of color; and women workers. Tomasa, Irena, and Marissa, while not the most exploited in their own contexts, nonetheless represent in their paid work as well as their household work the increasing *distancing* between production and consumption of food and a *flexibility* based on both spatial and temporal migration, contributing to a deepening *feminization of labor and of poverty*. All must move a certain distance to work to feed their families, whether it's Tomasa riding a truck to a plantation an hour away from her village, Marissa driving her car to a supermarket away from her suburban home, or Irena flying from Mexico to work in Canada as a summer farmworker. They must also move through time, adjusting their monthly, weekly, and daily schedules to the demands of either seasonal agricultural production or of just-in-time production of the retail commercial sector. Southern agribusinesses and northern supermarkets alike depend on the flexible labor of women workers, who must piece together paid jobs in both the formal and informal sectors with their unpaid domestic work.

While Marissa may appear to have the most privileged position of the three, owning a house and a car, she still must supplement her income. And both Tomasa and Irena have extended families to help with child care, and grown-up children to contribute to the family wage. Still, Irena most poignantly reflects the sacrifices that Mexican women in particular must make in order to survive, migrating for four months a year to work in Canada, then migrating to a nearby city when in Mexico, ironically, to support the family that she must leave behind in both cases.

On her return from visiting Irena on the Ontario farm, Marissa wrote me a nine-page letter reflecting on the visit. She was struck by the sacrifice that Irena made for her family, prioritizing their needs before personal comforts. Yet Marissa also makes sacrifices, as a part-time food worker, to be at home for her children a few days a week, and to work on the weekends that they are with their father. She recognizes the differences but also the similarities: "We're all just trying to survive." Survival in Mexico is a different challenge from what it is Canada, to be sure, but those who control the global economy have given women ever deepening and expanding pressures to be flexible enough to move not only across borders, but also through days and months and years, to meet corporate demands.

References

Appendini, Kirsten. 1995. "Revisiting Women Wage Workers in Mexico's Agro-Industry: Changes in Rural Labour Markets." *Working Paper* 95, no. 2. Copenhagen, Denmark: Centre for Development Research.

Barron, Maria Antonieta. 1999. "Mexican Women on the Move: Migrant Workers in Mexico and Canada." In Deborah Barndt, ed., *Women Working the NAFTA Food Chain: Women, Food, and Globalization*, pp. 113–26. Toronto: Second Story Press.

Basok, Tania. 1997. "Forms of Control Within the 'Split Labour Market': A Case of Mexican Seasonal Farm Workers in Ontario." Paper presented to the Rural Sociology Conference. August, Toronto.

Brecher, Jeremy, John Brown Childs, and Jill Cuder, eds. 1993. *Global Visions: Beyond the New World Order.* Montreal: Black Rose Books.

Dabat, Alejandro. 1994. *México y la globalización.* Cuernavaca, México: Universidad Nacional Autónoma de México, Centro Regional de Investigaciones Multidisciplinarias.

Hubbard, Ruth, and Margaret Randall. 1988. *The Shape of Red: Insider/Outsider Reflections.* San Fransisco: Cleiss Press.

Kainer, Jan. 1999. "Not Quite What They Bargained For: Female Labour in Canadian Supermarkets." In Deborah Barndt, ed., *Women Working the NAFTA Food Chain: Women, Food, and Globalization*, pp. 175–89. Toronto: Second Story Press.

Kneen, Brewster. 1993. *From Land to Mouth: Understanding the Food System.* Toronto: New Canada Publications.

Lara, Sara. 1994. "La Flexibilidad del Mercada Rural." *Revista Mexicana de Sociología* 54, no. 1 (January–February): 29–48.

Mitter, Swasti. 1986. *Common Fate Common Bond: Women in the Global Economy.* London: Pluto Press.

Personal interviews with Tomasa (pseudonym), Gomez Farias, April 1997; with Irena (pseudonym), Miacatlán, December 1997; with Marissa (pseudonym), Toronto, May 1997 and Bolton, October 1997.

Reiter, Ester. 1991. *Making Fast Food: From Frying Pan to Fryer.* Montreal: McGill Queen's.

Wall, Ellen. 1992. "Personal Labour Relations and Ethnicity in Ontario Agriculture." In Vie Satzewich, ed., *Deconstructing a Nation: Immigration, Multiculturalism, and Racism in '90s Canada*, pp. 261–75. Halifax: Fernwood Publishing.

Winson, Anthony. 1993. *The Intimate Commodity: Food and the Development of the Agro-Industrial Complex in Canada.* Toronto: Garamond Press.

Challenging, Contesting, and Transforming the Food System

33

The Chain Never Stops*

Eric Schlosser

American slaughterhouses are grinding out meat faster than ever—and the production line keeps moving even when the workers are maimed by the machinery.

> In the beginning he had been fresh and strong, and he had gotten a job the first day; but now he was second-hand, a damaged article, so to speak, and they did not want him. They had worn him out, with their speeding-up and their carelessness, and now they had thrown him away!
>
> Upton Sinclair, *The Jungle* (1906)

Kenny Dobbins was hired by the Monfort Beef Company in 1979. He was 24 years old, and 6 foot 5, and had no fear of the hard work in a slaughterhouse. He seemed invincible. Over the next two decades he suffered injuries working for Monfort that would have crippled or killed lesser men. He was struck by a falling 90-pound box of meat and pinned against the steel lip of a conveyor belt. He blew out a disc and had back surgery. He inhaled too much chlorine while cleaning some blood tanks and spent a month in the hospital, his lungs burned, his body covered in blisters. He damaged the rotator cuff in his left shoulder when a 10,000-pound hammer-mill cover dropped too quickly and pulled his arm straight backward. He broke a leg after stepping into a hole in the slaughterhouse's concrete floor. He got hit by a slow-moving train behind the plant, got bloodied and knocked right out of his boots, spent two weeks in the hospital, then returned to work. He shattered an ankle and had it mended with four steel pins. He got more bruises and cuts, muscle pulls and strains than he could remember.

Despite all the injuries and the pain, the frequent trips to the hospital and the metal brace that now supported one leg, Dobbins felt intensely loyal to Monfort and ConAgra, its parent company. He'd left home at the age of 13 and never learned to read; Monfort had given him a steady job, and he was willing to do whatever the company asked. He moved from Grand Island, Nebraska, to Greeley, Colorado, to help Monfort reopen its slaughterhouse there without a union. He became an outspoken member of a group formed to keep union organizers out. He saved the life of a fellow worker—and was given a framed certificate of appreciation. And then, in December 1995, Dobbins felt a sharp pain in his chest while working in the plant. He thought it was a heart attack. According to Dobbins, the company nurse told him it was a muscle pull and sent him home. It was a heart attack, and Dobbins nearly died.

*Originally published 2001

While awaiting compensation for his injuries, he was fired. The company later agreed to pay him a settlement of $35,000.

Today Kenny Dobbins is disabled, with a bad heart and scarred lungs. He lives entirely off Social Security payments. He has no pension and no health insurance. His recent shoulder surgery—stemming from an old injury at the plant and costing more than $10,000—was paid for by Medicare. He now feels angry beyond words at ConAgra, misused, betrayed. He's embarrassed to be receiving public assistance. "I've never had to ask for help before in my life," Dobbins says. "I've always worked. I've worked since I was 14 years old." In addition to the physical pain, the financial uncertainty, and the stress of finding enough money just to pay the rent each month, he feels humiliated.

What happened to Kenny Dobbins is now being repeated, in various forms, at slaughterhouses throughout the United States. According to the Bureau of Labor Statistics, meatpacking is the nation's most dangerous occupation. In 1999, more than one-quarter of America's nearly 150,000 meatpacking workers suffered a job-related injury or illness. The meatpacking industry not only has the highest injury rate, but also has by far the highest rate of serious injury—more than five times the national average, as measured in lost workdays. If you accept the official figures, about 40,000 meatpacking workers are injured on the job every year. But the actual number is most likely higher. The meatpacking industry has a well-documented history of discouraging injury reports, falsifying injury data, and putting injured workers back on the job quickly to minimize the reporting of lost workdays. Over the past four years, I've met scores of meatpacking workers in Nebraska, Colorado, and Texas who tell stories of being injured and then discarded by their employers. Like Kenny Dobbins, many now rely on public assistance for their food, shelter, and medical care. Each new year throws more injured workers on the dole, forcing taxpayers to subsidize the meatpacking industry's poor safety record. No government statistics can measure the true amount of pain and suffering in the nation's meatpacking communities today.

A list of accident reports filed by the Occupational Safety and Health Administration gives a sense of the dangers that workers now confront in the nation's meat-packing plants. The titles of these OSHA reports sound more like lurid tabloid headlines than the headings of sober government documents: Employee Severely Burned After Fuel From His Saw Is Ignited. Employee Hospitalized for Neck Laceration From Flying Blade. Employee's Finger Amputated in Sausage Extruder. Employee's Finger Amputated in Chitlin Machine. Employee's Eye Injured When Struck by Hanging Hook. Employee's Arm Amputated in Meat Auger. Employee's Arm Amputated When Caught in Meat Tenderizer. Employee Burned in Tallow Fire. Employee Burned by Hot Solution in Tank. One Employee Killed, Eight Injured by Ammonia Spill. Employee Killed When Arm Caught in Meat Grinder. Employee Decapitated by Chain of Hide Puller Machine. Employee Killed When Head Crushed by Conveyor. Employee Killed When Head Crushed in Hide Fleshing Machine. Employee Killed by Stun Gun. Caught and Killed by Gut-Cooker Machine.

The most dangerous plants are the ones where cattle are slaughtered. Poultry slaughterhouses are somewhat safer because they are more highly mechanized; chickens have been bred to reach a uniform size at maturity. Cattle, however, vary enormously in size, shape, and weight when they arrive at a slaughterhouse. As a result, most of the work at a modern beef plant is still performed by hand. In the age of the space station and the microchip, the most important slaughterhouse tool is a well-sharpened knife.

Thirty years ago, meatpacking was one of the highest-paid industrial jobs in the United States, with one of the lowest turnover rates. In the decades that followed the 1906 publication of *The Jungle*, labor unions had slowly gained power in the industry, winning their members good benefits, decent working conditions, and a voice in the workplace. Meatpacking jobs were dangerous and unpleasant, but provided enough income for a solid, middle-class life. There were sometimes waiting lists for these jobs. And then, starting in the early 1960s, a company called Iowa Beef Packers (IBP) began to revolutionize the industry, opening plants in rural areas far from union strongholds, recruiting immigrant workers from Mexico, introducing a new division of labor that eliminated the need for skilled butchers, and ruthlessly battling unions. By the late 1970s, meatpacking companies that wanted to compete with IBP had to adopt its business methods—or go out of business. Wages in the meatpacking industry soon fell by as much as 50 percent. Today meatpacking is one of the nation's lowest-paid industrial jobs, with one of the highest turnover rates. The typical plant now hires an entirely new workforce every year or so. There are no waiting lists at these slaughterhouses today. Staff shortages have become an industrywide problem, making the work even more dangerous. In a relatively brief period of time, the meatpacking industry also became highly centralized and concentrated, giving enormous power to a few large agribusiness firms. In 1970, the top four meatpackers controlled just 21 percent of the beef market. Today the top four—IBP, ConAgra, Excel (a subsidiary of Cargill), and National Beef—control about 85 percent of the market. While the meatpackers have grown more powerful, the unions have grown much weaker. Only half of IBP's workers belong to a union, allowing that company to set the industry standard for low wages and harsh working conditions. Given the industry's high turnover rates, it is a challenge for a union simply to remain in a meatpacking plant, since every year it must gain the allegiance of a whole new set of workers.

In some American slaughterhouses, more than three-quarters of the workers are not native English speakers; many can't read any language, and many are illegal immigrants. A new migrant industrial workforce now circulates through the meat-packing towns of the High Plains. A wage of $9.50 an hour seems incredible to men and women who come from rural areas in Mexico where the wages are $7 a day. These manual laborers, long accustomed to toiling in the fields, are good workers. They're also unlikely to complain or challenge authority, to file lawsuits, organize unions, fight for their legal rights. They tend to be poor, vulnerable, and fearful. From the industry's point of view, they are ideal workers: cheap, largely interchangeable, and disposable.

One of the crucial determinants of a slaughterhouse's profitability is also responsible for many of its greatest dangers: the speed of the production line. Once a plant is fully staffed and running, the more head of cattle slaughtered per hour, the less it costs to process each one. If the production line stops, for any reason, costs go up. Faster means cheaper—and more profitable. The typical line speed in an American slaughterhouse 25 years ago was about 175 cattle per hour. Some line speeds now approach 400 cattle per hour. Technological advances are responsible for part of the increase;

the powerlessness of meatpacking workers explains the rest. Faster also means more dangerous. When hundreds of workers stand closely together, down a single line, wielding sharp knives, terrible things can happen when people feel rushed. The most common slaughterhouse injury is a laceration. Workers stab themselves or stab someone nearby. They struggle to keep up with the pace as carcasses rapidly swing toward them, hung on hooks from a moving, overhead chain. All sorts of accidents— involving power tools, saws, knives, conveyor belts, slippery floors, falling carcasses— become more likely when the chain moves too fast. One slaughter-house nurse told me she could always tell the line speed by the number of people visiting her office.

The golden rule in meatpacking plants is "The Chain Will Not Stop." USDA inspectors can shut down the line to ensure food safety, but the meatpacking firms do everything possible to keep it moving at top speed. Nothing stands in the way of production, not mechanical failures, breakdowns, accidents. Forklifts crash, saws overheat, workers drop knives, workers get cut, workers collapse and lie unconscious on the floor, as dripping carcasses sway past them, and the chain keeps going. "The chain never stops," Rita Beltran, a former IBP worker told me. "I've seen bleeders, and they're gushing because they got hit right in the vein, and I mean they're almost passing out, and here comes the supply guy again, with the bleach, to clean the blood off the floor, but the chain never stops. It never stops."

Albertina Rios was a housewife in Mexico before coming to America nearly 20 years ago and going to work for IBP in Lexington, Nebraska. While bagging intestines, over and over, for eight hours a day, Rios soon injured her right shoulder. She was briefly placed on light duty, but asked to be assigned to a higher-paying position trimming heads, an even more difficult job that required moving heavy baskets of meat all day. When she complained about the pain to her supervisor, she recalls, he accused her of being lazy. Rios eventually underwent surgery on the shoulder, as well as two operations on her hands for carpal tunnel syndrome, a painful and commonplace injury caused by hours of repetitive motion.

Some of the most debilitating injuries in the meatpacking industry are also the least visible. Properly sutured, even a deep laceration will heal. The cumulative trauma injuries that meatpacking workers routinely suffer, however, may cause lifelong impairments. The strict regimentation and division of labor in slaughterhouses means that workers must repeat the same motions again and again throughout their shift. Making the same knife cut 10,000 times a day or lifting the same weight every few seconds can cause serious injuries to a person's back, shoulders, or hands. Aside from a 15-minute rest break or two and a brief lunch, the work is unrelenting. Even the repetition of a seemingly harmless task can lead to pain. "If you lightly tap your finger on a desk a few times, it doesn't hurt," an attorney for injured workers told me. "Now try tapping it for eight hours straight, and see how that feels."

The rate of cumulative trauma injuries in meatpacking is the highest of any American industry. It is about 33 times higher than the national average. According to federal statistics, nearly 1 out of every 10 meatpacking workers suffers a cumulative trauma injury every year. In fact, it's very hard to find a meatpacking worker who's not suffering from some kind of recurring pain. For unskilled, unschooled manual laborers, cumulative trauma injuries such as disc problems, tendonitis, and "trigger finger" (a syndrome in which a finger becomes stuck in a curled position) can permanently limit the ability to earn a decent income. Much of this damage will never be healed.

After interviews with many slaughterhouse workers who have cumulative trauma injuries, there's one image that stays with me. It's the sight of pale white scars on dark skin. Ana Ramos came from El Salvador and went to work at the same IBP plant as Albertina Rios, trimming hair from the meat with scissors. Her fingers began to lock up; her hands began to swell; she developed shoulder problems from carrying 30- to 60-pound boxes. She recalls going to see the company doctor and describing the pain, only to be told the problem was in her mind. She would leave the appointments crying. In January 1999, Ramos had three operations on the same day—one on her shoulder, another on her elbow, another on her hand. A week later, the doctor sent her back to work. Dora Sanchez, who worked at a different IBP plant, complained for months about soreness in her hands. She says the company ignored her. Sanchez later had surgery on both hands. She now has a "spinal cord stimulator," an elaborate pain-reduction system implanted in her body, controlled from a small box under the skin on her hip. She will need surgery to replace the batteries every six or seven years.

Cumulative trauma injuries may take months or even years to develop; other slaughterhouse injuries can happen in an instant. Lives are forever changed by a simple error, a wrong move, a faulty machine. Paul Lopez worked as a carpenter in Mexico, making tables, chairs, and headboards, before coming to the United States in 1995 to do construction work in Santa Fe, New Mexico. He was 20 years old at the time, and after laying concrete foundations for two years, he moved to Greeley and got a job at the Monfort Beef plant, where the pay was higher. He trimmed hides after they came up from the kill floor, cutting off the legs and heads, lifting them up with mechanical assistance, and placing the hides on a hook. It was one of the most difficult jobs in the plant. Each hide weighed about 180 pounds, and he lifted more than 300 of them every hour. He was good at his job and became a "floater," used by his supervisor to fill in for absent workers. Lopez's hands and shoulders were sore at the end of the day, but for two years and two months he suffered no injuries.

At about seven in the morning on November 22, 1999, Lopez was substituting for an absent worker, standing on a four-foot-high platform, pulling hides from a tank of water that was washing blood and dirt off them. The hides were suspended on hooks from a moving chain. The room was cold and foggy, and it was difficult to see clearly. There were problems somewhere up ahead on the line, but the chain kept moving, and Lopez felt pressure to keep up. One of his steel-mesh gloves suddenly got snagged in the chain, and it dragged him down the line toward bloody, filthy water that was three feet deep. Lopez grabbed the chain with his free hand and screamed for help. Someone ran to another room and took an extraordinary step: He shut down the line. The arm caught in the chain, Lopez's left one, was partially crushed. He lost more than three pints of blood and almost bled to death. He was rushed to a hospital in Denver, endured the first of many operations, and survived. Five months later, Lopez was still in enormous pain and heavily medicated. Nevertheless, he says, a company doctor ordered him back to work. His previous supervisor no longer worked at the plant. Lopez was told that the man had simply walked off the job and quit one day, feeling upset about the accident.

I recently visited Lopez on a lovely spring afternoon. His modest apartment is just a quarter mile down the road from the slaughterhouse. The living room is meticulously neat and clean, filled with children's toys and a large glass display case of Native American curios. Lopez now works in the nurse's office at the plant, handling files. Every day he sees how injured workers are treated—given some Tylenol and then sent back to the line—and worries that ConAgra is now planning to get rid of him. His left arm hangs shriveled and lifeless in a sling. It is a deadweight that causes severe pain in his neck and back. Lopez wants the company to pay for an experimental operation that might restore some movement to the arm. The alternative could be amputation. ConAgra will say only that it is weighing the various medical options. Lopez is 26 years old and believes his arm will work again. "Every night, I pray for this operation," he says, maintaining a polite and dignified facade. A number of times during our conversation, he suddenly gets up and leaves the room. His wife, Silvia, stays behind, sitting across from me on the couch, holding their one-year-old son in her arms. Their three-year-old daughter happily wanders in and out to the porch. Every time the front door swings open for her, a light breeze from the north brings the smell of death into the room.

The meatpacking companies refuse to comment on the cases of individual employees like Raul Lopez, but insist they have a sincere interest in the well-being of their workers. Health and safety, they maintain, are the primary concerns of every supervisor, foreman, nurse, medical claims examiner, and company-approved doctor. "It is in our best interest to take care of our workers and ensure that they are protected and able to work every day," says Janet M. Riley, a vice president of the American Meat Institute, the industry's trade association. "We are very concerned about improving worker safety. It is absolutely to our benefit."

The validity of such claims is measured best in Texas, where the big meatpackers have the most freedom to do as they please. In many ways, the true heart of the industry lies in Texas. About one-quarter of the cattle slaughtered every year in the United States—roughly 9 million animals—are processed in Texas meatpacking plants. One of the state's U.S. senators, Phil Gramm, is the industry's most powerful ally in Congress. His wife, Wendy Lee, sits on the board of IBP. The state courts and the legislature have also been friendly to the industry. Indeed, many injured meat-packing workers in Texas now face a system that has been devised not only to prevent any independent scrutiny of their medical needs, but also to prevent them from suing for on-the-job injuries.

In the early years of the 20th century, public outrage over the misfortune of industrial workers hurt on the job prompted legislatures throughout the United States to enact workers' compensation laws. Workers' comp was intended to be a form of mandatory, no-fault insurance. In return for surrendering the legal right to sue their employer for damages, injured workers were guaranteed immediate access to medical care, steady income while they recuperated, and disability payments. All 50 states eventually passed workers' comp legislation of one sort or another, creating systems in which employers generally obtained private insurance and any disputes were resolved by publicly appointed officials.

Recent efforts by business groups to "reform" workers' comp have made it more difficult for injured employees to obtain payments. In Colorado, the first "workers' comp reform" bill was sponsored in 1990 by Tom Norton, a conservative state senator from Greeley. His wife, Kay, was a vice president at ConAgra Red Meat at the time. Under Colorado's new law, which places limits on compensation, the maximum payment for losing an arm is $37,738. Losing a digit brings you anywhere from $2,400 to $9,312, depending on whether it's a middle finger, a pinkie, or a thumb.

The meatpacking companies have a vested interest in keeping workers' comp payments as low as possible. IBP, Excel, and ConAgra are all self-insured. Every dime spent on injured workers in such programs is one less dime in profits. Slaughterhouse supervisors and foremen, whose annual bonuses are usually tied to the injury rate of their workers, often discourage people from reporting injuries or seeking first aid. The packinghouse culture encourages keeping quiet and laboring in pain. Assignments to "light duty" frequently punish an injured worker by cutting the hourly wage and forbidding overtime. When an injury is visible and impossible to deny—an amputation, a severe laceration, a chemical burn—companies generally don't contest a worker's claim or try to avoid medical payments. But when injuries are less obvious or workers seem uncooperative, companies often block every attempt to seek benefits. It can take injured workers as long as three years to get their medical bills paid. From a purely financial point of view, the company has a strong incentive to delay every payment in order to encourage a less-expensive settlement. Getting someone to quit is even more profitable—an injured worker who walks away from the job is no longer eligible for any benefits. It is not uncommon to find injured workers assigned to meaningless or unpleasant tasks as a form of retaliation, a clear message to leave. They are forced to sit all day watching an emergency exit or to stare at gauges amid the stench in rendering.

In Texas, meatpacking firms don't have to manipulate the workers' comp system—they don't even have to participate in it. The Texas Workers Compensation Reform Act of 1989 allowed private companies to drop out of the state's workers' comp system. Although the law gave injured workers the right to sue employers that had left the system, that provision was later rendered moot. When a worker is injured at an IBP plant in Texas, for example, he or she is immediately presented with a waiver. It reads: "I have been injured at work and want to apply for the payments offered by IBP to me under its Workplace Injury Settlement Program. To qualify, I must accept the rules of the Program. I have been given a copy of the Program summary. I accept the Program."

Signing the waiver means forever surrendering your right—and the right of your family and heirs—to sue IBP on any grounds. Workers who sign the waiver may receive immediate medical care under IBP's program. Or they may not. Once they sign, ISP and its company-approved doctors have control over the worker's job-related medical treatment—for life. Under the program's terms, seeking treatment from an independent physician can be grounds for losing all medical benefits. If the worker objects to any decision, the dispute can be submitted to an IBP-approved arbitrator. The company has said the waivers are designed "to more effectively ensure quality medical care for employees injured on the job." Workers who refuse to sign the IBP waiver not only risk getting no medical care from the company, but also risk being fired on the spot. In February 1998, the Texas Supreme Court ruled that companies operating outside the state's workers' comp system can fire workers simply because they're injured.

Today, an IBP worker who gets hurt on the job in Texas faces a tough dilemma: Sign the waiver, perhaps receive immediate medical attention, and remain beholden, forever, to IBP. Or refuse to sign, risk losing your job, receive no help with your medical bills, file a lawsuit, and hope to win a big judgment against the company someday. Injured workers almost always sign the waiver. The pressure to do so is immense. An IBP medical case manager will literally bring the waiver to a hospital emergency room in order to obtain an injured worker's signature. Karen Olsson, in a fine investigative piece for the Texas Observer, described the lengths to which Terry Zimmerman, one of IBP's managers, will go to get a signed waiver. When Lonita Leal's right hand was mangled by a hamburger grinder at the IBP plant in Amarillo, Zimmerman talked her into signing the waiver with her left hand, as she waited in the hospital for surgery. When Duane Mullin had both hands crushed in a hammer mill at the same plant, Zimmerman persuaded him to sign the waiver with a pen held in his mouth.

Unlike IBP, Excel does not need to get a signed waiver after an injury in Texas. Its waiver is included in the union contract that many workers unwittingly sign upon being hired. Once they're injured, these workers often feel as much anger toward the union as they do toward their employer. In March, the Texas Supreme Court upheld the legality of such waivers, declaring that the "freedom of contract" gave Americans the ability to sign away their common-law rights. Before the waiver became part of the standard contract, Excel was held accountable, every so often, for its behavior.

Hector Reyes is one of the few who has managed to do something productive with his sense of betrayal. For 25 years, his father was a maintenance worker at the Excel plant in Friona, Texas, a couple of hours southwest of Amarillo. As a teenager, Reyes liked to work in the plant's warehouse, doing inventory. He'd grown up around the slaughterhouse. He later became a Golden Gloves champion boxer and went to work for Excel in 1997, at the age of 25, to earn money while he trained. One day he was asked to clean some grease from the blowers in the trolley room. Reyes did as he was told, climbing a ladder in the loud, steam-filled room and wiping the overhead blowers clean. But one of the blowers lacked a proper cover—and in an instant the blade shredded four of the fingers on Reyes' left hand. He climbed down the ladder and yelled for help, but nobody would come near him, as blood flew from the hand. So Reyes got himself to the nurse's office, where he was immediately asked to provide a urine sample. In shock and in pain, he couldn't understand why they needed his urine so badly. Try as he might, he couldn't produce any. The nurse called an ambulance, but said he wouldn't receive any painkillers until he peed in a cup. Reyes later realized that if he'd failed the urine test, Excel would not have been obligated to pay any of his medical bills. This demand for urine truly added insult to injury: Reyes was in training and never took drugs. He finally managed to urinate and received some medication. The drug test later came back negative.

On his fourth night in a Lubbock hospital, Reyes was awakened around midnight and told to report for work the next morning in Friona, two hours away. His wife would have to drive, but she was three months pregnant. Reyes refused to leave the hospital until the following day. For the next three months, he simply sat in a room at the Excel plant with other injured workers or filed papers for eight hours a day, then drove to Lubbock for an hour of physical therapy and an hour of wound cleaning before heading home. "You've already cost the company too much money," he recalls one supervisor telling him. Reyes desperately wanted to quit but knew he'd lose all his medical benefits if he did. He became suicidal, despondent about the end of his boxing career and his disfigurement. Since the union had not yet included a waiver in its Excel contract, Reyes was able to sue the company for failing to train him properly and for disregarding OSHA safety guidelines. In 1999, he won a rare legal victory: $879,312.25 in actual damages and $1 million in punitive damages. Under the current Excel contract, that sort of victory is impossible to achieve.

Federal safety laws were intended to protect workers from harm, regardless of the vagaries of state laws like those in Texas. OSHA is unlikely, however, to do anything for meatpacking workers in the near future. The agency has fewer than 1,200 inspectors to examine the safety risks at the nation's roughly 7 million workplaces. The maximum OSHA fine for the death of a worker due to an employer's willful negligence is $70,000—an amount that hardly strikes fear in the hearts of agribusiness executives whose companies have annual revenues that are measured in the tens of billions. One of President George W. Bush's first acts in office was to rescind an OSHA ergonomics standard on repetitive-motion injuries that the agency had been developing for nearly a decade. His move was applauded by IBP and the American Meat Institute.

The new chairman of the House Subcommittee on Workforce Protections, which oversees all legislation pertaining to OSHA, is Rep. Charles Norwood, a Republican from Georgia. Norwood was an outspoken supporter of the OSHA Reform Act of 1997—a bill that would have effectively abolished the agency. Norwood, a former dentist, became politically active in the early 1990s out of a sense of outrage that OSHA regulations designed to halt the spread of AIDS were forcing him to wear fresh rubber gloves for each new patient. He has publicly suggested that many workers get repetitive-stress injuries not from their jobs, but from skiing and playing too much tennis.

For Kevin Glasheen, one of the few Texas attorneys willing to battle IBP, the plight of America's meatpacking workers is "a fundamental failure of capitalism." By failing to pay the medical bills of injured workers, he says, large meatpackers are routinely imposing their business costs on the rest of society, much as utilities polluted the air a generation ago without much regard to the consequences for those who breathed it.

Rod Rehm, an attorney who defends many Latino meatpacking workers in Nebraska, believes that two key changes could restore the effectiveness of most workers' comp plans. Allowing every worker to select his or her own physician would liberate medical care from the dictates of the meatpacking companies and the medical staff they control. More important, Rehm argues, these companies should not be permitted to insure themselves. If independent underwriters had to insure the meatpackers, the threat of higher insurance premiums would quickly get the attention of the meatpacking industry—and force it to take safety issues seriously.

Until fundamental changes are made, the same old stories will unfold. Michael Glover is still awaiting payment from IBP, his employer for more than two decades. For 16 of those years, Glover worked as a splitter in the company's Amarillo plant. Every 20 to 30 seconds, a carcass would swing toward him on a chain. He would take "one heavy heavy power saw" and cut upward, slicing the animal in half before it went into the cooler. The job took strength, agility, and good aim. The carcasses had to be sliced exactly through the middle. One after another they came at him, about a thousand pounds each, all through the day.

On the morning of September 30, 1996, after splitting his first carcass, Glover noticed vibrations in the steel platform beneath him. A maintenance man checked the platform and found a bolt missing, but told Glover it was safe to keep working until it was replaced. Moments later, the platform collapsed as Glover was splitting a carcass. He dropped about seven feet and shattered his right knee. While he lay on the ground and workers tried to find help, the chain kept going as two other splitters picked up the slack. Glover was taken in a wheelchair to the nurse's station, where he went into shock in the hallway and fell unconscious. He sat in that hall for almost four hours before being driven to an outpatient clinic. A full seven hours after the accident, Glover was finally admitted to a hospital. He spent the next six days there. His knee was too badly shattered to be repaired; no screws would hold; the bone was broken into too many pieces.

An artificial knee was later inserted. Glover suffered through enormous pain and a series of complications: blood clots, ulcers, phlebitis. Nevertheless, he says, IBP pressured him to return to work in a wheelchair during the middle of winter. On snowy days, several men had to carry him into the plant. Once it became clear that his injury would never fully heal, Glover thinks IBP decided to get rid of him. But he refused to quit and lose all his medical benefits. He was given a series of humiliating jobs. For a month, Glover sat in the men's room at the plant for eight hours a day, ordered by his supervisor to make sure no dirty towels or toilet paper remained on the floor.

"Michael Glover played by IBP'S rules," says his attorney, James H. Woods, a fierce critic of the Texas workers' comp system. The day of his accident, Glover had signed the waiver, surrendering any right to sue the company. Instead, he filed for arbitration under IBP's Workplace Injury Settlement Program. Last year, on November 3, Glover was fired by IBP. Twelve days later, his arbitration hearing convened. The arbitrator, an Amarillo lawyer named Tad Fowler, was selected by IBP. Glover sought money for his pain and suffering, as well as lifetime payments from the company. He'd always been a hardworking and loyal employee. Now he had no medical insurance. His only income was $250 a week in unemployment. He'd fallen behind in his rent and worried that his family would be evicted from their home.

On December 20, Fowler issued his decision. He granted Glover no lifetime payments but awarded him $350,000 for pain and suffering. Glover was elated, briefly. Even though its workplace-injury settlement program clearly states that "the arbitrator's decision is final and binding," the company so far has refused to pay him. IBP claims that by signing the waiver, Glover forfeited any right to compensation for "physical pain, mental anguish, disfigurement, or loss of enjoyment of life." IBP has even refused to pay its own arbitrator for his services, and Fowler is now suing the company to get his fee. He has been informed that IBP will never hire him again for an arbitration.

Glover's case is now in federal court. He is a proud man with a strong philosophical streak. He faces the possibility of another knee replacement or of amputation. "How can this company fire me after 23-and-one-half years of service," he asks, "after an accident due to no fault of my own, and requiring so much radical surgery, months and months of pain and suffering, and nothing to look forward to but more pain and suffering, and refuse to pay me an award accrued through its own program?"

There is no good answer to his question. The simple answer is that IBP can do it because the laws allow them to do it. Michael Glover is just one of thousands of meat-packing workers who've been mistreated and then discarded. There is nothing random or inscrutable about their misery; it is the logical outcome of the industry's practices. A lack of public awareness, a lack of outrage, have allowed these abuses to continue, one after another, with a machine-like efficiency. This chain must be stopped.

34

Fast Food/Organic Food: Reflexive Tastes and the Making of "Yuppie Chow"[*]

Julie Guthman

Introduction

Hundreds of millions of people buy fast food every day without giving it much thought, unaware of the subtle and not so subtle ramifications of their purchases. They rarely consider where this food came from, how it was made, what it is doing to the community around them. They just grab their tray off the counter, find a table, take a seat, unwrap the paper, and dig in … They should know what really lurks behind those sesame-seed buns. As the old saying goes: You are what you eat. (From the introduction to *Fast Food Nation*, Schlosser 2001: 10)

The Slow Food movement is different from ecological movements and from gastronomy movements. Gastronomical movements don't defend the small producers and their products, and ecological movements fight the battles, but can't cook. You have to have both at the same time. (Spoken by Carlo Petrini, founder of the Slow Food movement at a 'convivium' held at Berkeley's Chez Panisse; Brennan 1999)

The recently published *Fast Food Nation* (Schlosser 2001) is an exposé of an industrialized food system *in extremis*. Deliberately building on the legacy of Upton Sinclair's *The Jungle*, Schlosser seeks to enrage people's hearts as well as their stomachs by describing both the social and the public health/environmental costs of a food sector gone awry. Hence, not only does he recount the epidemiology of *E. coli* 0157:H7, he drives home the point that the rise of fast food was inextricable from the de-skilling, racializing, and youthening of restaurant and food-processing work, making such work mindless at best and extraordinarily hazardous at worst.[1] Curiously, though, the desire for fast food is treated as somewhat of a given. Indeed, Schlosser treats taste as a purely biological phenomenon, unmediated by cultural and economic factors, claiming at several junctures that fast food simply tastes good. As but one consequence, he says, the USA has the highest rate of obesity in the industrialized world (Schlosser 2001: 240). The success of fast foods, he insinuates, depends on compulsive gluttony and unrefined taste, both of which are manifest in fat bodies.

Juxtaposed to fast food is what Bell and Valentine (1997) call ethical eating, a counter-trend (cf. Hollander, 2003) that includes vegetarianism, organic food, Fair Trade coffee, direct farmer-to-consumer marketing, and, most directly, the Slow

[*]*Originally published 2003*

Food movement. Social critics (including Schlosser himself), academics (e.g. Friedmann 1993; Miele and Murdoch forthcoming; Morgan and Murdoch 2000; Whatmore and Thorne 1997), diehard natural food consumers, and 'foodies' (e.g. Kraus 1991; McManus and Rickard 2000; Unterman 1998), most of all, read these trends as active opposition to industrialized food provision. In this view, consumption practices are driven by a *conscious* reflexivity, such that people monitor, reflect upon and adapt their personal conduct in light of its perceived consequences (Warde and Martens 2000: 199; also DuPuis 2000). In contrast to the fast food eater, the reflexive consumer pays attention to how food is made, and that knowledge shapes his or her 'taste' toward healthier food. That this consumer has a 'healthier' body is only implied.

Presumably the end point of the broadest set of alternative practices, organic food consumption, is treated in this literature as reflexive eating *par excellence.* To be sure, growth in organic production has been strongly correlated with increased consumer knowledge about mass-produced food, at times coming as 'food scares' but also with compelling evidence of some of the public health, environmental and moral risks involved with chemical-based crop production and intensified livestock manage-ment. Yet, a look at the growth in organic food in geographic and historical context shows that the explosion in organic food production and consumption was not entirely innocent of some of the very factors that were implicated in the growth of fast food. Indeed, the simultaneity of growth with the so-called McDonaldization of America raises the question of whether the arrival of organic foods truly represented a paradigmatic shift or was the just the other side of the same coin.

The moral positioning of organic food in binary opposition to fast food is equally problematic in this literature. For, if fast food is about common tastes, mass production and massive bodies, to construct an inverse of refined (or reflexive) taste, craft produc-tion and crafted bodies raises some class and gender issues that, at the very least, compli-cate the new politics of consumption. In regards to class, this dichotomy not only suggests that 'good' food is out of the economic and cultural reach of non-elites, it fails to bring to scrutiny the labour conditions under which such food is produced. In regards to gender, it not only effaces the links between convenience food and women's massive participation in the paid workforce, it contributes to the pervasive social nagging about body norms.

The purpose of this paper is, thus, two-fold. One is to examine the evolution of organic food from what Belasco (1989) called the 'counter-cuisine' to what organic growers call 'yuppie chow' to suggest that the success of the organic industry was largely wrapped up with gentrification—and the class differentiation that necessarily entailed. The other is to problematize the facile dichotomies between fast and slow, reflexive and compulsive, fat and thin, and, hence, good and bad eaters, to show where there is slippage and instability in these categories, in addition to this troubling poli-tics of class and gender. To these ends, I will showcase the provision of a particular commodity (organic salad mix, or *mesclun*) in a particular place: California.[2]

In important respects, salad mix gave a jump-start to the California organic sector, which then became what is likely the largest in the world in terms of crop value.[3] There-fore, the production complex around salad mix set a crucial standard in the evolution of the organic sector. Introduced by restaurateurs in the early 1980s, salad mix also helped establish organic food as precious, a 'niche' product not necessarily representing a critique of industrial food. So successful was organic salad mix as a high-end commodity that it induced major changes in the system of provision in the decade that followed. The growing disconnect between new forms of provision and the meanings organic farming originally embodied surely calls into question the positioning of organic farming and organic food as antidote to industrialized agriculture and fast food.

Making and Remaking Salad Mix[4]

While the organic farming movement has multiple geographic and philosophical origins (see, e.g., Harwood 1990; Peters 1979), California was always important to its formation (Guthman 1998, forthcoming). Tropes of nature and health were central to the California mythology (see, e.g., Baur 1959; Shrepfer 1983; Starr 1985), and the 1960s' counter-culture, with its stronghold in the San Francisco Bay Area, drew on these tropes, in addition to the oppositional politics of the so-called New Left. Many of the key institutions and figures of the movement were also California-based. For example, Alan Chadwick, a British-born Shakespearean actor, began the first university-run research and extension service devoted solely to organics at the University of California at Santa Cruz in 1967. The decidedly counter-cultural milieu of this programme set the idiomatic tone for organic farming for a long time to come, as many farmers were apprenticed in this programme. In addition, the first organic certification programme in the USA, California Certified Organic Farmers (CCOF), started in Santa Cruz in 1973, then a rag-tag group of fifty or so self-proclaimed hippie farmers. The annual 'gathering' of ecological farmers—now a major industry conference—made its home in Asilomar, California. The Capay Valley, a small offshoot of the Sacramento Valley, became an important enclave of subscription farms, where consumers buy in for a weekly box of produce. There are other examples. Most of the organic farmers involved in these formative institutions counter-posed their vision to fast, industrial food in some respect or another.

Nevertheless, organic agriculture *arrived* in a post-1970s', *post*-counter-cultural climate, in some ways contradicting the simple-living, tread-lightly message that some would argue is central to the organic critique. Indeed, this emergence was contingent on bridging the counter-cultural associations of organic food with a new class of eaters, a contingency that was similarly dependent on *where* it occurred: the San Francisco Bay Area—a curious *mélange* itself of a high-wage economy with a liberal-to-radical political climate (Walker 1990)—and a history of trend-setting in food.

From the heady days of the Gold Rush, the Bay Area was historically a high-wage economy (for whites), a centre for industries requiring high-skilled labour. The crucial juncture, for the purposes of this argument, was the explosive success of high-tech electronics in Silicon Valley and finance in San Francisco during the 1980s (Walker 1990). Riding the waves of financial crises and de-regulation that characterized the neo-liberal transition, many mini-fortunes were made in stock and real estate speculation, supplementing the already above-average wages of the professional working classes. No doubt, much of this wealth was a by-product of some of the same processes that made McDonald's the most financially successful restaurant chain in the world (e.g. tax roll backs, falling real wages). To be sure, the rapid growth in financial markets starting in the mid-1980s involved a sharpening of class divisions, so that a decade later, wealth in the USA was the most concentrated it had been since the 1920s (Henwood 1998: 66). Yet, as Walker notes, the Bay Area had long been a centre of personal innovation and indulgence, and cultural non-conformity, as well. It was a local social pundit, Alice Kahn, who coined the word 'yuppie' to connote the emerging group of young urban professionals who 'combin[ed] fierce upward mobility and strong consumerism with some remarkably progressive cultural and political interventions' (Walker 1990: 22).[5]

From the Gold Rush, San Francisco had also been a restaurant town, an early draw for immigrating French chefs. Unlike most of the rest of the USA, moreover, San Francisco did not shun *haute cuisine* in the era of what Levenstein (1988) calls 'culinary babbitry'. To the contrary, the Bay Area remained a haven of good food sense amid the downward spiral of dietary expectations and food quality that occurred in the middle third of the twentieth century. As anecdotal evidence, a survey of twelve Berkeley families, nine headed by professors, was taken in 1927. The surveyors noted that, 'the Berkeley diet emphasized fresh vegetables and fruits, especially the leafy and citrus varieties, milk products, and eggs, in contrast to the average urban diet which substituted the cheaper cereals and potatoes and spent relatively more for meat. The extraordinary amount of fresh fruits and vegetables were especially noteworthy' (Luck and Woodruff 1931; cited in Levenstein 1993). Proximity to the wine country of Napa and Sonoma counties, as well as prevalent truck gardens, contributed to relatively urbane food tastes.

It was a young woman from Berkeley who forged the unlikely connection between this early culinary history, the 1960s' counter-culture, and the *nouveau riche* of the 1980s. As a young adult, Alice Waters went to France and became enamoured with French rustic cooking. She returned to Berkeley to open a café in 1971 where she served simple meals to her friends. Within a few years of opening, she had pioneered the California version of *nouvelle cuisine*. Feeling that the best food was made from fresh, local and seasonal ingredients, she bought most of her produce from local farms. Warren Weber, of Star Route Farms in Bolinas, one of the original self-professed hippie farmers, began to sell cut organic baby greens to Waters in 1981, using the French term *mesclun*. A handful of others soon joined in, some calling it spring mix. All were garden-variety organic farmers—relatively small scale, independent and ideologically motivated—and, in Weber's words, 'employed the time-honored organic techniques of cover-cropping and composting'. So when Waters modified the noun *mesclun* with the word 'organic' on the menu in what came to be an upscale restaurant, she started an association that she was only part conscious of. Not only did Waters inspire a rash of imitation, and quite instrumentally contribute to the diffusion of organic consumption, she also, and in this way, unintentionally, institutionalized a certain set of meanings for organic.

Within a decade after opening, Chez Panisse had become a world-renowned culinary institution. Waters continued to buy local seasonal produce and highlight its organic origins. Many Bay Area chefs trained with Waters and went on to open their own restaurants and become 'celebrity chefs' in their own right. Many also made it a practice to form personal relationships with local farmers to ensure availability of the highest quality ingredients. Following Waters' lead, they wanted organic ingredients, although, crucially, only salad mix was regularly featured as organic. To draw emphasis to the farm–restaurant connection, some featured the name of the farm on the menu, Star Route Farms having received the most notoriety this way.

By the late 1980s, organic salad mix was on the menu of many upscale restaurants and certainly at those at the cutting edge. Green-leaf, a local Bay Area distributor, and Terra Sonoma, a consortium of small growers with personal connections to the restaurant business, made entire businesses out of selling speciality and organic produce directly to restaurants. Because restaurateurs were extraordinarily picky about what they would buy, they enforced a high appearance standard on growers so not to compromise their own reputations. The need for 'quality' became a major push for technical solutions to organic farming (and processing), at the same time it required an extraordinary amount of care. Growers were pushed to be delicate in their handling of organic produce and to discard (or separate) produce that did not conform to restaurant standards. In turn, organic shed the image of the twisted stunted carrot showing up at the local food-co-op to the splendid display of *mesclun* on a chef's dish.

The specificity of the farm–restaurant connection reinforced another attribute of organic salad mix: that it was necessarily expensive. Restaurants were willing to pay top dollar for the finest, freshest and eye-pleasing mix. Several growers interviewed harkened back to the rumours than had once circulated about restaurants paying $35 per pound for *mesclun*. One grower spoke of short-lived Kona Kai farms, situated on a small urban lot in Berkeley, whose owner had once boasted to have made the equivalent of $100,000 per acre in one year selling salad mix and herbs to nearby restaurants. Complaining that the data were 'heavily extrapolated' and based on 'counter-cultural economics', this grower confirmed that it had been widely circulated. So whether these prices were real or illusory, such talk contributed to the notion that organic salad mix was a precious commodity. Upscale supermarkets picked up on this discourse, selling their salad mix as 'custom-made' and pricing it upwards of $12 per pound (as observed by the author).

Although organic produce more generally had long been sold in health food stores, co-operatives and selected greengrocers, the *taste* for organic salad mix was mostly diffused through restaurants, as are many exotic tastes (Warde and Martens 2000). But *sales* of organic salad mix exploded when producers started to infiltrate more mainstream retail establishments. The domestication of salad mix began when two graduates of the University of California at Santa Cruz, Myra and Drew Goodman, who had been selling their own organic berries and lettuce to area restaurants like Chez Panisse, came up with the idea of bagging their lettuce mixes. Adopting the name of Earth-bound Farms, from 1986 to 1989 they were the only company selling washed, spun dried and re-sealable bagged salad mixes to supermarkets. Thereafter, others became involved in retail sales, some imitating the one-meal bags designed by Earthbound and others selling custom mixes in bulk to upscale supermarkets. The Aldicarb and Alar pesticide scares of 1986 and 1988, respectively, created a surge of growth in the California organic sector at large, with certified organic acres quadrupling in two years (Schilling 1995). Ultimately this cause of growth was outlasted by the expansionary activity around salad mix (Klonsky and Tourte 1995), suggesting that food safety was not the only impetus towards organic consumption, at least in this particular period. A leader in one major organic industry organization was later to quip, 'Salad mix has done more to reduce pesticide use in California than all the organizing around pesticide reform'.[6]

Meanwhile, the equation of organic with high value brought a rash of new growers into the sector. In the aftermath of the 1980s' farm crisis, many growers were looking for higher value cropping or marketing strategies, which occasionally led them to organic production. In California, commercial development pressure on farmland made organic farming especially attractive, a way to reap more crop value per acre in escalating land markets. Many growers simultaneously moved from commodity crops (such as cotton or sugar beets) into fresh vegetables. In the long run, these new entrants did a huge disservice to extant growers, who were eventually faced with unprecedented price competition (see Guthman forthcoming).

The gradual distancing of salad mix from its earlier movement roots was to have profound implications for the way it was produced. Todd Koons, a former chef at Chez Panisse who started his own brand of mixed greens (TKO), introduced a system of contracting with other growers for the different components of salad mix. Eventually, other salad mix marketers followed suit. Consequently, another set of growers were brought into organic production, this time because they were asked to, as marketers preferred the 'professionalism' and 'reliability' of conventional growers. Koons, along with other key growers, also improved post-harvest processes (washing, spin drying, and bagging), a key value-adding strategy but one that raised the cost of capitalization and, hence, barriers to entry.

Meanwhile, salad mix production began to stray from agro-ecological principles. Component contracting effectively encouraged mono-cultural production, at the same time it did not preclude suppliers from growing conventional crops on their other fields. Because baby salad greens are picked young, they had never wanted for pesticides. Fertility needs, however, were increasingly met with forms of soluble nitrogen such as Chilean nitrate, an allowed but contentious substance within the organic farming community, known to destroy soil micro-organisms and contribute to ground water pollution (Conway and Pretty 1991). Because baby greens could be grown quickly, growers could manage several crops per year, contributing to the logic of intensification that has characterized California's salad-growing regions. Component production could also move around the state (as well as into Mexico and Arizona), taking advantage of seasonal climatic variation, and allowing salad mix to be produced year-round. At the same time, vacuum packing increased storage life and allowed salad mix to be shipped all over the country and into Canada.

And what were working conditions like? Growers in the organic industry continued to rely on the 'time-honoured' exploitation of racialized and marginalized immigrant workers as documented in accounts of the California lettuce industry (Friedland, Barton, and Thomas 1981; Thomas 1985). Many were hired through labour contractors, a system that keeps wages low through structural over-supply and attempts to remove grower responsibility for ensuring that workers are documented (Martin 1989). To ensure 'care' in weeding, some growers encouraged use of the short-handled hoe, a practice that would have been banned in California were it not for the last minute lobbying of the organic and ornamental flower industries (CCOF 1995). As for the harvest, with hardier components (e.g. radicchio), labour could be partially mechanized, meaning that a conveyor belt was placed in the field, ensuring that each head was cut and packed at a brisk clip; more delicate components were often hand cut with stoop labour.

TKO itself was to go bankrupt in 1996, attributed to rapid expansion and misman-agement, but the future of salad mix was altered for good. Over the course of five years, organic salad mix had gone from a speciality commodity selling for over $12 per pound at retail, to just a commodity at $4 per pound. Extremely low prices squeezed many of the high-end 'niche' growers out of the market, many of whom diversified with other, newly exoticized crops. A later crackdown on food safety, after sixty-one illnesses were linked to bags of salad mix found to be tainted with *E. coli* H157:H7 (*Food Chemical News* 1998), forced others to get big (for returns to scale on more frequent inspections and more elaborate washing equipment) or get out. As a consequence, salad mix became the province of some of the largest grower–shippers in the state of California. Salinas-based Missionero and Earthbound took up the slack of TKO, buying up its land and taking on the growers it had cultivated, and developed a significant clientele of 'white table cloth chains' as well as bagged mix. Major multi-nationals such as Dole entered the retail salad mix market in force. Meanwhile, Earth-bound Farms continued to grow at a rate of at least 50 per cent a year until 1995, when a series of mergers began. Having more capital than organic market potential, Earth-bound and its new partners joined forces to create Natural Selection Foods. Thereafter, they became involved in a series of partnerships with major conventional vegetable growers, including Growers' Vegetable Express, and Tanimura and Antle. They continued to grow geographically, with at least 1,600 acres in production in Baja California where they grow off-season lettuce and tomatoes; they continued to grow in market share by buying out or contracting with some of their erstwhile competi-tors. By 2001, they had 7,000 acres in organic production; 2,000 more in transition; and were in contract with dozens of other large acre growers. Natural Selection had become the biggest supplier of speciality lettuces and the largest grower of organic produce in North America (www.ebfarm.com).

In short, salad mix was the medium of some dramatic shifts in the politics of organic production. With rampant growth in demand, the production of organic salad mix became increasingly industrialized, with scaled-up growers out-competing some of the earlier movement growers. Many of the practices they incorporated, while in keeping with organic regulations, were not in keeping with organic idioms. The association of organic salad mix with 'yuppieness' imparted even more political ambiguity to organic salad mix, here in the sphere of consumption.

Eating Salad Mix

In the early days of the organic movement, the shared meanings of organic food sup-pliers and eaters made for a reasonably coherent movement politics. Salad mix was arguably one of the factors that de-stabilized that coherence, as certain consumers began to see it as a speciality item, rather than a systemic alternative to industrialized food. Yet, it is not simply its earlier cost structure that made salad mix seemingly inaccessible to all but the privileged, a so-called niche product (cf. Allen and Sachs 1993; DeLind 1993). Eating organic salad mix was in some sense performative of an elite sensibility, albeit a rather unusual one. Organic salad mix was strongly coupled with—indeed helped to animate—the figure of the 'yuppie', the San Francisco Bay version of which was not wholly devoid of social conscience, having grown up in the tumultuous late 1960s and early 1970s, but not shorn of gentrified aspirations either. Thanks to the Alice Waters diaspora, and the introduction of ingredient-based menus, this new group of eaters obtained a keener interest in the constituent ingredients of food and how they were put together, in lieu of the haute cuisine pretension of named dishes (Kuh 2001). In that way among others, they helped usher in broader entitlement to luxurious eating. At the same time, they developed their own conceits about taste, and brought with them heightened concern with body image that in important respects mapped on to the idea of reflexive eating.

Historians of food have shown how the making of taste has been inextricably tied to the conditions and social processes that gave rise to inequitable distributions of food and variations in diet, so that varying levels and practices of food consumption have been shaped by social ranking and identity (Burnett 1966; Mennell 1986; Toussaint-Samat 1994). In that way, taste has come to play a role in defining social ranking and identity (Bourdieu 1984). In particular, taste as an aesthetic has become a sign of privilege, albeit the nature of this aesthetic has changed over time (cf. Korsmeyer 1999). So, for instance, eighteenth-century *nouvelle cuisine* helped usher the aesthetic shift to the visual, in particular 'the singularization of presentation' (Ferguson 1998: 606) that characterizes the so-called simplicity of extremely labour-intensive kitchen art (Mennell 1986).

Until the 1960s, dining out in the USA (except for the famed lunch counter or coffee shop) was largely the purview of the privileged, or the middle class enjoying a special occasion (Kuh 2001). Food habits gradually began to change in the late 1960s, with the expansion of chain restaurants, ethnic restaurants (operated by new migrants) and middle-class travel to Europe, creating new interest in fine food (Levenstein 1993). In its frequency, restaurant eating became much more democratized (Mennell 1986). Consequently, as Warde and Martens (2000) show for the UK, *where* to go and *what* to eat became the key indicators of class. And while dining out was never a conscious strategy for social display, the middle class were much more experimental and prone to evaluate the meals they enjoy in aesthetic terms. Brought to California from France by Alice Waters, new *nouvelle cuisine* or 'California cuisine' helped launch this trend in food experimentation, which evolved into a culinary eclecticism involving 'dizzying dives into novel combinations of exotic ingredients' (Levenstein 1993: 24). Northern California's young *nouveau riche* were the primary consumers of this new cuisine, indeed were in some sense defined by it, as reflected in much of the local humour of the time.[7]

Historians of food have also noted that as taste has become a performance of class, gender and nationality, the body has become a potent symbol of such difference, a way in which one's taste is displayed (Bourdieu 1984:190). For example, gastronomes—public arbiters of good taste—began to express concern about body weight as an affliction of gourmets in the early nineteenth century, contributing to the trend within *haute cuisine* towards simpler, lighter food and fewer courses (Mennell 1986: 37). Indeed, gastronomie was morally positioned as a model of discipline, control and moderation, counterpoised to the '*unreflective*' and excessive eating of the gourmand

(Ferguson 1998: 608–609, emphasis mine). During the Victorian era, the bourgeoisie emulated the aristocratic ideal of a graceful and slender body, disdainful of the need to display wealth and power ostentatiously. Women, in particular, were admonished to eat with delicacy, to take in as little as possible, and to display no desire, clearly reflecting extant mores about sexuality and establishing an early link between anorectic self-denial and privilege (Bordo 1993: 191). This is but one example by which good taste (and reflexivity) became wrapped up in self-surveillance.

Beginning in the 1960s, the links between body norms and taste found a new articulation, when breakthroughs in nutritional science combined with social changes to spur new concern over food intake, particularly in the USA. It is not only that fresh vegetables came to be routinely available on a mass-market basis, as did chicken, tofu and other so-called healthy foods (some of which were incorporated into fast food menus in not so healthy ways). New understandings of heart disease, diabetes, cancer, and so forth, coupled with a round of journalistic muck-raking, raised questions regarding the quality of the processed foods that dominated the early post-war era (Levenstein 1988). What Belasco (1989) called the counter-cuisine, which emerged out the counter-culture, emphasized the health-giving properties of relatively unprocessed food. With nutritional ideas increasingly emphasizing what should *not* be eaten, exhortations regarding excess weight shifted from the language of aesthetics to that of health (Levenstein 1993). As Levenstein argues, these new ideas about diet fit in well with the moral asceticism of the times, given newly found awareness of international poverty (e.g. Biafra, the 'other' America) and the climate of scarcity that pervaded during the early 1970s' energy crisis. Beginning in the late 1970s, body fat came to be relentlessly villainized in the popular media, to the point that 'food replaced sex as a source of guilt' (Levenstein 1993: 212).

Yet, it was more than health concerns (if notions of health can even be disassociated from other cultural constructs) that triggered a shift to near-impossible body ideals in the 1980s. Not only were the success-driven young urbanites helping to shape food tastes, they were also helping to define body ideals in ways that tended toward unprecedented self-surveillance. Indeed, it is arguable that ideologies of success were directly implicated in the new body ideal of muscular thinness. For example, some of the psychological roots of anorexia nervosa—an extreme form of self-surveillance—are over-achievement, the notion that autonomy, will, and discipline can lead to success, even the idea that toleration of pain is a sign of strength (Bordo 1993: 178; also Counihan 1999). In a striking piece, Price draws further parallels between new body norms and the political economy of the 1980s, juxtaposing the discourse of the tight, thin, sleek body to be made through diet and exercise with that of structural adjustment, e.g. 'tightening their belts', 'cutting the fat', 'shaping up' 'bloated' economies (2000: 92). This discourse was beginning to circulate at the same time that, according to Schlosser (2001), fast, cheap, convenience food was becoming the cornerstone of most working-class American diets and rates of obesity were beginning to soar, particularly among poorer people.

So it was also in this context that *nouvelle cuisine* offered such a 'spectacular challenge' to traditional restaurant cooking, with its emphasis on fresh ingredients, minimum preparation and an awareness of health considerations (Beardsworth and Keil 1997). When the exhortations of the new cuisine spilled over into North America, it is not coincidental that it was embraced by a new class of over-achievers. For a new generation of well-heeled American eaters, *nouvelle cuisine* was the perfect vehicle to mediate the deeply felt contradictions of food intake and simultaneously enjoy their new class position. It was expensive by nature of its use of the finest ingredients and labour intensiveness, a perfect combination for those whose moral sensibilities increasingly privileged environmental concerns over social ones. Simplicity of ingredients fit well with the asceticism yuppies grew up with, quite different from the stodgy *haute cuisine* of the old riche, at the same time that inventiveness satisfied the craving for difference. And as food came to be presented as art—a sensual *visual* experience—it made it possible for the body-obsessed to enjoy the dining out experience without admitting to the literally visceral sensual experience. In some sense, it made it possible to not be too rich or too thin, the phrase made famous by a New York socialite during the yuppie emergence (Levenstein 1993).

Considered this way, salad mix undoubtedly provided some interesting comfort. As *nouvelle cuisine in extremis* in its simplicity, perhaps it moderated the ambivalence of the new class position. Short of the ability to taste without swallowing (suggesting wine spit jars and aromatherapy lotions as the ultimate pleasures), salad, with its paucity of calories, was a good option for mediating body anxiety. The clincher, though, was organic food's idiomatic associations with health and environmental soundness, perhaps even opposition to fast food. As local food critic and restaurateur, Patricia Unterman (2000) was later to say, 'when you choose to buy and eat organic and sustainably raised produce, a little of this karma rubs off on you, which makes everything taste better. A lot of this local, organic stuff does taste better'. Eating organic salad mix connoted a political action in its own right, legitimizing a practice that few could afford. But the subtle conflation of aesthetic reflexivity (that of the gastronome) with political reflexivity added an extra ingredient of desire. It is surely telling that organic farmers themselves began to refer to salad mix as 'yuppie chow'.

One of the ironies of this connotation is that it necessarily limited market size to those who identified themselves in these terms. Consciously attempting to appeal to mass market tastes in order to expand the market, the major producers in the USA, including Natural Selection, started marketing non-organic salad mix under several other brand names, especially because prices no longer warranted the rigamarole of organic certification. Occasionally packaged with a packet of salad dressing, bagged salad mix was increasingly marketed as a convenience food. Pavich Family Farms, another major organic producer introduced organic iceberg lettuce, another way of de-coupling the notion of organic from yuppie. Curiously, only upscale restaurants continued to consistently modify the menu item of salad greens with the adjective 'organic', suggesting some persistence in the relationships between reflexivity, distinction and eating out.

Although only one organic commodity among many, salad mix nevertheless has borne some important changes in the politics of organic consumption. Diffused through restaurateurs, it was an elite commodity from the onset, playing into yuppie sensibilities, including the desire to control one's body shape. Then produced in relatively more ecologically sensitive ways, it is now produced largely by mass production methods, albeit reaching a broader group of consumers, many who simply want food grown without pesticides. Yet, when no longer labelled as organic, it loses all oppositional meaning. In short, the meaning and character of salad mix has become quite fractured, suggesting no easy oppositions to fast, mass-produced food.

Organic Oppositions?

Organic salad mix has come a long way from the aesthetic of the slow food gastronome, even further from the holey lettuce found at the local health food co-op. So it is striking that fast food and organic/slow food continue to be posed as binary, even organic assemblages, if you will, of taste, body type, social consciousness, class, mode of production, and so forth. Sometimes termed tendency and counter-tendency, sometimes hegemony and resistance, one of the problems with these oppositions is they impart a good deal of subjectivity on to the organic or slow food eater while the fast food eater is treated as mindless dupe. To be sure, Schlosser (also Ritzer 1993) makes the point that fast food is not an acquired taste; heavy doses of salt, fat, sugar— the stuff that rides easily on the tongue, along with the factory-made olfactory stimuli— gives it instant appeal, unreflexive appeal. In contrast, the discerning, organic food eater is imputed with much more individual agency, including the putative freedom to refuse food altogether. But who has the freedom to carve out what Ritzer calls these non-rationalized niches? At the very least, a binary framing should highlight the way in which privileged eating is intrinsically tied to impoverished eating; that what allows an aesthetic of food is disparity. The fact that many of those who eat organic food came into their wealth from some of the very processes that enabled the fast food industry's growth surely tightens the relationship between yuppie eaters and their fast food counterparts.

The uncomfortable parallel between the growth of organic food, particularly salad mix, and the contraction of particularly female body ideals provides more food for thought. Reminiscent of the opposition of gastronomy and gluttony, fast food has come to represent indulgent satiety, organic food a guiltless aesthetic. Yet, the suggestion that yuppie eaters have more control does not square with the psychopathology of anorexia nervosa that in some cases arises when sufferers cannot control their desire to control (Fraad, Resnick, and Wolff 1994). More broadly, the conflation of good taste and a slim body obtains a moral valence not in keeping with growing recognition that such body ideals often insist on neurotic self-surveillance, bulimia and/ or occasional plastic surgery for those who can afford it (Price 2000). Not only is body anxiety a questionable indicator of reflexivity, there is a good deal of slippage in eating patterns. Surely there are those who will eat a Jack N the Box® hamburger one day and a salad of *mesclun* the next. Fast food is often pitched to healthy eaters (e.g. Subway®'s advertising campaign suggesting you can lose weight and cut fat by eating fast food) and slow food is often made tasty by lavish uses of salt and butter. And while anorexia is more a stigma of the privileged, there is no easy mapping of body types on to taste or lifestyle, as Schlosser so flippantly posits.

Most importantly, to posit one assemblage as unwaveringly good and the other as altogether bad de-politicizes a potentially powerful politics of consumption. Little is it considered that organic production depends on the same systems of marginalized labour as does fast food. Or that organic salad mix led the way in convenience packaging, and is often grown out of place and out of season. Or that fast food serves women who work outside the home who are then blamed for depending on it to manage family and work. Or that slow food presumes a tremendous amount of unpaid feminized labour. Restaurants serve up their own contradictions. How else to explain the *haute* restaurant that serves organic *mesclun* and *foie gras*? The well-paid artisan cook working in tandem with the illegal immigrant bus boy? If the political importance of organic food/slow food is attention to the labour processes and ecologies by which food is produced, it is imperative to make sure that these valorized alternatives reflect alternative values.

Acknowledgements

This paper has been greatly improved thanks to the comments of Susanne Freidberg, Gail Hollander, Cindi Kurz, and for anonymous reviewers. Its final form remains the author's responsibility.

Notes

1. In an opposite logic to Fordism, the low-wage service economy, emboldened by fast food, made workers dependent on unfathomably cheap food and all of its consequences, including the food scares that could bring the entire edifice down.
2. Need I remind the reader that California was also the birthplace of the fast food industry?
3. Today California holds more organic farms than any other state in the USA (extrapolated from Klonsky and Tourte 1998), is second to Idaho in the amount of certified organic cropland, and grows 47 per cent of the certified organic vegetables and 66 per cent of certified fruit in the USA (Economic Research Service 2000).
4. Data in this section are drawn from a preliminary study done in 1995 (see Buck, Getz and Guthman 1997) and the author's dissertation research, which took place in 1997 and 1998 (Guthman 2000). The latter study included over 150 semi-structured interviews with both all-organic and mixed (i.e. both conventional and organic) growers in several regions of California. Approximately 20 per cent of these growers had at one time been involved in the production of organic salad mix. The research was supported by grants from the National Science Foundation (SBR-9711262) and the Association of American Geographers.
5. The author recognizes that in most places yuppie has come to refer to those who are wealthy, self-absorbed and *without* social conscience.
6. In actuality, pesticide use in California increased dramatically in the 1990s (Liebman 1997).
7. For example, Alice Kahn used to feature two yuppie characters named Dirk and Bree in her weekly column for Berkeley's *East Bay Express*. As Bree's name suggests, they were often the butt of food jokes. The San Francisco Mime Troupe's (misnamed given its tradition of oral political satire) show of 1988, *Ripped Van Winkle*, presents another example. Waking up from a deep sleep begun in the 1960s, the main character experiences a series of surprises in the new yuppie world of San Francisco. One of these was a menu being read by an upscale restaurant waiter with elaborate descriptions of the daily offerings.

References

Allen, P. and Sachs, C. (1993) Sustainable agriculture in the United States: engagements, silences, and possibilities for transformation, in Allen, P (ed.) *Food for the Future*. New York: John Wiley and Sons, pp. 139–167.
Baur, J.E. (1959) *The Health Seekers of Southern California, 1870–1900*. San Marino: Huntington Library.
Beardsworth, A. and Keil, T. (1997) *Sociology on the Menu*. London: Routledge.
Belasco, W.J. (1989) *Appetite for Change*. New York: Pantheon.

Bell, D. and Valentine, G. (1997) *Consuming Geographies: We Are Where We Eat*. London: Routledge.

Bordo, S. (1993) *Unbearable Weight: Feminism, Western Culture, and the Body*. Berkeley: University of California Press.

Bourdieu, P. (1984) *Distinction: a Social Critique of the Judgment of Taste*. Cambridge: Harvard University Press.

Brennan, G. (1999) 'Slow Food' followers target fast-food nation, *The San Francisco Chronicle*, 2 June.

Buck, D., Getz, C. and Guthman, J. (1997) From farm to table: the organic vegetable commodity chain of northern California, *Sociologia Ruralis* 37: 3–20.

Burnett, J. (1966) *Plenty and Want*. London: Nelson.

CCOF (1995) CCOF influences defeat of bill to ban hand weeding, *California Certified Organic Farmers Statewide Newsletter*, XII, Summer 1995: 9.

Conway, G.R. and Pretty, J.N. (1991) *Unwelcome Harvest: Agriculture and Pollution*. London: Earthscan Publications.

Counihan, C.M. (1999) *The Anthropology of Food and Body: Gender, Meaning, and Power*. New York: Routledge.

DeLind, L.B. (1993) Market niches, 'cul de sacs', and social context: alternative systems of food production, *Culture and Agriculture* 1993: 7–12.

DuPuis, M. (2000) Not in my body: rBGH and the rise of organic milk, *Agriculture and Human Values* 17: 285–295.

Economic Research Service (2000) *U.S. Organic Agriculture*. United States Department of Agriculture, <www.ers.usda.gov/whatsnew/issues/organic>.

Ferguson, P.P. (1998) A cultural field in the making: gastronomy in 19th-century France, *American Journal of Sociology* 104: 597–641.

Food Chemical News (1998) California gourmet salad processor charged with food safety violation, *Food Chemical News*, 19 January.

Fraad, H., Resnick, S. and Wolff, R. (1994) *Bringing it All Back Home: Class, Gender and Power in the Modern Household*. London: Pluto Press.

Friedland, W.H., Barton, A.E. and Thomas, R.J. (1981) *Manufacturing Green Gold*. Cambridge: Cambridge University Press.

Friedmann, H. (1993) After Midas's feast: alternative food regimes for the future, in Allen, P. (ed.) *Food for the Future*. New York: John Wiley and Sons, pp. 213–233.

Guthman, J. (1998) Regulating meaning, appropriating nature: the codification of California organic agriculture, *Antipode* 30: 135–154.

Guthman, J. (2000) Agrarian dreams? The paradox of organic farming in California, PhD dissertation, Department of Geography, University of California, Berkeley.

Guthman, J. (forthcoming) *Agrarian Dreams? The Paradox of Organic Farming in California*. Berkeley: University of California Press.

Harwood, R.A. (1990) A history of sustainable agriculture, in Edwards, C. (ed.) *Sustainable Agricultural Systems*. Ankeny: Soil and Water Conservation Society, pp. 3–19.

Henwood, D. (1998) *Wall Street: How it Works and for Whom*. London: Verso.

Hollander, G.M. (2003) Re-naturalizing sugar: narratives of place, production and consumption, *Social & Cultural Geography* 4(1): 57–72.

Klonsky, K. and Tourte, L. (1995) *Statistical Review of California's Organic Agriculture 1992–1993*. Davis: University of California Cooperative Extension.

Klonsky, K. and Tourte, L. (1998) Organic agricultural production in the United States: debates and directions, *American Journal of Agricultural Economics* 80: 1119–1124.

Korsmeyer, C. (1999) *Making Sense of Taste: Food and Philosophy*. Ithaca: Cornell University Press.

Kraus, S. (1991) Working the land with a sense of community, *San Francisco Chronicle*, 2 Oct.

Kuh, P. (2001) *The Last Days of Haute Cuisine: The Coming of Age of American Restaurants*. New York: Penguin.

Levenstein, H.A. (1988) *Revolution at the Table: The Transformation of the American Diet*. New York: Oxford University Press.

Levenstein, H.A. (1993) *Paradox of Plenty: A Social History of Eating in Modern America*. New York: Oxford University Press.

Liebman, J. (1997) *Rising Toxic Tide: Pesticide Use in California 1991–1995*. San Francisco: Californians for Pesticide Reform.

Luck, M.T. and Woodruff, S. (1931) *The Food of Twelve Families of the Professional Class*. Berkeley: University of California Press.

Martin, P.L. (1989) *The California Farm Labor Market*. Working Paper No. 4. Davis: California Institute for Rural Studies.

McManus, F. and Rickard, W. (eds) (2000) *Cooking Fresh from the Bay Area*. Hopewell: Eating Fresh Publications.

Mennell, S. (1986) *All Manners of Food: Eating and Taste in England and France from the Middle Ages to the Present*. New York: Basil Blackwell.

Miele, M. and Murdoch, J. (forthcoming) Fast food/slow food: differentiating and standardising cultures of food, in Almas, R. and Lawrence, G. (eds) *Globalisation, localisation and sustainable livelihoods*. Aldershot: Ashgate.

Morgan, K. and Murdoch, J. (2000) Organic vs. conventional agriculture: knowledge, power and innovation in the food chain, *Geoforum* 31: 159–173.

Peters, S. (1979) The land in trust: a social history of the organic farming movement, PhD dissertation, Sociology, McGill University, Montreal.

Price, P.L. (2000) No pain, no gain: bordering the hungry new world order, *Environment and Planning D: Society and Space* 18: 91–110.

Ritzer, G. (1993) *The McDonaldization of Society*. Thousand Oaks: Pine Forge Press.

Schilling, E. (1995) Organic agriculture grows up, *California Journal*, May: 21–25.

Schlosser, E. (2001) *Fast Food Nation: The Dark Side of the American Meal*. Boston: Houghton Mifflin Co.

Shrepfer, S. (1983) *The Fight to Save the Redwoods*. Madison: University of Wisconsin Press.

Sinclair, U. (1906) *The Jungle*. New York: Doubleday, Page & Co.

Starr, K. (1985) *Inventing the Dream: California Through the Progressive Era*. Oxford: Oxford University Press.

Thomas, R.J. (1985) *Citizenship, Gender, and Work*. Berkeley: University of California Press.

Toussaint-Samat, M. (1994) *History of Food*. Cambridge: Blackwell.

Unterman, P. (1998) Faith healing, *San Francisco Examiner*, 19 April.

Unterman, P. (2000) Fresh off the farm, *San Francisco Examiner*, 20 Aug.

Walker, R. (1990) The playground of US capitalism? The political economy of the San Francisco Bay Area, in Davis, M., Hiatt, S., Kennedy, M., Ruddick, S. and Sprinker, M. (eds) *Fire in the Hearth*. London: Verso, pp. 3–82.

Warde, A. and Martens, L. (2000) *Eating Out: Social Differentiation, Consumption, and Pleasure*. Cambridge: Cambridge University Press.

Whatmore, S. and Thorne, L. (1997) Nourishing networks: alternative geographies of food, in Goodman, D. and Watts, M.J. (eds) *Globalising Food: Agrarian Questions and Global Restructuring*. London: Routledge, pp. 287–304.

35

The Politics of Breastfeeding: An Advocacy Update*

Penny Van Esterik[1]

Introduction

Politics may be defined as the practice of prudent, shrewd and judicious policy. Politics is about power. How, then, can politics have anything to do with breastfeeding? When health, profits, and the empowerment of women are at stake, how could politics not be involved? Extraordinary changes in the way power is allocated in the world would be necessary for breastfeeding to flourish in this world. Many people believe such changes are impossible to make, that we have "advanced" too far into industrial capitalism to ever retreat into natural infant feeding regimes not based on profits. But even state policies influencing infant feeding practices can change, particularly when people begin to ask some very basic questions about child survival.

Advocacy on behalf of breastfeeding is incomplete and probably ineffective unless accompanied by a politically informed analysis of the obstacles to breastfeeding. These obstacles include the marketing practices of infant formula manufacturers, physician dominated medical systems, and the relationship between industry and health professionals. This relationship has resulted in widespread misinformation about breastfeeding, including false claims of the equivalence between breastmilk and artificial substitutes, and the devaluing of women's knowledge about the management of breastfeeding.

The purpose of this paper is to trace the development of infant feeding as a public policy issue over the last few decades, to examine the role of non-governmental groups (NGOs) in influencing public policy, and to place breastfeeding within the advocacy debates on the promotion of commercial breastmilk substitutes, with the modest goal of putting the voices of industry critics more directly into discussions of the politics of breastfeeding. The paper concludes with a call for anthropologists to include advocacy discourses as a valid addition to other modes of understanding and interpretation.

The Development of the Controversy

Women have always had choices about infant feeding methods. Throughout history, women have substituted animal milks or wetnursing for maternal breastfeeding.

*Originally published 1995, with updates in 2008, 2013

This is, however, the first time in history when many infants lived through these experiments long enough for others to measure the impacts on their health. This is also the first time that huge industries have promoted certain options for women, and profited from mothers' decisions not to breastfeed or to supplement breastmilk with a commercial product. It is this historical and economic fact that requires us to place breastfeeding in a broad political context.

An early presentation on the problem of bottle feeding may be traced to a Rotary Club address made by Dr. Cicely Williams in Singapore in 1939 entitled "Milk and Murder". She argued that the increased morbidity and mortality seen in Singapore infants was directly attributable to the increase in bottle feeding with inappropriate breastmilk substitutes, and the decline of breastfeeding. And she dared to call this murder—not something that happens to poor people over there, but murder. Her words were:

> If you are legal purists, you may wish me to change the title of this address to *Milk and Manslaughter*. But if your lives were embittered as mine is, by seeing day after day this massacre of the innocents by unsuitable feeding, then I believe you would feel as I do that misguided propaganda on infant feeding should be punished as the most criminal form of sedition, and that these deaths should be regarded as murder. (Williams, 1986:70)

Although conditions in other cities in the developing world may have been similar or worse than in Singapore, the voices of warning and reproach were hesitant, isolated, and easily ignored. Conditions in many inner city and Native communities in North America today may be little improved over the conditions Williams found in Singapore in 1939.

Occasionally, reports from missionaries and health workers would confirm the devastating effects of bottle feeding on infant morbidity and mortality. But these were single voices and never stimulated a social movement. And it was easy to assume that the "problem" was "over there" and thus was irrelevant to promotional practices of infant food manufacturers in developed industrial countries. Only recently has the full extent of the dangers of commercial infant formula been acknowledged or publicized (Cunningham, Jelliffe, and Jelliffe, 1991; Palmer, 1993:306–312; Walker, 1993).

From the 1930s, the promotion of breastmilk substitutes steadily increased, particularly in developed countries. In North America, competition between American pharmaceutical companies and the depression reduced the number of companies producing infant formula to three large firms—Abbott (Ross), Bristol-Myers (Mead-Johnson) and American Home Products (Wyeth) (cf. Apple, 1980). Food companies like Nestlé were already producing baby foods before the turn of the century. Both food- and drug-based companies producing infant formula expanded their markets during the post-World War II baby boom, as breastfeeding halved between 1946 and 1956 in America, dropping to 25% at hospital discharge in 1967 (Minchin, 1985:216). By that time, the birth rate in industrialized countries had dropped, and companies sought new markets in the rapidly modernizing cities of developing countries. As industry magazines reported "Bad News in Babyland" as births declined in the sixties in North America, their sales in developing countries increased, with only isolated and occasional protests from health professionals and consumer groups.

Other points of resistance to the increasing collaboration between infant formula manufacturers and health professions in North America came from mothers who wanted to breastfeed their infants and met with resistance or lack of support from the medical profession. These voices of resistance were not raised against the infant formula industry nor against the medical profession *per se*. Rather, they took the form of mother-to-mother support groups. The prime example is La Leche League, a group founded in 1956 in Chicago by breastfeeding mothers. The founding of La Leche League represented women's growing dissatisfaction with physician-directed bottle feeding regimes. While mother to mother support groups in some countries have lent support to infant food industry critics, it is important to remember that since its inception, La Leche League never directed its energies outward against infant formula companies, but rather inward toward the nursing couple. Only in recent years has the linkage been made between advocacy groups oriented towards consumer protests and mother support groups.

One phrase in a speech in 1968 by Dr. Derrick Jelliffe caught the attention of a much wider audience. He labelled the results of the commercial promotion of artificial infant feeding as "commerciogenic malnutrition." Like "Milk and Murder," this phrase grabbed headlines and became the focus for advocacy writing. By the mid-1970s, publications like the *New Internationalist* (1973) were bringing the problem to public attention. Reports such as Muller's *The Baby Killer* (1974) and the version by a Swiss group called *Nestlé Totet Babys* (Nestlé Kills Babies) prompted responses from Nestlé. In 1974, Nestlé filed libel charges in a Swiss court for five million dollars against the Third World Action Group for their publication *Nestlé Kills Babies*, leading to a widely publicized trial. The judge found the members of the group guilty of libel and fined members a nominal sum, but clearly recognized publicly the immoral and unethical conduct of Nestlé in the promotion of their infant feeding products. The libel suit and these popular publications provided focal points around which public opinion gradually developed, strengthening the efforts of advocacy groups in two complementary directions, the organization of a consumer boycott and drafting a code to regulate the promotion of baby foods (bottles, teats, and all breastmilk substitutes, not just infant formula).

Strategy for Change: Consumer Boycotts

Since the mid-1970s, a broad range of people from all walks of life, in many different parts of the world, have participated in a public debate known as the breast–bottle controversy or the baby food scandal. Changes in infant feeding practices do not occur spontaneously, nor as a result of health promotion campaigns. In North America, one catalyst for the "back to the breast" movement and a resurgence of interest in breastfeeding was a consumer movement organized by grass roots advocacy groups that drew attention to how the existence and advertising of commercial infant formula affected women's perceptions of their breasts, breastmilk, and breast-feeding. They demonstrated that there was a direct and specifiable link between changes in infant feeding practices and the promotion of commercial infant formula in developing countries. The participation of ordinary people in North America in this debate was mostly through the direct action of a consumer boycott. Without the social mobilization of the consumer boycott, the work to promote a code for the marketing of breastmilk substitutes would not have been as effective.

Both boycott groups and promoters of a code to regulate the way infant formula was being promoted and marketed argued that the decline in initiation rates and the duration of breastfeeding could be linked to the expanding promotion of breastmilk substitutes, usually by multinational food and drug corporations, and to bottle feeding generally. The boycott against Nestlé's products, and eventually those of other infant formula manufacturers generated the largest support of any grass roots consumer movement in North America, and its impact is still being felt in industry, governments, and citizen's action groups around the world. Women were the primary supporters of the boycott against Nestlé and other manufacturers of infant formula, although the movement in North America was strongly male dominated. Nevertheless, many women gained experience in analyzing the relations between corporate power and public health through their experience of working on the boycott campaign.

The groups that took on the task of challenging the infant formula companies were for the most part small, underfunded and in many cases ran on voluntary labor. While they were not the only people to recognize the problems of bottle feeding, they were the first to effectively mobilize to challenge the industries promoting it. Their success against the forces ranged against them, including powerful governments and multinational corporations, is a study in the power of co-operative networking. The importance of these small, non-governmental groups cannot be overstressed.

IBFAN (the International Baby Food Action Network) is a single-issue network of extraordinarily dedicated people—flexible, non-hierarchical, decentralized, and international in organization (Allain, 1991). IBFAN works to promote breastfeeding worldwide, eliminate irresponsible marketing of infant foods, bottles and teats, advocate implementation of the WHO/UNICEF International Code of Marketing of Breastmilk Substitutes, and monitor company compliance with the Code.

In North America and Europe, advocacy groups also formed around the issue—most notably the Interfaith Centre for Corporate Responsibility (ICCR), the Infant Formula Action Coalition (INFACT) in Canada and formerly in the United States, the Baby Milk Action Group in Britain, the Geneva Infant Feeding Association (GIFA), and the many groups in developing countries that formed part of the IBFAN network. Throughout the late 1970s and early 1980s, these groups provided evidence of the unethical marketing of infant formula in their communities. This evidence was critically important in convincing delegates to the World Health Assembly (WHA, the meetings of the World Health Organization) that a regulatory code of industry practices was necessary.

The New York based ICCR, formed in 1974, monitored multinational corporations, provided information to church groups on responsible corporate investments, and publicized cases such as the lawsuit filed by the Sisters of the Precious Blood against Bristol-Myers in 1976 for misleading stockholders about their infant formula marketing practices. Although the lawsuit was dismissed, information about the marketing of breastmilk substitutes circulated in church basements among groups interested in Third World development and justice issues, bringing a new constituency into the movement. Public education on the promotion of breastmilk substitutes often featured the 1975 film, *Bottle Babies*, a vivid portrayal of the tragic effects of bottle feeding in Kenya.

In 1977, several action networks began the campaign to boycott Nestlé products in North America. The American INFACT (later called Action for Corporate Accountability) grew out of a student group at the University of Minnesota, while the Canadian INFACT groups developed around justice ministries of the Anglican and United Churches, first in Victoria, British Columbia. These groups were linked together through IBFAN to represent the views of coalition members at international health policy meetings such as the World Health Assembly.

It was through these groups that the general public in North America was made aware of the infant formula controversy (or the breast–bottle controversy) through an increasingly sophisticated campaign involving public debates, newsletters, radio and TV shows, petitions, demonstrations, posters, buttons, and the first consumer boycott of Nestlé's products, which ended in 1984.

The advocacy position as defined by the boycott groups is quite straightforward. It argues that the makers of infant formula should not be promoting infant formula and bottle feeding in developing countries where breastfeeding is prevalent and the technology for adequate use of infant formula is absent. Advocacy groups claim that multinational corporations (like Nestlé), in their search for new markets, launched massive and unethical campaigns directed toward medical personnel and consumers that encouraged mothers in developing countries to abandon breastfeeding for a more expensive, inconvenient, technologically complex, and potentially dangerous method of infant feeding—infant formula from bottles. For poor women who have insufficient cash for infant formula, bottles, sterilization equipment, fuel, or refrigerators; who have no regular access to safe, pure drinking water; and who may be unable to read and comprehend instructions for infant formula preparation, the results are tragic. Misuse of infant formula is a major cause of malnutrition and the cycles of gastroenteritis, diarrhoea, and dehydration that lead eventually to death. Advocacy groups place part of the blame for this "commerciogenic malnutrition" on the multinational companies promoting infant formula.

The boycott groups have never advocated a ban on the sale of infant formula, although some have advocated its "demarketing" (Post, 1985). Nor were women to be pressured to breastfeed against their will, although critics of breastfeeding advocacy groups represented their aims in this light. "Better to bottle feed with love than breastfeed with reluctance" is a cliché cited by many different people convinced that protecting mothers from feelings of guilt for not breastfeeding is more important than removing obstacles to breastfeeding. The intentions of INFACT and other boycott groups are clearly stated in their demands:

1. An immediate halt to all promotion of infant formula.
2. An end to direct product promotion to the consumer, including mass media promotion and direct promotion through posters, calendars, baby care literature, baby shows, wrist bands, baby bottles, and other inducements.
3. An end to the use of company "milk nurses."
4. An end to the distribution of free samples and supplies of infant formula to hospitals, clinics, and homes of new mothers.

5. An end to promotion of infant formula to the health professions and through health care institutions.

The infant formula companies responded to the boycott groups by modifying their advertising to the public, but they were slow to meet all demands and certainly never met the spirit of the demands, namely, to stop promoting their products. They simply promoted new products such as follow-on milks for toddlers, developed new marketing strategies, and hired public relations firms to answer their critics and to improve their corporate image.

Nestlé's efforts were concentrated on trying to improve their tarnished public image by hiring a prestigious public relations firm, sending clergy glossy publications about Nestlé's contributions to infant health, and generally discrediting their critics as being merely uninformed opponents of the free enterprise system (Chetley, 1986:46, 53). Companies such as Nestlé continue their efforts to buy social respectability by sponsoring events at international medical and nutrition conferences, in addition to funding research on infant feeding.

Food boycotts have been a successful tool for social mobilization. Like all mass action social movements, the rhetoric used by advocacy groups oversimplifies the issue and seldom provides all the statistically significant evidence that both the infant formula industry and medical journals call for (cf. Gerlach, 1980). But that is the nature of advocacy communication used by all social mobilization groups. At one level of analysis, the issue is both clear and simple; it is made more complex by the many obstacles ranged against breastfeeding. Nevertheless, the words and sentiments voiced in the original advocacy documents still ring clear today.

Strategy for Change: Code Work

Another parallel stream of activities for advocacy groups concerned lobbying and attending drafting sessions on the development of a code to regulate the marketing of breastmilk substitutes. Health professionals called for establishing policy guidelines on infant feeding through United Nations groups such as the Protein-Calorie Advisory Group. In 1979, WHO and UNICEF hosted an international meeting to develop an international code regulating the marketing of breastmilk substitutes. That meeting enabled nine infant formula companies to form the International Council for Infant Food Industries (ICIFI) (Palmer, 1993:237), and to lobby UN agencies for guidelines least damaging to their profits. The code was drafted with the cooperation and consent of the infant formula industry and is very much a compromise, a minimal standard rather than the ideal.

North American advocacy groups in IBFAN "... had to divide their very scarce resources and energy between running a boycott of Nestlé and the expensive periodic visits to Geneva for the Code drafting sessions" (Allain, 1991:10). Work in the United States to document abusive marketing practices of infant formula companies was brought to a head in 1978 by the Congressional Hearings on the Marketing and Promotion of Infant Formula in the Developing Nations chaired by Edward Kennedy. During the hearings, Ballarin, a manager of Nestlé's Brazilian operations, claimed—to the amazement of the hearing—that the boycott and the campaign against the infant formula companies was really an "attack on the free world's economic system," led by "a worldwide church organization with the stated purpose of undermining the free enterprise system" (United State Congress, 1978:127).

In May of 1981, the World Health Assembly adopted a non-binding recommendation in the form of the WHO/UNICEF Code for the Marketing of Breastmilk Substitutes with a vote of 118 for, 3 abstentions, and one negative vote. The negative vote was cast by the United States, in spite of the fact that the members of the United States Senate proposed the idea of a Marketing Code and had actively participated in the drafting process. The American delegate to the WHA had been an enthusiast for the Marketing Code until shortly before the vote, when his government gave him direct orders to vote against its adoption. The Reagan White House had responded to direct lobbying from the infant formula industry (Chetley, 1986). The delegate who was ordered to reverse his nation's stance did so, and then resigned his post.

The Marketing Code is not a code of ethics but a set of rules for industry, health workers, and governments to regulate the promotion of baby foods through marketing. It covers bottles, teats, and all breastmilk substitutes, not just infant formula.

The code includes these provisions:

- No advertising of any of these products to the public.
- No free samples to mothers.
- No promotion of products in health care facilities, including the distribution of free or low-cost supplies.
- No company sales representatives to advise mothers.
- No gifts or personal samples to health workers.
- No words or pictures idealizing artificial feeding, or pictures of infants on labels of infant milk containers.
- Information to health workers should be scientific and factual.
- All information on artificial infant feeding, including that on labels, should explain the benefits of breastfeeding, and the costs and hazards associated with artificial feeding.
- Unsuitable products, such as sweetened condensed milk, should not be promoted for babies.
- Manufacturers and distributors should comply with the Code's provisions even if countries have not adopted laws or other measures.

Since then, subsequent WHA resolutions extended the ban on distribution of free and low-cost supplies to all parts of the health care system, addressed promotion to the general public, and spelled out the responsibilities of different groups in implementing the Code.

After the Code

Following the establishment of the Code, Nestlé and other infant formula companies publicly released special instructions to their marketing personnel to comply with the

Code, and asked the International Boycott Committee, a subgroup of IBFAN groups who were working on the boycott, to call it off. However, the boycott continued until 1984 when some means of monitoring company compliance with the Code could be established, and WHO member countries could draft national codes.

The advocacy groups, in the absence of national machinery, continued their monitoring role, recording and publicizing non-compliance with the Code (IBFAN, 1991). WHO and UNICEF have never monitored Code compliance, although they occasionally have taken individual companies to task. UNICEF's executive board extracted a promise that manufacturers would end all free supplies of infant formula to hospitals by the end of 1992. They did not comply. In the Philippines, for example, a law banning free supplies was passed, but was evaded by the company tactic of invoicing for milk supplies and not bothering to collect payment. In the face of this and other flagrant violations, a second boycott against Nestlé and American Home Products in the United States, and Nestlé and Milupa in Germany was launched in 1988 by groups who were part of the IBFAN network. Today, Nestlé remains under boycott because the company continues to violate the Code. However, in this era of internet communication, the boycott is more a global movement to draw attention to obstacles to breastfeeding than national campaigns.

In 1986, a World Health Resolution was adopted that acknowledged the detrimental effect of free or low-cost supplies and clarified the relevant Articles in the Code by banning such supplies. According to the resolution, free or low-cost supplies of infant formula were not to be given to hospitals. If supplies were donated to an infant, they were to be continued for as long as the infant required the milk. Hospitals that needed small quantities of infant formula for exceptional cases could buy them through the normal procurement channels. Thus, free supplies could no longer be used as sales inducements. Most of the major companies who were giving free supplies ignored the resolution, arguing that they would only stop distributing free supplies if governments brought in laws against them. However, the Code states that "Independently of other measures" manufacturers and distributors should take steps to ensure their conduct at every level conforms to the principles and aims of the Code.

At the World Health Assembly meeting in May of 1994, advocacy groups' successful lobbying reminded delegates that free and low-cost supplies of infant formula are marketing devices pure and simple, and not charity, a point made in 1989 by the Nigerian Minister of Health during the WHA. A few European countries including Ireland and Italy, and most forcefully, the United States delegation tried to defeat the resolution to end free supplies. But their efforts were thwarted by a block of African delegates and a very effective Iranian delegate who made it clear that the American position was the industry position as advocated by the International Association of Infant Food Manufacturers (IFM, the successor to ICIFI). The meeting ended with a consensus to withdraw all amendments and support the original text proposed by WHO's Executive Board to end donations of infant formula to all parts of the health care system worldwide. The question still remains how the Code and WHA resolutions can be implemented and monitored. Advocacy groups have continued to take up the challenge, and ensure that the issue does not quietly disappear from the world's conscience.

Allain refers to the "unholy alliance" (1991:15) between the medical profession and the baby food companies. Certainly the medical profession and medical associations followed rather than led the advocacy groups in their criticism of industry. Although there was resistance by some doctors to the promotion of commercial baby foods, only occasional voices of protest were heard from health professionals in the 1950s and 1960s, as infant feeding became more completely medicalized.

In the United States, continuing efforts by health professionals, including the late Derrick and Patrice Jelliffe and Michael Latham, continually brought the issue of breastfeeding and promotional practices of industry to the attention of health organizations. Internationally, the advocacy groups turned a number of physicians into more outspoken public advocates for breastfeeding, stimulating a medical consensus on the value of breastfeeding. But many university and medical school research projects on infant nutrition are funded by industry money. Doctors are beginning to speak out against practices in their own hospitals, but they may be criticized by the medical establishment for doing so. As researchers are increasingly being warned (Margolis, 1991), there is no such thing as a free lunch, nor do people bite the hand that feeds them.

For all their rhetoric, and what some have decried their so-called confrontational tactics, the advocacy groups deserve great credit for bringing about what decades of clinical observations alone failed to accomplish: public awareness and concern about the dangers of breastmilk substitutes. This struggle for corporate accountability is often recounted in development education workshops as well as marketing classes (Post, 1985). For the first time, non-governmental organizations like INFACT, IBFAN, and ICCR had a direct role in the deliberations at WHO and UNICEF in 1979 and in subsequent meetings regarding infant feeding policy. Chetley points out that in spite of industry's concerns about the "scientific integrity" of allowing popular organizations, mother's groups and consumer groups to participate, delegates to the international meetings were impressed with the contributions of the non-governmental organizations (1986:65–69). It is the NGOs that keep alive the underlying concern about corporate responsibility, human rights, and infant feeding as a justice issue.

Breastfeeding Advocacy Since the Nineties

In 1990, a global initiative sponsored by a number of bilateral and multilateral agencies resulted in the adoption of the Innocenti Declaration, which reads in part:

> As a global goal for optimal maternal and child health and nutrition, all women should be enabled to practice exclusive breastfeeding and all infants should be fed exclusively on breast milk from birth to 4–6 months of age. Thereafter, children should continue to be breastfed, while receiving appropriate and adequate complementary foods, for up to two years of age or beyond. . . . Efforts should be made to increase women's confidence in their ability to breastfeed. Such empowerment involves the removal of constraints and influences that manipulate perceptions and behavior towards breastfeeding, often by subtle and indirect means. This requires sensitivity, continued vigilance, and a responsive and comprehensive communications strategy involving all media and addressed to all levels of society. Furthermore, obstacles to breastfeeding within the health system, the workplace and the community must be eliminated. (Innocenti Declaration, 1991:271–272)[2]

This carefully worded statement is nothing less than a challenge to change the priorities of the modern world. The language stresses the empowerment of women rather than their duty to breastfeed, a change that should bring more advocates for women's health to support breastfeeding.[3]

Later in 1990, UNICEF convened a meeting to review progress on breastfeeding programs and concluded that if the Innocenti Declaration were ever to be implemented, work would have to be done by NGOs rather than governments alone. This led to the formation of an umbrella group called the World Alliance for Breastfeeding Action (WABA). WABA is a global network of organizations and individuals who are actively working to eliminate obstacles to breastfeeding and to act to implement the Innocenti Declaration. The groups include those who approach breastfeeding from different perspectives—from consumer advocates to mother support groups and lactation consultants.

As part of their social mobilization efforts to gain public support for implementing the Innocenti Declaration, WABA sponsors World Breastfeeding Week (WBW, August 1–7) to pull together the efforts of all breastfeeding advocates, governments, and the public. The first campaign, in 1992, focused on hospital practices, and was called the Baby Friendly Hospital Initiative (BFHI, 1994). This campaign established steps that hospitals should take to support breastfeeding and to implement the Innocenti Declaration, and was based on the WHO/UNICEF statement, Ten Steps to Successful Breastfeeding. By 2005, over 20,000 maternity facilities world-wide had been approved as baby-friendly (Van Esterik, 2006). The second campaign, in 1993, tackled the problem of developing Mother-Friendly Workplaces, where breastfeeding and work could be combined. The complexity of the integration of women's productive and reproductive work, and the relevant cultural and policy issues have been explored elsewhere (Van Esterik, 1992). Other WBW campaign themes have explored implementing the Code (1994), empowering women (1995), environmental linkages (1997), economic advantages of breastfeeding (1998), human rights (2000), exclusive breastfeeding (2005), complementary feeding (2006), and breastfeeding in the first hour (2007).

New Millenium: New Challenges

The public appeal of the infant formula controversy was that it was presented as a simple, solvable problem. People in North America were attracted to the campaign because it put many of their unspoken concerns about the power of multinational corporations into a clear, concrete example of exploitative behavior that could be acted upon. For some boycott groups, the solution to the problem of bottle feeding with infant formula was for multinational infant formula manufacturers to stop promoting infant formula in developing countries. When the companies agreed to abide by the conditions of the WHO/UNICEF Code and the boycott was lifted, this marked the end of the campaign, a victory of small grass roots organizations over huge corporations. As with other social movements, it was hard to sustain interest in the issue after a "victory" had been declared. But the advocacy groups and most breastfeeding supporters recognized that infant feeding decisions are not related to marketing abuse alone; rather, the issue was embedded in a set of problems that require rethinking broader questions about the status of women, corporate power over the food supply, poverty, and environmental issues, among others.

For example, the implications of bottle feeding have not been explored from an environmental perspective with the exception of the position paper by Radford (1992). The ecology and environmental justice movements have been slow to recognize breastfeeding as part of sustainable development and breastmilk as a unique under-utilized natural resource. The report of the World Commission on the Environment and Development, *Our Common Future* (1987), made no reference to nurturance or infant feeding, although economy, population, human resources, food security, energy, and industry are all discussed as part of sustainable development.

Sustainability refers to courses of action that continue without damaging the environment and causing their own obsolescence. A sustainable infant feeding policy must consider the impact of decisions a number of years in the future, rather than simply examining conditions at the present. If we compare breastfeeding and bottle feeding as modes of infant feeding, each has very different implications for sustainability; breastmilk is a renewable resource, a living product that increases in supply as demand increases. It reinforces continuity with women's natural reproductive phases and is a highly individualized process, adapting itself to the needs of infant and mother. The infant is actively empowered and "controls" its food supply.

By contrast, the bottle feeding mode—most commonly associated with infant formula even in developing countries—is a prime example of using a non-renewable resource that uses even more non-renewable resources to produce and to prepare it. It puts demands on fuel supplies and produces solid wastes—for every 3 million bottle fed babies, 450 million tins are discarded. It is a standardized product that does not take into consideration individual needs (although in practice it is not really standardized; it is commonly adulterated in its industrial production with insect parts, rat hairs, iron filings and accidental excesses of chlorine and aluminum, or adjusted by the preparer to individualize it by the addition of herbs and sugar). The bottle fed infant is passive, controlled by others, and becomes a dependent consumer from birth.

Recently scientists have identified intrinsic contamination of powdered infant formula itself. "Pathogenic micro-organisms" have been found in unopened tins and packages of powdered infant formula. In 2003, the Codex Alimentarius Commission of the FAO identified the presence of harmful bacteria such as *Enterobacter sakazakii* in powdered infant formula as a "known public health risk." The risk of potentially fatal infections appears to be highest for neonates in hospital settings.

A sustainable development policy for infant feeding must take careful note of the fact that women's capacity to breastfeed successfully is often a gauge for judging when our capacity to adapt to environmental stresses—air and water pollution, environmental toxins, radiation—has been overstrained. But women are not canaries or cows or machines. Breastfeeding promotion that treats women as mere milk producers is bound to fail, and the issue itself will be rejected by women's groups. For this reason, breastfeeding advocacy groups have been working closely with environmental groups and women's groups to reposition breastfeeding in their agendas (cf. Van Esterik 1994, 2002). For example, by agreeing on common language among different movements, we see fewer phrases like "mother's milk poisons infants," and "contaminated breastmilk" in newspaper headlines.

With our increasing knowledge about HIV/AIDS, comes another challenge for breastfeeding advocacy. HIV can be transmitted during pregnancy, childbirth, and breastfeeding by a mother who is HIV positive. Consequently in many parts of the world, women who tested positive for HIV were advised not to breastfeed, but instead to feed their newborns with artificial baby milks. But the risks of not breastfeeding were often greater than the risks of transmitting HIV; the risk that HIV can be passed through breastmilk should not undermine breastfeeding support for other mothers and infants. Combining breastfeeding and artificial baby milks appears to be the worst solution for infants. More recent evidence suggests that women who exclusively breastfeed can reduce the risk significantly, increasing HIV-free survival for their children (Iliff et al. 2005). Thus, breastfeeding advocates have to work closely with HIV/AIDS groups to ensure that policies around preventing mother to child transmission do not undermine local breastfeeding cultures.

Advocacy and Anthropology

Food advocacy is tiring work, and many anthropologists working in academic settings are not full-time activists or breastfeeding counsellors. Yet many of us have been drawn to research on breastfeeding by our personal experiences of mothering or by witnessing the commercial exploitation of women in different countries. Advocacy lessons are personal lessons because they require each and every one of us to put our values on the line—even occasionally to suspend academic canons of reserve and non-involvement, and respond emotionally to things we feel strongly about. In the study of breastfeeding, there is a convergence of different ways of knowing—a convergence of scientific knowledge, experimental knowledge, and experiential knowledge of generations of women, with moral and emotional values that all encourage action to support, protect, and promote breastfeeding. Few areas of research in anthropology encourage such integration. Further, advocacy lessons are never far from us, as advocacy action permeates different parts of our lives and links diverse causes—from the women's movement to environmental concerns.

In this climate of reflexive anthropology, and the increasing responsibility that the profession as a whole is taking in human rights debates, it is important that we clarify our relation to advocacy discourse and action as professional anthropologists and as citizens. Anthropology has a long history of applied work, but more recent and more problematic is the commitment of individual anthropologists to advocacy work (cf. Harries-Jones, 1985). But advocacy anthropology is still suspect to some in the profession. Advocacy refers to the act of interceding for or speaking on behalf of another person or group (Van Esterik, 1986), or promoting one course of action over another. This takes us beyond presentations, analyses, and discussion of evidence to recommend particular alternatives. Advocacy work draws some anthropologists into taking action with regard to well-defined goals that may best be implemented outside of academic settings. What has made this position acceptable in anthropology? First, the increasing numbers of anthropologists who have become involved in "causes" such as the rights of indigenous peoples, famine, AIDS, and women's rights, have made such commitment more visible within the profession. At the same time, the increasing involvement of indigenous peoples and special interest groups in advocating on their own behalf has resulted in anthropologists working with or for these groups.

Second, these individual and collective initiatives occurred at the same time as theoretical work arguing that there is no such thing as "scientific objectivity," and that many past examples of applied anthropology were both paternalistic and supportive of the status quo.

Third, feminist anthropology's epistemological stance on the lack of separation between theory and action justifies and even requires advocacy stances. Feminist methodology calls for explicit statements of the positionality of the author. The feminist axiom "the personal is political" breaks down past opposition between "emotional advocacy action" and "cool, detached scientific reasoning," and accepts experience and emotion as valid guides to moral stands. This is particularly true of food activism, where the line between objective and participatory approaches to food is blurred. But as advocacy groups remind us, it is politics that determines whose truth is heard.

Finally, all branches of anthropology continue to be involved in human rights debates. These efforts have changed the way that advocacy is integrated into anthropology.

Advocacy for breastfeeding is one enormous anthropology lesson. Breastfeeding is simultaneously biologically and culturally constructed, deeply embedded in social relations, and yet cannot be understood without reference to varying levels of analysis including individual, household, community, institutional, and world industrial capitalism. As much a part of self and identity as political economy; as personal as skin and as impersonal as the audit sheets of international multinational corporations, breastfeeding research requires a synthesis of multiple methods and theoretical approaches. At a time when anthropology hovers on the brink of self-reflexive nihilism and fragmentation on the one hand, and greater involvement in studying global change, internationalism, and public policy on the other (cf. Givens and Tucker, 1994), breastfeeding provides a challenging focus for holistic, biocultural, interdisciplinary research.

Notes

1. The most comprehensive history of the controversy is Andrew Chetley's, *The Politics of Baby Foods* (1986) and *Baby Milk: Destruction of a World Resource* from the Catholic Institute for International Relations (1993). I also review the history in my book, *Beyond the Breast-Bottle Controversy* (1989), and am using this opportunity to update that discussion. This update has benefited from the views and writings of Gabrielle Palmer and Elizabeth Sterken.

2. "The Innocenti Declaration was produced and adopted by participants at the WHO/UNICEF policy-makers' meeting on 'Breastfeeding in the 1990s: A Global Initiative,' co-sponsored by the United States Agency for International Development (A.I.D.) and the Swedish International Development Authority (SIDA), held at the Ospedale degli Innocenti, Florence, Italy, on 30 July–1 August 1990. The Declaration reflects the content of the original background document for the meeting and the views expressed in group and plenary sessions." (Innocenti Declaration 1991)

3. The detailed reports on the infractions of the Marketing Code by infant formula companies used to be available only in "fugitive literature"—letters and brief reports in newsletters in many languages. The violations are most accurately recorded in the "SOCs," red and blue folders published by IBFAN since 1988, documenting the State of the Code, by country and by company. Breastfeeding advocacy groups in individual countries now trace and publicize the violations on line. See for example INFACT Canada (www.infactcanada.ca), IBFAN (www.ibfan.org), and the Baby Milk Action Group in Britain (www.babymilkaction.org). WABA (www.waba.org.my) has links to these and other relevant websites. The back files of the campaign over the last thirty years are treasure troves for studying this social movement, but are not easily made to conform to academic standards of citation.

References

Allain, A. (1991). IBFAN: On the cutting edge. *Development Dialogue* offprint, April:1–36, Uppsala, Sweden.

Apple, R. (1980). To be used only under the direction of a physician: Commercial infant feeding and medical practice, 1870–1940. *Bulletin of the History of Medicine* 54:402–417.

Baby Friendly Hospital Initiative. (1994). Progress Report. See endnote 3.

Catholic Institute for International Relations. (1993). Baby Milk: Destruction of a World Resource. London: Russell Press.

Chetley, A. (1986). *The Politics of Baby Food*. London: Frances Pinter.

Cunningham, A.S., D.B. Jelliffe, and E.F.P. Jelliffe. (1991). Breast-feeding and health in the 1980s: A global epidemiologic review. *Journal of Pediatrics* 118(5):659–666.

Fildes, V. (1986). *Breasts, Bottles and Babies*. Edinburgh: Edinburgh University Press.

Gerlach, L.P. (1980). The flea and the elephant: Infant formula controversy. *Transaction* 17(6):51–57.

Givens, D., and R. Tucker. (1994). Sociocultural anthropology: The next 25 years. *Anthropology Newsletter* 35(4):1.

Harries-Jones, P. (1985). From cultural translator to advocate: Changing circles of interpretation. In *Advocacy and Anthropology*, edited by R.Paine, pp. 224–248. St. John's, Newfoundland: Institute of Social and Economic Research.

IBFAN. (1991). Breaking the rules. Penang. See endnote 3.

Iliff, P. et al. (2005). Early Exclusive Breastfeeding (EBF) reduces the risk of postnatal HIV-1 transmission and increases HIV-free survival. *AIDS* 19(7):699–708.

Innocenti Declaration. (1991). Innocenti declaration: On the protection, promotion and support of breastfeeding. Ecology of Food and Nutrition 26:271–273.

Margolis, L.H. (1991). The ethics of accepting gifts from pharmaceutical companies. *Pediatrics* 88(6):1233–1237.

Minchin, M. (1985). *Breastfeeding Matters*. Sydney, Australia: George Allen and Unwin.

Muller, M. (1974). *The Baby Killer*. London: War on Want.

Palmer, G. (1993). *The Politics of Breastfeeding*. London: Pandora Press.

Post, J. (1985). Assessing the Nestlé boycott: Corporate accountability and human rights. *California Management Review* 27(2):113–131.

Radford, A. (1992). *The Ecological Impact of Bottle Feeding*. WABA Activity Sheet #1. Penang, Malaysia.

Sussman, G.D. (1982). *Selling Mothers' Milk: The Wet-Nursing Business in France, 1715–1914*. Urbana, IL: University of Illinois Press.

UNICEF News Release. (1994). See endnote 3.

United States Congress. (1978). Marketing and promotion of infant formula in the developing nations. Washington, D.C.: U.S. Government Printing Office.

Van Esterik, P. (1986). Confronting advocacy confronting anthropology. In *Advocacy and Anthropology*, edited by R. Paine, pp. 59–77. St. John's, Newfoundland: Institute for Social and Economic Research.

—— (1989). *Beyond the Breast-Bottle Controversy*. New Brunswick, N.J.: Rutgers University Press.

—— (1992). *Women, Work and Breastfeeding*. Cornell International Nutrition Monograph No. 23. Ithaca, New York.

—— (1994). Breastfeeding and feminism. *International Journal of Gynecology and Obstetrics*. 47: S.41–54.

—— (2002). *Risks, Rights and Regulation: Communicating about Risks and Infant Feeding*. Penang: WABA.

Van Esterik, P. ed. (2006). *Celebrating the Innocenti Declaration on the Protection, Promotion and Support of Breastfeeding: Past Achievements, Present Challenges and Priority Action for Infant and Young Child Feeding*. Florence: UNICEF, Innocenti Research Centre.

Walker, M. (1993). A fresh look at the risks of artificial infant feeding. *Journal of Human Lactation* 9(2):97–107.

Williams, C. (1986). Milk and murder. In *Primary Health Care Pioneer: The Selected Works of Dr. Cicely Williams*, edited by N.Baumslag, pp. 66–70. Geneva, Switzerland: World Federation of Public Health Associations.

World Commission on Environment and Development. (1987). *Our Common Future*. New York: Oxford Press.

Addendum 2012

According to the World Health Organization (WHO), UNICEF and other medical bodies, breastfeeding is the ideal way to feed an infant. This directive emerges from the best evidence-based research to date, and is regularly reviewed and updated; the research evidence is often questioned, but nothing to date challenges the importance of breastmilk for optimal infant health. Babies should receive breastmilk exclusively for the first six months of life. After six months, they should be introduced to appropriate local complementary foods, with continued breastfeeding for two years and beyond. UNICEF's State of the World's Children report for 2011 estimates that among the 136.7 million babies born worldwide, only 32.6% are breastfeeding exclusively for the first six months of life, leaving 92 million babies who are not fed optimally.

Why are these 92 million babies not fed optimally? Why is the problem of breastfeeding still unresolved? There is no single intervention that could improve the health of more people in the world than extending or expanding exclusive breastfeeding. This is not expensive to implement; in fact it is among the most cost-effective interventions to end infant malnutrition (Jones et al. 2003).

Advocacy efforts to support breastfeeding continue, as outlined in the preceding paper. But this addendum documents the new obstacles that need to be overcome before women are fully supported to breastfeed. Even our language has to change. Advocates now avoid using the phrase, "breast is best," because it suggests that there is some other way of feeding that is almost as good as breastfeeding—much like saying that a bladder is best for storing urine, or ears are best for hearing.

The Nestlé boycott, started in 1976, remains the longest and most successful food boycott in North America. The campaigns to limit the promotion of commercial baby milks provide a clear example of how advocacy actions have moved beyond public awareness to actually change policies with regard to the role of the food industry. Breastfeeding advocates who monitor the baby food corporations have a long, successful history of engaging with the food industry. The boycott story is particularly relevant because it brought NGO players to UN policy meetings (FAO, WHO, UNICEF) and made industry participation in policy making and their strategies—particularly in relation to public–private partnerships to "solve" hunger problems—more visible. But in the 1970s and 80s, Nestlé was vulnerable to the threat to its brand image; it was relatively easy to demonize the unethical profit-driven promotional practices of the baby food industry. Today, the situation is more complex.

The Code of Marketing of Breast Milk Substitutes and subsequent World Health Assembly resolutions is still not legislated or implemented in many countries. IBFAN continues to monitor Code compliance. Advocates who lobbied for the protection of breastfeeding pressed for marketing codes rather than codes of ethics, on the assumption that industry codes of ethics in capitalist societies reflect corporate responsibility to stockholders. Codes of ethics assume that individuals in corporations are unethical if not outright evil in their intentions; instead many are trapped in conditions they cannot control. In the end, marketing codes helped corporations manage themselves better and improve their public relations work, guiding their efforts in the direction of corporate social responsibility (CSR).

The longevity of the Nestlé boycott campaign has strained NGO personnel. Groups recognize the need to educate the next generation, and have begun the process of replacing aging gray activists who got involved when they had babies many years ago, with younger people. Much of this work with youth is done on the internet.

Have direct action campaigns like boycotts and international legislation had any effects on breastfeeding rates? The food industry expects to make profits from the food it produces and markets to the general population, and baby food is no exception. Although breastfeeding advocates argue that foods for infants and young children should be exempt from market forces, realistically, this is unlikely. Clearly, boycotts and advocacy work have done little damage to the baby food industry. Their products are still actively promoted, and they are perceived as solving a variety of problems for women (better integration with mothers' work schedules, sharing child care with others, more sleep for mothers, etc.). Boycotts, however, have pushed baby food manufacturers into taking on more public corporate social responsibility work to rehabilitate their image, after boycott campaigns exposed their promotional techniques.

Global conditions of food production and distribution have increased households' access to breastmilk substitutes and baby foods; in spite of breastfeeding protection, support and promotion efforts by governments and civil society, the promotion and marketing of breastmilk substitutes and other commercial baby foods has not changed substantially. In fact, the market has increased in value and expanded since the 2001 *Euromonitor* report forecasted that the World Market for Baby Food would increase to nearly twenty billion US dollars by 2005. The estimates were a bit off. By 2006, the market was well over 25 billion US dollars and by 2011, it had grown to over 42 billion US dollars (*Euromonitor International* 2011, accessed November 8, 2011). The market has expanded at a rate that surprised even the economic experts.

While the baby food market has thrived, the same cannot be said about the financial security of households and NGOs in many parts of the global north and global south. The increase in the value of the baby food market, including the development of new product lines such as special milk products for older babies, iron-enriched formula or special formula for pre-term infants is somewhat surprising, given the emphasis on breastfeeding promotion and the financial problems of the last decade. Advocates need to resituate the infant formula controversy in the context of the global recession of 2008, and the struggle households, institutions and NGOs face during uncertain financial times. How do advocates operate in the current economic environment under changed economic conditions?

Since the recession of 2008, NGOs that support breastfeeding have had increasing difficulties raising funds. Advocacy groups like WABA and IBFAN have seen their bilateral and multilateral funding decrease dramatically over the past decade. The donor environment has changed with the growth of deregulation and the increasing influence of corporations on multilateral agencies. Now the World Bank partners with coalitions of food corporations, not with small local NGOs to solve the problems of child malnutrition. The increasing numbers of Public Private Partnerships with food corporations have drawn funding away from local infant and young child feeding support programs, and encouraged medicalized solutions to the problem of malnutrition, while discouraging humanitarian interventions that address the underlying root causes of poverty and hunger. This shift to technical interventions has resulted in the neglect of other community-based and social interventions (People's Health Movement 2011:251).

Consider GAIN (the Global Alliance for Improved Nutrition), a Public Private Partnership alliance of mostly food companies (over 600) that promote processed, fortified and ready to eat foods for the poor in developing countries. Companies such as Ajinomoto, Cargill, Coca Cola, Danone (the second largest baby food company), Kraft, Pepsico, and many others, offer "business solutions" and "enabling environments" for companies interested in nutrition for the poor. UNICEF has been particularly supportive of GAIN, lauding their "cost-effective food fortification initiatives that promise to improve the health and productivity of the poorest nations" (People's Health Movement 2011:256).

Other large coalitions between UN agencies, governments, donors, private industry, and academia such as Scaling Up Nutrition (SUN) offer even more technical solutions to the problem of malnutrition. The project, costing around 10 billion US dollars per year, is promoted through the World Bank. Of the 13 nutrition interventions in the package that national governments are encouraged to support, 10 involve commercial products such as vitamin and micronutrient supplements, and fortified foods (Horton et al. 2010:xx).These large well-funded coalitions are no longer accountable the way that a single corporation like Nestlé was. GAIN, SUN, and the UN agencies speak the same language; these business coalitions build new markets for "quick-fix" solutions such as micronutrient supplements; they also open the door to new and more complex conflicts of interest in the regulatory environment.

Many of the same food companies in GAIN and SUN have a significant influence on the Codex Alimentarius, a review committee of the UN's Food and Agriculture Organization (FAO) that sets food and infant food safety standards. At a meeting in November, 2011, 40% of meeting delegates were food industry, many representing BINGOs (business interest NGOs), and were part of (or heading) government delegations. For example, the Mexican delegation, which made many industry-friendly interventions, was 100% industry. GAIN lobbied the Codex Alimentarius to permit promotional health claims on infant food products. To curb well-documented abuses, advocates wanted more safeguards for baby foods, such as regulations that would prevent de-fatted cotton-seed flour or irradiated ingredients from being used in their manufacture; however, the industry-dominated meeting did not take up these suggestions (Press release, May 29, 2009, Baby Milk Action).

Breastfeeding advocates are becoming concerned about the increasing complexity of conflicts of interest obvious when pharmaceutical companies and food companies sit on regulatory bodies and participate in policy and research discussions. GAIN participates in UNICEF's policy making, although they have a clear conflict of interest in program implementation (People's Health Movement 2011:256). Industry funded articles, reviews of literature and ghost writing also have a strong impact on policy development. While consumer preferences for foods (not just baby foods) have always been shaped by commercial interests, breastfeeding advocates are concerned about the degree to which commercial interests are driving the marketing of new food products for infants.

Consider for example, the marketing of ready to feed therapeutic foods (RUTFs), like Plumpy'nut, a patented energy-dense peanut product made by Nutriset, a member of GAIN, for the treatment of severe acute malnutrition (SAM) of infants and young children. The products are very effective for the short-term clinic-based treatment of SAM. Advocates fear that these products are moving from therapeutic use to mass market products to prevent chronic malnutrition, before full consideration of how these products are likely to affect breastfeeding. There is evidence in places in West Africa where these "quick-fix" targeted interventions to end child malnutrition have been used, that there has been a decrease in exclusive breastfeeding, since support for breastfeeding is a low priority (People's Health Movement 2011:257). In addition, food activists ask why a French company, Nutriset, a member of GAIN, brings groundnuts from African countries, processes them in France into Plumpy'nut, sells the product to UN agencies such as UNICEF who distribute it back to infants with SAM in Africa, reaping an enormous profit in the process, instead of encouraging the local subsistence farming of ground nuts and their use for child feeding. The current compromise is to have local factories in Africa and elsewhere make some of the products where the patent is not registered. In 2009, India refused a shipment of Plumpy'nut from UNICEF because it was not consulted on the matter; local food advocates argued that Nutrimix, a micronutrient supplement product prepared in the community by womens' groups was found to be just as effective (People's Health Movement 2011:253). In the end, it is support for breastfeeding mothers that provides food security for infants throughout the world.

Food Safety

In addition to UN regulatory bodies like Codex Alimentarius, every national government has agencies to advise on the risks associated with the national food supply. While we would like to think that these food safety regulations are based on objective science, there is growing evidence of the influence of the food industry on these regulatory bodies. The International Life Sciences Institute (ILSI), an industry lobbying group for the food, chemical and pharmaceutical industry has a substantial presence on the European Food Safety Authority (EFSA), where ILSI members have encouraged industry-friendly policies concerning pesticides residues, genetically modified crops, the sweetener aspartame (made by Ajinomoto) and the use of a known endocrine disruptor, BPA (bisphenol A), in food containers (Holland et al. 2012).

Pesticides, chemical additives, and persistent organic pollutants (POPs) occur in both the general food supply and baby foods. As everyone carries chemical residues in their bodies, they also exist in breastmilk. This continues to be a concern to breastfeeding advocates, but with more collaborative work on message integration with environmental activists who understand the complexity of the issue, there are fewer sensationalist headlines about breastfeeding mothers downloading toxins into their infants. Of course, when buying processed foods, including baby foods, consumers cannot always rely on appearance, taste or smell to assess food safety; as a result we are very dependent on the independence and integrity of those who protect our food supply (cf. Kjernes et al. 2007).

The cultural perception that artificial infant feeding carries no risks is maintained very effectively by commercial marketing strategies. These strategies are more effective than campaigns that say there are no risks to eating beef or unpasteurized cheese products, for example; media amplification of risk scares many consumers away from consuming these products after they are alerted to recognize and respond to these publicized risks. Why are the risks from unpasteurized cheese more believable than risks associated with infant formula?

This is all the more difficult to understand when mothers are so sensitive to the quality of their own milk; these long standing fears have made women so skeptical of their own diet and body that they may "think" their way into insufficient milk. But at the same time, mothers may be so accepting of the quality of what they use to substitute for their breastmilk that they react to media scares by choosing another brand of infant formula, confident that the regulatory system will protect them from obvious defects like melamine in milk-based infant formula or arsenic levels in organic formula (Codex Alimentarius 2011).

Recall the bacteria, *Enterobacter sakazakii*, a pathogenic micro-organism found in unopened tins of powdered infant formula. It has not gone away, but in 2008, it was renamed *Cronobacter sakazakii*, named after Cronus, the king of the titans of Greek mythology who swallowed his own children. Recent outbreaks of infection have confirmed that the problem is not always in the mode of preparing and filling bottles, but may be intrinsic to the industrial processing of powdered infant formula itself. Infections caused by *Cronobacter sakazakii* bacteria can be fatal for newborns and young infants. In 2011, the Centers for Disease Control (CDC) were informed of 12 cases in the United States; in late November and early December, 2011, four cases were reported in four different states, resulting in two deaths and two illnesses. To date, the number of cases worldwide is unknown, since not all incidents are reported or attributed to *Cronobacter sakazakii*. The bacteria might enter infants by three routes: first, from the raw materials used in the production of the infant formula; second, from contamination following pasteurization; and third, during reconstitution. CDC laboratory tests of samples provided by the Missouri Department of Health and Senior Services found Cronobacter bacteria in an opened container of infant formula, an opened bottle of nursery water, and prepared infant formula. It is unclear how the contamination occurred, nor how many cases have been unrecognized or unreported. Walmart voluntarily recalled batches of Enfamil newborn powdered formula from 3000 stores in the United States, but as of January, 2011, the FDA had not ordered a recall. Mead Johnson Nutrition, the manufacturer, refused to disclose whether the lot was distributed to other stores. The company claims to test for *Cronobacter* in every batch. When the bacteria is found in unopened tins it is considered intrinsic contamination; when it is found in opened tins it is considered extrinsic contamination (FDA update 2011).

Testing the safety of infant formula is an ongoing process. Advocates are seeking strategies to address this problem. These include mandatory labels warning that powdered infant formula is not a sterile product; explaining how to prepare infant formula more safely by raising the temperature of water mixed with powdered infant formula; and making the dangers more widely known. Critics of breastfeeding advocacy claim that the risks of using infant formula are overblown; *Cronobacter sakazakii* and related bacteria are evidence that this criticism is unwarranted; there is no way to ensure safe formula feeding, only safer formula feeding.

Advocates for breastfeeding continue to face challenges in spite of the near universal policy support for breastfeeding in the global north and global south. In addition to lack of financial support for NGOs and health care facilities that support breastfeeding mothers, advocates must guard against creating additional pressure on mothers or make them feel guilty if they fail to breastfeed in the way they wanted, or in the manner WHO advised. This is not the intention of breastfeeding advocates who put as much attention on obtaining full maternity entitlements for women as on monitoring food companies.

Cyberactivism

What new activist strategies fit with these contemporary problems and new products? Are boycotts still effective? What is the best way to expose and reduce industry control over the marketing of baby foods? Advocacy is an ongoing process, and most work now occurs on the internet, with almost instant communication between activists in different parts of the world. Over the last decade, more advocacy work as well as breastfeeding support takes place in cyberspace. While list-serves, chat rooms, mommy blogs, and on-line journals make it easier for breastfeeding practitioners to keep in touch with each other and keep up to date with new research, material posted on-line may be unverified. Often infant formula ads and links to food companies pop up on screen while readers are searching for breastfeeding information.

Mommy blogs provide a means for sharing infant feeding experiences, as have social media sites such as Facebook. However, these sites are often full of complaints about problems faced by breastfeeding mothers. In addition, Facebook regularly removes breastfeeding photographs that women have posted of themselves, claiming the photos violate their strict nudity policy. They consider a fully exposed breast, which is rarely visible during breastfeeding, constitutes nudity. However, photos of tattooing a vagina have been spread all over the web and Facebook with no reports of warnings or removal. Following the removal of a Facebook photograph of a mother breastfeeding her two year old, breastfeeding supporters arranged a nurse-in at Facebook offices around the world in February, 2012. They argued that Facebook should be held accountable to the same community standards that allow women to breastfeed in public.

Many North American women consider breastfeeding in public to be a sensitive personal issue, and not all breastfeeding supporters care to fight for public breastfeeding or breastfeeding photographs on Facebook as a women's right. The issue underlined on-going efforts to create a breastfeeding friendly on-line community. The idea of covering up is a North American preoccupation, not one shared in other parts of the world. As one blogger suggested, "… if breastfeeding on-line offends you, put a blanket over your head".

Moving Forward with Breastfeeding Advocacy

Current advocacy work is much broader than boycotts, and includes developing the expertise to analyze and critique the broad economic conditions that underlie the food system. More young people need to commit their careers to solving the problems related to infant feeding through research as well as advocacy. Breastfeeding advocacy does not sound radical when it is treated as a personal lifestyle choice, deeply embedded in (western) maternal values. But improving conditions for mothers and infants requires altering priorities and shifting gender hierarchies in order to remove economic and social barriers to new mothers, and overturning entrenched capitalist corporate strategies that undermine breastfeeding and other nurturing relations. Denying parents the time to nurture their children, and then offering them expensive convenience foods to replace time-intensive caring practices like breastfeeding and child feeding does not "save time" for families. Breastmilk is the ultimate slow food, as local and sustainable as it gets. But sustaining breastfeeding requires radical change to the food system and the support system provided to new mothers. This is the ongoing challenge for the politics of breastfeeding advocacy.

Final Note

The following websites are regularly updated and provide the latest information on infant and young child feeding, as well as the efforts of international advocacy groups to address the newest corporate marketing techniques.
WABA, www.waba.org.my
IBFAN, www.ibfan.org
Baby Milk Action, http://info.babymilkaction.org
www.stakeholderforum.org
www.gainhealth.org
www.unicef.org

References

Codex Alimentarius. (2011). "Report of the fifth session of the codex committee on contaminants in food". The Hague, Netherlands.
FDA Update. (2011). "Joint statement by the FDA and CDC on Cronobacter Investigation", Dec. 30.
Holland, N. et al. (2012). *Conflicts on the Menu: A Decade of Industry Influence at the European Food Safety Authority (EFSA)*. Brussels: Corporate Europe Observatory.
Horton, S. et al. (2010). *Scaling Up Nutrition: What Will It Cost?* Washington, D.C.: World Bank.
Jones, G. et al. (2003). How many child deaths can we prevent this year? *Lancet* 362.9377:65–71.
Kjernes, U. et al. (2007). *Trust in Food: A Comparative and Institutional Analysis*. New York: Palgrave Macmillan.
People's Health Movement. (2011). *Global Health Watch 3*. London: Zed Press.

36

The Political Economy of Food Aid in an Era of Agricultural Biotechnology*

Jennifer Clapp

In 2002 the U.S. sent significant quantities of food aid, in the form of whole kernel maize, to southern Africa in response to the looming famine in the drought stricken region. It soon became apparent that the aid contained genetically modified organisms (GMOs), though the recipients had not been notified prior to the shipments being sent. Many southern African countries initially refused to accept the GM food aid, partly as a health precaution, and partly on the grounds that it could contaminate their own crops, thus hurting potential future exports to Europe. A number of the countries eventually accepted the food aid provided it was milled first, but Zambia continued to refuse even the milled maize. The U.S. argued that it could not supply non-genetically modified (GM) food aid, and it refused to pay for the milling. The U.S. then blamed Europe's moratorium on imports of GM foods and seed for contributing to hunger in southern Africa.

This incident highlights a new aspect of the recent global predicament over how the international movement of GMOs should be governed. While there has been much analysis of this question with respect to commercial trade in recent years, particularly regarding the adoption of the biosafety protocol[1], the literature on food aid has not kept up with these new developments. Recent academic analyses of food aid have paid little attention to the question of GMOs. The literature on food aid has focused mainly on the motivations for donating food aid, and its potential as a development tool. Some have argued that while economic and political considerations are present to some degree in the motivation for giving food aid, today it is mainly given as part of a development regime that aims primarily to promote food security and rural development rather than as a means to serve donor countries' domestic economic and political interests.[2]

In light of the changes in global agriculture over the past decade, especially the rise of the U.S. as a major producer of GM crops, it is important to re-examine the political economy of food aid. There appear to be strong economic motivations for the U.S. to pursue the food aid policy described above, as well as scientific motivations, not addressed by the earlier food aid literature. Both of these motivations are highly politicized. Europe has not followed the lead of the U.S. on GM food aid policy. The divergence of the policies of the EU and the U.S. on this issue may well lead to interesting politics in the years to come in the international battle over GMOs. Only this time, the

*Originally published 2005

debate looks set to be played out globally, with some of the world's poorest countries as unwitting participants in the conflict.

Why Revisit Food Aid Politics?

The modern era of food aid was instituted in the U.S. in 1954, with the passage of U.S. Public Law (PL) 480. Since that time food aid has been an important feature of U.S. assistance to developing countries, though its role has changed over time. In the 1950s food aid accounted for nearly a third of U.S. agricultural exports, whereas in the mid 1990s it was closer to 6 percent.[3] Food aid under PL 480 is given under different categories of assistance. Title I is government to government aid in the form of concessional sales with the express aim of opening new markets for U.S. grain. Title II is grant food aid distributed in emergencies. Such aid can be distributed via NGOs and the World Food Program. Title III is government to government grants of food aid for development activities.[4]

From its origins, U.S. food aid was largely seen as a multi-purpose tool. On the surface, the idea of the PL 480 was to provide the world's food deficit countries with food from the U.S., as part of a broader humanitarian effort. It was also clearly a mechanism for surplus disposal and export promotion in the U.S. It created a market for surplus food and as such it had the effect of raising U.S. domestic prices for grain. Further, shipping free or concessionally-priced U.S. grain to poor countries, it was hoped, would create new markets in the future for commercially traded U.S. grain.[5] U.S. food aid was, however, soon seen as a political tool as well. The U.S. had even gone so far as to amend PL 480 in the 1960s to explicitly tie the donation of food aid to political goals, in particular to favor non-communist countries.[6] Other countries followed the U.S. in giving food aid, including Canada, which began its program in the 1950s, and the European Economic Community, which began to give food aid in the late 1960s.[7] Canada and the European donors have been less overtly political and economic in their rationale for food aid, though some surplus disposal mechanism has been part of their food aid donations at various times.

The World Food Program (WFP) of the United Nations was set up in 1963 as a multilateral channel for food aid from donor countries. In its early years the WFP distributed around 10 percent of food aid, while today nearly 50 percent of all food aid is channeled through the WFP.[8] The Food Aid Convention (FAC) was first established in 1968 as part of the Kennedy Round of GATT negotiations, and was attached to the International Wheat Trade Convention.[9] The FAC members are the donor countries, and the agreement sets out minimum amounts of food aid per year to be given by each donor (denominated in tonnes of wheat). The FAC, re-negotiated periodically, now stipulates that food aid can be given either in-kind or in cash equivalent, and other commodities apart from wheat can be given (but they are still measured in wheat equivalents). Today the donor members of the FAC include Argentina, Australia, Canada, the European Community and its member states, Japan, Norway, Switzerland, and the United States.[10] From the early days of food aid to the present, the U.S. has remained the principal donor country, and gives its aid primarily in-kind. Other donors have over the past decade increasingly given their food aid in the form of cash, which is directed toward third country purchases or local purchases in the recipient region.

Since the 1980s food aid policies in the U.S. have been reformed significantly, with the overt political goals removed from the PL 480. And in the mid-1990s the surplus of grain in the U.S. diminished, making the surplus disposal element of food aid appear to be less significant than it was in the past.[11] In the European Union, food aid policies since the 1990s have focused on giving aid in the form of cash to finance food distribution programs with local or third party sources of the food, rather than in-kind. This policy has been reinforced by the EU's regulation requiring the shift toward cash-based food aid in 1996.[12] This policy on the part of the EU was largely in response to studies which showed that cash spent on local purchases of food in aid recipient regions boosts the local economies and allows for much more flexibility in terms of sourcing culturally appropriate foods.[13]

Because of these policy shifts, some have argued that food aid by the late 1980s and early 1990s had in fact become largely a development tool, with the motivations for donating food governed more by the existence of an international regime (and desire to cooperate) than by donor economic and political considerations, which is in line with a liberal institutionalist perspective on international relations.[14] In other words, a "depoliticized" food aid regime was seen to have emerged, which was not merely serving the interests of the donors, but rather was promoting international development. This was especially the case for European donors. Uvin argued that by the early 1990s most EU food aid and about 60 percent of food aid from the U.S. was clearly not driven by economic or political motivations.[15] Other, more recent studies have made similar arguments. Eric Neumayer, for example, argues that in the 1990s while U.S. economic and military-strategic interests had some influence on food aid donations for program, or longer term food aid, it is an insignificant influence on emergency relief.[16]

In light of the development of agricultural biotechnology in recent years, I argue that it is important to re-examine the political economy of food aid. Important factors influencing donor motivations in an age of agricultural biotechnology are not adequately considered in the food aid literature. Economic factors may once again be key motivating factors for food aid policy. These factors are especially important to consider given the growing corporate concentration in the agricultural biotechnology sector and its close ties with U.S. government agencies, as well as the U.S. dispute with the EU over its 1998–2004 moratorium on GMOs. Moreover, new factors that may influence food aid policy must also be considered, such as the scientific debates over the safety of genetically modified food. These factors appear to be influencing food aid policies on the part of both donors and recipients, and they are highly political.

GMOs in Food Aid

GMOs have been present in food aid since GM soy and maize were initially approved for production in the U.S. in the mid-1990s. Its presence in food aid was inevitable for a number of reasons. U.S. food aid is predominantly given in-kind and is made up of food (mainly wheat, corn and soy) grown in the U.S. The U.S. is by far the largest producer of GM crops, accounting for over 60 percent of the global acreage planted with GM varieties. Between 1996 and 2003 the global area planted with GM crops increased by 40 fold, in 2003 covering some 67.7 million hectares.[17] In 2002 some three-quarters of the soy and over a third of maize grown in the U.S. were GM varieties.[18] Moreover, there is not a segregated system for GM and non-GM crops in the U.S., and cross contamination has been widespread. This is important, as the U.S. accounts for 60 percent of all food aid donations.

Though negotiations began in 1995 on a protocol on biosafety under the Convention on Biodiversity to address the safety issues related to trade in GMOs, little attention was paid to their presence in food aid transactions at that time. It is not surprising, then, that when it was discovered that some food aid donations contained GMOs in 2000, many were caught unaware. Both USAID and the WFP had sent shipments of food aid containing GMOs, amounting to some 3.5 million tonnes per year.[19] Such shipments were often in contravention of the national regulations in the recipient country.

Ecuador was the first known developing country to receive food aid containing GMOs in a shipment of soy from the U.S. and channeled through the WFP. The product was eventually destroyed following complaints by Ecuador.[20] There were also cases of GMOs being sent in food aid shipments to Sudan and India in 2000. In 2001 GMO soy was found in food aid shipments sent to Columbia and Uganda. Food aid maize from the U.S. containing GMOs was also reportedly sent to Bolivia in 2002, despite the fact that the country had a moratorium in place on the import of GMO crops. The GMOs found in the Bolivian aid contained StarLink corn, which is a modified form of corn that was not approved in the U.S. for human consumption (it was approved as animal feed), but which nonetheless managed to find its way into the human food system in the U.S. in the fall of 2000. NGOs claim that despite the fact that when StarLink was found in the U.S. food supply it was immediately removed from the market, the U.S. did little to remove the maize from Bolivia. In 2002 Nicaragua and Guatemala were also sent GM corn seed as food aid from the WFP. This caused a stir in Nicaragua in particular, as that country is a centre of origin for corn.[21]

By mid-2002, there were enough incidents of GMO food aid to have made the donors fully aware of the issue. Recipient countries expressed concern about the potential health and environmental impacts of GMOs, including allergenicity, and out-crossing of GMOs with wild relatives (if the grains are planted rather than eaten) which could reduce biodiversity by contaminating and driving out local varieties. Once GMOs are released into an environment, they are difficult, if not impossible, to remove. Food aid, when given in whole grain form, is often planted by local farmers, who may have exhausted their seed supply as food in times of crisis.[22] The fact that GM crops have not been approved in many countries, including in the European Union which had placed a moratorium on their imports and new approvals of GM crops in 1998, fueled many of these concerns, especially for those countries which have export markets in the EU.

Until mid-2002 the food aid shipments identified as containing GMOs were mainly to areas, which, while in food deficit, were not facing an acute food shortage. This changed in mid-2002 with the looming famine in southern Africa. Some 14 million people in 6 countries faced imminent food shortages and famine at that time. The situation was seen to have been precipitated by a number of factors. Drought and floods were identified as one of the immediate causes. However, underlying factors were just as important. These include the high prevalence of HIV/AIDs in the region, as well as conflict in Angola (and refugees from Angola in neighbouring countries), domestic agricultural policies, as well as the impacts of trade liberalization under structural adjustment in some countries in the region.[23] It was the worst food shortage faced by the region in 50 years.

In response to this crisis the U.S. sent 500,000 tonnes of maize in whole kernel form to the region in the summer and fall of 2002 as food aid. It was estimated by the WFP that around 75 percent of food aid to the region at that time contained GMOs.[24] The countries that received the shipments were Zambia, Zimbabwe, Malawi, Swaziland, Mozambique and Lesotho. The aid was channeled through the WFP as well as NGOs. When the countries discovered that the aid contained GMOs, they were forced to consider whether they wanted to accept the aid. Zimbabwe and Zambia said they would not accept the food aid at all, while Mozambique, Swaziland and Lesotho said they would accept it if it was milled first. Malawi accepted it with strict monitoring to ensure that its farmers do not plant it. Zimbabwe eventually said it would accept it if it was milled and labelled first.[25]

Zambia stood firm in not accepting it for its own people. It did eventually accept it in milled form but only for the 130,000 Angolan refugees in camps within its borders, but not for the general population.[26] Zambia expressed its concern that any health problems that might arise from eating GMOs would be too costly for the country to address. Since the Zambian diet consists of far more maize than the diets of North American consumers, such health problems may not be foreseen. Moreover, Zambia does have some maize exports to Europe, and contamination of its maize with GMOs could affect its exports if the EU moratorium continues.[27] The WFP scrambled to find non-GMO aid for Zambia, which had some 3 million people at risk of starvation. In the end, the WFP was only able to source about one-half of the necessary 21,000 tonnes of maize needed for Zambia.[28]

The WFP responded by saying that it was impossible to mobilize non-GMO food aid fast enough. The WFP made it clear that it respected the right of the countries to refuse to accept the aid, and it did what it could to organize the milling of the maize for those countries that would accept it in that form, and to source non-GMO aid for Zambia. The WFP had to quickly arrange local milling, and in the case of Zambia, it had to remove shipments which had already been delivered. The milling did provide the WFP with the ability to fortify the grain to raise its micronutrient content, however, which was seen as an unexpected benefit. Further, the WFP did manage to solicit donations from non-traditional donors of aid for food, including a number of developing countries.[29]

The response of the U.S. was much more defensive. The U.S. refused to mill the maize before sending it to the region, claiming that it was too expensive to do so, raising the cost of the food by as much as 25 percent, and reducing its shelf life. It also initially refused to send non-GM varieties of corn to the region, claiming that it was impossible to source non-GM crops from the U.S. It refused to give cash instead of in-kind aid, on the grounds that it has traditionally given in-kind aid, and has done so for 50 years. The U.S. did, however, stress that it would respect the wishes of the countries that did not want GMO food aid sent to them. The U.S. position was clearly spelled out in a USAID website "questions and answers" on the GMO food aid crisis.[30]

The U.S. did eventually give Zambia a donation of GM-free maize of some 30,000 tonnes, however, after heavy international pressure to do so.[31]

The U.S. also blamed Europe for the crisis, saying that its moratorium on approval of seeds and foods containing GMOs was stalling efforts to promote food security.[32] In the midst of the African crisis the U.S. began to seriously consider launching a formal complaint at the WTO over the EU's moratorium on GMOs, claiming that it was in contravention of WTO rules. Though the WTO rules do allow countries to ban imports of a product on food safety concerns while the country seeks further scientific evidence, the U.S. argued that five years was plenty of time and that no such evidence had been gathered. The U.S. was concerned that this position of the EU was influencing too many countries, including those in Africa.[33]

Throughout the fall of 2002 and early in 2003 the U.S. put pressure on Europe to remove its moratorium. The U.S. finally launched the formal complaint against the EU at the WTO in May 2003. Argentina and Canada joined the formal challenge.[34] At the time U.S. President Bush stated: "European governments should join—not hinder—the great cause of ending hunger in Africa."[35] Egypt was initially listed as a co-complainant, but it pulled out. Though Egypt does have an active agricultural bio-technology research program, it withdrew from the dispute because Europe is a very important market for its exports of fresh fruits and vegetables. The U.S. had hoped that having Egypt on board would help it to drive the point home that GM crops are beneficial to Africa. The U.S. retaliated against Egypt for its withdrawal by pulling out of talks on a free trade agreement with that country.[36]

When the U.S. launched the dispute, the European Union issued a press release stating its regret over the U.S. decision to take action on this case. It criticized the U.S. for using the African countries' refusal of GM food aid to pressure the EU:

> The European Commission finds it unacceptable that such legitimate concerns are used by the U.S. against the EU policy on GMOs . . . Food aid to starving populations should be about meeting the urgent humanitarian needs of those who are in need. It should not be about trying to advance the case for GM food abroad.[37]

In the midst of the southern African crisis the European Commission specifically requested the WFP to only purchase non-GM maize as food aid with the money the EU donates for such assistance.[38]

In mid-2003, another dispute over GM food aid emerged. Sudan had been pressured by the U.S. to accept GM food aid, despite its recently passed legislation that requires food aid to be certified GM-free. In response to U.S. pressure, the Sudan issued a temporary six month waiver to this legislation in order to give the U.S. more time to source GM-free food aid. In March 2004, however, the U.S. threatened to cut the Sudan off from food aid completely.[39] This prompted the Sudan to extend the waiver to early 2005.

Unclear Rules on International Trade in GMOs

How is it that such massive shipments of GM food aid could have been sent without the recipients knowing about it before it was sent? The rules regarding trade in GMOs were unclear at both the global and local levels between the mid 1990s and 2003. This was the very period when much of the controversy over GMO food aid was at its highest.

As of mid-2002 when the southern African crisis erupted, only a few developing countries had any domestic legislation dealing with imports of GMOs, let alone GMO food aid. The only sub-Saharan African countries with biosafety laws in place at that time were South Africa and Zimbabwe, though a number have since begun to develop policies dealing with the import of genetically modified organisms. Zimbabwe had a Biosafety board to advise on GMOs, but it has not approved any GM crops for commercial release. South Africa is the only sub-Saharan African country which has approved the commercial planting of genetically modified crops. In July 2001 the Organization of African Unity (OAU, now the African Union) endorsed a Model Law on Safety in Biotechnology which takes a precautionary approach to biotechnology and calls for clear labeling and identification of imports of GMOs. This model legislation was designed as guidance for countries in formulating their own national laws on biosafety as well as a way to develop an Africa-wide system for biosafety. As of 2003, no countries in Africa had yet adopted the model law into its legislation.[40]

In response to the southern African crisis in 2002, the Southern African Development Community (SADC) established an advisory committee to set out guidelines for policy on GMOs in the region. These guidelines stipulate that "food aid that contains or may contain GMOs has to be delivered with the prior informed consent of the recipient country and that shipments must be labeled."[41] But such guidelines were not available at the time of the crisis. Other regional responses include efforts by the Common Market for Eastern and Southern Africa (COMESA) to develop a regional policy on GMOs, including food aid. And the New Partnership for Africa's Development (NEPAD) decided in mid-2003 to establish a panel to advise African countries on biosafety and biotechnology as a means to try to harmonize regulations on these issues across Africa.[42]

At the international level, rules on biosafety and trade in GMOs were also not all that clear prior to 2003. The Cartagena Protocol on Biosafety, which governs trade in GMOs, was negotiated between 1995 and 2000 (when it was adopted), but was not in legal force until September 2003.[43] The Protocol's rules state that GMOs (living modified organisms) intended for release into the environment (seeds) in the importing country, are subject to a formal Advanced Informed Agreement (AIA) procedure for the first international transboundary movement to a country. Importing countries can reject these if they wish, based on risk assessment. Genetically modified commodities (living modified organisms intended for food, feed or processing) are exempted from the formal AIA procedure, and instead are subject to a separate form of notification, in the form of a Biosafety Clearing House, an internet-based database where exporters are required to note whether shipments of such commodities "may contain GMOs." Importers can also reject such shipments, based on risk assessment. In both cases, parties are given the right to make decisions on imports on the basis of precaution in cases where full scientific certainty is lacking.[44] The food aid donations shipped prior to the Protocol's entry into force were not covered by these rules. And now that it is in force, these rules only apply to those countries that have signed and ratified the agreement. The U.S. and Canada, two of the major food aid donors which grow significant quantities of GMOs, have not yet ratified the Protocol, and thus are not bound by its rules.

The Codex Alimentarius Commission, which sets voluntary international guidelines on food standards, was from the late 1990s trying to address questions of biotechnology and food safety. In 1999 the Codex established a special Task Force on Biotechnology to address the wider concerns expressed about biotechnology and food safety, especially those related to risk analysis. The Task Force only released its guidelines in mid-2003. Though they are voluntary, the standards are considered a benchmark for international trade under the WTO. The biotechnology guidelines adopted include safety evaluations prior to marketing of GM products, and measures to ensure traceability in case a GM product needs to be recalled.[45] But because these guidelines were not in place at the time of the food crisis in southern Africa, nothing was done to ensure these guidelines were followed for food aid.

The WFP did not set an explicit policy on how to deal with GMOs until mid-2003. Its policy has long been to give food aid to countries in food deficit if the food met requirements for food safety by both the donor and the recipient. But if neither the recipient nor the donor had a policy of notification, it was difficult for the WFP to keep track of them. It defended its lack of a GMO policy prior to that date by stating that "none of the international bodies charged with dealing with foods derived from biotechnology had ever requested that the Programme handle GM/biotech commodities in any special manner for either health or environmental reasons."[46] Because of the media attention to the issue, and claims that the WFP was negligent, the WFP decided to establish a formal policy for dealing with GMOs in food aid in 2002, which was finalized in 2003. The new policy asks recipient country offices of the WFP to be aware of and comply with national regulations regarding GM food imports. It also maintains its original policy that it will only provide food as aid which is approved as safe in both donor and recipient nations. Countries that clearly state that they do not wish to receive GM food aid will have their wishes respected. The WFP stated that it will still accept GM food aid from donors, but will also respect the wishes of donors who give cash in lieu of in-kind aid if they request that the money not be spent on GM food.[47]

Unpacking Motivations for GM Food Aid Policy

What explains the widely divergent positions on GM food aid on the part of the donors, specifically the U.S. and the EU, and the rejections by the recipient countries? As mentioned above, much of the food aid literature sees the current donor motivation for giving food aid as being driven not so much by economic and political goals as had been the case in the past, especially in the case of emergency aid. In this section I argue that we need to revisit this issue. In an age of agricultural biotechnology, new issues must be considered as having an influence on food aid policy, primarily the scientific debate over the safety of GM food. Further, economic and political incentives, inextricably tied to corporate interests in agricultural biotechnology, appear once again to be important factors behind the U.S. position on GM food aid in particular.

Debates over the Science of GMOs: Differing Interpretations of Risk and Precaution

The southern African crisis fuelled an already existing scientific debate over the safety of GMOs and their role in promoting food security. The debate has largely been over whether there is sufficient risk associated with the planting and consumption of GM crops and foods to warrant precaution with respect to their adoption. In the media accounts of the GM food aid incidents in southern Africa, this scientific dimension has tended to dominate the explanations for the policies pursued by the donors and the recipients.

The North American position on the safety of GM foods and crops is that there is minimal risk attached to them, and that because of this a precautionary approach in their adoption is not warranted. In both the U.S. and in Canada, regulatory procedures for GMOs are built on the notion that if the developer of a genetically-modified crop or food can demonstrate that it is "substantially equivalent" to a conventional counterpart, the GM crop or food does not require an extensive risk assessment prior to its approval.[48] Ongoing scientific uncertainty with respect to the risks of GMOs does not automatically invoke a precautionary approach in these countries. In other words, agricultural biotechnology products are assumed to be innocent until proven guilty. It is further argued that the benefits of GM crops, in terms of higher yields and easier management of weeds, far outweigh the (known) risks associated with them.[49] The U.S. and Canada view their approach to the regulation of agricultural biotechnology as being firmly grounded in "sound science."

The approach to regulating agricultural biotechnology products is very different in the EU and in many developing countries. The EU's interpretation of the potential risks associated with GMOs is much more precautionary. It views the existence of scientific uncertainty with respect to the safety of agricultural biotechnology as enough reason to take more time to evaluate the full range of potential risks associated with these products prior to their approval. Before such products can be approved, they must be subject to a rigorous scientific risk assessment.[50] In this sense, agricultural biotechnology products are assumed to be guilty until proven innocent. Many developing countries lack a regulatory structure for approval of agricultural biotechnology products, and for this reason they have tended to favor the EU approach which applies precaution in the face of scientific uncertainty. Further, there is widespread sentiment in Europe and in many developing countries that the potential risks, such as the potential for out-crossing with wild relatives and creating new allergens, do not outweigh the possible benefits, which reinforces the pre-cautionary mood in those countries.

The different interpretations of the science and risks of GMOs go some way to explaining the widely divergent positions with respect to GM food aid amongst the U.S., the EU, and the recipient countries. The hostility on the part of the U.S. toward those countries that rejected the GM food aid, and placing of the blame on Europe, are partly products of these different viewpoints. In particular, the U.S. sees the EU's regulatory system, which is much more precautionary, as being too "emotional" and not scientifically based. The U.S. would much rather see its own regulatory style, rather than the EU approach, adopted in developing countries that currently lack a regulatory framework. This attitude on the part of the U.S. can be seen in the comments made by U.S. Senator Chuck Grassley, at a speech to the Congressional Leadership Institute in March 2003, just prior to the launch of the trade dispute against the EU:

> By refusing to adopt scientifically based laws regarding biotechnology, the EU has fed the myth that biotech crops are somehow dangerous . . . The European Union's lack of science based biotech laws is unacceptable, and is threatening the health of millions of Africans.[51]

The refusal of the GM food aid on the part of the southern African countries can also be seen as a reflection of their position in the scientific debate, as many of the comments made by African leaders when rejecting the aid made this specific link. For example, Zambian president Levy Mwanawasa expressed his concern that GM food aid was "poison", stating "If it is safe, then we will give it to our people. But if it is not, then we would rather starve than get something toxic."[52] The Zambian government did authorize a scientific delegation to study the issue, which was sponsored by the U.S. government and several European countries. This delegation traveled to South Africa, a number of European countries, and the U.S. The eventual report from the delegation, which came in the fall of 2002, cautioned against the acceptance of GMOs in Zambia, much to the disappointment of the U.S.[53]

Economic Motivations

While the different interpretations of risk and precaution are clearly relevant in explaining motivations for GM food aid policy, they are not the only important factors. In an age of agricultural biotechnology, it appears that economic considerations are re-emerging as explanatory factors for food aid policy, at least on the part of the U.S.

Throughout the history of food aid, surplus disposal has remained important for the U.S.[54] Because stocks have declined over the past 50 years, and over the past decade in particular, however, some say that surplus disposal is no longer as important as it once was.[55] But the advent of GM food aid may be reviving and reinforcing the surplus disposal aspect of U.S. food aid. The European moratorium on imports of GMOs has meant a significant loss of markets for U.S. grain. The U.S. has lost around U.S.$300 million *per year* in sales of maize to Europe, for example, since 1998.[56] Some 35 countries, comprising half of the world's population, have rejected GM technology, and this is also closing the market opportunities for GMO-producing countries to export their products. In addition to the European Union, Australia, Japan, China, Indonesia and Saudi Arabia, also refuse to approve most agricultural biotechnology for domestic use and import.[57] Because of the loss of these markets, the U.S. may well be looking for other outlets for its GM maize.

The inability to find export markets for its GM grain may well be a principal reason why the U.S. continues to insist on giving its food aid in-kind, rather than in the form of cash. Both the FAC and the WFP encourage food aid donations in cash rather than in-kind, and the EU has been pushing to have cash-only donations of food aid incorporated into WTO rules. In the case of southern Africa, the U.S. was the only donor that gave food aid in kind rather than as cash.[58] This may be in part due to the preferences of the strong grain lobby in the U.S. In a letter to the U.S. trade representative on this issue, the National Wheat Growers Association stated: "We wish to assure you that producers across the nation are strong supporters of humanitarian programs, but will not be willing to support cash-only programs."[59]

A second potential economic motivation for the U.S. in giving GM food aid, not unrelated to surplus disposal, is to subsidize the production and sale of GM crops, as well as the agricultural biotechnology sector more broadly, which is dominated by U.S. transnational corporations (TNCs). Some 80 percent of funds for the PL 480 program are in actual fact spent in the U.S.[60] In 2000 it was reported that Archer Daniels Midland and Cargill, two of the largest grain trading corporations, were granted a third of all food aid contracts in the U.S. in 1999, worth some U.S.$140 million.[61] The U.S. Department of Agriculture (USDA), which is responsible for regulating biotechnology in the U.S. and which also oversees the Title I food aid, works in close cooperation with the agricultural biotechnology industry.[62] One example of this is the 2002 U.S. Farm Bill which provided funding for the USDA to set up a biotechnology and agricultural trade program with the aim "to remove, resolve or mitigate significant regulatory non-tariff barriers to the export of United States agricultural commodities."[63] USAID, which is responsible for Title II and Title III food aid, also actively promotes the adoption of agricultural biotechnology in the developing world through educational programs, giving some U.S.$100 million for that purpose in recent years.[64] This includes USAID funding for private-public partnerships such as the African Agricultural Technology Foundation[65] and the Agricultural Biotechnology Support Project[66] both of which have heavy participation from TNCs in the agricultural biotechnology industry. These initiatives seek to promote the use of agricultural biotechnology in the developing world through research, education and training, and they also acknowledge that they hope such efforts will open new markets in the future.[67]

Critics see such efforts as a means by which the U.S. is trying to pave the way for the introduction of pro-GM legislation to facilitate the export of GM crops and seeds around the world.[68] For many the position of the U.S. in the southern African crisis, especially its refusal to mill the GM grain and its attack on Europe's regulatory structure, was seen as a deliberate strategy to spread GMOs as far and as wide as possible, in order to break the remaining resistance to the technology.[69]

Economic considerations in the EU must also be taken into account in unpacking donor motivations. The EU's position on GM food aid is very much tied up in the WTO trade dispute over GMOs more broadly. The U.S. had been pressuring the EU to lift its moratorium on approvals of GM crops and foods before the crisis hit in southern Africa, and so it is not surprising that the EU position was in opposition to that of the U.S. Tied up in this broader dispute is the question of export markets for the EU as well. It may be that the EU is seeking to solidify trade relations with developing countries by creating a non-GM market which would exclude the U.S. The EU has also been pushing for several years now for cash-only food aid to be written into WTO rules as part of the ongoing talks on the revision of the WTO's Agreement on Agriculture. The EU sees the U.S. in-kind food aid, and Title I sales of food aid, as unfair subsidies to the U.S. agricultural industry, and wishes to see these removed in exchange for its own subsidy reductions. This helps to explain the EU's criticism of in-kind food aid.[70]

On the recipient side, economic considerations are also important in helping to explain their acceptance or rejection of food aid. The southern African countries were concerned about their export prospects with the EU if they accepted GM food aid in whole grain form. If GM food aid were planted and crossed with local varieties, this could affect exports of maize. Zambia, for example, exports some maize to European countries, and Zambia and other countries in the region did not want to close the door to potential future markets in Europe for GM free maize exports.[71]

Conclusion

It is unfortunate that the debate over biotechnology has been played out in the developing world through the politics of food aid. It has profoundly affected the recipient countries, and their environments and future trade prospects may suffer from it. The literature on food aid has to date paid insufficient attention to the question of GMOs and the impact they have on the food aid regime.[72] I argue that it is time to insert the question of agricultural biotechnology squarely into the debates on food aid. The food aid regime is being influenced by a number of factors that are unique to an age of agricultural biotechnology. These include the scientific debate over the safety of GMOs, as well as economic considerations linked to markets for GM crops. Both of these factors appear to have had an important influence on the policies on GM food aid pursued by both donors and recipients. In many ways, these factors are hard to separate from one another, and both are highly political. The notion put forward in the early 1990s that the food aid regime had become largely "depoliticized" must today be questioned. It is clear that the advent of agricultural biotechnology has fundamentally changed the nature of the regime.

Jennifer Clapp is Chair of the International Development Studies Program and Associate Professor of Environmental and Resource Studies at Trent University in Canada. She would like to thank Peter Andrée, Derek Hall, Brewster Kneen, Marc Williams and three anonymous reviewers for useful comments. She would also like to thank Marcelina Salazar, Sam Grey, Chris Rompré and Kate Turner for research assistance, and the Social Science and Humanities Research Council of Canada for research support.

Notes

1. See, for example, Robert Falkner, "Regulation Biotech Trade: The Cartagena Protocol on Biosafety," *International Affairs*, 76, no.2, (2000); Peter Newell and Ruth Mackenzie, "The 2000 Cartagena Protocol on Biosafety: Legal and Political Dimensions," *Global Environmental Change*, 10, (2000); Cristoph Bail, Robert Falkner and Helen Marquard (eds), *The Cartagena Protocol on Biosafety: Reconciling Trade in Biotechnology with Environment and Development?* (London: Earthscan, 2002).
2. Peter Uvin, "Regime, Surplus and Self-Interest: The International Politics of Food Aid," *International Studies Quarterly*, 36, (1992), pp. 293–312; Raymond Hopkins, "Reform in the International Food Aid Regime: the Role of Consensual Knowledge," *International Organization*, 46, no. 1, (1992), pp. 225–264; Raymond Hopkins,

"The Evolution of Food Aid: Towards a Development-First Regime", in Vernan Ruttan (ed), *Why Food Aid?* (Baltimore: Johns Hopkins, 1993); Edward Clay and Olav Stokke (eds), *Food Aid and Human Security* (London: Frank Cass, 2000).

3. Cheryl Christiansen, "The New Policy Environment for Food Aid: The Challenge of Sub-Saharan Africa," *Food Policy*, 25, (2000), p. 256.

4. USAID, *Food Aid and Food Security Policy Paper* (PN-ABU-219) (Washington, D.C.: USAID, 1995).

5. Harriet Friedmann, "The Political Economy of Food: The Rise and Fall of the Postwar International Food Order", in M. Burawoy and T. Skocpol (eds), *Marxist Inquiries: Studies of Labour, Class and States*, supplement to *American Journal of Sociology*, 88, (1982) S248–86.; Vernan Ruttan, "The Politics of U.S. Food Aid Policy: Historical Review," in Vernan Ruttan (ed), *Why Food Aid?* (Baltimore: Johns Hopkins, 1993).

6. Mitchel Wallerstein, *Food for War—Food for Peace* (Cambridge, MA: MIT Press, 1980); Shlomo Reutlinger, "From 'Food Aid' to 'Aid for Food': Into the 21st Century," *Food Policy*, 24, (1999), p. 9.

7. See (on Europe), John Cathie, European Food Aid Policy (Aldershot: Ashgate, 1997); and (on Canada), Mark Charlton, *The Making of Canadian Food Aid Policy* (Montreal: McGill-Queens, 1992).

8. International Grains Council (IGC), *IGC Annual Report* (London: IGC, 2004).

9. International Wheat Council, *The Food Aid Convention of the International Wheat Agreement* (London:International Wheat Council, 1991).

10. Food Aid Convention, *Food Aid Convention* (London: International Grains Council, 1999).

11. See Christiansen, "The New Policy Environment for Food Aid: The Challenge of Sub-Saharan Africa".

12. See Christopher Barrett and D. Maxwell, *Food Aid After Fifty Years: Recasting Its Role* (London: Routledge, 2005);EU Council Regulation (ED) No. 1292/96.

13. See, for example, Edward Clay and Olav Stokke (eds), *Food Aid Reconsidered: Assessing the Impact on Third World Countries* (London: Frank Cass, 1991).

14. Uvin, "Regime, Surplus and Self-Interest: The International Politics of Food Aid"; Hopkins "Reform in the International Food Aid Regime: the Role of Consensual Knowledge," "The Evolution of Food Aid: Towards a Development-First Regime".

15. Uvin, "Regime, Surplus and Self-Interest: The International Politics of Food Aid," pp. 307–308.

16. Eric Neumayer, "Is the Allocation of Food Aid Free from Donor Interest Bias?" *Journal of Development Studies*, (forthcoming: 2004).

17. International Service for the Acquisition of Agri-Biotech Applications, Preview: *Global Status of Commercialized Transgenic Crops: 2003: Executive Summary, No.30*, pp. 3–4. Internet address: http://www.isaaa.org

18. See USAID, "United States and Food Assistance," *Africa Humanitarian Crisis* (3 July 2003). Internet address: http://www.usaid.gov/about/africafoodcrisis/bio_answers.html#8.

19. Geoffrey Lean, "Rejected GM Food Dumped on the Poor," *The Independent* (London), (18 June 2000); Fred Pearce, "UN is slipping modified food into aid," *New Scientist*, 175, no. 2361, (2003), p. 5.

20. Friends of the Earth International (FOEI), *Playing with Hunger: The Reality Behind the Shipment of GMOs as Food Aid* (Amsterdam: FOEI. April 2003), p. 5.

21. FOEI, *Playing with Hunger: The Reality Behind the Shipment of GMOs as Food Aid*, pp. 6–7; ACDI/VOCA. *Genetically Modified Food: Implications for U.S. Food Aid Programs* (2nd revision, April 2003), pp. 6–10. Internet address: http://www.acdivoca.org/acdivoca/acdiweb2.nsf/news/gmfoodsarticle

22. Genetic Resources Action International (GRAIN) "Better Dead than GM Fed?", *Seedling* (October 2002).

23. For a more detailed explanation of each of these factors, see Oxfam International, "Crisis in Southern Africa," *Oxfam Briefing Paper* 23, (2002), p. 6.

24. World Food Program (WFP), *Policy on donations of foods derived from biotechnology (GM/Biotech foods)*,WFP/EB.3/2002/4-C, (14 October 2002), pp. 4–5.

25. Institute for the Study of International Migration, *Genetically Modified Food in the Southern Africa Food Crisis of 2002–2003* (Georgetown: University School of Foreign Service, 2004), pp. 16–17.

26. Jon Bennett, "Food Aid Logistics and the Southern Africa Emergency," *Forced Migration Review*, 18, no. 5, (2003), p. 29.

27. The value of Zambia's exports of maize in 2002 was U.S.$2.23 million, according to the FAO. FAO, *FAO Statistical Database*. Internet address: http://faostat.fao.org.

28. Rob Crilly, "Children go Hungry as GM food rejected," *The Herald* (Glasgow), (30 October 2002), p. 12.

29. Bennett, "Food Aid Logistics and the Southern Africa Emergency," p. 29.

30. ACDI/VOCA, *Genetically Modified Food: Implications for U.S. Food Aid Programs*, p. 9; USAID "United States and Food Assistance."

31. Matt Mellen, "Who is Getting Fed?", *Seedling*, (April 2003). Internet address: http://www.grain.org/seedline/seed-03-04-3-en.cfm.

32. Chuck Grassley, "Salvation of Starvation? GMO food aid to Africa," *Remarks of Senator Chuck Grassley to the Congressional Economic Leadership Institute*, (5 March 2003).

33. Norman Borlaug, "Science vs. Hysteria," *Wall Street Journal*, (22 January 2003).

34. For an overview of the technical issues involved in the dispute, see Duncan Brack, Robert Falkner and Judith Goll, "The Next Trade War? GM Products, the Cartagena Protocol and the WTO," *Royal Institute of International Affairs Briefing Paper No.8*, (September 2003).

35. Quoted in Charlotte Denny and Larry Elliott, "French Plan to Aid Africa Could be Sunk by Bush," *The Guardian*, (23 May 2003).

36. Edward Alden, "U.S. Beats Egypt with Trade Stick," *Financial Times* (29 June 2002).

37. EU, *Press Release IP/03/681*, (13 May 2003).

38. EU, *Press Release IP/03/681*.

39. Africa Center for Biosafety, Earthlife Africa, Environmental Rights Action—Friends of the Earth Nigeria, Grain and Safe Age, *GE Food Aid: Africa Denied Choice Once Again?*, (4 May 2004).

40. Heike Baumüller, "Domestic Import Regulations for Genetically Modified Organisms and their Compatibility with WTO Rules," *Trade Knowledge Network*, pp. 13–15. Internet address: www.tradeknowledgenetwork.org/pdf/tkn_domestic_regs.pdf

41. FOEI, *Playing with Hunger: The Reality Behind the Shipment of GMOs as Food Aid*, p. 9.

42. Baumüller, "Domestic Import Regulations for Genetically Modified Organisms and their Compatibility with WTO Rules," p. 14.

43. For a history and analysis of these negotiations, see Bail, Falkner and Marquard (eds), *The Cartagena Protocol on Biosafety: Reconciling Trade in Biotechnology with Environment and Development?*; Falkner, "Regulation Biotech Trade: The Cartagena Protocol on Biosafety"; Newell and MacKenzie, "The 2000 Cartagena Protocol on Biosafety: Legal and Political Dimensions."

44. Text of the Cartagena Protocol on Biosafety.

45. Codex Alimentarius Commission, *Report of the Fourth Session of the Ad Hoc Intergovernmental Task Force of Foods Derived from Biotechnology ALINORM 02/34A* (Rome: FAO and WHO, 2003).

46. WFP, *Policy on donations of foods derived from biotechnology (GM/Biotech foods)*, p. 5.

47. World Food Program (WFP), *Policy on donations of foods derived from biotechnology*, WFP/EB.A/2003/5-0B/Rev.1, (2003).

48. Aseem Prakash and Kelly Kollman, "Biopolitics in the EU and the U.S.: A Race to the Bottom or Convergence to the Top?", *International Studies Quarterly*, 46, (2003), p. 625.

49. Robert Paarlberg, "The Global Food Fight," *Foreign Affairs*, 79, no.3, (2000), pp. 24–38.

50. Grant Isaac and William Kerr, "Genetically Modified Organisms at the World Trade Organization: A Harvest of Trouble," *Journal of World Trade*, 37, no. 6, pp. 1086–1090; Prakash and Kollman, "Biopolitics in the EU and the U.S.: A Race to the Bottom or Convergence to the Top?", p. 626.

51. Grassley, "Salvation of Starvation? GMO food aid to Africa."

52. Michael Dynes, "Africa Torn between GM aid and starvation," *The Times* (London), 6 August 2002), p. 12.

53. Rory Carroll, "Zambia Slams Door Shut on GM Food Relief," *The Guardian* (London), (30 October 2002); Institute for the Study of International Migration, *Genetically Modified Food in the Southern Africa Food Crisis of 2002–2003*, p. 20.

54. Polly Diven, "The Domestic Determinants of U.S. Food Aid Policy," *Food Policy*, 26, (2001), p. 471.

55. Christiansen, "The New Policy Environment for Food Aid: The Challenge of Sub-Saharan Africa," p. 257.

56. Brack, Faulkner and Goll, "The Next Trade War? GM Products, the Cartagena Protocol and the WTO," p. 3.

57. Katrin Dauenhauer, "Health: Africans Challenge Bush Claim that GM food is Good for Them," *SUNS: South-North Monitor*, #5368, (23 June 2003).

58. WFP official Richard Lee, Quoted in Greenpeace UK, *Statements on the Southern African Food Crisis* (November 2002).

59. National Association of Wheat Growers (NAWG), "Letter to Robert Zoellick," portions reprinted in the *NAWG Weekly Newsletter*, (13 February 2004). Internet address: http://www.wheatworld.org.

60. Oxfam America, *U.S. Export Credits: Denials and Double Standards* (Washington, D.C.: Oxfam, 2003), p.8.

61. Declan Walsh, "America Finds Ready market for GM food—The hungry," *The Independent* (London), (30 March, 2000), p. 18.

62. Katherine Stapp, "Biotech Boom Linked to Development Dollars, say Critics," *SUNS*, (3 December 2003).

63. Section 1543A of the Farm Bill, cited in ACDI/VOCA, *Genetically Modified Food: Implications for U.S. Food Aid Programs*, p. 5.

64. *The Ecologist*, 33, no.2, (March 2003), p. 46.

65. African Agricultural Technology Foundation (AATF), "Rationale and design of the AATF," *AATF Website*, (June 2002). Internet address: http://www.aftechfound.org/rationale.php

66. Agricultural Biotechnology Support Project II (ABSPII), "Scope and Activities," *ABSPII Website*, (2004). Internet address: http://www.absp2.cornell.edu/whatisabsp2/

67. Mellen, "Who is Getting Fed?"

68. Devlin Kuyek, "Past Predicts the Future—GM Crops and African Farmers," *Seedling*, (October 2002). Internet address: http://www.grain.org/seedling/seed-02–10–3–en.cfm; Mellen, "Who is Getting Fed?"

69. Dominic Glover, "GMOs and the Politics of International Trade," *Democratising Biotechnology: Genetically Modified Crops in Developing Countries Briefing Series*, Briefing 5, (Brighton, UK: Institute of Development Studies, 2003); Brewster Kneen, *Farmageddon* (Gabriola, B.C.: New Society, 1999); Kuyek, "Past Predicts the Future—GM Crops and African Farmers"; Mellen, "Who is Getting Fed?"

70. Jennifer Clapp, "WTO Agricultural Trade Battles and Food Aid," *Third World Quarterly*, (forthcoming).

71. Institute for the Study of International Migration, *Genetically Modified Food in the Southern Africa Food Crisis of 2002–2003*, pp. 18–19.

72. An exception to this is Barrett and Maxwell, *Food Aid After Fifty Years: Recasting Its Role*, who do incorporate some discussion of GMOs.

37

The Political Economy of Obesity: The Fat Pay All[1]*

Alice Julier

Recently, the Learning Channel (TLC) has entered the realm of Reality TV with a new program called "Honey, We're Killing the Kids." In each episode, a heterosexual family with children is chosen and visited by a nutritionist who does an "assessment" of the BMI and eating patterns of the kids. Using computer imaging, the ultra-thin blonde expert shocks the parents with a picture of their children as fat adults: the premise is, of course, that their current food habits and lifestyle put them on a collision course with obesity. TLC calls the program "a wake up call to parents" who will have a "dramatic reality check" when they see the future face of their children. The promotional ads show a mother in a supermarket checkout line, busy but absentmindedly acquiescing to her 8-year-old son's requests for candy—she looks up as she empties her cart to see him aged into a corpulent balding man. Along the way, the nutritional expert berates the parents for their bad behavior, gives them a prescription for changing their habits, and then checks back in three weeks on how they're managing. The family's reward is to see new computer images of how their children will turn out if they stick with the regime forever. As with many reality shows, there is spectacle, public chastisement, and repentance, but no absolution. The viewer wonders how soon after the surveillance ends that the family will fall off the anti-fat bandwagon. Given the prevailing belief in Westerners as undisciplined and self-indulgent, we suspect that a relapse is inevitable.

The show and its advertisements encapsulate much of the public and political anxiety about food and eating that is currently focused on what's been called "the obesity epidemic." It is a spectacle that, in the press, easily out-maneuvers the genocide in Darfur and the war in Iraq as threats to global stability.[2] Fears of an obese nation have led the last three Surgeon Generals as well as the current President to call for greater personal responsibility towards exercise and weight loss as part of the moral obligation of citizenship. Sociologists refer to this kind of event as a moral panic, where a collective fear of a group or its behavior is fomented by intense media coverage (Hunt 1997).

How We Got Fat

Although body size has engendered social concern and state policies in other historical moments, this particular moral panic in the United States builds on decades of

*Originally published 2008

what Kim Chernin calls "a tyranny of thinness," which ties a slender appearance to social virtue.[3] Its rise, however, was aided by the moral entrepreneurship of doctors, pharmaceutical companies, and public health professionals who, in the last two decades, began shifting obesity (a descriptor of a physical state) to a disease entity with the potential for contagion (Jutal 2006). In the mid-1990s, the *Journal of the American Medical Association* and other leading medical journals published key studies linking rising rates of obesity and mortality.[4] Around the same time, the World Health Organization issued a report that used new, lower BMI benchmarks for overweight and obesity.[5] In a critical convergence of science and collective framing, William Dietz and colleagues at the Centers for Disease Control published a Power-Point presentation of a series of U.S. maps over a ten-year period, showing rates of obesity spreading like an infection across the country, as more states crossed into the "red" zone of high BMI.[6] Calling obesity an epidemic frames it such that in 2005 the CDC even sent a team of specialists into West Virginia to investigate an "infectious outbreak" of obesity.

Like most contemporary social problems, groups of claimsmakers have developed on both sides of the issue: on one side, there are anti-fat scientists and activists who use science and the media to lambaste the food industry, Americans' sedentary lifestyles, and a variety of moral causes; on the other, there are fat acceptance researchers and activists, who question the links between body size and morbidity and advocate for "size acceptance" (Saguy & Riley 2005). Using a variety of critical, feminist, and postmodern approaches, social scientists have attempted to understand why body size, a seemingly personal and physical state, has become such a center point for collective outrage and concern.[7] By questioning the very construction of a moral panic around weight and the national diet, they take apart the categorical boxes that often manifest around the growing, producing, and eating of food. These critics try to dismantle the science behind the construction of obesity as a disease state and the vilification of women, poor people, and people of color, who are often seen to epitomize the problem. Feminist scholars offer a reclamation of the meaning of women's bodies as historically shifting, such that contemporary configurations, the constraints on women's body size are directly related to constraints on women's economic, social, and political power (Wann 1999, Bordo 2003). According to Thompson (1994), for lesbians, working class women, and women of color, the seemingly "disordered" relationship to food and eating is related to the stress of living in a sexist, racist, and classist society.[8] Others point to the continued and indeed growing numbers of people, especially women and children, in affluent societies who are food insecure; such debates about obesity draw attention away from the insufficiency of current food distribution and civil entitlements. Within the field of medical research, scientists debate the research methods and results. Even the Centers for Disease Control has been embedded in its own internal conflict about the links between obesity and mortality (Campos 2004).

Meanwhile, as scholars question the veracity of the scientific arguments about obesity as a public health crisis, the public belief in the correlation between fatness, deviance, and illness becomes more entrenched. The degree of media coverage of the obesity-morbidity relationship continues unabated, with some of the public health focus shifting slightly to an emphasis on physical activity rather than weight loss. At the same time, the stigmatization of fat remains perfectly acceptable in a culture that decries overt racial slurs.[9] As the rhetoric increases, fat activists engage in a difficult public legal battle to free body size from the realm of public health crisis, engaging scientific researchers whose work questions the methods and statistics generated by their anti-fat peers.

But sometimes, social problems are not solved by "more science," but rather by questioning the social uses and structural arrangements that go with the science. As Campos et al. (2005b) point out, "very few of those who have announced the arrival of the obesity epidemic have been satisfied with being mere messengers" (p. 6). While others with greater knowledge have the scientific authority to critique the problem on those grounds, I believe in these times, it might be good for some "soft scientists" to rough up the messenger a bit. We might better understand the persistence of this moral panic by applying a more conservative theoretical frame-work, illuminating how an obesity epidemic benefits some members of society. A political economy of obesity encourages us to look at the systemic distribution of power and rewards associated with this public health crisis. When fatness is conflated with irresponsible behavior, those who are not fat—who "treat" and construct a public agenda based on controlling the obese—gain status.

A Functional Analysis of Obesity

In the 1950s, functionalism was a dominant theoretical tool in American sociology. The theory's grand argument is that institutions have social functions that fill social and individual needs, integrating them into a larger system that remains relatively stable. Critiqued by a new generation of Marxist, feminist, critical race, and post-modern scholars who decried its adherence to the status quo, its presentation of "society" as a cohesive entity, and its inability to understand the changes wrought by the social movements of the time, functionalism fell out of favor with most scholars who unabashedly hoped to challenge persistent inequality, especially in affluent societies.

However, sociologist Herbert Gans has spent much of his distinguished career questioning the ways in which the poor and marginalized are demonized by the media, sociologists, and public policy experts, even in their choice of terminology. In his 1971 article "The Uses of Poverty: The Poor Pay All," Gans was engaged in a two-fold sociological and political act. The article was a continuation of his observation that the U.S. has a long history of casting off the poor and the needy and then blaming them for their own marginalization.[10] Gans' second concern was in making use of functionalism as an answer to conservative critics, arguing that, as scholars and citizens, if we do not deal with the *positive* functions of poverty—the ways in which some people benefit from the continued existence of inequality—then public policies would always be inadequately remedial. This way of thinking about the "functionality" of poverty is in many ways a preview of post-structuralist and constructionist theories that unpack the kinds of privileges and entitlements that accrue to wealth, whiteness, and maleness in unequal social systems. As Gans rightly points out, these entitlements remain entrenched because it is difficult to enact policies that ask people to give up or share benefits they perceive as rights.

We can apply Gans' analysis to the current framing of obesity as a social problem. I write as a public sociologist, using sociological frameworks to question how private issues are transformed into social problems and moral panics. Public sociology applies our skills, concepts, and theoretical tools to problems that are deeply and discursively defined by the media, public perception, and scientific ideologies. I use a functionalist lens in order to highlight why such discourses and frameworks dominate the debate.

In this paper, I will be using the terms "overweight," "obese," and "fat," although we need to question the facticity and utility of those categories, recognizing that they are moral and political designations rather than fixed states. Furthermore, such terms presume that people share experiences because of body size. Borrowing Gans' functional analysis of poverty, I ask what are we really concerned about when we talk about an "obesity epidemic"? Ideas about obesity parallel ideas about the poor and indeed, poverty and obesity are often conflated in much of the rhetoric and the science.[11] Although there are clearly relationships between weight and economic or social status, some researchers are actually surprised to see obesity typified as a problem related to poverty, racism, or sexism at the structural level; the ideologies that promote an individualization of economic mobility extend to physical appearance and health.[12] Others have talked about the general concern for "bodies out of bounds," and the nature of citizenship in consumer culture. While there are social constructionist critiques of the structural and institutional forces that place some people in a problematic relationship with food and consumption, it is extremely difficult even for critical frameworks to address the ideological depth of fat phobia and the medicalization of weight and body size.

Thirteen Economic, Political, and Cultural Functions

In his piece, Gans identifies thirteen economic, political, and cultural "functions" of poverty in the U.S. It is striking how easy it is to insert obesity rather than poverty in the statements and come up with roughly the same functions thirty-five years later. Using Gans' list, I draw upon examples from the copious news and academic studies on weight and social life.[13]

First, the existence of obesity—of a population of people identified visually and scientifically as being too fat—ensures that society's "dirty work" gets done. Every society has such work: physically dirty or dangerous, temporary, dead end or underpaid, undignified and menial jobs. A society can fill these jobs by paying higher wages than for "clean work" or it can force people who have no other choice to do the dirty work—and at low wages. Sociologists have amply demonstrated that two critical factors affecting economic mobility and stability are discrimination and social capital. People who are perceived to be overweight find it harder to get jobs, are paid less for the same jobs, and are less likely to be promoted (Roehling 1999). Using data from the National Bureau of Labor, Cawley (2000a) suggests that white women are most apt to experience a loss in wages and job opportunities when they are large. Women as a group already experience a measurable wage disparity as well as greater responsibility for unpaid domestic labor—we can surmise that large women are particularly targeted for the low end of the wage scale (Hebl & Heatherton 1998, Fikkan & Rothblum 2005).

Researchers at Yale's Rudd Center for Food Policy have compiled an array of studies suggesting that weight bias exists in populations across the life course, affecting student-teacher relations, college admissions, marital prospects, and job advancement.[14] Such biases have direct and indirect economic costs for citizens: one study suggests that one reason the wages for obese workers are lower than those for non-obese workers is because employers perceive a greater cost of providing health insurance for these workers (Bhattacharya & Bundorf 2005). Employers often pay them less; even when they have health insurance, obese workers pay a "wage penalty," calling into question the claims that the epidemic is costing citizens and employers in public health expenditures. Although often difficult to prove legally, obesity is often a criterion for screening people out of jobs (Brownell et al. 2005). As April Herndon (2002) writes, "the prospect of having one's body read as a text about slovenly behavior, inherent flaws, and abnormality—all narratives associated with fat people—robs them of a significant source of power" (p. 134). Fat discrimination becomes an accepted yardstick for measuring workers.

In both media reports and scientific studies, obesity is disproportionately associated with poor African Americans and Latinos, populations who also suffer discrimination in the job market and are increasingly asked to do the jobs that middle class white Americans don't want to do. Often lacking the type of social capital that whites use for employment advantages, people of color are routinely positioned in less desirable jobs.[15] Both academic and popular media focus on obesity among African American and Latino populations. In particular, the thesis is often that assimilation breeds overeating, causing second and third generation immigrants to gain weight in the United States (Popkin & Urdry 1997).[16] These issues become clearer when we look at the CDC's own stated concerns about the convergence between the growing numbers of overweight people and the "browning" of America.[17] Such conflation of marginal statuses plays out in debates about immigration and the reinforcement of national borders. Mainstream environmental organizations like the Sierra Club have a subset of members who see limits on immigration as an environmental issue, arguing that all newcomers quickly become superconsumers as they adapt to America (Knickerbocker 2004). Despite the rhetoric, it is certainly functional for the American middle and upper class to hire immigrants whose work subsidizes a standard of living made easier by relief from undervalued service and caring labor needed to support such families. Growing economic disparities in the U.S. mean that in general, the poor and working class subsidize economic growth for the wealthy by paying more for taxes, goods, and services, and consequently have a higher cost of living.

Second, *because the obese and overweight are working at lower wages and generally higher costs of living, they subsidize a variety of economic activities that benefit the affluent*. Those who are medicalized as obese support innovations in medical practice as patients in hospitals and as guinea pigs in medical experiments. Treatments to "normalize" the obese, such as surgeries and drugs, parallel other treatments to "cure" the deaf, the disabled, the intersexed, or differently embodied (Herndon 2004). The medical and pharmaceutical measures used to re-shape large bodies provide a testing ground for less risky versions of the same procedures for non-obese patients. In particular, the incredible media visibility and advertising of gastric bypass surgery and liposuction make such measures seem ordinary and accessible to a vast swath of

American society (Alt 2001, Salant & Santry 2005). Fatness is perceived as a "social emergency," because fat people literally don't fit. Since institutions are difficult to change, individuals are forced to adapt to the indignities of inappropriately shaped clothing, seats, tools, and other materials of everyday life. This lack of acceptance of a variety of embodiments contributes to a general cultural fascination with re-shaping. Television shows that illustrate "extreme" body makeovers normalize other more vol-untaristic body interventions. In one horrific reality show, a woman with a cleft palate was offered corrective surgery and, to complete her transformation, was given lipo-suction, breast implants, and a face lift. Although we cannot make a direct correla-tion, it is not surprising that the cosmetic surgery industry reports a 300% increase in cosmetic surgeries since 1997 (Williamson 2004). Rather than through doctor refer-rals, one of the main avenues for the recruitment of new bariatric surgical patients is through website advertisements (Jutel 2006)

Third, *labeling obesity an epidemic creates jobs for a number of occupations and pro-fessions that serve or "service" the diet, exercise, and health industries—and perhaps, "protect" the rest of society from the obese.* In sociological terms, obesity has been med-icalized, a historical and social process of framing through medical and physiological criteria that institutionalize and rationalize its meaning and treatment (Sobal 2005). Medical professionals (and their organizations and institutions) act as moral entre-preneurs who gain money and status from typifying obesity as a disease and, more recently, as an epidemic. Within the Centers for Disease Control, different researchers have challenged the methodological validity of early studies that over-estimated the population of overweight and obese, yet the official position of the CDC stands that current estimates "do not diminish the urgency of obesity as a public health crisis" (Saguy 2006). Although the pharmaceutical industry and health insurance industries also benefit financially, many segments of the medical profession gain a continued source of income and power from labeling obesity a disease. As a crisis, the obesity epidemic requires research funding, institutes and think tanks to study and solve the problem. *Business Week* recently suggested that biotech, drug, and medical device companies all stand to profit in the coming years of the epidemic (Gogoi 2006). Stan-ton Glantz recently graphed the way that the Robert Wood Johnson Foundation's funding for tobacco research has plummeted in proportion to the increase in their funding for obesity research (Saguy 2006). The International Obesity Task Force and the American Obesity Organization are both funded by pharmaceutical and weight loss companies (Oliver 2006). The obesity epidemic revitalizes the work of nutrition-ists, dieticians, and social workers, professional workers who, without a socially man-dated function as reformers, have less status than doctors and social policy analysts (Ouellette 2004, Biltekoff 2005). Even progressive projects focused on agriculture and food security, like the Yale Sustainable Food program, provide expert status and gain-ful employment to academics whose work focuses on eradicating obesity. The Rudd Institute embodies the contradictory messages concerning obesity: on the one hand, they suggest punitive public policies, like Kelly Brownell's now-famous idea of "hit-ting junk food junkies where it hurts: in their wallets" with a so-called junk food tax (Ball 1998). On the other hand, Brownell and his colleagues have co-authored numer-ous studies focused on de-stigmatizing weight. The moral "goodness" of these public-minded projects deflects collective questioning of what productive social labors would fill the experts' time if the obesity epidemic suddenly ended. Like many other social reform movements, the functional desire to "fix" social ills by curing dysfunctional members obscures the underlying structures of inequality that foster social problems. It also hides the locus of moral responsibility and social control behind the cloak of scientific neutrality (Zola 1986). In another influential article, Gans (1990) points out that by constructing universal and often denigrating terminology, sociologists and policy researchers often contribute to the social ills they hope to eradicate. Gans argues that using the term "underclass" to characterize the chronically poor lumps together a diverse group of people without regard for the possibility of movement in or out of such a rigid identity. Again, we can see a parallel in the use of "the obese" as a descriptor of an entire population, greatly compounded by the tendency to haphazardly extend weight-related risks to those designated "overweight."

Fourth, *the overweight and obese buy goods that others do not want and thus prolong the economic usefulness of such goods.* Consumer goods—including clothing, food, diet aids, drugs, and household items—are marketed to obese people. Entrepreneur magazine claims, "there are no market boundaries to the plus size clothing line," which is, as they put it, "morphing into regular size" (Penttila 2003). This occurs simultaneously with the production of clothing and other goods strategically limited to the very thin and the very wealthy. In particular, haute couture and high-end goods are constructed with the presumption that no one who is rich would ever be fat.

The food industry creates three times as many food products as we as a society need and spends billions of dollars selling endless variety and constructing new needs where none existed before. In American culture, food is ubiquitous—from gas stations to banks to department stores and schools, there is food for purchase everywhere, 24 hours a day. To speak of the economic usefulness of 25 kinds of Oreo cookies is to enter the realm of the absurd and yet the food industry depends upon the continued existence of that market while simultaneously providing the products for dieting. Low fat, and low carb products appear almost instantaneously as diet books and nutrition experts propose anew to answer the problem (Nestle 2002).

Consider how the intense marketing of processed food products to children co-exists in the same media that broadcast commercials exhorting kids to get exercise. On a typical television station, you can routinely see public service commercials for kids to "get out and move," whose animation blends seamlessly into the commercial for Cocoa Puffs that follows. For an even more concrete integration, McDonald's offers us Ronald McDonald on a snowboard during broadcasts of the Winter Olympics. The food industry uses a combination of unrestrained desire and one-shot solutions, which allows them to continue to produce, promote and distribute products that are clearly harmful while pushing the government to continue to subsidize the cost of farming and producing processed foods (Nestlé 2002). The links between poverty and obesity are compounded by such things as: food deserts in poor neighborhoods, the unequal distribution of good quality food for a decent price across socioeconomic areas, and the intense pressure for immigrant racial groups to assimilate by "eating American."

Market research that concludes poor people "prefer" Doritos and soda to organic lettuce allows the food industry to justify providing poor quality food in disadvantaged neighborhoods.[18] Overall, the number of food stores in poor neighborhoods is nearly one-third lower than in wealthier areas, and the quality of these stores, their size and physical condition, the range and nutritional content of their merchandise tends to be poorer. People in low-income areas pay more for nutrition and have less access to preventative health and medical services. The health risks and costs of diabetes for the poor may be greater simply because they lack access to health care.

Fifth, moving on to the social and cultural functions of obesity, we can suggest that one *major function of obesity is that the obese can be identified and punished as alleged or real deviants in order to uphold the legitimacy of conventional norms*. Stigma against fat is one of the most acceptable forms of overt prejudice. Erving Goffman's (1963) groundbreaking work Stigma provides an original and useful template for understanding how people confront a discredited condition like obesity. The cornerstone of weight bias is the belief that it is a self-induced state from which a self-disciplined individual can escape by hard work or, failing that, the purchase of the right diet book, foods, exercise equipment, or medical interventions. Cultural messages about status anxiety are reinforced by a consumer culture that offers a way out through the possession of consumer products or a commodified self. Failure to do so is moral lapse and deserves public response. Consider the four-year-old Mexican-American child who was taken away from her family by social service workers who labeled her obesity a form of child endangerment, despite the fact that her parents were actively seeking treatment for her abnormal growth patterns (Belkin 2001, Campos 2004). In what is probably an intentional parallel, in one ad for "Honey We're Killing the Kids," a Latina mother is shown throwing her son snacks the way a dog receives a treat—he shows her his report card or plays his trumpet and she distractedly tosses him a cookie which he catches in his mouth. Given the moral panic frame used by the show's producers, it's easy to see how they are equating Latinos with dogs, bad parenting with the off-handed training of a pet, and good grades with social rewards such as food. Campos et al. (2005b) find that news "articles (about the obesity epidemic) that reported on blacks and Latinos were over eight times more likely than articles that did not blame obesity on bad food choices and over 13 times more likely to blame sedentary life styles."

Another form of vilification comes in the shape of punitive public policies: the rise of various "snack taxes" which add to the cost of high sugar, high sodium snack foods neglects to take into account how these foods are distributed across the socioeconomic landscape. To see food as simply good or bad nutrition also medicalizes it, underplaying all the other reasons people eat. To justify the desirability of hard work, thrift, honesty, frugality, self-discipline, for example, the defenders of these norms must find people who can be accused of being lazy, self-indulgent, dishonest, and gluttonous. The "risky behavior" frame argues that fat bodies are read as evidence of both preventable illness and moral failings (Saguy & Riley 2005). Fat acceptance becomes tantamount to accepting bad behavior that knowingly contributes to ill health. Conservative commentator and anti-obesity writer Michael Fumento uses a number of these examples. He argues that "when somebody shows prejudice to an obese person, they are showing prejudice toward overeating and what used to be called laziness. It's a helpful and healthful prejudice for society to have" (Saguy & Riley 2005). Seeing fat people as lazy and ignorant supports an ideology of choice, increasingly popular in a time when governments are pulling back from collective services and obligations.

Sixth, despite the growing numbers of fat activists, *people stigmatized by body size lack the level of political and social power to correct the stereotypes that other people hold of them* and thus continue to be thought of as willing victims, engaged in bad personal decisions. The most obvious is the use of obese people as examples of moral failure (as in "fat jokes"). By unquestioningly connecting "obesity or overweight" to risky health behaviors, medical professionals and public health spokespersons categorize them as "preventable illnesses," which means that people who are fat are willfully creating the social and physical costs. Like blaming the poor for their lack of upward mobility, blaming the fat also takes our gaze away from the structural causes of food as a social emergency. It also misplaces the urgency: we may need a better food system for everyone, but to use "growing obesity" as the basis for food security and sustainability is problematic. As with all moral panics, once the emergency is gone, the funding, support, and moral obligation to support such systems disappears. Ironically, the same problems have operated in the typification and ensuing public policy related to hunger and food insecurity in the USA. As Jan Poppendieck (1998) has illustrated, while hunger remains a constant concern in North America, its visibility as a moral issue is tied to the construction of emergency aid rather than an examination of the underlying structural conditions.

Seventh, *the overweight and obese offer vicarious participation in indulgence to the rest of the population.* Gluttony may be a sin, but in consumer culture, there is a kind of envy of those who appear to consume without restraint. It parallels a history of mythologizing the "freedoms" that working class or poor people seem to have from the panopticon of self-control we expect from middle class citizens. Consider cultural voyeurism around eating a lot or taking pleasure in food. Although the winners of many eating contests in recent years are often tiny Japanese men and women, they are usually shown alongside corpulent American men wearing t-shirts and baseball caps (Berg 2003). In particular, women are defined by their appearance and subject to intense scrutiny about their bodies. Those who cannot or will not participate in the culture of slimness are more deeply scrutinized with a kind of prurient interest. People who focus aesthetic or positive attention on heavier women are seen as having deviant sexual interests.[19] Actor Leonard Nimoy, who recently published a photo art portfolio of large nude women, commented that he is constantly asked about his personal sexual preferences rather than about the subject within a richer vocabulary of representation.

Eighth, the obese serve a direct cultural function when, seen as a single group, their "culture" is adopted through icons, stereotypes and heroes. Consider the fat lady who sings at the end of the opera, the fat contestants on "American Idol", and any number of celebrity chefs on the food network. Author, commentator, and Man of Size, Daniel Pinkwater agrees that fat people are stereotyped as funny and jolly—and he claims, historically many of them are. He says, "There's a kind of joyousness to big, ponderous creatures."[20] However, because the media construction of the obesity epidemic is so intense, the cultural celebration of people of size has virtually disappeared except on food television.

One notable exception that begs deeper analysis is the black male comedian in drag and a fat suit. In the past, certain racial and ethnic groups have connected heaviness with power, status, sexiness, and beauty. In some strands of black culture, music and images celebrate a rounder, heavier aesthetic for women. This has taken an odd turn in a recent spate of films, where actors Martin Lawrence, Eddie Murphy, and Tyler Perry have all portrayed heavy people—usually women. The images ambiguously range from repulsion to adulation. In one film, Murphy seems to celebrate the fat professor as the more authentic and sexually attractive man, although his other characters, the heavyset family (particularly the grandmother and mother), never materialize as more than comic fodder. In a more recent film, Murphy more explicitly vilifies the fat black woman he embodies, making her a central object of ridicule, even as he plays opposite himself as her love interest. Perry's character of Medea, is questionably a positive source of folk wisdom, while her size, anger, and dragged-out femininity remain the locus of humor. As feminist race scholars have demonstrated, there is a problematic and lingering history of the image of a large black woman, "reminiscent of 'mammy' symbolizing comfort and reassurance with which many moviegoers want to connect" (Williams-Forson 2006). The Moynihan Report was only the first of many public and scholarly sources that pathologized black families as dysfunctional for relying on single mothers (stereotyped as large women) as the head of household in black communities. For black comedians to adopt this physical parody is a questionable route to power that needs to be examined more fully in light of the limited number of large black women who have cultural and iconic power, even as entertainers. The historical shift in accolades from Hattie McDaniel to Hallie Berry may be simultaneously liberating and constraining. Feminist race scholars have pointed out that recently, "the hegemony of white popular culture and upward class mobility has resulted in increased pressure on African American women to become slender" (Witt 1999, p. 188). This trend coexists uncertainly with the black male comedians' performance of "Big Mama."[21]

   Ninth, *seeing obesity as a master identity (and homogeneous grouping) helps guarantee the status of those who are not fat.* It is a way of distinguishing self from others. When fatness is conflated with bad nutrition, bad health, and sedentary lifestyles, those who are not fat gain status through that association. In hierarchical societies, someone (or, more likely, some group) ends up on the bottom. In American society, where social mobility and shifting status are important goals, people need visible signs as to where they stand. The obese function as a reliable measuring rod for status comparisons. This is true whether people accept a discourse that blames genetics or bad choices as the "cause" of obesity. Status is status, whether based on scientifically sanctioned predestination or the Protestant work ethic. At the same time, even epidemiologists who see genetics and environmental factors as key contributors to people's body size generally present the obese as a group with a singular lack of will to change. For example, websites advertising bariatric surgery often induce potential patients with the claim that obesity is a complex disease that is caused by genetic and environmental factors outside the individual's control. However, in the same sites, surgical failure is blamed on the individual's inability to conform to the maintenance routine necessary for weight stability (Salant & Santry 2005). The tinge of personal responsibility is almost impossible to expunge from medical and public health directives. At the same time, many studies relating mortality to body mass fail to control for other variables related to life chances, environment, or more broadly to lifestyle. Discursively, the fluidity of the body connects directly to the fluidity of social class: both are seen as real possibilities in the U.S., and yet there are incredible structural impediments to both weight loss and upward mobility that get masked by the belief in self-discipline. In this historical moment, thinness is an unequivocal visible sign of "health," an undefined value presumably shared by all. As April Herndon (2004) points out, it's incredibly important to recognize that "while there are some people for whom being large presents serious health and life problems . . . we cannot presume on scientific evidence that this is the case for all people of a certain body size or mass. Despite our comfort with statistical norms, there are no populations for whom material experiences are identical."

Tenth, *the obese also aid in the status mobility of those who are just above them in the hierarchy—those who were heavy and lose weight.* We are all familiar with the visibility of so-called "success stories"—Al Roker with his surgically clamped stomach; the endless diet ads with before and after pictures; Jared, the man who lost 100 pounds eating Subway sandwiches. They all profit from their disassociation with a stigmatized identity. Others also gain status by financing their own success from the change—becoming diet and exercise gurus, selling products and their own success. Kirstie Alley seemed to buck the trend in a short-lived TV series called "Fat Actress," but she's received more publicity—and money—for her weight loss through a national diet chain. The number of self-help and autobiographical books written by "former fat people" is astounding. Interestingly, people who lose weight are granted expert status generated from their own experiences, but those who are fat activists are often challenged on their ability to speak with authority about the lives of people of size. As Charlotte Biltekoff (2005) points out, "the pursuit of thinness may have more to do with its power as a signifier of self-control than with its promise of health."

Eleventh, *the obese keep the thin busy, particularly those who assimilate into thinness via diets and surgery, by becoming trainers, diet experts, and icons of what is right.* The existence of obesity provides the fuel behind much of the entertainment industry, both in terms of producing a steady stream of images dedicated to extreme thinness, but also in endless speculation on weight and body in the media. Oprah Winfrey, one of the most influential and richest people in America receives more attention for her "battle" to stay slim than for her other social and cultural endeavors. Those who assimilate into thinness are lauded like terminal disease patients who survive. Conservative commentator Michael Fumento calls obesity a "disease that is socially contagious," meaning that those who are not yet labeled overweight need to remain vigilant. For everyone, but for women in particular, the culture of fear keeps them engaged in endless acts of self-disciplining. Comparing disparate but interesting attitudinal surveys, one could surmise that the number of people worried about their weight at any given time is greater than the number of people worried about terrorist attacks.

Twelfth, *being relatively powerless to affect public policy and cultural production, the obese and overweight are made to absorb the costs of changes and growth in American society.* Fitness can signify physical health but also who is or who is not worthy of status within a society. In 2001, instigating a national war on obesity, former Health and Human Services director Tommy Thompson claimed that as their patriotic duty, all Americans should lose ten pounds. Communities vied to see which town could collectively lose the most weight and political candidates of both genders are now routinely evaluated for their "fitness" for the job, in terms of pounds as well as skills. As April Herndon (2004) illustrates, "In order to be a proper American one must meet a certain corporeal standard and take seriously the moral responsibility to be a patriotic citizen" (p. 128). However, the critical question becomes, "What kind of responsibilities are people being asked to take?" In this case, good citizenship means doing more to improve their own health, and presupposes that people have the capacity to do more. Indeed, the responsibility of citizens to lose weight coexists with encouragement to consume more as a form of patriotism, particularly post-9/11, where consumption was presented as a way of preserving "the American way of life."

Constructing the problem as an obesity epidemic functions as a means of chastising all who fall outside the confines of ideal citizenship. This is particularly noticeable when it becomes a means of talking indirectly about poverty, race, and immigration without appearing to be racist or classist. Saguy and Riley (2005) conclude that "the war against obesity targets a specific group of people who are already, in some sense, second-class citizens" (p. 129). New versions of racism and sexism are played out through national discourses and programs aimed at reducing fat rather than poverty. Fear of obesity is yet a new way to vent anxiety about changes in the gender or racial order without fear of reproach. When asked why people fear fat, Daniel Pinkwater said, "It can't be fat. Fat is too trivial for it to be about fat. Just think, people see you as a defenseless person."[22]

It is particularly disconcerting when the obesity epidemic is used as a justification for sustainable food projects, using the premise that it is morally right to secure school gardens and good institutional food by claiming obesity as the "problem" rather than the agro-industrial food system and the lack of government support for children's health. Critics move seamlessly from the suggestion that current industrial agricultural policies would be radically changed if we all consumed less to the idea that fat people are "overconsumers" whose behavior pushes the food industry to produce more food and the government to maintain agricultural subsidies (Cafaro et al. 2006). It seems contradictory to talk about people's "desire" for more food when the motivation for more cannot be separated from a capitalist system that fetishizes the market as an entity requiring endless development and promotion of new products, despite any discernable consumer demand. Movements aimed at changing food and agriculture must be careful to escape their historical roots in paternalistic and class-based reform movements designed to produce citizens according to a universalist and restrictive model.

Thirteenth, *the obese facilitate the American political process.* The "obesity epidemic" is more about social and political norms than about the scientific and medical realities of body size. American political institutions have embraced the rhetoric of personal responsibility undergirding the fears of a fat nation. This serves purposes beyond the care of citizenry or concerns about overall costs to a society. As Pinkwater aptly points out, it is about discrediting or disenfranchising people from visibility in the political process. We can see how this works in public condemnation, which is often focused on women. In the 1980s, Rush Limbaugh (not a thin person himself) famously called feminists "a bunch of fat cows who can't get dates." Conservative commentator and anti-obesity crusader Michael Fumento covers two bases with one insult by lambasting global environmental activist and physicist Vandana Shiva as being a "blubbery bourgeois hero." Anti-obesity activists, especially scientists, are often dismissive of fat activists because the vast majority of them are women. This framing of obesity is useful for those whose ideological commitments are focused on "individual responsibility" rather than universal health insurance. Using a historical analysis of American food reform movements, from domestic science to Alice Waters, Charlotte Biltekoff (2005) reminds us that this process has consistently "produced an equivalence between thinness and good citizenship and made the position of 'fat citizen' a conceptual impossibility." Most importantly, it shifts the focus away from structural and cultural reasons for obesity and allows some groups in society to scapegoat other groups, while avoiding questions about the nature of food distribution, poverty, lack of jobs at a livable wage, and a time bind that encourages people to work longer for less pay. To blame the individual for lack of willpower is to ignore the ways in which work has increased, pay has decreased, and avenues for fulfillment are structurally constrained for women, people in poverty, and racial-ethnic groups. Current entitlement programs focused on food security (such as food stamps) provide as little as $3.00 a day per individual. These programs have been chipped away to the extent that hunger relief is almost entirely governed by non-profit charitable organizations, supplemented by a backhanded and unsteady supply of federal funds (Poppendieck 1998). Such an approach makes good food, leisure, and physical exercise into commodities that are only affordable to those who have disposable income, time, and cultural capital. Despite Bush's recent public health initiatives for fitness, all of which are focused on "personal responsibility," there are major structural impediments that prevent people from gaining access to physical activity. Even a simple walk around the block or unstructured outdoor play is problematic in urban neighborhoods with high crime rates, in suburban areas without sidewalks, in school districts that must use their decreasing budgets to pay for "No Child Left Behind" rather than "specials" like physical education, art, or music. In 2000, the IRS passed regulations that allowed people willing to pay for their own bariatric surgeries to take a reduction in taxes (Herndon 2002, p. 133). Rather than come up with national health insurance or preventative health campaigns (supplementing gym memberships for everyone rather than extreme weight control for a few), the government rewards those who are willing to take on personal medical risks for the sake of some vague future reduction in public health costs.

The concept of responsibility has many meanings. By making public health promotion entirely about individual behavior, we limit people's autonomy regarding the vast number of reasons they choose to eat what they eat or lead their lives the way they do. As the Food Ethics council points out, we lose a great deal by valuing food for little but its nutrients, and, I would add, by valuing our citizens for little but their appearance. In *Deconstructing the Underclass*, Gans (1990) states:

> Those who argue that all people are entirely responsible for what they do sidestep the morally and otherwise crucial issue of determining how much responsibility should be assigned to people who lack resources, who are therefore under unusual stress, and who lack effective choices in many areas of their lives in which even moderate income people can choose relatively freely.

Pointing out the important functions of obesity does not intend to suggest that categorizing and stigmatizing people because of their size is a necessary condition for social life. As fat activists and sociologists have demonstrated, it is possible to suggest functional alternatives. Some things that might be more useful for all members of society might be: a different food system that provides access to good food to everyone, regardless of economic status; a wage system that compensates caregivers, food producers, service workers, and manual laborers in a more equitable fashion; dismantling the structures of racial and gender inequality; a food industry that focuses more on feeding people than profiting from their desires; a health care system that is available to all and offers a range of preventative care options; and a government that insures everyone's right to adequate food. There are certainly historical examples of an acceptance and even glorification of a variety of body sizes and shapes, of government programs that supplement individual responsibility with institutional support, and of corporations working for consumers. (Maybe there aren't any examples of that last point.) However, the "risky behavior" frame and the medicalization of food and eating make it extremely difficult to assert an alternative that would easily resonate with an already terrified population. This is particularly true in a time when there is a huge and growing gap between wealthy and poor citizens, both within the U.S. and across the globe. As Gans suggests, a functional analysis must conclude that the obesity epidemic exists because it fulfills a number of positive functions but also because many of the functional alternatives to the obesity epidemic would be quite dysfunctional for the affluent and privileged members of society, including many contemporary organizations, professionals (including academics and doctors), corporations, and institutions. Phenomena like the obesity epidemic can be eliminated only when it becomes dysfunctional for those who benefit from its construction or when the powerless obtain enough power to change society.

Notes

1. This piece is written with admiration for and deference to Herbert Gans. I am indebted to Tom Henricks for his excitement and quick thinking in applying Gans' article to the obesity debate as well as his encouragement in having me following the line of thought. The ideas for this paper were generated during a seminar sponsored by the Centers for Disease Control and the Academy for Educational Development in the fall of 2005. I would like to thank Peter Conrad, Jeff Sobal, Lisa Heldke, Tom Henricks and a host of ASFS conference participants for their invaluable feedback on the original talk. My thinking about morality, weight, and citizenship originated from talks with Charlotte Biltekoff, who points out numerous historical instances of moral reform played out through bodies and eating. This article was originally presented as my fourth and final presidential address for the joint conference of the Association for the Study of Food and Society and the Agriculture, Food, and Human Values Society. Boston, Mass. 2006.
2. Campos, P. (2004) *The Obesity Myth*, p. 3. Campos cites: "Obesity is America's Greatest Threat, Surgeon General Says." *Orlando Sentinel*, January 22, 2003.
3. For a history of body size and morality in countries like the U.S., see Stearns, P. (1997) *Fat History: Bodies and Beauty in the Modern West*. NY: NYU Press.
4. See, for example, Kuczmarski, R. et al. (1994) Increasing Prevalence of Overweight among U.S. Adults: The National Health and Nutrition Examination Surveys, 1960–1991, JAMA, 272. Campos points to the following four studies as being the most frequently cited as evidence for the link between increased morbidity and obesity: Manson, et al. (1995) Body Weight and Mortality Among Women. *New England Journal of Medicine* 3333; Allison, et al. (1999) Annual Deaths Attributable to Obesity, JAMA, 289; Fontaine, et al. (2003) Years of Life Lost to Obesity, JAMA 289; Calle et al. (2003) Overweight, Obesity, and Mortality from Cancer in a Prospectively Studied Cohort of U. S. Adults. *New England Journal of Medicine*, 248 (Campos, p. 255).
5. Oliver (2006) points out that the 1995 WHO Report on Overweight and Obesity was based on data from the International Obesity Task Force, a private research and policy organization funded by pharmaceutical companies with major stakes in weight-loss drug development (p. 29).

6. The maps and PowerPoint presentation are available to the public on the Centers for Disease Control and Prevention website, www.cdc.gov

7. For example, Campos et al. (2005) evaluate four of the central claims related to the obesity epidemic to argue that the rhetoric is far greater than the real or potential public health crisis. They find limited scientific evidence for the following claims: "that obesity is an epidemic; that obesity and overweight are major contributors to mortality; that higher than average adiposity is pathological and a primary cause of disease; and that significant long-term weight loss is both medically beneficial and a practical goal." For more in-depth analysis of the same issues, see Gard and Wright (2005).

8. Thompson, B. (1994) *A Hunger So Wide and So Deep: American Women Speak Out on Eating Problems*. Minnesota: Univ. of Minnesota Press. For social constructionist critiques, see Saguy and Riley (2005), Campos et al. (2006). For feminist critiques, see Chernin 1981; Orbach, 1988; Bordo, 2003; and most recently Braziel and LeBesco, 2001. Feminist analyses of the body and gender are wide-ranging, often encompassing the issue of size. See, for example the edited volume: Weitz, R. (2003) *The Politics of Women's Bodies: Sexuality, Appearance, and Behavior*. New York: Oxford Press. According to Gard and Wright (2005), "Central to contemporary feminist understanding of the body is the idea that what it means to be female is shaped by and in historical relations of power" (p. 154). For a blending of personal narrative and sociological analysis see also: Thomas (2005).

9. See for example: Fierstein, H. (2007) Our Prejudices, Ourselves. *New York Times*, April 13, 2007. Commenting on the firing of radio host Don Imus for a racist and sexist remark, Fierstein argues that American culture is selective in its outrage over hate speech, tolerating homophobia and fat prejudice while decrying racism and sexism—ignoring the way material discrimination against gays, people of color, women, and heavy people continues.

10. What Gans proposes is really a "radical functionalism," where social life is less beneficial to a singular entity and more so to privileged groups within. In this and other articles, he suggests that the idea of "society" is easily confused with the stability and well-being of its upper classes. He subtly argues that poverty is functional for the middle and upper groups; and the alternatives to it are dysfunctional for these same groups.

11. For example, Critser, G. (2003) *Fat Land: How Americans Became The Fattest People in the World*. New York: Houghton Mifflin.

12. See Crawford, R. (1980) Healthism and the medicalization of everyday life. *International Journal of Health Services* 10 (3). Crawford coins the term "healthism" to capture how new health movements draw upon existing medical frameworks, which situate problems, prevention, and solutions to health and disease at the level of the individual. Crawford argues that such an approach elevates health to a super-value, which de-politicizes health issues and encourages private, personal approaches to health rather than collective or structural strategies.

13. For an impressive compilation of recent studies of obesity, weight stigma, and the food industry, see the Rudd Center for Food Policy (www.yaleruddcenter.org); see also Sobal and Maurer (1999b) *Weighty Matters*. For the shift from physical condition to disease see Jutel (2006).

14. Brownell K. et al. (eds) (2005) *Weight Bias: Nature, Consequences, and Remedies*. New York: Guilford Publications; for articles on weight bias see www.yaleruddcenter.org

15. For an overview of the relationship between employment advantages, race, and social capital see the following: Smith, R. (2002) Race, Gender, and Authority in the Workplace: Theory and Research, *Annual Review of Sociology*; Mason, P. (2000) Understanding Recent Empirical Evidence on Race and Labor Market Outcomes in the U.S.A. *Review of Social Economics*, 58 (3).

16. See Saguy and Riley (2005) for a quantitative analysis of articles on race and obesity. See also Almeling, R. and Saguy, A. C. (2005, Aug.) Fat Panic! The "Obesity Epidemic" as Moral Panic. Paper presented at the annual meeting of the American Sociological Association, Marriott Hotel, Loews Philadelphia Hotel, Philadelphia, PA.

17. Source: Centers for Disease Control "Overview of the Obesity Epidemic" prepared for expert seminar at the Academy for Educational Development, Fall 2005.

18. Although most of these studies are done for market research, see an academic example in Chrzan, J. (2003) Performing the Good Pregnancy: Teen Mothers and Diet in West Philadelphia. Paper presented for the joint conference of the Association for the Study of Food and Society and the Agriculture, Food, and Human Values Society. Chrzan critiques the food deserts of the inner city but ultimately decries the bad food choices of low income women prior to pregnancy.

19. See, for example, Goode's (2002) interpretation of NAAFA as mainly "a dating service for men who like large women," and the critique articles that follow in the same issue. *Qualitative Sociology*, 25(4).

20. Interview with Marilyn Wann, www.fat!so.com

21. Witt suggests that black women are conspicuously absent in the national discourse on eating disorders while simultaneously being highly visible in the specularization of corpulence in U.S. culture (p. 189).

22. Ibid.

References

Allon, N. (1982) "The Stigma of Overweight in Everyday Life." In B. Wolman, ed., *Psychological Aspects of Obesity: A Handbook*. New York: Van Nostrand Reinhold.

Alt, S. J. (2001) "Bariatric Surgery programs growing quickly nationwide." *Health Care Strategic Management*, 19 (9).

Ball, M. (1998) "Brownell Calls for Food Tax to End 'Epidemic'." *Yale Herald Online*, February 18, 1998.

Belkin, L. (2001) Watch Her Weight. *New York Times*, July 8, 2001.

Berg, J. (2003) "Bringing Back the Belt: Nathan's Hot Dogs and American Nationalism." Unpublished paper presented at the Association for the Study of Food and Society/Agriculture, Food, and Human Values Society joint conference. June 11–13, 2003. Austin, Texas.

Bhattacharya, J. and Bundorf, M. (2005) "The Incidence of the Health Care Costs of Obesity." *National Bureau of Economic Research, Working Paper* No. 11303 May.

Biltekoff, C. (2005) "The Terror Within: Citizenship and Self Control in the Fat Epidemic." In *Hidden Hunger: Eating and Citizenship from Domestic Science to the Fat Epidemic*. Ph.D. thesis for the American Civilization Program. Brown University, Rhode Island.

Bordo, S. (2003) *Unbearable Weight: Feminism, Western Culture, and the Body*. Berkeley: University of California Press.

Braziel, J. and LeBesco, K. (eds) (2001) *Bodies out of Bounds: Fatness and Transgression*. Berkeley: University of California Press.

Brownell, K. D. and Horgan, K. B. (2003) *Food Fight: The Inside Story of the Food Industry, America's Obesity Crisis, and What We Can Do About It*. Chicago: Contemporary Books.

Brownell, K., Puhl, R., Schwartz, M. and Rudd L. (eds) (2005) *Weight Bias: Nature, Consequences, and Remedies*. New York: Guilford Publications.

Cafaro, P., Primack, R. and Zimdahl, R. (2006) "The Fat of the Land: Linking American Food Overconsumption, Obesity, and Biodiversity Loss." *Journal of Agricultural and Environmental Ethics*, 10.

Campos, P. (2004) *The Obesity Myth: Why America's Obsession with Weight is Hazardous to Your Health*. New York: Gotham Books.

Campos, P., Saguy, A., Ernsberger, P., Oliver, E. and Gaesser, G. (2005a) "Response: Lifestyle Not Weight Should be the Primary Target." *International Journal of Epidemiology*, 35 (1): 80–81.

Campos, P., Saguy, A., Ernsberger, P., Oliver, E. and Gaesser, G. (2005b) "The epidemiology of overweight and obesity: public health crisis or moral panic?" *International Journal of Epidemiology*, 35 (1): 55–60.

Cawley, J. (2000a) "Body Weight and Women's Labor Market Outcomes." *National Bureau of Economic Research, Working Paper* No. 7841 August.

Cawley, J. (2000b) "An Instrumental Variables Approach to Measuring the Effect of Body Weight on Employment Disability." *Health Services Research*, 35 (5).

Chernin, K. (1981) *The Tyranny of Slenderness*. London: Woman's Press.

Conrad, P. (2005) "The Shifting Engines of Medicalization." *Journal of Health and Social Behavior*, 46.

Cramer, P. and Steinvert, T. (1998) "Thin is good, fat is bad: How early does it begin?" *Journal of Applied Developmental Psychology*, 19 (3): 229–252.

Ferraro, K. and Holland, K. (2002) "Physician evaluation of obesity in health surveys: 'Who are you calling fat?'" *Social Science and Medicine*, 55.

Fikkan, J. and Rothblum, E. (2005) "Weight Bias in Employment." In Brownell, K. et al. (eds) *Weight Bias: Nature, Consequences, and Remedies*. New York: Guilford Publication.

Gans, H. (1971) "The Uses of Poverty: The Poor Pay All." *Social Policy*, 2 (2) (July/August): 20–24.

Gans, H. (1990) "Deconstructing the Underclass: The Term's Danger as a Planning Concept." *Journal of the American Planning Association*.

Gard, M. and Wright, J. (2005) *The Obesity Epidemic: Science, Morality, and Ideology*. New York: Routledge.

Goffman, E. (1968) *Stigma: Notes on the Management of Spoiled Identity*. London: Penguin Books.

Gogoi, P. (2006) "All Eyes on the Obesity Prize." *Business Week Online*, June 6, 2006.

Goode, E. (2002) "Sexual Involvement and Social Research in a Fat Civil Rights Organization." *Qualitative Sociology*, 25 (4).

Herndon, A. (2002) "Disparate but Disabled: Fat Embodiment and Disability Studies." *NWSA Journal*, 14 (3) (Fall).

Herndon, A. (2004) "Collateral Damage from 'friendly fire?' Race, Nation, and Class and The 'War Against Obesity'." *Social Semiotics*, 15 (2) (August).

Hesse-Biber, S. (1996) *Am I Thin Enough Yet?: The Cult of Thinness and the Commercialization of Identity*. New York: Oxford Press.

Hebl, M. and Heatherton, T. (1998) "The stigma of obesity in women: The difference is black and white." *Personality and Social Psychology Bulletin*, 24.

Hunt, A. (1997) "The 'Moral Panic' and Moral Language in the Media." *British Journal of Sociology* (online) 48 (4).

Jutel, A. (2006) "The emergence of overweight as a disease entity: measuring up normality." *Social Science and Medicine*, 63.

Knickerbocker, B. (2004) "A hostile takeover bid at the Sierra Club." *Christian Science Monitor*, January 20, 2004.

Kulick, D. and Meneley, A. (ed.) (2005) *Fat: The Anthropology of an Obsession*. New York: Tarcher/Penguin Publishing.

Lupton, D. (1993) "Risk as Moral Danger: The Social and Political Functions of Risk Discourse in Public Health." *International Journal of Health Services*, 23 (3).

Maurer, D. and Sobal, J. (1999) *Weighty Issues: Fatness and Thinness As Social Problems*. New York: Aldine de Gruyter.

Nestle, M. (2002) *Food Politics: How the Food Industry Influences Nutrition and Health*. Berkeley: University of California Press.

Oliver, J. (2006) *Fat Politics: The Real Story Behind America's Obesity Epidemic*. New York: Oxford Press.

Orbach, S. (1988) *Fat is a Feminist Issue*. London: Arrow Books.

Ouellette, L. (2004) Review of "Honey We're Killing the Kids." www.flowtv.org

Penttila, T. (2003) "Hot Market: Overweight." *Entrepreneur Magazine*, December 2003.

Popkin, B. and Urdry, J. (1997) "Adolescent Obesity Increases Significantly in Second and Third Generation U.S. Immigrants: The National Longitudinal Study of Adolescent Health." *Journal of Nutrition*, 128 (4): 701–706.

Poppendieck, J. (1998) *Sweet Charity: Emergency Food and the End of Entitlement*. New York: Penguin Putnam Books.

Powdermaker, H. (1997) "An Anthropological Approach to the Problem of Obesity" from the *Bulletin of the New York Academy of Medicine*, 36, May 5, 1960. (reprinted in Food and Culture, 1st edition, eds C. Counihan and P. Van Estrik.)

Roehling, M. (1999) "Weight-Based Discrimination in Employment: Psychological and Legal Aspects." *Personnel Psychology*, 52.

Saguy, A. (2006) "Are Americans Too Fat? Conversation with Stanton Glantz." *Context*s 5 (2) Spring.

Saguy, A. and Riley, K. (2005) "Weighing Both Sides: Morality, Mortality, and Framing Contests over Obesity." *Journal of Health Politics, Policy, and Law*, 5,

Salant, T. and Santry, H. (2005) "Internet Marketing of Bariatric Surgery: Contemporary Trends in the Medicalization of Obesity." *Social Science and Medicine*, 62 (14).

Sobal, J. (1995) "The Medicalization and Demedicalization of Obesity." In Maurer, D. and Sobal, J. (eds) *Eating Agendas: Food and Nutrition as Social Problems*. New York: Aldine de Gruyter.

Sobal, J. (2005) "Social Consequences of Weight Bias by Partners, Friends, and Strangers." In Brownell, et al. (eds) *Weight Bias: Nature, Consequences, and Remedies*. New York: Guilford Publication.

Sobal, J. and Maurer, D. (eds) (1999a) *Interpreting Weight: The Social Management of Fatness and Thinness*. New York: Aldine de Gruyter.

Sobal, J. and Maurer, D. (eds) (1999b) *Weighty Matters: Fatness and Thinness as Social Problems*. New York: Aldine de Gruyter.

Thomas, P. (2005) *Taking Up Space: How Eating Well and Exercising Regularly Changed My Life*. Nashville: Pearlsong Press.

Thompson, B. (1994) *A Hunger so Wide and so Deep: American Women Speak Out on Eating Problems*. Minnesota: University of Minnesota Press.

Wann, M. (1999) *Fat! So?: Because You Don't Have to Apologize for Your Size*. Berkeley: Tenspeed Press.

Wann, M. *Daniel Pinkwater and the Afterlife*: Interview. www.fat!so.com.

Williams-Forson, P. (2006) *Building Houses Out of Chicken Legs: Black Women, Food, and Power*. Chapel Hill: University of North Carolina Press.

Williamson, B. (2004) "The Surge In Surgery: Why Cosmetic Enhancements Are So Popular." *Elevate Magazine*, October 20, 2004.

Witt, D. (1999) *Black Hunger: Food and the Politics of U.S. Identity*. New York: Oxford Press.

Zola, I. (1986) "Medicine as an institution of social control." In P. Conrad & R. Kern (eds) *The Sociology of Health and Illness*. New York: St Martin's Press.

38

Want Amid Plenty: From Hunger to Inequality*

Janet Poppendieck

"Scouting has some unacceptables," the Executive Director of the Jersey Shore Council of the Boy Scouts of America told me, "and one of them is hunger."[1] We were talking in the entrance to the Ciba Geigy company cafeteria in Toms River, New Jersey, where several hundred Boy Scouts, their parents, grandparents, siblings, and neighbors were sorting and packing the 280,000 pounds of canned goods that the scouts of this Council had netted in their 1994 Scouting For Food drive. The food would be stored on the Ciba Geigy corporate campus, where downsizing had left a number of buildings empty, and redistributed to local food pantries to be passed along to the hungry. The scouting executive was one of several hundred people I interviewed as part of a study of charitable food programs—so called "emergency food" in the United States. In the years since the early 1980s, literally millions of Americans have been drawn into such projects: soup kitchens and food pantries on the front lines, and canned goods drives, food banks, and "food rescue" projects that supply them.

Hunger Has a "Cure"

What makes hunger in America unacceptable, to Boy Scouts and to the rest of us, is the extraordinary abundance produced by American agriculture. There is no short-age of food here, and everybody knows it. In fact, for much of this century, national agricultural policy has been preoccupied with surplus, and individual Americans have been preoccupied with avoiding, losing, or hiding the corporeal effects of over-eating. Collectively, and for the most part individually, we have too much food, not too little. To make matters worse, we waste food in spectacular quantities. A study recently released by USDA estimates that between production and end use, more than a quarter of the food produced in the United States goes to waste, from fields planted but not harvested to the bread molding on top of my refrigerator or the lettuce wilting at the back of the vegetable bin. Farm waste, transport waste, processor waste, wholesaler waste, supermarket waste, institutional waste, household waste, plate waste; together in 1995 they totaled a startling 96 billion pounds, or 365 pounds—a pound a day—for every person in the nation.[2]

The connection between abundant production and food waste on the one hand, and hunger on the other, is not merely abstract and philosophical. Both public and

*Originally published 2000

private food assistance efforts in this country have been shaped by efforts to find acceptable outlets for food that would otherwise go to waste. These include the wheat surpluses stockpiled by Herbert Hoover's Federal Farm Board and belatedly given to the Red Cross for distribution to the unemployed, the martyred piglets of the New Deal agricultural adjustment (which led to the establishment of federal surplus commodity distribution), and the cheese that Ronald Reagan finally donated to the needy to quell the criticism of mounting storage costs. Accumulation of large supplies of food in public hands, especially in times of economic distress and privation, has repeatedly resulted in the creation of public programs to distribute the surplus to the hungry. And in the private sphere as well, a great deal of the food that supplies today's soup kitchens and food pantries is food that would otherwise end up as waste: corporate over-production or labeling errors donated to the food bank, farm and orchard extras gleaned by volunteers after the commercial harvest, and the vast quantities of leftovers generated by hospital, school, government and corporate cafeterias, and caterers and restaurants. All of this is food that is now rescued and recycled through the type of food recovery programs urged by Vice President Al Gore and Agriculture Secretary Dan Glickman at their 1997 National Summit on Food Recovery and Gleaning. "There is simply no excuse for hunger in the most agriculturally abundant country in the world," said Glickman, who urged a 33 percent increase in food recovery by the year 2000 that would enable social service agencies to feed an additional 450,000 Americans each day.[3] For Americans reared as members of the "clean plate club" and socialized to associate our own uneaten food with hunger in faraway places, such programs have enormous appeal. They provide a sort of moral relief from the discomfort that ensues when we are confronted with images of hunger in our midst, or when we are reminded of the excesses of consumption that characterize our culture. They offer what appear to be old-fashioned moral absolutes in a sea of shifting values and ethical uncertainties. Many of the volunteers I interviewed for my study told me that they felt that their work at the soup kitchen or food pantry was the one unequivocally good thing in their lives, the one point in the week in which they felt sure they were on the side of the angels. Furthermore, they perceive hunger as one problem that is solvable—precisely because of the abundant production—one problem about which they can do something concrete and meaningful. "Hunger has a cure," is the new slogan developed by the Ad Council for Second Harvest, the National Network of Foodbanks. It is not surprising, then, that hunger in America has demonstrated an enormous capacity to mobilize both public and private action. There are fourteen separate federal food assistance programs, numerous state and local programs, and thousands upon thousands of local, private charitable feeding projects which elicit millions of hours of volunteer time as well as enormous quantities of donated funds and food. In one random survey in the early 1990s, nearly four-fifths of respondents indicated that they, personally, had done something to alleviate hunger in their communities in the previous year.[4]

The Seductions of Hunger

Progressives have not been immune to the lure of hunger-as-the-problem. We have been drawn into the anti-hunger crusade for several reasons. First, hunger in America shows with great clarity the absurdity of our distribution system, of capitalism's approach to meeting basic human needs. Poor people routinely suffer for want of things that are produced in abundance in this country, things that gather dust in warehouses and inventories, but the bicycles and personal computers that people desire and could use are not perishable and hence are not rotting in front of their eyes in defiance of their bellies. The Great Depression of the 1930s, with its startling contrasts of agricultural surpluses and widespread hunger, made this terrible irony excruciatingly clear, and many people were able to perceive the underlying economic madness: "A breadline knee-deep in wheat," observed commentator James Crowther, "is surely the handiwork of foolish men."[5] Progressives are attracted to hunger as an issue because it reveals in so powerful a way the fundamental shortcomings of unbridled reliance on markets.

Second, progressives are drawn to hunger as a cause by its emotional salience, its capacity to arouse sympathy and mobilize action. Hunger is, as George McGovern once pointed out, "the cutting edge of poverty," the form of privation that is at once the easiest to imagine, the most immediately painful, and the most far-reaching in its damaging consequences.[6] McGovern was writing in the aftermath of the dramatic rediscovery of hunger in America that occurred in the late 1960s when a Senate subcommittee, holding hearings on anti-poverty programs in Mississippi, encountered the harsh realities of economic and political deprivation in the form of empty cupboards and malnourished children in the Mississippi Delta. Hunger was in the news, and journalist Nick Kotz reports that a coalition of civil rights and anti-poverty activists made a conscious decision to keep it there. They perceived in hunger "the one problem to which the public might respond. They reasoned that 'hunger' made a higher moral claim than any of the other problems of poverty."[7] The anti-hunger movement—or "hunger lobby" that they initiated—was successful in enlisting Congressional support for a major expansion of food assistance and the gradual creation of a food entitlement through food stamps, the closest thing to a guaranteed income that we have ever had in this country.

The broad appeal of the hunger issue and its ability to evoke action are also visible in the more recent proliferation of emergency food programs. "I think the reason . . . that you get the whole spectrum of people involved in this is because it's something that is real basic for people to relate to. You know, you're busy, you skip lunch, you feel hungry. On certain levels, everyone has experienced feeling hungry at some point in the day or the year," explained Ellen Teller, an attorney with the Food Research and Action Center whose work brings her into frequent contact with both emergency food providers and anti-hunger policy advocates. The food program staff and volunteers I interviewed recognized the difference between their own, essentially voluntary and temporary hunger and hunger that is externally imposed and of unpredictable duration, but the reservoir of common human experience is there. Hunger is not exotic and hard to imagine; it stems from the failure to meet a basic and incontrovertible need that we all share.

Furthermore, the failure to eliminate hunger has enormous consequences. As the research on the link between nutrition and cognition mounts, the social costs of failing to ensure adequate nutrition for pregnant women and young children become starkly obvious. And this, too, contributes to the broad spectrum that Ellen Teller mentioned. There is something for everyone here—a prudent investment in human capital for those concerned about the productivity of the labor force of tomorrow, a prevention of suffering for the tender hearted, a unifying concern for would-be organizers, a blatant injustice for critics of our social structure. Many anti-hunger organizations with relatively sophisticated critiques of the structural roots of hunger in America have engaged with the "feeding movement," the soup kitchens and the food pantries, in the belief that, as the Bread for the World Institute once put it, "Hunger can be the 'door' through which people enter an introduction to larger problems of poverty, powerlessness, and distorted public values."[8] For those progressives seeking common ground with a wider range of American opinion, hunger is an attractive issue precisely because of the breadth of the political spectrum of people who are moved by it.

Third, progressive have been drawn into the hunger lobby by the utility of hunger as a means of resisting, or at least documenting the effects of, government cuts in entitlements. In the early 1980s, especially, when Ronald Reagan began his presidential assault on the nation's meager safety net of entitlement programs for the poor, progressives of all sorts pointed to the lengthening soup kitchen lines as evidence that the cuts in income supports, housing subsidies, food assistance, and a host of other public programs were cuts that neither the poor nor the society could afford. While Reagan and his team claimed that they were simply stripping away waste and fat from bloated programs, critics on the left kept track of mounting use of emergency food programs as a means of documenting the suffering caused by the erosion of the welfare state. The scenario is being replayed, this time amid an expanding economy, as soup kitchens and food pantries register the effects of "the end of welfare as we know it."

Finally, of course, progressive are drawn to the hunger issue by a sense of solidarity with those in need. Most of us became progressives in the first place because we cared about people and wanted a fairer society that would produce less suffering. Few of us can stomach an argument that says that we should leave the hungry to suffer without aid while we work for a more just future. "People don't eat in the long run," Franklin Roosevelt's relief czar Harry Hopkins is reported to have said; "they eat every day."[9] Many of the more activist and progressive people I interviewed in the course of my emergency food study articulated similar sentiments. A woman who worked in the early eighties helping churches and community groups in southern California set up soup kitchens and food pantries to cope with the fallout from the budget cuts in Washington recalled the dilemma as she had experienced it. "As far as I was concerned, the people in Washington had blood on their hands . . . but I wasn't going to stand by and watch people suffer just to make a political point." As one long-time left activist in Santa Cruz put it when questioned about her work as a member of the local food bank board, "There are numbers of people who are very compatible with my radical philosophy who also feel that foodbanking is very important, because the reality is that there are ever increasing homeless and poor, including working poor, who need to be fed . . . the need for food has increased and the resources for providing it haven't. And if there weren't foodbanks, I think a lot of people would starve."

It is easy to see why progressive people have been drawn into anti-hunger activity in large numbers, and why they have been attracted to the soup kitchens, food pantries, and food banks, despite misgivings about these private charitable projects. I, personally, have counted myself an anti-hunger activist since the nation rediscovered hunger in the late 1960s. Nevertheless, after three decades in the "hunger lobby," and nearly a decade of observing and interviewing in soup kitchens, food pantries, food banks, and food recovery projects, I would like to offer a caution about defining hunger as the central issue.

The Case Against Hunger

The very emotional response that makes hunger a good organizing issue, and the felt absurdity of such want amid massive waste, makes our society vulnerable to token solutions—solutions that simply link together complementary symptoms without disturbing the underlying structural problems. The New Deal surplus commodity distribution program, which laid the political and administrative groundwork for most subsequent federal food programs, purchased surplus agricultural commodities from impoverished farmers in danger of going on relief and distributed them to the unemployed already receiving public help. It responded to what Walter Lippmann once called the "sensational and the intolerable paradox of want in the midst of abundance," by using a portion of the surplus to help some of the needy, without fundamentally changing the basis for access to food.[10] As Norman Thomas put it in 1936, "We have not had a reorganization of production and a redistribution of income to end near starvation in the midst of potential plenty. If we do not have such obvious 'breadlines knee deep in wheat' as under the Hoover administration, it is because we have done more to reduce the wheat and systematize the giving of crusts than to end hunger."[11]

For the general public, however, the surplus commodity programs were common sense, and they made well-fed people feel better. Few asked how much of the surplus was being transferred to the hungry, or how much of their hunger was thus relieved. As the *New York Times* predicted in an editorial welcoming the program: "It will relieve our minds of the distressing paradox."[12] And with the moral pressure relieved, with consciences eased, the opportunity for more fundamental action evaporated. Thus the token program served to preserve the underlying status quo.

Something very similar appears to be happening with the private food rescue, gleaning, and other surplus transfer programs that have expanded and proliferated to supply emergency food programs since the early 1980s. The constant fund-raising and food drives that characterize such programs keep them in the public eye, and few people ask whether the scale of the effort is proportional to the scale of the need. With the Boy Scouts collecting in the fall and the letter carriers in the spring, with the convenient barrel at the grocery store door and the opportunity to "check out hunger" at the checkout counter, with the Taste of the Nation and the enormous array of other hunger-related fundraisers, with the Vice President and the Secretary of Agriculture assuring us that we can simultaneously feed more people and reduce waste through food recovery, with all this highly visible activity, it is easy to assume that the problem is under control. The double whammy, the moral bargain of feeding the hungry and preventing waste, makes us feel better, thus reducing the discomfort that might motivate more fundamental action. The same emotional salience that makes hunger so popular a cause in the first place makes us quick to relieve our own discomfort by settling for token solutions.

In the contemporary situation, the danger of such tokenism is even more acute. There is more at stake than the radicalizing potential of the contradictions of waste amid want. The whole fragile commitment to public income supports and entitlements is in jeopardy. Food programs not only make the well fed feel better, they reassure us that no one will starve, even if the nation ends welfare and cuts gaping holes in the food stamp safety net. By creating an image of vast, decentralized, kind-hearted effort, an image that is fueled by every fund-raising letter or event, every canned goods drive, every hunger walk, run, bike, swim, or golf-a-thon, every concert or screening or play where a can of food reduces the price of admission, we allow the right wing to destroy the meager protections of the welfare state and undo the New Deal. Ironically, these public appeals have the effect of creating such comforting assurances even for those who do not contribute.

Promoting hunger as a public issue, of course, does not necessarily imply support for the private, voluntary approach. There are undoubtedly social democrats and other progressives who support expanded food entitlements without endorsing the emergency food phenomenon. Unfortunately, however, much of the public makes little distinction. If we raise the issue of hunger, we have no control over just how people will choose to respond. As the network of food banks, food rescue organizations, food pantries, and soup kitchens has grown, so have the chances that people confronted with evidence of hunger in their midst will turn to such programs in an effort to help.

Many private food charities make a point of asserting that they are not a substitute for public food assistance programs and entitlements. Nearly every food banker and food pantry director I interviewed made some such assertion, and the national organizations that coordinate such projects, Second Harvest, Food Chain, Catholic Charities, even the Salvation Army, are on record opposing cuts in public food assistance and specifying their own role as supplementary. When it is time to raise funds, however, such organizations, from the lowliest food pantry in the church basement to national organizations with high-powered fund raising consultants or departments, tend to compare themselves with public programs in ways that reinforce the ideology of privatization. You simply cannot stress the low overhead, efficiency, and cost effectiveness of using donated time to distribute donated food without feeding into the right-wing critique of public programs in general and entitlements in particular. The same fund-raising appeals that reassure the public that no one will starve, even if public assistance is destroyed, convince many that substitution of charitable food programs for public entitlements might be a good idea.

Furthermore, as the programs themselves have invested in infrastructure—in walk-in freezers and refrigerated trucks, in institutional stoves and office equipment, in pension plans and health insurance—their stake in the continuation of their efforts has grown as well, and with it, their need for continuous fund raising, and thus for the perpetuation of hunger as an issue. While many food bankers and food recovery staff argue that there would be a role for their organizations even if this society succeeded in eliminating hunger, that their products also go to improve the meal quality at senior citizen centers or lower the cost of daycare and rehabilitation programs, they clearly realize that they need hunger as an issue in order to raise their funds. Cost effectiveness and efficient service delivery, even the prevention of waste, simply do not have the same ability to elicit contributions. Hunger is, in effect, their bread and butter. The result is a degree of hoopla, of attention getting activity, that I sometimes think of as the commodification of hunger. As Laura DeLind pointed out in her insightful article "Celebrating Hunger in Michigan," the hunger industry has become extraordinarily useful to major corporate interests, but even without such public relations and other benefits to corporate food and financial donors, hunger has become a "product" that enables its purveyors to compete successfully for funds in a sort of social issues marketplace.[13] It does not require identification with despised groups—as does AIDS, for example. Its remedy is not far off, obscure, or difficult to imagine—like the cure for cancer. The emotional salience discussed above, and the broad spectrum of people who have been recruited to this cause in one way or another, make hunger—especially the soup kitchen, food pantry, food recycling version of hunger—a prime commodity in the fund-raising industry, and a handy, inoffensive outlet for the do-gooding efforts of high school community service programs and corporate public relations offices, of synagogues and churches, of the Boy Scouts and the Letter Carriers, of the Rotarians and the Junior League: the taming of hunger.

As we institutionalize and expand the response, of course, we also institutionalize and reinforce the problem definition that underlies it. Sociologists have long argued that the definitional stage is the crucial period in the career of a social problem. Competing definitions vie for attention, and the winners shape the solutions and garner the resources. It is important, therefore, to understand the competing definitions of the situation that "hunger" crowds out. What is lost from public view, from our operant consciousness, as we work to end hunger? In short, defining the problem as hunger contributes to the obfuscation of the underlying problems of poverty and inequality. Many poor people are indeed hungry, but hunger, like homelessness and a host of other problems, is a symptom, not a cause, of poverty. And poverty, in turn, in an affluent society like our own, is fundamentally a product of inequality.

Defining the problem as hunger ignores a whole host of other needs. Poor people need food, but they also need housing, transportation, clothing, medical care, meaningful work, opportunities for civic and political participation, and recreation. By focusing on hunger, we imply that the food portion of this complex web of human needs can be met independently of the rest, can be exempted or protected from the overall household budget deficit. As anyone who has ever tried to get by on a tight budget can tell you, however, life is not so compartmentalized. Poor people are generally engaged in a daily struggle to stretch inadequate resources over a range of competing demands. The "heat-or-eat" dilemma that arises in the winter months, or the situation reported by many elderly citizens of a constant necessity to choose between food and medications are common manifestations of this reality.

In this situation, if we make food assistance easier to obtain than other forms of aid—help with the rent, for example, or the heating bill—then people will devise a variety of strategies to use food assistance to meet other needs. It is not really difficult to convert food stamps to cash: pick up a few items at the store for a neighbor, pay with your stamps, collect from her in cash. Some landlords will accept them, at a discounted rate of course, then convert them through a friend or relative who owns a grocery store. Drug dealers will also accept them, again at lower than face value, and you can resell the drugs for cash. The list goes on and on. Converting soup kitchen meals is almost impossible, but there are items in many pantry bags that can be resold. In either case, eating at the soup kitchen or collecting a bag from the food pantry frees up cash for other needs, not only the rent, but also a birthday present for a child or a new pair of shoes. By offering help with food, but refusing help with other urgent needs, we are setting up a situation in which poor people are almost required to take steps to convert food assistance to cash.

Conservative critics of entitlements will then seize on these behaviors to argue that poor people are "not really hungry." If they were really hungry, the argument goes, they would not resell items from the pantry bag or convert their food stamps. Such behavioral evidence fits into a whole ideologically driven perception that programs for poor people are bloated, too generous, and full of fraud and abuse; it allows conservatives to cut programs while asserting that they are preserving a safety net for the "truly needy." Progressives meanwhile are forced into a defensive position in which we argue that people are indeed "really hungry," thereby giving tacit assent to the idea that the elimination of hunger is the appropriate goal. In a society as wealthy as ours, however, aiming simply to eliminate hunger is aiming too low. We not only want a society in which no one suffers acute hunger or fails to take full advantage of educational and work opportunities due to inadequate nutrition. We want a society in which no one is excluded, by virtue of poverty, from full participation, in which no one is too poor to provide a decent life for his or her children, no one is too poor to pursue happiness. By defining the problem as "hunger," we set too low a standard for ourselves.

Where to?

The question of where we should direct our organizational efforts is inextricably tied up with the underlying issue of inequality. Above some absolute level of food and shelter, need is a thoroughly relative phenomenon. In an affluent society, the quality of life available at a given level of income has everything to do with how far from the mainstream that level is, with the extent to which any given income can provide a life that looks and feels "normal" to its occupants. In many warm parts of the world, children routinely go barefoot, and no mother would feel driven to convert food resources into cash to buy a pair of shoes, or to demean herself by seeking a charity handout to provide them. In the United States, where children are bombarded with hours of television advertising daily, and where apparel manufacturers trade on "coolness," a mother may well make the rounds of local food pantries, swallowing her pride and subsisting on handouts, to buy not just a pair of shoes, but a particular name brand that her child has been convinced is essential for social acceptance at the junior high school.

In this context, the issue is not whether people have enough to survive, but how far they are from the median and the mainstream, and that is a matter of how unequal our society has become. By every measure, inequality has increased in the United States, dramatically, since the early 1970s, with a small group at the top garnering an ever increasing share of net marketable worth, and the bottom doing less and less well. And it is this growing inequality which explains the crying need for soup kitchens and food banks today, even at a relatively high level of employment that reflects the current peak in the business cycle. Unfortunately, however, a concept like hunger is far easier to understand, despite its ambiguities of definition, than an abstraction like inequality. Furthermore, Americans have not generally been trained to understand the language of inequality nor the tools with which it is measured. Just what is net marketable worth, and do I have any? As the statistics roll off the press, eyes glaze over, and the kindhearted turn to doing something concrete, to addressing a problem they know they can do something about: hunger. Once they begin, and get caught up in the engrossing practical challenges of transferring food to the hungry and the substantial emotional gratifications of doing so, they lose sight of the larger issue of inequality. The gratifications inherent in "feeding the hungry" give people a stake in maintaining the definition of the problem as hunger; the problem definition comes to be driven by the available and visible response in a sort of double helix.

Meanwhile, with anti-hunger activists diverted by the demands of ever larger emergency food systems, the ascendant conservatives are freer than ever to dismantle the fragile income protections that remain and to adjust the tax system to concentrate ever greater resources at the top. The people who want more inequality are getting it, and well-meaning people are responding to the resulting deprivation by handing out more and more pantry bags, and dishing up more and more soup. It is time to find ways to shift the discourse from undernutrition to unfairness, from hunger to inequality.

Notes

1. All quotations not otherwise attributed come from the transcripts of interviews I conducted in conjunction with my study of emergency food. For a more extensive treatment, see Janet Poppendieck, *Sweet Charity? Emergency Food and the End of Entitlement* (New York: Viking, 1998).

2. Foodchain, the National Food Rescue Network, *Feedback* (Fall, 1997), 2–3.

3. Ibid.

4. Vincent Breglio, *Hunger in America: The Voter's Perspective.* (Lanham, MD: Research /Strategy/Management Inc., 1992), 14–16.

5. For a discussion of the so called paradox of want amid plenty in the great depression, see Janet Poppendieck, *Breadlines Knee Deep in Wheat: Food Assistance in the Great Depression.* (New Brunswick, NJ: Rutgers University Press, 1986).

6. George McGovern, "Foreword," in Nick Kotz, *Let Them Eat Promises: The Politics of Hunger in America.* (Englewood Cliffs, NJ: Prentice-Hall, 1969) viii.

7. Nick Kotz, "The Politics of Hunger," *The New Republic* (April 30, 1984), 22.

8. Bread for the World Institute, *Hunger 1994: Transforming the Politics of Hunger.* Fourth Annual Report on the State of World Hunger (Silver Spring, MD, 1993), 19.

9. Quoted in Edward Robb Ellis, *A Nation in Torment: The Great American Depression, 1929–1939.* (New York: Capricorn Books, 1971), 506.

10. Walter Lippmann, "Poverty and Plenty," Proceedings of the National Conference of Social Work, 59th Session, 1932 (Chicago: University of Chicago Press, 1932), 234–35.

11. Norman Thomas, *After the New Deal, What?* (New York: Macmillan, 1936), 33.

12. "Plenty and Want," editorial, *New York Times*, September 23, 1933.

13. Laura B. DeLind, "Celebrating Hunger in Michigan: A Critique of an Emergency Food Program and an Alternative for the Future," *Agriculture and Human Values* (Fall, 1994), 58–68.

39

Community Food Security "For Us, By Us": The Nation of Islam and the Pan African Orthodox Christian Church[*]

Priscilla McCutcheon

> If Black people could secure sufficient power to maintain a balance it might be possible for Black people and white people to live together as two separate peoples in one country. Black people must remain separate using the separateness that already exists as a basis for political power, for economic power, and for the transmission of cultural values. . . . The only hope for peace in America depends upon the possibility of building this kind of Black power. . . . A Black Nation within a nation must come into being if we are to survive. For the Black man everything must be judged in terms of Black liberation. There is but one authority and that is the Black experience. (Cleage 1972, xxxvii)

This excerpt is from *Black Christian Nationalism* written by Albert Cleage. In it he describes his beliefs and methods on how blacks should empower themselves in what he deems to be a white supremacist society. This book also provides an ideal starting point for exploring how two Black Nationalist religious organizations are using food not only as a means to address hunger, but also as a tool of empowerment among blacks. In 1999, the Pan African Orthodox Christian Church (PAOCC) completed the purchase of over 1,500 acres of farmland on the border of Georgia and South Carolina to build a self-sustaining community called Beulah Land Farms. Their land acquisition has now grown to over 4,000 acres. Albert Cleage (1972), the founder of the PAOCC, envisioned a place where members of the church would come together, but also a place where inner-city youth would be exposed to nature and farmland.

The Nation of Islam (NOI) purchased over 1,556 acres of rural South Georgia farmland in 1994, naming it Muhammad Farms. Its expressed purpose is to feed the forty million black people in America (Muhammad 2005). The NOI was founded by Master Farrad Muhammad and led for decades by Elijah Muhammad. Its most notable leader, Malcolm X, strongly believed in black landownership and its importance in achieving self-sufficiency. While both organizations' work around food and health is heavily influenced by their self-proclamation as Black Nationalist religious organizations, the NOI and the PAOCC define Black Nationalism in two *distinct* ways. Food is not simply used to address hunger, but also to build community among blacks. Food is a part of a larger ideology of Black Nationalism, in which self-reliance and the individual achievements of blacks are linked to the "black community" at large.

[*]*Originally published 2011*

Black Nationalism is one of the six political ideologies that Michael Dawson (2001) describes in his seminal work *Black Visions*. Dawson argues that "popular support for black nationalism continues to be based on the time-tested skepticism in black communities that, when it comes to race, America will live up to its liberal values" (Ibid., 86). Black Nationalism is the belief that race and racial discrimination are at the center of the black experience in America and must be addressed by blacks if this group is to ever achieve any tangible progress. Elijah Muhammad, one of the key founders and leaders of the NOI, fervently preached the need for blacks to look beyond the dream of integrating into a white society that devalued every aspect of black life. Instead, he asserted that blacks should develop their own racial identity, and effectively form a psychological and geographically separate nation from whites to promote the true liberation of blacks (Muhammad 1997a). Historically, the PAOCC does not define black liberation as a geographic separation from whites. Instead psychological separation is key so that blacks can develop their own institutions that serve their identities and interests (Cleage 1972). When blacks secure a sufficient amount of equality and power, Cleage argues that only then will it be possible for blacks and whites to live together in the United States but still utilize separate institutions. The recent philosophy of the PAOCC builds on the organization's historical belief of blackness as a unifying factor. The PAOCC asserts that blackness alone should not be the sole organizing factor, but issues including class must also be considered. Blackness then, is complicated and cannot be portrayed as simply white vs. black or us vs. them. Both the NOI and the PAOCC are using their work around food and agriculture to promote some aspects of Black Nationalism achievable through self-sufficiency.

The purpose of this chapter is to delve into the relationship between food and racial identity and religion through the lens of these two Black Nationalist religions. I intend to explore this concept of just sustainability by investigating the ways that race and racial identity are at the heart of the ideological justification and actions of both the NOI and the PAOCC's work around food and health. More important are the ways in which self-sufficiency and community contribute to just sustainability not only in both religious organizations but also among blacks as a collective. This chapter reflects archival and textual research for the NOI. I also engaged in archival and textual research for the PAOCC, but had the added opportunity to do participant observation at Beulah Land Farms. While my access to both organizations differs, the amount of textual information on each is extensive.

To begin, in the first section, I give a brief history of these organizations and their food programs ending with exploring why these two cases might offer unique insights into questions of race in alternative food movements. Second, I bring to light the insistence on self-reliance, borrowing the name FUBU to illuminate the For Us, By Us principle that guides these Black Nationalist religions' work around food and health. Third, I unpack the word *community*, keying in on how both groups define this term racially, socially, and spatially and noting both similarities and differences. I conclude by offering some recommendations on how the broader community's food movement might utilize these two examples in the quest to understand the linkage between race and food provisioning practices, which can only aid in efforts to diversify all levels of the movement.

Organizational Histories

Nation of Islam

The story about the founding of the NOI centers on "the prophet" who appeared on the streets of Detroit in 1930. Farrad Muhammad traveled from house to house initially using the Bible to teach blacks because this, to him, was the only religion that they knew. Food and health were central to the NOI's teachings from its inception. NOI members preached that blacks should not eat unhealthy food, equating such food to poison.

The NOI was founded during the Great Depression when racial barriers prevented progress, and some blacks felt that the black Christian church was not forceful enough in its stand against racial inequality. Elijah Muhammad was one of the first followers of Master Muhammad. He preached fervently about what blacks could do to gain freedom on this Earth. Malcolm X is perhaps the best-known member of the NOI. He was a vocal minister who furthered the message of the NOI preaching to masses of blacks both inside and outside of the NOI about self-sufficiency, the evilness of whites, and the importance of a geographically separate nation. Though Malcolm X eventually broke away from the NOI and changed his views on race drastically in his later years, the NOI and its teachings are often still associated with views he espoused earlier in its history (Lincoln 1994).

The NOI, commonly characterized as a Black Nationalist organization (Harris-Lacewell 2004; Squires 2002; West 1999; Dawson 1994), contends that the only path to black liberation is in forming an autonomous nation separate from whites (Marable 1998). The NOI rejects Christianity as a direct manifestation of white racism, which is appealing to many members. Even so, some of the NOI's teachings resemble those of some black churches and other groups that share its strict ethical and moral guidelines. The NOI has had a profound influence on the religious experience of blacks both inside and outside of this religious sect (Curtis 2006; Dawson 2001; Muhammad 1997a).

The NOI's teachings have received criticisms from blacks and non-blacks alike. During the 1950s and 1960s, some prominent black leaders denounced the NOI as hateful and divisive, and some black intellectuals ignored this group altogether in their discussion of black religious life. Despite this, the NOI has retained relationships with some black Christian ministers, politicians, and businessmen. Among blacks, the relationship with the NOI is a complicated one. Many acknowledge and often share the NOI's frustrations, but differ on their methods for achieving equality. The NOI's insistence on black unity to achieve progress appeals to some blacks both inside of and outside of the religious organization (Lincoln 1994).

Lincoln (1994) argues that most average whites know little about the NOI. "Those who learn of the movement tend to consider it an extreme and dangerous social organization" (172). Some even compare the NOI to the Ku Klux Klan. For the most part, the NOI is more concerned with its perception among blacks and expanding its membership to one day include all blacks. Any objection by whites to its teachings is seen as a natural extension of a white supremacist society.

Food plays a prominent role in the NOI's teachings. In the excerpt that follows from *How to Eat, How to Live*, Elijah Muhammad emphasizes the importance of food in maintaining physical, mental, and spiritual health among blacks. He preaches: "Many years [can] be added to our lives if we only knew how to protect our lives from their enemies . . . food keeps us here; it is essential that we eat food which gives and maintains life . . . we must protect our lives as well as possible from the destruction of food. If we eat the proper food, and eat at the proper time, the food will keep us living a long, long time" (Muhammad 1997b, 1).

The NOI's rhetoric articulates a clear connection between black liberation and the production and consumption of food. The NOI's religious and racial goals influenced its decision to produce and distribute food as a means to increase black autonomy. Elijah Muhammad speaks at length about the appropriate food intake needed to completely emancipate blacks from racial oppression. He admonishes black Christians for continuing to consume pork, alcohol, and tobacco, connecting their consumption to mental bondage, and argues that they are tools used to oppress the black community (Muhammad 1997b; Rouse and Hoskins 2004). According to scholars studying the NOI, proper consumption signifies purity and a commitment to the teachings of Allah (Curtis 2006; Rouse and Hoskins 2004; Witt 1999).

The current work and rhetoric of the NOI on food and health suggests a commitment to the principles of the organic food movement. The NOI believes that food should ideally be chemically free. Though the NOI is not currently farming organically, its Web site includes information about the dangers of pesticides, insecticides, genetically modified seeds and food, and the general danger of large agribusiness. The NOI's minister of agriculture, Dr. Ridgely Abdul Mu'min (Muhammad), states that monetary limitations and the lack of labor prohibit the NOI from growing solely organic produce ("Background of Farm" n.d.).

The NOI's goal of promoting black liberation is seen broadly in its priority of land ownership to increase food production and autonomy among blacks (Malcolm X 1965). Perhaps the most widespread effort of the NOI to promote self-reliance among blacks is the purchase of Muhammad Farms in Bronwood, Georgia to grow a variety of fruits and vegetables. Further investigation into the publicly available archives of Muhammad Farms reveals that its leaders' goals are to "develop a sustainable agriculture system that would provide at least one meal per day . . . [for] 40 million black people" (Muhammad 2005, 1). This land would not only be used to feed people, but also to eventually develop a separate nation for blacks. The NOI contends that much of the land in southern states was cultivated by black slaves and rightfully belongs to them. Though the majority of the NOI's membership is located in major cities including Chicago, Detroit, and Atlanta, the NOI purchased land that is generally outside of its reach to further members' efforts around food, health, and black autonomy. Food grown on this land is distributed mainly to NOI mosques in major cities and also to some black community members outside of the NOI located near mosques in these cities.

Pan African Orthodox Christian Church

The Pan African Orthodox Christian Church is a lesser-known organization founded in Detroit. Reverend Albert Cleage founded Central Congregational Church in 1956 while he was diligently working for racial equality in the city. Throughout the 1960s,

Cleage's religious ideology became increasingly Afrocentric, and he renamed the church the Shrine of the Black Madonna. He went on to form congregations in Atlanta and Houston (Shrine of the Black Madonna 1). Cleage is most known for developing black liberation theology as a Black Nationalistic tradition throughout Christianity. He argued that black people, particularly black ministers, were ordained to teach liberation theology and that the black experience should be central to the teachings of all black churches (Cleage 1972).

Central to Cleage's (1972) teachings are ideas of black nationhood as a way for blacks to cope with their marginalized position and exclusion from a white society. Cleage and the church support the notion that God believes in the freedom of black people, and Jesus is also called the black Messiah. The churches are named The Shrine of the Black Madonna to further emphasize that Jesus is black and to empower black women. Albert Cleage, the founder of the PAOCC, created Black Christian Nationalism. Among the many positions of Black Christian Nationalism is a rejection of the individualism that, in Cleage's opinion, permeates white society. According to an article written by the Holy Patriarch, Jaramogi Menelik Kimathi, communalism, when used in accordance to God's will, is key to helping the greatest number of people possible (Kimathi n.d.). Individualism is not useful to blacks and contradicts the communal nature of African religion, the black church in the United States, and the black nation more broadly. Authentic black liberation requires that black people recognize that race is the overarching way that they are defined in this country and take ownership of this definition. Their oppression is group oppression that cannot be overcome by the individual success of blacks or individual acts of kindness by whites. Cleage says:

> White people are in one group and Black people are in another, and the interests of the two groups are in basic conflict. You may be Black and confused and not realize that you are a part of a group, but if you are Black you are in the Black group. Everyone knows that but you. The whole white group . . . all work together to keep us powerless and they have no choice . . . White people have little value for black people other than the wealth that they can extract from us. (Cleage 1972, 84)

An important aspect of Cleage's explanation of Black Nationalism as a necessity is his discussion of power and group recognition. Despite the fact that some individual blacks may view themselves as better off economically or socially than other blacks, Cleage argues that all are in the struggle together. Equally important is Cleage's description of power and Black Christian Nationalism. Cleage does not argue that whites are inherently evil. He instead argues that the actions of the white power structure derive from power itself. Black people and white people are not different in nature, but rather the differences come from experience and environment. He argues that "white people have been ruthless in their use of power. Under the same circumstances the Black man *will* act the same way" (Cleage 1972, 102). He goes on to say that unless black people separately define a value system based on community, perceived equality will only bring forth similar individualized actions.

The PAOCC has recently expanded their philosophy. Kimathi notes that "blackness alone is no longer a sufficient basis for unity" (Kimathi n.d., 9) because we live in a world where class conflict and racism—to offer one example—cannot be divorced from one another. Blackness is still key, but it is complex, and a host of other complexities must be recognized.

It is useful here to quote Kimathi's article in more detail. He says, "Our struggle is not simply for Black power but also for righteousness, justice, communalism, and goodness-power that is used in compatibility with the will of GOD. We seek always to do the greatest good for the greatest number of people. . . . This is the evolution of Black theology." It is important that this evolution of theology does not signal a departure from the needs of black people, but rather, that these needs are understood within a global context that is interconnected with other important issues.

Beulah Land Farms has now grown to an approximately 4,000-acre lakefront site in Calhoun Falls, South Carolina, on the Georgia/South Carolina border. Its purpose is to promote communal living and self-sufficiency among blacks (New Georgia Encyclopedia 2006). It is a physical setting in which residents are removed from the stimuli of their normal environment to allow a spiritual and physical transformation to occur (Kimathi n.d.). The original tract of land was purchased by Albert Cleage and is now a productive farm. Members of the PAOCC describe it as a "multi-faceted agricultural complex" (PAOCC 2009, 1). On this land, members grow vegetables and fruit but also raise poultry and cattle, and use aquaculture. This land is also a retreat for members of the PAOCC. (Ibid., 1). The name *Beulah* itself is taken from the Book of Isaiah in the Holy Bible; it means to be married to the land. Biblically, Beulah is seen as an environment that stimulates a spiritual transformation and awakening (PAOCC 2009).

Why the NOI and PAOCC

Both the NOI's Muhammad Farms and the PAOCC's Beulah Land Farms are attempts, in distinct ideological and action-based ways, by Black Nationalist religious organizations to develop an idea of black nation-hood based on community.

Though the NOI has received a considerable amount of attention in the media, both it and the PAOCC have received limited scholarly attention. Even less recognition has been paid to their work around food and health. Dorris Witt (1999) discusses the NOI's focus on the dietary and spiritual harms that come from eating foods deemed impure. Witt focuses specifically on the connections that the NOI makes between food and agriculture and black male masculinity. Rouse and Hoskins (2004) describe the dietary guidelines that NOI members follow, including how improper dietary intake is attributed to poor health but also to "negatively valued modes of behavior" (Ibid., 237). Scholars have also investigated black settlements in the United States, including freedom farms after slavery and during the Civil Rights movement (Lee 1999). However, there are no works to date that specifically focus on both the NOI's and the PAOCC's actions around food and how they contribute to the formation of a community and race-based identity designed to influence not only their members but also blacks outside of these distinct religions and denominations.

Because of each group's existence as a Black Nationalist organization, it is unlikely that either the NOI or the PAOCC's work will ever gain widespread attention or appeal among the dominant food movements. This is not simply because some portions of Black Nationalism may be offensive to some, but also because, while in different ways, both the NOI and the PAOCC seem to desire to be somewhat on the outside of these movements. In very distinct ways, they aim to build self-sufficiency and a reliable food source for blacks in the United States. Furthermore, both groups aim to expand this self-sufficiency and ownership to even more institutions. The PAOCC is using its farm to grow cattle, but members also have the vision of one day producing an environmentally sustainable electricity source and already have their own water source. While both the NOI and the PAOCC are on the outskirts of the community food movement, many of their beliefs about the dangers of pesticide and genetically modified food are strikingly similar to the beliefs of the community food movement. I would argue that their reasoning is slightly different, often echoing race-based and black liberation-themed theology. The goal of both religions is to achieve a vision of community improvement and autonomy among blacks. Race and community are at the heart of both organizations' food work. Increasingly, antiracist practices and white privilege are becoming the focus of scholarly work on community food.

Both the NOI and the PAOCC are Black Nationalist religious organizations, which adds an interesting perspective to addressing whiteness and white privilege in the community food movement. Most groups in the community food movement assert that they are "colorblind" and do not view race as relevant to their work (Guthman 2008). Slocum (2006) finds that some of these groups are uncomfortable addressing white privilege, feeling that racism will always be a constant in society. Both the NOI and the PAOCC, to varying degrees, have been formed around race as one of their key group identifiers. These organizations obviously differ from many of the organizations that Slocum describes in her work, and not only address race directly, but also use it as a key organizing principle. In the PAOCC's case, blackness is not enough. Included in blackness is a concern for blacks across the world and for problems that affect a variety of different groups. I would argue that neither of these organizations see themselves as a part of a largely white community food movement or white society as a whole. And to be certain, the goal of neither organization is to be a part of a movement or society that they largely see as unjust and without true opportunities for blacks to succeed. Their intent is for food production to be a part of a broader goal of building community. Regardless, I argue that because the NOI and PAOCC do not want to assimilate into a broader and whiter movement, they can be useful for understanding the importance of racial identity in the community food movement.

When thinking about race and community food, the important question seems less how these two organizations should strive to become a part of the community food movement, but rather how the community food movement can transform itself *and* a broader society that thus far has not been inclusive. It would be easy to come to the conclusion that since these groups "peacefully" lie on the outskirts, there is no point in even investigating them alongside other groups within the movement. I argue that scholars should instead delve into both groups and the communities that they create to get a sense of what inclusion means to these two Black Nationalist organizations. This may in turn provide suggestions on how the broader community food movement can become more inclusive. These groups are not simply looking to provide sustainable food, but also a communal religious experience for blacks that is just and empowering. Both the NOI and the PAOCC in distinct ways are getting at deeper questions of race and racial identity in their community food work. Those looking to diversify the movement and bring marginalized groups in might use these two cases as examples that growing and distributing food is not enough. Social justice must be at the heart of community food work because the relations occurring in it are a microcosm of the relations occurring in society. It is in this tenor that I proceed to the next section on self-reliance. Specifically, I describe how this principle is evident in both the NOI's and the PAOCC's work around food and health.

The FUBU Principle

In 1992, five black men started FUBU (For Us, By Us), a shoe company geared toward inner-city youth but more important, one that is operated and was conceived of in the inner city (Nash 2010). The founders felt that inner-city American communities and cultures were being exploited and commodified by popular shoe companies without having a sense of ownership. They were concerned with the psychological benefits that a sense of ownership has within the concept of "the black community." While community food security could not be further away from the initial conceptualization of a hip hop sneaker company, the emphasis on self-reliance is central to conceptualizing both the NOI and the PAOCC's work around food and health.

Self-reliance is a key tenet of Black Nationalism. Put simply, its definition is ownership and control for blacks over economic, political, and social institutions within the black community. It is the need for blacks to look to themselves for their means of survival. Crucial to the concept of self-reliance is that it is not individualistic, but rather "self" is seen as a community made up of blacks (Dawson 2001). Melissa Harris-Lacewell brilliantly sums up the concept of self-reliance when she defines it as the belief that while many sectors of society may by law be integrated, no one is going to look out for the best interest of blacks but blacks themselves (Harris-Lacewell 2004).

Following slavery and as a result of segregation, many blacks developed their own institutions that included farms started by groups such as the NOI, black-led religious denominations, and black social organizations. (Dawson 2001). At the core of this emphasis on self-reliance is land, which Black Nationalist discourses relate directly to power. Dawson states that "many black nationalists of the modern era continue to promote Garvey's view that black liberation could only come with the reclaiming of the land and the creation of the revolutionary Afrikan state" (Ibid., 94). This concept of a black nation adds yet another layer to both organizations' work around food and health. The NOI believes that this black nation should be a geographically separate nation within the United States; the PAOCC argues that this separation is a mental separation that does not necessitate physical boundaries.

Preaching Self-reliance through the NOI's Muhammad Farms

Self-reliance is at the core of the NOI's teachings around food and health. The definition of self-reliance comes from the core belief that "any ideological perspectives are considered to be the tools of white oppression" (Dawson 2001, 88). Many Black Nationalist organizations believe that because of this, actions must be for blacks and by blacks. The NOI argues that blacks must take care to consume an appropriate diet, but more importantly, one that is grown by blacks that have the best interest of their own people in mind. In *How to Eat, How to Live,* Elijah Muhammad admonishes black Christians for continuing to consume poisonous foods (Muhammad 1997b). NOI doctrine and leaders argue that self-reliance first begins by purifying "one's own body and controlling the food that enters it." They contrast this self-reliance with the "slave diet" (Curtis 2006, 102) in which blacks could not control what they put into their body. Self-reliance then begins with limiting food intake and eliminating the consumption of poisonous food.

The NOI's understanding of self-reliance based on food also includes the establishment of grocery stores and restaurants in inner-city neighborhoods. One example is Salaam Restaurant in Chicago, which did not use white flour and served mainly fish. Jesse Jackson even used this establishment for weekly meetings of his "Operation Breadbasket." Some would argue that by doing this Jackson was making a regular statement that his organization's goal of feeding people was consistent with the NOI's focus on developing self-reliance and community building through food.

Perhaps the most widespread effort of the NOI to promote self-reliance among blacks is the purchase of farmland in Bronwood, Georgia. As a part of its "3-year economic savings program," the NOI purchased 1,556 acres of land to grow a variety of organic fruits and vegetables and to eventually provide adequate housing for blacks. Again, the goal of the NOI is to ensure that all 40 million black Americans are able to have one healthy meal a day ("3-Year Economic Savings Program" 2005). Dr. Ridgley Abdul Mu'min (Muhammad), the minister of agriculture for the NOI, argues that this will increase community autonomy among blacks. Knowledge plus land plus capital equals power (Muhammad 2005). He argues that at one point blacks were beginning to create a nation within a nation, citing black land ownership in the forty-five years following slavery.

The NOI's insistence on land ownership is consistent with many Black Nationalists. While Black Nationalists often debate over the location, many agree that it should be in the Black Belt of the South (Dawson 2001), known as the homeland for blacks in the United States. This is partially why the NOI acquired land in southern Georgia; it is a step toward eventually building this black nation. The NOI argues that since slaves labored on this land, it is rightfully theirs. They also cite black labor through sharecropping and free blacks' farm ownership in the south in the years following slavery. Due to the USDA's unfair lending practices, much of this land has been lost (Grant 2001).

Self-reliance and Beulah Land Farms

Albert Cleage, the founder of the Pan African Orthodox Christian Church, argues for black separation as one of the only avenues for blacks to achieve self-reliance. He acknowledges that this separatism has been forced upon blacks living in a segregated and unjust society. Blacks must however use the separation that already exists and take ownership of it. The promises of integration have not been fulfilled and only require blacks to reject their blackness and adopt all aspects of a white society (Cleage 1972). Self-reliance is one of the major themes of Black Christian Nationalism. Cleage preaches that in "desperation, we turn away from the white world and to that Black Nation for strength" (62). The ultimate goal of the PAOCC's Black Christian

Nationalism is Pan Africanism, but more specifically liberation. To do this, black "counter institutions must be built as a basis for black unity and power" (Ibid., 206). Such institutions enable the achievement of tangible liberation through mental and spiritual transformation.

Beulah Land Farms is a step in this spiritual transformation. The purpose of Beulah Land Farms is to build self-sufficiency and provide this spiritual transformation here on earth. Members of the PAOCC take a holistic approach to agricultural production, not only growing fruits and vegetables but also raising poultry and cattle. An interesting production method of the PAOCC is the use of aquaculture (PAOCC 2009, 1). Keeping in line with the spiritual aspects, Beulah Land Farms is seen as an environment that stimulates a spiritual transformation and awakening. Similar to the NOI, the PAOCC is using land to increase self-reliance among its members and eventually spread this message to all blacks. Self-reliance through a community of blacks is what members of Beulah Land Christian Center are attempting to achieve.

While Beulah Land Farms is a separate physical retreat for members of the PAOCC, the ideological beliefs of the PAOCC is Black Christian Nationalism, which does not insist on the need for a true physical separation of whites from blacks. Cleage argues that if one simply identifies with the promised land geographically, one is missing its true purpose. Instead, Beulah Land Farms is less about a geographic space, and more about a community of people that share common values and a common way of life (Cleage 1972). Therefore the first step to achieving this promised land is for blacks to ascribe to a communal way of life.

"Community" in the Nation of Islam and the Pan African Orthodox Christian Church

When describing how he believed blacks should develop a new consciousness, Stokely Carmichael says that "this consciousness might be called as sense of peoplehood, pride, rather than shame, in blackness, and an attitude of brotherly, communal responsibility among all black people for one another" (Carmichael and Hamilton 1967, vii). Though Carmichael had no official affiliation with either organization, his emphasis on community responsibility and collectivity is prevalent in the religious doctrine of both the NOI and the PAOCC. More important, both groups' take on communal values and responsibility are mirrored in their work around food and health. Who is involved in the community and what goals this community must have influence their actions. From the outset, it is clear that both groups have an expressed purpose of developing communal values among black people.

Minister Louis Farrakhan wrote in the most recent *Final Call News* that "we must accept our responsibility to build our community" (Farrakhan 2009, 1). This message of communal responsibility is a part of the NOI's insistence on acquiring land for food production to eventually build a separate nation for blacks. Part of the NOI's mission on Muhammad Farms is to expose all black people to healthy food. The NOI regularly attends conferences including the Federation of Southern Cooperatives, comprised of black farmers from throughout the southern region. According to one representative of Muhammad Farms, their message is not about conversion, but rather convincing blacks that healthy eating is essential to self-improvement (Muhammad 2005).

While much of the NOI's early rhetoric focused on condemning blacks who practiced Christianity and consumed alcohol and pork, later messages attempted to reach blacks where they are. This is not to suggest that the NOI is abandoning its belief that Islam is the true and only religion of black people, but rather members argue that they must reach blacks in black Christian churches along with the nonreligious. Food is an interesting avenue to build a more inclusive community of blacks who might one day become members of the NOI. Like many Black Nationalist teachings, there is a focus on *we* and *us* in describing the problems that black people still face. When the NOI speaks about using Muhammad Farms for the purpose of nation building, they are speaking of a black nation that will support the "masses of our people" (Muhammad 2005, 1). They even go on to describe blacks in urban centers including Atlanta and Cincinnati who are using their collective efforts to provide better communities for future generation of blacks. The NOI minister of agriculture ends this message by preaching that "now we must take the lessons from our past and use the courage from the faith in God and buy land, develop our skills, save and invest our money to build a glorious future for ourselves and our children" (Ibid.).

Community is also at the forefront of the PAOCC's race-based and religious messages around food. The mission of Beulah Land Farms is to "build a community for all people that is a microcosm of the Kingdom of God" (PAOCC 2009, 1). Beulah Land Farms was only recently completed, though the land has under the PAOCC's ownership for years. The farm includes a Christian Worship Center and camp for inner-city youth. On the Web site, they are insistent on Beulah Land Farms being a place where all are welcome. Furthermore, they work with federal agencies including the United States Department of Agriculture to secure training and funds to continue their work around agriculture and aquaculture (Maxwell n.d.).

The PAOCC is a lesser-known Black Nationalist religion. From reading the sermons and writings of their founder and first Holy Patriarch Albert Cleage, it is obvious that black pride and empowerment are at the center of this Christian community experience. Cleage, who passed away in 2000, argued that all black churches and ministers must recognize that black liberation *is* the true teaching of Jesus and should be taught in all black churches. He says that "the white man's declaration of the black inferiority has served to provide for Black people a unique experience" (Cleage 1972, xxxi). Cleage goes on to preach that this unique experience calls for blacks to develop their own set of values that are not based on individuals, but are rather community values that black people develop collectively. This is what is being done at Beulah Land Farms through a holistic approach geared toward having a transformative and communal spiritual experience for blacks on earth (PAOCC 2009).

I witnessed Beulah Land Farms as described earlier by participating in farm activities. All of the PAOCC workers live on the land. Communal activities include eating together at sunset and worshiping together. Individual growth is also crucial at Beulah. Members often use their time on the farm to reflect on their spirituality. In a publication written by the PAOCC, members described their experiences at Beulah Land Farms (Djenaba n.d.). One member (*Anonymous*) says that "Beulah Land is a red clay soil, fresh vegetables all the time, dusty pink sunrises, and having everyone show up for all assignments and meetings. It is also driving more than ten miles to the 'neighborhood grocery' store, not to mention the new-born calves almost daily and the sweet well water to drink. Above all it is the deep refreshing sleep at night." To this member, the land and the work are peaceful and somewhat removed from society.

Exploring aspects of community is a key focus of much scholarly work about blacks. Many scholars explore community through the concept of the black counterpublic. The Black Public Sphere Collective is a group of scholars who met and wrote a book about the experience of blacks within what they call the black public sphere of the black counterpublic. They describe the black counterpublic as "a sphere of critical practice and visionary politics, in which intellectuals can join with the energies of the street, the school, the church, and the city to constitute a challenge to the exclusionary violence of much public space in the United States" (Harris-Lacewell 2004, 5). There is this recognition that blackness is a political category that was formed based on exclusion from mainstream white society. Institutions were developed in response to this exclusion, and these institutions remain relevant today. Both the NOI and the PAOCC were formed partially in response to this exclusion, but also out of a desire to build institutions that would serve the needs of blacks and help develop a separate and community-based belief system. Their work around food and health reflects the desire to build this community on earth. This community is not simply reactionary, but is a community that must be built based on the specific needs and desires of blacks. There is agency among blacks in this formation of community through food. The NOI has been actively working to create a geographically separate nation from whites, while the PAOCC believes that nation building is key, but does not entail geographic separation. It is instead psychological in an attempt to develop and maintain black communal values. Reed (1999) takes on what he calls a "communitarian mythology," saying that it causes leaders to make generic appeals to race and is not important to blacks achieving economic, political, and social progress. Reed states that blacks must go beyond an empty racial identity and look at the processes that reify racial inequalities. This idea of community or nation building by the NOI and the PAOCC seems to be an effort to do just that. Their beliefs are not based on empty rhetoric but rather a strong belief that community building is necessary for blacks to survive in a white society. The NOI and the PAOCC are actually building the values and common interests that Reed suggests blacks do through their work around food.

Community in the Community Food Movement

In "Reweaving the Food Security Safety Net," Patricia Allen delves into the concept of community. She discusses this idea of "mythical community interests" that tend to dominate community food movements, which often ignore cultural differences and assume cooperation between different groups (Allen 1999, 121). The community food movement's sense of community elevates shared geographic boundaries. An insistence on community is complicated. Similar to Allen, I argue that a community is not simply geographic. Furthermore, the NOI and the PAOCC are examples of two groups that insist (in similar and different ways) that the cultural values of blacks should be central to these organizations' agricultural work. They are using a specific geographic space but appealing to a nationwide constituency of blacks far outside of the geographic boundaries of their respective farms.

Both the NOI and the PAOCC are attempting to build community based on the common identifier of race and racial identity. Both groups recognize that blacks are not a homogenous group but still see race as a common and important connector. Albert Cleage (1972) preaches that being an individual is a choice that does not exist for black people. This is what both the NOI and the PAOCC are attempting to do through these food programs. Their methods are slightly different, but they revolve around this notion of building a community based around food that not only acknowledges blackness but also uses it as a source of empowerment.

According to both organizations, justice and sustainability can only be achieved through building a self-sustaining community. Key to this community is its members' work around food and agriculture. The NOI argues on the one hand that this can only be done if blacks form a separate geographic nation through Muhammad Farms, because no black institution can truly sustain itself when geographically integrated into a white supremacist society. The PAOCC, on the other hand, wants to use the farm to build a just and sustainable community in which members provide for them-selves their own sources of water, food, energy, and peace. The food from this farm must be able to sustain black people if there are food shortages. Both groups are reconceptualizing just sustainability through their focus on racial identity in their food programs.

Conclusion

The Nation of Islam and the Pan African Orthodox Christian Church are two groups using food not only as a source of nourishment, but also as a means to define and uplift the black community. They have established farms in rural areas of South Caro-lina and Georgia with the intention of growing healthy food for their communities. Volunteers on the NOI's Muhammad Farms are largely NOI members who work to provide food for blacks in major cities throughout the nation. Those who work on the PAOCC's Beulah Land Farms are also largely members of this religious body who are working to address hunger worldwide and build community.

While both organizations have different religious ideologies, what ties them together is the thread of Black Nationalism and empowerment. The NOI argues that for blacks to truly achieve this power, they must form a separate geographic nation comprised only of black people in what is known as the Black Belt of the South (Muhammad 2005). The PAOCC, on the other hand, aim for peace on earth for blacks at Beulah Land Farms, and do not specifically advocate a geographic separation (New Georgia Encyclopedia 2006). Both groups are working to achieve self-reliance and feel that blacks must work as a community for this to truly be accomplished. Self-reliance is the belief that individual blacks must rely on each other to achieve true progress. The NOI and the PAOCC aim to do this through their food programs.

The food programs of the NOI and the PAOCC offer insight into the intersection of race, religion, and food. This is an important intersection that helps to illuminate the social justice components of these food programs. Future investigation is needed to determine how these food programs fit into the community food security movement as a whole. I am currently conducting interviews with individual members and engaging in participant observation at Beulah Land Farms. I hope to do the same at Muhammad Farms. The PAOCC and the NOI tell us a great deal, not only about the activities of two black religious food programs, but also how black people in these programs are addressing race and building on racial identity through food. There are undoubtedly other, similar food programs that exist that might contain differences, but also the threads of similarities. For now, these two programs offer a starting point to investigate this nuanced intersection of race, religion, and food.

Acknowledgments

This material is based in part on work supported by the National Science Foundation under award number 0902925 and also the Association of American Geographers through a Dissertation Research Grant. I would like to acknowledge participants at the 2008 Race and Food Conference at the University of California Santa Cruz, the 2009 Association of American Geographers Annual Meeting, and numerous professors at the University of Georgia for their willingness to talk these ideas through with me. Last, I would like to thank my family for their continuous support.

References

Allen, P. (1999). Reweaving the Food Security Safety Net: Mediating Entitlement and Entrepreneurship. *Agriculture and Human Values* 16 (2): 117–129.

"Background of Farm." n.d. *Visit Muhammad Farms.* <http://www.muhammadfarms.com/background_of_farm.htm#Background> (accessed January 2011).

Carmichael, S., and C. V. Hamilton. (1967). *Black Power: The Politics of Liberation in America.* New York: Random House.

Cleage, A. (1972). *Black Christian Nationalism.* New York: William Morrow & Company.

Curtis, E. E. (2006). *Black Muslim Religion in the Nation of Islam, 1960–1975.* Chapel Hill: The University of North Carolina Press.

Dawson, M. (1994). A Black Counterpublic? Economic Earthquakes, Racial Agenda(s), and Black Politics. *Public Culture* 7 (1): 195–223.

Dawson, M. (2001). *Black Visions: The Roots of Contemporary African-American Political Ideologies.* Chicago: The University of Chicago Press.

Djenaba. n.d. "I've Seen the Promised Land." *Shrine of the Black Madonna 4th Pan African Synod Souvenir Booklet.* Beulah Land: Fulfilling Our Founder's Vision.

Farrakhan, L. (2009). The Final Call. FinalCall.Com News. <http://www.finalcall.com/> (accessed March 2009).

Grant, G. (2001). Letter to Bush. *The Farmer.* March 29. http://www.muhammadfarms.com/Letter%20to%20Bush-Mar29.htm (accessed December 2007).

Guthman, J. (2008). If They Only Knew. *Colorblindness and Universalism in California Alternative Food* 60 (3): 387–397.

Harris-Lacewell, M. (2004). *Barbershops, Bibles, and BET: Everyday Talk and Black Political Thought.* Princeton, NJ: Princeton University Press.

Kimathi, M. n.d. Synod (2000): Great Transitions. Shrine of the Black Madonna 4th Pan African Synod Souvenir Booklet. Beulah Land: Fulfilling our Founder's Vision. Detroit: Pan African Orthodox Christian Church.

Lee, C. K. (1999). *For Freedom's Sake: The Life of Fannie Lou Hamer.* Urbana: University of Illinois Press.

Lincoln, C. E. (1994). *Black Muslims in America.* Boston: Beacon Press.

Malcolm X. (1965). *Malcolm X Speaks.* New York: Pathfinder Books.

Marable, M. (1998). *Black Leadership.* New York: Columbia University Press.

Maxwell, A. n.d. Beulah Land Farms Come to Life in Abbeville County. <http://www.sc.nrcs.usda.gov/news/beulahland.html> (accessed March 2009).

Muhammad, E. (1997a). Message to the Black Man in America. <http://www.seventhfam.com/temple/books/black_man/blkindex.htm> (accessed November 2007).

Muhammad, E. (1997b). How to Eat to Live. <http://www.seventhfam.com/temple/books/eattolive_one/eat1index.htm> (accessed November 2007).

Muhammad, R. (2005). The Farm Is the Engine of Our National Life. *The Farmer*. <http://www.muhammadfarms.com/Farmer-Feb28-2005.htm> (accessed November 2007).

Nash, S. N. (2010). FUBU Founder Daymond John Stages His Next Act. Daily Finance. <http://www.dailyfinance.com/story/fubu-founder-daymond-john-stages-his-next-act/19557498> (accessed January 2011).

New Georgia Encyclopedia. (2006). Shrine of the Black Madonna. The University of Georgia Press, Athens. <http://www.georgiaencyclopedia.org/nge/Article.jsp?id=h-1630> (accessed March 2009).

Pan African Orthodox Christian Church (PAOCC). (2009). Beulah Land Christian Center. <http://blcc20.com/> (accessed March 2009).

Reed, A. (1999). *Stirrings in the Jug: Black Politics in the Post-Segregation Era*. Minneapolis: University of Minnesota Press.

Rouse, C., and J. Hoskins. (2004). Purity, Soul Food, and Sunni Islam: Explorations at the Intersection of Consumption and Resistance. *Cultural Anthropology* 19 (2): 226–249.

Slocum, R. (2006). Anti-racist Practice and the Work of Community Food Organizations. *Antipode*. <http://www.rslocum.com/Slocum_Antipode_2006.pdf> (accessed February 2009).

Squires, C. (2002). Rethinking the Black Public Sphere: An Alternative Vocabulary for Multiple. *Public Spheres* 12 (4): 446–468.

"3 Year Economic Savings Program." (2005). The official site of the Nation of Islam. <http://www.noi.org/3year-econ.html> (accessed November 2007).

West, M. (1999). Like a River: The Million Man March and the Black Nationalist Tradition in the United States. *The Journal of Historical Sociology* 12 (1): 81–100.

Witt, D. (1999). *Black Hunger: Food and the Politics of U.S. Identity*. New York: Oxford University Press.

40

Learning Democracy Through Food Justice Movements[*]

Charles Z. Levkoe

Introduction

Food can be a powerful metaphor for the way we organize and relate to society. Beyond subsistence, food is a social and cultural expression of individuals. It acts as an entry point into larger debates and discourse around a multitude of issues. Through food we can better understand our histories, our cultures, and our shared future. Food connects us to ecological systems and can teach us about the world in which we live. We also use food as a way to get in touch with our deepest desires or to examine political and social relations within society. One of the most well-known examples of this type of analysis is George Ritzner's explanation of "McDonaldization," a term he uses to describe a process of social rationalization modeled on the fast food restaurant (Ritzner, 1996).

A major theme within the analysis of the global food system, along with the world it illuminates, is that our current course of progress and development is unsustainable and unjust. This stems from the increasing focus on people, not as citizens, but as consumers. The perspective of consumer implies an identity defined by a direct relationship with the market, one in which profit becomes the most important factor in economic, political, and social activity. This identity is with us from the first moments we encounter the world—from entry into the school system to the daily media. In response, there are resistance movements being waged internationally by those who refuse to accept the commodification of human relationships. It is a struggle to build a viable alternative system outside the neo-liberal, capitalist marketplace and to reclaim the ethos of democracy.

This food activism takes many forms and is manifested through a multitude of approaches. The term "food justice movement" has been used to represent the coming together of a wide range of activists, from farmers to eaters. They represent a diversified approach that brings together many critical issues in Canada and around the world with a focus on creating a just food system. In his work, Tim Lang (1996) outlines some of the founding ideologies of these movements:

- Consumers have rights which must be fought for rather than assumed
- Human and environmental health go hand in hand

[*]*Originally published 2006*

- There is no such thing as an average consumer
- What matters is not just "what" is eaten, but "how" it is produced and distributed
- Policies can be changed for the better, but this requires imagination, coalitions, and focused effort.

In this paper I will examine food justice movements as a valuable site for countering the identity of the person only as a consumer, and as a place for learning active democratic citizenship. Food offers a unique opportunity for learning because it has the power to galvanize people from diverse backgrounds and opinions. According to food policy analysts Welsh and MacRae, "Food, like no other commodity, allows for a political reawakening, as it touches our lives in so many ways … from the intimacy of breastfeeding to discussions at the World Trade Organization" (1998: 214).

Participation in food justice movements encourages the development of strong civic virtues and critical perspectives along with the necessary experience for shaping policy makers' decisions. Food justice activism has the ability to increase the confidence, political efficacy, knowledge, and skills of those involved. This has been evident in the case of The Stop Community Food Centre's (The Stop) Urban Agriculture program in Toronto, and shows how participation in food-based, grassroots organizations can foster transformative adult learning.

Through the community garden at The Stop, participants have the potential to gain a better understanding of their role as an active citizen. Together they can understand the challenges that face their local communities and develop strategies for engagement. They are able to take responsibility for a number of tasks and follow them through while recognizing their rights within a larger system. By working together on a common vision, participants directly witness the strengthening of their community. Their commitment and ownership establishes a greater sense of control and power over their lives. Participants in the community garden also are partaking in a wider process, one that de-links their community from the corporate system by taking steps to build sustainable alternatives (Starr, 2000). By reclaiming public space and growing organic vegetables, they are breaking dependencies on systems of charity and the market economy by producing their own food. The garden also serves as a model for the community of what can be collectively accomplished and how people can reconnect to each other and the earth.

In her work, Juliet Merrifield explains that although "learning through doing seems to be the key root to active citizenship … there is little hard evidence" (2001:8). This paper provides evidence in the form of a case study and joins other works in the field of social movement learning by linking existing theory with grounded practice (see for example Eyerman, 1991; Buttel, 1997; Foley, 1999; Gottlieb, 2001). Thus, I emphasize that organizing in pursuit of food justice affects not simply practical experiences, such as growing foods and building shared community spaces, but also instills civic experiences that foster participation and leadership in wider social justice activities.

This paper draws on my experience working with The Stop as researcher, volunteer, and staff member from December 2002 through June 2005. Evidence presented through this case study draws primarily on a participant–observer methodology, along with archival materials such as program reports and evaluations.

Food Justice vs. Food Power

One of the central struggles of food justice movements is to identify eaters primarily as citizens as opposed to consumers. This involves recognizing the current trends of the global food system and increasing corporate control. Graham Riches explains that the "giants of the transnational corporate agriculture and food industry have taken over local control of the production and distribution of nutritious food, and their bottom line is profit, not nutritional value or the health of the community" (1999b: 205). Relegating food solely to the whim of market forces directly threatens democracy, putting profits ahead of the people who are involved in its production, distribution, and consumption. Economic benefit takes precedence over people's need for survival. The corporate food economy has led to an increasing separation of people from the sources of their food and nutrition. In his work, Brewster Kneen (1993) describes this process as "distancing"—the disempowering and deskilling of people from producing their own food and being able to eat well.

Put simply, "citizens are being transformed into consumers (and [by] the illusion of choice this entails) and are being increasingly disconnected from the sources of their food" (Riches, 1999a: 208). For instance, in my experience working with urban children, many are shocked to discover that a carrot grows underground or that a hot dog comes from a living animal. Similarly, many adults increasingly prefer the ease and convenience of drive through fast food to taking the time to prepare and enjoy a healthy meal with friends and family (Schlosser, 2001). The market, once a place for interaction with those who produce our food, has been transformed into an anonymous super-market. Farm products are broken down and recombined into complex industrial foods different from anything that could be prepared in a kitchen. These foods are then patented and sold to us in packages by corporations.

Contrary to corporate ideology, food is more than just another commodity and people are more then just consumers. Anthony Winson explains that people's relationship with food goes far beyond commodification:

> In the process of [consuming food and drink] we take them inside our very bodies, a fact that gives them special significance denied such "externally" consumed commodities as refrigerators, automobiles, house paint or television sets. Moreover, unlike many other goods that we produce and consume in capitalist society, food is an **essential** commodity: we literally cannot live without it (although this is not to say that all of the processed food products for sale today are essential) (1993: 4).

As a growing force, food justice movements promote a strategy of food security where all people have access to adequate amounts of safe, nutritious, culturally appropriate food produced in an environmentally sustainable way and provided in a manner that promotes human dignity.[1] Various critical discourses have clashed attempting to understand this concept of food security and the ways it can be attained. The different discourses operate on different scales and have varied implications for activism. They also highlight many of the central debates within food justice movements. I will briefly examine three perspectives in order to set the context for discussing food justice activity and the nature of food systems work.

The "rights discourse" is one perspective that has been used to profile the unattained human right to food in Canada (see Riches, 1999a, b). Advocates primarily use international agreements between nations constructed through state agencies, and apply them to a multitude of political scales from municipality to national government. Proponents of this discourse focus on the individual. They contend that every citizen should have a right to feed him or herself as an essential attribute of the social rights within a democracy. Through rights, food, which is not often considered controversial, becomes a profoundly political matter, one that enables questions to be raised around the equality and justice of its production, distribution, and consumption. Using a rights discourse calls for accountability and places a significant amount of responsibility on governments to protect its citizens against hunger.

Human rights, although entrenched through international agreements, have little more than moral weight. Since there are no international enforcement mechanisms, they depend on local governments to support them through domestic law. The language of human rights, however, tends to focus on individual entitlement rather than on structural or political economic conditions. There is often little connection between hunger and poverty and other issues that contribute to food insecurity.

Second, overcoming food insecurity necessitates addressing structural barriers. Since the beginning of the recession in the early 1980s, food banks have been the traditional response to feeding hungry Canadians. Those within the food bank movement, along with many food security proponents, attribute the rising need for food directly to increasing poverty. They attempt to use their very existence as a marker of the inability of governments to achieve social equality. This "anti-poverty" discourse has taken on many of the issues ignored by the human rights approach. Although there have been different ways of framing their interests, most agree that the definition of food security must go beyond simply guaranteeing access to food.

By reframing hunger as an issue of poverty, it is argued that a strong social safety net and adequate income will enable marginalized people to make choices around the foods they purchase. Through these arguments, activists have attempted to frame issues of hunger as "food poverty" and to place them on municipal, provincial, and national agendas. Although the anti-poverty approach complements the use of a rights discourse, critics have shown that it can also be limiting. Looking at hunger solely from a perspective of poverty ignores the connection of food to the environment and the role that the global system as a whole plays in the production, distribution, and consumption of food.

The discourse of "Community Food Security" (CFS) is a third perspective. It encompasses both previous discourses and aims to engage a broader perspective including sustainability and community building. CFS emphasizes building local capacities for food production and marketing, equity, social justice, and ecological sustainability. Its objectives include food systems that are decentralized and environmentally sound in the long-term. CFS also aims to be supportive of the needs of the whole community and to assure equitable food access created through democratic decision-making (Fisher, 1997).

Unlike other approaches that focus their attention solely on governmental policy and regional or global change, CFS recognizes the importance of a strong safety net that can provide for those in need until conditions improve. Proponents work within smaller scales to build community and invest in projects that aim to create long-term self-sufficiency. CFS focuses primarily on neighborhoods and households and sees them as having the potential to initiate social change; at the same time, it recognizes the need for global coalitions. It draws upon both environmental sustainability and local economic development.

Through these perspectives we can analyze the nature of the food system as an important indicator of the broader picture. According to Tim Lang, "it is both a vignette and a microcosm of wider social realities" (1999: 218). Through food justice movements, a vision of food democracy has been adopted which directly challenges anti-democratic forces of control, exploitation, and oppression. Food democracy refers to the idea of public decision-making and increased access and collective benefit from the food system as a whole. It implies a reconnection to the earth and the process of growing, preparing, and eating food. According to Neva Hassanein,

> At the core of food democracy is the idea that people can and should be actively participating in shaping the food system, rather then remaining passive spectators on the sidelines.... [It is about] citizens having power to determine agro-food policies and practices locally, regionally, nationally and globally (2003: 79).

The transition to a food democracy requires that people develop the knowledge and skills necessary to actively participate in society and to have an impact on different political levels. Food justice movements, utilizing local grassroots initiatives, have the ability to provide this opportunity. Through organizations, collective groups of citizens are able to work together to raise awareness, put pressure on governments, and build viable alternatives to the current system. In the remainder of this paper, I will focus on the case of The Stop Community Food Centre's Urban Agriculture program, a Toronto-based, grassroots, non-profit organization that combines dignified direct service with capacity building and sustainable community development.

The Stop Community Food Centre

The Stop Community Food Centre works primarily with vulnerable populations in the Davenport West region, one of the poorest areas in Toronto, Canada. Similar to areas in other large urban centers, neighborhood residents face inadequate employment, low incomes, language barriers, and high rates of school dropout. Over half of the unattached adults live below the poverty line compared to the citywide rate of 37% (Urban Development Services, City of Toronto, 2003). These factors are compounded by the fact that there are few services in the community to meet local needs. A 2004 survey of The Stop's Food Bank (Bain and Company, 2004) shows a 20% increase in use of The Stop over the previous year and that 50% of recipients go hungry at least a couple of days each week.

Building on its strong history of community service, The Stop has grown to meet the needs of the existing community. The organization originally opened in the late 1970s, in St. Stephen-in-the-Fields Church in downtown Toronto, to work with people living on low incomes through the distribution of food. In 1985, once the food bank was well established, The Stop became involved with advocacy work by assisting people with landlord–tenant disputes and welfare and unemployment problems. By 2000, programs had expanded to include a community kitchen and dining programs, a morning and afternoon drop-in, a peri-natal support program, and the Urban Agriculture program. Currently, The Stop Community Food Centre has two central interconnecting ideologies. The first is that confronting hunger must go beyond handing out food to people struggling on low incomes. The second is that food access and food security are basic human rights.

In working to promote these ideas, The Stop's philosophy is reflected in its attempt to make food the focus of a larger project of a community center. By providing respectful emergency assistance through community development, social justice, and advocacy, The Stop is attempting to create a new model that takes a more holistic approach to issues surrounding hunger in all aspects of society. Operating within the discourse of Community Food Security (CFS), The Stop brings together many of the diverse perspectives in the food justice movement. In describing this approach, Nick Saul, The Stop's Executive Director, explains that "(t)oday, The Stop truly is a 'community food centre,' one that works on food access issues through a wide range of strategies—direct programming, education and advocacy" (Saul, 2001: 1). The new mission statement reflects these efforts, stating that The Stop strives to increase access to healthy food in a way that maintains dignity, builds community, and challenges inequality.

In its work, The Stop recognizes the interdependence of people's access to food and the health of the environment. The Urban Agriculture program has been a way to accomplish many interlocking goals, including environmental protection and protection of native species, environmental and food-based education, urban food production, waste reduction, and the development of strong social networks in the community. The program began in 1998, when a district supervisor with Toronto Parks and Recreation approached the organization's executive director and proposed jointly running an organic community garden in Earlscourt Park. Seen as an opportunity to gain access to fresh and healthy produce and to increase the community development aspects of their mandate, The Stop took on responsibility for the project. In 1999, a permanent staff person was hired to coordinate the garden activities.

Currently, the Stop maintains a number of community gardens in two main areas. The first area (in partnership with and located behind the Davenport Perth Neighbourhood Centre) is home to three smaller gardens: (1) a woodland teaching garden with plants native to the area; (2) a healing garden with medicinal herbs and flowers; and (3) a raised bed herb garden accessible to people with disabilities. The Stop also coordinates a wood-fired bake oven that was built in 2002 to enhance the public gathering space for both organizations. It is used primarily to facilitate weekly community pizza lunches.

The second focus of the Urban Agriculture program is Earlscourt Park, home to the Earlscourt Garden, which is currently maintained jointly with Toronto Parks and Recreation and local schools. As the largest of the gardens, it is over 8000 ft.^{2} and is run almost entirely by volunteers who contribute the majority of the produce to The Stop's food bank and community kitchens. In addition to increasing the amount of nutritious food available at the food bank, the Urban Agriculture program's main objectives are to teach the community about urban ecology and to provide an opportunity for community members from diverse backgrounds to work together. Not only does the garden serve as a model for how to reduce the amount of pesticides in soil and water, but it is also a magical green space in the center of downtown Toronto where people come to play, to rest, and to reflect.

Learning Democracy Through Food Justice Movements

Education is a key tool in building and maintaining a strong democracy. Strong civic virtues (to be an active, informed, and critical community member) and the rights and responsibilities associated with the status of citizenship are two vital areas of learning.

Juliet Merrifield (2001) outlines a scale of the different ways people learn democratic ideals and become active citizens. On the one hand, she discusses deep-rooted assumptions developed through socialization into political cultures through family and community. On the other, she examines formal, civic educational institutions that teach the knowledge, abilities, and dispositions of citizenship. In the middle and most pertinent to this study, she discusses the indirect learning that occurs through participation in groups. Although little study has been done in this area, many scholars have identified active participation in social movements as a necessary part of democratic learning. As emphasis is often placed on school and other formal institutions to teach civic responsibility, the role of informal learning through NGOs and community organizations has received limited attention in the literature on democratic citizenship.

In his work, Daniel Schugurensky identifies the informal learning sector, "together with the school, the family, media and community associations[,] as among the most powerful socialization agencies for the development of citizenship values and political competencies" (2003a). According to Derek Heater, "it is utterly artificial to treat the civic educative process as a school responsibility in isolation from the community at large and from the individual's experience as a citizen over his or her lifetime" (1999: 172).

Participation in social movements is a valuable way for citizens to learn about democracy through active participation. As opposed to simply studying civic activities, Schugurensky argues that "one of the best ways to learn democracy is by doing it and one of the best ways to develop effective civic and political skills is by observing them in the real world and exercising them" (2003a). Fred Rose (2000) views social movements as schools for democracy. In his work he engages discussion around social movements and suggests that, through participation, citizens have an opportunity to learn what they cannot understand from formal civics classes, television, or print media.

According to Schugurensky (2003b), learning acquired through participation in democracy has an "expansive effect." As people become more familiar with local democracy through their involvement, they become more interested and engaged in broader issues, which encourages them to work for the common good. Within social movements, learning is often incidental and informal, although many organizations increasingly include education and raising awareness as an important part of their work.

Food justice movements are an example of this as organizations from diverse sectors come together to work for progressive social change.

Learning from participation in food justice organizations can be organized into two broad and interconnecting categories: (1) individual learning, and (2) learning from the collective experience. In examining the intersection of individual and collective learning, I will draw upon the case of The Stop Community Food Centre's Urban Agriculture program. In my personal experience with the organization, its staff, and its community, I have witnessed how participants have gained increased knowledge, skill level, and a wider understanding of political issues.

Individual Learning Through Urban Agriculture

Individual learning through urban agriculture can happen in many ways, ranging from skill development to acquiring the knowledge and experience needed for democratic citizenship. By challenging the status quo and reframing the way we understand the current food system and new approaches to changing it, food justice movements present an opportunity for personal transformation. One way this is encouraged is through The Stop's focus on transformative or critical learning that "extends the learner, [moving] her beyond her current understanding" (Foley, 1999: 105). An example of this occurred during the summer of 2004 when Toronto Community Gardeners hosted the American Community Garden Association's 25th Anniversary Conference. Many of The Stop's Urban Agriculture volunteers worked with community groups from around the city to coordinate this massive endeavor.

The theme "Gardens of Diversity: Growing Across Cultures" was chosen to reflect the multi-cultural nature of the city and the gardens within it. Stop volunteers had the opportunity to reflect on this theme for over a year leading up to the conference, and eventually to attend workshops with people from around the world. Workshops all focused on community gardening and were connected to broader social and political issues. As part of an afternoon bus tour, a group visited the Earlscourt Garden. Volunteers spent time discussing their work with organic gardening and how it connected to their own community. These experiences enabled the garden volunteers to put their efforts into the context of a larger movement and understand their own work in a deeper way.

Over the regular garden sessions, volunteers have continually identified new skills and learning in the areas of gardening, environmentalism, problem solving, discovering other community resources, organics, and nutrition. Although some volunteers come to the program with gardening experience, many have never interacted with soil or seeds. The garden sessions provide ample opportunity to teach and share techniques. Harvests enable participants to taste and learn about new and healthy foods. Other Stop programming offers an opportunity to cook with produce in the community kitchen and share it with Stop members through the dining program and food bank.

Many of The Stop's programs encourage learning through workshops on environmental preservation, gardening techniques, creating value-added products, and cooking with fresh organic produce. Participants in food-based activities and popular education workshops often expressed "conscientisation" (Freire, 2000)—developing a critical understanding of reality in the form of "ah ha moments." This part of The Stop's pedagogical approach has been adapted from the work of Paulo Freire's work with Latin American social movements (2000). In one of these popular education workshops with the Sierra Club, participants were given the opportunity to make connections between food and issues relating to economics, politics, and culture. Through an interactive analysis, a critical understanding of the food system, its relation to individuals and the wider community, and concrete project ideas were developed for the group to take away.

Many of the programs relating to the garden have worked with participants to develop skills that have been lost in this modern era of technology and convenience. Relearning simple skills such as planting, growing, cooking, and eating can be an empowering act. Realizing that they can do these activities themselves helps people take steps towards understanding their dependence on corporations. This can be observed at weekly pizza lunches, which bring community members together around the brick oven to roll their own dough and pick fresh toppings. Participants have commented that the pizza is much better than that of any fast food restaurant and that it is simple and inexpensive. They are surprised to see that they can do things they did not expect and many have started baking pizza at home.

In the fall of 2003, The Stop developed a grade-ten curriculum on food security that is used at local high schools. The curriculum provides an opportunity for volunteer facilitation, student leadership, and learning. Consistently throughout the ten-week course a major transformation in the group can be witnessed. Using experiential and popular education techniques along with hands-on planting and cooking components, the group and facilitators are given the opportunity to acquire new knowledge, implement their learning, and reflect on their activities. In the fall of 2003, a number of "tough" boys were amazed at the living organisms in a sample of compost. While transplanting seedlings in the greenhouse, one boy adopted a worm he found, vowing to help it live by setting it free outside. This type of food-based education has been able to reach youth that have given up on school. In 2004/2005 the program expanded to involve over 1200 youth from kindergarten to grade 12.

Increasing participation in public life has also been a general theme observed within the Urban Agriculture program. One volunteer, who remembers gardening in his birth country of Jamaica, took great pleasure in educating local school children and even garden staff in ways to tend Callaloo.[2] Over the years, he has become the garden's "guardian angel," watching over the garden and making sure that visitors respect the area. During volunteer sessions, he is often the first to arrive and the last to leave, spending time with other participants and giving tips and assistance.

Participation in the community garden enables volunteers to invest in a long-term process to see the season through from beginning to end. They have repeatedly commented on the health benefits through stress reduction, physical fitness, and an increased understanding of nutrition and healthy eating. Through coordination with other Stop programming, further application of these skills is possible. Together with the community kitchen, garden volunteers participate in cooking workshops and learn to work with fresh organic produce. Later in the season, some of the volunteers take responsibility for teaching each other to cook with their own recipes. In the food bank, volunteers help prepare and distribute information about organic vegetables, including instructions on storing, preparing, and cooking fresh produce.

Another important aspect of participation in the garden has been the external impact and the ability of participants to educate others about the larger issues. Part of this has been done by talking to public figures who visit the garden about accessibility of healthy food and the necessity of green spaces in Toronto. Funders and supporters are also educated through their participation and through The Stop's publications about the holistic benefits of growing your own food and the environmental implications of urban agriculture. Open and critical discussion about where food comes from and the value of organic agriculture occurs regularly between garden volunteers and neighborhood residents. Volunteers continuously talk to passersby about their work, sharing experiences with each other through discussions. Many have also published articles, recipes, or gardening tips in the program's bi-annual publication, *The West End Gardener*. Furthermore, The Stop and its volunteers have become a model for community gardeners around the city by helping to initiate new projects.

Most importantly, participants learn that they have the ability to make change and influence larger policies. Many who have felt powerless in their lives recognize that through consciousness raising, knowledge, and skill development, they can make a difference. This is also fostered through The Stop's educational programming. In an ongoing partnership with the Justice for Workers' minimum wage campaign, Stop volunteers worked with community coalitions to raise awareness around low wages and worker exploitation. During lunchtime town hall style meetings, The Stop brings in speakers, educators, and politicians to facilitate interactive workshops. Although not directly related, workshops such as these have used the garden as a stepping-stone to bring people together, educate, and build a stronger community.

Finally, staff have also expressed elements of democratic learning through their participation in the Urban Agriculture program. Figuring out how to use community-organizing tools to encourage participation and ownership has been a central focus. In order to facilitate inclusiveness within the multitude of projects, participatory processes have been developed to organize and train individuals, foster positive leadership, and encourage democracy participation. A garden advisory committee and group evaluations have been used to encourage broad involvement. Some of the other strategies that have been implemented include hiring community members as seasonal part-time staff, creating an anti-harassment and discrimination policy, and organizing planning and evaluation sessions. The attempt to create a comfortable working environment has involved building a garden shed to store tools and personal belongings, providing transit tokens for volunteers, and having water and snacks available for breaks. Having a positive relationship between the knowledgeable and caring staff also provides a positive model for interactions with authority figures and helps to break down traditional, hierarchical power dynamics.

Beyond the specific skills acquired in the garden this learning is not unique to food justice movements. Other social movements also foster and have the potential to increase democratic learning. The diversity of food justice movements, however, enables citizenship learning in a wide array of areas and on various levels. Through participation, citizens gain knowledge and understanding of the social, legal, and political systems in which they live and operate. They gain skills and aptitudes to make use of this knowledge, acquiring important social values and dispositions, based on their democratic experience, to put their knowledge and skills to use.

Learning From Collective Experience

Learning also comes from participation in activities with others. Direct experience working with social change activities or with shifting public awareness on an issue can impact the political efficacy and the knowledge base of the individuals involved. Since democracy is something that necessitates community, democratic learning is enhanced in social spaces. According to Juliet Merrifield, "Learning is social, even though it occurs within an individual. It takes place in specific social contexts that shape what is learned, by whom and in what ways" (2001: 1). She suggests that learning in social situations is not simply a proficiency in a skill, but is a developmental process through engagement in a community.

Certain marginalized groups of people may have little exposure to such processes in the formal sector and, thus, may become alienated from politics. Therefore, social movements that operate in a democratic fashion and include mechanisms for diverse participation provide a unique and important forum for learning. By creating collective spaces and being involved in democratic practices, participants are able to directly experience, practice, and learn democracy (Schugurensky, 2003b). Grassroots organizations can serve as a model for what a healthy democracy could look like. Participants are given the opportunity for experimentation in a comfortable and supportive atmosphere and for public participation in the context of a smaller community. Numerous examples of this can be found within The Stop Community Food Centre's Urban Agriculture program.

The structure of the Urban Agriculture program has attempted to emulate a democratic society in various ways. Through the aforementioned advisory councils, feedback sessions, and collective decision-making, The Stop has become a place for participants to understand the opportunities for participation. In coordination with a staff facilitator, the advisory council is responsible for deciding how to organize the garden, what to plant, and how to organize various activities throughout the season. The garden is a safe place to experiment, take risks, and learn from mistakes. Most importantly, seasonal festivals and volunteer appreciation parties have created a space for celebration, appreciation, sharing, and fun. At the beginning of the 2003 growing season, a group of garden volunteers needed to make a decision on the layout of the garden. A spontaneous, collective decision-making process began which involved heavy negotiation and compromise. Eventually, the volunteers decided to plant a section of the garden in the shape of a peace sign as a response to the American invasion of Iraq. Whenever individuals or groups visited the garden, the volunteers would proudly explain the planning process.

Working in groups within the structure of a democratic, grassroots organization can be a valuable space to practice and enhance civic virtues. Such behaviors can range from responsibility, respect, and caring for others to taking pride in a community. For individuals who have little positive experience with social interaction, working democratically within the context of a controlled space can be "the ground" for learning. People can experiment with how they would like to be treated and how to treat each other. Within the garden, working with diverse individuals has resulted in breaking down stereotypes of race, class, and gender and has encouraged participants to embrace each other's differences. On many occasions, communities that have traditionally been in conflict have met face to face in the garden, in some cases developing friendships. Processes are being experimented with that increase accessibility and allow for the expression of all voices. The garden's anti-discrimination policy is one example of this. Another example is the path built in 2004 that makes the garden accessible to people who use wheelchairs.

The garden also provides volunteers with the ability to contribute to a neighborhood improvement project. A number of the volunteers are also users of the food bank, and gardening provides a rare chance for them to give something back to the community. As a result, participants continuously express feelings of connection to the space and a valuable sense of ownership. The lack of vandalism and theft from the garden speaks partially to these feelings within the larger community. Through the creation of green spaces in the center of a city, the garden is an opportunity for increased care for the commons. The aesthetic beautification of a local park has encouraged resident interaction and enjoyment of usable public space.

Over the years, participants have felt that they were making a change by contributing to organic agriculture in the city and by working to provide for themselves and their community. In 2004, over 2500 lbs of vegetables and herbs were harvested from the garden. By choice, the vast majority of the harvest was donated to The Stop's food bank and community kitchens. In the fall of 2004, due to the wet summer conditions, many of the tomatoes did not ripen. Fearing imminent frost, groups of volunteers picked as many as possible and researched green tomato recipes. That afternoon over 150 people dining at The Stop café learned about organic, heritage variety, green tomatoes while feasting on green tomato chutney and green tomato sweet pie. The proud volunteers answered questions and received many compliments.

At The Stop, many participants have expressed the value of feeling connected to something larger than themselves. This speaks to the power of working collectively. Cultural days and celebrations help participants teach and learn about the community and each other. In the fall of 2003, the community initiated an annual harvest festival complete with food, crafts, a parade, music, storytelling, and garden tours. At these events various community members, garden volunteers, and other Stop members gathered to celebrate the fruits of their labor. One year, two women who had volunteered in the garden realized that they were born in the same city in Mexico. Others shared stories and experiences around the different vegetables and herbs grown in the garden. After one of the festivals, an elderly woman commented that being in the parade that circled the neighborhood, and included a man on stilts, music, and costumes, was one of the best held memories of her life.

Social interaction is important for breaking down seclusion and individualism and for building a strong community. Giving volunteers the opportunity to interact with each other encourages mutual support and connects people to each other by creating social networks. Participants in the community garden continually express a heightened sense of self-esteem gained from sharing knowledge and skills with each other. For some of the volunteers, working in the garden is one of the few times in a week that they leave their home. During the weekly pizza lunch, some of the participants who routinely return to socialize at the oven do not even eat the pizza. The social atmosphere created by the garden activities gives volunteers the opportunity to meet new people and interact in a safe environment.

Through The Stop and other food justice movements, people are able to interact socially and recreate community. Coalitions are one further expression of collective activity that has provided an important learning space at The Stop. Groups of individuals and organizations come together on different levels, regionally, nationally, and/or internationally, and create networks that further enable connections to larger issues. For example, The Stop's Urban Agriculture program has been involved with the Toronto Community Gardening Network (regional), Plant-A-Row-Grow-A-Row (regional), the Food Justice Coalition (regional), the American Community Garden Association (North American), and the Canadian Food Security Assembly (national).

Through food justice movements, Hassanein shows how "building coalitions to work on particular issues increases citizen power and enables organizations to effect change that they could not achieve on their own" (2003: 82). This also encourages a deeper social analysis and broader understanding of issues. In the winter of 2005, The Stop hosted a gathering of over 40 Toronto-based community garden leaders in conjunction with the Toronto Community Gardening Network. During the meeting, collective brainstorming techniques were used to facilitate discussions around challenges and prospects for the upcoming season.

Conclusion

The case of The Stop Community Food Centre shows that food justice movements can be important sites of transformative learning. Learning from participation in activities can be a valuable way to reclaim community and public space. It also has the ability to empower people by increasing their political efficacy and overall knowledge base. The individual learning that can occur through food justice movements can be an important way to acquire valuable skills and the knowledge necessary for democratic citizenship. The learning from collective endeavors can be a valuable experience for groups to practice and understand the functioning of democracy. Although these activities do not solve the challenges of food insecurity, the learning enables individuals to contribute to building a stronger local community. Participation in small projects create changes in people that inspire and prepare them to participate in a wider society.

Acknowledgements

I would like to thank Dr. Gerda Wekerle for her encouragement and support in the preparation of this paper. I would also like to acknowledge the initial inspiration for this work that came from Dr. Daniel Schugurensky. This paper would not have been possible without the time and patience of the staff and members of The Stop Community Food Centre. Finally, I would like to express my gratitude to Laura B. DeLind along with the three anonymous reviewers who spent considerable time helping me strengthen this paper.

Notes

1. This definition of food security has been adapted from the Ontario Public Health Association's food security working group (www.opha.on.ca/workgroups/foodsecurity.html). This organization is comprised of individuals and constituent associations from various sectors and disciplines that have an interest in improving the health of the people of Ontario, Canada.
2. Callaloo is a dark-green leafy vegetable that resembles spinach and grows in the Caribbean. To the delight of the neighborhood, it also grows wild in The Stop's community garden.

References

Bain and Company (2004). "A community profile of The Stop's catchment area." Survey prepared for The Stop Community Food Centre. Toronto, Canada.

Buttel, F. H. (1997). "Some observations on agro-food change and the future of agriculture sustainability movements." In D. Goodman and M. J.Watts (eds.) *Globalizing Food: Agrarian Questions and Local Restructuring* (pp. 344–365). London, UK: Routledge.

Eyerman, R. (1991). *Social Movements: A Cognitive Approach*. Philadelphia, Pennsylvania: University Press.

Fisher, A. (1997). "What is community food security?" *Urban Ecologist* 2: 4. Accessed May 2004 at http://www. foodsecurity. org.

Foley, G. (1999). *Learning in Social Action*. New York, New York: Zed Books.

Freire, P. (2000). *Pedagogy of the Oppressed*. New York, New York: Continuum.

Gottlieb, R. (2001). *Environmentalism Unbound*: *Exploring New Pathways for Change*. Cambridge, Massachusetts: MIT Press.

Hassanein, N. (2003). "Practicing food democracy: A pragmatic politics of transformation." *Journal of Rural Studies* 19(1): 77–86.

Heater, D. (1999). *What is Citizenship?*. Cambridge, Massachusetts: Polity Press.

Kneen, B. (1993). *From Land to Mouth: Understanding the Food System, Second Helping*. Toronto, Canada: NC Press.

Lang, T. (1996). "Going public: Food campaigns during the 1980s and 1990s." In D. Smith (ed.) *Nutrition Scientists and Nutrition Policy in the 20th Century* London, UK: Routledge.

Lang, T. (1999). "Food policy for the 21st century: Can it be both radical and reasonable?" In M. Koc, R. McRae, L. Mougeot, and J. Welsh (eds.) *For Hunger Proof Cities: Sustainable Urban Food Systems* (pp. 216–224). Ottawa, Canada: International Development Research Centre.

Merrifield, J. (2001). "Learning from experience trust: A discussion paper prepared for Institute for Development Society For Participatory Studies Participation Group Research in Asia." Accessed September 2003 at http://www. commonwealthfoundation. com/documents/learning.pdf.

Riches, G. (1999a). "Advocating the human right to food in Canada: Social policy and the politics of hunger, welfare, and food security." *Agriculture and Human Values* 16: 203–211.

Riches, G. (1999b). "Reaffirming the right to food in Canada: The role of community based food security." In M. Koc, R. McRae, L. Mougeot, and J. Welsh (eds.) *For Hunger Proof Cities: Sustainable Urban Food Systems* (pp. 203–207). Ottawa, Canada: International Development Research Centre.

Ritzner, G. (1996). *The McDonaldization of Society*. Thousand Oaks, California: Pine Forge Press.

Rose, F. (2000). *Coalitions Across the Class Divide—Lessons from the Labour, Peace and Environmental Movements*. Ithaca, New York: Cornell Press.

Saul, N. (2001). "The name gain." *The Stop News* (The Stop Community Food Centre Newsletter) Fall.

Schlosser, E. (2001). *Fast Food Nation: The Dark Side of the All-American Meal*. Boston, Massachusetts: Houghton Mifflin.

Schugurensky, D. (2003a). "Three theses on citizenship learning and participatory democracy." Accessed September 2003 at http://fcis.oise.utoronto.ca/daniel_schugurensky/.

Schugurensky, D. (2003b). "Working paper #1: Citizenship learning and participatory democracy: Exploring the connections." Accessed September 2003 at http://fcis.oise.utoronto. ca/daniel_schugurensky/.

Starr, A. (2000). *Naming the Enemy: Anti-Corporate Movements Confronting Globalization*. New York, USA: Zed Books.

Urban Development Services, City of Toronto (2003). "Ward 17: Ward profiles, City of Toronto." Accessed February 2005 at http://www.city.toronto.ca.

Welsh, J. and R. MacRae (1998). "Food citizenship and community food security: Lessons from Toronto, Canada." *Canadian Journal of Development Studies* 19: 237–255.

Winson, A. (1993). *The Intimate Commodity*. Ontario, Canada: Garamond Press.

Contributors

Robert Albritton is Professor of Political Science at the University of Mississippi. He is co-editor of *Politics in the American States* and recipient of numerous grants for research and teaching in Thailand.

Anne Allison is Robert O. Keohane Professor of Cultural Anthropology and Professor of Women's Studies at Duke University. She is author of *Nightwork: Sexuality, Pleasure, and Corporate Masculinity in a Tokyo Hostess Club* (1994), *Permitted and Prohibited Desires: Mothers, Comics, and Censorship in Japan* (1996) and *Millennial Monsters: Japanese Toys and the Global Imagination* (2006). Currently, she is working on a book about precarious workers and the precarity of sociality as well as the hope (and hopelessness) surrounding futurity in twenty-first century Japan.

Deborah Barndt is a mother, popular educator, photographer, and Professor in the Faculty of Environmental Studies at York University in Toronto. She has brought her academic, artistic, and activist interests together around food issues in two books, an edited volume, *Women Working the NAFTA Food Chain* (1999) and *Tangled Routes: Women, Work and Globalization on the Tomato Trail* (2nd edition 2007).

Roland Barthes, teacher and writer, was appointed in 1976 as the first person to hold the Chair of Literary Semiology at the Collège de France. He pioneered the semiologic interpretation of foodways in articles including the preface of Brillat-Savarin's *Physiology of Taste*. He also authored the anti-autobiography *Roland Barthes by Roland Barthes*.

Susan Bordo holds the Otis A. Singletary Chair in the Humanities and is Professor of English and Gender Studies at the University of Kentucky. She is the author of the Pulitzer Prize nominated *Unbearable Weight: Feminism, Western Culture and the Body*; *The Male Body: A New Look at Men in Public and in Private*, and other influential books and articles on gender, culture, and the body.

Pierre Bourdieu was an active public intellectual of the late twentieth century. He became Chair of Sociology at the Collège de France in 1981. His main contribution was developing the concept of "cultural capital" in the article "The Forms of Capital" from 1986. Some of his book publications include *Distinction: A Social Critique of the*

Judgement of Taste; *Reproduction in Education, Society, and Culture*; and *Masculine Domination*. He died in 2002, at age 71.

Caroline Walker Bynum is Professor Emerita of Western Medieval History at the Institute for Advanced Study in Princeton. She is author of *Holy Feast and Holy Fast* (1987); *The Resurrection of the Body in Western Christendom* (1995); *Wonderful Blood* (2007); and *Christian Materiality* (2011). She is currently working on medieval devotional objects in comparative perspective.

Christopher Carrington is Associate Professor of Sociology and Sexuality Studies at San Francisco State University. He is author of *No Place Like Home: Relationships and Family Life among Lesbians and Gay Men* (2000). Dr. Carrington is currently finishing an ethnography entitled: *Circuit Boys: Into the World of the Gay Dance and Circuit Party Culture*.

Rossella Ceccarini holds a PhD in Global Studies (2010) from Sophia University, Tokyo, Japan. Currently (2012) she is an adjunct faculty member at the University of Trento, Italy, where she teaches a graduate class in "Culture and Globalization". She is the author of *Pizza and Pizza Chefs in Japan: A Case of Culinary Globalization* (Brill Academic Publishers, 2011).

Jennifer Clapp is Professor in the Environment and Resource Studies Department at the University of Waterloo. Her current research focuses on the interface of environmental sustainability and global food security. She has written widely on the global governance of food security, the political economy of food aid, agricultural trade politics, and corporate actors in global environmental and food politics. Her recent books include: *Hunger in the Balance: The New Politics of International Food Aid* (Cornell University Press, 2012); *Food* (Polity, 2012); *The Global Food Crisis: Governance Challenges and Opportunities* (co-edited with Marc J. Cohen, WLU Press, 2009), and *Corporate Power in Global Agrifood Governance* (co-edited with Doris Fuchs, MIT Press, 2009).

Dylan Clark is Assistant Professor of Anthropology at University of Toronto at Mississauga. His areas of expertise include gifts/commodities, anarchism, the youth subculture, Whiteness, punk, anti-globalization, and hegemony. He has had his work published in journals such as *Ethnology*; *Peace Review*; and *The Journal of Thought*.

Carole Counihan is Professor Emerita of Anthropology at Millersville University and has been Visiting Professor at Boston University, the University of Cagliari, and the University of Gastronomic Sciences (Italy). She is author of *The Anthropology of Food and Body* (1999), *Around the Tuscan Table: Food, Family and Gender in Twentieth Century Florence* (2004), and *A Tortilla Is Like Life: Food and Culture in the San Luis Valley of Colorado* (2009). She is co-editor with Psyche Williams-Forson of *Taking Food Public: Redefining Foodways in a Changing World* (2012) and is editor-in-chief of the scholarly journal *Food and Foodways*.

Mary Douglas was Professor of Anthropology at Cambridge University and held a number of other academic appointments, including the Avalon Foundation Chair at

Northwestern University. She was a trailblazer in the anthropological study of food, and her books include *Constructive Drinking*; *Purity and Danger*; and *Food in the Social Order*.

M.F.K. Fisher was a prolific essayist and memoirist whose writings centered on the pleasures of cooking and eating, principally in California and Southern France. She wrote about food with passion and brilliance, encapsulating the complex human relations centering on food. She was author of over sixteen volumes, including *The Art of Eating* and an acclaimed translation of Brillat-Savarin's *The Physiology of Taste*.

Jack Goody, formerly on the faculty of Anthropology at St. John's College, Cambridge University, is the author of *Cooking, Cuisine, and Class: A Study in Comparative Sociology*; *Production and Reproduction*; and *The Culture of Flowers*.

Julie Guthman is Professor of Social Sciences at the University of California at Santa Cruz, where she teaches courses on the politics of food, agriculture, and the body. She has published extensively on contemporary efforts to transform the way food is produced, distributed, and consumed, with a particular focus on voluntary food labels, community food security, farm-to-school programs, and "alternative food" more generally. Her publications include two award-winning books, *Agrarian Dreams: the Paradox of Organic Farming in California* (2004) and *Weighing In: Obesity, Food Justice, and the Limits of Capitalism* (2011).

Marvin Harris pioneered the cultural materialist interpretation of seemingly quirky human food habits in *Good to Eat: Riddles of Food and Culture* and co-edited *Food in Evolution* with Eric Ross. He was the author of many other books, including *Cultural Materialism*; *Cows, Pigs, Wars, and Witches*; and *The Rise of Anthropological Theory*.

Lisa Heldke is Professor of Philosophy and Sponberg Chair of Ethics at Gustavus Adolphus College, where she also teaches in the Gender, Women and Sexuality Studies program. She is the author of *Exotic Appetites: Rumination of a Food Adventurer*, and a co-editor of several works, including *Cooking, Eating, Thinking: Transformative Philosophies of Food*, and *Oppression, Privilege and Resistance*. Presently, she is the co-editor of the journal *Food, Culture and Society: An International Journal of Multidisciplinary Research*, and is writing a work with Ray Boisvert, called *Philosopher at Table*. In her fantasy life, she is a professional baker.

T.J.M. Holden is Professor of Mediated Sociology in the Department of Multicultural Studies at Tohoku University in Sendai, Japan. His research has been focused on advertising theory, semiotics, grounded studies of communication, and comparative sociology. He has co-edited the book *Medi@sia: Global Media/tion in and Out of Context* (2006) with Timothy J. Scrase.

Alice Julier is Program Director and Associate Professor of Food Studies at Chatham University. She is author of *Things Taste Better in Small Houses: Food, Friendship, and Inequality* (2010), co-editor of the *Food and Foodways* special issue on Food and Masculinity, and Past President of the Association of the Study for Food and Society.

Alison Leitch is a cultural anthropologist who currently teaches in the cultural sociology program in the Department of Sociology at Macquarie University in Sydney. Her research interests include investigating social and political movements of citizens, farmers, and consumers who are engaged with alternative visions of the consumption and production of food. She is also working on an ethnographic memoir based on her research over twenty-five years in the marble quarries of Carrara, in central Italy.

Claude Lévi-Strauss was a French cultural anthropologist best known for applying structuralism to the study of symbolism in mythology. He held the Chair of Social Anthropology at the Collège de France from 1959 until his retirement. His books include *Totemism*; *The Raw and the Cooked*; *The Origin of Table Manners*; and *The Story of the Lynx*. He died in 2009 at the age of one hundred.

Charles Z. Levkoe is currently a doctoral candidate at the University of Toronto in the Department of Geography and Program Planning after spending many years working within the food movement with non-profit organizations and as a community-based researcher. His participatory research works with provincial level organizations in Canada to engage the structures and strategies of cross-sector mobilization towards transforming food systems.

Priscilla McCutcheon is Assistant Professor with joint appointments in the Department of Geography and the Institute for African American Studies at the University of Connecticut. Dr. McCutcheon's primary research focus is on the intersection of agriculture/food, racial identity formation, and religion. Her dissertation examined these issues through the lens of three black religious food programs ranging from a black Protestant church's emergency food program to a Black Nationalist religion farming in southern Georgia. Dr. McCutcheon teaches Cultural Geography, Geography of the African American Experiences, and Race and Food. She is currently co-editing a special issue of *Geoforum* on Race and Food.

Margaret Mead was a cultural anthropologist and curator of ethnology at the American Museum of Natural History in New York. She carried out extensive fieldwork in Oceania, and during World War II, she was Executive Secretary of the Committee on Food Habits of the National Research Council. Some of her many books are *Coming of Age in Samoa*; *Growing Up in New Guinea*; *Sex and Temperament in Three Societies*; and *Male and Female*.

Sidney W. Mintz (Johns Hopkins University) has written on the roles of sugar and soybeans in a global food system. His books include *Sweetness and Power: The Place of Sugar in Modern History* (1985); and *Tasting Food, Tasting Freedom: Excursions into Eating, Culture, and the Past* (1996). His essay "Food, Energy, and Culture" introduces a new volume, *Food and Globalization*, edited by Alexander Nuetzenadel and Frank Trentmann. A collection of essays, *The World of Soy*, co-edited by Mintz, was published in 2008.

Gary Paul Nabhan co-authored one of the first technical articles relating the composition of slow release desert foods to the rise in Native American diabetes. He is author or editor of twenty books and founder of the Renewing America's Food Traditions campaign. For more of his work, see www.garynabhan.com.

Richard A. O' Connor is Biehl Professor of International Studies and Anthropology at Sewanee: The University of the South. He has held Fulbright, SSRC–ACLS, and NEH awards and fellowships at Kyoto University and the Institute of Southeast Asian Studies (Singapore). His early work was on Southeast Asian urbanism, Buddhist monasticism, and the cultural ecology of rice agriculture. In recent years, as a medical anthropologist, he has studied anorexia and breastfeeding as bio-cultural activities.

Fabio Parasecoli is Associate Professor and Coordinator of Food Studies at The New School in New York City. His work explores the intersections among food, media, and politics. Among his recent publications are: *Food Culture in Italy* (2004); *The Introduction to Culinary Cultures in Europe* (The Council of Europe, 2005); and *Bite me! Food in Popular Culture* (2008). He is general editor with Peter Scholliers of a six-volume *Cultural History of Food* (2012).

Jeffrey M. Pilcher is a Professor of History at the University of Minnesota. His most recent books are *Planet Taco: A Global History of Mexican Food* (2012) and the *Oxford Handbook of Food History* (2012). He also wrote *¡Que vivan los tamales! Food and the Making of Mexican Identity* (1998) and *Food in World History* (2006).

Janet Poppendieck is Professor of Sociology at Hunter College, City University of New York, and the author of *Free For All: Fixing School Food in America* (University of California Press, 2010), which was awarded the Outstanding Book Award for 2010 by the Association for the Study of Food and Society. She is also the author of *Breadlines Knee Deep in Wheat: Food Assistance in the Great Depression* (Rutgers: 1986); *Sweet Charity? Emergency Food and the End of Entitlement* (Viking, 1998, Penguin, 1999); and articles on hunger, food assistance, and public policy. She was selected for the James Beard Foundation Leadership Award in 2011.

Eric Schlosser is an award winning journalist, correspondent for *Atlantic Monthly*, and author of three national best-sellers including *Fast Food Nation* (2001), which analyzes how the fast food industry has changed American society. Schlosser has addressed the U.S. Senate about the dangers to the food supply from bioterrorism, as well as lectured at many universities around the country.

Rachel Slocum is Assistant Professor of Geography at the University of Wisconsin, La Crosse. She is a cultural geographer whose research concerns the way race is formed materially through engagements in food space. Exploring the imaginaries and practices of U.S. alternative food networks, she has written about the role of whiteness in these networks, anti-racism and emotionalism as part of the local food movement, and a review article, *Race in the Study of Food*. An edited collection, *Geographies of Race and Food: Fields, Bodies, Markets*, is under consideration for Ashgate's Critical Food Studies series.

Tulasi Srinivas is Assistant Professor of Anthropology at Emerson College. Her research focuses on the cultural politics of religion and the processes of cultural globalization through an inter-disciplinary and comparative analysis of ideology, experience, and subjectivity. Prior to joining the Emerson College faculty, she was a fellow at the Berkley Center for Religion, Peace and World Affairs at Georgetown University (2006–2007). In 1998 and 1999, Srinivas was the site director for India of a ten-nation study on cultural globalization undertaken by the Institute for the Study of Economic Culture at Boston University and the Harvard Academy of International and Area studies.

David Sutton is Professor of Anthropology at Southern Illinois University. He has been conducting research for over twenty years on the island of Kalymnos, Greece. His research interests include, cooking, restaurants, gender, the senses, and memory. Publications on these topics include *Remembrance of Repasts: An Anthropology of Food and Memory* and *The Restaurants Book: Ethnographies of Where We Eat.* When not thinking about food, he explores Hollywood movies, and with co-author Peter Wogan recently published *Hollywood Blockbusters: The Anthropology of Popular Movies.* He is currently working on an ethnography of everyday cooking practices on Kalymnos.

Rebecca Swenson is Assistant Professor of Agriculture, Food, and Natural Resource Communication at the University of Minnesota. Her dissertation, titled *Brand Journalism: Consumers, Citizens and Community* in Ford Times, examined how the Ford Motor Company used topics like food, travel, and outdoor exploration in their company magazine to connect with Americans during much of the twentieth century. She has also published essays and presented conference papers that look at General Mills' use of fictional brand icon Betty Crocker to build community among consumers by addressing women's roles as wives, mothers, friends, and patriots—in and outside the kitchen.

Penny Van Esterik is Professor of Anthropology at York University, Toronto. She teaches nutritional anthropology, advocacy anthropology, and feminist theory, and works primarily in Southeast Asia (Thailand and Lao PDR). Past books include *Beyond the Breast-Bottle Controversy*; *Materializing Thailand*; and *Taking Refuge: Lao Buddhists in North.* She is a founding member of WABA (World Alliance for Breastfeeding Action) and has been active in developing articles and advocacy materials on breastfeeding and women's work, breastfeeding and feminism, and contemporary challenges to infant feeding such as environmental contaminants and HIV/AIDS.

Richard Wilk is Provost Professor of Anthropology and Director of Food Studies at Indiana University. He has done research with Mayan people in the rainforest of Belize, in West African markets, and in the wilds of suburban California. His book on Belizean food is entitled *Home Cooking in the Global Village.* His most recent book is edited with Livia Barbosa, *Rice and Beans: A Unique Dish in a Hundred Places* (Berg Publishers).

Psyche Williams-Forson is Associate Professor of American Studies at the University of Maryland College Park and an affiliate faculty member of the Women's Studies and

African American Studies departments and the Consortium on Race, Gender, and Ethnicity. She authored the award-winning book (American Folklore Society), *Building Houses Out of Chicken Legs: Black Women, Food, and Power* (2006). Her new research explores the role of the value market as an immediate site of food acquisition and a project on class, consumption, and citizenship among African Americans by examining domestic interiors from the late nineteenth century to the early twentieth century.

Yungxiang Yan is Professor of Anthropology and Director of the Center for Chinese Studies at the University of California, Los Angeles. He is the author of *The Flow of Gifts: Reciprocity and Social Networks in a Chinese Village* (Stanford University Press, 1996); *Private Life under Socialism: Love, Intimacy, and Family Change in a Chinese Village, 1949–1999* (Stanford University Press, 2003); and *The Individualization of Chinese Society* (Berg publishers, 2009). His research interests include family and kinship, social change, the individual and individualization, and the impact of cultural globalization. Among other projects, he is currently writing a book on individualization and moral changes in post-Mao China.

Gisèle Yasmeen is Vice-President of Partnerships of the Social Sciences and Humanities Research Council of Canada. She was previously Senior Director of the Outreach, Communications and Research Directorate with Elections Canada and Regional Director (British Columbia/Yukon) of the Centre for Research and Information on Canada. She was also a French and English-language radio columnist with the CBC in Vancouver, and a consultant to the United Nations Food and Agriculture Organization, the Canadian International Development Agency, and the International Development Research Centre.

Credit Lines

Caroline Walker Bynum

Caroline Walker Bynum, "Fast, Feast, and Flesh: The Religious Significance of Food to Medieval Women" from *Representations* 11 (Summer 1985): 1–25. Copyright © 1985 by the Regents of the University of California. Reprinted with the permission of the University of California Press.

Christopher Carrington

Christopher Carrington, "Feeding Lesbigay Families" from *No Place Like Home: Relationships and Family Life among Lesbians and Gay Men*. Copyright © 1999 by The University of Chicago. Reprinted with the permission of The University of Chicago Press.

Rossella Ceccarini

Rossella Ceccarini, "Food Workers as Individual Agents of Culinary Globalization: Pizza and Pizzaioli in Japan" in *Globalization, Food and Social Identities in the Asia Pacific Region*, edited by James Farrer (Tokyo: Sophia University Institute of Comparative Culture, 2010). Copyright © 2010 by Rossella Ceccarini. Reprinted with the permission of the author.

Jennifer Clapp

Jennifer Clapp, "The Political Economy of Food Aid in an Era of Agricultural Biotechnology" from *Global Governance: A Review of Multilateralism and International Organizations* 11, no. 4 (2005): 467–485. Copyright © by Lynne Rienner Publishers, Inc. Used with the permission of the publisher.

Dylan Clark

Dylan Clark, "The Raw and the Rotten: Punk Cuisine" from *Ethnology* 43, no. 1 (2004): 19–31. Copyright © 2004 by the University of Pittsburgh. Reprinted with permission. This contains a figure "Lévi-Strauss' (1969) culinary triangle" which is adapted from Roy C. Wood, *The Sociology of the Meal* (Edinburgh: Edinburgh University Press, 1995): 11. Used by permission of Professor Roy C. Wood, NHTV Breda University of Applied Sciences.

Carole Counihan

Carole Counihan, "*Mexicanas'* Food Voice and Different Consciousness in the San Luis Valley of Colorado. Reprinted with the permission of the author.

Mary Douglas

Mary Douglas, "The Abominations of Leviticus" from *Purity and Danger: An Analysis of the Concepts of Pollution and Taboo*. Copyright © 1966 by Mary Douglas. Reprinted with the permission of Routledge.

M. F. K. Fisher

M. F. K. Fisher, "Foreword" from *The Gastronomical Me*. Copyright 1943 and renewed © 1971 by M. F. K. Fisher. Reprinted with permission.

Jack Goody
Jack Goody, "Industrial Food: Towards the Development of a World Cuisine" from *Cooking, Cuisine, and Class: A Study in Comparative Sociology.* Copyright © 1982 by Jack Goody. Reprinted with the permission of Cambridge University Press.

Julie Guthman
Julie Guthman, "Fast Food/Organic Food: Reflexive Tastes and the Making of 'Yuppie Chow' from *Social and Cultural Geography* 4, no. 1 (2003): 45–58. Copyright © 2003. Reprinted with permission.

Marvin Harris
Marvin Harris, "The Abominable Pig" from *Good to Eat: Riddles of Food and Culture.* Copyright © 1985, 1998 by Marvin Harris. Reprinted by permission of Waveland Press, Inc. All rights reserved.

Lisa Heldke
Lisa Heldke, "Let's Cook Thai: Recipes for Colonialism" in *Pilaf, Posole, and Pad Thai: American Women and Ethnic Food*, edited by Sherrie A. Inness. Copyright © 2001 by the University of Massachusetts Press. Reprinted by permission.

T.J.M. Holden
T.J.M. Holden, "The Overcooked and the Underdone: Masculinities in Japanese Food Programming" from *Food and Foodways* 13, nos. 1–2 (2005): 39–66. Copyright © 2005. Reprinted with permission.

Alice Julier
Alice Julier, "The Political Economy of Obesity: The Fat Pay All." Reprinted with the permission of the author.

Alison Leitch
Alison Leitch, "Slow Food and the Politics of 'Virtuous Globalisation'" in *The Globalization of Food*, edited by David Inglis and Debra Gimlin. Copyright © 2009. Reprinted with the permission of Berg Publishers.

Claude Lévi-Strauss
Claude Lévi-Strauss, "The Culinary Triangle" from *Partisan Review* 33, no. 4 (1966): 586–595. Reprinted with permission.

Charles Z. Levkoe
Charles Z. Levkoe, "Learning Democracy Through Food Justice Movements" from *Agriculture and Human Values* 23 (2006): 89–98. Copyright © 2006 Springer. Reprinted with permission.

Priscilla McCutcheon
Priscilla McCutcheon, "Community Food Security "For Us, By Us: The Nation of Islam and the Pan African Orthodox Christian Church" in *Cultivating Food Justice:*

Margaret Mead

Sidney W. Mintz

Gary Paul Nabhan

Richard A. O'Connor

Fabio Parasecoli

Jeffrey M. Pilcher

Janet Poppendieck

Eric Schlosser

Rachel Slocum

Index

Introductory Note

References such as "138–9" indicate (not necessarily continuous) discussion of a topic across a range of pages. Wherever possible in the case of topics with many references (but not in the case of cited authors), these have either been divided into sub-topics or only the most significant discussions of the topic are listed. Because the entire volume is about "food" and "culture", the use of these terms (and certain others occurring throughout the work) as entry points has been restricted. Information will be found under the corresponding detailed topics.

Food and Culture Editors Carole Counihan (left) and Penny Van Esterik (Right).
Photo taken by John Van Esterik at the Cape Cod Canal on March 4, 2012.